Smith & Keenan's
ENGLISH LAW

Also available:

BUSINESS LAW
Denis Keenan and Sarah Riches

Smith and Keenan's
LAW FOR BUSINESS

Smith and Keenan's
COMPANY LAW

Smith and Keenan's
COMPANY LAW
WITH SCOTTISH SUPPLEMENT

Visit the *English Law, fifteenth edition* Companion Website at
www.pearsoned.co.uk/keenan to find regular updates on major legal
changes affecting the book

Fifteenth Edition

Smith & Keenan's
ENGLISH LAW

Text and Cases

Denis Keenan
LLB(Hons) (Lond.), FCIS, CertEd

of the Middle Temple, Barrister
Formerly Head of Department of Business Studies and Law
at what is now Anglia Ruskin University

PEARSON

Longman

Harlow, England • London • New York • Boston • San Francisco • Toronto
Sydney • Tokyo • Singapore • Hong Kong • Seoul • Taipei • New Delhi
Cape Town • Madrid • Mexico City • Amsterdam • Munich • Paris • Milan

Pearson Education Limited

Edinburgh Gate
Harlow
Essex CM20 2JE
England

and Associated Companies throughout the world.

Visit us on the World Wide Web at:
www.pearsoned.co.uk

———————————

First published in Great Britain under the Pitman Publishing imprint in 1963
Second edition published 1966
Third edition published 1969
Fourth edition published 1973
Fifth edition published 1975
Sixth edition published 1979
Seventh edition published 1982
Eighth edition published 1986
Ninth edition published 1989
Tenth edition published 1992
Eleventh edition published 1995
Twelfth edition published 1998
Thirteenth edition published under the Longman imprint in 2001
Fourteenth edition published 2004
Fifteenth edition published 2007

ISBN 978-1-4058-4618-9

British Library Cataloguing-in-Publication Data
A catalogue record for this book is available from the British Library

10 9 8 7 6 5 4 3 2
11 10 09 08

Typeset by 35 in 9/12pt Stone Serif.
Printed by Ashford Colour Press Ltd., Gosport

The publisher's policy is to use paper manufactured from sustainable forests

CONTENTS

**PART 4
THE LAW OF PROPERTY**

**PART 5
CRIMINAL LAW**

PART 6
CASES AND MATERIALS

Supporting resources
Visit **www.pearsoned.co.uk/keenan** to find valuable online resources

Companion Website for students
● Regular updates on major legal changes affecting the book

For more information please contact your local Pearson Education sales representative or visit **www.pearsoned.co.uk/kennan**

PREFACE

The major feature of this fifteenth edition is the considerable amount of updating of the text required since the last edition was published in 2004. The volume of law that emanates from Parliament in terms of statues and Whitehall in terms of ministerial orders and the courts in terms of rulings in case law is enormous. A particular feature this time has been the full inclusion of the Constitutional Reform Act 2005 which has made the biggest and most far-reaching changes in the system of courts since Victorian times. Nevertheless my publishers and I have tried to keep the book very broadly within the page limits of the last edition. In regard to the problems of legal change I can only repeat what I have said in previous prefaces that it serves to accentuate the feeling always present in those who write legal textbooks and those who lecture in law and their students that they may diligently pursue but seemingly never overtake the fleeting vision of the Law!

What has this publication done to alleviate the problem?

- First there has been rigorous updating of the text so that the relevant law keeps us up to date to the end of February 2007.
- Secondly it will be noticed that as the text proceeds there is reference usually under a separate heading to reform. Here is set out reforms imminent in say the next 12 to 18 months.
- Finally this edition will, as has been the case with previous editions, receive updating three times a year through the companion website, details of which appear in the preliminary pages of the text.

A further distinctive feature of the book is to be found in the extensive cases and materials section which forms Part 6 and we have a new title 'English Law – Text and Cases'. Why is such an extensive treatment of case law included? The reasons are as follows:

- Long experience as a lecturer in both the public and private sectors of professional education led me to believe that other texts might be either too sketchy or too academic in their coverage of cases for the average student at the foundation stage of study. Far too often a case summary describes A selling goods to B, i.e. undefined persons in an undefined place at an undefined time (since the date of the case does not necessarily reflect the date of the facts which gave rise to it). Such summaries are often uninteresting for the reader and difficult to remember because there is no detailed description of the facts which may impress themselves upon the memory. This book therefore gives students ready access to the cases themselves.
- It was usual at one time for students to buy a leading text and a separate casebook. However, this has become an expensive exercise for students, particularly at foundation level where a number of legal topics must be studied at least in terms of the basic principles. This book includes both principles and cases.
- The case summaries in this text are detailed and the relevant circumstances identified and described, verbatim extracts from judgements often being given.
- The headnote to a case or group of connected cases also allows the student to study the Cases and Materials section separately from the main text and, in particular, to revise from this section when the text has been mastered.
- The extended case summaries are particularly useful where the teaching institution does not have an extensive law library or where there is great pressure upon the library

facilities. However, to assist in the use of a law library, the following page lists the law report abbreviations used in Part 6. Furthermore, an extended summary of a case for the student can represent a permissible economy of time, eliminating immaterial facts in the longer full report. It should be remembered that, particularly in the common law subjects, the cases are the authority for the points made in answers to examination questions and students should try to have an appreciation at least of the major cases.

■ The Cases and Materials section assists the lecturer by removing the chore of producing case summaries of the more extended kind, allowing the lecturer to fulfil the much more useful role of giving comment, discussion and criticism of a case.

An additional point is worth mentioning in regard to the Appendix. It is not just an appendix of cases but also of materials. It will be noticed that many of the more discursive aspects of a legal topic are contained in the materials surrounding the reported case. Some may ask why these are not in the text. The reason is that throughout its life the text has been used on a wide variety of courses pitched at different levels and with slightly differing requirements. To facilitate the suitability of the book for this role the text is written in terms of the basic law of the topic. This may be enough in some courses if the basic cases are read and studied. In other courses a little more strength may be required and where this is so attention can be directed as required to the material in the Appendix that pushes out the boundaries of knowledge a little more.

Finally I would like to thank Zoë Botterill, Acquisitions Editor; my Editor Elizabeth Rix and Cheryl Cheasley, Editorial Assistant for their help. I need a lot of it! I also thank those who set, printed and bound the book. A text with so many inevitable changes is not that easy to cope with.

We have once more had the invaluable assistance of my wife Mary in terms of the organisation of the sources of reference of new material for inclusion. No lawyer can survive without this service.

Naturally I take responsibility for any errors or omissions.

Denis Keenan
Maenan
1 March 2007

Courses on which this book is known to be used

AAT	CIMA Foundation
ACCA Foundation Stage	Edexcel Foundation Stage
AS and A2 Level Law	GCSE
BA Accounting and Finance	IComA
BA Business Studies	ICSA
BA European Business	ILEX
BA Estate Management	The Chartered Institute of Housing
BA Financial Services	CIPS
	LLB (English Legal System)

THE BOOK AT A GLANCE

Part 1 THE ENGLISH LEGAL SYSTEM

1	2	3	4
The nature and development of English law – the sources	**The courts of law** – including appeals	**Other courts and tribunals, judicial review, human rights and legal services** – statutory and domestic tribunals	**Criminal procedure** – magistrates' court and Crown Court
5	**6**	**7**	**8**
Civil procedure – a case in the High Court	**The law-making process I: UK legislation**	**The law-making process II: case law and the legislative organs of the European Union**	**Persons and the Crown**

Part 2 THE LAW OF CONTRACT

9	10	11	12	13	14
Making the contract I – formation	**Making the contract II** – consideration and legal intent	**Making the contract III** – formalities and capacity	**Reality of consent I** – mistake	**Reality of consent II** – misrepresenta-tion, duress and undue influence	**Contractual terms** – express and implied terms

15	16	17	18	19
Exclusion clauses and other unfair terms	**Illegality, public policy and competition law**	**Discharge of contract**	**Remedies and limitation of actions**	**Employment rights**

Part 3 THE LAW OF TORTS

20	21
The law of torts: general principles – including parties, vicarious liability and general defences	**Specific torts** – including torts against the person and goods, together with nuisance, negligence and defamation

Part 4 THE LAW OF PROPERTY

22
The law of property – including real and personal property generally, landlord and tenant, transfer of land and securities

Part 5 CRIMINAL LAW

23	24	25
Criminal law: general principles – including strict offences and corporate liability	**Specific offences** – including murder, manslaughter, wounding, and sexual offences	**Age and responsibility** – general defences – including insanity, automatism and self-defence

Part 6 CASES AND MATERIALS

LAW REPORT ABBREVIATIONS

The following table sets out the abbreviations used when citing the various series of certain Law Reports which are in common use, together with the periods over which they extend.

AC	Law Reports, Appeal Cases 1891–(current).
ATC	Annotated Tax Cases 1922–1975.
All ER	All England Law Reports 1936–(current).
All ER (Comm)	All England Law Reports (Commercial Cases) (current).
All ER (D)	All England Law Reports (Direct) (online) (current).
All ER Rep	All England Law Reports Reprint, 36 vols 1558–1935.
App Cas	Law Reports, Appeal Cases, 15 vols 1875–1890.
BCLC	Butterworths Company Law Cases 1983–(current).
B & CR	Reports of Bankruptcy and Companies Winding-up Cases 1918–(current).
Ch	Law Reports Chancery Division 1891–(current).
CLY	Current Law Yearbook 1947–(current).
CMLR	Common Market Law Reports 1962–(current).
Com Cas	Commercial Cases 1895–1941.
Cr App R	Cohen's Criminal Appeal Reports 1908–(current).
Crim LR	Criminal Law Review 1954–(current).
EHRR	European Human Rights Reports (current).
Fam	Law Reports Family Division 1972–(current).
ICR	Industrial Court Reports 1972–1974; Industrial Cases Reports 1974–(current).
IRLB	Industrial Relations Law Bulletin 1993–(current).
IRLR	Industrial Relations Law Reports 1971–(current).
ITR	Reports of decisions of the Industrial Tribunals 1966–(current).
KB	Law Reports, King's Bench Division 1901–1952.
LGR	Local Government Reports 1902–(current).
LRRP	Law Reports Restrictive Practices 1957–(current).
Lloyd LR or (from 1951) Lloyd's Rep	Lloyd's List Law Reports 1919–(current).
NLJ	New Law Journal.
P	Law Reports, Probate, Divorce and Admiralty Division 1891–1971.
P & CR	Planning and Compensation Reports 1949–(current).
PIQR	Personal Injuries and Quantum Reports.
QB	Law Reports Queen's Bench Division 1891–1901; 1953–(current).
Sol Jo	Solicitors' Journal 1856–(current).
STC	Simon's Tax Cases 1973–(current).
Tax Cas (or TC)	Tax Cases 1875–(current).
WLR	Weekly Law Reports 1953–(current).

TABLE OF CASES

Note: The number of the case in Part 6: Cases and Materials is printed in bold type; the page on which the case is cited in the main text is printed in *italic* type.

TABLE OF STATUTES

Part 1

THE ENGLISH LEGAL SYSTEM

THE NATURE AND DEVELOPMENT OF ENGLISH LAW

Classification of English law

The following are the main classifications of English law with which this book deals. The areas of law mentioned will be considered in more detail as relevant in the chapters which follow. They are given here merely as an overview of what is to come.

Private and public law

Private law is concerned with the legal relationships of ordinary persons in everyday transactions. It is also concerned with the legal position of corporate bodies and associations of persons the first of which are given a special form of legal personality. Private law includes contract and commercial law, the law of tort, family law (e.g. divorce, adoption and guardianship), trusts and the law of property which involves a consideration of the rights which can exist in property and how property can be transferred from one person to another.

Public law is concerned with the constitution and functions of the many different kinds of governmental organisations, including local authorities, such as county councils, and their legal relationship with the citizen and each other. These relationships form the subject matter of constitutional and administrative law. Public law is also concerned with crime which involves the state's relationship with the power of control over the individual.

There is also a division into *criminal and civil law*. Criminal law is concerned with legal rules which provide that certain forms of conduct shall attract punishment by the state, e.g. homicide and theft. Civil law includes the whole of private law and all divisions of public law except criminal law.

In order to understand the various branches of substantive private law which are considered in detail later, it is necessary to be able in particular to distinguish the following:

Contract

A contract is an agreement made between two or more persons which is intended to have legal consequences. Thus, if there is a breach of contract, the parties can go to court and obtain a remedy. We shall see in the chapters on contract which agreements the courts will enforce, under what conditions they are enforceable, and what remedies are available to injured parties. It should be noted that the parties to a contract in general enter voluntarily into their obligations; the function of the law is merely to act in an impartial way in order to settle any disputes which may arise between the parties to the contract.

It is, however, worth noting even at this early stage that not all contractual obligations are undertaken voluntarily. In order to protect the consumer, certain obligations are implied into some contracts by statute and cannot in some cases be removed, e.g. an undertaking that the goods are of satisfactory quality in consumer sales where the Sale of Goods Act 1979 applies.

Tort

A tort, on the other hand, is a civil wrong independent of contract. It arises out of a duty imposed by law, and not by agreement, and a person who commits a tortious act does not voluntarily undertake the liabilities which the law imposes on him. There are many kinds of tort with a common characteristic: injury of some kind inflicted by one person on another. Nuisance, inflicting injury by negligence, trespass, slander and libel are well-known civil wrongs. The typical remedy in this branch of the law is an action for damages by the injured party against the person responsible for the injury. Such damages are designed not to punish the wrongdoer but to compensate the injured party.

Crime

A crime is in a different category. It is difficult to define a crime, but it is basically a public offence against the state, and, while an individual may be injured, the object of a criminal charge is to punish the offender, not to compensate the victim, though under the provisions of the Powers of Criminal Courts (Sentencing) Act 2000 compensation orders can be made. Criminals are prosecuted, usually by a Crown Prosecutor, and if found guilty receive the appropriate punishment.

Crimes and civil wrongs distinguished

The distinction does not lie in the *nature of the act* itself. For example, if a railway porter is offered a reward to carry A's case and runs off with it, then the porter has committed a crime, that of theft, and two civil wrongs, i.e. the tort of conversion and a breach of his contract with A. Again, a railway signalman who carelessly fails to operate the signals so that a fatal accident occurs will have committed one crime, i.e. manslaughter, if persons are killed, and two civil wrongs, the tort of negligence in respect of those who die and those who are merely injured and a breach of his contract of service with the employer in which there is an implied term to take due care. It should also be noted that in this case the right of action in tort and the right of action in contract would be brought by different persons. However, although the example is valid, it should be noted that an employer who has been successfully sued for damages by those injured by the signalman's act is unlikely in modern law to try to recoup them from the employee by an action for breach of contract because this upsets industrial relations and is strongly resisted by trade unions.

The distinction does depend on the *legal consequences* which follow the act. If the wrongful act is capable of being followed by what are called criminal proceedings, that means that it is regarded as a *crime*. If it is capable of being followed by civil proceedings, that means that it is regarded as a *civil wrong*. If it is capable of being followed by both, it is both a crime and a civil wrong. Criminal and civil proceedings are usually easily distinguishable; they are generally brought in different courts, the procedure is different, the outcome is different and the terminology is different.

Terminology and outcome of criminal and civil proceedings

In *criminal proceedings* a prosecutor *prosecutes* a defendant. If the prosecution is successful, it results in the *conviction* of what is now the offender. After the conviction the court may deal with the offender by giving him a custodial sentence, e.g. prison; or a non-custodial sentence, e.g. a community sentence. In rare cases the court may discharge the defendant without sentence.

As regards *civil proceedings*, a claimant *sues* (brings a claim against) a defendant. If the claimant is successful, this leads to the court entering judgment ordering the defendant to pay a debt owed to the claimant or money damages. Alternatively, it may require the defendant to transfer property to the claimant or to do or not to do something (injunction) or to perform a contract (specific performance). Some of these remedies are legal and others equitable. The matter of remedies for breach of contract and for torts will be dealt with in more detail in the chapters on those topics.

Trusts

A trust arises where one or more persons holds property, e.g. shares, for the benefit of other persons. People often wish to provide for their children or grandchildren when they die. They may leave some of their property on trust, particularly where, as in the case of grandchildren, they are minors, i.e. under the age of 18 years. They can appoint trustees who will take over the ownership of the property but they will not themselves benefit from that ownership since the capital and/or income of the trust will be used for the benefit of the children or grandchildren who are called the beneficiaries. It is, however, necessary to include a charging clause in the trust instrument or will to allow payment of fees where the trustees are professional persons or a trust corporation. Trusts may also be set up by living persons. The characteristics of a trust are that the trustees own the trust property but the beneficiaries get the benefits.

The development and sources of English law – generally

Our present legal system began, for all practical purposes, in the reign of Henry II (1154–89). When he came to the throne justice was for the most part administered in local courts, i.e. by local lords to their tenants in the feudal courts, and by the County Sheriffs, often sitting with the Earl and the Bishop, in the courts of the Shires and Hundreds. A Shire was a territorial division of England equivalent in many ways to what we would call a county. A Hundred was an administrative division of a Shire supposed originally to have contained 100 families. They administered the law in their respective areas and decided the cases which came before them on the basis of local custom. Many of these customary rules of law were the same or similar in all parts of the country, but there were some differences. For instance, primogeniture, the right of the eldest son to inherit the whole of his father's land where there was no will, i.e. on intestacy, applied almost universally throughout England; but in Kent there existed a system of landholding called gavelkind tenure whereby on intestacy all the sons inherited equally; while in Nottingham and Bristol, under the custom of Borough-English, the property passed to the youngest son. These customs were finally abolished by s 1 and Part IV of the Administration of Estates Act 1925, and replaced by the rule that land goes to those administering the deceased's estate for distribution to near relatives – in most cases spouse and children.

A Royal Court existed called the Curia Regis (King's Council) but this was in general available only to high-ranking persons to whom the King had granted interests in large estates.

In addition, the Curia Regis followed the person of the King and those wishing to complain to the court had to incur the expense, delay and frustration of pursuing the King in his constant movements about the country and abroad. It seems that one claimant followed the King through England and France for five years before his case was heard.

However, s 17 of the Statute of 1215, Magna Carta, provided that what is now the High Court should not follow the King but should be held 'in some certain place'. This turned out to be Westminster and so what is now the High Court became centred in London. It is now in the Strand.

Steps were also taken to ensure that royal justice would go out to the shires and be open to all. This began with the General Eyre which also was instrumental in unifying the law. This is considered below.

The common law

The administrative ability of the Normans began the process destined to lead to a unified system of law which was nevertheless evolutionary in its development. The Normans were not concerned to change English customary law entirely by imposing Norman law on England. Indeed, many charters of William I giving English boroughs the right to hold courts stated that the laws dispensed in those courts should be laws of Edward the Confessor, which meant that English customary law was to be applied.

Attempts were made to ensure a greater uniformity in English law and the chief means by which this was achieved was the introduction of the General Eyre (which simply means 'a journey') whereby representatives of the King were sent from Westminster on a tour of the Shires for the purpose of checking on the local administration. During the period of their visit they would sit in the local court and hear cases, and gradually they came to have a judicial rather than an administrative function and were then called the Justices in Eyre.

Henry II took steps to formalise the jurisdiction of the General Eyre by the Assize of Clarendon (1166) and the Assize of Northampton (1176). These provided that in relation to the criminal law there should be 12 men in every county to be responsible for presenting to the sheriff those suspected of serious crimes. The accused were then brought before the General Eyre when it arrived in the area. As regards the civil law, a new civil remedy called the Assize of Novel Disseisin (lately dispossessed) was offered to persons who complained that their land had been wrongly seized. From this remedy grew a range of civil actions which were brought before the General Eyre. Thus, royal and more uniform justice began to come to the country as a whole.

The General Eyre disappeared in the reign of Richard II (1377–99), but a system of circuit judges from what is now the High Court took its place, the first circuit commission being granted in the reign of Edward III (1327–77). The Justices in Eyre were replaced by more formally trained lawyers over the period 1327–77. By selecting the best customary rulings and applying these outside their county of origin, the circuit judges gradually moulded existing local customary laws into one uniform law 'common' to the whole kingdom. Thus, customs originally local ultimately applied throughout the whole of the realm. Even so, there was no absolute unification even as late as 1389, and in a case in what is now the High Court in that year, a custom of Selby in Yorkshire was admitted to show that a husband was not in that area liable for his wife's trading debts, though the common law elsewhere regarded him as liable.

Furthermore, the right to make a will of personal property, e.g. jewellery, was not universal in England until 1724 when it finally extended to the City of London. Before that time half of the personalty (i.e. property unconnected with land), 'the dead man's part', went to the church and the other half to the wife and children. Land could still not be left by will but descended to the heir at law, though it later became possible, as it is today, to leave land by will.

However, many new rules were created and applied by the royal judges as they went on circuit and these were added to local customary law to make one uniform body of law called 'common law'. Thus, the identity between custom and the common law is not historically true, since much of the common law in early times was created by the judges, who justified their rulings by asserting they were derived from the 'general custom of the Realm'. Thus, in *Beaulieu* v *Finglam* (1401) YB 2 Hen 4, f 18, pl 6, it was said that a man who by his negligence failed to control a fire so that it spread to his neighbour's house was liable in damages according to 'the law and custom of the realm', though it is not easy to see which customary rule the court based its decision on.

The Royal Commissions

The circuit judges from what is now the Queen's Bench Division came eventually to derive their authority from Royal Commissions, the granting of which marked the real beginning of the assize system. The Commissions were:

Commission of oyer and terminer

This commission, which dates from 1329, directed the judges to 'hear and determine' all complaints of grave crime within the jurisdiction of the circuit. It was given to persons by now referred to as circuit judges.

General gaol delivery

This commission, which dates from 1299, gave the judges power to clear the local gaols and try all prisoners within the jurisdiction of the circuit. It was originally given to the Justices in Eyre to formalise the purpose of their visits to the Shires.

Other criminal cases were heard by Justices of the Peace either summarily or sitting in quarter sessions (now abolished) and the circuit judges were also made Justices of the Peace so as to increase their jurisdiction.

Commission of Assize for Civil Actions

Civil actions were usually heard at Westminster but under the Statute of Westminster II, 1285, the Justices in Eyre and later the circuit judges heard *civil cases* under provisions known as *nisi prius* which required the local sheriff to send a jury to London *unless before* the appointed time the royal justices came to hear the case locally, which in practice they always did. Thus, civil cases were opened in London, tried by a circuit judge and jury in the locality and the verdict recorded in London. This lasted until the nineteenth century when a Commission of Assize for Civil Actions was granted to assize judges on circuit.

The Courts Act 1971

The system, which lasted for many years, was brought to an end by the Courts Act 1971, s 1(2) which provided that all courts of assize were abolished and commissions to hold any court of assize would not be issued. This section, having achieved its purpose, was repealed by Sch 7 to the Supreme Court Act 1981.

Stare decisis

Initially the system was held together by the doctrine of *stare decisis*, or standing by previous decisions. Thus, when a judge decided a new problem in a case brought before him, this became a new rule of law and was followed by subsequent judges. In later times this practice crystallised into the form which is known as the binding force of judicial precedent, and the judges felt bound to follow previous decisions instead of merely looking to them for guidance. By these means the common law earned the status of a system. Indeed it was possible for Bracton, Dean of Exeter and a Justice Itinerant of Henry III, to write the first exposition of the common law before the end of the thirteenth century – *A Treatise on the Laws and Customs of England*. There was also an earlier treatise ascribed to Ranulph de Glanvill in 1187, but this was not so comprehensive as the work of Bracton. Nevertheless, the number of writs which Bracton describes as being available in the Royal Courts is much in excess of those described by Glanvill and shows the rapid growth of the system in its first 100 years.

To sum up, the common law is a judge-made system of law, originating in ancient customs, which were clarified, *much* extended and universalised by the judges, although that part of the common law which concerned the ownership of land was derived mainly from the system of feudal tenures introduced from Europe after the Norman Conquest. It is perhaps also worth noting that the term 'common law' is used in four distinct senses, i.e. as opposed to (*a*) local law; (*b*) equity; (*c*) statute law; and (*d*) any foreign system of law.

Equity

The growth of the common law was rapid in the thirteenth century but in the fourteenth century it ceased to have the momentum of earlier years. As a legal profession came into existence the judges came to be chosen exclusively from that profession instead of from a wider variety of royal officials as had been the case in the thirteenth century. The common law courts became more self-conscious about what they were doing and attempted to become more systematic. There was much talk about the proper way of doing things, of not being able to do this or that and much clever reasoning. Reports of cases in the Year Books, the nearest we have to law reports at this time, show a considerable concern with procedural points and niceties, a reluctance to depart from what had become established, a close attention to the observance of proper forms and much less concern with what the circumstances of a particular case demanded if it was to be settled in an appropriate way.

Defects of the common law

As a result of this hardening up of the system, complaints were made by large numbers of people about the inadequacy of the service provided by the courts and the defects of the common law. The main defects were as follows:

The writ system

Writs (now claim forms) were issued by the clerks in the Chancellor's office, the Chancellor being in those days a clergyman of high rank who was also the King's Chaplain and Head of Parliament. In order to bring an action in one of the King's courts, the party wishing to do so had to obtain from the Chancery a writ for which he had to pay. A writ was a sealed letter issued in the name of the King, and it ordered some person, Lord of the Manor, Sheriff of the County or the defendant, to do whatever the writ specified.

The old common law writs began with a statement of the plaintiff's (now claimant's) claim, which was prepared in the Royal Chancery (or office) and not by the claimant's advisers as is the statement of case today. Any writ which was new, because the claimant or his advisers

THE NATURE AND DEVELOPMENT OF ENGLISH LAW | 9

had tried to draft it to suit the claimant's case, might be abated, i.e. thrown out by the court. Thus, writs could only be issued in a limited number of cases, and if the complaint could not be fitted within one of the existing standard writs, no action could be brought.

For example, the writ of trespass to land was available. However, trespass is a *direct* wrong, e.g. actually being on the land. *Indirect* activity affecting enjoyment of land was not covered, e.g. nuisance from smelly pigs or smoky bonfires. There was *at that time* no writ to deal with this type of indirect harm. The common law came to expand its writs to cover an action for damages in this situation, but in the meantime equity had carved out a jurisdiction and had an ideal remedy to deal with nuisance, i.e. the issue of an injunction requiring the defendant to cease the activity or pay a fine or be imprisoned for contempt of court. Moreover, writs were expensive, and their cost could deprive a party of justice. In some cases the cost of the writ was more than the amount of the claimant's claim so he did not bother to sue.

However, a practice grew up under which the clerks in Chancery provided new writs even though the complaint was not quite covered by an existing writ, thus extending the law by extending the scope of the writ system. This appeared to Parliament to be a taking away of its powers as the supreme lawgiver. Further, it took much work away from the local courts into the Royal Courts, thus diminishing the income of the local barons who persuaded Parliament to pass a statute called the Provisions of Oxford in 1258, forbidding in effect the practice of creating new writs to fit new cases. This proved so inconvenient that an attempt to remedy the situation was made by the Statute of Westminster II in 1285 which empowered the clerks in Chancery to issue new writs *in consimili casu* (in similar cases), thus adapting existing writs to fit new circumstances. The common law began to expand again, but it was still by no means certain that a writ would be forthcoming to fit a particular case, because the clerks in Chancery used the statute with caution at first.

Procedure

Other difficulties arose over the procedure in the common law courts, because even the smallest error in a writ would avoid the action. If X complained of the trespass of Y's mare, and in his writ by error described the mare as a stallion, his action could not proceed and he would have to start again. Furthermore, some common law actions were tried by a system called 'wager of law', and the claimant might fail on what was really a good claim if a defendant could bring more people to say that the claim was false than the claimant could get to support it.

The system worked well in local courts where the witnesses (called 'oath helpers') knew the parties and circumstances of the case. However, in cases brought at Westminster it fell into disrepute because 'oath helpers' who would support any case could be hired outside court for a few pence a head.

Defences and corruption

In common law actions the defendant could plead certain standard defences known as *essoins* which would greatly delay the claimant's claim. For example, the defendant might say that he was cut off by floods or a broken bridge. He might also plead the defence of sickness which could delay the action for a year and a day. In early times these defences were checked by sending four knights to see the defendant, but at a later stage there was no checking and the defences were used merely to delay what were often good claims. There were also complaints about the bribery, corruption or oppression of juries, the bias of sheriffs in favour of the powerful and the inability of a successful claimant to enforce a judgment or recover property from his more powerful neighbour.

Remedies

The common law was also defective in the matter of remedies. The only remedy the common law had to offer for a civil wrong inflicted on a claimant was damages, i.e. a payment of money, which is not in all cases an adequate compensation.

For example, if A trespasses each day on B's land, B is unlikely to be satisfied with damages. He would rather stop A from trespassing which equity could do by its remedy of injunction. The common law could not compel a person to perform his obligations or cease to carry on a wrong, though it is not true to say that the common law was entirely lacking in equitable principles, and even in early times there were signs of some equitable development; but generally the rigidity of the writ system tended to stifle justice.

Trusts and mortgages

Furthermore, the common law did not recognise the 'concept of the trust or use' and there was no way of compelling the trustee to carry out his obligations under the trust. Thus, if S conveyed property to T on trust for B, T could treat the property as his own and the common law would ignore the claims of B. In addition, the main right of a borrower (or mortgagor) is the right to redeem (or recover) the land he has used as a security for the loan. Originally at common law the land became the property of the lender (or mortgagee) as soon as the date decided upon for repayment had passed, unless during that time the loan had been repaid. However, equity regarded a mortgage as essentially a security, and gave the mortgagor the right to redeem the land at any time on payment of the principal sum, plus interest due to the date of payment. What is more important, this rule applied even though the common law date for repayment had passed. This rule, which still exists, is called the equity of redemption.

Many people, therefore, unable to gain access to the King's courts, either because they could not obtain a writ, or because the writ was defective when they got it, or because they were caught in some procedural difficulty, or could not obtain an appropriate remedy, began to address their complaints to the King in Council. For a time the Council itself considered such petitions, and where a petition was addressed to the King in person, he referred it to the Council for trial. Later the Council delegated this function to the Chancellor, and eventually petitions were addressed to the Chancellor alone.

The Chancellor began to judge such cases in the light of conscience and fair dealing. He was not bound by the remedies of the common law and began to devise remedies of his own. For example, the Chancellor could compel a person to perform his obligations by issuing a decree of *specific performance* or could stop him from carrying on a wrong by the issue of an *injunction*. The Chancellor also recognised interests in property which were unknown to the common law, in particular the concept of the trust (as it became known) under which persons might be made the legal owners of property for the use or benefit of another or others. As we have seen, the common law did not recognise the interests of the beneficiaries under a trust, but allowed the legal owner to deal with the property as if no other interests existed. Equity, however, enforced the beneficial interests.

In order to bring persons before him, the Chancellor issued a form of summons, called a *subpoena*, which did not state a cause of action but merely told the recipient to appear in Chancery. There were no rules of evidence and the Chancellor's Court did not sit in a fixed place; some hearings were even held in the Chancellor's private house. Equity was thus not cramped by anything like the writ system or the excessive formality of the common law. Eventually, as new Chancellors took over, and Vice-Chancellors were appointed to cope with the increasing volume of work, uncertainty crept into the system, and conflicting decisions were common.

At this stage in its development equity adopted the practice of following previous decisions (or *stare decisis*) which had proved so powerful a force in unifying the diverse systems of local custom under the common law. This was precipitated by the Reformation and by the appointment in 1530 of Sir Thomas More as Chancellor. More was a common lawyer and not a cleric. From then on non-clerical Chancellors were drawn from the ranks of the common lawyers and naturally followed the system of precedent which they had seen used in the common law courts. Lord Ellesmere (1596–1617) began to apply the same principles in all cases of the same type, and later, under Lord Nottingham (1673–82), Lord Hardwicke (1736–56) and Lord Eldon (1807–27), equity developed in scope and certainty.

Relationship of law and equity

Although law and equity eventually operated alongside each other with mutual tolerance, there was a period of conflict between them. This arose out of the practice of the Court of Chancery which issued 'common injunctions' forbidding a person on threat of imprisonment from bringing an action in the common law courts, or forbidding the enforcement of a common law judgment if such a judgment had been obtained.

Thus, if X by some unfair conduct, such as undue influence (see further Chapter 13), had obtained an agreement with Y, whereby Y was to sell X certain land at much below its real value, then, if Y refused to convey the land, X would have his remedy in damages at common law despite his unfair conduct. However, if Y appealed to the Chancellor, the latter might issue a common injunction which would prevent X from bringing his action at common law unless he wished to suffer punishment for defiance of the Chancellor's injunction. Similarly, if X had already obtained a judgment at common law, the Chancellor would prevent its enforcement by ordering X, on threat of imprisonment, not to execute judgment on Y's property.

However, the common law courts retaliated by waiting for the Chancellor to imprison the common law litigant for defiance of the injunction, and then the common law would release him by the process of *habeas corpus*, which was and still is a type of writ used to obtain the release of a person who has been unlawfully detained in prison or elsewhere (see further Chapter 21).

This period of rivalry culminated in the *Earl of Oxford*'s Case in 1615 when Lord Coke, representing the common law courts, offered a direct challenge to the Court of Chancery's jurisdiction. The challenge was taken up and James I, on the advice of Lord Bacon, then his Attorney-General and later Lord Chancellor, gave a firm decision that, where common law and equity were in conflict, equity should prevail. This principle now appears in s 49 of the Supreme Court Act 1981, having appeared in a number of earlier Judicature Acts.

After that the two systems settled down and carved out separate and complementary jurisdictions. Equity filled in the gaps left by the common law, and became a system of case law governed by the binding force of precedent. However, it also lost much of its earlier freedom and elasticity. It is certainly no longer a court of conscience.

Many reforms were still to come. Equitable and legal remedies had to be sought in different courts, but this in due course was rectified by the Judicature Acts, 1873–75, which brought about an amalgamation of the English courts. Since then both common law and equitable remedies have been available to a litigant in the same action and in the same court.

Before leaving the topic, a final characteristic of equity should be noted which is that equity never says the common law is wrong but merely provides alternative solutions to legal problems. This is illustrated by certain cases in the Law of Contract. For example, the decision in *Central London Property Trust Ltd* v *High Trees House Ltd* (1947) (see Chapter 10) shows how modern equity sometimes adopts a different solution from that provided by the common law. Equity is not, therefore, a complete system of law. It complements the rules of the common law but does not replace them.

> The *Earl of Oxford*'s Case, 1615 – Relationship of law and equity (1)

Legislation

In early times there were few statutes and the bulk of law was case law, though legislation in one form or another dates from AD 600. The earliest Norman legislation was by means of Royal Charter, but the first great outburst of legislation came in the reign of Henry II (1154–89). This legislation was called by various names: there were Assizes, Constitutions, and Provisions, as well as Charters. Legislation at this time was generally made by the King in Council, but sometimes by a kind of Parliament which consisted in the main of a meeting of nobles and clergy summoned from the shires.

In the fourteenth century parliamentary legislation became more general. Parliament at first asked the King to legislate, but later it presented a bill in its own wording. The Tudor period saw the development of modern procedure, in particular the practice of giving three readings to a Bill.

From the Tudor period onwards Parliament became more and more independent and the practice of law making by statute increased. Nevertheless, statutes did not become an important source of law until the last two centuries, and even now, although the bulk of legislation is large, statutes form a comparatively small part of the law as a whole. The basis of our law remains the common law, and if all the statutes were repealed we should still have a legal system of sorts, whereas our statutes alone would not provide a system of law but merely a set of disjointed rules.

Parliament's increasing involvement with economic and social affairs increased the need for statutes. Some aspects of law are so complicated or so novel that they can only be laid down in this form; they would not be likely to come into existence through the submission of cases in court. A statute is the ultimate source of law, and, even if a statute is in conflict with the common law or equity, the statute must prevail. It is such an important source that it has been said – 'A statute can do anything except change man to woman', although in a purely legal sense even this could be achieved. No court or other body in the UK can question the validity of an Act of Parliament.

However, the validity of an Act of Parliament can be challenged before the European Court of Justice (ECJ) on the ground that it is in conflict with the Treaty of Rome. Reference should be made to *Factortame Ltd* v *Secretary of State for Transport (No 2)* (1991) (Case **34**, below) where a successful challenge to the validity of the Merchant Shipping Act 1988 in the ECJ was successful and resulted in the repeal by the UK government of certain sections of that Act.

It should also be noted that the Human Rights Act 1998 permits UK courts to make declarations of incompatibility where a UK Act of Parliament is found to violate the European Convention on Human Rights. However, UK courts cannot disapply Acts of Parliament on this ground in contrast to the situation where a challenge is made on the ground of violation of Community law.

Statute law can be used to abolish common law rules which have outlived their usefulness, or to amend the common law to cope with the changing circumstances and values of society.

Once enacted, statutes, even if obsolete, do not cease to have the force of law, but common sense usually prevents most obsolete laws from being invoked. In addition, statutes which are no longer of practical utility are repealed from time to time by Statute Law Repeal Acts. Nevertheless, a statute stands as law until it is specifically repealed by Parliament. This may take place by implication as where an earlier Act is repealed by a later one which is inconsistent with it.

An Act of Parliament is, in general, binding on everyone within the sphere of its jurisdiction, though it may not be binding if it infringes the Treaty of Rome, as the *Factortame* case shows, but all Acts of Parliament can be repealed by the same or subsequent parliaments; and this is a further exception to the rule of the absolute sovereignty of Parliament – it cannot bind itself or its successors.

> *Cheney* v *Conn*, 1968 – The court cannot in general declare a statute to be invalid (2)
>
> *Prince of Hanover* v *Attorney-General*, 1957 – A statute remains law until repealed (3)
>
> *Vauxhall Estates Ltd* v *Liverpool Corporation*, 1932 – Repeal by implication (4)

Repeal of statutes and the European Communities Act 1972

As regards the power of Parliament to abolish or alter statute law by a later Act, an interesting situation arises in connection with our membership of the European Community.

Since this is the first time we have met the expression 'European Community' it would perhaps be desirable to consider whether the expression 'Community' or 'Union' should be used. The parts of the European co-operation arrangements include: the European Community (economic co-operation – the old EEC); the European Atomic Energy Community (EURATOM); the European Coal and Steel Community (ECSC); and the Maastricht areas (new areas of co-operation such as political, foreign affairs, defence and conventions (for instance, on drugs)).

When referring to all of them, the correct legal reference is to the European Union, and the same is true when referring only to the Maastricht area of co-operation. Otherwise, the correct references are to the European Community or EURATOM or ECSC as the context requires.

The European Court of Justice has no automatic jurisdiction in the Maastricht areas and so rightly continues to call itself the Court of Justice of the European Communities, though confusingly the Council calls itself the Council of the European Union even when passing EC legislation! The Treaty of Amsterdam, which was agreed at the European Council in Amsterdam in June 1997 and which was incorporated into UK law by the European Communities (Amendment) Act 1998, has relevance to the legal system in that it extends the powers of the ECJ in regard to action by the Union on asylum and immigration and co-operation on police and judicial matters.

Those in business tend to use the term 'Union' at all times and there is no harm in this. Practising lawyers would no doubt feel that they had to be precise.

The obligation of the British Parliament on entry to the European Community was to ensure that Community law was paramount. The view of the European Court is that Community law overrides English law where the latter is inconsistent with it. Section 3 of the European Communities Act 1972 binds our courts to accept this principle and talks of applying the principles of Community law with the idea that it prevails. Section 2(4) of the 1972 Act states that a UK statute should be construed so as to be consistent with Community law. However, many authorities on constitutional law see this obligation as a dilemma in the sense that Community law cannot be paramount when like the rest of our law the 1972 Act is at the mercy of any future Act of Parliament which must, under the fundamental rule of our constitution, prevail over any pre-existing law whatsoever. In other words, Community law is paramount as the result of the European Communities Act 1972, which could be repealed by a future Act of Parliament. It would seem to be the duty of our courts to accept that repeal.

Delegated legislation

Many modern statutes require much detailed work to implement and operate them, and such details are not normally contained in the statute itself, but are filled in from some other source. For example, much of our social security legislation gives only the general provisions of a complex scheme of social benefits, and an immense number of detailed regulations have had to be made by civil servants in the name of, and under the authority of, the appropriate Minister. This method of legislating is increasingly common in the field of business law, where companies, insolvency and consumer statutes give a large number of powers to government ministers to make rules and orders to flesh out the statute. These regulations, when made in the approved manner, are just as much law as the parent statute itself. This form of law is known as delegated or subordinate legislation.

The major difference between an Act of Parliament and delegated legislation is that the courts can declare the latter to be invalid and inapplicable because it was made beyond the powers given in the parent statute and/or the proper procedures were not followed in its enactment as where consultation required by the parent statute was not carried out (see further Chapter 6).

Custom

In early times custom was taken by the judges and turned into the common law of England, and it is still possible, even today, to argue the existence of a local or trade custom before the courts. Local customs consist in the main of customary rights vested in the inhabitants of a particular place to use, for various purposes, land held in the private ownership of another: for example, to take water from a spring (*Race* v *Ward* (1855) 24 LJQB 153) and for fishermen to dry their nets on private land (*Mercer* v *Denne* [1905] 2 Ch 538). A local custom can also affect the terms of a contract as is illustrated by *Hutton* v *Warren*, 1836 (see Chapter 14). As a present-day source of law, however, custom is of little importance.

The law merchant

Mercantile law, or *lex mercatoria*, is based upon mercantile customs and usages, and was developed separately from the common law. The Royal Courts did not have a monopoly of the administration of justice and certain local courts continued to hear cases long after the Royal Courts were established. One notable area was that involving mercantile and maritime disputes. Disputes between merchants, local and foreign, which arose at the fairs where most important commercial business was transacted in the fourteenth century, were tried in the courts of the fair or borough, and were known as 'courts of pie powder' (*pieds poudrés*) after the dusty feet of the traders who used them.

These courts were presided over by the mayor or his deputy or, if the fair was held as part of a private franchise, the steward appointed by the franchise holder. The rules applied were the rules of the European law merchant developed over the years from the customary practices of merchants and the jury was often made up of merchants. The fair or borough courts were supplemented for a time by 'Staple Courts' which sat in the staple towns. These towns, which were designated by Edward III (1327–77) as the exclusive centres of trade for such commodities as wine, wool, leather and tin, were required to hold courts to decide the trading disputes of merchants and again the customary practices of merchants were used.

Maritime disputes were heard by maritime courts sitting in major ports such as Bristol. These, too, applied a special European customary law developed from the customary practices of seamen.

The common law courts were slow to show an interest in dealing with commercial matters. In part this was due to the idea that their jurisdiction had a geographical limit and was restricted to matters which had arisen in England between English citizens. Foreign matters, and many of these commercial disputes did involve either a foreign merchant or a contract made or to be performed abroad, were left to some other body, especially if it could raise questions about the relations between the King and foreign sovereigns where the King's Council might be a more appropriate body. To some extent also it was due to the fact that the common law courts and the common law had come into existence at a time when land was the most important commodity and the procedures and concerns of the common law courts were adapted to problems arising from disputes about the possession and ownership of land. They were formal, slow and ill-adapted to the needs of merchants who required a speedier justice administered according to rules with which they were familiar.

When the Court of Admiralty developed, it took over much of the work of the merchants' courts, but from the seventeenth century onwards the common law courts began to acquire the commercial work, and many rules of the law merchant were incorporated into the common law. This was achieved partly by fiction. For example, to get over the fact that technically it still lacked jurisdiction over matters arising abroad the Court accepted allegations that something that had occurred abroad had in fact occurred in England within its jurisdiction, e.g. by using the fiction that Bordeaux was in Cheapside.

Lord Mansfield and Lord Holt played a great part in this development, in particular by recognising the main mercantile customs in the common law courts without requiring proof of them on every occasion. Perhaps the most important mercantile customs recognised were that a bill of exchange was negotiable and that mere agreements should be binding as contracts. In this way the custom of merchants relating to negotiable instruments and contracts including the sale of goods became part of the common law, and later, by codification, of statute law in the Bills of Exchange Act 1882, and the Sale of Goods Act 1979.

International conventions

Where the UK has signed up to an international convention, the convention really represents the customary consensus of the states signing up to it in terms of rulings to be given on certain matters such as the carriage of persons and goods by sea and air. These conventions become part of UK law and the common law cannot override them. An example is provided by *Sidhu* v *British Airways plc* [1997] AC 430. The claimants sued the airline for damages at common law for breach of contract and negligence following delays in their flight when the plane they were on landed in Kuwait and the delays arose out of arrests made by the authorities of themselves and other passengers. The House of Lords, in the eventual appeal, rejected their claim. The matter was governed by the Warsaw Convention on International Carriage by Air 1929 which the UK had signed up to and under which only two years were allowed for a claim against the six years allowed by the common law. The claimants were out of time under the Convention.

Canon law

A brief mention should be made of the ecclesiastical or church courts since prior to 1857 they dealt not only with offences against church doctrine and morality but also with other matters such as matrimonial causes, legitimacy and the inheritance of property when a person died. Many of the rules laid down by these courts were derived from Roman law and were inherited by the civil courts to which these matters were eventually transferred. In 1970 the civil courts concerned were amalgamated into the Family Division of the High Court (see Chapter 2).

The present position is that the church courts remain to deal with certain matters, e.g. decoration, alteration and use of churches.

Since disciplinary hearings against clergy receive more publicity these days, it is worth noting that the church courts only heard disciplinary matters where the clergy involved were incumbents, i.e. those appointed to livings within the Church of England. Those who hold appointments as priest-in-charge were not covered by these procedures but are subject to a disciplinary hearing before a Bishop under what are called the Canons of the Church of England. There has been reform also even in regard to disciplinary matters affecting incumbents where the Consistory Courts (see below) are replaced by a system of clerical tribunals on the lines of those existing for doctors and lawyers, i.e. domestic tribunals (see p 78).

The court of first instance is that of the diocesan chancellor, called a Consistory Court. He must be a member of the Church of England and is usually a practising barrister. Appeal lies from him to the Court of Arches in the province of Canterbury, and to the Chancery Court of York in the northern province. On matters concerning conduct, there is a further appeal to the Judicial Committee of the Privy Council and on other matters, e.g. the suitability of a Henry Moore altar in a Wren church (*Re St Stephen Walbrook* [1987] 2 All ER 578), there may be an appeal to the Court of Ecclesiastical Cases Reserved. The church courts are not courts of common law and the prerogative orders (see Chapter 3) – which operate as a valuable check on the abuse of power by other courts and tribunals – do not apply to them.

Legal treatises

One last source remains to be considered – namely, legal treatises. Throughout the centuries great English jurists have written books, some in the nature of legal textbooks, which have helped to shape the law and inform the legal profession.

We have already mentioned Bracton whose *Treatise on the Laws and Customs of England* was written in the thirteenth century and was probably based on the decisions of Martin de Pateshull, who was Archdeacon of Norfolk, Dean of St Paul's and an Itinerant Justice from 1217 to 1229, and on those of William de Raleigh who was the Rector of Bratton Fleming in Devon and an Itinerant Justice from 1228 to 1250.

Sir Edward Coke, who lived from 1552 to 1634, is a celebrated name. His *Institutes* covered many aspects of law. For example, his *First Institute*, published in 1628, was concerned with land law. His *Second Institute*, published in 1642, was concerned with the principal statutes. The *Third Institute*, published in 1644, dealt with criminal law, while the *Fourth Institute*, also published in 1644, was concerned with the jurisdiction and history of the courts, this work containing bitter attacks on the Court of Chancery. Although at first sight 'Institute' may seem an odd word to use to describe a legal text, it is derived from the Latin *Institutio* which means 'instruct, arrange, make order of'.

During his lifetime Coke occupied the offices of Recorder of London, Solicitor-General, Speaker of the House of Commons, Attorney-General and finally Chief Justice of Common Pleas.

Sir William Blackstone, who lived from 1723 to 1780, published his *Commentaries on the Laws of England* in 1765. These are concerned with various aspects of law and are based on his lectures at Oxford. He was a Judge of the Common Pleas and was also the first Professor of English Law to be appointed in any English university.

In addition to older treatises such as those mentioned above, the works of modern writers, sufficiently eminent in the profession, are sometimes quoted when novel points of law are being argued in the courts.

Boys v *Blenkinsop*, 1968 – Textbooks as a source of law (**5**)

THE COURTS OF LAW

The Royal Courts of Westminster developed out of the *Curia Regis* (or the King's Council). The Court of Exchequer was the first court to emerge from the *Curia Regis* and dealt initially with disputes connected with royal revenues. The Court of Common Pleas was set up in the time of Henry II to hear disputes between the King's subjects. The Court of King's Bench was last to emerge and initially was closely associated with the King himself, hearing disputes between subjects and the King.

As the system developed the Court of Chancery was added and there was also a Court of Admiralty. The Court of Probate and the Divorce Court developed from the old ecclesiastical courts which formerly dealt with these matters. Each of these courts had its own jurisdiction, sometimes overlapping and sometimes conflicting. This was particularly true with regard to the common law courts and the Court of Chancery. For example, in *Knight* v *Marquis of Waterford* (1844) 11 Cl & Fin 653 the appellant was told by the House of Lords, after 14 years of litigation in equity, that he had a good case but must begin his action again in a common law court. It is useful to refer at this point to *Wood* v *Scarth* (1858) (see Chapter 12). This case is a further illustration of the delays which resulted from the administration of law and equity in separate courts. Anyway, this was how the English legal system entered the nineteenth century and it was this inheritance that the Victorians set out to rationalise into the form with which we are familiar.

The Supreme Court of Judicature

In order to rationalise the system, the Supreme Court of Judicature was established. Under the Judicature Acts 1873–75 the High Court was divided into five divisions: Queen's Bench, Common Pleas, Exchequer, Chancery, and Probate, Divorce and Admiralty, the number being reduced to three by an Order in Council in 1881 when the Common Pleas and Exchequer Divisions were merged into the Queen's Bench Division. The Court of Appeal was given jurisdiction over appeals.

The House of Lords

The House of Lords was not included in the Supreme Court of Judicature by the Judicature Acts because of Parliament's opposition to its then hereditary character. Its jurisdiction as a final court of appeal was established by the Appellate Jurisdiction Act 1876 which also provided the House with trained judges, i.e. Life Peers with legal training. The Judicature Acts 1873–75 were consolidated in the Supreme Court of Judicature (Consolidation) Act 1925.

This Act is now repealed by the Supreme Court Act of 1981, s 1, reaffirming the previous position by providing that the Supreme Court of England and Wales shall consist of the Court of Appeal, the High Court of Justice and the Crown Court, and that the Lord Chancellor shall be the President of the Supreme Court. The Employment Appeal Tribunal is not included, even though it is staffed in part by High Court judges and appeals lie to the Court of Appeal.

The above material will be significantly altered when the relevant sections and Schedules of the Constitutional Reform Act 2005 are brought into force. The reason is that the House of Lords is renamed by that Act as the Supreme Court so that the present sets of courts currently forming the Supreme Court cannot continue under this nomenclature. They will remain as now but be retitled the Senior Courts of England and Wales. These moves cannot be made until 2009 because the new Supreme Court has no place in which to conduct its hearings. The Middlesex Guildhall in Parliament Square has been chosen but needs refurbishment, which is scheduled to be completed by 2009.

It is also worth noting that, as the CRA 2005 comes into force, the Supreme Court Act 1981 will be renamed as the Senior Courts Act 1981.

The courts today

In recent times far-reaching changes have been made in the structure and jurisdiction of the civil and criminal courts by various reforming statutes. The present system of courts exercising both civil and criminal jurisdiction is set out in Figures 2.1 and 2.2 respectively and the main routes of appeal indicated.

Administration of the courts

Under s 1 of the Courts Act 2003, the Lord Chancellor is under a statutory duty to secure an efficient and effective administration system and other services such as enforcement services to support the current Supreme Court of England and Wales (i.e. the Court of Appeal, the three Divisions of the High Court and the Crown Court) and also the county courts and magistrates' courts business. The Lord Chancellor chose an executive agency called Her Majesty's Courts Service, which began operating in April 2005. The new system brings all the courts in the current Supreme Court and the county courts and magistrates' courts under one administrative roof.

It is worth noting again that s 59 of the Constitutional Reform Act 2005 (CRA 2005) will, as it comes into force, rename the current Supreme Court of England and Wales as the Senior Courts of England and Wales, the House of Lords being then replaced by the Supreme Court of England and Wales, with the current Law Lords constituting its judiciary (but as new appointments are made this link will not continue).

Section 1 of the Courts Act 2003 continues in force but the statutory duty referred to will, as the CRA 2005 comes into force, rest upon the Secretary of State for Constitutional Affairs in consultation with the Lord Chief Justice, who becomes the head of the judiciary.

Magistrates' courts

Although, as we shall see, the Crown Court tries the most serious criminal cases (all those in fact which are tried on indictment with a jury), the great bulk of the criminal work of the country is performed in the magistrates' courts.

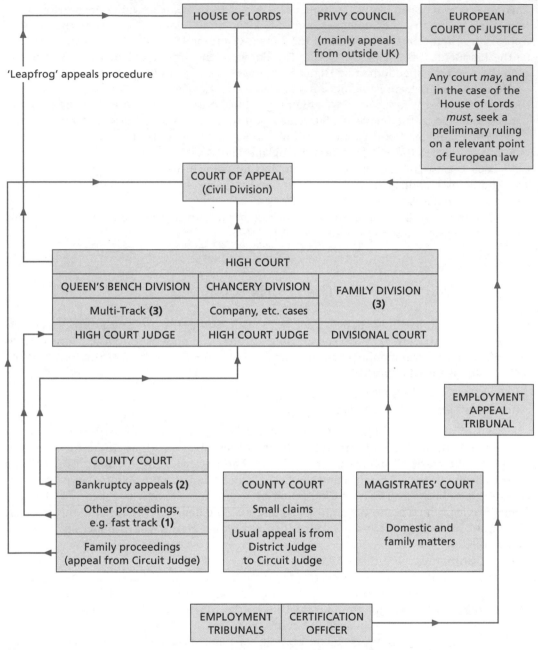

Figure 2.1 System of courts currently exercising civil jurisdiction

Notes

1 If heard by a circuit judge.

2 If heard by a district or circuit judge.

3 If heard by a High Court judge.

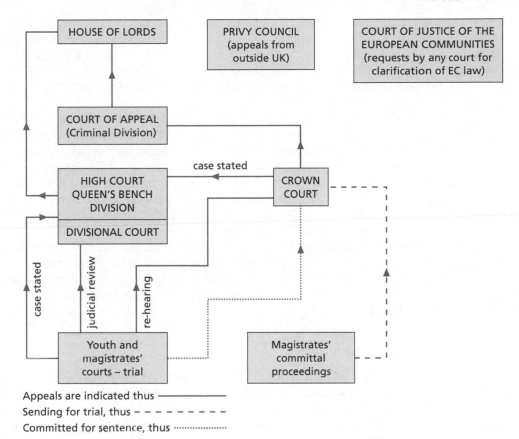

Figure 2.2 System of courts currently exercising criminal jurisdiction

Types of magistrates

Magistrates may be of several kinds as follows:

(a) Lay magistrates. These are appointed by the Lord Chancellor on behalf of, and in the name of, the Queen under s 10 of the Courts Act 2003. The Lord Chancellor is required to assign each lay justice to one or more local areas. The Lord Chancellor is currently empowered to make rules regarding the training of magistrates.

Under the CRA 2005, as it comes into force, s 10 of the Courts Act 2003 will continue but the assignment of lay justices becomes a matter for the Lord Chief Justice after consultation with the Lord Chancellor. It is important here to note that s 19 of the CRA 2005 allows the Lord Chancellor by Order to divest himself of functions to another person. Therefore, as the CRA 2005 comes into force, the functions of the Lord Chancellor will be transferred. There are the following options according to Orders made: to transfer mainly to the Lord Chief Justice with the right of consultation with the Lord Chancellor retained; to transfer to the Lord Chief Justice with consultation rights in the Secretary of State; or abolition in favour of the Lord Chief Justice.

(b) District judges (magistrates' courts) and deputy district judges (magistrates' courts). These are full-time magistrates who sit in various areas of the country. They were formerly called stipendiary magistrates. The area to which an appointment is made is entirely a matter for the Lord Chief Justice. From 6 April 2006 they are appointed by the Queen on the recommendation of the Lord Chief Justice and must have a seven-year general advocacy qualification within the meaning of s 71 of the Courts and Legal Services Act 1990. Appointments have been made, e.g. in the West Midlands, Greater Manchester, Merseyside and in London – in courts such as Bow Street and Tower Bridge. There was a limit on these appointments but this was removed by the Access to Justice Act 1999 with, perhaps, the object of making more appointments in order to reduce the number of courts staffed by lay magistrates.

The Justices of the Peace Act 1997 established a national bench of district judges (magistrates' courts). The authority for appointment is now s 22 of the Courts Act 2003. The national bench is lead by the Senior District Judge (or Chief Magistrate). A district judge is assigned to a local justice area but may be directed by the Department for Constitutional Affairs through the senior district judge to sit in any court in England and Wales as required. A main difference between a district judge (magistrates' court) and a lay justice is that the district judge sits alone in criminal cases. District judges (magistrates' courts) can exercise the jurisdiction of the Crown Court (s 65 Courts Act 2003).

The Judicial Studies Board undertakes the training of district judges and gives initial and continuing training. Some district judges (magistrates' courts) may be designated by the senior district judge to deal with certain kinds of specialist work, such as youth court cases, extradition and applications for further detention under terrorism legislation. The judges are addressed as 'Sir' or 'Madam'.

Justices' clerks and legal advisers

Section 27 of the Courts Act 2003 (as amended by Sch 4 to the CRA 2005) provides for a justices' clerk and assistant justices' clerks in magistrates' courts. These individuals must have had a right of audience in relation to all proceedings in a magistrates' court for five years, or be a barrister or solicitor who has served for not less than five years as an assistant to a justices' clerk or has previously been a justices' clerk.

The justices' clerk manages a team of advisers who may be engaged by contract under s 2(4) of the Courts Act 2003. Powers are delegated to the legal advisers to give legal advice to magistrates: assistant clerks may also be engaged by contract under s 2(4). Most of the advisers are barristers or solicitors. Magistrates are not bound to accept the advice given. However, it is accepted practice that they should do so, otherwise the proceedings may be appealed.

Legal advice should be given in open court. Advice given in the justices' retiring room which has not been discussed in open court is given on a provisional basis only. The advice should be repeated in open court so that the parties may make representations.

There has in the past been much case law relating to situations where clerks have given legal advice in the retiring room and not in open court and on appeal the court has said that, in the absence of any indication or suspicion that the clerk had taken part in making the decision, the conviction must stand. However, it is doubtful whether such convictions would now be allowed to stand. The Human Rights Act 1998 has impacted on this area and transparency of communications between magistrates and their clerks and advisers is stressed in current Practice Directions, which are rules governing particular aspects of court procedure. Certainly, consultations out of court must be limited so that Art 6 of the European Convention on Human Rights (the right to a fair trial) is observed.

Justices' clerks can perform duties that are authorised to be done before one magistrate. These include issue of summons, allowing adjournment of trials where the parties agree, and granting criminal defence representation orders. A justices' clerk may delegate these functions to a legal adviser. This means that the clerk or adviser can consider the above matters while the magistrates deal with other matters.

Administration of magistrates' courts

The Courts Act 2003 unifies the Supreme Court *as it is currently constituted*, the county courts and the magistrates' courts into one system called Her Majesty's Court Service. The same Act makes provision for the practice and procedure in those courts and for accommodation for the court house and offices and staff. An important provision of the 2003 Act is to set up Courts Boards to be concerned with Crown Courts, county courts and magistrates' courts based on police authority areas. The members of these Boards are:

- a judge, e.g. a district or circuit judge;
- two lay justices from the area of the Board;
- at least two members being persons who have knowledge and experience of the work of courts in the area of the Board;
- at least two members who are representative of people living in the area of the Board.

The Board will keep under review the suitability or otherwise of the provision being made for local justice and consider, for example, the reallocation of court houses.

Section 6 of the Courts Act 2003 abolishes the former magistrates' courts, committees which used to carry out administrative functions.

Classification of criminal offences

Before discussing the powers of magistrates in regard to criminal prosecutions, it is necessary to classify criminal offences for procedural purposes. Proceedings are regulated by the Magistrates' Courts Act 1980 in the main. Criminal jurisdiction falls into three classes of offence listed in the Criminal Law Act 1977 (as amended) as:

(*a*) offences triable only on indictment before a judge and jury;
(*b*) offences triable only summarily by the magistrates;
(*c*) offences triable either way.

Some examples

Examples of crimes which fall into the relevant categories appear below.

Offences triable only summarily
- driving without insurance;
- careless or inconsiderate driving;
- speeding;
- being drunk and disorderly in a public place.

Offences triable either way
- theft;
- burglary without violence or threat to a person;
- aggravated vehicle taking (this occurs, e.g. where after the taking a person is injured by the driving);
- assault occasioning actual bodily harm;
- dangerous driving.

Offences triable only on indictment
- murder and manslaughter;
- robbery, which involves a taking by force;
- rape.

The nature of proceedings

Summary offences are tried only in a magistrates' court. Offences triable either way may be tried by magistrates (see below). Indictable only charges cannot be dealt with at a magistrates' court and are sent to the Crown Court under s 51 of the Crime and Disorder Act 1998. By reason of s 41 of and Sch 3 to the Criminal Justice Act 2003 as it comes into force, committal proceedings which are used to send charges of either way offences to the Crown Court will be abolished so that all indictable and either way cases that have been allocated for Crown Court trial will be sent to the Crown Court under amendments to s 51 of the Crime and Disorder Act 1998.

Sending for trial

Where an adult defendant is brought before the magistrates charged with an indictable-only offence, the magistrates must send him forthwith for trial in the Crown Court. The magistrates' functions are only to determine whether what is charged is an indictable-only offence and to consider legal aid. The court will set the time for the first hearing in the Crown Court and will remand the defendant in custody or on bail to appear at the Crown Court. These proceedings can be heard by one magistrate.

A juvenile offender (i.e. a person under the age of 18) is not liable to be sent to the Crown Court for an indictable-only offence unless he is charged for that offence jointly with an adult, when he or she may be sent with the adult to the Crown Court if the magistrates think that it is in the interests of justice that he or she should be tried jointly with the adult.

The juvenile offender hearing should be before two or more magistrates and a Crown prosecutor must be present. The hearing will normally take place at the next available sitting of the court after the defendant has been charged.

Offence triable either way

These offences can be tried either in a magistrates' court or in the Crown Court before a judge and jury. Of major importance here is the requirement to have disclosure of the prosecution's case to the defendant. Rule 21 of the Criminal Procedure Rules applies. The 2005 Rules require the prosecution to supply a written statement containing the facts and matters which the prosecutor proposes to bring in as evidence during the proceedings. This includes evidence by video. All of this is to assist the defendant and his advisers with a decision as to the mode of trial or whether to plead guilty or not guilty. There are the following possibilities at the hearing:

- the magistrates may decide that the case is not suitable for summary trial. The defendant then has no choice and the case will be adjourned to a future date so that committal proceedings may take place. In reaching their decision, the main considerations will be whether, were there to be a conviction, the sentencing powers of the court would be adequate. If not, the magistrates will not accept the case but will send it to the Crown Court;
- if the magistrates are prepared to hear the case, the defendant must make his decision:
  - if he consents to be tried by magistrates and pleads guilty, his case will be dealt with immediately;
  - if he consents to be tried by magistrates and pleads not guilty, the case will be adjourned to a later date for trial;
  - if he asks for a trial in the Crown Court, he will not be asked to plead and there will be an adjournment to a later date for committal proceedings to take place. The defendant cannot be denied a jury trial.

Summary trial

Disclosure by prosecution and defence

As regards the prosecution, the Criminal Procedure and Investigations Act 1996 applies. Disclosure applies where the defendant pleads not guilty and the court proceeds to summary trial. The defence is not entitled to disclosure where the defendant has pleaded guilty. The prosecution must disclose any prosecution material which has not previously been disclosed and which might reasonably be considered capable of undermining the case for the prosecution or assist the case for the defence.

There is also a duty under the Criminal Procedure and Investigations Act 1996 for the prosecution to make available to the defence *any unused material* relating to the case on which it does not intend to rely. This applies where there is a not guilty plea. If there is no such material, the prosecution should confirm in writing that this is so. This could include, e.g. material casting doubt on a confession or the reliability of a witness. Where the prosecution has made the above primary disclosure, the defence may in a not guilty plea give a defence statement setting out in general terms the defence and disclosure of details of any alibi. The defendant is not required to make this statement but if he does so, the prosecution is required to make further disclosure of relevant and undisclosed prosecution material, e.g. in the light of the defence. The prosecution has a continuing duty of disclosure until the defendant is convicted or acquitted. It should be noted that the right to a fair trial as set out in the European Convention on Human Rights reinforces the need for maximum disclosure by the prosecution.

Further details of the trial procedure appear in Chapter 4, but it is enough here to note that the magistrates' verdict is by a majority and if the defendant is found guilty, the magistrates will proceed to sentence. An outline of the available sentences is also given in Chapter 4.

Committal proceedings

Offences which are triable either way and not tried by the magistrates as described above are currently the subject of committal proceedings before a magistrates' court. The purpose of these proceedings is to decide whether there is a case for the defendant to answer in the Crown Court.

As already noted, under s 41 of and Sch 3 to the Criminal Justice Act 2003, as they come into force, committal proceedings for either way cases allocated for trial in the Crown Court will be *sent for trial* in the Crown Court in line with the current procedure for indictable offences and committal proceedings will be abolished. (See further p 26.)

Types of committal proceedings

There are two types of committal proceedings as follows:

- committal without consideration of the evidence under s 6(2) of the Magistrates' Courts Act 1980; and
- committal with consideration of the evidence under the Magistrates' Courts Act 1980, s 6(1).

Section 6(2) committals

The prosecution can offer the defence a committal without consideration of the evidence. This is made in almost all cases usually by letter. The prosecution will serve the relevant bundle of prosecution documents on the defence and the defence solicitor will consider with his client what they contain. In most cases the defence will accept the prosecution's offer, though it may request a contested committal on the grounds that there is no case to answer that could be put to a jury. In s 6(2) committals the magistrates' function is mainly administrative and the proceedings will take only a few minutes since the magistrates do not at any stage read the evidence which is in the prosecution statements. The defendant is committed for trial to the Crown Court and a date is set for the first hearing in the Crown Court. Legal aid and bail will also be dealt with.

Section 6(1) committals

In these cases the evidence for the prosecution is either read out aloud at the hearing or, if the court directs, it will be orally summarised. At the end of the case for the prosecution the defence may submit that there is no case to answer, e.g. that the case against the defendant is so unreliable that a jury could not convict the defendant on it. If no submission is made or if, being made, it is rejected, the magistrates will commit the defendant for trial in the Crown Court. If, in the very unlikely event that the magistrates decide that there is no case to answer, they will discharge the defendant. Where the defendant is committed for trial, a date will be set for the first hearing in the Crown Court and the matter of legal aid and bail will be considered.

It should be noted that if the prosecution requires a committal with consideration of evidence, the defence has no choice and must accept, but since the prosecution can no longer use such proceedings to test its own witnesses by requiring them to give oral evidence, it is very unlikely to require a s 6(1) committal.

Effect of the Criminal Justice Act 2003

Before considering the substantial changes that will be made by the Criminal Justice Act 2003 as it comes into force, it should be borne in mind that s 41 and Sch 3, which carry the changes, are not yet in force, although it is over three years since Royal Assent. Therefore, at the present time the material referred to above is the procedure that is followed. When the relevant parts of the 2003 Act are in force, the material set out below will take the place of the above material in terms of the trial of each way offences. The rules under which the magistrates send for trial in the Crown Court forthwith in indictable offences will be covered by the CJA 2003 procedures but these will be substantially the same as those applying at present. The trial of each way offences will change significantly. The purpose of the changes is to encourage defendants to accept the opinion of the magistrates that the case is more suitable for summary trial and to achieve that result by minimising uncertainties about the sentence.

Committal proceedings as described above will be overtaken by the CJA 2003 provisions and the current expression of 'committal for trial' in the Crown Court will become 'sending for trial' in the Crown Court.

Allocation and transfer of offences triable either way

Section 41 of the Criminal Justice Act 2003 introduces Sch 3 of the Act and deals with the allocation of offences triable either way and transfer of cases to the Crown Court. The magistrates must decide whether cases triable either way should be tried summarily or on indictment. The provisions are aimed at ensuring that only cases that need to go to the Crown Court are sent there. Paragraphs 5 and 6 of Sch 3 deal with the preliminary stages of an either-way case including the defendant's plea before venue and allocation of the case. A single justice may hear the plea, *called a plea before venue*, but cannot conduct a contested case following a plea of not guilty. He or she may hear a guilty plea but cannot impose sentence on the defendant.

Paragraph 5 enacts a new s 19 of the Magistrates' Courts Act 1980 to provide the procedure to be followed by magistrates when deciding whether a case triable either-way where the defendant has not entered a guilty plea should be tried summarily or on indictment.

The new procedure differs from the former procedure in that the magistrates must be informed about and take account of previous convictions of the defendant in assessing whether the sentencing powers available to magistrates are adequate. The court must have regard not only (as before) to representations made by the prosecution or defence but also to allocation guidelines that may be issued by the Sentencing Guidelines Council under s 170 of the 2003 Act (see further Chapter 4). *These new procedures are referred to as allocation procedures.*

Cases suitable for allocation for summary trial

Paragraph 6 of Sch 3 substitutes a new s 20 of the Magistrates' Courts Act 1980 which sets out a procedure to be followed by magistrates when they decide that a case is suitable for summary trial. This is as follows:

- defendants will be told that they can consent to be tried summarily or if they wish on indictment;
- when making that decision defendants (and their advisers) are likely to be influenced by the knowledge that it is not possible for the magistrates to commit them to the Crown Court for sentence. Once the magistrates have accepted jurisdiction to try summarily, they cannot give a sentence beyond their powers. Under s 154 of the CJA 2003, as it comes into force, the magistrates can impose custodial sentences of up to and including 12 months in regard to any one offence and up to 65 weeks in regard to two or more offences to be served consecutively. The current provisions appear on p 28. Clause 139 gave the Secretary of State power to increase these limits by order up to 18 months in regard to any one offence and 24 months in regard to two offences to be served consecutively. *This clause was not enacted.*
- defendants have the opportunity to request an indication from the magistrates whether, if they plead guilty at that point, the sentence would be custodial or not;
- the magistrates have a discretion whether or not to give an indication. Where an indication is given, defendants may reconsider their plea;
- where a defendant then decides to plead guilty, the magistrates will proceed to sentence. A custodial sentence will only be available if such a sentence was indicated, and if so, the magistrates will not have the option of committal to the Crown Court for sentence;
- where the defendant declines to reconsider his plea indication or where the magistrates do not give a sentence indication, the defendant has the choice of accepting summary trial or electing for trial on indictment;
- where an indication of sentence is given and the defendant does not plead guilty because of it, the sentence indication is not binding on the magistrates who later proceed to summary trial or on the Crown Court if the defendant elects for trial on indictment.

Cases suitable for trial on indictment

Paragraph 7 amends s 21 of the Magistrates' Courts Act 1980. Under this amendment, where the magistrates decide that a trial on indictment would be more suitable, they will proceed forthwith to send the case for trial in the Crown Court under s 51(1) of the Crime and Disorder Act 1998 (see below).

There is currently no power for magistrates, having started to hear a case summarily, to switch to committal proceedings. There is a new power in the CJA 2003 for the prosecution to apply for an either-way case that has been allocated for summary trial to be tried on indictment instead.

Sending for trial procedure

Amendments effected by the Criminal Justice Act 2003

The sending for trial procedure will apply to either-way cases allocated for trial on indictment. Furthermore, committal of defendants by the magistrates to the Crown Court will no longer be available where the magistrates have accepted jurisdiction in an either-way offence whether as a contested case or guilty plea. Where a guilty plea has been indicated at plea before venue as distinct from at allocation and the magistrates deal with the case summarily, *the power to commit to the Crown Court for sentence will be available to the magistrates.*

Disclosure in criminal cases to assist trial management

Part 5 of the Criminal Justice Act 2003 amends the provisions of the Criminal Procedure and Investigations Act 1996 which govern disclosure of material. These provisions are now substantially in force, with some exceptions, and are included in the disclosure material in this Chapter (see p 25). They are now part of the 1996 Act, which is the authority for them.

The duty solicitor

The duty solicitor scheme is concerned to provide an emergency service to defendants appearing in magistrates' courts who might otherwise be unrepresented. Representation is free. A duty solicitor can make bail applications, apply for adjournments and present pleas in mitigation. Duty solicitor schemes are staffed by local solicitors in practice who are paid hourly rates from the Legal Aid Fund.

Magistrates – sentencing powers

Unless there is a lower maximum for a given offence, the magistrates may only impose a custodial sentence on an adult of up to six months unless that adult is convicted of two or more either-way offences. In such a case the maximum becomes 12 months. The minimum sentence is five days, although there is a power to impose detention for one day as a sentence or for non-payment of a fine (see s 135 of the Magistrates' Courts Act 1980). The common practice is to express the sentence in months, but when the provisions of the CJA 2003 come into force (see below), a sentence will have to be expressed in weeks. The maximum fine that can be imposed generally is £5,000. However, in certain cases, for example, under s 35 of the Food Safety Act 1990 for the offence of selling food not of the nature or substance or quality demanded, the maximum custodial sentence is six months but the maximum fine is £20,000.

For individuals under 18, the maximum fine is £1,000 and for those under the age of 14 it is £250.

In addition, it should be noted that if the magistrates are trying an either-way offence summarily and feel that the circumstances are such that the defendant should be given a greater sentence than can be given in a magistrates' court, they may transfer the defendant to the Crown Court for sentence under s 38 of the Magistrates' Courts Act 1980. Further details are given at the sentencing section which appears in Chapter 4.

The Criminal Justice Act 2003, as it comes into force, increases the magistrates' general sentencing powers from six months to 12 months in regard to any one offence and up to 65 weeks in regard to two or more offences to be served consecutively. The Secretary of State's power to increase these limits by order was not in the end enacted with the Act. It is felt that this increased sentencing power will encourage magistrates to retain and hear more either-way cases thus keeping them out of the Crown Court and within the cheaper regime of the magistrates' court.

Civil jurisdiction

The magistrates and civil debt

The magistrates have power to make an order, on complaint, for the payment of any money which is recoverable as a civil debt. On making the order the court may require immediate payment or give time for payment or allow payment by instalments. If payment is not made as required, the magistrates may issue a distress warrant under which the bailiff service may enter the debtor's premises and remove goods for sale in order to pay the debt.

Family proceedings

The magistrates also have a limited civil jurisdiction which includes what are known as family proceedings hearing applications for matrimonial relief, such as maintenance orders sought by women for themselves and/or children who do not initially opt for divorce on breakdown of marriage. They can also deal with questions regarding the custody of children, and so far as parents and other relatives are concerned, they can decide the place of residence of a child and rights of contact with him or her. There is also power to order a violent spouse to leave the home in order to protect the other spouse and children (if any). They may also consent to the marriage of a minor of 16 or 17 years of age who is not a widow or widower, where other relevant consents, e.g. those of parents, are not forthcoming. These family matters are dealt with in separate branches of the magistrates' court known as the family proceedings court and family panels (see the Children Act 1989, s 92 and Sch 11). The magistrates also deal with matters relating to the enforcement of the Council Tax and VAT. Where a foreign state wants an alleged criminal living in England and Wales to be returned, the request for extradition is heard under the provisions of ss 67 and 137 of the Extradition Act 2003 by a district judge (magistrates' court).

Appeals

Appeals from the magistrates in family proceedings are to the Divisional Court of the Family Division. As regards criminal offences, appeal may be to the Crown Court or to the High Court as follows:

(a) Crown Court. An appeal to the Crown Court may be made by the accused only, provided he did not plead guilty. The appeal may be against conviction or sentence on law or fact and no permission is required. If he pleaded guilty, he may appeal against sentence only. Appeals against conviction and/or sentence take the form of a re-hearing. Where the appeal is against conviction, all the evidence will be heard but, if it is against sentence the prosecution will outline the facts of the case to the court, which will decide what the appropriate sentence is after offering the defendant an opportunity to address the court in mitigation of sentence.

The Crown Court may confirm, reverse or vary the decision of the magistrates and can give any sentence which may be heavier or lighter than that given by the magistrates but it must be within the powers of the magistrates, e.g. in general a custodial sentence of up to six months or a fine of up to £5,000. Defendants should therefore be informed that an appeal to the Crown Court may result in the sentence being increased up to the maximum sentencing powers of the magistrates who first dealt with the case.

On appeal to the Crown Court the judge will sit with two magistrates who did not participate in the hearing in the magistrates' court.

(b) High Court. An appeal to the High Court may be made by either the accused or the prosecution by means of *case stated*. This means that the magistrates must set out in writing their findings of fact together with the arguments put forward by the parties and their decision and the reasons for it. The appeal questions the decision of the magistrates on the ground that it is wrong in *law* (Magistrates' Courts Act 1980, s 111). Issues of *fact* should not be appealed against by way of case stated (*James* v *Chief Constable of Kent, The Times*, 7 June 1986). It is available to a person who has pleaded guilty. The procedure for the appeal is not a re-hearing. The appeal is decided after hearing legal arguments put forward by the parties on the relevant points of law. If the lower court or the House of Lords (as the Constitutional Reform Act 2005 comes into force the Supreme Court) gives leave, there may be a further appeal to the House of Lords, (which will become the Supreme Court as the CRA 2005 comes into force) but the lower court must certify that the case raises a matter of law of public importance.

Proceedings by way of case stated by magistrates or the Crown Court are regulated by the Supreme Court Act 1981, s 28A (becomes the Supreme Courts Act 1981). The High Court is now given the task of dealing with case stated proceedings and is also given the necessary powers to amend the stated case and to make any final orders on the application. In particular, it may reverse, affirm or amend the decision of the magistrates and may order a rehearing. As regards the constitution of the High Court, for these appeals a case stated is heard by a Divisional Court of Queen's Bench and at least two judges must sit on the appeal. If their opinions are divided, the appeal fails (*Flannagan* v *Shaw* [1920] 3 KB 96).

(c) Judicial review. Whenever a court, including, obviously, a magistrates' court, acts without jurisdiction, or fails to observe the rules of natural justice (see further Chapter 3) or makes an important procedural error (as where there is inadequacy of disclosure of material to the defence) any person affected, and obviously a defendant, may apply to the High Court to review the decision of the magistrates and issue a quashing order, as it is called, to make ineffective the decision of the magistrates (see further Chapter 3). These types of defects in a magistrates' court must be challenged by judicial review and not by case stated (*R* v *Wandsworth Justices, ex parte Read* [1942] 1 All ER 56).

(d) The European Court. The magistrates may refer matters to the European Court. Thus, in *R* v *Marlborough Street Stipendiary Magistrate, ex parte Bouchereau* [1977] 3 All ER 365, the magistrate indicated that he proposed making a recommendation for the deportation of B, but it was said that the magistrate had no such power since B was a migrant worker protected by Article 39 (now 33) of the Treaty of Rome. The magistrate decided to refer the matter to the European Court under Article 234 (now 307) of the Treaty and this was held to be in order by a Divisional Court which decided also that legal aid legislation allows a magistrates' court to order legal aid for the purposes of proceedings before the European Court of Justice.

(e) Rectification of mistakes by the magistrates themselves. Section 142 of the Magistrates' Courts Act 1980 (as amended by s 26 of the Criminal Appeal Act 1995) provides an alternative to appeal to the Crown Court or High Court. The section gives magistrates the power to re-open a case to rectify their mistake, regardless of the plea made by the defendant at the relevant proceedings, but only if the defendant has been found guilty, not if he has been acquitted. The power may be used, e.g., to deal with a sentence passed in excess of the court's powers and also where the defendant asks for a review of his sentence on the grounds that it is too harsh. The prosecution or the defence may institute a review and it would seem that the magistrates may do so of their own volition. The magistrates may vary, rescind or replace a sentence imposed at the relevant proceedings.

An inspectorate

Part 5 of the Courts Act 2003 sets up an inspectorate known as Her Majesty's Inspectorate of Courts Administration. The inspectorate has power to inspect the system that supports the carrying on of the business of all magistrates' courts, county courts and the Crown Court.

Youth courts

The magistrates also have a part to play in regard to children over 10 but under 14 and young persons who are 14 or over but have not attained the age of 18. Criminal proceedings cannot generally be brought against a person under the age of 10. For this purpose the magistrates sit as a youth court. This court must sit in a different building or room from that in which other courts are held or else must sit on a different day. The court consists of not more than three magistrates who are drawn from a special panel of persons who need no longer be under 65 years of age and it is usual for one or more female magistrates to be present. The public is excluded from these courts and there are strict controls on press reports. In particular, the restrictions relate to not identifying the defendant and this may also be applied to other juveniles concerned in the case, e.g. witnesses. The court also has power to order the juvenile's parent or guardian to attend. This applies also in the adult court and the Crown Court where relevant. Youth courts have a range of sentences at their disposal including custodial measures (see further Chapter 4). In general defendants under the age of 18 must be dealt with in a youth court (but see further p 136).

The county court

The magistrates' courts deal with most of the less serious criminal matters in this country. At something like the same level, but dealing exclusively with civil cases, is the county court. County courts were created by the County Courts Act 1846, to operate as the chief lower courts for the trial of civil disputes, and a large number of cases are heard in these courts annually. They are now governed by the County Courts Act 1984. Section references are to that Act unless otherwise stated.

A county court is presided over by a circuit judge. The judge usually sits alone, though, under ss 66 and 67, there is provision for a trial by a jury of eight persons in some cases, e.g. where fraud, libel, slander, malicious prosecution or false imprisonment is alleged. The judge is assisted by a district judge who acts as clerk of the court and may try certain cases. A district judge may try:

- claims with a financial value of not more than £5,000 (or a larger sum if all parties consent to allocation to what is known as the small claims track);
- matters relating to attachment of earnings orders so that a creditor with a judgment may receive payment directly from the debtor's employer through the payroll;
- matters relating to the appointment of receivers so that a judgment creditor can collect rents from the debtor's tenants;
- the conduct of case management conferences in multi-track cases;
- the approval of settlements out of court for minors and mental patient claimants;
- undefended cases.

Cases where the claim is not for a set amount (i.e. an unliquidated sum), as in a claim for damages for the tort of nuisance (see further Chapter 21), where, unless the claimant states in his particulars of claim that the amount is likely to exceed £5,000, it will be regarded as worth less than that amount and will normally be allocated to a district judge for decision. There is a right of appeal to a circuit judge from the decision of a district judge.

Assistant district judges may be appointed for carrying out the work of the court. Deputy district judges may also be appointed as a temporary measure to dispose of business in the county court. An assistant district judge and a deputy district judge have the same powers as the district judge. District judges, assistant district judges and deputy district judges are appointed from persons who have a seven-year general advocacy qualification within the meaning of the Courts and Legal Services Act 1990. (See ss 6–9 of the 1984 Act (as amended by the Courts and Legal Services Act 1990).)

Jurisdiction

Generally

Under s 15(1), the county court has a virtually unlimited jurisdiction in most contract and tort cases. There are some exceptions including, most importantly, cases of libel and slander unless such cases are commenced in the county court by consent of the parties or having been commenced in the High Court a particular case is transferred to a county court from the High Court under s 15(2). In contrast to the above common law jurisdiction, the equity juris-diction of the county court, e.g. in regard to matters concerning mortgages, has remained at a maximum of £30,000 for many years.

Proceedings for a specified or unspecified sum of money in regard to a claim which does not include a claim for death or personal injury must be commenced in the county court unless the value of the claim is *more* than £15,000. It is likely to be tried there, though the High Court would also have jurisdiction in respect of it. The procedure regarding the alloca-tion of cases is dealt with in Chapter 5. However, the claimant's solicitor knows at least that the claim must commence in the county court.

If the proceedings include a claim for death or personal injury, a claim for *less* than £50,000 must be commenced in the county court though, again, the High Court would also have jurisdiction and allocation will decide ultimately in terms of where the trial takes place. There is an exception in regard to medical claims which includes claims in respect of dental and nursing treatment. Such proceedings can be brought in the High Court even if the claim is less than £50,000. *There is thus a remaining distinction between the High Court and the county court which is that claims should not be brought in the High Court unless the above limits are exceeded.*

Human rights jurisdiction

The county court has no jurisdiction to hear applications that Acts of Parliament or statutory instruments are incompatible with the Convention on Human Rights (s 3 of the Human Rights Act 1998) (see further Chapter 3), and transfer to the High Court would be required if such a point arose in a county court case. County courts do have jurisdiction in other human rights cases such as proceedings against education authorities and the police.

Choice of court

Where, as in the case of a claim for breach of contract or in tort not involving death or per-sonal injury the value of the claim is, say, £40,000, the claimant has the choice of issuing the claim in the High Court or the county court. Then, by reason of a Practice Direction to Part 7 of the Civil Procedure Rules 1998 (SI 1998/3132), a claim should be started in the High Court if because of:

- the financial value of the claim and the amount in dispute; and/or
- the complexity of the facts, legal issues, remedies or procedures involved; and/or
- the importance of the claim to the public in general;

the claimant's solicitor believes that the claim should commence in the High Court, then he should commence it there.

In summary, therefore, there is a presumption of trial in a county court but this presumption can be rebutted:

- by the financial value of the claim in some cases (see above); and/or
- by one of the grounds mentioned above, such as complexity of facts or high value of the claim.

These matters are also taken into account when the court is considering the transfer of a case from one court to another.

Territorial limits

The territorial limits of the county court have been largely swept away, but the following material should be noted.

A claimant in a default action may sue out of any county court he wishes regardless of the defendant's place of residence or business or where the cause of action arose. A default action is one where the *only* relief claimed is the payment of money, e.g. a liquidated sum such as a debt for goods sold but not paid or an unliquidated sum such as a claim for damages for personal injury. However, if in a liquidated claim the defendant files a defence, this will generally result in the case being transferred to the defendant's home court and the defendant has a right to apply for a transfer to his home court in unliquidated claims. In actions in which there is a claim for relief other than the payment of money, e.g. a possession order for land or the recovery of goods or an injunction to restrain a nuisance, the general rule is that the claimant must bring his action in the court of the district where the defendant dwells or carries on business, or that for the district in which the cause of action wholly or mainly arose, and where land is involved, the action is generally brought in the court of the district in which the land is situated. Under s 3 of the Courts and Legal Services Act 1990 the county court has the same jurisdiction as the High Court to grant an injunction or a declaratory judgment setting out the rights of the parties, in respect of, or relating to, any land or the possession, occupation, use or enjoyment of any land. This jurisdiction applies only where the capital value of the land or interest in land does not exceed £30,000.

Apart from this, a county court can give the same remedies as the High Court although the orders of *mandamus, certiorari* and prohibition (now referred to as mandatory orders, quashing orders and prohibiting orders respectively) are available only in the High Court (see further Chapter 3). County courts are also prohibited – patent court apart – from granting a search order or a freezing injunction (see further Chapter 18). A freezing injunction is an order which restrains a party from moving his assets, for example, overseas so that they are not available to meet any judgment made against him. A search order is an order requiring the defendant to allow his premises to be searched by the agents of the claimant for documents or property. If the injunction or the order is asked for in a county court, the matter must be heard by a High Court judge. This involves a temporary transfer to the High Court after which the proceedings return to the county court.

The general jurisdiction of county courts and the procedure therein are governed by the County Courts Act 1984, the Courts and Legal Services Act 1990 and the High Court and County Courts Jurisdiction Order 1991 (SI 1991/724 (L5)) (as amended by the High Court and County Courts Jurisdiction (Amendment) Order 1999 (SI 1999/1014)) and the Civil Procedure Rules 1998 (SI 1998/3132). The latter are in the form of delegated legislation. In general terms, the extent of the jurisdiction apart from contract and tort, is as follows:

Other jurisdictions

(a) Equity matters, e.g. mortgages and trusts where the amount involved does not exceed £30,000, unless the parties agree to waive the limit. Under this heading would be found requests for repossession orders by building societies against mortgage defaulters.

(b) Actions concerning title to land, and actions for recovery of possession of land, where the capital value of the land or interest in land does not exceed £30,000. There is unlimited jurisdiction in cases involving residential tenancy security issues (see, e.g., s 40 of the Housing Act 1988), or by agreement between the parties.

Proceedings under the Leasehold Reform Act 1967, the Leasehold Reform, Housing and Urban Development Act 1993 and the Commonhold and Leasehold Reform Act 2002 are also covered. These Acts give tenants of leasehold *houses* the right, in certain circumstances, to acquire the freehold or an extended lease while the Act of 1993 (as amended and extended by the 2002 Act) allows *flat* owners collectively to enfranchise, i.e. purchase the freehold of the block and for individual flat owners to obtain a new lease if this is required as where, e.g. collective enfranchisement is not required by all residents in the block. (See further Chapter 22.)

(c) Bankruptcies. Here there is unlimited jurisdiction in terms of the value of the debtor's estate, though not all county courts have a bankruptcy jurisdiction. The appropriate court in which to commence proceedings is defined in the Insolvency Rules 1986.

Normally it will be the court for the district in which the debtor has resided or carried on business for the longest period during the previous six months. In the London Insolvency District the court will be the High Court and proceedings will be issued out of the Bankruptcy Registry which is part of the Chancery Division. Outside London it will be a county court which has a bankruptcy jurisdiction for the relevant area.

Under s 375 of the Insolvency Act 1986 appeal from a first instance decision whether made in the county court or by a Registrar of the High Court now lies to a single judge of the High Court and from the decision of that judge lies with leave of the judge or the Court of Appeal to the Court of Appeal. There is no further appeal to the House of Lords.

(d) Company winding-up. Where the paid-up share capital of the company does not exceed £120,000, the county court of the district in which the company's registered office is situated has concurrent jurisdiction with the High Court, provided that the relevant county court has a bankruptcy jurisdiction (ss 117 and 416 of the Insolvency Act 1986). A relatively small number of petitions are issued in the county court.

(e) Probate proceedings, where the value of the deceased's estate is estimated to be £30,000 or less. These proceedings could include the case where the court is being asked for a decree confirming that a will is valid or invalid where it is alleged to have been made under duress. In addition to the £30,000 monetary limit, only county courts in places where there are Chancery District Registries can hear a case. There are, for example, such Registries in Birmingham, Bristol, Cardiff, Leeds, Liverpool, Manchester, Newcastle-upon-Tyne and Preston.

(f) Admiralty matters. For the avoidance of doubt, county courts have lost their Admiralty jurisdiction. Admiralty proceedings, such as payment for salvage cases, must now be brought in the High Court, i.e. Queen's Bench Division.

(g) Matrimonial and family proceedings. The jurisdiction of county courts in matrimonial causes is derived mainly from s 33 of the Matrimonial and Family Proceedings Act 1984, and the Children Act 1989. The Civil Procedure Rules 1998 do not apply. Family proceedings are governed by their own rules.

A county court designated by the Lord Chancellor as a 'divorce county court' has jurisdiction in certain matters relating to any undefended matrimonial cause, but may *try* such a cause only if further designated as a court of trial. Every matrimonial cause must be commenced in a divorce county court and is to be heard and determined there, unless transferred to the High Court, e.g. under s 39 of the 1984 Act (i.e. on the application of a party or on the court's own motion).

Thus, the divorce process generally takes place in the divorce county court. Divorce county courts are now divided into two, i.e. the divorce county court and the Family Hearing Centre. If in a divorce case where the parties have children an application is made for an order under s 8 of the Children Act 1989 (e.g. a residence order settling the arrangements to be made as to the person with whom the child is to live), then the s 8 application must be dealt with at a family hearing centre by a nominated circuit judge. Otherwise, what is referred to as the Special Procedure is used, whereby decrees in undefended cases are pronounced without hearing oral evidence. This is the most usual method of disposing of these cases.

As regards cases concerning children, the coming into force of the Children Act 1989 has reinforced the philosophy that children cases should be heard by a judiciary who by reason of their experience and training are specialists in family work. Accordingly the Lord Chancellor has, under the Courts and Legal Services Act 1990 with the agreement of the President of the Family Division, nominated certain circuit judges to deal with family proceedings and child care cases. There are special arrangements in London where jurisdiction is given to nominated district judges of the Family Division.

(h) Civil partnerships. There is now a class of county courts known as civil partnership proceedings courts. These have a similar status to divorce county courts. They derive from the coming into force of the Civil Partnership Act 2004. In brief this allows homosexual and lesbian couples to get rights similar to those of heterosexual married couples by registering their partnership in a civil ceremony at a register office. These partnerships can be dissolved on the grounds of unreasonable behaviour but not until after one year. Other grounds are separation for two years with the agreement of both parties or, failing that, separation for five years or more. These designated county courts will deal with dissolution proceedings and children of the civil partners either adopted or from previous heterosexual relationships.

(i) Small claims. A major jurisdiction of the county court is in regard to small claims allocated to what is known as the small claims track. The types of claims dealt with on this track are as follows:

- straightforward claims where the financial value is not more than £5,000 (or a greater sum if all parties consent to a small claims track allocation);
- cases which do not require a considerable amount of preparation;
- cases that will not lead to large legal costs since, in general, no costs are recoverable by the parties one against the other. Each side pays its own costs (but see below).

A claimant may limit the claim to bring it within the financial limits of the small claims track even if this is less than the proper value of the claim (see *Khiaban* v *Beard* [2003] 3 All ER 362 – a ruling of the Court of Appeal).

As regards personal injury claims, there are special rules under which the financial limit of the whole claim must not be more than £5,000 and that part of it which is for general damages, i.e. pain and suffering, not more than £1,000. The rest of the £5,000 claim will be made up of what are called special damages, e.g. loss of earnings. Claims by tenants against their landlords for an order to carry out repairs are a maximum of £1,000 for the necessary works plus a further £1,000 for any additional damages, e.g. for inconvenience. Fast track proceedings are not available where the tenant complains of harassment and/or unlawful eviction.

Small claims – involvement of lawyers and experts
Very few small claims are conducted by solicitors from the beginning of the case to the end. The procedure is designed to allow a party to conduct his own case and assistance from the

court is available. Initial advice from a solicitor is normally required in terms of the merits of bringing or defending a claim. Some firms of solicitors will do this for a fixed fee for, say, an hour's consultation or less. No form of expert evidence is allowed in a small claims hearing unless with the permission of the court.

The court may be prepared to allow expert evidence in the form of a report where, in a claim for breach of contract, it is necessary to decide whether an article purchased failed because of a breach of contract by the seller/defendant or because the claimant failed to follow the seller's instructions. An expert's report may also be allowed where it might lead to the parties settling the case.

Small claims – costs

Generally speaking, only the fixed costs of issuing the claim are recoverable from the losing party. However, the court has a discretion to order payment of court fees, experts' fees (not exceeding £200 per report), travelling expenses and loss of earnings for the parties and any witnesses up to £50 a day maximum. In addition, the court may penalise a party in costs where he has 'behaved unreasonably' as in *Wright* v *Ryder* [1995] CLY 3985 where the defendant had lied in relation to his involvement in a road traffic accident which was the subject of the claim.

Small claims – the judiciary

Small claims are usually tried by a district judge with appeal to the circuit judge. A circuit judge may consent to hear a small claim, though, if he does, appeal is to a High Court judge.

Small claims – appeal grounds

There are rather few appeals against small claims judgments. The reason for this is that appeal can only be made on the grounds that:

- there is a serious irregularity affecting the proceedings; or
- the court has made a mistake of law.

Mistakes of law are unlikely, but if the district judge failed to take into account that a guarantee of a loan had to be evidenced in writing (see Chapter 11), this would be a ground of appeal to the circuit judge. As regards irregularity, a party may allege that he or she was not given adequate time to cross-examine a witness. The amount of time for cross-examination is fixed by the court before the hearing so that it is not difficult to see whether the time laid down has not been allowed.

Costs and representation on small claims appeals

The 'no costs' rule does not apply on a small claim appeal. In addition, lay representatives have no right of audience as they have on the initial hearing, though a party can still take his own case as he could at the initial hearing.

Small claims and counterclaims

In deciding whether a case is heard on the small claims track, the value of any counterclaim made by the defendant must be taken into account (see further Chapter 5). Thus, if the claim is for £3,000 but there is a counterclaim for £8,000, the case is a fast-track case unless the parties and the procedural judge at allocation agree otherwise.

Pre-trial review

The matter of a pre-trial review to consider the final programme for the trial is now part of the new Civil Procedure Rules 1998 which deal with the allocation of a case to a track. These rules are considered in Chapter 5. There is power to hold a preliminary hearing in small claims track cases, but it is unlikely to be necessary since the issues are not normally complex and district judges can fix a simple timetable for the case.

(j) Patents county court. Part VI of the Copyright, Designs and Patents Act 1988 provides for the setting up of patents county courts with a countrywide jurisdiction to hear and determine proceedings relating to patents and designs and matters ancillary thereto. Concern about the high cost of resolving patent disputes in the High Court led the Oulton Committee in its report of November 1987 to recommend the creation of specialist county courts as a solution to the problem. The Edmonton County Court was designated as the first patents county court. The Patents County Court (Designation and Jurisdiction) Order 1994 (SI 1994/1609) has established a patents county court at the Central London County Court and closed the one at Edmonton. Other than this, a patents court is set up as part of the Chancery Division of the High Court.

(k) Miscellaneous matters. The county court derives an important part of its jurisdiction from social legislation, e.g. adoption of children, guardianship of infants, legitimacy, claims other than those relating to employment, under sex, race and disability discrimination, and the enforcement of legislation concerning landlord and tenant.

(l) Exclusive jurisdiction. Although in many matters the county court has concurrent jurisdiction with the High Court, there are certain matters over which the county courts have *exclusive* jurisdiction so that actions concerning them cannot be commenced in the High Court: e.g. all regulated consumer credit agreements or hire agreements. Section 2 of the Consumer Credit Act 2006 removes the financial limit for the regulation of consumer credit and consumer hire agreements. Formerly, it was only where the credit provided or the hire payments did not exceed £25,000 that these agreements were regulated. Under the 2006 Act all such agreements are regulated and the county court has exclusive jurisdiction to hear disputes.

The earlier rules giving the county court exclusive jurisdiction to open what were called 'extortionate credit bargains' have been replaced under the 2006 Act by rules relating to 'unfair relationships' between debtors and creditors. The county court has exclusive jurisdiction in these proceedings. The court is given a number of powers to deal with unfairness, for example to require the creditor to repay in whole or in part any sum paid by the debtor or a guarantor by reason of the unfair relationship.

Furthermore, where the lender on mortgage is seeking to take possession of land and the mortgage includes a dwelling house and no part of the land is in Greater London, the county court has exclusive and unlimited jurisdiction (County Courts Act 1984, s 21, as amended). In addition, the Attachment of Earnings Act 1971, s 1 gives the county court alone the power to order attachment of earnings for ordinary civil debt.

Enforcement of judgments

As regards the enforcement of judgments, the High Court and County Courts Jurisdiction (Amendment) Order 1999 (SI 1999/724) provides that county court judgments for the payment of sums of money of £5,000 or more *must* be enforced, e.g. by procedures leading to execution on property, as by obtaining a distress warrant to allow bailiffs to take the defendant's moveable property in payment, in the High Court and *may* be enforced in the High Court if they are for £600 or more (see SI 1996/3141). Below that they *must* be enforced in the county court.

In the case of county court judgments of £600 or more but less than £5,000, the judgment creditor can choose whether to issue execution in the High Court or the county court.

The advantage of proceeding in the High Court where there is a choice is that the judgment will attract interest under the Judgments Act 1838 once it has been registered in the High Court. Judgments for less than £5,000 do not attract interest in the county court unless the enforcement is in connection with a debt under the Late Payment of Commercial Debts (Interest) Act 1998 (see further Chapter 18).

Appeal

In the usual case of a small claim the hearing will be before a district judge. There is an appeal to the circuit judge. If the circuit judge dismisses the appeal *but without an oral hearing*, the appeal from the circuit judge is to a High Court judge and there is no further right of appeal.

If the circuit judge dismisses the appeal *following an oral hearing*, there is a further appeal to the Court of Appeal. This is known as a 'second appeal' and is granted sparingly.

Where a small claim allocated to the small claims track is heard (exceptionally) by a circuit judge, appeal is to the High Court with a second appeal to the Court of Appeal.

What is meant by permission?

Permission may be granted either by the lower court at the hearing at which the decision to be appealed was made or by the appeal court. If the appeal court refuses an appeal *without an oral hearing* because no sufficient ground is shown in the notice of appeal, a request may be made for an oral hearing. If at that oral hearing the appeal court refuses permission to appeal, then no further right of appeal exists and that brings the matter to a close.

Alternative dispute resolution (ADR)

The Civil Procedure Rules specifically recognise the advantages of ADR. This will receive a more extended treatment in Chapter 5. Mechanisms include *mediation* where a neutral intermediary encourages the parties to reach a settlement using a kind of 'shuttle diplomacy' between the parties. There is also *conciliation* which is similar but the conciliator is more pro-active and may put forward the terms of a possible settlement. Under the Civil Procedure Rules the court will encourage ADR and may stop proceedings for this to be considered but cannot enforce ADR on the parties unreasonably. If one of the parties to the dispute declines unreasonably to co-operate, the court may take this into account when awarding costs.

> *Dunnett v Railtrack plc*, 2000 – Rejection of ADR: costs refused to successful party (**5A**)

Online court service: money claims online (MCOL)

A website introduced by the Court Service allows undefended debt claims to be processed online without the claimant or defendant having to appear in court.

The site can deal with claims of up to £100,000 for all kinds of debt repayment from rent arrears and hire purchase payment to suppliers of goods and services who have not been paid.

Under the system the claimant registers initially by creating a password and typing in details of the money owed. The court fee is automatically calculated and can be paid online by credit card.

The claimant can then check the progress of the case and whether the defendant has filed a defence at any time. The claimant need not at any stage collect the forms from the court or even download them from the court website. Any defence of a claim has to be filed in person or by post which will then lead to a trial.

The website can be accessed at **www.hmcourt-service.gov.uk/mcol/index-htm**, where you can set out your claim to start the process in not more than 1,080 characters including spaces and punctuation.

Fortunately the MCOL screen has a character counter. The claim is issued through the county court at Northampton.

Failure to submit a defence leads to judgment in favour of the claimant without trial so that the judgment can be enforced through the bailiff service (see Chapter 5: enforcing a judgment).

The Crown Court

The Crown Court is a superior court of record created by the Courts Act 1971. The Crown Court system replaced Courts of Assize and Quarter Sessions. It deals in the main with criminal work.

Classification of Crown Court business

For the purposes of trial in the Crown Court, offences are classified as follows:

Class 1 (main offences): (a) treason; (b) murder; (c) genocide; (d) torture and hostage taking; (e) offences under the Official Secrets Acts; (f) manslaughter; (g) soliciting, incitement, attempt or conspiracy to commit any of the above offences.

Class 2. In summary, these are rape, including oral penetration, and various forms of sexual abuse of children under 13 or with mental disorders, and family sex (formerly incest), such as sexual intercourse between a father and his daughter, though the definition is wider than this and covers intercourse between blood relatives and adoptive parents and those they have adopted.

Class 3. These are all other offences not listed in classes 1 or 2, e.g. wounding or causing bodily harm.

The Class 2 and 3 offences include soliciting, incitement, attempt or conspiracy to commit the main offence.

Allocation of business to judges

Cases in Class 1 can only be tried by a High Court judge, or a circuit judge or deputy circuit judge, provided that in all cases, except attempted murder, such judge is authorised by the Lord Chief Justice to try murder cases or in the case of attempted murder to try murder or attempted murder cases and also that the presiding judge (see Chapter 3) has released the case for trial by such a judge.

Cases in Class 2 can be tried by a High Court judge, a circuit judge or deputy High Court judge or deputy circuit judge or a recorder, provided that in all cases such judge is authorised by the Lord Chief Justice to try Class 2 offences and the case has been assigned to the judge by or under the direction of the presiding judge.

Cases in Class 3 can be tried by a High Court judge or, in accordance with guidance given by the presiding judge, a circuit judge, a deputy circuit judge or a recorder. A case in Class 3 should not be listed for trial by a High Court judge except with the consent of the presiding judge. The functions of a recorder can be carried out as required by an assistant recorder.

Involvement of magistrates on appeals from magistrates' courts

Appeals to the Crown Court from magistrates' courts are heard by a circuit judge or an experienced recorder or deputy circuit judge approved by the presiding judge for the purpose. In addition, between two and four magistrates sit with the judge or recorder. Where a judge of the High Court, circuit judge, or recorder, sits with magistrates, he or she presides and:

(i)   the decision of the Crown Court may be a majority decision; and

(ii) if the members of the court are equally divided, the judge of the High Court, circuit judge, or recorder shall have a casting vote (Supreme Court Act 1981, s 73(3), which becomes the Senior Courts Act 1981 as the CRA 2005 comes into force).

Section 79 of the Access to Justice Act 1999 removes the former provision in the Supreme Court Act 1981 (see above) that where the Crown Court sits on the hearing of committal proceedings for sentence from the magistrates' court the court must be composed of magistrates as well as the Crown Court judge. Now a judge can deal with a committal for sentence without magistrates, and administrative overheads are reduced and time to make appointments with magistrates is saved. The main situation in which magistrates will sit with a Crown Court judge is thus where that court hears an appeal following a trial and conviction in a magistrates' court.

Appeal from the Crown Court: defendant

In the case of a trial on indictment, there is an appeal by the defendant only against conviction and/or sentence, though leave of the Court of Appeal (Criminal Division) is required before that court will hear the appeal, unless the trial judge has, in each case, issued a certificate of fitness for appeal. The Attorney-General may ask the Court of Appeal to clarify a point of law in a case and may refer cases to the Court of Appeal where the sentence is unduly lenient. These matters are further considered when dealing with the Court of Appeal. Where the Crown Court has heard an appeal from magistrates, there is a further appeal to the High Court by way of case stated by either the prosecutor or the defendant on a point of law or excess of jurisdiction.

Appeal from the Crown Court: prosecution

The Criminal Justice Act 2003 gives the prosecution a right of appeal to the Court of Appeal. The defendant has a right of appeal at the end of the trial and sentence (as described above) but the prosecution had no equivalent right of appeal against the decision of a judge to stop the trial. Part 9 (ss 57–74) of the CJA 2003 corrects the imbalance by introducing a prosecution right of appeal against a ruling of a Crown Court judge that has the effect of terminating the trial either at a pre-trial hearing or during the trial at any time up to the conclusion of the prosecution evidence. Such a ruling could be that there is no case to answer.

The judge or the Court of Appeal must give leave to appeal. The judge will decide, according to the circumstances of the case, whether the appeal will follow an expedited route and if so adjourn the trial until the appeal is concluded or a non-expedited route in which case where any jury has been empanelled it may be discharged. In any case the judicial ruling terminating the trial or a decision to acquit the defendant will not take place while the prosecution is considering an appeal or if an appeal is required until the conclusion of the appeal or its abandonment. When making an appeal the prosecution must agree to the acquittal of the defendant for the offence(s) concerned should the appeal not proceed or the outcome is that the proceedings against the defendant should not continue.

The Court of Appeal may confirm, reverse or vary the ruling that is the subject of the appeal and can order the acquittal of the defendant on the offence(s) involved. If it reverses or varies the judge's ruling, the Court of Appeal may, if it is thought to be in the interests of justice, order that the proceedings in the Crown Court should continue or order a fresh trial. The prosecution and the defence may appeal to the House of Lords (Supreme Court from 2009, as the CRA 2005 comes into force) on a point of general public importance.

The CJA 2003 provides for reporting restrictions on the proceedings relating to the appeal and the appeal itself until the trial is concluded. The object is to ensure that if the appeal is successful matters prejudicial to the trial are not reported. Failure to observe the restricted reporting rules is a criminal offence punishable by fine.

Judicial review

Decisions taken at a trial on indictment in the Crown Court are not subject to judicial review (*R* v *Harrow Crown Court, ex parte Perkins* [1998] Current Law 96).

Jurisdiction

All indictable offences are triable in the Crown Court, as are either-way offences committed (currently) for trial by magistrates. An indictment is a formal statement of a serious crime prepared for a trial by jury. The Court also determines questions of bail and legal aid, and hears appeals from magistrates and committals for sentence from the magistrates (see p 28). It also hears appeals from youth courts and for this purpose forms a youth appeals court. This consists of a circuit judge plus two magistrates drawn from the youth court panel and chosen so that one is a man and one a woman.

Judge-only trials

Sections 44–50 of the Criminal Justice Act 2003 make provision for trials on indictment without a jury. The Act permits the prosecution in the Crown Court to apply to the court to have the trial heard by a judge sitting alone. The prosecution may make an application to the court for a judge-only trial where the case is likely to be affected by jury tampering, which is a real and substantial risk. Further details of judge-only trials appear in Chapter 4: Criminal procedure.

Section 43, which provides for judge-only trials in complex fraud cases, will not now be brought into force but the government is, at the time of writing, contemplating further legislation.

The Central Criminal Court

Before leaving the subject of the Crown Court, special mention should be made of the Central Criminal Court, otherwise referred to as the 'Old Bailey'. This court continues as a Crown Court sitting in the City of London. The judiciary is the same as that found in any other Crown Court, with the addition of the Recorder of London and the Common Serjeant, which is a special judicial office for London.

The High Court – generally

Under s 4 of the Supreme Court Act 1981 (as amended by Sch 4, para 117 of the CRA 2005, which is in force) the High Court consists of the Lord Chief Justice, the President of the

Queen's Bench Division, the President of the Family Division, the Chancellor of the High Court and not more than 108 justices known as *puisne* judges (pronounced 'puny'). The *puisne* judges of the High Court are styled 'Judges of the High Court'. The number of *puisne* judges may be increased by Order in Council, the latest being SI 1999/3138 which increased the number of *puisne* judges from 98 to 106, mainly in anticipation of the increase of work expected to come from the Human Rights Act 1998. Appointment is from those with a 10-year High Court qualification, i.e. from those who have had a right of audience (or advocacy) in relation to all proceedings in the High Court for at least 10 years. Also eligible are circuit judges who have held that office for at least two years (s 10(3) of the 1981 Act as amended by s 71 of the Courts and Legal Services Act 1990).

The CRA 2005, Sch 11, para 1 will, as it comes into force, rename the Supreme Court Act 1981 as the Senior Courts Act 1981.

The Queen's Bench Division has the largest staff, generally between 60 and 70 *puisne* judges. The court is presided over by the President of the Queen's Bench Division. As regards jurisdiction, every type of common law civil action, e.g. contract and tort, can be heard by the Queen's Bench Division at the Royal Courts of Justice in the Strand. In addition, the judges of this division staff the Crown Court and sit in the Court of Appeal (Criminal Division) as well as the Divisional Court of Queen's Bench and the Central Criminal Court. Admiralty business is now assigned to a separate court called the Admiralty Court within the Queen's Bench Division. The same is true of commercial business which is heard by a separate court called the Commercial Court within the Queen's Bench Division. The Commercial Court also provides an arbitration service (see below).

The Chancery Division currently has 17 *puisne* judges and is presided over by the Chancellor (a new post under the CRA 2005). Company business is assigned to a separate court called the Companies Court within the Chancery Division. Apart from company work, the Chancery Division deals with partnership matters, mortgages, trusts, revenue matters, rectification of deeds and documents, the administration of estates of deceased persons and contentious probate. The bulk of the bankruptcy work of the Chancery Division is performed by Registrars in Bankruptcy who deal with cases arising in the London insolvency district, provincial bankruptcies being dealt with by the local county court. The Patents Court forms part of this Division and deals with cases which are outside the jurisdiction of the patents county court.

The Family Division currently has 19 *puisne* judges and is presided over by the President of the Family Division. The court deals with all aspects of family law including family property and children in terms for example of adoption, guardianship and wardship. A more recent acquisition of jurisdiction arises under the Human Fertilisation and Embryology Act 1990 where the Family Division may, e.g., make an order providing for a child to be treated in law as the child of the parties to a marriage if the child has been carried by a woman other than the wife as a result of the placing in her of an embryo (s 20). All High Court business under the Child Support Act 1991 goes to the Family Division.

The Family Division has acquired jurisdiction under the Gender Recognition Act 2004. This Act aims to provide transsexual people with legal recognition in their acquired gender. This recognition follows from the issue of a full gender recognition certificate by the Gender Recognition Panel. The Panel consists of legal members and medical members. Before issuing a certificate, the Panel must be satisfied that the applicant has, or has had, gender dysphoria and has lived in the acquired agenda throughout the preceding two years and intends to continue to live in that gender until death.

An applicant may appeal to the Family Division under s 8 of the 2004 Act on a point of law where the Panel has rejected the application.

Divisional courts

Each of the three divisions of the High Court has divisional courts. These are constituted by not less than two judges.

(a) Divisional Court of Queen's Bench. This court has a supervisory jurisdiction under which it exercises the power of the High Court to discipline inferior courts and to put right their mistakes by means of judicial review through mandatory orders, prohibiting orders and quashing orders (formerly the orders of *mandamus*, prohibition and *certiorari*). When dealing with applications for these orders, the court is designated the Administrative Court.

Under s 28A of the Supreme Court Act 1981, the court has jurisdiction in cases stated and *habeas corpus* applications to the High Court and in some cases these functions may be carried out by a single judge of that court.

(b) Divisional Court of the Chancery Division. This court hears appeals in bankruptcy cases from county courts outside London, the Bankruptcy Court of the Chancery Division hearing bankruptcy appeals from London.

(c) The Divisional Court of the Family Division. This court hears appeals from magistrates' courts in family proceedings.

The Commercial Court

Since 1964 the High Court has operated a Commercial Court. Section 6 of the Supreme Court Act 1981 now constitutes, as part of the Queen's Bench Division, a Commercial Court for the trial of causes of a commercial nature, e.g. insurance matters. The judges of the Commercial Court are such High Court judges as the Lord Chief Justice may, after consulting the Lord Chancellor, from time to time nominate to be Commercial judges. They are, in practice, drawn from those who have spent their working lives in the commercial field.

They combine the general work of a Queen's Bench Judge with priority for commercial cases. The Act merely continues formal independence to the Commercial Court. Commercial litigation has since 1895 been dealt with in the Queen's Bench Division on a simplified procedure and before a specialist judge, the intention being to overcome the reluctance of those in business, who prefer the privacy of arbitration, to resort to the machinery of the courts.

Two specific steps were proposed in the Administration of Justice Bill 1970 to attract such customers: first a power was to be taken to allow the court to sit in private and to receive evidence which would not normally be admissible in an ordinary court, and second, High Court judges were to be allowed to sit as arbitrators. The first of these proposals was rejected by the House of Commons at the Report Stage but the second was passed into law and is now to be found in s 93 of the Arbitration Act 1996 which enables a judge of the Commercial Court to take arbitrations. Before doing so he must obtain clearance from the Lord Chief Justice. However, given their court commitments it is unlikely that a commercial judge would be made available. Arbitrators are most often experts familiar with the industry or commercial area in which the dispute has arisen.

Thus, although in theory the court has no wider power than other courts of the Queen's Bench Division, there is, in practice, a general discretion for departures in procedure and admission of evidence where the parties consent or where the interests of justice demand it or where it is necessary to expedite business. The power to hold hearings in private is restricted, but s 12 of the Administration of Justice Act 1960 gives a power which could be used if, for example, trade secrets were involved. Commercial cases may be tried by a judge alone, or by a judge and a jury. It was once a special jury in that it consisted of persons who had knowledge of commercial matters. An ordinary jury is now used since s 40 of the Courts Act 1971 abolished special juries.

Where a judge of the Commercial Court is acting perhaps rarely as an arbitrator, he sits in private and in any place convenient to the parties. There is no requirement for such arbitrations to take place in the law courts. The conduct of the hearing should be as informal as any other arbitration. In addition, the award is made privately to the parties and not published like a judgment.

The Commercial Court sits in London and there are separate mercantile lists in Bristol, Birmingham, Cardiff, Leeds, Manchester, Liverpool and Newcastle for cases involving commercial transactions. The Commercial Court publishes a 'Guide to Commercial Court Practice' which gives guidance on matters of practice in that court.

Practice Statements encourage the use of alternative dispute resolution in commercial cases, particularly where the costs of conventional litigation are likely to be wholly disproportionate to the amount at stake. The Clerk to the Commercial Court keeps a list of individuals and bodies that offer mediation, conciliation and other ADR services (see further Chapter 5).

Additionally, of course, the Civil Procedure Rules 1998 encourage the use of ADR in all civil disputes.

The Companies' Court

This is really a court of the Chancery Division where company matters are tried before a single judge whose special concern is with company work. The work of the court is divided into company liquidation proceedings, and other company matters.

The Bankruptcy Court

The bulk of the bankruptcy work of the Chancery Division is performed by Registrars in Bankruptcy who deal with cases arising in the London insolvency district, provincial bankruptcies being dealt with by those county courts with bankruptcy jurisdiction.

The Court of Protection

The present Court of Protection is concerned to protect and administer the property and effects of those who are by reason of mental disorder not able to manage these matters for themselves. In practice, the Public Trustee's Office carries out the administrative functions of the Court of Protection.

Part VII of the Mental Health Act 1983 deals with Court of Protection matters. The judges of the Chancery Division are nominated under s 93(1) to act. There is also a Master and two Assistant Masters nominated under s 93(4) who carry out the work of protection matters. Very little work is in practice referred to a nominated judge.

The usual remedy is to appoint a receiver to look after the patient's property and affairs. It is usual for a near relative, e.g. a spouse, to apply and be appointed.

Reform

Section 45 of the Mental Capacity Act 2005 will, as it comes into force, set up a new superior court also called the Court of Protection. It has been given a comprehensive jurisdiction over the health, welfare and financial affairs of those who lack capacity. The new court has been given the same powers, rights, privileges and authority as the High Court. The existing Court of Protection, which dealt only with the patient's property and affairs, is abolished by the 2005 Act. The new court may make decisions on behalf of the patient and where a more general supervision of a patient's affairs is required may appoint persons called deputies. The appointment of receivers is abolished by the 2005 Act.

The jurisdiction of the court will be exercised by one judge who is either:

■ the President of the Family Division;
■ the Chancellor of the High Court;
■ a *puisne* judge of the High Court; or
■ a circuit judge or district judge.

There will be a President of the Court of Protection and a Senior Judge of the Court of Protection, the latter having administrative responsibilities.

Technology and Construction Court

This court was formerly known as the Official Referees' Court. A claim before the court is one which involves matters that are technically complex, e.g. cases involving civil or mechanical engineering, building, other construction work and professional negligence claims in those fields. Allocation to this court is equivalent to allocation to the multi-track and there is no need for normal allocation procedures (see further Chapter 5). The judges are circuit judges who sit as judges of the High Court. It is comparable in importance with the Commercial Court.

Restrictive practices

The Restrictive Practices Court was abolished by the Competition Act 1998 which came into force on 1 March 2000. Further details of enforcement of the current competition laws contained in the Competition Act 1998 and the Enterprise Act 2002 appear in Chapter 16. However, for enforcement of domestic (UK law) infringements the Office of Fair Trading and trading standards departments of local authorities have power to ask the High Court or county court for an enforcement order against the trader to stop the infringement. If the trader fails to do so, he or she is in contempt of court and can be fined or imprisoned for up to two years. Those suffering loss from a prohibited practice can make a claim to the Competition Appeals Tribunal (CAT) for damages. Claims by way of class actions can be brought on behalf of two or more consumers by, e.g., consumers' associations. Appeal from the CAT is to the Court of Appeal (Civil Division).

A new s 58A of the Competition Act 1998 (inserted by the Enterprise Act 2002 s 20) makes clear that there may also be proceedings before a civil court in which damages may be claimed, e.g. in relation to a breach of the prohibitions in the 1998 Act.

The Court of Appeal – generally

The Court of Appeal consists of two divisions:

(a) the Civil Division which exercises the jurisdiction formerly exercised by the former Court of Appeal; and

(b) the Criminal Division which exercises the jurisdiction formerly exercised by the Court of Criminal Appeal.

Appeals up to the Civil Division

Consideration has already been given to the route of appeal in small claims cases. It is convenient to consider the route of appeal in fast-track and multi-track and specialist cases in terms of the track and the judiciary involved bearing in mind that what are referred to as 'second appeals' are much restricted.

Appeals from fast-track claims

- Where the decision is made by a district judge the circuit judge is the appeal court. Permission to appeal is required for such an appeal. It should be noted that when permission to appeal is used in this text it means that permission may be given by the court against whose decision the appeal is to be made or to the court to which the appeal will be made. Permission of the court making the decision should be asked for first, and if there is failure to do this or that court refuses permission, the permission of the court to which the appeal will be made should be sought.
- Where a circuit judge dismisses an appeal at a hearing the Court of Appeal is the appeal court. Such an appeal is a 'second appeal'. Where a circuit judge refuses permission to appeal to him without a hearing, a request may be made for an oral hearing. It at the oral hearing the circuit judge refuses permission to appeal to himself, no further right of appeal exists.
- Where a circuit judge hears a fast-track appeal from a district judge, an appeal from the circuit judge is to the Court of Appeal. Permission is required and such an appeal is a 'second appeal'.
- Where a circuit judge himself hears a fast-track claim, appeal is to a High Court judge. Permission is required for such an appeal. Where the High Court refuses permission without a hearing, a request may be made for an oral hearing. If at the oral hearing permission is refused, no further right of appeal exists.
- Where a High Court judge hears a fast-track appeal from a circuit judge, the Court of Appeal is the appeal court. Permission is required but such an appeal is a 'second appeal'.

Appeal in multi-track claims and specialist proceedings, e.g. patents court business

- Where a district judge or circuit judge in a county court or a master (see Chapter 3) or a High Court judge in the High Court gives a final decision in a multi-track claim, the Court of Appeal is the appeal court. A final decision is one that disposes of the issue in the case or part of it, e.g. as by deciding liability or the assessment of damages or both of these matters. The same route of appeal applies in specialist proceedings such as patents, commercial court business, Technology and Construction Court business and proceedings under legislation relating to registered companies. Permission is required for these appeals.

■ Where the decision is not final as where e.g. it relates to costs or a case management decision or a claim to strike out an action so that a trial will not take place the route of appeal depends upon the judge whose decision is being appealed as follows:

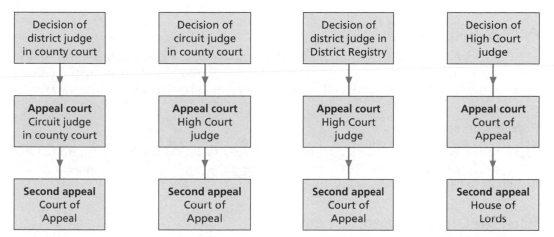

Note: under the CRA 2005, as it comes into force, the second appeal from a decision of a High Court judge will be to the Supreme Court.

Permission is required for the above appeals. Furthermore, if the appeal court refuses permission without a hearing, a request may be made for an oral hearing. If there is refusal at that hearing, no further right of appeal exists. Where the appeal is to the Court of Appeal, permission to appeal is *only* from the Court of Appeal itself. A strict test must be satisfied, i.e. that the Court of Appeal considers that the second appeal raises an important point of legal principle or practice or that there is some other compelling reason for the Court of Appeal to hear it.

Family proceedings

The circuit judge is the appeal court where the decision was made by a district judge sitting in a county court. The Court of Appeal is the appeal court where the decision is that of a circuit judge sitting in the county court. The same is true where the decision is that of a High Court judge or a circuit judge or High Court judge on appeal from a district judge.

Insolvency proceedings

A single High Court judge is the appeal court from a bankruptcy or other insolvency decision by a district judge or a circuit judge in a county court and permission is not required. Appeal from the single judge lies to the Court of Appeal with the permission *only* of the Court of Appeal. Where the decision is by a High Court judge but not on appeal, the Court of Appeal is the appeal court. Permission is required either from the High Court judge or the Court of Appeal.

Leapfrog appeals

Under ss 12 and 13 of the Administration of Justice Act 1969 an appeal from a High Court judge may be made to the House of Lords (under the CRA 2005, as it comes into force, the Supreme Court), if all the parties consent and the judge gives a certificate to the effect that the case raises a point of law of public importance relating wholly or mainly to a statute or statutory instrument. The House of Lords (going forward the Supreme Court), must also give leave. This procedure is most often used in tax and patent appeals where the meaning of statutes is often very involved.

Appeals from tribunals

The Court of Appeal hears appeals from a number of tribunals, e.g. the Employment Appeal Tribunal and the Lands Tribunal (see further Chapter 3). It also hears appeals from the Competition Appeal Tribunal in matters arising from competition law (see further Chapter 16).

Permission to appeal

As we have seen, the main test for granting permission to appeal is whether the appeal has any real prospect of success. This would not necessarily apply to leapfrog appeals where matters of public importance are involved.

What the Court of Appeal may do

The court may, on appeal, uphold or reverse the judge below or substitute a new judgment. Exceptionally, it may order a new trial as it did, e.g. in *Gilberthorpe* v *News Group Newspapers* [1995] 2 CLY 3885 where fresh evidence had become available. A retrial was also ordered in *Gabriel* v *Kirklees Metropolitan Council* (2004) *The Times*, 12 April, where on appeal from the county court in a case of alleged negligence it appeared that the judge had not made thorough findings of fact, so that her judgment for the defendants was flawed.

Hearing the appeal

Under the provisions of the Access to Justice Act 1999 the Court of Appeal (Civil Division) may consist of any number of judges depending on the importance and complexity of the case. Where there are two judges and they cannot agree, the case may have to be re-argued before a new court of three or the original two plus a third. Some appeals are heard by a single judge.

Reopening a final judgment

The Court of Appeal ruled in *Taylor* v *Lawrence (Appeal: Jurisdiction to Reopen)* (2002) *The Times*, 8 February that it had a power to re-open appeal proceedings in order to avoid real injustice in exceptional circumstances. Lawrence asked the Court of Appeal to re-open an appeal relating to a boundary dispute which he had brought and which had been dismissed. He alleged bias in a judge where the solicitor for the claimant Taylor had, it later appeared, been engaged to amend a will for the judge the day before judgment was announced. The court ruled that it had jurisdiction to re-open the appeal but declined to do so in this case because it did not accept that the judge would have been influenced by this.

Comment We are here considering the rehearing of the appeal and not the ordering of a fresh trial.

The judiciary

The work of the Civil (and Criminal) Division is currently carried out by a maximum of 37 Lords or Lady Justices of Appeal (SI 2002/2837). This number can be increased by statutory instrument. The court is presided over by the Master of the Rolls, who is appointed by the Prime Minister, who is in turn advised by the Lord Chancellor. The qualification for a Lord or Lady Justice of Appeal is a 10-year High Court qualification, i.e. having had a right of audience in relation to all proceedings in the High Court for at least 10 years or having been a *puisne* judge (which is the normal route) (Supreme Court Act 1981 (going forward the Senior Courts Act 1981), s 10(3)(b), as amended). It should be noted that also included in the judiciary in the Civil Division are, under s 2 of the Supreme Court Act 1981 (going forward the Senior Courts Act 1981) (as amended by the CRA 2005), any person who was Lord Chancellor before 12 June 2003, the Lord Chief Justice, the Master of the Rolls, the Presidents of the Queen's Bench Division and the Family Division and Chancellor of the High Court. Currently, the Law Lords are included (going forward Judges of the Supreme Court). The Lord Chief Justice may also request judges of the High Court to sit. However, under s 56 of the Supreme Court Act 1981 (to be renamed (see above)) a judge may not sit on an appeal to the Court of Appeal if he sat at the hearing of the case in the lower court. This applies to both civil and criminal cases.

The Criminal Division

The work of the Criminal Division is carried out by the Lord Chief Justice and the same Lord and Lady Justices of Appeal, who also sit in the Civil Division. It should also be noted that the Lord Chief Justice may ask any judge of the High Court to sit in the Criminal Division. The normal court consists of three judges but sometimes, though rarely, a full court of five will sit if the case is a difficult one. Under s 55 of the Supreme Court Act 1981 (to be renamed (see above)) a court of two may sit to deal with appeals against sentence. A single judge may carry out some functions, e.g. grant leave to appeal against conviction or sentence (Criminal Procedure Rules 2005, rule 68). The success rate in terms of the ordinary prisoner seeking leave to appeal against *conviction* is negligible, though thousands of appeals against *sentence* are heard annually.

As regards the Criminal Division, it should be noted that following the bringing into force of s 52 of the Criminal Justice and Public Order Act 1994 senior circuit judges may sit as judges of that division but not of the Civil Division. Only one circuit judge can sit as part of a full court. Circuit judges cannot act as single judges and could not sit as part of a court reviewing a case tried by a High Court judge in terms of conviction or sentence. This restriction is removed by Sch 10 to the Courts Act 2003. The request to sit is made by the Lord Chief Justice.

Jurisdiction – generally

The Criminal Division hears appeals from the Crown Court against conviction and sentence and may dismiss or allow the appeal or order a new trial. Further details appear in the section on the Crown Court. In addition, the Home Secretary could refer a case to the Criminal Division under s 17(1)(a) of the Criminal Appeal Act 1968. An example is to be found in *R v Maguire* [1992] 2 All ER 433. All the appellants had, following an IRA bomb attack on a Birmingham pub, been convicted of knowingly having in their possession or under their control an explosive substance namely nitro-glycerine, under such circumstances as to give rise to a reasonable suspicion that it was in their possession or control for an unlawful object. Following a reference to the Court of Appeal by the Home Secretary, the convictions were quashed, on the ground that they were unsafe and unsatisfactory because the possibility of innocent contamination of the appellants' hands could not be excluded. An expert prosecution witness had failed to disclose this at the trial.

Now that the Criminal Cases Review Commission (see below) has been set up, s 17 of the 1968 Act is repealed by s 3 of the Criminal Appeal Act 1995 and this abolishes the Home Secretary's power to refer cases to the Court of Appeal. Instead, under s 5 of the 1995 Act, the Court of Appeal is enabled to commission investigations to be carried out by the Commission, which will report its findings to the court. Under s 14 of the 1995 Act (and rule 68.25 of the Criminal Procedure Rules 2005), a reference regarding a conviction, verdict finding or sentence may be made to the Commission with or without an application by the person to whom it relates.

Furthermore, the Attorney-General may refer for an opinion on a point of law arising from a charge which resulted in an acquittal (Criminal Justice Act 1972, s 36(1) and rules 69.1 and 69.5 of the 2005 Rules). An example is to be found in *Attorney-General's Reference (No 2 of 1982)* [1984] 2 WLR 447, where two directors, A and B, were alleged to have committed theft of the company's property leaving it without funds to pay its creditors. They were also the only shareholders. Since theft requires a taking from some other person without that person's consent, the trial judge held that the offence of theft had not been committed and A and B were acquitted. On the reference of the Attorney-General, the Court of Appeal held that since a company was a separate person at law (see further Chapter 8), A and B could steal from it. Furthermore, although the consent of the directors would often be imputed to the company, it was irrational to do so here when A and B were alleged to be acting dishonestly in relation to the company. The Court of Appeal was of the opinion that A and B could be legally charged with theft. It should be noted that the Court of Appeal's opinion has no effect upon the outcome of the original trial. The acquittal stands.

Jurisdiction – retrial for serious offences

The Criminal Justice Act 2003 sets out the cases that may be retried under the *evidence* exception in the Act to the *normal rule against double jeopardy*. The procedure is contained in Part 10 of the Act. There is provision for retrial of 'qualifying offences'. These include murder, rape, armed robbery and causing explosions, drugs offences and a variety of terrorist offences and conspiracy. The provisions apply where *new evidence* comes to light after a first acquittal which strongly indicates that the person acquitted is guilty and it is right in all the circumstances to hold a second trial.

The Director of Public Prosecutions must consent to a suspect being re-investigated. The prosecution must then apply to the Court of Appeal Criminal Division for the original acquittal to be quashed. Only one application in regard to a particular person can be made and therefore only one retrial is possible.

The problem presented by this removal of the double jeopardy rule is in the main that a person whose original acquittal is overturned may find that the presumption of his innocence in the retrial is affected so that it may well be difficult for the alleged offender to get a fair trial.

The government made a declaration under Art 55 of the Schengen Convention which allows an exception to the normal rule against double jeopardy within member states of the EU where the offence took place in the home state. This will ensure that the Act is compatible with the Convention. The above provisions will assist further trials now that DNA evidence is available.

Appeals in cases of death

Section 7 of the Criminal Appeal Act 1995 inserts a new s 44A into the Criminal Appeal Act 1968 under which the Court of Appeal may approve an application to conduct an appeal on behalf of a convicted person who has died. This is particularly important where the deceased has been fined and has died before an appeal could be heard. Before the enactment of this section his estate would have had to pay the fine even though if there had been an appeal the court may have quashed the conviction and the fine.

Power to increase sentence

Section 36 of the Criminal Justice Act 1988 allows the Attorney-General to refer a case for increased sentence if it appears that the judge in the Crown Court has been too lenient. The section applies only to trials on indictment. The Court of Appeal must give leave before the reference can be heard and has power on hearing the reference to give any sentence which the original court could have given. Thus the sentence may be increased or reduced. The section is an attempt to deal with public disquiet over lenient sentences.

It should be noted that the Court of Appeal is not bound to give leave to refer and did refuse leave in *Attorney-General's Reference (No 14 of 2003), R v Sheppard* (2003) *The Times*, 18 April, where Nicola Sheppard had pleaded guilty in Bristol Crown Court to a charge of laundering the proceeds of criminal conduct. She was sentenced by the recorder to a community punishment order of 120 hours. The Court of Appeal refused the Attorney's reference because it did not take into account mitigating circumstances pleaded before the recorder on Ms Sheppard's behalf.

New trials

The court may order a new trial under s 7 of the Criminal Appeal Act 1968 as amended by s 54 of the Criminal Justice Act 1988. The power is quite extensive and a retrial can be ordered if the Court of Appeal is satisfied that it is in the interests of justice to do so. It is intended in the main to prevent unmeritorious defendants from escaping justice because of some technical mistake at the original trial. It does not cover retrials on new evidence (see above).

There is also a power to order a new trial at common law where there has been a fundamental defect in the trial so that it was a nullity. Thus, in *R v Ishmael* [1970] Crim LR 399, the accused had been sentenced to life imprisonment having pleaded guilty at his trial to an offence under s 3 of the Malicious Damage Act 1861 (arson of buildings, punishable by life imprisonment) thinking he was charged with an offence under s 7 of the 1861 Act (arson of goods, punishable by 14 years' imprisonment). The Court of Appeal held that he must be tried again.

These provisions survive the provisions of the Criminal Justice Act 2003. The power is not restricted to the qualifying offences of the 2003 Act. It is a procedure that the court can perhaps adopt instead of dismissing an appeal. *Retrial is ordered when an appeal is made to the court* which may allow the appeal but because of the circumstances order also a retrial. The Criminal Justice Act 2003 applies even when all appeal procedures have been exhausted.

Criminal Cases Review Commission

Sections 8 to 25 of the Criminal Appeal Act 1995 provide for a body to investigate and report on cases of possible wrongful conviction or sentence. The Commission consists of not less than 11 persons one-third of whom must be legally qualified. The other two-thirds must have knowledge or experience of some aspect of the criminal justice system. Cases are referred to the Commission by the Court of Appeal and it is to that court that the Commission's report is made. In addition the Commission may, with or without an application by the person to whom it relates, investigate and refer to the Court of Appeal any conviction or sentence in any case which has been tried summarily or on indictment in England and Wales.

Where the Criminal Cases Review Commission refers a case to the Court of Appeal, the Criminal Appeal Act 1968, s 23 allows the court to receive fresh evidence, e.g. DNA evidence that was not adduced at the trial. Although DNA evidence may be adduced *by the offender* to point to another person as guilty, it may be brought in by the Crown as showing the guilt of the offender.

The Crown is not restricted to adducing fresh evidence under s 23 only in order the rebut fresh evidence adduced by the defendant on appeal. Thus in *R* v *Hanratty* [2002] 3 All ER 534 the prosecution, i.e. the Crown, was allowed to adduce DNA evidence proving conclusively that H was guilty of the crime of murder for which he had been convicted and hanged, on an appeal brought in an attempt to clear his name, even though the DNA evidence did not address the grounds of the appeal that there were alleged procedural defects in the investigation and at the trial. The court did not accept that the investigation or trial was flawed or that the conviction was unsafe.

Vice-presidents

Under s 3(3) of the Supreme Court Act 1981 (Senior Courts Act 1981 going forward) (as amended) the Lord Chief Justice may, after consulting the Lord Chancellor, appoint one of the ordinary judges of the Court of Appeal as Vice-President of both Divisions of that court, or one of those judges as Vice-President of the Criminal Division and another of them as Vice-President of the Civil Division. The Vice-President will preside in the absence, for example, of the Lord Chief Justice (Criminal Division) or the Master of the Rolls (Civil Division).

Assistance for transaction of judicial business in the Supreme Court

Section 9 of the Supreme Court Act 1981 (becomes Senior Courts Act 1981) brings together a number of provisions enabling assistance to be given by judges, former judges and deputy judges in terms of the business of the Supreme Court at the request of the Lord Chief Justice.

A judge of the Court of Appeal is competent to act on request in the High Court and the Crown Court. A person who has been a judge of the Court of Appeal is competent to act in the Court of Appeal, the High Court and the Crown Court. A *puisne* judge of the High Court is competent to act in the Court of Appeal. A person who has been a *puisne* judge of the High Court is competent to act in the Court of Appeal, the High Court and the Crown Court. A circuit judge is competent to act in the High Court.

By reason of s 58 of the Administration of Justice Act 1982, a recorder is competent to act in the High Court.

Under s 9(4) of the Supreme Court Act 1981, if it appears to the Lord Chief Justice that it is expedient as a temporary measure to make an appointment in order to facilitate the disposal of business in the High Court or the Crown Court, he may appoint a person qualified for appointment as a *puisne* judge of the High Court to be a deputy judge of the High Court during such period or on such occasions as the Lord Chief Justice thinks fit.

Where there is a vacancy in the office of Lord Chief Justice or he or she is unable for any reason to fulfil the above roles, they will be carried out by the Master of the Rolls.

The House of Lords

Current constitution

The court is constituted by the Lords of Appeal in Ordinary (or Law Lords). There are at any one time between nine and 12 Law Lords, two of whom normally come from the Scottish judiciary. The Law Lords are life peers and each of them is appointed by the Queen on the Prime Minister's advice, who is in turn advised by the Lord Chancellor, from among persons who have a Supreme Court qualification, i.e. a right of audience in relation to all proceedings in the Supreme Court. No number of years is stated. (See Appellate Jurisdiction Act 1876, s 6, as amended by the Courts and Legal Services Act 1990, Sch 10.) Normally the appointments are made from the Lords Justices of Appeal. A minimum of three law lords is required to constitute a court, but in practice five normally sit to hear an appeal. The decision is by majority judgment.

Jurisdiction

(a) Civil. On the civil side the House of Lords hears appeals from the Court of Appeal (Civil Division), the Court of Session in Scotland, when one or two Scottish Law Lords sit, and the Supreme Court of Northern Ireland when a Law Lord from Northern Ireland sits. In all cases the lower court must certify that a point of law of general public importance is involved and either the lower court or the Appeal Committee of the House of Lords consisting of three Law Lords must give leave. In addition, there is a direct appeal from the High Court to the House of Lords by what is referred to as the 'leapfrogging method'. This phrase is used because the appeal goes straight to the House of Lords and not through the Court of Appeal. As we have seen all parties must consent and the appeal must raise a point of law of public importance relating wholly or mainly to a statute or statutory instrument. The trial judge must certify the importance of the case and the House of Lords must give leave. This 'leapfrogging' procedure is most likely to be used in revenue appeals and patent matters where construction of statutes is often very involved.

(b) Criminal. On the criminal side the court hears appeals from the Court of Appeal (Criminal Division) and the Queen's Bench Division of the High Court under the case stated procedure. In both cases the lower court must certify that a point of law of general public importance is involved and either the lower court or the Appeal Committee of the House of Lords must give leave. The House of Lords is not a final appellate tribunal for Scotland in criminal matters, but the Scottish Court of Criminal Appeal is.

Attorney-General's references, including those on sentence, may reach the House of Lords. The proceedings in the House of Lords are surprisingly informal. The Law Lords are not robed but sit in dark suits generally in panels of five at a table in one of the committee rooms in the Houses of Parliament at Westminster.

Effect of the Human Rights Act 1998

The House of Lords has played a vital part in the development of UK law on human rights (see further Chapter 3) where, as the final appeal court in the UK, it may sometimes clash with government by ruling that an Act of Parliament operates contrary to the Act and requires amendment. The former Lord Chief Justice, Lord Bingham, was appointed to head the 12 Law Lords. As senior Law Lord, the person involved is influential in deciding the composition of the panels of judges who hear appeals. This could be helpful in dealing with the potentially difficult relationship between the government and the judiciary as the 1998 Act continues to bite. The post of Lord Chief Justice was filled by the Master of the Rolls and that appointment was filled by a Lord Justice of Appeal. Further judicial appointments were made at the more junior level of judiciary in preparation for the Act and wide-ranging training of the judiciary was instigated.

Reform: the Supreme Court

The Constitutional Reform Act 2005 includes the creation of a new Supreme Court to replace the House of Lords Judicial Committee (the Law Lords), which currently fulfils the role of highest appeal court. The Supreme Court will be the highest appeal court in the UK. The provisions of the Constitutional Reform Act 2005 (CLRA), which are described below, will not be fully in force until 2009. The problem has been the setting up of the Supreme Court courthouse. The matter has been resolved and the Middlesex Guildhall in Parliament Square, London has been chosen. It is undergoing refurbishment and will not be ready until 2009. At that time the other courts formerly constituting the Supreme Court of which the House of Lords Judicial Committee is not a part will be categorised as the Senior Courts under the Senior Courts Act 1981, as described in material earlier in this Chapter.

However, other changes have been made: for example, the Lord Chief Justice is President of the Courts in England and Wales in place of the Lord Chancellor. The office of Lord Chancellor is not abolished, as originally proposed, but is being modified. The Lord Chancellor is no longer head of the judiciary or a judge and is no longer the Speaker of the House of Lords. It is no longer necessary for him or her to be a member of the House of Lords or a lawyer.

The Supreme Court

(Section references are to the CRA unless otherwise stated.)

Under s 23 the Supreme Court will consist of 12 judges appointed by the Queen on the recommendation of the Prime Minister, but the Prime Minister can only recommend a person notified to him or her by the Lord Chancellor following selection by a selection commission set up by the Lord Chancellor. The Prime Minister has no discretion (s 26).

The number of judges may be increased by Order in Council. The Queen may appoint by letters patent one of the 12 judges to be President of the Court and one to be Deputy President of the Court. Recommendation is again by the Prime Minister, who can only recommend a person notified to him or her by the Lord Chancellor following selection by a selection commission. Other judges are called Justices of the Supreme Court.

First members of the court

Under s 24, and when s 23 is brought into force, persons who were immediately before that commencement Lords of Appeal in Ordinary (Law Lords) become Justices of the Supreme Court and the Senior Lord of Appeal in Ordinary becomes President of the Court. The person who immediately before the commencement is the second senior Lord of Appeal in Ordinary becomes the Deputy President.

Judiciary: qualifications for appointment

To be qualified for appointment as a judge of the Supreme Court, a person must under s 25 have:

- held high judicial office for at least two years; or
- been a qualifying practitioner for at least 15 years; in other words a person who has had a right of audience in relation to all proceedings in what becomes known as the Senior Courts, e.g. Court of Appeal and High Court.

High judicial office will include the senior courts of Scotland and Northern Ireland. Those who have practised before those courts as advocates for at least 15 years are also included. In practice, members of the Supreme Court are likely to be appointed from the Court of Appeal in England and Wales and from the top judiciary in Scotland and Northern Ireland.

Selection of members of the court: selection commissions

Schedule 8 deals with these commissions, which must be convened by the Lord Chancellor when a vacancy is required to be filled in the Supreme Court judiciary. A selection commission consists of the following members:

- the President of the Supreme Court;
- the Deputy President of the Supreme Court and one member of each of the following bodies:
  - the Judicial Appointments Commission;
  - the Judicial Appointments Board for Scotland;
  - the Northern Ireland Judicial Appointments Commission.

A selection commission is dissolved when the Lord Chancellor notifies a selection made by the commission to the Prime Minister for appointment.

Process of selection

Section 27 requires a commission to consult:

- senior judges who are not members of the commission and are not willing to be considered for selection;
- the Lord Chancellor;
- the First Minister in Scotland;
- the Assembly First Secretary in Wales;
- the Secretary of State for Northern Ireland.

Selection must be on merit (which is not defined). The commission must have regard to any guidance by the Lord Chancellor as to matters to be taken into account in making a selection and only one person can be selected.

Report

Having completed the selection process, the commission must submit a report to the Lord Chancellor stating who has been selected and state the senior judges consulted under s 27. The commission must supply any further information required by the Lord Chancellor. On receipt of the report, the Lord Chancellor must consult with those required to be consulted by the selection commission except, of course, himself or herself.

The report: Lord Chancellor's options

Under ss 30 and 31, the Lord Chancellor may:

- reject the person selected;
- the commission cannot put that person forward again;
- ask the commission to reconsider a person's selection;

- if after that reconsideration the commission puts forward the same person as before, the Lord Chancellor may notify or reject that person and that decision to reject is final and binding on the commission;
- if after reconsideration the commission selects a different person, the Lord Chancellor can notify for appointment that person or the person whom he or she asked to be reconsidered. This effectively amounts to a power to correct his request for reconsideration which has led to non-selection.

Terms of appointment

At an early date after appointment, members of the Supreme Court must take an oath of allegiance to the Queen and the judicial oath, which in summary is to the effect that they will do right by all manner of people after the laws and usages of the realm without fear or favour, affection or ill will.

As regards *tenure of office*, s 33 provides that a judge of the Supreme Court holds office during good behaviour but may be removed at the request of both Houses of Parliament. Salaries are determined by the Lord Chancellor with the agreement of the Treasury. The President, Deputy President and judges of the Supreme Court can resign at any time by giving written notice to the Lord Chancellor (s 35). There is also power for the Lord Chancellor to dismiss on the grounds of incapacity (s 36).

Acting judges

At the request of the President, a person who holds office as a senior territorial judge may act as a judge of the Supreme Court. A senior territorial judge is an appeal court judge in England and Wales, Scotland and Northern Ireland. In addition, a member of the supplementary panel may act (s 38). The supplementary panel contains members of the Judicial Committee of the Privy Council and those who ceased to be members of the Privy Council in the last five years and members of the House of Lords who have held high office in the last five years but no longer do so and have not reached the age of 75 years (s 39).

Jurisdiction of the Supreme Court

Section 40 and Sch 9 define the jurisdiction of the Supreme Court as follows:

- Appeals from the Court of Appeal (Civil and Criminal Divisions) in England and Wales but only with permission of the Court of Appeal or the Supreme Court.
- Appeals from the Scottish Court of Session in civil matters. The Supreme Court is not a final appellate court for Scotland in criminal matters but the Scottish Court of Criminal Appeal is.

Schedule 9 transfers the 'leapfrog' appeal arrangements from the House of Lords to the Supreme Court and the case stated appeal arrangements described on page 29. The Supreme Court will take appeals from Northern Ireland from the Court of Judicature of Northern Ireland (renamed and not in the future to be called the Supreme Court of Judicature of Northern Ireland) and takes over the devolution jurisdiction of the Judicial Committee of the Privy Council. These issues will arise from matters concerned with the devolution of certain central government functions to Scotland, Wales and Northern Ireland. When appeals are heard from Scotland and Northern Ireland, the President of the Supreme Court will normally request a judge or judges from the relevant appellate court in the relevant country to sit as acting judge or judges which they are qualified to be.

As before, appeal to the Supreme Court must involve a matter of public importance and be certified as such by the Supreme Court or the appellate court from which the case comes.

The composition of the Supreme Court

Under s 42 the Supreme Court is duly constituted when:

- the court consists of an uneven number of judges;
- there are at least three judges;
- more than half of the judges are permanent judges and not acting judges.

The quorum of three is to avoid a vote equal on each side: casting votes would be inappropriate. The above provision means that, where there are three judges, two must be permanent judges of the Supreme Court.

Specially qualified advisers

Under s 44, if the Supreme Court thinks fit, it may hear and dispose of the proceedings wholly or partly with the assistance of one or more specially qualified advisors appointed by it. The court will decide on the advisor's remuneration and this will form part of the costs of the proceedings.

The advisor is a new concept and has implications for counsel instructed by the parties, since the matter before the court can be disposed of wholly or partly with the assistance of the advisor.

Photography

Section 47 is important because photography is currently banned in the courts of England and Wales and Northern Ireland. Section 47 indicates that the Supreme Court will be excluded from the general prohibition. This could lead to the ban being removed in general.

Chief executive

Section 48 provides for the Supreme Court to have a chief executive to undertake the non-judicial functions of the court under the direction of the President of the court. The President appoints other court officers and staff with the number of these to be decided by the Chief Executive with the agreement of the Lord Chancellor.

Accommodation and other resources

The Lord Chancellor must ensure that the Supreme Court is provided with a courthouse and offices and other accommodation as are appropriate for the carrying out of its business.

This has been a major problem and has delayed the coming into force of the Supreme Court provisions. The Middlesex Guildhall has now been chosen, but refurbishment is required, with completion by 2009.

Annual report

At the end of each financial year the chief executive is required by s 84 to prepare an annual report about the business of the Supreme Court during that year. The Lord Chancellor must lay a copy of the report before Parliament. A copy is also to be sent to the First Minister in Scotland and in Northern Ireland and to the First Secretary of the Welsh Assembly.

The Judicial Committee of the Privy Council

The Privy Council is a lineal descendant of the ancient King's Council, and was originally a sort of cabinet advising the Crown. The Judicial Committee, which is not part of the Supreme Court, is a final court of appeal in civil and criminal matters from the courts of some Commonwealth and Colonial territories, but the changes which have taken place in the Commonwealth have restricted the number of cases coming before it, many Commonwealth countries preferring to hear appeals within their own judicial systems. However, some aspects of this jurisdiction survive. For example, Malaysia and New Zealand retained the Privy Council as a final appeal court, in spite of their constitutional independence. The Australia Act Commencement Order of 1986 abolished appeals to the Privy Council from Australia. In October 2003 MPs in New Zealand voted in legislation to abolish appeals to the Privy Council. Under this legislation, which came into force in July 2004, the New Zealand Supreme Court of five judges became the country's final court of appeal.

Even in those countries where a general right to appeal to the Privy Council exists, a particular statute in that country may exclude appeal. Specific words are not necessary. The expression in a statute that an appeal to a national court 'is final' rules out appeal to the Privy Council (see *Sears* v *AG of New Zealand* (1997) *The Times*, 4 November).

The court is still the final court of appeal on criminal and civil matters from the Channel Islands and the Isle of Man, and also from those islands and colonies, such as Gibraltar and Belize, whose independence is not a viable proposition. There is strictly speaking no right of appeal, but it is customary to petition the Crown for leave to appeal. It is also the final court of appeal from English ecclesiastical courts, and here it is assisted by the Archbishops of Canterbury and York who, as assessors, advise on ecclesiastical matters. It also hears appeals from disciplinary bodies for dentists, opticians and professions relating to medicine.

The Judicial Committee of the Privy Council has jurisdiction under the Northern Ireland Act 1998, the Scotland Act 1998 and the Government of Wales Act 1998 to decide the competence and functions in a legal sense of the Scottish Parliament and the Northern Ireland and Welsh assemblies. A question of the legal competence of those bodies to make laws within the powers given to them would be raised before the Judicial Committee.

Composition

The Judicial Committee (or the Board as it is called) is comprised of the Lord President of the Council, the Lord Chancellor, the Lords of Appeal in Ordinary, Lords Justices of Appeal (if Privy Councillors) and all Privy Councillors who have held high judicial office in the United Kingdom, together with Commonwealth judges who have been appointed members of the Privy Council. It does not actually decide cases, but advises the Crown which implements the advice by an Order in Council. This advice used to be unanimous, but since March 1966 dissenting members of the Privy Council who were present at the hearing of the appeal may express their dissent, giving reasons therefor. The court is not bound by its own previous decisions.

Reform

It has already been noted that the functions of the Privy Council in matters arising from devolution of some central government powers to devolved governments or assemblies in Scotland, Wales and Northern Ireland will be transferred to the Supreme Court as it comes into being. Other jurisdiction as described above will be taken over by a newly constituted court called, as before, the Judicial Committee of the Privy Council, which will be governed by Sch 16 to the CRA 2005 and the law relating to the Judicial Committee will be confined to that Schedule. The Judicial Committee is in effect reconstituted by Sch 16, which substitutes a new s 1 to the Judicial Committee Act 1833. It will comprise holders and former holders of high judicial office who are also privy councillors. High judicial office includes former membership of the Supreme Court, membership or former membership of the Court of Appeal in England and Wales and membership or former membership of the appellate courts in Scotland and Northern Ireland. The Judicial Committee Act 1881 will be repealed by the CRA 2005.

THE COURTS OF LAW

Judicial appointments and discipline

The Judicial Appointments Commission and Ombudsman

The following materials relate to the appointment of the judiciary and the role of the Judicial Appointments Commission and the provisions relating to the setting up of a Judicial Appointments and Conduct Ombudsman to hear complaints of maladministration by the Judicial Appointments Commission or the Lord Chancellor. All of the following sections and schedules are in force unless otherwise stated.

The Judicial Appointments Commission

Section 61 introduces Sch 12 to the CRA 2005, which is about the commission and establishes the commission. The JAC is a body corporate. The membership is a lay chairman and 14 other commissioners. There are five judicial members plus a tribunal member and a lay justice, together with two professional members and five lay members. They are appointed by the Queen on the recommendation of the Lord Chancellor. The commission will normally work through selection panels having four members.

Appointments

General provisions

Section 63 states that selection for membership of the judiciary must be solely on merit. Further, a person must not be selected unless the selecting body, be it the JAC or a panel of the JAC, is satisfied that the person is of good character. There is no definition of 'merit'. Section 64 goes on to state that the selecting body must have regard to the need to encourage diversity in the range of persons available for selection for judicial appointments. Section 64 is subject to s 63, which means that diversity should be achieved without diluting the principle of merit. Sections 65 and 66 give the Lord Chancellor power to issue guidance about procedures for the performance by the commission or a selection panel of its functions.

Selection of Lord Chief Justice and Heads of Divisions

Section 67 gives the detail by providing that ss 68–75 (see below) apply to a recommendation for appointment to one of the following offices:

- Lord Chief Justice;
- Master of the Rolls;
- President of the Queen's Bench Division;
- President of the Family Division;
- Chancellor of the High Court.

Duty to fill vacancies

Section 68 states that the Lord Chancellor must make a recommendation to fill any vacancy in the office of Lord Chief Justice (LCJ) and any other vacancy listed in an office listed above. However, the section allows the LCJ to keep a Head of Division vacant by agreement with the Lord Chancellor. The Lord Chancellor's recommendation for appointment is to the Queen, who makes the appointment. There is no longer any involvement of the Prime Minister.

Request for selection for appointment to the s 67 offices

The Lord Chancellor may request the commission for a person to be selected for recommendation for appointment but there must be consultation with the LCJ. Thus, the section leaves the initiative for a selection to the Lord Chancellor. The Lord Chancellor may withdraw or modify the request for selection, but only if the LCJ agrees. The JAC does not have to respond to a withdrawal if the Lord Chancellor has already accepted a selection. The Lord Chancellor must give reasons for withdrawing a request.

The selection process

On receiving a request, the JAC must appoint a selection panel. A panel is a committee of the JAC. The panel has four members: normally a senior Supreme Court Judge (currently a Law Lord); the LCJ; the Chairman of the JAC; and a lay member (i.e. two judicial members and two lay members, the Chairman of the JAC being a lay person).

Panel report

The selection panel submits a report to the Lord Chancellor stating who has been selected (s 72). The Lord Chancellor then has the following options:

- to accept the selection;
- to reject it;
- ask the selection panel to reconsider the selection (the selection panel must be given the Lord Chancellor's written reasons for rejecting or requiring reconsideration of a selection).

Where the Lord Chancellor has asked for reconsideration the panel may select the same person or a different person, but where there has been a rejection and a request for reconsideration the panel may not select the person rejected.

Where the Lord Chancellor has asked for a reconsideration and the panel puts forward another person, the Lord Chancellor must accept that person *unless* he or she selects the person whose selection the panel had been asked to reconsider rather than the different person the panel has put forward. In other words, there may be a change of mind.

Selection of Lords Justices of Appeal

Sections 76 to 84 apply. The procedures follow a similar pattern to those listed above for Lord Chief Justice and Heads of Division.

Selection of puisne (High Court) judges

Sections 85 to 94 apply similar procedures to those listed above in connection with the Lord Chief Justice and Heads of Divisions, and Lords Justices of Appeal, with a major exception which is that when the Lord Chancellor gives the JAC notice of a request for the selection of a High Court judge, the Commission must seek to identify persons it considers would be suitable in advance of any judicial or other recommendation.

Other appointments

These can be filled by advertisements placed by the JAC as follows.

Circuit judge
Appointment is by the Queen on the recommendation of the Lord Chancellor following selection by the JAC. Qualification is a 10-year Crown Court or county court advocacy qualification.

Recorder
This is a part-time appointment by the Queen on the recommendation of the Lord Chancellor following selection by the JAC from those with a 10-year Crown Court or county court advocacy qualification.

2

Assistant recorders

There are also part-time but are appointed by the Lord Chancellor following selection by the JAC from persons with a 10-year Crown Court or county court advocacy qualification.

Common Serjeant (City of London Old Bailey)

Appointment is by the Queen on the recommendation of the Lord Chancellor following selection by the JAC. The qualification is the same as that for recorders and assistant recorders.

District judges (county courts)

Appointment is by the Queen on the recommendation of the Lord Chancellor following selection by the JAC from persons with a seven-year general advocacy qualification.

Deputy district judges (county courts)

Appointment and qualifications follow the same pattern as for a district judge.

District judges (magistrates' courts)

Appointment is by the Queen on the recommendation of the Lord Chancellor following selection by the JAC.

Deputy district judges (magistrates' courts)

Appointment is by the Lord Chancellor following selection by the JAC from those with a seven-year general advocacy qualification.

The advertisements of the JAC always make clear that selection is on merit by open competition and that the JAC encourages a wide variety of applicants to satisfy the diversity principle. An application pack is issued to applicants, who are required to submit a essay indicating why they are suitable for the relevant post.

The main function of the Lord Chief Justice in these appointments is consultation by the Lord Chancellor with the Lord Chief Justice. Importantly, as head of the judiciary in England and Wales the Lord Chief Justice allocates the appointee to particular courts in particular areas.

Complaints about appointments

Section 62 provides for the appointment of a Judicial Appointments and Complaints Ombudsman. Under s 125, a complaint is one of maladministration by the JAC or a committee of the JAC by a person who claims to have been adversely affected as an applicant for selection or as a person selected by the maladministration complained of. Complaints can be made:

- to the Commission;
- to the Lord Chancellor; or
- to the ombudsman.

The Lord Chancellor may refer a complaint to the Ombudsman.

Where the complaint or reference is to the Ombudsman, he or she must make a report. This may uphold the complaint in whole or in part or not uphold it. He or she may make recommendations including the payment of compensation where there is loss.

A copy of the draft report is sent to the JAC and the Lord Chancellor and to the complainant.

Under s 105, the JAC and the Lord Chancellor must provide the Ombudsman with such information as may reasonably be required for the investigation of the complaint.

Discipline

Disciplinary powers over the judiciary are given to the LCJ and/or the Lord Chancellor. A power of suspension from office is included. The LCJ exercises his powers only with the agreement of the Lord Chancellor. The latter, who need no longer be a Lord or a lawyer, can act alone and may veto the disciplinary acts of the LCJ.

Applications for review and references

Application may be made to the Ombudsman by an interested party for a review of the exercise of a regulated disciplinary function on the grounds of failure to follow proper procedures or some other form of maladministration. 'Interested party' obviously includes the judge being disciplined but apparently also any person who has made a complaint under prescribed procedures. The complaint must be made within 28 days beginning with the latest failure or other maladministration alleged by the applicant.

The Ombudsman has power to recommend payment of compensation or set aside a decision of the LCJ or Lord Chancellor.

The Lord Chancellor or the LCJ may make a reference to the Ombudsman relating to a disciplinary matter.

Reports on reviews

The Ombudsman must send a draft copy of a conduct report to the Lord Chancellor and in this case also to the LCJ. The report must state the Ombudsman's proposed response to the review. The Lord Chancellor and the LCJ may make proposals and the Ombudsman must consider whether to change the report to give effect to the proposal or not. The final report goes to the Lord Chancellor and the LCJ and to the applicant but the applicant's report must not contain information relating to an identified or identifiable individual other than the applicant nor must the applicant's copy contain information that would be a breach of confidence.

The Ombudsman is also required to make a report where the investigation has been made on a reference by the Lord Chancellor or the LCJ.

Removal and retirement of judges

Section 17(4) of the Courts Act 1971 (as amended) contains the only formal power to remove a judge. The power relates to circuit judges and states that the Lord Chancellor may, if he thinks fit, and if the Lord Chief Justice agrees, remove a circuit judge from office on the ground of incapacity or misbehaviour. Recorders, assistant recorders, and magistrates are governed by similar provisions. Other judges can only be removed by a motion approved by both Houses of Parliament.

As regards retirement, the Judicial Pensions and Retirement Act 1993 imposes a general obligation on the judiciary at all levels to retire at 70. Those who were appointed before the Act may retain their former retirement age, which is 75 for judiciary in the High Court and above and 72 below High Court level, e.g. circuit judges and recorders. Removal by the Parliamentary procedure has never been used for an English judge since its creation in 1701. The power to remove circuit judges was exercised by the Lord Chancellor, Lord Hailsham, who removed Judge Campbell after he had admitted smuggling whiskey and cigarettes into this country. Judges who have been convicted of drink-driving can expect to be removed.

High Court judges, who are rarely removed, are persuaded to resign by the Lord Chancellor and/or the appeal judiciary. This happened in 1998 when Mr Justice Jeremiah Harman was persuaded to resign after his intolerable delay in producing a judgment.

Arbitration

Arising from contract

Not uncommonly commercial contracts, for example contracts of insurance, contain a provision under which the parties agree to submit disputes arising under the contract to an arbitrator who need not be a lawyer but might in, say, a building dispute, be a surveyor who has knowledge and experience of the subject matter of the dispute.

Arbitration proceedings differ from court proceedings in two main ways: first, they are private in that there need be no publicity (e.g. a public hearing followed by a law report), and second, the arbitrator will have special experience of the particular trade or business which a judge would not have. Privacy is usually the determining factor in the choice by the parties of commercial arbitration rather than litigation.

Arbitration is no longer cheap since experienced arbitrators can command daily fees of several hundred pounds, and the lawyers who appear before the arbitrators charge the same fees as for litigation in the courts. There is no guarantee of a quick resolution because it may be several months before the parties can agree upon the identity of the arbitrator(s) and also the parties are dependent in arranging the arbitration on the availability of the arbitrator, whose diary may be as full as the waiting lists in the ordinary courts.

The Unfair Terms in Consumer Contracts Regulations 1999 (SI 1999/2083) apply in regard to the possible abuse of clauses which businesses may put into their contracts with consumers. The Arbitration Act 1996, s 89 (as amended by SI 1999/2167) applies the provisions of the regulations to arbitration clauses and an unfair clause cannot be enforced against a consumer who may, therefore, use the civil court system where there is, say, a breach of contract by a supplier, provided the amount involved is £5,000 or less. Section 90 of the 1996 Act applies the rules relating to unfair arbitration clauses to cases where the consumer is a company. The 1999 Regulations are considered further in Chapter 15.

Other arbitrations

Arbitration also occurs under codes of practice prepared by various trade associations with the assistance of the Office of Fair Trading. The arbitration service for a particular code of practice is usually provided by the Chartered Institute of Arbitrators. The trade associations concerned, e.g. the Association of British Travel Agents and the Motor Agents Association, make a substantial contribution to the cost of administration but the consumer has to pay a fee. This is normally refunded if the consumer is successful.

Arbitration in the High Court

Arbitration in the Commercial Court, which is part of the High Court, has already been considered. There are now no arbitration arrangements in the county court, claims of £5,000 or less being referred to the small claims track.

Conciliation

Sometimes a dispute is settled following an initiative by an outside agency. For example, the Advisory, Conciliation and Arbitration Service (ACAS) is, under ss 18 and 19 of the Employment

Tribunals Act 1996, given a role in settling matters which are, or could be, the subject of proceedings before an employment tribunal.

When a complaint or claim is presented to an employment tribunal, say, for equal pay or sex discrimination, a copy is sent to the conciliation officer. It is his duty to try to settle the dispute so that it need not go to an employment tribunal. He *must* do this if asked to by the person making the complaint or the person against whom it is made, but *may* do so on his own initiative where he thinks there is a good chance of a settlement.

During the course of conciliation the parties can speak freely with the conciliation officer because anything which is said to the conciliation officer during the course of an attempted settlement is not admissible in evidence if the matter goes to an employment tribunal unless the person who made the statement agrees.

Tribunals

These are considered in detail in Chapter 3, which is concerned with tribunals and legal services.

The Court of Justice of the European Communities

This court, which is often referred to as the European Court, sits in Luxembourg, and is charged with ensuring that Community law is observed in regard to the interpretation and implementation of the Treaties. Its decisions must be accepted by the courts of member states and there is no right of appeal. The major decisions of the court are disposed of by a full court though the court can sit as a Grand Chamber of 13 judges.

At present the court consists of 25 judges, one from each member state. There is a Registry in Luxembourg, and there are information offices in Luxembourg, London, Cardiff, Edinburgh and Belfast. The court is assisted by a number of Advocates-General who give an unbiased Opinion of the case for consideration by the court. The members of the court are appointed by the unanimous agreement of the governments of the member states. They serve for six years, although the appointment is renewable. There is no requirement of professional law practice and the court consists of professional judges, academic lawyers and public servants. A judge may be removed during a period of office only by unanimous decision of the other judges.

Procedure

There is more emphasis upon submissions in writing rather than oral argument. The proceedings are more inquisitorial and the judges play a more active role in terms of asking questions during hearings.

As we have seen, there are a number of Advocates-General. They assist the court and they give an independent view of the proceedings before the publication of the decision of the court. The court does not always follow the opinion of the Advocates-General.

The court gives a single judgment and no dissenting views are given. Enforcement of judgments is through the national courts of member states.

An important function of the court is under Article 234 of the Treaty of Rome to hear references from national courts for a ruling on the interpretation of provisions of Community law. The court is mainly concerned with actions alleging failure to fulfil the obligations of the Treaty by member states in terms of the free movement of goods, equal pay and sex and disability discrimination, and free movement of persons, which includes recognition of professional qualifications and diplomas obtained in one state of the EC as entitling the holder to practise a profession in another. The Treaty of Amsterdam extends the jurisdiction (see p 221).

Under various other Articles of the Treaty of Rome the court may deal with the following types of actions:

(*a*) actions by the Commission against member states for failure to fulfil Treaty obligations (Art 249);

(*b*) actions by one member state against another for failure to fulfil Treaty obligations (Art 227);

(*c*) actions by a member state or an individual or company against the Council or Commission for acting in breach of the Treaty (Art 230);

(*d*) actions by a member state against the Council or Commission for failure to act (Art 233).

Enforcement of judgments

Where a member state fails to comply with a judgment, infringement proceedings may be brought against it by the Commission (see further Chapter 7) before the court under Art 228. Therefore, the burden of ensuring that a judgment is complied with falls mainly on the Commission. However, the Commission succeeds in most cases in persuading the member states to comply without bringing court proceedings.

Court of First Instance

The European Communities (Amendment) Act 1986 was the UK Parliament's ratification of the Single European Act under which a new court of first instance was set up by a decision of the Council of Ministers of the EC in 1988. It consists of 25 judges, one from each member state, and deals with certain categories of case to relieve pressure on the Court of Justice, in particular, appeals against Commission Decisions in competition cases (see further, Chapter 16) and disputes between the Community and its employees. Appeal is to the European Court on a point of law only.

The judges of the court are appointed for a period of six years by unanimous agreement of the member states. There are no Advocates-General appointed to the court but judges can be asked to act as Advocates-General and, if so, must not participate in the deliberations of the court.

The role of the European Court at Luxembourg

It was decided by the Court of Appeal in *Bulmer* v *Bollinger* [1974] 2 All ER 1226 that the High Court and the Court of Appeal have a jurisdiction to interpret Community law and that they are not obliged to grant a right of appeal to the European Court of Justice. However, if the case goes to the House of Lords (going forward the Supreme Court) on appeal, the House of Lords (going forward the Supreme Court) is bound to refer the matter to the European Court of Justice if either or both of the parties wishes this. The decision in *Bulmer* was based upon an interpretation of Art 234 of the Treaty, which provides, in effect, that although any court or tribunal of a member state *may* ask the European Court to give a ruling, only the final court of appeal, in our case the House of Lords (becomes the Supreme Court) is *bound* to ask for a ruling if a party requests it.

In the case Bulmer had marketed products for many years under the name of 'Champagne Cider' and 'Champagne Perry'. Bollinger claimed that this was contrary to an EC regulation which restricted the use of the word 'champagne' to wine produced from grapes grown in the Champagne district of France. The Court of Appeal decided that since cider was made from apples and perry was made from pears, there was no infringement of the regulation. The court also refused to refer the matter to the European Court.

In the course of his judgment Lord Denning, MR laid down certain guidelines to assist judges in deciding whether to refer a case to the European Court or not. The main guidelines are as follows:

(a) **The time to get a ruling**. The length of time which may elapse before a ruling can be obtained from the European Court should always be borne in mind. It is important to prevent undue protraction of proceedings. The English judge should always consider this delay and the expense to the parties. However, in *Customs & Excise Commissioners* v *APS Samex* [1983] 1 All ER 1042, Bingham, J, while accepting that a reference should not be made in, say, the High Court, simply because if it was not made one of the parties would go on making appeals, it might be that if the High Court did make the reference, thus preventing further appeals to English courts, it would be cheaper for the parties in the long run.

(b) **The European Court must not be overloaded**. Thus, if there are too many references, the court would not be able to get through its work. However, in more recent times practitioners have appeared happier with the performance of the senior court, though there have been significant delays at the Court of First Instance level.

(c) **The reference must be on a question of interpretation only of the Treaty**. It is a matter for the national courts to find the facts and apply the Treaty, though the way in which the national court has interpreted the Treaty can then be a matter for reference.

(d) **The difficulty of the question of Community law raised**. Lord Denning was of opinion that unless the point raised was 'really difficult and important' it would be better for the English judge to decide it himself. However, in *APS Samex* (above) Bingham, J took the view that in some cases, even though the point raised might not be of great difficulty, the European Court should receive a reference because it was in a better position, among other things, to make the sort of decision which would further the orderly development of the Community. These statements by Bingham, J (who is now the Lord Chief Justice), in this case are to be welcomed because they show a greater willingness in the judiciary to take matters to Luxembourg and not to make too many decisions themselves thus to some extent shutting out the European Court.

In regard to criminal matters, a circuit judge presiding over a criminal trial on indictment has a discretion conferred on him by Art 234 of the Treaty of Rome to refer any question of interpretation of the Treaty to the European Court. It was held by the House of Lords in *R* v *Henn* [1980] 2 All ER 166 that it can seldom be a proper exercise of the presiding judge's discretion to seek a preliminary ruling before the facts of the alleged offence have been ascertained, since this could result in proceedings being held up for several months. It is generally better, said the House of Lords, that the judge should interpret the Treaty himself in the first instance and his interpretation can be reviewed thereafter if necessary through the hierarchy of the national courts, any of which may refer to the European Court.

In general terms, therefore, the House of Lords (becomes the Supreme Court) has an obligation to make a reference under Art 136. Lower courts *may* do so but if they think that the relevant Community law is sufficiently clear to be applied to the case straightaway they will not refer. This is known as the doctrine of *acte clair*. The provision of European law must, however, be directly applicable as is the case with Art 141 (Equality of Treatment) which is often applied in equal pay cases (see Chapter 19).

The International Criminal Court

This court came into being on 1 July 2002. All the European Union members are among the 73 nations that have ratified the Rome statute of 1998 that forms the basis of the court.
  Its jurisdiction and staff is as follows:

- the court will try persons accused of genocide, war crimes, crimes against humanity and (when defined) crimes of aggression; those who are heads of state as well as soldiers and civilians may be tried;
- the cases taken by the court will be cases that have not been tried or investigated by the country of the person accused and only crimes committed after 1 July 2002 can be tried;
- there are 18 judges elected by those countries that have ratified the Rome statute. They are of different nationality and they together with a chief prosecutor serve for a term of nine years;
- cases can be referred by:
    - any country that has ratified the Rome statute and has had crimes committed within its territory by foreigners or its own nationals;
    - the court prosecutor following approval by a panel of three judges;
    - the United Nations Security Council.

The ICC will make a difference since for the first time persons will be held criminally responsible for crimes against humanity. The ICC will complement existing national jurisdictions and will be able to prosecute where states are unwilling or unable to do so.

International Criminal Court Act 2001

This UK Act gives effect to the Statute of the International Criminal Court and makes provision for e.g. the arrest and delivery up of persons in the UK to the jurisdiction of the ICC, together with enforcement of sentences of imprisonment in the UK under orders of the ICC.

The European Court of Human Rights

This court, which sits in Strasbourg, was set up by the Convention for the Protection of Human Rights and Fundamental Freedoms to ensure the observance of the engagements undertaken by contracting states under the Convention. The United Kingdom is one of the states which have accepted the court's jurisdiction. The jurisdiction of the court in contentious matters extends to all cases concerning the interpretation and application of the Convention. The court can now be approached directly by the person alleging a human rights violation, by bringing an action against the state responsible. A panel of three judges then decides whether the case should be heard. If so, a ruling is given by a chamber of seven judges with an appeal to a Grand Chamber of 17. Since its creation in 1959 it has dealt with a wide variety of problems, including compulsory sex education in state primary schools in Denmark, where it was found that there was no violation of the Convention, and punishment by birching in the Isle of Man, where one or more breaches of the Convention were found to exist. More recently, the court decided against Britain by regarding the caning of schoolchildren against the wishes of their parents as a breach of the Convention. The court has power to grant 'just satisfaction' of a pecuniary nature to the injured party.

The court has decided that certain members of the UK armed forces who were discharged because of their homosexuality had been subjected to a violation of their human rights under the European Convention (see *Lustig-Prean and Beckett* v *United Kingdom* (1999) *The Times*, 11 October). The decision meant that the armed forces had to revise their policy on homosexuals, but the case has no binding effect on private business, only on 'emanations of the state'. The ruling is not *directly applicable* to business, but it is binding on public authorities. It will, of course, be influential in terms of future legislation on discrimination.

The Human Rights Act 1998 incorporates the Convention into UK law, enabling enforcement of Convention rights by UK residents in UK courts.

Since the most usual channel of complaint under the Act will be against public authorities by way of judicial review, the Act is considered in more detail in Chapter 3.

3

OTHER COURTS AND TRIBUNALS, JUDICIAL REVIEW, HUMAN RIGHTS AND LEGAL SERVICES

All of the famous writers on constitutional theory have drawn attention to the dangers of any system which takes away from the citizen, in his dealings with government and other officials, the protection of the law functioning in its traditional setting, i.e. the courts of law, which were considered in a previous chapter.

However, one of the most significant developments of this century is the considerable increase in what might be called broadly administrative justice dispensed in special courts outside of the ordinary system.

This has arisen from the great extension in the functions of government which has taken place over the years. For example, the government pays pensions to various classes of persons and a wide variety of social security benefits, and in order to further schemes of social welfare, it is often necessary for a public body to acquire land by compulsory purchase.

Obviously, disputes arise between individuals and the state. People may claim benefits to which the state suggests they are not entitled, and landowners are often aggrieved by the compulsory purchase of their land. Tenants complain about increases in rent and other charges by landlords. The settlement of such disputes might have been given over to the ordinary courts of law, but instead increasing use has been made of an administrative court of one kind or another.

Lord Denning, in *Freedom under the Law*, has said of these tribunals:

> They are a separate set of courts dealing with a separate set of rights and duties. Just as in the old days there were ecclesiastical courts dealing with matrimonial cases and the administration of estates and just as there was the Chancellor dealing with the enforcement and administration of trusts so in our day there are the new tribunals dealing with the rights and duties between man and the State.

It should not be assumed, however, that all administrative tribunals are concerned with disputes between a person and the state. Some deal with disputes between individuals. The Rent Assessment Committees set up under the Rent Act 1977 to deal with rent and other questions arising under statutory provisions relating to the letting of houses, are an example of a situation in which the government has provided a specialised court to deal with certain disputes between landlord and tenant rather than give the particular jurisdiction to the ordinary courts of law.

Furthermore, administrative justice is not always meted out in a permanent independent tribunal. For example, the local planning authority may grant planning permission with or without conditions or may refuse permission or fail to notify their decision within the period laid down. In the case of a grant with conditions, or a refusal to grant, or delay in notification, the applicant may appeal to the Secretary of State through the Department of the Environment. The decision of the Secretary of State is final, though there may be an appeal by the authority or the applicant to the High Court on the grounds set out in s 288(1) of the Town and Country Planning Act 1990, e.g. that the order is not within the provisions of that Act.

We shall now consider in more detail the way in which certain of these tribunals work.

Administrative tribunals

It is not appropriate in a book of this nature to deal with all the tribunals in this field but consideration will be given to some important ones as examples.

Social Security Tribunals – the Appeals Service

The procedure is governed by the Social Security Act 1998 and previous arrangements have been wound-up. Where the payment of social security benefits is refused, appeal is to an appeals tribunal.

The members of the tribunal

The members of the relevant appeal tribunals are made up from a panel of doctors, lawyers, those with experience of disability and those with financial specialisms, e.g. accountants. One of the members of the tribunal must be legally qualified and will normally act as the chair of the tribunal.

Rules made under the Social Security Act 1998 apply and the following types of tribunals are available to hear appeals as appropriate:

- a three-member tribunal being a lawyer, a doctor and a person with experience of disability hears appeals for disabled persons' tax credits, disability living allowance, and attendance allowance;
- a two-member panel, i.e. a lawyer and a doctor, hears appeals regarding incapability to work;
- a two or three-member tribunal, i.e. a lawyer and one or two doctors, hears appeals regarding industrial injuries or severe disablement. Where the appeal involves difficult financial issues, a financial specialist, e.g. an accountant, is substituted for one of the doctors.

Appeals

There is an appeal to the Social Security Commissioner if the tribunal has made an error of law as where the tribunal misunderstood a particular benefit rule or where there is a breach of natural justice as where the tribunal refuses to postpone a hearing even though the appellant had a good reason for not being able to attend and told the tribunal about it. This would offend against the rule that the appellant had a right to be heard.

There is a further appeal to the Court of Appeal from the Commissioner only on a error of law. Leave of the Commissioner or the Court of Appeal is required. It is also possible in some cases to challenge the decisions made by judicial review, such as on a refusal to give a right of appeal by a tribunal chair. The above rights of appeal are possessed also by the provider of the benefit, e.g. a local authority.

3

Human rights

Arguments based on the Human Rights Convention can be raised throughout the above procedures.

Valuation and use of Lands Tribunal

Another important tribunal is the *Lands Tribunal* which deals with disputes arising over the valuation and compensation payable on compulsory acquisition of land by public authorities under a variety of statutes, together with appeals from local valuation courts on the value of property for various purposes. An important function of the Lands Tribunal is that it can discharge or modify restrictive covenants over land. These normally restrict the use to which the land can be put and are not always welcomed by business developers. An application to the Lands Tribunal may be made in these circumstances. It does not follow that the Lands Tribunal will discharge or modify a particular covenant (see further Chapter 22).

The tribunal has a President, who is either a person who has held high judicial office or a person who holds a seven-year general qualification within s 71 of the Courts and Legal Services Act 1990, and other members, of the same standing, or persons experienced in the valuation of land. The jurisdiction of the tribunal may be exercised by any one or more of its members. Procedure is governed by rules made after consultation between the Lord Chief Justice and the Lord Chancellor and these are published by statutory instrument. The tribunal ordinarily sits in public and travels round the country, and there is a right of audience and legal representation. The decisions of the tribunal are written and reasoned, and appeal lies to the Court of Appeal on points of law. Either party can require the tribunal to state a case for consideration by the Court of Appeal. Legal representation is available in respect of proceedings in the Lands Tribunal. Legal aid is not available (see Sch 2 of the Access to Justice Act 1999).

Employment tribunals

These consist of employment tribunals from which there is an appeal to the Employment Appeal Tribunal. Neither the Employment Appeal Tribunal nor an employment tribunal has the jurisdiction to decide whether legislation is incompatible with the Convention on Human Rights since neither tribunal falls within the definition of a 'court' within s 4(5) of the Human Rights Act 1998 (see *Whittaker* v *P & D Watson* (2002) *The Times*, 26 March).

Employment tribunals

Employment tribunals are constituted under the Employment Tribunals Act 1996 and the Employment Tribunals (Constitution and Rules of Procedure) Regulations 2004 (SI 2004/1861). Some changes were made by the Employment Act 2002 but these were by way of changes in the 1996 Act.

The jurisdiction of these tribunals includes, for example, disputes arising out of the contract of employment or unfair dismissal, redundancy, equal pay and sex, race and disability discrimination. (See further Chapter 19.)

Tribunals, which usually consist of a chairman, and two lay members one from each panel (see below), are drawn from three panels as follows:

■ a chairman who is appointed by the Lord Chancellor following selection by the Judicial Appointments Commission and who must have a seven-year qualification. Appointments may be full-time or part-time;

- persons appointed by the Secretary of State for Trade and Industry after consulting representatives of employers; and
- persons so appointed after consultation with organisations representative of employees.

Members drawn from the two lay panels immediately above are referred to as 'lay members' and all serve part-time. The tribunals sit at suitable centres throughout the United Kingdom.

A full tribunal consists of a member from each panel. However, certain types of proceedings must be heard by a tribunal consisting of a chairman sitting alone unless a chairman, who need not necessarily be the same person who is to hear the case, directs to the contrary (ETA 1996, s 4). Some important categories of case are:

- applications for unlawful deductions from wages;
- applications regarding written particulars of employment and itemised pay statements, guarantee payments and redundancy payments;
- proceedings where the parties have given written consent to a hearing before the chairman alone whether or not consent was subsequently withdrawn;
- proceedings where the defendant or all defendants, if more than one, did not contest the claim at first or later.

These claims are explained in Chapter 19.

If a sum of money awarded by a tribunal is not paid over to the claimant, he can apply to the county court for a warrant of execution (see Chapter 5).

Legal aid is not available for a lawyer to represent a claimant before a tribunal, but legal advice may be given in respect of employment matters. This can include the drafting of documents in relation to the proceedings and assistance with the way in which the case is to be presented to the tribunal. A legal aid lawyer can attend the tribunal hearing with his client but cannot speak or argue on his behalf. If legal representation is required at the hearing, the party concerned must take responsibility for payment subject to recovery of costs, which are only exceptionally awarded (see below).

An applicant to a tribunal may be able to obtain legal assistance including representation in the tribunal from a variety of sources, e.g. a trade union or from the Equal Opportunities Commission (in sex discrimination claims) or the Commission for Racial Equality (in race discrimination claims) and the Disability Rights Commission (in disability discrimination claims). Under the Equality Act 2006 the above Commissions will, over a period of time, be brought together under the single Commission for Equality and Human Rights. Small employers responding to claims may also seek assistance from the Commissions and this may also be provided by a trade association.

The claim form for a case to be heard by an employment tribunal is ET1. It can be obtained from job centres and most advice centres or from the tribunals' website **www.employmenttribunals. gov.uk.** In England and Wales the claim should be presented to the tribunal office in the postal district where the claimant is or was employed. The claim can be delivered by hand, sent by post, or fax or completed online at the above website or by other means of electronic communication, such as email.

The person against whom the claim is being made will receive a copy of the claim from the tribunal secretariat. If he or she wishes to defend the claim, a response form (ET3) must be completed and returned within 28 days of the date on which the copy of the claim was sent. The response must be in writing.

Employment tribunals have power to request the parties to give each other particulars of the grounds which are relied upon and to grant disclosure of documents.

Hearings before employment tribunals normally take place in public, though there may be a private hearing where, in the opinion of the tribunal, this would be appropriate, as where evidence is to be presented which relates to national security.

3

As regards costs, an employment tribunal does not normally make an award but may do so, for example, where in its opinion a party to any proceedings has acted frivolously or vexatiously, as where an employer or employee refuses to take any part in the proceedings, or has acted abusively or disruptively – so the parties must behave!

The only situation in which a tribunal *has a duty to make a costs order* is when in an unfair dismissal complaint the employee claimant has expressed a wish to be reinstated or re-engaged and has told the employer this at least seven days before the hearing and yet the hearing has had to be postponed because the employer has failed, without special reason, to adduce reasonable evidence as to the availability of the job from which the employee was dismissed or of comparable or suitable employment where he can be re-engaged. Under the 2004 regulations a tribunal can now also make a *preparation time order* where either the claimant or the defendant makes a payment in respect of the preparation time of the other. Such an order may be made where the party who receives payment was not legally represented at the hearing or where the proceedings were determined without a hearing. An hourly rate of £26 per hour is applied from 1 April 2006 and goes up by £1 an hour every year. A maximum of £10,000 can be awarded. The provision may help, for example, small employers who may face claims from employees who are backed by trade unions and the employer deals with his or her own defence. These payments do not depend upon who succeeds at a hearing.

Also under the 2004 regulations a tribunal may make a *wasted costs order* against a person representating either party where the representative's unreasonable or negligent act or omission has affected the conduct of the proceedings. These orders can be applied to lawyers and other representatives such as trade unions, employers' associations and law centres.

The decision is made by a majority and is given orally at the hearing or, if necessary, reserved and given at a later date. In any case it is recorded in a document which is signed by the chairman and contains reasons for the decision. The parties each receive a copy. It should also be noted that where an employee has died tribunal proceedings may be started or continued by his personal representatives.

An employment tribunal can review and change its decision afterwards where, for example, new evidence has become available which could not have been known of or foreseen at the original hearing.

The Employment Appeal Tribunal (EAT)

Appeal from an employment tribunal lies only on questions of law. The determination of the facts by an employment tribunal cannot be challenged on appeal and it is, therefore, most important that the facts are properly presented to the tribunal at the hearing. In this connection an EAT decision serves as a warning to employers who fail to turn up at tribunal hearings. The EAT has ruled that evidence that was not placed before an employment tribunal because the employer decided not to attend the hearing could not be raised on appeal (see *Taylor* v *John Webster Buildings Civil Engineering* [1999] ICR 561). Under s 9 of the Trade Union and Labour Relations (Consolidation) Act 1992 it will also hear an appeal from the ACAS Certification Officer by a trade union aggrieved by his refusal to issue it with a certificate that it is independent. The major legislative privileges are given to those trade unions which are independent of the employer and not, for example, to employer-dominated staff associations. The Certification Officer adjudicates upon the matter of independence under s 6 of the Trade Union and Labour Relations (Consolidation) Act 1992.

The Employment Appeal Tribunal is a superior court of record with an official seal. Although the central office of the tribunal is in London, it may sit at any time and in any place in Great Britain. It may also sit in one or more divisions.

Appeals are usually heard by a judge of the High Court or a circuit judge or a recorder and either two or four appointed members who do not belong to the judiciary but have special knowledge or experience of industrial relations, either as representatives of employers or workers. The reason why the judge will usually sit with either two or four appointed members is so that in either case there are an equal number of persons whose experience is as representatives of employers and of workers. The decision need not be unanimous but may be by a majority. Each member of the court, including the judge, has a vote so that the judge could be outvoted, but this is extremely rare. Exceptionally, if the parties to the proceedings consent, a case may be heard by a judge and one or three appointed members. Legal aid for advice and representation is available to individuals for appeals from employment tribunals (see Access to Justice Act 1999, Sch 2).

Appeals to the Employment Appeal Tribunal are commenced by serving on the tribunal within 42 days of the date on which the document recording the decision or order appealed against was sent to the person appealing, a notice of appeal. The appropriate form is set out in the Employment Appeal Tribunal Rules.

The hearing will normally take place in public but the tribunal may sit in private to hear evidence where, for example, it relates to national security or could cause substantial injury to an organisation appearing before it, as where a company's trade secrets might be revealed. The EAT usually consists of a High Court judge and two lay members. A practice has developed under which circuit judges or recorders sit in the EAT regularly. For cases of major importance the EAT may be composed of a presiding judge with four lay members maintaining the balance between employer representatives and those of workers. There may be one or three lay members if the parties consent.

The Employment Appeal Tribunal may review and change any order made by it on a similar basis to the provisions already mentioned in regard to employment tribunals. Appeal lies on any question of law, decision, or order of the Employment Appeal Tribunal, either with leave of the Tribunal or of the Court of Appeal to the Court of Appeal. Legal aid would be available on such appeal according to the usual rules. There may then be a further appeal to the House of Lords (becomes Supreme Court) under the usual rules.

Section 28 of the Employment Tribunals Act 1996 provides that EAT proceedings in an appeal against the decision of an employment tribunal consisting of a chairman sitting alone are to be heard by a judge sitting alone, unless he or she directs otherwise.

Reporting restrictions

Sections 11, 12, 31 and 32 of the Employment Tribunals Act 1996 (ETA) allow employment tribunals and the EAT to make restricted reporting orders in cases involving sexual misconduct (e.g. sexual harassment) and disability cases. These orders prevent those who make or are affected by such allegations from being identified in media reports of the case. Persons have in the past been put off bringing such cases before tribunals because of the publicity which they attracted.

Contractual breach

Section 3 of the ETA 1996 and SI 1994/1623 (made under previous legislation) give the employment tribunals power to hear and determine claims for damages for breach of the contract of employment, in addition to their usual jurisdiction for breach of employment rights. It is now possible to claim unfair dismissal and damages for wrongful dismissal, i.e. dismissal without due notice, before the same tribunal. Formerly, the wrongful dismissal aspect of the claim would have had to be carried on in a county court or the High Court. These courts are still available for those who wish to pursue a claim for wrongful dismissal in them. The employment tribunal limit on damages is £25,000 and the claim must be brought, if a tribunal is used, within three months from the date the employment ceased. The main disadvantage of bringing wrongful dismissal claims in employment tribunals is that legal aid is not available, whereas it may be in the ordinary civil courts. Furthermore, the limitation of claims in the ordinary courts is six years and not the shorter period of three months allowed for tribunal claims.

Claims for statutory unfair dismissal must be brought before an employment tribunal. As noted above, contractual claims for wrongful dismissal can also be brought before an employment tribunal but the damages are capped at £25,000, even when the claimant's loss is known to be greater.

What is the position where a tribunal hears a case for wrongful dismissal and while accepting that the claimant's loss is greater, makes an award of £25,000 being governed by its cap? Can the claimant proceed with a claim in the county court or the High Court for the balance between the capped award and the actual loss?

The Court of Appeal dealt with this situation in *Fraser* v *HLMAD Ltd* [2006] IRLR 687. F was dismissed by the administrative receivers of HLMAD Ltd, which was insolvent. F claimed unfair dismissal and wrongful dismissal before a tribunal. In his claim initiating proceedings in the tribunal he stated that he reserved the right to pursue a claim in the High Court for damages in excess of the £25,000 cap.

Later, F commenced an action for the alleged wrongful dismissal in the High Court but did not withdraw the wrongful dismissal claim from the tribunal, which went on to make an award for unfair dismissal and £25,000 for the wrongful dismissal. HLMAD Ltd, through its administrative receivers, asked the High Court to strike out F's claim for wrongful dismissal, which it did. F appealed to the Court of Appeal, which agreed with the High Court and affirmed the striking out.

The civil procedure rule of merger applied. The effect of a judgment for the claimant absorbs any claim which was the subject of that action into the judgment so that the claimant's rights are then confined to enforcing the judgment. The claim for the excess over £25,000 was not a separate cause of action and could not be split into two causes of action, one for damages up to £25,000 and another for the balance. A claimant who expected to recover more than £25,000 should bring the claim in the ordinary courts. Merger of the claim in this case was not prevented by the express statement made in the tribunal claim form that F reserved his right to bring High Court proceedings for the excess over £25,000.

Appeals in health and safety matters

Where a health and safety inspector has served an improvement notice requiring improvements to be made in the procedures of a business, or a prohibition notice under which activity must cease, appeal is to an employment tribunal and from that tribunal to a Divisional Court of Queen's Bench and not the EAT.

Alternative dispute resolution

The work of tribunals has increased greatly and, in line with the movement in the ordinary courts towards more ADR, the *Report of the Tribunal System Taskforce*, issued in 2002, recommended a greater emphasis on the resolution of disputes by the Advisory, Conciliation and Arbitration Service (ACAS), following experiments through pilot schemes.

It is also relevant to mention here that s 32(2) of the Employment Act 2002 states that a claimant cannot put a claim before a tribunal if he or she has not followed paras 6 or 9 of Sch 2 to the 2002 Act. These provisions are designed to reduce tribunal applications by requiring would-be claimants to raise a grievance internally before going to a tribunal. Problems have emerged with this legislation, which receives further treatment in Chapter 19.

Administrative inquiries

As we have seen in some areas of administrative action, e.g. planning, there is in general no right of appeal from the initial decision of the government or a local authority to an independent tribunal. The relevant Acts of Parliament normally provide for an opportunity to put a case against the decision at a public inquiry conducted before an inspector who is normally a Ministry official. The inspector makes a report to the Ministry concerned and the decision is made by the Minister himself or a senior civil servant on his behalf.

Advantages of tribunals

As a method of deciding disputes tribunals and administrative inquiries have advantages. For example, the tribunals and inquiries generally specialise in a particular field, and can thus acquire a detailed knowledge of disputes in that field. The procedure of tribunals is simple and informal, and it is often suggested that this puts those appearing before them at ease so that they are better able to present their case. Certainly such justice is cheaper and there are in general no court fees and costs, though if the assistance of a lawyer is required he will have to be paid and there is no legal aid in this field except in the Employment Appeal Tribunal.

However, appellants who are not represented by lawyers may take full advantage of the rights of appeal given, though sometimes this results in references to tribunals which are frivolous by nature. Generally speaking, administrative tribunals and inquiries give quick decisions, and appellants are not subjected to the delays which are sometimes met with in ordinary courts of law. Tribunals and inquiries are usually local by nature; they are, therefore, able to acquaint themselves with local conditions, and can carry out inspections of property and sites where this would assist them in their decision.

The Tribunals and Inquiries Acts

Criticism of administrative tribunals led to the setting up of a Committee on Administrative Tribunals and Inquiries under the chairmanship of Sir Oliver Franks which reported in 1957. The main areas of disquiet were that tribunals did not give reasons for their decisions and furthermore that those decisions were not subject to appeal to the High Court on a point of law.

The majority of the proposals of the Franks Committee were accepted by Parliament and enacted in the Tribunals and Inquiries Act 1958. This Act, together with certain changes and additions in subsequent legislation was re-enacted as the Tribunals and Inquiries Act 1971. This was later consolidated into the Tribunals and Inquiries Act 1992.

The implementation of Franks led to the following main changes:

(a) A Council on Tribunals now gives advice to the Lord Chancellor on the working of tribunals and reports to Parliament from time to time on its work.

(b) The chairmen of the various tribunals are selected by the Ministers in whose fields they work from a panel of persons appointed by the Lord Chancellor. The chairmen are usually lawyers.

(c) A tribunal must normally allow a party who wants it to have a lawyer to represent him.

(d) All material facts are disclosed to all parties before a tribunal hearing and the hearing is in public unless, e.g., public security is involved.

(e) Reasons for decisions are given if requested.

(f) Appeals lie from most tribunals to the Divisional Court of Queen's Bench.

Unfortunately, governments have often set up new tribunals without proper consultation with the Council on Tribunals to see whether an existing tribunal might take on the work. This has resulted in a proliferation of tribunals with a bewildering multiplicity of separate jurisdictions. That apart, the implementation of most of the Franks' Committee recommendations means that there are no longer any major reasons for dissatisfaction with the powers and duties of tribunals.

There are those who have argued for appeal to a special Administrative Division of the High Court and, as we shall see as the chapter proceeds, control of administrative tribunals by means of judicial review is exclusively within the jurisdiction of the High Court and claims are heard by an Administrative Court within the Queen's Bench Division.

Reform

The former Lord Chancellor's Department that now has the title of Department of Constitutional Affairs is poised for a huge expansion to involve the takeover of tribunals in England and Wales which are now scattered among several departments as is revealed by the above materials. The proposals contained in the Leggatt Report of 2001 bring under the Department the tribunals now split between such departments as Employment, Social Security and the Inland Revenue (see *Tribunals for Users: Report of Sir Andrew Leggatt* published in August 2001). The Report is the culmination of a 10-month review of the tribunal system, the first since the Franks Committee reported 44 years before. Ministers are looking to 2006/07 for unification of the tribunals service.

Inquiries Act 2005

This Act is included for the sake of completeness but is not concerned with the solving of disputes between the citizen and the state as the above material is. The Act replaces the little used Tribunals of Inquiry (Evidence) Act 1921, which applied where both Houses of Parliament had resolved that it was expedient that a tribunal be established for inquiring into a matter of urgent public importance. The 2005 Act now covers these situations and the power to establish an inquiry is vested in ministers of the various departments of state that are relevant to the problem.

The Act provides a useful framework for the conduct of future public inquiries but it does contain provisions that are potentially inimical to the conduct of an independent and free inquiry, in that it reserves to the relevant minister the power to stop the inquiry or publish only a limited report.

The inquiry is undertaken by a chairman alone or with other members of an inquiry panel appointed by the relevant Minister in writing.

Legal aid

Legal aid in tribunals has been reviewed from time to time but it was felt appropriate to recommend that it should be available only for proceedings in the Lands Tribunal and the Employment Appeal Tribunal. In fact, advocacy before the Lands Tribunal is no longer the the subject of legal aid, having been excluded by Sch 2 of the Access to Justice Act 1999. Legal aid is still available for proceedings before the Employment Appeal Tribunal. Many still regard the present position as unreasonable.

In particular, it is felt that legal aid is appropriate in cases heard before, e.g. the Social Security Commissioners. In addition, there is no reason why legal aid should not be extended to some of the domestic tribunals, e.g. in respect of hearings before the Professional Standards Committees of the Institute of Chartered Accountants in England and Wales (see below). Extension of legal aid to these proceedings is unlikely for the present at least.

Domestic tribunals

Another area in which persons or groups of persons or other public agencies exercise judicial or quasi-judicial functions over others is to be found in the system of domestic tribunals. These are, in general, disciplinary committees concerned with the regulation of certain professions and trades, some having been set up by statute and others merely by contract between members and the association concerned. Examples of tribunals regulating professions are what might be referred to broadly as the disciplinary committees of the General Medical Council, Architects' Registration Council, The Law Society, the Professional Standards Committees of the ICAEW, and the Inns of Court. As regards the regulation of the investment industry and the City of London, there is the Financial Services Authority operating under the Financial Services and Markets Act 2000 and the Panel on Take-overs and Mergers, together with recognised investment exchanges, e.g. The London Stock Exchange.

Because domestic tribunals are not *public* authorities but *private associations based on contract,* the courts cannot control the decisions which these tribunals make by the process of judicial review leading to the issue of a mandatory order, a prohibiting order or a quashing order (*Law* v *National Greyhound Racing Club Ltd* [1983] 3 All ER 300).

At one time members were bound by the rules of these tribunals no matter how unreasonably or unfairly they might operate. For example, if the rules allowed expulsion there was no remedy against this even though a person so expelled might be unable to work if he was not a member of the association.

The breakthrough came in the decision of the Court of Appeal in *Lee* v *Showmen's Guild of Great Britain* [1952] 1 All ER 1175 which brought domestic tribunals under the control of the courts. Mr Lee ran a roundabout. He occupied the same pitch each year at Bradford Summer Fair. Another Guild member, Mr Shaw, claimed the pitch and a committee of the Guild found that Mr Shaw was entitled to have it and that Mr Lee was guilty of unfair competition. It fined Mr Lee £100. He then brought an action claiming a declaration that the committee's decision was invalid. The Court of Appeal upheld Mr Lee's claim in the main because it was at last accepted that the contract associations could not by that contract rule out the jurisdiction of the court because no contract intended to bind the parties to it could oust that jurisdiction (see further Chapter 16).

Since that time the courts have intervened to see that the rules of these associations are correctly interpreted and that the principles of natural justice are observed. They have developed a jurisdiction to redress wrongful expulsion; wrongful refusal to admit to membership; refusal to admit women and restrictive activities in terms of what members can do. Thus, in *Pharmaceutical Society of Great Britain* v *Dickson* [1968] 2 All ER 686 the House of Lords decided that the Society could not by its rules restrict chemists in terms of what they sold in their shops.

In *R* v *Panel on Take-overs, ex parte Datafin plc* [1987] 1 All ER 564, the Court of Appeal decided that having regard to the *public* consequences of non-compliance with the code, e.g. that a bid by one company for another could be declared invalid if the procedures of the code were infringed, application for judicial review of Panel decisions would be available in an appropriate case. This represents a considerable extension of the law to allow judicial review of domestic bodies where their decisions have effect upon the non-member public. However, it is doubtful whether the *Datafin* decision could be extended to purely domestic tribunals, e.g. the disciplinary bodies of the various professions whose proceedings affect only their members and not to any significant effect the public who are not members.

The *Datafin* decision was distinguished in *R (On the application of Sunspell Ltd)* v *Association of British Travel Agents* [2000] All ER (D) 1368. The High Court ruled that unlike the Panel the government did not seek to regulate the travel industry through ABTA. The power that ABTA possessed arose entirely from the truly voluntary submission of its members to its authority. It was not a public or governmental body in its nature.

A person aggrieved by the decision of a domestic tribunal can, however, ask the court for the remedy of a *declaration* of his rights or an *injunction*. These have proved quite powerful remedies as a means of controlling purely domestic tribunals.

Judicial control over inferior courts and tribunals

We must now consider what *control* the ordinary courts of law have over administrative action as expressed in the decisions of tribunals and inquiries and what *methods* are used to exercise that control.

Control by the judiciary is exercised as follows:

(a) by statutory rights of appeal from the tribunal;

(b) by application of the doctrine of *ultra vires*;

(c) by the use of the principal administrative law remedies, i.e. injunctions, declarations, and the prerogative orders of *certiorari*, prohibition, and *mandamus*, through an application under the Civil Procedure Rules for judicial review. The application to the court may additionally include a claim for damages. Claims are dealt with by the Administrative Court in London or Cardiff (where the matter relates to a public authority in Wales).

These methods of control will now be considered in more detail. However, before proceeding further it should be noted that by reason of a Practice Note issued by the Lord Chief Justice (see [2000] 4 All ER 1071), an order for *mandamus* is now known as a mandatory order, an order for prohibition is known as a prohibiting order and an order of *certiorari* is known as a quashing order.

Statutory right of appeal

Where, as in the case of the Lands Tribunal, the Act of Parliament setting up or controlling the tribunal gives a right of appeal to the ordinary courts of law, the courts are entitled to re-hear the whole case and are not limited to a consideration of the reasons given by the tribunal for its decision. The court can consider the whole matter afresh, and can substitute a new decision for that of the tribunal.

It should be noted that the existence of a right of statutory appeal does not necessarily prevent a successful application for judicial review. Thus, in *R v Wiltshire CC, ex parte Lazard Bros Ltd* [1998] CLY 95 the local authority resolved to make an order under the Wildlife and Countryside Act 1981 designating a road through a village as a by-way open to all traffic. Lazard Bros, who were owners of a farm in the village, successfully applied to the High Court for an order quashing the resolution. The court said that the fact that there was a statutory remedy of public inquiry and statutory appeal thereafter did not negate the court's jurisdiction to entertain an application for judicial review.

Ultra vires

No public authority may lawfully make a decision and take action on it unless it is authorised by law to do so or the act is construed as being reasonably incidental to its authorised activities. An act which does not conform with the above is treated by the courts as void under the doctrine of *ultra vires* (beyond the powers of).

The doctrine applies to bodies and individuals such as Ministers exercising judicial, quasi-judicial, legislative or administrative functions, including local authorities, tribunals, government departments and other public authorities, though Parliament's legislative powers are unlimited (see Chapter 1).

Typically, the *ultra vires* method of control is used where the decision taken is unauthorised by the powers given to the authority. However, even when the authority acts within its powers, the court can review the decision if it is unreasonable to a high degree (*Associated Provincial Picture Houses Ltd v Wednesbury Corp* [1947] 2 All ER 680). Subsequent case law has moved away from the 'reasonableness' test in favour of saying that the decision is disproportionate to the result to be achieved (see p 85).

> *Attorney-General v Fulham Corporation*, 1921 – The *ultra vires* method of control (6)

Prerogative orders and judicial review

Where no right of appeal is given, it may be possible to challenge the decision of an inferior court or public tribunal by having recourse to the supervisory jurisdiction of the High Court. The procedure is available in civil and criminal matters.

This jurisdiction is exercised exclusively by the High Court by means of the orders known as *mandatory orders, prohibiting orders* and *quashing orders*. These orders, which are not available as of right but at the discretion of the court, were formerly prerogative writs, which a subject might obtain by petitioning the Crown.

The Sovereign has no such power today, the control being exercised by the Administrative Court as part of the Queen's Bench Division, the former writs being now called orders (Supreme Court Act 1981, s 29: becomes Senior Courts Act 1981).

A person cannot normally invoke the supervisory jurisdiction of the High Court if other more appropriate procedures for appeal exist.

Order 53 of the Rules of the Supreme Court (becomes Senior Court Rules) which is attached as a schedule to the Civil Procedure Rules 1998 Part 50, introduces a comprehensive system of judicial review. A statutory basis for this procedure also appears in s 31 of the Supreme Court Act 1981 (becomes Senior Courts Act 1981). It allows an application to cover under one umbrella, as it were, all the remedies of *mandatory orders, prohibiting orders* and *quashing orders*, and also declaration and injunction. There is no need to apply for one of these remedies individually. Any combination of them is available under the one claim for judicial review. Damages may also be claimed on an application for judicial review (1981 Act, s 31(4)). No application for judicial review may be made without leave. Application is made for this to a single judge in what was called the Crown Office, but which is now called the Administrative Court. This is to eliminate frivolous claims. As regards the title of the action, proceedings are taken in the name of the Crown as in criminal proceedings. Thus, there is the citation as, e.g., *R v Barchester County Council, ex parte Bloggs* (since July 2000 the citation is e.g. *R (On the application of Bloggs) v Barchester County Council*). If permission to apply for judicial review is obtained from the single judge, the application is made in a criminal cause or matter to the Divisional Court of Queen's Bench and in a civil cause or matter to a single judge of the High Court. These applications are not governed by the track allocation procedures under the Civil Procedure Rules 1998 (see further Chapter 5).

There have been difficulties in the past as to whether a person had the necessary *locus standi*, i.e. interest, to bring an action for one of the administrative remedies. *Locus standi* is dealt with in Order 53 and s 31(3) of the 1981 Act which lay down a simple test which is that the applicant must have 'a sufficient interest in the matter to which the application relates'. The test is, of course, rather vague, but Lord Denning, in discussing the remedy of judicial review in *The Discipline of Law*, states:

> The court will not listen to a busybody who is interfering in things which do not concern him, but it will listen to an ordinary citizen who comes asking that the law should be declared and enforced, even though he is only one of a hundred, or one of a thousand, or one of a million who are affected by it. As a result, therefore, of the new procedure, it can I hope be said that we have in England an *actio popularis* by which an ordinary citizen can enforce the law for the benefit of all – as against public authorities in respect of their statutory duties.

However, it should not be assumed that judicial review is available to redress any decision which might be regarded in a broad sense as 'unfair'. The House of Lords made it clear in *Puhlhofer v Hillingdon LBC* [1986] 1 All ER 467 – an attempt to challenge a decision not to house the applicant – that persons seeking judicial review must base their case on one of the accepted principles of review, e.g. *ultra vires* or procedural irregularity.

As we have seen, decisions taken at a trial on indictment in the Crown Court are not subject to judicial review (see *R v Harrow Crown Court, ex parte Perkins* [1998] Current Law 96).

R v Brighton Justices, ex parte Robinson, 1973 – Judicial review not generally available where appropriate procedures for appeal exist (7)
IRC v National Federation of Self-Employed and Small Businesses Ltd, 1981 – Judicial review: the need for *locus standi* (8)

Grounds on which a quashing order lies

The only grounds on which such an order lies are as follows:

(a) Want or excess of jurisdiction. This exists where the inferior court or body has adjudicated on a matter which it had no power to decide, i.e. where it is acting beyond its powers (*ultra vires*).

A quashing order is not the only remedy which may be used to control *ultra vires* acts. Note, for example, the use of an injunction in the *ultra vires* situation seen in *A-G v Fulham Corporation*, 1921 (Case 6).

(b) Denial of natural justice. The principle is that, although a tribunal should not be required to conform to judicial standards, but should be free to work out its own procedures, nevertheless it must observe the rules of natural justice, i.e. there must be no bias and both sides should be heard.

(i)   *Bias*. This may be pecuniary bias but other forms of bias are relevant as where, for example, the chairman of magistrates states that he always prefers the evidence for the prosecution given by the police. It was held in *Seer Technologies Ltd* v *Abbas* (2000) *The Times*, 16 March that it was inconceivable that any legitimate objection could be taken against a judge purely on grounds of religion, ethnic or national origin, gender, age or sexual orientation. This is obviously right, since it would allow the issue of bias to be brought in many cases particularly as women and black lawyers begin to be appointed to the judiciary. A defendant cannot be allowed to say, e.g., 'The judge was biased. He is black and I am white', or 'The judge is a woman and I am a man'. The situation would, of course, be different if actual bias could be shown as where a female or black judge was shown to have a pecuniary interest in the outcome of a case.

The Court of Appeal ruled in *Kjell Tore Skjevesland* v *Geveran Trading Co Ltd* [2003] 1 All ER 1 that the requirement that judges be free from bias may not always apply to advocates. The petitioner was not entitled to a retrial of bankruptcy proceedings on the ground that his barrister had been acquainted with the wife of the debtor for six years.

However, the House of Lords did find procedural bias in *Lawal* v *Northern Spirit Ltd* [2004] 1 All ER 187, where a barrister who had previously sat as a part-time judge in the Employment Appeal Tribunal appeared for the employer on appeal by the claimant to the EAT in a situation where one of the lay members of the EAT had previously sat with the barrister when he was taking appeals as a part-time judge. L contended that this could have been instrumental in the loss of his claim for racial discrimination. The House of Lords agreed that there was procedural bias.

(ii) *The right to be heard*. There is no inherent right to an oral hearing; written evidence may be acceptable. However, the right to be heard (*audi alteram partem*) implies that notice of the hearing or other method of stating one's case must be given together with notice of the case which is to be met (see *R* v *Wear Valley DC, ex parte Binks* (1985) and *R* v *Board of Governors of London Oratory School, ex parte R* (1988) at p 687). In addition, though the law is not entirely free from doubt, it is the better view that a reasonable opportunity to cross-examine witnesses is part of the *audi alteram partem* principle. Thus, in *Nicholson* v *Secretary of State for Energy* (1977) 76 LGR 693, the right of cross-examination at a public inquiry into the siting of an opencast mine was upheld on the basis that the denial of that right was a breach of natural justice.

Legal representation is also part of the *audi alteram partem* principle. Public tribunals under the Tribunals and Inquiries Act 1992 will normally allow a party who wants it to have a lawyer to represent him. As regards a domestic tribunal, the Court of Appeal in *Enderby Town Football Club Ltd* v *The Football Association Ltd* [1971] 1 All ER 215 laid down the following broad principles:

(1) If the rules of the organisation say nothing about it, the matter is basically within the discretion of the tribunal.

(2) If the case involves difficult points of law, it is better for the parties to use the ordinary courts and get a declaratory judgment setting out their rights. If, however, a tribunal is used, legal representation should be allowed and the court will intervene on the grounds of public policy to see that it is.

(3) A rule forbidding legal representation altogether is probably invalid. A tribunal should always be given a discretion.

However, it seems that in *disciplinary cases* where it is necessary to reach decisions quickly, it might well be appropriate to refuse legal representation. Thus, in *Maynard v Osmond* [1977] 1 All ER 64, the Court of Appeal held that natural justice did not require that a police constable should have legal representation at a hearing before the chief constable on a disciplinary matter involving an allegation that a sergeant had falsely stated that PC Maynard had been asleep while on duty. Furthermore, the House of Lords decided in *R v Board of Visitors of the Maze Prison, ex parte Hone and McCarten* [1988] 1 All ER 321 that a prisoner charged with a disciplinary offence is not entitled, as of right, to legal representation at the disciplinary hearing.

Whether a decision is judicial, quasi-judicial or administrative, or disciplinary, the rules of natural justice need not necessarily be applied if national security is involved.

(c) Effect of failure to comply with rules. In recent times the courts have made it clear that anything done by a tribunal in breach of natural justice (or *ultra vires*) is void. If action has been taken on the decision of a tribunal which is void that action is also void. If the decision was merely voidable action taken on it prior to the court quashing it would be valid.

(d) Error of law on the face of the record. A quashing order lies to quash a decision the record of which discloses an error of law. According to Lord Denning in *R v Northumberland Compensation Appeal Tribunal, ex parte Shaw* [1952] 1 All ER 122, the record consists of 'the document which initiates the proceedings, the pleadings (if any), and the adjudication, but not the evidence or the reasons unless the tribunal chooses to incorporate them'. As we have seen, the Tribunals and Inquiries Act 1992 requires reasoned decisions in cases coming before tribunals and inquiries so that there should now normally be a record giving reasons which will assist the High Court in exercising its supervisory jurisdiction. In addition, if a reasoned decision is required by the 1992 Act a mandatory order lies to compel the tribunal or inquiry to give one.

However, the above provisions do not apply to magistrates' courts. If an order of a magistrates' court does not contain reasons for the making of the order, then, provided the magistrates have stayed within their jurisdiction and observed the rules of natural justice, a quashing order does not lie on the order under this heading.

R v London County Council, ex parte Entertainments Protection Association Ltd, 1931 – Quashing orders and *ultra vires* (**9**)

Dimes v Grand Junction Canal, 1852 – Monetary bias (**10**)

R v Bingham Justices, ex parte Jowitt, 1974 – Other bias (**11**)

R v Secretary of State for Home Department, ex parte Hosenball, 1977 – Natural justice and national security (**12**)

Ridge v Baldwin, 1963 – Effect of failure to comply with rules of natural justice and *ultra vires* (**13**)

A prohibiting order lies to prevent an inferior tribunal from exceeding its jurisdiction, or infringing the rules of natural justice. It is governed by similar principles to a quashing order, except that it does not lie once a final decision has been given (a quashing order is then the appropriate order). The object of a prohibiting order is to prevent an inferior tribunal from hearing and deciding a matter which is beyond its jurisdiction. A prohibiting order and a quashing order are available against the Crown and public authorities but not against private persons or bodies, e.g. the big industrial conglomerates and trade unions.

Applications for quashing and prohibiting orders are often brought together, e.g. to quash a decision already made by a tribunal, and to prevent it from continuing to exceed or abuse its jurisdiction.

A prohibiting order may be issued to any person or body (not necessarily an inferior court, since it might be issued to a local authority). It commands him or them to carry out some public duty. Once again, it is not available against private persons or bodies.

It might be used to compel an administrative tribunal to hear an appeal which it is refusing to hear, or to compel a local authority to carry out a duty lying upon it, e.g. to produce its accounts for inspection by a council tax payer (*R* v *Bedwellty UDC* [1943] 1 KB 333). A mandatory order lies to compel the exercise of a duty and of a discretionary power, though in the case of the latter not in a particular way.

It is not available against the Crown itself, but it may issue against Ministers or other Crown servants to enforce a personal statutory duty.

The High Court has power to issue the above orders under s 29(3) of the Supreme Court Act 1981 (becomes Senior Courts Act 1981) in respect of all decisions of the Crown Court (with the exception of matters relating to trial on indictment) where such orders are normally appropriate, e.g. where an error of law appears on the face of the record in, say, a licensing decision as where the Crown Court appears to have misinterpreted statutory provisions (*R* v *Exeter Crown Court, ex parte Beattie* [1974] 1 All ER 1183). Appeals from trials on indictment are to the Court of Appeal, Criminal Division.

Injunction and declaratory judgment

The High Court can also exercise control over the decisions of inferior tribunals by granting, at its discretion, an injunction to prevent, for example, the implementation of a decision made by an inferior tribunal which does not observe the rules of natural justice. The remedy is not *normally* available against the Crown (*Factortame Ltd* v *Secretary of State for Transport* [1989] 2 All ER 692), but see Chapter 8. Defiance of an injunction amounts to contempt of court. In many ways the remedy is like a prohibiting order. However, it is rarely used against public tribunals. It is more commonly brought into play against domestic tribunals.

A *declaratory judgment* may be asked for by a person aggrieved by the decision of an inferior tribunal so that the High Court can state the legal position of the parties. Defiance of a declaratory judgment is not a contempt of court and there is no method by which it can be enforced, but parties usually observe it. However, disobedience could lead to a later action for an injunction or damages in which the law would already have been decided leaving only the facts to be proved. A declaration by the court that an administrative act was *ultra vires* will make it void and of no effect. It is particularly useful in respect of complaints against the actions of government departments and Ministers.

It is important to note here that in *R* v *Secretary of State for Employment, ex parte Equal Opportunities Commission*, 1994 (see Chapter 19) the House of Lords gave a declaratory judgment to the effect that UK employment law on part-time working was incompatible with the Treaty of Rome and the EC Equal Pay Directive. In doing so they were, in effect, saying that what was then the government's Employment Protection (Consolidation) Act 1978 was not correct. Their Lordships also made two decisions of great importance as follows:

(*a*) that the judicial review procedure is available to deal with defects in the government's interpretation of EC employment law. This is a much quicker way of sounding out the possible application of EC law than a reference to the European Court of Justice;

(*b*) that the Equal Opportunities Commission had the necessary *locus standi* (right to be heard) in this case. In other words, the EOC was qualified to act on behalf of a group of workers, i.e. part-timers. This principle was previously in doubt and the House of Lords did not feel that it was prevented from making this decision by *IRC* v *National Federation of Self-Employed and Small Businesses Ltd*, 1981 (see Case 8), though the case was not overruled. The decision strengthens the power of pressure groups, as does the judicial review ruling.

Damages

Although a public authority has acted unlawfully in the sense of being *ultra vires*, a person affected, such as Shell UK in *R* v *Lewisham BC, ex parte Shell UK* (see Case **6**: Comment (ii)), cannot recover damages against the wrongdoer unless he can base his claim on breach of contract, or a tort, or alleges infringement of a property right (*O'Reilly* v *Mackman* [1983] 2 AC 237). It was held in *R* v *Knowsley Metropolitan Borough Council, ex parte Maguire* (1992) *The Independent*, 19 June (High Court) that there was no general right to damages against a local authority for maladministration.

Where on an application for judicial review it appears that there is a case, e.g. a breach of contract, for which damages might be available, the court may, instead of refusing the application, order the proceedings to continue as if begun by claim form under the Civil Procedure Rules 1998 and may give directions either allocating the proceedings to a case management track or providing for allocation questionnaires or an allocation hearing (see further Chapter 5).

R v *Commissioner of Police of the Metropolis, ex parte Blackburn*, 1973 – Mandatory orders and discretionary powers (**14**)

R v *Secretary of State for Social Services, ex parte Grabaskey*, 1972 – Mandatory orders may be issued against Ministers (**15**)

Laker Airways v *Department of Trade*, 1977 – Declaratory judgments: actions of government departments and Ministers (**16**)

Judicial review – delay

It was decided in *R* v *Dairy Produce Quota Tribunal for England and Wales, ex parte Caswell* [1989] 3 All ER 205 that if application for judicial review was not made promptly or within three months at the latest as prescribed by Order 53 of the Rules of the Supreme Court, the judge had to refuse leave to continue an action unless the applicant had a good reason for the delay.

Judicial review and infringements of human rights

When reviewing the decision-making powers of public authorities the court has sometimes used the *Wednesbury* reasonable test (see p 80) under which the court has quashed the decision of a public authority not on the basis that it did not have the power to make it but that it was an unreasonable decision. The court is saying in effect that no reasonable decision-maker could have made the decision that the court is being asked to review.

However, where the decision is also an infringement of an individual's human rights the House of Lords in *R* v *Secretary of State for the Home Department ex parte Daly* [2001] 2 WLR 1622 has substituted a test of 'proportionality'. Thus in a human rights case the court will not ask whether it would have made the decision (a merits-based test) nor whether the decision was so unreasonable that no reasonable decision-maker could have made it (*Wednesbury*). Instead the test will be proportionality. This means that the court needs to look at the legitimate decision of a public authority in terms of whether there is a *fair balance* between the protection of individual rights and the interests of the public at large.

The proportionality test has always been the approach of the European Court of Human Rights and an example from that court is to be found in *Open Door Counselling and Well Woman* v *Ireland* [1993] 15 EHRR 244 where the court found that an injunction preventing the publicising of information about abortion was disproportionate to the aim of protecting morals because it was framed as an absolute ban, i.e. it prevented information being given even where there might be serious medical need.

Although the proportionality test has arisen in connection with human rights claims there have been statements by the senior judiciary that it should be recognised in all cases of judicial review. It will obviously be difficult to combine the *Wednesbury* reasonable test with the test of proportionality and it is likely that the proportionality test will take over from *Wednesbury*.

In the *Daly* case the Home Secretary had introduced a blanket policy allowing cell searches in prisons and examination of correspondence between the prisoner and his lawyers in the prisoner's absence. The House of Lords ruled that the policy infringed the prisoner's right to legal professional privilege at common law and was contrary to the Human Rights Convention, Art 8 (right to privacy). The infringement was greater than could be shown to be justified by the aim, e.g. of revealing and prosecuting crime successfully. In other words, the House of Lords was saying that the policy was disproportionate.

There is some difference between the tests, the proportionality test being more *objective*. The *Wednesbury* test does involve the court in saying that no reasonable decision-maker could have made it and yet as we know some religious groups are opposed to abortion and some of them are decision-makers. Indeed, some governments are pro-life and yet have been elected by a wide franchise. Are all the decisions of such a government to be declared unreasonable where they follow pro-life policies? The proportionality test is more objective and less personal in its approach though it will often produce the same effect as *Wednesbury*.

Judicial review – a commercial context

The remedy of judicial review has traditionally operated mainly in the field of public law in terms, for example, of the review of decisions made by local and central government or Ministers. More recently the remedy has been extended into a more commercial context. Thus in *Interbrew SA v Competition Commission and the Secretary of State for Trade and Industry* [2001] All ER (D) 305 the Belgian brewer Interbrew had tried to acquire Whitbread the UK brewer but the Competition Commission exercising powers under the Competition Act 1998 had decided that in view of the fact that Interbrew had already acquired Bass Brewers, the makers of Carling and Tennants lager, the acquisition of Whitbread would be contrary to the public interest as creating abuse of a dominant position in terms of supply. The Commission ruled that if Whitbread was acquired Interbrew must sell off Bass. Interbrew claimed that the Commission had not given it a fair hearing in terms of other solutions put forward to it by Interbrew, but the Secretary of State had followed the decision of the Commission. The Administrative Court found for Interbrew and quashed the decision of the Secretary of State.

Other controls on decision making

Ministers of the Crown and the courts

Sometimes an Act of Parliament places a Minister in a supervisory role over, for example, the decisions of local authorities, and where this is so he must act judicially and not administratively in respect of that supervisory role. If he does not exercise the supervisory role in the way envisaged by the Act which gave it to him, the Minister's directions are themselves subject to review by the court. This is, of course, in addition to the parliamentary question and the rule of ministerial responsibility to Parliament.

> *Secretary of State for Education and Science v Tameside Metropolitan Borough Council*, 1976 – Courts can examine executive action (**17**)

3

The Ombudsman

It has become a popular idea to give the citizen safeguards against maladministration which are in addition to the traditional ones of application to a court or tribunal, by the setting up in various areas of administration of Ombudsmen, so called because the system is modelled upon the Scandinavian office of Ombudsman. Some examples appear below.

The Parliamentary and Health Service Commissioner

A further check on abuse of power by government departments was created by the appointment of the Parliamentary Commissioner for Administration (or 'Ombudsman') (now the Parliamentary and Health Service Commissioner) under the provisions of the Parliamentary Commissioner Act 1967 (whose jurisdiction has been extended by the Parliamentary Commissioner Act 1994). The Commissioner is appointed by the Crown and has the same security of tenure as a judge of the Supreme Court. He is also a member of the Council on Tribunals. His function is to investigate complaints relating to the exercise of administrative functions. However, investigation of central government departments is made only at a Member of Parliament's request and a citizen who wishes to have a complaint investigated must first bring it to the MP's notice.

Unfortunately, the Commissioner is very often limited to a consideration of the *administrative procedures* followed and is powerless to act if the correct procedure has been followed even though the decision is bad. Furthermore, he cannot investigate personnel matters. Nevertheless, each year sees a steady rise in the number of complaints referred to him, though the Commissioner and his functions are still not well enough known and he is at the present time less effective than his counterparts in other countries. In fact, Britain is alone among the countries with national ombudsmen in not allowing the Ombudsman to initiate his own investigations. Most of the complaints involve government departments in constant contact with the public, more complaints being levied against the Department of Social Security, followed by the Inland Revenue, than any other department. In this connection, there is now a Revenue adjudicator to whom taxpayers can complain. Those who are not satisfied with the adjudicator's decision may still ask their MPs to take up the complaint with the Parliamentary Ombudsman.

The Commissioner's jurisdiction under the Act of 1967 is limited to certain aspects of Central Government administration but the Parliamentary Commissioner (Consular Complaints) Act 1981 extends the jurisdiction of the Parliamentary Commissioner to complaints about the conduct of United Kingdom consular officers abroad. The Parliamentary and Health Service Commissioners Act 1987 extends the jurisdiction of the Parliamentary Commissioner to non-departmental bodies etc. listed in Sch 1, e.g. the Information Commissioner under the Data Protection Act 1998. Section 110 of the Courts and Legal Services Act 1990 extends the jurisdiction of the Commissioner to administrative acts of the administrative staff of courts and tribunals. This does not include review of the acts of the judiciary or tribunal members.

There is also a Health Service Commissioner for England and Wales to investigate complaints about certain aspects of the National Health Service. The Commissioner is the Parliamentary Commissioner who, therefore, combines the two offices and takes the title of Parliamentary and Health Service Commissioner.

Under the Act of 1967 the Parliamentary Commissioner is given discretion whether to investigate a complaint or not. It was held in *R v Parliamentary Commissioner, ex parte Dyer* [1994] 1 All ER 375 that there was nothing in either the Commissioner's role or statutory framework which placed him beyond judicial review, but because of the largely discretionary nature of his duties the court would not readily interfere with his exercise of those discretions. In consequence, a prohibiting order will not issue to him since he has no duty to hear a complaint (*Re Fletcher's Application* [1970] 2 All ER 527). Furthermore, there is no way of enforcing the findings of the Ombudsman and there are those who feel that it would improve matters if the courts had power to enforce these findings. Judicial review is available against the decisions of local commissioners (see *R v Local Commissioner for Administration for the South, the West, the West Midlands, etc.* [1988] 3 All ER 151).

Commissions for Local Administration

In addition, there are two Commissions for Local Administration in England and Wales each consisting of Local Commissioners appointed by the Secretary of State plus the Parliamentary Commissioner. A Local Commissioner may investigate a written complaint made by a member of the public who claims to have sustained injustice in consequence of maladministration in connection with action taken by or on behalf of a local authority, joint board, police authority or water authority, being action taken in the exercise of administrative functions. The complaint will normally be made in writing either through a member of the local authority complained against *or* with evidence that a member has been asked to refer it but has not done so. Furthermore, it must be made within a time limit of 12 months. Any one of the Local Commissioners has the same powers as the High Court to require the attendance of witnesses and production of documents when he is conducting an investigation. He must report the results of any investigation to the person who referred the complaint to him, to the complainant and to the authority concerned which must make copies available for public inspection. If he finds that injustice has been caused, the authority concerned must consider his report and notify him of what action they have taken. The greatest number of complaints relates to activities of local housing and planning authorities. Certain matters, such as the conduct of legal proceedings, action taken to prevent crime, or action concerning the giving of instruction or discipline in schools, are excluded from the jurisdiction of a Local Commissioner.

Legal Services Ombudsman

Sections 21–26 of the Courts and Legal Services Act 1990 set up the office of Legal Services Ombudsman. The object is to help people who have a genuine cause for complaint against members of the legal profession but have not been able to sort their problems out. The Ombudsman has power to investigate the handling of complaints by the Law Society, the Bar Council and the Council for Licensed Conveyancers, reinvestigate the complaints and recommend remedies. He reports annually to the Lord Chancellor and Parliament.

Under s 49 of the Access to Justice Act 1999 the powers of the Ombudsman are widened and binding awards of compensation can be made, but the jurisdiction does not extend to alleged overcharging as such. Bad work is a main ground of complaint. Under the provisions of s 50 of the 1999 Act the Lord Chancellor can require the relevant professional bodies to pay contributions to the Ombudsman's expenses, which goes some way to making the ombudsman scheme self-funding.

Other Ombudsmen

The Financial Services Authority has set up a company called The Financial Services Ombudsman Scheme to operate an arrangement capable of resolving disputes between, e.g.

independent financial advisers regulated by the FSA and consumers. The Financial Services Ombudsman has appointed three ombudsmen to deal with banking, insurance and investment services. Compensation up to £100,000 (currently) can be awarded with an additional £1,000 where the complainant has suffered distress and inconvenience. If a regulated firm has not dealt with a consumer's complaint within eight weeks, the consumer can go to the Ombudsman. These complaints can, of course, be brought in the ordinary courts since they will usually be based on negligence and/or breach of contract. Section 225 of the Financial Services and Markets Act 2000 contains the necessary powers for the FSA to set up an ombudsman service.

Sections 150–160 of the Pensions Act 1995 provide for a Pensions Ombudsman to adjudicate in disputes between an individual and a pension scheme or provider. In addition, the Institute of Chartered Accountants in England and Wales has appointed an ombudsman called the 'Receiver of Complaints' to review complaints against its members.

Under Article 195 of the EC Treaty, the European Parliament is enabled to appoint an ombudsman to investigate maladministration by Community institutions including the non-judicial functions of the EC courts. The Ombudsman may be approached directly or through an MEP, or may investigate of his own motion. He holds office for the duration of the Parliament and can only be dismissed by the European Court at the request of the Parliament.

The Human Rights Act 1998

The materials discussed so far in this chapter have been concerned with the operation of various controls on authority of one sort or another. The Human Rights Act 1998 (HRA) which came into force on 2 October 2000 represents the most massive vehicle for control of authority, whatever called, in its day-to-day activities. The following is an outline of its effects upon English law.

New legislation

Under s 19 the HRA provides that, in respect of new legislation, the Minister in charge of it must make a statement that the relevant Bill is compatible with the rights of the European Convention on Human Rights, most of which it incorporates into UK law. This statement, which must be made before the Second Reading of the relevant Bill, also appears on the front of the Bill and on the Explanatory Notes and Financial Memorandum which accompany it. The object is to concentrate the mind of government on the matter of compatibility. It also informs Members of Parliament that human rights are relevant in debates on the Bill. Finally, it reminds the judiciary of the need to give the Bill, when it passes into law, a compatible interpretation, although s 3 requires this anyway. If a Bill is not compatible with the Convention, the appropriate Minister must give reasons during Parliamentary debate.

A new rule of statutory interpretation

Section 3 provides that so far as it is possible to do so, Acts of Parliament and delegated legislation must be interpreted in a way which is compatible with Convention rights. This introduces a new rule of construction (see further Chapter 6) and has a significant effect on the rule of precedent in that for example a Crown Court could be obliged to refuse to follow a previous decision of the Court of Appeal or even the House of Lords on the meaning of an Act of Parliament if this was required to give effect to Convention rights. Thus, if a piece of legislation can be interpreted in two ways, one compatible with the Convention and one not, the court is required to choose the compatible interpretation. Nevertheless, the section makes clear that if the only possible interpretation is contrary to the Convention, it must be applied and remains valid.

Section 3 applies to past as well as future legislation. This rule of construction is not unique in that our courts and tribunals are already required to interpret the provisions of English domestic law in order to be compatible with European law.

Method of interpretation

Under s 2 UK courts must take into account relevant case law of the European Court of Justice and the Commission of Human Rights when determining a question of human rights, but the relevant decisions are not binding on UK courts. The UK courts will, in having regard to Convention cases, have to use Convention techniques of interpretation. Since the general theme of the European approach is that human rights are always developing and that the Convention is a 'living document' a practical effect will be that UK courts will be less inclined to have regard to older UK case law. Nevertheless, it is only the Convention that binds UK courts and not the interpretive case law. Clearly the UK Human Rights Act 1998 must be interpreted in a way compatible with Convention rights.

Declaration of incompatibility

Under s 4 where a 'designated court', e.g. the House of Lords, the Judicial Committee of the Privy Council, the Court of Appeal or the High Court, is satisfied that primary or secondary legislation is incompatible with Convention rights and cannot be interpreted to be otherwise, it may (not must) make a declaration of 'incompatibility'. This does not affect the validity of the provision nor is it binding on the parties to the case in which it is made and it operates only as a notification to Parliament that a measure has been found incompatible.

The ability to make a declaration of incompatibility in the case of subordinate legislation applies where the primary legislation under which it was made prevents the removal of that incompatibility. If not, delegated legislation can be struck down by the court or merely disapplied. This is not possible with primary legislation (see s 3(2)). This is a major extension of the *ultra vires* rule discussed earlier in this chapter.

It should be noted that common law case law has no protection under the HRA as has legislation, particularly primary legislation. The common law must be developed in a way compatible with the Convention.

Public authorities

Section 6 provides that it is unlawful for a public authority to act in a way which is incompatible with Convention rights. There is no full definition of 'public authority'. It was felt by Parliament to be better to leave this to the courts as cases came before them. However, s 6 expressly excludes both Houses of Paliament and expressly includes courts and tribunals. Beyond that, it includes 'any person certain of whose functions are functions of a public nature'.

Proceedings against public authorities

Section 7 provides that anyone who claims that a public authority has acted or proposes to act in a way incompatible with rights in the Convention may:

- bring proceedings against that authority; or
- join in proceedings brought by someone else where the person joining the proceedings is a 'victim', e.g. a person whose Convention rights have been violated.

Freedom of expression

Section 12 applies and was inserted into the HRA at a late stage. The main object is to protect the freedom of the press.

Freedom of thought, conscience and religion

Section 13 was also a late amendment inserted mainly to deal with problems posed by religious groups which felt that the Act might lead to interference with doctrinal matters, such as requiring churches to marry homosexual couples.

Remedial orders

A remedial order is by reason of s 20(1) a statutory instrument. The provision relating to such order is contained in s 10. These orders amend legislation in order to remove any incompatibility with Convention rights. When faced with a judicial declaration of incompatibility Parliament will generally legislate to remove it. There are three major safeguards on the use of the power as follows:

- there must be a finding of incompatibility by the judiciary;
- the Minister involved must feel that there are 'compelling reasons' for making a remedial order; and
- there must be Parliamentary approval in line with Sch 2.

A Minister may infer incompatibility from a decision of the European Court of Human Rights, but it must be a decision containing a judgment against the UK and, therefore, binding on the UK in international law. Judgments against other contracting parties to the Convention will not suffice, even though they reveal incompatibility in UK legislation.

Commission for Equality and Human Rights

However, the Equality Act 2006, which received the Royal Assent on 16 February 2006, will set up the Commission for Equality and Human Rights (CEHR). The Commission will take over the existing duties of the Equal Opportunities Commission, the Commission for Racial Equality and the Disability Rights Commission. It will promote equality and combat unlawful discrimination also in the new areas of sexual orientation, religion or belief and age, and it will promote understanding of human rights and encourage public authorities to comply with the Human Rights Act 1998.

The CEHR will be established in October 2007 for areas other than racial equality. This area transfers by March 2009.

Further details of this legislation appear in Chapter 19.

Remedies

Section 8 gives the court a general discretion as regards remedies and an award of damages is included. However, the court must have power to award damages so that criminal courts cannot make such an award. They may, however, quash a conviction. As regards action against public authorities, the court could quash a decision made by such an authority, or award damages. In a criminal matter, the court may also order the exclusion of evidence. Loss of earnings is recoverable and awards of damages have been made by the ECHR (European Court of Human Rights) for 'permanent and deep anxiety' caused by violation of Convention rights as where civil proceedings have been unduly prolonged. High awards of damages have been made for police misconduct and wrongful detention and for unfair trials, e.g. non-attendance of the claimant's lawyer after a decision to let the trial proceed. High awards have also been made for interference with rights of privacy and in child care cases where a parent has been denied contact with a child. Environmental issues, as where pollution has caused illness, distress or inconvenience, have also received high awards.

Limitation period

Under s 7(5) the limitation period for bringing claims against public authorities is one year from the doing of the act complained of. Otherwise, no limitation period is imposed by the HRA. In addition, of course, a court may find that an over-short limitation period is a violation of human rights.

Companies

Although the Convention rights are seen initially at least as a tool for the relief of individuals against arbitrary acts of the state, the HRA does not preclude claims by companies if they are victims of human rights abuse. It is also worth noting that the City Panel on Take-overs and Mergers which operates self-regulatory controls in company take-over situations is a public body and potentially within human rights law as is the Financial Services Authority which controls, under the statutory authority of the Financial Services and Markets Act 2000, almost the whole of the financial services industry.

The EU experience

It is not possible in a book of this nature to go into the detail of Convention case law so far. However, the following headings indicate the main areas involved.

- *The right to a fair trial in civil proceedings*. This has included unfair arbitration clauses, short limitation periods, legal aid and admissibility of evidence, burden and standard of proof, expert witnesses who are over-biased in favour of a client and are sometimes referred to as 'hired guns'. Enforcement of judgments and rights of appeal are included.
- *The right to life and physical integrity*. Here are included abortion, euthanasia, the death penalty, torture, and medical care and access to health information.
- *Police powers*. This includes fingerprinting, search and seizure, entrapment, arrest and detention and discrimination.
- *Mental health*. This includes detention and the right of periodic review.
- *Family life*. This includes adoption, embryology and surrogacy, lesbian and gay couples and transsexuals, divorce and separation, and domestic violence.
- *Children*. This concerns parental control, corporal punishment, detention and abuse.
- *Freedom of expression*. This includes defamation proceedings and access to information.
- *Workplace rights*. This covers the right to form a trade union and the right to join or not to join one, industrial action and privacy at work, including security vetting.

There have also been rulings in the fields of immigration and asylum, prisoners' rights, education, housing planning and the environment, welfare benefits, protest and public order, property rights, thought, conscience and religion, and discrimination.

The UK experience

Many cases in which the Convention has been raised have come before UK courts and it is therefore reasonable to expect students to be able to quote some of these as examples of the use of the Articles of the Convention by claimants. As an introduction, however, it has emerged from the case law that if a human rights point is taken it should be taken properly and not thrown into the case as a makeweight. Advocates wishing to rely on the Convention are under a duty to the court to make available any material in terms of decisions of the European Court of Human Rights on which they could rely or that might assist the court (see *Barclays Bank plc* v *Ellis and Another* (2000) *The Times*, 24 October).

An advocate should also consider carefully whether the 1998 Act and Convention add anything to the argument (*Daniels* v *Walker* [2000] 1 WLR 1382) and should not use court hearings as an international seminar on human rights (*Williams* v *Cowell* [2000] 1 WLR 187).

Finally, although the Court of Appeal has found certain of the provisions of the Consumer Credit Act 1974 incompatible with the Convention (see below), the impact of the Act of 1998 to date has not been as far-reaching as some commentators said it would be. This is hardly surprising. It would be rather odd if UK law was found to be full of serious deficiencies. What we have seen is many challenges to substantive law by reference to the Act and Convention. This process is likely to continue.

Case law Art 6: right to a fair trial of disputes

Wilson v First County Trust (No 2) [2002] QB 74

In this case the Court of Appeal held the absolute bar on the enforcement of a consumer credit agreement in s 127(3) of the Consumer Credit Act 1974 which provides that such an agreement is unenforceable if it fails to contain the terms prescribed under s 61 of the 1974 Act, infringed the trader's rights for the purposes of Art 6. He was unable to recover a loan and interest simply because the agreement had misstated the amount owing in the loan agreement. The court made a declaration of incompatibility of the relevant sections of the 1974 Act.

The above ruling of the Court of Appeal was reversed by the House of Lords in *Wilson* v *First County Trust (No 2)* (2003) *The Times*, 11 July. The House of Lords ruled that although s 127(3) of the Consumer Credit Act 1974 led automatically and inflexibly to a ban on a court making an enforcement order if a regulated agreement did not comply with the statutory requirements about the form and content of the agreement, it was open to Parliament to decide as a matter of social policy that despite the severity of its effect that was an appropriate way to protect consumers. Therefore, s 127(3) was compatible with the Human Rights Convention.

Comment The Consumer Credit Act 2006 repeals s 127(3) of the Consumer Credit Act 1974 but not the whole section. The result is that, for the future, the previous bars to a court granting an enforcement order in respect of an agreement that is improperly executed have gone. The court is left with a discretion under s 127(1) to refuse an enforcement order if it considers it just to do so and according to the degree of prejudice to any party or person. This is in line with the thinking in the House of lords in *Wilson* because their Lordships may well have regarded s 127(3) as contrary to the Convention if all credit agreements were non-regulated. At the time of the action, a credit agreement was non-regulated only if the credit exceeded £25,000. Section 2 of the 2006 Act removes the limits so that all agreements for credit or hire will be regulated under the 1974 Act though there are exemptions, e.g. credit over £25,000 to large businesses. In future, situations like *Wilson* would be decided under the just and equitable principle of s 127(1) and there would be no absolute bar to the court granting an enforcement order so that the 1974 Act, after amendment by the 2006 Act, is not contrary to Art 6.

R (on the application of Fleurose) v Securities and Futures Authority [2002] IRLR 297

Here the House of Lords held that it was justifiable for the SFA to require stock market traders to answer its questions and that the traders could not invoke the privilege against self-incrimination (a general rule in legal proceedings) because this would prevent the SFA from carrying out its duty to protect the public against infringements of the Authority's rules. In this case those involved had been manipulating prices in the stock market to make a profit. The Financial Services Authority took over from the SFA at the end of November 2000 with similar powers and protection by this case.

Case law Art 9: freedom of thought, conscience and religion

The Court of Appeal has ruled against a high school which sent home a pupil Shabina Begum for wearing a jilbab, i.e. a gown covering the whole of her body except her hands and face.

R (on the application of SB) v Headteacher and Governors of Denbigh High School [2005] 2 All ER 396

The relevant provision of the Convention on Human Rights reads as follows:

Article 9: Freedom of thought, conscience and religion
(1) Everyone has the right to freedom of thought, conscience and religion; this includes freedom to change his (or her) religion or belief and freedom either alone or in community with others and in public or private to manifest his (or her) religion or belief in worship, teaching, practice and observance.
(2) Freedom to manifest one's religion or beliefs shall be subject only to such limitations as are prescribed by law and are necessary in a democratic society in the interests of public safety for the protection of public order, health or morals or for the protection of the rights and freedoms of others.

The Court of Appeal ruled that the school had infringed Miss Begum's freedom to manifest her beliefs by taking the view that a shalwar kameez was acceptable for the majority of Muslims and that she accept this garment which showed more of the body.

Lord Justice Scott Baker said: 'Every shade of religious belief if genuinely held is entitled to due consideration under Art 9.'

Comment The school could have considered whether a limitation of Miss Begum's right was justified under Art 9(2) (above), but since it had not done so, it was impossible to conclude what the result would have been. The House of Lords reversed this decision (see [2006] 2 All ER 887).

Case law Art 10: freedom of expression

Steen v HM Attorney-General (2001) The Times, 30 March

In this case the Court of Appeal ruled that the proviso to an injunction preventing disclosure of any information obtained by any member of the Security Service in the course of his employment that required a person wishing to publish material within the terms of the injunction to get clearance from the Attorney-General was a restriction on the freedom of the press out of proportion to any public interest and was thus ineffective as being contrary to Art 10.

V and Another v News Group Newspapers Ltd and Others [2001] 1 All ER 908

This case may well be the most well-remembered case to date on human rights law. Jon Venables and Robert Thompson who were convicted of murder at the age of 11 took action against Newsgroup Newspapers and Associated Newspapers for an injunction to protect information that might lead to them being identified on release from detention. The High Court upheld their claim. In exceptional circumstances individuals who were seriously at risk of death or injury if their identity or whereabouts became public knowledge could be protected by an injunction as an exception to the defendant's right to freedom of expression.

Coroners' courts

These courts, which commenced in 1194, are amongst the oldest English courts still in existence. Their chief function is to inquire into cases of violent, unnatural or suspicious death, including suicide, together with cases of sudden death without apparent cause. They also inquire into deaths in prison.

A coroner has jurisdiction to hold an inquest on a body lying within his jurisdiction even though the death and cause of death have not occurred in England and Wales. Thus, in *R v West Yorkshire Coroner, ex parte Smith* [1982] 3 All ER 1098 the Court of Appeal decided that the coroner was obliged under what is now s 8 of the Coroners Act 1988 to hold an inquest into the death of a nurse who had died in Saudi Arabia but whose body had been brought back to this country. However, the coroner faces special difficulties in such a case because he cannot summon witnesses from abroad or request the production of documents (see further Chapter 5).

The procedure is that of an inquest or inquiry; it is not a trial. The object is to find out the identity of the deceased, the cause of his death, and where the death took place. It is not the purpose of an inquest to apportion blame (*R v Coroner for North Humberside and Scunthorpe, ex parte Jamieson* (1994) *The Times*, 28 April). The coroner's officer, a serving police officer, collects evidence before the inquest begins. All witnesses are under oath, but the rules of evidence are not applied as strictly as they are in other courts. The coroner decides what constitutes relevant and admissible evidence, and has much discretion at all stages of the investigation.

The coroner's jury

In cases such as suspected murder or death in prison, the coroner may summon a jury of from seven to 11 persons, and he may accept the verdict of the majority so long as there are not more than two dissentients. He is required to summon a jury under s 8(3) of the Coroners Act 1988 where the death with which he is concerned occurred in circumstances the continuance or possible recurrence of which is prejudicial to the health or safety of the public or any section of the public. An example from earlier legislation is the decision of the Court of Appeal in *R v Hammersmith Coroner, ex parte Peach* [1980] 2 All ER 7, where it was held that the suspicious or unauthorised use by a police officer of a lethal weapon was a matter coming within s 8, and accordingly it was compulsory to have a jury. Section 8(3) also requires a coroner to summon a jury where the deceased was in police custody or death resulted from an injury caused by a police officer in the purported exercise of his duty.

Section 9 of the 1988 Act provides that a person is not qualified to serve as a juror at an inquest held by a coroner unless he is for the time being qualified to serve as a juror in the Crown Court, the High Court, and the county court (see further Chapter 4). The Act also provides criminal penalties for evasion of service on a coroner's jury.

The coroner can require a *post mortem*, and the attendance of medical and other witnesses who may be examined on oath. He can also invite an expert to sit with him (*R v HM Coroner for Surrey, ex parte Wright* (1996) *The Independent*, 5 July).

If the court finds that a death was a result of murder, manslaughter or infanticide, this does not operate to convict the person said to be responsible, and a coroner can in no case charge a person with those offences.

It may happen that before the end of the inquest a person is charged with an offence, e.g. murder or manslaughter, in connection with the death of the deceased. On being informed of this by, e.g., a clerk to magistrates, the coroner must adjourn the inquest until after the conclusion of the relevant criminal proceedings and if he has summoned a jury he may, if he thinks fit, discharge them. This is to prevent inquests turning into, in effect, murder trials as they sometimes did in the 1920s.

After the conclusion of the relevant criminal proceedings the coroner may resume the adjourned inquest if, in his opinion, there is sufficient cause to do so. If he does resume an inquest, the finding of the inquest as to the cause of death must not be inconsistent with the outcome of the relevant proceedings (Coroners Act 1988, s 16(7)).

Under s 1 of the Coroners Act 1988 coroners are appointed for each coroner's district in a Metropolitan County or Greater London and for each Non-Metropolitan County and for the City of London by the relevant Councils. Appointment is from persons with a five-year general qualification within s 71 of the Courts and Legal Services Act 1990 or legally qualified medical practitioners who have had at least five years in practice.

Section 6 of the 1988 Act provides that every coroner must appoint a deputy coroner and *may* appoint an assistant deputy provided in each case that the approval of the Chairman of the relevant Council is obtained. This is to ensure continuity in the office where a coroner dies or retires. The qualifications for a deputy or assistant deputy are as for a coroner himself. All the appointments referred to above are generally part-time and there can be dismissal for inability or misbehaviour. The Lord Chief Justice and the judges of the High Court are by reason of holding that office also coroners *ex officio* as it is referred to.

Reform

The Home Office independent review group that reported in 2003 recommends that mandatory inquests into suicides, deaths at work and road accidents should be abolished. This says the report would respect the sensitivities of families in these cases. The report recommends that the circumstances of death should be settled administratively in private and without publicity and with respect for family privacy. Legislation will be required to effect the reforms.

At the time of writing there has been no implementation of the above proposals.

Treasure

The jurisdiction of coroners referred to in s 30 of the Coroners Act 1988 is exercisable in relation to anything which is treasure for the purposes of the Treasure Act 1996.

Treasure is any object which when found is at least 300 years old and if not a coin has a metallic content of silver or gold of at least 10 per cent by weight. This applies to coins which are at least 300 years old if they are one of at least two coins which taken together have the above percentage of gold or silver. Furthermore, if a coin is at least 300 years old and is one of at least 10 coins in the same find, it is treasure regardless of its metallic composition. A coin found on its own is not treasure.

Objects which are part of the same find whether found at the same time or earlier are also treasure so, for example, the pot (or whatever) in which the treasure is found is also treasure. The Secretary of State has a power to designate other types of objects as treasure, provided they are at least 200 years old. The power is exercisable by statutory instrument. Ownership of treasure will in general terms vest in the Crown. This ownership applies without regard to the place where it was found or the circumstances in which it was left. The Act removes the need to establish that the relevant objects were hidden with a view to their being later recovered. A new criminal offence of non-declaration of treasure is created. The finder must notify the coroner within 14 days from the date of the find or from the date when the finder believes or has reasonable grounds to believe that the object is treasure. The coroner's inquest held to decide whether what has been found is treasure may be held without a jury. If it is not treasure the finder, and not the Crown, acquires a good title to it.

If it is treasure (and so vests in the ownership of the Crown) and is to be transferred to a museum, the Secretary of State must decide whether a reward is to be payable by the museum prior to transfer. Under the old law a reward if payable was paid only to the person who found the treasure – often a person with a metal detector who made the discovery as a trespasser. The 1996 Act gives landowners and occupiers a right to a share and a right to be informed of finds which have been reported and are on their land. There is to be a code of practice which will deal among other things with how rewards will be paid and shared.

In the spring of 2006 the government issued a consultation paper containing proposals to speed up treasure handling by transferring administration of the process from the Department for Culture, Media and Sport to the British Museum. Currently, those finding treasure have to deal with both institutions at different stages of the process. The DCMS will retain its function to decide on valuations after being advised by the Treasure Valuation Committee. The consultation paper is entitled *Amendments to the Treasure Act 1996 Code of Practice* and can be accessed at **www.culture.gov.uk**.

Reform

The government has announced its intention to reform the law relating to treasure. The reform is aimed at clamping down on treasure hunters and dealers who sell items recovered without asking the landowner's consent to the excavation. Previous attempts have failed because of lack of parliamentary time. There is still no implementation of the above proposals.

Adjournment in event of judicial inquiry

Under s 17A of the Coroners Act 1988 (as inserted by s 71 of the Access to Justice Act 1999) coroners' inquests will normally be adjourned where a public inquiry is to be held which, in the opinion of the Lord Chancellor, will adequately investigate the death. At the end of the public inquiry the Lord Chancellor is required to inform the coroner, who will certify the facts ascertained at the inquiry as if they had been found at the inquest. The section reduces the possibility that inquests and inquiries may lead to conflicting findings of fact or lead to problems of self-incrimination.

Reform

The coroners' system is set for considerable reform under a draft Coroner Reform Bill. The main change relates to the families of the deceased person who is the subject of the inquest. Families will have the right to ask the coroner for a 'second opinion' on a death certificate about which they have concerns, together with a right to challenge coroners' rulings. A complaints system will be established.

All coroners will have to be legally qualified and will be given new powers to call evidence. The Department for Constitutional Affairs has stated that this means that no more solely medically qualified coroners will be appointed but the changes will not be retrospective and doctors without legal qualifications already in post will continue to act.

The right to seek a *review* of coroners' decisions will be easy to access and will not require the hiring of lawyers.

There will be a Chief Coroner for England and Wales to provide leadership and guidance to coroners in much the same way as the Lord Chief Justice does for the judiciary. The Chief Coroner will hear appeals against coroners' rulings, oversee their training and bring in judges to deal with complex matters. The Chief Coroner will be supported by a Coronial Advisory Council, which will act as a further check on standards and will advise on what service and strategic issues may require further scrutiny.

In addition, all coroners will be full-time appointments. Co-ordination between coroners will be improved and a 'Coroners' Charter' will be published, laying down the standard of service that bereaved family members can expect.

A suggested flaw in the draft Bill is that it does not provide legal aid to families to have legal representation *at inquests*. Thus, in a complicated inquest the coroner will have the benefit of advice from legal counsel and medical advice but the family will not have these benefits legally aided.

Legal services

Generally

Under the current regulatory system there are, for our purposes, six forms of legal service that are subject to statutory control mainly under the Courts and Legal Services Act 1990 as amended by Part III of the Access to Justice Act 1999. These services are:

- **The right to conduct litigation**. This is in the main the function of solicitors and legal executives.
- **The right of audience**. This is the right to be heard on a client's behalf by a judge. Barristers, solicitors and legal executives have these rights, with some restrictions on legal executives.
- **Certain probate services**. e.g. the right to draw up or prepare any papers in regard to the obtaining or opposing of the grant of probate of a will or letters of administration where there is no valid will. Probate or letters are necessary to effectively administer the estate of a deceased person.
- **The preparation of the documents required to convey land** from the ownership of one person into that of another.
- **Notorial services**. This is explained below.
- **Acting as a commissioner for oaths**, where the law requires that to validate a particular document a person must swear an oath before a commissioner as to its truth.

As regards the fitness of individuals to act in the above areas, this is left to authorised bodies, such as the Bar Council and the Law Society, which are concerned, in addition to other functions, with the education and training of those who are called to the Bar as barristers or entered on the Rolls as a solicitor or admitted to membership of the Institute of Legal Executives. There are a number of higher level regulators over the professional bodies, such as the Secretary of State for Constitutional Affairs (formerly the Lord Chancellor), the Master of the Rolls, who may refuse entry on the Rolls, and the Office of Fair Trading in regard, for example, to anti-competitive practices by the primary regulators such as the Bar Council and the Law Society.

Rights of audience

In order to understand current arrangements, it is necessary only to know that barristers have for many years been advocates presenting cases in court, whereas solicitors have been engaged, so far as actions in a court of law were concerned, in pre-trial work and briefing barristers to appear in court to present the case – something which they could not, in general do, at least at the level of the High Court and above. In today's environment, advocacy is still the work of barristers, but since the 1990 Act pre-trial work is called litigation and has been, and is, carried out by solicitors.

The position today is that, subject to satisfying the rules of the Bar Council (barristers) and the Law Society (solicitors), solicitors and barristers can appear and be advocates in all proceedings in every court and solicitors retain their function as litigators. However, the Bar Council has set up a scheme known as BARDIRECT under which, from 2003, people needing legal services including other professionals are able to bypass solicitors and engage a barrister direct. The barrister will then do both the litigation and advocacy elements of the case. The move is in response to threats from the Office of Fair Trading to stop restrictive practices that are not in the public interest.

A further and important development for users of legal services has resulted from the approval by the Secretary of State for Constitutional Affairs of a change in the Bar Council's code of conduct under which barristers who have been called to the Bar for at least three years and have practised for that time are able to liaise directly with the public without the need for a solicitor to act as intermediary. Before barristers can accept any direct access instructions, they must have attended a training course designated by the Bar Council. The move will cut costs in the more straightforward cases. In complicated claims, clients may still need the services of a solicitor.

Employed lawyers of either profession who are qualified as advocates can appear in court for their employers, but not for clients or customers of their employers.

The Institute of Legal Executives may make regulations under which legal executives, who are in general employed by solicitors, may conduct litigation, i.e. pre-trial work and advocacy, having a right of audience in civil and family proceedings in county counts and magistrates' courts. There is a proposal to extend their advocacy rights in criminal proceedings in the magistrates' and youth courts.

Overriding duties of advocates and litigators

These are as follows:

- to act with independence in the interests of justice; and
- to comply with rules of conduct.

Rights of audience and the employees of the Crown Prosecution Service

This is a special case because of the problems of impartiality. Nevertheless, the Crown Prosecution Service can now put its own advocates into court instead of, e.g., briefing barristers at the Bar at some expense. The CPS is now able to train its own employed advocates and put them into trials in the Crown Court and above. The hope is that they will not be swayed by a need for higher conviction rates. The reforms take effect under the Access to Justice Act 1999.

Conveyancing services

Sections 34–52 of the Courts and Legal Services Act 1990 are concerned to develop legal services by providing a wider choice of persons who may practise conveyancing which involves the preparation of the document (conveyance) which transfers a freehold interest in land after sale and the necessary documentation involved.

A sole regulatory body is set up by the 1990 Act. It is called the Authorised Conveyancing Practitioners Board and it is given the task of authorising, supervising and disciplining practitioners authorised for conveyancing work. Previously such work was restricted to solicitors, barristers and licensed conveyancers. They now face competition from authorised conveyancing practitioners.

A conveyancing ombudsman scheme to investigate complaints against authorised practitioners is set up and rules regulating the scheme are made by the Board. The Ombudsman can make compensation orders against practitioners including sums of money to represent inconvenience and distress as well as loss.

There is also the Council for Licensed Conveyancers which was set up under the Administration of Justice Act 1985, Part II to grant licences to practitioners of conveyancing services. This continues under the regulator, the Authorised Conveyancing Practitioners Board, but s 53 of the 1990 Act extends the powers of the Council so that it can extend the licences given to licensed conveyancers to allow them to undertake probate work, i.e. to get formal proof of a will, which must be applied for when the person making the will dies, or to get letters of administration to wind up the estate when there is no will, and to grant some rights of audience and rights to conduct litigation.

Probate services

Formerly, it was an offence for any person other than a solicitor or barrister to draft or prepare *for payment* the papers leading to a grant of probate or letters of administration. However, under ss 54 and 55 there is machinery by which bodies may apply for approved status under which their members could become 'probate practitioners' (s 55) (as the Institute of Chartered Accountants in England and Wales has already successfully done). The employees of banks, building societies and insurance companies can also do so under s 54.

Administration of oaths and the taking of affidavits

It is sometimes necessary for a person to make a statement on oath as to the truth of what is said in a document. If the statement in the document is false to the knowledge of the person giving the oath, that person commits the crime of perjury and can be prosecuted and may be fined or imprisoned. Every solicitor with a practising certificate can administer oaths and take affidavits (see below), but now s 113 provides that in the interests of competition authorised litigators and advocates may do so and may use the title 'Commissioner for Oaths', as can Licensed Conveyancers.

The Commissioners for Oaths (Prescribed Bodies) Regulations 1995 (SI 1995/1676) empower members of the Institute of Legal Executives to administer oaths and take affidavits (i.e. where the oath is administered in connection with the verification of the contents of a document) (and see also the notary public, at p 110).

Legal services: business structures

There are currently some statutory restrictions on the type of business structures through which legal services may be provided. These include a prohibition on lawyers entering into partnership with non-practising lawyers, other types of lawyers and non-lawyers, e.g. accountants. There are also restrictions on unregulated persons being formally involved in the management of a regulated legal practice and also on unregulated persons having a stake in the ownership of a legal practice. Thus, in general terms neither different types of lawyers, e.g. barristers and solicitors, nor lawyers and non-lawyers can work together in legal partnerships.

Legal services: consumer complaints

A complaint by a consumer of legal services must first of all be taken up with the legal practice concerned. Where the complaint is not resolved by the practice, the consumer can contact the relevant regulator, e.g. the Law Society. If the complaint is not resolved, the consumer may refer the complaint to the Legal Services Ombudsman. The Ombudsman will investigate the way in which the regulator handled the complaint and the response from the professional body. If the Ombudsman is not satisfied that the complaint has been handled properly, then he or she will recommend that the professional body look at the matter again.

Reform: the Legal Services Bill

Following a review of the provision of legal services by Sir David Clementi in 2004/05, the government has published the Legal Services Bill. It will be put before Parliament in the session 2006/07. Its main provisions are:

- To enable different types of lawyers and other professionals such as accountants to work together to provide legal and other services.
- To allow external investment in businesses offering such services.
- To create a Legal Services Board to regulate the legal profession. The majority of the Board will consist of non-lawyers. This new regulator will provide consistent oversight of the front-line regulators, such as the Bar Council and the Law Society with power to devolve day-to-day regulatory responsibilities to them subject to their competence and governance arrangements.
- To set up an Office for Legal Complaints to carry out independent investigation of complaints.
- To establish a consumer panel to represent consumer interests to the Legal Services Board.

Several companies, including the Co-op and the AA, have stated that they will set up provision of legal services once the Bill becomes law.

Payment for legal services

Conditional fees

In the past any form of contingency fee arrangement between a lawyer and a client, e.g. to give the lawyer a share of the damages or an increased fee if successful but nothing on failure, was unenforceable in English law. The position is now governed by ss 58, 58A and 58B of the Courts and Legal Services Act 1990 (as inserted by the Access to Justice Act 1999). These sections authorise:

- no-win, no-fee arrangements for lawyers and their clients; and
- discounted fee arrangements where a case is lost; and
- similar arrangements for those who fund litigation.

These arrangements are available for all claims except family cases, cases relating to children and criminal cases. The relevant agreements must be in writing.

At the present time the law allows a conditional fee arrangement under which the lawyer involved receives no fee if the client loses the case, but receives a fee enhanced by a success fee of up to a further 100 per cent if the client wins (see the Conditional Fee Agreements Order 1995 (SI 1995/1674)).

When a client approaches a solicitor for a conditional fee arrangement, it will be discovered that before an action can be commenced, a single premium after the event insurance policy must be entered into by the client to pay the other side's costs if the client loses and the client's court fees, though obviously the client will not have to pay the lawyer. In this context it should be noted that for, e.g., a personal injury claim of an estimated £100,000 the one premium insurance could be quite high, and this and the success fee were not recoverable from the other side even where the client won the case.

Under amendments made to the Courts and Legal Services Act 1990 as indicated above, the success fee is now recoverable from the losing side as is the insurance premium.

With regard to discounted fee arrangements, there is no element of success fee here. The lawyer takes his normal fee if the client wins but agrees to, say, discount the fee by 30 per cent if the case is lost. The lawyer's normal fee is, of course, recoverable from the losing party as costs in the normal way.

Regarding conditional fees, the initial premium remains a problem for some claimants even though it is recoverable if the case is won. However, it may be possible to negotiate with an insurance company so that the premium is only paid if the claimant wins. If the case is lost, the insurance company merely pays the agreed costs and the other side's claim where the insurance is, in addition to a cost insurance, a liability insurance as well, though it need not be a liability insurance. In the above situation, the insurance company is, in effect, working on a 'you pay only if you win' basis.

Costs funded by non-parties

In many cases the cost of legal representation of one party, be it the claimant or the defendant, may be funded by a non-party, e.g. a trade union or an insurance company, especially in road accident cases. If the case is lost, the non-party pays the costs. If the claim or defence succeeds, the non-party will be able to recover the usual full reasonable costs.

Callery v *Gray* (2001) and other case law

Now that legal aid for personal injury claims (except clinical negligence) has been abolished, the risk of losing a claim is borne either by after the event insurance (ATE) and the claimant's solicitors or by before the event insurance (BTE). Case law is now beginning to give guidelines as to what is involved.

The case law is arising because the insurers of the losing party have become involved in actions where they have disputed the size of the premium on the other party's ATE or BTE insurance that they are having to pay as part of the costs. The following cases are illustrative.

Callery v *Gray (No 2)* (2001) *The Times*, 24 October is a decision of the Court of Appeal. It was a straightforward claim for damages arising out of a road accident – a whiplash injury, in fact. Damages were agreed but costs were not, hence the litigation. The claimant's solicitors argued for a success fee of 98 per cent and the recovery of a premium of £350 for ATE insurance. The defendant's insurers appealed against recovery of these sums particularly because the matter never came to trial because the defendant settled by admitting liability within the three-month Pre-Action Protocol period. The Court of Appeal ruled that the ATE premium was recoverable because 'it did not seem unreasonable in terms of the service it offered'. However, as regards the success fee in a straightforward case such as this settled out of court, a 20 per cent success fee was all the court would allow.

Personal injury lawyers were not too pleased with this ruling but were less pleased with the ruling of the Court of Appeal in *Halloran* v *Delaney* (2002) 146 Sol Jo 815 where the court ruled that in a straightforward road traffic case involving personal injury and settled out of court a success fee of only 5 per cent was appropriate. The judgment in *Halloran* was delivered by Brooke LJ who sat in the *Callery* case.

Sarwar v *Alam* [2001] 4 All ER 541 is also instructive. It decided that a claimant could recover an ATE premium even though he had a BTE insurance as part of his motor insurance, because the ATE insurance gave additional service. Nevertheless, the Court of Appeal advised solicitors involved in this type of litigation to see whether the client had BTE insurance and as to its adequacy. Failure to do this said the court could lead to ATE insurance taken out in addition being disallowed as a head of costs.

Intervention of the Civil Justice Council

The ruling in *Halloran*, in particular, had affected the willingness of lawyers to take on the large number of road traffic injuries cases where settlement without trial is common. The Civil Justice Council, set up by s 6 of the Civil Procedure Act 1997 to keep the civil justice system under review, then brokered a deal with the legal profession for road accident cases that are settled out of court for up to £10,000. Lawyers handling these cases will receive a basic fee of £1,400 plus an additional fee on a sliding scale, examples of which are as follows: £1,000 for a case settling for £1,000, £1,200 for a case settling for £2,000 and £1,950 for a case settling for £6,000. The Civil Justice Council consists of the Master of the Rolls, judges, lawyers, consumers of legal services to give lay advice and litigant representatives.

Advocates' fees

What is said above relates to the fees of the solicitor and court fees. If it is thought that the services of a barrister will be required, further negotiations will be expected with a member of the Bar. There is no compulsion for members of the Bar (or solicitors) to enter into conditional fee arrangements. Since September 1999, all barristers and solicitors have acquired full rights of audience on call to the Bar or admission to the Rolls (of solicitors), subject to satisfying the Bar or Law Society requirements. Thus, it may not be necessary to brief a barrister but to use a solicitor/advocate throughout the case. It may be necessary to seek the services of a barrister in a difficult case and in such cases the barrister is not likely to be prepared to enter into conditional fee arrangements.

Conditional fees – rights of defendant/claimant

The claimant must disclose the amount of the success fee to the defendant within seven days of entering into such an agreement or the commencement of proceedings. The conditional fee agreement may, of course, be entered into later than the commencement of proceedings. The basic fact of the claimant's insurance but not its details must also be disclosed to the defendant within seven days of commencement of the claim or of entering into the insurance (if later). The defendant (through his insurance company) can challenge the cost of the insurance on final assessment of costs. The above rules apply to disclosure and challenge by a claimant to a defendant where the latter has entered into a conditional fee agreement.

Payment of solicitors by hourly rates

Section 98 of the Courts and Legal Services Act 1990 provides for agreements between a solicitor and client relating to the hourly rate which the solicitor will charge. The agreement must be in writing and the court may set it aside if it is unfair or unreasonable. The intention here is to widen the number of situations in which a solicitor will agree the terms of business in advance with a client.

Legal aid

The availability of state-funded legal aid for litigation and legal advice in criminal and civil proceedings is considered in the chapters on Procedure. However, under the Access to Justice Act 1999 the Community Legal Service replaces the civil Legal Aid Scheme in the provision of funding for civil cases. It is administered by the Legal Services Commission which replaces the Legal Aid Board. CLS funding will not normally be available in cases that could be financed by a conditional fee agreement and will, in any case, not be available for personal injury claims, except for clinical negligence. The result of these changes will be a decrease in the number of cases where a party to a civil claim has the benefit of representation by state-funded legal aid.

It is worth noting here that more than 300 barristers including 60 QCs (see below) have agreed to offer their services free to the public through a scheme launched by the Bar. It is called the Bar Pro Bono Unit and will help people who have what are described as 'deserving' legal problems and who cannot afford legal advice. A register has been compiled of barristers willing to offer up to three free days on such a case.

The Bar Pro Bono Unit (alternatively called the Free Representation Unit) has extended its field of operation to litigants at the Employment Appeal Tribunal, in general to employees. Incidentally, the Lord Chief Justice Lord Woolf suggests that the expression *pro bono* should be rendered 'law for free'. The translation is 'for the public good' (*pro bono publico*).

The main legal professions

Although the changes in the provision of legal services effected by the Courts and Legal Services Act 1990 are immense the *main* participants in such provision will continue to be barristers and solicitors, the latter being assisted by legal executives. The nature of these professions is considered in outline below.

Barristers

Barristers conduct cases in court, and generally draft the statement of case which outlines the manner in which the case is to be conducted. They also give opinions on difficult legal problems.

There is, of course, nothing to stop a party presenting his own case, though when it comes to an appeal to the House of Lords, unless leave has been granted by the Court of Appeal, it is necessary for two Queen's Counsel to certify that it is reasonable to bring the case to appeal.

Call to the English Bar is the prerogative of the four Inns of Court – Lincoln's Inn, Gray's Inn, the Inner Temple and the Middle Temple. The Inns of Court are unincorporated societies governed by Masters of the Bench (benchers), who are judges or senior barristers, and call to the Bar is by the benchers.

Education and training

There are three parts to the course of training to be a barrister as follows:

- *The academic stage*. Most students complete this stage by studying for a law degree. Some may prefer to take other degrees and must then take a one-year conversion course in law called the Common Professional Examination course. This is offered by the Inns of Court School of Law in London and at a number of teaching institutions throughout the country. Possession of a degree with at least lower second class honours plus the Common Professional Examination, where appropriate, constitute the minimum requirement for entry to the vocational stage which is not easy to achieve.
- *The vocational stage*. This involves completion of a one-year full-time Bar Vocational Course at an approved institution which gives practical training in the special skills and knowledge required by a barrister. This training is provided by the Council of Legal Education and by some universities. After successfully completing the vocational course students are called to the Bar by their Inn.
- *Pupillage*. Those intending to practise as a barrister in independent practice or to exercise rights of audience as an employed barrister are required to do pupillage for an aggregate of 12 months, six months of which must be spent in the chambers of a private practitioner (but see below). This period is non-practising. For the remainder of the period of 12 months, the pupil can do some practising work but not as part of an independent practice. A final certificate is given after 12 months which allows the barrister to enter independent practice.

Students who enter employment may undergo the whole period of pupillage as an employee. All practising barristers are required to undertake continuing professional development courses.

With effect from September 2008, pupillage will become mandatory not only for the purposes of practising but also to obtain the professional qualification and title of barrister. It is not easy to find a pupillage and, from 2008, those who have completed the Bar Vocational Course (which continues) but have failed to find a pupillage will not be able to benefit from the title of barrister. In other words, if you have completed pupillage you are a barrister, if you have not you go away without a professional qualification in a netherworld of part-qualification. The shortfall in pupillages in relation to BVC graduates will deter applicants.

Legal Services Consultative Panel

Section 35 of the Access to Justice Act 1999 puts in place the Legal Services Consultative Panel. This panel advises the Secretary of State for Constitutional Affairs on various issues including the education and training and conduct of lawyers in general.

Employed barristers

Provided an employed barrister has complied with the conditions set out above, he or she may appear in court but only for the employer.

Circuits

After call, a barrister intending to practise generally will join what was known as a Circuit but is now called a Region and will then practise within that Region though cases may be taken on others. There were six Circuits in England and Wales, i.e. Midland; North Eastern; Northern; South Eastern; Wales and Chester; and Western.

The structure of HM Court Service has changed and the six Regions are currently: Midland, North East, North West, London and South East, Wales and Cheshire, and South West.

There are no partnerships at the Bar, and one barrister cannot employ another, but it is usual though not essential for counsel to group together by taking a tenancy in chambers and employ a clerk who is responsible for the administration of the chambers, fees, appointments and instructions. There is, however, no objection to what is called 'purse-sharing' under which a particular chamber pools all its fees and each barrister draws the same monthly 'salary'. From the end of 2002 all pupil barristers are entitled to a minimum annual payment of £10,000 per year plus travelling expenses. This scheme received the statutory approval of the Lord Chancellor and is a step towards opening the Bar to a wider range of entrants regardless of their financial support from other sources, e.g. family. Vacancies must now be advertised.

Under a Bar Council code of conduct barristers are allowed to advertise, work without clerks and open chambers where they like. They are no longer restricted to setting up chambers in or near the Inns of Court.

Queen's Counsel

Experienced barristers may apply to 'take silk', i.e. to become Queen's Counsel which gives the entitlement to wear a silk gown in court. There is now a new appointments procedure for the appointment of QCs. A selection panel oversees and selects from applicants those whom the Queen will appoint as QCs. The Lord Chancellor has no power of veto on who is selected. Applications are invited once a year. The selection panel has legal and lay members. Applicants must outline how they meet a set of competencies and provide referees from the legal profession to back up the competencies. Applicants must pay a processing fee and a further appointment fee if they are successful. After appointment as Queen's Counsel, a barrister will not, in general, appear without a junior, i.e. another barrister who is not a QC, and his practice henceforth tends to be restricted to the more important cases requiring two counsel, i.e. a junior to deal with less difficult but time-consuming procedural matters and the drafting of pleadings, leaving the QC to concentrate on advocacy.

Until 1977 the rules of conduct laid down by the Bar *prevented* a QC from working without a junior. The rule was dropped following a report by the Monopolies Commission that the practice was contrary to the public interest. However, most QCs still claim that they need the assistance of a junior, and the scheme to avoid duplication of service appears to have failed.

There is, in general, no need to employ a QC, though only a QC can lead for the defence in a trial for murder.

Solicitor-Advocates may also apply to take silk.

Briefing and negligence

A barrister can, but will not always, deal directly with a client and will often be briefed by a solicitor, and then he cannot sue for his fees, though a solicitor who fails to pay over to counsel fees received from a client is liable to disciplinary action, and indeed under an arrangement between the Law Society and the Bar a briefing solicitor is personally liable, except in legal aid cases, to pay counsel's fees even if the solicitor has not received them from the client. However, s 61 of the Courts and Legal Services Act 1990 now allows a barrister to enter into a contract with a client for the provision of services and payment of fees. As we have seen more recently, the Bar Council has approved proposals which allow direct access to barristers by other professions, e.g. accountants and the public. Thus the usual route through a solicitor need not always be followed.

As regards fees, barristers are entitled to a 'brief fee' which covers preparation of the case plus the first day of the trial (if any). Added to this is a sum called a 'refresher' payable for the second and each subsequent day of the trial for however long it continues. The costs of one side for a week in court on, say, a contested personal injury case with a QC can run into several thousands of pounds on top of which fees are also payable to the firm of solicitors involved in preparatory work.

As regards the liability of advocates, both barristers and solicitors, an ancient principle of the common law had in its developed state prevented advocates from being sued in negligence. The case of *Rondel* v *Worsley* [1969] 1 AC 19 upheld the immunity on considerations of public policy and confined it to acts closely concerned with the conduct of litigation in court. In *Rondel* the House of Lords thought that the possibility of claims being brought against advocates might undermine their willingness to carry out their duties to the court. A later case of *Saif Ali* v *Sydney Mitchell & Co* [1980] AC 198 confirmed the *Rondel* rule and applied the immunity to solicitors when acting in court as advocates. This development of immunity ended with the decision of the House of Lords in *Arthur J S Hall & Co (a firm)* v *Simons* [2000] 3 WLR 543. Section 62 of the Courts and Legal Services Act 1990 gave statutory confirmation of the common law position but, since the common law position is now changed, the effect of the Act is spent.

> *Hall* v *Simons*, 2000 – Advocates: liability in negligence (**18**)

Conduct

In matters of conduct, counsel is under an obligatory duty to pursue his case in a proper manner. He must inform the court of all the relevant statutes and precedents, and, where a legal authority is against his argument, he must not suppress it, though he may attempt to distinguish or criticise it. In *Copeland* v *Smith* (1999) *The Times*, 20 October the Court of Appeal reaffirmed the importance of an advocate being aware of and bringing to the attention of the court all recent authorities and to be familiar with the Weekly Law Reports and the All England Reports but not necessarily others. The statement of Lord Justice Brooke in this regard is of interest. He said: 'By "recent authority" I am not necessarily referring to authority which is only to be found in specialist reports, but authority which has been reported in the general law reports. If a solicitors' firm or a barristers' chambers only take one set of the general reports, for instance the *Weekly Law Reports* as opposed to the *All England Law Reports* (or vice versa) they should at any rate have systems in place which enable them to keep themselves up to date with cases which have been considered worthy of reporting in the other series.' He must also ensure that his client has a fair hearing. If a prosecuting counsel in a criminal case is aware of facts which support the case for the accused, or lessen the gravity of the offence, he must state them. Counsel may not plead guilty for a client, but may persuade him to do so if it is in the client's interest.

In addition, barristers are required to act for any client whether legally aided or not in any field in which they profess to practise. This is called the 'cab-rank' rule which is referred to in s 17(3)(c) of the Courts and Legal Services Act 1990 as a matter for consideration in approving an application by, e.g., a professional body for authorisation of its members as advocates.

Special advocates

In cases involving national security, it is the practice to use lawyers as special advocates to present to the court secret evidence which is not made available to the defendant or his lawyers. The evidence is put before the court at a closed hearing. The object is to allow disclosure where the public interest and the interests of those supplying the information are at risk but only to the court through the special advocate.

In a major departure from previous practice, the House of Lords has ruled in favour of the appointment of a special advocate in a case not affecting national security.

In *Roberts* v *Parole Board* [2005] 2 AC 738, Harry Roberts, a police killer, was sentenced to life imprisonment in 1966. The term required to satisfy that sentence was 30 years. This had expired but he had not been released because an informant had alerted the authorities as to his involvement in drug dealing in prison. Roberts asked for parole. The witness statement of the informant in terms of the drug dealing was regarded as secret evidence and was not made available to Roberts' lawyers. It was presented to the Parole Board by an appointed special advocate and heard by the Board in closed session.

The House of Lords ruled by a majority of three to two that this evidence could be used by the Board to deny Roberts parole and keep him in prison.

The ruling has been criticised. The reform group JUSTICE intervened in the case on the ground that the use of the special advocate procedure was contrary to Art 5(4) of the Convention on Human Rights (the right for a prisoner to have detention fairly reviewed). Nevertheless, the House of Lords ruling stands.

Solicitors

The profession of solicitor is derived from three former branches of the legal profession. The early stages of litigation in the King's Bench and Common Pleas was conducted by *attorneys*; in the Court of Chancery by *solicitors*, so called because cases in Chancery could go on for years and the only way of getting the case moving was to employ a person to '*solicit*' or cajole the court into action, and in the Ecclesiastical Courts and Admiralty by *proctors*. These three branches fused in 1831 to form the Law Society, though their functions were not fused under the one name of solicitor until 1875. The Law Society is responsible for prescribing the qualifications and setting the examinations, issuing practising certificates and preserving minimum standards of behaviour. It also runs a compensation fund for those who have suffered from the wrongful acts and defaults of solicitors, supervises the charges made by solicitors for their work and provides a complaints system through the Office for the Supervision of Solicitors that reports to the Council of the Law Society.

Today a solicitor is in some respects a businessperson who advises his clients on legal, financial and other matters. His work is not all of a legal nature, but most of it requires legal training. Much of the work of a solicitor is concerned with property. He investigates title to land, prepares contracts of sale, conveyances and wills, and often acts as executor and trustee. He also assists promoters in company formation. As we have seen, since the passing of the Administration of Justice Act 1985 and the Courts and Legal Services Act 1990 practising solicitors no longer have a monopoly of conveyancing, which may now be done also by licensed conveyancers who need not be qualified as solicitors.

There is a Practice Rule under which a solicitor should not, in general, act for both parties to a transaction though there are exceptions, e.g. where both parties are established clients. A solicitor is also entitled to act for both parties, even where their interests may conflict, if they consent after being fully informed of the difficulties that may emerge (*Clark Boyce (a firm)* v *Mouat* (1993) 143 NLJ 1440). In addition, it was decided by the Court of Appeal in *Re a firm of Solicitors* (1991) 141 NLJ 746 that a firm of solicitors will not be allowed to act for a present client against a former client if it was reasonable to anticipate that there was a danger that information gained by the firm while acting for a former client would be used against that former client.

The House of Lords has ruled that a solicitor does have a duty to disclose information to a later client which was obtained during the course of working for another client where this was likely to and has caused loss to the later client. A solicitor may be held liable in damages for breach of contract for the loss.

Thus, in *Hilton* v *Barker, Booth & Eastwood* [2005] 1 WLR 567, H engaged the defendants to act for him in the purchase of a development site on which he was to build flats and then sell the developed property to another client of the defendants. The defendants did not disclose that they were lending the client the deposit for the purchase, nor that the client/purchaser had been declared bankrupt and convicted of fraud. The bankrupt client failed to complete the purchase and the property was sold by a bank which had also lent the purchaser money on mortgage. The claimant's business collapsed and the court found that if the claimant had known of the matters which were not disclosed he would not have become involved in the transaction. The amount of damages was left to be assessed by a judge if the claimant and the defendants could not agree on the amount.

Their Lordships remarked that in such a situation it would be best for the solicitor not to act for the later client but advise that other solicitors be used.

In future the distinction between solicitors and barristers in the matter of advocacy in court will not be so marked as it has been in the past. As we have seen under arrangements set up by the Courts and Legal Services Act 1990 (as inserted by the Access to Justice Act 1999), solicitors, who wish to do so, are able to acquire wider rights of advocacy before our courts. However, many will continue to follow their traditional role as litigators involved in pre-trial work where their functions will be to prepare the case, ascertain the facts, arrange for the presence of the necessary witnesses and any documents which may be required, and conduct any disputes over costs which have been awarded after judgment.

Solicitors who have had experience in advocacy, either as part-time judges or as having formerly practised as barristers, are allowed to appear in the higher courts immediately; but most solicitors are required to complete Law Society training courses before being able to appear in the Crown Court, High Court, the Appeal Courts and the House of Lords. The Lord Chancellor has, however, ordered that they cannot wear wigs.

A number of solicitors have been given rights of audience in the Crown Court and High Court and beyond to the higher civil and criminal courts. In addition, these solicitor-advocates have been allowed to apply to be appointed Queen's Counsel and some have been appointed. Appointments have also been made to the High Court bench, and Court of Appeal positions which were formerly the prerogative of members of the Bar.

The normal route of qualification as a solicitor is a law degree followed by a one-year Legal Practice Course. Non-law graduates and mature entrants must follow a one-year educational stage before embarking on the LPC. This is followed by a two-year period as a trainee with a firm of solicitors. Under current proposals of the Law Society all training will be done in the practice thus cutting out the Legal Practice Course provided by various educational establishments and organisations. After this application must be made to the Law Society for admission as a solicitor, and admission must be approved by the Master of the Rolls, since a solicitor is an officer of the court. A person may then practise alone, or as a member of a partnership, and every practising and some employed solicitors must take out an annual practising certificate. Section 9 of the Administration of Justice Act 1985 allows solicitors to form incorporated practices. A number of solicitors are employed in local and central government departments and by commercial firms.

Lawyers' practising certificates

Section 46 of the Access to Justice Act 1999 gives the Bar Council the power to require barristers to hold a practising certificate in order to practise and the power to require payment by applicants for these certificates. The money received by the Bar Council is expended on education and training, as under s 47 is part of the money raised by the issue of solicitors' practising certificates.

Disciplining the legal profession

Under s 48 and Sch 7 of the Access to Justice Act 1999, the powers of the Law Society to discipline solicitors and investigate misconduct are extended. For example, the Law Society is given further powers to examine a solicitor's files or require details of bank accounts connected with the practice or of any trust of which he is or was a trustee.

Sections 51 and 52 set up the office of Legal Services Complaints Commissioner to oversee the handling of complaints against the legal profession. The power will be used if the Lord Chancellor feels that the relevant professional body e.g. the Law Society is not handling complaints against its members effectively. The Commissioner has power to investigate complaints, make recommendations as to how to handle them and ask the professional body to produce a plan to deal with complaints. If the professional body fails to do this, or to deal with a complaint as requested, the Commissioner may impose a fine.

Legal executives

The Institute of Legal Executives which was established in 1963 gives professional status to the unadmitted staff employed, e.g. in solicitors' offices. There are two examinations: the first leads to Associate membership of the Institute and the second, which is of higher standard, leads to Fellowship. Legal executives frequently carry heavy responsibilities in connection with the business of the firm. A great deal of the routine work in connection with, e.g., conveyancing also falls on them. Under arrangements put in place by the Courts and Legal Services Act 1990 (as amended by the Access to Justice Act 1999) legal executives are able to acquire wider rights in terms of (a) audience in our courts, and (b) pre-trial work as litigators. In this connection, some legal executives have qualified as advocates under the 1990 Act having passed appropriate tests and received advocacy certificates approved by the ILEX Rights of Audience Committee. Those concerned have extended rights of audience in civil and matrimonial proceedings in county and magistrates' courts. Legal executives are also approved persons to give legal advice to a worker who is entering into a compromise with an employer to compromise, e.g. an unfair dismissal claim (see further Chapter 19).

The Commissioners for Oaths (Prescribed Bodies) Regulations 1995 (SI 1995/1676) empower members of the Institute to administer oaths and take affidavits (i.e. where the oath is administered in connection with the verification of the contents of a document). This adds to the scope of their activities and means that solicitors and notaries are not the only persons who can administer oaths.

Notary public

A notary public is an officer of the law who is appointed by the Court of Faculties of the Archbishop of Canterbury. He is a civil lawyer empowered to verify, e.g., the signature of documents and authenticate the contents of documents. He may also administer oaths and declarations. In other words, his main function is to substantiate evidence of human activities. A notary will often also be a solicitor but this is not essential since there is a separate professional body called The Notaries Society.

Community justice centres: the community judge

The United Kingdom's first judge to sit in what are called community justice centres was appointed in October 2004. The appointee is a district judge and a former solicitor. He sits in the pilot 'one-stop justice centre' in Liverpool and deals with cases of anti-social behaviour and low level crime. He also monitors the progress of offenders and oversees rehabilitation programmes. The centre is based on successful New York models and is a joint initiative between the Home Office, the Department of Constitutional Affairs and the Crown Prosecution Service.

Law centres

Since 1970 when the North Kensington law centre was set up there has been a growth in such centres which are sources of legal advice. They employ lawyers and some supporting lay staff and are funded by the local authority for the area in which they are situated and by legal aid income and sometimes by private donations. They work mainly in the fields of housing, employment and immigration. In recent times they have been desperately under-funded and some have closed. Nevertheless, where they do exist, they provide a vital legal service in some of our poorer communities.

A further development is the setting up of two legal advice centres by the College of Law in London. The centres are staffed by students supervised by lecturers of the College. It is hoped that this type of centre will extend to other parts of the country with staffing by lecturers and students from the university law schools.

Information and advice from non-lawyers

Those in business can obtain information and advice on legal matters from non-lawyers. Accountants are highly competent in the law of taxation and also in company law. Government departments can be helpful – for example the Department of Work and Pensions is prepared to advise on employment legislation, as HM Revenue and Customs is on tax and VAT regulations. There are also government-sponsored organisations which provide information and advice such as the Equal Opportunities Commission on sex discrimination. Those in business may also obtain useful information and advice from a relevant trade association and, of course, from their own professional institutes and associations. Advice on social matters such as rent reduction, security of tenure of property and social benefits can be obtained from Citizens' Advice.

Some other important judicial offices

The Lord Chancellor

The Office of Lord Chancellor continues to exist, but with radical changes effected in the main by the Constitutional Reform Act 2005. The object was to achieve what is known as the separation of powers, Montesquieu's French concept, which he thought was a characteristic of the British Constitution in the early eighteenth century but in fact was not.

This involves the separation of the judiciary from the executive and the legislature. The following are the consequences of that objective:

■ On 12 June 2003 the Lord Chancellor's Department was renamed the Department for Constitutional Affairs. The Lord Chancellor, Lord Falconer, remained in that office but was also appointed by the Queen as Secretary of State for Constitutional Affairs. It was also announced that the Lord Chancellor would not sit as a Law Lord, nor would he hold office as the Speaker of the House of Lords and in fact a new Speaker has been elected by the Lords, i.e. Baroness Hayman.

■ The Lord Chancellor will not in future be a member of the Cabinet. It so happens that in the transistional period Lord Falconer is holding the office of Lord Chancellor and is also a minister, in that he is the Secretary of State for Constitutional Affairs, and in that capacity can carry on Cabinet service.

Qualifications

Under s 2 of the Constitutional Reform Act 2005, a person may not be recommended for appointment as Lord Chancellor unless he appears to the Prime Minister to be qualified by experience. In this sense, the Prime Minister may take into account any of the following:

■ experience as a Minister of the Crown;
■ experience as a member of either House of Parliament;
■ experience as a qualifying practitioner, i.e. a practitioner who has the 10-year senior courts' qualification to appear in the High Court, Court of Appeal and House of Lords (becomes Supreme Court) in relation to all proceedings, or an advocate or a solicitor in Scotland entitled to appear in the Court of Session and the High Court of Justiciary, or a member of the Bar of Northern Ireland, or a solicitor of the Court of Judicature of Northern Ireland;
■ experience as a teacher of law in a university;
■ other experience the Prime Minister considers relevant.

Under s 3 of the CRA 2005, the Lord Chancellor, other ministers of the Crown, and all with responsibility for matters relating to the judiciary or otherwise in the administration of justice must uphold the continued independence of the judiciary.

Functions

The Lord Chancellor has an important part to play, along with the Judicial Appointments Commission, in the appointment of the judiciary (see p 59). The Lord Chancellor is also responsible for a very large number of appointments of Presidents and members of tribunals, e.g. the President and members of the Lands Tribunal. The Lord Chancellor also retains the function of custody and use of the Great Seal of the United Kingdom. The Lord Chancellor retains functions under the Insolvency Act 1986, including the power to exclude a county court from having a jurisdiction to wind up companies and in connection with the making of insolvency rules which govern practice and procedure. There are still a number of functions in relation to judicial appointments where the appointment is made by the Lord Chief Justice but after consultation with the Lord Chancellor. An example is the appointment of members, judicial and lay, of the Employment Appeal Tribunal. The full list, which is much too long to be reproduced here, is set out in Sch 7 to the Constitutional Reform Act 2005.

Head and deputy head of civil justice

Section 62 of the Courts Act 2003 (as inserted by the Constitutional Reform Act 2005) states that there is to be a Head of Civil Justice who is the Master of the Rolls or, if the Lord Chief Justice appoints another person, that person. The Lord Chief Justice may also appoint a Deputy Head of Civil Justice. In the case of the Lord Chief Justice's appointments, consultation with the Lord Chancellor is required and the persons appointed by the Lord Chief Justice must be either the Chancellor of the High Court or an ordinary judge of the Court of Appeal. The Lord Chief Justice can delegate the above function to a senior judge, e.g. the Master of the Rolls or a Lord Justice of Appeal. It has been recognised that there is a need for a Head of Civil Justice to provide an overview of the system and give it consistency.

The Attorney-General and the Solicitor-General

The Attorney-General and the Solicitor-General are known as the Law Officers. The appointments are political and change with the government. As a rule, the Law Officers are not members of the Cabinet.

The Attorney-General

The Attorney-General is appointed by Letters Patent under the Great Seal, and is usually a member of the House of Commons. He represents the Crown in civil matters and can prosecute in important criminal cases. He is the Head of the English Bar, and points of professional etiquette are referred to him. He also advises government departments on legal matters, and advises the court on matters of parliamentary privilege. He can institute litigation on behalf of the public, e.g. to stop a public nuisance or the commission of a crime and to enforce or regulate public charitable trusts, because he acts on behalf of the public as a whole. Individuals do not have sufficient interest (or *locus standi*) to bring actions in these cases.

Where a person does not have sufficient *locus standi* to initiate proceedings himself, he may ask the Attorney-General to take proceedings. If the Attorney-General does act at the relation of a private individual, the action is known as a 'relator action' and the relator is responsible for the costs incurred. If the Attorney-General refuses to act, no court can compel him to do so.

The Solicitor-General

The Solicitor-General is the subordinate of the Attorney-General, and sometimes gives a joint opinion with him when asked by government departments. In spite of his title, he is a member of the Bar and he need not, strictly speaking, be in the House of Commons. His duties are similar to those of the Attorney-General and he is in many ways his deputy. Both Law Officers are precluded from private practice. The Law Officers Act 1997 provides that any functions authorised or required to be discharged by the Attorney-General may be discharged by the Solicitor-General.

The reason that the Solicitor-General is a barrister is merely a constitutional convention based on the fact that formerly only barristers had a right of audience in the higher courts. Since this is no longer the case, a future appointment may be of a solicitor with advocacy rights.

> *Gouriet* v *Union of Post Office Workers*, 1977 – Law Officers: Attorney-General's enforcement of the law in the public interest (**19**)

Masters

Many matters arise for decision between the time of issue of the claim form and the trial of the action, e.g. what documents must be shown by one side to the other; what time should be allowed for putting in the statements of case and defences. In summary, a master is concerned with the management of a case pre-trial. Case management matters are, under the Civil Procedure Rules 1998, conducted at the appropriate Civil Trial Centre (see Chapter 5). These conferences are generally dealt with by a master (or district judge) particularly in multi-track cases (see further Chapter 5).

Taxing officers

These are salaried officers of the Supreme Court. They fix the costs which one party is directed to pay to the other. 'Taxation' of costs is an old expression, and the function of the taxing officer is described in the Civil Procedure Rules as the detailed assessment of costs. The title of taxing officer is retained.

The Official Solicitor and Public Trustee

The Official Solicitor is an officer of the Supreme Court who acts in litigation to protect the interests of persons suffering under mental disability. He is also concerned to protect the interests of children in adoption matters and those of persons imprisoned for contempt of court.

As the title suggests, the Official Solicitor and Public Trustee will also act as a trustee for those wishing to set up trusts during their lifetime or after death by will.

The Official Solicitor must have a 10-year general advocacy qualification but the right to act as a litigator is preserved by s 90(3A) of the Supreme Court Act 1981 (as inserted by the Courts and Legal Services Act 1990). Section 54 of the 1990 Act also makes clear that the Official Solicitor can apply for probate.

Circuit Administrators

The Royal Commission on Assizes and Quarter Sessions (Beeching Commission) recommended the appointment of a Circuit administrator in each of the six Circuits (now Regions) into which England and Wales is divided. A legal qualification is not essential. Their function is to a large extent managerial and they took over from Clerks of Assize, Clerks of the Peace, and other officers of the numerous different courts who previously had to try to provide the public and the legal profession with a court service. There is now one person entitled Regional Director at each High Court and Crown Court Centre to whom all involved can turn in respect of administrative problems.

Presiding Judges

Under s 72 of the Courts and Legal Services Act 1990 the Lord Chief Justice with the agreement of the Lord Chancellor appoints 12 High Court judges, known as Presiding Judges, who are assigned to each of the six Circuits (now Regions) in England and Wales. They spend substantial periods of time in the area and have general responsibility for the local High Court and Crown Court Centre. They see to the convenient and efficient distribution of judges in the area, and give support and guidance to the Circuit administrator on these matters.

Under the same section the Lord Chief Justice also appoints a Lord Justice as a Senior Presiding Judge to oversee all the Circuits. His function is to provide the Presiding Judges with a Senior Lord Justice to whom they can turn for advice rather than to the Lord Chief Justice himself, and to relieve the Lord Chief Justice of some of the administrative work in which he would otherwise be involved both in and out of London.

CRIMINAL PROCEDURE

Having described the system of major criminal courts and tribunals existing in England and Wales, we shall now consider the procedure in the major courts which leads to a prosecution and conviction for crime.

Criminal procedure – generally

The system of trial in this country is accusatorial in that a trial is a contest between two persons. As regards crime, these persons are normally the Queen (on behalf of the community) and the person accused of the crime.

Advocates representing the prosecution and the defence each put forward evidence to the court so that a decision may be made on the question before the court which is, did the accused commit the offence with which he is charged?

It should also be noted in particular that a person accused of crime is presumed innocent until proved guilty and is given certain protections in regard to the proof of his guilt as follows:

(a) The Code of Practice on the Detention, Treatment and Questioning of Suspects by the Police (Code C). This code is prepared by the Home Office under powers given by s 66 of the Police and Criminal Evidence Act 1984 (PACE). The codes are revised from time to time, the latest version came into force on 1 January 2006. The code ensures that a person cannot be trapped by questioning into an admission of guilt. A main safeguard of the code is the caution. A caution must be given to a suspect by a police officer as follows:

> You do not have to say anything. But it may harm your defence if you do not mention when questioned something which you later rely on in court. Anything you do say may be given in evidence.

Where a person is questioned without a caution where one should have been given, any admissions made by that person are likely to be inadmissible in evidence.

Basically, a caution has to be given to a person in respect of whom there are grounds to suspect of an offence before any questions or further questions are put. In addition a caution is required:

- on or immediately before arrest;
- when detention is authorised by a custody officer;
- before an interview; and
- following a break in questioning if there is any doubt as to whether the suspect realises that he or she is still under caution.

At any subsequent trial, anything said by a suspect or indeed his or her silence may be used for or against his or her case.

A person need not be cautioned if the questions are just to establish the ownership of a vehicle or the person's identity or in the furtherance of a proper and effective conduct of a search, provided that the questions do not relate to the person's involvement in a criminal offence.

Under the revised code it is not now generally permissible to conduct interviews and questioning except at a police station or other authorised place of detention *once a decision to arrest has been taken*. Tape recording of interviews is then a requirement under s 60 of PACE, except in cases concerning purely summary offences, e.g. driving without insurance. In practice, it is usual for all interviews to be tape recorded, even though it is not technically required. If an interview is conducted at a place other than a police station, which it may be on the ground of 'necessity' (mainly on the ground of non-co-operation), the suspect must be asked to verify the notes of the interview 'unless it is impracticable'. The police also have a duty to keep a record of any unsolicited comments and ask the suspect to verify these as well. The suspect should write his agreement on the relevant record as soon as is practicable. Where legal advice has been requested, verification should await the arrival of a solicitor.

In addition, where legal advice has been asked for by a suspect, he or she may not be interviewed or continue to be interviewed until he/she has received legal advice. Following charge, no further questions relating to the offence may be put except, e.g. if these are necessary to clear up an ambiguity in a previous answer or statement.

The above matters are considered in further detail later in this chapter.

(b) The Human Rights Act 1998. The Human Rights Act 1998 makes it even more important to comply with PACE and its codes of practice. The ruling in *R* v *Aspinall* [1999] 2 Cr App R 115 is to the effect that a breach of Code C is fundamental in affecting the fairness of any evidence obtained.

(c) The burden of proof. Once in court, the prosecution must prove its case beyond all reasonable doubt. The magistrates or jury need not be *certain* of the accused's guilt, but they must in effect be *sure* that he has committed the crime (and see *Woolmington* v *DPP* (1935) (Case **506**)).

The prosecutor

Here we are concerned in effect with the parties to the prosecution of a criminal offence.

Attorney-General

We have already considered the part played by the Attorney-General in Chapter 3. In particular, he/she appoints the Director of Public Prosecutions (see below) who acts under the superintendence of the Attorney-General. He/she can also bring prosecutions where no member of the public would have *locus standi* (no right to be heard) (see *Gouriet* v *Union of Post Office Workers* (1977), Case **19**)).

In addition, some criminal charges require the consent of the Attorney-General before a prosecution can be commenced. Examples are:

■ conspiracy; and
■ contempt of court where the contempt is in a publication such as a newspaper.

Director of Public Prosecutions

The duties of the Director (DPP) are to be found in s 3 of the Prosecution of Offences Act 1985. Major duties are:

- to institute and conduct criminal proceedings because of the importance or difficulty of the case;
- to appear for the prosecution if the court so directs in appeals from the Crown Court to the Court of Appeal (Criminal Division) and from there to the House of Lords and appeals from the High Court to the House of Lords in criminal cases;
- to consent or refuse consent to a prosecution where an Act of Parliament states that a prosecution may not proceed without it.

Some offences requiring the consent of the DPP are:

- under s 38 of the Health and Safety at Work etc. Act 1974 prosecutions relating to health and safety offences, e.g. by employers: an inspector of the Environment Agency may give consent instead of the DPP; and
- child abduction under the Child Abduction Act 1984.

Crown Prosecution Service

The CPS was set up by the Prosecution of Offences Act 1985. The DPP is its head. The Service is divided into areas coinciding with the boundaries of the various police forces. The CPS London covers the Metropolitan Police and the City of London Police. The CPS is not subject to instruction by the police but takes over prosecutions from the police by deciding whether proceedings should be instituted or, if already instituted, discontinued. The CPS also determines what charges should be preferred.

Serious Fraud Office

The Serious Fraud Office was put in place by the Criminal Justice Act 1987. Its head is the Director who is appointed by and works under the superintendence of the Attorney-General. The SFO's functions are to investigate suspected offences appearing to involve serious or complex fraud and to initiate and conduct criminal proceedings that relate to such fraud. The SFO may also take over existing prosecutions. The major difference between the SFO and the DPP is that the former has investigatory powers whereas the CPS has not. In addition, the staff of the SFO includes fraud investigators and accountants in contrast to the CPS which is staffed by lawyers only.

Other bodies involved in prosecutions

The following are important in terms of business:

- the Department of Trade and Industry, for breaches of company legislation;
- the Inland Revenue for cases of tax evasion;
- Customs and Excise for VAT frauds; and
- the Information Commissioner for breaches of data protection legislation.

Private prosecutions

Individuals may bring private prosecutions but the DPP may take these over and having done so may discontinue them but not where there is evidence to support the prosecution. Where in a private prosecution the accused is committed for trial the police can be required to make available all statements and exhibits which they have.

Getting the accused into court

It is obviously necessary to the success of a criminal prosecution that the law provides a method for getting the accused before the court. The following materials are relevant:

Arrest

The accused may be arrested without a warrant and charged with the offence at the police station and released on police bail to attend a magistrates' court on a specified date to answer to the charge. Where there is no bail the defendant comes before the court to answer the charge while still in police custody.

Laying an information

If there is no arrest, the prosecution is currently initiated by the laying of an information before a magistrate or a magistrates' clerk. The information must be laid by a named person who disclosed his or her identity. Often informations are laid by the police in the name of the Chief Constable or a senior officer. The information will ask for a summons to be issued requiring the attendance of the defendant to appear before magistrates to answer the charge or a warrent for arrest so that the defendant can be brought before the magistrates to answer the charge.

The information process differs from the arrest and charge because the individual against whom the information is laid is at liberty and is not detained at a police station while the charge is investigated and drawn up. The information is to secure the attendance of the individual at court. An information is laid when it is received by the justices' chief executive for the relevant area.

Issue of summons

The magistrate before whom the information was laid has power to issue a summons which is usually served upon the defendant by post.

Issue of a warrant

The magistrate before whom an information is laid has power to issue a warrant for the arrest of the person named in it provided in this case that the information is made on oath and the offence is an indictable offence or punishable by imprisonment or the defendant's address is not well enough established to serve a summons.

Since many offences carry a power of arrest without warrant, it is not usual to issue warrants in the way described above.

Reform

A major reform effected by s 4 of the Criminal Justice Act 2003 is to enable the immediate grant of bail from the scene of arrest if there is no immediate need to deal with the person arrested at a police station. The police have a discretion to decide when and where an arrested person should attend a police station for interview. This type of bail is referred to as 'street bail'.

At the time of writing, s 4 of the 2003 Act was not in force.

New method of instituting proceedings

Section 29 of the Criminal Justice Act 2003 provides for a new method of instituting criminal proceedings which is available to a public prosecutor as defined in subsection (5). This method replaces the laying of an information and issue of a summons. Public prosecutors include the police, the CPS and the Director of the Serious Fraud Office. In practice, prosecuting lawyers from the CPS are taking over the job of charging suspects because of evidence that this reform could reduce the number of trials that collapse. The procedure consists in the issue to the person to be prosecuted of a *written charge together with a written requisition* for him or her to appear before a magistrates' court to answer to the charge. The written charge and the requisition must be served on the person named and copied to the court. Subsection (4) prohibits public prosecutors from laying an information for the purpose of obtaining the issue of a summons. They may still do so, however, for the purpose of obtaining the issue of a warrant (see above). Section 31 removes the need for warrants to be substantiated on oath.

At the time of writing, ss 29 and 31 were not in force.

Procedure at the police station

At the beginning of criminal proceedings a person is a suspect and this section deals, among other things, with the law relating to the detention, treatment and questioning of a suspect by the police. References in this section are, unless otherwise indicated, to the Police and Criminal Evidence Act 1984 (PACE).

Arrestable and serious arrestable offences: abolition

This text up to the 14th edition used to refer to arrest without warrant for an arrestable or a serious arrestable offence. An arrestable offence was one punishable with a maximum of five years' imprisonment or more. It became a serious arrestable offence if it led to the death of any person or serious injury or serious financial loss and that which was done was intended or likely to lead to the relevant result. Sections 24 and 116 of PACE applied.

Radical changes have been made to PACE by the Serious Organised Crime and Police Act 2005 and new PACE Code G. Powers of arrest have been completely overhauled to give the police the power to arrest for any offence subject only to a necessity requirement. Additionally, the concepts of 'arrestable offence' and 'serious arrestable offence' have been abolished. The effective date for the abolition of these pre-conditions for the exercise of police powers was 1 January 2006.

Thus, all offences are arrestable and certain other police powers other than arrest which applied only where a serious arrestable offence had taken place (e.g. the power to set up road blocks) now apply only to the committal of indictable offences.

The above powers do represent, as Code G states, an obvious and significant interference with the right to liberty guaranteed by the Human Rights Act 1998 and the Convention on Human Rights Art 5. The Code does, however, stress that the use of the power must be fully justified and those exercising the power should consider if the necessary objectives can be achieved by other less intrusive means and that arrest must never be used simply because it can be used.

Attendance at a police station

Let us now follow the progress of John Doe through the relevant procedures. He has stolen £500 from an elderly pensioner who was leaving a building society having threatened her with a knife. He is known to the police for this kind of street crime. There are two ways in which John may arrive at a police station:

- *As a volunteer*, assisting the police with their inquiries following a call at his home by police: in this situation s 29 applies and John must be allowed to leave at will unless he is arrested and informed that this is so. Arrest may occur if police questioning gives rise to a reasonable suspicion that John may be guilty of the offence.
- *By being arrested* away from the police station, in which case, under s 30 he must be taken to a police station as soon as is reasonably practicable after arrest. The 1984 Act requires that prisoners who will be detained, or are likely to be detained, for more than six hours must be taken to a 'designated' police station. Such a police station is one designated by the Chief Officer of Police as having enough facilities to detain arrested persons. Those who come to the police station following arrest must be taken before a custody officer who must hold at least the rank of sergeant. Under s 37 the custody officer is required to see whether there is enough evidence to charge John, and he may detain him for such period as is necessary to be able to make that decision. Except, perhaps, in those cases where a suspect has been caught in the act before witnesses, which is not the case here, there is unlikely to be enough evidence to charge John at this stage.

Incidentally, in *DPP* v *L* [1999] Crim LR 752 the Divisional Court of Queen's Bench ruled that a custody officer is not required to inquire into the legality of the arrest and if it is found subsequently to have been unlawful the decision to detain will not be invalidated. Where the custody officer knows that the arrest has been unlawful he or she should consider whether detention can be justified especially in view of the Human Rights Act 1998.

John will, therefore, be released with or without bail, though the custody officer may keep him at the police station without being charged in order to get more evidence, e.g. (1) by searching John's premises, or (2) to take samples in, e.g., alleged sex offences or, (3) as is most often the case, to carry out further questioning. John may, therefore, be detained for the first or third reasons in the circumstances of our case. A custody record must be kept by the custody officer and a legal representative attending the suspect can inspect it and a copy must be given to the suspect or his legal representative, on request, when the suspect goes before a court or is released from the police station.

Detention without charge

The basic detention periods without charging John are as follows:

- The general maximum period is 24 hours from arriving at the police station or from arrest whichever is the earlier.
- Where there is an indictable offence, as John's offence would seem to be, further detention of up to 36 hours from arrival can be authorised by a superintendent under s 42.

Section 7 of the Criminal Justice Act 2003 (as amended by the Serious Organised Crime and Police Act 2005, Sch 7) extends the time for which a person may be detained without charge under the authority of a superintendent, from 24 to 36 hours for *any* indictable offence. This will assist the police in dealing effectively with offences such as robbery (seemingly robbery under s 8 of the Theft Act 1968) from a bank or building society with or without the use of a firearm or imitation firearm. These cases are sometimes extremely difficult or impossible to complete in terms of the necessary investigation processes within 24 hours.

- Detention beyond 36 hours requires that the offence is an indictable offence and the grant of a warrant of further detention by a magistrates' court under s 43. The grounds for granting an extension up to and beyond 24 hours – either by a superintendent or the magistrates – are that detention is necessary to secure or preserve evidence or obtain evidence through questioning (which is the most common ground) or that the investigation is being conducted diligently and expeditiously.
- A magistrate's warrant may initially be granted for a period not exceeding 36 hours, but can be extended by further periods until 96 hours from arrival at the police station have expired. *This is the maximum period for detention without charge* except in cases of terrorism.
- A different regime applies to terrorism investigations. The periods of time differ, i.e. 48 hours instead of 36 hours for initial detention, 14 days instead of 96 hours for the maximum period, and the authority for detention beyond the initial period is given by a 'designated judicial person', e.g. a district judge (magistrates' courts), rather than by magistrates (Terrorism Act 2000). The above periods are changed by the Terrorism Act 2006. The initial period becomes seven days from arrest, the period of 14 days becomes 28 days, but any extension beyond 14 days must be authorised by a High Court judge and the detention must be supervised by a High Court judge.

Detention review

An inspector (or a rank above) must carry out a detention review within six hours of the first authorisation and thereafter at intervals of nine hours. The purpose is to ensure that the grounds for initial detention still apply. The custody record must give details of these reviews.

Bail after charge

We will assume that John has been charged. If there are no reasons relating to the investigation for detaining him further, s 38 provides that he be released from police detention either on police bail or without bail, unless there are grounds for detention after charge. These are, e.g., that the suspect's name and address have not been ascertained or it is reasonably thought that he may have given a false name and address or that he may not be at that address long enough for a summons to be served or that he may not answer to bail or may commit an offence while on bail (s 38). The bail decision is taken by the custody officer.

Section 25 of the Criminal Justice and Public Order Act 1994 provides that bail cannot be granted where a person is charged with murder, manslaughter, rape or attempted rape, *if he/she has been convicted of any of these offences,* unless there are exceptional circumstances.

Rights in connection with legal advice

The position is as follows:

- **Volunteers**. These have an absolute right to legal advice in private or to get in touch with anyone outside the station at any time. These rights are conveyed to the suspect by a notice which is given to him on arrival. The duty solicitor can give this advice if the suspect requires it.

■ *Those under arrest*. The basic provision is to be found in s 58 of PACE, which states that a person arrested and held in custody at a police station or other premises is entitled, if he so requests, to consult a solicitor privately at any time. Code C para 6 states that detainees may consult and communicate with a solicitor in person or in writing or by telephone and that free independent legal advice is available from the duty solicitor. A revision of the Code adds a Note 6J, which states that this right to consult or communicate in private is fundamental. These suspects then are informed by the custody officer that they have a right to free legal advice and to have a person informed of the arrest and of the right to consult the PACE codes of practice. These rights are set out in a notice given to the suspect.

The suspect then signs the custody record to indicate whether or not he requires advice. Advice may be from his own solicitor if available or alternatively the duty solicitor.

Duty solicitor

The duty solicitor scheme operates throughout all areas of the country and ensures that a solicitor is available on a 24-hour basis to go to police stations to advise suspects who are being detained. The advice is free, regardless of the suspect's means, and the solicitor is paid at a fixed hourly rate by the Criminal Defence Service, which is an arm of the Legal Services Commission.

As regards competence, this is a matter for the Legal Services Commission's accreditation scheme. In broad terms, accreditation requires that duty solicitors must be competent to do the relevant work and have relevant experience. In addition, they must have attended both an advocacy course and a course for police station advisers.

The LSC has introduced a new method of delivering police station duty solicitor services through CDS (Criminal Defence Service) Direct. Under the scheme, a request for a duty solicitor goes to CDS Direct unless the offence is indictable only or the time at which the suspect will be interviewed is known. The CDS will give initial advice and decide whether attendance by a duty solicitor is required. If so, the case goes to a solicitor providing criminal defence services. In addition, where the service is for telephone only advice, all duty solicitor services are handled by CDS Direct.

Denying access to advice

Where the suspect is in detention for an indictable offence, the right to legal advice may be suspended for up to 36 hours if a superintendent authorises it. The period in the case of terrorism is 48 hours. Those who have not committed such offences have an unqualified right to advice (s 58). A superintendent may authorise suspension where, for example, there are reasonable grounds to believe that the suspect or another person has benefited from the criminal conduct (aimed mainly at drug trafficking) and the recovery of the value of the property constituting that benefit will be hindered (as where, perhaps, the pensioner's money has not been recovered). There are also grounds for delay with terrorism suspects, where, for example, there are reasonable grounds for believing that it will interfere with the gathering of information relating to terrorist activities. The right to have a friend or relative notified of the arrest may be delayed for the same reason.

Interviews – generally

All interviews at police stations other than those relating to purely summary offences, e.g. driving without insurance, should be tape-recorded. Two tapes are used. One is sealed and signed by the suspect or interviewing officer. The other tape is a working copy to which the defence has a right of access. Interviews other than at the police station may be off-tape. Normally the suspect must be given the chance to read the record and to sign it as correct or to indicate any parts which he thinks are incorrect.

The 2006 revision of Code E alters all references to 'tape' to 'recording' and adds a new definition of recording media as 'any removable, physical audio recording medium (such as magnetic tape, optical disc or solid state memory) which can be played and copied'. It would now be permissible to refer to this procedure as audio recording.

Interviews – suspect protection

There are the following main safeguards for the suspect:

- the suspect must be reminded of the availability of free legal advice;
- a caution must be given. This is set out at the beginning of this chapter;
- the suspect must not be unfit through drink or drugs so that he cannot appreciate the significance of the questions;
- a juvenile, i.e. a person under 17, must have an 'appropriate person' at the interview. This may be a parent or guardian of the juvenile or if one is not available or is unsuitable, as where that person is also involved in the offence, a social worker, solicitor or duty solicitor at the station may act.

The right to silence restricted

Section 34 of the Criminal Justice and Public Order Act 1994 deals with the failure by a suspect to mention facts when questioned or charged. Provided the suspect was under caution, charged or officially informed that he/she may be prosecuted at the time, the court at his subsequent trial can draw adverse inferences from the failure to disclose. So in John's case, if he does not answer a question relating to his whereabouts at the time of the offence but at the trial raises a defence of alibi, i.e. that he was at home at the relevant time, the court can draw adverse inferences from the fact that John did not mention this in answer to the question. Essentially, it means that the court may not believe John and think that the alibi has been made up after the event.

Under s 58 of the Youth Justice and Criminal Evidence Act 1999 inferences from silence are not permissible where the defendant has not had prior access to legal advice.

The trial of criminal proceedings

There are some preliminary considerations as follows.

Time-limits

- *Summary offences*. The magistrates cannot deal with the prosecution of a case if the information (see below) is laid more than six months after the alleged offence was committed. An information is laid when it is received at the court office by an authorised officer (s 127, Magistrates' Courts Act 1980).
- *Indictable offences* (including offences triable either way). There are no statutory time limits for commencing criminal proceedings (s 127, MCA 1980). Defendants have, however,

a common law right to be protected against undue delay and a court may dismiss proceedings for undue delay amounting to an abuse of the process of the court. The defendant must normally show unjustifiable delay or the prosecution's bad faith. Both are, in fact, difficult to establish.

■ *Some road traffic offences*, such as dangerous driving and careless or inconsiderate driving, cannot proceed to conviction unless a notice of intented prosecution is served on the defendant within 14 days of the offence (s 1, Road Traffic Offenders Act 1988).

This does not apply where, in addition to the nature of the driving, an accident has occurred of which the driver was aware.

Commencing the prosecution

There are two ways to commence a prosecution, i.e. by charge or by summons.

Charge

There are two possibilities as follows.

■ *Where the defendant has been charged and bailed*. Here a Crown Prosecution Service lawyer at the police station will after a police officer has signed the charge sheet look into the police files and decide how the matter will be heard. There are two possibilities as follows:

(a) *a simple guilty plea hearing*: here the defendant admits all the elements of the offence and the offence does not involve complex issues which means in general that there are not more than two defendants and three key witnesses. These pleas will be listed before a full bench so that the defendant can be sentenced that day though the case can be adjourned for pre-sentence reports. The prosecution is conducted by a non-qualified CPS representative.

Where the offence is a summary offence for which the defendant cannot be sent to prison for more than three months, the 'statement of facts' procedure may be used. The appropriate summons will have been served on the defendant with a 'statement of facts' and a form of explanation allowing the defendant to plead guilty and make a plea in mitigation in his or her absence. The clerk will inform the prosecution of the guilty plea and on proof of service on the defendant the statement of facts and the plea in mitigation is read out in court. No further facts of evidence may be given;

(b) *an early administrative hearing*: where a not guilty plea is expected, the defendant's first appearance before the magistrates will be at an early administrative hearing under s 50 of the Crime and Disorder Act 1998. Except in the case of indictable-only offences, the hearing may be before a single justice or the justices' clerk. The prosecutor is a lawyer from the CPS. The EAH will deal with legal aid and make arrangements for the defendant to consult a solicitor. Where the offence is an either-way offence arrangements can be made for the advance disclosure of the case for the prosecution. The case will then be adjourned. The single justice may remand the defendant on bail or in custody. The clerk cannot remand in custody and will, therefore, take 'bail' hearings. Legal representation is allowed at both simple guilty plea and EAH proceedings by the defendant's own solicitor or the duty solicitor in either case free of charge. Following the EAH the defendant will be remanded to a pre-trial review (see below) or to the appropriate mode of trial, i.e. summary or on indictment.

For guilty pleas the expectation is that the case will be dealt with on first appearance before magistrates.

■ *Where the defendant has been charged and detained*. In this situation the defendant will remain in custody and be taken before a magistrates' court as soon as is practicable. In this connection, s 57 of the Crime and Disorder Act 1998 provides for the use of live television links at preliminary hearings where the accused is detained in custody. This reduces delays in proceedings and the number of escapes on the way to and from court. The magistrates' court will decide how the case will proceed.

Summons

As regards less serious offences, such as careless or inconsiderate driving, where there will not normally have been an arrest, the prosecution will lay an information. This tells a magistrate or the clerk of the offence alleged and asks for the issue of a summons. An information is usually in writing. A summons is normally served by posting it to the defendant's usual or last known address. An example of a summons appears later in this chapter. As regards the commencement of the prosecution, this is done by the person who lays the information. The prosecution will then normally be taken over by the relevant prosecuting body, which in the case of police officers will be the Crown Prosecution Service. Under the Criminal Justice Act 2003 (as it comes into force) this procedure is replaced by the written charge and requisition though an information can still be laid for a warrant to arrest.

Pre-trial reviews

These are provided for by s 49 of the Crime and Disorder Act 1998. They can be conducted by one justice or the clerk. The object is to provide better management of cases through the court. They provide an opportunity for the prosecution to amend the charges; the defence to enter different pleas; the issue to be identified; there may be clarification as to witnesses who need to attend and an estimate of the time the trial will take.

These reviews are not compulsory but magistrates will normally hold such procedures before trial. The decision whether or not to hold a review is for the members of the court.

The duration of remands

There are three possible situations as follows:

■ *Remand before conviction or committal for trial*. Here the general rule is that the defendant may not be remanded in custody for more than eight clear days at a time, i.e. eight days excluding the day on which the remand was made and the day on which it ends. If remand is on bail, and subject to the defendant's consent, there is no time limit (s 128, Magistrates' Courts Act 1980). If there are successive remands in custody, the defendant need only be brought to court on every fourth remand if he has given and not withdrawn his consent, and has a solicitor acting for him – who need not be present in court (MCA 1980, s 128(3A)). A court can under s 128A, MCA 1980 remand the defendant in custody for up to 28 days if it has previously remanded him in custody for the same offence and he is in court, and can remand him to the next stage in any proceedings, and this may be within the 28-day period.

It should also be noted that magistrates have power to remand a person who has been charged with offences to police custody for up to three days the purpose being to allow questioning about other offences (see s 128(7) of the Magistrates' Courts Act 1980).

- **Remand after conviction**. Here s 10(3) of the MCA 1980 applies and states that a magistrates' court may for the purpose of enabling inquiries to be made, e.g. medical reports, before sentence adjourn after convicting the defendant for a successive period of four weeks if on bail, but if in custody for not more than successive periods of three weeks.
- **Remand following committal to the Crown Court**. The defendant if committed to the Crown Court for trial or sentence is remanded on bail or in custody until the case is due to be heard.

Time limits for the trial to commence

The Prosecution of Offences Act 1985 enables the Home Secretary to make regulations imposing time limits for the completion of various stages in the criminal process as follows:

- **Magistrates' courts**: the Prosecution of Offences (Custody Time Limits) (Amendment) Regulations 1999 (SI 1999/2744) provide for a maximum magistrates' court custody time limit from first appearance to the start of the trial of 56 days in regard to those charged with summary offences. In the case of an offence triable either way, the maximum period of custody between the accused's first appearance and the start of summary trial or the time when the court decides whether or not to commit the accused for trial in the Crown Court is 70 days. If the court decides to proceed to summary trial, it must do so within 56 days. In the case of the trial of indictable-only offences, the maximum period of custody between first appearance and the decision to commit for trial in the Crown Court is 70 days.
- **Crown Courts**: the Prosecution of Offences (Custody Time Limits) (Amendment) Regulations 2000 (SI 2000/3284) provide for a maximum Crown Court custody time limit of 182 days less any period previously spent in custody of a magistrates' court for the offence.
- **Youth courts**: the Prosecution of Offences (Youth Court Time Limits) Regulations 1999 (SI 1999/2743) provide for the following time periods in regard to the three stages of youth court proceedings:
  - persons must be brought to trial within 99 days (the overall time limit) of the date of first appearance;
  - where they have been arrested, persons must first appear in court within 36 days (the initial time limit) of the date of arrest;
  - persons convicted should be sentenced within 29 days of the date of conviction.

The above regulations have a procedure under which the prosecution may apply for the overall and the initial time limits to be extended.

Funding the defence – legal aid

Part I of the Access to Justice Act 1999 applies. It sets up the Legal Services Commission, the members of which are appointed by the Lord Chancellor. The Commission administers the Community Legal Service (for civil legal aid, see Chapter 5) and the Criminal Defence Service (CDS) for legal aid in criminal cases. There is power in the Act to make these bodies separate and self-managing.

As regards the repayment of aid provided in criminal cases, an assisted individual may not be required to make any contribution except where aid is provided in the Crown Court and the judge orders payment to be made.

Franchising

As regards solicitors, only those firms who have contracts with the CDS and fulfil quality of service criteria are able to represent assisted clients. Defendants in criminal cases have a right to choose among firms who have contracts. Following the granting of a contract, there will be quality monitoring of firms through the Commission and a charge is made upon the firms for this purpose. Private solicitors may undertake publicly funded criminal defence work only if they have a contract with the Criminal Defence Service.

All advocacy assistance before magistrates' courts is currently granted without reference to financial resources, so there is no means test.

The Criminal Defence Service Act 2006, ss 1–4 will, as it comes into force, re-introduce means testing and the Legal Services Commission will become responsible for administering payments (see further p 104).

Payments to lawyers

Payments to solicitors are made under their contract arrangements but the Access to Justice Act provides for rules to be made by the Lord Chancellor under which the Commission may make payments to non-contracted persons. This deals with payments to barristers who, by tradition, do not contract for their services. There have been statements by the Lord Chancellor that barristers should consider offering services by contract franchising.

Criteria for the grant of a right to representation

The following are the main factors that will be taken into account when deciding whether representation is in the interests of justice (see Access to Justice Act 1999, Sch 3):

- whether the individual concerned would, as a result of the proceedings, be likely to lose his liberty or livelihood or suffer serious damage to his reputation;
- whether the determination of any matter arising in the proceedings may involve consideration of a substantial question of law;
- whether the individual may be unable to understand the proceedings or state his own case.

Bail

The place of bail as part of the pre-trial process has already been considered. More detail on the somewhat complex matter of bail appears below.

(a) Bail elsewhere than at a police station. Section 4 of the Criminal Justice Act 2003 as it comes into force amends s 30 of PACE to allow police officers to grant bail to persons following their arrest without the need to take them to a police station. This gives the police more flexibility and allows them to remain on patrol if there is no immediate need to take the person concerned to a police station. However, the CJA 2003 makes clear that the basic principle set out in PACE remains and that a person arrested by a police officer must be taken to a police station as soon as practicable. The arresting officer is required to release a person he has arrested and is taking to a police station where the officer is satisfied that there are no grounds for keeping him under arrest or releasing the person under the street bail arrangements.

A police officer can delay taking an arrested person to a police station or releasing him on street bail if that person's presence elsewhere is required for the purposes of investigation. The reasons for the delay must be recorded on eventual arrival at a police station or at the time of release on street bail. Where a constable is taking a person arrested to a police station that person may be released before arriving at the station and released on bail but must be required to attend a police station at a later time. No other conditions may be imposed on the person as a condition of bail.

A person who is street bailed must be given a notice prior to release stating the offence for which he was arrested and the police station the person is to attend and when. The grounds for arrest must also be included in the notice. The CJA 2003 makes clear that a person released on street bail may be rearrested if new evidence comes to light. Those who fail to attend at a police station as the notice requires may be arrested without warrant.

(b) Bail at a police station (police bail). Under s 47 of PACE the custody officer (see above) must, after charges have been laid, consider whether the detention conditions (see above) apply. If not, he must order the release of the accused on bail in accordance with the Bail Act 1976 (see below) or without bail. An accused who is not released must be brought before the magistrate as soon as practicable (see above). Under s 3A of the Bail Act 1976 a custody officer who has granted bail (or another custody officer at the same police station) may vary the conditions of the bail at the request of the person to whom it was given. Under Part IV of PACE a constable may arrest without warrant a person who has failed to answer to police bail.

(c) By magistrates. When an accused person comes before magistrates, e.g. on committal proceedings, the magistrates have to decide at the end of the proceedings whether to remand the accused in custody, in one of the remand prisons for persons awaiting trial, or release him on bail.

Under s 154 of the Criminal Justice Act 1988 the magistrates are obliged to consider bail on each successive remand but *are not obliged to hear argument* in support of a bail application unless there are new circumstances or circumstances not previously brought before them. They are not obliged to review matters previously considered. They are, however, obliged to hear argument in support of bail at the first hearing and at the next if they have refused bail at the first.

The granting of bail is covered by the Bail Act 1976, which is applied also to those in customs detention by s 150 of the Criminal Justice Act 1988. Section 4 of the 1976 Act contains a statutory presumption in favour of granting bail, though this does not apply in breach of bail and 'no-bail' cases (see below). Under the section a person accused of crime must be granted bail unless:

- he is charged with, or convicted of, an offence which is punishable with imprisonment and the court is satisfied there are good grounds for believing that, if released on bail, he would fail to appear at a subsequent hearing or commit an offence while on bail or obstruct the course of justice by intimidating witnesses; or
- the court is satisfied that he ought to remain in custody for his own protection or, if he is a juvenile, for his own welfare; or
- there has not been enough time to obtain information about the defendant for the court to reach a decision; or
- the defendant has been convicted of an imprisonable offence and remanded for enquiries or, say, a medical report, and it seems to the court that it is not practical to complete the enquiries or make the report unless the defendant is kept in custody;
- where the defendant is on bail at the time of the alleged offence, that is a mandatory ground to refuse bail. Under the CJA 2003 where a defendant was on bail in criminal

proceedings on the date the alleged offence was committed, *particular weight can be given to this fact* when the court is deciding release on bail. There is no longer a mandatory bar. This provision applies where the present offence, the offence for which the defendant was already on bail, or both are imprisonable;

- the defendant is in custody under the sentence of a court;
- having been released on bail in connection with proceedings for the offence, he has been arrested for absconding or breaking conditions of bail;
- drug users restrictions. Under s 19 of the CJA 2003 an alleged offender charged with an imprisonable offence will not be granted bail – unless the offender can demonstrate that there is no significant risk that he or she will commit an offence while on bail – where the following conditions exist:
  - there is evidence from a drug test that the person has a specified Class A drug, e.g. cocaine, in his or her body;
  - the court is satisfied that there are substantial grounds for believing that the misuse of a specified Class A drug caused or contributed to that offence or provided its motivation; and
  - the person does not agree to undergo an assessment as to dependency upon or propensity to misuse specified Class A drugs or has undergone such an assessment but does not agree to participate in any follow-up offered.

If an assessment or follow-up is proposed, it will be a condition of bail that they be accepted, provided that appropriate assessment and treatment facilities are available in the area.

Section 25 of the Criminal Justice and Public Order Act 1994 provides that there is to be no bail, other than in exceptional circumstances, for a person charged with murder, attempted murder, rape, attempted rape or manslaughter, where the person concerned has a previous conviction for any of those offences and, in the case of a previous conviction for manslaughter, was sentenced to imprisonment or detention. It is not necessary that the previous conviction be for the same offence as the current charge before the court.

The prosecutor may ask the court to reconsider its decision to grant bail on the basis of new information which was not available to the court or the police (in the case of police bail) when the original decision was taken.

Where the defendant is charged with, or convicted of, an offence which is not punishable with imprisonment, the grounds for refusing bail are much more restricted. However, such a person can be refused bail if he has previously failed to answer bail and if the court believes, in view of that failure, that he will again fail to surrender to custody if released on bail. Conditions may be imposed on the granting of bail, e.g. the handing in of a passport or regular reporting to the police.

Appeals against refusal of bail

As regards appeals, an unconvicted defendant could, under s 22 of the Criminal Justice Act 1967, appeal to a High Court judge against a refusal by the magistrates or the Crown Court to grant bail. Under s 60 of the Criminal Justice Act 1982 he could, as an alternative to the High Court judge, go to a Crown Court judge in chambers for bail. Section 17 of the CJA 2003 abolishes the duplicate appeal to the High Court so that appeal is now to the Crown Court *only* from a magistrate's refusal of bail, and there is a consequent repeal of s 22 of the 1967 Act. Appeals from a Crown Court refusal are to the High Court. Section 29 of the 1982 Act gives the Crown Court the power to grant bail pending an application to the Court of Appeal for leave to appeal against sentence, or pending an appeal to that court against conviction on indictment.

In addition, under the Bail (Amendment) Act 1993 the prosecution may appeal against a magistrates' decision to grant bail. Appeal is to a judge of the Crown Court. The accused must be charged with or convicted of taking a vehicle without consent, or aggravated vehicle taking under ss 12 and 12A of the Theft Act 1968, or an offence punishable with imprisonment or, in the case of a child or young person, be so punishable if it had been done by an adult (but see below). Bail must have been opposed initially.

Power to appeal to the Crown Court

Section 16 of the CJA 2003 creates a new right of appeal to the Crown Court against the imposition by magistrates of certain conditions of bail. The conditions that may be challenged are requirements relating to residence, provision of a surety (see below), or giving a security, curfew or electronic monitoring or non-contact with a particular person or persons. Such an appeal can only be made where application to vary has been made to the magistrates. This complements the removal by s 17 of the former power of the High Court to entertain such appeals.

Section 18 of the CJA 2003 amends the Bail (Amendment) Act 1993 so that the prosecution's right of appeal to the Crown Court against a decision by magistrates to grant bail is extended to cover *all imprisonable offences*.

Surrender to bail and sureties

Section 3 of the 1976 Act imposes a duty upon a person granted bail to surrender to custody. This duty is enforceable by the creation of the offence of absconding in s 6. Security for surrender into custody and sureties may not be required nor conditions imposed on the grant of bail except as provided by s 3. Thus, for example, a deposit of a sum of money or a surety or sureties may be required if it is believed the person will abscond. A previous restriction that security or surety could be required if it was thought the person would leave the country has gone. The court may ask for sureties other than the defendant to provide an additional guarantee to secure the defendant's surrender to custody. As regards conditions, the section makes it plain that these are only to be imposed to ensure the defendant's surrender to custody, that he does not commit a further offence while on bail, that he does not interfere with the course of justice, as by intimidating witnesses, and that he makes himself available for the purposes of enabling enquiries or a report to be made. The section also provides for the parent or guardian of a juvenile to stand as surety in a sum not exceeding £50 to ensure that the juvenile complies with the requirements attached to the grant of bail.

Section 6 also creates the offence of failing, without reasonable cause, to surrender at the time and place appointed. The offence is punishable in a magistrates' court by a maximum of three months' imprisonment and/or a fine, and in a superior court, such as a Crown Court, if committed for sentence by the magistates after conviction, with 12 months' imprisonment and/or a fine. Section 7 provides for the arrest of a defendant who fails to surrender himself to custody at the appointed time and place or who breaches any of the conditions attached to the grant of bail.

Suitability of sureties and indemnities

If the court requires sureties under s 3, s 8 provides for the first time in statutory form some matters which should be taken into account in deciding the suitability of sureties. The list, which is neither mandatory nor exhaustive, relates to the financial resources, character (including previous convictions) and proximity to the defendant (in terms of blood relationship, dwelling, or otherwise) of the proposed surety. In addition, the section enables a person who is not accepted as a surety to apply to a court to have the matter reconsidered. Section 9 creates the offence of agreeing at any time and regardless of whether or not a person in fact becomes a surety, to indemnify that person against his liability as a surety. Thus, if A asks B to stand as a surety for C and tells B that he (A) will pay to B any sum which B has to pay into court because C absconds, then A commits this s 9 offence. The penalties for this offence are the same as those for the offence of absconding. No proceedings may be instituted under this section without the consent of the Director of Public Prosecutions.

Where a person who has stood surety for a defendant's bail cannot be blamed for his failure to surrender, as where the surety has not been told when the defendant was required to appear, then the surety should not forfeit his recognisance (*R* v *Reading Crown Court, ex parte Bello* (1990) *The Times*, 10 December). However, the matter is at the discretion of the court and lack of blame on the part of the surety will not necessarily mean that there will be no forfeiture though the court may reduce the amount payable if there has, e.g., been police negligence (*R* v *Crown Court at Maidstone, ex parte Lever* [1995] 2 All ER 35).

Funding is available for defendants who wish to be represented in actions relating to whether they are entitled to bail or not.

Bail hostels

Before leaving the subject of bail, the provision of bail hostels is worthy of consideration. These hostels, often run by the probation service, give an accused person an address so that he need not necessarily be remanded in custody because he has no fixed abode, which is still a ground under s 1(4) of the Magistrates' Courts Act 1980, though persons of no fixed abode are not bound to be refused bail. The Secretary of State is given power to approve bail hostels and to provide a system of inspection under s 49 of the Powers of Criminal Courts Act 1973 (as amended by the Criminal Justice Act 1982, Schs 11 and 16). Before this statutory measure there was only a limited number of such hostels provided by voluntary organisations.

On granting bail the court may impose a condition that the defendant reside at a bail hostel and abide by its rules so that a remand in custody can result if the defendant misbehaves (Criminal Justice Act 1988, s 131, amending Bail Act 1976, s 3).

Criminal trials and the Human Rights Act 1998

Before considering trial procedure, the effect of the Human Rights Act 1998 must be briefly looked at. In this connection the Act does not require Convention issues to be taken into consideration at any particular stage of criminal proceedings. However, under the Convention the charge or indictment could be challenged before trial, and at the trial attempts may be made under the Convention to exclude evidence allegedly obtained in breach of the Convention or questioning the drawing of adverse inferences from the silence of the defendant. On appeal the defence may ask that a conviction be quashed where it is alleged that it was obtained in breach of the Convention. Since the court itself is a public authority required to comply with the Convention, it may of its own volition take points relating to breaches of the Conventions. Articles 5 and 6 of the Convention are especially applicable. The former deals with rights in relation to criminal proceedings, while the latter is concerned with the right to a fair hearing.

The law relating to arrest involves Art 5, which provides that everyone has a right to liberty and security of the person. Article 5 is also relevant to detention. If the conditions of detention amount to inhumane or degrading treatment there could be a breach of Art 3, i.e. freedom from torture or inhumane or degrading treatment.

Summary trial before magistrates (other than in a youth court)

Since the majority of summary trials before magistrates relate to motoring offences, such an offence has been chosen as an example of the form of summary trial.

The position in regard to the disclosure of the prosecution's case, which is not a legal right in summary trials and the disclosure of unused material together with the defence statement, have been considered in Chapter 2, but should be looked at again by way of revision.

The alleged offence

Let us suppose that on 29 March 2007 Freda Jones was driving her car along George Road, Barchester, and that her attention was distracted by the sun so that she ran into the back of a stationary delivery van which was parked at the kerbside in an area where there were no parking restrictions.

Freda is to be prosecuted under s 3 of the Road Traffic Act 1988 for careless or inconsiderate driving. This offence is classified as summary only. The maximum penalty is a fine of £2,500 with discretionary disqualification and an obligatory endorsement of three to nine penalty points. The offence is defined as driving '. . . a mechanically propelled vehicle on a road or other public place without due care and attention, or without reasonable consideration for other persons using the road or place . . .'.

The summons

Freda will receive a summons containing the following materials. The content of a summons is set out in Rule 7.7 of the Criminal Procedure Rules 2005 as follows:

1. It is addressed to Freda Jones and must be signed by the magistrate issuing it or state his or her name and if it does the latter the signature must be authenticated by the signature of the clerk to the magistrates' court.
2. The summons requiring a person to appear before a magistrates' court to answer an information or complaint must state shortly the matter of the information or complaint in Freda's case as follows:
   That you on 29 March 2007 at George Road, Barchester drove a motor vehicle without due care and attention contrary to section 3 of the Road Traffic Act 1988.
   Note: Rule 7.2 states that an information is sufficient if it describes the offence with which the defendant is charged. It is not necessary for it to state all the elements of the offence.
3. Rule 7.7 requires a summons to state the time and place at which the defendant is required to appear before the court as follows:
   You are hereby summoned to appear on 7 May 2007 at 10 a.m. before the Magistrates' Court at The Law Courts, High Street, Barchester to answer the information.
4. The summons is dated.
   Note: Rule 7.7(4) states that where a signature is required an electronic signature incorporated into the document will suffice.

The summons will be accompanied by (1) a notice explaining the guilty plea procedure and (2) a statement of the facts of the offence (but see below) as follows:

IF YOU INFORM THE CLERK TO THE MAGISTRATES COURT that you wish to plead guilty to the offence set out in the summons, without appearing before the Court, and the Court proceeds to hear and dispose of the case in your absence under s 12 of the Magistrates' Courts Act 1980, the following Statement of Facts will be read out in open Court before the Court decides whether to accept your plea. If your plea of guilty is accepted the Court will not, unless it adjourns the case after convicting you and before sentencing you, permit any other statement to be made by or on behalf of the prosecutor with respect to any facts relating to the offence.

STATEMENT OF FACTS
On 29 March 2007 at 10.00 hours you were the driver of a Suzuki Vitara car reg. no FJ 123, travelling north on George Road, Barchester. On approaching the junction with Marks Road you collided with a Ford delivery van N113 PJC which was parked at the kerbside. When asked by the Police Reporting Officer what had happened you said: 'I had the sun in my eyes. I did not see the van.'

Signed *Peter Green*
(on behalf of the Prosecutor)

Freda will be advised that under s 8 of the Road Traffic Offenders Act 1988 her driving licence must be at the court by the date of the hearing and that failure to comply could lead to the suspension of the licence and a fine.

Freda is unlikely to get legal aid for a lawyer to defend her (see criteria earlier in this chapter). Many magistrates are reluctant to give legal aid in motoring offences. This contrasts with persons pleading not guilty in the Crown Court. They are likely to get legal aid whatever the offence.

Effect of the Magistrates' Courts (Procedure) Act 1998

When considering summary trial before magistrates (other than in a youth court), the provisions of the Magistrates' Courts (Procedure) Act 1998 should be addressed. It amends the Magistrates' Courts Act 1980. The Act revises the procedure of pleading by post. Previously many defendants did not respond to the summons. In other words, they did not take the opportunity to plead guilty by post which the summons gives. Where guilt was not admitted in this way, the case had to be adjourned in order that the Crown Prosecution Service could obtain detailed statements from witnesses or make arrangements for them to attend the court. The 1998 Act contains provisions under which the police *may* prepare witness statements rather than a mere statement of the facts and serve these with the summons. The witness statements are then admissible as evidence, provided the defendant does not object. Thus, where a defendant does not plead guilty by post and does not attend court to plead not guilty, the magistrates can try the defendant in his or her absence and the prosecution may base its case on the witness statements which have been served on the defendant as described above. As the example given in the text indicates, the procedure of pleading guilty by post is usually used for certain driving offences. In this connection, the 1998 Act makes provision for the Driver and Vehicle Licensing Agency to supply a printout, which is admissible as evidence of the defendant's previous convictions, and there is no need to give the defendant advance notice of the intention to refer to previous convictions.

The trial

Freda could plead guilty by letter since the offence is summary only and imprisonment is not involved (Magistrates' Courts Act 1980, s 12). In fact, as we have seen, it is punishable only by a fine (subject also of course, to discretionary disqualification and penalty points). If Freda does plead guilty by letter she must, under s 8 of the Road Traffic Offenders Act 1988 give notification of her date of birth and sex. However, on the assumption that Freda is to attend court and plead not guilty, the main aspects of the procedure are as set out below.

The charge. Freda appears in answer to the summons and the first thing that happens is that the clerk to the magistrates or a legal adviser identifies Freda as the defendant and then reads out the offence with which she is charged and asks her if she pleads guilty or not guilty.

Election to trial by jury. This does not arise in Freda's case because the offence of careless or inconsiderate driving under s 3 of the Road Traffic Act 1988 cannot be tried on indictment before a jury. However, if the police had decided to charge her with dangerous driving under s 2 of the Road Traffic Act 1988, the question of trial on indictment would have arisen because the offence is triable either way.

Attendance of defendant. We shall assume that Freda having refused to plead not guilty by letter will actually attend court to plead not guilty. If she does not and has not given a reasonable explanation for her absence, the matter may be heard without her attending. If there is a reasonable explanation, the case is adjourned.

Freda's plea. Since Freda's case will be dealt with summarily by the magistrates, the clerk or legal adviser will, as we have seen, ask her whether she pleads guilty or not guilty. If Freda pleads guilty, such a plea in itself constitutes a conviction and the magistrates have the power to sentence her without hearing evidence, though they also have the power to decide that even on a guilty plea it is desirable in the circumstances to hear evidence on oath.

The plea of guilty must be unambiguous, i.e. 'guilty'. The court sometimes receives an equivocal plea, e.g. in a trial for theft the defendant may answer, 'Guilty but I had no intention of stealing'. Since this strikes at the heart of the offence, because intention is required, the defendant should be advised to make an unequivocal plea. If he still does not do so, the magistrates can enter a plea of guilty on the defendant's behalf.

The prosecution's case. Since we know that Freda will plead not guilty, the prosecution will have to prove its case. If the prosecution opens the case, the prosecutor will give a succinct outline of the facts and a succinct summary of the law, particularly if a technical defence is expected. The prosecution will then call its evidence, which may be oral evidence and/or written evidence. If oral evidence is called, the prosecution asks questions of witnesses (called examination-in-chief). It is then open to Freda or her solicitor to cross-examine the witnesses for the prosecution and the prosecution may re-examine them.

The defence. When the case for the prosecution has been presented the defence may:

(*a*) submit that there is no case to answer; or
(*b*) proceed to open the case for the defence.

The choice in (*a*) above could be taken where, for example, the prosecution has failed to establish a main ingredient of the offence, or where the prosecution's evidence is so weak that the court could not reasonably convict Freda on it. Freda's solicitor may support his submission of no case to answer by a speech in which he may draw the attention of the court to inconsistencies and omissions in the prosecution's case. Since these are matters of law, the prosecution may reply.

The court will then consider the submission and may retire in order to do so. Should the court accept the submission the case is dismissed. If it finds that there is a case to answer, the defence proceeds. On the assumption that the court does not accept the submission of no case to answer, defence witnesses may be called or their statements admitted in the same way as the prosecution evidence was. If oral evidence is given by witnesses for the defence and by the defendant, they may be examined by the prosecution and may be re-examined by the defence. The defence may make the closing speech provided that the defence has not opened the case which the defence rarely does because then the right to make a closing speech is lost. The prosecution does not make a closing speech as such but may reply on disputed points of law raised by the defence in the closing speech, but the defence will always address the court last.

Decision and sentence. When the case for the defence is closed, the court must consider whether to convict the defendant or dismiss the information. In general, a magistrates' court has no power to return a verdict of not guilty as charged in the information but guilty of a lesser offence (*Lawrence* v *Same* [1968] 2 QB 93). There are exceptions under s 24 of the Road Traffic Offenders Act 1988 where, e.g. the offence charged is dangerous driving an alternative verdict is careless or inconsiderate driving. The court decides by a majority and lay justices do not normally give reasons for their findings, though some district judges (magistrates' courts) do. There is no need for unanimity and if magistrates are equally divided a new trial is ordered. The justices may ask their clerk to give them advice privately on matters of law (and see *R* v *Uxbridge Justices, ex parte Smith* (1985), Chapter 2), but they must not ask for or listen to the views of the clerk on issues of fact, and it is certainly improper for them to ask the clerk to retire with them when no issues of law arise in the case.

If the magistrates decide to convict, they will then enquire whether the accused has any previous convictions or breaches of court orders recorded against her and may hear both the prosecution and the defence as to her character. The matter of previous convictions is governed by s 151 of the Powers of Criminal Courts (Sentencing) Act 2000, which provides that in considering the seriousness of any offence the court may take into account any previous convictions of the offender or any failure to respond to a previous sentence, e.g. probation. The defendant may ask the court to take into account other offences with which he or she has not been charged but wishes to confess to and be sentenced for. This does not arise in Freda's case. The defence may also address the court in what is called mitigation. This could consist, for example, of an address outlining the defendant's domestic stress, perhaps in Freda's case, that her boyfriend had recently been severely injured in a road accident. The court will then decide upon the sentence and announce it. Once the court has done this, or has dismissed the summons, it will not normally change its decision. However, as we have seen, magistrates' courts are given the power to re-open a case to rectify a mistake in any order they have made within 14 days. The court on the second occasion must be constituted in the same way as it was on the first occasion or with a majority of the same justices. This procedure could be used, for example, where the magistrates had omitted to order the endorsement of a defendant's driving licence. (See also Chapter 2.)

If Freda's defence has failed, the magistrates can fine her. They have a discretion as to whether to disqualify her from driving, though an endorsement of her licence is obligatory (Road Traffic Offenders Act 1988, Sch 2).

Section 152 of the Act of 2000 gives the court a discretion to impose a lesser sentence where the defendant has pleaded guilty and saved a trial particularly but not only where there was an early guilty plea. If the court gives a reduction it must say so in open court. There is no obligation on the court to say what the sentence might otherwise have been. This discretion does not apply in Freda's case because she pleaded not guilty.

Admissibility of previous convictions and bad character evidence

Although s 151 of the Powers of Criminal Courts (Sentencing) Act 2000 remains in force, the CJA 2003 in Chapter I of Part 11 gives the prosecution power to bring evidence to show that the defendant has committed the offence such as evidence of previous convictions *before the court finds the defendant guilty or not* (see s 98). The 2003 Act also abolishes the restrictions on the admissibility of previous convictions before verdict that were contained in the common law (see s 99). The same procedure can be used by the prosecution in regard to *witnesses*. In the case of the defendant such evidence can be excluded by the court if it thinks that the adverse effect it would have on the fairness of the proceedings requires this and as regards witnesses the permission of the court is required. Evidence as to 'bad character' is also admissible before verdict and is also provided for by the CJA 2003 under similar provisions. There are provisions preventing admission of pre-age 14 offences.

In *R v Hanson and others* [2005] 1 WLR 3169 the Court of Appeal stated that since the object of the 2003 Act was to assist in the *evidence-based* conviction of the guilty without putting at risk those who were not guilty it was to be hoped that the prosecution would not *routinely* make application to admit bad character and previous conviction evidence.

Costs

Freda may also be ordered to pay all or part of the costs of the prosecution. A court order will specify the sum.

Proceedings in the youth court

Apart from the specific exceptions listed below, no charge against a person who is under 18 (i.e. between 10 and 17) can be heard anywhere other than in a youth court. In consequence, juveniles are not given the option of electing to be tried by a jury. The public does not have access to youth courts and there are restrictions on press reporting. For this reason, a news story may carry a piece that says that the defendant or another person, e.g. a parent, cannot be identified 'for legal reasons'.

Under s 24 of the Magistrates' Courts Act 1980 there are the following instances where a person under the age of 18 years must be tried in the Crown Court on indictment or where the magistrates have a discretion to deal with the juvenile or commit him or her for trial:

- if the juvenile is charged with homicide, i.e. murder or manslaughter, the trial must be on indictment in the Crown Court;
- if a juvenile is charged with an indictable offence, e.g. causing grievous bodily harm, and the youth court or magistrates' court considers that its sentencing powers are insufficient, it may commit the juvenile for trial on indictment;
- if a juvenile is charged jointly with an adult who is to be tried on indictment, the magistrates may, if it is in the interests of justice, commit the juvenile for trial with the adult.

Sentences in a youth court

The sentences available to a youth court, both custodial and non-custodial, appear in the section of this chapter devoted to that subject (see p 151 and subsequently).

Youth Justice Board

Section 41 of the Crime and Disorder Act 1998 sets up the Youth Justice Board. The Board has the duty, among other things, of monitoring the system of youth justice and is, therefore, concerned with the proceedings in youth courts. The Board consists of between 10 and 12 members appointed by the Secretary of State for the Home Department. The members have extensive experience of the system of youth justice and are appointed for a fixed period of five years. They may be re-appointed but the total length of service cannot exceed 10 years.

Trial on indictment in the Crown Court

Defendants will have reached the Crown Court for trial on indictment by a jury in two ways as follows:

- by being *sent for trial* by the magistrates where the offence is triable only on indictment e.g. murder (there are no committal proceedings for indictable offences); or
- by being *committed for trial* by the magistrates where the offence is triable either way.

Reference should be made to the relevant material in Chapter 2 for further details.

Obviously, the accused will have appeared before the magistrates and may have been remanded in custody or on bail. Issues of bail or no bail will have been decided and the accused will have been instructed how to apply for legal aid and given the necessary form. The usefulness of the duty solicitor at this stage has already been described.

Legal aid

Legal aid in criminal proceedings is given only to those charged with offences and is not available to persons wishing to bring a prosecution.

The Criminal Defence Service Act 2006 will, by reason of ss 1–3, set up a new regime for the funding of Criminal Defence Services. It makes changes in the arrangements for the public funding for representation in criminal cases. Under the old system of legal aid in criminal cases, which was established by the Legal Aid Act 1988, legal aid was granted only by following a means test to decide whether a person was eligible and also whether he or she should make any contribution towards the cost. This scheme was abolished by the Access to Justice Act 1999. This meant that there was no means test and legal aid was granted as of right in criminal cases.

The 2006 Act provides for the power to grant rights to representation to be conferred on the Legal Services Commission instead of the court. The Act also introduces a test of financial eligibility for the grant of funding and where there is eligibility contributions based on means.

The Commission manages the Criminal Defence Service and Criminal Defence Solicitors must work within the general criminal contract in order to carry out CDS functions. The Act gives the Lord Chancellor power to make regulations giving precise schemes for eligibility but these had not been approved at the time of writing. However in a Framework Document issued in 2005 there were proposals for a means test based on gross income as follows:

- any defendant with a gross income of £27,500 or more will be automatically ineligible;
- any defendant with a gross income of £15,000 or less will be eligible;
- between £15,000 and £27,500 there will be allowances made for any partner, dependants and housing costs;
- there is no test of capital assets in the scheme;
- any defendant receiving income support, job seekers allowance or pension credit will qualify automatically with no further assessment.

Court staff under contract to the Commission will process applications.

What is an indictment?

An indictment is a document setting out a list of charges (or one charge) made against the defendant to which he must plead guilty or not guilty. The alleged offences are set out separately in what are called counts and each count must allege only one offence. An indictment is usually drafted by the prosecution. It is then delivered to the Crown Court where it is signed by an officer of the Crown Court. Until the indictment is signed, it is called a bill of indictment. Delivery to the Crown Court is known as preferment of a bill of indictment.

Reporting

There are restrictions on the reporting of adult committal proceedings. There are also restrictions on reports of proceedings in which children or young persons up to 18 are concerned. Matters such as name, address and school cannot be published. There are also restrictions on the publication of the name of the complainant in rape trials.

Although committal proceedings usually take place in open court and the press may be present, any report in adult proceedings is restricted by s 8 of the Magistrates' Courts Act 1980 to the formal part of the proceedings, i.e. the names of the defendants and witnesses, the offence charged and the result of the proceedings. The object of these restrictions is to prevent a jury from being prejudiced by anything it may read in the newspapers so that in the Crown Court the jury will have to decide the case on the evidence presented to it there. It is for this reason that the press is not allowed to report the evidence given at committal proceedings. A defendant or any one of several defendants can require the reporting restrictions to be lifted and may do this, for example, if publicity may lead to the tracing of a vital witness whose identity is not known. An example of the infringement of the above restrictions is provided by *The Eastbourne Herald Case* (see below).

The Eastbourne Herald Case, 1973 – Criminal proceedings: excessive reporting (20)

Alibi

Section 5 of the Criminal Procedure and Investigations Act 1996 is designed to prevent the use of 'sprung' or late alibis which were once so widespread in criminal trials. The section provides that, in general, notice of alibi must be given in advance of a trial on indictment. This is not required in summary trials, though it may appear in the defence statement, because of the ease with which the prosecution can ask for an adjournment where the defendant 'springs' an alibi on the prosecution at the last moment.

It must be made clear by a warning to the defendant that he will not be allowed to bring in evidence of an alibi, i.e. that he was somewhere else when the offence was committed, unless notice of it is given to the solicitor for the prosecution either as part of the committal proceedings or within seven days of the end of them.

Although this warning need not be given if it seems unnecessary having regard to the nature of the offence charged, it should as a general rule be given where there is any doubt, because the Act provides that failure to give it will allow the defendant to introduce a last-minute alibi at his trial.

There is a discretion in the trial judge to allow alibi evidence to be heard even though particulars of it were not given within seven days, provided the prosecution has been given time to investigate the alibi before the trial started (*R* v *Sullivan* [1970] 2 All ER 681). It is unusual for the defence to give notice of an alibi at the committal proceedings.

Place and time of trial

Under s 7 of the Magistrates' Courts Act 1980 a magistrates' court transferring proceedings for trial in a Crown Court has to specify the Crown Court centre at which the accused is to be tried and in selecting that centre must have regard to:

(*a*) the convenience of the defence, the prosecution and the witnesses;

(*b*) the expediting of the trial;

(*c*) any directions regarding the distribution of Crown Court business given by the Lord Chief Justice or by an officer of the Crown Court with the concurrence of the Lord Chancellor under s 4(5) of the Courts Act 1971.

Under s 76 of the Supreme Court Act 1981 (becomes Senior Courts Act 1981) the Crown Court may alter the place of any trial on indictment by substituting some other place for the place specified by the magistrates or in a previous decision on the matter by a Crown Court. Under the 1981 Act the defendant or the prosecutor, if dissatisfied with the place of trial as fixed by the magistrates or by the Crown Court, may apply to the Crown Court to vary the place of trial. The Crown Court may deal with the application as it sees fit. An application under the 1981 Act must be heard in open court by a High Court judge.

The above materials relate to the *place* of trial but when committing *an either-way case* for trial in the Crown Court, the magistrates will fix a date for what is known as a *plea/directions hearing* in the Crown Court. The hearing must take place:

(1) within four weeks of committal where the defendant is in custody; or

(2) within six weeks of committal if the defendant is on bail.

The defendant will be required to plead to the charge(s) at the hearing. If he pleads guilty, he may be sentenced at the hearing. If he pleads not guilty, the judge will require certain information to enable him *to set a date for the trial*. This includes the number of witnesses together with a summary of the issues involved, any facts which are admitted and any alibi, the estimated length of the trial and the date of availability of witnesses and advocates.

When sending *an indictable-only offence* and defendant to the Crown Court for trial, the first hearing is called a *preliminary hearing* and allows a defendant to apply to the Crown Court for bail and allows the judge, following consultation with the prosecution, to set a date by which the prosecution should serve its case on the defence and to set the date for a plea and directions hearing as above. In this case, the first Crown Court appearance must take place:

■ within eight days of the receipt of a notice from the magistrates specifying the charges on which the defendant is sent for trial;

■ within 28 days of receipt of the above notice where the defendant is given bail.

The magistrates' notice must be given within four days of sending for trial.

The above provisions are designed to bring an accused person to trial as quickly as possible. However, the prosecutor and the accused and his advisers must be given time in which to prepare the case properly. Accordingly, s 77 of the Supreme Court Act 1981 (as amended) (becomes Senior Courts Act 1981) provides for the laying down under Crown Court Rules of the minimum period from the date of committal when the trial shall commence. These minimum periods cannot be *shortened* without the consent of the accused and the prosecutor or *lengthened* without an order of the Crown Court.

The offence and indictment

Let us suppose that Jim Green has recently and successfully objected to the granting of planning permission to Fred Brown, his neighbour, which has prevented Fred from using part of his land for car-breaking. Let us also suppose that on the evening of 25 February 2007, Jim left home for work and shortly afterwards in a lane not far from his home he was attacked by Fred who was wearing a black balaclava over his head and had, on the evidence to be called, planned the attack. Fred attacked Jim with a knife. Jim suffered serious injuries requiring five stitches in his cheek, six on his right hand, and 16 in his stomach. Jim was detained in hospital for several days.

Fred is now to be tried on indictment for the offence. An indictment is a printed accusation of crime made at the suit of the Queen and read out to the accused at the trial. In Fred's case the main contents of the indictment will state the court of trial and be set out as follows:

INDICTMENT

No. 123456

The Crown Court at Barchester

The Queen – *v* – Frederick Brown

FREDERICK BROWN

      IS Charged as follows:

COUNT 1 STATEMENT OF OFFENCE
Wounding or Causing Grievous Bodily Harm with Intent contrary to s 18 of the Offences Against the Person Act 1861.

PARTICULARS OF OFFENCE
Frederick Brown on the 25 February 2007 wounded James Green with intent to cause grievous bodily harm.

Signed *J. Bloggs*
Officer of the Court

In this case there is only one offence, but if there had been more, each would have appeared in a separate paragraph. Each paragraph is referred to as a 'count'.

There may be a motion by the defence to quash the indictment. This is quite rare because such a motion is appropriate only where there is an error apparent on the face of the indictment. A possible ground to quash the indictment is that a count set out in it is bad for duplicity, as where assault and theft are charged in the same count.

Arraignment

When the day of Fred's trial arrives the clerk of the court will confirm Fred's identity, read out the indictment and ask Fred whether he is guilty or not guilty. This is called the arraignment.

If Fred pleads guilty, counsel for the prosecution will give the court a summary of the evidence together with details of Fred's background and record. The defence will put in a plea for mitigation of sentence and sentence will then be passed. In this situation, it will not be necessary to empanel a jury to hear the evidence.

Fred may, while intending to plead 'not guilty' to the s 18 offence, be prepared to plead 'guilty' to a lesser offence which is not on the indictment. In this case Fred may be prepared to plead guilty to unlawful wounding under s 20 of the Offences Against the Person Act 1861. This carries a maximum period of five years' imprisonment, whereas the s 18 offence carries a maximum term of imprisonment for life. This is known as 'plea-bargaining'. The proper practice in such a case is for the defence lawyer to tell the prosecution in advance of Fred's intention or willingness to plead guilty to the lesser offence not appearing on the indictment. If the prosecution accepts the plea, the lawyers concerned in the case must explain to the judge why they think this course of action is appropriate, and the judge must approve the course of action proposed.

If the prosecution (or the judge) refuses to accept the plea to the lesser offence, the trial will continue, and if Fred is acquitted, he cannot be sentenced on the basis of his guilty plea to the lesser offence (*R* v *Hazeltine* [1967] 2 All ER 671) which is regarded as withdrawn if not accepted by the prosecution or judge. It should be noted that a trial judge may allow a defendant to change his plea to not guilty at any time before sentence is passed, even though a formal verdict of guilty has been returned by the jury on the direction of the judge after the trial has begun (*R* v *Drew* [1985] 1 WLR 914).

Some persons may, of course, be too mentally disordered to plead at all. This is referred to as 'unfitness to plead' and is further considered in Chapter 25.

We will assume that Fred pleads not guilty and in this case a jury must be sworn in.

Jury trial

The membership of the jury

As regards membership of a jury, s 321 of and Sch 33 to the Criminal Justice Act 2003 substitutes new provisions into the Juries Act 1974 under which *every* person is qualified to serve as a juror in the Crown Court, the High Court and county courts and is liable to attend for jury service if summoned if:

- they are registered as a parliamentary or local government elector and not less than 18 nor more than 70 years old;
- they have been ordinarily resident in the UK, the Channel Islands or the Isle of Man for any period of at least five years since attaining the age of 13;
- they are not mentally disordered persons; and
- they are not disqualified for jury service.

The definition of mentally disordered persons appears in a new Sch 1 to the Juries Act 1974. It includes persons suffering from mental illness, psychopathic disorder, mental handicap or severe mental handicap and who are resident in hospital or other institution or are under treatment by a medical practitioner or under guardianship or subject to a receivership order made by a judge of the Court of Protection.

Persons disqualified are set out in the new Sch 1 and are:

- persons who have at any time been sentenced in the UK, the Channel Islands or the Isle of Man:
  - to imprisonment for life, detention for life, imprisonment for public protection, an extended sentence under s 227 of the CJA 2003 or to a term of imprisonment, youth custody or detention of five years or more; or
  - to be detained during Her Majesty's pleasure or during the pleasure of the Secretary of State.
- persons who at any time in the last 10 years have in the UK or the Channel Islands or the Isle of Man:
  - served any part of a sentence of imprisonment, youth custody or detention; or
  - been detained in a young offender institution; or
  - had passed on them or (as the case may be) made in respect of them a suspended sentence of imprisonment or order for detention; or
  - had made in respect of them a community service order, a community punishment order or community order as defined in s 160 of the CJA 2003.
- persons who at any time in the last five years have in the UK or the Channel Islands or the Isle of Man had made in respect of them a probation order or a community rehabilitation order.

The various sentences are considered later in this chapter.

There are also provisions under which full-time serving members of the Forces may be excused on a certificate from the appropriate commanding officer that their absence would be prejudicial to the efficiency of the service.

Many well-known previous exemptions, e.g. for lawyers, are repealed.

The court has power to excuse a person from jury service where it is felt that the particular juror would not be able to perform the duties properly as where a person has a conscientious objection to jury service. (See *R* v *Guildford Crown Court ex parte Sinderfin* [1989] 3 All ER 7.)

Furthermore, since the widening of the base for jury service, a Practice Direction has been issued by the Lord Chief Justice stating that with more professionals and others with public service commitments being available judges should be alert to excuse or discharge a juror should the need arise.

The Juries Act 1974 also provides for exemptions to be granted administratively for prior jury service; previously only the trial judge could grant exemption. Under s 5 of the Juries Act 1974 the defence has a right to see the names, and in London the addresses as well, of the jury panel. This could assist 'jury nobbling' but it remains a right at the present time (but see below).

Under s 61 of the Administration of Justice Act 1982 questions may be put to a prospective juror to ascertain whether he is qualified for jury service *at any time*, and not just when he attends following a jury summons. If a juror refuses without reasonable excuse to answer, or knowingly or recklessly gives a false answer to the questions which are customarily set out in the jury summons, he will commit an offence punishable with a fine. This applies also to a juror who pretends to have a disqualification which he does not have in order to try to avoid jury service.

As regards disabilities, the 1974 Act provides that the court may also exclude anyone from jury service because physical disability or insufficient understanding of English makes his ability to act effectively as a juror doubtful. However, s 18 provides that no judgment after verdict should be reversed by reason, amongst other things, that any juror was unqualified or unfit to serve. Thus, in *R* v *Chapman* (1976) 63 Cr App R 75 where, after a trial at which both defendants had been found guilty by a unanimous verdict, it was discovered that one juror had been deaf so that he was unable to follow the proceedings, it was held that that did not make the verdict unsafe or unsatisfactory and was a situation covered by the Juries Act 1974, s 18. However, a judge has a discretion *to discharge* a juror *during the trial*, e.g. for bias, as where on a charge of shoplifting from a store a juror reveals that she is employed by that store (*R v Morris* (1991) *The Times*, 24 January).

Under s 3 of the 1974 Act the responsibility for summoning jurors is placed upon the Lord Chancellor. The court's administration at each centre acts as summoning officer. However, selection from the electoral register is now effected randomly by computer at the Central Summoning Bureau at Blackfriars in London. Juries are paid travelling and subsistence allowances and are compensated for loss of earnings and other expenses.

Advantages and disadvantages of jury trial

Some take the view that the verdict of a jury is more acceptable to the public than the verdict of a judge, and certainly the jury system gives ordinary persons a part to play in the administration of justice. It is perhaps better that lay men and women should decide matters of fact and the credibility of witnesses. The jury system also tends to clarify the law, in that the judge has to explain the more important points arising at the trial in clear and simple terms, so that the jury may arrive at a proper verdict.

On the other hand, juries may be too easily swayed by experienced advocates and the random method of selection sometimes produces a jury which is not as competent in intellectual terms as it might be in weighing the evidence and following the arguments presented. It has been suggested that trial by, say, three judges would be better, particularly where difficult issues are involved.

There is also the possibility that a member or members of a jury may be subjected to threats by organised crime or by delinquent associates of the accused or his family to achieve an acquittal. Therefore, the prosecution will, in some cases, ask for police protection of the jury, which the judge may grant. The prosecution's application is not made in court but to the judge in the presence of the defendant and his lawyer(s).

Indictable offences are triable before a jury of 12 persons. A panel of more than 12 jurors is brought into court and the clerk will select 12 jurors by a ballot.

Challenge

The names of the jury as selected by the clerk's ballot are called out on selection and each person goes into the jury box to be sworn. Under s 118 of the Criminal Justice Act 1988 the right to challenge jurors without cause (reasons), in proceedings for the trial of a person on indictment, is abolished.

Now a challenge must be supported by reasons. The defence may, before a potential juror is sworn, say 'Challenge for cause' in order, e.g., to challenge the inclusion of a man who has published anti-semitic articles where the defendant is of the Jewish faith. The cause should not be stated in the presence of the potential juror and the other potential jurors who are waiting to be sworn: they should be excluded from the court while the matter is argued before the judge. Jurors may also be challenged because they know the defendant.

The prosecution can also challenge for cause. However, it has, in effect, a right to challenge without cause under the 'stand by' procedure. The prosecution may call on a juror to 'stand by for the Crown', i.e. to be excluded unless it is impossible for a jury to be empanelled without calling on him. In practice, such persons are not called again. This right should not be used to ensure a pro-prosecution jury.

Jury vetting

Following judicial decisions, particularly perhaps that of the Court of Appeal in *R* v *Mason* [1980] 3 All ER 777, that it was not only lawful but necessary and a 'commonsense' precaution, for the police to vet jurors' criminal records and pass information to the prosecution so that challenge could be made, the Attorney-General has issued guidelines on jury checks. In the first place, the guidelines state that a person will in general be disqualified or ineligible for a jury only as provided by the Juries Act 1974 (as amended). However, where the case involves national security and part of the evidence is likely to be heard *in camera* (i.e. the court closed to the public and the news media), or in terrorist cases, extra precautions may be necessary. However, no check on the records of police special branches will be made except on the authority of the Attorney-General following a recommendation from the DPP. Furthermore, checks involving so-called strong political motives will not be made except in terrorist cases or where national security is involved and the court is expected to sit *in camera*. There is, of course, no reason why routine police checks on criminal records for the purpose of ascertaining whether or not a jury panel includes any person disqualified under the Juries Act 1974 should not continue.

It was held in *R* v *Ford* [1989] 3 All ER 445 that fairness in the composition of a jury was best achieved by random selection and a trial judge had no power to interfere with the make up of a jury in order to get a racially mixed jury on the trial of a black defendant charged with reckless driving. The Court of Appeal also ruled in *R* v *Smith (Lance Percival)* (2003) *The Times*, 3 March that judges cannot influence the racial composition of juries and that the Juries Act 1974 is not incompatible with the Human Rights Act 1998 because it fails to provide for multi-racial juries. Mr Smith, who is a black man, appealed against his conviction by an all-white jury for causing grievous bodily harm with intent and possessing a firearm with intent in an incident at a night club in a town where almost all of the residents were white. His appeal failed.

Again, in *R* v *Tarrant (James Nicholas)* (1997) *The Times*, 29 December Tarrant appealed against his conviction of conspiracy to possess cannabis resin with intent, contending that his trial was a nullity because the judge, who thought that jurors might be intimidated, had ordered that the jury be selected from outside the area. The appeal to the Court of Appeal succeeded because the jury had not been randomly selected.

The oath

The 12 persons who survive the selection procedure are then sworn, by each holding a Bible in his right hand and reading the following oath:

I swear by Almighty God that I will faithfully try the defendant and give a true verdict according to the evidence.

Christians are sworn on the New Testament and those of the Jewish faith on the Old Testament. Other faiths may be sworn upon a holy book of their choice. For example, Hindus are sworn on the Vedas, and Muslims are sworn on the Koran.

The affirmation which jurors may select if non-Christian or of no religion or belief is as follows:

I do solemnly, and sincerely and truly declare and affirm that I will faithfully try the defendant and give a true verdict according to the evidence.

All jurors must take the oath in the presence of each other. The jury is then addressed by the clerk who explains the charges and tells the jurors that having heard the evidence they must decide whether the defendant is guilty or not, and the trial begins officially at this point (*R* v *Tonner* [1985] 1 All ER 807).

Juror personation

It may be that a person who receives a jury summons will get someone to stand in for them. This is known as juror personation and there are legal consequences. A notice is included in all jury summonses. It says:

> Impersonation of Jurors: It is an offence for any person to impersonate a juror and serve on a jury on his or her behalf. As a matter of routine, court staff may need to verify the identity of a juror. Those attending for jury service are therefore requested to have with them some form of personal identification.

Trials on indictment without a jury

Part 7 of the Criminal Justice Act 2003 sets out (ss 43–50) the circumstances in which a trial on indictment may take place in the Crown Court before a judge sitting alone.

Defendant's application

Defendants being tried in the Crown Court may make an application to the court to have the trial heard by a judge sitting alone instead of by a judge and jury. Unless other defendants also being tried object to the application (or any one of them does) or there are exceptional circumstances applying leading the judge to believe that a trial before a jury would be in the interests of justice or necessary in the public interest, the judge *must* make an order granting trial by a judge alone. The Act does not specify what are to be regarded as 'exceptional circumstances'.

Prosecution application

The prosecution can apply for a judge-only trial on the following grounds:

- *The length or complexity of the trial.* The case must be so long or complex (or both) that the trial would be burdensome upon the jury to the extent that it is necessary in the interests of justice to conduct the trial without a jury, or the trial would be likely to place an excessive burden on the life of a typical juror. The trials that come to mind are those concerning business fraud where transactions and/or records of a financial or commercial nature or relating to property are involved. However, consideration must be given, always, to ways in which steps could be reasonably taken to reduce the length and complexity of the trial to allow it to be conducted before a jury. (Fraud trial provision not enacted.)
- *The real and present danger of jury tampering* so that the trial should be *conducted* without a jury or *continued* without a jury and the jury discharged. The court must be satisfied that the level and duration of police protection that would be required for the jury would be excessively burdensome to a typical juror or that jury tampering would remain a high threat even if maximum possible police protection was given so that it is in the interests of justice to conduct a judge-only trial. In trials already in progress where the jury has been discharged because of tampering the trial will continue without a jury unless the judge thinks it is necessary in the interests of justice to terminate the trial. In such a situation the judge may order a retrial and has the option of ordering that the retrial will take place without a jury.

The issue as to whether there should be a jury or whether the trial should continue without a jury or retried without a jury will be considered at a preparatory hearing or a separate hearing.

There are *rights of appeal* to the Court of Appeal for both prosecution and defence against the decision of a court on application for a judge-only trial and against a court order to continue a trial in the absence of a jury or to order a retrial without a jury because of jury tampering.

Where a trial is conducted or continued without a jury and a defendant is convicted the court must give its reasons for conviction.

Judge-only trials: present position

There were problems over the provisions of Part 7 of the CJA 2003 when the Bill was before Parliament. Trial by jury is a major feature of the legal system in England and Wales and many MPs felt strongly that it should be retained and available in trials on indictment. In order to get the Bill through Parliament, a compromise was reached and the 2003 Act regarding complex issues such as fraud trials was not enacted. The only judge-only trials under the 2003 Act are in relation to cases involving threats to and intimidation of juries. The government has said, however, that it will try to legislate again in the future on the complex fraud trial issue.

The judge

Criminal offences are divided into three classes for the purpose of trial in a Crown Court. The classifications are set out on p 39 and should be referred to. Fred's offence is in Class 3 and can be tried by a High Court judge, a circuit judge, a deputy circuit judge or a recorder or assistant recorder. As will be seen from the material at p 39, it is unlikely to be a High Court judge and will probably be a recorder or assistant recorder.

Trial and evidence

The advocate appearing for the prosecution will make an opening speech outlining the case to the court and will then call witnesses to confirm the facts. However, before doing so he must tell the jury that the burden of proof rests on the prosecution to establish that the defendant is guilty beyond a reasonable doubt. A witness will first take the oath appropriate to his religion or affirm if he has no religious belief. The Christian oath is most often used. It is: 'I swear by Almighty God that the evidence I shall give shall be the truth, the whole truth and nothing but the truth.' Contrary to popular belief, it does not end with 'so help me God'.

Leading of witnesses and hearsay evidence

During the examination-in-chief, counsel for the prosecution must not lead his witnesses, i.e. must not suggest a particular answer to his question. Thus, counsel for the prosecution cannot ask one of his witnesses, say, a police officer, 'Did the defendant punch you when you arrested him?' He must instead say, 'What happened when you arrested the defendant?'

Also, in examination-in-chief counsel must not contradict his own witness by referring to a prior inconsistent statement made in, say, committal proceedings, unless the witness becomes 'hostile', i.e. as where he is now showing bias against the person calling him. In addition, hearsay evidence is not admissible. A witness must give evidence only as to what he himself saw or heard. Thus, evidence given by a witness either for the prosecution or the defence in the form: 'Alice told me that she saw Bill in the pub on Wednesday' would be inadmissible, unless the provisions of s 114 of the Criminal Justice Act 2003 are satisfied, e.g. that the court has given leave that the evidence be admitted where the court is satisfied that it would not be contrary to the interests of justice to admit the evidence even though there is some difficulty in challenging the statement since Alice is not present.

After counsel for the prosecution has carried out his examination-in-chief of a witness, counsel for the defence can cross-examine the witness. In this situation he can lead and say, for example, 'My client was upset by the circumstances of his arrest, wasn't he? There was no need to have called him a lying swine, was there?' Counsel for the defence can also refer to prior inconsistent statements of the witness.

When the prosecution has called all its witnesses, the defence will present its case and call witnesses to support it. These witnesses are examined-in-chief, cross-examined, and sometimes re-examined. More rarely, defence counsel may, before calling his witnesses, try to bring the trial to an end by endeavouring to persuade the judge that there is no case to answer, e.g. that the prosecution has not produced sufficient evidence to warrant the trial proceeding. This argument takes place without the jury. If the judge agrees with defence counsel, he will call the jurors back and tell them to give a formal acquittal. Otherwise the trial proceeds.

Bad character evidence and evidence of previous convictions

Part 11 of the Criminal Justice Act 2003 removes previous common law rules regarding the admission before verdict of evidence of bad character of the defendant and any previous convictions. The new rules apply also to non-defendants such as witnesses. The permission of the court is required before such evidence can be given. This provision has led to some concern in that it may encourage the police to focus investigations on those with previous convictions, past acquittals or a history of arrests.

The defendant's evidence: defendant's silence

The defendant may give evidence on oath or by affirmation on his own behalf, though he is not obliged to give evidence at all. This is affirmed by s 35 of the Criminal Justice and Public Order Act 1994. However, under s 35 of that Act the silence of the accused at a trial allows the judge or jury in determining guilt to draw such inferences as appear proper from the failure of the accused to give evidence at all or to answer a particular question or questions, unless there is good cause. Under s 34 of the Act the same is true of the failure to answer police questions when a suspect, but police officers must tell suspects that silence could go against them in court and then repeat the question. For example, John is arrested on suspicion of theft having been found by the police standing near a broken shop window from which items of jewellery are missing. The police, suspecting that John has been involved (probably with others) in the theft, ask him to account for his presence near the shop window. John does not reply. He is told this may go against him but still does not reply. The court may draw the inference that John is guilty on the grounds that if he could have explained his presence in terms that he was not guilty of the theft he would have done so.

Under the Youth Justice and Criminal Evidence Act 1999 inferences from silence are not permissible where the defendant has not had prior access to legal advice *provided that the accused was at an authorised place of detention*, such as a police station, at the time of failure to answer questions or a particular question. The provision is to be found in s 34(2A) of the 1994 Act as inserted by the 1999 Act. The inferences that may be drawn where there is a failure to answer questions at a trial apply only where the trial is of a person who has attained 14 years of age (s 35 Criminal Justice and Public Order Act 1994).

Home Office Reports state that the provisions of the 1994 Act, before the passing of which the court could not draw adverse inferences from the defendant's silence, have not led to more convictions.

Section 72 of the Criminal Justice Act 1982 abolishes the right of an accused person to make an unsworn statement from the dock without being subject to cross-examination. However, the accused may address the court or jury if he has no legal representation and may make a statement in mitigation of sentence without being sworn. If he gives evidence on oath in the ordinary way, he may be cross-examined but there can be no cross-examination where a mere statement is made, though the making of a statement in this way often leads to the suggestion that the defendant has something to hide.

After the defence witnesses have been heard, the prosecution makes its closing speech, followed by the defence, which always has the last word.

Summing up

The judge will then explain his role to the jury. He will say that he will tell them what the law is and that the law is a matter for him but that they are the only judges of the facts in the case. He will repeat that it is for the prosecution to prove guilt. The judge will then sum up the evidence on both sides and will define the law of the offence. If he misleads the jury on this, the accused may well have grounds for a successful appeal. The judge will also explain that although Fred is charged under s 18 of the Offences Against the Person Act 1861 of wounding with intent to cause grievous bodily harm, the jury may acquit him of that offence and yet find him guilty of the lesser offence of unlawful wounding under s 20 of the Offences Against the Person Act 1861. The judge may then explain to the jury that it must endeavour to reach a unanimous verdict (but see below), though whether he does so or not is a matter of discretion (*R* v *Watson* [1988] 1 All ER 897). The judge will then leave the court and the jury, escorted by a bailiff, will retire to a jury room where it will try to reach a verdict. If a verdict is not reached on the day the jury retires, the jurors may be taken to a hotel to spend the night.

However, under s 13 of the Juries Act 1974 (as substituted by s 43 of the Criminal Justice and Public Order Act 1994), if on the trial of any person for an offence on indictment the court thinks fit, it may at any time (whether before or after the jury has been directed to consider its verdict) permit the jury to separate.

In this connection, *R* v *Rankine* (*Elliston*) [1997] CLY 1330 is of interest. In that case Rankine appealed against a conviction for unlawful wounding on the ground that the judge should not have invited the jury to consider its verdict without retiring. The Court of Appeal held that, as a matter of law, it was permissible for a judge to ask a jury if it wished to consider its verdict without retiring, and that an appeal court should intervene only if it felt that this put pressure on the jury to reach a verdict. Rankine's appeal on the retirement point failed.

The verdict

If the jury is unanimous in finding Fred guilty, it will tell the jury bailiff that it is ready to come back into court. The judge and counsel return and the jury files in. A court usher will ask the foreman of the jury what their verdict is. We assume that the jury has found Fred guilty of the s 18 offence; the foreman says so.

At this stage Fred's previous convictions, if any, will be handed to the judge who may refer to some of them openly in court. It will be appreciated that under the Criminal Justice Act 2003 evidence of previous convictions and bad character would already have been given in evidence if the court had permitted this (see p 147). Counsel for the defence will then normally put in a plea in mitigation, saying, perhaps, that Fred has not been in trouble before or at least not for some time, according to his record, in the hope that this plea will lead to a lighter sentence.

The judge will then address the defendant and pass sentence, which, in view of the violence involved in Fred's case, is likely to be a term of imprisonment.

Majority verdicts

The Juries Act 1974 provides for majority verdicts of juries in criminal proceedings. Section 17 provides that the verdict of the jury in criminal proceedings need not be unanimous if:

(a) in a case where there are not less than *eleven* jurors, *ten* of them agree on the verdict. In the case of an ordinary jury of 12, this means that the judge can accept a verdict of 11 to one or 10 to two; and

(b) in a case where there are *ten* jurors, *nine* of them agree on the verdict. If there are only nine jurors, the verdict must be unanimous (see below).

A court must not accept a majority verdict of guilty unless the foreman of the jury has stated in open court the number of jurors who respectively agreed to and dissented from the verdict. No such statement is required if the verdict is one of not guilty so that it will not be known that a verdict of not guilty was by a majority.

Furthermore, a court must not accept a majority verdict unless it appears to the court that the jury has had not less than two hours' deliberation or such longer period as the court thinks reasonable, having regard to the nature and complexity of the case.

The judge cannot accept a majority verdict after less than two hours' deliberation and if the jury is not unanimous after two hours, he should send it back, at least once more, to try to reach unanimity. If the jury still cannot, he should send the jurors back to see if they can reach a decision by the necessary majority, having directed them on the law relating to majority verdicts.

When the jury returns to the courtroom, the judge will ask whether the required majority has agreed on a verdict. If so, the verdict is accepted *provided*, according to a Practice Direction, that at least two hours and *ten minutes* have elapsed between the time at which the last juror left the jury box to go to the jury room and the time when the judge asked whether the jury had reached a verdict by the required majority.

Before the judge asks whether the jury has reached a majority verdict, the senior officer of the court present must announce the deliberation time which the jury has had. The extra 10 minutes was added in order to reduce the number of appeals made to the Court of Appeal on the ground that majority verdicts had been accepted, although the deliberation time had been less than two hours, as for example where the jury had returned to put a question to the court during the deliberation period.

The majority provision is, of course, a controversial one because the principle of the unanimous decision was an old and much-respected feature of English law, indeed the requirement for a jury to be unanimous first appeared in a case in 1367. The main reason for the change was the growing problem of deliberate corruption or intimidation of jurors to secure an acquittal. The majority of 10 to two was chosen because it was felt that it would be difficult to find more than one or two who were susceptible to bribery or intimidation, particularly in view of the fact that those with criminal records are excluded from jury service under the Juries Act 1974 (as amended by the Criminal Justice Act 2003). It should be noted that what happens in a jury room is not supposed to be disclosed. This is reinforced by s 8 of the Contempt of Court Act 1981. This makes it an offence for a juror to reveal the discussions in the jury room and for a newspaper or any other organisation or person to try to find out by interviewing a juror.

Thus, in *AG v Associated Newspapers* [1994] 2 WLR 277 the House of Lords found the *Mail on Sunday* newspaper, through its editor and publisher, to be in contempt of court for revealing the deliberations of a jury in a criminal trial. The informant was also in contempt.

It should be noted that in cases where jury tampering is present a trial could, under the Criminal Justice Act 2003, be *conducted* or be *carried on* by a judge alone. This procedure is more effective than majority verdicts in appropriate cases.

Alternative verdicts

The common law, as restated by s 6(3) and (4) of the Criminal Law Act 1967, provides for alternative verdicts, which means that a jury can convict an accused of an offence other than the one with which he is charged. Although the wording of s 6 appears wider than the common law rule, subsequent cases seem to indicate that a jury cannot convict of an offence different in *character* from the offence charged. The power is limited to a conviction for an offence involving *the same criminal act* but with a lesser degree of aggravation. As we have seen, in Fred's case it would have been possible for the jury to bring in a verdict of unlawful wounding under s 20 of the Offences Against the Person Act 1861, although the charge was wounding with intent to cause grievous bodily harm under s 18 of the 1861 Act.

Where there exists an alternative and less serious offence to the one charged, the judge *must* direct the jury on the lesser offence if there is evidence to support it (*R v Fairbanks* [1986] 1 WLR 1202), but not apparently if the main offence is very serious and the alternative offence is trifling. So in a case of robbery, the judge is not bound to direct the jury on the alternative offence of theft (*R v Maxwell* [1990] 1 All ER 801).

Victims' advocate

The government has outlined plans for the introduction of victims' advocates and is carrying out pilot schemes in England and Wales. A victims' advocate will be able to address the court before sentence in a murder or manslaughter case. The advocate could be a family member or a third party and while the address is not intended to impact on sentence, it will give the advocate the chance to highlight how the crime has affected those close to the victim.

Numbers of jurors

The number of jurors will normally be 12 unless the number has been reduced in accordance with s 16 of the Juries Act 1974. The section provides for the continuation of criminal trials where a juror dies or is discharged by the court, whether through illness or for any other reason.

If the number of members of the jury is not reduced below nine, the trial may proceed and the verdict may be given accordingly.

However, in a trial for any offence formerly punishable with death, e.g. treason, this rule only applied if assent in writing was given by or on behalf of both the prosecution and the accused, or each of the accused if there were more than one. The rule is now obsolete.

Moreover, the court has discretion in any criminal trial to discharge the jury if it sees fit to do so when its numbers are depleted.

Committal to the Crown Court for sentence

As we have seen, there are times when the Crown Court sits to sentence persons convicted of offences before the magistrates. This happens where the magistrates have found a particular defendant guilty and have had access to his previous convictions showing, shall we say, a very bad record, and feel that the defendant should receive a greater sentence than they can give. In such a situation they will commit the defendant to the Crown Court for sentence. The Crown Court may then deal with the defendant as if he had been convicted on indictment.

The Crown Court may sit solely for the purpose of sentencing and if so consists of a judge (either a High Court judge or circuit judge or recorder). Under s 74 of the Supreme Court Act 1981 (as amended by s 79 of the Access to Justice Act 1999) magistrates do not, as before, sit with the judge or recorder in sentencing cases. The judge or recorder deals with sentencing appeals by himself.

Under the Criminal Justice Act 2003 there is a limited power for magistrates to commit to the Crown Court for sentence. This will occur where a defendant is charged with a number of either-way offences and pleads guilty to one of them at plea before venue and is sent by the magistrates for trial in the Crown Court on the others. In such a case if the magistrates feel that having accepted jurisdiction on the guilty plea there are circumstances in which the defendant should be sent to the Crown Court for sentence then the magistrates may do so under s 4 of the Powers of Criminal Courts (Sentencing) Act 2000.

Appeal in criminal cases

A person who has been convicted and sentenced by a criminal court has rights of appeal. These have already been considered in Chapter 2.

Contempt of Court Act 1981

Under s 4 of the 1981 Act the trial judge may make an order imposing restrictions on the reporting of a trial in, e.g., newspapers. The section gives the court power to order the postponement of publication of reports of a trial or part of a trial where it appears necessary to avoid a substantial risk of prejudicing that trial or other proceedings pending or imminent, as where witnesses or potential witnesses might be intimidated.

Section 11 gives the court power to prohibit the publication of any name or other matter in connection with the proceedings where the court has allowed the name or other matter to be withheld from the public when the proceedings were before the court.

Sentencing

The matters to be taken into account in sentencing and the purposes of sentencing are set out in ss 142–146 of the Criminal Justice Act 2003.

■ *Matters to be taken into account* are the purposes of sentencing (see below), the seriousness of the offence, whether the defendant pleaded guilty and whether the offence was aggravated by race or religion.
■ *The purposes of sentencing* that are set out in statute for the first time are, punishment, public protection, crime reduction and reparation.

Custodial sentences: generally

The courts are given power to impose custodial sentences. Before doing so the courts must be satisfied that the circumstances are such, in terms particularly of the seriousness of the offence, that only a custodial sentence will suffice.

A custodial offence is:

- a sentence of imprisonment;
- a sentence of detention; and
- a detention and training order.

General restrictions on imposing custodial sentences

Section 152 of the CJA 2003 states that a court cannot impose a custodial sentence except where the offence, taken in combination with any past offences, merits it. Section 152(1) excludes from the above principle those offences which are punishable under ss 225 to 228 of the CJA 2003. These are:

- *Life sentence or imprisonment for public protection for serious offences (s 225)*. This sentence of life (or unspecified term of imprisonment) can be passed by a court only if the offender is convicted of a sexual or violent offence specified in Sch 11, e.g. rape or wounding with intent to cause grievous bodily harm, *carrying a sentence of 10 years or more* and the court considers that the offender is in its opinion *a significant risk to members of the public*. Where the offence carries a maximum sentence of life imprisonment, as wounding with intent to cause grievous bodily harm does, the court must pass a life sentence if the offence is serious enough to warrant it. In other cases s 228(1) requires the court to impose a sentence of imprisonment for public protection if it considers that no other sentencing options are adequate to protect the public.
- *Serious offences committed by those under 18 (s 226)*. This section applies the above principles to those aged under 18 as are applied to adults except that the sentence is not imprisonment but detention, in such place as the Secretary of State or a person authorised by him may decide.
- *Extended sentence for certain violent and sexual offences: persons 18 or over (s 228)*. This section makes provision for an extended sentence for sexual and violent offenders. The offender must have committed a sexual or violent crime specified in Sch 15. It must carry *a maximum sentence of less than 10 years*, e.g. assault occasioning actual bodily harm (where the maximum sentence is five years) and the offender must be judged by the court to pose *a significant risk of serious harm to the public*. The sentence is in two parts, the first part being *'the appropriate custodial term'*, and the second part being an *'extension period'*. The custodial period reflects the seriousness of the offence and must be at least 12 months. During the second half of the custodial period the offender may be released on the recommendation of the Parole Board. The court must also specify an *'extended period' of supervision on licence* to be added to the custodial period to protect the public. The extension period may be up to five years for violent offenders and nine years for sexual offenders. The total of the extended sentence must not be more than the maximum sentence for the offence in question. In the example given above the maximum extended period following a custodial sentence for assault occasioning actual bodily harm would be five years.
- *Extended sentence for certain violent or sexual offenders: persons under 18 (s 228)*. This section applies the extended sentence regime to those aged under 18 in the same way as for adults but the appropriate custodial term is limited to 24 months.

Also excluded are the offences in ss 110 and 111 of the Powers of Criminal Courts (Sentencing) Act 2000. These are:

- *Minimum of seven years for third class A drug trafficking offence (s 110)*. This section requires a court to pass a custodial sentence of at least seven years if the offender is aged 18 or over and has been convicted of at least two previous and separate class A drug trafficking offences. The court is not required to pass a seven-year sentence if there are particular circumstances that would make this unjust.

■ *Minimum of three years for third domestic burglary (s 111).* Under these provisions the court has a statutory duty to impose a custodial sentence of at least three years on a person who has been convicted of domestic burglary and who has been convicted on two previous occasions of domestic burglary unless there are particular circumstances that would make this unjust.

Section 152(2) of the CJA 2003 states that a custodial sentence must only be imposed if the offence is so serious that neither a fine nor a community sentence would be adequate punishment for it.

Section 152(3) makes clear that this does not prevent a court from passing a custodial sentence on an offender who does not consent to requirements imposed as part of a community sentence where consent is required or if he refuses to provide samples for the purposes of drug testing.

Length of discretionary custodial sentences: general provision (s 153, CJA 2003)

This section directs the court to impose the shortest term of custody that is commensurate with the seriousness of the offence. There are exceptions where the sentence is fixed by law, i.e. as in the case of an offence such as murder that carries a mandatory life sentence, and for the case of the new sentences for dangerous offenders in ss 225 to 226 (see above).

Restrictions where offender not legally represented (s 83, POCC(S)A 2000)

Under this section the court cannot impose a sentence of imprisonment on an offender who has not been legally represented at some time after being found guilty and before sentence is passed, unless representation has been offered and refused or withdrawn because of conduct or there has been failure to apply.

The pre-sentence report

Section 156 of the CJA 2003 deals with pre-sentence reports for community and custodial sentences. Where the court is considering whether to impose a discretionary custodial sentence and if so what its duration should be or whether to impose a community sentence and what restrictions to impose on the liberty of the offender as part of the sentence it must obtain a pre-sentence report (PSR). These reports are, in the case of adults, written by the probation service and are based on interviews with the offender and his or her history of offending and needs. The report contains advice as to punishment and what rehabilitative work would be likely to reduce the risk that the offender will re-offend. The court need not obtain a PSR if it thinks that it is unnecessary to do so in an individual case. Where the offender is under 18, the court must *not* decide that a PSR is unnecessary unless it has access to a report that relates to the offender. No sentence is invalid because the court did not obtain and consider a PSR even in the case of custodial and community sentences (see above).

Where an offender appeals, a PSR must be obtained unless the appeal court believes that the lower court was justified in not obtaining one. On appeal by offenders under 18, a PSR is required and the appeal court cannot decide that the lower court was justified in not obtaining a PSR or that a PSR is not necessary unless there is a previous PSR regarding the offender and the appeal court has access to it.

There are special provisions in s 157 CJA 2003 for reports on *mentally disordered offenders.* A qualified medical practitioner must be consulted to give a medical report unless a custodial sentence is fixed by law, i.e. a mandatory life sentence for murder where the court has no choice as to sentence.

Under s 158, CJA 2003 the PSR for an adult is, as we have seen, made by an officer of the local probation board. Where the offender is under 18 the PSR may be made by a probation officer, social worker or member of a youth offending team (see p 161).

Under s 159, CJA 2003 copies of the PSR go to the offender or his legal representative and the prosecutor though the court may consider that it is not appropriate for the prosecutor to have one. Where an offender is under 17 and is not legally represented the court may give the PSR to his or her parent or guardian if present in court.

Under s 160, CJA 2003 *other reports* that are not PSRs can be given to the offender and his legal representative or as set out above to a parent or guardian and the court. These will be designed to help the court to determine the appropriate sentence and will have been written by the probation service or a youth offending team.

Pre-sentence drug testing

Section 161, CJA 2003 provides that pre-sentence drug testing is available to assist the court when considering a community sentence.

Financial circumstances

Under s 162, CJA 2003 the court can before sentence make a financial circumstances order under which the offender must report his financial circumstances to the court. There are penalties for failure to make a report or to render a false report.

Is the offence serious?

Section 143, CJA 2003 gives certain principles that the court must follow when required to determine whether an offence is serious. The court must consider:

- the offender's culpability in committing the offence and the harm (or risk of harm) caused by the offence (or intended to be caused by the offence);
- any previous convictions, if recent and relevant, should be regarded as an aggravating factor that should increase the severity of the sentence;
- the fact that the offence was committed while the offender was on bail should also be regarded as an aggravating factor.

Reduction in sentence for guilty pleas

Section 144, CJA 2003 makes provision for the reduction of sentences for *early* guilty pleas. This is designed to encourage offenders who are guilty not to take up court time and trouble victims and witnesses unnecessarily.

Increase in sentence for racial or religious aggravation

Section 145, CJA 2003 provides that the court must treat the fact that the offence was religiously or racially aggravated as increasing the seriousness of the offence and must say so in court. There is an exception in the case of racially or religiously aggravated assaults because under the Crime and Disorder Act 1998 these offences already have a racial or religious ingredient and carry special penalties for this.

Human rights concerns

Article 3 of the European Convention on Human Rights (freedom from torture or inhuman or degrading treatment) has relevance in that an exceptionally severe sentence may raise an issue under the Article. This is implicit in the judgment of the European Court of Human Rights in *Weeks* v *UK* (1987) 10 EHRR 293 where it was ruled that to sentence a person of 17 to life imprisonment for robbery (which is the maximum sentence) for punitive reasons would potentially raise the issue of violation of Art 3. Article 7 (protection from any retrospective effect of the criminal law) may also be raised in an appropriate case in that no heavier penalty shall be imposed than the one applicable when the offence was committed bearing in mind that there is in general no limitation of actions where prosecution for crime is concerned.

Custodial sentences: the mandatory life sentence

We have already considered the discretionary life sentence for public protection in violent or sexual offences under s 225 of the CJA 2003. The following material is concerned with the *mandatory life sentence for murder*. An offender aged 21 or over who is convicted of murder must be sentenced to imprisonment for life under s 1(1) of the Murder (Abolition of the Death Penalty) Act 1965. There is no right of appeal against this sentence.

The Home Secretary has statutory power under s 29 of the Crime (Sentences) Act 1997 to intervene and fix a tariff going beyond the recommendation of the court even to the extent of a whole life sentence. The House of Lords ruled in *R* v *Lichniak* [2000] UKHL 47 that the imposition of a mandatory life sentence for murder was not contrary to the Convention on Human Rights. However in *R (on the application of Anderson)* v *Secretary of State for the Home Department* [2002] 4 All ER 1089 their Lordships ruled that the Home Secretary's power to intervene and set tariffs was incompatible with Art 6(1) of the Convention (right to have sentence imposed by an independent tribunal). The Home Secretary was not independent of the executive. The House of Lords declared s 29 of the 1997 Act incompatible with the Convention.

The Home Secretary accepted the judgment but introduced sentencing principles into the Criminal Justice Act 2003 as follows:

- *Whole-life terms: offender will die in jail (adults)*. Multiple murderers (two or more) with a high degree of premeditation or murders of a child involving abduction or involving sexual or sadistic conduct, terrorist murder, offenders with a previous conviction for murder.
- *Sentence of 30 years (adults)*. Murder of a police or prison officer in the course of duty, murder involving the use of a firearm or explosive, killing done for gain, burglary, robbery or contract killing, murder with a racial, religious or sexual motive, single sadistic or sexual murder of an adult, multiple murders not covered by the whole-life category.
- *Sentence of 15 years*. All other murders.
- *Murderers aged 10 to 17* have a 15-year starting point and *murderers aged 18 to 20* have a starting point of 15 or 30 years.

The sentences described above, other than, obviously, the whole-life sentence are *starting-point sentences* on which the judge can build to give an appropriate sentence.

Sentencing Guidelines Council

Sections 167 to 173 of the CJA 2003 set up the Council in March 2004 that produces a set of sentencing guidelines for all criminal courts and also guidelines on the allocation of cases between courts (see p 146). The guidelines will be starting points on which the court can build to give an appropriate sentence in a particular case. Further, legal practitioners and the public will know what the starting point for a given offence is. The existing Sentencing Advisory Panel continues and will give its advice to the Council from time to time. The courts are obliged to take the Council's guidelines into account when deciding on a sentence.

The members of the Council are drawn from the police, probation and prison services, victims of crime and the legal profession and those responsible for sentencing in magistrates' courts, Crown Courts and the Court of Appeal.

Further information on the Council and the Guidelines can be accessed at **www.sentencing-guidelines.gov.uk.**

Reasons for sentence

Section 174 of the CJA 2003 provides for a duty upon the court to provide reasons for the sentence and explain it in ordinary language. The court must refer to relevant guidelines when giving its reasons. Section 175 expands the existing duty on the Home Secretary in s 95 of the Criminal Justice Act 1991 to *publish information* on the effectiveness of sentencing.

Community orders

Sections 177–180 of the CJA 2003 provide for community orders for offenders aged 16 or over. Previously there were various different community orders, e.g. community rehabilitation orders. The CJA 2003 creates a *single community sentence* that combines all of the requirements previously available under the different and separate community sentences.

The requirements that may be placed on a community sentence are:

- compulsory (but unpaid) work;
- participation in specified activities;
- programmes aimed at changing offending behaviour;
- prohibition from certain activities;
- curfew;
- exclusion from certain areas as specified in the order;
- residence requirements;
- mental health treatment (where the offender consents);
- drug treatment and testing (with the consent of the offender);
- alcohol treatment (if the offender consents);
- supervision, e.g. by a member of the local probation service or a member of the youth offending team;
- attendance centre requirements, i.e. attendance at a specified centre at specified times to take part in specified activities (for under 25s).

Restrictions on imposing a community sentence

Section 148 makes provision in regard to when it is appropriate to impose a community sentence. Where the offence or the history of offending is not serious enough for a community sentence a fine or conditional or absolute discharge would be appropriate. The requirements of the community order must be suitable for the offender and restrictions on liberty, as by curfew, must be in line with the seriousness of the offence.

An exception will be provided by s 151 when in force where the offence does not in itself merit a community sentence but where the offender has committed several similar offences in the past. Under the section an offender aged 16 or over who has been fined on at least three previous occasions for similar offences may receive a community sentence even though the current offence does not in itself merit it. Of course, the previous convictions may lead the court to impose a custodial sentence if they go to the seriousness of the current offence. The section does not interfere with the courts' power in this regard.

Under s 149 where a community sentence is passed on an offender who has been remanded in custody the time on remand counts towards the length of the community sentence as does the time spent considering the appropriate form of community sentence in terms of its restrictions.

Under s 150 community sentences are not available where the sentence is fixed by law nor in respect of dangerous offenders (see ss 205 to 208 above).

Prison sentences of less than 12 months

Section 181 carries provisions to ensure that in general terms all prison sentences of less than 12 months will consist of *a short period of custody* followed by *a longer period on licence* during which time the offender must comply with requirements fixed by the court as part of the sentence. The length of the custodial period must be between two and 13 weeks and the licence period at least 26 weeks. There is provision for sentences to run consecutively where the total period of imprisonment must not exceed 15 months. The licence conditions may include electronic monitoring.

Under s 183 where the sentence is under 12 months the court may give a sentence of *intermittent custody* where the offender serves a period of time in custody and a period of time on licence. These periods are predetermined by the court when giving the sentence.

Suspended sentences

A custodial sentence can be suspended for between one and two years provided that the offence merits custody and the suspension is justified by the exceptional circumstances of the case. A suspended sentence can be combined with a fine or compensation order but not with a community sentence though a supervision order can be attached. The custodial sentence is activated by the committal of another imprisonable offence. Sections 189 to 193 of the CJA 2003 create a new form of suspended sentence as an addition to the above procedure. The court may suspend a short custodial sentence (see s 181 above) for between six months and two years on condition that the offender undertakes activities in the community. These activities are chosen by the court from the community sentence list. Commission of a further offence during the whole period of the suspended sentence will count as a breach and the court will deal with the suspended sentence when sentencing the offender for the new offence.

Deferred sentences

Here the court does *not sentence the offender*. It defers the passing of sentence on the basis of the good behaviour of the offender if the offender consents and the court believes that a deferred sentence is in the interests of justice. If the offender commits another offence during the period of deferment the court will deal with both offences at the same time. Under sections 1–1D of the Powers of Criminal Courts (Sentencing) Act 2000 more is required of an offender on a deferred sentence. The court may impose requirements as to his conduct and he may have to complete tasks in the community as set by the court including reparation to the community. This aspect of the sentence is monitored, e.g. by the probation service (now supplied by the National Offender Management Service) with a view to a report to the court for early sentence if the report is unsatisfactory. The commission of a further offence during the deferred period activates the deferred sentence and both offences can be dealt with in terms of sentence.

Release of offenders from custody

Sections 244 to 253 of the CJA 2003 provide for the release of offenders from custody. Under this framework offenders serving sentences of 12 months or more are released automatically on licence *at the half way point of their sentence*. The licence period is subject to conditions a general one being good behaviour and specific ones such as curfew and electronic monitoring. Breach of the licence conditions may result in recall to prison. Supervision is by the probation service and that service plus the prison service will make the recall not the Parole Board as formerly. The offender may appeal against recall to the Parole Board and the Board scrutinises the decisions to recall.

Fines

The imposition of a fine is the most common penalty in the criminal courts and is in effect an order requiring the offender to pay a sum of money to the state. The fine should reflect the seriousness of the offence.

The main principle is a requirement to investigate and take into account the financial circumstances of the offender and as we have seen the court may order a statement as to the offender's financial circumstances. There are penalties for failing to provide a statement or providing a false one.

There is a standard scale of maximum fines for summary offences (see s 37(2) of the Criminal Justice Act 1982) as follows:

Level	Amount
1	£200
2	£500
3	£1,000
4	£2,500
5	£5,000

Where the offender is under 18 the fine must not exceed £1,000 (s 135, POCC(S)A 2000) and if under 14 must not exceed £250 (s 135(2)). The court may order a parent or guardian of a person under 18 to pay the offender's fine, costs or compensation to the victim (s 137, POCC(S)A 2000) and may order a statement as to the financial circumstances of the parent or guardian.

Fines: reform

The Courts Act 2003 in ss 36 and 37 deals with the problems created by the fact that for some time large numbers of fines imposed by the courts have remained uncollected. The Act provides for the Lord Chancellor to designate *fines officers* whose role will be to manage the collection and enforcement of fines. Schedule 2 of the Act specifies new powers available to the courts and fines officers to enforce payment of fines. The following are some examples:

■ persons struggling to pay fines may contact the fines officer with a view to a variation of payment terms before payment is due and afterwards, in favour of the person required to pay the fine;

■ on the other hand, in appropriate cases, a fine may be increased on payment default as an incentive for offenders to pay their fines promptly;

■ in regard to fines for illegally parked cars that have been clamped the court will have power to order that on failure to pay the relevant vehicle be sold and the fine deducted from the selling price. This type of action may be appropriate for persistent offenders.

Absolute discharge

Section 12 of the POCC(S)A 2000 gives the court power to grant an absolute discharge. This procedure may be used in all criminal courts irrespective of the age of the offender. When used it normally reflects the trivial nature of the offence, the circumstances in which the offender came before the court or some special factors regarding the offender himself or herself.

Conditional discharge

Section 12 also applies and this procedure may be used in all criminal courts regardless of the age of the offender. There is only one condition which is that the offender does not commit any further offences for which he is convicted by a court in Great Britain, during the period of the discharge that the court has fixed. This period must not exceed three years. Where there is a relevant conviction, the court may sentence the offender for the original offence (s 13(6), POCC(S)A 2000).

Binding over to keep the peace

Section 1 of the Justices of the Peace Act 1361 gives power to bind over to be of good behaviour to magistrates, the Crown Court and the Court of Appeal. Section 115 of the Magistrates' Courts Act 1980 and the common law give the magistrates power to bind over to keep the peace or be of good behaviour. The court involved may take a recognisance in its discretion. This involves the payment of a sum of money on failure to comply. The court cannot impose a custodial sentence for failure to comply.

Binding over of a parent or guardian

Section 150 of the POCC(S)A 2000 applies and here a recognisance may be imposed on a parent or guardian of a child or young person for up to three years or until the offender has reached 18 whichever is the shorter. The recognisance comes into effect and the sum payable under it becomes payable if the parent or guardian fails to take proper care and control over the offender or ensure that he or she complies with a community sentence.

Travel restriction orders

Section 33 of the Criminal Justice and Police Act 2001 allows the court to make a travel restriction order where an offender receives a sentence for drug trafficking of four years or more. The order may be imposed for a minimum period of two years from release from custody. Surrender of a UK passport may also be ordered.

Compensation orders

Section 130 of the POCC(S)A 2000 applies and empowers a court before which a person is convicted of an offence to make a compensation order requiring the offender to pay compensation for any 'personal injury, loss or damage' resulting from the offence or any offence that is taken into consideration. A compensation order may be made in addition to any other form of sentence or as the only sentence for the offence. If a court does not make a compensation order where it has power to do so it must give reasons.

Anti-social behaviour orders

A court including a youth court may make an anti-social behaviour order (ASBO) where an offender is convicted of an offence. (See s 1C of the Crime and Disorder Act 1998, as amended by the Serious Organised Crime and Police Act 2005). The 1998 Act in this regard came into force at the end of 2002.

The court must consider that the offender has acted in a manner likely to cause harassment, alarm or distress to one or more persons not of the same household as the offender. The court must also take the view that an ASBO made on conviction is necessary to protect persons in any place in England and Wales from further anti-social acts committed by the defendant. The order is in fact a civil order but the criminal standard of proof (beyond a reasonable doubt) applies in satisfying the above criteria. Although it is a civil order there are criminal penalties if it is breached. The order may take effect immediately or be suspended, e.g. until the offender completes a custodial sentence. The order must last for a minimum of two years, although it can be discharged earlier by the court if, for example, the Director of Public Prosecutions consents. It contains only prohibitions, i.e. things the defendant must not do rather than positive requirements. The maximum period for an order is five years.

As regards penalties, if the offender does any of the things forbidden by the order, the offender is guilty of an offence triable summarily and punishable by imprisonment up to a maximum of six months or a fine up to the statutory maximum (currently £5,000) or both.

Youth crime and disorder: sentencing

In terms of the sentencing of youth offenders the following materials are relevant:

Custody of young offenders

Three forms of custodial sentence are available as set out below.

Detention during Her Majesty's Pleasure

This is restricted to cases of murder and s 90 of the POCC(S)A provides for a mandatory sentence in this form for an offender who is under 18 at the time of the offence. A person receiving this sentence will be detained at a place and under such conditions as directed or arranged by the Home Secretary (s 92(1), POCC(S)A 2000).

Detention for a specified period

Section 91 of the POCC(S)A 2000 applies and relates to persons under 18 who are convicted of serious offences listed in s 91.

An example is provided by the offence of sexual assault on a female or a male under s 3 of the Sexual Offences Act 2003 which is a triable either way offence, imprisonment following trial on indictment being for a maximum of 10 years.

Under s 91(3) the offender may be detained for such period not exceeding the maximum term of imprisonment for the offence if there is no other suitable way of dealing with the case.

Detention and training orders

Section 100 of the POCC(S)A 2000 applies. It provides for custodial sentences for offenders aged between 10 and 18. The period of such an order can be 4, 6, 8, 10, 12, 18 or 24 months. The period of detention and training is half the period of the order, the other half being a supervision and training arrangement. Supervision is by an officer of the local probation board or a social worker or a member of the youth offending team. *A youth offending team* consists of at least one of the following, namely, a probation officer, a social worker, a police officer, a person nominated by the local health authority and a person nominated by the chief education officer of the relevant local authority. These teams are set up by the Chief Constable and probation service under powers given in the Crime and Disorder Act 1998.

Under s 104(1) and (3) of the POCC(S)A 2000 failure to comply with the requirements of the supervision section of the order leads to an appearance before a youth court and the court may order detention for a period not exceeding the shorter of three months or the remainder of the term of the order or a fine not exceeding level 3 on the standard scale.

Youth community orders

Under the CJA 2003 a 'Youth Community Order' means any of the following orders.

Curfew order

As we have seen, these orders may be made in regard to an offender of any age but where the offender is on conviction under 16 the maximum period of the order is three months as opposed to six months in other cases. The order requires the offender to remain for the period specified at a specific place usually his or her home. The period must be not less than two hours a day and not more than 12 hours a day.

Attendance centre order

These orders are available for offenders who are at least 10 years old and under 25. The order requires attendence at a specified attendence centre to take part in specified activities. An order may be made for example requiring attendance at a centre for say three hours on a number of Saturday afternoons resulting in deprivation of peak leisure time. Consent of the offender is not required.

The aggregate number of hours for which an offender may be required to attend at an attendance centre must not be less than 12 nor more than 36. A child under 14 may be ordered to attend for less than 12 hours if the court is of the opinion that 12 hours would be excessive and in any case such persons cannot be required to attend for more than 12 hours.

Supervision order

These orders may be made where the offender is under 18. In essence, they are the equivalent for children and young persons of the old probation order. The offender's consent is not required. No minimum period is specified and the maximum period is three years. Supervision is by an officer of the local authority or of the local probation service or by a member of a youth offending team. The offender may be required to live at a specified place or places and there may be a night restriction for not longer than 10 hours on any one night. Breach of the order may lead to a fine of up to £1,000 or a curfew order. The court may also revoke the supervision order and deal with the offender for the offence committed.

Action plan orders

These can be applied to offenders aged 10 to 17 inclusive. Under the provisions the offender must comply with a three-month action plan placing him or her under the supervision of an officer of the local probation board, a social worker or a member of the youth offending team. An action plan is essentially an intensive programme of work with the offender and the parents to tackle the causes of offending at an early age. The plan imposes requirements regarding the offender's whereabouts and behaviour. Youth offending teams and their membership have already been considered (see p 161).

The order cannot be made if the court proposes to impose a custodial sentence or an attendance centre order or supervision order or referral order (see below).

Reparation order

These orders require the offender to make reparation for the offence other than by the payment of compensation. They may be made in respect of an offender under the age of 18. The court may make the order along with other orders, e.g. a fine. Reparation may consist, for example, of writing a letter of apology or apologising in person or removing litter or graffiti. Reparation of up to 24 hours in all must be made within three months of the making of the order. The period of reparation is supervised, e.g., by an officer of the local probation board.

For breaching an action plan order or a reparation order or a curfew order or an attendance centre order, the penalties are a fine not exceeding £1,000. A major sanction for the court is to discharge the order and deal with the offender in regard to the offence committed.

Referral orders

This involves referral to a youth offender panel and is intended to trigger an inquiry into the reasons for the offending behaviour and to impose on the offender, who must be under 18, the principle of restorative justice. This involves making restoration to the victim and reintegration into the law-abiding community and taking responsibility for the consequences of the offending behaviour. The panel concerned with a referral draws up a programme entitled a 'youth offender contract' that gives effect to the above objectives and with which the offender must comply. A court making the order can make a parenting order to run alongside the referral order. Where the court decides to make a parenting order with a referral order, the court must obtain a report by a probation officer, or a social worker or a member of the youth offending team. The report will indicate what the requirements of the parenting order might include with reasons. If the offender is under 16, information about the family's circumstances and the likely effect of the order on those circumstances is included.

A *youth offender panel* must be distinguished from a *youth offending team*. A youth offender panel is set up under a referral order for *that particular offender*, and consists of a member of the local youth offending team and two members who are not from that team but are volunteers from the local community. In regard to referral orders, the youth offending team is responsible for providing administrative support, accommodation and other facilities required by the youth offender panel. The team also arranges for the supervision of the youth offender contract and the member of the team who is on the panel keeps records of compliance or non-compliance.

Parenting orders

A parenting order requires the parent(s) to comply for a period not exceeding 12 months with such requirements as are specified in the order and to attend for a concurrent period not exceeding three months and not more than once in any week such counselling and guidance sessions as may be specified by the responsible officer, i.e. an officer of the local probation board, or a social worker or a person appointed by the chief education officer or a member of the youth offending team. The requirements shall as far as practicable avoid conflict with the parents' religious beliefs and with their normal working times. The requirements of the order are in general terms to involve the parents in the supervision of the child with the aim of preventing a recurrence of criminality or truancy. Breach of a parenting order can result on prosecution to a fine not exceeding level 3 on the standard scale i.e. £1,000.

Restitution of property in criminal cases

Restitution orders

Restitution orders may also be made in regard to property which is the object of an offence under ss 148 and 149 of the Powers of Criminal Courts (Sentencing) Act 2000. Restitution orders may also be made in respect of an offence which the accused asks to have taken into consideration. A restitution order and a compensation order may be made in respect of the same goods if recovered in a damaged condition.

Restitution and money-laundering legislation

As part of the law relating to restitution in criminal cases note should be taken of the Proceeds of Crime Act 2002. This is the most important of the legislative measures for business in terms of its wide scope and effect on commercial undertakings though there are measures covering particular areas, e.g. the Prevention of Terrorism Act 2005.

The money-laundering provisions of the 2002 Act are as follows:

- it creates the Assets Recovery Agency to investigate and recover wealth that has been obtained through criminal conduct;
- it gives a right of recovery at civil law which enables the Agency to recover property that was obtained through criminal conduct, including the right to recover property from third parties not involved in the criminal conduct. The Agency is only required to prove its case on the civil standard of proof, i.e. that the property was 'probably' the result of crime, and can apply to the High Court for an interim freezing order in regard to suspect property to prevent the movement of the property which will be managed by a receiver;
- the Agency has a right to exercise the functions of the Inland Revenue and tax the suspected proceeds of a crime without identifying the source of the income as the Revenue must do;
- it creates new powers of investigation including customer information orders. These require banks and other financial institutions to identify accounts that are held by persons connected with an investigation. There is also power to monitor accounts. A code of practice provides guidance on how these functions are to be exercised;
- it creates new obligations to report where there are reasonable grounds to know or suspect that a person is engaged in money laundering.

Some concerns have been expressed in regard particularly to the civil burden of proof and that offences can be committed even where money laundering, e.g. by a customer, is suspected or where it *should* have been suspected. It is now essential that firms, particularly those involved in financial services, review their procedures especially the 'know your customer' procedures to ensure that they do not commit, by mere negligence, a money-laundering offence.

Injury compensation in criminal cases

The compensatory awards set out above are ineffective if the offender is never caught or if when caught he has no money or property with which to pay compensation. In consequence, there is, under the Criminal Injuries Compensation Act 1995, a scheme of state compensation operated by the Criminal Injuries Compensation Authority under a Scheme Manager.

The Authority may make discretionary payments to those suffering personal injury which is attributable to certain criminal offences, e.g. rape and assault under s 47 of the Offences Against the Person Act 1861. Payments are not made for offences against property unless it was a physical aid to the victim, e.g. glasses, a hearing aid or a wheelchair. Dependants of a person who dies as a result of a relevant crime may claim. There are rights of appeal to Adjudicators appointed by the Secretary of State. The Authority can, having made an award, seek to reimburse itself by a claim against the offender. Those who cannot show the need for this sort of compensation may, of course, make an application under s 130 of the Powers of Criminal Courts Act 1973 if possible. Compensation is based on a tariff or scale of payments up to £500,000 together with additional payments for special expenses and loss of earnings for those who are incapacitated for at least 28 weeks.

The government issued a consultation paper in 2005 in which it is proposed that the current maximum payment of £500,000 be increased for serious injuries but no compensation for less serious injuries, only more practical and emotional support. It seems clear that there will be no extra money for victims of crime.

Rehabilitation of Offenders Act 1974 – non-disclosure of sentence

The provisions of this Act are an attempt to give effect to the principle that when a person convicted of crime has been successful in living down that conviction and has avoided further criminal activities, common justice demands that his efforts should not be prejudiced by the unwarranted disclosure of that earlier conviction.

All sentences are subject to rehabilitation except imprisonment for life and custodial sentences of more than 30 months. After the expiry of certain defined periods the offender is rehabilitated as follows:

- an absolute discharge   6 months
- a conditional discharge   1 year or for the period of the order if longer
- an attendance centre order   1 year after the order expires
- a fine or community sentence   5 years
- a custodial sentence up to 6 months 7 years
- a custodial sentence between 6
  and 30 months   10 years

In the case of those who were under 18 at the date of conviction, the rehabilitation periods are halved.

So far as the employment of persons with previous convictions is concerned, it should be noted that any questions seeking information as to a person's pervious convictions shall be treated as not relating to spent convictions and any obligation on any person to disclose matters shall not require him to disclose a spent conviction, and a spent conviction or failure to disclose a spent conviction is not a proper ground for dismissing or excluding a person from or prejudicing him in any occupation or employment. There is an exception (see SI 1986/1249) where the employment allows contact with persons under 18, e.g. in care, leisure and recreational activities. Here questions can be asked designed to reveal spent convictions particularly those with a sexual connotation. Such spent convictions are a ground for dismissal which will not, for that reason alone, be unfair.

In this connection, the Protection of Children Act 1999 makes changes to the law with the object of creating a framework for *identifying* people who are unsuitable for work with children and to compel or, in some cases, to allow employers to access a single point for checking the names of people they propose to employ in a post involving the care of children. This involves the check of names against criminal records and two lists of people considered unsuitable for work with children. The Department of Health and the Department of Work and Pensions maintain the lists to be made available via the Criminal Records Bureau under Part V of the Police Act 1997. These disclosures, via the records and lists, provide exceptions to the Rehabilitation of Offenders Act 1974. The above procedures are a response to the increasing number of cases involving the employment of paedophiles in local authority and other children's homes.

Another exception occurs under the Financial Services and Markets Act 2000. One of the primary purposes of the Act is to protect the public from the activities of unscrupulous and dishonest people who may find their way into the investment business. For example, those who are authorised to conduct investment business are under a duty to take reasonable care not to employ or continue to employ unsuitable persons. In this connection, the Act of 2000 provides that the 1974 Act does not apply to a spent conviction for fraud or dishonesty or to an offence under companies legislation such as insider dealing or under legislation relating to building societies, friendly societies, insurance, banking or other financial services, insolvency, consumer credit or consumer protection. There exceptions are now contained in the Police Act 1997 (see below).

The Police Act 1997 provides for access to criminal records for the purposes of employment and spent convictions are not to be included in the conviction certificate. However, spent convictions can be shown under the Financial Services and Markets Act 2000 where the conviction is, e.g., for fraud or dishonesty and where the certificate is required by an individual who will be working on a regular and unsupervised basis with children or is seeking appointment as a judge or magistrate.

Further exceptions are made from time to time by statutory instrument. For example, the Rehabilitation of Offenders Act 1974 (Exceptions) (Amendment) Order 2002 (SI 2002/441) adds to the exceptions where disclosure is required to those seeking employment with Customs and Excise, those who wish to be involved with work concerning vulnerable adults and those concerned with monitoring Internet communications for the purposes of child protection.

In addition, certain employees are excluded from the 1974 Act and their convictions can be disclosed. Included are doctors, chartered accountants and chartered certified accountants, insurance company managers and building society officers (see SIs 1975/1023 and 1986/2268).

5

CIVIL PROCEDURE

In this chapter we shall consider the way in which a civil action is brought and concluded in the High Court.

For the purposes of our High Court claim, we shall consider a case of alleged breach of contract on the lines of the case of *Mitchell (George) (Chesterhall) Ltd* v *Finney Lock Seeds Ltd* (1983) (see below Case **187**).

The claim is for breach of contract by reason of the supply by the defendant company of defective cabbage seed. The amount of the claim is an estimated alleged loss of £100,000. The defendant will defend the claim mainly on the basis of an exemption clause in the contract.

Initial considerations

The following matters will be considered by the claimant's solicitor before a claim form to commence the claim is served.

Time-bars

The Limitation Act 1980 (as amended) sets out a number of fixed periods of time for issuing a claim form to commence proceedings. In cases of our kind, i.e. breach of contract, the claimant has six years from the date on which the claim accrued, i.e. when the defective seed was delivered, or (as in our case, where there was latent damage not emerging until the defective seed had grown) there is a period of three years from knowledge of the defect if this period expires after the six-year period. It is unlikely that our claimant has left his claim for so long and limitation of claims rules should not affect him.

Cutting short liability

The Court of Appeal has ruled in *Granville Oil and Chemicals Ltd* v *David Turner & Co Ltd* [2003] 1 All ER (Comm) 819 that when a business is dealing with another business, but not a non-business consumer, the six-year period for contract claims can be reduced by a term in the contract. This leads to earlier ascertainment of potential liability. The facts were briefly that it was a standard condition of a freight forwarder's contract that the freight forwarder would be discharged of all liability arising if a claim in respect of alleged liability was not commenced by the customer within nine months of the provision of the relevant service. The condition could equally have been applied to alleged liability in respect of goods.

The condition was challenged in the Court of Appeal on the basis that it was an unfair term and unreasonable under the Unfair Contract Terms Act 1977. However, the Court of Appeal ruled that the condition was not void under the Act of 1977 after taking into account the fact that the parties had equal bargaining strength and that the condition had been brought to the attention of the customer. Furthermore, it was practical to commence a claim in that time since any damage could be ascertained on delivery of the goods by the carrier.

Comment The Court of Appeal stressed the value of the Act of 1977 to consumers and their protection and would not it seems have decided the case as it did unless both parties were in business and of equal bargaining strength. The court was not, however, so keen to allow the Act of 1977 to intrude into contracts between commercial parties such as these. They should, said the court, be capable of reaching agreements of their own choosing and should expect to be bound by them.

Defendant's finances

There is no point in making a claim against an individual who is insolvent nor against a company which is in a terminal insolvency procedure, such as liquidation. A search of the company's file at Companies' House, Cardiff, which is online, should be made. For individuals, the matter is not so straightforward and may require the services of an inquiry agent.

The cost effectiveness of the claim

Consideration should be given to the cost of the claim and the possibility of a successful outcome must be discussed, i.e. does the claim merit the bringing of civil proceedings which cannot be guaranteed to be successful?

Alternative approaches

These could include arbitration where the contract contains an arbitration clause or alternative dispute resolution.

The remedy

There is a variety of remedies which a claimant may ask for from the court. These are considered as we proceed through the chapters on substantive law, e.g. contract and tort. However, in our case, the claimant will be asking for damages on the ground that the defendant has caused loss by reason of his failure to perform his obligations under the contract. The object of the damages in this situation is to put the claimant in the position he would have been in, at least financially, if the contract had been properly performed. In our case, where the remedy sought is money damages, the court may award interest on the sum outstanding. The rules are further considered in Chapter 18. It is enough to say here that a claimant suing for interest must claim it specifically in the statement of case, which gives particulars of the claim.

Funding the claim – generally

Under the Access to Justice Act 1999 the Community Legal Service (CLS) replaces the former civil Legal Aid Scheme in regard to the provision of funds for civil cases. The CLS is administered by the Legal Services Commission (LSC), which replaced the Legal Aid Board.

The two levels of service which are of most importance are:

- initial advice and assistance referred to as legal help; and
- representation in the court should litigation ensue referred to as help at court.

The above categories of aid are available subject to what is said below to claimants and defendants. However, the matter of the success or failure of the claim is relevant in the granting of aid for representation.

In broad terms, it will be available:

- where the prospects of success are very good (80 per cent or more) – that the damages are likely to exceed the estimated cost;
- where there is a good chance of success (between 60 per cent and 80 per cent) – that the applicant expects to recover a sum at least three times the likely costs; and
- where the case has only a moderate chance of success (between 50 per cent and 60 per cent) – that the applicant expects to recover a sum of at least four times the likely costs.

By way of explanation of the above, the point is that if the claim is more risky in terms of success, the LSC will not finance it unless it will produce considerable funds if it is successful.

The following points should also be noted:

- funding by the CLS will not normally be available where the case could be funded by a conditional fee agreement; and
- it is not available for personal injury cases, except those for medical negligence.

Since personal injury claims were a large part of the state funding arrangements and since these claims lend themselves to conditional fee arrangements, the amount of state aid for civil matters has considerably decreased.

Financial eligibility

The solicitor involved will assess financial eligibility. The position for individuals is set out below.

Legal help

Income. The solicitor will take the actual gross income in the past month of the client and partner if any. If this exceeds £2,288 the client will not be eligible. A higher limit applies if there are more than four dependent children in the client's family for whom child benefit is received. Where the gross income is £2,288 or less, the solicitor will calculate the disposable income (see below) and if the disposable income exceeds £632 per month the client is not eligible.

Capital. The solicitor will work out the client's and any partner's disposable capital and if this exceeds £8,000 the client is not eligible.

Clients who are in receipt of income support, income-based jobseekers' allowance or guarantee state pension credit will be eligible on income and capital.

Where the client qualifies, it is not necessary for him or her to pay a contribution from income or capital.

Legal representation

Income. If the gross monthly income of the client and any partner exceeds £2,288, the client will not be eligible for funding. The rule regarding four or more children, however, applies (see above). If the gross monthly income is £2,288 or less, the solicitor will assess disposable income (see below) and if this is £632 or less, the client will qualify on income for all types of representation.

Capital. If the client's and any partner's disposable capital is £8,000 or less, the client qualifies for all types of legal representation on capital.

Even when a client qualifies, it may be necessary to pay a contribution to costs e.g. where the monthly disposable income is £273–£400 the contribution is one-quarter of income in excess of £268.

As will be seen, the provision of legal aid is irrelevant in the normal commercial case such as ours and the figures are only included to give a flavour of the paucity of the state provision in this area for non-business clients. In this connection, government consultation papers and statements suggest that matters relating to financial provision will get worse rather than better.

Family cases

Since these are not subject to conditional fee arrangements in terms of their suitability, they continue as state-aided civil matters. In fact, as a broad generalisation, it may be said that in the developed future only family lawyers will be doing civil legal aid work to any degree. In this connection funding is available for family mediation and general family help until the solicitor's fees have reached a certain level the highest in mediation being £350 and in family help £1,500.

Franchising of firms of solicitors

Additionally, legal aid work can be carried on only by those firms of solicitors which are accredited by the Legal Services Commission as being competent to provide the relevant service. The Commission also monitors the accredited firms to see that the appropriate range of experience is maintained, with the resulting withdrawal of some firms from legal aid capacity.

Reform

Following proposals outlined in Lord Carter's initial review of legal aid published in February 2006, the Legal Services Commission has consulted on a national *preferred supplier scheme*, which will radically change the way in which it administers legal aid. Approved suppliers will have to meet stringent entry requirements and will have to deliver consistently good quality advice to clients and take greater responsibility for managing their own performance. Solicitors and advice agencies can expect to benefit from greater autonomy, simpler processes and lower transaction costs. Ultimately, the LSC will be working with fewer larger organisations by the time the proposals are fully implemented in 2009.

These arrangements are seen as a move forward from the franchising scheme outlined above.

Conditional fee agreements

Under these arrangements, the client's solicitor will receive no payment if the client's claim fails. However, usual or higher than usual fees are payable where the client succeeds. Section 27 of the Access to Justice Act 1999 applies, together with statutory instruments made to support it. The section inserts ss 58 and 58A into the Courts and Legal Services Act 1990. Section 29 of the 1999 Act allows the recovery of insurance premiums from the losing side (see below).

These agreements can be made in regard to any civil litigation matter, but matrimonial cases are excluded. No such agreement can be made if the client is legally aided.

CFA with success fee

If the fees are to be higher than usual if the client is successful, as is the case with a conditional fee agreement, the maximum permitted percentage increase is 100 per cent. The Access to Justice Act 1999 allows recovery of the normal fees and the success fee by a successful client against his opponent.

In *Designers Guild Ltd* v *Russell Williams (Textiles) Ltd* [2003] 1 Costs LR 128 the House of Lords granted a success fee of 100 per cent in a case where leading counsel had advised that the chances of success were no more than evens. The claimant had succeeded at first instance but had lost in the Court of Appeal. The case is important because it gives an example of a dispute in which a 100 per cent success fee was merited and also because previously it was doubtful whether CFAs were permissible in the House of Lords since the Civil Procedure Rules do not specifically apply to proceedings in the Lords. This case rules that they are because, said the House of Lords, CFAs are authorised by the Courts and Legal Services Act 1990 and do not derive validity from the Civil Procedure Rules.

In effect, in this sort of agreement the maximum fees payable to the solicitor comprise two parts: the base or normal fee usually calculated by reference to hourly rates in terms of time spent on the case, and a success fee expressed as a percentage of the base or normal fee. In the case therefore of a 100 per cent success fee, the solicitor's fees would be double the base or normal fee. Therefore and in general terms, a client who loses will pay no fees and a client who wins will pay both the base or normal fees and the success fee. The defendant may be ordered to pay the fees as part of costs awarded against him including the success fee. If there is an appeal on the matter of costs, the appeal court can reduce the success fee (see *Callery* v *Gray* [2001] 1 WLR 2112 and 2142).

Contingency fees (or CFA without success fee)

The 1999 Act provides also for a contingency fee agreement, i.e. one where there is no success fee but either all or part of the solicitor's fees are payable only if the client wins the case and not at all if he loses. An example would be a fee reduction of 30 per cent if the case is lost and the usual fee if it is won.

It is still unlawful for a contingency fee to provide for the recovery by the lawyer of a percentage of any damages awarded to the client, e.g. 'There will be no fee if you lose but if you win I shall take 40 per cent of your damages'. Such an agreement is contrary to public policy (see Chapter 16) as being champertous. Champerty is the maintenance of any person in a legal claim upon condition to have part of the property or money recovered. The statutory provisions for conditional and contingency fees are, of course, exceptions to the common law rule.

Contingency fees in assessment of damages

Agreements to receive a percentage of damages by those who have assisted a client in ascertaining the size of the claim AFTER liability has been established in court do not necessarily fall foul of the public policy rules mentioned above. Thus in *Regina (Factortame Ltd and Others)* v *Secretary of State for Transport, Local Government and the Regions (No 8)* (2002) *The Times*, 9 July, the accountants Grant Thornton were paid 8 per cent of the final settlement in this case under an agreement with the claimant and this was not, said the Court of Appeal, a void agreement as contrary to public policy and was recoverable by the claimant against the defendants as costs. The Court of Appeal did however stress the following points as relevant in arriving at their ruling:

- when the agreement was made the claimant had already succeeded on the issue of the defendant's liability; and
- the accountants had not played any part in the proceedings leading to the establishment of that liability.

Comment The decision is of importance to experts such as accountants who are often engaged to provide back-up services of this kind in litigation.

Insurance

Obviously, the law does not allow a person to proceed with a claim against another under conditional or contingency arrangements unless he can pay the other side's costs if he loses. Therefore, a solicitor will always ask whether a client has an insurance policy covering litigation. This type of insurance may be purchased separately or may be part of a household policy. This is called 'before the event' insurance. It may well be possible to purchase 'after the event' insurance. The premium payable will be related to the strength of the applicant's case, a more difficult case to win attracting a higher premium. As we have seen, this premium may be recovered from the losing party (but see below). The payment of what may be a large initial premium for a personal injury claim worth, say, £100,000 can be a problem, but it may be possible in a claim which is likely to succeed to negotiate with an insurance company so that a client only pays the premium if he wins. If the client loses, the insurance company pays the costs of the other side and the smaller share of costs of the claimant and that is that. Clearly, there are no lawyers' fees to pay for the client's side.

The role of the insurance company

It is important that clients understand the role of the insurance company and its interest in the case. The claimant's insurer, like his lawyer, is only interested in whether the case is won. If it is, the lawyer gets the success fee and the insurer will have received a premium and not had to pay out. In the insurance deal, therefore, it will be a requirement of the insurer that the solicitor inform the insurance company if the defendant makes an offer to settle or makes a payment into court. These matters are explained later in this chapter but, as an example, if the claim is for £20,000 and the defendant offers to settle by a payment of £16,000, the insurance contract may require the claimant to accept the offer to avoid possible loss of the case if it goes to trial with consequent expense to the insurer. Failure to accept an offer, if required by the insurer, can, under the contract of insurance, lead to withdrawal of cover so that the claimant who wishes to try for more money may have to do so at his own expense.

Payment by insurers

The system of conditional fees has suffered because of the tactics of insurance companies who having entered into insurance commitments have used tactics such as arguing in court over the way in which fees have been calculated and even whether the conditional fee provisions are valid, all to delay payment. However, in a number of cases such as *Hollins* v *Russell* (2003) 147 Sol Jo 602 the Court of Appeal gave a firm ruling that technical challenges on compensation by insurers should not in general be allowed. Brooke LJ referring to the 'trench warfare' that had broken out between solicitors and insurers said that provided there was no serious breach of the legal rules and a claimant was not adversely affected the no-win, no-fee agreement plus insurance was valid and would be enforceable.

It is also worth noting here that the Court of Appeal decided in *Callery* v *Gray* [2001] 1 WLR 2112 and 2142 that the cost of after the event insurance was recoverable even when as in this case proceedings were only in contemplation and in fact never took place.

Sarwar v *Alam* [2001] 4 All ER 541 is also worth noting because in it the Court of Appeal allowed, as part of recovery of costs, the premium on an after the event insurance even though the claimant had before the event insurance (which was recoverable) because the ATE insurance provided additional benefits in that it was custom built for the particular road traffic claim. However, the court warned that all solicitors conducting these no-win, no-fee claims should inquire after and investigate the adequacy of any BTE insurance before advising ATE insurance. This could involve asking the client to bring in any relevant motor policy. Failure to take advantage of an adequate BTE insurance could result in the ATE premium being disallowed as a head of recoverable costs.

Finally, an attempt by the defendant's insurer to refuse to pay an ATE insurance premium as costs in the cause because the premium was not payable at the time the ATE was entered into but only on conclusion of the case if the claim was successful (which it was) was a credit agreement and was void because the formalities of the Consumer Credit Act 1974 had not been observed failed. The ATE was an insurance contract not falling within the statutory framework applicable to credit agreements (see *Tilby* v *Perfect Pizza Ltd* (2002) 152 NLJ 397).

Other disbursements

It is also important that clients understand that, in addition to the insurance premium, there are other 'up-front' payments that will have to be made and which will only be recovered if they win. These include medical reports, experts' fees, accident reports and court fees, which may run into a few hundred pounds. Where the claim has a very good chance of success, the solicitor may cover these payments, but is in no way obliged to do so.

Environmental Protection Act 1990 cases

Conditional fee agreements are available for proceedings under the 1990 Act, s 82 which allows those aggrieved by a statutory nuisance to ask the court for an order to put that nuisance right. An example would be the failure of a landlord to maintain rented housing in a habitable condition. It should be noted, however, that there is no success fee here. The lawyer gets his usual fee if he wins the case for the client but no more and, of course, nothing if he loses.

Formalities

Conditional and contingency agreements between clients and solicitors must be in writing and signed by both parties. Importantly, also an agreement for a success fee must briefly set out the reasons for setting the percentage increase at the level stated. Regulations also require a conditional fee agreement to include a term that a solicitor may not recover from a client any part of the success fee disallowed by the court (see below).

Costs

When it comes to recovery of the success fee from the losing side, it should be borne in mind that the court in assessing costs may reduce it on the ground that it was set at an unreasonable level, given the level of risk of failure of the client's case. The amount of the success fee in the agreement is thereby also reduced so that the client does not pay the balance up to the original success fee. An unreasonably high insurance premium might also be reduced where better terms might reasonably have been obtained. Here the client will have to pay the balance of the premium from his own funds.

Barristers and their involvement

It should be noted that the above materials relate to the fees of the solicitor in the case. The terms agreed between solicitor and counsel may be on conditional fee terms either with or without success fees. If not on such terms the solicitor is personally liable to pay counsel's proper fees whether or not the proceedings are successful and whether or not the solicitor has been put in funds by the client. If it is thought necessary to brief a barrister, negotiations will be required with the barrister. There is no compulsion upon members of the Bar (or solicitors for that matter) to enter into conditional or contingent fee agreements. However, since September 1999, all barristers and solicitors have acquired full rights of audience on call to the Bar or admission to the Rolls, subject to meeting the requirements of the Bar Council or Law Society. Thus, it may not be necessary to brief a barrister, the solicitor/advocate carrying the case right through. A barrister may be required in a difficult case where, of course, it is unlikely that the barrister will be prepared to enter into conditional or contingency fee arrangements.

Alternatives to a claim in court

There are three major alternative procedures to a claim before a court of law as set out below.

Arbitration

Where the dispute relates to a contract, it may be found that the contract contains an arbitration clause requiring the parties to submit any dispute to an arbitrator rather than to a court of law. In other cases the parties must first agree to proceed by arbitration and then choose an arbitrator. The procedure has already been considered in Chapter 2, to which reference should be made. The procedure is useful where money awards are required, but certain equitable remedies, such as an injunction, are not available if this route is chosen.

The party who obtains an award can apply to the High Court under s 66 of the Arbitration Act 1996 for leave to enforce the award as if it were a judgment of a court. The various methods of enforcing a judgment appear at the end of this chapter. It is currently a defect of the alternative dispute resolution procedures described below that there is no such enforcement of the solution reached if a party does not comply with it.

Alternative dispute resolution (ADR)

Generally

ADR consists in the resolving of disputes by using an independent third party. The object is to help the parties reach their own solution since the third party cannot, as a judge can, impose a solution upon them. The parties can withdraw from the process at any time and they do not have to accept the solution to the problem that was reached.

When ADR is inappropriate

The ADR procedure should *not* be considered in the following situations:

- where an injunction is required;
- where there is no dispute between the parties, as in a case where a debt is owed. In these cases the creditor should issue a claim form (see later in this chapter) or, if the debt is unlikely to be paid in full, consider insolvency proceedings;
- where the law is unclear, so that a ruling by a court is required.

Types of ADR

Mediation and conciliation. In a mediation (also referred to as conciliation) a third party whom the parties have accepted as mediator will receive written statements from the parties and after that the mediator will discuss the case with the parties. The mediator will not disclose confidential matters which one or other party may reveal to him. The discussions are on a 'without prejudice' basis, which means that the matters discussed cannot be raised before a court, should the case end up there on the mediation failing. The discussions do not have to take place at a meeting but may be dealt with in correspondence or by telephone. The purpose of the discussions with the mediator is for the parties to reach a satisfactory solution to the problem without resort to a court. In some types of conciliation, the conciliator may be more pro-active and put forward his own solutions to the parties' disagreement.

Mediation-arbitration. Here the parties agree to submit a dispute to mediation but agree also to refer the matter to arbitration if the mediation is unsuccessful. The parties may agree to use the mediator as an arbitrator should the mediation fail. However, this may not be desirable since the mediator may have confidential information that was supplied to him by the parties and this may compromise him as an arbitrator. The agreement for 'Med-arb', as it is called, should, therefore, contain a right in both parties to object to the mediator taking on the role of arbitrator, should the mediation fail.

Structured settlement procedure

This is sometimes referred to as a mini-trial. The parties appoint a representative each to sit with a neutral chairman. The tribunal will hear or read the submissions of both parties and the representatives will agree a solution with the assistance of the neutral chairman.

Other methods

The most important of these are set out below:

- *Judicial appraisal*. The Centre for Dispute Resolution in London provides a scheme under which former members of the judiciary and senior barristers are available to give a speedy initial view on the legal position having heard the parties' representations. The parties may or may not accept the conclusions.
- *Expert determination by contract*. Here the parties select an expert and agree to be bound by his ruling. If a party fails to accept the ruling, he can be sued for breach of contract, *so there is a sanction*. In view of the contract, the expert will have a duty of care to each party and can, therefore, be sued in negligence if his award is affected by negligence.
- *Employment disputes*. ADR has been available for some considerable time in employment disputes. The Advisory, Conciliation and Arbitration Service (ACAS), which was set up in 1974, has as its objectives the prevention and resolution of disputes, conciliation in actual and possible complaints to employment tribunals, the provision of information and advice and the promotion of general good practice.

Contractual ADR

What has been considered above is a situation in which the parties have reached the point of litigation before deciding to try ADR first. It makes sense, however, to include a provision in a contract that in the case of any dispute it should be resolved by a form of ADR. This is particularly the case where the contract already contains an arbitration clause. In such a case, the contract could provide that ADR be undertaken before proceeding to arbitration if, and only if, ADR has failed to provide an acceptable solution.

In this connection, the Commercial Court has ruled that an agreement to use ADR is binding and enforceable by the courts. In the ruling which was given in *Cable & Wireless plc* v *IBM United Kingdom Ltd* [2002] 2 All ER (Comm) 1041 the court rejected the claimant's argument that an agreement to refer disputes to ADR was simply an agreement to negotiate. The court saw no difference between the reference to ADR and an agreement to arbitrate both of which could be enforced by staying the court proceedings so that the parties could proceed with ADR or arbitration.

ADR and the Civil Procedure Rules

Before leaving the topic of ADR, it is worth noting that under the Civil Procedure Rules 1998, enacted post-Woolf, the courts actively encourage parties to resolve their disputes by some form of ADR and *may refuse a party some of his costs even when he wins his case in court* if he has previously and unreasonably refused to embark upon an ADR procedure.

In this connection, reference could usefully be made to the case of *Dunnett* v *Railtrack plc* (2002) and the cases appearing in the Comment at p 716.

Offers to settle and Part 36 payments in

A defendant (or a claimant where there is a counterclaim, see later in this chapter) may make an offer to settle the claim. Part 36 of the Civil Procedure Rules 1998 applies. The matter is best dealt with by an example. Suppose that our defendant makes an offer to settle the claim for £80,000 believing that our claimant will not be able to prove damage to his business of £100,000. Let us further suppose that our claimant refuses to accept that offer or any other offer that the defendant might make and issues proceedings. Our defendant should then pay the sum of £80,000 into the court office under Part 36 of the Rules. This gives our claimant a problem. If he proceeds to a full trial and does not get more than the offer (a penny would do), he will be likely to have to pay his costs and the defendant's from the time of payment in. The claimant's representatives are informed of the payment in at the time it is made so the possible problems as to costs are known. The judge, in making an award of damages, is *unaware* of the amount of the payment in. The same is true if the claimant decides to accept the payment in before the trial begins or before its termination. Once again, the claimant will have to pay the costs of both sides from payment in to the date of his acceptance of the offer. Permission of the court is required prior to the acceptance of a payment in. The above rules would apply also to the defendant if he had made a counterclaim (see below) and the claimant had made an offer on this. The moral is to accept an offer when it is made if there is a reasonable doubt about a party being able to recover in full his alleged loss.

Written offers

In *Crouch* v *King's Healthcare NHS Trust* [2005] 1 All ER 207 the Court of Appeal ruled that if a written offer is genuine and contains all the relevant information and the defendant is 'good for the money' at the time the offer is made, the written offer should be treated in the same way as a payment into court under Part 36 of the Civil Procedure Rules. There is no need to support the written offer by a payment. In this connection the Department for Constitutional Affairs has consulted on changes to be made to Part 36 to allow a written offer from certain defendants, e.g. NHS Trusts, in a money claim to be treated as a payment into court.

The commencement of proceedings

If we now assume that our claimant has sufficient funds to proceed with the claim or has arranged a conditional fee funding and is not prepared to accept ADR, the dangers in terms of recovery of costs having been explained to him, and that no offer of settlement has been made or is acceptable, then our claimant will proceed to trial.

The claim form

A party wishing to issue proceedings must complete a claim form (formerly called a writ or a summons). This should be taken or sent to the court office. These forms are issued by the Court Service and the appropriate court office is stated on the form. The relevant offices are county courts designated as civil trial centres – there are some 58 of them in England and Wales or feeder county courts which, in relation to multi-track claims, will transfer the case to a civil trial centre after allocating to track (see later in this chapter) and giving case management directions.

Contents of the claim form

The claim form states:

- the name of the claimant;
- the name of the defendant (or defendants) and the address;
- brief details of the claim and the remedy sought;
- the value of the claim.

The value of the claim is necessary in order to assist the court in deciding to which track to allocate the case. Allocation is considered later in this chapter but, as we saw in Chapter 2, claims which are not worth more than £5,000 will usually be allocated to the small claims track; claims worth more than £5,000 but not more than £15,000 will be allocated to the fast track; and claims for more than £15,000 will be allocated to the multi-track. Also, a fee is payable on issue of the claim form, and this is based on the value of the claim.

Particulars of claim

On the back of the claim form is a section for particulars of the claim. This gives a concise statement of the facts on which the claimant relies. In our case we shall be claiming that the seed supplied was not of satisfactory quality or fit for the purpose, and we shall give particulars of what happened, e.g., the cabbages had no heart and so on, as the details in Case **187** show. The consequences to our claimant will be described and the particulars of loss and damage stated. A claim for interest on the sum involved will be made.

Where the particulars of the claim are not included in or with the claim form, they will be served separately.

Statement of truth

The particulars of claim conclude with a statement of truth. This states: 'I believe the facts stated in these Particulars of Claim are true'. It is signed by the claimant or his solicitor and the address of the firm of solicitors involved is given.

Business claims – the parties

- **Sole traders**. A sole trader must *sue* in his or her own name and not a business name. A sole trader can *be sued* in his or her own name or a business name.
- **Partnerships**. A partnership may *sue* in the firm name or in the names of individual partners. A partnership may *be sued* in the firm name or the names of individual partners.
- **Companies**. A company can *sue* in its corporate name, and can *be sued* in its corporate name.

Service of claim form

If the court serves the claim form on the defendant, it will normally use first-class mail and delivery is deemed effective on the second day after posting. The court will send the claimant a notice which includes the date when the claim form is deemed to be served. If the claimant serves the claim form, he must file a certificate of service with the court within seven days of deemed service of the claim form. If no such certificate of service is filed, there can be no judgment in default (see later in this chapter).

Service may be *personal service* where the claim form is left, e.g., at the principal place of business of an organisation or, in the case of a registered company, at its registered office or a branch of the company at which, e.g., the contract under dispute was made.

Where, as is usual, a solicitor is authorised to accept service on behalf of his client, the claim form must be served on the solicitor.

It is important to note that it is proper procedure for the claimant to send the defendant a letter of claim or other form of advanced warning of his or her involvement in litigation. Failure to do so may result in a penalty in terms of the costs awarded in the case (see *Phoenix Finance Ltd* v *Federation International De L'Automobile (Costs)* (2002) *The Times*, 27 June). Furthermore, the deemed date of delivery mentioned above is not rebuttable by evidence that the defendant did not in fact receive the claim form on the deemed date (see *Anderton* v *Clwyd CC* [2002] 8 Current Law 70). In addition, the court has power under the Civil Procedure Rules to dispense with service of a claim form in appropriate circumstances (*Godwin* v *Swindon BC* [2002] 1 WLR 997).

The consent of the defendant or his representative is required before service by fax is effective (see *Kuenyehia* v *International Hospitals Group Ltd* (2006) *The Times*, 17 February).

The defendant's response to the claim

The defendant will also receive what is called a 'Response Pack' with Notes. These explain how the defendant may deal with the claim form. There are five possibilities as listed below.

- **Acknowledging service**. If the defendant is not ready to file a defence, he must acknowledge service of the claim form within 14 days of service. If the claimant has chosen to send his particulars of claim separately, acknowledgement is within 14 days of receipt of the particulars.

- *Filing a defence*. Where the defendant wishes to defend the claim, he must file a defence within 14 days of service of the particulars of claim or, where service has been acknowledged, within 28 days of service of the particulars of claim. The forms which the defendant can use form part of the Response Pack. Where a solicitor is being used, a defence is normally prepared as a separate document. The time for filing a defence can be extended by agreement between the parties by a further period of up to 28 days, but the court must be informed. Our defendant company will deny that it is in breach of contract and will say that the seed supplied was of satisfactory quality and fit for the purpose. As regards the exclusion clause, a phrase such as the following might be used:

  > Further or alternatively, if (which is not admitted) the Claimant has suffered the loss and damage claimed it is within the Defendant's exclusion clause in paragraph X of the contract.

- *Example*. If the defendant is served with particulars of claim on Monday, 3 September and is ready to file a defence he or she must do so by Monday, 17 September. Defendants wishing to acquire time must file an acknowledgement by that date. These defendants will then have until Monday, 1 October to file a defence.

- *Filing an admission*. An admission may be for the full amount of the claim, in which case, the claimant will ask the court for judgment. There may also be an admission for part only of the claim. In this case, the claimant may reject what is, in effect, an offer and proceed with the full claim. Alternatively, he may accept the offer and ask for judgment.

  As regards service and timing, an admission of the claim where the claim is for a specified sum of money is sent to the claimant. In other cases, e.g. admission of part of the claim, the form of admission is sent to the court. An admission of claim must be made to the claimant or the court as the case may be within 14 days of service of the claim form if it has on it or accompanying it particulars of claim. Where particulars of claim are served later, an admission may be made within 14 days of service of the particulars of claim.

- *Defendant fails to respond – the default judgment*. If, following service of proceedings, the defendant fails to acknowledge the same or to file a defence within the time scales allowed, the claimant may ask the court for a judgment in default against the defendant. Such a judgment will be obtained without a trial of the issues involved. There are several situations in which *default judgments cannot be obtained*, e.g., in claims for delivery of goods under a Consumer Credit Act 2006 regulated agreement, such as a hire-purchase agreement and mortgage claims. The court will need to be satisfied that the claim form and particulars of the claim have been served on the defendant and that he has not made a response. A defendant against whom a default judgment has been made can apply to the court to have it set aside.

- *Counterclaim*. The defendant may make a counterclaim against the claimant. This will not arise in our case, but if our claimant had not paid in full for the cabbage seed but merely paid a deposit, the defendant may well claim for the balance of the purchase price. Particulars of a counterclaim may be filed with the defence. Where this is done, the permission of the court to file a counterclaim is not required. It will be required if the counter-claim is made *after* the defence has been filed. The claimant need not acknowledge a counterclaim, but must file a defence within 14 days. This may be extended by agreement of the parties to 28 days over and above the initial 14-day period.

  A counterclaim is a statement of case and must be prepared as such. Furthermore, if the claim is in the county court a statement of value must be included to ascertain the whole value of the claim and counterclaim.

Reply to the defence

The claimant is not under an obligation to reply to the defence and, if he does not do so, it is not to be taken as admitting anything which is raised in the defence. The most usual reply to a defence is a counterclaim and this may also include a reply as where the claimant wishes to allege facts in answer to the defence which were not contained in the particulars of claim. In general, therefore, a reply should be limited to a statement of new facts the claimant intends to prove to defeat the defence.

Requests for further information

If the information given by a party about his case is unclear, a request for further information can be made under Rule 18 of the Civil Procedure Rules 1998. The request can be made:

- *by the court* if the court feels the need for more information;
- *by a party.* Initially, a party should make the request in writing to the other party, but, if a satisfactory reply is not forthcoming, the party aggrieved should apply to the court for an order. Failure to comply with a request by the court is a contempt punishable by fine or imprisonment.

Statements of case

The above materials starting with the claim form and going through to the Request are referred to in the Civil Procedure Rules of 1998 as 'statements of case'. Before 1998 the documents described were known as 'pleadings' and doubtless this expression will continue in use by practitioners for some time to come. It will be appreciated that the main purpose of pleadings or statements of case is to enable the court and the parties to define and identify the issues in dispute before a trial begins.

Case management and allocation of cases

Throughout the following section we shall be referring to what 'the court' may do. Which court is concerned? Case management and track allocation is a matter for designated *civil trial centres* across England and Wales. These centres will also be the venue for multi-track trials and a portion of fast-track trials. They are, in fact, county courts which operate as civil trial centres. Other county courts are designated as feeder centres and will normally transfer multi-track claims to a civil trial centre after allocating the case to track and giving case management instructions. Multi-track cases may also be heard in the High Court. Those where the value of the claim is £50,000 or more will be held there. Cases where the value is less than £50,000 are also likely to be held in the High Court if they are in the following list:

- professional negligence claims (see Chapter 21);
- fatal accident claims (see Chapter 20);
- fraud or undue influence claims (see Chapter 13);
- defamation claims (see Chapter 21);
- claims for malicious prosecution or false imprisonment (see Chapter 21);
- claims against the police, and where a will is contested.

Our claimant will, because of the size of the claim and the possible complexity of expert evidence, normally be heard in the High Court as a multi-track case.

Striking out

Before proceeding to the mechanics of allocation, it should be noted that the court has power to strike out a claim (or a defence) rather than allocate it for trial. Rule 3 of the Civil Procedure Rules 1998 applies and, for example, all or part of a statement of case (or defence) can, if it discloses no reasonable grounds for bringing or defending the claim, be struck out. If, e.g., the claim is that Fred gave his friend Freda bad advice on the purchase of investments while they were having a drink in the local pub, a claim by Freda in negligence will normally be struck out because it is unlikely that in the casual circumstances of the case there is a duty of care owed by Fred to Freda. This is essential if a claim in negligence is to have a chance of success, and represents a common reason for striking out. The requirement of a duty of care is considered in detail in Chapter 21. Equally, a defence prepared without legal advice which said merely 'I deny I owe the money' would be struck out.

The court may, itself, strike out or it may do so on the application of a party. Where a claim is struck out, the claimant will either abandon his claim or see if it can be based on some other principle(s) of law. Where a defence is struck out, the claimant can apply to the court for judgment, though he may have to wait for up to three days if the court gives the defendant time to submit a full defence.

Allocation – generally

This next stage of case management *begins where a defence has been filed*. On receipt of a defence, the court serves each party with an allocation questionnaire. The parties must return it within 14 days and pay a fee. It is desirable that the parties' lawyers co-operate in the completion of the questionnaires.

The allocation form

The form will ask the parties whether they wish for a stay of proceedings (for up to one month) to try to settle the case without an action in court. The general principle of the Civil Procedure Rules 1998 is for out of court settlement wherever possible. The court will extend the time if any of the parties so requests for a period of four weeks, but further extensions may be granted.

The parties are then asked under the questionnaire which track they consider to be the most suitable for the case. As we have seen, the value of the claim is an important factor. In this connection, where there is a counterclaim, the highest of the value of the claim and counterclaim is taken. Thus, where the claim is for £12,000 but there is a counterclaim for £25,000, the value of the counterclaim governs the case.

Where the allocation questionnaire is not filed

The position is broadly as follows:

■ *If all parties fail to file*. Here the judge will, after the 14-day filing period, order that all claims and counterclaims be struck out unless the questionnaires are filed within three days.
■ *If some only of the parties fail to file*. Here the court will allocate on the information available, or will call an allocation hearing where more information is required and then allocate the case. A party not attending the allocation meeting may be required to meet the costs of any party who has attended it.

Allocation to track

Claims not exceeding £5,000 will normally be allocated to the small claims track. They will normally be heard in the county court by a district judge, with appeal only where there is a serious irregularity affecting the proceedings, to a circuit judge unless a circuit judge hears the case when there may be an appeal to a High Court judge. A serious irregularity could exist where the district judge had, e.g., failed to allow a party to cross-examine a witness.

Claims over £5,000 but not exceeding £15,000 will normally be allocated to the fast track where the trial will take place within 30 weeks of allocation. The length of the trial will be no more than one day and there is a cap on lawyers' advocacy costs.

Where the claim is over £15,000, it will normally be allocated to the multi-track.

However, the track allocation is not purely a matter of the size of the claim and a request can be made at the allocation stage for allocation to a track that is not the normal one. A request for a different allocation may be made by the lawyer representing a party where, e.g., he or she submits that the trial will last for two days because of a counterclaim and the need for oral expert evidence on the matter of liability. This could move a claim for more than £5,000 but less than £15,000 from the fast track to the multi-track.

The case management conference

Where the case has been allocated to the multi-track, the court:

- may give directions as to the management of the case and set a timetable for the various stages to be completed before the trial;
- alternatively, it may fix a case management conference or a pre-trial review or both to consider matters such as which documents should be disclosed and what expert evidence can be reasonably required. The court will fix a trial date or a period of time in which it is to take place. There is no restriction of 30 weeks as in the fast track cases.

Pre-trial review

A pre-trial review will be necessary in multi-track cases if they deal with complex matters involving numerous parties and/or are likely to last for a significant period of time, to ensure that all conference issues have been dealt with. The judge (usually the trial judge) will consider the updated cost estimates and set a budget and a final programme for the trial, including parameters for its length.

Pre-action protocols

These are, in effect, codes of practice for various types of claim and, in general, they provide for more contact and discussion between the parties from the beginning of the dispute so that they can better cope in general and more quickly with, e.g., the case management conference. Up to now, protocols have been issued for guidance, for example, in personal injury cases and medical negligence, construction and engineering disputes, defamation and professional negligence (see p 568), but others will follow. A feature of the first protocols is that a joint expert acceptable to the parties should be instructed. This saves much time (and sometimes confusion) which can be the case where a number of experts appear to give evidence for the parties.

Allocation of track and court for our case example

Because our case example, in terms of claim and defence, involves the law of contract, particularly the sale of goods and exclusion clauses, it is not on the list of cases suitable for the High

Court, but the value of the claim, i.e. £100,000, takes it to the High Court in the Queen's Bench Division.

Court enforcement of timetables

5

Two recent cases indicate in relation to experts and their availability, that the courts are stressing the need to keep to timetables when fixing cases for hearing and that the expert witness, who is a professional person, owes an overriding duty to the court and not merely to his client. In *Linda Rollinson* v *Kimberley Clark Ltd* [1999] 7 Current Law 37 the claim was for damages for an injury sustained at work. The defendant sought to change the dates fixed for the trial because one of its expert witnesses was not available. The Court of Appeal dismissed the application. It was wholly inappropriate, said the court, for a solicitor to instruct an expert without regard to the expert's availability. Again, in *Matthews* v *Tarmac Bricks and Tiles Ltd* [1999] 7 Current Law 55 the defendant had caused difficulties by failing to give details of when expert witnesses would be available. The matter was, nevertheless, listed for trial. The Court of Appeal dismissed an appeal by the defendant. Lord Woolf's judgment includes a further point: that those holding themselves out as expert witnesses should be prepared to arrange or rearrange their affairs to meet the requirements of the court.

The trial

The parties and their witnesses will assemble for the trial.

Attendance of witnesses

As regards witnesses (except expert witnesses), it is not wise to assume that they will attend voluntarily, and their attendance should be encouraged by service on them of a witness summons. This is issued by the court and it requires a witness to attend court and give evidence or produce documents to the court. It should be served at least seven days before attendance is required. Failure to comply with a witness summons is a contempt of court punishable by fine and/or imprisonment.

Trial bundles and skeleton arguments

Except where the court rules otherwise, the claimant must prepare and file in court a trial bundle not more than seven days nor less than three days before the start of the trial. The bundle will include the documents relevant to the trial such as the claim form and statements of case and witness statements, together with a case summary indicating what points are or are not in issue and the nature of the argument on disputed matters. This summary is referred to in some courts, such as in the Chancery Division, as a skeleton argument.

The contents of the bundle should be agreed between the parties and if agreement cannot be obtained on all of the contents, a summary of points of difference should be included. Either party may, e.g., not agree on the inclusion of a document or documents. Bundles should be supplied for the trial judge, all the parties and for the use of witnesses. The advocates can then refer to the contents of the bundle as required during the trial.

Order of proceedings

Counsel for the claimant may, if allowed by the judge or the timetable for the case, make an opening speech giving the background to the case and the facts which are in issue. If such an opening speech is allowed at all, it must be very concise. The court may, however, proceed with the evidence, and, if so, the case begins with the claimant and his witnesses giving evidence.

The court requires that evidence be given on oath (or affirmation by a person who objects to swearing on the Bible). Documentary evidence such as a letter is not normally admissible and the writer must be called and give evidence on oath unless it is difficult or impossible to call him.

As in a criminal trial counsel for the claimant cannot ask his own witnesses 'leading questions'. A leading question suggests the answer, and, in our case, could consist of asking the claimant 'Did the defendant supply you with seed which was not of satisfactory quality or fit for the purpose?' An acceptable question to elicit facts would be: 'Tell the court the condition of the seed supplied to you by the defendant.' Nor is hearsay evidence admissible unless the provisions of the Civil Evidence Act 1995 are followed, which involves giving the other party notice of the intention to introduce hearsay evidence and, if requested, giving particulars of it. Hearsay evidence may be an oral or written statement made outside of court which is repeated by a party or a witness in order to prove that it is true. Thus, in our case, if the claimant were to say in evidence: 'My neighbour, Joe Bloggs, bought seed from the defendants and he told me he had the same problems as I did', this evidence should be given by Joe Bloggs since, if it is not, there is no chance for the defendant's advocate to cross-examine Joe Bloggs as he is not there. After the examination-in-chief the witnesses for the claimant may be cross-examined by counsel for the defence, the object being to discredit their evidence. After cross-examination counsel for the claimant may re-examine a witness.

Sometimes a witness will give an account of events which is totally different from that in the statement he gave to the claimant's solicitors; counsel for the claimant is not allowed to discredit his own witness unless the judge gives leave as he may do if he feels that the witness is prejudiced against the person who called him. Such a witness is called a hostile witness and his examination-in-chief is more like a cross-examination since it is designed to discredit his evidence.

At the end of the claimant's case it is the turn of counsel for the defence to produce evidence to refute it. The claimant does not have to prove his case beyond a reasonable doubt, as the prosecution in a criminal trial does, but must show that what he alleges is probably the right version, i.e. proof on a balance of probabilities. The court must be satisfied that it is more likely than not (or more probable than not) that the relevant fact is established (*R v Swaysland*, *The Times*, 15 April 1987).

The defence need not necessarily produce evidence. If the claimant's case is weak the defence may submit to the judge that there is no case to answer. In practice such a submission would very rarely be made because the court will usually 'put the defendant to his election'. This means that the judge will only hear the submission of no case to answer if the defendant elects not to call evidence to support his case. The judge is not forced to do this and may hear a submission of no case to answer; if he finds that there is a case to answer he may allow the defence to continue its case. Otherwise, the judge may allow the defence to make its submission of no case to answer and if the judge agrees, he will enter judgment for the defendant. If he does not, then, in effect, the claimant succeeds and will have judgment entered in his favour. Counsel for the defence can ask the judge to clarify the position before proceeding or not proceeding with the reasons why it is alleged there is no case to answer.

If there is no submission of no case to answer, the defence will call its witnesses who will be examined, cross-examined and re-examined.

Counsel for the defence then makes a closing speech showing how in his view the claimant's case has failed. The claimant's counsel then presents his view. Both will give an indication of what they think the damages should be. Either party may make a final Response, as it is called. This is on a matter of law only and may be with leave of the judge or by his invitation. Thus, a party may say, 'My learned friend referred to the case of *Bloggs* v *Snooks* on which I have not addressed you. I would be grateful if you would allow me to address you on that point.' Sometimes the judge will say to a party, 'What do you say about [a point raised by the other party in closing his case], Mr Taylor [counsel]?'

The judge will have remained largely silent during the trial, though he may have asked for an obscure point to be clarified. In fact a judge should not be too 'active' and interfering and if he is his decision may be overturned in an appeal court. The classic statement of the trial judge's function was given by Lord Denning in a civil appeal, *Jones* v *National Coal Board* [1957] 2 All ER 155 where he said:

> The judge's part in all this is to hearken to the evidence, only himself asking questions of witnesses when it is necessary to clear up any point that has been overlooked or left obscure; to see that the advocates behave themselves seemly and keep to the rules laid down by law; to exclude irrelevancies and discourage repetition; to make sure by wise intervention that he follows the points the advocates are making and can assess their worth; and at the end to make up his mind where the truth lies.

The statement is not confined to civil trials though in a criminal trial 'the truth' is a matter for the jury.

After the closing speeches, the judge considers the evidence and will then give judgment stating the grounds on which it is based, though if a judge requires more time to consider the case he may reserve judgment and give it at a later date. The judge will also decide the amount of damages unless there is a jury as there may be in an action for defamation (see below).

Civil jury

Section 69 of the Supreme Court Act 1981 (becomes Senior Courts Act 1981) gives the court discretion with regard to juries in civil cases, though a jury must be empanelled at the request of the defendant where fraud is alleged, or at the request of either party in cases of libel, slander, malicious prosecution and false imprisonment. If the trial is likely to involve long and detailed examination of documents or accounts or scientific evidence, the court has the discretion to refuse a jury trial even in these cases. There is also an exception in the case of libel and slander under the Defamation Act 1996 which introduces a summary (or fast track) procedure which gives sweeping powers of disposal to the court and provides for assessment of damages by a judge without a jury whether or not the parties consent (see further Chapter 21). Not all defamation cases are suitable for disposal by this 'fast track' method and trials for libel and slander in front of a jury will continue in those cases. In particular, libel actions involving issues or persons of national importance should be tried with a jury, even if complex documents are involved (*Rothermere* v *Times Newspapers* [1973] 1 All ER 1013). The percentage of jury trials in civil actions is very small and outside of the above areas the court is not likely to exercise its discretion to allow a jury. In *H* v *Ministry of Defence* (1991) *The Times*, 1 April, for example, the Court of Appeal held that it was normally inappropriate to order trial by jury for the assessment of damages in actions for personal injuries since the damages were based on consideration of conventional scales of damages known to the judiciary but not to a jury.

Juries are not used in Admiralty cases but there is a power to summon a jury in the Chancery Division. This power is, in practice, neglected.

A civil jury consists of 12 persons, though the parties may, in a particular case, agree to proceed with less. There is a right, under s 66 of the County Courts Act 1984, to ask for a jury of eight persons in a county court, where the case is an appropriate one, as where, for example, fraud, or malicious prosecution, or false imprisonment are alleged. These rights are rarely exercised. In addition, a coroner must, under s 8(3) of the Coroners Act 1988, summon a jury of 7 to 11 persons in some cases, e.g. where the deceased was in police custody, or death was the result of an injury caused by a police officer in the purported execution of his duty, and may accept the verdict of the majority if the dissentients are not more than two. Where there is no jury the judge determines the facts as well as the law.

Apart from a coroner's jury, a civil jury formerly had to be unanimous. However, under s 17 of the Juries Act 1974, the verdict of the jury in civil proceedings in the High Court need not be unanimous if:

(a) where there are not less than 11 jurors, 10 of them agree on the verdict; and
(b) where there are 10 jurors, nine of them agree on the verdict.

The verdict of a jury of eight persons in a county court need not be unanimous if seven of them agree on the verdict. The two hours' deliberation necessary for a criminal jury before a majority verdict is permissible is not required for a civil jury. It is enough if it appears to the court that the jury had such period of time for deliberation as the court thinks reasonable, having regard to the nature and complexity of the case. In civil cases the court may accept a verdict by *any* majority so long as both parties consent (s 17(5) of the 1974 Act).

Appeals

Consideration has already been given in Chapter 2 to the rights of appeal in civil cases.

Enforcing a judgment

Let us assume that the judge has given judgment to our claimant on his claim for a sum of money thought appropriate in the circumstances of the case. Let us suppose that the defendant is not prepared to pay these sums. How can a party to an action get the money the court has awarded him? Some of the more important methods available to *judgment* creditors are set out below.

(a) Execution. A claimant can ask the High Court to institute execution, which orders the sheriff's officer of the county in which the debtor's goods are located to seize through bailiffs the defendant's goods and sell them by public auction in order to pay the claimant. In the county court there is a similar procedure but it is based upon a warrant of execution issued to the court bailiff.

(b) The charging order. The court may make such an order over, say, the defendant's land or other property such as shares. If the money is not paid the claimant can have the property sold and recover his damages from the proceeds of sale. The Charging Orders Act 1979 defines the type of property in respect of which a charging order may be made. The 1979 Act widened the scope of property which may be made the subject of an order so that, for example, a charging order may now be made over a debtor's beneficial interest under a trust.

(c) **The garnishee order** (now called a third-party debt claim for procedural purposes). If the creditor knows that the debtor is owed money by a third party – where, for instance, there is a credit balance on the debtor's bank account or building society account – the creditor may wish to divert the payment away from the debtor to himself. This can be done by applying to the court for a garnishee order *nisi*. The order is addressed to the third party, e.g. the bank, forbidding it to pay the debt to the debtor and requiring a representative to attend before the court to show why the money (or part of it) should not be paid over to the judgment creditor.

The order is served at least seven days before the next court hearing on the matter and if at that hearing no cause has been shown as to why payment should not be made to the judgment creditor, the court can make a garnishee order absolute, requiring payment by the bank to the judgment creditor.

(d) **Attachment of earnings.** Where the defendant is in employment the claimant can obtain an attachment of earnings order through the county court. Under such an order the defendant's employer is required to deduct a specified sum from the defendant's wages or salary and pay the money into court for the claimant. The court sends the money to the claimant. Attachment is not available against the profits of the self-employed.

It will have been noted that, so far as (*a*) to (*d*) above are concerned, each of the ways of enforcing the judgment is aimed at a different aspect of the defendant's finances, that is:

(i)   goods owned (order and warrant of execution);
(ii) wages or salary (attachment of earnings);
(iii) savings (garnishee order);
(iv) property (charging order).

Details of a defendant's finances can be obtained by what is known as 'oral examination' through the court.

(e) **Equitable execution.** The court may appoint a *receiver* where, for example, the defendant owns property. The receiver can take over income such as rent and apply it in order to pay the claimant. The judgment creditor of a person who is a partner can, under s 23 of the Partnership Act 1890, obtain an order charging that partner's interest in the partnership property and profits with payment of the judgment debt. If the judgment creditor feels that he will experience difficulty in getting the firm to pay over, e.g. the profit share of the partner concerned, he can ask for the appointment of a receiver.

The enforcement of a non-money judgment, such as an injunction, is by means of the offence of contempt of court. If a defendant fails to obey an injunction, he is in contempt of court and the court may, if the claimant applies, punish him. It may make, for example, an order for committal under which if the defendant still refuses to comply with the injunction, he may be imprisoned. Alternatively, the court may issue a writ of sequestration. This writ, which is directed by the court to commissioners, usually four in number, commands them to enter the lands and take the rents and profits and seize the goods of the person against whom it is directed. Thus, the court can in effect take control of the defendant's property until the defendant has complied with the court's order.

(f) **Bankruptcy or insolvency proceedings.** Where as here the debt exceeds £750, bankruptcy or company insolvency proceedings could be considered. This would at least ensure that an insolvency practitioner (generally an accountant) would be put in charge of the debtor's assets and ensure a fair and legal distribution of the assets between creditors as well as effectively preventing the debtor from dealing with them. These procedures are not available to a person who has registered a charging order because by so doing he has made himself a secured creditor and only unsecured creditors can petition for bankruptcy or company winding-up.

Insolvent individuals and companies may try to avoid bankruptcy or liquidation by proposing to creditors, who must agree by a majority of three-quarters *in value, a voluntary arrangement*. This will not get the creditor all his money but will get him at least some of it. The arrangement operates under a supervisor who is usually an accountant and allows for so many pence in the pound to be paid over an agreed time span.

Enforcement outside of the UK

In these days of global trade, a claimant may wish to enforce an English judgment abroad. There are two situations as follows:

- *Enforcement within the EU*. Article 26 of the Brussels Convention of 1968 was incorporated into English law by the Civil Jurisdiction and Judgments Act 1982. The Convention requires all member states to recognise and enforce the judgments of other member states.
- *Enforcement outside the EU*. The Administration of Justice Act 1920 and the Foreign Judgments (Reciprocal Enforcement) Act 1933 apply to the countries covered, which are mainly Commonwealth states. Elsewhere as, e.g., in the USA, it is a matter for the courts of the country where enforcement is sought.

Enforcing a judgment – reform

In March 2003 the government published a White Paper entitled *Effective Enforcement* that is designed to introduce in due course legal rules to improve the process for recovering civil debt. The proposals include most importantly:

- *a new court order* known as a data disclosure order that would oblige debtors to give their creditors personal information such as their full real name, address and credit details. The government feels that this will make it easier for creditors to track down those who go missing when ordered to pay their debts. The orders will strike a balance between the interests of creditors and respect for individuals' privacy;
- *in regard to attachment of earnings*, the system for recovery from pay packets is to be made faster, fairer and more effective, though there will be no application of a similar remedy to operate against the incomes of the self-employed. There will be powers for the courts to track down and redirect the orders against those who change their jobs;
- *there are also proposals to clean up the image of the civil enforcement industry* by licensing court bailiffs and freelance operators who should be able to offer debtors advice on court orders and discuss repayment options rather than operating as 'hired heavies' as some do;
- *there are proposals to streamline charging orders* and to protect vulnerable individuals who suffer anxiety from believing that their homes will of necessity be repossessed.

There is no timescale for any required legislation.

6

THE LAW-MAKING PROCESS I:
UK LEGISLATION

The word 'source' has various meanings when applied to law. One may treat the word 'source' as referring to the *historical or ultimate origins of law* and trace the *development* of the common law, equity, legislation, delegated legislation, custom, the law merchant, canon law and legal treatises, as we have done in Chapter 1. But on the other hand, one may treat the word 'source' as referring to the *methods by which laws are made or brought into existence*, and consider the current processes of legislation, delegated legislation, judicial precedent and, to a limited extent, custom. In this chapter we shall be concerned with the *methods by which laws are made*, i.e. the *active* or *legal* sources of law and in particular the laws which are made by the Westminster Parliament and how they are interpreted by the judiciary.

The United Kingdom

There are within the United Kingdom two parliaments and two assemblies. However, for our purposes, there is one parliament and one assembly to consider. This text is concerned with the law of England and Wales and so no reference is made to the powers of the Scottish Parliament or the Northern Ireland Assembly.

The Welsh Assembly

The Government of Wales Act 1998 provides for an Assembly for Wales. It creates for the first time an all-Wales elected government. It has 60 members sitting in Cardiff. Elections are held every four years on a basis of proportional representation. Forty members are elected from Welsh Westminster parliamentary seats with a top-up of 20 from five electoral regions, four from each. The Assembly has a budget of several billion pounds (though only about one-half of the Scottish budget) and there are no taxing powers. Its legislative powers are currently confined to *subordinate legislation* for Wales. The Government of Wales Act 2006 will from May 2007 give the Assembly power to make *statutes* for Wales which, if approved by Parliament, will become part of the statute book. The First Minister will be appointed by the Queen following nomination by the Assembly. The Queen will also approve the First Minister's choice of other ministers, bringing the governance of Wales more into line with the Westminster model.

It has control over:

- health and education;
- training policy;

- local government and social work;
- housing and planning;
- economic development and financial assistance to industry;
- tourism;
- some aspects of transport;
- environment and national heritage;
- agriculture, forestry and fisheries;
- food standards;
- the arts.

The members of the Assembly are called Assembly Members (or AMs).

The Westminster Parliament

The Westminster Parliament consists of two chambers: the House of Commons and the House of Lords.

The House of Commons

This consists of 659 members, called MPs, who meet in London at Westminster. Elections are held at least every five years and all MPs are elected on a first-past-the-post basis. There is, in theory, a five-day week, but for MPs with constituencies outside London it is, in effect, a four-day week to allow them to return to those constituencies to conduct, e.g., surgeries for constituents. Most business is conducted between 11am and 7pm, except on certain days when debates start at 9.30am. The Commons sits for between 30 and 35 weeks a year and has a budget well in excess of £300 billion. Perhaps obviously, it has taxing powers limited only by the sanction that the electorate would not return a Parliament which adopted draconian taxing policies.

The House of Lords

This is the Second Chamber of Parliament and used to consist, in the main, of hereditary peers, though under the Life Peerages Act 1958 there has been added a number of persons from various walks of life who hold life peerages but whose descendants have no right to a seat when the life peers die, as the descendants of hereditary peers have. These peers are called the Lords Temporal. Then there are the Lords Spiritual, e.g., the Archbishops of Canterbury and York and certain other bishops of the Church of England. From 2009, when the Supreme Court becomes effective, the Law Lords will become the first judges of the Supreme Court but subsequently the link between that court and the House of Lords will end. In the meantime, the Law Lords do not take part in the legislative functions of the House of Lords.

Reform of the House of Lords

The system of hereditary peers was deemed to be undemocratic in that these peers followed on taking a seat in the Lords by inheritance, and were never subjected to election. There are also some arguments to suggest that the life peerage system is undemocratic in that it has been used by prime ministers to elevate to a life peerage certain of those who have lost an election, in some cases where they have lost a subsequent by-election or, in one classic case, where the life peer had as prospective MP lost two subsequent by-elections! In other words, having been rejected by the people once or even twice or three times, the ex-MP returned to the legislature via a life peerage.

The House of Lords Act 1999 received the Royal Assent on 11 November 1999. It effects the removal of the right of hereditary peers to sit and vote in the Lords. For the time being,

75 have been elected by their peers to remain until further reforms are agreed. The Conservatives won 42 seats, the crossbenchers 28, the Liberal Democrats three and Labour two. The proposals of the Royal Commission under Lord Wakeham were:

- a new 550-member (there are currently some 700) mainly nominated, partly elected second chamber;
- three options for the number of elected members – 65, 87 or 195;
- election through a regional voting system on the basis of proportional representation;
- an appointments commission to select suitable figures and maintain the political balance of the chamber;
- a minimum 20 per cent of independent crossbenchers;
- members to receive a daily attendance rate rather than expenses;
- increased powers to delay secondary legislation, e.g. statutory instruments, and to oversee constitutional legislation;
- the chamber's link with the peerage to end;
- representation from all Christian denominations and non-Christian faiths;
- the Law Lords will continue to sit in the chamber.

The above proposals have not been implemented but a committee of MPs and peers was formed and charged by the Prime Minister to put together a further compromise on Lords' reform. However, the committee reached the conclusion that there was no point in continuing its complicated work after the Prime Minister expressed his preference for a fully appointed second chamber. Accordingly, the committee decided to wind itself up. In July 2003 the government stated its intention to put in place a fully appointed (not voted) second chamber. The government has committed itself to removing the remaining hereditary peers and keeping the rest of the chamber much as it is. The government statement is as follows:

> There is no consensus about the best composition for the second chamber. For the time being the Government will concentrate on making the House of Lords work as effectively as possible in fulfilment of its important role. It remains the Government's policy, as set out in its White Paper in November 2001, that the remaining hereditary peers should be removed from the House.

The Department for Constitutional Affairs has undertaken to reform the Appointments Commission that handles new peerages and look again at the matter of how long a peer should serve in the House.

The Westminster Parliament has control of:

- foreign policy;
- defence and national security;
- the civil service;
- stability of fiscal economic and monetary system;
- border control;
- drug policy;
- common markets for UK goods and services;
- electricity, coal, oil, gas and nuclear energy;
- transport safety and regulations;
- social security policy and administration;
- employment legislation;
- abortion;
- broadcasting;
- equal opportunities.

The Westminster Hall debates

The House of Commons has another chamber sited in the Grand Committee Room off Westminster Hall. It sits in the morning and is designed to be non-confrontational and a forum for a reasoned discussion on select committee reports and to allow MPs to raise issues relating to their constituencies by seeking to get them on the agenda. Instead of the face-to-face arrangement of the Commons benches, this parallel chamber seats MPs in a semi-circle. The proceedings are presided over by the deputy speaker and the quorum is three. About one-and-a-half hours are given to a topic and cover such subjects as police numbers and issues of law and order in rural areas, together with ancient woodlands and tourism. The list is potentially endless.

The Westminster Hall debates have become more popular in recent times and sometimes there are more MPs at these debates than in the Commons chamber which of course is seldom well-attended except where matters such as the Budget are considered and for Prime Minister's Questions or where an international crisis is looming. In particular, debates have been initiated by the opposition parties and in terms of business MPs have used the system to initiate debates on, e.g. the government's action in putting Railtrack into the insolvency procedure of administration – somewhat hurriedly some thought, to the disadvantage of its shareholders.

From now on, in this and other chapters of the text, a reference to 'Parliament' means the Westminster Parliament.

Future developments

The Regional Assemblies (Preparations) Act 2003 received the Royal Assent on 8 May 2003. It makes provision for the holding of referendums about the establishment of elected assemblies for regions of England (except London). It implements the first stage of the White Paper, *Your Region, Your Choice: Revitalising the English Regions*, May 2002. It could lead to the setting up of assemblies in e.g. the North-East, the West Midlands and the South-West, among other regions. The Act does not itself permit the creation of elected regional assemblies. This will require further legislation.

Types of Bills

A session of Parliament normally lasts for one year commencing in October or November. During that time, a large number of Bills become law, most of which are *government Bills*. An Act of Parliament begins as a Bill, which is the draft of a proposed Act. The government is formed by the parliamentary party having an overall majority, or at least the greatest number, of members in the House of Commons, or more rarely by a formal coalition of, or more informal arrangement between, two or more parties who between them can command such a majority. The government is led by a Prime Minister who appoints a variety of other Ministers, such as the Chancellor of the Exchequer, the Home Secretary, the Foreign Secretary, and others to manage various departments of state. A small group of these Ministers, called the Cabinet, meets frequently under the chairmanship of the Prime Minister and formulates the policy of the government. An important part of this policy consists of presenting Bills to Parliament with a view to their becoming law in due course. Such Bills are usually presented by the Minister of the department concerned with their contents.

Queen's Speech

The legislative intentions of the government are given in outline to Parliament at the commencement of each session in the Queen's Speech. This is read by the Queen but is prepared by the government of the day. Most government Bills are introduced in the House of Commons, going later to the House of Lords and finally for the Royal Assent. However, some of the less controversial government Bills are introduced in the House of Lords, going later to the Commons and then for the Royal Assent. Money Bills, i.e. those containing provisions relating to finance and taxation, e.g. the annual finance Bill, and other Bills with financial clauses must start in the Commons.

Private members' Bills

Members of either House whether government supporters or not have a somewhat restricted opportunity to introduce *private members' Bills*. Such Bills are not likely to become law unless the government provides the necessary parliamentary time for debate. Some, however, survive to become law – for example, the Murder (Abolition of Death Penalty) Act 1965. Those that are lost usually fail to be debated fully because influential and anonymous objectors work behind the scenes to ensure that they are taken towards the end of the session when parliamentary time is at a premium. In addition, the severe restriction of debating time for private members' Bills makes such time as is available an ideal stamping ground for the determined filibuster who wishes to talk the Bill out. In spite of all this, many more private members' Bills have reached the statute book in recent times.

Prorogation and its effect

A session of Parliament is brought to an end by the Monarch by prorogation and a Bill which does not complete the necessary stages and receive the Royal Assent in one session will lapse. It can be introduced in a subsequent session but must complete all the necessary stages again. This lapse is not, however, inevitable since there is a procedure under which the government of the day can by negotiation with the Opposition allow a Bill to carry on with its remaining stages in the next session. This procedure was used, e.g., with the Financial Services and Markets Act 2000 when it was at the Bill stage. The Bill was of great length and dealt with fundamental changes in the regulation of the financial services industry and the City of London as a financial market. By agreement it was carried over after the end of the 1998/9 session to the 1999/2000 session in order to complete its stages. Bills also lapse when Parliament is dissolved prior to a General Election. The above provisions do not apply to *private Bills* (see below) which because of the costs involved in promotion can complete their remaining stages in a new session. The sittings of Parliament within a session are divided by periods of 'recess'. Bills do not lapse when Parliament goes into recess.

Public and private Bills

Bills are also divided into *public* and *private* Bills. *Public Bills*, which may be government or private members' Bills, alter the law throughout England and Wales and extend also to Scotland and Northern Ireland unless there is a provision to the contrary. *Private Bills* do not alter the general law but confer special local powers. These Bills are often promoted by local authorities where a new local development requires compulsory purchase of land for which a statutory power is needed. Enactment of these Bills is by a different parliamentary procedure.

The Speaker of the House of Commons rules whether a Bill is public or private if there is doubt as where, e.g., the Bill might affect areas beyond that of the local authority concerned, as would be the case if a seaport authority forbade the export of live animals from the port.

Enactment of Bills

A public Bill and a private members' Bill follow the same procedure in Parliament. These Bills may be introduced in either House, though, as we have seen, a money Bill, which is a public Bill certified by the Speaker as one containing provisions relating to taxation or loans, must be introduced in the Commons by a Minister and not a private member. The following procedure relates to a public or private members' Bill introduced in the Commons.

The various stages

On its introduction the Bill receives a purely formal first reading. Only the title of the Bill is read out by the Clerk of the House. The purpose of this stage is to tell members that the Bill exists. It is then printed and published. Later it is given a second reading, at which point its general merits may be debated, but no amendments are proposed to the various clauses it contains. There is an alternative procedure for the second reading stage of *Public Bills in the Commons*, which is designed to save parliamentary time. A Minister may move that the Bill be referred to a Standing Second Reading Committee of between 30 and 80 MPs. They report to the Commons recommending with reasons whether or not the Bill should be read a second time. The report of the Committee must be put to the House for a vote without debate or amendment. This procedure does not apply if 20 Members rise in their seats to object. Private members' Bills are automatically referred to the Second Reading Committee.

The Second Reading Committee procedure has saved a lot of parliamentary time and assisted the passing of many non-controversial Bills for which the government would otherwise have had to find debating time. There is also a rule limiting speeches in second reading debates in the Commons to 10 minutes which also saves time.

Having survived the second reading, the Bill passes to the Committee stage. Here details are discussed by a Standing Committee chosen in proportion to the strength of the parties in the House of Commons. The number of members varies but is in general between 20 and 30. Amendments to the clauses are proposed, and, if not accepted by the government, are voted on, after which the Bill returns to the House at the Report stage. The Committee mentioned may be a Committee of the Whole House, if the legislation is sufficiently important. Certain Bills in the Commons may be sent to a Special Standing Committee which is given power to hear evidence from outsiders, thus following to some extent the procedure for private Bills (see below).

At the Report stage the amendments may be debated, and the Bill may in some cases be referred back for further consideration. It is then read for the third time, when amendments may strictly speaking be moved but in practice only verbal alterations are taken.

After passing the third reading, the Bill is said to have 'passed the House'. It is then sent to the House of Lords where it goes through a similar procedure and must pass through all stages successfully *in the same session of Parliament*. If the Lords propose amendments, the Bill is returned to the Commons for approval. At one time the House of Lords had the power to reject Bills sent up by the Commons. Now, under the provisions of the Parliament Acts 1911 and 1949, this power amounts to no more than an ability to delay a public Bill (other than a money Bill) for a period of one year; a money Bill may be delayed for one month only (and see below). The supremacy of the Commons stems from the fact that it is an elected assembly, responsible to its electors and coming periodically at intervals of not more than five years before the public for re-election. The Lords may veto a private Bill and have retained the power to reject a Bill which attempts to extend the duration of Parliament beyond five years.

Parliament Acts 1911 and 1949 – the procedure

The procedure involved where the Commons wishes, in effect, to pass legislation without the consent of the Lords is as follows:

Money Bills. Where a money bill has passed the Commons, it shall receive the Royal Assent without the approval of the Lords unless it has been passed by the Lords within one month of being sent to the Lords, provided that the Bill was sent to the Lords at least one month before the end of the relevant session.

Other public Bills. If a Bill has been passed by the Commons and then rejected in the Lords, and *in the next session of Parliament* it is again passed by the Commons but the House of Lords does not pass it without amendments (except those that are approved by the Commons), the Commons has the power to send the Bill for the Royal Assent, despite the opposition by the Lords. However, it is also provided that at least one year must have elapsed between the second reading of the Bill in the Commons in the first session and the third reading in the Commons in the second session.

As we have seen, the power of the Lords to veto any Bill which attempts to extend the life of Parliament beyond five years remains.

Parliament Acts 1911 and 1949 – a challenge

A challenge to the validity of the Hunting Act 2004, which banned hunting with dogs, reached the House of Lords, where an instructive judgment was given on the validity of Acts passed into law without the consent of the Lords. The Hunting Act 2004 did not receive the consent of the Lords (see *R (Jackson and others)* v *Attorney-General* [2005] 2 WLR 866).

The government contended that the 2004 Act was valid, since it was passed under procedures laid down in the Parliament Act 1911, as amended by the Parliament Act 1949. The 1911 Act was passed by the Lords largely because the King promised he would create, if necessary, sufficient new peers who would support its passage through the Lords.

As we have outlined, s 2(1) of the 1911 Act provided that, after a period of two years had elapsed, a Bill that had still not received the consent of the Lords, being a public Bill other than a money bill or a Bill to extend the maximum duration of a Parliament beyond five years, could become an Act of Parliament without being passed by the Lords. The 1949 Act amended the 1911 Act by reducing the period of two years to one year. The provisions of the Parliament Act 1911 as amended were used to enact the 1949 Act.

The claimants seeking to make void the ban on hunting with dogs under the Hunting Act 2004 said that the 1911 Act was passed by the Lords and could only be lawfully amended with the consent of the Lords. Thus, since the 2004 Act was passed under the amended 1911 Act, and since the amending Act of 1949 was unlawful, the 2004 Act was also unlawful.

Their Lordships did not agree. The basis of their ruling that the 2004 Act was valid was based in the main on the fact that the Parliament Act 1949 was valid because it did not fundamentally change the relationship between the Commons and the Lords. A Bill could, as before, under the 1911 Act, be enacted without the consent of the Lords. It was merely that the period in the procedure had been reduced from two years to one year. The Lords' delaying power was maintained, but for a shorter period.

Other challenges to the Hunting Act 2004 were made in *R (on the application of Countryside Alliance and others)* v *Attorney-General* (2005) *The Times*, 3 August (judicial review) and in the House of Lords on appeal from a failed judicial review in the Divisional Court of Queen's Bench and the Court of Appeal in *R (on the application of Jackson) and others* v *Attorney-General* [2006] 1 AC 262. The claimants failed in both hearings and the Hunting Act 2004 remains valid.

Private Bills – a judicial stage

The main difference between the enactment of a *private Bill* and a *public Bill* is that the committee stage of a private Bill may be judicial. Any person whose interests are specifically affected by the Bill, normally in relation to property or business interests, may lodge a petition against the Bill in accordance with the procedure set out in Standing Orders. In such a situation the Bill is referred to an Opposed Committee consisting of four MPs of all parties appointed by the House. They must be entirely disinterested in a material sense, in the matters with which the Bill is concerned. The Committee hears both the petitioner and the promoter, who usually appear by counsel. If the petition succeeds the Bill is amended to take account of it. There is no appeal against the decision of the Committee. Since this is a somewhat lengthy procedure, some statutes allow Ministers to grant special powers to local authorities by what is called a Provisional Order. Such an order does not take effect unless and until it is embodied (usually along with others) in a Provisional Order Confirmation Bill which is passed by Parliament and given the Royal Assent. There are also radical proposals to change the Private Act of Parliament procedure because the parliamentary timetable is becoming clogged up by the number of these Bills, many of which are concerned, e.g., with new powers for docks and harbours. The suggestion is that power of approval be given to local authorities and/or public inquiries followed by a parliamentary debate only. This could well be an improvement since public inquiries are more accessible than the Private Bill procedure though the above proposals have not, as yet, been taken further.

Royal Assent

When a Bill has passed through both the Commons and the Lords, it requires the Royal Assent. It is not customary for the Monarch to consent in person, and in practice consent is given by a committee of three peers, including the Lord Chancellor. The Royal Assent Act 1967 provides that an Act is duly enacted and becomes law if the Royal Assent is notified to each House of Parliament, sitting separately, by the Speaker of that House or the acting Speaker.

The former Bill is then referred to as an Act or a statute, and may be regarded as a *literary* as well as a *legal* source of law. However, an Act may specify a future date for its coming into operation, or it may be brought into operation piecemeal by ministerial order. The courts have no power to examine proceedings in Parliament in order to determine whether the passing of an Act or delegated legislation has been obtained by means of any irregularity or fraud.

> *British Railways Board* v *Pickin*, 1974 – The courts and parliamentary proceedings (**21**)

Short title – numbering and citation

It should be noted that, as well as having a title setting out what its objects are, each Act has, under the provisions of the Short Titles Act 1896, a short title to enable easy reference to be made. Each Act has also an official reference. The Law of Property Act 1925, is the short title of an Act whose official reference is 15 & 16 Geo 5, c 20, which means that the Law of Property Act 1925 was the twentieth statute passed in the session of Parliament spanning the fifteenth and sixteenth years of the reign of George the Fifth.

The Acts of Parliament Numbering and Citation Act 1962 provides that chapter numbers assigned to Acts of Parliament passed in 1963 and after shall be assigned by reference to the calendar year and not the session in which they are passed. For example, the official reference of the Sale of Goods Act 1979 is 1979, c 54.

Statute law and case law distinguished

The essential differences between statute law and case law are apparent from the definition of a statute. It is:

> an express and formal laying down of a rule or rules of conduct to be observed in the future by the persons to whom the statute is expressly or by implication made applicable.

Thus a statute openly creates new law, whereas a judge would disclaim any attempt to do so. Judges are, they say, bound by precedent and merely select existing rules which they apply to new cases (but see Chapter 7). A statute lays down general rules for the guidance of future conduct; a judgment merely applies an existing rule to a particular set of circumstances. A judgment gives reasons and may be argumentative; a statute gives no reasons and is imperative.

6

Delegated legislation

Modern statutes may require much detailed work to implement and operate them. In such a case the Act is drafted so as to provide a broad framework, the details being filled in by Ministers by means of delegated legislation. For example, much of our social security legislation gives only the general provisions of a complex scheme of social benefits and an immense number of detailed regulations have had to be made by civil servants in the name of and under the authority of the appropriate Minister. These regulations when made in the approved manner are just as much law as the parent statute itself. This form of law is known as *delegated* or *subordinate* legislation.

Advantages

A number of advantages are claimed for delegated legislation as follows.

(a) It saves Parliamentary time in that Ministers are left, with the civil service, to make the detailed rules, Parliament concerning itself solely with the broad framework of the legislation.

(b) Speed. The Parliamentary procedure for enacting Bills is slow whereas rules and orders can be put more rapidly into law, particularly in a time of national emergency.

(c) Parliament cannot foresee all the problems which may arise after an Act has become law. Delegated legislation can deal with these if and when they arise.

(d) Delegated legislation is less rigid in that it can be withdrawn quickly by another statutory instrument if it proves impracticable.

(e) The aptitude of the legislature is limited and experts in the departments of state can better advise a Minister on the technicalities of a certain branch of law. It would be difficult to give this kind of advice to the Lords or Commons as a whole.

Disadvantages

However, there are disadvantages as follows.

(a) Parliamentary control over legislation is undoubtedly reduced. However, the power to make delegated legislation must be given by an Act of Parliament (sometimes referred to as the enabling statute) and so Parliament is to that extent in broad control because it must pass the enabling statute.

Beyond that much depends upon what the enabling statute says about reference to Parliament when instruments are made. There are different requirements and the inclusion of one rather than another in an enabling statute does not appear to be based upon any detectable principle.

The enabling Act may require:

(i)   that the instrument be merely laid before Parliament. Where this is so, MPs and Peers have no right to change it but laying before Parliament does, at least, inform them that the instrument exists, and in any case there is a scrutiny committee. In some cases the instrument is already in force. However, Members may ask Parliamentary questions about instruments laid for information only;

(ii) that Parliament may annul the instrument, e.g. within 40 days of laying. Where this is so a resolution of either House to annul the instrument is effective, but if there is no such resolution the instrument passes into law. However, whether there is a debate leading to a resolution to annul, the instrument is entirely dependent upon the initiative of an MP or Peer to engineer the debate since the government is not obliged to find time for it;

(iii) that each House of Parliament must pass a resolution approving the instrument. Where this is so, the government must obviously find time for a debate and a resolution approving the instrument must be made in each House, otherwise it will not become law;

(iv) that the instrument be laid in draft before Parliament and may only be issued if an affirmative resolution is passed by each House in its favour;

(v)   that the instrument be laid in draft without reference to affirmative resolutions, in which case by s 6 of the Statutory Instruments Act 1946 it may be made law after a period of 40 days if no resolution is passed during that period by either House against it.

It should be noted that if it is essential that an instrument comes into operation before copies of it can be laid before Parliament, then it may do so provided notification is sent to the Lord Chancellor and the Speaker of the House of Commons explaining why copies could not be laid before the instrument came into operation.

There is a special procedure for what are called Deregulation Orders. Part I of the Deregulation and Contracting Out Act 1994 gives power to amend or repeal by ministerial order primary legislation, i.e. Acts of Parliament, that impose an unnecessary burden on business. This somewhat extraordinary power is exercisable only after special scrutiny procedures have been followed. The 1994 Act provides a two-stage process for the parliamentary scrutiny of deregulation orders. A document containing the proposal is laid before Parliament under s 3(3) of the Act in the form of a draft of the order, together with explanatory material; and the Deregulation Committee in the Commons and the Select Committee on the Scrutiny of Delegated Powers in the Lords have 60 days in which to consider and report on it. The government then lay under s 1(4) of the 1994 Act a draft order, either in its original form or amended to take account of the views of the two Committees, for approval by resolution of each House. In the Lords a motion to approve a draft order can only be moved after the Lords Committee has made a second report on it. Thus, although the power to repeal or amend an Act of Parliament in this field rather than the requirement elsewhere to use another Act of Parliament seems to some a potentially dangerous and undemocratic process, the controls as listed above are very strict.

There are also other controls both by the judiciary and by Parliament itself (see below).

The 1994 Act has not been as successful as it might have been in removing red tape from business, because the Act provides that proposed changes to simplify procedures *must not impose fresh burdens of any kind*. If, therefore, it was decided to simplify an employment law procedure currently not applying to, say, employers with 20 or fewer employees, then if the proposal to simplify would only work if the simplified proposals were extended to all employers to save the complication of dealing with some employers as exceptions, it would not be possible to make the change because a new burden, albeit a simplified one, would be placed on the relevant small employers. Parliament has expressed an intention to remove the restriction, but it requires primary legislation and none is, as yet, forthcoming.

While on the matter of red tape, note can be taken of the *Better Regulation Task Force* that was set up in 1997 and published its initial programme of work at the end of that year. The task force is an independent advisory body appointed by a government Minister and the Chancellor of the Duchy of Lancaster. Its terms are to advise the government on improving the effectiveness and credibility of government regulation by ensuring that it is necessary, fair, affordable and simple to understand and administer, taking particular account of small businesses and ordinary people.

(b) It is said that there is too much delegated legislation so that it is difficult to know what the law is, particularly in view of the fact that little publicity is given to statutory instruments whereas most important Acts of Parliament are referred to at one time or another in the press. The difficulty is that a defendant's *ignorance of the law is no excuse*, though s 3(2) of the Statutory Instruments Act 1946 protects a person in respect of a crime contained in a statutory instrument *if the instrument has not been published*, unless it is proved that reasonable steps have been taken for the purpose of bringing the content of the instrument to the notice of the public or of persons likely to be affected by it or the person in fact charged. The section does not protect if the instrument has been published but a particular defendant does not know of its existence.

A way of dealing with the mass of delegated legislation is to introduce *'sunset' clauses* into regulations so that they would have to be reviewed or die after a specified period. This method is used in the United States with some degree of success and the UK government is looking at it and may introduce it here.

(c) The dangers of sub-delegation are on occasions quite real. One can find in some cases a pedigree of four generations of instrument emanating from a statute as follows:

(i)   regulations made under the statute;
(ii)   orders made under the regulations;
(iii) directions made under the orders;
(iv)   licences issued under the directions.

When this happens it does reduce very seriously the control by Parliament of the making of new laws since Parliament would only see the parent statute and the first set of regulations.

Types of delegated legislation

In modern statutes delegated powers are exercisable by four main vehicles as follows:

(a) Statutory instruments. Most powers conferred on Ministers in modern statutes are exercisable by ministerial or departmental regulations or orders, called collectively statutory instruments.

(b) Orders in Council. Powers of special importance relating to constitutional issues, e.g. emergency powers, are conferred on the Queen in Council. These powers are in fact exercised by the Cabinet who are all Privy Councillors by means of an order in council.

(c) By-laws of local authorities. These are made by local authorities under powers given to them in Acts of Parliament and require the approval of the appropriate Minister.

(d) Rules of the Supreme Court and County Court. These are made by Rules Committees set up by statute specifically to make rules concerning the practice and procedure of the courts. The Rules Committees are made up of judges and senior members of the legal profession.

Judicial control

Delegated legislation takes effect as if it were part of the enabling statute. Therefore, it has statutory force and, as we have seen, the courts cannot declare a statute *ultra vires*. However, delegated legislation does not acquire statutory force unless it is *intra vires*, i.e. properly made in accordance with the terms of the enabling Act. The courts can declare delegated legislation *ultra vires* in this sense. There are two approaches to the *ultra vires* rule as regards delegated legislation as follows:

(a) Substantive *ultra vires*. This means that the Minister has exceeded the powers given to him in the parent statute. If a Minister is authorised to make regulations as to road traffic, clearly if he purports to make regulations under the same parent statute concerning rail traffic, they would be held by the courts to be *ultra vires* and invalid.

(b) Procedural *ultra vires*. This means that the instrument is invalid because the Minister has failed to follow some mandatory procedural requirement specified in the parent Act. For example, much social security legislation requires the Minister to consult various advisory bodies before making rules and orders. If a rule or order was made without the necessary consultation, then it would be *ultra vires* in procedural terms and invalid.

> *Hotel and Catering Industry Training Board* v *Automobile Proprietary Ltd*, 1969 – Delegated legislation and *ultra vires* (**22**)

Henry VIII (or ouster) clauses

Sometimes a section of an Act will give a Minister or the Queen in Council very wide powers so that it is difficult to say that any instrument made or decision taken under it is *ultra vires*. These are referred to as 'Henry VIII Clauses' after the way in which that monarch used to legislate in arbitrary fashion by a proclamation. A more modern expression is an 'ouster clause', i.e. a clause attempting to prevent a decision being reviewed by the court. For example, s 4(7) of the Parliamentary Constituencies Act 1986 provides that 'The validity of any Order in Council purporting to be made under this Act . . . shall not be called in question in any legal proceedings whatsoever.' It was at one time thought that the courts were powerless to intervene to review any order made under such a provision. However, in more recent times the courts have taken power to overcome ouster clauses by saying, in effect, that if the exercise of such a power is not in accordance with the law, as where it is, e.g., *ultra vires* or made by misinterpreting the power given, the Minister or tribunal has lost jurisdiction and the court can intervene. In other words, the jurisdiction is to decide correctly but not incorrectly. An illustration is provided by the decision of the House of Lords in *Anisminic Ltd* v *Foreign Compensation Commission* [1969] 1 All ER 208. A Ltd applied to the Commission for compensation for property seized by Egypt in 1956 at the time of the Suez crisis relating among other things to the blocking of the Suez canal. The Foreign Compensation Act 1950 was relevant. It said that decisions of the Commission 'shall not be called into question in any court of law'. The Commission decided that A Ltd was not entitled to compensation but in doing so misinterpreted the statute. This said the House of Lords made the decision *ultra vires* and void. It was, therefore, not a 'decision' and the court could question it. Being merely asked to say what the law was the court gave a declaratory judgment that the decision was void.

Parliamentary control

The main Parliamentary control is through a Joint Committee on Statutory Instruments between the House of Commons and the House of Lords. The Joint Committee is appointed to consider statutory instruments with a view to determining whether the special attention of Parliament should be drawn to the legislation on various grounds. The grounds, briefly, are that the legislation:

(*a*) imposes a tax on the public;

(*b*) is made under an enactment containing specific provisions excluding it from challenge in the courts;

(*c*) purports to have retrospective effect where there is no express authority in the enabling statute;

(*d*) has been unduly delayed in publication or laying before Parliament;

(*e*) has come into operation before being laid before Parliament and there has been unjustifiable delay in informing the Speaker of the delay under s 4(1) of the Statutory Instruments Act 1946;

(*f*) may be beyond the powers given by the parent statute or makes some unusual or unexpected use of those powers;

(*g*) calls for better explanation as to its meaning.

As regards law coming from the European Union, there is also a system of three standing committees consisting of 10 MPs to examine the proposals of the Union in terms of legal matters and to question Ministers about them. There are also Commons debates before the twice-yearly EU summit meetings to give MPs a chance to air their views on the agendas for the summit meetings.

By-laws of local authorities

These must be *intra vires*, i.e. within the powers given to the local authority in the enabling statute, and also reasonable. Thus, in *Kruse* v *Johnson* [1898] 2 QB 91 a local authority by-law making it an offence to sing within 50 yards of a dwelling house was upheld but the court decided that unreasonableness could be a ground for invalidating by-laws.

Burnley Borough Council v *England*, 1978 – By-laws: challenge in court (**23**)

Interpretation of statutes by the judiciary

The main body of the law is to be found in statutes, together with the relevant statutory instruments, and in case law as enunciated by judges in the courts. But the judges not only have the duty of declaring the common law, they are also frequently called upon to settle disputes as to the meaning of words or clauses in a statute.

Parliament is the supreme lawgiver, and the judges must follow statutes (but see *Factortame Ltd* v *Secretary of State for Transport (No 2)* (1991) 1 All ER 70). Nevertheless, there is a considerable amount of case law which gathers round Acts of Parliament and delegated legislation since the wording sometimes turns out to be obscure. Statutes were at one time drafted by practising lawyers who were experts in the particular branch of law of which the statute was to be a part. Today, however, statutes are drafted by parliamentary counsel to the Treasury, and, although such persons are skilled in the law, the volume of legislation means that statutes are often obscure and cases continue to come before the courts in which the rights of the parties depend upon the exact meaning of a section of a statute. When such a case comes before a judge, he must decide the meaning of the section in question. Thus even statute law is not free from judicial influence.

The judges have certain recognised *aids to interpretation*, and these are set out below.

Statutory aids

Judges may get some guidance from statute law.

(*a*) The Interpretation Act 1978, which is itself a statute, defines terms commonly used in Acts of Parliament, e.g. that 'person' includes a corporation as well as a human being.

(*b*) A complex statute will normally contain an interpretation section, defining the terms used in the particular Act, e.g. ss 735–744A of the Companies Act 1985 define, among other things, 'accounts' and 'director', and the judges have recourse to this.

(*c*) Every Act of Parliament used to have what was known as a preamble, which set out at the beginning the general purpose and scope of the Act. The preamble was often quite lengthy and assisted the judge in ascertaining the meaning of the statute. Modern public Acts do not have this type of preamble, but have instead a long title which is not of so much assistance in interpretation. For example, the Sex Discrimination Act 1975, which contains 87 sections and a number of schedules, says merely: 'An Act to render unlawful certain kinds of sex discrimination and discrimination on the grounds of marriage, and establish a Commission with the function of working towards the elimination of such discrimination and promoting equality of opportunity between men and women generally; and for related purposes.' All private Acts must have a preamble setting out the objects of the legislation, and this preamble must be proved by the promoters at the Committee stage in the House of Lords. So far as private Acts are concerned the preamble may be of assistance.

Hutton v Esher UDC, 1973 – Statutory interpretation and the Interpretation Act (**24**)

General rules of interpretation evolved by judges

There are a number of generally recognised rules or canons of interpretation, and some of the more important ones are now given.

The mischief rule

This was set out in *Heydon*'s Case (1584) 3 Co Rep 7a. Under this rule the judge will look at the Act to see what was its purpose and what mischief in the common law it was designed to prevent.

Broadly speaking, the rule means that where a statute has been passed to remedy a weakness in the law the interpretation which will correct that weakness is the one to be adopted.

The literal rule

According to this rule, the working of the Act must be construed according to its literal and grammatical meaning whatever the result may be. The same word must normally be construed throughout the Act in the same sense, and in the case of old statutes regard must be had to its contemporary meaning if there has been a change with the passage of time.

The Law Commission, in an instructive and provocative report on the subject of interpretation (Law Com 21), said of this rule that 'to place undue emphasis on the literal meaning of the words of a provision is to assume an unattainable perfection in draftsmanship'.

The rule, when in operation, does not always achieve the obvious object and purpose of the statute. A classic example is *Whiteley* v *Chappell* (1868–9) 4 LRQB 147. In that case a statute concerned with electoral malpractices made it an offence to personate 'any person entitled to vote' at an election. The defendant was accused of personating a deceased voter and the court, using the literal rule, found that there was no offence. The personation was not of a person entitled to vote. A dead person was not entitled to vote, or do anything else for that matter. A deceased person did not exist and could therefore have no rights. It will be seen, however, that the literal rule produced in that case a result which was clearly contrary to the object of Parliament.

The golden rule

This rule is to some extent an extension of the literal rule and under it the words of a statute will as far as possible be construed according to their ordinary plain and natural meaning, unless this leads to an absurd result. It is used by the courts where a statutory provision is capable of more than one literal meaning and leads the judge to select the one which avoids absurdity, or where a study of the statute as a whole reveals that the conclusion reached by applying the literal rule is contrary to the intentions of Parliament.

Thus, in *Re Sigsworth* [1935] Ch 89 the court decided that the Administration of Estates Act 1925, which provides for the distribution of the property of an intestate amongst his next of kin, did not confer a benefit upon the person (a son) who had murdered the intestate (his mother), even though the murderer was the intestate's next of kin, for it is a general principle of law that no one can profit from his own wrong.

The ejusdem generis rule

This is a rule covering things of the same genus, species or type. Under it, where general words follow particular words, the general words are construed as being limited to persons or things within the class outlined by the particular words. So in a reference to 'dogs, cats, and other animals', the last three words would be limited in their application to animals of the domestic type, and would not be extended to cover animals such as elephants and camels which are not domestic animals in the UK.

Expressio unius est exclusio alterius

(The expression of one thing implies the exclusion of another.) Under this rule, where specific words are used and are not followed by general words, the Act applies only to the instances mentioned. For example, where a statute contains an express statement that certain statutes are repealed, there is a presumption that other relevant statutes not mentioned are not repealed.

Noscitur a sociis

(The meaning of a word can be gathered from its context.) Under this rule words of doubtful meaning may be better understood from the nature of the words and phrases with which they are associated.

Gardiner v *Sevenoaks RDC*, 1950 – The mischief rule (**25**)

Keene v *Muncaster*, 1980 – The golden rule (**26**)

Lane v *London Electricity Board*, 1955 – The *ejusdem generis* rule (**27**)

R v *Immigration Appeals Adjudicator, ex parte Crew*, 1982 – The rule of *expressio unius* (**28**)

Muir v *Keay*, 1875 – The rule of *noscitur a sociis* (**29**)

Compatibility with Convention on Human Rights

As we have seen in the overview of the Human Rights Act 1998, in Chapter 3, s 3 of that Act provides that, as far as it is possible to do so, both primary and subordinate legislation must be read and given effect in a way which is compatible with Convention rights. The section applies to past as well as future legislation and the court is not bound by previous interpretations of past legislation in terms of Convention rights. This has implications for the rule of precedent (see Chapter 7) under which judges generally follow previous decisions. It may be that a Crown Court will be obliged to refuse to follow a previous ruling of the Court of Appeal or the House of Lords where this is required in order to give effect to Convention rights. It is expected that the courts will in almost all cases be able to interpret UK legislation compatibly with Convention rights.

Other considerations and presumptions

In addition to the major rules of interpretation, there are also several other considerations which the court will have in mind.

Use of *Hansard*

In general terms, the court will concern itself only with the wording of the Act and will not go to *Hansard* to look at the reports of debates during the passage of the Act.

There is here some conflict with the mischief rule, since it might be thought there is no better way to ascertain what mischief the Act was designed to prevent than by reference to the Parliamentary debates in *Hansard*. Nevertheless, the Law Commission in their deliberations on the matter of statutory interpretation had decided against the use of *Hansard* since they doubted the reliability of statements made in Parliamentary debates.

The general rule that *Hansard* should not be referred to as an aid to interpretation was relaxed in *Pepper* v *Hart* [1993] 1 All ER 42. The House of Lords held that reference to *Hansard* should be allowed where:

(*a*) the legislation is ambiguous or obscure or where a literal interpretation would lead to an absurdity. The House of Lords subsequently made it clear that this condition must exist before reference to *Hansard* can be made and that the judiciary has no general power to refer (see *R* v *Secretary of State for the Environment, ex parte Spath Holme Ltd* [2001] 1 All ER 195);

(*b*) the material which is referred to consists of statements by a Minister or other promoter of the Bill together with such other Parliamentary material as is necessary to understand the statements and the effects of them;

(*c*) the statements relied upon are clear.

Their Lordships held that the above references would not contravene parliamentary privilege.

The House of Lords decided in *Davis* v *Johnson* [1978] 1 All ER 1132 that it is now permissible for the court to refer to reports by such bodies as the Law Commission and committees or commissions appointed by the government or by either House of Parliament from which the reform of the law stems.

However, according to the judgments, e.g. that of Lord Diplock, 'Where legislation follows on a published report of this kind the report may be used as an aid to identify the mischief which the legislation is intended to remedy but not for the purpose of construing the enacting words . . .'. In other words, the relevant report can assist in terms of what the legislation was designed to do but not whether the words it uses achieve it.

Of course, it may be the case that a reference to *Hansard* will not clarify the position. For example, in *R* v *Deegan (Desmond Garcia)* [1998] 1 CLY 966 the defendant appealed against his conviction for possessing a bladed knife in a public place. The issue was whether the type of knife he was carrying came within the scope of s 139 of the Criminal Justice Act 1988 under which he was charged. On referring to *Hansard*, it was discovered that ministerial statements were not consistent and of no assistance, so knives of a type described in earlier case law relating to bladed articles were followed, and the defendant's appeal to the Court of Appeal failed.

No retrospective effect or alteration of existing law

A statute is presumed not to alter the existing law unless it expressly states that it does. There is also a presumption against the repeal of other statutes and that is why statutes which are repealed are repealed by specific reference.

In the absence of any express indication to the contrary, a construction which would exclude retrospective effect is to be preferred to a construction which would not. Thus in *Alexander* v *Mercouris* [1979] 3 All ER 305, where the claimant sued the defendant for alleged defective workmanship in the conversion of two flats, the claimant tried to bring his case under the Defective Premises Act 1972 (see further Chapter 21) which came into force on 1 January 1974. However, it appeared that the defendant commenced the work in November 1972 and it was held by the Court of Appeal that no claim could be brought under the Act as the Act could not be construed as having retrospective effect. Some Finance Acts do have retrospective effect in terms of taxation.

Miscellaneous rules

When a statute deprives a person of property, there is a presumption that compensation will be paid. Unless so stated it is presumed that an Act does not interfere with rights over private property. There is a rebuttable presumption against alteration of the common law. Any Act which presumes to restrict private liberty will be very strictly interpreted, though the strictness may be tempered in times of emergency. It is presumed that an Act does not bind the Crown on the ground that the law, made by the Crown on the advice of the Lords and Commons, is made for subjects and not for the Crown. Furthermore, as we have seen, the courts lack the power to examine proceedings in Parliament in order to determine whether the passing of an Act has been obtained by means of any irregularity or fraud (see *British Railways Board* v *Pickin* (1974)).

Purposive interpretation

However, the Law Commissioners have recommended that more emphasis should be placed on the importance of interpreting a statute in the light of the *general purposes behind it and the intentions of Parliament*. This is referred to as a purposive interpretation. Thus in *Fletcher* v

Budgen [1974] 2 All ER 1243 the Divisional Court of Queen's Bench decided that under the Trade Descriptions Act 1968 a buyer of goods, in this case a car dealer, could be guilty of the offence of falsely describing goods when he told a private seller that his car was almost worthless, bought it, repaired it and sold it at a considerable profit. Lord Widgery, CJ said that although he had never thought of the Act as applying to buyers of goods, it was necessary in the public interest that it should, at least in the case of expert buyers, and that in his view such decision 'is not in any sense illogical and is not likely to run counter to any intention which Parliament may have had'.

In *Knowles* v *Liverpool City Council* [1993] 1 WLR 1428 a council employee was injured while handling a defective flagstone. He was awarded damages under the Employers' Liability (Defective Equipment) Act 1969. The council appealed on the grounds that a flagstone was not 'equipment' under the Act; the matter reached the House of Lords which said that it was equipment. The purpose of the Act was to protect employees from exposure to dangerous materials.

Again, in *Inco Europe Ltd* v *First Choice Distribution* [2000] 1 WLR 586 the House of Lords discovered a drafting error in the Arbitration Act 1996 which prevented a right of appeal from a decision of the High Court. The House of Lords ruled that the Act should be interpreted as allowing the appeal since this was the intended purpose of the legislature.

However, as Lord Scarman said in *Shah* v *Barnet London Borough Council* [1983] 1 All ER 226 at p 238: 'Judges may not interpret statutes in the light of their own views as to policy. They may, of course, adopt a purposive interpretation if they can find in the statute read as a whole or in material to which they are permitted by law to refer as aids to interpretation an expression of Parliament's purpose or policy.'

Rules of interpretation tend to some extent to cancel each other. Thus by using one or other of these rules judges can be narrow, reformist, or conservative. In fact Pollock, in his *Essays in Jurisprudence and Ethics*, suggests:

> English judges have often tended to interpret statutes on the theory that Parliament generally changes the law for the worse and that the business of the judges is to keep the mischief of its interference within the narrowest possible bounds.

It must be said that this comment applies particularly to judicial interpretation of welfare law where they have sometimes been reluctant to fill in gaps in order to make the law work, whereas if the Act is in the field of 'lawyers' law, then they have been prepared to do precisely this in order, for example, to convict a guilty person of a crime. This is, however, not surprising since judges are the product of a legalistic training and are clearly ill-equipped to pronounce upon welfare law, whereas in crime, for example, they are dealing with rules which they better understand so that they feel less reluctant to fill in gaps. There is now, of course, a much wider training of the judiciary that may overcome this problem.

Explanatory Notes

The Department of State sponsoring the Bill now produces Explanatory Notes at least for major Bills. These are available for purchase through the Stationery Office and state clause by clause and in ordinary language the provisions of the Bill. However, the Notes are prefaced with the warning that they are not part of the Bill and have not been endorsed by Parliament. They are not judgemental and are in no sense binding on a court in terms of the interpretation of the Bill once it becomes law. Nevertheless, they are useful to professionals and those in business as a means of understanding quickly the aims and intentions of the legislation.

7

THE LAW-MAKING PROCESS II: CASE LAW AND THE LEGISLATIVE ORGANS OF THE EUROPEAN UNION

We are concerned in this chapter to explain the methods by which the judiciary become involved in the law-making process and the effect of European Union legislation – how it is made and interpreted, together with the official bodies involved in law reform.

Case law or judicial precedent

Case law still provides the bulk of the law of the country, although Parliament is becoming much more active in making new laws and statute law may come to dominate the common law. This trend is, of course, encouraged by the existence of the Law Commission which is constantly putting forward proposals to codify the law by statute. Some case law states the law itself, and some is concerned as we have seen with the interpretation of statutes. We will examine here case law which is law in its own right. Case law is built up out of precedents, and a precedent is a previous decision of a court which may, in certain circumstances, be binding on another court in deciding a similar case. This practice of following previous decisions is derived from custom, but it is a practice which is generally observed. As Park, CJ said in *Mirehouse v Rennell* (1833) 1 Cl & Fin 527, 'Precedent must be adhered to for the sake of developing the law as a science.' In more modern times attention to precedent is essential because without it no lawyer could safely advise his client and every quarrel would lead to a law suit. Even in early times the itinerant judges adopted the doctrine of *stare decisis* (abiding by precedent), and this doctrine has been developed in modern times so that it means that a precedent binds, and must be followed in similar cases, subject mainly to the power to distinguish cases in certain circumstances, though there are other exceptions listed later in this chapter.

The modern doctrine of the binding force of judicial precedent only fully emerged when there was (*a*) good law reporting, and (*b*) a settled judicial hierarchy. By the middle of the nineteenth century law reporting was much more efficient, and the Judicature Acts 1873–75 created a proper pyramid of authority which was completed when the Appellate Jurisdiction Act 1876 made the House of Lords the final Court of Appeal. Judicial precedents may be divided into two kinds:

- binding precedents;
- persuasive precedents.

Before we explain the precise meaning of these terms, we have still to find out where these precedents are to be found. The answer is in the law reports, and, as we have seen, the doctrine of judicial precedent depends upon an accurate record being kept of previous decisions.

Law reports

Since 1865 law reports have been published under the control of what is now called the Incorporated Council of Law Reporting for England and Wales, which is a joint committee of the Inns of Court, the Law Society and the Bar Council. They are known simply as the Law Reports, and they have priority in the courts because the judge who heard the case sees and revises the report before publication. Nevertheless, private reports still exist, and of these the All England Reports, published weekly and started in 1936, are the only *general* reports existing in the private sector. These reports are now revised by the judge concerned with the case. The All England series now includes specialist reports entitled *Commercial Cases*, also *European Cases*, together with the *All England Direct* online service. The citation of the first reports is, e.g. [2000] 1 All ER 10 (Comm), the second is cited, e.g. [2000] All ER (EC) 10, and the online reports are cited, e.g. [2000] All ER (D) 10.

In 1953 the Incorporated Council began to publish reports on a weekly basis and these are known as the Weekly Law Reports. *The Times* newspaper publishes summarised reports of certain cases of importance and interest on the day following the hearing, as do other newspapers, e.g. the *Financial Times*, the *Independent* and the *Guardian*, and there are also certain specialised series of reports covering, for example, the fields of taxation, shipping, company law and employment law. In a Practice Direction in 1990 (see *The Times*, 7 December 1990) the Master of the Rolls stated that in the House of Lords and the Court of Appeal the general rule was that the Law Reports published by the Incorporated Council of Law Reporting should be cited in preference to other reports where there was a choice. It is not absolutely essential that a case should have been reported in order that it may be cited as a precedent, and very occasionally oral evidence of the decision by a barrister who was in court when the judgment was delivered may be brought.

Citation of unreported cases

The issue of the citation of unreported cases was raised by Lord Diplock in the House of Lords in *Roberts Petroleum* v *Bernard Kenny* [1983] 1 All ER 564, and Sir John Donaldson, MR in *Stanley* v *International Harvester* (1983) *The Times*, 7 February. These have become readily available since the Lexis Computer Retrieval System, among others, came into use. Lexis records, for example, 3,000 Court of Appeal decisions a year. Of these only some 350 are reported in any of the major series such as All England, and Weekly Law Reports. These, as we have seen, are edited by the judge(s). Both judges seemed determined to discourage the growing resort by counsel to unreported cases. Indeed, in the *Stanley* case the view was that counsel should beware of citing to the courts cases which are of no great novelty or authority, but which are supplied in unnecessary profusion by computers.

Also relevant is a Practice Statement issued in May 1996 by the Master of the Rolls. It states that leave to cite unreported cases before the Court of Appeal will not usually be granted unless counsel can assure the court that the trial transcript in question contains a relevant statement of legal principle not found in reported authority and that among other things the unreported authority is not being cited as an illustration of an established legal principle.

In this connection, the case of *Hamblin* v *Field* (2000) *The Times*, 26 April is instructive. In hearing a bankruptcy case, the judge had been given a summary of what was a recent case. There was later an appeal to the Court of Appeal which commented on the citing of such summaries. The one in question was a Lawtel summary. Lord Justice Peter Gibson said that the object of these summaries was merely to give practitioners notice via computer that a particular case in a particular area of law had been decided. It did not appear from the summary whether the judgment was summarised by a professional lawyer still less a member of the Bar (as is usual). The intention was that Lawtel should be contacted to obtain a copy of the complete judgment. The practice of using such summaries should not be tolerated.

Reference to decided cases

Decided cases are usually referred to as follows: *Smith* v *Jones*, 1959. This means that, in a court of first instance, Smith was the claimant, Jones the defendant, and that the case was published in the set of reports of 1959, though it may have been heard at the end of 1958. This is called the 'short citation'. A longer citation is required if the report is to be referred to, and might read as follows: *Smith* v *Jones* [1959] 1 QB 67 at p 76. The additional information means that the case is to be found in the first volume of the Reports of the Queen's Bench Division, the report commencing on page 67, the number 76 being used to indicate the page on which an important statement is to be found. Where the date is cited in square brackets, it means that the date is an essential part of the reference, and without the date it is very difficult to find the report in question. For many years now the Incorporated Council's reports have been written up in a certain number of volumes each year. It will be seen that a mere reference to Vol 1 of the Queen's Bench Division will not be sufficient unless the year is also quoted. The same procedures are followed in the All England Reports.

The early reports by the Incorporated Council and other collections did not use the year as a basic item of the citation, but continued to extend the number of volumes regardless of the year. So a case may be cited as follows: *Smith* v *Jones*, 17 Ch D 230. It can be found by referring to Vol 17 of the Chancery Division reports, and it is not necessary to know the year in which the report was published, though this will be ascertained when the report is referred to. Where the date is not an essential part of the citation, it is quoted in round brackets. The abbreviations used in the Official Reports for the various divisions are: QB for Queen's Bench, Ch for Chancery, Fam for Family, and AC for the House of Lords and Privy Council (Appeal Cases). The reports of decisions of the Court of Appeal appear under the reference of the division in which they were first heard. As regards the case title petitions for leave to appeal and appeals to the Court of Appeal carry the same title as that which obtained in the court of first instance. This results in the claimant being shown first in the title whether he or she be the petitioner/appellant or respondent in the Court of Appeal. Since a Practice Note of 1974 ([1974] 1 All ER 752), this is now true of the House of Lords so that appeals to the House of Lords now carry the same title as that which obtained in the court of first instance, though in the Official Reports the reference AC is still used in House of Lords and Privy Council cases.

Media-neutral citations

Decided cases in the High Court and above are now given what are called media-neutral reference numbers. Examples are EWHC (QB) or (Ch) or (Fam) 103, say. These numbers cover the three divisions of the High Court in England and Wales and sometimes (Admin) may be found to indicate the Administrative Court. For the Court of Appeal the references are EWCA Civ 289, say, for the Civil Division and Crim for the Criminal Division. For the House of Lords the citation is EWHL 421, say. In all cases the year of the case is in square brackets, i.e. [2007].

The numbers are media neutral because they do not relate to a publication such as *The Times* or the *All England Law Reports* and so on. However, if the case is reported in a publication such as *The Times* or the *All England Law Reports* that reference appears after the media-neutral one. These numbers do not relate in any way to a computer or other report of the case but would assist in identifying a case in court records or for identifying a transcript. It is an advance on the citation '(unreported)'.

A practitioners' text would be expected to include these media-neutral citations. However, since they are of no assistance in ascertaining the facts of the case in themselves and will assist only those who wish to purchase expensive transcripts, they are not included in this text.

Precedent – generally

We are now in a position to refer to a decided case but we still have to find out where the precedent is to be found, since the whole of the case is reported, and the judge may have said things which are not strictly relevant to the final judgment. We must know what to take as precedent, and what to ignore, so that we can find what is called the *ratio decidendi*. The doctrine of precedent declares that cases must be decided in the same way when their *material* facts are the same. The *ratio* is therefore defined as the *principle* of law used by the judge to arrive at his *decision* together with his *reasons* for doing so. To take an example from contract law, in *Household Fire Insurance Company* v *Grant* (1879) (see Chapter 9) the court *decided* that a letter of acceptance took effect when it was posted, the *reason* behind this *principle* being that the Post Office was the common agent of the parties.

The *ratio decidendi* of a decision may be narrowed or widened by a subsequent judge before whom the case is cited as an authority. Although a judge will give reasons for his ruling, he is neither concerned nor obliged to formulate *all* the possibilities which may stem from it. Thus, the eventual and accepted *ratio decidendi* of a case may not be the *ratio decidendi* that the judge who decided the case would himself have chosen, but the one which has been approved by subsequent judges. This is inevitable, because a judge, when deciding a case, will give his reasons but will not usually distinguish in his remarks, in any rigid or unchangeable way, between what we have called the *ratio decidendi* and what are called *obiter dicta*. The latter are things said in passing, and they do not have binding force. Such statements of legal principle are, however, of some persuasive power, particularly the *dicta* of cases heard in the House of Lords.

The reason why *obiter dicta* are merely persuasive is because the prerogative of judges is not to make the law by formulating it and declaring it (this is for the legislature) but to make the law by applying it to cases coming before them. A judicial decision, unaccompanied by judicial application, is not of binding authority but is *obiter*. A judge does sometimes indicate which of his statements are *obiter dicta*. For example he may say: 'If it were necessary to decide the further point, I should be inclined to say that . . .'. What follows is said in passing.

It may, therefore, be said that the *ratio decidendi* of any given case is an abstraction of the legal *principle* from the *material* facts of the case and the *decision* which the judge made thereon, together with his *reasons* for so doing. Of course, the higher the level of abstraction, the more circumstances the *ratio decidendi* will fit. Let us take the following fact situation: 'At 12 noon on a Saturday A, a woman aged 30, drove a car through the centre of Manchester at 80 mph. She mounted the pavement and injured B, an old man of 90. B sued A and the judge found that she was liable.' If a subsequent judge thinks that the principle in *B* v *A* should be restricted he will tend to retain many of the facts of the case as material. If he thinks that the principle should be extended, he will not regard many of the facts of the situation as material and so produce a broad principle of wide application. Thus, a very narrow *ratio* would be as follows: 'If a woman aged 30 by the negligent driving of a car injures an old man of 90, she is liable to compensate him in damages.' However, the law of negligence is a much wider principle and the *ratio* is: 'If A, by negligence injures B, A is liable to compensate B in damages.'

The same principles of abstraction apply when a judge chooses to follow *obiter dicta*. This is well illustrated by the way in which the decision of the House of Lords in *Donoghue* v *Stevenson*, 1932 was developed to produce the modern doctrine of negligence (see further Chapter 21).

Binding force – generally

It is now necessary to examine which precedents are binding, and this depends also upon the level of the court in which the decision was reached. It would be useful to consider again at this point the diagrams in Chapter 2 which deal with the structure of the civil and criminal courts.

The House of Lords

The Supreme Court will take over from the House of Lords as the final court of appeal in 2009. The rules regarding precedent that apply to the House of Lords will apply to the Supreme Court. The House of Lords was bound by its own decisions (*London Street Tramways* v *London County Council* [1898] AC 375), except, for example, where the previous decision had been made *per incuriam*, i.e. where an important case or statute was not brought to the attention of the court when the previous decision was made. However, in July 1966, the House of Lords abolished the rule that its own decisions on points of law were absolutely binding upon itself. The Lord Chancellor announced the change on behalf of himself and the Lords of Appeal in Ordinary in the following statement:

> Their Lordships regard the use of precedent as an indispensable foundation upon which to decide what is the law and its application to individual cases. It provides at least some degree of certainty upon which individuals can rely in the conduct of their affairs, as well as a basis for orderly development of legal rules.
>
> Their Lordships nevertheless recognize that too rigid adherence to precedent may lead to injustice in a particular case and also unduly restrict the proper development of the law. They propose therefore to modify their present practice and, while treating former decisions of this House as normally binding, to depart from a previous decision when it appears right to do so.
>
> In this connection they will bear in mind the danger of disturbing retrospectively the basis on which contracts, settlements of property and fiscal arrangements have been entered into and also the special need for certainty as to the criminal law.
>
> This announcement is not intended to affect the use of precedent elsewhere than in this House.

A Practice Direction issued in March 1971 by the Appeal Committee of the House of Lords requires lawyers concerned with the preparation of cases of appeal to state clearly in a separate paragraph of the case any intention to invite the House to depart from one of its own decisions.

The declaration was not used for over 20 years to overrule decisions in the field of criminal law. It has now been used in the context of crime. For example, in *R* v *Howe* [1987] 2 WLR 568, the House of Lords overruled its previous decision in *DPP for Northern Ireland* v *Lynch* [1975] 1 All ER 913 which had decided that duress could be a defence in a prosecution for murder. *R* v *Howe* removes the defence of duress from the law relating to murder altogether so that the defence is now never available to any participant in murder.

> *Schorsch Meier Gmbh* v *Hennin*, 1975 – A case leading to the use of the 1966 declaration (**30**)
>
> *Miliangos* v *George Frank (Textiles) Ltd*, 1975 – The declaration applied (**31**)

The Court of Appeal

On the next rung of the hierarchy there is the Court of Appeal (Civil Division), and this court is bound by its own previous decisions, as well as by those of the House of Lords (*Young* v *Bristol Aeroplane Co* [1944] 2 All ER 293). There are, however, two main exceptions to the above rule.

(*a*) If there are two conflicting decisions of its own on the case before it the court may choose which one to follow.

The court may follow the most recent decision but this is not necessarily the rule. Where the *ratio* of an earlier decision is directly applicable to the circumstances of the case currently before the court but that decision has been wrongly distinguished in a later decision of the Court of Appeal, it is in principle open to the Court of Appeal to apply the ratio of the earlier decision and to decline to follow the later one (see *Starmark Enterprises Ltd* v *CPL Distribution Ltd* [2001] All ER (D) 472. A case concerned with whether a notice required to be served under a rent review clause in a lease had been served in sufficient time to make the rent review valid).

(*b*) The court will not follow a decision of its own if that decision is inconsistent with a decision of the House of Lords or the Judicial Committee of the Privy Council. Thus, *Re Polemis* [1921] 3 KB 560, a Court of Appeal decision which said that in negligence all *direct* harm was actionable even if not foreseeable, was disapproved of by the Privy Council in *The Wagon Mound* (1961) (see Chapter 20) and was not subsequently followed by the Court of Appeal.

The decisions of the Court of Appeal (Civil Division) are binding on the lower civil courts, i.e. the High Court and the county court.

On the criminal side, the Court of Appeal (Criminal Division) is bound by the decisions of the House of Lords and normally by its own decisions and those of the former Court of Criminal Appeal and the earlier Court for Crown Cases Reserved. However, an ordinary court of three judges in the Criminal Division may deviate from previous decisions more easily than the Civil Division because different considerations apply in a criminal appeal where the liberty of the accused is at stake and in any case a full court of the Criminal Division can overrule its own previous decisions.

In this connection, a court of five judges including the Lord Chief Justice declined to follow and overruled a previous decision of the Court of Appeal Criminal Division stating in particular that the decision could create problems if allowed to stand and bind the Criminal Division because in criminal cases there were many situations where in practice there was little prospect of an appeal to the House of Lords (see *R* v *Simpson* (2003) *The Times*, 26 May).

A full court generally consists of five judges instead of three as is usual in an ordinary sitting. A decision of the Civil Division is not binding on the Criminal Division and vice versa. Decisions of the Criminal Division are binding on lower criminal courts, i.e. the Crown Court and magistrates' courts.

It is perhaps worth noting that Lord Denning in *Davis* v *Johnson* [1978] 1 All ER 841 took the view that the Court of Appeal should take for itself guidelines similar to those taken by the House of Lords in 1966 to depart from a previous decision of its own where that decision was clearly wrong. However, Lord Denning does not appear to have received sufficient support for this view and a declaration on the lines he suggested has not been made.

However, it was decided in *Williams* v *Fawcett* [1985] 1 All ER 787 that the Court of Appeal could depart from one of its own previous decisions where that decision was felt to be wrong in law and there was unlikely to be an appeal to the House of Lords by a person whose liberty was at stake.

R v Gould, 1968 – Precedent in criminal appeals (**32**)

Divisional Courts

Divisional Courts are, in civil cases, bound by the decisions of the House of Lords, the Court of Appeal (Civil Division) and generally by their own previous decisions. However, a Divisional Court of Queen's Bench decided in *R v Greater Manchester Coroner, ex parte Tal* [1984] 3 All ER 240 that a Divisional Court would normally follow a previous decision of another Divisional Court but could in rare cases exercise its power to refuse to follow a previous Divisional Court decision if the court was convinced that the previous decision was wrong. In criminal cases there is, under ss 12–15 of the Administration of Justice Act 1960, an appeal from the Divisional Court of the Queen's Bench Division straight to the House of Lords, and the Divisional Court is not bound by the decisions of the Criminal Division of the Court of Appeal. The decisions of Divisional Courts are binding on judges of the High Court sitting alone and on magistrates' courts but not on Crown Courts (see below).

The High Court

At the next lower stage, a High Court judge, although bound by the decisions of the Court of Appeal and the House of Lords is not bound by the decisions of another High Court judge sitting at first instance (*Huddersfield Police Authority v Watson* [1947] 2 All ER 193). Nevertheless, such a judge will treat previous decisions as of strong persuasive authority. If a judge of the High Court refuses to follow a previous decision on a similar point of law, the Law Reports will contain two decisions by judges of equal authority and the cases will remain in conflict until the same point of law is taken to appeal before a higher tribunal whose decision will resolve the position (and see the statement of Nourse, J in the *Colchester Estates* case considered later in this chapter).

The Crown Court

A judge sitting in the Crown Court, the jurisdiction of which is largely confined to criminal cases, is bound by decisions made in criminal matters by the House of Lords and Court of Appeal (Criminal Division) but not apparently by decisions of the Divisional Court of the Queen's Bench Division (*R v Colyer* [1974] Crim LR 243). A judge sitting in the Crown Court and exercising a civil jurisdiction, e.g. licensing, is bound by the decisions of the House of Lords, Court of Appeal and the High Court.

Magistrates' courts and county courts

These courts are bound by the decisions of the higher courts. Their own decisions are not reported officially and have no binding force on other courts at the same level.

The Employment Appeal Tribunal (EAT)

As regards this tribunal, only the decisions of the Court of Appeal and the House of Lords on matters of law are binding, though the decisions of the earlier Industrial Relations Court and the High Court in England are of great persuasive authority and the tribunal would not lightly differ from the principles which are to be found in those decisions (*per* Bristow, J in

Portec (UK) Ltd v *Mogensen* [1976] 3 All ER 565 at p 568). These remarks remain valid even though the *Portec* case was overruled in terms of its decision by *Wilson* v *Maynard Shipbuilding Consultants AB* [1978] 2 All ER 78. Nevertheless, Wait, J, who as President of the EAT presided in *Anandarajah* v *Lord Chancellor's Department* [1984] IRLR 131, ruled that no assistance could be derived from precedent in deciding whether a dismissal was unfair (see further Chapter 19).

The EAT is not bound to follow its own decisions and the decision of an employment tribunal binds no one except the parties to the dispute.

The Judicial Committee of the Privy Council

The decisions of the Judicial Committee of the Privy Council are in general not binding, either on the Committee itself or on other English courts, save the Ecclesiastical and Prize Courts. Its decisions are technically only of persuasive authority in English law, and this derives from the fact that the Judicial Committee hears appeals from overseas territories. Thus, when it hears an appeal from Belize, it may not apply a rule of law used (say) in a previous appeal from the Channel Islands.

As regards the relationship of the Judicial Committee and the House of Lords, where the law applicable to the case is English, the Committee will feel bound to follow a relevant decision of the House of Lords but not otherwise (*Tai Hing Cotton* v *Liu Chong Hing Bank* [1985] 2 All ER 947).

Although in general terms the decisions of the Privy Council are persuasive only, there may rarely be cases where a decision of the Privy Council can overrule a decision of the House of Lords. This occurred in a case concerning provocation as a defence to a charge of murder which, if accepted by the court, can reduce the charge to one of manslaughter. The difficulty, as Chapter 24 will further illustrate, is whether in the act put forward as a provocation any special characteristics of the defendant can be taken into account as leading him or her to be provoked when a person without those characteristics would not. In *R* v *Smith (Morgan James)* [2000] 4 All ER 289, the House of Lords ruled that the defendant's depressive illness could be taken into account. In *Attorney-General for Jersey* v *Holley* [2005] 2 AC 580 the Privy Council ruled that alcoholism could not. The matter came before the House of Lords in *R* v *James* [2006] 1 All ER 759. James had killed his wife after they had separated and psychiatric evidence was adduced and James sought to regard this as a special characteristic, though the killing was not spontaneous. Should the House of Lords follow *Holley* or *Smith*, bearing in mind that the Privy Council in *Holley* had said *Smith* was wrongly decided?

The House of Lords followed *Holley*. Why? Because the Privy Council which heard the *Holley* case consisted of nine of the Lords of Appeal in Ordinary: a very strong court. We have seen that the House of Lords can overrule its own decisions and in effect surely that is what it was doing here under the guise of the Privy Council.

Could it happen once the Supreme Court is in place? Under the Constitutional Reform Act 2005, the judges of the Privy Council are those who have held high judicial office and former holders who are privy councillors. Since the judges of the Supreme Court and former judges of the court are within this category, the answer is yes, if the Privy Council had a high percentage of Supreme Court judges and/or former judges on the bench when the relevant decision was made.

General exceptions to the rule of binding precedent

Having examined the relationship of the above courts with regard to the rule of binding precedent, it should be noted that a court is not always bound to follow a precedent which according to the rules outlined above ought to be binding on it. It is by avoiding the following of precedents that judges can, and do, make law.

Thus, when the court in question is invited to follow a binding precedent, it may refuse to do so, for example:

(a) by distinguishing the case now before it from the previous case on the facts. A case is *distinguished* when the court considers that there are important points of difference between the facts of the case now before it and a previous decision which it is being invited to follow. As Lord Halsbury said in *Quinn* v *Leatham* [1901] AC 495:

> Every judgment must be read as applicable to the particular facts proved, or assumed to be proved, since the generality of the expressions which may be found there are not intended to be expositions of the whole law but govern and are qualified by the particular facts of the case in which such expressions are found.

This process of narrowing down the implications of the *ratio decidendi* of a previous case by 'distinguishing' is a device often used by a court which does not wish to follow an earlier decision which would otherwise be binding on it.

If a court deems that an earlier case was wrongly decided but cannot overrule it because the *ratio decidendi* of the case now before it does not cover all the matters raised in the earlier case, it may, by way of *obiter dictum*, *disapprove* the earlier case which is then to some extent affected as a precedent. Examples of distinguishing are to be found by comparing the decisions in *Ingram* v *Little* (1961) and *Lewis* v *Averay* (1971) (see Chapter 12);

(b) by refusing to follow the previous case because its *ratio* is obscure. Thus, in *Harper* v *NCB* [1974] 2 All ER 441 the Court of Appeal refused to follow the decision of the House of Lords in *Central Asbestos Co* v *Dodd* [1972] 2 All ER 1135 because the majority of three to two judges who found for Dodd left behind no discernible *ratio*. It was unclear whether the decision that Mr Dodd, who brought an action against his employers because he contracted an industrial disease in the course of his employment after the time limit of three years had elapsed, succeeded (i) because he knew that the injury arose from his employment but did not know that he could sue; or (ii) because he knew he could sue but not that the disease arose from his employment;

(c) by declaring the previous case to be in conflict with a fundamental principle of law, as where, for example, the court in the previous case has not applied the doctrine of privity of contract (see *Beswick* v *Beswick* (1967) (see further Chapter 10));

(d) by finding the previous decision to be *per incuriam*, i.e. where an important case or statute was not brought to the attention of the court or ignored (see view of Bristow, J in *Miliangos*) when the previous decision was made;

(e) because the previous decision is one of several conflicting decisions at the same level. In this connection, the comments of Nourse, J in *Colchester Estates (Cardiff)* v *Carlton Industries* [1984] 2 All ER 601 are of interest. He said that as a general rule, a judge faced with two conflicting authorities of judges of the same rank should feel himself bound by the later of them. This would not, however, be the rule if it appeared to the judge deciding the case that the later judgment was wrong in not following the first, as, for example, where some other binding authority had not been cited to the earlier judge or judges;

(f) because the previous decision had been overruled by statute.

(g) effect of the Human Rights Act 1998. We have already noted that the courts will not be bound by previous interpretations of statute law that does not take account of Convention rights. This is true also of the common law that must also be developed so as to be compatible with the Convention. Furthermore, there is no protection for the common law as there is for primary legislation where the courts can only declare primary legislation incompatible and then it is a matter for Parliament to decide how to deal with the matter.

(h) references to the European Court of Justice (ECJ). The Court of Appeal ruled in *Trent Taverns Ltd* v *Sykes* (1999) *The Times*, 5 March that it could, in the exercise of its discretion, make a reference to the ECJ in a case where the relevant point of Community law had already been decided by the Court of Appeal since the ordinary rules of precedent did not apply to such references.

It should be noted that when a reference is made to the European Court, it is to rule on the law not the facts of the case. If the European Court does give a contrary ruling on the facts in reaching its decision, a national court can refuse to follow it. This arose in *Arsenal Football Club plc* v *Reed* [2003] 1 All ER 137. Arsenal claimed that Mr Reed was passing off his merchandise as official Arsenal merchandise from his stall outside the ground. Mr Reed displayed a disclaimer saying that his goods were not official Arsenal merchandise. In the High Court Mr Justice Laddie ruled that there was no passing off because *of the fact of the disclaimer*. The ECJ ruled that there was *in spite of the fact of the disclaimer*. The ECJ therefore took a different view of the facts from Laddie J and he refused to follow the ECJ. The matter was resolved by the Court of Appeal in *Arsenal Football Club plc* v *Reed* (2003) *The Times*, 22 May. The Court of Appeal *accepted the view of the facts* taken by the ECJ that in spite of the disclaimer there had been a passing off by Mr Reed. Nevertheless, the case is still a valid and almost singular illustration of a judge refusing to apply an ECJ ruling.

(i) Some miscellaneous rulings. In *R (on the application of Kadhim)* v *Brent LBC Housing Benefit Board* [2001] QB 955 the Court of Appeal ruled that a precedent may be departed from where the previous court had assumed the correctness of the precedent without hearing argument. Furthermore, in *Bakewell Management Ltd* v *Brandwood* (2002) *The Times*, 19 April the High Court ruled that a High Court judge ought not to regard himself or herself as able to depart from an applicable Court of Appeal decision on the basis that a new argument not presented to the Court of Appeal had been presented to him or her. That was all the more so where the House of Lords had refused leave to appeal against the earlier Court of Appeal decision.

Cases heard in the county court and in the magistrates' courts are not generally reported, and for this reason do not create binding precedents. It would not be desirable to report such cases, for English law already possesses such a large number of reported cases that decisions are sometimes made in which relevant precedents are not cited or considered, and may therefore be *per incuriam*. Some judges feel that this position is exacerbated by unreported cases stored in computers (see above).

Persuasive precedents

These consist of decisions made in lower courts, and generally in the Judicial Committee of the Privy Council of *obiter dicta* at all levels and also decisions of Irish, Scottish, Commonwealth, and United States courts, the reason being that these nations also base their law on the common law of England and Wales, though some parts of the law of Scotland are derived from Roman law. Cases coming to the House of Lords from Scotland do not bind English courts. They are only persuasive unless the legal principles involved are the same in both systems of law. The House of Lords normally gives a direction as to the binding nature of such decisions; for example, *Donoghue* v *Stevenson* (1932) (see Chapter 21), which is a fundamental case on the law of negligence, is binding on both jurisdictions, although it was an appeal from the Scottish Court of Session.

In the absence of any persuasive authority from the above sources, the court may turn to textbooks and sometimes to Roman law. The weight which a court will give to persuasive authority may depend upon the standing of the judge whose decision or *dictum* it was and whether it was a reserved judgment, i.e. a case in which the court took time to consider the judgment. Reserved judgments are highly regarded. Undefended cases in which the issues have not been fully argued on both sides do not carry great weight.

Declaratory and original precedents

One further classification of precedents must be noted. They may be either 'declaratory' or 'original':

- *a declaratory precedent* is one which is merely the application of an existing rule of law;
- *an original precedent* is one which creates and applies a new rule. Original precedents alone develop the law; declaratory precedents are merely further evidence of it. Thus, if a judge says: 'The matter before us is not covered by authority and we must decide it on principle . . .' an original precedent is indicated.

Reversing, overruling and *res judicata*

It often happens that when a case has been decided in (say) the High Court, a decision is taken to appeal to an appellate court, in this case the Court of Appeal. The Court of Appeal will re-examine the case and, if it comes to a different conclusion from the judge in the High Court, it reverses his decision. Reversal, therefore, applies to a decision of an appellate court in the same case. Sometimes, however, the case which comes before the appellate court has been decided by following a previously decided case, the judge having followed precedent. In this case, if the appellate court decides to differ from the decision reached in the lower court, it is said to overrule the case which formed the basis of the precedent.

In this connection, it was held to be in order for a court, in this case a county court, to adjourn proceedings pending a ruling by the House of Lords on a similar issue on which the Court of Appeal had already ruled instead of following the Court of Appeal ruling (see *Kingcastle Ltd* v *Owen-Owen* (1999) *The Times*, 18 March).

Reversal affects the parties, who are bound by the decision of the appellate court, and it affects precedent because lower courts will in future be bound to follow the decision. *Overruling affects precedent*, but does not reach back to affect the parties in the original case now regarded as wrongly decided, and it is not necessary, for example, for a successful claimant to return his damages. Furthermore, the case could not be tried again because the rule of *res judicata* would apply. So the rule of *res judicata* (a matter which has been adjudicated on) protects defendants against a multiplicity of actions in regard to the same issues.

Res judicata does not apply where the decision is affected by *judicial bias*. This is illustrated by the various proceedings brought in connection with the application for extradition of General Pinochet, the former head of the state of Chile, to Spain to face charges of murder of Spanish citizens in Chile and the taking of such citizens as hostages and the torturing of them. On the basis of these allegations, the House of Lords ruled in 1998 (see *R* v *Bow Street Metropolitan Stipendiary Magistrate, ex parte Pinochet* [1998] 3 WLR 1456) that Pinochet was not entitled to immunity as an ex-head of state. However, lawyers acting for him discovered that one of the Law Lords, who was part of the court that heard the case, had been the chairman and an unpaid director of Amnesty International, which had been allowed to intervene in the appeal and was vigorously seeking Pinochet's extradition. In 1999 (see *R* v *Bow Street Metropolitan Stipendiary Magistrate, ex parte Pinochet* [1999] 1 WLR 272) the House of Lords re-heard the case with a different court and set aside the 1998 ruling, although the matter was in a sense *res judicata*.

The rule of *res judicata* can in modern law be divided into what is called cause of action estoppel and issue estoppel. Cause of action estoppel prevents a party to an action from suing again on the same matter in order to try to overturn the earlier decision. The earlier decision must stand once all rights of appeal have been exhausted or abandoned. The matters in issue must be the same, otherwise the rule does not apply. Thus, the failure or settlement of a claim for unfair dismissal (see Chapter 19) does not prevent a claim being made for unpaid wages (see *Dattani* v *Trio Supermarkets* [1998] ICR 872 – a ruling of the Court of Appeal).

A claimant is also barred by cause of action estoppel from bringing a claim which could have been brought at the same time as another claim brought by a *different claimant* having the same cause of action against the same defendant. Thus, in *Talbot* v *Berkshire County Council* [1993] 4 All ER 9, Talbot and his passenger were injured when his car ran into water on the highway and went off the road. The passenger sued Talbot and the Council, and damages were awarded to her as to two-thirds against Talbot for his negligence and one-third against the Council for its negligence. Talbot, who had been unaware of the claim against the Council because of the involvement of insurance companies, then tried to claim against the Council. The Court of Appeal said he could not. Talbot's claim could have been brought at the same time as the passenger's and was, therefore, barred by cause of action estoppel.

Issue estoppel is different and the court may in some cases allow an issue which was dealt with in an earlier action between the parties to be litigated again in a later claim between them.

Arnold v *National Westminster Bank plc*, 1990 – Cause of action and issue estoppel (**33**)

Advantages and drawbacks of case law

The system of judicial precedent has several *advantages*. Up to a point it can claim the *advantage of certainty*, since it is possible to predict the ruling of a court because judicial decisions tend to be consistent. Nevertheless judges have a habit of distinguishing cases on the facts and, as we have seen, avoiding the following of cases in a variety of other ways. This means that the claim to certainty has to be taken with reservations. Another claim put forward in favour of case law is its *power of flexibility and growth*. New decisions are constantly being added as new cases come before the courts. In this way the law tends to keep pace with the times and can adapt itself to changing circumstances. Judicial precedent covers a *wealth of detail*. There is a case in point for every rule, and there is a *practical character* to judicial rulings. Legal rules are made only as the need arises, and the law is not made in advance on the basis of theory. When a case arises, a decision is taken and the ruling is usually recorded, so that when a similar case arises again the law will be there to be applied.

Case law has certain *drawbacks*. These drawbacks are in some cases merely the converse aspects of the advantages. For example, Jeremy Bentham criticised *the principle of the 'law following the event'*, and applied the epithet 'dog's law' to the system. 'It is', he says, 'the judges that make the common law. Do you know how they make it? Just as a man makes laws for his dog. When your dog does something you want to break him of, you wait till he does it then beat him. This is the way you make laws for your dog: this is the way the judges make law for you and me.'

A further criticism is that *the binding force of precedent limits judicial discretion*. It has been said that judges are engaged in 'forging fetters for their own feet'. This can be illustrated by the doctrine of common employment, which was laid down by the House of Lords in *Priestley* v *Fowler* (1837) 3 M & W 1. This doctrine said that if an employee was injured by a fellow employee whilst both were acting within the scope of their employment, their employer was not liable vicariously for that negligence. The rule operated in a most unjust fashion during the period of great industrial development, but it continued to bind judges for over a century until it was finally abolished by the Law Reform (Personal Injuries) Act 1948. All the judges could do in the meantime was to try to limit its scope.

Limiting the scope of a decision may lead to the court's making *illogical distinctions*. Judges and counsel pay attention to differences in cases which are fundamentally similar, in order to uphold the doctrine of precedent and still not feel bound to follow an inconvenient rule. Often these distinctions have real substance, but occasionally they are illogical and serve to complicate the law.

Difficulties of the kind outlined above may not now arise in such an acute form because, as we have seen, the House of Lords is no longer bound by its own decisions, though this tends to detract from the element of certainty.

A further criticism must be noted – that of *bulk and complexity*. The number of reported cases is so large that the law can be ascertained only by searching through a large number of reports. This search has been eased somewhat where case law has been codified by statute in order to produce a rational arrangement. The Bills of Exchange Act 1882, the Sale of Goods Act 1893 (now 1979), and the Law of Property Act 1925 have to a large extent produced order in what might have been called chaos, but case law still tends to develop even around a codifying statute, and its sections soon have to be read in the light of interpretative cases.

Finally, it is a major criticism of our system of case law that only the House of Lords gives the ultimate authoritative judicial ruling on a matter. However, whether this happens depends upon the litigants or, at least, the losing party footing the bill to get to the House of Lords or, increasingly more unlikely these days, legal aid doing so. It would be an improvement if we had a system under which the High Court or Court of Appeal could refer a question of law to the House of Lords at public expense, rather on the lines of Art 177 (now 234) of the EC Treaty which allows reference to the Court of Justice by domestic courts on matters involving Community law.

Precedent in the European Court

In line with the normal Continental approach, there is no doctrine of binding precedent, though the body of decisions which the court is making in the interpretation of the Treaty are having strong persuasive influence. These decisions are cited before the court in argument and are also quoted in judgments. In terms of the interpretation of legislation, the European Court has much broader powers than those which English courts have. There is no question of being restricted, for example, to the words of the Treaty or regulations. The court may consider the reasons for enactment and the general objectives and policy of the Communities. It can have regard to *travaux préparatoires*, i.e. statements and publications made prior to enactment and *doctrine*, i.e. views of learned writers as to what the law should be.

The European Union

On 1 January 1973 the United Kingdom became a member of the European Community (now the European Union) and in consequence subject to an additional source of law.

Membership of the EU

Twenty-five countries are now members of the European Union. They are: France, Germany, Italy, Belgium, the Netherlands, Luxembourg, the United Kingdom, the Republic of Ireland, Denmark, Greece, Spain, Portugal, Sweden, Finland, Austria, Cyprus, the Czech Republic, Estonia, Hungary, Latvia, Lithuania, Malta, Poland, Slovenia and Slovakia. Bulgaria and Romania plan to join in 2007 and Turkey has applied to join.

Union or Community?

The parts of the European co-operation arrangements include:

(a) The European Community (economic co-operation: the old EEC);
(b) The European Atomic Energy Community (EURATOM);
(c) The European Coal and Steel Community (ECSC); and
(d) The Maastricht areas referred to above.

As we have seen, when referring to all of them the correct legal reference is to the European Union and the same is true when referring to the Maastricht areas of co-operation. Otherwise, the correct reference is to the European Community, which took over from the earlier EEC, or to EURATOM or ECSC as the context requires.

The European Court has no automatic jurisdiction in the Maastricht areas and so rightly continues to call itself the Court of Justice of the European Communities, although confusingly the Council of Ministers calls itself the Council of the European Union, even when passing EC legislation!

The expressions 'Community' and 'Union' are used indiscriminately in this book as they are in real life and if the reader is more at home with 'Union' then there is no reason why that expression should not be used throughout.

The European Economic Area (EEA) Agreement came into force on 1 January 1994. It extends the EC's Single Market to Austria, Finland, Iceland, Norway and Sweden. Some 1,500 EC measures, such as the rules on competition, will apply to these countries and, as we have noted, Austria, Finland and Sweden now have full membership of the EU, while Norway has decided not to join. The EEA was implemented in the UK by the European Economic Area Act 1993.

The institutions of the Union

The five basic institutions of the Union are:

- the Parliament
- the Council
- the Commission
- the Court of Justice
- the Court of First Instance.

Consideration has already been given to the courts listed above.

The Parliament

This is a large assembly that currently has 732 members directly elected by their member states. *It is important to note that it is not the legislature of the Union.* In this sense it differs from Parliaments modelled on the Westminster Parliament. However, the powers of the Parliament have been extended by the Single European Act of 1986 and the Treaty on European Union

1992 (the Maastricht Treaty). These extensions have in some ways remedied the defect that critics had of the Parliament in that *the unelected Council is the primary legislature*.

The Treaty of Amsterdam extended its powers in the field of co-decision (see below). The Parliament now has a legislative role at a number of levels as follows.

Advisory and consultative. This procedure represents the only original involvement of the Parliament in legislation. Under this procedure the Commission puts forward proposals to the Council for consideration. At this stage the Parliament has a right to be *consulted* and can give *an opinion*. The final decision is taken by the Council. This procedure is retained for matters concerned with the Common Agricultural Policy.

Co-operation. Under this procedure the Parliament has the opportunity to express an opinion and propose amendments:

■ when a proposal of the Commission is submitted to the Council; and
■ when the Council has considered the opinion of the Parliament and reached what is called a 'Common Position'. The procedure is a right to influence but not veto. The procedure is restricted to matters concerning economic and monetary union.

Co-decision. This procedure is the same as the co-operation procedure to the point where a Common Position is reached. After that it changes and the Parliament may approve the Common Position in which case the Council will adopt it. In the case of rejection, the matter is referred to a *Conciliation Committee* of 12 persons from the Council and 12 MEPs charged to reach an agreement acceptable to both sides. If there is no such agreement or the agreement is unacceptable to the Parliament, the proposal lapses. The Parliament may propose amendments to the Common Position, and then:

■ the Council and the Commission will consider the amendments;
■ the Council may, if it approves all the amendments, adopt the measure as amended; or
■ find the amendments or some of them unacceptable (in this case the Conciliation Committee is convened; if a joint approach is agreed between the two sides of the Committee, the measure must be adopted within six weeks by the Council and Parliament);
■ if the Committee cannot agree, the proposal will lapse, though it could be adopted unilaterally by the Council subject in this case to a power of veto in the Parliament.

This procedure applies to the majority of single-market proposals, culture and public health and importantly consumer protection.

Assent. The assent procedure applies in regard to applications for membership of the Union and agreements between the Union and other states, or international organisations. The Council may only adopt a proposal by the Commission through this procedure by obtaining the formal assent of the Parliament.

The Council

If the Union can be said to have a legislature this is it. It is a body composed of one minister to represent each member state. These persons change in accordance with the subject under discussion. For example agricultural ministers attend when agricultural policies are involved and finance ministers where economic issues are under discussion or review. This body is not to be confused with the European Council which meets twice a year at least with the Commission President, foreign ministers and a Commissioner.

The main function of the Council is to ensure that the treaty objectives are attained. It acts normally on a proposal from the Commission. Because it is not a permanent body the day-to-day work of looking into Commission proposals is delegated to COREPER (the

Committee of Permanent Representatives) that consists of more junior representatives of the member states.

The Commission

The Commission is the central administrative and policy making body of the Union. It consists of 25 members one for each member state. The nominee commissioners are approved by the Parliament and one of them acts as President.

Functions. The Commission initiates legislation and the Council legislates following proposals by the Commission. The Council can, however, ask the Commission to undertake research and submit proposals in the relevant area. It is a very powerful body in view of this power of initiation of proposals. The Commission also enforces the treaty obligations of the member states and can take such a state before the Court of Justice if it fails to comply. It can also impose penalties and fines on those in breach of competition law who ignore decisions against them. The Commission has extensive powers of investigation in the furtherance of its functions.

The Executive of the Commission executes the decisions of the Commission. In regard to the external policies of the Union the Commission is the negotiator. The agreements that it makes are concluded by the Council after consultation with the Parliament if this is a treaty requirement.

Types of Union law

Primary legislation: the Treaty of Rome

The Treaty of Rome (as amended) contains primary legislation in the following areas:

- free movement of goods (Arts 30–31);
- agriculture (Arts 32–38);
- free movement of persons, services and capital (Arts 39–60);
- visas, asylum, immigration (Arts 61–69);
- transport (Arts 70–80);
- common rules on competition, taxation and approximation of laws (Arts 81–97);
- economic and monetary policy (Arts 98–124);
- employment (Arts 125–130);
- common commercial policy (Arts 131–134);
- customs co-operation (Art 135);
- social policy, education, vocational training and youth (Arts 136–150);
- culture (Art 151);
- public health (Art 152);
- consumer protection (Art 153);
- trans-European networks (Arts 154–156);
- industry (Art 157);
- economic and social cohesion (Arts 158–162);
- research and technological development (Arts 163–173);
- environment (Arts 174–176);
- development co-operation (Arts 177–181).

Although we refer to the above as 'legislation', the relevant Articles are, in the main, defining legislative objectives and require implementing secondary legislation to firm up the objectives. This is the task of the Council and the Commission through the exercise of their powers under the treaty.

Secondary legislation

This is as follows:

Regulations

These are generally applicable throughout the Union so that they may give rise to rights and obligations for states and individuals without the need for further national legislation. Regulations in the areas of agriculture and transport are examples of this type of legislation.

Directives

These are binding in terms of the result to be achieved, e.g. reform of company law. However, the member states must enact national laws to achieve the required effect. The UK's response to many Directives on company law is included in the Companies Act 1985.

Decisions

These are of more particular application and also are immediately operative. Decisions may be addressed to a state or individual or a corporation and an example would be a Commission ruling that a company was adopting restrictive practices in its operations within the Union contrary to Arts 81/82 of the treaty (see Chapter 16). Such a Decision could also impose a fine. Decisions have the force of law but affect the recipient only.

Union law: direct effect in the UK

The position is as follows:

Primary law (or legislation)

This is law contained in treaty Articles. If they are sufficiently precise, they are effective in the UK. They then have what is known as *vertical effect*, i.e. they create rights against 'emanations of the state', e.g. government departments, local authorities and hospital trusts. They also have *horizontal effect* in that rights are created in individuals against other individuals and organisations in the private sector of industry. An example is provided by Art 141 on equal pay that is directly applicable in a vertical and horizontal sense in the UK.

If an Article is not sufficiently precise to be enforced as such it is not directly applicable at all in the UK and requires national legislation to implement it.

Secondary legislation

Here the position is as follows:

Regulations. These are usually directly applicable with vertical and horizontal effect.

Directives. These are not directly applicable in that normally the member state has to pass legislation to implement them. If there is no such implementation after the expiry of the deadline set to member states for implementation, a Directive can be directly applicable if it is sufficiently precise but only in a vertical sense in creating rights against emanations of the state.

Decisions. These are binding upon the person or organisation to which they are addressed.

A EU constitution

In December 2000 there was a meeting of heads of state and government at Nice, where it was concluded that enlargement of the EU would require constitutional reform. In 2001 the European Council adopted a Declaration on the Future of the European Union. This led to the setting up of a European Convention to develop a draft treaty to establish a Constitution for Europe. The draft constitution was published in full in 2003.

This draft is not, at the present, a profitable area for study. It requires approval by all member states and has been turned down by France and the Netherlands. Whether in these circumstances there will be a referendum in the UK remains to be seen, although it would appear to have only a marginal chance of success.

Those who wish to pursue this matter further should access **http://europa.eu.int.** This is Europa, the EU's gateway, which carries most of the relevant sites.

Application of EC law in UK cases

Section 3 of the European Communities Act 1972 requires our courts to take note of the provisions of the EC Treaty and also the decisions of the European Court.

Although arguments about the subject rage on, there can be little doubt now that EC law is supreme and that the sovereignty of the UK Parliament is thereby reduced.

> *Factortame Ltd* v *Secretary of State for Transport (No 2)*, 1991 – Supremacy of EC law (**34**)

Monetary union – impact of the euro

Our concern is purely that of the effect of the introduction of the euro on UK law, in particular, on business law. The arrival of the euro on 1 January 1999 (though not in the UK) could affect contracts in terms that they might be frustrated by impossibility of performance and so discharged (see further Chapter 17). This could occur where payment under the contract is required to be, say, in French francs and yet this has become impossible by the eventual takeover of this and other currencies by the euro, payment in French francs being no longer possible. The Maastricht Treaty introduced the solution by providing that, in the absence of a contrary intention by the parties, the introduction of the euro will not:

- affect any term of the contract;
- discharge or excuse performance under any contract; or
- on its own give any party the right unilaterally to alter or terminate any contract.

These matters will be considered as necessary in relevant parts of the text.

Law reform

It should be noted that a number of official bodies exist to consider and make proposals for *law reform*, and the work of these bodies can have a considerable influence on the development of statute law. The most important of these bodies is the *Law Commission*, which was set up by the Law Commissions Act 1965. Section 1 of the Act establishes the Commission to promote the reform of English law and deals with the constitution of the Commission. The Lord Chancellor appoints the members of the Commission, on a full-time basis, from among persons holding judicial office, experienced barristers and solicitors and university teachers of law. Section 3 states the duty of the Commission to be to keep under review the whole of English law with a view to its systematic development and reform, including the codification of such law, the elimination of anomalies, the repeal of obsolete enactments and generally the simplification and modernisation of the law. The programme of the Law Commission includes the codification of the law of contract. In this connection, and of major importance to business is the Contracts (Rights of Third Parties) Act 1999, which stems from Law Commission Report No 242 and provides for major and far-reaching changes in the privity of contract rule (see further Chapter 10).

In arriving at its programme, the Commission consults with the chairmen of the Home Secretary's Criminal Law Revision Committee and the Lord Chancellor's Law Reform Committee, which are bodies set up on a part-time basis to consider specific matters of law reform which he may refer to them in the fields of criminal and civil law respectively. The work of the Commission and the Committees may be regarded as a source of law in that it is a *historical source* of the law contained in the statute which implements its proposals. Thus, the proposals of the Law Commission may be regarded as a historical source of the Criminal Law Act 1967.

There is also the *Civil Justice Council* set up under s 6 of the Civil Procedure Act 1997. Under s 6(2) it must include members of the judiciary appointed by the Lord Chief Justice after consultation with the Lord Chancellor, and the legal professions, together with civil servants concerned with court administration and persons with experience in and knowledge of consumer affairs and the lay advice sector, e.g. Citizens' Advice Bureaux and representatives of employers and employees and business generally appointed by the Lord Chancellor after consultation with the Lord Chief Justice. Its functions are set out in s 6(3) as follows:

- keeping the civil justice system under review;
- considering how to make the civil justice system more accessible, fair and efficient;
- advising the Lord Chancellor and the Lord Chief Justice and the judiciary on the development of the civil justice system;
- referring proposals for changes in the civil justice system to the Lord Chancellor and the Lord Chief Justice and the Civil Procedure Rules committee; and
- making proposals for research.

8

PERSONS AND THE CROWN

In law a *person* possesses certain rights and owes certain duties. There are two categories of persons as follows:

(a) Natural persons. These are human beings who are referred to as natural persons. An adult human being has in general terms a full range of rights and duties. However, even in regard to human beings, the law distinguishes between certain classes and gives to them a *status* which may carry with it a more limited set of rights and duties than are given to the normal adult. These classes include minors, persons of unsound mind, bankrupts and aliens, and the significance of belonging to these categories will be more fully examined in connection with the chapters on substantive law, such as contract, tort and crime. Non-human creatures are not legal persons and do not have the full range of rights and duties which a human being acquires at birth. However, animals may be protected by the law for certain purposes, e.g. conservation (see Wildlife and Countryside Act 1981).

(b) Juristic persons. Legal personality is not restricted to human beings. In fact various bodies and associations of persons can, by forming a corporation to carry out their functions, create an organisation with a range of rights and duties not dissimilar to many of those possessed by human beings. In English law such corporations are formed by charter, statute or registration under the Companies Act 2006 or previous Acts; there is also the common law concept of the corporation sole.

Natural persons

Here we shall consider some of the more important general principles of law relating to minors, persons of unsound mind, bankrupts and aliens together with the rules governing a natural person's domicile and nationality and the general principles of law preventing discrimination against natural persons.

Minors

The Family Law Reform Act 1969, s 1(1) reduced the age of majority from 21 to 18 years. There is also a provision in the Act which states that a person attains a particular age, i.e. not merely the age of majority, at the first moment of the relevant birthday, though this rule is subject to any contrary provision in any instrument (i.e. a deed) or statute (s 9).

Section 1(2) provides that the age of 18 is to be substituted for 21 wherever there is a reference to 'full age', 'infancy', 'minor', 'minority' in:

(*a*) any statutory provision made *before or after* 1 January 1970;
(*b*) any deed, will or other instrument made *on or after* that date.

This sub-section draws a distinction between statutory provisions and private dispositions. In the case of the former the new age of 18 is substituted. Thus, in s 164 of the Law of Property Act 1925 which uses the word 'minority' to deal with restrictions on the accumulation of income in a trust as where the income is reinvested and not given to a beneficiary, references to 'minority' will be construed as applying to persons under 18 years of age. However, in the case of private dispositions such as deeds, wills and settlements the Act does not apply retrospectively. Accordingly, if in a deed made before 1 January 1970 a person X (say, a grandchild of the maker of the deed) is to take property 'on attaining his majority', he will take it at age 21 years. If the deed was on or after 1 January 1970, he would take it at 18 years. The reason for this rule is that where persons in the past have arranged their affairs in reliance on the law as it stood, it would be unjust to interfere. The following general matters relating to minors can be considered at this point.

(*a*) A minor cannot contract a valid marriage under the age of 16 years and requires the consent of his parents or if the parents are divorced or separated, the one with custody, or if one parent is dead, the survivor (or on failure that of a magistrates' court) to marry under 18 years of age.
(*b*) A person under 18 years cannot vote at elections and must be 21 before he can sit in Parliament or be a member of the council of a local authority.
(*c*) With regard to civil litigation, a minor sues through a 'litigation friend', i.e. an adult who is liable for the costs (if any) awarded against the minor in the action, though the minor must indemnify him. A minor defends an action through a 'litigation friend' who is not liable for costs. The minor's father or mother often acts as 'litigation friend'.
(*d*) A person of 16 or over can give valid consent to medical treatment and it is not necessary as before to obtain the consent of a parent or guardian (Family Law Reform Act 1969, s 8). However, the court can override a minor's refusal to consent to medical treatment (*Re W* (1992) 142 NIJ 1124).
(*e*) The Tattooing of Minors Act 1969 makes it an offence, punishable by fine, for a person other than a duly qualified medical practitioner to tattoo a person under the age of 18. The person charged with the offence will have a defence if he can show that at the time he had reasonable cause to believe that the person tattooed was 18 years of age or over.

The position in contract, tort and criminal law is set out in Chapters 11, 20 and 25 respectively.

The protection of children

The Children Act 1989 introduced a new regime to ensure the safety and protection of children. Of major importance are two orders provided for by Part V of the Act. The first is an emergency protection order.

Under s 44 an emergency protection order will only be made if the court which is asked to grant it is satisfied that:

(*a*) there is reasonable cause to believe that the child is likely to suffer significant harm; or
(*b*) enquiries are being made by the relevant local authority and these are being frustrated by denial of access to the child where such access is urgently required; or
(*c*) the applicant is an authorised person such as a local authority or the National Society for the Prevention of Cruelty to Children and the applicant has reasonable cause to suspect that a child is suffering or likely to suffer significant harm and the enquiries of the authorised person are being frustrated by lack of access.

It will be seen that an emergency protection order will be granted only on the basis of hard evidence.

However, s 43 provides for child assessment orders and these allow a local authority or authorised person to apply to the court to take the child away from home, if necessary, for assessment in cases which are not necessarily emergencies. Here the court must be satisfied that the child is suffering or is likely to suffer 'significant harm' and that an assessment is needed which would not otherwise be likely to take place. This order is not designed for absolute emergencies but could be asked for following a case conference of interested professionals which had considered a case where a child had, e.g., suddenly ceased to attend a day nursery in suspicious circumstances or where neighbours had reported repeated screaming.

Also of importance is the concept of 'parental responsibility' introduced by ss 2, 3 and 12 of the 1989 Act. The court may make a parental responsibility order. This involves maintenance of the child and seeing to its education and providing accommodation, medical attention and so on. This is no longer a matter for the natural parents. Parental responsibility can now be held by others, e.g. grandparents and even the local authority. It can be held by several people concurrently. Every person who has parental responsibility can act alone in most cases to ensure the welfare of the child. In many cases, therefore, there will be a small army of persons including relatives and the local authority who will be able to intervene legally for a parental responsibility order if the natural parents are found wanting in terms, e.g., of the welfare of the child.

The 1989 Act also provides for the making of *contact orders*. Where the parents of a child are divorced or separated, an application may be made for a contact order (normally by the man) where access cannot be achieved by arrangement between the parents. The court will refuse such an order to prevent direct contact between a father and his child where the father is, e.g., violent and/or has an alcohol problem.

The effect of adoption

The material that follows is not concerned with the procedure for adoption but only with the effects of adoption on the individual adopted in the law once adoption has taken place.

An adopted person is to be treated in law as if born as the legitimate child of the adopters or adopter whether the adopters or adopter are married or unmarried (s 67 Adoption and Children Act 2002). This principle applies in interpreting wills, settlements made during lifetime and intestacies. Where questions of seniority arise, ss 69 and 70 of the 2002 Act provide that the adopted child is deemed to have been born on the date of the adoption and if adoptive parents adopt two or more children on the same day they are regarded as born on that day in the order of the actual dates of their births. For example, we may take a gift in the will of a testator 'to the eldest son of X'. Suppose that X had a natural child (A) in 1975 and in 1976 adopted a child (B) then aged 10, it appears that the natural child (A) takes the gift although B is biologically the elder.

However, the above rules do not affect a document where there is reference to the age of a child (s 69 of the 2002 Act).

Thus, if a testator gave his estate 'to the children of X at 25', it is clear that an adopted child would take the gift when he in fact attained that age and not 25 years after his adoption. It also seems that a gift to 'the first son of X to attain 25' would go to an adoptive child if he attained 25 before X's natural born children, although, as we have seen, he would not take as X's 'eldest son' in the example given above.

Adopted persons may, on reaching the age of 18, have a copy of their birth certificate as of right and not as formerly only by leave of the court (s 60 Adoption and Children Act 2002).

Under s 63 of the 2002 Act when information such as a birth certificate is supplied the registration authorities must tell the applicant that counselling services are available and from whom, e.g. a local authority. The Registrar must also maintain a register of relatives of adopted persons who wish to make contact. A person supplied with information about his natural parents may have access to this register if he wishes.

Persons suffering from mental disorder

We shall be giving fuller consideration to the position of mentally disordered persons in contract, tort and crime in the chapters which follow. However, the following general points can be noted now.

If a person suffering from mental disorder goes through a ceremony of marriage but cannot understand the nature of marriage, i.e. the responsibilities and change of status involved, the marriage will be void.

In connection with mental disorder, it is of interest to note the existence of the Court of Protection which under the Mental Capacity Act 2005 is concerned with proper management of a mental patient's property. The court operates through deputies who are, in many cases, close relatives of the patient. The court can administer the patient's property and make a will for the patient or make lifetime gifts of that property on the application of the patient's deputy.

Undischarged bankrupts

Bankruptcy procedure is set out in the Insolvency Act 1986. Bankruptcy proceedings which involve asking the court to make a bankruptcy order may be taken against a debtor by his creditor(s). The debtor's affairs will then be taken over by an insolvency practitioner who is generally an accountant in practice though in the case of many bankruptcies the estate is too small for this and a state official called the Official Receiver (OR) does the work. A petition to the court for a bankruptcy order is most usually presented by a creditor who must be owed £750 or more. Two or more creditors (none of whom is owed as much as £750) may present a joint petition if they are together owed £750 or more by the debtor as where creditor A is owed £280 and creditor B is owed £600.

As regards the disabilities of an undischarged bankrupt, he is disqualified from being an MP and cannot be a member of a local authority council. This, however, applies under ss 265–267 of the Insolvency Act 1986 (as amended) only to those bankrupts who are the subject of a bankruptcy restriction order (BRO). These are made by the court and are intended for 'culpable bankrupts', such as those who have not kept proper accounting and other business records. The restrictions also apply to those culpable bankrupts who have not waited for the court to make a BRO but have offered a BRO to the Secretary of State who has accepted the undertaking. Under s 360 of the 1986 Act he is guilty of an offence punishable by a maximum of two years' imprisonment and/or an unlimited fine if either alone or jointly with another person he obtains credit of £500 or more unless he tells the person giving it that he is an undischarged bankrupt – in general he will not then get the credit. Under s 11 of the Company Directors Disqualification Act 1986 it is an offence for an undischarged bankrupt to act as a company director or to promote or form or manage a company without the permission of the court which made the bankruptcy order.

The position is as follows.

■ there is automatic discharge from bankruptcy on the 12-month anniversary of the bankruptcy order. This will be the end of the bankruptcy disabilities, e.g. there is no credit restriction;

- for the culpable bankrupt there will normally be a BRO in place that imposes such restrictions as are contained in the order, e.g. the credit restriction (the length of a BRO can be any period between two and 15 years);
- many non-culpable bankrupts may be discharged even sooner than the 12-month period following a small investigation by the Official Receiver following which the OR may file a certificate in court discharging the bankrupt.

Any money owed by the debtor which has not been paid at the date of discharge is no longer payable by the debtor, who can then go back into business legally free of his or her old debts and with no restriction on credit. This does not apply where there is a BRO.

However, damages awarded against all bankrupts for personal injury caused by negligence or nuisance, money payable under maintenance and other matrimonial orders, and fines and debts incurred by fraud are not discharged and remain payable, as does money due under the Child Support Act 1991.

Domicile – generally

The basis of jurisdiction and the law to be applied in many matters coming before English courts, e.g. wills, matrimonial causes and taxation, may depend on the domicile of the parties. A person's domicile is the country which he regards as his permanent home, and thus contains a dual element of actual residence in a country and the intention of remaining there. Where a country has within its national boundaries several jurisdictions, the person's domicile must be determined with reference to a particular jurisdiction, e.g., there is no such thing as domicile in the United States of America, though a person may be domiciled in a particular state. England and Wales, Scotland, Northern Ireland, the Channel Islands, and the Isle of Man are distinct jurisdictions within the British Isles. A person must always have a domicile, and he can only have one domicile at a time. It should be noted that the concepts of domicile and nationality are, as appropriate, applied to corporate bodies.

IRC v *Bullock*, 1976 – Domicile and taxation (**35**)

Domicile of origin

The domicile of origin of a child is that of its father at the date of the child's birth if the father is alive at that date and is married to the child's mother, i.e. if the child is legitimate (for example, the Nova Scotia domicile of Mr Bullock in *IRC* v *Bullock* (1976)). If the child is illegitimate or, though legitimate, the father is not alive when it is born, it takes its domicile of origin from that of its mother at the date of the child's birth. Foundlings take their domicile of origin from the place where they were found.

Dependent domicile

The concept of dependent domicile applies as follows:

Minors (i.e. persons under the age of 18 years)

(a) **At common law.** The domicile of a legitimate, legitimated or adopted child is dependent on, and changes with, that of its father or adoptive father, and after the father's death with that of its mother or adoptive mother. The domicile of an illegitimate child depends on, and changes with, that of its mother.

(b) Under statute. Sections 3 and 4 of the Domicile and Matrimonial Proceedings Act 1973 are concerned with the domicile of minors. Where previously the domicile of a minor had to follow that of his father until the age of majority, a minor can under the Act acquire an independent domicile at the age of 16, or under that age if he marries before then. This latter principle cannot, of course, apply to any marriages in this country, but it may apply to those in this country, e.g. Nigerians, who may be married under 16 according to their domiciliary law. The provision referred to above, which is in s 3 of the Act, avoids the previous possibility of a father leaving this country and establishing a domicile elsewhere, thus changing the domicile of his minor son who had remained in this country. Furthermore, it had always been uncertain whether, after the divorce of the parents, a child's domicile continued to follow his father's or followed that of his mother with whom the child was living. Now s 4(2) of the 1973 Act provides that the child's domicile where he is under 16 or has not set up an independent domicile and his father and mother are alive but living apart shall be that of his mother if:

(*a*) he then has his home with her and has no home with his father; or

(*b*) he has at any time had her domicile by virtue of (*a*) above and has not since had a home with his father.

The section also deals with other possible situations: for example, where the mother is dead and the child has not returned to his father, he will keep the domicile he acquired under s 4(2).

Married women

By s 1 of the Domicile and Matrimonial Proceedings Act 1973, the domicile of a married woman is not bound to be determined by that of her husband, as was the case at common law. She is capable of acquiring a separate domicile in exactly the same manner as her husband. By s 1(2) of the 1973 Act a married woman is treated as retaining the domicile of her husband (as a domicile of choice if it is not one of origin) at the coming into force of the Act unless and until it is changed in accordance with common law rules for determining such change.

Certain consequences regarding jurisdiction in divorce proceedings follow from the general principles enacted by the above section. As a wife can now acquire a separate domicile from that of her husband, jurisdiction is now based upon the domicile of either party in England and Wales at the time of the proceedings or on the ground that either party was habitually resident in those countries for one year before the proceedings commenced (but see below). The court has power to stay proceedings where courts in two countries have jurisdiction. This would prevent, for example, divorce proceedings being taken in an English court and a Scottish court contemporaneously as where the husband had an English domicile but his wife had acquired one in Scotland.

The rules on jurisdiction in matrimonial cases set out above are now governed by the European Communities (Matrimonial Jurisdiction and Judgments) Regulations 2001. Jurisdiction in matrimonial suits is now available where:

- both parties are habitually resident here (period irrelevant);
- both parties were last habitually resident here and one still is (period irrelevant);
- the respondent is habitually resident here (period irrelevant);
- the petitioner is resident here and has been for at least 12 months;
- the petitioner is domiciled here and has resided here for at least six months; or
- both parties are domiciled here (no matter where they may reside).

On the matter of 'habitual residence', the High Court ruled in *Ikimi v Ikimi (Divorce: Habitual Residence)* [2001] 1 FLR 913 that where a person had two residences and occupied both from time to time even though for only short periods in one of them that person could be regarded as 'habitually resident' in both.

Domicile of choice

A person, other than a minor under 16, can change his domicile of his own volition. To do so he must be in the new country, and have a 'fixed and settled intention' to abandon his domicile of origin or choice, and to settle instead in the new country.

A person retains his domicile of origin until he acquires a domicile of choice, and since a person must always have a domicile, there can be no abandonment of the domicile of origin unless a domicile of choice is acquired instead. However, having acquired a domicile of choice, a person who abandons it without acquiring a fresh domicile of choice, reverts to his domicile of origin.

The country in which a person resides is on the face of it the country of his domicile. Where it is claimed that a domicile of origin has been changed for one of choice, the onus of proof is on the party claiming that such a change has taken place. Examples of evidence which suggest a change of domicile are oral or written declarations to this effect, letters, wills as in *IRC* v *Bullock*, the adoption of a new name, as where a German living in England changes his name to Richmond from Reichman, an application for naturalisation, the purchase of land, or a grave, or of a home or a business in the new country. It was decided in *Plummer* v *IRC* [1988] 1 All ER 97 that it is not enough merely to express an intention eventually to live and work in the new country. Furthermore, it was held in *Cramer* v *Cramer* [1987] 1 FLR 116 that domicile is not established by an *intention to marry* a person resident in the new country at some time in the future even where the intention to marry is reciprocated by the other party.

> *Tee* v *Tee*, 1973 – Reverting to domicile of origin (**36**)
> *Steiner* v *IRC*, 1973 – Evidence of change of domicile (**37**)

Residence

The residence of a person is important for certain purposes, e.g. liability for income tax, and a person who is not domiciled in the UK may nevertheless be liable to UK tax if he is regarded as resident here in the year of assessment. The matter is of considerable importance to international high-earners since income tax is charged broadly on the world income of UK residents. Non-residents are liable to UK tax only on income that arises in the UK. Furthermore, the jurisdiction of magistrates in matrimonial matters is based on the residence of the parties and not their domicile, as is the right to vote in a particular constituency at an election under s 1(1) of the Representation of the People Act 1983. On the other hand, the jurisdiction of the High Court in matrimonial proceedings is based either on domicile or habitual residence for one year (Domicile and Matrimonial Proceedings Act 1973, s 5). Domicile must, therefore, be distinguished from residence.

The term residence imports a certain degree of permanence, and must not be casual or merely undertaken as a traveller. In *Fox* v *Stirk* [1970] 3 All ER 7, the Court of Appeal decided that two undergraduates were resident at their universities and entitled to have their names on the electoral register for that constituency although their parental homes were elsewhere. On the other hand, in *Scott* v *Phillips* 1973 SLT (Notes) 75 it was held that the claimant, who lived mainly at his house in Inveresk but had a cottage on lease in Berwickshire in which he spent $3^1/_2$ months each year, was not resident in Berwickshire and therefore not entitled to have his name included on the electoral roll for that county. Obviously, residence can be changed at any time by moving to a new home. Temporary absences abroad while on holiday or on business do not create a gap in the period of residence, which is determined on the facts of the case.

Racial and Religious Hatred Act 2006

The Public Order Act 1986 (see below) is amended by the Racial and Religious Hatred Act 2006 to create offences which involve stirring up hatred on racial and/or religious grounds. The offences cover: use of words or behaviour or display of written material; publishing or distributing written material; the public performance of a play; distributing, showing or playing a recording; broadcasting programmmes; and possession of inflammatory material. There are powers of entry to property and seizure of material. The Act makes clear that freedom of speech is protected in terms of discussion and also, for example, criticism. The police have powers of arrest but there is no power for a citizen's arrest. The Act does not apply to reports of parliamentary or judicial proceedings. Offences are triable either way and a conviction on indictment attracts a penalty of a maximum of seven years' imprisonment or an unlimited fine or both. On conviction before magistrates the maximum imprisonment is six months and/or a fine of up to £5,000. The bringing of proceedings requires the consent of the Attorney-General.

Discrimination

We shall now consider the rules of law which are designed to prevent discrimination against natural persons. Discrimination in employment is dealt with in Chapter 19.

Racial discrimination

The Race Relations Act 1976 and the Public Order Act 1986 are designed to deal with discrimination on racial grounds and with relations between different racial groups. It should be noted before considering the main provisions of the Acts that under s 72 of the 1976 Act a term in a contract which purports to exclude or limit any provisions of that Act is unenforceable by any person in whose favour the term would operate.

The Race Relations Act 1976

Discrimination to which the Act applies

Section 1 provides that it is *direct discrimination* to treat a person less favourably on racial grounds and *indirect discrimination* where there is some requirement or condition, e.g. of employment, which, although it applies to all potential employees, is discriminatory since a smaller proportion (or none) of black applicants can comply with it than white. Thus a rule insisting that bus conductors wear company caps could be *indirect discrimination* against Sikh applicants, who were held to be a protected ethnic group by the House of Lords in *Mandla v Dowell Lee* [1983] 1 All ER 1062.

Section 2 deals with *discrimination by way of victimisation* of a person who has, for example, brought or given evidence in proceedings under the Act against a discriminator or alleged discriminator. Thus if A brings proceedings against his employer, B, for alleged discrimination and as a consequence A's landlord, C, will not allow A to use a goods lift provided for common use in the block of flats where A lives, then C could be guilty of victimisation under s 2. Under s 3, 'racial grounds' means colour, race, nationality, or ethnic or national origins, and 'racial group' means a group of persons defined by reference to colour, race, nationality, or ethnic or national origin.

For example in *Commission for Racial Equality* v *Dutton* (1988) *The Times*, 29 July, the Court of Appeal held that gypsies were a racial group for the purposes of the Act. They were not, however, synonymous with 'travellers' so that a notice in a public house saying 'sorry, no travellers' did not directly discriminate against them. It did, however, indirectly discriminate against them. However, in *Crown Suppliers (PSA)* v *Dawkins* [1993] IRLR 284, the Court of Appeal decided that Rastafarians are not a group defined by ethnic origin within the meaning of the 1976 Act. Therefore, a van driver who was turned down for a job because he would not cut his hair had not been discriminated against. Rastafarians were a religious sect not an ethnic group. The Act still permits discrimination on grounds of religious belief unless that constitutes racial discrimination, as it would if the religion was Jewish but not if it was Catholic or Protestant since the last two named are not matters of race.

As regards *harassment*, the Race Relations Act 1976 did not contain an express definition of harassment. Case law has found a remedy for harassment by regarding it as a 'detriment' within the terms of the 1976 Act. The Race Relations Act 1976 (Amendment) Regulations 2003 introduce a new test for racial harassment that is applied also to harassment on the grounds of sexual orientation or religion or belief and is applied to disability discrimination from 1 October 2004. For these purposes, harassment is defined as occurring where – on grounds of race or ethnic or national origins or sexual orientation or religion or belief or for a reason that relates to a person's disability **A** engages in unwanted conduct which has the purpose of:

- violating **B**'s dignity; or
- creating an intimidating, hostile, degrading, humiliating or offensive environment for **B**.

The conduct is deemed to have the required effect if having regard to all the circumstances including, in particular, the perception of **B** it should reasonably be considered as having that effect.

Areas of racial discrimination not relating directly to the contract of employment appear below.

Partnerships

Section 10 of the 1976 Act extends protection against discrimination to partnerships as regards failure to offer a partnership or the terms on which it is offered, including benefits, facilities and services. Thus discrimination would exist if a partner was refused a cheap loan for house purchase under the firm's scheme or was refused the use of a firm's car. The section applied only to firms of six or more partners. The exemption for partnerships of fewer than six partners was removed by the Race Relations Act 1976 (Amendment) Regulations 2003. The section also covers discrimination in cases where persons are preparing to form themselves into a partnership.

Trade unions, etc.

Section 11 renders unlawful discriminatory practices by trade unions, employers' associations and professional trade bodies. Surprisingly, individual discriminatory action by shop stewards is not covered by the Act. Thus if a shop steward discriminates with the authority of his union, the union will be liable, but if he acts without authority, no one is liable. This appears to be a defect in the Act since it is well known that white organised labour has in several areas of the country held back black development in employment.

Qualifying bodies

Section 12 provides that it is unlawful for an authority or body which can confer an authorisation or qualification which is needed for, or facilitates employment in, a particular trade or profession, e.g. the General Medical Council, to discriminate against a person in terms of conferring that authorisation or qualification.

Discrimination in education

Sections 17–19 make it unlawful for responsible bodies, e.g., governing bodies of educational establishments including both state and private schools, to discriminate on racial grounds as regards, for example, allocation of places or dress. These matters are also often covered by the Convention on Human Rights, which can be used as a basis for complaint to the court (see *R (on the application of SB) v Headteacher and Governors of Denbigh High School* [2005] 3 All ER 396).

Discrimination in provision of goods, facilities or services

Under s 20, discrimination by, for example, shops, hotels, boarding houses and banks is outlawed as is discrimination in clubs which have 25 or more members. When membership of a club reaches 25 or more a licence to serve intoxicating liquor must be sought. Clubs with membership of less than 25 members are excluded and may discriminate.

In terms of public authorities, the 1976 Act was weak because it protected against racial discrimination only in terms of the provision of goods, facilities and services and its application to the police required strengthening. Public authorities not only supply goods, facilities and services, they make *decisions*, e.g. in the field of planning permission where there could be discrimination. The 2000 Act inserts new sections and amends Sch 1 of the 1976 Act to achieve the wider coverage. A police authority is covered and chief officers of police are made vicariously liable (see Chapter 20) for acts of racial discrimination by police officers. Direct and indirect discrimination is covered. The making of Orders by the UK and Scottish Parliaments is covered as is the Welsh Assembly and the enforcement agencies such as Customs and Excise, which are now on the same footing as a bank or building society.

Discrimination in the disposal or management of premises

Section 21 states that discrimination on racial grounds by a seller of property in terms of the buyer or by, say, a brewery in terms of who shall manage a public house, is unlawful. The section does not apply to owner-occupiers of houses who sell the property without employing an estate agent or advertising it for sale (s 21(3)). There is also an exemption for the letting of accommodation in premises where the occupier or a near relative of his resides and intends to continue to reside on the premises which are 'small premises' under s 22(2), e.g. where there is not room for more than six persons in addition to the occupier and members of his household. Section 23 provides for exemptions allowing discrimination where a person takes into his home and treats as a member of his family a child, an elderly person or a person requiring a special degree of care and attention. Thus discrimination on racial grounds in the choice of foster children is not unlawful. Section 24 provides that where a tenant requires the licence or consent of the landlord to assign or sublet to another person it is unlawful for that licence or consent to be withheld in a discriminatory way, as where a landlord will not allow a tenant to assign to a black tenant.

As we have seen, discrimination in clubs with 25 or more members is unlawful but s 26 provides an exemption for organisations whose main object is to confer benefits on ethnic or national groups and does not exclude others. Thus the London Welsh Club is still a lawful association but must not exclude black Welshmen.

By s 27 the Act applies only to benefits, facilities and services in Great Britain. However, it does extend outside Great Britain in some cases. For example, discrimination in Great Britain in regard to the provision of facilities for travel is unlawful even though the facilities are to be supplied outside Great Britain.

Discrimination in the legal profession

The Race Relations Act 1976 did not make unlawful discrimination on the grounds of race either by or within barristers' chambers or by solicitors in relation to barristers approached to take on cases. The Courts and Legal Services Act 1990 inserts a new section, s 26A, into the 1976 Act making it unlawful for a barrister or a barrister's clerk to discriminate against current or prospective pupils or members of chambers on the grounds of race. It also makes it unlawful to discriminate on the grounds of race in regard to the giving or withholding of instructions to a barrister.

Discriminatory practices

Under s 28 there may be a discriminatory practice, even where there is no victim. Thus a factory which has discriminatory recruiting procedures may be regarded as discriminating even during a recession when there has been no recruitment for some time. However, proceedings under s 28 can be brought only by the Commission for Racial Equality.

Advertisements

Section 29 makes discriminatory advertisements unlawful, as in *Commission for Racial Equality* v *Dutton*, 1988, unless, as in an employment advertisement, there is, for example, a GOQ (genuine occupational qualification), e.g. being Chinese is a GOQ for employment in a Chinese restaurant, but not a take-away.

Instructions, pressure or inducement to discriminate

Under ss 30 and 31 it is unlawful to instruct a person to discriminate or to put pressure on a person to discriminate in a way which the 1976 Act makes *unlawful*. The act must be unlawful so instructions by a landlord to his tenant not to take black foster children would not be unlawful. Under s 32 an employer is vicariously liable (see Chapter 20) together with the offending employee for any act done by the employee in course of employment, whether the act was done with the knowledge or approval of the employer or not. Similarly, principals will be liable for the *authorised* acts of their agents but in neither case does vicarious liability extend to criminal proceedings. An employer (not a principal) is given a defence if he can show that he took such steps as were reasonably practicable to prevent his employee doing discriminatory acts. Under s 33 those who assist others to do unlawful acts are also liable.

> *The Commission for Racial Equality* v *Imperial Society of Teachers of Dancing*,
> 1983 – Inducement to discriminate (**38**)

Charities

Section 34 makes it clear that any provision in an existing or future charitable instrument, e.g. a trust, which confers benefits on persons of a different colour is void. Further, it is unlawful to do any act in Great Britain to give effect to such a provision.

General exceptions

Certain general exceptions from liability are set out in Part IV of the Act. Under s 35 acts done to meet the special needs of racial groups with regard, for example, to education, training and welfare, such as special language training for groups whose first language is not English, are not unlawful. Sections 37 and 38 allow positive discrimination in favour of particular racial groups by training bodies, employers and trade unions, employers' associations, and professional and trade associations, by encouraging members of those groups to take work by giving special talks and guided tours of factories and premises. Under s 39 the selection of sports teams on the basis of nationality, place of birth, and length of residence is exempted from the provisions of the Act. Thus a country may continue to select its football teams from among those born in the country but cannot refuse to select a person otherwise willing and able who was born in the country but of parents born elsewhere.

Equality Act 2006

Before considering the Commission for Racial Equality, it should be appreciated that the Equality Act 2006 creates the Commission for Equality and Human Rights (CEHR) to take over and build on the work of the existing bodies, i.e. the Equal Opportunities Commission (EOC), the Commission for Racial Equality (CRE) and the Disability Rights Commission (DRC). The CEHR will be established in 2007 but the CRE will continue until April 2009, when its functions will also transfer to the CEHR.

The Commission for Racial Equality

Section 43 sets up the Commission (CRE) which is to work towards the elimination of discrimination, to promote equality of opportunity and good relations between different racial groups, and to keep under review the working of the Act. Under s 47 the CRE has issued codes of practice giving guidance on ways of achieving equality of opportunity and eliminating discrimination in the employment field and in housing including rented housing. Sections 48–52 give the CRE power to conduct formal investigations, for example into alleged discriminatory employment practices, in order to carry out its duties. The court may prevent such an investigation going ahead on the grounds, e.g., that the concern to be investigated has not been given an opportunity to make representations of its own position (*R v Commission for Racial Equality, ex parte Prestige Group plc* [1983] IRLR 408).

Section 47 empowers the Commission for Racial Equality to issue *codes of practice* in the field of employment. While such codes are not binding in law, they are taken into account in the decisions of employment tribunals concerned with racial discrimination in employment.

Enforcement

The enforcement provisions which are set out in Part VIII are of two types:

(a) Complaints by an individual who is the subject of unlawful conduct other than 'discriminatory practices', advertising or pressures or instructions to discriminate. In employment cases the complaint goes to an employment tribunal (s 54) (see below). Complaints of discrimination in education and in the provision of goods, facilities and services and in housing may be made to the county court (s 57). Complaints that a responsible body in an educational establishment has discriminated must be notified to the Secretary of State for Education who must be given a maximum of two months to consider the matter before court proceedings can be commenced (s 57(5)). It should be noted that an individual is now given direct access to courts and tribunals in race relations matters; under previous legislation only the Race Relations Board (now abolished) could institute proceedings.

No compensation will be awarded for indirect discrimination on the grounds of race if the defendant proves that he did not *intend* to treat the claimant unfavourably (s 57).

(b) Enforcement by the CRE. This involves: (i) the issuing of a non-discrimination notice (s 58); (ii) proceedings in the county court or employment tribunal where there are discriminatory practices, advertisements or pressures or instructions to discriminate (s 63); (iii) proceedings in the county court for an injunction where there has been persistent discrimination (s 62); (iv) assisting individual complainants in certain matters of principle or complexity or other special considerations (s 66).

It should be noted that a non-discrimination notice will require a person not to commit any further discriminatory acts and, where in order to comply with this it is necessary to change practices or arrangements, to inform the CRE that the changes have been effected and bring these changes to the attention of other persons concerned. There is a right of appeal within six weeks against such a notice to an employment tribunal which may modify or quash the notice (s 59). If an appeal against a notice is dismissed, the notice becomes final and is entered on the CRE's Register of Notices (s 61).

Sex discrimination

The three main Acts of Parliament involved here are the Sex Discrimination Acts 1975 and 1986 and the Equal Pay Act 1970, to which amendments have been made by the Equal Pay (Amendment) Regulations 1983. Some provisions of the above legislation relate to the field of employment and are dealt with in Chapter 19.

Sex Discrimination Act 1975

The form of drafting used in the Race Relations Act 1976 was based on the Sex Discrimination Act 1975, and the reader will recognise many similar features.

Under the Act of 1975 it is unlawful to treat anyone, on the grounds of sex, less favourably than a person of the opposite sex is or would be treated in the same circumstances. Once again, a term in a contract which purports to exclude or limit any provision of the Act is unenforceable by any person in whose favour the term would operate (s 73(3)).

Sex discrimination defined

There are two kinds of discrimination as follows:

(a) **Direct** discrimination which involves, for example, treating a woman less favourably than a man because she is a woman *or because of marital status*.

(b) **Indirect** discrimination which occurs where conditions are applied which favour, quite unjustifiably, one sex more than the other, as where a firm advertises for clerical workers who must be six feet tall.

It should be noted that although the Act is written in terms of discrimination against women, it applies equally to discrimination against men either because they are men *or because of marital status*. Thus in *Jepson and Dyas-Elliott* v *The Labour Party* (1996) 543 IRLB 10 it was held that the Labour Party's policy of shortlisting only women as prospective parliamentary candidates in some constituencies was unlawful direct sex discrimination against two men who but for their sex would have been considered.

Areas of discrimination

Areas of sexual discrimination not relating directly to the contract of employment appear below.

(a) **Partnerships.** The sex discrimination provisions were extended to all partnerships regardless of the number of partners by the Sex Discrimination Act 1986. The provisions cover failure to offer a person a partnership on grounds of sex or to offer it but on worse terms or to refuse benefits or give inferior benefits, facilities and services to a partner on the grounds of sex.

(b) **Trade unions and qualifying bodies.** The provisions relating to sex discrimination are applied as they are for racial discrimination with the necessary changes being made.

(c) **Education.** Co-educational schools, colleges, and universities may not discriminate in the provision of facilities or in their admissions. Thus it would be unlawful to refuse a girl admission to a metalwork class because she is a girl. In addition, the Careers Service must not discriminate in the advice and assistance offered to girls and boys, though single-sex schools are still permissible.

Local education authorities are required to provide secondary education without discriminating on the grounds of sex. In *R* v *Birmingham City Council, ex parte Equal Opportunities Commission* [1989] 1 All ER 769 it appeared that the Council provided considerably fewer grammar school places for girls than for boys. The House of Lords approved a declaration that the Council's arrangements were unlawful.

(d) Housing, goods, facilities and services. In general, no one providing housing, goods, facilities or services to the public may discriminate because of sex. There are some exceptions where discrimination will not be unlawful; these include, for example, situations where it is necessary to preserve decency and privacy, e.g. public lavatories.

Discrimination must not be used in the buying or renting of accommodation and a hotel, boarding house or restaurant may not refuse accommodation or refreshment on the grounds of sex.

In addition, a bank, building society, finance house or other credit business must offer credit, a mortgage or loan on the same terms that it would offer the facilities to someone of the opposite sex.

> *Gill* v *El Vino Co Ltd*, 1983 – Sex discrimination: facilities and services (**39**)
> *Quinn* v *Williams Furniture Ltd*, 1981 – Sex discrimination: credit (**40**)

(e) Advertising. Advertisements with job descriptions such as 'salesgirl, waiter, stewardess, postman' are deemed to discriminate unless they contain an indication that both men and women are eligible, though it should be noted that only the Equal Opportunities Commission (EOC) can bring proceedings in matters to do with advertising.

Victimisation

The provisions here are similar to those set out in the Race Relations Act 1976, so that the law will protect a person if they are victimised for bringing a complaint under the Sex Discrimination Act 1975.

The Equal Opportunities Commission

The Equal Opportunities Commission was set up to ensure effective enforcement of the Sex Discrimination Act and the Equal Pay Act (see Chapter 19) and to promote equal opportunity between the sexes. The Commission has power to hold formal investigations, and if satisfied that practices are unlawful, can issue non-discrimination notices requiring that they cease. When holding a formal investigation, either on its own initiative or because it has been asked to do so by the Secretary of State, the Commission has power to require any person to furnish information and to attend hearings to give evidence.

The Commission has power to help individuals in the preparation and conduct of complaints in both courts and tribunals, and as well as investigating areas of inequality between the sexes, the Commission has a duty to make recommendations to the government about the operation of existing law. It is also empowered to undertake or assist others to undertake research and educational work and generally to advise people as to their rights.

The Race Relations Act 1976 made minor amendments in the Sex Discrimination Act. In particular, the EOC was given power to issue codes of practice giving practical guidance on equality of opportunity and the elimination of discrimination between men and women, i.e. powers matching those given to the CRE. This was achieved by adding s 56A to the Sex Discrimination Act 1975.

Enforcement

The provisions, which are similar to those of the Race Relations Act 1976, are as follows:

(a) Individuals' rights. Complaints in the employment field may be made to employment tribunals (see further Chapter 2).

Complaints in all other fields may be made to a county court and if the court finds in favour of the complainant it may award: (i) an order declaring the rights of the parties as e.g. in *Gill* v *El Vino Co Ltd* (1983) 1 All ER 398 (Case **39**); (ii) an injunction; or (iii) damages which may include loss of earnings and also compensation for injured feelings. The Sex Discrimination and Equal Pay (Miscellaneous Amendments) Regulations 1996 (SI 1996/438) give power to make an award of compensation in cases of unintentional indirect discrimination. This does not apply to race discrimination cases where no such award can be made unless a tribunal is satisfied that the defendant intended the discriminatory consequences of the imposition of the relevant condition or requirement.

(b) The Equal Opportunities Commission. The functions of the EOC in regard to enforcement are as follows:

(i) the Commission may conduct formal investigations into any matter in order to carry out its duties and where it discovers conduct which contravenes the Sex Discrimination Act or the Equal Pay Act it is empowered to issue a non-discrimination notice. The result of issuing such a notice is the same as that under the Race Relations Act 1976;

(ii) the Commission can institute legal proceedings in respect of persistent discrimination, including judicial review (*R* v *Birmingham City Council, ex parte EOC* (1989) (see above);

(iii) the Commission has the sole right to institute legal proceedings in respect of discriminatory practices in advertisements, and instructions and pressure to discriminate;

(iv) the Commission has power to assist individual complainants in preparing their case on, e.g., difficult aspects of the law.

The effect of the Equality Act 2006 has already been noted (see p 72).

(c) Qualifying bodies. Where a qualifying body is required by law to satisfy itself as to the good character of an applicant for the authorisation or qualification it can confer, it must have regard, in deciding whether or not to issue, renew or extend the authorisation or qualification, to any evidence tending to show that the applicant, or any of his past or present employees or agents, has practised unlawful discrimination in, or in connection with, the carrying on of any profession or trade. Discrimination by persons who require such authorisations or qualifications to carry on their profession or trade may therefore be drawn to the attention of the appropriate qualifying body, e.g. the Law Society. An additional example would be an allegation against a person in the consumer credit or hire business, for which a licence from the Office of Fair Trading is required. Such an allegation may be referred to the Director-General who is required to have regard to evidence of discrimination when considering the fitness of a person to hold a licence under s 25 of the Consumer Credit Act 1974 as amended by the Consumer Credit Act 2006.

Disability discrimination

To those forms of discrimination which relate to race and sex must now be added discrimination against the disabled. The Disability Discrimination Acts 1995 and 2005 apply and the main employment provisions will be considered in Chapter 19. Other provisions are considered below.

What is disability?

Section 1 of the 1995 Act defines a disabled person as a person who has a physical or mental impairment which has a substantial and long-term effect on his or her ability to carry out normal day-to-day activities. Section 3 allows the Secretary of State to issue guidance. However Sch 1 states that impairment is of long-term effect if it has lasted for 12 months or is likely so to last or is likely to last for life. A severe disfigurement is included as is a progressive condition such as HIV, multiple sclerosis and cancer. Under the Disability Discrimination Act 2005 there is now no need to show current substantial effect and disability dates from diagnosis. Section 2 covers a person 'who has had a disability' even though he or she may no longer be disabled as in the case of a cancer which has gone into remission. This follows a government pledge that those with a history of disability should be covered.

Meaning of discrimination

In terms of access to goods, facilities and services, a person discriminates against a disabled person if for a reason which relates to the disabled person's disability he treats him less favourably than he treats or would treat others to whom that reason does not nor would not apply *and* he cannot show that the treatment in question is justified (s 20(1)(a) and (b)).

Provision of goods, facilities or services

Part III of the Act (ss 19–28) makes it unlawful for those who provide goods, services and other facilities, to the public or a section of the public, to discriminate against disabled persons by treating them less favourably for a reason relating to their disability than they treat or would treat others.

Thus providers must take reasonable steps:

(1) to change any practice, policy or procedure which makes it unreasonably difficult or impossible for a disabled person to make use of a service which is provided to other members of the public;
(2) to alter or remove any physical barrier which makes it unreasonably difficult or impossible for a disabled person to make use of such a service or to provide *alternative* means of making the service accessible; and
(3) to provide other aids or services which would make it easier for disabled people to use their services.

A *code of practice* has been issued on rights of access to goods, facilities and services to help suppliers to make reasonable adjustments to comply with the law. The code is not legally binding but breach of its provisions may be taken into account by any court or tribunal when considering whether a breach of the 1995 Act has taken place. The code also gives examples of possible breaches of the law as follows:

■ a hotel refusing to take a booking from a schizophrenic, saying that the hotel is fully booked when it is not;
■ a fast-food outlet telling a person with a severe facial disfigurement to sit at a table out of sight of other customers, even though other tables are free; and
■ a bookshop refusing to order a large print book for a visually impaired person, even though it does order books for other persons.

Giving the disabled more favourable treatment is not in general prevented by the Act, says the code.

There has been some confusion in business as to whether the 1995 Act applies to company meetings. It would seem that the Act will apply if a company meeting can be sensibly described as a meeting involving the public. In the case of a public company whose shares are listed on the Stock Exchange and are widely held, the annual general meeting might well be regarded as a public meeting so that consideration should be given to access for disabled members and possibly as regards the provision of accounts in braille, together with systems designed to enable, e.g., the deaf to participate in the meeting and so on. However, since private unlisted companies are by far the major form of corporate structure in the UK, many with five or fewer members, it is unlikely that the Act would apply in that context except in employment situations (see Chapter 19). Of course, it does a company no harm to give proper consideration to its disabled members and there is an overriding rule of the common law that states in regard to all meetings that the organisers must ensure that all those attending can participate fully in the proceedings.

It is also unlawful under ss 22–24 of Part III to discriminate against a disabled person in regard to the sale, letting and management of premises in the sense, e.g., of refusing to sell or rent a property to a disabled person or offering it on worse terms than would be offered to anyone else, unless the less favourable treatment can be justified on grounds stated in s 24, e.g. on the grounds of health and safety, so that it is reasonable for the person selling or letting the property to apply the less favourable treatment. Thus it may justifiable to refuse to let a flat to a disabled person if that person is unable to negotiate stairs safely or use the fire escape in an emergency. Thus in *Rose v Bouchet* [1999] IRLR 463 the landlord was held to be justified in refusing to let premises to a blind person because of the difficulty he would have in negotiating steps leading to them where a handrail was missing. It should be noted that in the context of selling of premises there is no duty to make reasonable adjustments to the property.

The Disability Discrimination Act 2005 amends the 1995 Act to bring in the letting of premises and a requirement to make adjustments, but not if this requires altering the physical features of the premises. For example, a landlord might be required to provide a clip-on receiver which vibrates when the door bell rings where the tenant is deaf. There would not in the case of a relevant disability be a requirement to provide a wheelchair where the tenant needed one for general purposes and not only for getting around the house. A tenant with mobility difficulties may have to be allowed to deposit rubbish in another place if it is too difficult to access the designated place. These changes would not apply where the letting was in the landlord's own home.

Disabled access to the Internet

Access to websites is included in the scope of the Disability Rights Commission's Code of Practice and the 1995 Act. Website proprietors must therefore take reasonable steps to ensure that their websites are accessible to persons with a wide range of disabilities. Thus text-only versions of documents must be made available to allow visually impaired users access using a braille reader. New contracts for design and maintenance of websites should contain detailed provisions regarding compliance with the supplier's obligations to ensure that the website meets the requirements of the law. Changes to existing websites should also be made if this is necessary to comply with the legislation.

Enforcement

Claims under Part III must be brought in the county court and the remedies available are the same as those which would be available in the High Court. The court may award damages and include an element of compensation for injury to feelings. There is no upper limit on the damages.

Discriminatory advertisements

These were not included in the 1995 Act but are now following insertion of provisions by the 2005 Act. Where the publisher of the advertisement relies upon a statement by the person placing the advertisement that it is not discriminatory and it is reasonable for him to do so, the publisher will not commit an offence but the person placing the advertisement will. The matter is triable summarily and can result in a fine of up to £5,000.

Education

The education of children with special educational needs and of students with learning difficulties is consolidated in the Education Act 1996. The Disability Discrimination Act 1995 made some modest changes to legislation existing in 1995 requiring governing bodies and local authorities to provide *information* as to arrangements made and facilities for disabled pupils and students. These provisions are now to be found in the Education Act 1996 (see s 528 (duty to publish disability statements)).

Public transport

Transport facilities are limited to access improvements provided this does not involve altering the physical features of the vehicle and, with rail, the changes relating to access do not take effect until 2020. Other forms of transport, e.g. by aircraft, may be brought in at some time in the future by regulations.

The Disability Rights Commission

The Disability Rights Commission Act received the Royal Assent on 27 July 1999. It sets up the Disability Rights Commission. The DRC will:

- work towards eliminating discrimination against disabled people;
- promote equal opportunities for disabled people;
- provide information and advice in particular to disabled people, employers and service providers;
- prepare codes of practice and encourage their use;
- review the working of the Disability Discrimination Act 1995;
- investigate discrimination and ensure compliance with the law;
- arrange for a conciliation service between service providers and disabled people to help resolve disputes on access to goods and services.

The major powers of the Disability Rights Commission are as follows:

- *The conduct of formal investigations*. The Commission may conduct a formal investigation into alleged discrimination and it may be *required* to do so by the Secretary of State.
- *The issue of non-discrimination notices*. If after a formal investigation the Commission is satisfied that a person is committing or has committed an unlawful act, it may issue a non-discrimination notice which may include recommendations as to action which the person concerned could reasonably be expected to take to comply with the law. The notice may also require the drawing up of an *action plan* by the person who is the subject of the notice to change procedures, practices and policies or other arrangements which have caused or contributed to the breach of law.
- *Non-discrimination agreements*. As an alternative to setting up an investigation or issuing a non-discrimination notice the DRC may make an agreement with the person concerned that no action will be taken if there is an agreement that the person concerned will take such action as may be specified in the agreement.

Non-compliance with a non-discrimination notice, agreement or action plan makes the offender liable to a fine of up to £5,000.

Disability: reform

The Disability Discrimination Act 1995 (Amendment) Regulations 2003 came into force on 1 October 2004. They extend the Disability Discrimination Act 1995 to cover partnerships, qualifying bodies, vocational training, employment agencies, barristers and advocates and the police. The regulations also remove the small employer exemption. Employers with less than 15 employees were not covered though associated organisations were taken into account such as the total number of employees in a holding company and its subsidiary.

Additional areas of discrimination

Regulations as indicated have brought in new areas of discrimination consequent upon EU directives as follows:

- *The Employment Equality (Religion or Belief) Regulations 2003 (SI 2003/1660)*. These regulations that came into force in December 2003 make it unlawful to discriminate on grounds of religion or belief in employment and vocational training. They prohibit direct and indirect discrimination and harassment on the grounds of any religion, religious belief or similar philosophical belief. There is the usual general occupational requirement defence and a special one allowing bias where the employer has an ethos based upon religion or belief.
- *The Employment Equality (Sexual Orientation) Regulations (SI 2003/1661)*. These regulations make it unlawful to discriminate on the grounds that a person is gay, heterosexual or bisexual in employment and vocational training. They prohibit direct and indirect discrimination, victimisation and harassment. There is a GOR that provides an exemption in the case of an organised religion to avoid conflict with the religious convictions of a significant number of its followers.

The areas of non-employment discrimination broadly follow those already considered in sex, race and disability discrimination.

However, they are not given by the regulations but appear in the Equality Act 2006 for religion or belief. The same Act gives power to make regulations to cover the non-employment areas for sexual orientation. At the time of writing these had not been made.

- *The Employment Equality (Age) Regulations 2006.* These regulations, which came into force on 1 October 2006, outlaw age discrimination in employment and vocational training only.

The Gender Recognition Act 2004

Under the provisions of this Act, transsexual persons are given all the rights and responsibilities appropriate to the acquired gender. Gender Recognition Panels will grant recognition in the new gender. Once this has been obtained, a person will be treated as a person of the acquired agenda so, for example, a male-to-female transsexual will be able to marry as a woman and obtain a birth certificate showing that she is a woman. State benefits and pension benefits will be given as a woman. Female-to-male transsexuals are also included.

It is not necessary for transsexuals to have had surgery, but they must have lived for at least two years in the new gender and intend to continue to live in it. They must also meet medical criteria, so that gender dysphoria must be diagnosed. Rights and obligations under the former gender are retained, e.g. as a mother or a father.

The Civil Partnership Act 2004

This Act allows same-sex partners to give notice of their intention to register their civil partnership at a Register Office. UK law restricts the registration of a marriage to heterosexual couples. Of most importance so far as the general law is concerned is to note the areas where the word 'spouse' is used to give rights or duties to heterosexual married couples and where civil partners acquire those rights and duties. For example, there is a duty to provide reasonable maintenance for a partner and the partner's children. There is also an equality of treatment in life assurance and pension benefits. There is recognition under the intestacy rules where a partner dies without leaving a will and access to fatal accident compensation. Thus, where a negligent act results in the death of a partner, the right to claim in the same way as a spouse can now be enjoyed by a same-sex registered partner. For tax purposes, civil partners will be treated in the same way as married couples so that, for example, no inheritance tax will be payable on property coming to a partner on the death of the other partner.

The Act allows couples who have entered into legally recognised overseas partnerships to be treated as civil partners in the UK.

Persons and legal relationships

The law recognises and defines certain common relationships. The following, in particular, have relevance to the various branches of substantive law dealt with in later chapters.

Agency

It is quite common to find parties having the relationship of principal and agent. Sometimes a person (the principal) wishes to have certain tasks carried out – he may wish to sell a house or buy shares in a company. He therefore employs an estate agent or a stockbroker to carry out his purposes. Sometimes an agent is a specialist who carries out a limited range of duties, e.g. an auctioneer who sells a wardrobe put into an auction. Sometimes he has wider powers, and may even be able to bind the principal in all the ways the principal could bind himself, as where the agent has a power of attorney.

An agent may be specifically appointed as such, but in some cases an agent acquires his status without specific authority being given to him, and such an agent may bind his principal by what is called usual authority. If P appoints A to be the manager of a hotel, A may be able to bind P in a contract although he had no actual authority to make it, for the law is not solely concerned with the actual authority of an agent but regards him as having the usual powers of an agent of his class. It follows that the usual powers of a hotel manager will be relevant in deciding the sort of agreement which A can make on behalf of P. The doctrine of usual authority does not apply where the third party knows that the agent has no authority to make the contract.

An agent's powers may also be extended in an emergency. If A is a carrier of perishable goods for P, he may be able to sell them on behalf of P if the goods are deteriorating and he cannot get P's instructions with regard to disposal. A becomes an agent of necessity for the purpose of sale, though his actual authority is to carry the goods. Agency may also arise out of conduct resulting in apparent authority. If a husband pays the debts which his wife incurs with the local dressmaker, he may be liable to pay for an expensive article of clothing which she buys without his consent, because the husband has, by his conduct, led the dressmaker to believe that the wife has power to bind her husband in contracts of this nature. This type of agency is not peculiar to the relationship of husband and wife and could arise wherever P holds out A as having authority to make contracts on P's behalf. It is also possible in certain circumstances for a principal to ratify, i.e. adopt, the contracts of his agent, even though the agent had no actual authority when making the contract.

At one time, if a person appointed an agent to manage his or her affairs, the appointment became invalid when the person making the appointment lost mental capacity. However, under the Mental Capacity Act 2005 it is possible to enter into an agency agreement called a Lasting Power of Attorney which does not terminate on the principal's loss of mental capacity.

Bailment

A bailment arises when one person (the bailor) hands over his property to the care of another (the bailee). The reasons for such a situation are many. The bailee may have the custody of the property by way of loan or for carriage. The article may be pledged, or left with another to be repaired or altered. Sometimes the bailee has the mere custody of the goods; sometimes he may use the property, as when he 'purchases' a radio set under a hire-purchase (or consumer credit) agreement or borrows a lawn mower. In all cases of bailment, the property or ownership remains with the bailor; the possession with the bailee.

A bailment is an independent legal transaction and need not necessarily originate in a contract. When X hands his goods to Y under a bailment Y has certain duties in regard to the care of the goods even though the bailment is not accompanied by a contract. Thus Y may be held liable for negligent damage to the goods even though he had not been promised any money or other benefit for looking after them. Bailment is considered in more detail in Chapter 22.

Lien

A lien is a right over the property of another which arises by operation of law and can be independent of any contract. In its simplest form it gives a creditor, such as a watch repairer, the right to retain possession of a debtor's property, in this case his watch, until he has paid or settled the debt, incurred in this case as a result of repairing the watch. Lien is considered in more detail in Chapter 22.

Juristic persons

As we have seen, the concept of personality is not restricted to human beings and we shall now consider corporate personality in terms of the nature and types of corporations.

The registered joint stock company

The enormous increase in industrial activity during the industrial revolution of the last century made necessary and inevitable the emergence of the registered joint stock company and the concept of limited liability. For the first time it was possible for the small investor to contribute to the capital of a business enterprise with the assurance that, in the event of its failure, he could lose no more than the amount he had contributed or agreed to contribute. The principles of 'legal entity' and 'perpetual succession' apply, whereby the joint stock company is deemed to be a distinct legal person, able to hold property and carry on business in its own name, irrespective of the particular persons who may happen to be the owners of its shares from time to time.

The concept of corporate personality is capable of abuse and where, for example, the concept has been used to evade legal obligations, the courts have been prepared to investigate sharp practice by individuals who are trying to hide behind a corporate mask or front.

Salomon v Salomon & Co, 1897 – The concept of legal personality (**41**)
Gilford Motor Company v Horne, 1933 – Looking behind corporate personality (**42**)

Joint Stock Companies are formed by registration under the Companies Act 2006 or previous Acts. The main current controlling statute is the Companies Act 2006. It provides for two types of registered companies: the public limited company and the private company. A registered company is fully liable for its debts but the liability of the members may be limited either to the amount unpaid on their shares, i.e. *a company limited by shares*, or to the amount they have agreed to pay if the company is brought to an end (wound up), i.e. *a company limited by guarantee*. Some companies are *unlimited* and the members are fully liable for the unpaid debts of the company if, and only if, the company goes into liquidation.

The allotted capital of a public limited company, which must before it can trade or borrow money be at least £50,000 with 25 per cent of the nominal value and the whole of any premium paid up, is usually raised by the public subscribing for its shares, which are issued with varying rights as to dividends, voting powers, and degrees of risk. Shares are freely transferable and are almost invariably but not necessarily listed on a recognised investment exchange such as the London Stock Exchange. When making a public issue of shares, the company is under a statutory obligation to publish full particulars of the history, capital structure, loans, profit record, directors, and many other matters calculated to assist the intending shareholder to assess the possibilities of the company. Such a document is called Listing Particulars or a Prospectus, and the directors are liable to penalties for fraud, misrepresentation or failure to disclose the material information as required by the Prospectus Regulations 2005 (SI 2005/1433) for listed securities. Part VI of the 2005 Regulations applies to unlisted securities on the Alternative Investment Market maintained by the Stock Exchange, together with the rules of a recognised investment exchange such as the London Stock Exchange.

The Listing Rules are now under the control of the Financial Services Authority: the City of London regulator which derives its authority from the Financial Services and Markets Act 2000.

The minimum number of members is usually two. However, s 123 of the Companies Act 2006 provides for the registration of private limited companies with only one member. Existing multi-member companies may also convert to one-member status. There is no upper limit.

Incorporation of companies is achieved by making an application to the Registrar of Companies at Companies House, of which the main office is in Cardiff.

The application for registration must give:

- the name of the company;
- the situation of the registered office, i.e. England and Wales or Wales (for Welsh companies if the promoters wish);
- the status of the company, i.e. whether it is to be public or private;
- a statement of initial shareholdings and a statement of capital (these two documents are required where the company is to have a share capital);
- a statement of guarantee where the company is to be limited by guarantee as where the members agree to pay a certain sum to the liquidator if the company is wound up (or is brought to an end).

The application must also state the company's proposed officers and the intended address of the registered office. It must be accompanied by a copy of the proposed articles (unless the company intends to use the model articles issued by the Secretary of State currently for Trade and Industry). There must also be a copy of the company's memorandum and a statement of compliance with the requirements of the Companies Act 2006.

The relevant documents can be delivered online as well as paper. The above requirements appear in ss 9–13 of the Companies Act 2006.

As regards the memorandum, this used to be the main constitutional document but it now serves to carry the names of those who wish to form the company and is merely a formation document. The main constitutional document is now the articles of association and all companies have unlimited objects unless the members wish to restrict the objects by a clause in the articles.

If the application satisfies legal requirements, the Registrar will issue a certificate of incorporation which is conclusive evidence that the company was properly formed. Thus, in the UK, the activities of a company cannot be challenged even if there was a defect in the formation procedures.

The directors of a company stand in the fiduciary position of agents towards the company whose money they control, and many of the provisions of the Companies Act 2006 are framed to ensure the maximum possible degree of disclosure by the directors of information calculated to keep the members acquainted with the affairs of the company.

The Memorandum and Articles of Association are public documents which must be deposited with the Registrar of Companies at Companies House in Cardiff and are open to public inspection along with other records relating to charges on the company's property, and copies of important resolutions. Each year the company's Annual Return, giving particulars of share capital, debentures, mortgages and charges, list of members, particulars of directors and secretary, is sent by the Registrar of Companies to the company for checking and, if necessary, alteration if there have been changes, before return to the Registrar. In addition, the company's accounts and the directors' and auditors' reports are filed with the Registrar within nine months (private company) and six months (public company) of the end of the accounting period to which they relate. Under ss 477 to 479 of the Companies Act 2006 small private companies whose annual turnover does not exceed £5.6 million need not appoint auditors, so they would not file an auditors' report if they had taken advantage of the exemption. Any person may inspect the Register of Members at the Registered Office of the company.

The private company, for which the usual minimum is two members (but see above) and no maximum number, is now a firmly established feature of the business world. The private company is barred by the Financial Services Authority Prospectus Rules 2005 from going to the general public for subscriptions for its securities. As we have seen, under the Companies Act 2006, a private company limited by shares or guarantee may be formed with only one member or allow its membership to fall to one.

Dissolution of a registered company usually takes place by the company being put into liquidation, as a result of the process of winding-up.

Other types of corporation

Incorporation may also be achieved by a *Royal Charter* granted by the Crown. The procedure is for the organisation desiring incorporation to address a petition to the Privy Council, asking for a grant of a charter and outlining the powers required. If the Privy Council consider that the organisation is an appropriate one, the Crown will be advised to grant a charter. Charter companies were formerly used to further the development of new countries, e.g. the East India Company and the Hudson Bay Company, but now they are usually confined to non-commercial corporations, e.g. the Institute of Chartered Accountants in England and Wales and the Institute of Chartered Secretaries and Administrators. Universities are also incorporated in this way. It is possible for the liability of members to be limited, and a chartered company, sometimes known as a 'Common Law Corporation', has the same powers as an individual person in spite of limitations in its charter. However, it is said that the Crown may forfeit the charter if the company pursues *ultra vires* activities, and certainly a member can ask the court to grant an injunction preventing the company from carrying out *ultra vires* activities.

Jenkin v Pharmaceutical Society, 1921 – Charter companies: acts inconsistent with charter (**43**)

Companies have also been created by special Act of Parliament, and governed by their special Acts and also by Acts which apply to statutory companies generally, which are known as 'Clauses Acts'. These Acts together define and limit their activities. The purpose of statutory companies was to promote undertakings of the nature of public utility services, e.g. gas and electricity, where monopolistic powers and compulsory acquisition are essential to proper functioning. The liability of members could be limited. Many of the former statutory public utility companies were nationalised by other statutes and operated on a national basis. In more recent times these undertakings have been privatised and run as public limited companies, e.g. gas and electricity.

All the forms of incorporation which we have discussed have one feature in common, i.e. they produce corporations aggregate having more than one member. However, English law recognises the concept of the *corporation sole*, i.e. a corporation having only one member. A number of such corporations were created by the common lawyers. They were concerned because land did not always have an owner, and there could be a break, however slight, in ownership. Church lands for example were vested in the vicar of the particular living, and at higher levels in other church dignitaries, such as the bishop of the diocese. When such persons died, the land had no legal owner until a successor was appointed, so the common lawyers created the concept of the corporation sole whereby the office of Vicar or Bishop was a corporation, and the present holder of the office the sole member of that corporation. The death of the office holder had thereafter no effect on the corporation, which never dies, and each successive occupant of the office carries on exactly where his predecessor left off. The Bishop of London is a corporation sole, and the present holder of the office is the sole member of the corporation. The Crown is also a corporation sole. A private *registered* company can have one member but is not a corporation sole.

It does not seem likely that any further corporations sole will be created by the common law, but they may still be created by statute. For example, the Public Trustee Act 1906 sets up the office of Public Trustee as a corporation sole. The Public Trustee (who is also the Official Solicitor) works as part of the Public Trust Office in London, and is prepared to act as executor or trustee, when asked to do so, and much property is vested in him or her from time to time in the above capacities. It would be most inconvenient to transfer this property to the new holder of the office on the death or retirement of the current one, and so the person who holds the office of Public Trustee is the sole member of a corporation called the Public Trustee, and the property over which he has control is vested in the corporation, and not in the individual who is the holder of the office.

Unincorporated associations

Having considered juristic personality, we will now turn to organisations which have no personality separate and distinct from the members. Many groups of people and institutions exist which carry on their affairs in much the same way as incorporated associations, but which are in fact non-charitable unincorporated associations. Examples are cricket clubs, tennis clubs, and societies of like kind. Such associations have no independent legal personality, and their property is treated as the joint property of all the members. The main areas of legal difficulty arising in regard to these associations are as follows:

Liability of members in contract. This rests on the principles of the law of agency. Thus a member who purports to make a contract on behalf of his club is usually personally liable. The other members will only be liable as co-principals if they had authorised the making of the contract. This would be the case if, for example, the rules of the club so provided. Alternatively, the members may ratify the contract after it is made. However, it appears that no member has authority to make a *purchase on credit* (*Flemyng* v *Hector* (1836) 2 M&W 172) unless he is specifically authorised to do so. Membership of a club usually involves payment of an annual subscription and nothing more. Consequently, it is expected that everything needed by the club will be paid for from existing funds. If more money is needed, a meeting of members should be called so that subscriptions might be raised rather than pledge the credit of the members.

Liability of members in tort. A person is liable if he committed the tort and in addition may be liable vicariously for the tort of his employee (see Chapter 20). These principles have been applied to clubs in two main types of case, viz.:

(a) Where a person has been injured as a result of the dangerous condition of the club premises. The Court of Appeal held in *Robertson* v *Ridley* [1989] 2 All ER 474 that at common law membership of the committee of a members' club did not of itself carry with it any duty of care towards the members. However, this rule could be changed by the rules of the club which could create a duty of care in the committee in regard to the safety of club premises. It was, however, held in *Jones* v *Northampton Borough Council* (1990) *The Times*, 21 May, that if a member of a club or of its committee is given a task to do on behalf of the other members he owes them a duty of care to warn them of any circumstances of which he becomes aware which give rise to the risk of injury. In this case A who was the chairman of a sports club booked accommodation for a six-a-side football match in premises which to his knowledge had a leaking roof making the floor slippery. He was held liable to a member of the team who was injured because of this.

(b) Where a person has been injured as a result of the negligence of an employee of the club. The tendency here is to find that the employee is employed by the officer or committee or trustees who appointed him (*Bradley Egg Farm Ltd* v *Clifford* [1943] 2 All ER 378).

Rights of members in the assets of the association. While a club is functioning the individual members have no separate rights in its property. They do, however, acquire realisable rights when the club is dissolved. On dissolution the general rule is that the assets are sold and after liabilities have been discharged any surplus is divided equally among those persons who are members at the time of dissolution regardless of length of membership or of subscriptions paid (*Re GKN Bolts & Nuts Ltd Sports & Social Club, Leek and Others* v *Donkersley and Others* [1982] 2 All ER 855), subject, of course, to any contrary provision in the rules of the club. It should be noted that a club is not dissolved simply because it changes its name and constitution with the express or implied consent of the members (*Abbatt* v *Treasury Solicitor* [1969] 3 All ER 1175).

Rights of members under the rules. The rules of an unincorporated association constitute a contract between the members of the association and the court will grant an injunction to a member who is denied a right given under the rules, e.g. the right to vote at meetings (*Woodford* v *Smith* [1970] 1 All ER 1091), or if he is expelled either where there is no power of expulsion under the rules, or if the power exists it has not been exercised properly as where the principles of natural justice (see Chapter 3) have not been observed.

Procedure. If only a few of the members are liable no problems arise since they can all be sued personally. If, however, it is intended to allege that all the members are liable this procedure is impracticable since all would have the right to be individually defended and represented. In this sort of case a representative action is available. Under the Rules of the Supreme Court and the county court rules the claimant may ask for a *representative order* to be made against certain members of the association and sue them. If he is successful these members will be liable to pay the damages but may also be entitled to an indemnity from the funds of the association, and in this way the claimant is in effect paid from the association's funds. Similarly, some members of an unincorporated association can sue for wrongs done to the association by means of the representative order procedure.

Trade unions

As regards the status of trade unions, the Trade Union and Labour Relations (Consolidation) Act 1992 is the governing statute and ss 10 and 12 provide that a trade union shall not be treated as if it were a body corporate but it is capable of making contracts; the property of the trade union is vested in trustees on trust for the union; it is capable of suing and being sued in its own name, whether in proceedings relating to property or founded on contract or tort or any other cause of action whatsoever; proceedings for any offence alleged to have been committed by it or on its behalf may be brought against it in its own name and any judgment made in proceedings of any description brought against a trade union are enforceable, e.g. by way of execution against the property held in trust for the union as if the union were a body corporate.

Section 127(2) extends the identical provisions to an employers' association where it is unincorporated. However, an employers' association may be a body corporate.

Under s 20 the liability of trade unions is as follows:

Industrial action against the employer of its members (primary action)

In an official strike the union would at common law be liable for torts committed during the dispute. The most usual tort is interfering with contracts of employment by organising the strike. There may be other torts for which it is liable, e.g. damage to the employer's property.

A trade union has immunity, however, in regard to the tort of interference with contracts of employment only if the industrial action is preceded and supported by a ballot of members and the action is commenced within four weeks of the ballot taking place, or such longer duration, not exceeding eight weeks, as is agreed between the union and the members' employer, unless under s 234 the union was prevented from calling action during that period by, e.g., a court injunction when the union can apply to the court for an order that the period of injunctive restraint shall not count towards the relevant period. The rationale behind the provision allowing the union and the employer to agree a period beyond four weeks and up to eight weeks is that the shorter period might pressurise the union into calling industrial action before the end of four weeks. This can prejudice continuing post-ballot negotiations.

However, a ballot becomes ineffective in any case after the end of a period of 12 weeks beginning with the date of the ballot. The employer is entitled to seven days' notice of strike action. The majority of those voting must vote in favour of the action. Under the 1992 Act the ballot must be secret, and there must be separate ballots for each place of work where there are separate workplaces. An official scrutineer must supervise the way in which voting papers are drawn up and sent to members to prevent ballot-rigging. Under s 62 balloting is extended to self-employed members of a trade union. Section 229 requires the voting papers for industrial action ballots to say who can call for such action if there is a vote in favour. The statutory immunity of the trade union will not apply unless the action is called by the specified person.

If there is no ballot the union can be sued for an injunction and damages which are limited according to the number of members it has.

Under provisions of the Employment Relations Act 1999, which inserted those provisions into the 1992 Act, it is automatically unfair (see Chapter 19) to dismiss employees or select them for redundancy for the first eight weeks of their participation in an official and otherwise lawfully organised, protected industrial action. Dismissal during unofficial action is not protected and action is not protected if it involves unlawful secondary action.

Action which is not against the employer (secondary action)

Basically, secondary action is a term used to describe industrial action taken by workers where the real dispute is not between themselves and their own employer. A major example is a 'sympathy strike'.

Under s 224 virtually all forms of secondary action are unlawful and the union is liable for torts including interfering with contracts of employment and there is no immunity by reason of a ballot. An injunction and damages may be awarded and again the damages are limited according to the membership of the union involved.

Unofficial industrial action

Section 20 makes a trade union legally responsible for the acts of its committees and officials including shop stewards and other officials regardless of whether they are authorised by the rules of the union to act on its behalf. This means that a trade union is potentially liable for industrial action organised by any of its officials or committees unless the union takes steps to repudiate the call for action. Section 20 contains a requirement that the union must 'do its best' to give individual written notice to the members involved.

Contracts made by a trade union are normally enforceable in accordance with the general principles of the law of contract. However, under s 179 collective agreements, i.e. with an employer in regard to wages, hours and conditions of work of a group of workers, are presumed *not* to be intended to be legally enforceable *unless* they are in writing and contain a provision to that effect.

Political strikes

A political strike is not a trade dispute. Strikes against government policy are not covered by the statutory immunity. In *Beaverbrook* v *Keys* [1978] IRLR 34 the TUC's 'Day of Action' against the then Conservative government and its policies was ruled unlawful.

Citizen's right

Under s 235A of the 1992 Act any individual who is deprived or likely to be deprived of goods or services because of an unlawfully organised form of industrial action can bring proceedings before the High Court to restrain the unlawful action. Such an individual can apply to the Commissioner for Protection against Unlawful Industrial Action for assistance at his office in Warrington.

Essential workers

In contrast to some other European countries UK law does not impose more stringent restrictions on its essential workers such as firefighters. It once did but the criminal sanctions as they were became repealed shortly after the Second World War.

Human rights law

Article 11 of the Convention which is given direct effect in the UK by the Human Rights Act 1998 gives a right of association which extends to membership of and protection by trade unions. However, Art 11 does not expressly include a right to strike and the European Court of Human Rights has not implied one. Contracting states are left a choice as to how the freedom of trade unions can be safeguarded.

The partnership

A partnership is defined in s 1 of the Partnership Act 1890 as 'the relationship which subsists between persons carrying on a business in common with a view of profit'. It will be noted that there must be a business; that it must be carried on in common by the members (whether by all of them, or by one or more of them acting for the others, will depend on the agreement subsisting between them); and that there must be the intention to earn profits. An association of persons formed for the purpose, say, of promoting some educational or recreational object to which the whole of the funds of the association shall be devoted, and from which no advantage in the nature of a distribution of a profit shall accrue to the members, is not a partnership.

Sharing profits

Participation in the profits of a business may be regarded as *prima facie* evidence of a partnership, but it is not conclusive – the intention of the parties must be examined. Thus, an employee whose remuneration is based on a share of profits, or the widow or child of a deceased partner receiving an annuity in the form of a share of profits, would not legally be deemed to be partners. Neither does the common ownership of property constitute a partnership (see further Chapter 22), nor the lending of money in consideration of an agreement to pay the interest, or to repay the capital, as a share or percentage of profits as they accrue. (But in such a case the lender should take the precaution of having the agreement embodied in writing, signed by all the parties, and setting out clearly the fact that he is not to be considered a partner.)

Citation as partner

The question of citation as a partner is of great importance because the existence of a partnership, if such is proved, will involve all parties cited as partners in unlimited liability for the debts of the firm. Partners are agents for the firm, and can bind the other partners in contracts concerning the business of the firm whether they are specifically authorised to make them or not.

No formalities

Two or more persons can combine to form a partnership, which can be brought into existence in a highly formal or a very casual manner. *No legal formalities are required*, but it is desirable and usual for the rights and liabilities of the partners to be defined in a formal Deed of Partnership, or at least in a written Partnership Agreement. On the other hand, a mere oral agreement is equally binding, and in extreme cases a relationship of partnership may be inferred from the conduct of the parties. The partners are at liberty to vary the arrangements made between them and, where the conduct of the parties has for a lengthy period been inconsistent with the terms as originally agreed, it will be presumed that they intend that the new arrangements shall be binding on them. The Partnership Act 1890 makes provisions as to contribution of capital, division of profits, rights of partners to participate in active management, and so on, but these only apply in so far as they are not varied by agreement between the partners.

Number of partners

Section 716 of the Companies Act 1985 prohibited the formation of a partnership consisting of more than 20 persons for the purpose of carrying on any business for gain. The Banking Act 1979, s 51(2) and Sch 7 applied the usual limit of 20 to banking partnerships.

Now the Regulatory Reform (Removal of 20 Member Limit in Partnerships etc.) Order 2002 applies and disapplies the above sections. It therefore removes entirely the 20-member limit from all unlimited and limited partnerships. The restriction did not apply to limited liability partnerships. The order is a Regulatory Reform Order. These orders can be used to reform any legislation, even a statute, that imposes a burden on business. There is no need for primary legislation.

Capacity to contract

There is no limitation on the activities of partners, provided that these are legal, nor is there any limit to the liability of the individual partners for the debts of the firm, each partner being liable to the full extent of his personal estate for any deficiencies of the partnership. However, provision is made for the introduction of limited partners whose liability is limited to the amount of capital they have introduced, though there must always be at least one general partner who is fully liable for the debts of the firm. Such a partnership must be registered as a limited partnership under the Limited Partnerships Act 1907 (and see below).

Partnership as a business organisation

The partnership was the normal form of business organisation for operations on a fairly large scale before the advent of the joint stock company, but it is now largely restricted to the type of enterprise requiring intimate personal collaboration between the members, or where incorporation is not possible or desirable, as among doctors, though the increasing control over companies including, in particular, private companies, may see some revival of the partnership as a more general business organisation. However, in the legal and accounting professions particularly, negligence liability is encouraging a move towards incorporation of firms to achieve limited liability or the formation of limited liability partnerships (see below).

Lack of continuity

One of the defects of the partnership is its lack of continuity. On the death of a partner the continuing partners must account to his personal representatives for the amount of his interest in the firm. This difficulty may be met to some extent by providing funds out of the proceeds of an insurance policy on the deceased partner's life, or by arranging for the balance of his capital account to be left in the business as a loan, but failing these measures the sudden withdrawal of a large amount of capital may well cause serious dislocation of the smaller business, or even end its operations. The most serious defect of a partnership, however, is the difficulty of providing additional funds for expansion, and this may induce partners to admit new members for the sake of their capital, regardless of their fitness for taking an active part in controlling the business.

Not a persona at law

A *partnership firm is not a* persona *at law*; a partnership is an aggregate of its members. In the matter of procedure, the Rules of the Supreme Court make it possible for the firm to sue and be sued in its own name, but this does not confer upon it a legal personality as is possessed by a corporation. This makes the holding of property more difficult in the partnership. For example, land cannot be conveyed to the firm. Instead it is conveyed to some or all of the partners as legal owners who declare a *trust of land* for all the partners in equity.

Limited liability partnerships (LLPs)

The Limited Liability Partnerships Act 2000 creates a new kind of partnership arrangement that is of major importance to those in the professions and in business generally. Its provisions are set out below. Registration began on 1 April 2001.

Section 1

This provides that an LLP is a legal person. It is a body corporate formed by incorporation (see below). It has an unlimited capacity and is able to undertake the full range of business activities which an ordinary partnership can undertake. The matter of *ultra vires* transactions will not therefore arise. An LLP is separate and distinct from its members. However, the members may be liable to contribute to its assets if it is wound-up. The extent of that liability is set out in regulations. Since an LLP will be a corporate body partnership law will not in general apply to an LLP. The basic principles of corporate law and the Companies Act 1985 apply with appropriate modifications. Clause 14 however provides that elements of partnership law may be applied to LLPs by regulations.

Comment The new LLP is not confined to those practising a profession but is open to other persons who may wish to use it as a business organisation. The new form of limited liability partnership also addresses liability of the partners individually in terms of their private estate. The members of the new organisation will benefit from limited liability because the LLP is a separate person. Thus the LLP and not its members personally will be liable to third parties. However, under the general law a professional person owes a duty of care to a third party or may do. Therefore negligent advice given to a client will result in liability of the LLP and may result in the professional giving the advice having personal liability but the other members will not be personally liable. Where the person injured by negligent advice is not a client, then, provided there is a duty of care when the advice was given and it was in the course of business, the LLP will be liable and the professional giving the advice will be personally liable but not the other members.

This is a principal aim of LLPs, i.e. to provide protection against 'Armageddon' legal claims, as they are called, that are capable of bringing even a substantial practice to its knees in terms of insolvency as the result of a negligent act by *one* of the partners, since in the ordinary partnership liability for such acts lies also with the other partners under the rule of joint *and several* liability.

Personal liability of the partners

It should be noted that an outsider may not find it easy to establish this personal liability. There will have to be evidence that the partner concerned was not merely acting as an agent for the firm but was also assuming personal liability to the outsider, e.g. a client. This could occur where the partner (or member as they may be called) has signed letters and documents in a personal capacity and not merely as an agent in the firm's name or on behalf of the firm. There is at the moment no specific case law, though company directors who performed a professional service on behalf of the company, e.g. a valuation have escaped personal liability for a negligent performance where it was made clear that they were acting on behalf of the company as an agent (see *Williams* v *Natural Life Health Foods Ltd* [1998] 2 All ER 577).

However, where the evidence shows that the partner or even a qualified employee has signed documents and conducted certain business apparently in a personal capacity without indicating that he or she was acting as an agent of the firm there may be personal liability (see *Merrett* v *Babb* [2001] QB 1174: a case involving an ordinary partnership that is nevertheless applicable to the LLP situation). This attempt to make an individual partner or member liable will arise crucially where the firm is insolvent and there are no liability insurance arrangements to cover the loss.

Incorporation

Section 2

This sets out the conditions to be met for the incorporation of an LLP. There must be at least two people who subscribe to a document called an 'incorporation document'. This document must be delivered to the Registrar of Companies.

The incorporation document must contain various items of information: name; whether the registered office is to be situated in England or Wales; in Wales or in Scotland; the address of the registered office; the names of the persons who are to be members on incorporation and whether some or all of them are to be designated members. Designated members are responsible for the LLP's conduct, including matters of compliance. If there are no designated partners, all partners are responsible.

Section 3

This provides that when the Registrar receives the incorporation document he will retain and register it. Once the document has been registered, the Registrar will issue a certificate that the LLP is incorporated by the name specified in the incorporation document. The certificate is evidence that all requirements have been complied with.

Membership

Section 4

This provides that the first members of an LLP are those signing the incorporation document. Following incorporation any person can become a member of an LLP by agreement with the existing members. A person may cease to be a member in accordance with any agreement with the other members.

Section 5

This deals with the relationship between the members. The rights and duties of the members of an LLP to one another and to the LLP are governed by the provisions of any agreement between the members subject to the provisions of the incorporation document. The Act does not require the members to have such an agreement and there is no requirement to publish it. There is a provision under which when an LLP comes into being it is bound by the terms of any agreement that is entered into by the persons who sign the incorporation document before incorporation. This avoids the problems presented, to some extent, in company law by pre-incorporation contracts. (But see now the Contracts (Rights of Third Parties) Act 1999 – Chapter 10.)

Section 6

Under these provisions each member of the LLP is an agent of it and may represent and act on its behalf in all its business. However, the LLP is not bound by the non-authorised acts of a member provided that the person who deals with the member knows this or is not aware that the member was a member of the LLP. A transaction entered into by a person who is no longer a member of the LLP is nevertheless valid and binding on the LLP unless the other party has been told that the person is no longer a member or the Registrar has received notice to that effect, in which case the person is deemed to know that the person he has dealt with is not a member of the LLP. Notice is constructive.

Section 7

This section is concerned with the situation in which a person ceases to be a member of an LLP or his interest in the LLP is transferred to someone else as, e.g., by assignment. A former member, the member's personal representative or trustee in bankruptcy or liquidator (in the case of a corporate member), or the trustees under a trust deed for the benefit of his creditors or assignee may receive any amount to which the former member would have been entitled but may not interfere in the management or administration of the LLP.

Section 8

Where the incorporation document states who the designated members are, they will become designated members on incorporation. Other members may become designated by agreement with the other members and may cease to be designated members in the same way. There must be at least two designated members. Every member may, however, be a designated member. An LLP may at any time notify the Registrar that all persons who may from time to time be members are to be designated members and on notification they will be. The notification will be in a form specified by the Registrar and must be signed by a designated member. A person who ceases to be a member of the LLP will also cease to be a designated member.

Designated members have additional responsibilities such as signing the accounts and delivering them to the Registrar of Companies and preparing, signing and delivering the annual return together with appointing an auditor (unless the audit exemption applies).

Registration of membership changes

Section 9

This section provides that if a person ceases to be a member or a designated member, the Registrar must be notified within 14 days and a change in the name and address of a member must be notified in 21 days. Where all the members are designated, members' notice is required only of the fact that the person who is concerned has ceased to be a member. Failure to comply with the notice requirements is a criminal offence, but it is a defence to show that all reasonable steps were taken to comply. Punishment is by fine.

Taxation

Section 10

Under this section members of an LLP carrying on business are treated for income tax and capital gains tax purposes as if they were partners even though an LLP is a body corporate. Also the property of an LLP will be treated as partnership property. This means that, like partners, members will be individually liable to tax on their shares of the profits of the LLP.

For capital gains tax purposes, the assets of the LLP are treated as partnership assets. This means that members will be individually liable for chargeable gains when LLP assets are disposed of. An acquisition or disposal will not therefore be treated as made by the LLP.

Section 11

This clause inserts a new section in the Inheritance Tax Act 1984. This provides that for the purposes of IHT the members of an LLP are treated as members of a partnership. Thus IHT will be charged in respect of members' interests in an LLP as for a partnership and business relief will be available on that basis.

Section 12

This provides for relief from stamp duty on an instrument transferring property from a partnership to a newly incorporated LLP. The relief is conditional on the membership of the partnership and the LLP being the same and on the members' interest in the property being the same.

It should be noted that s 12 of the LLP Act 2000 gives this concession for only 12 months from incorporation. This is important to those who may register an LLP for future operation of an existing business.

Regulations

Section 13

This gives regulation-making powers in regard to insolvency by incorporating with modifications various parts of the Insolvency Act 1986. This will ensure that procedures relating to company voluntary arrangements, administration, receivership and voluntary and compulsory winding up are available as suitably modified.

The section also contains regulation-making powers in regard to the insolvency and winding-up of an overseas LLP. There will be separate consultation on and before the exercise of this power.

Sections 14 to 18

These sections give general rule-making powers in regard to LLPs.

Names

Schedule to the Act

The name of an LLP must end with 'limited liability partnership' or llp or LLP. There are equivalents in Welsh where the registered office is situated in Wales. An LLP cannot have a name which is already used by a registered company nor one that the Secretary of State thinks constitutes a criminal offence or is offensive. A name may not be registered if it gives the impression that it is connected with central or local government authorities. An LLP may change its name at any time. If it has been registered in a name which is the same or similar to a registered name, the Secretary of State may direct a change within 12 months of registering the name. Where the LLP has given misleading information to obtain a sensitive name such as 'charity', the Secretary of State may direct a change within five years of it being registered and where it is misleading and likely to cause harm to the public the Secretary of State can direct a change *at any time* but the LLP may appeal to the court.

The above matters are for all practical purposes like those rules for company names.

Registered office

An LLP must have a registered office at all times and this must be situated in either England and Wales, Wales or Scotland. The details, e.g. the address of the registered office, must appear in the incorporation document. On change of address of the registered office, the Registrar must be notified on the approved form to be signed by a designated member. For the next 14 days documents may be validly served at the old address.

Disclosure and audit

The extent to which disclosure of financial and other information is required depends upon regulations (see the Limited Liability Partnerships Regulations 2001) and this is also the case with audit. However, the audit exemption for small companies is applied as appropriate (see earlier in this chapter).

The need for a membership agreement

The need for the LLP to have a carefully drafted agreement covering all eventualities cannot be over-stressed. Although the LLP regulations apply many Companies Act 1985 provisions it must be remembered that an LLP is not a species of company. Section 1(1) of the LLP Act 2000 states 'There shall be a new form of legal entity . . .'. Furthermore, the law relating to ordinary limited partnerships (see below) does not apply. Section 1(5) of the LLP Act 2000 states that in general terms and unless there is a provision in statute law to the contrary the law relating to partnerships does not apply to an LLP.

The general internal procedures of a registered company are governed by special articles or Table A which is a statutory instrument designed for companies. Ordinary partnerships are governed by more extensive fall-back provisions in the Partnership Act 1890 that apply in the absence of partnership articles. There is no equivalent support for the LLP and so an agreement is vital to determine the internal governing rules that are to apply.

Limited partnerships

It is possible for the liability of partners in certain circumstances to be limited. This is in the case of limited partnerships which are formed under the Limited Partnerships Act 1907. While this might appear attractive, limited partnerships are not commonly used in the *generality* of business (but see **Reform** below).

Limited partnerships must have one or more partners (called general partners) who are liable for all of the debts and obligations of the firm and may then have one or more persons (called limited partners) who are only liable for the debts and obligations of the firm to the stated amount of the value of capital or property contributed by them to the firm at the outset. As already noted, the Regulatory Reform (Removal of 20 Member Limit in Partnerships etc.) Order 2002 removes the 20-member limit in all limited and ordinary partnerships.

The limited partners must not then either directly or indirectly draw out or receive back any part of that contribution; if they do then they are liable for the debts of the firm up to the amount so drawn out or received back.

Limited partners must not take any part in the management of the business of the firm: if they do they can be made liable for all debts and obligations of the firm incurred while they were doing so. Any person may, subject to the general requirements as to capacity of a partner mentioned before, be a limited partner and this includes a body corporate.

In this connection, it is a not uncommon misconception that if a limited company is introduced as a partner the firm must of necessity convert into a limited partnership. This is not the case since a limited company is, like an individual, fully liable for its debts so long as it has assets to pay them. It is the liability of the members that is limited. Thus when the company's assets have been exhausted in the payment of its debts the members cannot be called upon to meet the deficit provided of course they have paid for their shares in full.

If therefore, other individuals join a limited partnership as members of a limited company, the liability of all the partners is limited and yet the partnership would comply with the law. The company as the general partner would be liable to the full extent of its assets for the debts of the firm but the individual members having paid for their shares in full would not be. This assumes that there is no fraud which might convince a court to ignore the corporate separate entity rule and make individual members liable.

The other main points to note as regards a limited partnership are:

(a) a limited partner has no power to bind the firm;
(b) any question arising as to ordinary business matters may be decided by a majority of the general partners;
(c) a new partner may be introduced without the consent of the existing limited partners; and
(d) a limited partner is not entitled to dissolve the partnership by notice.

Limited partnerships must be registered under the Act with the Registrar of Companies. If they are not so registered then every limited partner loses the benefit of that status and is deemed to be a general partner. There are forms to be filed giving the necessary details and changes in those details must also be notified to the Registrar. A certificate of registration is issued. There are various other detailed formalities that need to be followed.

Reform

The Law Commission and the Scottish Law Commission have published a joint consultation paper on the Limited Partnerships Act 1907. It can be accessed at **http://www.scot-lawcom.gov.uk**. Limited partnerships are increasingly used by institutional investors such as insurance companies and pension funds that are wholly or partially exempt from tax. These investors can invest jointly with others that are liable to tax without losing their own tax status. Limited partnerships are also used extensively by venture capitalists. The view of the Law Commissions is that current legislation requires updating to maintain the UK's competitive position in the venture capital market.

There is currently no legislation on this.

The Crown

The Crown consists of the Monarch and her Ministers, together with the central government departments staffed by civil servants, the armed forces, and the Privy Council which retains some powers, e.g. to arrange for the coronation of the Monarch. The police are not servants of the Crown.

Until 1947 the Crown was not liable for the tortious acts of its servants, and was liable only to a limited extent in contract, though the person who did the wrongful act could be sued and the Crown often stood behind him and paid the damages against him. Actions in contract could only be started by an awkward procedure known as a Petition of Right, with the consent of the Crown given on the advice of the Attorney-General.

The rather anomalous position at common law which has been outlined above arose out of the ancient maxim, 'The King can do no wrong', which was extended to cover the activities of the Departments of State and their servants. The Crown Proceedings Act 1947, and the Rules of the Supreme Court (Crown Proceedings) Act 1947, which were required to support the Act in the matter of procedure, came into force together on 1 January 1948, to rectify the matter.

The general effect of this legislation is to abolish the rule that the Crown is immune from legal process, though s 40 preserves the immunity of the Monarch in a personal capacity from any liability in law, and to place the Crown as regards civil proceedings in the same position as a subject. Proceedings by Petition of Right are abolished, and all claims which might before the Act have been enforced by Petition of Right can be brought by ordinary action in accordance with the Act.

Contractual claims

The Crown is now liable in contract where a Petition of Right could have been brought before, and also in tort. Regarding contractual claims, there are some limitations upon the rights of the other party, viz:

Executive necessity

In *Rederiaktiebolaget Amphitrite* v *R* [1921] 3 KB 500, a neutral shipowner's vessel was detained in England, although the British Legation in Stockholm had given an undertaking that it would not be. The basis of Rowlatt, J's decision for the Crown was that the government cannot by contract hamper its freedom of action in matters which concern the welfare of the state. This statement has been regarded as much too wide and is probably of very limited application.

The main result of the ruling of Rowlatt, J is that contracts with the government normally contain cancellation clauses which provide for compensation. In practice, the Crown does not invoke the *Amphitrite* rule to avoid liability for such compensation.

Parliamentary funds

In *Churchward* v *R* [1865] 1 QB 173, a contract to carry mail for 11 years was terminated by the Crown in the fourth year. Shee, J, in deciding for the Crown, held that it was a condition precedent of the contract that Parliament would allocate funds and if they chose not to there was no claim. This decision came under criticism in subsequent cases and the better view is that it is limited to cases where Parliament has *expressly* refused to grant the necessary funds.

This rule does, of course, cause hardship to contractors with the government but it must be continued if the control of Parliament over public expenditure is to be maintained.

Freedom to legislate

In *Reilly* v *R* [1934] AC 176, a barrister who was employed by the Canadian government had his contract terminated by legislation. The Privy Council found for the Crown on the ground that the Crown cannot by contract restrict its right to legislate.

Contracts of employment

Here the position is as follows:

(a) **Military personnel.** Military employees cannot successfully claim against the Crown for breach of contract (*Dickson* v *Combermere* (1863) 3 F & F 527) nor can they claim arrears of pay (*Leaman* v *R* [1920] 3 KB 663). Thus, although they have a statutory right to claim unfair dismissal (see below) they cannot bring a claim for wrongful dismissal which is based on breach of contract.

(b) Civil servants. It was the position *at common law* that civil servants were dismissible at pleasure (*Shenton* v *Smith* [1895] AC 229) but could claim arrears of pay (*Kodeeswaran* v *Attorney-General of Ceylon* [1970] 2 WLR 456). The general rule that those in Crown service might be dismissed at the Crown's pleasure could be varied by legislation. A well-known example is the provision under which judges of the High Court and the Court of Appeal hold their offices during good behaviour (Supreme Court Act 1981, s 11(3)).

However, in *R* v *Lord Chancellor's Department, ex parte Nangle* [1991] IRLR 343 a Divisional Court of Queen's Bench held that a civil servant is employed under a contract of service based upon the Civil Service Pay and Conditions of Service Code. This sets out conditions regarding, e.g., pay, pensions, holidays and so forth. Admittedly para 14 of the code says that a civil servant does not have a contract of employment enforceable in the courts but the court held in this case that para 14 must be seen in context. It could not be said that all the carefully prepared terms and conditions of service in the code were to be regarded as purely voluntary. Mr Nangle could sue for damages for breach of contract if, as he alleged, his employers, the Crown, had failed to follow a code of practice when transferring him to another department with a loss of a salary increment following allegations that he had assaulted and sexually harassed a female colleague. Section 191 of the Employment Rights Act 1996 extends most of the *statutory employment rights* to those in Crown employment including the right to claim unfair dismissal. They are not, however, covered by the provision relating to minimum periods of notice (because of the rule that employment by the Crown is terminable at will) and redundancy (although redundancy payments are made to civil servants as appropriate). The legislation relating to sex, racial and disability discrimination is applied to Crown servants.

The armed forces enjoy, by reason of s 192 of the Employment Rights Act 1996, the employment rights relating to a written statement of employment particulars, itemised pay statements, remuneration while on medical suspension, time off for ante-natal care, maternity leave, written statement of reasons for dismissal, unfair dismissal and the ability to complain to an employment tribunal. However, members of the armed forces are required to exhaust internal grievance procedures before going to a tribunal. In addition, ss 21–27 of the Armed Forces Act 1996 enable service men and women to complain to an employment tribunal in regard to sex and racial discrimination or equality of treatment provided the appropriate services' redress of complaints procedures have been followed first. These are provided for by s 20 of the Armed Forces Act 1996. These matters are further considered in Chapter 19.

Actions in tort will lie against the Crown for the torts of its servants or agents committed in the course of their employment; for breach of duty owed at common law by an employer to his servants; for breach of the duties attaching to the ownership, occupation, possession or control of property; and for breach of statutory duties, e.g. breaches of the duty of fencing dangerous machines under factory legislation.

The law as to indemnity and contribution under the Civil Liability (Contribution) Act 1978 applies to Crown cases so, if the Crown is a joint tortfeasor, it can claim a contribution from fellow wrongdoers, which may, under s 2(2) of the 1978 Act be a complete indemnity, so that where the Crown is led into publishing a libel, it may claim an indemnity against the party responsible (see further Chapter 20). The Law Reform (Contributory Negligence) Act 1945 also applies to Crown cases (see further Chapter 21).

Under s 10 of the Crown Proceedings Act 1947 both the Crown and any member of the Armed Forces were immune from liability in tort in respect of the death of, or personal injury to, another member of the Armed Forces on duty, provided that the death or injury arose out of service which ranked for the purpose of pension. This section was repealed in regard to acts or omissions causing injury after 15 May 1987 (see Crown Proceedings (Armed Forces) Act 1987). It follows that any claim by members of the armed forces for injury or death occurring between 1947 and 1987 is barred. In this connection, claims relating to injury for exposure to asbestos dust during that period have come before the courts alleging that Art 6 (fair trial) and Art 2 (right to life) of the Human Rights Convention were infringed by s 10 of the 1947 Act. The House of Lords ruled that there was no infringement of the Convention since s 10 created an issue of procedure not substantive law to which the Convention could be applied (see *Matthews* v *Ministry of Defence* [2003] 2 WLR 435). However, this does not mean that service men and women will necessarily win a claim against the Crown. Thus in an action against the Crown for injury caused by negligence the person making the claim will, as a civilian would, have to prove that there was a duty of care owed to him or her which was breached (see further Chapter 21). Thus in *Mulcahy* v *Ministry of Defence* (1996) *The Times*, 27 February the claimant was a soldier serving in the Gulf War who suffered damage to his hearing when a fellow soldier fired a shell from a howitzer. He lost the case because the Court of Appeal decided that there was no duty of care between service personnel in battle conditions.

Actions under the Act may be brought in the High Court or a county court, and under ss 17 and 18 of the 1947 Act the Treasury is required to publish a list of authorised government departments for the purposes of the Act, and of their solicitors. Actions by the Crown will be brought by the authorised department in its own name, or by the Attorney-General. Actions against the Crown are to be brought against the appropriate department, or, where there is doubt as to the department responsible or appropriate, against the Attorney-General.

In any civil proceedings by or against the Crown, the court can make such orders as it can make in proceedings between subjects, except that no injunction or order for specific perform-ance can normally be granted against the Crown (but see below). The court can, in lieu thereof, make an order declaratory of the rights of the parties in the hope that the Crown will abide by it. No order for the recovery of land, or delivery up of property, can be made against the Crown, but the court may instead make an order that the claimant is entitled as against the Crown to land or to other property or to possession thereof. No execution or attachment will issue to enforce payment by the Crown of any money or costs. The procedure is for the successful party to apply for a certificate in the prescribed form giving particulars of the order. This is served on the solicitor for the department concerned, which is then required to pay the sum due with interest if any. The above exceptions show that, in spite of the Act, the rights of the subject against the Crown are still somewhat imperfect.

However, injunctions can be granted against officers of the Crown personally, even though acting in their official capacity. Thus, in *M* v *Home Office* [1993] 3 WLR 433, a mandatory injunction was issued against the Home Secretary for contempt of court, to achieve the return to this country of a person deported while his case for political asylum was still under review by the court.

Following the decisions of the House of Lords in *M* v *Home Office* (see above) and *Factortame* v *Secretary of State for Transport (No 2)* (1991) 1 All ER 70 it would appear that while a perman-ent injunction cannot be granted against the Crown injunctive relief by way of interim relief can be given, e.g. to suspend the operation of legislation said to be inconsistent with Community law.

For historic, constitutional and procedural reasons also, the Crown cannot be prosecuted for crime. Once again a nominated defendant is put forward; e.g. for a road traffic offence, such as using a lorry with a defective tyre, the principal transport officer of the Department concerned would probably be nominated. Unfortunately, this practice results in the officer con-cerned acquiring a long record of motoring convictions in a personal capacity. Accordingly,

8

in *Barnett* v *French* [1981] 1 WLR 848, the Court of Appeal suggested the use of the name 'John Doe' for the nominated defendant who, for the purpose of criminal records, would be shown as having a date of birth 'circa 1657'. The name 'John Doe' was used in civil actions from about that time onwards as part of a very elaborate procedure to prove the title to land. The procedure is no longer in use.

The general rule that statutes do not bind the Crown unless by express words or necessary implication is contained in s 40 of the 1947 Act. It produced an absurd result when it was decided that public health and hygiene legislation did not apply to National Health Service hospital kitchens. This anomaly was abolished by the National Health Service (Amendment) Act 1986 though the general immunity in other areas given by s 40 was preserved.

Crown privilege in civil proceedings

As we have seen, either party to a civil action can, amongst other things, ask the court to order the other party to produce any relevant documents for inspection: a process called disclosure (see Chapter 5). Under s 28 of the Crown Proceedings Act 1947, this right lies against the Crown though the Crown could refuse to obey the order if production of the document(s) would be injurious to the public interest. It had been felt for some time that Ministers whose departments were involved in civil litigation had abused this right. Undoubtedly, some claimants failed in an action against the Crown because even the judge could not obtain access to documents necessary to support the claim. As a result of a number of cases of this kind, the House of Lords decided, in *Conway* v *Rimmer* [1968] 1 All ER 874, that even though a Minister certifies that production of a particular document would be against the public interest, the judge may nevertheless see it and decide whether the Minister's view is correct. If the judge cannot accept the Minister's decision, he may overrule him and order disclosure of the document to the party concerned. Thus the decision of the Minister is no longer conclusive though it is unlikely that a judge would order disclosure if there was a danger of real prejudice to the national interest.

However, despite *dicta* in *Conway* v *Rimmer* that claims to privilege on grounds of confidentiality could not expect sympathetic treatment, the courts vary in their interpretation of this view.

> *Norwich Pharmacal Co* v *Commissioners of Customs and Excise*, 1973 – Crown or public interest privilege: documents (**44**)
>
> *Alfred Crompton Amusement Machines* v *Customs and Excise Commissioners (No 2)*, 1973 – Non-disclosure of documents: privilege (**45**)

Privilege in civil proceedings – the public interest ground

Privilege extends beyond cases against the Crown. Thus in *D* v *NSPCC* [1977] 1 All ER 589 the House of Lords held that the NSPCC or a local authority is entitled to privilege from disclosing the names of its informants in relation to child neglect or ill-treatment.

The House of Lords decided in *British Steel Corporation* v *Granada Television* [1980] 3 WLR 774 that the information media and their journalists do not have immunity from the obligation to disclose their sources of information when disclosure is necessary in the interests of justice. Their Lordships went on to say, however, that the remedy is equitable and may be withheld in the public interest.

Public interest privilege has really replaced the older Crown privilege. However, the latter has been included as a separate head of privilege to show the historical development.

Legal professional privilege

Two kinds of legal professional privilege protect some communications from disclosure to other parties to legal proceedings as follows:

- *legal advice privilege* which protects communications between solicitor and client where the purpose is to obtain legal advice regardless of whether litigation is pending or in contemplation; and
- *litigation privilege* which protects communications between solicitor and client and a third party where the primary purpose for which the document was brought into existence was, from the beginning, its use in pending or contemplated litigation.

Legal advice privilege was affirmed by the House of Lords in *R* v *Special Commissioner, ex parte Morgan Grenfell & Co Ltd* [2002] STC 786. Their Lordships ruled that documents in the taxpayer's possession but prepared for the purpose of seeking legal advice from solicitors on tax matters were subject to legal professional privilege and need not be disclosed to an inspector of taxes whether they were in possession of the solicitor or the client.

The privilege is confined to lawyers and so whether communications between accountants and their clients is privileged presents a difficulty. However, in such a case the client may be able to claim successfully the right to privacy in Art 8 of the Human Rights Convention in order to justify refusal to produce tax advice given to the client by accountants to the tax authorities under a Revenue notice to do so.

Some difficulties have arisen in connection with legal advice given by lawyers in the presentation of legal advice to a public or other inquiry where litigation is not necessarily in view. However, in *Three Rivers DC* v *Bank of England* [2005] 1 AC 610 the House of Lords affirmed that such advice did come within legal advice privilege. The case arose from legal advice given in an inquiry into the collapse of the Bank of Credit and Commerce International.

8

Part 2

THE LAW OF CONTRACT

9

MAKING THE CONTRACT I

A contract may be defined as an *agreement*, enforceable by the law, between two or more persons to do or abstain from doing some act or acts, their intention being to create *legal relations* and not merely to exchange mutual promises, both having given something, or having promised to give something of value as consideration for any benefit derived from the agreement. As regards the requirement that consideration must be supplied by a party to a contract, this is subject to a number of exceptions, including arrangements made under the Contracts (Rights of Third Parties) Act 1999.

The definition can be criticised in that some contracts turn out to be unenforceable and, in addition, not all legally binding agreements are true contracts. For example, a transaction by deed derives its legally binding quality from the special way in which it is made rather than from the operation of the laws of contract, e.g. a deed is enforceable even in the absence of valuable consideration. In consequence, transactions by deed are not true contracts at all. Nevertheless, the definition at least emphasises the fact that the basic elements of contracts are (i) an agreement, (ii) an intention to create legal relations, and (iii) valuable consideration. It should be noted that even in the exceptional case where a third party who has not supplied consideration can claim under the contract, that underlying contract must be supported by consideration given one to the other by the parties unless it is a deed.

The essentials of a valid contract

The essential elements of the formation of a valid and enforceable contract can be summarised under the following headings:

(*a*) There must be an offer and acceptance, which is in effect the agreement.
(*b*) There must be an intention to create legal relations.
(*c*) There is a requirement of written formalities in some cases.
(*d*) There must be consideration (unless the agreement is by deed).
(*e*) The parties must have capacity to contract.
(*f*) There must be genuineness of consent by the parties to the terms of the contract.
(*g*) The contract must not be contrary to public policy.

In the absence of one or more of these essentials, the contract may be void, voidable, or unenforceable.

Classification of contracts

Before proceeding to examine the meaning and significance of the points set out above, the following distinctions should be noted.

Void, voidable and unenforceable contracts

A *void* contract has no binding effect at all, and in reality the expression is a contradiction in terms. However, it has been used by lawyers for a long time in order to describe particular situations in the law of contract and its usage is now a matter of convenience. A *voidable* contract is binding but one party has the right, at his option, to set it aside. An *unenforceable* contract is valid in all respects except that it cannot be enforced in a court of law by one or both of the parties should the other refuse to carry out his obligations under it. This sounds strange but property or money which has passed from one party to the other under the contract can be retained by that party. The contract can be used as a *defence* if the party brings a claim to recover the property or money. So the contract has some life; it is not void. Contracts of guarantee are unenforceable unless evidenced in writing (see further Chapter 11).

Executed and executory contracts

A contract is said to be *executed* when one or both of the parties have done all that the contract requires. A contract is said to be *executory* when the obligations of one or both of the parties remain to be carried out. For example, if A and B agree to exchange A's scooter for B's motor cycle and do it immediately, the *possession* of the goods and the *right* to the goods are transferred *together* and the contract is *executed*. If they agree to exchange the following week the *right* to the goods is transferred but not the *possession* and the contract is *executory*. Thus an *executed* contract conveys a *chose in possession*, while an *executory* contract conveys a *chose in action* (see Chapter 22).

Specialty contracts

Specialty contracts are also called deeds.

The general law of contract *requires* a deed in the case of a lease of more than three years, which must be made as a deed if it is to create a legal estate (see further Chapter 22). In addition, a transfer of property, e.g. a conveyance, which imposes covenants (or agreements) in regard, for example, to the use of the land, is a contract and must also be by deed. In addition, a conveyance is an agreement by the vendor of land to convey his title or ownership and the agreement of the purchaser to take it.

As regards the *form* of a deed the Law of Property (Miscellaneous Provisions) Act 1989 is now relevant. Section 1 requires, as before, that a deed must be in writing but gets rid of the requirement for sealing where a deed is entered into by an individual. The signature of the individual making the deed must be witnessed and attested. Attestation consists of a statement that the deed has been signed in the presence of a witness.

The section also provides that it must be made clear on the face of the document that it is intended to be a deed. The usual form to satisfy this requirement and attestation is: 'signed as a deed by AB in the presence of XY'.

As far as companies are concerned, s 44 of the Companies Act 2006 provides that while a company may continue to execute documents by putting its common seal on them it need not have such a seal. Any document signed by an authorised signatory such as a director and the secretary of the company if it has one, or by two directors and said to be executed by the company will be regarded as if the seal had been put on it. Once again, it must be made clear on the face of the document that it is intended to be a deed and the form here could be as follows: 'signed as a deed: AB director and CD secretary (or another director) – for and on behalf of Boxo Ltd'.

A deed has certain characteristics which distinguish it from a simple contract:

(a) Merger. If a simple contract is afterwards embodied in a deed made between the same parties, the simple contract merges into, or is swallowed up by the deed, for the deed is the superior document. The deed is then the only contract between the parties. But if the deed is only intended to cover part of the terms of the previous simple contract, there is no merger of that part of the simple contract not covered by the deed.

(b) Limitation of actions. The right of action under a specialty contract is barred unless it is brought within 12 years from the date when the cause of action arises on it, i.e. when the deed could first have been sued upon, which is in general when one party failed to carry out a duty under it. For example, A and B make a contract by deed on 1 March. B is due to pay money under it on 1 April and fails to do so. Time runs from 1 April not 1 March as regards a claim by A. A similar right of action is barred under a simple contract after only six years.

However, it would appear from a ruling of the Court of Appeal that when a business is dealing with another business of broadly equal negotiating power as distinct from a consumer the above period, certainly of six years, can be much reduced thus shortening the period of potential liability for breach of contract (see *Granville Oil and Chemicals Ltd* v *Davis Turner & Co Ltd* (2003) (unreported)). In that case a simple contract stated that action was barred nine months after the provision of a service. The Court of Appeal ruled that the period must be adhered to. It was not an unfair term (see further Chapter 18).

(c) Consideration is not essential to support a deed, though specific performance, which requires a party in default to actually carry out the contract as distinct from paying damages, will not be granted if the promise is gratuitous (see Chapter 18). Simple contracts must be supported by consideration.

(d) Estoppel. Statements in a deed tend to be conclusive against the party making them, and although he might be able to prove they were not true, the rule of evidence called 'estoppel' will prevent him from doing this by excluding the very evidence which would be needed. In modern law, however, a deed does not operate as an estoppel where one of the parties wishes to bring evidence to show fraud, duress, mistake, lack of capacity or illegality.

Simple contracts form the great majority of contracts, and are sometimes referred to as parol contracts. This class includes all contracts not by deed, and for their enforcement they require consideration. Simple contracts may be made orally or in writing, or they may be inferred from the conduct of the parties; but no simple contract can exist which does not arise from a valid offer and a valid acceptance supported by some consideration. When these elements exist, the contract is valid in the absence of some defect such as lack of capacity of one of the parties, lack of reality of consent, or illegality or impossibility of performance.

The formation of a contract

In order to decide whether a contract has come into being, it is necessary to establish that there has been an *agreement* between the parties. In consequence, it must be shown that an *offer* was made by one party (called the offeror) which was *accepted* by the other party (called the offeree) and that *legal relations* were intended.

Agreement

A contract is an agreement and comes into existence when one party makes an offer which the other accepts. The person making the offer is called the offeror, and the person to whom it is made is called the offeree. An offer may be express or implied. Suppose X says to Y – 'I will sell you this watch for £5', and Y says – 'I agree'. An express offer and acceptance have been made; X is the offeror and Y the offeree. Alternatively, Y may say to X: 'I will give you £5 for that watch'. If X says: 'I agree', then another express offer has been made, but Y is the offeror and X is the offeree. In both cases, the acceptance brings a contract into being. In order to find out who makes the offer and who the acceptance, it is necessary to examine the way in which the contract is negotiated.

Offer and invitation to treat

An offer is an undertaking by the offeror that he will be bound in contract by the offer if there is a proper acceptance of it. An offer may be made to a specific person or to any member of a group of persons, and in cases of an offer embracing a promise for an act designed to produce a unilateral contract, to the world at large.

Carlill v *Carbolic Smoke Ball Co*, 1893 – Offer: the unilateral situation (**46**)

Invitation to treat – auctions

Problems relating to contractual offers have arisen in the case of *auction sales* but the position is now largely resolved. An advertisement of an auction is not an offer to hold it. At an auction the bid is the offer; the auctioneer's request for bids is merely an invitation to treat. The sale is complete when the hammer falls, and until that time any bid may be withdrawn (*Payne* v *Cave* (1789) 3 Term Rep 148).

Where an auction is expressly advertised as subject to a 'reserve price' the above rules are not applied and there is no contract unless and until the reserve price is met and this is so even if the auctioneer knocks the goods down below the reserve price by mistake (*McManus* v *Fortescue* [1907] 2 KB 1). The auctioneer is not liable for a breach of warranty of authority to sell at the price knocked down because the sale is advertised as being subject to a reserve and this indicates to those attending the sale that the auctioneer's authority is limited.

The position when the auction is without reserve is not absolutely certain because it has never been clearly decided whether an advertisement to sell articles by auction without any reserve price constitutes an offer to sell to the highest bidder. It is at any rate clear that s 57(2) of the Sale of Goods Act 1979 prevents any *contract of sale* coming into existence if the auctioneer refuses to accept the highest bid. There remains the possibility once the auction of an item has begun that the auctioneer may be liable in damages on the basis of a breach of warranty that he has authority to sell, and will sell, the goods to the highest bidder. This device appears to be sanctioned by *obiter dicta*, i.e. statements made by the court which were not part of its decision (see further Chapter 7), of the Court of Exchequer Chamber in *Warlow* v *Harrison* (1859) 1 E & E 309.

Harris v *Nickerson*, 1873 – Invitation to treat: the auction situation (**47**)

Invitation to treat – price indications: price lists and catalogues

If I expose in my shop window a coat priced £50, this is not an offer to sell. It is not possible for a person to enter the shop and say: 'I accept your offer; here is the £50.' It is the would-be buyer who makes the offer when tendering the money. If by chance the coat has been wrongly priced, I shall be entitled to say: 'I am sorry; the price is £100', and refuse to sell. An invitation to treat is often merely a statement of the price and not an offer to sell.

The same principles have been applied to prices set out in price lists, catalogues, circulars, newspapers and magazines.

Pharmaceutical Society of Great Britain v *Boots Cash Chemists (Southern) Ltd*,
1953 – Price indications (**48**)

Partridge v *Crittenden*, 1968 – Magazines and circulars (**49**)

Company prospectuses/advertisements in connection with sale of securities

A prospectus/listing particulars issued by a company in order to invite the public to subscribe for its shares (or debentures, i.e. loan capital) is an invitation to treat, so that members of the investing public offer to buy the securities when they apply for them and the company, being the acceptor, will only accept the proportion of public offers which matches the shares or debentures which the company wishes to issue. If there are more offers than shares, the issue is said to be over-subscribed. Some applicants then get no shares at all or only a proportion of what they applied for. The conditions of issue also allow the company to make a binding contract by a *partial* acceptance in this way. Normally acceptance must be absolute and unconditional.

A prospectus is used where the shares are offered on say the Alternative Investment Market and listing particulars are used where the company has a full listing on the main London Stock Exchange.

Other situations

In other cases, such as automatic vending machines, the position is doubtful, and it may be that such machines are invitations to treat. However, it is more likely that the provision of the machine represents an implied offer which is accepted when a coin is put into it. However, it does seem that if a bus travels along a certain route, there is an *implied offer* on the part of its owners to carry passengers at the published fares for the various stages, and it would appear that when a passenger puts himself either on the platform or inside the bus, he makes an *implied acceptance* of the offer, agreeing to be bound by the company's conditions and to pay the appropriate fare: *per* Lord Greene *obiter* in *Wilkie* v *London Passenger Transport Board* [1947] 1 All ER 258.

Price indications

The court may find in a variety of circumstances that an alleged offer is a mere price indication.

Harvey v *Facey*, 1893 – Offers and price indications (**50**)

Those in business clearly require to contract on somewhat firmer ground than is indicated by the above materials. It is therefore common in business contracts to indicate clearly by a clause in the contractual documents that a particular document is not an offer and to omit this information when the relevant document is an offer. Nevertheless, a study of the above materials is necessary in order to understand why certain matters are contained in business contracts.

Acceptance – generally

Once the existence of an offer has been proved, the court must be satisfied that the offeree has accepted the offer, otherwise there is no contract. An agreement may nevertheless be inferred from the conduct of the parties.

The person who accepts an offer must be aware that the offer has been made. Thus if B has found A's lost dog and, not having seen an advertisement by A offering a reward for its return, returns it out of goodness of heart, B will not be able to claim the reward. He cannot be held to accept an offer of which he is unaware. However, as long as the acceptor is *aware* of the making of the offer, his motive in accepting it is immaterial (see *Carlill* v *Carbolic Smoke Ball Co* (1893)).

It should be noted that an acceptance brings the offer to an end because the offer then merges into the contract.

> *Brogden* v *Metropolitan Railway*, 1877 – Acceptance by conduct (**51**)

Conditional assent

An acceptance must be absolute and unconditional. One form of conditional assent is an acceptance 'subject to contract'. The law has placed a special significance on these words, and they are usually construed as meaning that the parties do not intend to be bound until a formal contract is prepared.

In the past the main practical use of this phrase was in correspondence relating to sales of land and agreements for leases of land, to indicate that the correspondence between the parties was part of a process of negotiation and not in itself contractual. Under the Law of Property (Miscellaneous Provisions) Act 1989 a contract for the sale or other disposition of land must now be in writing in a document incorporating all the terms which the parties have expressly agreed and must be signed by each party. Solicitors and conveyancers are thus no longer at risk that pre-contract correspondence signed only by one party might amount to enforceable evidence of the contract itself, which was a possibility before. The practice of heading correspondence 'subject to contract' in the above context has therefore lost its former importance. However, the practice may well continue in case litigation on the 1989 Act provisions reveals an unsuspected trap as a result of its omission.

In addition, the form of words is well established in case law as indicating mere negotiation and there is no reason why it should not be used in pre-contractual correspondence in other fields where the parties wish to indicate that they will not be bound by statements in such correspondence unless they later appear in a formal contract.

It is worth noting that the House of Lords decided in *Walford* v *Miles* [1992] 2 WLR 174 that an agreement to continue negotiations until an agreement was reached was not enforceable as having no legal content. So if A and B agree with each other that they will continue to negotiate with each other in regard to the sale of property belonging to A until they reach a binding agreement, the agreement to negotiate will have no legal effect and B will have no successful claim if, in the course of negotiations between himself and A, A decides to sell the property to C.

However, a negative undertaking by the vendor that he will not for a given period deal with anyone else once the purchaser has agreed to buy and is getting on with the exchange of contracts, is enforceable even if oral. Section 2 of the 1989 Act does not apply. The agreement is not for the sale or disposition of land but only a 'lock-out' agreement not to deal with another for a stated period after which, if contracts are not signed, the vendor can deal with and sell to another. If he does sell within the stated period, he is liable in damages to the would-be purchaser.

Pitt v *PHH Asset Management Ltd*, 1993 – Effect of lock-out agreement (**52**)

Counter-offer

A counter-offer is a rejection of the original offer and in some cases has the effect of cancelling it. Where the counter-offer *introduces a new term*, the original offer is cancelled, though the counter-offer may be accepted either expressly or by implication. However, a simple request for information where the offeree merely *tries to induce a new term* may not amount to an actual counter-offer.

Hyde v *Wrench*, 1840 – Effect of counter-offer (**53**)

Stevenson v *McLean*, 1880 – Request for information (**54**)

Butler Machine Tool Co v *Ex-Cell-O Corporation*, 1979 – Accepting a counter-offer (**55**)

Acceptance in the case of tenders

In the case of an invitation to submit tenders for the purchase of specific goods, as in *Spencer* v *Harding* (1870) where the defendants were selling off a business and issued a circular inviting submission of tenders to buy specific goods listed, the person or company which asks for the tender will usually be regarded as making an invitation to treat. The tender is the offer and the person who asks for it may accept it or reject it as he thinks fit. If tenders are asked for an indefinite amount of goods, e.g. 'coal as required during 2001 not exceeding 100,000 tonnes', the 'acceptance' of such a tender results in a standing offer by the supplier to supply the goods set out in the tender as and when required by the person accepting it. Each time the buyer orders a quantity, there is a contract confined to that quantity; but if the buyer does not order any of the goods set out in the tender, or a smaller number than the supplier quoted for, there is no breach of contract. Conversely, if the person submitting the tender wishes to revoke his standing offer, he may do so, except in so far as the buyer has already ordered goods under the tender. These must be supplied or the tenderer is in breach of contract.

Great Northern Railway v *Witham*, 1873 – The tender as a standing offer (**56**)

Incomplete (or inchoate) agreements

A contract will not be enforced unless the parties have expressed themselves with reasonable clarity on the matter of essential terms. A situation may therefore exist in which the parties have gone through a form of offer and acceptance but this has left some terms unclear so that if either party wishes to avoid the contract he may claim to do so on the basis that he does not know precisely what to do in order to perform his part of it. The concept of the inchoate contract normally arises as a defence to an action for breach of contract.

In such a case it may be possible for the court to complete the contract by reference to a *trade practice* or *course of dealing* between the parties. Sometimes the agreement itself may provide a method of completion as where it contains an arbitration clause. However, if the court cannot obtain assistance from these sources, it will not usually complete the contract for the parties, and the contract, being *inchoate*, cannot be enforced. However, a covenant in a conveyance that the purchaser should be given 'the first option of purchasing . . . at a price to be agreed upon' certain adjoining land imposes an obligation on the vendor at least to offer the land to the purchaser at a price at which he is willing to sell or, in other words, give him first refusal (*Smith* v *Morgan* [1971] 2 All ER 1500).

However, it is necessary to distinguish between a term which has yet to be agreed by the parties and a term on which they have agreed but is in the event meaningless or ambiguous. In the first case, no contract exists unless the deficiency can be made good by the methods outlined above. In the second case, it may be possible to ignore the term and enforce the contract without it. However, if the term is still being negotiated the contract will be inchoate and unenforceable. In addition, the term must be *clearly* severable from the rest of the contract, i.e. it must be possible to enforce the contract without it.

> *Hillas & Co Ltd* v *Arcos Ltd*, 1932 – Inchoate agreements: a course of dealing (**57**)
> *Foley* v *Classique Coaches Ltd*, 1934 – Inchoate agreements: an arbitration clause (**58**)
> *Scammell* v *Ouston*, 1941 – Where the agreement is inchoate (**59**)
> *Nicolene* v *Simmonds*, 1953 – A meaningless term is ignored (**60**)

Communication of acceptance

An acceptance may be made in various ways. It may be made in writing or orally, or at an auction by the fall of the hammer, but it must in general be communicated and communication must be made by a person authorised to make it. Silence cannot amount to acceptance except sometimes where there is the prior consent of the offeree which is, for example, implied in circumstances such as those in *Carlill*'s case (see Case **46**). Thus if P says to Q: 'If I do not hear from you before noon tomorrow, I shall assume you accept my offer', he will find he is unable, at least without Q's consent to this method of making a contract, to bind Q in this way, and Q need take no action at all.

This rule of the common law goes some way towards preventing inertia selling, though protection is now given by the Unsolicited Goods and Services Acts, 1971 and 1975. The Acts provide for fines to be made on persons making demands for payment for goods which they know are unsolicited. If the demand is accompanied by threats a higher scale of fines applies. Furthermore, under s 1 of the 1971 Act, unsolicited goods may be kept by the recipient without payment *after a period of 30 days* provided the recipient gives notice to the sender asking that they be collected, or *after six months* even if no such notice has been given. It should be noted that the Acts are designed to protect the consumer and do not apply where the goods are acquired in the context of a trade or business, i.e. they do not apply to a business recipient.

> *Felthouse* v *Bindley*, 1862 – Silence does not amount to acceptance (**61**)

Waiver of communication

There are some cases in which the offeror is deemed to have waived communication of the acceptance. This occurs in the case of *unilateral contracts* such as promises to pay money in return for some act to be carried out by the offeree. Performance of the act operates as an acceptance, and no communication is required (*Carlill* v *Carbolic Smoke Ball Co* (1893), see Case **46**). In addition, acceptance need not necessarily be communicated if the post is used (see below).

Mode of communication prescribed by offeror

The offeror may stipulate the mode of acceptance, e.g. to be by letter so that there will be written evidence of it. In such a case, however, the offeror could still waive his right to have the acceptance communicated in a given way and agree to the substituted method.

In addition, an acceptance made in a different way may be effective if there is no prejudice to the offeror, as where the method used is as quick and reliable as the method prescribed.

Thus although the method of communication may be prescribed by the offeror very clear words are required to make the court treat that method as essential.

Yates Building Co v *R J Pulleyn & Sons (York)*, 1975 – Prescribed mode of acceptance: the matter of prejudice (**62**)

Oral acceptances

If the offeror has not stipulated a method of acceptance, the offeree may choose his own method, though where acceptance is by word of mouth it is not enough that it be spoken, it must actually be heard by the offeror. In this connection an interesting development occurs with the use of the telephone, teleprinter and, presumably, fax and e-mail. Since these are methods of instantaneous communication, it is held that the contract is not complete unless the apparent communication takes place.

Entores Ltd v *Miles Far Eastern Corporation*, 1955 – Acceptance by telex and telephone (**63**)

Use of post in offer and acceptance

If the post is the proper method of communication between the parties, then acceptance is deemed complete immediately the letter of acceptance is posted, even if it is delayed or is lost or destroyed in the post so that it never reaches the offeror. Nevertheless, the letter of acceptance must be properly addressed, stamped and properly posted and the court must be satisfied that it was within the contemplation of the parties that the post might be used as a method of communicating acceptance. Thus in *Henthorn* v *Fraser* [1892] 2 Ch 27 the post was the proper method of accepting an offer, which the offeror had, in fact, handed to the offeree, because the parties lived in different towns.

The rule relating to acceptance by post is a somewhat arbitrary one seeming to favour the offeree and is in practice kept within narrow confines. For example, if the statements of the parties appear to exclude the rule then the court will not apply it. Where there is a misdirection of a letter containing an offer, then the offer is made when it actually reaches the offeree, and not when it would have reached him in the ordinary course of the post.

In contrast with the rule regarding acceptance by post, a letter of revocation is not effective until it actually reaches the offeree, whereas a letter of acceptance is effective when it is posted (see *Byrne* v *Van Tienhoven* (1880)).

The better view is that, in English law, an acceptance cannot be recalled once it has been posted even though it has not reached the offeror. Thus, if X posted a letter accepting Y's offer to sell goods, X could not withdraw the acceptance by telephoning Y and asking him to ignore the letter of acceptance when it arrived, and Y could hold X bound by the contract if he wished to do so. This is obvious, the rules being what they are, since otherwise Y would be bound when the letter was posted, and X would be reserving the right to withdraw his acceptance during the transit of the letter even though Y was still bound.

There is some controversy as to whether agreement can result from *identical cross-offers*. For example, suppose X by letter offers to sell his bicycle to Y for £50, and Y, by means of a second letter, which crosses X's letter in the post, offers to buy X's bicycle for £50. Can there be a contract? The matter was discussed by an English court in *Tinn* v *Hoffman* (1873) 29 LT 271, and the court's conclusion was that no contract could arise, though this is regarded as too strict a view of the position. The matter is still undecided by the judges and it is possible to hold the view that today a contract would come into being where it appears that the parties have intended to create a legally binding agreement on the same basis.

Household Fire Insurance Co v *Grant*, 1879 – Effect of posting an acceptance (**64**)
Holwell Securities Ltd v *Hughes*, 1974 – The postal rule of acceptance excluded (**65**)
Adams v *Lindsell*, 1818 – A misdirected offer (**66**)

The post rule and e-mail

Legal opinion is divided on the effect of an acceptance by e-mail and clearly the best approach is for those making offers by website or e-mail to stipulate methods of acceptance and when they will be regarded as having concluded a contract. However, where there is no such indication, the better view would seem to be that the post rule does not apply to e-mail acceptances. After all an offeree can always ascertain whether the e-mail has been successfully delivered. Most e-mail software allows for request of delivery receipts and it would seem reasonable to expect this to be used.

Termination of offer

We shall now consider the ways in which an offer may be terminated.

Revocation – generally

The general rule is that *an offer may be revoked at any time before* it is accepted (*Payne* v *Cave* (1789) 3 Term Rep 148). Once an offer has been accepted, it cannot be withdrawn merely because the offeror made a mistake, provided the offeree was not aware of that mistake. Thus in *Centrovincial Estates* v *Merchant Investors Assurance*, *The Times*, 8 March 1983 it was held by the Court of Appeal that a landlord who offered to grant a tenancy at a stated rent of £65,000, which the tenant accepted, could not withdraw the offer merely because he made a mistake in the offer and had intended to ask for a rent of £126,000. If the offeree knows that the offeror is mistaken the contract may be void for unilateral mistake (see Chapter 12).

Sometimes there is what is known as an option attached to the offer, and time is given to the offeree in which to make the decision whether to accept the offer or not. If the offeror agrees to give seven days, then the offeree may accept the offer at any time within seven days, or he need not accept at all. However, the offeror need not keep the offer open for seven days but can revoke it unless the offeree has given some consideration for the option, or the option is made by deed, though even in such a situation the offeror can still revoke the offer but will in that event be liable to the offeree in damages for breach of the option.

Revocation, to be effective, must be communicated to the offeree before he has accepted the offer. The word 'communication' merely implies that the revocation must have come to the knowledge of the offeree.

Presumably the offeree cannot ignore facts suggesting an attempt to communicate a revocation. If A offers B a car and before B accepts A posts a letter of revocation which B receives but, recognising A's handwriting, does not open until he has written and posted a letter of acceptance, it would seem unfair to regard A as bound in contract and he would probably not be. In addition, it appears from statements made in the House of Lords in *Eaglehill Ltd* v *J Needham (Builders) Ltd* [1972] 3 All ER 895, where their Lordships were discussing notice of dishonour of a bill of exchange, that an offer would be revoked when the letter of revocation 'was opened in the ordinary course of business or would have been so opened if the ordinary course of business was followed'.

Communication may be made directly by the offeror or may reach the offeree through some other reliable source. Suppose X offers to sell a car to Y and gives Y a few days to think the matter over without actually giving him a valid option. If, before Y has accepted, X sells the car to Z and Y hears from P that X has in fact sold the car, it will be of no use for Y to purport to accept and try to enforce the contract against X, provided P is a reliable source.

Routledge v *Grant*, 1828 – Revocation where there is an option (**67**)

Byrne v *Van Tienhoven*, 1880 – Communication of revocation (**68**)

Dickinson v *Dodds*, 1876 – Communication of revocation by third parties (**69**)

Revocation – unilateral contracts

Where the offer consists of a promise in return for an act, as where a reward is offered for the return of lost property, the offer, although made to the whole world, can be revoked as any other offer can. It is thought to be enough that the same publicity be given to the revocation as was given to the offer, even though the revocation may not be seen by all the persons who saw the offer.

A more difficult problem arises when an offer which requires a certain act to be carried out is revoked after some person has begun to perform the act but before he has completed it. If, for example, X offers £1,000 to anyone who can successfully swim the Channel, and Y, deciding he will try to obtain the money, starts his swim from Dover, can X revoke his offer from a helicopter when Y is half-way across the Channel? One view is that he cannot on the grounds that an offer of the kind made by X is two offers in one, namely (i) to pay £1,000 to a successful swimmer and (ii) something in the nature of an option to hold the offer open for a reasonable time once performance has been embarked upon, so that the person trying to complete the task has a reasonable time in which to do so.

Other lawyers reach the same conclusion by distinguishing between the acceptance of the offer and the consideration necessary to support it. As regards the latter, the completion of the act involved is necessary before the offeror can be required to pay any money because until the act is completed the necessary consideration has not been supplied. However, acceptance may be assumed as soon as the offeree has made a beginning on the performance of the contract and proof of the fact that he has made a beginning makes revocation impossible. The problem could have arisen in *Carlill*'s case if the company had tried to revoke its offer after Mrs Carlill had started to perform the contract by using the smoke ball.

The matter also came before the Court of Appeal in *Errington* v *Errington* [1952] 1 All ER 149. In that case a father bought a house for his son and daughter-in-law to live in. He paid the deposit but the son and daughter-in-law made the mortgage payments after the father gave the building society book to the daughter-in-law, saying, 'Don't part with this book. The house will be your property when the mortgage is paid.' The son left his wife who continued to live in the house. It was held by the Court of Appeal that neither the father nor the claimant, his widow, to whom the house was left by will, could eject the daughter-in-law from the property. As Lord Denning said: 'The father's promise was a unilateral contract – a promise of the house in return for their act of paying the instalments. It could not be revoked by him once the couple entered on the performance of the act . . .' The court went on to decide that the son and daughter-in-law would be fully entitled to the house once they had made all the mortgage repayments.

Lapse of time

If a time for acceptance has been stipulated, then the offer lapses when the time has expired. If no time has been stipulated, then the acceptance must be within a reasonable time. What is reasonable is a *matter of fact* for the judge to decide on the circumstances of the case.

Ramsgate Victoria Hotel Co v *Montefiore*, 1866 – Offer and lapse of time (**70**)

Conditional offers

An offer may terminate on the happening of a given event if it is made subject to a condition that it will do so, e.g. that the offer is to terminate if the goods offered for sale are damaged before acceptance. Such a condition may be made expressly in the contract as where, e.g., a seller offers to sell goods by tender from time to time subject to a condition that the seller can himself obtain adequate supplies. It may also be implied from the circumstances.

Financings Ltd v *Stimson*, 1962 – Conditional offers (**71**)

Effect of death of a party

The effect of death would appear to vary according to the type of contract in question, whether the death is that of the offeror or the offeree, and whether death takes place before or after acceptance.

Death of offeror before acceptance

It would seem that if the contract envisaged by the offer is not one involving the personality of the offeror, the death of the offeror may not, until notified to the offeree, prevent acceptance.

However, there is a contrary point of view based on an *obiter dictum* in the judgment of Mellish, LJ in *Dickinson* v *Dodds* (1876) where he said, 'it is admitted law that, if a man who makes an offer dies, the offer cannot be accepted after he is dead . . .'. However, the decision in *Bradbury* v *Morgan* (1862) (see below) suggests that the offer can be accepted until the offeree is told of the offeror's death. The matter is therefore unresolved pending a further decision. If the contract envisaged by the offer does involve a personal relationship, such as an offer to act as agent, then the death of the offeror certainly prevents acceptance.

Death of offeree before acceptance

Once the offeree is dead, there is no offer which can be accepted. His executors cannot, therefore, accept the offer in his stead. The offer being made to a living person can only be accepted by that person and assumes his continued existence. The rule would seem to apply *whether the proposed contract involves a personal relationship or not.*

Death of parties after acceptance

Death after acceptance has normally no effect unless the contract is for personal services, when the liability under the contract ceases. Thus, if X sells his car to Y and before the car is delivered X dies, it would be possible for Y to sue X's personal representatives for breach of contract if they were to refuse to deliver the car. But if X agrees to play the piano at a concert and dies two days before the performance, one could hardly expect his personal representatives to play the piano in his stead.

> *Bradbury* v *Morgan*, 1862 – Where the offeror dies before acceptance (**72**)
> *Re Cheshire Banking Co*, 1886 – Where the offeree dies before acceptance (**73**)

Offer and acceptance not identifiable

Sometimes the usual processes of offer and acceptance are not easily identifiable and yet a contract is deemed to exist (*The New Zealand Shipping Co Ltd* v *AM Satterthwaite & Co Ltd* (1974) – see Chapter 15). There are also situations of collateral contract. These derive from another main contract, and for purposes of illustration reference should be made to the case law and comment as indicated below.

> *Rayfield* v *Hands*, 1958 – The concept of the collateral contract (**74**)

Trading electronically

Electronic trading or electronic commerce (e-commerce) is trading carried on by electronic means. In its simplest form it involves an exchange of e-mails instead of letters, and the law to be applied is presumably that applied to instantaneous communications like telex (see *Entores* v *Miles Far East Corporation* (1955)), but there are more complex forms in which a contract can be concluded by communication between two or more computers without any immediate human intervention. The means by which e-commerce is conducted is the Internet.

Open e-commerce

This occurs where the parties have contracted through the means of an Internet website on which a supplier is, say, offering goods for sale.

Whilst the legal rules relating to this form of trading are largely a matter of informed surmise and largely untested in the courts, the following matters should be borne in mind.

If demand exceeds supply. The seller will wish to avoid actions for breach of contract by reason of his inability to meet orders from customers responding to the seller's website. In these circumstances every website should make clear that the seller is not making an offer to supply the goods but inviting offers from potential customers (i.e. an invitation to treat). If this is done, the website should be regarded in law as a mere shop window.

Customer's orders. Since we are dealing with instantaneous communication, customer's orders must be received by the seller. This may not happen, given the occasional vagaries of e-mail, which may lead to the loss of or the scrambling of the order. The website should carry a cut-off date for receipt of orders. If the acceptance is via a website, the position is likely to be clearer, since the seller and the customer can immediately identify whether or not communication has broken down.

Whose terms apply? Sellers will normally be using standard terms for each customer and to ensure that the seller's terms apply the potential customer should be asked to scroll through the terms to indicate his agreement to them. This should be done before the contract is made.

Conflict of laws. In terms of international trading, the seller should state the law which applies to the contract, e.g. English law. Sometimes, however, the law of the customer's state may override the adoption of foreign law for international agreements and a careful check should be made and legal advice taken before embarking on international sales. If there is uncertainty as to foreign law or the seller does not wish to become involved, orders from a particular country or countries which might raise applicable problems of law should be declined.

A problem that has faced those wishing to engage in e-commerce is that the law has not recognised the validity of electronic signatures so that there was, e.g., no way in which a deed could be made by electronic means. However, the Electronic Communications Act 2000 makes provision for this by changing all those laws which require an actual signature so that an electronic signature is now acceptable. Digital signatures can now be used.

A significant impact of the 2000 Act is for property lawyers who are now able to use electronic conveyancing and in this context it is worth noting that the Law of Property (Miscellaneous Provisions) Act 1989 already contains provisions allowing the use of electronic signatures in land deals – a forward looking piece of legislation. The 1989 Act is considered in Chapter 11.

Contract formation and call centres

A caller to a call centre may well enter into a contract for the call centre's client's goods or services. The client needs to look at the way in which contract law governs the formation of such a contract. The position is as follows:

- the caller will normally be the offeree and the call centre operator the offeror;
- if the call centre operator does not receive the message of acceptance through no fault of his own though the caller thinks he has, there is not likely to be a contract (*Entores Ltd* v *Miles Far East Corporation* (1955));

■ if, however, it is the call operator's fault that he did not receive the acceptance, e.g. because he did not hear it and failed to ask that it be repeated, he may be estopped or precluded from denying that he did receive it and a contract will come into being;

■ it is always necessary to attend to the matter of consideration and intention to create legal relations, though these matters should not normally provide a problem in the call-centre context.

9

10

MAKING THE CONTRACT II

In this chapter we continue the study of those elements of contract law which go to making a mere agreement into a contract which is at least potentially binding on the parties. Consideration and intention to create legal relations are looked at here.

Consideration

Definition and related matters

Consideration, which is essential to the formation of any contract not made by deed was defined in *Currie* v *Misa* (1875) LR 10 Ex 153 as:

> Some right, interest, profit or benefit accruing to one party, or some forbearance, detriment, loss or responsibility given, suffered or undertaken by the other.

Paying (or promising to pay) money in return for the supply of goods or services constitutes the most common form of consideration.

Consideration may be *executory*, where the parties exchange promises to perform acts in the future, e.g. C promises to deliver goods to D and D promises to pay for the goods; or it may be *executed*, where one party promises to do something in return for the act of another, rather than for the mere promise of future performance of an act. Here the performance of the act is required before there is any liability on the promise. Where X offers a reward for the return of his lost dog, X is buying the act of the finder, and will not be liable until the dog is found and returned.

The definition in *Currie* v *Misa* suggests that consideration always refers to the type called executed consideration since it talks of 'benefit' and 'detriment', whereas in modern law executory contracts are enforceable. Perhaps the definition given by Sir Frederick Pollock is to be preferred:

> An act or forbearance of one party, or *the promise thereof*, is the price for which *the promise* of the other is bought, and *the promise* thus given for value is enforceable.

This definition, which was adopted by the House of Lords in *Dunlop* v *Selfridge* (1915), fits executory consideration as well as executed. The 'promise for a promise' concept really means that consideration can consist in a promise to act in the future, e.g. to deliver goods or to pay for goods.

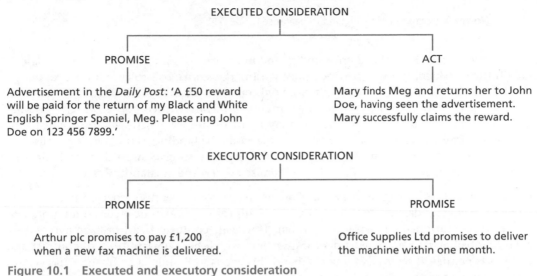

Figure 10.1   Executed and executory consideration

Consideration in relation to formation of a contract – generally

There are a number of general rules governing consideration in terms of the formation of a contract:

(a) Simple contracts must be supported by consideration. This has a long history, but in practical terms it is the common law's way of limiting the number of agreements which can be brought before the courts for enforcement. Other legal systems have required, e.g., part performance by one or other of the parties or that the contract be made in writing and, if so, no consideration is required. The effect of the consideration rule is that in English law an agreement, even if the parties intend legal relations, is not a contract unless it is supported by consideration or made by deed.

(b) Consideration need not be adequate, but must have some value, however slight. The courts do not exist to repair bad bargains, and though consideration must be present, the parties themselves must attend to its value. However, where the consideration for a transaction is of very small value, it may raise a suspicion of fraud, duress or undue influence on the part of the person gaining the advantage. However, what is offered by way of consideration must be capable of expression in terms of economic value or at least the giving up of some right. That apart, acts or omissions even of a trivial nature may be sufficient to support a contract.

> *Thomas* v *Thomas*, 1842 – Adequacy of consideration (**75**)
>
> *Chappell Co Ltd* v *Nestlé Co Ltd*, 1959 – Adequacy: a commercial application (**76**)
>
> *White* v *Bluett*, 1853 – Economic value required (**77**)

Although there were once arguments to the contrary, it is now accepted that an express or implied forbearance to sue may be adequate consideration. It is not necessary to show that the action would have succeeded but merely that if it had been brought to trial it might have done. Thus the court would be unlikely to accept that a bookmaker could supply consideration by forgoing a claim against a client for stake money. Such an action, being based on an illegal transaction, could have no hope of success.

Horton v *Horton*, 1961 – Implied forbearance to sue (**78**)

A self-seeking act in itself may not suffice, and in the case of *Carlill* v *Carbolic Smoke Ball Co* (1893) the consideration was provided not by using the smoke ball to cure influenza, but by the unpleasant method of its use. A gift promised conditionally may be binding, if the performance of the condition causes the promisee trouble or inconvenience, e.g. 'I will give you my old car if you will tow it away.' So too may a gift of property with onerous obligations attached to it, e.g. a promise to give away a lease would be binding, if the donee promised to perform the covenants to repair and pay rent. A promise to give away shares which were partly paid up would be good, if the donee promised to pay the outstanding calls.

(c) Bailment. The concept of *bailment* gives rise to problems because a person may be held liable for negligent damage to or loss of goods in his care, although he received no money or other consideration for looking after them. However, confusion can best be avoided by regarding bailment as an independent transaction, which has characteristics of contract and tort but is neither. It seems that when X hands his goods to Y under a bailment Y has certain duties in regard to the care of the goods, whether the bailment is accompanied by a contract or not.

Of course, the court may be invited to refuse a claim on the contract by a person who has given inadequate consideration by invoking the doctrine of inequality of bargaining power (see further Chapter 13). However, at the present time the basis of this doctrine, which was applied in particular by Lord Denning, is somewhat vague and has not, as yet, received much direct judicial support.

Gilchrist Watt and Sanderson Pty v *York Products Pty*, 1970 – Bailment and consideration (**79**)

(d) Consideration must be sufficient. Sufficiency of consideration is not the same thing as adequacy of consideration, at least in law. The concept of sufficiency arises in the course of deciding whether the acts in question *amount to consideration at all*. This situation arises where the consideration offered by the promisor is an act which he is already bound to carry out. Thus, the discharge of a *public duty* imposed by law is not consideration nor is the performance of a *contractual duty* already owed to the defendant. However, where the contractual duty is not precisely coincident with the public duty but is in excess of it, performance of the contractual duty may provide consideration and the actual performance of an outstanding contractual obligation may be sufficient to support a promise of a further payment by a third party.

Collins v *Godefroy*, 1831 – Sufficiency and public duties (**80**)
Stilk v *Myrick*, 1809 – Sufficiency and contractual duties (**81**)
Glasbrook Bros Ltd v *Glamorgan County Council*, 1925 – Sufficiency: public duty exceeded (**82**)
Shadwell v *Shadwell*, 1860 – Sufficiency: payments by third parties (**83**)

(e) Consideration must be legal. An illegal consideration makes the whole contract invalid (see further Chapter 16).

(f) Consideration must not be past. Sometimes the act which one party to a contract puts forward as consideration was performed before any promise of reward was made by the other. Where this is so, the act in question may be regarded as past consideration and will not support a contractual claim. This somewhat technical rule seems to be based on the idea that the act of one party to an alleged contract can only be regarded as consideration if it was carried out in response to some promise of the other. Where this is not so, the act is regarded as gratuitous, being carried out before any promise of reward was made.

However, there are exceptions to this rule:

(i)   Where services are rendered at the express or implied request of the promisor in circumstances which raise an implication of a promise to pay. This exception is not entirely a genuine one since the promisor is assumed to have given an implied undertaking to pay at the time of the request, his subsequent promise being regarded as deciding merely *the actual amount* to be paid. In this situation the act, which follows the request but precedes the settling of the reward, is more in the nature of *executed consideration* which, as we have seen, will support a contract.

(ii)   A debtor or his duly authorised agent can make a written acknowledgement of the debt to the creditor or his agent (Limitation Act 1980, s 29). Time begins to run again from the date of acknowledgement. However, once a debt is statute barred it cannot be revived in this way (s 29(7) of the 1980 Act) (see further Chapter 18). Again, this exception is not wholly genuine since the Limitation Act 1980 does not provide that past consideration will support the subsequent acknowledgement of debt. The Act simply states that *no consideration of any kind* need be sought.

(iii) Section 27 of the Bills of Exchange Act 1882 provides that an antecedent debt or liability will support a bill of exchange or cheque. This genuine exception was probably based on a pre-existing commercial custom. This is essential particularly in the case of cheques many of which are based on a form of past consideration. Thus, if S sells goods to B, a debt comes into being payable in legal tender (i.e. bank notes or coins – see further Chapter 17) when the contract is made. So when B decides to pay S by cheque, which he may do provided S is agreeable, the cheque is based upon a previous or antecedent debt or liability and is for past consideration. Nevertheless, this type of consideration will support the cheque should an action be brought on it.

> *Re McArdle*, 1951 – Consideration must not be past (**84**)
> *Re Casey's Patents, Stewart* v *Casey*, 1892 – The effect of a previous request (**85**)

(g) The Contracts (Rights of Third Parties) Act 1999 has no direct effect on the concepts of adequacy, sufficiency and past consideration discussed above. The 1999 Act has an effect where A contracts with B to give a benefit to C. In these circumstances C may have rights under the 1999 Act to sue A for failure to perform the contract. However, if the consideration moving between A and B does not conform with the above rules (or there is no consideration), the contract is not enforceable by B or C (or A for that matter) and the 1999 Act does not change that situation.

(h) Consideration must move from the promisee, i.e. the person to whom the promise is made (the promisee) must give some consideration for it to the promisor. From this arises the doctrine of privity of contract which is considered below.

Privity of contract

This means that in general third parties cannot sue for the carrying out of promises made by the parties to a contract. Thus, if a contract between A and B requires B to benefit C, the privity rule prevents C from suing B. However, A may sue B if B breaks the contract, and the court may award A damages or may grant a decree of specific performance under which B must perform the contract for the benefit of C. If A and C are, in fact, both parties to the contract with B then C still cannot sue B unless he has provided some consideration. Merely being a party to the contract is not enough. Even though C may be named in the document, if any, which records and constitutes the contract between A and B, or may be a party to their oral deliberations, if he does not undertake anything in return for a promise from A or indeed from B, then he is not participating in a bargain with A and/or B and is not a party to the contract. This view is based upon the belief that the 'privity' rule is merely an aspect of the rule that 'consideration must move from the promisee'. The position is different if A, B and C are parties to a deed. C can then sue B for damages if B fails to carry out his promises in the deed. Deeds do not require consideration.

> *Tweddle* v *Atkinson*, 1861 – Privity of contract illustrated (**86**)
> *Dunlop* v *Selfridge*, 1915 – Privity: a further application (**87**)
> *Jackson* v *Horizon Holidays*, 1975 – Remedies of the promisee: damages (**88**)
> *Beswick* v *Beswick*, 1967 – Remedies of the promisee: specific performance (**89**)

Main exceptions to the privity rule

There are cases in which a person is allowed to sue upon a contract to which he is not a party as follows.

The Contracts (Rights of Third Parties) Act 1999

This important piece of legislation provides a major exception to the law of privity of contract. It received the Royal Assent on 11 November 1999. For six months from that date it only applied where its provisions were said expressly to apply in the contract. After that it applies to nearly all categories of agreement unless expressly excluded.

The Act provides for a major and far-reaching method of preventing the application of the privity rule. The Act brings English law into line with the position in Scotland, in most member states of the European Union and in many of the common law countries of the world, including the USA. The harmonisation of business law in this way is of benefit to the business community.

The Act implements the recommendations of the Law Commission in Report No 242, *Privity of Contract: Contracts for the Benefit of Third Parties*, published in July 1996. Before looking at its provisions, it should be noted that there is no change to the rule of law which states that a burden cannot be imposed on a third party without his consent. Thus, in general terms, a person can assign the right to receive money owed to him but cannot without the consent of all parties assign the burden of paying his debts. The Act deals only with the conferring of benefits on third parties.

Section 1

This section is at the heart of the Act. It deals with the circumstances in which a third party may have the right to enforce a term of a contract. He will have that right:

- where the contract contains an express term saying so;
- where a term of the contract purports to confer a benefit on him.

This part of s 1 will not apply if it appears on a true construction of the contract that the contracting parties did not intend the third party to have a right to enforce it. Thus, if a contract confers a benefit on a child, it may also provide specifically that any claim in respect of it should be brought by either of its parents and in such a case the child could not bring a claim under the Act. The parents would have the third-party rights. In order to acquire the third-party right, the party concerned must be expressly identified in the contract but need not be identified by name. It is enough if the third party is identified as a member of a class, e.g. 'both of my children'.

In addition, so long as the third party is adequately described, that party need not be in existence when the contract is made. It might, therefore, be in the business context, that a company as yet not incorporated but to be incorporated may take benefits under a contract made by its promoter.

Remedies available to the third party will be the same as those available to a party to a contract bringing an action for its breach and the rules relating to damages, injunctions, specific performance and other relief will apply, as will mitigation of loss. Section 1 also defines 'promisor' and 'promisee' as used in the Act. The *promisor* is the person against whom the contractual term is enforceable by the third party. The *promisee* is the contracting party by whom the term is enforceable against the promisor. Thus in a contract by A with B for the benefit of C, A is the promisor and B is the promisee. C sues under third-party rights. Section 1 also makes it clear that the third party may take *advantage* of any exclusion or limitation clause in the contract.

Section 2

This restricts the way in which the contracting parties can alter the third party's entitlement under the contract without his consent once the third party has the right to enforce the term. There may be no variation or cancellation of the contract after the third party has accepted the term as by written notice to the promisor or relied on it when the promisor knows of or can reasonably be expected to have foreseen that reliance. Suppose A, a wealthy businesswoman, sells one of the many businesses that she owns to B in return for the payment of an annuity of £15,000 a year to her favourite nephew Sam, by B. So long as Sam has not accepted the payment term, A and B could alter it to, say, £12,000 a year, but once Sam has accepted it or, say, B has made a payment under it and can be assumed to expect that Sam will rely on getting future payments, the term cannot be altered without Sam's consent. If he never accepts or if there is no evidence of reliance, Sam is still entitled to the payment, but it could be altered without his consent. Acceptance by post is not effective until received by the promisor. This is contrary to the general rules of contractual acceptance by post. In keeping with the Act's preservation of the freedom of the parties to make their own contract, the above rules relating to third-party consent may be displaced by an express term of the contract providing that the contract can be cancelled or varied without the third party's consent. Where the consent of the third party is required, the court may on the application of both parties to the contract dispense with that consent where:

- it cannot be obtained because his or her whereabouts are unknown; or
- he or she is mentally incapable of giving consent.

This will enable the parties to the contract to change the third-party beneficiary or to remove the contract term so that there are not third-party rights in it.

The courts having power to make the variation are the High Court and county court.

Section 3

This deals with the defences, set-offs and counterclaims available to the promisor in proceedings by a third party to enforce a term of the contract. Illustrations are as follows:

- The third party cannot enforce the contract if it is void as where it is affected by agreement mistake or illegality or has been discharged as where the promisor has performed the contract, e.g. by making a payment or supplying goods under it, or is unenforceable as where the third party is given rights on a contract of guarantee which is not evidenced in writing (see Formalities in Chapter 11. This provision follows from the fact that in the circumstances the promisee could not enforce it either (s 3(2)).

■ A (the promisor) contracts with B (the promisee) that B will sell goods to A, who will pay the price of the goods, to C (the third party). If B delivers sub-standard goods to A in breach of contract and A is sued by C for the price, then A is entitled to counterclaim to reduce or extinguish the price by reason of B's breach of contract. B could also be faced by this counterclaim if he or she were to sue A (s 3(2)).

■ A and B make a contract under which A will pay C if B transfers his car to A. B already owes money to A under a different and unrelated contract, say, in connection with the previous sale of a van. A and B agree to an express term (as the Act requires) in the contract which states that A can raise against a claim by C any matter which would have given A a defence or set-off to a claim by B. Thus, in a claim by C for the money, A can set-off what he is owed by B (s 3(3)).

Section 3 also makes it clear that the promisor also has available any defence or set-off and any counterclaim not arising from the contract with B but which is specific to the third party. Illustrations are as follows:

■ A contracts with B to pay C £2,000, C already owes A £600. A may set-off against any claim by C the £600 and need only pay C £1,400.

■ C induces a contract between A and B by misrepresentation of which B is unaware. A has a defence or a counterclaim for damages when sued by C which he or she would not have had against B (s 3(4)).

The agreement may specifically provide e.g. that A will not raise set-off or counterclaim in an action by C (s 3(5)).

Section 4
This states that the Act does not affect the rights of the promisee A to enforce any term of the contract including the term which benefits the third party. Thus B can sue on behalf of C.

Section 5
This states that if the promisee B has already recovered a sum by way of damages for the promisor's breach, then in a claim by the third party C this sum will be taken into account in terms of any sum recovered by C. This is to prevent A from suffering a double liability.

Section 6
This excludes certain types of contract from the operation of the Act. Main examples are:

■ A third party is prevented from suing an employee for a breach of his contract of employment. Without this exception there could be a risk that workers taking lawful industrial action might be sued and restricted from doing so in unexpected ways. It is worth noting here that the Trade Union and Labour Relations (Consolidation) Act 1992 gives individuals the right to bring proceedings to halt *unlawful* industrial action which deprives them of goods and services.

■ The s 6 provisions also prevent third-party rights arising from the 'deemed' contracts under s 14(1) of the Companies Act 1985 under which the memorandum and articles of a registered company constitute a contract between the company and its members in respect of their rights as such. The special nature of these deemed contracts makes them unsuitable for enforcement by a third party under the 1999 Act, which is a general reform.

Also excluded are contracts for the carriage of goods by sea, as are contracts for the international carriage of goods by road, rail or air, which are covered by international conventions. Nevertheless, the Act allows third parties to enforce exclusion or limitation of liability clauses in the above contracts. For example, the person who charters a ship may make a contract with the owner of the goods being carried that the shipowner is not liable for damage resulting from negligent stowage. The Act enables the shipowner as a third party to rely on that exclusion clause should the owner of the goods sue him. The business application is that the price of the carriage will be cheaper if the shipowner knows he can rely on the clause. In a similar way, exclusions and defences available to the carrier of goods can be extended to employees' agents and independent contractors such as stevedores engaged in loading and unloading, and will be effective without the legal gymnastics seen in *New Zealand Shipping Co Ltd* v *A M Satterthwaite & Co Ltd* (1975) (Case **181**).

Contracts contained in a bill of exchange, promissory note or other negotiable instrument are also excluded.

Section 7

This preserves any rights or remedies which may be available to a party at common law or by statute apart from the Act, for example, by making ineffective a contractual provision which tries to exclude liability for personal injury or death. However, the section ensures that a third party cannot use the 'reasonableness' test under s 2(2) of the Unfair Contract Terms Act 1977 to try to defeat a clause excluding liability for other damage caused by negligence on the ground that the exclusion is unreasonable. (See Chapter 15.) The policy of the Act is to let the parties decide to what extent they should be sued by the third party. The opposing view that the policy of the law should be against unreasonable terms in contracts whoever relies on them and in whatever situation did not prevail.

Effect on business

The Act has significant implications for almost all kinds of contract. All businesses should review their standard form and other contracts to see where advantage may be taken of the new law and to decide where its effects might be excluded for it is possible to opt out. In particular businesses may wish to look again at those contracts where devices such as agency and trust law have been used to get round the privity rule.

The following areas will be of benefit in company law and company formation:

- *Group purchasing companies*. In many situations one company in a group of companies will enter into a contract to purchase goods or services which will be used by other companies in the group. Formerly the other group companies had no right to enforce the contract directly and it was difficult for the contracting group company to recover for loss suffered by other group companies (see *Jackson* v *Horizon Holidays* (1975) (Case **88**)). The contracting group company can now use the Act to give the other group companies a right to enforce the contract directly.
- *Directors' and officers' insurance*. Companies are allowed by the Companies Act 1999 to take out insurance against liability of directors and officers. The 1999 Act allows the company to confer direct rights on the directors and officers concerned to enforce the insurance contract themselves instead of the company having to do so on their behalf.
- *Pre-incorporation contracts*. The promoters of companies may use the Act to give direct rights to newly formed companies to enforce contracts made on their behalf prior to their incorporation. Under the 1999 Act the third party does not have to be in existence when the contract is made.
- *Exclusion*. The effects of the Act are likely to be uncertain and far-reaching and until there is defining case law it is likely (and sensible) for those in business to exclude, at least in the generality of contracts, the application of the Act as the Act permits.

10

Agency

A principal, even if undisclosed, may sue on a contract made by an agent. This exception is perhaps more apparent than real, because in fact the principal is the contracting party who has merely acted through the instrumentality of the agent.

Cheques and bills of exchange

Bills of exchange provide an exception. Suppose A buys goods from B but does not wish to pay immediately; then, if B agrees, a period of credit can be achieved by using a bill of exchange. A takes the goods and B draws up a bill of exchange on a standard form under which A (the drawee) agrees to pay the bill at some time in the future, say three months from the date on the bill. B (the drawer) can make himself or another person the payee. Let us suppose he makes himself the payee. B has now a choice: he can wait three months and get the money from A; or he can discount the bill with a bank, so that the bank will present the bill for payment by A after three months; or B can sign it (indorse it) over to someone else. Suppose he indorses it over to his daughter C as a birthday present. Can C sue A if she presents him with the bill for payment on the due date and he does not pay it? The answer is 'yes' because, although C gave no consideration to A or B, s 27 of the Bills of Exchange Act 1882 gives C a statutory right to sue. In order to make bills as negotiable as possible, the technical rule of privity is not applied. C could not sue B on the bill because, as between immediate parties, consideration is required.

It used to be possible to give an indorsed cheque as an example but this is impractical since the passing of the Cheques Act 1992. This makes clear that a cheque crossed 'account payee' or 'a/c payee', with or without the word 'only', is not transferable. The banks are now printing these words on cheques issued to customers and reinforcing the non-transferability rule by removing the words 'or order' after the payee's name and inserting 'only'. However, the example given is quite valid as regards bills of exchange other than cheques, since these remain transferable unless crossed 'a/c payee', but this is a matter for the parties and bills of exchange which are not so crossed remain transferable.

The Contracts (Rights of Third Parties) Act 1999 does not apply to these instruments.

Insurance

Section 11 of the Married Women's Property Act 1882 provides that if a man insures his life for the benefit of his wife and/or children, or a woman insures her life for the benefit of her husband and/or children, a trust is created in favour of the objects of the policy, who, although they are not parties to the contract with the insurance company, can sue upon it. In addition the policy moneys are not liable for the deceased's debts.

Bankers' commercial credits and performance bonds

As regards bankers' commercial credits, it is common commercial practice for an exporter, E, to ask the buyer of the goods, B, to open, with his banker, a credit in favour of E, the credit to remain irrevocable for a specified time. B agrees with his banker that the credit should be opened and, in return, promises to repay the banker, and usually gives him a lien over the shipping documents. The banker will also require a commission for his services. B's banker then notifies E that a credit has been opened in his favour, and E can draw upon it on presentation of the shipping documents.

It will be seen that E and B's banker are not in privity of contract. It might be thought that this could give rise to problems in the unlikely event that the banker did not pay. However, this is not so. In fact the buyer/customer of the bank cannot stop payment. In *Malas (Hamzeh) v British Imex* [1958] 1 All ER 262 the claimants, who were buyers of goods, applied to the court for an injunction restraining the sellers (who were the defendants in the case) from drawing under a credit established by the buyer's bankers. The Court of Appeal refused to grant this injunction and Jenkins, LJ said: 'The opening of a confirmed letter of credit constitutes a bargain between the banker and the vendor of the goods which imposes on the banker an absolute obligation to pay . . .'. Sellers, LJ said that there could well be exceptions where the court could exercise a jurisdiction to grant an injunction, as where there was a fraudulent transaction. However, in other situations the binding nature of the banker's commercial credit is an exception to the doctrine of privity of contract.

There have been similar developments making performance bonds enforceable by commercial custom so that where a bank guarantees performance of an export contract by the supplier a claim may be made against the bank if the contract is not performed. The leading authority for this is *Edward Owen Engineering Ltd* v *Barclays Bank International Ltd* [1978] 1 All ER 976.

There is no reason why the right of exporters to sue the relevant bank should not be contained in the contract between B and his banker providing the credit under the Contracts (Rights of Third Parties) Act 1999. However, the rule that the bank always pays (fraud apart) is such a part of international commerce that the case law rules may well be felt sufficient in themselves.

Assignment

If A owes B £10 B may assign the right to receive the money to C and provided that assignment is a legal assignment (as distinct from an equitable one) C may sue A without the assistance of B as a party to the claim. The matter of assignment is considered more fully in Chapter 22.

Land law – generally

The position in land law is that benefits and liabilities attached to or imposed on land may in certain circumstances follow the land into the hands of other owners.

> *Smith and Snipes Hall Farm Ltd* v *River Douglas Catchment Board*, 1949 –
> Exceptions to the privity rule: passing of benefits (**90**)
> *Tulk* v *Moxhay*, 1848 – The passing of burdens (**91**)

Land law – leases

The rule of privity of contract had an unfortunate effect on leases of land in the sense that if the original tenant under the lease assigned his tenancy to another tenant with the landlord's consent the original tenant, being in privity with the landlord, could not get rid of the duties under the lease. If, therefore, the person to whom the lease was assigned did not, for example, pay the rent the original assignee could be required to do so and this remained the case where there were further assignments to other assignees. The Landlord and Tenant (Covenants) Act 1995 abolished this liability in the original tenant so that the landlord will only be able to sue the tenant for the time being unless there is an authorised guarantee agreement in force. Under the Act a landlord may require an assigning tenant to enter into a guarantee with the landlord as a condition of the landlord giving his assent to the lease being assigned. Under such an agreement the outgoing tenant would guarantee the performance of the terms of the lease, e.g. payment of rent by his immediate (but not subsequent) assignee. The rules relating to leases are, as we have seen, contained in the Landlord and Tenant (Covenants) Act 1995 which applies to the exclusion of the Contracts (Rights of Third Parties) Act 1999.

Privity and claims against insolvent businesses

If an employee is injured by his employer's negligence and the employer is, for example, a company that goes into liquidation, the Third Parties (Rights Against Insurers) Act 1930 allows the injured employee to make a claim against the company's insurers directly, thus avoiding a proof in the company's liquidation which might only produce a small payment covering only part of the claim.

However, the claim against the insurer is not straightforward since the insurer is only liable to indemnify the company, so that the victim must sue the company to establish its liability before the insurance company is obliged to pay. This may mean an action at law to restore the company to the register if it has been struck off on liquidation and another action to establish its liability. It may then be necessary to bring a legal action against the insurance company if it fails to pay for some reason. The Law Commission published a consultation paper in the spring of 1998 suggesting legislative changes to enable claims to be dealt with in one set of proceedings. As yet, there is no legislation.

Consideration viewed in relation to the discharge or variation of a contract

All that has so far been said in regard to consideration relates to the *formation* of a contract. As we have seen, there must be consideration in order to bring a contract into existence, deeds apart. The rules are rather different where a contract is to be *discharged* or *varied*. There are a number of ways in which a contract may be discharged, all of which will be dealt with later. However, the one with which we are now concerned is *discharge by agreement* under which contract A is to be discharged or varied by a new contract, B, the question being to what extent does contract B require consideration? The attitude of the common law is different from that of equity, as we shall see.

Common law – the rule of accord and satisfaction

At common law if A owes B £10 and wishes to discharge that obligation by paying B £9, he must:

(*a*) obtain the agreement (accord) of B; and

(*b*) provide B with some consideration (satisfaction) for giving up his right to £10 unless the release is by deed.

This is the common-law rule of accord and satisfaction. The rule is an ancient one and an early example of it is to be found in the judgment of Brian, CJ in *Pinnel*'s Case (1602) 5 Co Rep, 117a. Pinnel sued Cole in debt for what would now be £8.50 which was due on a bond on 11 November 1600. Cole's defence was that at Pinnel's request he had paid him £5.12 on 1 October and that Pinnel had accepted this payment in full satisfaction of the original debt. Although the court found for Pinnel on a technical point of pleading, it was said that:

(*a*) payment of a lesser sum on the due day in satisfaction of a greater sum cannot be any satisfaction for the whole; but

(*b*) payment of a smaller sum at the creditor's request before the due day is good consideration for a promise to forgo the balance for it is a benefit to the creditor to be paid before he was entitled to payment and a corresponding detriment to the debtor to pay early.

The first branch of the rule in *Pinnel's* Case was much criticised but was eventually approved by the House of Lords, and the doctrine then hardened because of the system of binding precedent.

Exceptions to the rule

The practical effect of the rule is considerably reduced under common law by the following exceptions which have been made to it:

(a) Where there is a dispute as to the sum owed. If the creditor accepts less than he thinks is owed to him the debt will be discharged. For example, A says that B owes him £11. B says it is only £9. A agrees to take £10. Then, even if it can be proved that A was owed £11, he cannot recover the £1. He has compromised his claim.

(b) Where the creditor agrees to take something different in kind, e.g. a chattel, the debt is discharged by substituted performance. Thus, if A gives B a watch worth £5 and B is agreeable to taking it, then the debt of £10 will be discharged. The legal theory here seems to be that the article given may be worth more than the balance of the debt and the court is not prepared to be a valuer. In this connection it should be noted that a cheque for a smaller sum no longer constitutes substituted performance.

(c) The payment of a smaller sum before the larger is due gives the debtor a good discharge. This is the second branch of the rule in *Pinnel's* Case.

(d) If a debtor makes an arrangement with his creditors to compound his debts, e.g. by paying them 85p in the £1, he is satisfying a debt for a larger sum by the payment of a smaller sum. Nevertheless, it is a good discharge, the consideration being the agreement by the creditors with each other and with the debtor not to insist on their full rights.

(e) Payment of a smaller sum by a third party operates as a good discharge.

Foakes v *Beer*, 1884 – *Pinnel's* Case: House of Lords approves (**92**)

D & C Builders v *Rees*, 1965 – Cheque not substituted performance: extinguishing rights (**93**)

Good v *Cheesman*, 1831 – Compositions with creditors (**94**)

Welby v *Drake*, 1825 – Payments by third parties (**95**)

Equity – the rule of promissory estoppel

There has always been some dissatisfaction with the common-law rule of accord and satisfaction. After all, if A owes B £10 and B agrees to take £9, as he must before there can be any question of discharging the obligation of A to pay £10, why should B be allowed afterwards to break his promise to take £9 and succeed in an action against A simply because A gave him no consideration?

It was to deal with this sort of situation that the equitable doctrine of promissory estoppel was propounded, first by Lord Cairns in *Hughes* v *Metropolitan Railway* (1877) 2 App Cas 439 and later by Denning, J (as he then was) in the *High Trees* case (1947) (see below) and later by the House of Lords in *Tool Metal Manufacturing Co Ltd* v *Tungsten Electric Co Ltd* (1955) (see below).

The doctrine of estoppel is basically a rule of evidence under which the court, surprisingly enough, is not prepared to listen to the truth.

It occurs at common law out of physical conduct. Suppose A and B go into a wholesaler's premises and A asks for goods on credit. The wholesaler, who knows that B is creditworthy, but has no knowledge of A, is not prepared to give credit until A says, 'Do not worry, you will be paid, B is my partner'. If B says nothing and A receives the goods on credit and does not pay, then B could be sued for the price, even though he can produce evidence that he was not in fact A's partner. This evidence will not be admitted because the wholesaler relied on a situation of partnership created by B's conduct and the statement is concerned with *existing fact* which is essential at common law (see *Jorden* v *Money* (1854) 5 HL Cas 185). A statement about *future conduct* is not enough at common law.

Promissory estoppel in equity is very little different except that the equitable estoppel arises from a *promise* and not from *conduct*. The common law does not recognise an estoppel arising out of a promise, or a statement about *future conduct*, but equity does.

Ingredients of promissory estoppel

The doctrine of promissory estoppel has the following ingredients:

(a) It arises from a promise made with the intention that it should be acted upon. The promise must be clear and unambiguous to the effect that strict legal rights will not be enforced. It must also be unconscionable to allow the promise to be disregarded. It is difficult to say when this might be the case. However, the courts may very well, in practice, decide (i) that it is unconscionable, in equity, to revoke any agreement modifying an obligation unless it is done quickly and before any action has been taken on it so that if a tenant actually pays a lower rent under a promise that he may do so it will not be possible to recover the rent forgiven though the payment of the full rent can be required for the future if the landlord gives reasonable notice (see the *High Trees* case below) or (ii) unless the promise to modify was extorted under duress as in *D & C Builders* v *Rees* (1965).

(b) It was once thought that the person who had received the promise must do something to show that he had relied on it. If A, a landlord, said B could pay only half his usual rent while he was unemployed, it was thought that B would have to show, for example, that he had spent what should have been the rent money on travelling expenses to find work in the district. Reliance upon the promise in this way is not, it would appear, a necessary requirement. All that would seem to be necessary is that the debtor has made the part-payment; he need not do anything else.

(c) It relates only to variation of a contract by agreement and does not affect the requirement of consideration on formation of contract.

(d) So far as the rule has been developed in cases, it *merely* suspends rights but does not totally discharge them because it does not preclude enforcement of the original contract after reasonable notice has been given. Thus it does not create a binding variation for the future (see *Tool Metal Manufacturing Co Ltd* v *Tungsten Electric Co Ltd* below).

(e) The promise must be freely given and not extorted by threats (see *D & C Builders* v *Rees* (1965) above).

(f) Of considerable importance is a *dictum* by Lord Denning in *D & C Builders* v *Rees* (1965) (see above) that the rule could be developed to the point at which it operated, not merely to suspend rights, but to preclude enforcement of them. If this point is reached, then if A owes £10 and B agrees to take £9, A will be discharged from his obligation to pay £10 without the need for consideration.

Such a situation would involve a virtual overruling of *Foakes* v *Beer* (1884) (see above) and would put an end to the first branch of the rule in *Pinnel's* Case which is that payment of a lesser sum on the day due in satisfaction of a greater sum cannot be any satisfaction for the whole. Although in the past a number of *dicta* by Lord Denning have been incorporated into the *ratio* of subsequent decisions, the position outlined here has not yet been reached.

The High Trees case, 1947 – The rule of promissory estoppel (**96**)

Tool Metal Manufacturing Co Ltd v *Tungsten Electric Co Ltd*, 1955 – Promissory estoppel merely suspends rights (**97**)

Alan v *El Nasr*, 1972 – No need for reliance on promise (**98**)

Combe v *Combe*, 1951 – Rule not applicable to formation of contract (**99**)

Discharge of contract by performance – relevance of the *High Trees* case

10

The rule of equitable estoppel has relevance in discharge of a contract by performance (see Chapter 17). Although the agreed date of delivery must usually be complied with in a contract of sale, the buyer may waive the condition relating to the date of delivery and accept a later date. Such a waiver may be binding on him whether made with or without consideration. It was held by Lord Denning in *Charles Rickards Ltd* v *Oppenhaim*, 1950 (see Chapter 17) that the binding nature of a waiver without consideration might be based on the *High Trees* case (i.e. a promissory estoppel to accept a later delivery date). Alternatively, the seller may rely on s 11(2) of the Sale of Goods Act 1979, which states: 'Where a contract of sale is subject to any condition to be fulfilled by the seller, the buyer may waive that condition.'

Equitable estoppel – other applications

The principle of equity on which promissory estoppel is based is one of general application and may be applied whenever the court feels it is necessary in the interests of justice to do so.

Durham Fancy Goods v *Michael Jackson (Fancy Goods) Ltd*, 1968 – Equitable estoppel: use other than in discharge or variation of contract (**100**)

Intention to create legal relations

The law will not necessarily recognise the existence of a contract enforceable in a court of law simply because of the presence of mutual promises. It is necessary to establish also that both parties made the agreement with the intention of creating legal relations so that if the agreement was broken the party offended would be able to exercise legally enforceable remedies. The subject can be considered under two headings as follows.

Cases where the parties have not expressly denied their intention to create legal relations

Advertisements

Most advertisements are statements of opinion and as such are not actionable. Thus, unless the advertisement makes false statements of specific verifiable facts, which is rare, the court will not enforce the claims made for the product on a contractual basis. However, where a company deposits money in the bank against possible claims, the court is likely to hold that legal relations were contemplated (*Carlill* v *Carbolic Smoke Ball Co* (1893)), though a deposit is not essential (*Wood* v *Lectric Ltd* (1932) – see Chapter 9).

Family agreements

Many of these cannot be imagined to be the subject of litigation but some may be. The question is basically one of construction and the court looks at the words and the surrounding circumstances. The two basic divisions of family agreements are set out below.

(a) Husband and wife. With regard to agreements between husband and wife, it is difficult to draw precise conclusions. However, the following situations have appeared in decided cases.

(i)   Where husband and wife were living together in amity when the agreement was made, the agreement is not enforceable as a contract because legal proceedings are an inappropriate method of settling purely domestic disputes.

(ii) Where husband and wife were living together but not in amity or were separated altogether when the agreement was made, the court may enforce it.

(iii) If the words used by the parties are uncertain, the agreement will not be enforced – the uncertainty leading to the conclusion that there was no intention to create legal relations. Thus in *Gould* v *Gould* [1969] 3 All ER 728 a contractual intention was negatived where a husband on leaving his wife undertook to pay her £15 per week 'so long as I can manage it'. The uncertainty of this term ruled out a legally binding agreement.

Agreements of a non-domestic nature made between husband and wife are enforceable, e.g. in *Pearce* v *Merriman* [1904] 1 KB 80 it was held that a husband may be his wife's tenant and as such could be made to pay the rent.

(b) Other family and personal relationships. The question of intention to create legal relations arises for consideration here as well but it seems that the less close the relationship between the parties the more likely it is that the court *will presume* that legal relations were intended. However, in these cases also uncertainty as to the terms of the agreement normally leads to the conclusion that there was no contractual intention.

Other cases

There may well be other areas where intention to create legal relations is doubtful but which have not been the subject of cases in court. Again, the matter is one of fact for the court. However, in the case of clubs and societies many of the relationships which exist and promises which are made are enforceable only as moral obligations. They are merely *social agreements*. For example, the decision in *Lens* v *Devonshire Club*, *The Times*, 4 December 1914, would suggest that if a person competes for a prize at a local golf club and is the winner, he or she may not be able to sue for the prize which has been won if it is not otherwise forthcoming.

However, in *Peck* v *Lateu* (1973) *The Times*, 18 January, two ladies attended bingo sessions together and had an arrangement to pool their winnings. One of them won an additional

'Bonanza' prize of £1,107 and claimed it was not covered by the sharing arrangements. Pennycuick, VC held that there was an intention to create legal relations and to share all prizes won. The claimant was entitled to a share in the prize.

It should also be borne in mind that quotations and estimates may be passed from one person to another without any intention that they should be legally binding *at that stage.*

Balfour v *Balfour*, 1919 – Husband and wife living in amity (**101**)

Merritt v *Merritt*, 1970 – Effect of separation (**102**)

Simpkins v *Pays*, 1955 – Intention in family relationships (**103**)

Jones v *Padavatton*, 1969 – Family relationships and uncertainty (**104**)

Cases where the parties expressly deny any intention to create legal relations

By contrast with family arrangements, agreements of a commercial nature are *presumed* to be made with contractual intent. Furthermore, the test applied by the court is an *objective* one so that a person cannot escape liability simply because *he did not* have a contractual intention. The presumption is a strong one and it was held in *Edwards* v *Skyways Ltd* [1964] 1 All ER 494 that the use of the words *ex gratia* in regard to an airline pilot's contractual redundancy payment did not displace the presumption, so that the airline had to make the payments and did not have a discretion whether to make them or not.

However, the Court of Appeal has held more recently that a court need not necessarily presume intention to create legal relations just because the parties are in business.

Kleinwort Benson Ltd v *Malaysian Mining Corporation, Berhad*, 1989 – Business contracts: intention usually but not always assumed (**105**)

Some agreements where the court would normally assume an intention to create legal relations may be expressly taken outside the scope of the law by the parties agreeing to rely on each other's honour. This is a practice which appears to be allowable to pools companies who are especially subject to fraudulent entries but should not be allowed to spread into other areas of *standardised* contracts, i.e. contracts where the consumer has no choice of supplier as where he requires electrical services laid on which can only be provided by a monopoly corporation.

There is no such objection where business persons reach agreements at arm's length, and if the parties expressly declare, or clearly indicate, that they do not wish to assume contractual obligations, then the law accepts and implements their decision.

Jones v *Vernon's Pools Ltd*, 1938 – Business agreements: contractual intent may be excluded (**106**)

Rose and Frank Co v *Crompton (JR) & Bros Ltd* 1925 – An honourable pledge clause (**107**)

Statutory provisions

Sometimes an Act of Parliament renders an agreement unenforceable. Thus under s 1 of the Law Reform (Miscellaneous Provisions) Act 1970, a contract of engagement, which is, in effect, an agreement to marry, is not enforceable at law since there is a statutory presumption that there was no intention to create legal relations. Thus actions for breach of promise are no longer possible.

In addition, under s 29 of the Post Office Act 1969, the acceptance of ordinary letters and packets for transmission does not give rise to a contract between the Post Office and the sender.

Finally, under s 179 of the Trade Union and Labour Relations (Consolidation) Act 1992, collective agreements between trade unions and employers (or employers' associations) concerning industrial conditions such as hours, wages, holidays, procedures in disputes and so on, are presumed *not* to be intended to be legally enforceable unless they are in writing and contain a provision to that effect.

However, under s 70A and Sch A1 of the 1992 Act, as inserted by the Employment Relations Act 1999, arrangements between an employer and a trade union in regard to recognition for the purposes of collective bargaining have effect as legally binding agreements, specific performance being the only remedy for breach.

11

MAKING THE CONTRACT III

In this chapter we shall conclude the study of those elements of contract law which go to making a *mere agreement* into *a binding contract*. *Formalities (or the need for writing)* and the requirement that the parties must have capacity in law to make the contract are considered here.

Formalities

In most cases a contract made orally (or by parol, which is an alternative expression) is usually just as effective as a written one. Exceptionally, however, written formalities are required as follows.

Contracts which must be made by deed

A lease of *more* than three years should be made by deed otherwise no legal estate is created (see ss 52 and 54 of the Law of Property Act 1925). If there is no deed then there is in equity a contract for a lease. This is an estate contract under s 2(3) of the Law of Property Act 1925. It is enforceable against third parties who acquire the freehold from the landlord only if it has been registered at the Land Registry. Registration gives notice to the whole world. Failure to register makes the contract void against a later purchaser of the freehold from the landlord for a consideration, even though in fact the purchaser *knows* the lease exists (Law of Property Act 1925, s 199(1)). The purchaser could turn out the tenant if the lease was not registered. However, where it is registered the tenant is protected.

It should be noted, however, that the Court of Appeal decided in *Crago v Julian* [1992] 1 All ER 744 that a distinction must be made between the *creation* of a lease and its *assignment*. If tenant A wishes, say, to sell his lease to B, the assignment from A to B must be by deed, even though the original lease given to A was oral and for three years or less. This arises from ss 52 and 53 of the Law of Property Act 1925, which deal with the transfer of interests in land.

As regards the form of a deed, the Law of Property (Miscellaneous Provisions) Act 1989 is now relevant and was considered in Chapter 9.

Estoppel and deeds

Because the deed is the most formal and considered form of contract making the deed is subject to the rule of estoppel that says that a party who executes a deed, i.e. signs it, cannot say in a court of law that the deed is not true as to the facts stated in it. Thus, although a deed was not signed in the presence of a witness, although it was signed by a witness, the Court of Appeal ruled that a person who had agreed by the deed to be personally liable for a debt owed by a bank of which he was a director could not deny his liability because he had signed the deed even though not in the presence of the witness as the law requires (see *Shah* v *Shah* [2002] QB 35).

Comment A deed requires attestation and the form required to satisfy this requirement is 'signed as a deed by AB in the presence of CD'. So, because the deed says that *as a fact* it must be regarded as correct even if it is not.

Contracts which must be in writing

For example, the following simple contracts are required by statute to be in writing, otherwise they are affected in various ways:

(a) By reason of amendments to the Consumer Credit Act 1974 made by the Consumer Credit Act 2006, all consumer credit agreements of any amount are covered by the legislation, although there is an exemption for lending over £25,000 to large businesses. The amount refers to the credit provided. If these agreements are not in appropriate written form they cannot be enforced by the dealer, unless the court thinks it is fair in the circumstances to allow him to enforce the contract.

(b) Contracts of marine insurance, which must be embodied in a written policy, otherwise the contract is not effective, being inadmissible in evidence unless embodied in a written policy signed on behalf of the insurer (Marine Insurance Act 1906, s 22).

(c) Contracts for the sale or other disposition of land are required by statute to be in writing, otherwise they are invalid, i.e. there is no contract. Section 2(1) of the Law of Property (Miscellaneous Provisions) Act 1989 provides that a contract for the sale or other disposition of an interest in land can only be made in writing and only by incorporating all the terms which the parties have expressly agreed in one document or, where contracts are exchanged, in each contract. The document must be signed by each party. As regards the requirement that the parties must sign a copy of the agreement, it was held by the Court of Appeal in *Firstpost Homes* v *Johnson* [1995] 4 All ER 355 that the word 'signed' in the 1989 Act meant that the parties must sign their names in their own hand. A typed signature was not enough even though earlier cases on the requirements of writing under previously applicable legislation had decided that a typed signature was acceptable.

There are some exceptions to the above requirements as follows:

(i) leases for three years or less where the tenant takes possession can be granted orally;
(ii) sales at public auctions are excluded and the contract is regarded as made when the auctioneer's hammer falls. There is thus no requirement of writing at all at auction sales;
(iii) section 2(5) of the 1989 Act provides that the requirements of the Act do not prevent the creation of implied trusts over land where these arise orally. Thus, in *Yaxley* v *Gotts* [1999] EGCS 92 there was an oral agreement between the freehold purchaser of a property and a builder that if the builder would convert the property into flats the freeholder would grant him a long lease of the ground floor flat. The builder carried out the work supplying services and materials. The freehold owner then refused to grant him a lease of the flat and claimed that the agreement for it was unenforceable since it was not in writing. The Court of Appeal said that the circumstances had created a constructive trust over the flat in favour of the builder and since such trusts do not require writing and s 2(5) provides for this in the context of the case, the builder could enforce the oral trusts. The court granted him a 99-year lease.

Since the document must now contain all the terms agreed by the parties and be signed by both parties, solicitors and conveyancers are no longer at risk that pre-contract correspondence signed by only one party might amount to a contract itself as was a possibility before. The practice of heading correspondence 'subject to contract' can now be brought to an end but some lawyers may advise its retention in case a judicial interpretation reveals an unexpected trap in its omission. Also, there should not be a problem as to whether the parties to a sale or other disposition of land intended legal relations because there will be a formal contract.

Contracts which must be evidenced in writing

Here we are concerned with contracts of guarantee where the Statute of Frauds 1677 requires writing which, though not essential to the formation of the contract, is needed as evidence if a dispute about it comes before a court. The court will not enforce the guarantee in the absence of written evidence.

The provision in the Statute of Frauds applies to guarantees and not to indemnities. It is therefore necessary to distinguish between these two. In a contract of indemnity the person giving the indemnity makes himself primarily liable by using such words as 'I will see that you are paid'.

In a contract of guarantee the guarantor expects the person he has guaranteed to carry out his obligations and the substance of the wording would be: 'If he does not pay you, I will'. An indemnity does not require writing because it does not come within the Statute of Frauds: a guarantee requires a memorandum.

An additional distinction is that it is an essential feature of a guarantee that the person giving it is totally unconnected with the contract except by reason of his promise to pay the debt. Thus a *del credere* agent who, for an extra commission, promises to make good losses incurred by his principal in respect of the unpaid debts of third parties introduced by the agent, may use the guarantee form 'if they do not pay you I will' but no writing is required. Such a promise is enforceable even if made orally because even where a person does promise to be liable for the debt of another that promise is not within the Statute of Frauds where it is, as here, an incident of a wider transaction, i.e. agency.

> *Mountstephen v Lakeman*, 1871 – Guarantee and indemnity distinguished (**108**)

The memorandum in writing to satisfy the court need not exist when the contract is made but must be in existence when an action, if any, is brought for breach of the guarantee. A guarantee cannot be proved orally – writing is required as evidence. The memorandum must identify the parties, normally by containing their names. The material terms must be included, e.g. that it is a guarantee of a bank overdraft facility limited to £50,000. The memorandum must also contain the signature of the party to be charged or his agent properly authorised to sign. However, the law is not strict on this point and initials or a printed signature will do (contrast the position under the Law of Property (Miscellaneous Provisions) Act 1989, above). The 'party to be charged' is the proposed defendant and there may be cases where one party has a sufficient memorandum to commence an action whereas the other may not since the memorandum does not contain the other party's signature. This could happen where the memorandum was in a letter written by Bloggs to Snooks. The letter would presumably be signed by Bloggs but not by Snooks. It would therefore be a good memorandum for an action by Snooks but not by Bloggs. Section 3 of the Mercantile Law Amendment Act 1856 dispenses with the need to set out the consideration in the memorandum but it must exist. It is normally the extension of credit by A to B in consideration of C's guarantee of B's liability if B fails to pay.

Signatures and electronic trading

A problem which has faced those wanting to engage in electronic commerce is the fact that the law did not recognise the validity of electronic signatures so that e.g. there was no way in which a deed could be made by electronic means. However, the Electronic Communications Act 2000 is now in force. Among the main provisions is one to introduce measures to promote the legal recognition of electronic signatures. In this connection the Law of Property (Miscellaneous Provisions) Act 1989 has abolished the previous rule that a deed must be written on paper, thus clearing the way for the making of deeds by electronic means. The Act provides that digital signatures be given legal force and will set up a voluntary licensing system for trusted third parties that offer signature and encryption services. Existing laws (as set out in this chapter) which require the use of paper will be swept away. Digital signatures are forgery-resistant computer codes which are used to prove someone's identity.

Delegated legislation will be required to make the Act of 2000 fully effective. There are so many instances, e.g. in the law of real property, where paper documents with signatures on them are required. Areas for change are being identified prior to legislation.

An electronic signature need not be in the form of a code. For example, an e-mail which is signed off 'yours faithfully, J. Bloggs' is a valid electronic signature. However, the High Court ruled in *J Pereira Fernandes SA* v *Mehta* [2006] 2 All ER 891 that a guarantee was unenforceable because the only thing approaching a signature in the e-mail which set out the guarantee was the automatic insertion of the sender's e-mail address after the e-mail had been transmitted by an internet service provider. An e-mail address, said the court, was not a signature but in the view of the court more like a phone or fax number.

Capacity to contract

Adult citizens have full capacity to enter into any kind of contract but certain groups of persons and corporations have certain disabilities in this connection. The most important groups for our purposes are dealt with below.

Minors

The Family Law Reform Act 1969, s 1, reduced the age of majority from 21 to 18 years. Contracts made by minors were governed by the common law (including parts of sale of goods legislation) as amended by the Infants Relief Act 1874 and the Betting and Loans (Infants) Act 1892. The Minors' Contracts Act 1987 repealed the relevant parts of the 1874 and 1892 Acts so that minors' contracts are now governed by the rules of common law (including the Sale of Goods Act 1979) as amended by the Minors' Contracts Act 1987.

Valid contracts

These are as follows:

(a) Executed contracts for necessaries. These are defined in s 3(3) of the Sale of Goods Act 1979 as 'Goods suitable to the condition in life of the minor and to his actual requirements at the time of sale and delivery'. If the goods are deemed necessaries, the minor may be compelled to pay a reasonable price which will usually, but not necessarily, be the contract price. The Sale of Goods Act does not, of course, cover necessary *services* such as, for example, a series of treatments by an osteopath. However, the common law applies and follows the Sale of Goods Act by requiring the minor to pay a reasonable price. The minor is not liable if the goods, though necessaries, have not been delivered or the service has not yet been rendered, i.e. there is no claim for breach of contract. This, together with the fact that he is only required to pay a reasonable price, illustrates that a minor's liability for necessaries is only quasi-contractual.

If the goods (or services) have a utility value, such as clothing, and are not merely things of luxury, e.g. a diamond necklace, then they are basically in the category of necessaries. Whether the minor will have to pay a reasonable price for them depends upon:

(i) the minor's income which goes to his condition in life. If he is wealthy, as where he has a good income from a trust, then quite expensive goods and services may be necessaries for him, provided they are useful;

(ii) the supply of goods which the minor already has. If the minor is well supplied with the particular articles then they will not be necessaries, even though they are useful and are well within his income.

(b) Contracts for the minor's benefit. These include contracts of service, apprenticeship and education.

However, trading contracts of minors are not enforceable no matter how beneficial they may be to the minor's trade or business. The theory behind this rule is that when a minor is in trade his capital is at risk and he might lose it, whereas in a contract of service there is no likelihood of capital loss.

> *Nash* v *Inman*, 1908 – What are necessaries? (**109**)
>
> *Roberts* v *Gray*, 1913 – Contracts which are beneficial (**110**)
>
> *Mercantile Union Guarantee Corporation* v *Ball*, 1937 – Trading contracts not 'beneficial' (**111**)

Contracts not binding unless ratified

These are as follows:

(a) Loans. These are not binding on the minor unless he ratifies the contract of loan after reaching 18 which he may now legally do. No fresh consideration is now required on ratification.

(b) Contracts for non-necessary goods. Again, these are not binding on the minor unless he ratifies the contract after reaching 18, as he may now legally do. Once again, no fresh consideration is required on ratification.

It should be noted that in spite of the fact that the contracts in (*a*) and (*b*) above are not enforceable against the minor, he gets a title to any property which passes to him under the arrangement and can give a good title to a third party as where, for example, he sells non-necessary goods on to someone else (who takes in good faith and for value). This was decided in *Stocks* v *Wilson* [1913] 2 KB 235. Furthermore, any money or property transferred by the minor under the contract can only be recovered by him if there has been a total failure of consideration (see below).

Contracts binding unless repudiated

These are usually contracts by which the minor acquires an interest of a permanent nature in the subject matter of the contract. Such contracts bind the minor unless he takes active steps to avoid them, either during his minority or within a reasonable time thereafter. Examples of voidable contracts are shares in companies, leases of property and partnerships.

Steinberg v *Scala (Leeds) Ltd*, 1923 – Minors: voidable contracts (**112**)

Consequences of the defective contracts of minors

We must now have a look at what happens where there has been some performance of a contract with a minor which is either not binding unless ratified or binding unless repudiated.

Recovery by minor of money paid

Where a minor has paid money under these defective contracts he cannot recover it unless total failure of consideration can be proved, i.e. that the minor has not received any benefit at all under the contract. The court is reluctant to say that no benefit has been received. This can be seen in the context of a contract not binding unless ratified in *Pearce* v *Brain* (see below) and in the context of a contract binding unless repudiated in *Steinberg* v *Scala* (see above).

Pearce v *Brain*, 1929 – Recovery of money paid or property transferred (**113**)

Effect of purchase by minor of non-necessary goods

As we have seen, the minor acquires a title to the goods and can give a good title to a third party who takes them *bona fide* and for value (*Stocks* v *Wilson* [1913] 2 KB 235). The tradesman who sold the goods to the minor cannot recover them from the third party.

However, as regards recovery from the minor, if he still has the property, s 3 of the Minors' Contracts Act 1987 provides that the court can order restitution, for example, of non-necessary goods to the tradesman, where the minor is refusing to pay for them. As we know, he cannot be sued for the price.

The question of recovery in any particular case is left to the court which must regard it as just and equitable to allow recovery, though a restitution order can be made whether the minor is fraudulent, as where he obtained the goods by overstating his age, *or not*. Fraud is no longer a requirement for restitution. Money will be virtually impossible to recover because it will normally be mixed with other funds and not identifiable. However, the minor could be made under s 3 to offer up any goods acquired in exchange for the non-necessary goods. The tradesman recovers the goods in the state he finds them and cannot ask for compensation from the minor if they are, for example, damaged.

Thus, if Ann, a minor, buys a gold necklace and does not pay for it, the seller can recover the necklace from Ann. If Ann exchanges the necklace for a gold bangle, the seller can recover the gold bangle from Ann. If Ann sells the necklace for £500, it is not clear whether the seller can get restitution of the money unless it has been kept separate from Ann's other funds or can be identified in a fund containing other money of Ann's, for example, a bank account into which she has paid her salary. Section 3 says that the seller can recover the article passing under the contract 'or any property representing it'. It is at least arguable that Ann's general funds do not solely represent the necklace in the way that the bangle does. Judicial interpretation is required.

Guarantees

Section 2 of the Minors' Contracts Act 1987 provides that a guarantee by an adult of a minor's transaction shall be enforceable against the guarantor even though the main contractual obligation is not enforceable against the minor. Thus, if a bank makes a loan to a minor or allows a minor an overdraft and an adult gives a guarantee of that transaction, then although the loan or overdraft cannot be enforced against the minor, the adult guarantor can be required to pay.

Mental disorder and drunkenness

11

Where the property and affairs of a person who lacks capacity under the Mental Capacity Act 2005 are placed under the management of the Court of Protection by means of a court appointed person called a 'deputy' (formerly a 'receiver'), that person has no capacity to contract as regards that property but the deputy has. In other cases, s 1 of the 2005 Act states that a person must be assumed to have capacity unless it can be established, normally to the satisfaction of the court, that he or she lacks capacity, in which case there is no contract. The burden of proof falls on the person who says that capacity is lacking. Section 7 of the 2005 Act deals with necessary goods and services and provides that, if necessary goods or services are supplied to a person who lacks capacity to contract for the supply, he or she must pay a reasonable price for them. The section goes on to define 'necessaries' as goods or services suitable to a person's condition in life and to his or her actual requirements at the time of supply. The common law rule that a person who makes a contract while lacking capacity can ratify it at a later stage if he or she recovers sufficiently to understand the transaction would seem to survive and continue to apply.

As regards persons who make contracts while drunk, the common law applies and the position is as follows:

(a) A contract made by a person who by reason of drunkenness is incapable of understanding what he is doing is valid unless he or she can prove:

(i) that he or she did not understand the nature of the contract; and
(ii) that the other party knew this to be the case.

(b) A contract made by such a person is binding on him or her if he or she afterwards ratifies it at any time when the state of mind is such that the person can understand what he or she is doing.

(c) Where necessaries are sold and delivered to a person who by reason of drunkenness is incompetent to contract, he or she is bound to pay a reasonable price (Sale of Goods Act 1979, s 3(2)). This is also true of services, but by reason of the common law.

(d) Necessaries are 'goods suitable to the condition in life of such person and to his actual requirements at the time of the sale and delivery' (1979 Act, s 3(3)). The common law defines necessary services in the same way. Therefore the principle of 'necessaries' is applied to persons who are drunk in the same way as it is to minors and s 7 of the Mental Capacity Act follows this.

> *Imperial Loan Co* v *Stone*, 1892 – Contract and mental disorder (**114**)
> *Matthews* v *Baxter*, 1873 – Contracts with drunkards (**115**)

Lasting powers of attorney

Professionals in practice, such as solicitors and accountants, may have clients who are of advancing years and whose sanity may come into doubt at a future time and where there is a desire to avoid the cost and delay of deputy proceedings through the court. In this connection the Mental Capacity Act 2005 makes it possible for the ageing person to enter into an agreement with, say, a younger member of the family (or the practitioner) being the agent. Such an agreement does not terminate on the client's loss of capacity as other forms of agency do. Thus an application for a deputy is avoided as are the uncertainties that may arise from not knowing precisely when or if the client/principal actually became mentally incapable. The instrument creating the power must be in the form prescribed by the 2005 Act. Lasting powers of attorney are wider in scope than the former enduring powers of attorney. The latter related mainly to financial affairs, whereas the lasting power extends also to things such as healthcare and general welfare of the person who gives the power.

Corporations

We have seen that regardless of the method by which it is formed, a company on incorporation becomes a *legal person*, acquires an identity quite separate and distinct from its members, and carries on its activities through agents (see Chapter 8). In carrying out those activities and making contracts companies and their agents are to some extent restrained by the *ultra vires* rule. *Ultra vires* acts are those which are *beyond the powers* of the company. Our main concern here is to look at that rule as it affects registered companies.

Ultra vires rule – statutory and registered companies

The powers of statutory corporations are contained in the statute setting them up and these powers are sometimes increased by subsequent statutes or by delegated legislation. Acts beyond these powers are *ultra vires* and *void*, i.e. of no effect.

Before proceeding to discuss the contractual capacity of the registered company after the intervention of the Companies Act 2006 and previous legislation, the reader should refer to the *Ashbury* case (see below) for a classic example of the *ultra vires* rule at common law as a way of appreciating the statutory changes.

> *Ashbury Railway Carriage & Iron Co* v *Riche*, 1875 – The *ultra vires* rule before the intervention of Parliament (**116**)

By way of explanation of the decision in the *Ashbury* case, it should be said that the *ultra vires* rule was brought in by the courts in earlier times to protect shareholders. It was thought that if a shareholder X bought shares in a company which had as its main object publishing and allied activities then X would not want the directors of that company to start up a different kind of business because he wanted his money in publishing.

In more recent times it has been noted that shareholders are not so fussy about the kind of business the directors take the company into so long as it makes money to pay dividends and raises the price of the company's shares on the stock market thus giving a capital gain. In these days of the conglomerates it is doubtful whether any investor invests in a company because of only one facet of its trading.

The legal position today

Section references are to the Companies Act 2006.

Section 39 – A company's capacity

This section provides that the acts of a company are not to be questioned on the ground of lack of capacity because of anything in the constitution of the company and so contracts beyond the company's powers (where the articles, and not as before the memorandum, contain restrictions on business) are valid and enforceable by the company and the other party. Post the coming into force of the Companies Act 2006, new companies requiring restrictions will put them in a clause in the articles of association and where an existing company has restrictions in the memorandum these will be deemed to be in the articles. The articles can be altered by a resolution of the members.

There is no power, as there was in previous law, giving members the right to restrain acts of the directors beyond the company's powers or their own because under the provisions of the Companies Act 2006, companies will normally have unrestricted objects so that such a power would be pointless. Where there are restrictions in the articles on the company's powers or on the directors' powers, there are provisions in the Companies Act 2006 for the company to have civil remedies against the directors, e.g. to recoup for the company any loss it has suffered from the directors involved.

Section 40 – Power of directors to bind the company

For those dealing with the company in good faith, the power of the directors to bind the company or authorise others (agents) to do so is deemed not to be constrained by the company's constitution. External parties need not enquire whether there are any limitations on the powers of the directors, nor are they affected by actual knowledge that the directors have no power. External parties must, however, be 'dealing with the company', which will normally require involvement with some commercial transaction such as the buying and selling of goods or the provision of services.

Section 41 – Constitutional limitations: directors and their associates

Company insiders such as directors and their associated persons, e.g. husband or wife, do not have the protection of s 40 so that the relevant transaction can be avoided by the company and not enforced against it.

Insiders and any authorising directors are liable to account to the company for any gain made by them and to indemnify the company for any loss or damage caused to it even though the contract was avoided by the company, e.g. legal costs not recoverable by the company in connection with the avoidance.

Insiders who are not directors may be able to avoid the abovementioned liability if they did not know when entering into the transaction with the company that the directors were acting beyond their powers and so an associated or connected person, such as a husband or a wife, may not always be liable.

Transactions will not be avoidable if restitution of the company's property is not possible, as where the company's money has been spent by a director on a cruise (and there is no restitution against the cruise company unless it was in some way involved in the director's breach of duty) or the company has been indemnified or the company through its members has affirmed (or approved) of the transaction.

Section 42 – Charities

This section provides that, for companies that are charities, the rules relating to the capacity of the company and the power of its directors to bind it shall not apply to an external party unless that party did not know that the company was a charity when the act was done or the charity receives full consideration in regard to the act done and the external party did not know that the act was beyond the powers of the company and therefore beyond the powers of its directors to bind it.

Charitable companies cannot affirm a transaction so as to make valid those acts infringing the above rules without the prior written consent of the Charity Commissioners.

The above rules would not apply so as to invalidate an illegal act as where the directors issue shares at a discount, i.e. a share with a nominal value of £1 for 80 pence, because this is forbidden by the Companies Act 2006.

12

REALITY OF CONSENT I

In this chapter we begin a study of the various factors which can affect an agreement once it has been formed. We begin by dealing with the law relating to mistake which affects the true consent of one or both parties so that one or both of them may be asked to be released from their contractual obligations.

Introduction

A contract which is regular in all respects may still fail because there is no real consent to it by one or both of the parties. There is no *consensus ad idem* or meeting of the minds. Consent may be rendered unreal by mistake, misrepresentation, duress and undue influence. There are also instances of inequality of bargaining power where it would be inequitable to enforce the resulting agreement.

It is particularly important to distinguish between mistake and misrepresentation because a contract affected by mistake is void, whereas a contract affected by misrepresentation is only voidable. As between the parties themselves, this makes little difference since in both cases goods sold and money paid can be recovered. However, the distinction can be vital so far as third parties are concerned. If A sells goods to B under circumstances of mistake and B resells them to C, then C gets no title and A can recover the goods from him or sue him for damages in conversion. If, on the other hand, the contract between A and B was voidable for misrepresentation, then if B sold the goods to C who took them bona fide and for value before A had rescinded his contract with B, then C would get a good title and A would have a remedy only against B.

Agreement mistake in general

Mistake, to be operative, must be of *fact* and not of *law*. Furthermore, the concept has a technical meaning and does not cover, for example, errors of judgment as to value. Thus, if A buys an article thinking it is worth £100 when in fact it is worth only £50, the contract is good and A must bear the loss if there has been no misrepresentation by the seller. This is what is meant by the maxim *caveat emptor* (let the buyer beware).

The various categories of mistake will now be considered, beginning with the rather special case where a document is signed by mistake.

Documents mistakenly signed

If a person signs a contract in the mistaken belief that he is signing a document of a different nature, there may be a mistake which avoids the contract. He may be able to plead *non est factum* ('it is not my deed'). This is a defence open to a person who has signed a document by mistake. Originally it was a special defence to protect those who could not read who had signed deeds which had been incorrectly read over to them. At one time the defence was available only where the mistake referred to the *kind* of document it was and not merely its contents. Now the defence is available to a person who has signed a document having made a *fundamental* mistake as to the kind of document it is or as to its contents. However, the defendant must prove that he made the mistake despite having taken all reasonable care. If he is negligent he will not usually be able to plead the defence.

Since the courts have taken the view that merely to sign a document without knowing its contents is in itself negligent, the plea will rarely be successful, though it may be where the document is commonly regarded as confidential, such as an alleged will where the signer believes he signs in the capacity of a witness but in fact appears to incur liability on the document which is not in fact a will as in *Lewis* v *Clay* (1898) 77 LT 653.

> *Saunders* v *Anglia Building Society*, 1970 – Documents mistakenly signed: the legal effect (**117**)

Unilateral mistake

Unilateral mistake occurs when one of the parties, X, is mistaken as to some fundamental fact concerning the contract and the other party, Y, knows, or ought to know, this. This latter requirement is important because if Y does not know that X is mistaken the contract is good.

The cases are mainly concerned with mistake by one party as to the *identity* of the other party. Thus a contract may be void for mistake if X contracts with Y thinking that Y is another person, Z, and if Y knows that X is under that misapprehension. Proof of Y's knowledge is essential but since in most cases Y is a fraudulent person, the point does not present great difficulties.

> *Higgins (W) Ltd* v *Northampton Corporation*, 1927 – Relevance of knowledge of the mistake (**118**)
> *Cundy* v *Lindsay*, 1878 – Mistake as to identity (**119**)

There were difficulties where the parties contracted face to face because in such a case the suggestion could always be made that whatever the fraudulent party was saying about his identity, the mistaken party must be regarded as intending to contract with the person in front of him, whoever he was. Thus in this situation, the court might find on the facts of the case that the contract was voidable for fraud or sometimes void for mistake.

However, the position is now a little clearer as a result of the decision in *Lewis* v *Averay* (1971) (see below) where it was said that if the parties contracted face to face the contract will normally be voidable for fraud but rarely void for mistake. However, much depends upon the facts of the case and if the court is convinced on the evidence that identity was vital then even a 'face to face' contract will be regarded as void for mistake, as *Ingram* v *Little* (1961) (see below) shows.

> *Lewis* v *Averay*, 1971 – Mistake as to identity when the parties are face to face (**120**)
> *Ingram* v *Little*, 1961 – Another approach (**121**)

Effect of unilateral mistake in equity

If the claimant is asking for an equitable remedy, such as rescission of the contract or specific performance of it, then equitable principles will apply. As far as unilateral mistake is concerned, equity follows the principles of the common law and regards a contract affected by unilateral mistake as void and will therefore rescind it or refuse specific performance of it. Rectification of the contract is also available.

> *Webster* v *Cecil*, 1861 – Unilateral mistake: the equitable approach (**122**)

12

Bilateral identical (or common) mistake

This occurs where both parties are mistaken and each makes the same mistake. In other words it is a *shared mistake*. There is no general rule that common mistake affects a contract and in practice only common mistakes as to the existence of the subject matter of the contract or where the subject matter of the contract already belongs to the buyer will make the contract void at common law. The principles applied are considered below.

(a) Cases of *res extincta*. Here there is a common mistake as to the existence of the subject matter of the contract. Thus, if S agrees to sell his car to B and unknown to both the car had at the time of the sale been destroyed by fire, then the contract will be void because A has innocently undertaken an obligation which he cannot possibly fulfil. It should be noted that the goods may actually exist but the rule of *res extincta* applies if they are not in the condition envisaged by the contract.

(b) Cases of *res sua*. These occur where a person makes a contract about something which already belongs to him. Such a contract is void at common law.

> *Couturier* v *Hastie*, 1856 – An example of *res extincta* (**123**)
> *Cochrane* v *Willis*, 1865 – *Res sua* illustrated (**124**)

(c) Other cases – mistakes as to quality. These occur when the two parties have reached agreement but have made an identical mistake as to some fact concerning the quality of the subject matter of the contract. Suppose, for example, that X sells a particular drawing to Y for £5,000 and all the usual elements of agreement are present, including offer and acceptance and consideration, and the agreement concerns an identified article. Nevertheless, if both X and Y think that the drawing is by a well-known Victorian artist when it is in fact only a copy worth £25, then the agreement is made in circumstances of common mistake.

At common law a mistake of the kind outlined above has no effect on the contract and the parties would be bound in the absence of fraud or misrepresentation. The case law shows how reluctant the courts have been to establish a general rule of common mistake.

> *Bell* v *Lever Bros Ltd*, 1932 – Mistakes as to quality (**125**)
> *Leaf* v *International Galleries*, 1950 – Quality mistakes: a further illustration (**126**)

Effect of identity bilateral (or common) mistake in equity

The position in equity is as follows.

(a) Cases of *res extincta* and *res sua*. Equity treats these in the same way as the common law, regarding the agreement as void. The equitable remedy of specific performance is not available for such an agreement which may also be rescinded.

(b) Other cases. Equity could apparently regard an agreement affected by common mistake as voidable even though the case was not one of *res extincta* or *res sua*. The above statement derives from the decision of Lord Denning in *Solle* v *Butcher* [1950] 1 KB 671. In the case Lord Denning advanced the view that a contract affected by common mistake as to quality, although unaffected at common law, could be rescinded in equity. The case concerned the lease of a flat where the parties had assumed that the rent was controlled to a maximum by rent control legislation whereas by reason of improvements that the landlord had made to the premises a higher rent could have been charged. Lord Denning said that although the common law would ignore the common mistake as to quality that the flat had a controlled rent thus leaving the fortunate tenant to pay only the controlled rent equity could rescind the lease and in effect put the tenant out unless the parties could renegotiate the terms. This development was brought to an end by the House of Lords in *Great Peace Shipping Ltd* (see below).

> *Cooper* v *Phibbs*, 1867 – Equity and *res sua* (**127**)
> *Great Peace Shipping Ltd* v *Tsavliris Salvage (International) Ltd*, 2002 – Mistake as to quality, no general power of rescission (**128**)

(c) Rectification. If the parties are agreed on the terms of their contract but because, for example, of drafting or typing errors certain terms are set out incorrectly, the court may order equitable rectification of the contract so that it properly represents what the parties agreed. Thus, if A orally agrees to give B a lease of premises for 99 years and in the subsequent written contract the term is expressed as 90 years by mistake, then if A will not co-operate to change the lease, B may ask the court to rectify it by substituting a term of 99 years for 90 years. In order to obtain rectification it must be proved:

(i) that there was complete agreement on all the terms of the contract or at least continuing intention to include certain terms in it which in the event were not included. It is not necessary to show that the term was intended to be legally binding prior to being written down;

(ii) that the agreement continued unchanged until it was reduced into writing. If the parties disputed the terms of the agreement, the written contract may be taken to represent their final position;

(iii) that the writing does not express what the parties had agreed. If it does, then there can be no rectification.

Rectification is available for both common and unilateral mistake.

> *Joscelyne* v *Nissen*, 1970 – Rectification: no need for previous binding agreement (**129**)
>
> *Frederick Rose (London) Ltd* v *William Pim & Co Ltd*, 1953 – Rectification where writing is what the parties agreed (**130**)
>
> *Thomas Bates & Sons Ltd* v *Wyndham's (Lingerie) Ltd*, 1981 – Rectification available for unilateral mistake (**131**)

Non-identical bilateral (or mutual) mistake

In a situation where A intends to buy real pearls but the seller intends to sell imitation pearls, and in the absence of misrepresentation by the seller, there is a bilateral mistake that is non-identical. It will be remembered that in the previous category the mistake was bilateral but both parties had made an identical mistake. Here we have what may be described as a *mutual misunderstanding*. Confusion of this non-identical bilateral kind generally exists in the mind of one party only and may therefore have no effect on the contract (see below).

Effect of non-identical bilateral (or mutual) mistake at common law

The contract is not necessarily void because the court will try to find the 'sense of the promise'. This usually occurs where, although the parties are at cross purposes, the contract actually *identifies* a credible (or believable) agreement.

If the parties are at cross purposes and the contract does *not identify* a credible (or believable) agreement, it is void.

The basis of the 'sense of the promise' rule is that the court does not ascertain contractual intention from what is in the minds of the parties, i.e. *a subjective intent*, because the parties are confused. Instead the court decides contractual intention in an *objective way* by looking at the parties dealings to see if these identify a contract. If they do, the court will enforce it; if not, the transaction is void.

Effect of non-identical bilateral (or mutual) mistake in equity

Equity also tries to find the sense of the promise as identified by the contract, thus following the law. However, equitable remedies are discretionary and even where the sense of the promise as identified by the contract can be ascertained equity will not necessarily grant specific performance if it would cause hardship to the defendant.

> *Wood* v *Scarth*, 1858 – The sense of the promise: the hardship rule (**132**)
>
> *Raffles* v *Wichelhaus*, 1864 – Where there is no sense of the promise (**133**)

Trading electronically

Mistake is a matter that should concern online traders. Suppose purchasers wanting to buy advertised goods of one company through its website visit the website of a company with a similar name in a similar line of business. Would such purchasers be entitled to return the goods or reject the services and obtain a refund once the mistake was realised? A mistake as to identity is fundamental as we have seen and may negate the consent of the purchasers.

12

REALITY OF CONSENT II

In this chapter we continue a study of further situations in which a contract can be affected by lack of proper consent. Topics considered to complete the study of consent problems are misrepresentation, duress, undue influence, economic duress and unconscionable bargains.

Misrepresentation

Misrepresentation is an expression used to describe a situation in which there is no genuineness of consent to a contract by one of the parties. The effect of misrepresentation on a contract is less serious than that of mistake because the contract becomes *voidable and not void*. This means that the party misled can ask the court to rescind the contract, i.e. to put the parties back into the positions they held before the contract was made. Thus in a sale of goods the goods would be returned to the seller and the money to the buyer.

However, the effect on third parties is more fundamental because if A sells goods to B under circumstances of misrepresentation by B and before A has a chance to rescind the contract B sells the goods to C, who takes them for value without notice of the misrepresentation, C has a good title and A cannot recover the goods or sue him in conversion. His remedy is against B and the type of remedy available will depend upon the nature of B's misrepresentation, i.e. whether it was fraudulent, negligent or innocent.

Meaning of representation

A representation is an inducement only and its effect is to lead the other party merely to make the contract. A representation must be a statement of some specific existing and verifiable fact or past event. It becomes a misrepresentation, of course, when it is false.

However, a statement which is not entirely false but a half-truth may be a misrepresentation. Thus in *Dimmock* v *Hallett* (1886) LR 2 Ch App 21 it was held that a statement that a property was let, and therefore producing income, was a misrepresentation because it was not revealed that the tenants had given notice (see also *Curtis* v *Chemical Cleaning and Dyeing Co* (1952) in Chapter 15).

There are three ingredients: (1) a statement, (2) of specific existing and verifiable fact or past event, and (3) that the statement induces the contract.

There must be a statement

In consequence, silence or non-disclosure has no effect except in the following circumstances.

(a) Failure to disclose a change in circumstances. Where the statement was true when made but became false before the contract was made there is a duty on the party making the statement to disclose the change and if he does not do so his silence can amount to an actionable misrepresentation.

(b) Where the contract is *uberrimae fidei* **(of utmost good faith)**, such as a contract of insurance (see further p 324).

(c) Where there is a confidential or fiduciary relationship between the parties, as where they are solicitor and client. Here the equitable doctrine of constructive fraud may apply to render the contract voidable.

Although this branch of the law is closely akin to undue influence, which will be considered later, there is a difference in the sense that in undue influence the person with special influence, such as a solicitor over his client, is often the prime mover in seeking the contract. Constructive fraud, however, could apply where the client was the prime mover in seeking a contract with his solicitor. In such a case if the solicitor remains silent as regards facts within his knowledge material, say, to the contract price, then the client could rescind the contract for constructive fraud.

(d) Where statute requires disclosure, as does the Financial Services and Markets Act 2000 under which a number of specified particulars must be disclosed in an advertisement/prospectus issued by a company to invite the public to subscribe for shares or debentures. The particulars must give all such information as investors and their professional advisers would reasonably require and reasonably expect to find in the advertisement/prospectus for the purpose of making an informed assessment as to whether to buy the securities.

The provisions of the Financial Services and Markets Act 2000 apply to companies which have a full listing on the Stock Exchange. Similar disclosures are required in relation to prospectuses that are used for issues of unlisted securities that are quoted on the Alternative Investment Market. These provisions are contained in the Offers of Securities Regulations 1995 and 1999.

(e) In cases of concealed fraud, following the case of *Gordon* v *Selico Co Ltd* (1986) *The Times*, 26 February. In that case a flat in a block of flats which had recently been converted by a developer was taken by the claimant on a 99-year lease. Soon after he moved in dry rot was discovered. Goulding, J, who was later upheld by the Court of Appeal, decided that deliberate concealment of the dry rot by the developer could amount to fraudulent misrepresentation whereupon damages were awarded to the claimant. Silence can, therefore, amount to misrepresentation in the case of concealed fraud.

> *With* v *O'Flanagan*, 1936 – Where circumstances change (**134**)

Specific existing and verifiable fact or past event

The representation must be a statement of some specific, existing and verifiable fact or past event, and in consequence the following are excluded.

(a) Statements of law. Everyone is presumed to know the law which is equally accessible to both parties and on which they should seek advice and not rely on the statements of the other party. Thus, if A has allowed B, a tradesman, to have goods on credit and C has agreed orally to indemnify A in respect of the transaction, then if A enters into a second contract with B under which A is to receive two-thirds of the price of the goods from B in full settlement on B's representation that C's indemnity is unenforceable at law because it is not in writing, then the second contract would be good because A cannot deny that he knows the law because of the maxim 'ignorance of the law is no excuse'.

(b) Statements as to future conduct or intention. These are not actionable, though if the person who makes the statement has no intention of carrying it out, it may be regarded as a representation of fact, i.e. a misrepresentation of what is really in the mind of the maker of the statement.

(c) Statements of opinion. Again, these are not normally actionable unless it can be shown that the person making the statement held no such opinion whereupon the statement may be considered in law to be a misstatement of an existing fact as to what was in the mind of the maker of the statement at the time. However, in *Bissett* v *Wilkinson* [1927] AC 177 it was held that a vendor of land was not liable for stating that it could support 2,000 sheep, because he had no personal knowledge of the facts, the land having never been used for sheep farming. The buyer knew this so that it was understood by him that the seller could only be stating his opinion.

Nevertheless, the expression of an opinion may involve a statement of fact. Suppose A writes a reference for B to help B get a house to rent and A says to C, the prospective landlord: 'B is a very desirable tenant'. A is doing two things: first he is giving his opinion of B, but also he is making a statement of fact by saying that he *believes* B to be a very desirable tenant. If in fact therefore A actually believes B to be a bad tenant he is lying as to what is in his mind.

(d) Sales talk, advertising, 'puffing' (or what is called these days 'hype'). Not all statements in this area amount to representations. The law has always accepted that it is essential in business that a seller of goods or services should be allowed to make some statements about them in the course of dealing without necessarily being bound by everything he says. Thus, if a salesman confines himself to statements of opinion such as 'This is the finest floor polish in the world' or 'This is the best polish on the market', there is no misrepresentation. However, the nearer a salesman gets to a statement of specific verifiable fact, the greater the possibility that there may be an action for misrepresentation. Thus a statement such as 'This polish has as much wax in it as Snooks' wax polish' may well amount to a misrepresentation if the statement is not in fact true.

> *Edgington* v *Fitzmaurice*, 1885 – Statements as to future conduct or intention (**135**)
>
> *Smith* v *Land and House Property Corporation*, 1884 – Opinion may be construed as fact (**136**)

The statement must induce the contract

It must therefore:

(a) have been relied upon by the person claiming to have been misled who must not have relied on his own skill and judgment or some other statement.

Thus in *Attwood* v *Small* (1838) 6 Cl & Fin 232 the purchaser of a mine elected to verify exaggerated (but not fraudulent) statements of its earnings by commissioning a report from his agents. This failed to reveal the defects in the original statement and the purchaser bought the mine. It was later *held* that he could not rescind the contract because he had relied on the report, not on the statement. It should be noted that relief is not barred simply because there has been an unsuccessful attempt by the misled person to discover the truth where the misrepresentation was fraudulent (*Pearson* v *Dublin Corpn* [1907] AC 217);

(b) have been material in the sense that it affected the claimant's judgment;

(c) have been known to the claimant. The claimant must always be prepared to prove that an alleged misrepresentation had an effect on his mind, a task which he certainly cannot fulfil if he was never aware that it had been made.

Thus in *Re Northumberland and Durham District Banking Co, ex parte Bigge* (1858) 28 LJ Ch 50 a person who bought shares in a company asked to have the purchase rescinded because the company had published false reports as to its solvency. Although these reports were false, the claimant failed because, among other things, he was unable to show that he had read any of the reports or that anyone had told him what they contained;

(d) have been addressed to the person claiming to have been misled.

Peek v *Gurney*, 1873 – The statement must induce the contract: the common law approach (**137**)

13

Knowledge that statement is untrue

If the person to whom the false statement was made knew that it was untrue then he cannot sue in respect of it because he has not been misled. However, it is not an acceptable defence to an action for misrepresentation that the representee was given the means of discovering that the statement was untrue.

Redgrave v *Hurd*, 1881 – No need to check on a statement (**138**)

Did the statement influence the representee's decision?

The law requires that a misrepresentation must have operated on the mind of the representee. If it has not, as where the representee was not influenced by it, there is no claim.

Smith v *Chadwick*, 1884 – Was the statement material? (**139**)

Types of actionable misrepresentation and remedies in general

Innocent misrepresentation

A purely innocent misrepresentation is a false statement made by a person who had reasonable grounds to believe that the statement was true, not only when he made it but also at the time the contract was entered into. As regards reasonable grounds, the representer's best hope of proving this will be to show that he himself had been induced to buy the goods by the same statement, particularly where he is not technically qualified to verify it further (see *Humming Bird Motors Ltd* v *Hobbs* (1986) and *Oscar Chess Ltd* v *Williams* (1957)). The party misled can ask the court to rescind the contract but has no right to ask for damages. However, the court may at its discretion award damages instead of rescission (Misrepresentation Act 1967, s 2(2)). Rescission in effect cancels the contract and the court may in some cases regard this as a drastic remedy, particularly where there has been misrepresentation on a trivial matter, such as the quality of the tyres on a car. Suppose the seller of a car in a private sale says: 'The previous owner fitted new tyres at 26,000 miles'. If that statement is false but the seller was told this by the previous owner, the court could award damages instead of rescission, thus leaving the contract intact but giving the party misled monetary compensation. Statements by dealers, however, are often taken to be terms of the contract (see Chapter 14).

There has been uncertainty as to whether damages could be awarded under s 2(2) of the Misrepresentation Act 1967 if the remedy of rescission was no longer available as where a third party had acquired rights in the subject matter of the contract. However, in *Thomas Witter* v *TBP Industries Ltd* [1996] 2 All ER 573 the High Court ruled that damages could be awarded under s 2(2), provided that the right to rescind had existed *at some time*. It was not necessary said the High Court for the right to exist at the time of the judgment. This seems a reasonable interpretation of the sub-section because the remedy of rescission is lost so quickly that it is unlikely to exist at the time of trial because of, among other things, the passage of time (see later in this chapter).

The same ruling was given again by the High Court in *Zanzibar* v *British Aerospace (Lancaster House) Ltd* (2000) *The Times*, 28 March and would seem to be firmly established.

Negligent misrepresentation

A negligent misrepresentation is a false statement made by a person who had no reasonable grounds for believing the statement to be true. The party misled may sue for rescission (see below) and/or damages, and the requirement to prove that the statement was not made negligently but that there were reasonable grounds for believing it to be true is on the maker of the statement (or representer) (Misrepresentation Act 1967, s 2(1)).

The sub-section recognises only a claim for damages and says nothing about rescission. However, in *Mapes* v *Jones* (1974) 232 EG 717 a property dealer contracted to lease a grocer's shop to the claimant for 21 years but in fact did not have sufficient interest in the property himself to grant such a lease, the maximum period available to him being 18 years. Despite constant requests, no lease was supplied as originally promised and the claimant shut the shop and elected to treat the contract as repudiated. Willis, J held that the claimant was entitled to rescission for misrepresentation under s 2(1) of the 1967 Act. He also found that the defendant's delay in completion was a breach of condition which *also* allowed the claimant to repudiate the contract. As we have seen, s 2 claims can extend to statements of opinion (see *BG plc* v *Nelson Group Services (Maintenance) Ltd* [2002] EWCA Civ 547.

Gosling v Anderson, 1972 – Negligent misrepresentation illustrated (140)

Fraudulent misrepresentation

A fraudulent misrepresentation is a false representation of a material fact made knowing it to be false, or believing it to be false, or recklessly not caring whether it be true or false.

Mere negligence is not enough. An element of dishonesty is required. For example, if Mr Tidbury in the *Gosling* case had *known* that there was no planning permission for the garage but had nevertheless gone on to state that there was, then the element of dishonesty would have been present and he would have been guilty of fraud. The party misled may sue for rescission and/or damages. As regards the action for damages, the claimant sues not on the contract but on the tort of deceit.

In this connection, it is worth noting that when a person is sued upon the tort of deceit he or she will not be able to defend the claim on the basis that although the contract was induced by deceit it would not have been if the claimant had done more checking and not been perhaps careless in accepting the fraudulent inducement. Why? – because the defence of contributory negligence does not apply where the claim is for fraud (see *Standard Chartered Bank* v *Pakistan National Shipping Corp (No 2)* [2002] 3 WLR 1547).

> *Derry* v *Peek*, 1889 – Fraudulent misrepresentation defined (**141**)

Compensation under the Financial Services and Markets Act 2000

13

Under this Act, where the directors of a company with a full Stock Exchange listing publish an advertisement or prospectus containing false statements made innocently they may have to pay a form of damages called compensation.

This will occur where they have issued listing particulars or a prospectus that is inaccurate. In general terms, errors of omission or commission in listing particulars or a prospectus will render any party responsible such as the directors of the company liable for loss caused thereby to anyone acquiring the securities covered by the document.

Those responsible such as the directors can escape liability if they made such enquiries as were reasonable and reasonably believed that the statement was true when the document was submitted to the Financial Services Authority (as Listing Authority for the UK) for approval provided that at the time the securities were *subsequently* acquired:

- they continued in that belief;
- it was not reasonably practicable to bring the correction to the attention of those likely to acquire them;
- they had taken all reasonable steps to bring the correction to their attention; or
- they ought reasonably to be excused because they believed it when dealings commenced and now too much time has elapsed.

Where the statement is in a report by an expert such as an engineer or accountant the directors are not liable for it provided they had a reasonable belief in the competence of the expert.

Experts, such as accountants, are liable under the Act for false statements in their reports which are included in the listing particulars or prospectus. Again, the defence of lack of responsibility is available, as where the expert has not consented to the inclusion of his report in the prospectus. However, given that he accepts responsibility for the inclusion of his report, he has a defence if he can show that he had reasonable grounds for believing the statement to be true. Presumably, he could sustain this defence by showing, amongst other things, that the false statement came from an official document. Furthermore, whether or not a professional person has reasonable grounds will almost always depend upon the steps taken to *verify* the statement. If these are reasonable the professional person will not be liable even if the statement is wrong.

Agent's breach of warranty of authority

Under the law of agency where an agent misrepresents himself as having authority he does not possess, the third party will not obtain a contract with the principal and if he suffers loss as a consequence he may sue the agent for breach of warranty of authority, the action being for damages and brought in *quasi-contract*. Quasi-contract is based on the idea that a person should not obtain a benefit or unjust enrichment or cause injury to another with impunity merely because there is no obligation in contract or another established branch of law which will operate to make him account. The law may in these circumstances provide a remedy by implying a *fictitious promise* to account for the benefit of the enrichment or to compensate for damage caused.

Negligence at common law

The tort remedy in general

Where the parties concerned were not in a *pre-contractual relationship* when the statement was made, s 2(1) of the Misrepresentation Act 1967 will not apply. However, an action for damages for negligence will lie in tort, provided the false statement was made negligently. The law relating to tortious negligent misstatements is considered in more detail in Chapter 21. However, the leading case is looked at now.

> *Hedley Byrne & Co Ltd* v *Heller & Partners Ltd*, 1963 – Negligent misstatements: the tort remedy (**142**)

Use of the tort remedy in contract cases

In *Esso Petroleum* v *Mardon* [1976] 2 All ER 5 the court held that the principle in *Hedley Byrne* could apply even where the parties concerned were in a pre-contractual relationship and in addition that the person who had made the statement need not necessarily be in business to give advice, provided it is reasonable for one party to rely on the other's skill and judgement in making the statement. Mr Mardon was awarded damages for a negligent misstatement by a senior sales representative of Esso in regard to the amount of petrol he could expect to sell per year from a petrol station which he was leasing from Esso. The facts of *Mardon* pre-dated the 1967 Act and the court could not use it. The decision is obviously important but where the facts have occurred since 1967 the Misrepresentation Act is likely to prove more popular to claimants who have been misled *into making contracts*, since they can ask the representer to show he was not negligent. In *Hedley Byrne* claims the burden of proof is on the claimant to prove negligence.

There is a very obvious use, however, for the tort of negligence claim even where the careless misstatement has induced a contract. The tort claim allows an action for a misleading *opinion or falsely stated intention*, whereas misrepresentation in all its forms requires a misstatement of *fact*, not opinion or intention. The use of *Hedley Byrne* would today make the legal gymnastics seen in *Edgington* v *Fitzmaurice* (1885) and *Smith* v *Land and House Property Co* (1884) unnecessary.

Use of the tort remedy for inaccurate company securities advertisements

As regards actions against directors and experts in respect of statements in an advertisement for the sale of securities or in a prospectus, there is as we have seen a statutory claim under the Financial Services and Markets Act 2000 and under *Hedley Byrne* at common law. The claim against directors under *Hedley Byrne* is specifically preserved by the Financial Services and Markets Act 2000 in s 87(9). A claim under the Misrepresentation Act 1967 is against 'the other party to the contract', i.e. the company or issuing house, and not against directors or agents.

It will be recalled that in *Esso Petroleum Co Ltd* v *Mardon* (1976) (see above) the court held that it was too restrictive to limit the duty in *Hedley Byrne* to persons who carried on or who held themselves out as carrying on the *business* of giving information or advice. The acceptance of these views means that the duty can apply more widely and brings in company directors in terms that they could be liable on a personal basis for negligence.

In any case, it is a requirement as part of admission of the shares to a full Stock Exchange listing or AIM (Alternative Investment Market) listing that the advertisement or prospectus shall state that the directors have taken reasonable care to ensure that the facts stated in it are true and accurate, that there are no misleading omissions and that, accordingly, all the directors take responsibility for the prospectus.

In view of this statement, it is likely that a duty of care is owed only by the individuals involved in the making of the statements and not by the company as such. If this is so, no claim can be made against the company. This would accord with the general principle of capital maintenance inherent in the prospectus remedies, i.e. it is difficult to get one's money back from the company and easier to get compensation from directors or experts, leaving capital contributed with the company.

In view of this it would seem that an action for rescission of the contract (see below) against the company will not in the company law context be a likely remedy. In any case it is very quickly lost as we shall see.

Remedy of rescission

As we have seen, this remedy is available to a party misled by innocent, negligent or fraudulent misrepresentation. It restores the status quo, i.e. it puts the parties back to the position they were in before the contract was made. However, the remedy may be lost:

(a) By affirmation. If the injured party affirms the contract he cannot rescind. He will affirm if with full knowledge of the misrepresentation he expressly affirms the contract by stating that he intends to go on with it or if he does some act from which an implied intention may properly be deduced. In the company situation this could, for example, be attending a company meeting to complain about an inaccurate prospectus.

(b) By lapse of time. This is a form of implied affirmation and applies as follows:

(i) In innocent and negligent misrepresentation the position is governed by equity and the passage of a reasonable time, even without knowledge of the misrepresentation, may prevent the court from granting rescission: *Leaf* v *International Galleries* (1950) – see Chapter 12.

(ii) In fraudulent misrepresentation the position is governed by s 32 of the Limitation Act 1980 and lapse of time has no effect on rescission where fraud is alleged as long as the action is brought within six years of the time when the fraud was, or with reasonable diligence could have been, discovered.

(c) Where status quo cannot be restored. Rescission is impossible if the parties cannot be restored to their original positions as where goods sold under a contract of sale have been consumed.

(d) Where a third party has acquired rights in the subject matter of the contract. Thus if X obtains goods from Y by misrepresentation and pawns them with Z, Y cannot rescind the contract on learning of the misrepresentation in order to recover the goods from Z. Nor can he sue Z in conversion (*Lewis* v *Averay* (1971) – see Chapter 12).

It should be noted that the third party must have supplied consideration, as in *Lewis*. If the third party has received the property as a gift, it can be recovered from him.

> *Long* v *Lloyd*, 1958 – Application of the affirmation rule (**143**)
> *Clarke* v *Dickson*, 1858 – Inability to restore status quo (**144**)

Rescission and contractual debt

The fact that a party to a contract rescinds it because, e.g., of non-performance by the other party does not mean that the party rescinding has thereby abandoned an action for debts owed under the contract. Thus in *Stocznia Gdanska SA* v *Latvian Shipping* [1998] 1 All ER 883 S rescinded a contract with L to build two ships because of L's failure to pay the first instalment of the price when due. The House of Lords later decided that a claim by S for the unpaid instalment which represented the cost of the design and laying of the keel of a ship was recoverable.

Contracts *uberrimae fidei* (utmost good faith)

Silence does not normally amount to misrepresentation. However, an important exception to the rule occurs in the case of certain contracts where from the circumstances of the case one party alone possesses full knowledge of all the material facts and in which therefore the law requires him to show utmost good faith. He must make full disclosure of all the material facts known to him, otherwise the contract may be rescinded. The contracts concerned are as follows.

At common law

Contracts of insurance provide the only true example of a contract *uberrimae fidei*. There is a duty on the person taking up the insurance to disclose to the insurance company all facts of which he is aware which might affect the premium or acceptance of the risk. Failure to do so renders the contract voidable at the option of the insurance company. This could happen, for example, where a person seeking insurance did not disclose that he had been refused insurance by another company. Where there is a failure to disclose, the insurance company is not required by law to meet the claim but must return the premiums. In other words, the contract is rescinded. A leading decision that this is so is *Banque Keyser Ullmann SA* v *Skandia (UK) Insurance Co* [1989] 3 WLR 25.

In addition, most proposals for insurance may require the proposer to sign a declaration in which he warrants that the statements he has made are true and agrees that they be incorporated into the contract as terms. Where this is so any false statement which the proposer makes will be a ground for avoidance of the contract by the insurance company, even though the statement was not material in terms of the premium.

> *Dawsons Ltd* v *Bonnin*, 1922 – The contract may widen the duty of disclosure (**145**)

By statute

As regards contracts to take shares in a company with a listing or quotation on the Stock Exchange, there is a duty on the directors or its promoters, under the Financial Services and Markets Act 2000, to disclose various matters essential to an informed assessment as to whether an investor should purchase the securities. These provisions, and those in earlier statutes which preceded them, had to be put into law by Parliament because the judiciary had always refused to regard the sale of securities by a company as a contract *uberrimae fidei*. They did not, therefore, require the advertisement or prospectus under which the shares were issued necessarily to disclose all the material facts.

In equity – fiduciary relationships

In contracts between members of a family, partners, principal and agent, solicitor and client, guardian and ward, and trustee and beneficiary, the relationship of the parties requires that the most ample disclosure should be made. The duties of disclosure arising from the above fiduciary relations recognised by equity are not situations of *uberrimae fidei*. In contracts *uberrimae fidei* it is the nature of the contract, i.e. insurance, which requires disclosure regardless of the relationship of the parties. In the fiduciary situation it is the relationship of the parties and not the particular contract which gives rise to the need to disclose.

> *Gordon* v *Gordon*, 1819 – Disclosure in a family situation (**146**)

13

Duress

Duress will affect all contracts and gifts procured by its use. Duress, which is a common-law concept, means actual violence or threats of violence to the person of the contracting party or those near and dear to him. The threats must be calculated to produce fear of loss of life or bodily harm.

Threats of violence

A contract will seldom be procured by actual violence but threats of violence are more probable. The threat must be illegal in that it must be a threat to commit a crime or tort. Thus to threaten an imprisonment, which would be unlawful if enforced, constitutes duress, but not, it is said, if the imprisonment would be lawful. However, the courts are unlikely to look with favour on a contract obtained by threatening to prosecute a criminal. A contract procured by a threat to sue for an act which was not a crime, e.g. trespass, would not be affected by duress.

Welch v *Cheesman*, 1973 – Duress by threats of violence (**147**)

Threats to property

In *Skeate* v *Beale* (1840) 11 Ad & El 983 a tenant owed £19 10s in old money and agreed to pay £3 7s 6d immediately and the remaining £16 2s 6d within a month if his landlord would withdraw a writ of distress under which he was threatening to sell the tenant's goods. The tenant later disputed what he owed and the landlord tried to set up the agreement and sued for the remaining £16 2s 6d. It was held that the landlord was entitled to £16 2s 6d under the agreement which was not affected by duress since the threat was to sell the tenant's goods. However, more recently the courts have been moving away from the view that threats to property cannot invalidate contracts. In *The Siboen and The Sibotre* [1976] Lloyd's Rep 293 it was said that duress could be a defence if a person was forced to make a contract by the threat of having a valuable picture slashed or his house burnt down.

Duress probably renders a contract voidable

This, at least, is the view expressed in Cheshire & Fifoot's *Law of Contract* (a leading text on contract law), though other writers have argued that the effect of duress is to render a contract void. However, the judgments of the Privy Council in *Barton* v *Armstrong* [1975] 2 All ER 465 and *Pao On* v *Lau Yiu Long* [1979] 3 All ER 65 suggest that duress has the same effect as fraud, i.e. it renders a contract voidable. The issue is an important one for third parties, since if B procures goods from A by duress and sells the goods to C, who has no knowledge of the duress, A will be able to recover the goods from C if the contract is void, but will not be able to do so if it is voidable. On the authorities to date, therefore, A would have no claim against C.

Undue influence and associated equitable pleas

The doctrine of undue influence was developed by equity. The concept of undue influence is designed to deal with contracts *or gifts* obtained without free consent by the influence of one mind over another.

If there is no special relationship between the parties undue influence may exist, but must be proved by the person seeking to avoid the contract.

Where a confidential or fiduciary relationship exists between the parties, there is a presumption of undue influence and the party in whom the confidence was reposed must show that undue influence was not used, i.e. that the contract was the act of a free and independent mind. It is desirable, though not essential, that independent advice should have been given.

There are several confidential relationships which are well established in the law, namely parent and child, solicitor and client, trustee and beneficiary, guardian and ward, and religious adviser and disciple. In these cases there is a presumption of undue influence by the parent, the solicitor, the trustee and so on. There is no presumption of such a relationship between husband and wife, nor, according to the Court of Appeal in *Mathew* v *Bobbins* (1980) 256 EG 603, between employer and employee. This was affirmed by Millett, LJ in *Credit Bank Nederland* v *Burch* (1996) *The Independent*, 27 June. He did, however, state that the relationship could develop into one of trust and confidence on the facts of a particular case but it was not a relationship where undue influence would necessarily be presumed. The facts must show it to exist. The Court of Appeal held that undue influence did exist between an employer and employee on the facts of the case. The employee B agreed to mortgage her flat to the bank as security for the debts to the bank of a travel company by which she was employed. She had no independent advice. When the company went into liquidation the bank tried to enforce the mortgage by a sale of her flat. The Court of Appeal set the mortgage aside because B had entered into it by reason of her employer's undue influence and the bank should have been put on enquiry because of the relationship of employer and employee of which they were aware and where undue influence might come to exist. However, a presumption of undue influence may be made between husband and wife where there are special circumstances such as the lack of sufficient mental capacity in either party to resist the influence of the other leading to gifts of property which are quite out of character with the donor's normal inquiring disposition when disposing of property (*Simpson* v *Simpson* (1988) *The Times*, 11 June). The fiduciary relationship between parent and child ends usually, but not necessarily, on reaching 18 or on getting married.

> *Lancashire Loans Ltd* v *Black*, 1934 – Undue influence: parent and child (**148**)
> *Allcard* v *Skinner*, 1887 – Undue influence: religious adviser and disciple (**149**)

However, there may be a presumption of undue influence even though the relationship between the parties is not in the established categories outlined above. In *Re Craig (Deceased)* [1970] 2 All ER 390 Ungoed-Thomas, J ruled that presumption of undue influence arose on proof:

(*a*) of a gift so substantial or of such a nature that it could not on the face of it be accounted for on the grounds of the ordinary motives on which ordinary men acted, and

(*b*) of a relationship of trust and confidence such that the recipient of the gift was in a position to exercise undue influence over the person making it.

> *Hodgson* v *Marks*, 1970 – Undue influence: outside the special categories (**150**)

Effect of undue influence on third parties

A contract between A and B procured by undue influence cannot be avoided by rescission against third parties who acquire rights for value without notice of the facts. Where this has happened the party suffering the undue influence, say, A, will have to rely on tracing the proceeds of sale into the original purchaser's, i.e. B's, assets. The contract may be avoided and the property recovered from third parties for value with notice of the facts and also against volunteers (i.e. persons who have given no consideration) even though they were unaware of the facts.

Effect of undue influence on the parties to the contract

Undue influence renders the contract voidable so that it may be rescinded. However, since rescission is an equitable remedy, there must be no delay in claiming relief after the influence has ceased to have effect. Delay in claiming relief in these circumstances may bar the claim since delay is evidence of affirmation. This is illustrated by the case of *Allcard* v *Skinner* above.

Economic duress

Apart from the old concepts of duress and undue influence, the courts are developing in modern times wider rules to protect persons against improper pressure and inequality of bargaining power as it affects contracts. This development was perhaps best described by Lord Denning in *Lloyds Bank* v *Bundy* [1974] 3 All ER 757 where he said, having discussed duress and various forms of undue pressure in contract:

> Gathering all together, I would suggest that through all these instances there runs a single thread. They rest on 'inequality of bargaining power'. By virtue of it, the English law gives relief to one who, without independent advice, enters into a contract on terms which are very unfair or transfers property for consideration which is grossly inadequate, where his bargaining power is grievously impaired by reason of his own needs or desires, or by his own ignorance or infirmity coupled with undue influence or pressures brought to bear on him by or for the benefit of the other.

Economic duress is within this concept. Suppose A agrees to build a tanker for B by an agreed date at an agreed price and B enters into a contract with C under which the tanker is to be chartered to C from the agreed completion date or shortly afterwards. If A then threatens not to complete the contract by the agreed date unless B pays more and B makes an extra payment because he does not want to be liable in breach of contract to C, then the agreement to pay more is affected by economic duress. (See the judgment of Mocatta, J in *North Ocean Shipping Co Ltd* v *Hyundai Construction Co Ltd, The Atlantic Baron* [1978] 3 All ER 1170.)

The decision of the House of Lords in *Universe Tankships Inc of Monrovia* v *International Transport Workers' Federation* [1982] 2 All ER 67 is instructive in that it affirms the existence of the doctrine of economic duress. In that case a ship called the *Universe Sentinel*, which was owned by Universe Tankships, was 'blacked' by the respondent trade union, the ITF, which regarded the ship as sailing under a flag of convenience. ITF was against flag-of-convenience ships and refused to make tugs available when the ship arrived at Milford Haven to discharge her cargo. The blacking was lifted after Universe Tankships had made an agreement with ITF regarding improvements in pay and conditions of the crew and had paid money to ITF which included a contribution of $6,480 to an ITF fund known as The Seafarers' International Welfare Protection and Assistance Fund. Universe Tankships sued for the return of the $6,480 on the basis of economic duress, and the House of Lords held that they were entitled to recover it. It appears from the judgments that the effect of economic duress is to make the contract voidable and to provide a ground for recovery of money paid as money had and received to the claimant's use – a form of quasi-contractual claim.

The decision in *Universe Tankships* was applied by the Court of Appeal in *B & S Contracts & Design* v *Victor Green Publications* [1984] IGR 419 where A agreed to erect stands for B who was doing a presentation at Olympia. A's employees threatened to strike unless they received extra money which they had demanded and to which they were not entitled. A said that the contract could not proceed unless these extra sums were paid by B as an increase in the contract price. B paid the extra sums to get the work done and then recovered them in this action. The money was paid under economic duress.

It should also be noted that where extra contractual payments have been arranged under circumstances of economic duress they cannot be recovered in a claim before a court. Thus in *Atlas Express* v *Kafco* [1989] 1 All ER 641 Atlas, a national road carrier, made a contract to deliver cartons of basketware to Woolworths stores for Kafco who were a small company importing and distributing the basketware. A price of £1.10 per carton was agreed but the first load had fewer cartons than had been anticipated and Atlas told Kafco that they would not carry any more without a minimum payment per trip regardless of the number of cartons carried. Kafco could not find another carrier quickly and, being worried about their contract with Woolworths if the latter did not get their supplies, Kafco agreed to the new terms but later refused to pay the new rate, only the per carton rate. The High Court held that the claim of Atlas for the minimum rate must be dismissed. The circumstances amounted to economic duress and there was no proper consent by Kafco.

Unconscionable bargains

The court will, in what it regards as an appropriate case, set aside a contract which is affected by improper pressure by one party or where there is inequality of bargaining power. However, mere inequality is not in itself enough: the court will look at all the circumstances of the case.

> *Lloyds Bank* v *Bundy*, 1974 – Unconscionable bargains illustrated (**151**)

Further examples of inequality of bargaining power may be found in *Clifford Davis Management* v *WEA Records* [1975] 1 All ER 237 where A, an experienced manager, obtained a contract with a pop star, B, who had little or no business experience, under which B gave A the copyright in all his compositions for a period of years. It was held that B could avoid the contract because A had exploited his superior bargaining power.

13

No general rule that all contracts must be fair

There is no rule of law which states that a fair price must be paid in *all* transactions and some unfair contracts will be held binding provided the parties were of equal bargaining strength. In *Burmah Oil Ltd* v *The Governor of the Bank of England* (1981) *The Times*, 4 July, Burmah was in financial difficulties and sold a large holding of shares which it had in British Petroleum to the government at a price below the Stock Exchange price. Burmah then brought an action to set the contract aside. The court refused to do so. Although there was authority to set aside a transaction where one party had acted without independent advice, or where the bargaining strength of one party was grievously impaired, neither of those situations existed in this case. The relationship was purely commercial and the contract for the sale of shares must stand.

Cases such as *Burmah Oil* indicate that the broad principle of 'inequality of bargaining power' can be misleading. A further example is provided by *Alec Lobb* (*Garages*) *Ltd* v *Total Oil GB Ltd* (1985) where directors of a company which was desperate to raise money negotiated a disadvantageous mortgage over its property which was nevertheless upheld as valid. Lawful business pressure seems to be justified no matter how much inequality of bargaining power may exist particularly where, as in this case, the loan was given in extremely risky circumstances to rescue Lobb which was in danger of collapse. The more recent case of *Leyland Daf Ltd* v *Automotive Products plc* (1993) *The Times*, 9 April, is also of interest. The Court of Appeal decided that Automotive was entitled to withhold supplies of brake and clutch systems to Leyland, which owed Automotive £758,955, until this was paid. Leyland was in administrative receivership and the receivers urgently needed the supplies to carry on the company's trade in the hope of finding a buyer for it. The court also decided that Automotive was not in breach of Art 86 of the Treaty of Rome (abuse of a dominant position) (see further Chapter 16).

14

CONTRACTUAL TERMS

We shall now consider the contents of the contract by explaining the types of terms express or implied which may be found in a contract.

Inducements and terms generally

Even where it is clear that a valid contract has been made it is still necessary to decide precisely what it is the parties have undertaken to do in order to be able to say whether each has performed or not performed his part of the agreement.

In order to decide upon the terms of the contract it is necessary to find out what was said or written by the parties. Furthermore, having ascertained what the parties said or wrote, it is necessary to decide whether the statements were mere inducements (or representations) or terms of the contract, i.e. part of its actual contents. The distinction in diagrammatic form together with an indication of remedies appears in Figure 14.1 at p 331.

The distinction is less important than it was since the passing of the Misrepresentation Act 1967. Before the Act became law there was often no remedy for a misrepresentation which was not fraudulent, and in such a case the claimant's only hope of obtaining a remedy was to convince the court that the defendant's statement was not a mere inducement but a term of the contract of which the defendant was in breach and for which damages might be obtained. As we have seen, under the Misrepresentation Act 1967 the new form of negligent misrepresentation which did not exist before will now give rise in many cases to an action for damages even in respect of a mere misrepresentation or inducement.

Written contracts and outside evidence

It is a general rule of the common law that outside (or extrinsic) evidence cannot be brought to vary a written contract (*Goss v Nugent* (1833) 5 B & Ad 58). This is known as the parol (oral) evidence rule. However, the courts have been prepared to admit outside evidence if it can be shown that the written contract was not intended to express the whole agreement of the parties. Thus in *Walker Property Investments (Brighton) Ltd v Walker* (1947) 177 LT 204 a prospective tenant under a written tenancy agreement was allowed to add an oral agreement to the tenancy under which, as he satisfied the court, he was entitled to the use of two basement rooms and the garden. Reference to this right had been omitted from the tenancy agreement.

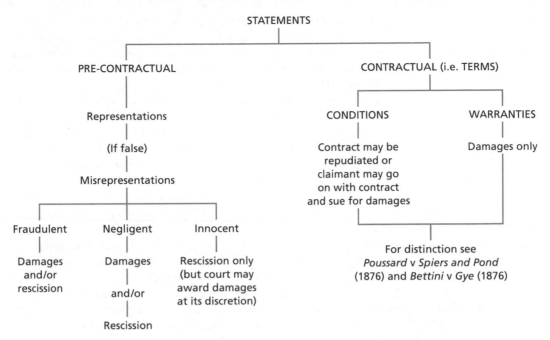

Figure 14.1 Distinction between pre-contractual and contractual statements

Inducements and terms distinguished

Nevertheless, it is still necessary to consider the main tests applied by the courts in order to distinguish between a mere misrepresentation and a term of the contract, bearing in mind always that the question whether a statement is an inducement or a term and, if a term, whether a condition or warranty *is a matter of fact for the judge*. Fact decisions of this sort vary widely according to the circumstances of each case, so that it is virtually impossible to predict with absolute accuracy what the outcome of a particular case will be. However, by way of illustration the following headings contain the major guidelines which are applied.

The statements and intentions of the parties

The court will always be concerned to implement the intentions of the parties as they appear from statements made by them. Thus in *Gill & Duffus SA v Société pour l'Exportation des Sucres SA* [1985] 1 Lloyd's Rep 621 the defendants agreed to sell sugar to Gill. A term of the contract (not specified as a condition or warranty) said that the defendants were to name a port at which the sugar was to be loaded by 14 November 'at latest'. The defendants did not nominate a port by that time and so Gill refused to take any sugar from the defendants and regarded the contract as cancelled. The defendants then tried to make a nomination of a port but Gill refused to accept it saying that they had repudiated the contract because of the defendants' breach of condition (or repudiatory breach). Following a decision unfavourable to them at arbitration, Gill appealed. Leggatt, J said that there were no words in the English language by which a deadline could be appointed more concisely, more precisely, or with more finality than 'at latest'. They meant what they said and the judge had no doubt that the intention of the parties as gathered from the contract itself would be best carried out by treating the promise not as a mere warranty but as a condition precedent by the failure to perform which the other party was relieved of liability. Gill's contention was accepted. There was a repudiatory breach of condition. Where in a contract the parties have indicated that a particular undertaking is to be a term of the contract, the courts will in general abide by the wishes of the parties. However, the court will not slavishly follow the parties' statements and where, for example, the parties appear to have regarded a trivial matter as a vital term of the agreement, the court may still take the view that it is not.

Thus, so far as a written contract is concerned, the court may disregard a statement by the parties that a particular undertaking is a condition and say instead that it is a warranty. So far as wholly oral contracts are concerned, the court may ignore the statements of the parties and decide that a particular undertaking is a condition, a warranty, or a mere inducement.

Thus in *L Schuler AG v Wickham Machine Tool Sales* [1973] 2 All ER 39 the claimants entered into a contract for four years with the defendants giving them the sole right to sell panel presses in England. A clause of the contract provided that it should be a condition of the agreement that the defendants' representatives should visit six named firms each week to solicit orders. The defendants' representatives failed on a few occasions to do so and the claimants claimed to be entitled to repudiate the agreement on the basis that a single failure was a breach of condition giving them an absolute right to treat the contract as at an end. The House of Lords said that such minor breaches by the defendants did not entitle the claimants to repudiate. The House of Lords construed the clause on the basis that it was so unreasonable that the parties could not have intended it as a condition giving Schuler a right of repudiation, but rather as a warranty. Thus Schuler were themselves in breach of contract leaving Wickham with a claim for damages against Schuler.

This case is also an example of the court trying to give redress in regard to an unconscionable bargain and to correct unscrupulous commercial conduct.

The nature of the statement

A statement is likely to be an inducement rather than a term if the person making the statement asks the other party to check or verify it, e.g. 'The car is sound but I should get an engineer's report on it'.

In addition, a statement is likely to be a term rather than a mere inducement if it is made with the intention of preventing the other party from looking for defects and succeeds in doing this, e.g. 'The car is sound, you need not look it over'.

The importance of the statement

If the statement is such that the claimant would not have made the contract without it, then the statement will be a term of the contract and not a mere inducement.

Bannerman v White, 1861 – Representations and terms: a vital undertaking (**152**)

The timing of the statement

A statement made during preliminary negotiations tends to be an inducement. Where the interval between the making of the statement and the making of the contract is distinct then the statement is almost certain to be an inducement. Thus in *Routledge v McKay* [1954] 1 All ER 855 the claimant and the defendant were discussing the possible purchase and sale of the defendant's motor cycle. Both parties were private persons. The defendant, taking the information from the registration book, said, on 23 October, that the cycle was a 1942 model. On 30 October a written contract of sale was made. The actual date of the cycle was later found to be 1930. The buyer's claim for damages for breach of warranty failed in the Court of Appeal. In this case the interval between the negotiations and the contract was well marked and the statement was not a term. However, the interval is not always so well marked and in such cases there is a difficulty in deciding whether the statement is an inducement or a term.

Oral statements later put into writing

If the statement was oral and the contract was afterwards reduced to writing, then the terms of the contract tend to be contained in the written document and all oral statements tend to be pre-contractual inducements. Even so the court may still consider the apparent intentions of the parties and decide that they had made a contract which was part oral and part written (see *Evans* v *Merzario* (1976) in Chapter 15).

Special skill and knowledge or lack of same

Where one of the parties has special knowledge or skill with regard to the subject matter of the contract, then the statements of such a party will normally be regarded as terms of the contract. In addition, it will be difficult for an expert to convince the court that a person with no particular knowledge or skill in regard to the subject matter has made statements which constitute terms of the contract.

> *Oscar Chess Ltd* v *Williams*, 1957 – Effect of special skill and knowledge (**153**)

14

Conditions and warranties

Having decided that a particular statement is a term of the contract and not a mere inducement, the court must then consider the importance of that statement in the context of the contract as a whole. Not all terms are of equal importance. Failure to perform some may have a more serious effect on the contract than failure to perform others. The law has applied special terminology to contractual terms in order to distinguish the vital or fundamental obligations from the less vital, the expression *condition* being applied to the former and the expression *warranty* to the latter. A condition is a fundamental obligation which goes to the root of the contract. A warranty on the other hand is a subsidiary obligation which is not so vital that a failure to perform it goes to the root of the contract.

This distinction is important in terms of remedies. A breach of condition is called a repudiatory breach and the injured party may elect either to repudiate the contract or claim damages and go on with the contract.

It should be noted that the claimant must go on with the contract and sue for damages if he has affirmed the contract after knowledge of a breach of condition. He may do this expressly as where he uses the goods, or by lapse of time as where he simply fails to take any steps to complain about the breach for what in the court's view is an unreasonable period of time. A breach of warranty is not repudiatory and the claimant must go on with the contract and sue for damages.

Whether a term is a condition or warranty is basically a matter for the court which will be decided on the basis of the commercial importance of the term. As we have seen, the words used by the parties are, of course, relevant, but are not followed slavishly by the court which may still decide differently from the parties on the basis of the commercial importance of the term.

It should be noted that the word *warranty* is sometimes used in a different way, e.g. by a manufacturer of goods who gives a *warranty* against faulty workmanship offering to replace parts free. The term *warranty* is used by the manufacturer as equivalent to a guarantee. We are concerned here with its use as a term of a contract.

> *Poussard* v *Spiers and Pond*, 1876 – Condition: a vital commercial undertaking (**154**)
>
> *Bettini* v *Gye*, 1876 – Warranty: a collateral undertaking (**155**)

Innominate terms

In modern law there are also terms which the parties call conditions and where the breach has *in fact* had a serious result on the contract. The court will then agree that the breach should be treated as a breach of condition and the contract can be repudiated. There are also terms which the parties call warranties and where the breach has *in fact* not been serious. The court will then agree that the breach shall be treated as a breach of warranty and the contract cannot be repudiated. The parties must go on with it though the person injured by the breach has an action for damages.

There are also what are called *innominate terms*. The effect of these on the contract will depend upon how serious the breach has turned out to be *in fact*. If the breach has turned out to be serious the court will then treat the term as a condition, so that the contract can be repudiated. If *in fact* the breach has not had a serious effect on the contract, the court will treat it as a breach of warranty, so that the parties must proceed with the contract, though the injured party will have an action for damages.

Thus, if Dodgy Motors advertises a car for sale as having done 32,000 miles, this statement is likely to be a warranty giving an action for damages only if in fact the car has done, say, 34,000 miles. If, however, the car had done 60,000 miles the court would be likely to regard the statement as a condition allowing repudiation of the contract.

> *The Hansa Nord*, 1975 – The innominate term illustrated (**156**)

Implied terms – generally

Before leaving the topic of the contents of the contract it must be appreciated that in addition to the express terms inserted by the parties, the contract may contain and be subject to implied terms. Such terms are derived from custom or statute, and in addition a term may be implied by the court where it is necessary in order to achieve the result which in the court's view the parties obviously intended the contract to have.

Customary implied terms

A contract may be regarded as containing customary terms not specifically mentioned by the parties.

> *Hutton* v *Warren*, 1836 – A contract containing a customary term (**157**)

Judicial implied terms

Implication according to parties' intentions

The court may imply a term into a contract whenever it is necessary to do so in order that the express terms decided upon by the parties shall have the effect which was presumably intended by them. This is often expressed as the giving of 'business efficacy' to the contract, the judge regarding himself as doing merely what the parties themselves would *in fact* have done in order to cover the situation if they had addressed themselves to it.

> *The Moorcock*, 1889 – When the court implies a term (**158**)

Implication as a matter of law

Sometimes, however, the courts imply a term which is quite complex so that the parties would not, *in fact*, have addressed themselves to it. Here the judge is saying *as a matter of law* how the contract should be performed. This is illustrated by *Liverpool City Council* v *Irwin* [1977] AC 239 where the House of Lords held that it was an implied term of a lease of a maisonette in a block of properties owned by the Council that the landlord should take reasonable care to keep the common parts of the block in a reasonable state of repair, although the obligation to do so would *not* have been accepted by the landlord.

When *Irwin*'s case was in the Court of Appeal, Lord Denning, in deciding that there should be an implied term regarding maintenance, rejected the business efficacy test as the only test, saying that the court could imply a term whenever it was *just and reasonable* to do so, whether the term was strictly *necessary* to the performance of the contract or not. Although the House of Lords implied a term relating to maintenance, it did not go along with the view of Lord Denning that the test should be reasonableness regardless of necessity. The Court of Appeal returned to the 'necessary' approach in *Mears* v *Safecar Security* [1982] 2 All ER 865 and refused to imply a term into a contract of service that payment should be made to an employee during sickness. Stephenson, LJ was of opinion that the term could not be implied because, although it might be *reasonable* to imply a term relating to sick-pay, it was not *necessary* in a contract of employment. The term relating to maintenance in *Irwin* was in a sense not absolutely vital to performance of the contract in that the tenants could have walked up the stairs, even in the dark, to their flats if lift and light maintenance had not been carried out, but it was much closer to being necessary to *performance* of the contract than was the sick-pay term in *Mears*.

The Court of Appeal also decided in *Morley* v *Heritage plc* (1993) 470 IRLB 11 that a contract of employment does not contain an implied term that an employee will receive pay in lieu of unused holiday entitlement. A claim that the term should have been implied on the basis of custom and practice failed because there was no such custom or practice in the company. If there had been, the claim might well have succeeded.

The decision in *Morley* was distinguished in *Janes Solicitors* v *Lamb-Simpson* (1996) 541 IRLB 15. In that case the Employment Appeal Tribunal decided that there was an implied contract term to pay accrued holiday pay. Ms Lamb-Simpson had not been given written particulars of her employment as required by the Employment Rights Act 1996 (see Chapter 19) and the EAT felt able to imply the term. In *Morley* there was a detailed written contract between the parties which dealt with holiday entitlement and holiday pay but said nothing about accrued holiday pay. It seemed therefore that the parties had addressed themselves to the relevant area and if something was not covered it was because it was not intended.

14

It should be noted that payment for accrued holiday leave is now payable under the Working Time Regulations 1998 (see further Chapter 19). The maximum leave under the regulations is currently four weeks so the above materials have application where a claim is made for accrued holiday pay beyond four weeks.

Implied terms in consumer law – sale of goods

The law relating to the sale of goods is to be found in the Sale of Goods Act 1979 (as amended). This is a consolidating measure bringing together a number of previous Acts, but in particular the Sale of Goods Act 1893. Also relevant are rules of the common law not dealt with by legislation. Section references are to the Sale of Goods Act 1979 (as amended) unless otherwise indicated.

Title

The rules governing title are as follows.

Implied condition as to title

Section 12(1) provides that, unless the circumstances show a different intention, there is an implied condition on the part of the seller that in the case of a sale he has the right to sell the goods, and that in the case of an agreement to sell, he will have the right to sell the goods at the time when the property (ownership) is to pass.

Usually the ownership of goods passes to the buyer when the contract is made, but in an agreement to sell it does not. For example, a contract for goods yet to be made is an agreement for sale.

Rowland v *Divall*, 1923 – Section 12 and total failure of consideration (**159**)

The decision in *Rowland*, which has been applied in subsequent cases (see *Karflex Ltd* v *Poole* [1933] 2 KB 251), produces an unfortunate result in that a person who buys goods to which the seller has no title is allowed to recover the whole of the purchase price even though he has had some use and enjoyment from the goods before he is dispossessed by the true owner. It is thus difficult to suggest that there has been total failure of consideration. The Law Reform Committee (see 1966 Cmnd 2958, para 36) has recommended that, subject to further study of the law relating to restitution, an allowance in respect of use and enjoyment should be deducted from the purchase price and the balance returned to the claimant. It should be noted that the 1979 Act does not deal with this matter.

Section 12(1) might be construed as meaning that the seller must have the power to give ownership of the goods to the buyer, but if the goods can only be sold by infringing a trade mark, the seller has no right to sell for the purposes of s 12(1).

Niblett Ltd v *Confectioners' Materials Co Ltd*, 1921 – A sale which infringed a registered mark (**160**)

Implied warranties as to title

Section 12(2) provides that there is:

> An implied warranty that the goods are free, and will remain free until the time when the property is to pass, from any charge or encumbrance not disclosed or known to the buyer before the contract is made, and that the buyer will enjoy quiet possession of the goods except so far as it may be disturbed by the owner or other person entitled to the benefit of any charge or encumbrance so disclosed or known.

This does not apply where a limited interest is sold, but ss 12(4) and 12(5) do and contain similar provisions (see below).

It is not easy to see what rights this sub-section gives over those in s 12(1). The law does not recognise encumbrances over chattels unless the person trying to enforce them is in possession of the goods or in privity of contract with the person who is in possession (*Dunlop* v *Selfridge* (1915) – see Chapter 10). Thus, if A uses his car as security for a loan from B then:

(*a*) if B takes the car into his possession, the charge will be enforceable if necessary by a sale of the vehicle;

(*b*) the charge is equally enforceable against the car while it is still in A's possession, though if A sells it to C, B will be prevented by lack of privity of contract from enforcing any remedies against the vehicle once it is in the possession of C.

Thus, if situation (*a*) above applied, the sub-section is unnecessary since A could not deliver the vehicle even if he sold it and would therefore be liable in damages for non-delivery to C. If situation (*b*) above applied, then the encumbrances would not attach to the vehicle once C had taken possession. C would not, therefore, require a remedy.

However, the usefulness of s 12(2) is illustrated by the decision of the Court of Appeal in *Microbeads AC* v *Vinhurst Road Markings Ltd* [1975] 1 All ER 529. In this case A sold road-marking machines to B. After the sale C obtained a patent on the machines so that their continued use by B was in breach of that patent and C was bringing an action against B in respect of this. In a claim by A against B for the purchase price, B wished to include in their defence breach of ss 12(1) and 12(2). It was held by the Court of Appeal that they could include breach of s 12(2) but not breach of s 12(1). There had been no breach of s 12(1) at the time of the sale so that A had not infringed that sub-section but since B's quiet possession had been disturbed after sale, A was in breach of s 12(2).

Sales under a limited title

Under s 12(3), the sale of a limited interest is now possible. Where the parties intend only to transfer such a title as the seller may have, there is an implied warranty that all charges or encumbrances known to the seller and not known to the buyer have been disclosed to the buyer before the contract is made (s 12(4)), and an implied warranty that the buyer's quiet possession will not be disturbed (s 12(5)). There is an action by the buyer for breach of these warranties if, for example, he is dispossessed by the true owner. Furthermore, the seller is not able to contract out of this liability.

Sales under a limited title are common where the sale is of goods taken in execution by the bailiffs to satisfy a judgment debt.

14

Sales by description

Section 13(1) provides that, where there is a contract for the sale of goods by description, there is an implied condition that the goods shall correspond with the description.

(*a*) A sale is by description where the purchaser is buying on a mere description having never seen the goods. A classic example occurs in the case of mail-order transactions.

(*b*) A sale may still be by description even though the goods are seen or examined or even selected from the seller's stock by the purchaser, as in a sale over the counter, because most goods are described if only by the package in which they are contained. Therefore a sale in a self-service store would be covered by s 13 though no words were spoken by the seller.

> *Beale* v *Taylor*, 1967 – Application of s 13 where the goods are seen (**161**)

If s 13 applies it is enforced strictly, and every statement which forms part of that description is treated as a condition giving the buyer the right to reject the goods, even though the misdescription is of a minor nature. There is no such thing as a 'slight breach' of condition.

Buyers have been allowed to reject goods on seemingly trivial grounds, e.g. misdescriptions of how the goods are packed, and regardless of the fact that no damage has been suffered.

> *Moore & Co* v *Landauer & Co*, 1921 – Packaging is part of the description (**162**)

However, if the defect is a matter of quality and/or condition of the goods rather than an identifying description, s 14 (see below) rather than s 13 applies. Although the Sale of Goods Act applies in the main to sales by dealers, s 13 applies even where the seller is not a dealer in the goods sold (*Varley* v *Whipp* [1900] 1 QB 513).

There can be no contracting out of s 13 at all where a business sells to a consumer or the contract is between persons in a private capacity. In a non-consumer sale contracting out is allowed to the extent that it is 'fair or reasonable' (see further Chapter 15).

Where the sale is by sample as well as by description, s 13(2) provides that the bulk must correspond with both the sample and the description. Thus in *Nichol* v *Godts* (1854) 10 Ex 191 a purchaser bought by sample 'foreign refined rape oil'. It was held that the goods must not only correspond with the sample, which they did, but also be in fact 'foreign refined rape oil' and not a mixture of rape and hemp oil which was inferior.

Sale by description and misrepresentation distinguished

It should be noted that the description must be an identifying description to come under s 13 as in *Beale* v *Taylor* (above). Statements regarding the state of a car's tyres, e.g. 'they were fitted 5,000 miles ago', are concerned more with quality and/or condition of the goods and s 13 probably does not apply, the claim being for misrepresentation. If s 13 did apply, then every trivial statement about the goods would be a breach of condition and the law relating to misrepresentation would have no place – a rather unlikely situation.

Statements such as the one above do not identify the goods. Suppose I were to say to a student: 'The notes you require are in the boot of my car. Here are the keys. My car is the one which had new tyres fitted 5,000 miles ago.' How would the student find the car? Not easily: the statement does not identify the vehicle!

Sales in the course of a business

Although ss 12 and 13 of the 1979 Act apply to private sales as well as business sales, the s 14 implied terms of fitness and satisfactory quality apply only to sales *in the course of a business*. A problem may, therefore, arise where a milkman sells his old float in order to buy a new one. If the float is not fit for the purpose and/or of satisfactory quality, to what extent will the implied terms of s 14 (see below) be available to the person who has bought the float? Is it a private sale or a sale in the course of a business? It was decided by the Court of Appeal that it could be in the course of a business and that s 14 should be interpreted widely (see *Stevenson* v *Rogers* [1999] 1 All ER 613). Earlier statute law on sale of goods had confined s 14 to situations where the seller *dealt* in the goods, but the 1979 Act, following recommendations of the Law Commission, required only that the goods be sold *in the course of a business*, so that even an irregular sale of business property could be included and carry the implied conditions of fitness and satisfactory quality. If the sale is integral to the business, that is enough, even though the goods are not routinely sold by the business. Thus in *Stevenson* the sale by a person in business as a fisherman of one of his boats was within the 1979 Act and the condition of satisfactory quality applied. The decision in *Stevenson* runs contrary to the decision of the Court of Appeal in the *R & B Customs Brokers* case (1988) (see Chapter 15) where, because the purchase of a car by a business was irregular and not an integral part of the business, the company was treated as a consumer for the purpose of exclusion clauses. The Court of Appeal considered this case in *Stevenson*, but said that since it was an interpretation of the Unfair Contract Terms Act 1977, it could stand in that field, but the reasoning was not to be applied to the Sale of Goods Act 1979.

14

Implied conditions as to fitness

Section 14(3) lays down the following conditions.

Where the seller sells goods in the course of a business and the buyer (or debtor in a credit sale) expressly, or by implication, makes known (a) to the seller, or (b) to the dealer in a credit sale any particular purpose for which the goods are being bought, there is an implied condition that the goods supplied under the contract are reasonably fit for that purpose whether or not that is a purpose for which such goods are commonly supplied, except where the circumstances show that the buyer (or debtor) does not rely, or that it is unreasonable for him to rely, on the skill or judgement of that seller or dealer.

There is no need for the buyer to specify the particular purpose for which the goods are required when they have in the ordinary way only one purpose, e.g. a hot-water bottle. If ordinary goods in everyday use are required for a particular purpose, this must be made known to the seller.

> *Priest* v *Last*, 1903 – Where the goods have only one purpose (**163**)
> *Griffiths* v *Peter Conway Ltd*, 1939 – Where the goods must cope with the claimant's abnormalities (**164**)

Fitness for the purpose: meaning of reliance

In these days of national advertising under brand names it is somewhat unrealistic to assume that the buyer very often relies on the seller's skill and judgement. However, in order to make the law work, reliance will readily be implied even to the extent of saying that, at least in sales to the general public as consumers, the buyer has gone to the seller because he relies on the seller having selected his stock with skill and judgement. The buyer must show that he has made known the purpose for which the goods are being bought. Reliance will then be presumed, unless it can be disproved, or if the seller can show that reliance was unreasonable.

The court has to decide what amounts to 'unreasonable reliance'. However, presumably the seller can disclaim responsibility. For example, suppose B goes into S's general stores and sees some tubes of glue. If he then asks whether the glue will stick metal to plastic and S says: 'I am not expert enough to say', then if B buys the glue and it does not stick metal to plastic it would surely be unreasonable for B to suggest that he relied on S's skill and judgement.

There will in general be no implication of reliance where the buyer knows that the seller deals in only one brand of goods, e.g. where a public house sells only one brand of beer.

> *Grant* v *Australian Knitting Mills Ltd*, 1936 – Reliance on seller's skill and judgement readily implied (**165**)
>
> *Wren* v *Holt*, 1903 – Position where seller obliged to sell only one product (**166**)

Fitness: application to non-manufactured goods

The rules relating to fitness for the purpose under s 14(3) apply also to non-manufactured goods. Thus in *Frost* v *Aylesbury Dairy Co Ltd* [1905] 1 KB 608 the defendants who were retailers of milk were held liable under s 14(3) when they sold milk containing germs which caused the claimant's wife to die of typhoid fever.

Fitness: second-hand goods

In deciding the matter of fitness for the purpose in the case of second-hand goods the buyer must expect that defects are likely to emerge sooner or later. However, if defects occur fairly quickly after sale this is strong evidence that the goods were not reasonably fit at the time of sale.

> *Crowther* v *Shannon Motor Company*, 1975 – Fitness and second-hand goods (**167**)

Fitness and satisfactory quality distinguished

Before proceeding to consider satisfactory quality, we must distinguish the two heads of liability, i.e. fitness and satisfactory quality. Under s 14(2) an article is regarded as not satisfactory because of a manufacturing defect so that a perfect article would have served the purpose, or in other words it is the right article but it is faulty. Under s 14(3) an article is regarded as not fit for the purpose because of its design or construction. It may be perfect in terms of its manufacture but its construction or design does not allow it to fit the purpose and consequently no amount of adjustment or repair will ever make it right. In other words, it is a perfect article but the wrong article for the purpose.

> *Baldry* v *Marshall*, 1925 – Where goods not fit but satisfactory (**168**)

Satisfactory quality

By s 14(2) (as amended by the Sale and Supply of Goods Act 1994) *where the seller sells goods in the course of a business* there is an implied condition that the goods supplied under the contract are of satisfactory quality, except that there is no such condition:

(*a*) as regards defects specifically drawn to the buyer's attention before the contract is made; or
(*b*) if the buyer examines the goods before the contract is made, as regards defects which that examination ought to reveal.

If the seller does not normally deal in goods of the type in question, there is no condition as to fitness (nor as to satisfactory quality unless the sale is by sample which is dealt with below). The *only* condition in such a case is that the goods correspond with the description. This arises because s 14(1) provides that except as provided by s 14 and s 15 (sale by sample), and subject to any other enactment, there is no implied condition or warranty about the quality or fitness for any particular purpose of goods supplied under a contract of sale. If, therefore, S (who is not a dealer) sells a car to B with no express terms as to quality and fitness, the court is prevented by s 14 from implying conditions or warranties, even though S seems, from the circumstances, to have been warranting the car in good order.

The s 14 provision regarding satisfactory quality applies where the sale is by a dealer who does not ordinarily sell goods of precisely the same description. Thus if B ordered an 'X' brand motor bike from S who has not formerly sold that make, s 14 applies if the motor bike is unfit or unsatisfactory.

There is no need under s 14(2) for the buyer to show that he relied on the seller's skill and judgement, and the seller is liable for latent defects even though he is not the manufacturer and is merely marketing the goods as a wholesaler or retailer. Such a seller can, however, obtain an indemnity from the manufacturer if the buyer successfully sues him for defects in the goods.

Sales through an agent

Section 14(5) is concerned with the problem of a private seller who sells through an agent. The sub-section provides that the implied conditions of fitness and satisfactory quality operate if the agent is selling in the ordinary course of business unless the principal is not acting in the course of business and the buyer is aware of this, or reasonable steps have been taken to bring it to his notice. Thus, for example, an auctioneer acting for a private seller could exclude these sections by making it clear that the principal was a private seller.

Examination of the goods

The buyer is not obliged to examine the goods but if he does do so he will lose the protection of s 14(2) if he fails to notice obvious defects, at least in respect of such defects as where a new washing machine is examined and the buyer misses a rather obvious scratch on the front of the machine. The buyer can also lose his right to complain where the seller actually points out the defects.

The price paid

The interpretation of the word 'merchantable' (now 'satisfactory') has often been discussed in the courts. Section 14(6) provides: goods of any kind are of merchantable (now satisfactory)

14

quality within the meaning of this Act if they are as fit for the purpose or purposes for which goods of that kind are commonly bought as it is reasonable to expect having regard to any description applied to them, the price (if relevant) and all the other relevant circumstances.

The price paid by the buyer is therefore a factor to be taken into account. Goods (provided they are not defective) are not unsatisfactory simply because their resale price is slightly less than that which the buyer paid, though they may be if the difference in purchase and resale price is substantial.

> *B S Brown & Son Ltd* v *Craiks Ltd*, 1970 – Satisfactory quality and the resale price (**169**)

How were the goods described?

As regards the description applied to the goods, old cars or other mechanical items which are sold and described as scrap need not be of satisfactory quality. Furthermore, 'shop-soiled', 'fire-damaged', 'flood-salvage' and so on might imply non-satisfactory lines. In addition, old items, such as antiques and curios would not presumably be required to be in perfect working order. However, as we have seen it was held in *Cavendish-Woodhouse* v *Manley* (1984) 82 LGR 376 that the phrase on an invoice 'bought as seen' merely confirms that the purchaser has seen the goods. It does not exclude any implied terms as to quality or fitness.

Duration of satisfactory quality

As regards the time during which the goods must be satisfactory, the law is not clear. So far as perishable goods are concerned, the decision in *Mash and Murrell* v *Joseph I Emmanuel* [1961] 1 All ER 485 is relevant. In that case potatoes, though sound when loaded in Cyprus, were rotten by the time the ship arrived in Liverpool, though there was no undue delay. It was held by Diplock, J that the sellers were liable under s 14(2) because the goods should have been loaded in such a state that they could survive the normal journey and be in satisfactory condition when they arrived. In addition, the seller is liable for defects inherent in the goods when they are sold and will not escape merely because the defects do not become apparent until a later time. Circumstances such as those seen in *Crowther* v *Shannon Motor Co* (1975) provide an illustration of this situation.

Goods partially defective

Where part only of the goods is unsatisfactory it seems to depend on how much of the consignment is defective. In *Jackson* v *Rotax Motor and Cycle Co Ltd* [1910] 2 KB 937 the claimants supplied motor horns to the defendants and one consignment was rejected by the defendants who alleged they were unmerchantable (now unsatisfactory). Half the goods were dented and scratched because of bad packing and the Court of Appeal held that the buyers were entitled to reject the consignment.

In this connection we have already considered s 15A of the Sale of Goods Act 1979 (as inserted by the Sale and Supply of Goods Act 1994) under which a consumer can reject goods where the breach is slight but a business buyer will, where the breach is slight, have to take delivery and sue for any loss. Clearly in the *Jackson* case s 15A would have allowed rejection in a business context as well as a consumer context. The breach was hardly slight!

Satisfactory quality: the current test

Section 1 of the Sale and Supply of Goods Act 1994 inserts in s 14 of the Sale of Goods Act 1979 a reformed definition of the concept of quality, and merchantable quality has gone. There was always doubt about its scope and minor defects were not necessarily covered. Thus in *Millars of Falkirk Ltd* v *Turpie* 1976 SLT 66 it was decided that a new car with a slight leak of oil in the power-assisted steering was even so of merchantable quality. Similarly, a scratch on the dashboard of a new car would not prevent it from being merchantable.

Now a sale in the course of business carries an implied condition that the goods are of 'satisfactory quality'. To be of such quality the goods must meet the standard that a reasonable person would regard as satisfactory taking into account any description, price and other relevant circumstances. This is a general test but the section then explains that the quality of the goods includes their state and condition and gives specific and non-exhaustive aspects of quality:

- fitness for the purpose for which the goods are commonly supplied;
- appearance and finish;
- freedom from minor defects;
- safety;
- durability.

As before, defects specifically brought to the buyer's attention before the contract or if the buyer has examined the goods those he ought to have noticed are not covered. Nevertheless, many more defects will now be covered, and the Law Commission, in Working Paper 85 (which advocated the satisfactory quality test), took the view that in the *Millars* case the car would have failed the new test which it proposed.

The above rules also apply to goods supplied under a contract for work and materials, e.g. an oil filter supplied when servicing a car (see further later in this chapter).

14

Fitness and satisfactory quality

Private sales

The rules as to fitness for purpose and satisfactory quality do not apply to private sales of second-hand goods and there is still a fairly wide application of the maxim *caveat emptor* (let the buyer beware). In practice only manufacturers, wholesalers, retailers and dealers in new or second-hand goods will be caught by the implied conditions. The courts cannot imply conditions and warranties into private contracts similar to those implied by the Act into sales by dealers, because, as we have seen, s 14(1) forbids it.

Extension to items supplied with goods

The implied terms relating to fitness and satisfactory quality extend also to other items supplied under the contract of sale of goods, e.g. containers, foreign matter and instructions for use.

Geddling v *Marsh*, 1920 – Fitness and satisfactory quality: returnable bottles (**170**)

Wilson v *Rickett, Cockerell & Co Ltd*, 1954 – Where foreign matter is supplied with the goods (**171**)

Wormell v *RHM Agriculture (East) Ltd*, 1986 – Application to instructions for use (**172**)

Injury to third party, purchaser's indemnity

It should be noted that if a retailer sells goods which are faulty and in breach of s 14 he is obliged to indemnify the purchaser if the faulty goods injure a third party to whom the purchaser is found liable. However, no such indemnity is payable if the purchaser has continued to use the goods having become aware that they are faulty and dangerous.

> *Lambert* v *Lewis*, 1981 – Where goods are used by the buyer after knowledge of defects (**173**)

Usage of trade

Section 14(4) provides that an implied warranty or condition as to quality or fitness for a particular purpose may be attached to a contract of sale by usage. Where the transaction is connected with a particular trade, the customs and usages of that trade give the context in which the parties made their contract and may give a guide as to their intentions. Thus, in a sale of canary seed in accordance with the customs of the trade it was held that the buyer could not reject the seed delivered on the grounds that there were impurities in it. A custom of the trade prevented this but allowed instead a rebate on the price paid (*Peter Darlington Partners Ltd* v *Gosho Co Ltd* [1964] 1 Lloyd's Rep 149).

Sale by sample

Section 15(1) states that a contract of sale is a contract of sale by sample where there is a term in the contract, express or implied, to that effect. The mere fact that the seller provides a sample for the buyer's inspection is not enough: to be such a sale either there must be an express provision in the contract to that effect, or there must be evidence that the parties intended the sale to be by sample.

There are three implied conditions in a sale by sample.

(a) *The bulk must correspond with the sample in quality* (s 15(2)(a)).

(b) *The buyer shall have a reasonable opportunity of comparing the bulk with the sample* (s 15(2)(b)). The buyer will not be deemed to have accepted the goods until he has had an opportunity to compare the bulk with the sample, and will be able, therefore, to reject the goods, even though they have been delivered, if the bulk does not correspond with the sample. He is not left with the remedy of damages for the breach of warranty.

(c) *The goods shall be free from any defect, making their quality unsatisfactory, which would not be apparent on reasonable examination of the sample* (s 15(2)(c)).

The effect of s 15(2)(c) is to exclude the implied condition of satisfactory quality if the defect could have been discovered by reasonable examination of the sample whether or not there has in fact been any examination of the sample. This is presumably based upon the premise that the seller is entitled to assume that the buyer will examine the sample. The provision is in contrast with s 14(2) where the implied condition of satisfactory quality is not excluded unless an examination has actually taken place.

A reasonable examination for the purpose of a sale by sample is such an examination as is usually carried out in the trade concerned.

> *Godley* v *Perry*, 1960 – When a sale is by sample (**174**)

Implied terms in consumer law – the supply of goods and services

Having looked at the implied terms in a contract of sale of goods, we can now move on to consider the law relating to contracts for work and material, e.g. car repairs where goods and services are supplied *together* and the goods are used or supplied in such a process as distinct from being *sold on their own* (which would be a sale of goods), and for the supply of services and the implied terms therein.

Supply of goods other than by sale

As regards the rights of those who purchase goods, we have seen that the Sale of Goods Act 1979 applies and that ss 12–15 of that Act imply terms to which a buyer may resort if the goods are faulty, defective or unsuitable. Those who take goods on hire-purchase are similarly protected by ss 8–11 of the Supply of Goods (Implied Terms) Act 1973.

As regards contracts for work and materials, the supply of goods (or the materials used) is governed by Part I of the Supply of Goods and Services Act 1982. The services supplied (or the work element) are governed by Part II of the 1982 Act.

Contracts of exchange or barter, hire, rental or leasing are governed by Part I of the 1982 Act, while contracts for services only, e.g. a contract to carry goods or advice from an accountant or solicitor, are governed by Part II of the 1982 Act. The relevant provisions of the Act are dealt with in detail below. Section references are to the 1982 Act unless otherwise indicated.

The 1982 Act was amended by the Sale and Supply of Goods Act 1994. The relevant amendments are included in the material appearing below.

Contracts for the transfer of property in goods

The contracts concerned are dealt with in s 1(1) which provides that a contract for the transfer of goods means a contract under which one person transfers, or agrees to transfer to another, the property in goods, unless the transfer takes place under an excluded contract. These excluded contracts are set out in s 1(2). They are contracts for the sale of goods, hire-purchase contracts, and those where the property in goods is transferred on a redemption of trading stamps. (These are governed by the Trading Stamps Act 1964.) Transfer of property rights in goods by way of mortgage, pledge, charge or other security is excluded, as are gifts.

There must be a contract between the parties. If not, the statutory implied terms cannot be relied upon if the goods supplied prove to be defective. Thus a chemist supplying harmful drugs under a National Health Service prescription will not come within the Act. This is because the patient does not provide consideration. The chemist collects the prescription charge for the government and not for himself. The payment to the chemist does not come from the patient unless it is a private prescription where the patient has paid the full amount. Otherwise an action against the chemist would have to be framed in the tort of negligence.

As regards promotional free gifts, e.g. the giving away of a radio to a purchaser of a television set, the free gift may not be within the 1982 Act. The matter is not free from doubt, but s 1(2)(d) excludes contracts for the supply of goods which are enforceable only because they are made by deed which would seem to exclude other gifts. Furthermore, the Law Commission Report (No 95 published in 1979) on which the Act is based concludes that gifts are outside the scope of the Act.

Contracts for work and materials

It is impossible to provide a complete list of contracts for work and materials but they fall under three broad heads as follows:

(a) Maintenance contracts. Here the organisation doing the maintenance supplies the labour and spare parts as required. An example would be a maintenance contract for lifts.

(b) Building and construction contracts. Here the builder supplies labour and materials. An example would be the alteration of an office or workshop involving the insertion of new windows and extending the central heating system.

(c) Installation and improvement contracts. Here the contractor does not have to build or construct anything but, for instance, fits equipment into an existing building or applies paint to it. Examples are the fitting of an air-conditioning system, or painting and decorating an office or workshop.

The terms implied

Title

Section 2 implies terms about title. Under s 2(1) there is an implied condition that the supplier has a right to transfer the property in the goods to the customer. Under s 2(2) two warranties are implied:

(*a*) that the goods are free from any charge or encumbrance which has not been disclosed to the customer; and

(*b*) that the customer will enjoy quiet possession except when disturbed by the owner or other person whose charge or encumbrance has been disclosed.

The customer would have an action here if he suffered loss as a result of the true owner reclaiming or suing in conversion where the materials fitted had been stolen. Sections 2(3), (4) and (5) are concerned with sales under a limited title. If under the contract the supplier is to give only such title as he may possess, s 2(1) does not apply but warranties are implied that the supplier will disclose all charges and encumbrances which he knows about and that the customer's quiet possession of the goods will not be disturbed by, for example, the supplier or the holder of an undisclosed charge or encumbrance.

Cases involving bad title have occurred not infrequently in the sale of goods but the problem seems to have arisen only rarely in contracts for work and materials.

Description

Under s 3 there is an implied condition that where a seller transfers property in goods by description, the goods will correspond with the description. If the goods are supplied by reference to a sample as well as a description they must correspond with the sample as well as the description. Section 3 applies even where the customer selects the goods.

Section 3 will operate, for example, where a person is having his house or business premises extended and agrees with the contractor a detailed specification which describes the materials to be installed. It will not operate in some types of maintenance contract where the materials to be replaced are unknown until the maintenance is carried out. The materials fitted in the course of such a contract will not be described *before* the contract is made but probably only in an invoice *after* it has been made, which is too late to apply s 3. It should be noted that ss 2 and 3 apply to supplies in the course of a business *and* to a supply by a person other than in the course of a business, e.g. a milkman 'moonlighting' by doing the odd decorating job, provided there is a contract. They would not apply to a mere friendly transaction without consideration.

Quality and fitness

The first implied term in this area is in s 4 and it relates to *satisfactory quality* (s 4(2)). Satisfactory quality is defined in s 4(9) which states that the goods must be as fit for the purpose for which they are commonly supplied as it is reasonable to expect, having regard to their description, price and other relevant circumstances. This condition of satisfactory quality does not apply to defects:

(*a*) drawn to the customer's attention before the contract is made; or
(*b*) which any prior examination the customer *has actually made* ought to have revealed.

Thus, if the materials used are dangerous, unsafe, defective or faulty, and will not work properly under normal conditions, the supplier is in breach of s 4(2).

However, if the materials are described as 'seconds' or 'fire-damaged', the customer cannot complain if the materials are of lower quality than goods not so described.

As regards defects which ought to have been revealed where the customer has examined the goods, it is not likely that materials used in a contract for work and materials will be identified before the contract or that the customer will examine them. If they are examined, the customer should ensure that it is done properly so that obvious defects are seen and the goods rejected.

The second implied term in s 4 relates to *fitness for the purpose* (s 4(5)). Where a customer makes known, either expressly or by implication, to the supplier any particular purpose for which the goods are being acquired, there is an implied condition that the goods are reasonably fit for the purpose. This condition does not apply where the customer does not rely on, or it is not reasonable for him to rely on, the skill or judgement of the supplier.

If, for example, a factory process requires a lot of water supplied under high pressure, e.g. to clean special equipment, and the factory owners ask for the installation of a system of pressure hoses and a pump, revealing to the contractor precisely what the requirements are, then the contractor will be in breach of s 4(5) if the pressure is inadequate. This will be so even though the pressure hoses and pump are of satisfactory quality and would have been quite adequate for use in a different type of installation.

Of course, the way out of the fitness problem for the supplier is for him to make it clear to the customer that he has no idea whether the equipment will be suitable for the customer's special requirements. In such a case he will not be liable, though he may put some customers off by his unhelpful attitude.

Sample

If under the contract there is a transfer of the property in goods by reference to a sample, then under s 5 there is an implied condition that:

(*a*) the bulk will correspond with the sample in quality;
(*b*) the customer will have a reasonable opportunity of comparing the bulk with the sample; and
(*c*) there will not be any defect making the goods unsatisfactory which would not have been apparent on a reasonable examination of the sample.

Except as provided by ss 4 and 5, no conditions or warranties as to quality or fitness are to be implied into contracts for the transfer of goods. Sections 4 and 5 apply only to a supply of goods in the course of a business, and not to a supply by those such as the moonlighting decorator.

Remedies

In so far as the implied terms are conditions and are broken by the supplier, then the customer can treat the contract as repudiated. The customer is discharged from his obligation to pay the agreed price and may recover damages. The breach of implied warranties gives the customer only the right to sue for damages.

Exchange and barter

The most likely transactions to emerge here are the exchange of goods for vouchers and coupons as part of promotional schemes. Part I of the 1982 Act applies and the retailer who supplies the goods under a contract to the customer is the one who is liable if they are in breach of, for example, the implied terms of fitness and/or satisfactory quality. The manufacturer will be liable to the retailer, of course.

An exchange transaction in which goods are simply exchanged is not a sale but is covered by the 1982 Act. Where part of the consideration is money, as in a part-exchange of an old car for a new one with a cash difference, the contract is presumably a sale of goods because money is at least part of the consideration. It does not really matter now whether it is a sale or a supply, because the implied terms are almost identical.

Often where there has been a sale of faulty goods the seller exchanges them for other goods of the same type, although he is under no legal duty to do so unless a particular contract expressly provides. What happens if the other goods are faulty? The substitute goods must comply with the implied terms as to title, description, quality and fitness, and there is no longer any point in going into legal niceties as to whether the exchange is a sale or supply.

The terms implied

The implied terms in exchange or barter are the same as those implied in a contract for work and materials, i.e. s 2 (title), s 3 (description), s 4(2) (satisfactory quality), s 4(5) (fitness) and s 5 (sample).

Contracts for the hire of goods

The main areas of hiring (or renting or leasing) are as follows:

(a) *office equipment*, e.g. office furniture and a variety of machines, including telephones;
(b) *building and construction plant and equipment*, e.g. cranes and earth-moving equipment, such as JCBs;
(c) *consumer hiring*, e.g. cars, televisions and videos.

Under s 6(1) a contract for the hire of goods means a contract under which one person bails, or agrees to bail, goods to another by way of hire. There must be a contract, so that when the next-door neighbour makes a free loan of his lawnmower the Act does not apply. Also excluded are hire-purchase agreements. A contract is a contract of hire whether or not services are also provided. This would be the case where a supplier rented a television to a customer and also undertook to service it.

The terms implied

Title

Section 7 deals with title. It reflects s 2 except that being a contract of hire it makes provision only for the transfer of possession and not for the transfer of ownership. There is an *implied condition* on the part of the supplier that he has the right to transfer possession of the goods to the customer by hiring for the appropriate period. There is also a *warranty* that the customer will enjoy quiet possession of the goods except where it is disturbed by the owner or other person entitled to the benefit of any charge or encumbrance disclosed to the customer before the contract was made.

If, for example, the undisclosed true owner retakes possession so that the supplier is in breach of s 7, then the customer will have an action for damages. These will reflect the value he had had under the contract before the goods were taken from him. Thus, if C pays S £120 for the year's rent of a television but the undisclosed true owner takes it back after, say, two months, the damages would, on the face of it, be £100.

Neither of the terms in s 7 prevents the supplier from taking the goods back himself provided the contract allows this, as where it provides *expressly* for the repossession of the goods on failure to pay the rental or the court is prepared to *imply* that it does.

Description

Section 8 is the equivalent of s 3. Where the supplier hires or agrees to hire the goods by description, there is an implied condition that the goods will correspond with the description. If the goods are hired by reference to a sample as well as by description, they must correspond with the description as well as the sample. Section 8 applies even where the customer selects the goods. If the goods do not match the description, the customer will be able to reject them and recover damages for any loss.

Quality and fitness

Section 9 enacts the same provisions for hiring contracts as s 4 does for contracts of work and materials and exchange and barter. Except as provided by ss 9 and 10 (hire by sample), there are no implied terms regarding quality or fitness for any purpose of goods hired.

There are two terms in s 9 as follows:

(a) An implied condition that the goods hired are of satisfactory quality. There is no such condition where a particular defect has been drawn to the customer's attention before the contract was made or to defects which he should have noticed *if he actually examined* the goods.

(b) An implied condition that the goods hired are reasonably fit for any purpose to which the customer is going to put them. The purpose must have been made known to the supplier, expressly or by implication. The condition does not apply if the customer does not rely on the skill of the seller or if it is unreasonable for him to have done so.

Once again, where goods are to be hired for a special purpose, the supplier should make it clear that the customer must not rely on him if he wishes to avoid the implied condition of fitness. This has rather special application to those who supply DIY equipment on hire. A supplier in this area should certainly not overestimate the capacity of, for example, power tools, in order to get business. If he does he certainly faces s 9 liability.

Where the goods are leased by a finance house, it is responsible for breach of the implied terms in the hiring contract. It is in effect the supplier. This is also true of hire-purchase where the implied terms of the Supply of Goods (Implied Terms) Act 1973 apply against the finance company.

As regards fitness for the purpose, it is enough to involve the finance company in liability if the customer has told the distributor of the purpose. Generally, of course, the finance house will have an indemnity against the distributor under which it may recover any damages it has to pay, so it will all get back to the distributor in the end.

The above conditions relate to the state of the goods at the beginning of the hiring and for a reasonable time thereafter. It does not impose upon the supplier a duty to maintain and repair. This must be provided for separately in the contract.

Thus in *UCB Leasing Ltd* v *Holtom* (1987) 137 NLJ 614 the Court of Appeal decided that where a car was the subject of a long leasing agreement, the owner was not under an obligation to provide a vehicle which was fit for the purpose during the whole period of the leasing. Instead, rather like a sale of goods, the obligation is to provide a vehicle which is fit at the outset of the agreement. If it is not, the hirer must rescind quickly if he wishes to return the car. If he does not do so, he cannot return the vehicle but is entitled to damages only.

Sample

Section 10 applies and is in line with s 5 (above). Section 10 states that in a hiring by sample there is an implied condition that the bulk will correspond with the sample in quality; that the customer will have a reasonable opportunity to compare the bulk with the sample; and that there will be no defects in the goods supplied rendering them unsatisfactory which would not have been apparent on a reasonable examination of the sample.

As with ss 4 and 5 (above), the terms of ss 9 and 10 are implied only into contracts for hiring entered into in the course of a business. Thus, if there is a hiring for value with a private owner, or a mere friendly lending without consideration, s 9 of the Act would not apply. Incorrect and express statements by a private owner would be actionable in the common law of contract provided that there was consideration. In a friendly lending there could be an action for negligent misstatements made by the owner about the goods if they cause damage (see *Hedley Byrne* v *Heller & Partners* (1963)).

Exclusion clauses – supply of goods

Section 11 of the 1982 Act applies the provisions of the Unfair Contract Terms Act 1977 to exclusion clauses in work and materials, barter and exchange, and hiring contracts. The effect of this is set out below.

(a) Consumer transactions. In a contract covered by Part I of the Act, the rights given by the implied terms under ss 3–5 and ss 8–10 of the 1982 Act cannot be excluded or restricted. The circumstances in which a person deals as a consumer are described in Chapter 15.

(b) Business contracts. In these circumstances the supplier can only rely on an exclusion clause if it is reasonable. However, the obligations relating to title in s 2 of the 1982 Act cannot be excluded in a business dealing relating to work and materials and barter and exchange any more than they can in a consumer dealing (see Unfair Contract Terms Act 1977, s 7, as amended by s 17(2) of the 1982 Act).

However, the term in s 7 relating to the right of possession in the case of a hiring can be excluded in a consumer or business contract if reasonable.

The supply of services

The main areas of complaint in regard to services have been the *poor quality of service*, e.g. the careless servicing of cars; *slowness in completing work*, where complaints have ranged over a wide area from, for example, building contractors to solicitors; *the cost of the work*, i.e. over-charging. Part II of the Act is concerned to deal with these matters.

The contracts covered

Under s 12(1) a contract for the supply of a service means a contract under which a person agrees to carry out a service. A contract of service (i.e. an employment contract) or apprentice-ship is not included, but apart from this no attempt is made to define the word 'service'. However, the services provided by the professions, e.g. accountants, architects, solicitors, and surveyors, are included.

Section 12(4) gives the Secretary of State for Trade and Industry power to exempt certain services from the provisions of Part II. Of importance here is the Supply of Services (Exclusion of Implied Terms) Order 1982 (SI 1982/1771) which exempts services rendered by a director to his company, thus retaining existing common-law liability in this area. This is largely because more time is needed to consult the relevant interests and decide what sort of liability there should be in the areas referred to.

Part II applies *only to contracts*. If there is no contract there cannot be implied terms. This will exclude work done free as a friendly gesture by a friend or neighbour. If, however, injury is caused to a person who is not in a contractual relationship with a supplier as a result of the negligence of the supplier, there may be an action in the tort of negligence at common law (see Chapter 21).

Duty of care and skill

This duty applies to contracts which are purely for service, e.g. advice from an accountant or solicitor, and also to the service element of a contract for work and materials. Section 13

14

provides that where the supplier of a service is acting in the course of a business there is an implied term that the supplier will carry out that service with reasonable skill and care. This means that the service must be performed with the care and skill of a reasonably competent member of the supplier's trade or profession. In other words, the test is objective, not subjective. Thus an incompetent supplier may be liable even though he has done his best. A private supplier of a service, e.g. a moonlighter, will not have this duty.

There is no reference to conditions and warranties in regard to this implied term. Generally, therefore, the action for breach of the term will be damages. In a serious case repudiation of the contract may be possible. This is rather like the intermediate term concept discussed at p 334.

Cases such as *Woodman* v *Photo Trade Processing Ltd* and *Waldron-Kelly* v *British Railways Board*, which were brought on the basis of the common-law tort of negligence, would now be brought under the 1982 Act (see further Chapter 15).

Time for performance

Section 14 provides that a supplier who acts in the course of a business will carry out the service within a reasonable time. This term is only implied where the time for performance is not fixed by the contract, but left to be fixed in a manner agreed by the contract, or determined by the dealings of the parties. Section 14 states that what is a reasonable time is a question of fact. A claimant can claim damages for unreasonable delay. Of course, if a time for performance is fixed by the contract, it must be performed at that time and the question of reasonableness does not arise. Time is of the essence in commercial contracts unless the parties expressly provide otherwise or there is a waiver (see further Chapter 17).

The charges made for the service

Under s 15 the customer's obligation is to pay 'a reasonable charge' which is, again, a matter of fact. This obligation is not implied where the charge for the service is determined by the contract, left to be determined in a manner agreed by the contract, or determined by the dealings of the parties. The section in essence enacts the common-law rule of *quantum meruit* (see Chapter 18); it protects both the supplier and the customer, and applies to a supply in the course of a business and to a supply by a moonlighter.

Exclusion clauses – supply of services

Section 16 of the 1982 Act applies the provisions of the Unfair Contract Terms Act 1977 to exclusion clauses in regard to services. Section 2 of the 1977 Act is concerned with liability for negligence. There can be no exclusion of liability if death or personal injury is caused. In other cases an exclusion clause may apply if reasonable.

Section 3 of the 1977 Act is concerned with liability for breach of contract. Broadly speaking, there can be no exclusion of liability for breach of contract, or a different performance or non-performance, unless reasonable (see further Chapter 15). The terms implied by the 1982 Act cannot be excluded in a consumer transaction. They can in a non-consumer deal if reasonable. The criteria relating to bargaining power and so on apply only to the exclusion of implied terms in a non-consumer transaction relating to goods, but they will no doubt be applied by analogy to contracts under the 1982 Act.

The Sale and Supply of Goods to Consumers Regulations

This statutory instrument (SI 2002/3045) came into force on 31 March 2003. It implements the 1999 Directive of the EU entitled Directive on the Sale of Consumer Goods and Associated Guarantees. Now that we have completed a study of other UK sale and supply of goods legislation we are in a position to deal with these regulations that give new rights to consumers buying and hiring goods.

A consumer is defined as 'a natural person acting for purposes outside his trade or profession'.

Current law

The implied conditions of other existing legislation that goods are of satisfactory quality and fit for the purpose continue.

The regulations

These can be dealt with under the following heads.

Conformity to the contract

This provision states that where goods sold or hired to a consumer do not conform to the contract of sale or hiring at any time within the period of *six months* beginning with the date on which the goods were delivered to the buyer they must be taken not to have so conformed at that date. This is achieved by inserting a new s 48A into the Sale of Goods Act 1979. Similar provisions are inserted into legislation relating to hire and hire-purchase but the main treatment is in terms of a sale.

The provision in s 48A does not apply if:

■ it is established that the goods did so conform on that date; or
■ if its application is incompatible with the nature of the goods themselves.

Thus grocery retailers may escape in many ways since for example a dozen eggs will inevitably prove to be defective after six months. The section will not therefore apply.

The effect of the section is that for the first six months after purchase/delivery the burden of proof when reporting faulty goods will be on the seller and thus reversed in the buyer's favour.

If the seller can show that the goods were perfect when delivered and so satisfies the burden of proof and the buyer cannot prove they were defective the buyer could resort to the Sale of Goods Act 1979, for example, by alleging that if the goods were perfect at sale/delivery then they should have lasted longer. This is a possible head of claim under the 1979 Act. After the first six months then only the 1979 Act claims are available.

Repair or replacement

The regulations insert a new s 48B into the 1979 Act. It applies within the first six months' period and if within that period a defect is discovered the seller must, at his own expense, repair or replace the goods at the request of the consumer within a reasonable period of time and without causing any significant inconvenience to the consumer. The seller is not obliged to repair or replace the product if it can demonstrate that replacement or repair is impossible

14

or that it would be disproportionate to do so. Determining whether such repair or replacement would be disproportionate will rest mainly on whether it would impose unreasonable costs upon the seller in comparison to those arising from any other remedy that might be available to the buyer. The courts will have to work these provisions out through case law but it can be seen straightaway that it is often not worthwhile to repair the cheaper goods so that a replacement would satisfy the requirements on the seller even if the only such products the seller has left are green and the consumer wanted and originally had red!

The court has power to order specific performance in respect of repair or replacement but also has a discretion to order an alternative remedy e.g. damages if that is deemed reasonable in the circumstances.

Reduction of purchase price or rescission

If a problem arises in a consumer contract within the first six months then s 48C (inserted by the regulations) provides that the buyer may require the seller to reduce the purchase price of the goods by an appropriate amount or in the alternative rescind the contract. This remedy is subject to the condition that the buyer has required the seller to repair or replace the goods but the seller has failed to do so within a reasonable time and without significant inconvenience to the buyer. Furthermore, once the buyer has embarked upon price reduction or rescission he cannot ask also for repair or replacement.

If the buyer rescinds the contract any reimbursement to the buyer may be reduced on account of any use which the buyer has had from the goods since delivery.

Consumer guarantees

Suppliers will be affected by the concept under the regulations of consumer guarantees. Sellers and suppliers are not bound to give guarantees but if *any undertaking* is given to a consumer to repair the goods or refund their cost if they fail to meet the specification in the guarantee or in any relevant advertising it will come within the consumer guarantee provision. The guarantee does not have to be given by the supplier and could, e.g. be given by the manufacturer or a distributor or by a salesperson. It takes effect on delivery as a contractual obligation on the organisation giving the guarantee. The consumer can require that the guarantee be put into writing in intelligible language and if the guarantee is given by the manufacturer the request can be made to the supplier. Where the goods are offered within the UK the guarantor must ensure that it is given in English.

Amendment of Unfair Contract Terms Act 1977

If an accountant bought a commercial cooker for his private use the protection of the 1977 Act in terms of reasonable exclusion clauses did not apply because the goods were not ordinarily supplied for private use or consumption. The Act now applies in this situation. Individuals who buy new (not secondhand) goods at auction or by competitive tender are also now treated as consumers for the purpose of the Act of 1977.

Passing of risk

Relevant legislation is now amended so that when a buyer of goods deals as a consumer the goods will remain at the seller's risk until they are delivered to the consumer. Furthermore, the parties cannot effectively change this rule even in cases where title may have passed before delivery under contractual arrangements.

Application of the regulations

Equivalent changes are made to the Supply of Goods and Services Act 1982 in regard to the hiring of goods and in the Supply of Goods (Implied Terms) Act 1973 in regard to goods taken on hire-purchase.

14

15

EXCLUSION CLAUSES
AND OTHER UNFAIR TERMS

In this chapter we shall look at the rules which decide whether an exclusion clause which purports to exclude liability for breach of contract and other civil damage is valid.

Exclusion clauses – the issue of communication

A contract may contain express terms under which one or both of the parties excludes or limits liability for breach of contract or negligence. Although such express terms are permissible, both the courts and Parliament have been reluctant to allow exclusion clauses to operate successfully where they have been imposed on a weaker party, such as an ordinary consumer, by a stronger party, such as a person or corporation in business to supply goods or services.

The judges have protected and continue to protect consumers of goods and services against the effect of exclusion clauses in two main ways, i.e. by deciding that the exclusion clause never became part of the contract, and by construing (or interpreting) the contract in such a way as to prevent the application of the clause.

It is still important to consider the judicial contribution because even though an exclusion clause can now, under the Unfair Contract Terms Act 1977 (see below), be regarded as not applying if it is unreasonable, there is no need to consider the matter of unreasonableness if the clause has not been communicated or does not apply under the rules of construction (see below). As important is the fact that even if an exclusion clause is acceptable as reasonable, it will not apply if it has not been communicated or cannot survive the judicial rules of construction.

Was the clause part of the contract?

The court will require the person wishing to rely on an exclusion clause to show that the other party agreed to it at or before the time when the contract was made, otherwise it will not form part of the agreement. In this connection:

(a) Where a contract is made by signing a written document the signer will in general be bound by everything which the document contains, even if he has not read it, unless the signature was induced by misrepresentation as to the effect of the document. An exception is the rule of *non est factum*, provided the signer is not negligent.

L'Estrange Ltd v *Graucob (F)*, 1934 – Where the document containing the clause is signed (**175**)

Curtis v *Chemical Cleaning and Dyeing Co*, 1951 – Where the claimant was misled as to the extent of the clause (**176**)

(b) Where the terms are contained in an unsigned document, the person seeking to rely on an exclusion clause must show that the document was an integral part of the contract which could be expected to contain terms. However, if the document is contractual in the sense outlined above, the clause will apply even though the claimant did not actually know about the exclusion clause in the sense that he had not read it. Communication may be constructive so long as the document adequately draws the attention of a reasonable person to the existence of terms and conditions.

Thompson v *LMS Railway*, 1930 – A constructive communication (**177**)

Chapelton v *Barry UDC*, 1940 – Where the document is not contractual (**178**)

This rule of constructive communication will not necessarily be applied if the term in the contract is particularly burdensome for the other party. In such a case the law may require that the burdensome clause is actually brought to the attention of the other party. This results from the decision of the Court of Appeal in *Interfoto Picture Library Ltd* v *Stiletto Visual Programmes Ltd* [1988] 1 All ER 348. In that case Interfoto sent some transparencies to Stiletto for it to make a selection. The delivery note, which is a contractual document, contained a clause that if the transparencies were not returned within 14 days, Stiletto would pay £5 per day for each transparency retained after that. Stiletto delayed returning the transparencies for three weeks and ran up a bill of some £3,783. When Stiletto was sued for this sum the court said that it could not be recovered by Interfoto because the clause was not specifically drawn to the attention of Stiletto. The court awarded damages of £3.50 per transparency per week but would not apply the clause.

(c) As regards previous dealings, where the defendant has not actually given the claimant a copy of conditions or drawn his attention to them when making a particular contract, the doctrine of constructive notice will not apply, at least in consumer transactions, in order to enable the defendant to rely on previous communications in previous dealings, unless, perhaps, the dealings have been frequent. Thus in *Hollier* v *Rambler Motors* [1972] 1 All ER 399 it appeared that the claimant had had his car repaired five times in five years (i.e. infrequently) by the defendants and had signed a form containing a clause stating 'the company is not responsible for damage caused by fire to customers' cars on the premises'. On the occasion in question the claimant was not required to sign a form when leaving his car for repair. In the event the car was damaged by fire caused by the defendants' negligence. In an action by the claimant the defendants pleaded the clause. It was held by the Court of Appeal that the claimant succeeded and that the clause did not apply. Previous dealings were not incorporated and in any case as a matter of construction the wording was not sufficiently plain to exclude negligence. However, where the parties are, for example, large corporations, terms used in previous dealings between the parties themselves or *in the trade generally* may be incorporated.

Thus in *British Crane Hire Corporation Ltd* v *Ipswich Plant Hire Ltd* [1974] 1 All ER 1059 the defendants hired a crane from the claimants who were the owners. The agreement was an oral one, though after the contract was made the defendants received a printed form from the claimants containing conditions. One of these was that the hirer of the crane was liable

15

to indemnify the owner against all expenses in connection with its use. Before the defendants signed the form the crane sank into marshy ground, though this was not the fault of the defendants. The claimants were put to some cost in repairing the crane and now sued the defendants for an indemnity under the contract. The defendants argued that the indemnity had not been incorporated into the oral contract of hire. It was held that the bargaining power of the defendants was equal to that of the claimants and the defendants knew that printed conditions in similar terms to those of the claimants were *in common use in the business*. The conditions had therefore been incorporated into the oral contract on the basis of the common understanding of the parties and the claimants' action for an indemnity succeeded.

(d) Any attempt to introduce an exclusion clause after the contract has been made is ineffective because the consideration for the clause is then past.

(e) An exclusion clause may be made ineffective by an inconsistent oral promise.

> *Olley* v *Marlborough Court Ltd*, 1949 – Belated notice of a exclusion clause (**179**)
> *J Evans & Son (Portsmouth) Ltd* v *Andrea Merzario Ltd*, 1976 – An inconsistent promise (**180**)

(f) At common law the rule of privity of contract may also prevent the application of an exclusion clause. Thus, if A, the owner of a road haulage company, excludes his own and his employees' liability for damage to the goods of his business customers by a properly communicated clause, an employee who causes damage to the goods will be liable under common law, although his employer will not be, provided the clause is reasonable under the Unfair Contract Terms Act 1977, because the employee has not supplied consideraton for the contract which is between his employer and the customers.

Reference should, however, be made to the case of *NZ Shipping* v *A M Satterthwaite* (see below) where by application of the common law rules relating to acceptance in unilateral contracts and the performance of existing contractual duties owed to a third party the court was able to hold that a stevedore could take the benefit of an exclusion clause in the shipping company's contract of carriage.

> *The New Zealand Shipping Co Ltd* v *A M Satterthwaite & Co Ltd*, 1974 – An exclusion clause avoids privity rule at common law (**181**)

It has already been noted in Chapter 10 that exclusions and defences available to a carrier of goods can under the Contracts (Rights of Third Parties) Act 1999 be extended to employees, agents and independent contractors that will be effective without the ingenious application of common law rules seen in the *New Zealand Shipping* case, though the common law rules will be helpful to such persons where the main contract does not extend exclusion rights to them and is, therefore, construed as not applying to them even by implication.

The position of the third party under the 1999 Act

The Contracts (Rights of Third Parties) Act 1999, s 7(2) may apply. A may enter into a contract with a builder to build a house for his daughter Jane to live in. A may name Jane as having third-party rights under the contract. Let us suppose that the contract contains an exclusion clause exempting the builder from liability caused by his negligent building. There is a provision in s 7(2) of the 1999 Act that can best be understood by an example. The builder's negligence results in death or personal injury to A or his daughter Jane. Any exclusion clause inserted by the builder in his contract with A is void and of no effect in so far as it tries to exclude liability for death or personal injury. The 1999 Act leaves this untouched. The 1977 Act outlaws such clauses. However, if by reason of negligence by the builder a wall collapses and A's car is damaged he can sue the builder successfully unless the builder can show that the exclusion clause is reasonable. However, because of s 7(2) of the 1999 Act, if it is Jane's car which is damaged the clause, even if unreasonable, will be effective to exclude the builder's liability to her.

There are those who think that unreasonable exclusion clauses should be void even in regard to Jane's (the third-party's) loss but the 1999 Act does not reflect this view.

Construction of exclusion clauses

Rules of construction (i.e. interpretation) of contract may, when applied, prevent the application of an exclusion clause. The major rules of construction are as follows.

The *contra proferentem* rule

Under this rule, if there is any ambiguity or room for doubt as to the meaning of an exclusion clause, the courts will construe it in a way unfavourable to the person who put it into the contract. An example of the application of this rule is to be seen in *Hollier* v *Rambler Motors* because the Court of Appeal, having decided that previous dealings were not incorporated, went on to use the rule by saying that the wording in the form was not sufficiently plain to exclude negligence. That ambiguity had therefore to be construed against the defendants who put it into the contract. Those who wish to exclude liability for negligence must use clear words, said the House of Lords in *Smith* v *South Wales Switchgear* [1978] 1 All ER 18.

Alexander v *Railway Executive*, 1951 – The *contra proferentem* rule (**182**)

The repugnancy rule

This rule says in effect that the exemption clause is in direct contradiction to the main purpose of the contract and is therefore repugnant to it. Where such repugnancy exists the exemption clause can be struck out. Thus, if A makes a contract to supply oranges to B but includes a clause which allows him to supply any sort of fruit, the clause is repugnant to the main purpose of the contract and could be struck out. Thus, A would be liable in breach of contract if he supplied B with apples and could not rely on the clause to excuse his breach of contract.

The four corners rule

Under this rule exemption clauses only protect a party when he is acting within the four corners of the contract. Thus he is liable for damage which occurs while he is deviating from the contract and he would not be protected by the exclusion clause.

Pollock & Co v *Macrae*, 1922 – Where the clause is repugnant (**183**)

Thomas National Transport (Melbourne) Pty Ltd v *May and Baker (Australia) Pty Ltd*, 1966 – The four corners rule (**184**)

The doctrine of fundamental breach

This doctrine (or rule) was usually invoked where a claimant sought a remedy on a contract containing exemption clauses which had been adequately communicated. The doctrine said, in effect, that where one party had fundamentally broken his contract, i.e. done something fundamentally different from what he had contracted to do, an exclusion clause could not protect him, and that this was a *rule of law* and *not a rule of construction*, so that the court had no discretion in the matter.

After some years of differing judicial opinion regarding this, the House of Lords eventually affirmed that there was no rule by which exclusion clauses had become inapplicable to exclude liability for a fundamental breach of contract. It was in each case a question of construction whether in fact the clause covered the breach which had taken place.

Fundamental breach, which survives as a rule of construction, is only a simple presumption that exclusion clauses are not intended to apply where there is a very serious breach of contract. This presumption can be rebutted, as in *Photo Production* (below) and is not *automatically* applied.

> *Photo Production Ltd v Securicor Transport Ltd*, 1980 – Fundamental breach: no automatic application (**185**)

The approach of Parliament to exclusion clauses

Parliament has tried to prevent the widespread use of exclusion clauses by the passing of various statutes, the main one being the Unfair Contract Terms Act 1977.

The strongest protection is given by the Act to persons who deal as consumers (C), though those dealing otherwise than as consumers, e.g. where the goods are bought for use in a business, are covered. To be a consumer one must be dealing as a *private buyer* with a *person in business* (B). In addition, as the 1977 Act was originally enacted, the contract had to be for the supply of goods ordinarily supplied for private use or consumption and not obtained at an auction or by competitive tender (but see below). Thus a contract between a *private buyer* and a *private seller* is not a consumer deal.

However, in *R & B Customs Brokers Co Ltd v United Dominions Trust Ltd* [1988] 1 All ER 847 the Court of Appeal decided that when a business buys goods it may still take advantage of consumer law applying to an ordinary member of the public if the transaction concerned is not a regular one. The facts of the case were that R & B Customs bought a car for the use of a director. The contract excluded an implied term under s 14(3) of the Sale of Goods Act 1979 that the goods be fit for the purpose. Such an exclusion does not operate if the sale is between a person in business and a consumer. It was held that R & B Customs must be treated as a consumer. The purchase of the car was not a frequent transaction and unless regularity could be established the transaction could not be regarded as an integral part of the business and was not therefore in the course of business. (See as a contrast *Stevenson* v *Rogers* [1999] 1 All ER 613 in Chapter 14.)

Changes effected by the Sale and Supply of Goods to Consumers Regulations

As already noted, if a private person bought a commercial cooker for his or her private use, the protection of the Unfair Contract Terms Act 1977, in terms that any exclusion clause had to be reasonable or it would not be effective, did not apply because the goods were not ordinarily supplied for private use or consumption. The 1977 Act now applies in this situation and exclusion clauses are ineffective unless reasonable. Individuals who buy new (not second-hand) goods at auction or by competitive tender are now treated as consumers for the purposes of the 1977 Act.

Clauses rendered ineffective by the Unfair Contract Terms Act

These are as follows:

(a) Any exclusion clause contained in a contract or notice by which B tries to exclude or restrict his liability for death or personal injury resulting from negligence is wholly ineffective (ss 2 and 5). However, in *Thompson* v *Lohan* [1987] 2 All ER 631 A hired plant together with operatives to B. The contract contained a clause stating that B was liable for the negligence of the operatives who were A's employees. This clause was held by the Court of Appeal not to be contrary to s 2 of the Unfair Contract Terms Act. It was not designed to restrict or exclude liability to those who might be injured by the negligence of the operatives but merely decided whether A or B was to bear the liability.

(b) A manufacturer's guarantee cannot exclude or restrict the manufacturer's liability for loss or damage arising from defects in goods if used by a consumer which results from negligence in manufacture or distribution (s 5). The section is concerned with actions either in negligence or on the collateral contract (see further Chapter 9) which the guarantee can create against the manufacturer who is not the seller of the goods to the customer. The section is not concerned with a contractual relationship between the seller and the customer which is covered by ss 6 and 7. Thus, a manufacturer's 12-month guarantee for a vacuum cleaner which said that the goods would, if defective, be replaced or repaired free of charge but ended with a phrase such as: 'This guarantee is in lieu of, and expressly excludes, all liability to compensate for loss or damage howsoever caused' would not prevent a claim by the purchaser against the manufacturer if he/she was electrocuted by the cleaner (see *Donoghue* v *Stevenson* (1932), Chapter 21).

As regards *consumer guarantees*, the Sale and Supply of Goods to Consumers Regulations 2002 provide that such guarantees whoever gives them in the supply chain take effect on delivery as a contractual obligation on the part of the organisation giving them and there would be no need for the consumer to resort to the collateral contract or negligence approach. The claim would normally be for breach of the contract of guarantee, and exclusions would not apply in a claim on the guarantee.

(c) A clause under which B tries to exclude his liability, whether by guarantee or otherwise, to C for breach of the implied terms in the Sale of Goods Act 1979 (on a sale) or the Supply of Goods (Implied Terms) Act 1973 (as amended) (on a hire-purchase transaction), e.g. that the goods are fit for the purpose or of satisfactory quality, is wholly ineffective, as is a clause which tries to exclude against the consumer the implied terms in the Supply of Goods and Services Act 1982 in a contract of pure hiring, e.g. of a car, or a contract for work and materials, as in the repair of a car (Unfair Contract Terms Act 1977, ss 6(2) and 7(2)).

Section 6 also applies to non-business liability. However, since the implied terms requiring satisfactory quality and fitness for the purpose do not apply to non-business transactions, only s 13 of the Sale of Goods Act 1979 (sale by description) can be implied. However, s 13 cannot be excluded in a non-business transaction with a consumer.

15

Exclusion clauses applicable if reasonable

General

These are as follows:

(a) Any clause by which B tries to exclude or restrict his liability for loss arising from negligence other than death or personal injury (s 2(2)).

Such a clause may be raised successfully to defeat a claim by a third party who has acquired rights under the Contracts (Rights of Third Parties) Act 1999 whether the clause is reasonable or not. Even an unreasonable clause would be effective. The reasonableness test would be applied in an action between the original promisor and promisee. The relevant provision is contained in s 7(2) of the 1999 Act.

(b) Any clause by which B tries to exclude or restrict his liability to a non-consumer for breach of the implied terms in the Sale of Goods Act 1979, the Supply of Goods (Implied Terms) Act 1973, and the Supply of Goods and Services Act 1982 relating, for example, to contracts of hiring and work and materials (ss 6(3) and 7(3)).

(c) Any clause by which B tries to exclude his liability for breach of contract if the contract is with a consumer or, in the case of a non-consumer contract, the agreement is on B's written standard terms (s 3(1) and (2)(a)). There is no definition of 'written standard terms' in the 1977 Act, but it obviously covers cases in which the seller requires that all (or nearly all) of his customers purchase goods on the same terms with no variation from one contract to another. An example is provided by *L'Estrange* v *Graucob* (1934). This section applies also to cases where the clause purports to allow B to render a substantially different performance, as where a tour operator tries to reserve the right to vary the accommodation or itinerary or reserves the right to render no performance at all (s 3(2)(b)).

Section 3 of the 1977 Act which applies, as we have seen, between contracting parties where one 'deals as a consumer' to prevent the other from excluding or restricting any liability of his or hers for breach of contract extends to *contracts of employment* said the High Court in *Brigden* v *American Express Bank Ltd* (2000) 631 IRLB 13. Thus a clause in a contract of employment that excluded or restricted the employer's liability for wrongful dismissal would not apply by reason of the 1977 Act.

(d) As regards indemnity clauses in consumer transactions, B may agree to do work for C only if C will indemnify B against any liability which B may incur during performance of the contract, e.g. an injury to X caused by B's work (s 4). B may, for example, be a builder who takes an indemnity from C, the owner of a property on which B is to do work in regard to any injuries which B's work might cause to third parties. Such an indemnity will be unenforceable by B unless reasonable. Such clauses are unlikely to be found reasonable and B will have to cover himself by insurance. The section does not cover non-consumer situations and the indemnity found in *British Crane Hire* would still be enforceable (and see also *Thompson* v *Lohan* (1987)).

Inducement liability

Any clause purporting to exclude liability for misrepresentation applies only if reasonable, whether the transaction is with a consumer or a non-consumer (Misrepresentation Act 1967, s 3, as substituted by s 8(1) of the Unfair Contract Terms Act 1977). Thus, an estate agent would not be able to exclude his liability for falsely representing the state of a house unless the court felt that it was reasonable for the agent to exclude his liability, as it might be if the property was very old and there had been no survey.

However, the matter of reasonableness is a matter for the court in each case and will depend upon the circumstances. Thus an estate agent may be allowed to enforce a disclaimer in the case of a high value property where the client is a more sophisticated person whereas in the case of a property of less value and a less sophisticated client the court may take the view that enforcement of a disclaimer by the agent is unreasonable. (Contrast *McCullagh* v *Lane Fox* with *Smith* v *Eric S Bush*: Chapter 21.)

It is also worth noting that the Property Misdescriptions Act 1991 makes it a criminal offence to make a false or misleading statement about property matters in the course of an estate agency or property development business.

Section 3 also applies to non-business liability. A private seller cannot exclude his liability for misrepresentation unless he can show that the exclusion clause concerned satisfied the test of reasonableness.

> *Walker* v *Boyle*, 1982 – When liability for misrepresentation cannot be excluded (**186**)

Reasonableness

The burden of proof

The burden of proving that the clause is reasonable lies upon the party claiming that it is – usually B, the person in business (s 11(5)).

Meaning of reasonableness

Although the matter is basically one for the judge, the following guidelines appear in the 1977 Act.

(a) The matter of reasonableness must be decided on the circumstances as they were when the contract was made (s 11(1)).

(b) Where a clause limits the amount payable regard must be had to the resources of the person who included the clause and the extent to which it was possible for him to cover himself by insurance (s 11(4)). The object of this rule is to encourage companies to insure against liability in the sense that failure to do so will go against them if any exclusion clause which they have is before the court. However, in some cases it may be right to allow limitation of liability, e.g. in the case of professional persons such as accountants where monetary loss may be caused to a horrendous amount following negligence and be beyond their power to insure against.

(c) Where the contract is for the supply of goods, i.e. under a contract of sale, hire-purchase, hiring, or work and materials, the criteria of reasonableness are laid down by s 11(2) of and Sch 2 to the 1977 Act. They are:

(i)   strength of the bargaining position of the parties. Thus if one party is in a strong position and the other in a weaker in terms of bargaining power, the stronger party may not be allowed to retain an exclusion clause in the contract;

(ii) availability of other supplies. Again, if a seller is in a monopolistic position so that it is not possible for the buyer to find the goods readily elsewhere, the court may decide that an exclusion clause in the contract of a monopolistic seller shall not apply;

(iii) inducements to agree to the clause. If the goods have been offered for sale at £10 without an exemption clause but at £8 with the inclusion of the clause, the court may see fit to allow the clause to apply at the lower price because there has been a concession by the seller in terms of the price;

(iv) buyer's knowledge of the extent of the clause. If the clause had been pointed out to the buyer and he is fully aware that it reduces the liability of the seller, this will be relevant in deciding whether the seller should be allowed to rely on the clause. If a buyer is reasonably fully informed and aware of the seller's intentions as regards exclusion of liability, the buyer may have to accept the clause;

(v) customs of trade and previous dealings. If, for example, exclusion clauses are usual in the trade or have been used by the parties in previous dealings, the court may decide that an exclusion clause should apply. It should be noted that previous dealings do not seem relevant in consumer transactions, unless quite regular, but they are in this area where one is considering a non-consumer situation;

(vi) whether the goods have been made, processed or adapted to the order of the buyer. Obviously if the seller has been required by the buyer to produce goods in a certain way, then it may well be fair and reasonable for the seller to exclude his liability in respect of faults arising out of, for example, the buyer's design which he insisted was used. It would probably be reasonable to exclude the implied term under the Sale of Goods Act 1979 that the goods were fit for the purpose (see further Chapter 14).

Although the above criteria are, strictly speaking, confined to exclusion of statutory implied terms in, for example, the Sale of Goods Act 1979, they are being applied in other situations. For example, Judge Clarke in the *Woodman* case (see below) felt it was right to use them where what was at issue was a negligent service. The Supply of Goods and Services Act 1982 has not changed the law regarding the exclusion of liability of a supplier of services. Services are not specifically mentioned in the 1977 Act but they fall within the ambit of ss 2 and 3 which deal with negligence and breach of contract respectively.

Mitchell (George) (Chesterhall) Ltd v Finney Lock Seeds Ltd, 1983 –
Reasonableness: the tests to be applied (**187**)

Reasonableness – other case law

The following is a selection of other case law on the 1977 Act to illustrate its application.

Section 2(2) came up for consideration in two county court cases which were brought under the Act. In *Woodman* v *Photo Trade Processing Ltd*, heard in the Exeter County Court in May 1981, Mr Woodman took to the Exeter branch of Dixons Photographic for processing a film which carried pictures of a friend's wedding. The film was of special value because Mr Woodman had been the only photographer at the wedding, and he had said he would give the pictures as a wedding present. Unfortunately, the film was lost and when Dixons were sued they relied on an exclusion clause which, it appeared, was standard practice throughout the trade and had been communicated. The clause read as follows: 'All photographic materials are accepted on the basis that their value does not exceed the loss of the material itself. Responsibility is limited to the replacement of film. No liability will be accepted consequently or otherwise, however caused.' His Honour Judge Clarke found in the county court that the customer had no real alternative but to entrust his film to a firm that would use such an exclusion clause and that, furthermore, Dixons could have foreseen that the film might be irreplaceable and although they could argue that the exclusion clause enabled them to operate a cheap mass-production technique, it could not be regarded as reasonable that all persons, regardless of the value of their film, should be required to take their chance of the system losing them. The judge therefore granted compensation of £75 to Mr Woodman and held that the exclusion clause was unreasonable.

In *Waldron-Kelly* v *British Railways Board*, which was heard in the Stockport County Court in 1981, the claimant delivered a suitcase to Stockport railway station so that it could be taken to Haverfordwest station. The contract of carriage was subject to the British Railways Board general conditions 'at owner's risk' for a price of £6. A clause exempted the Board from any loss, except that if a case disappeared then the Board's liability was to be assessed by reference to the weight of the goods, which in this case was £27 and not to their value, which in this case was £320. The suitcase was lost whilst it was in the control of British Rail. In the county court Judge Brown held that the claimant succeeded in his contention that the exclusion clause was unreasonable and therefore of no effect. The judge held that in the case of non-delivery of goods the burden of proof to show what had happened to the goods was on the bailee. British Rail had failed to show that the loss was not its fault, and in any case the fault and loss were not covered by the exclusion clause because it did not satisfy the test of reasonableness.

Further, in *Stag Line Ltd* v *Tyne Ship Repair Group Ltd* [1984] 2 Lloyd's Rep 211 Staughton, J, in finding that exclusion clauses inserted into the contract by the defendants were not fair and reasonable, said:

> The courts would be slow to find clauses in commercial contracts made between parties of equal bargaining power to be unfair or unreasonable, but a provision in a contract, which deprived a ship owner of any remedy for breach of contract or contractual negligence unless the vessel were returned to the repairer's yard for the defect to be remedied would be unfair and unreasonable because it would be capricious; the effectiveness of the remedy would depend upon where the ship was when the casualty occurred and whether it would be practical or economic to return the vessel to the defendants' yard.

Also in *Rees-Hough Ltd* v *Redland Reinforced Plastics Ltd* [1984] Construction Industry Law Letters 84, His Honour Judge Newey QC decided that it was not fair and reasonable for the defendants to rely on an exclusion clause in their standard terms and conditions of sale. They had sold pipes to the claimants which were not fit for the purpose for which the defendants knew they were required, nor were they of merchantable (now satisfactory) quality under the Sale of Goods Act 1979 (see further Chapter 14) and the clause excluded liability for this. Clearly, then, it is difficult to apply exclusion clauses which try to prevent liability for supplying defective goods.

Where there is no contract, as in the *Hedley Byrne* situation where a bank used a 'without responsibility' disclaimer, s 2(2) of the Act applies the 'reasonable' test to the disclaimer (see further Chapter 21).

Provisions against evasion of liability

General

If an attempt is made to exclude or restrict liability in contract X by a clause in a secondary contract Y, then the clause in Y is ineffective (s 10). For example, C buys a television set from

B. There is an associated maintenance contract. The sale of a television would be within s 6 of the 1977 Act and so there could be no exclusion of B's implied obligations. Any attempt to exclude or restrict these obligations in the maintenance contract would also fail. If the transaction was a non-consumer one the 'reasonable' test would have to be applied.

Nor can the Act be excluded by a clause which states that the contract is to be governed by the law of another country which does not outlaw exclusion clauses, at least if it is part of an evasion scheme, or if the contract is with a United Kingdom consumer and the main steps in the making of the contract took place in the UK (s 27).

The Act does not apply to insurance contracts, nor to contracts for the transfer of an interest in land (s 1(2) and Sch 1, para 1(a) and (b)). House purchase is therefore excluded though inducement liability cannot be excluded unless reasonable (see above). Nor does it apply to certain contracts involving the supply of goods on an international basis because these are covered by conventions. Furthermore, it should be noted that a written arbitration agreement will not be treated as excluding or restricting liability for the purposes of the 1977 Act and such an agreement is valid (s 13(2)).

Office of Fair Trading and the Enterprise Act 2002

The Office of Fair Trading is empowered to deal with infringements (i.e. conduct) that harms the collective interests of consumers (ss 211 and 213, EA 2002). In addition to its enforcement powers, s 7 of the EA 2002 gives the OFT the function of making proposals to any Minister of the Crown on amongst other things proposed changes in the law. It was under a similar provision in earlier legislation that the Consumer Transactions (Restrictions on Statements) Order 1976 (SI 1976/1813) as amended by SI 1978/127 was passed to make it a criminal offence to sell or supply goods and purport that the implied terms in sale of goods and hire-purchase legislation can be excluded in a consumer sale since this might suggest to the customer that he has no rights so that he will not bother to try to enforce them.

Unfair contract terms regulations

The Unfair Terms in Consumer Contracts Regulations 1999 (SI 1999/2083) now implement the EC Directive on Unfair Terms in Consumer Contracts (93/13/EEC).

Terms covered (reg 3)

The Regulations apply to any term in a contract between a seller or supplier who is acting for purposes relating to his business and a consumer, i.e. a natural person (not a company) who is acting for purposes outside of business where the term has not been individually negotiated. Although the Regulations apply to oral contracts, it is businesses which use pre-printed contract terms, the substance of which cannot be influenced by the consumer, which are most affected by the Regulations.

No assessment is made of the fairness of terms which identify the goods or services to be supplied or the price or remuneration involved, provided such terms are in plain intelligible language. The fact that some terms of a contract have been negotiated will not prevent the contract being unfair if on an overall assessment it is found to be a pre-formulated standard contract. The seller or supplier must prove that a term in dispute was individually negotiated.

Under Sch 1 certain contracts and their terms are excluded from the scope of the Regulations, e.g. employment contracts and contracts relating to the incorporation and organisation of companies and partnerships. In addition, a contract that complies with other relevant UK legislation, e.g. the Package Travel Regulations will not be further tested under the Unfair Terms Regulations. Sales by auction are not excluded.

Unfair terms (reg 4)

An unfair term is any term which, contrary to the requirement of good faith, causes a significant imbalance in the rights and obligations of the parties under the contract, to the detriment of the consumer. The concept of good faith is thus introduced more widely into English law, having really only applied before to the disclosure requirement in a contract of insurance, which is a contract of utmost good faith.

Schedule 2 sets out matters which go to deciding whether the contract meets the requirement of good faith. These are:

- the strength of the bargaining positions of the parties;
- whether the consumer had an inducement to agree to the term, e.g. where the goods were cheaper if the term was included, it might survive;
- whether the goods or services were sold or supplied to the special order of the consumer, e.g. where goods were made to a consumer's design or adapted to the consumer's requirements, it might be fair to include a term relating to the possible unfitness of the goods for the intended purpose;
- the extent to which the seller or supplier has dealt fairly and equitably with the consumer.

Schedule 3 gives an indicative and non-exhaustive list of terms which may be regarded as unfair. This does not mean that they are automatically unfair. There are 17 examples including clauses:

15

- excluding or limiting the liability of a seller or supplier in the event of the death or personal injury of or to a consumer resulting from an act or omission of that seller or supplier;
- requiring any consumer who fails to meet his obligations to pay a disproportionately high sum in compensation. This could include, e.g., a non-refundable deposit;
- enabling the seller or supplier to alter the contract unilaterally;
- limiting the consumer's rights in the event of total or partial non-performance by the seller or supplier;

and so on.

It is worth noting here the somewhat unfortunate overlap between the 1999 Regulations and the Unfair Contract Terms Act 1977. The first example in the above list which is 'unfair' under the Regulations is actually totally barred by the 1977 Act in s 2(1). The other examples given in Sch 3 would probably be regarded as inapplicable because they do not satisfy the 'reasonableness' test of the 1977 Act. The government did not feel able to align the 'reasonableness' test and the 'fairness' test but did announce in the Final Consultation Document in September 1994 that the Regulations would not limit the 1977 Act, so we can take it that our first example is totally outlawed so that there is no need to apply the 'fairness' test.

There are differences between the two pieces of legislation. The Act applies to exclusion clauses in consumer contracts but can extend to business contracts, negotiated contracts and exclusion notices. The Regulations apply only to consumer contracts where the terms were not individually negotiated and in that sense are narrower but, since they are not limited to exclusion clauses, their effect may be much wider. Regulation 4 also states that an assessment of the unfair nature of a term should take into account: (a) the nature of the goods or services for which the contract was concluded; (b) the circumstances attending the conclusion of the contract; and (c) the other terms of the contract or of another contract on which it is dependent.

Consequences of inclusion of unfair terms (reg 5)

An unfair term is not binding on the consumer but the contract will continue to bind the parties if it is viable without the unfair term.

Construction of written contracts (reg 6)

Standard form contracts offered to consumers must be expressed in plain intelligible language. If there is any doubt about the meaning of a term the interpretation most favourable to the consumer shall prevail. This rule of construction applies only if the term under review is regarded as unfair. It does not apply to other terms not so regarded.

Enforcement by the Office of Fair Trading (OFT)

The Regulations and the Enterprise Act 2002 impose on the OFT a duty to consider complaints that contracts which have been drawn up for general use are unfair unless the complaint appears to be vexatious or frivolous. The OFT may apply to the court for an enforcement order against persons who appear to be recommending or using unfair terms in contracts with consumers. The OFT may also arrange for the dissemination of information and advice concerning the operation of the Regulations.

The Director-General of Fair Trading (see now Office of Fair Trading) achieved a substantial victory for borrowers in the Court of Appeal where the court gave the first authoritative guidance on the regulations (see *Director-General of Fair Trading* v *First National Bank plc* (2000) *The Times*, 14 March where the court ruled in favour of the Office of Fair Trading which had taken exception to a provision in a lending contract, apparently common to most banks in the UK, under which the lender was entitled to contractual interest on outstanding capital even after obtaining a judgment against the defaulting debtor until payment, which goes against the 'no interest' protection normally applied by court orders in this type of case, i.e. no interest accrues on the debt after judgment. An injunction (now an enforcement order) to stop the practice was granted against the bank.

Wider enforcement

The Regulations and Enterprise Act 2002 allow specified bodies referred to as 'qualifying bodies' or enforcers to consider complaints and apply for enforcement orders to restrain the use of unfair terms. The qualifying bodies include for example the various industry regulators and the Consumers' Association.

Terms affected

Examples are provided by an *Office of Fair Trading Case Report Bulletin*, as follows:

- *a mobile phone company* that required the consumer to pay for call charges even after giving the supplier notification of the loss/theft of the phone – *changed* so that call charges only payable up to the time of notification;
- *airline recruitment and training company* that gave itself the right to alter course venues, dates and times – *changed* to allow a full refund if changes not suitable;
- *a package holiday business* that allowed retention of prepayments on a sliding scale to 100 per cent loss of deposit on cancellation two weeks before departure – *changed* so that scale taper lengthened with full loss of deposit only in final week;
- *a property letting company* that had a financial penalty of £5 per day when payment was in arrears – *this was withdrawn altogether*.

Reform

The Law Commission has published proposals for a reform of the law relating to unfair contract terms. The intention is to replace the current legislation with new legislation extending the protection of the law to businesses particularly small and medium-sized enterprises including companies.

Trading electronically

Organisations selling online need to take into account the provisions of the law relating to unfair terms in the same way as other traders. The relevant legislation as described in this chapter applies.

15

16

ILLEGALITY, PUBLIC POLICY AND COMPETITION LAW

In this chapter we are concerned to describe the effect of illegality and public policy on the freedom of contract. The more commercial aspects of restraint of trade and restrictive practices are treated in greater depth as is competition law.

Introduction

Freedom of contract must always be subject to overriding considerations of public policy.

Public policy has been ascertained as follows:

(a) At common law by the judiciary. At one time the judiciary had wide powers of discretion in the matter of creating new categories of public policy but this view is now unacceptable. In *Fender* v *Mildmay* [1937] 3 All ER 402 the House of Lords declared against the extension of the heads of public policy, at least by the judiciary. However, up to then the judiciary had created a number of categories of public policy. These fell into two areas as follows:

(i) *Illegal contracts*. These involve some degree of moral wrong and contracts to commit crimes or to defraud the Revenue fall into this category.

(ii) *Void contracts*. In these cases there is not in any strict sense blameworthy conduct; the contracts are rendered void because if enforced by the courts they could produce unsatisfactory results on society. Examples are contracts in restraint of trade, e.g. an agreement under which an employee covenants with his employer that on the termination of his contract he will not work for a rival firm or start a competing business, and contracts prejudicial to marriage, e.g. a contract under which a person promises not to marry at all.

(b) By Parliament. Parliament expresses its view as to what is public policy by Acts of Parliament and rules and orders made by Ministers under Acts of Parliament.

The two main areas requiring consideration here are:

(i) *Wagering contracts*, which will be dealt with later; and

(ii) *The prevention of restrictive practices*. Here the Competition Act 1998 applies and prohibits, e.g., resale price agreements between suppliers of goods and retailers who agree not to sell below the minimum resale price agreed by the suppliers. This is covered by Prohibition 1 of the 1998 Act and any agreement that infringes the Chapter 1 prohibition is void and unenforceable.

The European Court of Justice confirmed in *Courage* v *Crehan* [2002] QB 507 that EU law required national courts to award relief, including damages, to any person suffering as a result of infringements of EU competition law. Under s 60(6)(b) of the Competition Act 1998 courts are required to follow this ruling when deciding what remedies to award in regard to infringements of UK competition law. Therefore, damages and injunctions should now be available to those who have suffered as a result of infringements of the UK Competition Act 1998. The provisions of the Competition Act 1998 and the Enterprise Act 2002, including third-party rights, are considered in more depth later in this chapter.

Crehan in the Lords

As a result of the ECJ ruling the UK Court of Appeal later awarded Bernie Crehan damages of £131,336, having decided that a lease agreement between a brewer and a publican Mr Crehan which tied him to buying beer at more expensive prices than other local pubs contravened Art 81. The Court of Appeal followed as a precedent a European case involving Whitbread which had a beer-tie with its tenant.

The brewer appealed to the House of Lords against the ruling of the Court of Appeal (see *Inntrepeneur Pub Company* v *Crehan* [2006] 4 All ER 465). The House of Lords ruled that beer-ties *did not infringe Art 81* and that Mr Crehan was not entitled to any damages. The Lords' judgment shows that an English court is entitled to consider all evidence before it and does not have to follow an ECJ decision which presented similar facts but in which Mr Crehan was not involved. However, the House of Lords did state, perhaps rather helpfully, that a party to an agreement that *does infringe Art 81* has a right to sue for damages.

Public policy – the contribution of the judiciary: illegal contracts

16

Illegal contracts

These contracts involve some form of moral weakness which society in general seeks to control. They are as follows:

(a) Contracts to commit crimes or civil wrongs. Thus a contract between an agent and his client whereby the agent was to receive a double commission would be illegal because it has as its object the commission of a fraud on the principal, since if the agent takes a double commission there is a conflict of interest.

(b) Contracts involving sexual immorality. Agreements for future illicit cohabitation are void, because the promise of payment might encourage immoral conduct in a person who otherwise would not have participated. However, a contract under which a person promises to pay another money in return for past illicit cohabitation is not illegal because it does not necessarily encourage future immorality between the parties. Such a contract will, however, be unenforceable unless made by deed because it is for past consideration. Furthermore, contracts which are on the face of it legal may be affected if *knowingly* made to further an immoral purpose. Immorality seems to refer only to extra-marital sexual intercourse.

It may be asked whether legally enforceable rights of maintenance may be created by a contract between cohabitants, i.e. persons who live together as husband and wife though unmarried. Certainly, a contract could be made, but its enforceability is doubtful. It was the view of the House of Lords in *Fender* v *St John Mildmay* [1937] 3 All ER 402 that the courts could not enforce an immoral promise between a man and a woman such as the payment of money or some other consideration in return for an immoral association. However, much depends upon the view a court would now take of this. The older cases, such as *Fender*, tended to regard the payment of money as a reward for and to induce the sexual aspect of the relationship. It may be that the courts would enforce a maintenance agreement which was entered into as part of a stable relationship between cohabitants, and which could not be seen as mere payment for a sexual relationship.

Nevertheless, in *H v H The Times*, 22 April 1983, the court refused to enforce maintenance support provisions in what was in effect a wife-swapping contract intended by the four parties to be permanent. Thus the matter of enforceable maintenance by contract must remain doubtful in terms that it may be contrary to public policy. In addition, the court may not enforce it on the basis that the parties did not intend to create legal relations, a concept which may affect contracts between members of a family or friends. This is unlikely to be a problem where the contract is in writing or by deed and especially so if the agreement is made following legal advice.

(c) Pre-nuptial agreements. In *M v M* (2002) 152 New Law Journal 696 the High Court held that a pre-nuptial agreement signed in Canada provided useful information as to the parties' intentions but went on to award a much higher sum to the wife. The judge could also have awarded less if the circumstances had required it. English law is at odds with many other jurisdictions in Europe and the English-speaking world in terms of the enforceability of these agreements. Individuals of high net worth coming to live in the UK should be advised that our courts are not impressed with such agreements and may regard the financial provisions as on the low side particularly if there are children or the marriage has lasted for some years. As we have noted, the judiciary is not obliged to enforce such agreements because they are contrary to public policy. The view is that they provide encouragement to violate the marriage tie that might be injurious to the public generally (*Fender* v *St John Mildmay* (1937) above). The judgment of Mr Justice Thorpe in *F v F* [1995] 2 FLR 45 is also relevant. He described pre-nuptial agreements as having 'a very limited significance in this jurisdiction'. A government Green Paper in 1998 supported such agreements but legislation has not been forthcoming.

(d) Contracts prejudicial to good foreign relations. This category includes contracts to carry out acts which are illegal by the law of a foreign and friendly country, since to enforce such contracts would encourage disputes.

(e) Contracts prejudicial to the administration of justice. Thus, a contract tending to defeat the bankruptcy laws is illegal at common law.

(f) Contracts tending to corruption in public life. A contract to procure a title or honour is illegal under this head.

(g) Contracts to defraud the Revenue. This applies to frauds in connection with national taxes or local business rates.

Dann v *Curzon*, 1911 – A contract to commit a crime (**188**)

Pearce v *Brooks*, 1866 – The prostitute's carriage (**189**)

Regazzoni v *KC Sethia*, 1958 – A contract to avoid apartheid sanctions (**190**)

John v *Mendoza*, 1939 – An attempt to avoid a bankruptcy (**191**)

Parkinson v *College of Ambulance*, 1925 – Buying a title (**192**)

Napier v *National Business Agency Ltd*, 1951 – A tax fiddle that failed (**193**)

Consequences

The consequences of illegality in the above cases depend upon whether the contract was unlawful on the face of it, i.e. there was no way in which lawful performance could be achieved, or whether the contract was lawful on the face of it, i.e. it could have been performed in a lawful manner.

(a) Contract unlawful on face of it. This includes all the categories mentioned above except some contracts involving sexual immorality. The consequences where the contract is unlawful on the face of it are as follows:

(i) The contract is void and there is no action by either party for debt (see *Dann* v *Curzon*, 1911), damages, specific performance or injunction.

(ii) Money paid or property transferred to the other party under the contract is irrecoverable (see *Parkinson* v *College of Ambulance* (1925)) unless:

(1) The claimant is relying on rights other than those which are contained in the contract. Thus, if A leases property to B for five years and A knows that B intends to use the property as a brothel, A cannot recover rent or require any covenant to be performed without pleading the illegal lease. However, at the end of the term A can bring an action for the return of his property as *owner* and not as a landlord under an illegal lease. In addition, if the action is to redress a wrong which, although in a sense connected with the contract, can really be considered independent of it, the law will allow the action.

(2) The claimant is not *in pari delicto* (of equal wrong). Where the contract is unlawful on the face of it, equal guilt is presumed but this presumption may be rebutted if the claimant can show that the defendant was guilty of fraud, oppression or undue influence.

(3) The claimant repents provided that the repentance is genuine and performance is *partial* and not *substantial*.

> *Bowmakers Ltd* v *Barnet Instruments Ltd*, 1944 – Where the claimant sues as owner (**194**)
>
> *Edler* v *Auerbach*, 1950 – An action independent of the illegal contract (**195**)
>
> *Hughes* v *Liverpool Victoria Legal Friendly Society*, 1916 – A contract induced by fraud (**196**)
>
> *Bigos* v *Bousted*, 1951 – Where repentance is not genuine (**197**)
>
> *Taylor* v *Bowers*, 1876 – A partial performance (**198**)
>
> *Kearley* v *Thomson*, 1890 – A substantial performance: no redress (**199**)

16

(b) Contract lawful on face of it. The result here is as follows:

(i)   Where both parties intended the illegal purpose. There is no action by either party for debt, damages, specific performance or injunction (see *Pearce* v *Brooks* (1866)) or to recover money paid or property transferred under the contract.

(ii) Where one party was without knowledge of the illegal purpose. The innocent party's rights are unaffected and he may sue for debt, damages, specific performance or injunction, or to recover money paid or property transferred.

(iii) The party who would have performed the contract in an unlawful manner has no action on it nor can he recover property delivered to the other party under the contract.

Fielding and Platt Ltd v *Najjar*, 1969 – An action by an innocent party (**200**)

Cowan v *Milbourn*, 1867 – Where the claimant intended unlawful performance (**201**)

Berg v *Sadler and Moore*, 1937 – Unlawful performance: no recovery of money or property (**202**)

Public policy and the judiciary – void contracts

These contracts do not involve any type of moral weakness but are against public policy because they are inexpedient rather than unprincipled. The contracts concerned are contracts to oust the jurisdiction of the courts, contracts prejudicial to the status of marriage and contracts in restraint of trade. These are dealt with individually below.

Contracts to oust the jurisdiction of the courts

A contract which has the effect of taking away the right of one or both of the parties to bring an action before a court of law is void, though it may be possible to *sever* the offensive part of the contract and enforce the rest. This rule does not make void honourable pledge clauses because in such cases the parties do not intend to be bound by the contract at all. If the contract is to be binding, however, then the parties cannot exclude it from the jurisdiction of the courts. Furthermore, arbitration clauses are not affected. Many commercial contracts contain an arbitration clause, the object being to provide a cheaper or more convenient remedy than a court action. An arbitration clause in a contract is not void if the effect of it is that the parties are to go to arbitration *first* before going to court. An arbitration clause which denies the parties access to the courts completely is, of course, invalid.

Goodinson v *Goodinson*, 1954 – Severing an unlawful promise (**203**)

Contracts prejudicial to the status of marriage

A contract in absolute restraint of marriage, i.e. one in which a person promises not to marry at all, is void. Partial restraints, if reasonable, are said to be valid, e.g. a contract not to marry a person of a certain religious faith, or not to marry for a short period of time. However, there are no recent cases and it may be that even a partial restraint would be regarded as void today. Marriage brokage contracts, i.e. contracts to introduce men and women with a view to their subsequent marriage, are also void on the ground that third parties should not be free to reap financial profit by bringing about matrimonial unions.

As regards separation agreements, these are invalid if made for the future, as where a husband promises that he will make provision for his wife if she should ever live apart from him, unless the agreement is made as part of a reconciliation arrangement. In this case the agreement is valid, although it may make provision for a renewed future separation. If the parties are not living in amity or are actually separated, then a separation agreement is valid. Once it is apparent that the parties cannot live together in amity, it is desirable that a separation which has become inevitable should be concluded upon reasonable terms.

The special case of the pre-nuptial agreement has already been considered.

Contracts in restraint of trade

Originally all contracts in restraint of trade were regarded as void but in the seventeenth century the courts began to allow certain of them to operate if reasonable, apparently because of the reluctance of masters to train apprentices unless they were able to restrain those apprentices in some way on the completion of the apprenticeship.

Because of the obvious importance of this area of the law, together with restrictive practices generally, the remainder of this chapter will be devoted to this subject.

Contracts in restraint of trade – generally

Such contracts are *prima facie* void and will only be binding if reasonable. Thus the contract must be reasonable between the parties which means that it must be no wider than is necessary to protect the interest involved in terms of the area and time of its operation. It must also be reasonable as regards the public interest. Finally, the issue of reasonableness is a matter of law for the judge on the evidence presented to him which would include, for example, such matters as trade practices and customs.

Even where the employee receives a special payment to accept the covenant, it must still be reasonable and justified by the employer. (See *Turner* v *Commonwealth & British Minerals Ltd* (1999) *The Independent*, 29 November.)

Wyatt v *Kreglinger and Fernau*, 1933 – Restraint of trade and the public interest (**204**)

16

Voluntary contractual restraints of trade on employees generally

Here the contract is entered into voluntarily by the parties and as regards employees it should be noted that there are only two things an employer can protect:

(a) Trade secrets. A restraint against competition is justifiable if its object is to prevent the exploitation of trade secrets learned by the employee in the course of his employment. In this connection it should be noted that the area of the restraint must not be excessive. Furthermore, a restraint under this heading may be invalid because its duration is excessive.

(b) Business connection. Sometimes an employer may use a covenant against solicitation of persons with whom the employer does business. The problem of area is less important in this type of covenant, though its duration must be reasonable. The burden on the employer increases as the duration of the restraint is extended, though in rare situations a restraint for life may be valid.

Forster & Sons Ltd v *Suggett*, 1918 – A restraint in regard to trade secrets (**205**)
Home Counties Dairies v *Skilton*, 1970 – A restraint preventing customer solicitation (**206**)
Fitch v *Dewes*, 1921 – A client restraint for life (**207**)

Restraint in the City of London

The problems involved in holding on to key staff in City of London financial institutions has been a matter of much publicity in recent times.

An important Court of Appeal decision gives some protection against poaching. It held that a provision in a company manager's service contract prohibiting him during employment, and for one year after leaving, from offering a partnership or employment to any person who had at any time during the manager's employment also been employed by the company as a director or senior employee of the company, was a reasonable restraint and enforceable. A clause which prohibited the poaching of any employee, regardless of status, was struck down as too wide. (See *Dawnay Day & Co Ltd* v *D'Alphen* [1997] IRLR 442.)

The managers concerned were acting as inter-dealer brokers with Dawnay Day, an investment bank. The managers had also entered into a joint venture with Dawnay Day but non-solicitation of staff clauses in the shareholder's agreement were held to be in unreasonable restraint of trade because they were too wide, since they applied to all staff from top to bottom of the company.

The importance of the case lies in the fact that there were conflicting decisions in previous case law as to whether an employer had a legitimate interest in maintaining a stable, trained workforce.

This case takes the line that there is a legitimate interest which can be protected. It is of great importance to the City since, if there was no legitimate interest in retaining the senior workforce, a competitor could take senior staff into his own organisation, in effect taking over the former employer's business without actually paying for it. It is important to note that the case does not cover the situation where an employee leaves because a job is advertised in the other organisation, for which he applies. The basis of the case is *solicitation* of employees.

Contractual restraints on employees through the period of notice

In recent times the court has had to consider the validity of contracts of service with restrictively long periods of notice which have sometimes been given to able and ambitious executives. Typically such contracts provide that if the employee leaves he must give notice of, say, one year and during that time the employer can suspend him from work but agrees to give him full pay and other benefits. The contract will normally also provide that the employer may exclude the employee from the workplace so that he cannot after serving his notice obtain any further information which might be of benefit to the new employer nor can he work for the new employer during the period of notice without being in breach of contract. He can either do nothing or pursue his hobbies. This is why the period of notice has been called 'garden leave'.

A specific provision in the contract is essential if the employee is to be excluded from work. *William Hill Organisation* v *Tucker* [1998] IRLR 313 decides that otherwise the employee has the right to work.

A 'garden leave' contract typically does not contain a restraint clause but the employee can be restrained from competing, during what is usually a long period of notice, because he is still employed during the notice period and so owes *a duty of fidelity to his employer at common law* not to compete. The 'garden leave' contract is an alternative to a restraint clause and allows the court to adopt a more flexible approach in that the employer may be granted an injunction to prevent competition during the period of notice if, *on the facts*, it is reasonable to do so, as where the competition is serious. This happened in *GFI Group Inc* v *Eaglestone* (1994) 490 IRLB 2 where the High Court held that an injunction could be granted to prohibit a highly-paid foreign exchange options broker from working for a rival firm during his notice period of 20 weeks, so that for that period of time he could not assist a competing organisation to deal with the business connections of his employer. If the competition is not so serious, a claim for damages can be brought, as the Court of Appeal decided in *Provident Financial Group plc* v *Whitegates Estate Agency* [1989] IRLR 84.

If, however, a restraint clause is put into a severance package when the employee leaves, the clause must satisfy the general test of reasonableness. The duty of fidelity at common law does not exist since the former employee is no longer employed. Thus, if the clause is too wide, the court cannot give any protection even if, *on the facts*, the competition is severe, as the Court of Appeal decided in *JA Mont (UK) Ltd* v *Mills* [1993] IRLR 172. For example:

(a) A surveyor with a firm of estate agents is on 'garden leave' and takes a job with a major competing estate agency in the same town. The court may well grant an injunction on the grounds of the surveyor's breach of the duty of fidelity at common law. However, if the court feels that injunctive relief is unreasonable, a claim for damages could be allowed. If the surveyor went to work for a firm of estate agents in the next town, the court might decide on the facts that no relief of any kind should be given.

(b) If the surveyor had left his job and as part of a severance package he was restrained from working for a firm of estate agents anywhere in the UK for five years, the restraint would obviously be too wide and wholly void. That being so the court could not give the employer any relief, even if the surveyor went to work for a rival firm of estate agents next door to his former employer!

Payments in lieu of notice (PILON) – effect on employee restraints

An employer who is in breach of contract may not be able to enforce agreements in restraint of trade. Thus an employer who, without cause, dismisses an employee without notice is in breach of contract and the court would be unlikely to uphold any post-employment restraints on the employee. The authority for this is *Atkins* v *General Billposting* [1909] AC 118. Where the contract contains a PILON clause and the employer makes such a payment then he or she is not in breach of contract and post-employment restraints can be enforced if reasonable. There was doubt as to the position where although the contract did not contain a PILON clause the employer nevertheless dismissed without notice but made a payment in lieu. The possibility was that the employer was in breach of contract and that the payment was a non-contractual payment of damages. In these circumstances did post-employment restraints become unenforceable?

In *Mackenzie* v *CRS Computers Ltd* [2002] Emp LR 1048 the Employment Appeal Tribunal ruled that a payment in lieu, not provided for by the contract, was not a repudiation of the contract provided the employer paid the ex-employee a sum representing his salary and loss of any relevant benefits. Therefore, *Atkins* did not apply and other clauses, including presumably restraint clauses, would apply if reasonable. In this case the clause that survived related to the fact that the ex-employee should pay settlement charges on the lease of a company car provided to him if he left, as here, during the first year of employment. There is another important aspect of *MacKenzie* because where there is a PILON clause, the payment is contractual and tax is payable on it. A payment without a PILON clause is, on the face of it, in the nature of damages and may be entitled to tax relief, up to £30,000, on compensation for loss of employment. The *MacKenzie* ruling allows the employee to have that benefit and the employer to retain rights under the contract. However, the Inland Revenue may challenge non-PILON payments particularly if, in the organisation, a payment in lieu of notice is always made even though there is no PILON clause.

Non-contractual restraints on employees: confidential information

The position is different where the employee has no restraint of trade clause in his contract and is not on 'garden leave'. Thus, in *Faccenda Chicken Ltd* v *Fowler* [1986] 1 All ER 617, Mr Fowler was sales manager for Faccenda Chicken Ltd for seven years and set up a van sales operation whereby refrigerated vans travelled around certain districts offering fresh chicken to retailers and caterers. He left the company and set up his own business selling chickens from refrigerated vans in the same area. Eight of the company's employees went to work for him. Each of the salesmen in the company knew the names and addresses of the customers, the route and timing of deliveries, and the different prices quoted to different customers.

The company unsuccessfully brought an action for damages in the High Court, alleging wrongful use of confidential sales information and was also unsuccessful in a counterclaim for damages for breach of contract by abuse of confidential information in Mr Fowler's action against the company for outstanding commission.

It is generally the case that rather more protection in terms of preventing an employee from approaching customers can be obtained by an express term which is reasonable in terms of its duration. In the absence of an express term, it is clear from this decision of the Court of Appeal that confidential information of an employer's business obtained by an employee in the course of his service may be used by that employee when he leaves the job unless, as the Court of Appeal decided, it can be classed as a trade secret or is of such a confidential nature that it merits the same protection as a trade secret. For example, there would have been no need for a term in the contract of service in *Forster* v *Suggett* (1918). The court could have prevented use of the secret process for a period without this. It should, however, be noted that in *Faccenda* the Court of Appeal did say that if the employees had written down lists of customers, routes, etc., as distinct from having the necessary information in their memories, and presumably being unable to erase it, short of amnesia, they might have been restrained for a period from using the lists. This follows the case of *Robb* v *Green* [1895] 2 QB 315 where the manager of a firm dealing in live game and eggs copied down the names of customers before leaving and then solicited these for the purposes of his own business after leaving the employment of the firm. He was restrained from soliciting the customers. In this connection, the High Court granted an injunction in regard to a one-year non-solicitation of customers clause in the contract of a manager in a company of insurance brokers who was dealing with small business clients. He had not set out to learn the client information to use it in competition with his employer but the High Court held that as regards confidentiality *Faccenda Chicken* did not *rigidly* draw a distinction between deliberate and innocent learning. Confidential information was confidential regardless of how it came into the employee's memory (see *SBJ Stevenson Ltd* v *Mandy*, High Court, 30 July 1999).

In the *Mandy* case there was a restraint in the contract of employment. It is hard to see how any such contractual restraint could work if memory matters were excluded. The situation may be different where there is no contract but the claimant is proceeding under the implied duty of confidentiality. Here mere innocent learning may not always be enough to create an enforceable restraint.

In addition, the courts prefer a written contractual restraint in confidentiality matters. Many of the cases are based on complex technical facts and a written contract can assist the court in deciding what is the confidential technical information that is in issue.

In this connection, the Court of Appeal ruled in *Pocton Industries Ltd* v *Michael Ikem Horton* [2000] Lawtel CCH New Law 200059503 that although an electro-plating apparatus was capable of protection under an implied duty of non-disclosure there was no contractual provision regarding which part of the employee's knowledge was to be regarded as confidential and the plating process was only part of a number of pieces of information the employee could not help but acquire from his duties. The claim to restrain use of the knowledge acquired failed.

Whistle-blowing

When discussing an employee's duty of confidentiality, mention should be made of the provisions of the Public Interest Disclosure Act 1998 which inserted some new sections into the Employment Rights Act 1996. The Act protects workers from being dismissed or penalised for disclosing information about the organisation in which they work that they reasonably believe exposes financial malpractice, miscarriages of justice, dangers to health and safety, and dangers to the environment. Disclosure may be made to an employer, but where the disclosure relates to the employer or there is danger of victimisation, it may be made e.g. to a regulator such as the Financial Services Authority for City frauds. Whistle-blowers who are dismissed or otherwise victimised may complain to an employment tribunal and make appeals to higher courts.

In this connection the Court of Appeal ruled in *Woodward* v *Abbey National plc* [2006] IRLR 677 that the protection under s 47B of the Employment Rights Act 1996 against whistleblowers being subjected to detriment because of making a protected disclosure is not restricted to the duration of the contract of employment but extends also to a detriment imposed by an ex-employer on an ex-employee after leaving employment. In this case the detriment was that Abbey would not provide a reference for Mrs Woodward after she had left employment with Abbey having made protected disclosures relating to Abbey's alleged failure to comply with certain legal obligations.

Is it a trade secret?

The Court of Appeal has held that an ex-employee who made negative remarks about the financial situation and management of the company from which he had resigned as managing director did not owe an implied duty of confidentiality with regard to the information disclosed about the ex-employer.

The information, it said, did not come within the category of a 'trade secret' (see *Brooks* v *Olyslager OMS (UK) Ltd* [1998] 601 IRLB 6).

When Mr Brooks resigned from the company, it was under a compromise agreement giving him three months' salary in three monthly instalments. Immediately following his resignation, he telephoned an investment banker who had an interest in the company. During the conversation, he intimated that the company's management was autocratic, the company was insolvent and would only last a month, its budgets were over-optimistic and that it would be taken over by its holding company.

When it heard about these remarks, the company refused to pay the salary instalments and claimed that Mr Brooks was in breach of an implied duty of confidentiality. He claimed damages in the lower court and was awarded them.

The issue in the Court of Appeal related mainly to the duty of confidentiality. The court did not agree that there was such a duty in this case and in respect of the information disclosed. There was no evidence that knowledge of the company's financial affairs was not already in the public domain. Also, Olyslager had not sought to show that what Mr Brooks had said was untrue or malicious, nor that his statements had caused any financial loss. The company's case was based on its desire to prevent Mr Brooks from disclosing the reasons why he had resigned and from making statements that were in any way detrimental to its interest.

There was no such broad right in law. Accordingly, Mr Brooks was entitled to his damages for breach of the compromise agreement and the company was not entitled to an injunction to prevent further disclosures of the kind put forward in this case. They were not trade secrets.

Employee restraints arising from agreements between manufacturers and traders

The courts are concerned to prevent an employer from obtaining by indirect means restraint protection which he could not have obtained in an express contract with the employee.

Kores Manufacturing Co Ltd v *Kolok Manufacturing Co Ltd*, 1958 – Employee restraints between employers (**208**)

Restraints imposed on the vendor of a business

In allowing restraints to protect the goodwill of the business sold, e.g. that customers will continue to buy from it, the law is only responding to commercial necessity. Unless the vendor (seller) was legally able to undertake not to compete with the purchaser, no one would buy the business. However, such a restraint will be void unless it is required to protect the business sold and not to stifle competition.

It should be noted, however, that the protection of the business sold may in rare situations involve a world-wide restraint.

British Reinforced Concrete Co v *Schelff*, 1921 – Restraints against mere competition not allowed (**209**)

Nordenfelt v *Maxim Nordenfelt Guns and Ammunition Co*, 1894 – An exceptional world-wide restraint (**210**)

Restrictions on shareholder-employees

The courts will generally allow wider restraints in the case of vendors of businesses than in the case of employees. However, what is the position where the employee is also a shareholder and therefore also a proprietor of the business?

Systems Reliability Holdings plc v *Smith*, 1990 – Where the employee is also a shareholder in the employing company (**211**)

Restrictions accepted by distributors of merchandise

In order to increase the efficiency of distribution, a manufacturer or wholesaler may refuse to make merchandise available for distribution to the public unless the distributor accepts certain conditions restricting his liberty of trading. This is the main purpose of the solus agreement used by petrol companies. Such agreements are void unless reasonable.

There is an important distinction here between a garage proprietor who borrows money on mortgage of his own property from a petrol company and a garage proprietor who agrees to sell only that company's products for a period of time. The rule relating to unreasonable restraints of trade applies to the mortgage. However, if the petrol company is the owner of the land and garage premises and grants a lease to a tenant who will run the garage then the rule relating to unreasonable restraints of trade does not apply to an agreement in the lease to take the petrol company's products.

> *Esso Petroleum Co Ltd* v *Harper's Garage (Stourport) Ltd*, 1967 – Restraint in a
> mortgage (**212**)
> *Cleveland Petroleum Co Ltd* v *Dartstone Ltd*, 1969 – A restraint in a lease (**213**)

Involuntary restraints of trade

We have so far considered, subject to an exception in the case of confidential information, restrictions against trading contained in contracts. However, the doctrine is not confined to these voluntary restraints. It extends to involuntary restraints imposed by trade associations or professional bodies upon their members. Such restraints are void unless reasonable.

> *Pharmaceutical Society of Great Britain* v *Dickson*, 1968 – Restraints imposed
> by a professional body (**214**)

Consequences where the contract is contrary to public policy: severance

Where a contract is rendered void by the judiciary, it is enforceable only in so far as it contravenes public policy. Thus lawful promises may be severed and enforced. A contract of service which contains a void restraint is not wholly invalid and the court will sever and enforce those aspects of it which do not offend against public policy. Thus an employee who has entered into a contract of service which contains a restraint which is too wide can recover his wages or salary.

The court will not add to a contract or in any way redraft it but will merely strike out the offending words. What is left must make sense without further additions, otherwise the court will not sever the void part in order to enforce what is good. For example, A agrees 'not to set up a competing business within ten miles' in a covenant when he sells his business. If we suppose that five miles would be reasonable, the court will not in fact substitute 'five' and then enforce the covenant because this would mean making a contract for the parties.

It is important also to note that the court will not delete the invalid part of a restraint clause if it is the major part of the restraints imposed.

Thus in *Attwood* v *Lamont* [1920] 3 KB 571 the heads of each department in a business of a general outfitter were required to sign a contract agreeing, amongst other things, after leaving the business not to be engaged in 'the trade or business of a tailor, dressmaker, general draper, milliner, hatter, haberdasher, gentlemen's, ladies' or children's outfitters, at any place within a radius of ten miles of the employers' place of business at Regent House, Kidderminster . . .'. Lamont, who was employed as cutter and head of the tailoring department, left and began to compete, doing business with some of his former employer's customers. The employer then tried to enforce the above restraint which was drawn too wide in terms of the various departments covered, since Lamont had never been concerned with departments other than the tailoring department. The court refused to sever the tailoring covenant from the rest because that would have meant severing almost the whole of the restraint in order to leave the restraint regarding tailoring.

A contrast is provided by *Goldsoll* v *Goldman* [1915] 1 Ch 292. In that case the defendant sold imitation jewellery and when he sold his business he agreed 'not for two years to deal in real or imitation jewellery in any part of the United Kingdom'. The court was prepared to sever the words 'real or' in order to make the restraint valid and restrict the defendant from competing in imitation jewellery. Only two words needed to be deleted and this was a very small part of the restraint as a whole.

No severance of widely drawn clause

It is not appropriate said the Court of Appeal in *Wincanton Ltd* v *Cranny* [2000] IRLR 716 for a court to sever an unenforceable restraint so that it becomes enforceable if it is clear that it has been drawn intentionally wide. The clause involved stated that the employee should not for a period of 12 months following the termination of his employment be 'directly or indirectly engaged, concerned or interested in any capacity . . . in any business of whatever kind in the UK which is wholly or partly in competition with any business carried on by the company . . .'. The Court of Appeal would not contemplate a possible severance.

Public policy: the contribution of Parliament

Some contracts are prohibited by statute in terms that they are illegal, the words 'unlawful' being used in the statute concerned. In this context 'statute' includes the orders, rules and regulations that Ministers of the Crown and other persons are authorised by Parliament to issue.

The statutory prohibitions with which we are concerned may be express or implied.

Implied statutory prohibition

In these cases the statute itself does not say expressly that contracts contravening its provisions are necessarily illegal. The statute may affect the formation of a particular contract as where a trader does business without taking out a licence. In some cases the statute may affect the manner of performance of the contract as where a trader is required to deliver to a purchaser a written statement such as an invoice containing, for example, details of the chemical composition of the goods.

In either case whether failure to comply with a statutory provision renders the contract illegal is a matter of construction of the statute and is for the judge to decide.

If, in the opinion of the judge, the Act was designed to protect the public then the contract will be illegal. Thus in *Cope* v *Rowlands* (1836) 2 M&W 149 an unlicensed broker in the City of London was held not to be entitled to sue for his fees because the purpose of the licensing requirements was to protect the public against possibly shady dealers. Furthermore, in *Anderson Ltd* v *Daniel* [1924] 1 KB 138 a seller of artificial fertilisers was held unable to recover the price of goods which he had delivered because he had failed to state in an invoice the chemical composition of the fertilisers which was required by Act of Parliament.

On the other hand, if in the opinion of the judge the purpose of the legislation was mainly to raise revenue or to help in the administration of trade, contracts will not be affected. Thus in *Smith* v *Mawhood* (1845, 14 M&W 452 it was held that a tobacconist could recover the price of tobacco sold by him even though he did not have a licence to sell it and had not painted his name on his place of business. The purpose of the statute involved was not to affect the contract of sale but to impose a fine on offenders for the purpose of revenue. In addition, in *Archbolds (Freightage) Ltd* v *Spanglett Ltd* [1961] 1 QB 374 a contract by an unlicensed carrier to carry goods by road was held valid because the legislation involved was only designed to help in the administration of road transport.

Express statutory prohibition

Sometimes an Act of Parliament may expressly prohibit certain types of agreement. For example, the Competition Act 1998 in s 2(2)(a) prohibits agreements, decisions or practices that directly or indirectly fix purchase or selling prices, and this would include resale price maintenance agreements. *As regards the remedies* available to an organisation affected by an anti-competitive practice, it may complain to the Office of Fair Trading or if the infringement has a European Union dimension it may complain to the EU Commission in Brussels. Interim relief may be asked for in urgent cases. However, the final outcome will be an infringement decision and a large fine on the offending organisation. *This will not produce damages for the organisation if it has lost profits because of the offending organisation's activities.*

Organisations wishing to pursue claims against the offender may go through the ordinary courts of law. Actions for damages and injunctions are clearly available to those who have suffered loss as a result of infringements of the 1998 Act (see *Courage* v *Crehan* [2002] QB 507: a ruling of the ECJ).

Organisations suffering loss may wait for the OFT to investigate and make a finding of infringement. When the appeals process has been exhausted the organisation may rely on the infringement decision and this will be beneficial because there will be no need to produce evidence that there has been an infringement to the court again. Obviously, matters of causation and quantification of damages may arise but the claim will be made easier. These are called *'piggyback' claims* and have been introduced by the Enterprise Act 2002 inserting a new s 58A into the Competition Act 1998.

Finally, if there is difficulty in pleading before the ordinary courts because of their unfamiliarity with competition issues the Enterprise Act 2002 has expanded the jurisdiction of the Competition Appeals Tribunal (a specialist tribunal) so that *it can hear actions for damages following domestic competition infringement decisions by the OFT and the EU Commission regarding infringements of EU law.* These will be 'piggyback' claims.

16

Wagering contracts: insurance and dealing in differences

In essence, for a wager to exist it must be possible for one party to win and one party to lose and there must be two persons or two groups opposed to each other in their views as to a future event. Thus, where S, Y and Z each put £5 into a fund to be given to the party whose selected horse wins a given race, there is no wager. The only commercial importance of the concept of wagering and the only reason why it is introduced in a book of this nature relates to insurance and dealing in differences (see below). A contract is not a wager if the person to whom the money is promised on the occurrence of the event has an interest in the non-occurrence of that event, e.g. where a person has paid a premium to insure his house against destruction by fire. Such an interest is called an *insurable interest* and is not a wager. However, to insure someone else's property would be a wager and not a valid contract of insurance.

The Gaming Act 1845 renders wagering contracts void so that there is no action for the bet or for the winnings. However, it should be noted that if the bet or the winnings have actually been paid over they cannot be recovered. Payment operates as waiver of the Act and the payment over of the money confers a good title to that money upon the person to whom it is paid.

It has become more common in recent times for persons to deal in differences, i.e. to bet on the future rises or falls in selected stock exchange indexes. No securities are bought or sold, the only transaction being the payment by one party to the other of the eventual difference in the indexes according to the accuracy or otherwise of the gambler's predictions.

It was decided in *City Index Ltd* v *Leslie* [1991] 3 All ER 180 that such a contract was validated by s 63 of the Financial Services Act 1986 so long as it was made 'by way of business'. The claimants offered clients a differences service and recovered £34,580 plus interest from the defendant whose predictions of rise and fall had not been successful.

Competition law

Competition law has become extremely complex and a detailed study of it can only be of benefit to the specialist practitioner. Nevertheless, it is important for all students in those disciplines that require a grounding in the law to have an environmental knowledge of current competition law. The following materials are designed to provide that environmental knowledge.

Setting the scene

Current competition law is based mainly on the Competition Act 1998, the Enterprise Act 2002 and Arts 81 and 82 of the EU Treaty of Rome.

We begin with the Competition Act 1998 the major provisions of which came into force in March 2000. It contains a system of public regulation of competition law that mirrors to a large extent EU competition law. Section 2 of the CA 1998 introduces the Chapter I Prohibition which has the objective of preventing co-ordinated market behaviour between undertakings, e.g. to fix prices. This policy was formerly carried out by the repealed Restrictive Trade Practices Act 1976 and the Resale Prices Act 1976. Prohibition I is modelled closely upon Art 81 of the Treaty of Rome.

Section 18 of the CA 1998 introduces the Chapter II Prohibition which controls any conduct in a market by one or more undertakings that amounts to an abuse of a dominant position in that market. Prohibition II is modelled closely upon Art 82 of the Treaty of Rome.

Finally, s 60 of the CA 1998 provides that in the absence of any relevant differences interpretation of the Prohibitions should be designed to achieve consistency with EU law.

Practices and provisions which infringe the Chapter 1 Prohibition

The 1998 Act sets out in s 2 a non-exhaustive list of practices and provisions that will infringe Prohibition I. There is a similarity with Art 81. The list is as follows:

- directly or indirectly fixing purchase or selling prices or other trading conditions. This includes attempts to fix resale prices (or resale price maintenance);
- limiting or controlling production markets, technical development or investment;
- agreements to share markets or sources of supply or doing so in practice;
- discrimination by applying different conditions to equivalent transactions with other trading parties so that they are at a competitive disadvantage;
- making the conclusion of contracts subject to the acceptance by the other parties of supplementary obligations which are unconnected with the subject matter of those contracts either by their nature or according to their commercial use.

Chapter 1 exclusions

These include:

- Mergers which have been cleared under previous legislation such as the Fair Trading Act 1973 which are allowed to continue.
- Agreements controlled by other legislation such as the acquisition of a controlling interest in a public listed company. This is controlled by the Financial Services Authority as the UK Listing Authority under the Financial Services and Markets Act 2000 and the City Code on Take-overs and Mergers. The same is true in regard to the general control of contracts between a company and its directors under the Companies Act 1985.
- Agreements which under previous law were not sent for investigation by the Restrictive Practices Court by the Secretary of State because they were not considered significant. There is, however, a 'claw-back' provision under which the Office of Fair Trading can reconsider them if they appear to infringe the Chapter I Prohibition which is unlikely.
- Vertical agreements are excluded so long as they are not price-fixing agreements. A vertical agreement is one entered into by organisations operating at different levels of the market such as an agreement between a manufacturer and a distributor. A horizontal agreement is normally one made between organisations operating at the same level in the market as in the case of an agreement between manufacturers or an agreement between distributors.
- Agreements concerning land, i.e. agreements that create or transfer estates in land such as restrictive covenants over land restricting its use. A major effect is to exempt leases where, for instance, there is a covenant restricting use of the property and forbidding car-breaking on the premises by the tenant. However, covenants protecting the landlord's *business* as distinct from the *land* may be affected by the Chapter I Prohibition as where a landlord leases property for use as a shop but includes a covenant forbidding the sale of goods that are sold by his own shop that is nearby. The Chapter II Prohibition does apply to land as where the owner of an airport refuses to grant a lease at the airport to a bookseller in order to protect a rival bookseller.

The Secretary of State has order-making powers that may be used to prevent adverse effects on competition in terms of access to facilities such as marinas and taxi-ranks.

16

Reform

Although the exclusion for vertical agreements is still in force European developments are to the effect that vertical agreements are within Art 85. Therefore, s 209(3) of the Enterprise Act 2002 gives the Secretary of State power to remove the exclusion as soon as it is reasonable to do so. In addition, the rules of professional bodies such as the Law Society were excluded under the Competition Act 1998. Now s 207 of the EA 2002 repeals that provision and professional rules are no longer excluded.

Chapter I exemptions

There are three exemptions as follows:

(a) an individual exemption granted by the Office of Fair Trading (OFT) where it can be shown that the agreement will contribute to improving production or distribution or promote technical or economic progress and allows consumers a fair share of the resulting benefit. Furthermore, any restrictions must be indispensable and there must be no elimination of competition. Potentially exempt agreements should be notified to the OFT and the OFT may also give guidance without formal notice as to whether the agreement might or might not be exempted;

(b) a block exemption given by the Secretary of State on the recommendation of the OFT covering particular classes of agreement which satisfy the criteria for individual exemption;

(c) agreements which are the subject of individual or block exemption under Art 81 are automatically exempt under the 1998 Act.

Abuse of a dominant position – the Chapter II Prohibitions

The prohibition on the abuse of a dominant position appears in Chapter II of the 1998 Act and is closely modelled on Art 82 of the EC Treaty of Rome.

Chapter II prohibits:

- any conduct on the part of one or more undertakings;
- which amounts to an abuse;
- of a dominant position in the market; and
- which may affect trade within the UK or *any* part of it.

In the same way as Art 82, the 1998 Act sets out a non-exhaustive list of the types of conduct which can amount to an abuse. The list includes:

- the imposition of unfair purchase or sale prices, e.g. unfairly high selling prices or unfairly low purchase prices and predatory pricing;
- the limitation of production, markets or technical developments to the prejudice of consumers, such as restricting output with a resulting rise in prices or refusal to supply;
- the imposition of unfair trading conditions over and above pricing, e.g. quality of products and service;
- applying dissimilar conditions to equivalent transactions thereby placing some organisations at a competitive disadvantage;
- tying, i.e. making the conclusion of a contract depend on the acceptance by other parties of obligations which have no connection with the subject matter of the contracts, e.g. A, a manufacturer, requires a retailer not to stock the products of a rival manufacturer, B. Conversely, a retailer might prevent a manufacturer from supplying rival outlets.

ILLEGALITY, PUBLIC POLICY AND COMPETITION LAW | 387

Article 82 is not followed entirely since the Art 82 provision refers to a *substantial* part of the Community, whereas Chapter II refers to *any part* of the UK, so that localised markets are covered, e.g. the provision of bus services in local areas.

What is dominance?

The 1998 Act does not set out thresholds for defining dominance but EU law cases will apply and these show that dominance has been found to exist where market shares have been in excess of 40 per cent in some cases and 45 per cent in others. This is also the Commission's view. The OFT Guidance note, however, quotes a lower market share, i.e. 20–40 per cent.

Exemptions and exclusions

As with Art 82, there are no exemptions from Chapter II. There are exclusions which are similar to the exclusions provided in regard to the Chapter I Prohibition.

It is possible to notify the OFT in regard to conduct that may amount to a Chapter II Prohibition for guidance or decision as to whether the prohibition does or does not apply.

Monopolies and mergers

This area of competition law was covered by the Fair Trading Act 1973. The Competition Act 1998 left the provisions of the 1973 Act in place. A major feature of the 1973 Act was that monopolies and mergers in terms of their undesirability had to be evaluated in terms of a 'public interest' test, i.e. did they operate or could they operate against the public interest? Section 84 of the FTA 1973 (now repealed) gave matters to which regard must be paid, e.g. the desirability of promoting, through competition, the reduction of costs and the development of new techniques and new products. The test was imprecise and was criticised for that. Control was by the Monopolies and Mergers Commission. This became the Competition Commission under the CA 1998. The Competition Commission, as the Monopolies and Mergers Commission before it, continues under the Enterprise Act 2002 but originally could be required to investigate and report in relevant areas of business following a reference to it by the Director-General of Fair Trading (a position that is now defunct). There were two types of monopoly situation as follows:

- *the scale monopoly* where one company or other organisation supplied or purchased 25 per cent or more of all goods or services of a particular type in the UK; or
- *the local monopoly* as above but the purchase or supply was only in a part of the UK; or
- *the complex monopoly* where a group of organisations acting together controlled 15 per cent of the market.

The Competition Act 1998 retained the above monopoly provisions.

The Enterprise Act 2002 changes

The main changes made by the Act of 2002 are the removal (with some exceptions, e.g. public interest cases affecting e.g. defence contracts) of the Secretary of State's role and the substitution of a 'substantial lessening of competition' test for the former general 'public interest' test.

There are also *new monopoly tests* called jurisdictional tests that replace the earlier tests. The primary requirements are:

- that two or more enterprises cease to be distinct; and
- that the value of the turnover in the UK of the enterprise being acquired, i.e. the target enterprise exceeds £70 million; or
- that in relation to the supply of goods or services of any description at least one-quarter of all the goods or services of that description that are supplied in the UK are supplied by or to one and the same person.

The first test is referred to as the *'turnover test'* and the second the *'share of supply test'*. The supply test means in practice that the merging parties will together supply or receive the relevant percentage of goods and services.

Media mergers

The most important of these are newspaper and TV channel monopolies and mergers. These are left untouched by the Enterprise Act 2002 and are dealt with by the Communications Act 2003. Part V of the Act applies and gives the Office of Communications (OFCOM) concurrent jurisdiction with the OFT under the Competition Act 1998 in relation to the application of the Chapter I and II Prohibitions to the relevant industries. It also has power in regard to market investigation references (see below).

The institutional structure in competition law

As we have seen the CA 1998 abolished the Restrictive Practices Court but the central authority in the enforcement of the CA 1998 was the Director-General of Fair Trading supported by the Office of Fair Trading's staff. The decisions of the Director-General, e.g. that a Prohibition of the Act had been infringed and any penalty imposed were capable of appeal to the Competition Commission Appeals Tribunal and from there to the Court of Appeal on matters of law. The Director-General also intitiated monopoly inquiries. The CA also reconstituted the Monopolies and Mergers Commission as the Competition Commission.

The EA 2002 abolishes the office of Director of Fair Trading and his functions become those of the Office of Fair Trading. The office is under the governance of a chairman and four other members appointed by the Secretary of State for Trade and Industry. Appointment is for a period of five years. There is also a chief executive appointed by the Secretary of State for Trade and Industry after consultation with the chairman of the Commission. References in legislation to the Director-General are to be taken as a reference to the OFT. The Competition Commission becomes the Competition Appeals Tribunal.

Civil remedies of third parties to recover loss

As regards the remedies available to an organisation affected by an anti-competitive practice, it may complain to the Office of Fair Trading or if the infringement has a European Union dimension it may complain to the EU Commission in Brussels. Interim relief may be asked for in urgent cases. However, the final outcome will be an infringement decision and a large fine on the offending organisation. *This will not produce damages for the organisation if it has lost profits* because of the offending organisation's activities. Organisations wishing to pursue claims against the offender may go through the ordinary courts of law. Actions for damages and injunctions would seem to be available to those who have suffered as a result of infringements of competition law (see *Courage* v *Crehan* [2002] QB 507: a ruling of the ECJ). The House of Lords has said that damages are available 'in an appropriate case' but were not required to give damages in the event because they ruled that pub beer-ties were not in the

Crehan case contrary to Art 81 of the Treaty of Rome (see *Inntrepeneur Pub Company* v *Crehan* [2006] 4 All ER 465 at p 371).

Organisations suffering loss may wait for the OFT to investigate and make a finding of infringement. When the appeals process has been exhausted the organisation may rely on the infringement decision and this will be beneficial because there will be no need to produce evidence that there has been an infringement to the court again. Obviously matters of causation and quantification of damages may arise but the claim will be made easier. These are called 'piggyback' claims and have been introduced by the Enterprise Act 2002 inserting a new s 58A into the Competition Act 1998.

Finally, if there is difficulty in pleading before the ordinary courts because of their unfamiliarity with competition issues, the Enterprise Act 2002 has expanded the jurisdiction of the Competition Appeals Tribunal (a specialist tribunal) so that it can hear actions for damages following domestic competition infringement decisions by the OFT and the EU Commission in regard to infringements of EU law. These will be 'piggyback' claims.

Complaints

Under the provisions of the CA 1998 any person may complain to the OFT in regard to alleged breaches of the CA 1998 Prohibitions. These provisions are retained but the EA 2002 makes provision for designated consumer bodies to make 'super complaints' where there are market features that may be harming consumers to a significant extent. An example is provided by certain complaints made by the Consumers' Association asking for an investigation into practices in the private dentistry market. The complaint must relate to the market as a whole and not merely the conduct of individual businesses.

Relationship with EU law

The prohibitions set out in the Competition Act 1998 mirror more directly Arts 81 and 82 of the Treaty of Rome. The Articles are in general directly effective in the UK where there is in, say, the case of a restrictive practice 'an effect on trade between member states'. In the absence of such an effect, EU law is not applicable. Where the practice called into question affects only trade in the UK it is the UK Prohibitions of the CA 1998 that apply but even here UK law is required to be interpreted in line with European Law (see s 60, CA 1998). Thus UK courts will be expected to reach similar conclusions in UK cases to those reached in the European Court EXCEPT where there is a 'relevant difference'.

Other main changes and innovations of the Enterprise Act 2002

Part 4 provides for market investigations by the Competition Commission (CC). This regime is designed to inquire into markets where the structure of the market or the conduct of the suppliers or customers is harming competition. The OFT may make references as may other regulators such as the Rail Regulator.

Part 5 provides for rules of procedure in the Competition Commission.

Part 6 has been the cause of much controversy in that it sets up a new *criminal offence for people engaged in cartels* and gives the OFT investigatory powers. A person is liable to criminal prosecution if he or she dishonestly engages in prohibited cartel activities, e.g. price-fixing or limitation of supply or production. The OFT can issue no-action letters to those who although they have been involved in the cartel give the OFT information about it. A kind of reward for whistleblowing. The maximum term of imprisonment where trial is on indictment is five years. Instead or in addition to this term there may be an unlimited fine.

Part 7 importantly gives a new power to disqualify company directors for serious breaches of competition law.

Part 8 deals with procedures for making 'super-complaints'.

Part 9 is concerned with disclosure of information by public authorities; *Part 11* is concerned with the bringing into force and application of the Act. *Part 10* makes significant changes to insolvency law that are not relevant here.

The European Community approach to restrictive practices

Under Articles 81 and 82 of the Treaty of Rome all agreements between business organisations which operate to prevent or restrict competition in the Market are void.

Restrictive trading agreements and the Treaty of Rome generally

We have already considered the position under English domestic law with regard to restrictive trading agreements. Some consideration must now be given to the position under Community law.

Policy and source of law

The provisions of the Treaty, which have been part of our law since January 1973, are based, as UK law is, on the protection of the public interest. The basis of the competition policy is to be found in Arts 81 and 82 of the Treaty. These ban practices which distort competition between members of the Community (Art 81), and prohibit the abuse of a monopolistic position by an organisation within the Market (Art 82). There is an additional aim of raising living standards.

Application of Arts 81 and 82, Treaty of Rome

It is perhaps inappropriate in a non-specialist book of this nature to go through the many illustrative cases on the above articles of the Treaty of Rome which have been heard by the European Court of Justice. However, by way of illustration and to show the application of the Articles in English cases before English courts we can consider the following.

When doing so, it is worth noting that, following the judgment of the European Court in *BRT* v *SABAM* [1974] ECR 51 that Arts 85 (now 81) and 86 (now 82) have direct effect in the UK, our courts have shared responsibility for the enforcement of Community competition law, as the cases illustrate.

They also provide examples of situations that might come before UK courts under Prohibitions I and II of the 1998 Act. Now under the Competition Act 1998 UK courts are dealing with the Prohibitions set out in Chapters I and II of the 1998 Act and so are applying English law which is now substantially the same as the Treaty of Rome provisions. In addition, the interpretation of the prohibitions will follow the line taken by European courts so that there will be a fusion of rulings. (See the governing principles provision (above) of s 60 of the 1998 Act.)

Article 81

Of interest here is the case of *Cutsforth* v *Mansfield Inns* [1986] 1 All ER 577. C supplied coin-operated machines to 57 Humberside public houses owned by Northern County Breweries. M acquired Northern and requested all the tenants of the old Northern public houses to operate equipment supplied by M's list of nominated suppliers. M refused to put C on that list. This was held to be an infringement of Art 81 and an injunction was granted preventing M from interfering with C's agreements with the tenants of the 57 public houses and from taking any action to limit the freedom of those tenants to order machines from C. M was not infringing Art 82 because they were not in a dominant position in the market.

Article 82

An illustration of the use of Art 82 in an English court of law is provided by *Garden Cottage Foods Ltd* v *Milk Marketing Board* [1983] 2 All ER 770. Garden Cottage (the company) was a middle-man transferring butter from the Board to traders in the bulk market in Europe and the UK taking a cut of the price. In March 1982 following some packaging problems which the company appeared to have overcome, the Board refused to supply direct. It said that supplies must be obtained from one of four independent distributors nominated by the Board.

These distributors were the company's competitors. The company would have to pay more to them for its supplies than if it bought direct from the Board. Therefore, it could not compete on price, and would be forced out of business.

The company alleged that the Board was in breach of Art 82 of the Treaty of Rome. This provides: 'Any abuse by one or more undertakings of a dominant position when in the Common Market or in a substantial part of it, shall be prohibited as incompatible with the Common Market in so far as it may affect trade between Member States . . .'.

The Court of Appeal, and later the House of Lords (see *Garden Cottage Foods Ltd* v *Milk Marketing Board* above), decided that there had been a breach of Art 82.

As regards remedies the court was asked to grant an injunction restraining the Board from refusing to maintain normal business relations contrary to Art 82. The case was dealt with on that basis. However, the House of Lords was of the opinion that the remedy of damages was available for breach of the Treaty but there is still some uncertainty about this. UK courts have not as yet clarified precisely what remedies are available in this area.

It will be recalled that more recently the Court of Appeal decided in *Leyland Daf Ltd* v *Automotive Products* (1993) that Automotive was not in breach of Art 82 when it refused to supply goods to Leyland unless Leyland paid £758,955 which Leyland owed to Automotive (see also Chapter 13).

Enforcement by European Commission

The responsibility for enforcement of the Articles lies with the European Commission. The Commission is able to levy fines of up to 10 per cent of worldwide turnover as a penalty for infringement. The classic decision of the Commission was in the *Tetra Pak II* (1992 OJ L72/1) case where the Commission levied a fine of 75 m ECU (£52 m) on an organisation for abuses of Art 86 (now 82).

EC Merger Regulation

Mergers which potentially set up monopolistic undertakings are dealt with under UK competition rules where the merger has only a UK dimension. Where there is an impact on other European states, the rules of the EC must be taken into account.

Under the EC Merger Regulation, which came into force on 21 September 1990, 'concentrations' (mergers) involving a combined worldwide turnover of more than 5 billion ECU (£3.9 bn), and in which at least two of the parties also have a European turnover exceeding 250 million ECU (around £200 m), and not more than two-thirds of the aggregate Community-wide turnover of the undertakings concerned are in one and the same member state, fall to the European Commission for assessment as the *exclusive* competition authority. Such mergers must be formally notified to the EC Commission not more than one week after the conclusion of the agreement or the announcement of the public bid or the acquisition of a controlling interest (whichever of these is the earliest). Article 223 of the EC Treaty allows member states to take measures to protect essential security interests and remove such mergers from the Commission's jurisdiction. In recent times a proposed acquisition of British Aerospace was removed from the Commission's jurisdiction by the UK government.

Changes were made to the above regulations by Council Regulation No 1310/97, which came into force on 1 March 1998. The old system, as outlined above, remains in place but the notification requirements have been extended to a wider category of transactions and, in addition to the above thresholds, mergers must also be filed in Brussels if:

- the aggregate combined worldwide turnover of the undertakings concerned is more than 2.5 billion ECU;
- in each of at least three member states the combined aggregate turnover of all the undertakings involved is more than 100 million ECU;
- in each of at least three member states identified above, aggregate turnover of each of at least two of the undertakings involved is more than 25 million ECU; or
- the aggregate Community-wide turnover of each of at least two of the undertakings concerned is more than 100 million ECU. However, if each of the undertakings involved in the transaction achieves more than two-thirds of its aggregate Community-wide turnover in one and the same member state, the EC Merger Regulation will not apply and the parties will have to make any required filings under national law.

EU merger reform

EU merger rules are currently undergoing reform. Major features of the reform that will be by way of a new directive are:

- a proposal for companies to request a 'cooling off' period of two weeks before probes into mergers and takeovers. This extra time will enable companies to discuss and present concessions that could help to get mergers and acquisitions approved.
- The concept of 'dominance' is to be replaced by the US and UK test of 'substantial lessening of competition'.

17

DISCHARGE OF CONTRACT

In this chapter we shall consider the four methods by which a contract can be discharged or terminated.

The discharge of a contract means in general that the parties are freed from their mutual obligations. A contract may be discharged in four ways: *lawfully* by agreement, by performance or by frustration, and *unlawfully* by breach.

Discharge by agreement

Obviously, what has been created by agreement may be ended by agreement. Discharge by agreement may arise in the following ways.

Out of the original agreement

Thus the parties may have agreed at the outset that the contract should end automatically on the expiration of a fixed time. This would be the case, for example, with a lease of premises for a fixed term. Alternatively, the contract may contain a provision entitling one or both parties to terminate it if they wish. Thus a contract of employment can normally be brought to an end by giving reasonable notice. This area of the law is, of course, subject to statutory minimum periods of notice laid down by s 86 of the Employment Rights Act 1996. They are one week after one month's service, two weeks after two years' service and an additional week for each year of service up to 12 weeks after 12 years' service. Section 86 provides that the employee must, once he has been continuously employed for one month, give at least one week's notice to his employer to terminate his contract of employment. This is regardless of the number of years of service. Individual contracts may provide for longer periods of notice both by employer and employee.

Change of control clauses

When entering into a contractual arrangement many companies will have carried out research into the ability of the other party to carry through the contract in terms of finance and general stability. These matters can, of course, be badly affected by a change in the shareholder control of the other party particularly where the contract is a continuing one for, e.g., the supply of goods over a period. Therefore, the contract when made could be drafted to allow one party to terminate the agreement where the controlling shareholder (if any) in the other party is changed by a transfer of shares. Such a clause would not normally operate to automatically discharge the contract but it does give the party who may be adversely affected the right to terminate if he so desires. Such a clause *which operates as a discharge by agreement* is particularly useful if the new controlling shareholder is a corporate competitor.

Out of a new contract

If the contract is *executory*, i.e. a promise for a promise, and there has been no performance, the mutual release of the parties provides the consideration and is called bilateral discharge. The only difficulty here is in relation to the form of the release. The position is as follows:

(a) contracts which are required to be in writing under the Law of Property (Miscellaneous Provisions) Act 1989 (see further Chapter 11), i.e. contracts involving a sale or other disposition of land, can be wholly discharged (or rescinded) by an oral agreement but variation requires a written document containing the variation and signed by both parties. For example, a revised completion date on the sale of a property requires a written document containing the variation and signed by both parties (as decided in *McCausland* v *Duncan Lowrie* (1996) *The Times*, 18 June);

Under the provisions of the Electronic Communications Act 2000 the relevant signatures may be electronic signatures and will increasingly be so in the developed future.

(b) written contracts other than the above may be rescinded or varied by an oral agreement (see *MSAS Global Logistics Ltd* v *Power Packaging Inc* (2003) *The Times*, 25 June);

(c) deeds may be rescinded or varied orally;

(d) contracts required to be evidenced in writing, i.e. guarantees, may be totally discharged by oral agreement but variations must be in writing.

If the contract is executed as where it has been performed or partly performed by one party, then the other party who wishes to be released must provide consideration for that release unless it is effected by deed. This is referred to as unilateral discharge. In other words, the doctrine of accord and satisfaction applies. This matter has already been dealt with and is really an aspect of the law relating to consideration (see Chapter 10).

Discharge by performance generally

A contract may be discharged by performance, the discharge taking place when both parties have performed the obligations which the contract placed upon them. Whether performance must comply exactly with the terms of the contract depends on the following.

Construction of the contract as entire

According to the manner in which the court construes the meaning, the contract may be an entire contract. Here the manner of performance must be complete and exact.

Bolton v *Mahadeva*, 1972 – Where the contract is entire (**215**)

Entire agreement clauses

In addition to the possibility that the court will *construe* a contract as entire, the parties may seek to achieve an entire contract by the use of entire agreement clauses that are *set out expressly* in the contract. A typical clause has two parts as follows:

- an express statement that the written agreement (and often other documents that the agreement expressly refers to) contain the whole agreement of the parties regarding the transaction and supersedes all previous agreements;
- an acknowledgement by the parties that they have not relied on any representation that is not set out in the agreement.

These clauses are subject to interpretation by the courts in terms of what exactly they cover and, for example, the second limb is unlikely to exclude liability for fraudulent misrepresentation.

There is obviously some hardship when the entire contract rule is applied because sometimes work is done by A for B which B does not pay for and certain other approaches have been worked out by the judiciary as follows.

Substantial performance

If the court construes the contract in such a way that precise performance of every term by one party is not required in order to make the other party liable to some extent on it, the claimant may recover for work done, though the defendant may, of course, counterclaim for any defects in performance. In this connection it should be noted that in construing a contract to see whether a particular term must be fully performed or whether substantial performance is enough, the court will refer to the difference between conditions and warranties. A condition must be wholly performed whereas substantial performance of a warranty is often enough. (*Poussard* v *Spiers and Pond* (1876) and *Bettini* v *Gye* (1876) – see further Chapter 14.)

> *Hoenig* v *Isaacs*, 1952 – Where there is substantial performance (**216**)

Acceptance of partial performance

If, for example, S agrees to deliver three dozen bottles of brandy to B and delivers two dozen bottles only, then B may exercise his right to reject the whole consignment. But if he has accepted delivery of two dozen bottles he must pay for them at the contract rate (Sale of Goods Act 1979, s 30(1)). It is worth noting here that s 30(2A) of the Sale of Goods Act 1979 (inserted by the Sale and Supply of Goods Act 1994) provides that a commercial buyer as distinct from a consumer may not reject goods for the delivery of the wrong quantity where the seller can show that the excess or shortfall is so slight that it would be unreasonable to do so. In the above example the shortfall is not slight and a commercial buyer (as well as a consumer) could reject the goods.

However, the mere conferring of a benefit on one party by another is not enough; there must be evidence of acceptance of that benefit by the party upon whom it was conferred. The acceptance must arise following a genuine choice.

17

> *Sumpter* v *Hedges*, 1898 – Has partial performance been accepted? (**217**)

Full performance prevented by the promisee

Here the party who cannot further perform his part of the contract may bring an action on a *quantum meruit* (a claim for a payment for work done) against the party in default for the value of work done up to the time when further performance was prevented.

> *De Barnardy* v *Harding*, 1853 – Where full performance is prevented (**218**)

Time of performance

Section 41 of the Law of Property Act 1925 provides that stipulations as to the time of performance in a contract are not construed to be of the essence of the contract and therefore need not be strictly complied with, unless equity would have regarded them as such. There are the following exceptional situations in which time was of the essence even in equity.

(a) The contract fixes a date and makes performance on that date a condition.

(b) The circumstances indicate that the contract should be performed at the agreed time. These cases are:

- *contracts for the sale of land or a business* because uncertainties as to ownership of land have traditionally been regarded as undesirable and uncertainties as to the ownership of a business can affect its goodwill;
- *commercial contracts* such as a sale of goods;
- *contracts for the purchase of shares* because share values are often volatile, which could affect the price at which it was agreed to sell them.

(c) Where the time of performance was not originally of the essence of the contract or has been waived but one party has been guilty of undue delay, the other party may give notice requiring that the contract be performed within a reasonable time.

> *Bowes* v *Shand*, 1877 – Sale of goods: time is of the essence (**219**)
> *Chas Rickards Ltd* v *Oppenhaim*, 1950 – Waiver of time of delivery (**220**)

Tender

With regard to the manner of performance, the question of what is good tender arises. Tender is an offer of performance which complies with the terms of the contract. If goods are tendered by the seller and refused by the buyer the seller is freed from liability, given that the goods are in accordance with the contract as to quantity and quality. As regards the payment of money, this must comply with the following rules.

(a) It must be in accordance with the rules relating to legal tender. By s 1(2) and (6) of the Currency and Bank Notes Act 1954 a tender of a note or notes of the Bank of England expressed to be payable to bearer on demand is legal tender for the payment of any amount. A tender of notes of a bank other than the Bank of England is not legal tender, though the creditor may waive his objection to the tender if he wishes. As regards coins, s 2 of the Coinage Act 1971, as amended by the Currency Act 1983, provides that coins made by the Mint shall be legal tender as follows:

(i)   Certain gold coins for payment of any amount. We are referring here to the gold sovereign. These are legal tender if struck after 1837. Even though the sovereign contains just under $\frac{1}{4}$ ounce of gold it is valid only for £1 although it is worth much more as a collector's item.

(ii) Coins of cupro-nickel or silver of denominations of more than 10 pence, i.e. 20p, 50p, £1 and £2 coins are legal tender for payment of any amount not exceeding £10.

(iii) Coins of cupro-nickel or silver of denominations of not more than 10 pence (in practice, the 5p and 10p coins) are legal tender for payment of any amount not exceeding £5.

(iv) Coins of bronze, i.e. the 2p and 1p coins, are legal tender for payment of any amount not exceeding 20 pence.

There is power of proclamation to call in coins which then cease to be legal tender or to make other coins legal tender.

(b) There must be no request for change.

(c) Tender by cheque or other negotiable instrument or by charge card or credit card is not good tender unless the creditor does not object. It should be noted that if a proper tender of money is refused the debt is not discharged, but if the money is paid into court the debtor has a good defence to an action by his creditor and the debt does not bear interest.

In connection with payment by credit card or charge card, the consumer normally discharges his obligation to the seller by payment in this way. If the card company cannot pay the seller as where that company is insolvent, the seller has no redress against the consumer subject always to the terms of the contract (*Re Charge Card Services* [1988] 3 All ER 702).

Discharge by receipt

A method of proving payment is by a receipt signed by or on behalf of the person paid. Proof may, however, be given orally and a court may be satisfied with this. A receipt is not conclusive evidence of payment and oral evidence is acceptable to the court to prove, e.g., that it was given in circumstances of fraud. In addition, a receipt given in 'full discharge' does not release the person paid unless there is 'accord and satisfaction'. Receipts are not normally given in business today since the passing of s 3 of the Cheques Act 1957 which provides that 'an unendorsed cheque which appears to have been paid by the bank on whom it is drawn is evidence of the receipt by the payee of the sum payable by the cheque'. This, again, is not conclusive evidence and, since banks do not return used cheques with monthly statements these days, evidence of payment through the clearing system would have to be sought from the bank, e.g. by a certified copy of the cheque. The receipt is thus in many ways more straightforward.

Appropriation of payments

In connection with performance, it is important to consider the rules governing appropriation of payments. Certain debts are barred by the Limitation Act 1980 and money which has been owed for six years under a simple contract or 12 years under a specialty contract without acknowledgement may not be recoverable by an action in the courts. Where a debtor owes several debts to the same creditor and makes a payment which does not cover them all, there are rules governing how the money should be appropriated. These are as follows.

(a) The debtor can appropriate either expressly by saying which debt he is paying or by implication as where he owed £50 and £20 and sends £20.

(b) If the debtor does not appropriate, the creditor can appropriate to any debt, *even to one which is statute-barred* (see further Chapter 18). However, if the statute-barred debt is £50 and the creditor appropriates a payment of £25 to it, the balance of the debt is not revived and cannot be sued for (*Mills* v *Fowkes* (1839) 5 Bing NC 455).

(c) Where there is a current account, there is a presumption that the creditor has not appropriated payments to him to any particular item. The major example is a bank current account. Appropriation here is on a chronological basis, i.e. the first item on the debit side of the account is reduced by the first item on the credit side: a first in first out principle. This follows from the rule in *Clayton's* Case (1816) 1 Mer 572.

Deeley v *Lloyds Bank*, 1912 – *Clayton*'s Case applied (**221**)

Discharge by frustration generally

If an agreement is impossible of performance from the outset, it is void at common law (*Couturier* v *Hastie* (1856) – see Chapter 12). This is also at the root of s 6 of the Sale of Goods Act 1979 which provides that where there is a contract for the sale of specific goods and the goods, without the knowledge of the seller, have perished at the time when the contract is made, it is void. However, some contracts are possible of performance when they are made but it subsequently becomes impossible to carry them out in whole or in part and they are then referred to as frustrated.

The judges developed the doctrine of discharge by frustration, which applies, as the House of Lords decided in *Davis Contractors Ltd* v *Fareham UDC* [1956] 2 All ER 145, in the restricted set of circumstances where there has been such a change in the significance of the obligation that the thing undertaken would, if performed, be a different thing than that contracted for. The subject is considered under the following heads.

Contracts for personal service

Such a contract is discharged by the death of the person who was to perform it; thus if A agrees to play the piano at a concert and dies before the date on which the performance is due, his personal representatives will not be expected to go along and play in his stead.

Incapacity of a person who has to perform a contract may discharge it. However, temporary incapacity is not enough unless it affects the contract in a fundamental manner (*Poussard* v *Spiers and Pond* (1876) – see Chapter 14).

If a contract of employment has been brought to an end by reason of frustration, the parties cannot agree afterwards that the contract continues to exist. Thus, in *G F Sharp & Co Ltd* v *McMillan* [1998] IRLR 632 a joiner lost the use of his left hand and could never work for the employer as a joiner again. Nevertheless, the parties agreed to keep him 'on the books' so that he could get access to greater pension benefits. The Employment Appeal Tribunal ruled that this did not amount to a continuation of his contract of employment. The contract had been terminated by his injury. In consequence, he was not entitled to notice from the employer or a payment in lieu of notice.

The doctrine of frustration will usually only apply where there is no fault by either party. Where performance of the contract is prevented by the fault of one party, that party is in breach of contract and that is the proper approach to the problem.

Storey v *Fulham Steel Works*, 1907 – Illness did not frustrate the contract (**222**)

Norris v *Southampton City Council*, 1982 – Frustration and breach in a personal service contract (**223**)

Government interference

In times of national emergency the government may often requisition property or goods in the national interest. This will have the effect of frustrating relevant contracts.

Re Shipton, Anderson & Co and Harrison Bros' Arbitration, 1915 – Frustration by government action (**224**)

17

Destruction of the subject matter of the contract

Physical destruction of the subject matter of the contract operates to frustrate it.

Taylor v *Caldwell*, 1863 – A fire at a concert hall (**225**)

Non-occurrence of an event

Where the taking place of an event is vital to the contract, its cancellation or postponement will, in the absence of a contrary provision, frustrate it. However, if the main purpose of the contract can still be achieved, there will be no frustration.

Krell v *Henry*, 1903 – A coronation is cancelled (**226**)

Herne Bay Steamboat Co v *Hutton*, 1903 – Cancellation of a naval review (**227**)

Commercial purpose defeated

Physical destruction of the subject matter is not essential to frustration. It extends to situations where although there is no physical destruction the essential commercial purpose of the contract cannot be achieved – a rule referred to as 'frustration of the common venture'.

> *Jackson* v *Union Marine Insurance Co*, 1874 – A ship is stranded (**228**)

Situations in which the doctrine does not apply

It is now necessary to consider the three situations where the application of the rules relating to frustration are limited.

Express provision in the contract

In such a case the provisions inserted into the contract by the parties will apply. Thus in some of the coronation seat cases, e.g. *Clark* v *Lindsay* (1903) 19 TLR 202, the contracts provided that if the procession was postponed the tickets would be valid for the day on which it did take place or that the parties should get their money back with a deduction for the room owner's expenses. These took effect to the exclusion of the principles of frustration.

Self-induced events

The rules relating to frustration do not apply where the event making the contract impossible to perform was the voluntary act of one of the parties.

Leases and contracts for the sale of land

Judicial opinion has been divided as to whether leases and contracts for the sale of land can be frustrated since these create an interest in land which survives any frustrating event.

> *Maritime National Fish Ltd* v *Ocean Trawlers Ltd*, 1935 – Effect of a self-induced frustration (**229**)
>
> *Cricklewood Property and Investment Trust Ltd* v *Leighton's Investment Trust Ltd*, 1945 – Frustration where a title to land is acquired (**230**)

The Law Reform (Frustrated Contracts) Act 1943

This important statute has laid down the conditions which will govern the rights and duties of the parties when certain contracts are frustrated.

Before 1943

The common-law doctrine of frustration did not make the contract void *ab initio* (from the beginning) but only from the time when the frustrating event occurred. Thus money due and not paid could be claimed and money paid before the frustrating event was not recoverable.

Chandler v *Webster*, 1904 – A startling application of the common-law rules (**231**)

After 1943

The position under the Act is as follows:

(a) Money paid is recoverable.

(b) Money payable ceases to be payable.

(c) The parties may recover expenses in connection with the contract or retain the relevant sum from money received, if any.

(d) It is also possible to recover on a *quantum meruit* (a reasonable sum of money as compensation) where one of the parties has carried out acts of part performance before frustration, provided the other party has received what the Act calls 'a valuable benefit' under the contract other than a money payment 'before the time of discharge', i.e. to the time of the frustrating event. There are difficulties in regard to the expression 'valuable benefit', particularly where the work is destroyed, since the Act is not clear as to whether a sum can be recovered by the person conferring the benefit where there has been destruction of his work. In *Parsons Bros* v *Shea* (1965) 53 DLR (2d) 86 a Newfoundland court, in dealing with an identical provision under the Newfoundland Frustrated Contracts Act 1956, held that the carrying out of modifications to a heating system in a hotel subsequently destroyed by fire could not be regarded as conferring any 'benefits' upon the owner. However, in *BP Exploration Co (Libya)* v *Hunt (No 2)* [1982] 1 All ER 125 the claimants were engaged to develop an oil field on the defendant's land and were to be paid by oil from the wells. After the wells came on stream but before BP had received all the oil which the development contract provided they should have, the wells were nationalised by the Libyan government which gave the defendant some compensation. The contract was obviously frustrated but Goff, J, who was later affirmed by the Court of Appeal and the House of Lords, gave BP a sum of 35 million dollars as representing the 'benefit' received by the defendant prior to the frustrating event.

Clearly, here there was a surviving benefit conferred before the frustrating event and at the time of it, i.e. the value of the oil already removed by Mr Hunt before nationalisation and, of course, his claim for compensation against the Libyan government. None of these things would have been available to him before BP's discovery and extraction of oil on his land. Since the benefit conferred up to the time of frustration clearly survived the frustrating event, i.e. the nationalisation, the case does not resolve the problems posed by *Parsons Bros* v *Shea* (above) where the benefit did not survive the frustrating event.

However, it is the better view that there is no need for the benefit conferred to survive the frustrating event. The court can make an award provided benefit was once conferred. The fact that it did not survive the frustrating event can be taken into account by the court when assessing (and probably reducing) how much it gives to the claimant.

The *force majeure* clause

It is unwise in business to rely on the court to declare that a contract is frustrated. If the court rules that there is no frustration, the defendant may be required to pay damages for breach to the other party. It is common, therefore, to include in business contracts what are known as *force majeure* clauses. The expression means 'irresistible compulsion or coercion' and a typical clause will contain events likely to impede performance such as strikes, accidents to machinery,

17

government restrictions in terms of licences, wars, epidemics and so on. The contract will go on to provide that the parties may suspend the contract or cancel it should one or more of the events happen and there will be no frustration. Why? – because as Lord Denning said in *The Eugenia* [1964] 1 All ER 161, 'The contract must govern'.

Discharge by breach

This occurs where a party to a contract fails to discharge it lawfully but instead breaches one or more of the terms of the contract. There are several forms of breach of contract as follows:

(*a*) Failure to perform the contract is the most usual form as where a seller fails to deliver the goods by the appointed time or where, although delivered, they are not up to standard as to quality or quantity.

(*b*) Express repudiation which arises where one party states that he will not perform his part of the contract.

(*c*) Some action by one party which makes performance impossible.

Any breach which takes place before the time for performance has arrived is called an *anticipatory breach*. Thus the situations described in (*b*) and (*c*) above are anticipatory breaches.

Where the breach is anticipatory the aggrieved party may sue at once for damages. Alternatively, he can wait for the time for performance to arrive and see whether the other party is prepared at that time to carry out the contract.

> *Hochster* v *De la Tour*, 1853 – An express repudiation (**232**)
>
> *Omnium D'Enterprises and Others* v *Sutherland*, 1919 – An implied repudiation (**233**)
>
> *White and Carter (Councils) Ltd* v *McGregor*, 1961 – Anticipatory breach: where a party carries on with the contract (**234**)

Anticipatory breach and supervening events

It may be dangerous to wait for the time of performance to arrive since the contract may, for example, have become illegal, thus providing the party who was in anticipatory breach with a good defence to an action.

> *Avery* v *Bowden*, 1855 – Anticipatory breach: where the second breach was excused (**235**)

Effect of breach on contract

Not every breach entitles the innocent party to treat the contract as discharged. It must be shown that the breach affects a vital part of the contract, i.e. that it is a breach of condition rather than a breach of warranty (contrast *Poussard* v *Spiers and Pond* (see Chapter 14) with *Bettini* v *Gye* (see Chapter 14)) or that the other party has no intention of performing his contract as in *Hochster* v *De la Tour* (see above) or has put himself in a position where it is impossible to perform it as in *Omnium D'Enterprises and Others* v *Sutherland* (see above).

Other matters relevant to breach

Two further points arise in connection with breach of contract. The first is that the concept of contributory negligence does not apply. In *Basildon District Council* v *J E Lesser* (*Properties*) *Ltd* [1985] 1 All ER 20 the claimant sued for breach of contract in regard to the building of dwellings which had become unfit for habitation without repair. There was a defence that the damages payable should be reduced on the basis that the council's officers were guilty of contributory negligence. It was said that they should have noticed the lack of appropriate depth in foundations on seeing the building contractors' original drawings. It was decided by the High Court that the defence of contributory negligence did not apply in contract but only in tort.

It should be noted, however, that the obligation in the above case was entirely contractual. If the claimant could have sued, either in contract or in tort, as where the damage arises from a breach of contract and a tort, then even if the injured party decides to sue for breach of contract only the damages can be reduced if he is contributorily negligent (see *Forsikrings Vesta* v *Butcher* [1988] 2 All ER 43).

The Law Commission in its report made in 1993 entitled *Contributory Negligence as a Defence in Contract* recommends that the availability of apportionment of damages for breach of contract should be extended from the field of tort to cases where the claimant who complains of breach of contract has contributed to his own loss.

Second, the Drug Trafficking Act 1994, s 50 brought in what is called a 'laundering' offence under which anyone knowingly assisting with the retention, control or investment of drug-trafficking proceeds could be liable to a term of imprisonment. Banks, building societies, accountants, solicitors and other advisers are given protection by the Act if they disclose their suspicions about their client's finances if these seem to be connected with drug trafficking. However, the Act ensures that they cannot be sued for breach of contract if they pass on to the appropriate authorities their suspicions that any funds or investments may be connected with drug trafficking. Section 50 is repealed and replaced by provisions in the Proceeds of Crime Act 2002.

17

Impact of the introduction of the euro

The immediate problem to be looked at is that of ensuring that commercial contracts affected by the arrival of the euro in much of the EU on 1 January 1999 do not operate where required beyond that date. The main reason for this will be that, as we have seen, a wide variety of contracts governed by English law provide that where a party is unable to perform his contractual obligations through factors beyond his control (such as in this case the abolition (eventually) of the currency in which he is required to tender payment), the contract is automatically discharged by frustration – a concept which has no direct equivalent in the rest of the EU, where law is based on Roman Law – or under a *force majeure* clause. The Maastricht Treaty deals with this by providing that, in the absence of an express contrary intention by the parties, the introduction of the euro will not:

- alter any term of the contract;
- discharge or excuse performance under any contract; or
- on its own give any party the right unilaterally to alter or terminate any contract.

The parties can, by expressing a contrary intention, agree that the introduction of the euro will end the original contractual intention.

Nevertheless, for contracts continuing beyond 1 January 1999, there will have to be some renegotiation to establish the equivalence of value between the originally contracted currency and the euro.

18

REMEDIES AND LIMITATION OF ACTIONS

In this chapter we shall consider the various remedies which exist both in common law and equity to deal with losses arising from contractual relationships and the rules which govern the recovery of money compensation through damages together with the time limits which are placed on the bringing of claims.

Damages generally

This is the main remedy for breach of contract and the rules of law relating to an award of damages are considered below.

Liquidated damages

In some cases the parties foreseeing the possibility of breach may attempt in the contract to assess in advance the damages payable. Such a provision for *liquidated* damages will be valid if it is a genuine pre-estimate of loss and not a penalty inserted to make it a bad bargain for the defendant not to carry out his part of the contract. The court will not enforce a penalty but will award damages on normal principles used in the assessment of unliquidated damages (see below).

Certain tests are applied in order to decide whether or not the provision is a penalty. Obviously, extravagant sums are generally in the nature of penalties. Where the contractual obligation lying on the defendant is to pay money, then any provision in the contract which requires the payment of a larger sum on default of payment is a penalty because the damage can be accurately assessed. Where the sum provided for in the contract is payable on the occurrence of any one of several events, it is probably a penalty for it is unlikely that each event can produce the same loss. If the sum agreed by the parties is regarded as liquidated damages, it will be enforced even though the actual loss is greater or smaller.

Ford Motor Co (England) Ltd v Armstrong, 1915 – No genuine pre-estimate of loss (**236**)

Cellulose Acetate Silk Co Ltd v Widnes Foundry Ltd, 1933 – Liquidated damages where the loss is smaller (**237**)

Unliquidated damages

Assessment

Unliquidated damages are intended as compensation for the claimant's loss and not as punishment for the defendant. Thus where no loss has been suffered, as where a seller fails to deliver the goods but the buyer is able to purchase elsewhere at no extra cost, the court will award *nominal* damages, i.e. an award of a small sum, e.g. £2, to reflect the view that any loss or damage is purely technical.

Exemplary or punitive damages which exceed the actual loss suffered by an amount intended to punish the offending party are not awarded for breach of contract. The intention is that the claimant should be placed in the same situation as if the contract had been performed.

Thus in an action by an employee for wrongful dismissal, the court will base its award on 'net' wages, i.e. after deduction of income tax and national insurance contributions. An award based on 'gross' wages or salary would make the employee better off than if the contract had continued.

> *Beach* v *Reed Corrugated Cases Ltd*, 1956 – Damages are compensatory (**238**)

Type of loss recoverable

Damages can include compensation for financial loss, personal injury and damage to property. Also there may be included a sum by way of compensation for disappointment, vexation and mental distress.

> *Jarvis* v *Swans Tours Ltd*, 1973 – Damages for mental distress (**239**)

Remoteness

Apart from the question of *assessment*, the matter of *remoteness of damage* arises. The consequence of a breach of contract may be far reaching and the law must draw a line somewhere and say that damages incurred beyond a certain limit are too remote to be recovered. Damages in contract must therefore be proximate.

The modern law regarding remoteness of damage in contract is based upon the case of *Hadley* v *Baxendale* (see below), as further explained in *The Heron II* (see below). These cases are authority for the statement that damages in contract will be too remote to be recovered unless they arise naturally, i.e. in the usual course of things, or if they do not arise naturally they are such that the defendant, as a reasonable man, *ought* to have had them in contemplation as likely to result. Damage which does not arise naturally and which would not have been in the contemplation of the reasonable man can only be recovered if the defendant was made aware of it *and* agreed to accept the risk of the loss.

> *Hadley* v *Baxendale*, 1854 – Where damages are too remote (**240**)
>
> *The Heron II*, 1967 – Where damages are in contemplation (**241**)
>
> *Horne* v *Midland Railway Co*, 1873 – Has the defendant agreed to be liable for the loss? (**242**)
>
> *Victoria Laundry Ltd* v *Newman Industries Ltd*, 1949 – Where loss arises naturally from the breach (**243**)

Mitigation of loss

The injured party has a duty to *mitigate* or minimise his loss, i.e. he must take all reasonable steps to reduce it. Thus a seller whose goods are rejected must attempt to get the best price for them elsewhere and the buyer of goods which are not delivered must attempt to buy as cheaply as possible elsewhere. Loss arising from failure to take such steps cannot be recovered.

> *Brace* v *Calder*, 1895 – There must be a mitigation of loss (**244**)

However, the claimant is not under a duty to mitigate his loss before there has been a breach of contract which the claimant has accepted as a breach. No doubt this is logical but it can produce startling results (see *White and Carter (Councils) Ltd* v *McGregor* (1961), Chapter 17). More recently the requirement of a 'legitimate interest' in keeping the contract going has made the position more equitable (see, for example, *Clea Shipping* (1984)).

Provisional damages for personal injury

The Administration of Justice Act 1982, s 6 makes provision for a court to award provisional damages for contractual claims for personal injury. Thus, in an action for a fracture to the hip caused to a passenger in an accident involving a negligently driven bus, the court can make an order for damages payable at once for the fracture and an award of provisional damages in case in the future chronic arthritis affects the injured passenger. If it does, but not otherwise, the provisional damages may also be recovered without another visit to the court to prove the damage.

Damages Act 1996

18

Section 3 of the Damages Act 1996 provides that where a claimant dies of his injuries after receiving a provisional award his dependants will not be prevented from claiming as *dependants* for loss of dependency. This is a separate claim made by the executors of the deceased on behalf of all those who were dependent on him, e.g. a wife. The claim will extend only to losses not covered by the original award. Since there is also a potential claim by the deceased's estate in such a case, the Act makes clear that dependants' claims will be preferred, if there are any, thus preventing double recovery by the dependants and then by the estate.

Structured settlements

In more recent times the courts have set up a system of structured settlements. The settlement of a damages claim is by means of a permanent income instead of a single lump sum. These settlements are confined to personal injury cases and are particularly suitable where the injuries are serious and the claimant is a young person.

An example is provided by the case of *Kelly* v *Dawes* (1990) *The Times*, 27 September. Catherine Kelly, a young nurse, was a passenger in a car which was involved in an accident by reason of the negligence of the defendant who died in the crash. She was awarded, in effect against the insurance company involved, a structured settlement with monthly payments guaranteed for her lifetime or for 10 years, whichever proved the longer, and inflation proofed. Because of a favourable tax treatment by the Inland Revenue, the payments were not subject to income tax. It follows that claimants who receive structured settlements do not have to concern themselves with investment or inflation, and if they live longer than expected the money will still be there. They are also protected against their own extravagance and against payment of tax.

These settlements are most likely to be found in actions for tort, e.g. negligence in terms of road accidents. Nevertheless, there are situations where the claimant has a claim in contract and tort as where A is a passenger on a bus and is injured by an accident caused by the driver's negligence. The claim here is for the tort of negligence and breach of contract for which one award is made, but the structured settlement rules are applied (or may be) to the contract claim as well as the tort claim.

Interest on debt and damages

Under the provisions of the Administration of Justice Act 1982, s 15 and Sch 1, which inserted s 35A of the Supreme Court Act 1981 and s 69 of the County Courts Act 1984, the court has power to award interest on debt or damages at the end of the trial or where judgment is obtained in default, i.e. where there is no defence and no trial. Interest may also be awarded where the defendant settles after service of claim form but before judgment. Interest is not available where a person settles *before* service of claim form no matter how long he has kept the other party waiting. High Court judgments carry interest at a rate that is fixed from time to time by statutory instrument. Since 1 April 1993 the rate has been fixed at 8 per cent per annum (Judgment Debts (Rate of Interest) Order 1993 (SI 1993/564)).

County court judgments of £5,000 or more also carry interest and once again the rate is 8 per cent per annum. County court judgments under £5,000 do not carry any interest unless the debt attracts contractual or statutory interest under the Late Payment of Commercial Debts (Interest) Act 1998 (see below).

Recovery of debt

Where one party has performed his part of the contract but the other has failed to pay, e.g. following a supply of goods complying with the contract requirements, the claim of the supplier is for *debt* rather than *damages*. The main point to be considered here is the possibility of recovering interest on unpaid debts. The topic may be considered by looking at the business procedure which involves the use of a default interest clause in the contract and then by looking at statutory provisions.

Default interest clauses

A default interest clause can be included in support of any obligation to pay a sum of money by a given date. A rate of 3 or 4 per cent over the Bank of England base rate is common and this is payable from the stated due date until payment. The court would enforce such a clause, but any attempt to make an interest charge except during the period for which the debt was due may very well be unenforceable as a penalty.

Late payment of commercial debts legislation

The Late Payment of Commercial Debts (Interest) Act 1998 gives creditors a statutory right to claim interest from debtors on debts relating to commercial contracts for the supply of goods and services. The Act was brought into force by stages. However, on 7 August 2002 the final phase of the implementation was made and the Act now applies to ALL businesses and public sector bodies.

Application of the Act

The Act applies to contracts for the supply of goods or services where the purchaser and the supplier are acting in the course of a business. It does not apply to consumer credit agreements or to any contract that operates by way of a security, for instance a mortgage, pledge, or charge.

What is the rate of interest?

Interest is calculated at 8 per cent above the Bank of England base rate. To simplify matters and avoid an ever changing rate, interest is calculated at 8 per cent above the base rate in force on 30 June for interest that starts to run between 1 July and 31 December or the base rate in force on 31 December for interest that starts to run between 1 January and 30 June. Thus where the base rate is, say, 4 per cent on the applicable date, the late payment rate will be 12 per cent. The Act gives suppliers an entitlement to simple interest only and not compound interest, i.e. interest on interest. From 1 January 2006, and in view of the then Bank of England base rate, the rate is 12.5 per cent.

From when does interest run?

Interest starts to run from the day after the due date for payment or, where no such date has been agreed, when 30 days have elapsed from the delivery of the goods or the carrying out of the services or notice being given to the purchaser of the amount of the debt, whichever is the later.

Recovering the costs

In addition to interest, a business can claim reasonable debt recovery costs, but only where the contract concerned was made on or after 7 August 2002.

The costs that are allowed are as follows:

- debt of less than £1,000: recovery costs £40;
- debt between £1,000 and £10,000: recovery costs £70;
- debt of more than £10,000: recovery costs £100.

A major problem in enforcement

A major problem in terms of the enforcement of the Act by small and medium enterprises against the larger organisations and public authorities is the fear that enforcement will lead to the loss of contracts. Some assistance is given by the Late Payment of Commercial Debts Regulations 2002 (SI 2002/1674). The regulations give a right to trade and other bodies representing SMEs to challenge on their behalf express contractual terms in regard to payment and interest that are unfair to SMEs (see below).

Express terms for payment of interest

The Act does not rule out contractual terms that have been agreed by the parties for payment of interest but unless they are 'substantial' the court will regard them as void and apply the provisions of the Act. It does not follow that because the contractual provision is less generous than the Act that it will be regarded as void but, among other things, the strength of the bargaining power of the parties is relevant. This may render void a less generous clause imposed on a small or medium-sized enterprise by a conglomerate. However, the conglomerate's less generous clause may be binding where the supplier has received an inducement to accept the term, such as a longer-term contract to supply goods or services.

EU developments

EU industry ministers have reached agreement on a European-wide Directive to combat late payment of debt. Progress is now being made towards the adoption of the Directive. The Directive entitled *Combating the Late Payment of Commercial Debt* is to provide interest at 6 per cent above the Bank of England or European Central Bank base rate in the event of late payment. The parties will retain freedom of contract to decide when debts should be paid, but interest would start to accrue 30 days after the date for payment. Member states may introduce provisions more favourable to creditors. *The advantage of the Directive will be that small and medium entities in the UK can be sure of rights similar to those in the UK wherever they do business in the EU.*

Equitable remedies

Damages are the common law remedy for breach of contract. However, in some situations equity will provide more suitable remedies and these will now be considered.

A decree for specific performance

This is an equitable remedy which is sometimes granted for breach of contract, where damages are not an adequate remedy or where specific performance is regarded by the court as a more appropriate remedy (see *Beswick* v *Beswick* (1967), Chapter 10). It is an order of the court and constitutes an express instruction to a party to a contract to perform the actual obligations which he undertook in a contract. For all practical purposes the remedy is now confined to contracts for the sale of land, though it may be a more appropriate remedy in the case of a contract to pay an annuity because the exact value of the annuity will depend on how long the annuitant lives and this cannot be known at the time of the breach (see *Beswick* v *Beswick* (1967), Chapter 10). It is not normally granted in the case of contracts for the sale of goods because other goods of a similar kind can be purchased and the difference assessed in money damages. In addition, it should be noted that specific performance will not be granted if the court cannot adequately supervise its enforcement. Thus contracts of a personal nature, such as employment, which rely on a continuing relationship between the parties, will not generally be specifically enforced because the court cannot supervise performance on the day-to-day basis which would be necessary. However, if constant supervision by the court is not required, a decree of specific performance may be made of a personal service undertaking. Thus in *Posner* v *Scott-Lewis* [1986] 3 All ER 51 Mervyn-Davies, J decided that the tenants of a block of flats could enforce by specific performance an undertaking in their leases that the defendant landlords would employ a resident porter to keep the communal areas clear. The court had only to ensure that the appointment was made. The claimants were not asking the court to supervise the porter's day-to-day work. Furthermore, specific performance will not be awarded either to or against a minor because a minor's contracts cannot in general be enforced against him and those which can, i.e. beneficial contracts (see Chapter 11), are in the nature of contracts of personal service. Equity requires equality or mutuality as regards its remedies and this does not exist in the case of minors' contracts.

An injunction

This is an order of the court used in this context to direct a person not to break his contract. The remedy has a somewhat restricted application in the law of contract and will be granted to enforce a negative stipulation in a contract where damages would not be an adequate remedy. Being an equitable remedy it is only ordered on the same principles as specific performance, so that it will not normally be awarded where damages are an adequate remedy (but see *Garden Cottage Foods Ltd v Milk Marketing Board* (1983), Chapter 16). Its main use in the contractual situation has been as an indirect means of enforcing a contract for personal services but a clear negative stipulation is required. The court will not imply one.

> *Warner Brothers Pictures Incorporated v Nelson*, 1937 – Enforcing a negative stipulation (**245**)
>
> *Whitwood Chemical Co v Hardman*, 1891 – A negative stipulation will not be implied (**246**)

Freezing injunction

This remedy, which can be of assistance to a party suing for breach of contract, has developed considerably over recent times. It was formerly known as a Mareva injunction but is now called a freezing injunction under the Civil Procedure Rules 1998 that followed the Woolf reforms of civil procedure. In general terms a court will not grant an injunction to prevent a person disposing of his property merely to assist a person suing, for example, for a debt, to recover his money. However, the freezing injunction is an exception to that general rule and is granted to restrict removal of assets outside the jurisdiction, often by a foreign defendant, where this is a real and serious possibility. The injunction took its original name from the second case in which it was awarded, i.e. *Mareva Compania Naviera SA v International Bulk Carriers SA* [1975] 2 Lloyd's Rep 509. However, the power of the High Court to issue a freezing injunction is now recognised by s 37 of the Supreme Court Act 1981 which makes it clear that the power applies to domestic as well as foreign defendants, whether the latter are residents in this country or not (*The Siskina* [1977] 3 All ER 803). However, the power is only to freeze assets within the jurisdiction of the English court. It cannot be used to freeze assets abroad. An order of a local court must be obtained (*Babanaft International Co SA v Bassante* (1988) 138 NLJ 203). It is, however, a valuable addition to existing contractual remedies, particularly when business is now so often conducted on an international scale.

A search order

This is an order that may be issued under the Civil Procedure Rules 1998. It permits the representatives of a claimant to enter the defendant's premises to inspect and remove vital material or evidence where it is contemplated that there is a risk that the defendant might destroy or otherwise dispose of them. It was previously referred to as an Anton Pillar order from the title of the case in which it was first granted.

Rescission

This is a further equitable remedy for breach of contract. The rule is the same when the remedy is used for breach as it is when it is used for misrepresentation. If the contract cannot be

18

completely rescinded, it cannot be rescinded at all; it must be possible to restore the status quo. All part payments must be returned. In this connection the fact that a claimant has rescinded the contract does not prevent that claimant from bringing an action for debts owed under the contract prior to rescission. These are not regarded as abandoned by the order of rescission (see *Stocznia Gdanska SA* v *Latvian Shipping Co* [1998] 1 All ER 883).

Refusal of further performance: a self-help remedy

If the person suffering from the breach desires merely to get rid of his obligations under the contract, he may refuse any further performance on his part and set up the breach as a defence if the party who has committed the breach attempts to enforce the contract against him.

Claims for restitution: quasi-contract

Quasi-contract is based on the idea that a person should not obtain a benefit or an unjust enrichment as against another merely because there is no obligation in contract or another established branch of the law which will operate to make him account for it. The law may in these circumstances provide a remedy by implying a fictitious promise to account for the benefit or enrichment. This promise then forms the basis of an action in quasi-contract.

In practice the following two areas are important.

Claims on a *quantum meruit*

This remedy means that the claimant will be awarded as much as he has earned or deserved. The remedy can be used contractually or quasi-contractually as follows.

(a) Contractually. Here it may be used to recover a reasonable price or remuneration where there is a contract for the supply of goods or services but the parties have not fixed any precise sum to be paid. This area is also covered by statute law in the case of a sale of goods by s 8 of the Sale of Goods Act 1979, and in the case of a supply of goods, e.g. a new distributor in a car repair contract, or the mere supply of a service by s 15 of the Supply of Goods and Services Act 1982.

(b) Quasi-contractually. A claim on this basis may be made where, for example, work has been done under a void contract. The claimant cannot recover damages for breach because no valid contract exists, but he may in some circumstances recover on a *quantum meruit*.

> *Craven-Ellis* v *Canons Ltd*, 1936 – A claim on a *quantum meruit* (247)

Total failure of consideration: actions for money had and received

Of particular importance here is the action for total failure of consideration. A total failure will result in the recovery of all that was paid. A common reason for total failure of consideration arises where A, who has no title, sells goods to B and B has to give up the goods to the true owner. B can then recover the whole of the consideration from A, his action being based upon the quasi-contractual claim of money had and received.

It should be noted that the action is based on failure of consideration and not its absence. Thus money paid by way of a gift cannot be recovered in quasi-contract. As we have seen, the decision in *Rowland* v *Divall* (1923) would appear to have been based on total failure of consideration (see Chapter 14).

Payments made under a mistake

This is a further aspect of restitution by use of an implied promise in the recipient to repay the sum(s) involved.

Payment under a mistake of fact

A claim lies (derived from the old action for money had and received) where money has been paid under a mistake of fact. The error may arise from an error in calculation as where defective arithmetic causes a debtor to pay more than he owes the creditor or where there is duplication of an item again in the debtor's accounts so that he pays it twice.

Payment under mistake of law

Until recent times, there was no claim for money paid under mistake of law. However, the House of Lords overturned this old rule in *Kleinwort Benson Ltd* v *Lincoln City Council* [1998] 4 All ER 513 where their Lordships ruled that money paid under a contract which was *ultra vires* or beyond the legal powers of the Council was nevertheless recoverable by the claimant who had made the payment.

Limitation of actions

Contractual obligations are not enforceable for all time. After a certain period the law bars any remedy in the main because evidence becomes less reliable with the passage of time. Time is the greatest enemy of the truth! The Limitation Act 1980 lays down the general periods within which an action may be brought. They are as follows.

(a) An action on a simple contract may be brought within six years from the date when the cause of action accrued.

As we have already noted, where the parties are broadly of equal bargaining power the above period of six years can be reduced by a term of the contract, in the relevant case to nine months after the provision of a service (see *Granville Oil and Chemicals Ltd* v *Davis Turner & Co Ltd* (2003) (unreported), Chapter 9). The case is not on its facts applicable to deeds.

(b) An action upon a contract made by deed may be brought within 12 years from the date when the cause of action accrued.

Where the claimant's claims include a claim for damages in respect of personal injury, the period is three years.

A person may suffer personal injury the extent of which only comes to light more than three years after the breach of contract which caused it. For example, A is a passenger on B's coach and B's careless driving causes an accident as a result of which A suffers injury consisting of bruising of the face. Four years later A goes blind as a result of the accident. Under the Limitation Act 1980, A has three years from his knowledge of the blindness to sue B and the court's permission is not required. The court may extend this period at its discretion, though in this case application must be made to the court for the extension.

A right of action 'accrues' from the moment when breach occurs, not from the date when the contract was made. Thus, if money is lent today for four years, the creditor's right to recover it will not expire until 10 years from today.

18

If when the cause of action accrues the claimant is under a disability by reason of minority or unsoundness of mind, the period will not run until the disability is ended or until his death, whichever comes first. Once the period has started to run, subsequent insanity has no effect.

If the claimant is the victim of fraud or acts under a mistake or deliberate concealment, the limitation period will not begin to run until the true state of affairs is discovered or should with reasonable diligence have been discovered.

> *Lynn* v *Bamber*, 1930 – Limitation of actions where there is fraud, etc. (**248**)

The Limitation Act does not truly discharge a contract, which is why it has been dealt with separately here. The Act merely makes the contract unenforceable in a court of law and if the defendant does not plead the statutes of limitation, the judge will enforce the contract. In addition, where the contractual claim is not for damages but for a debt or other liquidated (i.e. ascertained) demand, time for making a claim can be extended by a subsequent payment of money not appropriated by the debtor, because, as we have seen, the creditor can appropriate it, or by the debtor or his duly authorised agent making a written acknowledgement of the debt to the creditor or his agent. Time begins to run again from the date of the acknowledgement. However, once a debt is statute-barred, it cannot be revived by acknowledgement in this way (Limitation Act 1980, s 29). Electronic acknowledgement by telex was held valid by the Court of Appeal in *Good Challenger Navegante SA* v *MetalExportImport SA* [2004] 1 Lloyd's Rep 67.

Equitable remedies, i.e. specific performance or an injunction, are not covered by the ordinary limitation periods but will usually be barred much earlier under general equitable rules. An equitable remedy must be sought promptly and, according to the nature of the contract, a short delay of weeks or even days may bar the remedy.

Finally, the enforcement of a judgment debt does not become statute-barred by lapse of time under s 24 of the Limitation Act 1980 so that a judgment once obtained can be enforced, e.g. by a sale of the defendant's goods even though the relevant statutory period has elapsed. The amount of interest recoverable from the judgment until payment is similarly not limited to the relevant period but is limited to six years before the judgment is executed. Thus, if A obtains a judgment against B in 1998, he can still execute it to take the defendant's property for sale even though he leaves it until, say, 2005 to execute it. However, he can only recover interest on the judgment for six years prior to 2005 (*Lowsley* v *Forbes* (1996) *The Times*, 5 April).

Reform

In 2001 the Law Commission issued a report entitled *Limitation of Actions*. The report recommends a single regime of periods of limitation to be applied to all claims. There would be:

- *A primary limitation period of three years* from the date on which the claimant knew or ought reasonably to have known the relevant facts with a long stop period of ten years starting from the date on which the relevant events occurred.
- *Exceptionally personal injury claims* would only be subject to the three-year limitation period and not the 10-year period. The court would then have a discretion to disapply the primary period in appropriate cases.
- *Claims to recover land* would not fall under the main regime but would be subjected to a 10-year limitation period that will run from the date on which the cause of action accrued.

At the time of writing, no further action has been taken.

19

EMPLOYMENT RIGHTS

An ever-increasing feature of contract law is the way in which particular contracts are controlled by legislation to which the general principles of contract law yield; nowhere is this more obvious than in the contract of employment. Accordingly, the main features of this legislation, which are so important in all walks of business life, are given below.

Recruitment and selection of employees

Here the prospective employer must take account of discrimination legislation. The Equal Opportunities Commission set up under the Sex Discrimination Act 1975 (SDA) has the duty to work towards the elimination of discrimination on the grounds of sex. The Race Relations Act 1976 (RRA) sets up the Commission for Racial Equality with powers much the same as the Equal Opportunities Commission. The Disability Rights Commission set up under the Disability Discrimination Act 1995 (DDA) has similar powers. The government intends to create one commission to deal with all of the ever growing areas of discrimination liability. This has been initiated by the Equality Act 2006. It provides for the setting up of the Commission for Equality and Human Rights. The government has stated that the new Commission will become operative in 2007 with all Commissions and matters of discrimination being incorporated in 2008/09.

It is unlawful for a prospective employer (and an employer) to discriminate between applicants for jobs on the grounds of sex or marital status, colour, race, nationality or ethnic or national origins or on the grounds of sexual orientation, religion or belief, gender reassignment or age.

It is also unlawful to publish an advertisement which could be interpreted as discriminatory. Thus job descriptions such as 'waiter' and 'salesgirl' have largely disappeared from our newspapers. However, one still sees advertisements which are clearly intended to attract female employees which are nevertheless within the law, e.g. 'publishing director requires sophisticated PA/secretary with style and charm who can remain cool under pressure'.

Under the SDA it is unlawful for a person to discriminate against another on grounds of sex or on grounds of marital status when determining who will be offered a job and in regard to the terms and conditions of the job. There are exceptions where the sex or marital status of the person required is a genuine occupational qualification (GOQ), e.g. for reasons of physiology (as in the employment of a model) or for reasons of decency or privacy (as in the case of an attendant in a public lavatory) or where the job is one of two held by a married couple, as where the woman is to be a housekeeper living in with her husband who is to be employed as a gardener or a married couple is required to manage a club and live in.

Sex and race discrimination

Discrimination may be direct or indirect.

Direct discrimination. There is direct discrimination against a person if on the ground of race or sex that person is treated less favourably than a white or male person would be. This covers the usual scenario though, of course, both white and male persons can be discriminated against, but there is little case law on this.

Indirect discrimination. This occurs, e.g., where an employer has applied requirements or conditions to a job but the ability of some persons to comply because of sex, marital status or race is considerably smaller and cannot be justified.

Examples

- A company wishes to appoint a black woman to supervise a call centre but changes its mind when some of the white operators object. *This is direct racial discrimination.*
- A firm wishes to appoint a woman to a post as senior manager but she will be dealing mainly with one particular client who says he would prefer to work with a man. The firm, therefore, appoints a man instead. *This is direct sexual discrimination by the employer.*
- A company has a strict office rule that women way not wear trousers in the office. A Muslim woman who applies for a job with the company is unable to comply with this rule because religion and custom forbid the wearing of skirts and she must cover her legs. The proportion of the members of her racial group who can comply is considerably smaller than the proportion of other persons who can comply, although religious discrimination as such is not forbidden. *This is indirect discrimination* under the RRA but also now the discrimination rules relating to religion or belief.

An employer need not take the above applicants into work, but if he does not, he faces a claim for compensation. There may also be a genuine occupational qualification (see below).

However, s 7(4) of the SDA imposes a duty on employers to take reasonable steps to avoid relying on GOQ exceptions, so that where the employer already has sufficient female staff in a department store to, say, measure women for clothing, it may be unlawful not to employ a man for other duties in the relevant department of the store, e.g. in the women's shoe section or even in the clothing department if the job does not include intimate contact with the customers.

It should be noted that it is unlawful in *all* partnerships to discriminate on the grounds of race in regard to the selection of new partners and benefits, facilities, or services given to partners, unless a GOQ applies. Sex discrimination is unlawful in partnerships of all sizes and sex and race discrimination is unlawful in all companies and by sole traders, no matter how small the workforce.

It is also contrary to law to give unfavourable treatment to a person by way of *victimisation*. This occurs where, e.g., the person has taken proceedings in respect of discrimination or has threatened to do so, as where an employer refuses a job to a female applicant because she is involved in an unresolved sexual harassment case as in *Cornelius v Manpower Services Commission* (SXD 36117/86).

As regards race, it is lawful to discriminate where there is a GOQ for the job as, for example, in the employment of a West Indian social worker or probation officer to deal with problems relating to young persons of West Indian extraction. Other instances are dramatic performances or other entertainment, artists or photographic models and employment in places serving food or drink to be purchased and *consumed* on the premises by the public. Thus, being Chinese is a GOQ for employment in a Chinese restaurant, but not necessarily in a 'take-away'.

Exceptions

(a) Work outside Great Britain. Race, sex and disability discrimination legislation does not apply to work which is done wholly outside Great Britain.

However, under discrimination regulations passed to implement the EU Equal Treatment Directive a person who works or is to work wholly outside Great Britain will be able to use the discrimination laws if:

- the employer has a place of business at an establishment in Great Britain; and
- the work is for the purposes of that business; and
- the employee is ordinarily resident in Great Britain at the time when he applies for or is offered the employment or is so resident at any time during the employment.

(b) Under s 5 of the Employment Act 1989. Under these provisions the appointment of head teachers in schools and colleges may be restricted to members of a religious order where such a restriction is contained in a trust deed or other relevant instrument setting up the school or college. This is still the case in spite of the rules rendering unlawful discrimination on the grounds of religion or belief.

Enforcement

As regards enforcement, those who believe they have been discriminated against may complain to an employment tribunal within three months of the date of the act complained of. A conciliation officer of the Advisory Conciliation and Arbitration Service will try to settle the complaint without the need for a tribunal hearing.

In addition, it is possible once in employment for an employer and employee to settle a dispute by a binding agreement, called a compromise contract or agreement, in which the employee waives the right to bring or continue with a claim before an employment tribunal relating to the dispute in question. However, it is essential that the employee has received independent legal advice before entering into the contract.

If the matter goes to a tribunal, the tribunal may make an order declaring the rights of the parties in relation to the complaint. In addition, it may make an order for compensation, without limit as to amount, which could cover loss of prospective earnings and injured feelings. It may also recommend that the employer take, within a specified period, action which appears to the tribunal to be practicable for the purpose of obviating or reducing the adverse effect of any act of discrimination on which the complaint is based. Proceedings (relating for example to discriminatory advertisements and instructions to discriminate) will in future only be instituted by the Commission for Equality and Human Rights.

Johnson v *Timber Tailors (Midlands)*, 1978 – Racial discrimination (**249**)
Sisley v *Britannia Security Systems*, 1983 – A matter of decency (**250**)

Trade union members and non-members

Discrimination against job applicants on the ground of trade union membership or non-membership is dealt with in much the same way as other forms of discrimination. It is unlawful to refuse employment to a person because he or she is or is not a member of a trade union or is unwilling to become or remain a member. Application to a tribunal must be made within three months of the date of refusal and there is no cap on awards.

Discrimination against the disabled

The Disability Discrimination Act 1995 applies as follows.

Applicants for employment

It is unlawful to discriminate against disabled persons in deciding whom to interview, whom to give the job to and the terms of the offer. The potential employer has a defence if he believes on reasonable grounds that the nature of the disability will substantially affect the disabled person's ability to carry out the required task(s).

Employers are required to make reasonable adjustments in the working conditions and the workplace to accommodate disabled persons, but cost may be taken into account in deciding what is reasonable.

Reasonable adjustments include changes to the physical environment, such as widening a doorway to allow for wheelchair access. Also included are changes to arrangements in the workplace, such as flexible working hours, purchasing specialised equipment and allowing time off for treatment. If the employer rents his premises, the landlord cannot reasonably refuse permission to accommodate the disabled person(s), however, the landlord may require that the premises be returned to their original condition when vacated. Unreasonable refusal to make changes by a landlord can result in a claim for discrimination before an employment tribunal which can recommend steps to be taken by the landlord, refusal to take these steps resulting in increased money compensation.

These provisions have effect on the GOQ rules that apply more clearly in other areas of discrimination. With a disabled person the occupational qualification, i.e. for a non-disabled person can often be overcome by making adjustments in the workplace.

Exceptions

The 1995 Act only applies to employers who employ 15 or more people. This exception is removed from 1 October 2004 by the Disability Discrimination Act 1995 (Amendment) Regulations 2003. The disability discrimination rules will from then on apply to all employers, though it does not apply to operational staff in the prison service or fire service. Complaints must be made to a tribunal within three months of the act complained of and monetary compensation can be awarded. There is no cap upon the amount.

Disability defined

The 1995 Act defines disability as 'a physical or mental impairment which has a substantial and long-term adverse effect on a person's ability to carry out normal day-to-day activities'. Impairment includes things such as blindness, deafness or learning disabilities and mental illness. 'Substantial' means more than a minor or trivial problem. 'Long-term' means effects that have lasted at least 12 months or are likely to last for the rest of the person's life. Persons are covered by the Act if they have a severe disfigurement, even though it may not have any effect on the ability to carry out normal activities.

'Day-to-day' activities are defined as activities that involve moving from place to place, manual dexterity, physical co-ordination, continence, the ability to lift, carry or move objects, speech, hearing or eyesight, memory or the ability to concentrate, learn or under-stand and being able to recognise physical danger. The definition includes persons who have had a disability in the past, even if they no longer have it. This follows a government pledge to include those with a history of disablement. Medication or equipment that helps the disabled person is ignored, but glasses or contact lenses are not. It is the disability *with* the glasses or contact lenses which is considered.

The Disability Discrimination Act 2005 extends the definition of 'disability' specifically to cover those with HIV infection, cancer and multiple sclerosis *from the time of diagnosis*. The 1995 Act required that they had reached a significantly disabling point. Furthermore, the requirement in the DDA 1995 that a mental illness must be 'clinically well recognised' is removed.

The DDA 2005 also carries provisions relating to discriminatory advertisements which were not in the DDA 1995.

Enforcement

This is by application to an employment tribunal within three months of the discriminatory act. Damages for financial loss or hurt feelings is recoverable with no cap on the award.

Discrimination against transsexuals

The decision of the ECJ in *P* v *S and Cornwall CC* [1996] IRLR 347 was to the effect that the SDA 1975 should be applied to discrimination in connection with gender reassignment. The decision was confined to the public sector on the basis of the direct effect of EU law on 'emanations of the state'. However, in *Chessington World of Adventure Ltd* v *Reed* [1997] IRLR 556 the Employment Appeal Tribunal ruled that it was possible to interpret the SDA 1975 as applying to prohibit discrimination in connection with gender assignment in the private sector. The position now is that the Sex Discrimination (Gender Reassignment) Regulations 1999 (SI 1999/1102) have inserted s 2A into the SDA 1975 and this prohibits direct discrimination against a person on the grounds that he or she intends to undergo, is undergoing or has undergone gender reassignment. *This provision regulates equal pay in this area rather than the Equal Pay Act 1970.*

Section 2A does not protect against indirect discrimination but the EU Equal Treatment Directive would appear to do so. In addition, s 2A applies only in the context of employment and vocational training. In view of the probable contravention of the Equal Treatment Directive, UK law may require further amendment.

Restricted reporting orders

It is, of course, important in the above cases that confidentiality be preserved. In this connection, procedural rules for cases in the High Court allow for restricted reporting orders to be made. There is now *specific* power to make such orders in current rules relating to tribunals.

Genuine occupational qualifications

The SDA 1975, as amended, provides for GOQ exceptions to this form of discrimination. However, the alleged GOQ must be accepted by the court or tribunal. For example the Court of Appeal decided in *A* v *Chief Constable of West Yorkshire* [2003] 1 All ER 593 that a person who had declared to the employer on interview that she was a male to female transsexual was discriminated against on the grounds of sex when she was refused a post as a woman police officer because by law certain searches had to be conducted by a person of the same sex. The claimant was prepared to declare the gender change at the time of search.

On the facts of this case a person who had become the acquired gender after following the procedures set out in the Gender Recognition Act 2004 would be discriminated against without court approval because the SDA 1975 is amended by the 2004 Act to give statutory recognition to the acquired gender.

Human rights

Although transsexuals have some protection as regards employment and vocational training under UK discrimination legislation, the European Court of Human Rights is extending protection by applying the Convention on Human Rights. Thus in *Goodwin* v *UK* [2002] IRLR 664 the ECHR considered the case of a male to female transsexual who complained of discrimination in that she was still regarded as a man for the purposes of retiring age, i.e. 65 not 60 and the requirement to pay national insurance contributions after age 60. Such contributions cease on reaching state retirement age. The ECHR ruled that Art 8 of the Convention (right to respect for private and family life) had been infringed.

Discrimination on the grounds of sexual orientation

The Employment Equality (Sexual Orientation) Regulations 2003 (SI 2003/1661)

They apply from 1 December 2003. The regulations make it unlawful to discriminate on the grounds that a person is gay, heterosexual or bisexual in employment and vocational training. They prohibit direct and indirect discrimination in recruitment and victimisation and harassment once in employment. All partnerships of whatever size are covered.

Genuine occupational requirements (GORs). The regulations use the expression 'genuine occupational requirement' rather than a reference to a 'genuine occupational qualification'. The practical effect is the same. Importantly the regulations make clear that a GOR can exempt an otherwise unlawful discrimination. There is a specific GOR for the purposes of 'an organised religion' that would allow such a religion to exclude, e.g., gay clergy.

Positive discrimination. The regulations allow positive discrimination in regard to training where it reasonably appears to the person initiating the positive discrimination that it will prevent or compensate for disadvantages linked to sexual orientation suffered by persons of that sexual orientation doing certain types of work or likely to take it up. This substitutes for the test in other areas which is that workers covered are under-represented in the workforce which would not be easily ascertainable in terms of sexual orientation.

Marital status. The regulations do not prohibit anything such as a term of employment that prevents access to a benefit by reference to marital status. Obviously discrimination on the grounds of marital status is unlawful under the SDA 1975 so that it would be unlawful to exclude married persons from benefits. However, only persons who are married according to law can regard themselves as within the protection of marital status. Persons of the same sex living together are not within the protection offered by marital status.

Pensions. It is unlawful for an employer to discriminate against a person on the grounds of sexual orientation in relation to membership of a pension scheme. The regulations do not extend protection to the trustees and the managers of schemes. Provisions covering these persons have now been made and are in force.

Claims jurisdiction. Claims may be brought before employment tribunals in line with the time limits set for other discrimination claims. There is no cap on compensation.

Direct and indirect discrimination: definitions. Although the Religion and Belief Regulations are considered more fully below, it is convenient to deal with the definitions here because they are similar to those for sexual orientation.

Direct discrimination. The SDA, the RRA and the Sexual Orientation and the Religion and Belief Regulations all use the same method for identifying direct discrimination, i.e. less favourable treatment by comparing the treatment of the alleged victim with that of an actual or hypothetical comparator not of the same sex, race or sexual orientation or not of the same religion or belief.

Indirect discrimination. The Sexual Orientation and the Religion and Belief Regulations both use the same basic test and state that a person (A) discriminates against another (B) if: A applies to B a provision, criterion or *practice* which he applies or would apply equally to persons not of the same sexual orientation or religion or belief but which –

- puts or would put persons of the same sexual orientation or religion or belief as B at a particular disadvantage when compared with other persons;
- puts B at that disadvantage; and
- A cannot show this to be a proportionate means of achieving a legitimate aim.

No doubt tribunal case law will soon start to interpret the above provisions. It is, however, worth noting that *informal practices* can be indirectly discriminatory under the test as well as contractual requirements.

Discrimination on the grounds of religion and belief

The Employment Equality (Religion and Belief) Regulations 2003 (SI 2003/1660) apply from 2 December 2003. Prior to the coming into force of the regulations some religious groups have been able to claim protection under the RRA 1976, e.g. Jews and Sikhs. However, the Religion and Belief Regulations introduce for the first time a general protection from discrimination on the grounds of religion or belief. This is defined by the regulations as any religion, religious belief or philosophical belief. It is thought that political beliefs will not fall within the regulations. As to what is a religion or belief, it is likely that tribunals will see the need for factors such as collective worship, a clear belief system and/or a profound belief affecting a person's way of life and view of the world when deciding whether in the circumstances the regulations should be applied.

19

Direct and indirect discrimination. These matters have already been considered when dealing with the sexual orientation regulations. There is, however, a specific instance of indirect discrimination regarding Sikhs. Under this provision the requirement that those on construction sites must wear helmets would, by excluding Sikhs, be a form of indirect discrimination against them. It would be a requirement that they could not meet because of a religious requirement to wear a turban. The regulations here are consistent with s 11 of the Employment Act 1989 that exempts Sikhs generally from requirements to wear safety helmets on construction sites.

Genuine occupational requirements. There is a general GOR provision in regard to the Religion or Belief Regulations that is the same as the GOR for sexual orientation and has already been considered. There is also an additional GOR that applies where being of a particular religion is a *proportionate* requirement for the job.

Positive discrimination. The regulations contain an exception to allow positive discrimination on the lines of the Sexual Orientation Regulations.

Pensions. The government has taken the same position here as it has for sexual orientation.

Claims jurisdiction. The Religion and Belief Regulations take the same position as regards the forum for claims as do the Sexual Orientation Regulations. Once again, there is no cap on compensation.

The Equality Act 2006 makes amendments in the 2003 regulations as follows:

■ The regulations are extended to cover discrimination against those who lack religion or belief and the requirement that a philosophical belief be similar to a religious belief is dropped.

■ There is also an amendment to the regulations to make clear the fact that direct discrimination can occur even if it is another person's religion or belief and not the victim's which constitutes the grounds for discrimination, as where a manager discriminates against an employee on the basis that the victim associates with a person of a particular religion or belief. For example, an anti-semite manager may discriminate unlawfully against an employee who associates with a member of the Jewish community.

Some case law

Some examples of claims under the regulations are coming before tribunals. Thus, in *Williams-Drabble* v *Pathway Care Solutions Ltd* [2005] IDS Brief 776 an employment tribunal ruled that where an employer changed a Christian employee's hours so that she had to work on Sundays there was indirect religious discrimination under the Religion or Belief Regulations. It was a condition of working that made it difficult for Ms Drabble to comply with since she could not attend Sunday service. The employer was on notice that she was a practising Christian.

In *Brooks* v *Findlay Industries Ltd* [2005] IDS Brief 784 Mr Brooks, a homosexual, was employed by Findlay. He did not want his homosexuality to be known to his fellow workers. His line manager, who knew, informed the human resources manager in order to joke with him about this and rumour spread among the workforce and Mr Brooks was subjected to inappropriate and insulting remarks. A tribunal held that Mr Brooks had been subjected to conduct which fell within the sexual orientation regulations. The acts constituted direct discrimination against Mr Brooks.

Discrimination on the grounds of age

The Employment Equality (Age) Regulations 2006 (SI 2006/1031) came into force on 1 October 2006.

The regulations generally

The regulations follow the existing regulations on sex, race, religion or belief and sexual orientation:

■ Direct and indirect discrimination on the grounds of age are unlawful and so is victimisation and harassment.

■ There is an exception where there is a genuine occupational requirement where 'possessing a characteristic related to age' is concerned, provided it is proportionate to apply that requirement in a particular case – for example, if a person is producing a play which has parts for older or younger characters. Thus, a 60-year-old who was turned down for the part of Peter Pan could hardly claim discrimination!

- Positive action is allowed to encourage 'persons of a particular age' to take advantage of employment opportunities where this 'prevents or compensates for disadvantages linked to age suffered by persons of that age who do the work'.
- Claims may be brought in employment matters before an employment tribunal and potential claimants may serve a questionnaire to obtain information from a potential defendant. The county court will take claims in non-employment areas, e.g. discrimination in further or higher education.
- Post-termination discrimination is covered as where the ex-employer refuses a reference.
- Employees are obviously covered but also the self-employed, partners in a partnership, contract workers, office holders, members of trade organisations and those in vocational training are included.

The regulations apply in the case of age discrimination in terms both of recruitment and once in employment.

Exceptions

Regulation 3 provides that discriminatory treatment may be justified if it is a proportionate means of achieving a legitimate aim. This applies to direct and indirect discrimination. Examples given are:

- The setting of age requirements to ensure the protection or promote the vocational integration of people in a particular age group. This could include the health, welfare and safety of the individual, including protection of young people or older workers.
- The fixing of a minimum age to qualify for certain advantages linked to employment or an occupation so as to recruit or retain older people where perhaps these are under-represented in the workforce. This could include travel facilities and gift vouchers.
- The fixing of a maximum age for recruitment which is based upon the training requirements of the post or the need for a reasonable period in post before retirement. This is a general rule but the regulations provide more specifically that where a person is older than the employer's normal retirement age or will be within six months, or 65 if the employer does not have one, the employer may refuse to recruit that person.

Regulation 26 gives a further exception where employers must comply with other legislation, e.g. the law that prohibits under-18s from being employed in bars where alcoholic drinks are sold.

Default retirement at age 65

It will not amount to age discrimination if employers retire employees at or above age 65 where it is a genuine retirement. Employers are able to continue the employment of people beyond the default age. A retirement age below 65 will in general be unlawful. A lower age will be permitted, but only if the employer can satisfy the objective justification test.

In this connection the ruling of the EAT in *Payne* v *Royal and Sun Alliance Group plc* [2005] IRLR 848 is instructive although not a case brought under the Age Regulations. Mr Payne's contract provided for him to retire at age 65. The employer changed the retirement age, unilaterally and without Mr Payne's consent, to 62 and then terminated Mr Payne's contract at that age. Mr Payne successfully claimed wrongful and unfair dismissal by reason of breach of contract by the employer in terminating his contract at 62 and therefore not in accordance with its terms. The EAT agreed with the tribunal ruling in an area where there has previously been no clear authority that the normal retirement age cannot be earlier than the contractual retirement age unless the employee consents. Mr Payne's claim was not prevented by s 109(l)(a) of the Employment Rights Act 1996 (no claim by those who have reached retirement age).

Comment The case is of importance under the Age Regulations because under the regulations a retirement below 65 is forbidden unless the employee consents or the employer can justify it on objective grounds. The *Payne* case shows what will happen if employers do unilaterally retire workers below age 65 and cannot justify it.

Fair dismissal only on planned retirement date

The upper limit for bringing unfair dismissal claims which was 65 has been removed. However, reg 29 states that it will not be unlawful to dismiss an employee who is over 65 where the reason for the dismissal is retirement. For a dismissal on the planned retirement date to be fair regardless of the employee's age an employer who intends to dismiss for retirement must:

- give the employee not more than one year's and not less than six months' notice of the intention to retire him or her; and
- comply with a new duty under Sch 7 to the Age Regulations to notify the employee that he or she has a right to make a request not to retire on the intended date;
- consider a request by an employee to continue working, and meet with the employee within a reasonable time to discuss the request.

If the employer refuses a request to continue working, the employee has a right of appeal and another meeting must be held before the retirement dismissal takes effect. The employee's request must be in writing and made no more than six months nor less than three months before the retirement date. The employee must specify whether the request is to stay on indefinitely, or for a stated period or until a stated date. An employee can make only one request. At the meeting to consider the request the employee has a right to be accompanied by a fellow worker but not a trade union representative. If the fellow worker is not available the employee can postpone the meeting to a date convenient to the parties and within seven days of the date set by the employer. The employer is under no obligation to give a reason for rejecting a request to stay on. It is advisable, however, to do so, since failure to do so may lead to challenges under other discrimination laws, e.g. disability.

Where an employer fails to follow the above procedures, the employee may claim compensation of up to eight weeks' pay, currently capped at £310 per week but normally revised upward every 12 months.

Service-related pay and benefits

Older employees are more likely to qualify for these benefits, e.g. extra holiday entitlement, which might be regarded as discrimination against those of a younger age. To cover this, the Age Regulations include specific exemptions and one general provision as follows:

- nothing will prevent an employer from using length of service up to a maximum of five years as a criterion for awarding benefits, those with less service being denied them;
- the benefits must, however, be awarded to all employees who meet the length of service requirement and whose circumstances are not materially different;
- there is a general exception for all other service-related benefits provided that the employer reasonably believes that awarding benefits in this way fulfils a business need.

Where an employer is following statutory benefits based on age, this is lawful or where he or she is following more generous benefits in the statutory situation based on length of service, this will be lawful. This will apply in particular to statutory redundancy payments or more generous contractual redundancy payments. The exception covers only benefits based on length of service and not pay or other differentials on the ground of age nor does it extend to experienced-based criteria which may indirectly discriminate and which employers will have to justify objectively.

Other employee rights

- There is now no upper or lower age limit for claiming redundancy payments. The statutory formula will be calculated as before on a 20-year maximum service. These changes are further considered later in this chapter when dealing with redundancy.
- Age discrimination in recruitment will be permitted where candidates have reached 65 or will do so within six months of application.
- As regards pensions, there are special rules in Sch 2 to the Age Regulations so that, for example, it will not be unlawful to fix an age for admission to a pension scheme or for benefits to have different contribution requirements.
- Whenever the dismissal is other than for retirement the statutory dismissal and grievance procedures will apply.

Finally, the Department of Trade and Industry envisages a future where there will be no default retirement age because of trends in life expectancy, and it will review the matter again in 2011.

Asylum and Immigration Act 1996

This Act is relevant in terms of recruitment. It contains provisions designed to prevent illegal working by immigrants, overstayers and those breaching their immigration conditions. Employers must take steps to check the existence (but not the authenticity) of documents such as birth certificates or certificates of registration or naturalisation to prevent illegal working. If such checks have been carried out but nevertheless illegal working occurs, the employer is not liable. Failure to check regarding this responsibility can lead to a fine on the employer of up to £5,000. In the case of a corporate employer, directors and other officers and management of the company may be similarly prosecuted if they have connived at the offence or it has been committed as a result of their neglect. There is no need to check existing employees, who were employed when the legislation came into force.

The Immigration, Asylum and Nationality Act 2006 introduces a scheme of civil penalties including fines on the employer of up to £2,000 per illegal employee and a possible two-year custodial sentence and unlimited fine for those who have knowingly used or exploited illegal workers. This has manifested itself particularly in the cockle picking trade.

The Act does not apply to employees under the age of 16 or to the self-employed or to the clients of agencies in terms of agency workers. Furthermore, the transferee employer is not required to check the status of employees who come to the organisation following a transfer of undertakings.

Criminal records

The government has set up the Criminal Records Bureau (CRB) under the provisions of ss 112–127 of the Police Act 1997. It is put forward as a one-stop shop for those going through recruitment procedures to access a variety of information sources to ascertain criminal records.

19

There are *standard* disclosures and *enhanced* disclosures and these are wider and intended for those employing persons where the job involves regular contact with children and/or vulnerable persons. There are also *basic* disclosures for all other employments.

Employers have to register with the CRB and there is a charge for each request. This can be paid either by the would-be employer or the applicant. The standard and enhanced disclosures are sent to the applicant and to the employer. Basic disclosures are sent only to the applicant. It is then a matter for the applicant whether he/she shows them to the potential employer. An offer of employment can be legally withdrawn or a promotion refused if there is failure to disclose. Advertisements should state that a request for disclosure will be made. Employers who are registered with the CRB must abide by a code of practice and have a policy with regard to the employment of ex-offenders.

Protection during employment

Once an employee has taken up employment, there are the following safeguards.

The contract of employment

The Employment Rights Act 1996 (ERA) provides that an employee is entitled to one week's notice after one month or more of service. After two years' service, the minimum notice is increased to two weeks, and for each year of service afterwards it is increased by one week, to a maximum of 12 weeks after 12 years' service. The statutory minimum period of notice which an employee must give is one week, irrespective of the period of employment, provided he has been employed for one month. No other period of service is required.

In addition, an employer must give his employee written information about the terms of employment. The statement must be given to employees within two months of starting work but not if the job is for less than one month unless in fact it lasts for more than one month. This statement must contain the names of the employer and the employee; the date when the employment began; whether employment with a previous employer is to be counted as part of the employee's 'continuous period of employment' and, where this is so, the date on which it began (this is important to the employee, for example, in terms of redundancy payments and unfair dismissal); the title of the job, though under the ERA the employer can give a brief job description instead; the scale or rate of remuneration or the method of calculating remuneration; the intervals at which remuneration is paid; any terms and conditions relating to the hours worked, entitlement to holidays and holiday pay, sickness or injury and sick pay, pensions and length of notice. The rules for calculating continuous employment, normal hours and a week's pay are in the ERA.

There must also be a note specifying any disciplinary rules, the name of a person to whom the employee can apply in case of any disciplinary decision or grievance; and the disciplinary and grievance procedures. These procedures are now governed by the Employment Act 2002 and regulations made under it. All employers must include disciplinary and grievance procedures in the statement. These may be the employer's own or the statutory procedures but in any case the statutory procedures will apply and can be used by employees normally where the employer's procedures are inferior. A typical statutory procedure is set out on the facing page.

DISCIPLINARY PROCEDURE

(a) The employer must set out in writing the employee's alleged conduct or characteristics or other circumstances which lead him/her to contemplate dismissing or taking disciplinary action against the employee.

(b) The employer must send the statment, or a copy of it, to the employee and invite the employee to attend a meeting to discuss the matter.

Meeting

(c) The meeting will take place before action is taken except in the case where the disciplinary action consists of suspension.

(d) The meeting must not take place unless –
   (i) The employer has informed the employee what the basis was for including in the statement referred to above the ground or grounds that he/she has given in it, and
   (ii) the employee has had a reasonable opportunity to consider his response to that information.

(e) The employee must take all reasonable steps to attend the meeting.

(f) After the meeting the employer must inform the employee of his/her decision and notify him/her of the right to appeal against the decision if he/she is not satisfied with it.

Appeal

(g) If the employee does not wish to appeal he/she must inform the employer.

(h) If the employee informs the employer of his/her wish to appeal the employer must invite him/her to attend a further meeting. The employee must take all reasonable steps to attend the meeting.

(i) The appeal meeting need *not* take place before the dismissal or disciplinary action takes effect.

(j) After the appeal meeting the employer must inform the employee of the final decision.

GRIEVANCE PROCEDURE

(a) The employee must set out in writing the grievance and send the statement or copy of it to the employer.

Meeting

(b) The employer must invite the employee to attend a meeting to discuss the grievance.

(c) The meeting must not take place unless –
   (i) the employee has informed the employer what the basis for the grievance was when he/she made the above statement, and
   (ii) the employer has had a reasonable opportunity to consider his/her response to that information.

(d) The employee must take all reasonable steps to attend the meeting.

(e) After the meeting the employer must inform the employee of his/her decision as to his/her response to the grievance and notify him/her of the right to appeal against the decision if he/she is not satisfied with it.

Appeal

(f) If the employee does not wish to appeal, he/she must inform the employer.

(g) If the employee informs the employer of his/her wish to appeal the employer must invite him/her to attend a further meeting.

(h) The employee must take all reasonable steps to attend the meeting. After the appeal meeting the employer must inform the employee of his/her final decision.

19

As regards hours worked, it should be borne in mind that the Working Time Regulations 1998 provide for a maximum 48-hour working week averaged over 17 weeks, except where an individual employee has specifically opted out (see below).

Further particulars are required as follows:

(a) the duration of temporary contracts;

(b) work location or locations;

(c) collective agreements with trade unions affecting the job;

(d) where the job requires work outside the UK for more than one month, the period of such work; the currency in which the employee will be paid; and any other pay or benefits provided by reason of working outside the UK. Employees who begin work outside the UK within two months of starting the job must have the statement before leaving the UK.

Particulars can be given by instalments, provided all are given within two months. However, there must be a 'principal statement' in one document giving the following information:

(a) the identities of the parties;

(b) the date when the employment began;

(c) where the employment counts as a period of continuous employment with a previous one, a statement that this is so and the date when it began;

(d) the amount and frequency of pay, e.g. weekly or monthly;

(e) the hours of work;

(f) holiday entitlement;

(g) job title (or description);

(h) work location.

Certain particulars can be given by reference to a document, e.g. a collective agreement with a trade union, but any such document must be readily accessible to the employee. These particulars are pension arrangements, sickness provisions, notice entitlement and details of disciplinary matters and grievance procedures.

An employee who does not receive written particulars or who wants to dispute their accuracy or sufficiency may refer the matter to an employment tribunal. The tribunal may then make a declaration that the employee has a right to a statement and what particulars should be included in it or amended within it. The statement approved by the tribunal is then deemed to have been given by the employer to the employee and will form the basis of his rights.

Section 38 of the Employment Act 2002 provides for tribunals to award monetary compensation to an employee where on a claim being made, e.g. for unfair dismissal it appears that the particulars the employee has received are incomplete or inaccurate. Where this is so the tribunal may increase any award made against the employer by between two and four weeks' pay according to whether the statement is merely inaccurate or has never been issued at all. One or two weeks' pay is also to be awarded where compensation is not a remedy for the particular complaint or is not a remedy chosen by the tribunal as where it awards reinstatement in the job. Formerly there was no monetary penalty on the employer where particulars were incomplete, inaccurate or non-existent.

Exemptions from the written particulars requirements

There are some situations under the ERA where the employer does not have to give the written particulars. Those which may be found in the average business are as follows:

- employees with fully written contracts or letters of engagement containing all the necessary items need not be given also the written particulars;
- as already briefly noted it is not necessary to give an employee written particulars if he or she is employed for a specific job e.g. to clear a backlog of office work which is not expected to last more than one month. If it does last for more than one month, the worker is entitled to written particulars.

It should be noted that the former exception that there was no need for particulars where the employee was the husband or the wife of the employer is repealed as is the exemption formerly available to employers with fewer than 20 employees in regard to particulars of disciplinary procedures. All employers have now to state these in the particulars and the statutory ones are available anyway.

Working time

The Working Time Regulations 1998 (SI 1998/1833) came into force on 1 October 1998. They enact the European Working Time Directive (93/104). From that date there are detailed rules which govern hours of work and entitlement to paid holidays as set out below:

- a maximum 48-hour working week, averaged over 17 weeks, or 26 weeks in some cases (see below);
- at least four weeks of paid annual leave;
- a daily rest period of at least 11 consecutive hours between each working day;
- a weekly rest period of at least 24 hours in each seven-day period. This may be averaged over a two-week period, i.e. a worker is entitled to 48 hours' rest in 14 days, or two periods of 24 hours rest in 14 days;
- an in-work rest break of 20 minutes for those working more than six hours a day. This should not be taken at either the start or the end of a working day and should not overlap with a worker's daily rest period;
- the normal hours of night workers should not exceed an average of eight hours for each 24 hours over a 17-week period.

Who is a worker?

Generally speaking, a worker is a person employed under a contract of service, but the majority of agency workers are included as are trainees who are engaged on work experience. The Regulations also apply in part to domestic employees, though the working time limits do not apply but they are entitled to the rest breaks, rest periods and paid annual leave. Those who are genuinely self-employed are not covered. However, those businesses that take on self-employed workers for contracts of some length could be obliged to offer them holiday pay (see *Wright* v *Redrow Homes (Yorkshire) Ltd* [2004] 3 All ER 98, where self-employed bricklayers engaged by Redrow succeeded in a claim for holiday pay, having been engaged in some cases for a seven-month period). Developers and contractors would appear to be most involved.

Partners are not included since they own the firm. Salaried partners are if, as is usually the case, they are regarded in law as employees.

What is working time?

Working time is defined by the Working Time Regulations (WTR) as when a worker is working at his employer's disposal and carrying out his duty or activities. *Training time* is included but, according to DTI Guidance, time when a worker is 'on call' but is otherwise free to pursue

19

his own activities or is sleeping would not be working time. Lunch breaks spent at leisure would not be working time, but working lunches and working breakfasts would be. Travelling to and from a place of work is unlikely to be working time. The Regulations usefully allow workers or their representatives and employers to make agreements to add to the definition of working time.

Following the ruling of the ECJ in *Sindicato de Médicos de Asistencia Pública (Simap)* v *Conselleria de Sanidad y Consumo de la Generalidad Valenciana* Case C-303/98 [2001] All ER (EC) 609, it can be taken that overtime is working time and so is on call time where workers are obliged to be at their place of work to be ready to provide services immediately to the undertaking.

Can the WTR apply to a non-worker?

In *Kigass Aero Components* v *Brown* [2002] IRLR 312 the Employment Appeal Tribunal ruled that an employee who had been off work for a considerable time with a longstanding back injury was entitled under the 1988 Regulations to be paid the statutory holiday pay due to him *even though his entitlement had accumulated while he was not working*. It appeared from this decision that so long as workers are on the payroll they can build up holiday-pay entitlement even though they are not actually at work.

However, in *Inland Revenue Commissioners* v *Ainsworth* [2005] IRLR 465 the Court of Appeal held that *Kigass* was wrongly decided and was overruled. A worker on long-term sick leave is not entitled to four weeks' annual leave in a year when he or she has not been able to work, so that a claim for holiday pay must fail.

The 48-hour week

The law does not say that employees cannot work more than 48 hours in any one week. The 48-hour limit is averaged over a 'reference period' which will generally be a 17-week rolling period, in the absence of any other agreement. This gives a certain amount of flexibility for businesses to cope with surges in demand, so long as the average over the whole reference per period is not exceeded.

The reference period may be increased to 26 weeks if the worker is a special case, as in hospital work, or where there is a foreseeable surge of activity as in agriculture, tourism and postal services. The reference period can be increased to 52 weeks by a workforce agreement (see below) or by individual agreement with the employer (see below).

A High Court judge has ruled that all contracts of employment should be read as providing that an employee should not work more than an average of 48 hours in any week during the 17-week working time reference period, unless the relevant employee has opted out in writing. The judge also ruled that if the average hours are equalled or exceeded during the reference period, an employee may refuse to work *at all* during the remainder of the period until the working hours come down to the required level (see *Barber and Others* v *RJB Mining (UK) Ltd* [1999] 613 IRLB 16).

Mr Justice Gage gave his ruling in a case brought by five members of the pit deputies' union NACODS against RJB Mining, their employer. They had all been required to carry on working, although they had all worked in excess of 816 hours in the 17-week reference period. The judge also granted them an injunction (breach of which by the employer could lead to sanctions of contempt of court) to the effect that they could refuse to work any more during a 17-week reference period where the 48-hour average had been equalled or exceeded. The decision could present a number of employers with major problems, particularly in terms of staff in key areas. They could face the prospect of a number of workers being able to refuse to do any more work until their hours came down to the required level.

Paid annual leave

The entitlement is to four weeks of paid leave. Leave under the Regulations is not additional to contractual entitlements so that taking contractual paid leave in a particular leave year counts against the worker's entitlement under the Regulations. In the absence of any agreement, the employer can require a worker to take all or any of the leave at specified times, subject to giving the worker notice of at least twice the period of the leave to be taken. The worker is also required to give notice to the employer of the wish to take leave. The notice period must again be at least twice the period of leave to be taken.

A week's leave is the equivalent to the time a worker would work in a week. A full-time worker working five days a week is entitled to 20 days' leave. A part-time worker working two days a week would have a right to eight days of leave. Where the work is expressed in hours, annual leave may be so expressed, e.g. a worker works 24 hours a week and gets 96 hours leave entitlement. The leave cannot be replaced with a payment in lieu except on termination of employment.

Furthermore, the ECJ has decided that workers who do not take all of their minimum four weeks' leave during a given year must be allowed to carry it forward to the next year. In the same case the ECJ gave a confirmatory ruling that to give pay in lieu of minimum holiday leave is illegal. The basis of the rulings is that minimum leave must actually be taken for health and safety reasons (see Case C-12/405 *Netherlands Federation of Trade Unions* v *Dutch Government*).

Leave in the first year

The four weeks (or 20 days) of leave accrue during the first year of employment. After six months of the leave year therefore an employee is entitled to 10 days' paid leave and fractionally less at earlier stages of employment.

Leave in advance of entitlement

There is no harm in allowing employees to take leave in excess of the accrued entitlement but unless there is a provision in the contract of employment an employer cannot recover holiday pay where the relevant leave has been taken in advance of accrued entitlement and the worker resigns before he or she has accrued the necessary leave to match the leave actually taken (see *Hill* v *Chapell* (2002) EAT/1250/01).

Miss Hill gave in her resignation after taking 15 days holiday in six months of the leave year. Her contract had no provision about recovery of holiday pay in this situation and the EAT turned down the employer's claim for it.

This is an aspect of the WTR that should be considered by employers when making employment contracts. It is often convenient to allow leave to be taken in advance of entitlement. However, the contract of employment should allow recovery of any excessive sum of holiday pay where, e.g. the employee resigns before completing the necessary entitlement period.

If a worker's employment ends he/she has a right to be paid for leave accrued but not taken. This applies even where an employee is fairly dismissed (see *Witley and District Men's Club* v *Mackay* [2001] IRLR 595) where the dismissal was for dishonesty.

It should be noted that leave does not accrue on a pro-rata basis after the first year. All this means is that the worker is not obliged to wait until holiday has accrued before being allowed to take it. Of course, problems such as those seen in the *Hill* case above will arise but may be provided for in the contract of employment.

19

Paying a rolled-up rate

Calculating the various leave entitlements of a workforce is a time-consuming job for the employer and some have resorted to paying a rolled-up rate by including a proportion of holiday pay with the weekly or monthly basic pay.

In a number of conjoined appeals from the UK Court of Appeal, the ECJ ruled that rolled-up pay was unlawful. However, where the employer has *before the ruling* operated a system of rolled-up pay and the payments have been made in a transparent and comprehensible manner so that the worker can identify what is pay and what is holiday pay, the pay can be set off against future leave entitlement. However, *after that* an employer must not proceed with further rolled-up pay payments. The Department of Trade and Industry has also issued a statement to a similar effect: contracts must be renegotiated for the future.

The ECJ ruling is to be found in *Robinson-Steele* v *RD Retail Services Ltd*; *Clarke* v *Frank Steddon Ltd*; *Caulfield* v *Marshalls Clay Products Ltd* [2006] All ER (D) 195 (Oct).

Length of night work

Night work is presumed to be work between 11 pm and 6 am, unless otherwise defined by agreement.

Excluded sectors

The Regulations, other than those parts which apply to young workers (see below), were not applied to workers employed in the following sectors:

- air transport;
- rail;
- road transport;
- sea transport;
- inland waterway and lake transport;
- sea fishing;
- other work at sea, e.g. offshore work in the oil and gas industry.

In this connection, the *Working Time (Amendment) Regulations 2003 came into force on 1 August 2003*. They cover the above sectors but disapplying the following in regard to them:

- the average 48 hour working week;
- four weeks' paid annual holiday;
- rest breaks;
- health assessments for night workers; and
- an eight-hour limit on night working;
- the 1998 regulations are disapplied in their entirety in the case of seafarers, workers on board sea-going fishing vessels and workers on certain ships and hovercraft on inland waterways.

Although the WTR are applied to the police and armed services there will clearly be times when their working time cannot be measured or predetermined and in these situations they will be exempt from the WTR under the derogation mentioned below.

Other derogations

As regards road transport, the Road Transport (Working Time) Regulations 2005 now give working time protection for all mobile workers (in general, drivers and crew travelling in vehicles that are subject to tachograph requirements), such as goods vehicles over 3.5 tonnes, coaches and inter-urban bus services. The Regulations cover mobile workers in the haulage industry and those who work for companies with their own transport section and agency drivers.

Employees whose working time is not measured or predetermined are exempt from the provisions relating to the 48-hour week, daily and weekly rest periods, rest breaks and limits on night work but not the holiday provisions. Examples given in the WTR include 'managing executives or other persons with autonomous decision making powers, family workers and ministers of religion'. This seems to be a very limited exception that will only cover individuals who can choose the hours which they work. It is not likely to cover professional staff who have core hours but work additional hours as required. Since the definition is not entirely clear, employers would be advised to make the position clear by agreement.

A salaried partner, although a 'worker', may well be exempt under this head since he/she will not normally have core hours.

Collective and workforce agreements

The Regulations allow employers to modify or exclude the rules relating to night work, daily and weekly rest periods and rest breaks and extend the reference period in relation to the 48-hour week – *but not the 48-hour week itself* – by way of agreement as follows:

- a collective agreement between an independent trade union and the employer (or an employers' association);
- a workforce agreement with representatives of the relevant workforce *or if there are 20 workers or fewer the agreement may be with a majority of the workforce which obviates the need to elect worker representatives*. As regards worker representatives, these may be representatives elected for other purposes, e.g. health and safety consultation;
- for, e.g., technical reasons or reasons concerning the organisation of work the 17-week averaging period may be extended by up to 52 weeks by a collective workforce agreement;
- individuals may also choose to agree with their employer to work in excess of the 48-hour weekly time limit. *This is all that an individual agreement can cover*;
- this individual agreement must be in writing and must allow the worker to bring the agreement to an end. The agreement may specify a notice period of up to three months and if no period of notice is specified, only seven days' notice by the employee is required. The worker must give written notice to the employer;
- in addition, a workforce agreement may apply to the whole of the workforce or to a group of workers within it.

These agreements can only last for a maximum of five years before renewal.

Records

In outline the position is as follows:

- An employer must keep adequate records to show that he has complied with the weekly working time limit. The records must be kept for two years. It is up to the employer to determine what records must be kept. Pay records may adequately demonstrate a worker's working hours.
- Similar provisions apply in regard to records showing that the limits on night work are being complied with. Records need not be kept in regard to rest periods and in-work rest breaks nor in regard to paid annual leave.

- Amendments have been made to the record keeping requirements to relieve the burden on business (see SI 1999/3372 in force 17 December 1999). The amending Regulations:
  - remove the need to keep records for staff who have opted out. (Formerly, where a worker had agreed to work in excess of the 48-hour weekly working limit, the employer was required to keep records of the number of hours that the worker had worked.);
  - provide that *unpaid* time which workers have agreed to work over and above their contracted hours are disregarded in terms of records.

Compensatory rest

Employers who make use of the derogations or who enter into collective or workforce agreements must provide an equivalent period of rest or, if this is not possible, give appropriate health and safety protection. Thus the Regulations allow, through agreement, flexibility in the way its rights are delivered, but they do not allow those rights to be totally avoided.

Health and safety assessments

An employer must offer a free health assessment to any worker who is to become a night worker. Employers must also give night workers the opportunity to have further assessments at regular intervals.

Young (or adolescent) workers

The Regulations also apply rights to persons over the minimum school-leaving age but under 18.

The Regulations have been amended by the Working Time (Amendment) Regulations 2002 (SI 2002/3128) that came into force on 6 April 2003. The position under the WTR as amended is as follows:

- *weekly working hours* are limited to 40;
- there is a *prohibition on night work* between 10 pm and 6 am or 11 pm and 7 am;
- *daily working time* is limited to eight hours;
- *health assessments for night workers*: adolescent workers are entitled to a health and capacity assessment if they work during the period 10 pm to 6 am. Such an assessment for an adolescent worker differs in that it considers issues like physique, maturity and experience and takes into account the competence to undertake the night work that has been assigned;
- *weekly rest*: for young workers the general requirement is two days off per week;
- *in-work rest breaks*: for young workers the general provision is 30 minutes if the working day is longer than $4^1/_2$ hours;
- *paid annual leave*: adult and young workers are treated the same.

The restrictions are subject to various exceptions relating to particular occupations and circumstances, e.g. hospitals, agriculture, retail trading and hotel and catering work (but not in restaurants and bars), bakeries, postal and newspaper deliveries subject to certain conditions, e.g. compensatory rest. Young workers in the seafaring and sea fishing industries and the armed forces are excluded from the provisions.

Other young workers rules

SI 2000/2548, reg 2 limits the number of hours a child of school age can work – in any week during which he or she is required to attend school – to 12.

Enforcement and remedies

The weekly working time limit, the night work limit and health assessments for night workers are enforced by the Health and Safety Executive or local authority environmental health officers. The usual criminal penalties for breach of the health and safety law apply. In addition, workers who are not allowed to exercise their rights under the Regulations or who are dismissed or subjected to a detriment – whether a pay cut, demotion or disciplinary action – for doing so will be entitled to present a complaint to an employment tribunal. In view of the abolition on the ceiling of awards for unfair dismissal, employment tribunal claims could be much more expensive than health and safety fines.

The following case gives an example of a situation which gave rise to a claim. In *Brown* v *Controlled Packaging Services* (1999) unreported, a fork-lift truck driver was told when interviewed for a job that he would have to work overtime on occasions. On commencing work, he discovered that the amount of overtime he was expected to do conflicted with an evening part-time job which he had. His manager indicated that his services were not required in the business if he did not sign the opting-out agreement. Mr Brown took this as a dismissal and left. He later claimed unfair dismissal and the tribunal ruled that the main reason for the dismissal was his refusal to sign the agreement and that his dismissal was automatically unfair.

Pay

In business organisations the duty of the employer to pay his employees and the rate or amount of pay is decided as follows: (a) by the contract of employment; or (b) by the terms of what is called a collective agreement made between a trade union and the employer. The terms of this agreement, including the part on pay, are then assumed to be part of the individual contracts of employment of the members. The employer must also comply with the National Minimum Wage Act 1998 (see below).

The pay which the worker is to get should nearly always be definite because it is included in the written particulars, which we have just dealt with, and also because the ERA requires itemised pay statements.

19

Itemised pay statements

Under the ERA, an employee is entitled to an itemised pay statement, containing the gross amount for wages or salary; the amounts of any variable and fixed deductions and the reasons for them; and the net amount of wages or salary payable. As only gross and net amounts and deductions are required, it is apparently unnecessary for workers to be informed as to details of their basic rates, overtime payments or shift premiums. The fixed deductions can be aggregated so long as the employee is issued with a statement of fixed deductions which is reissued every 12 months, and he is notified of any alterations when they are made. If an employee does not receive a pay statement or if he receives one that is inadequate, he may refer the matter to an employment tribunal. The employment tribunal will make a declaration which will include answers to questions relating to the employer's failure to give particulars or his failure to give accurate amounts. The declaration then determines these matters. Where there have been unnotified deductions from pay during the previous 13 weeks, the tribunal may order the employer to pay to the employee a sum not exceeding the total unnotified deductions. It can do this even where the employer was entitled to make the deductions under the terms of the contract.

The compensation is intended to act as a penalty on the employer for non-compliance and it is payable even where the employer has accounted for the sums deducted to the Inland Revenue and therefore ends up paying twice (*Cambiero* v *Aldo Zilli & Sheenwalk Ltd t/a Signor Zilli's Bar*) (1998) 586 IRLB 11).

If the particulars are complete and in accordance with the law but the employee wishes to question the *accuracy* of the amounts deducted, this is a matter for the county court though it can be dealt with by an employment tribunal if the employee has left work.

Contractual sick pay

There is no presumption that a contract of employment contains an implied term that sick pay will be paid.

Mears v *Safecar Security*, 1982 – No presumption about sick pay (**251**)

Statutory sick pay

Employers are required to provide what is called *statutory sick pay* (SSP) on behalf of the government. It is not necessary in a book of this nature to go into detail in regard to the scheme but the main principles are that when an employee falls sick he or she gets a weekly amount from the employer and not from the Department of Social Security. As regards reimbursement of employers who have paid SSP, there is now no distinction between small employers whose annual National Insurance Contributions bills do not exceed £45,000 and other employers. Under the Statutory Sick Pay Percentage Threshold Order 1995 (SI 1995/512) all employers recover SSP on the 'percentage threshold scheme'. This works as follows: the employer takes the figure of NIC (employer's and employee's contributions) paid in any given tax month. The employer then finds out the SSP paid in that same month. If this is more than 13 per cent of the NIC figure he recovers the excess.

SSP can go on for 28 weeks and since the vast majority of employees are not sick for anything like as long as this, employee sickness benefit is, in effect, now paid by the employer. It is not possible to avoid the SSP provisions and any clause in a contract of employment which sets out to do this is void.

The current single rate of SSP is £70.05. The amount is reviewed annually.

Exceptions

There are some exceptions. Examples are:

- employees over pension age, though women who continue to work between the ages of 60 and 65 are eligible for SSP;
- persons employed for a fixed period of not more than three months unless the contract is extended beyond three months;
- an employee whose average weekly earnings are less than the lower earnings limit (currently £84 a week) is not entitled to SSP but there is no service requirement.

The national minimum wage

The National Minimum Wage Act 1998 received the Royal Assent on 31 July 1998. It is in part an enabling Act and its order- and Regulation-making powers came into force on 31 July. Remaining provisions were in force by 1 April 1999 (see SI 1998/2574). This section combines the main provisions of the Act with those of Regulations so far issued under it. Section references are to the 1998 Act, unless otherwise indicated.

The Act provides workers with a floor below which their wages will not fall, regardless of the size of the employer's business. Those who work part time will benefit most.

Entitlement

Those entitled must be 'workers' who work or ordinarily work in the UK under a contract of employment and are over compulsory school leaving age (ss 1(2) and 54(3)). Casual workers are included, as are agency workers (s 34) and home-workers (s 35).

Regulations may exclude any age group below 26 and prescribe different rates for different age groups below 26 (s 3). The self-employed are excluded, when providing services to a client or business customer, and there are other exclusions in ss 43–45, e.g. voluntary workers defined in s 44. These include charity workers, who are e.g. either unpaid or receive only reasonable travel and out-of-pocket expenses.

Also excluded are au pairs and nannies and companions who are treated as a member of their employer's family with free accommodation and meals.

Owner-managed businesses

The 1998 Act applies to directors of owner-managed businesses. Thus, a person who works as a director of his company, but takes no salary (or very little) *relying on dividends* as income, falls foul of the Act and must receive the minimum wage. The same is true of directors *who receive nothing* in the first months of the new company's life. The alternative is to remain a creditor and pay when the company can afford to do so.

A further solution for directors is not to have a contract of employment so that they are not employees. This is accepted by the National Minimum Wage Office (part of HM Revenue and Customs (HMRC)) which is the enforcing agency and by the Department of Trade and Industry which has confirmed that it will not challenge such an arrangement on the basis that the director has an *implied* contract of employment.

Level

The levels of the NMW are currently as follows:

- adult minimum wage £5.35;
- rate for age 18 to 21 £4.45;
- rate for age 16 to 17 £3.30.

The above are hourly rates.

Increases in level

This depends upon the advice of the Low Pay Commission (LPC) and the economic situation, and is not automatic.

Extensions

There is power to apply the Act to those who do not fit the current definition of a 'worker' (s 41). This could be used to deal with changes in working practices and to close loopholes which bad employers may exploit.

Calculation

The Regulations set out the averaging period to be used in calculating whether a worker has been paid the NMW. It is set at a month (i.e. a 'calendar month') except where workers are

19

currently paid by reference to periods of shorter than one month, e.g. a week, a fortnight or four weeks. In the latter cases, the pay reference period for NMW purposes will be the worker's existing pay period. In addition, the hourly rate for those who are paid annual salary will be calculated on an average basis. Therefore, the lowest salary for a 35-hour week would be: the current rate per hour × 35 × 52.

What counts as remuneration?

The Regulations deal with a number of instances of what does and does not count towards discharging an employer's obligation to pay the NMW. Examples of things which do not count are advances of wages, pensions, redundancy payments and benefits in kind. However, deductions are allowed where the employer provides accommodation, but only up to a fairly low limit.

Service charges, tips, gratuities or cover charges *not paid through the payroll* are not included. Tips pooled under an employees' informal scheme and distributed are not included. However, where tips are pooled by the employer and paid through the payroll, they do count as remuneration.

Basically tips given in cash to the worker belong to him or her and do not count towards NMW. Where the workers pool the tips and distribute them themselves the tips belong to the workers and do not count. Additions to the bill where payment of the whole account is made to the employer then this is his or her money and can be used to pay the basic wage and is not an addition to it (see *Nerva* v *UK* [2002] IRLR 815).

Enforcement

The Secretary of State appoints enforcement officers (s 13) and HM Revenue and Customs is responsible for enforcement by checking employers' records to ensure compliance. Complaints by employees will be investigated and spot checks will be made on employers.

The National Minimum Wage (Enforcement Notices) Act 2003

This Act ensures that the Inland Revenue can issue enforcement notices to require the payment of the NMW to *former* employees as well as current employees. The Act closes a loophole that was revealed by the decision of the EAT in *IRC* v *Bebb Travel plc* [2002] 4 All ER 534. In the *Bebb* case the EAT ruled that under s 19(2) of the National Minimum Wage Act 1998 an enforcement notice could be issued in regard to a previous failure to pay the NMW if the notice also contained a requirement that the employer pay the NMW *in the future*. Thus former employees could not claim merely for past failures to pay. The 2003 Act adds s 19(2A) to the 1998 Act which allows the service of an enforcement notice where it is of opinion that a worker who qualifies has 'at any time' not received the minimum wage. The 2003 Act is retrospective. Workers may bring claims under it to an employment tribunal, a county court or through HMRC's enforcement unit.

In this connection, enforcement officers can disclose information obtained from the employer to the worker and similarly disclose information obtained from the worker to the employer. Enforcement notices can be withdrawn or replaced as can penalty notices.

Organisations that refuse to pay the NMW will face daily fines of twice the NMW for each employee (s 21). If defiance continues, the fine goes up to a maximum of £5,000 for each offence (s 31). Workers have the right to recover the difference between what they have been paid and the NMW before a tribunal as an unlawful deduction from wages (s 17). There is no limit of time on back claims.

Access to tax records

The inspectors required to enforce the NMW have access through the Inland Revenue to relevant tax records.

Records

The record-keeping obligations were eased following consultation and it is now merely provided that an employer has to keep records 'sufficient to establish that he is remunerating the worker at a rate at least equal to the national minimum wage'. The records may be in a format and with a content of the employer's choosing and must be capable of being produced as a single document when requested either by an employee or the Inland Revenue. The DTI publishes guidance on the kinds of records that will be regarded as sufficient.

Corporate offences

Where a relevant offence is committed by a company, its directors and other officers are jointly responsible with the company where they have consented to or connived at the offence or been neglectful in regard to it (s 32).

Contracting out

Section 29 makes void any agreement to exclude or limit the Act's provisions or to prevent a complaint from being made to a tribunal, unless there has been conciliation by a conciliation officer or a valid compromise agreement.

Victimisation and unfair dismissal

Section 23 gives workers the right not to be subject to any detriment e.g. failure to promote because they have asserted rights under the 1998 Act. Under s 25, employees who are dismissed or selected for redundancy for similarly asserting rights will be regarded as automatically unfairly dismissed so that a complaint may be made to a tribunal even by those who do not have one year's service.

Low Pay Commission

The government has asked the Low Pay Commission, which was put on to a statutory footing when ss 5–8 of the National Minimum Wage Act 1998 came into force on 1 November 1998, to report on a number of matters e.g. to monitor and evaluate the impact of the NMW in terms of pay, employment and competitiveness in low-paying sectors and small businesses, and the effect on pay differentials.

Method of payment and deductions from pay

Employees no longer have a right to be paid in cash. The matter is now left to be decided by the contract of employment. The Truck Acts 1831–1940, which used to give this right, have been repealed. Payment may still, of course, be made in cash, but an employer can if he wishes pay the employee, for example, by cheque or by crediting the employee's bank account. It should be noted, however, that if a worker was paid in cash before 1986 when the new provisions came into force, the method of payment may only be changed if the worker agrees to a variation of the contract of service.

Under Part II (ss 13–17) of the ERA deductions from pay are unlawful unless they are (a) authorised by Act of Parliament, such as income tax and National Insurance deductions; or (b) contained in a written contract of employment, or the worker has signed a written statement containing his agreement or consent to the making of them. Such a statement is ineffective if made *after* the need to make the deductions arises. Once there are shortages, the employee is under much more pressure to sign a document to agree to make them good in order to save his job, even though he might not be responsible for them. This was decided in *Discount Tobacco and Confectionery Ltd* v *Williamson* [1993] IRLR 327. As regards (*b*), deductions from the wages of workers in the retail trade, e.g. petrol station cashiers, for stock and cash shortages are limited to 10 per cent of the gross wages and deduction may be made on any pay day, but only in respect of shortages within the period of 12 months from the date when the employer knew or ought to have known of the shortage. Deductions may be made by instalments and no limit is placed on the amount which may be deducted from a final pay packet when employment is terminated. These provisions are enforceable by the employee against the employer exclusively in employment tribunals (see *Franks Investment Management Ltd* v *Robertson* (1996) *The Times*, 12 November).

Equal treatment in terms and conditions of employment as between men and women in the same employment

The Equal Pay Act 1970, as amended, implies a term into men's and women's contracts of employment which requires equal treatment in terms of pay, holidays, sick pay and hours of work.

The Equal Pay Act 1970 provides that all contracts of employment are regarded as containing an equality clause which operates on pay when a woman is employed on 'like work' or on work 'rated as equivalent' to that of a man, e.g. by a job evaluation study.

Under the Equal Pay (Amendment) Regulations 1983, there is a further instance when equality is to have effect, i.e. where a woman is employed on work which is, in terms of the demands made on her, for instance under such headings as effort, skill and 'decision', of equal value to that of a man in the same employment. In addition, under the Regulations a complaint may go before an employment tribunal, even if the two jobs under comparison have already been shown to be unequal in a job evaluation study. However, the tribunal must find the study unsatisfactory either on the grounds of sex bias or other grounds.

Even if the two jobs are wholly dissimilar a claim may be made if the jobs are of 'equal value'. A case in point is *British Coal Corporation* v *Smith* [1996] 3 All ER 97 where women canteen workers and cleaners employed in the coal industry claimed that their work was of equal value to that of surface mineworkers and, in some cases, clerical workers employed at their own and at separate workplaces. The House of Lords decided that the women could use the above categories of worker as comparators. It was a matter for a court or tribunal to decide what was a relevant class of employees.

In addition, under directly applicable EC law (i.e. Art 141 of the Treaty of Rome), a person may rely on a successor to the post as a comparator as in *Hallam Diocese Trustee* v *Connaughton* [1996] IRLR 505 or a predecessor as in *Macarthys* v *Smith* [1980] ICR 672.

The Act applies to all forms of full-time and part-time work. There are no exemptions for small firms or in respect of people who have only recently taken up the employment, although the Act does not apply, for example, to those who work wholly outside Great Britain. Both the complainant and the comparator must be employed at an establishment or establishments in Great Britain. The Act also applies to pay discrimination against men but in practice claims have usually been made by women.

The comparison is with the pay of a comparator of the opposite sex and in the case of part-timers with part-time comparators. The 1970 Act is not concerned with fair wages generally but only between those of opposite sex. Thus, for a woman a male comparator is required, and vice versa.

Equal pay questionnaires

Under s 7B of the Equal Pay Act 1970 (as inserted by s 42 of the Employment Act 2002) an employee who believes that she/he may not be receiving equal pay can use a questionnaire to request key information from the employer when deciding whether to bring an equal pay claim. If it is decided to go to a tribunal the information elicited from the employer will be admissible as evidence and will help the complainant to formulate and present the case. A tribunal will be able to draw inferences from a deliberate refusal to answer or from an evasive reply. This includes an inference that the employer is contravening the implied equality clause in the employee's contract. While it is not necessary for the employer to reveal the names of persons on higher pay but only pay there are those in industry who feel that, particularly in the smaller organisation, it will be possible to make identification so that the employer may be in breach of confidence by revealing salaries of other employees though an employer should have a good defence because he or she is carrying out a statutory requirement.

Under the Employment Tribunals (Constitution and Rules of Procedure) (Amendment) Regulations 2004 (SI 2004/2351), a tribunal may order an employer to grant access to his or her premises to an expert where one has been appointed by the tribunal or to the claimant or his or her representative in order to question certain employees, e.g. alleged comparators.

Non-employees

Rights are given to persons who are not employees in the ordinary sense. The EPA definition includes persons who work under a contract to execute any work or labour, e.g. those who provide consultancy services under a contract for services.

Effect of successful claim

The complainant has a contractual right to the higher pay and/or the other contract terms enjoyed by the comparator. The tribunal can also award compensation in respect of the disparity.

19

Time limits

The Equal Pay Act 1970 (Amendment) Regulations 2003 (SI 2003/1656) apply and affirm the law laid down by the ECJ in *Levez* v *TH Jennings (Harlow Pools) Ltd* [1999] IRLR 36 and *Preston* v *Wolverhampton Healthcare NHS Trust* [2000] IRLR 506 by making appropriate amendments to the Equal Pay Act 1970. The time limit for bringing a claim is six months after the claimant was employed in the employment. However, where there is a succession of contracts at regular intervals forming part of a stable employment relationship the period of six months runs from the end of the last such contract. As regards compensation, the limit now relates to a six-year period before the date on which the proceedings were commenced.

Part-time workers

The *Part-time Workers (Prevention of Less Favourable Treatment) Regulations 2000*, which came into force on 1 July 2000, and are not retrospective, enable part-timers to claim equal treatment without the need to prove sex discrimination.

A part-time worker will not normally be able to use a full-time worker as a comparator where it is the *job* that gives rise to the different conditions and not *gender* (*Lynn* v *Rokeby School Board of Governors* [2001] All ER (D) 440 (Mar)).

Pensions

The matter of equality in pension rights exists but is dealt with by the Pensions Act 1995 and supporting Regulations.

Sections 62–66 require all occupational pensions schemes to provide equal treatment for men and women with regard to:

- the terms on which they become members of the scheme; and
- the terms on which members are treated in relation to any pensionable service.

Equality in this context means that claims for pension rights must be made within six months of leaving service or where there is a series of contracts forming a stable employment relationship six months from the end of the last contract. Service for pension entitlement may be calculated for service back to 8 April 1976 if there has been a stable employment relationship for that period of time and the claim has been brought in time. The date of 8 April 1976 is based upon the date of the ECJ decision in Case 149/77 *Defrenne* v *Sabena* [1978] ECR 1365 that decided pensions were pay for the purposes of EU law and *Barber* v *Guardian Royal Exchange Assurance Group* [1990] 2 All ER 660 which decided that equality clauses must be implied in pension schemes.

Community law

A claim can be brought under UK legislation only if the complainant and the comparator are or have been employed at the same time. However, any gaps or exceptions in UK legislation can be overridden by Community law. Article 141 of the Treaty of Rome establishes the principle that men and women are entitled to equal pay for work of equal value. As we have seen the EAT ruled that an employment tribunal could hear a claim for equal pay under what is now Art 141 where the applicant relied on a male comparator appointed *after* her resignation (see *Hallam Diocese Trustee* v *Connaughton* [1996] IRLR 505). In *Macarthys* v *Smith* [1980] ICR 672 the ECJ ruled that the complainant's *predecessor* was a valid comparator.

The above rulings on the basis of EC law provide good examples of the effect of European rulings on English law, in this area.

Employer's defences

One obvious defence is that the two jobs cannot be regarded as being 'like work'. Equal value is more difficult but here there may be resort to a job evaluation exercise to resolve the matter. The employer will not normally be able to argue the defence that the woman and the comparator are not in the same employment, where associated employers are included so that employees can find comparators in a holding company or a fellow subsidiary in a group situation. The material factor defence is more difficult and examples appear in the case law and comment that follows.

> *Capper Pass* v *Lawton*, 1976 – An equal pay claim succeeds (**252**)
> *Navy, Army and Air Force Institutes* v *Varley*, 1977 – An equal pay claim fails (**253**)

Part-time workers

The Part-time Employees (Prevention of Less Favourable Treatment) Regulations 2000 came into force on 1 July 2000 with the object of further extending the rights of part-time workers.

Although the rights of part-time employees have been extended in recent years so that, for example, claims for unfair dismissal can be brought by part-timers with one year's service, their rights are not the same in some remaining areas. The Regulations are intended to put this right. The provisions are set out below:

- *Pay*. Part-time employees should receive the same hourly rate of pay as comparable full-time workers. A lower rate may be justified on objective grounds as where, e.g., there is performance-related pay.
- *Overtime*. Part-time employees should receive the same hourly rate of overtime pay as comparable full-time employees once they have worked more than the full-time hours.
- *Contractual sick pay and maternity pay*. Part-time employees should not be treated less favourably than full-time employees in terms of the rate of contractual sick pay or maternity pay; the length of service required to qualify for payment and the length of time the payment is received. The benefits which a part-timer will receive are to be pro rata which means that where a comparable full-time employee receives or is entitled to receive pay or any other benefit a part-time employee is to receive or be entitled to receive not less than the proportion of that pay or other benefit that the number of his weekly hours bears to the number of weekly hours of the comparable full-time employee.
- *Occupational pensions*. Employers must not discriminate between full-time and part-time employees over access to pension schemes unless different treatment is justified on objective grounds. Calculation of benefits from the pension scheme for part-time staff should be on a pro rata basis of the calculation for full-time employees.
- *Access to training*. Employers should not exclude part-time staff from training simply because they work part-time.
- *Leave/holiday/breaks: annual leave, maternity, adoption and parental leave, career breaks*. The contractual holiday entitlement of part-time staff should be pro rata to that of full-time employees. Contractual maternity leave, adoption leave and parental leave should be available to part-time employees as well as full-time employees. Career break schemes should be available to part-time employees in the same way as for full-time employees, unless their exclusion is objectively justified on grounds other than their part-time status.
- *Redundancy*. The criteria used to select jobs for redundancy should be objectively justified and part-time employees must not be treated less favourably than comparable full-time workers in regard to selection for redundancy.

The Regulations cover not only workers but extend also to homeworkers and agency workers. In the case of homeworkers, they will have to find a comparator which may not be easy. Full-time workers who switch to part-time work can make a comparison with the benefits provided in their full-time contract. This may assist women wishing to convert to part-time work after maternity leave, though some employers may regard this as a further burden. It may, therefore, be counter-productive. A worker's request to the employer for change must be made in writing and the employer has 21 days to respond before a claim is made to an employment tribunal. This is intended to produce a reconciliation of the position. If not, a claim may be made to an employment tribunal within three months of the act of discrimination. This time scale does not seem to matter since failure to comply with the requirement to up-rate conditions in relation to a full-time comparator is a continuing

19

source of complaint so time will stop running in regard, e.g., to back pay only when the part-timer's rights are equalised. There is no limit on the money aspect of the award in terms of a back-pay claim.

Qualifying periods

There is no requirement that the claimant should have any minimum period of service. Also, the upper limit of normal retirement age, or if there is none at the workplace 65 years of age, does not apply. This is the first sign of laws prohibiting discrimination on the ground of age.

Effect on employers

Many employers follow the above practices and will not be affected. If not, they will be because there are likely to be comparators who are full-time.

Some small businesses may not be affected at all, either because they do not provide the contractual benefits set out above or because all the staff are part-time and so no pro rata comparison can be made with full-time staff.

> *Matthews* v *Kent and Medway Towns Fire Authority*, 2006 – Part-time firefighters: pensions and sick pay (**253a**)

Workers on fixed-term contracts

The Fixed-Term Employees (Prevention of Less Favourable Treatment) Regulations 2002 apply. The main provisions are set out below.

Definition

A fixed-term contract will generally be a contract of employment that terminates at the end of a specified term fixed in advance or automatically on completion of a particular task.

Comparators

Both individuals must be employed by the same employer and be engaged in the same or broadly similar work having regard to whether they have a similar level of qualifications and skills.

Less favourable treatment

This can be in regard to levels of pay, pension and other benefits such as bonuses. However, admission to a pension scheme may not be viable in the case of a short fixed-term contract.

Written statements

A fixed-term employee who thinks that he/she has been treated less favourably has a right to ask the employer for a written statement of reasons. This must be provided within 21 days.

A tribunal claim

A fixed-term employee who thinks that he/she has been treated less favourably may present a claim to an employment tribunal normally after having exhausted all internal procedures.

Vacancies for permanent employment

The Regulations give fixed-term employees a right to be informed of available vacancies for permanent employment.

Transfer to permanent employment

The Regulations provide that where an employee is on a fixed-term contract that has been renewed or where there is a re-engagement on a new fixed-term contract and where the employee has been employed for at least four years (excluding any period before 10 July 2002) the renewal of the contract will take effect as a permanent contract. The period of four years must be an unbroken one as where one fixed-term contract has immediately followed the previous one. The Regulations may not therefore correct the abuse seen in *Booth* v *United States* [1999] IRLR 16 where the US government employed men on fixed-term contracts at its UK base. There were intervals of two weeks between each contract. The claimant was not entitled to a claim for unfair dismissal or redundancy because his service was not continuous for the requisite period, nor would he have had four years of continuous service to trigger the permanent contract arrangements in the regulations. However, the employer's conduct in *Booth* may have been actionable under the Regulations if it had been based on 'detriment'.

In this connection it is worth noting that the first fixed-term workers became eligible to take advantage of the permanent contract provisions on 10 July 2006.

Dismissal and detriment

Dismissal where the Regulations have been infringed is automatically unfair so that there is no service requirement for a claim. This would overcome the major obstacle to a claim that emerged in *Booth* in terms of the claim itself. Fixed-term workers are also protected against a detriment for trying to enforce the Regulations.

Remedies

A tribunal may order compensation or recommend that reasonable action be taken to remove or reduce the effect of an employer's practice where less favourable treatment is found.

Discrimination once in employment

We have already considered the law relating to discrimination in the formation of the contract of employment, i.e. in recruitment and selection. Here we are concerned with discrimination during the course of employment.

As we have seen discrimination on the grounds of sex, marital status, race, disability, sexual orientation, religion and belief, transsexuality and age are unlawful. As regards employees, it is unlawful to discriminate as regards opportunities for promotion, training or transfer to other positions or in the provision of benefits, facilities or services or by selection for redundancy or dismissal.

The following kinds of discrimination apply:

- direct discrimination;
- indirect discrimination;
- victimisation; and
- harassment.

Direct and indirect discrimination bear the same definitions in the employment context as they do in recruitment. Victimisation and harassment are normally found, if at all, once employment has commenced and require treatment in this section of the text.

In direct and indirect discrimination a genuine occupational qualification or requirement if acceptable to the tribunal can be a defence for the employer. In the case of disability discrimination, however, the employer is required where possible to make reasonable adjustments to overcome individual difficulties with the job.

Some general illustrative case law

The concept of discrimination is wider than the relationship of employer and employee under a contract of service or apprenticeship. It includes employment 'under a contract personally to execute any work or labour' and no period of service is required before a claim can be brought. Rights are also given to partners in all partnerships.

An example of the broad nature of discrimination law is provided by *Harrods Ltd* v *Remick; Harrods Ltd* v *Seely; Elmi* v *Harrods* [1996] ICR 846. In that case the three complainants were dismissed by their employers from 'shops within a shop' at Harrods because Harrods said they were in breach of the Harrods dress code, for example in Mrs Seely's case the wearing of a nose stud. Although their contract of employment was not with Harrods that store was liable for sex discrimination when their employers dismissed them because Harrods threatened to withdraw the 'shop within a shop' concession. They were 'doing work for Harrods' and were ultimately under Harrods' control in view of the power to withdraw the concession.

Nor is discrimination liability confined to the discriminatory acts of the employer or those of his employees. In *Burton* v *De Vere Hotels Ltd* [1997] ICR 1 the EAT ruled that an employer can be regarded as having subjected employees to harassment, in this case racial harassment, by allowing a third party to inflict racial abuse on them in circumstances in which he could have prevented the harassment or reduced the amount of it. The complainants were two black women who were employed as waitresses at a Round Table function at a hotel in Derby and were subjected to racially offensive remarks by Mr Bernard Manning, a guest speaker, for example, about the sexual organs of black men and their sexual abilities. The employer did not withdraw them from the room at once as he should have done and was liable.

The House of Lords discredited this ruling in *MacDonald* v *Advocate General for Scotland; Pearce* v *Governing Body of Mayfield School* [2004] 1 All ER 339. In the above cases the claims were brought for discrimination against homosexual people but it is the last part of their Lordships' ruling that has most significance. Although the matter did not arise directly and the decision is technically not binding, the House of Lords stated that an employer would no longer be liable for failing to protect employees from the acts of third parties such as Mr Manning for whose acts the employer is not vicariously liable unless that failure is in itself less favourable treatment on discriminatory grounds.

It appeared that the manager would not have withdrawn white waitresses from a situation involving sex discrimination. In fact, he said in evidence that the matter of withdrawing the waitresses never occurred to him. So the employer is liable only for his or her own discrimination in this situation as where employees are left in a discriminatory situation because the employer, in effect, wishes to see them embarrassed or does not care whether they are.

An employer is also liable for the acts of his employees 'in the course of employment'. Employers have tried to defend themselves by saying that their employees were not employed to discriminate but in *Jones* v *Tower Boot Co Ltd* [1997] NLJR 60 the Court of Appeal rejected this defence saying a purposive interpretation must be put on 'in course of employment' for discrimination purposes. The case involved the harassment of a 16-year-old black youth who was called 'Baboon', 'Chimp' and 'Monkey' and was branded with a hot screwdriver. An employer has a defence where he or she can show that best endeavours were used to prevent the conduct. That was not the case in *Jones*. All reasonable steps to prevent the abuse were not used.

Victimisation in employment

Under discrimination legislation it is unlawful to treat a person less favourably than another because that person asserts rights under anti-discriminatory legislation or is or has helped another to do so. Damages can be awarded where victimisation has occurred. An example is to be found in *Cornelius* v *Manpower Services Commission* (SXD 36117/86) where the Commission refused to consider C for a permanent post for which she had applied because one of the references which she supplied indicated that she was involved in an unresolved sexual harassment case.

Harassment: generally

Most complaints of harassment have involved sexual harassment though *Jones* v *Tower Boot Co Ltd* (1997) provides a particularly bad situation of racial harassment.

There is now a separate head of liability for harassment in regard to sex, race, disability, sexual orientation and religion or belief. It is no longer an aspect of detriment as it has been for many years. The definition which results from the new Regulations in these areas described earlier in this chapter is defined as follows.

'Harassment occurs where on grounds of sex, race or ethnic or national origins or sexual orientation or religion or belief or for a reason which relates to a disabled person's disability – A engages in **unwanted conduct** which has the purpose or effect of (a) **violating B's dignity**; or (b) **creating an intimidating, hostile, degrading, humiliating or offensive environment** for B. The conduct is deemed to have the required effect if having regard to all the circumstances including in particular the **perception of B**, it should reasonably be considered as having that effect (author's emphasis). Obviously tribunals will be concerned to interpret this definition but it is likely that many of the cases on 'detriment' will fit the new definition.

Harassment and case law

There are numerous cases of mainly sexual harassment. Most of these provide different *fact* situations of such harassment and cannot, because of their number, be reproduced here. However, a leading case containing guidance from the EAT that can be applied in other cases

19

even under the new definition of harassment is *Driskel* v *Peninsular Business Services Ltd* [2000] 636 IRLB 12.

Mrs Driskel was an adviceline consultant with Peninsula. She claimed that she had been sexually harassed by the head of her department. She alleged that she had been subject to sexual banter and comments and that at an interview for promotion he had suggested that she wear a short skirt and a see-through blouse showing plenty of cleavage. This advice was not accepted. She then refused to return to work unless the head of department was moved elsewhere. She was then dismissed and made a claim to an employment tribunal. Her claim was rejected because the incidents looked at *in isolation* were not enough. She appealed and the EAT substituted a finding of sexual harassment and in doing so stated:

- the tribunal should have looked at the *total or overall effect* of the acts complained of;
- a woman's failure to complain at times throughout the conduct should not necessarily be taken as significant;
- sexual 'banter' between heterosexual men cannot be equated with, so as to excuse, similar comments towards a woman.

Harassment: other legislation

When harassment is intended and studied the Criminal Justice and Public Order Act 1994 creates a criminal offence of intentional harassment. It appears as s 4A inserted into the Public Order Act 1986. The penalty on conviction by magistrates is imprisonment for up to six months and/or a fine of up to £5,000.

It is clear from the wording of s 4A that harassment in the workplace is covered. This means that employees who are harassed at work are able to report the matter to the police.

The Protection from Harassment Act 1997 is also relevant. The Act is very wide ranging and covers discriminatory harassment and bullying at work. It is also possible to bring civil proceedings against offenders under the Act.

Enforcement

As regards enforcement by employees, those who believe that they have been discriminated against may make a complaint to an employment tribunal within three months of the date of the act complained of. A conciliation officer may be called in to see whether the complaint can be settled without going to a tribunal. If, however, a tribunal hears the complaint, it may make an order declaring the rights of the employee and employer in regard to the complaint, the intention being that both parties will abide by the order for the future. The tribunal may also give the employee money compensation, with no overall limit, and including aggravated damages in severe cases (see *HM Prison Service* v *Johnson* (1997) 567 IRLB 13), and may additionally recommend that the employer take, within a specified period, action appearing to the tribunal to be practicable for the purpose of obviating or reducing discrimination.

Damages can also be awarded for personal injury caused by unlawful discrimination according to the ruling of the Court of Appeal in *Sheriff* v *Klyne Tugs (Lowestoft) Ltd* (1999) 625 IRLB 6 where a ship's engineer suffered racial abuse leading to a nervous breakdown. This power obviates to need to pursue a personal injuries claim in the county court.

Coleman v *Skyrail Oceanic Ltd*, 1981 – A direct discrimination (**254**)
Price v *The Civil Service Commission*, 1977 – An indirect discrimination (**255**)

Discrimination after the end of work relationship

The relevant discrimination Regulations prohibit discrimination after the end of an employment (or partnership) relationship if the act of discrimination is closely connected to the relationship, e.g. unreasonable refusal to give a reference.

Of significance here is the case of *Woodward* v *Abbey National plc* (2006) 790 IRLB 16. In that case the Court of Appeal ruled that the statutory protection under s 47B of the Employment Rights Act 1996 against being subjected to a detriment because of the making of a protected disclosure (or whistleblowing) is not restricted to the duration of the contract of employment but extends to a detriment imposed by an employer on an employee who has left the employment, in this case the failure by Abbey to give Ms Woodward a reference after she disclosed to management that the company was failing to comply with certain legal obligations.

The importance of the ruling is that, as regards whistleblowing, there is no specific legislation giving post-employment rights. This was said by the Court of Appeal to be a purposive interpretation to make the legislation fulfil what must have been its purpose. The ruling may be of wider application because there are no specific post-employment protections in health and safety, maternity, parental or adoption leave working time and flexible working cases. There may well be however if the *Woodward* ruling is followed.

Guarantee payments

Employees with not less than four weeks' continuous service are entitled under Part III of the ERA to a guarantee payment if they are not provided with work on a normal working day, e.g. because of a proposed power cut as in *Miller* v *Harry Thornton (Lollies) Ltd* [1978] IRLR 430. The amount of the guarantee payment is reviewed from time to time by statutory instrument and is currently £19.60 per day. This guarantee is, under the ERA 1996, limited to five workless days in any three-month period. The provisions do not apply if the failure to provide work is due to a trade dispute, or if the employee has been offered suitable alternative work but has refused it.

An employee may present a complaint to an employment tribunal that his employer has failed to pay the whole or any part of a guarantee payment to which the employee is entitled. The employment tribunal may make an order to pay the employee the amount of guarantee payment which it finds is due to him.

The employee must apply to the tribunal within three months of the workless day for which no payment has been made or within such longer period as the tribunal thinks reasonable if it is satisfied that it was not reasonable or practical for the employee to present the claim within three months.

Suspension from work on medical grounds

An employee with not less than four weeks' continuous service who is suspended from work under the provisions of an Act of Parliament (e.g. the HASAWA) or a code of practice, not because he is ill but because he is exposed to a health hazard at his work and may become ill if he continues at work, is entitled to be paid normal wages while suspended for up to 26 weeks. This could occur, for example, where there was a leak of radioactivity at the workplace.

An employee may present a complaint to an employment tribunal within three months of the day in respect of which the claim is made (ERA, s 70) that his employer has failed to pay the whole or any part of remuneration to which he is entitled on suspension, and the tribunal may order the employer to pay the employee the remuneration due to him.

Family-friendly provisions

Suspension on maternity grounds

The ERA provides for suspension on maternity grounds. Formerly, a pregnant woman could be fairly dismissed if because of her condition she could not do her work, e.g. because of health and safety hazards, and either there was no suitable alternative work or she had refused it. The ERA substitutes suspension on grounds of pregnancy, recent childbirth or breastfeeding, while the health and safety hazards continue. There is no 26-week limit. The employee may complain to a tribunal if she is not offered available and suitable alternative work. Suspension continues even if such an offer is refused but pay ceases. For those who have not refused an offer, e.g. because it was not possible for the employer to make one, normal pay continues during the suspension. Those who are not paid, though entitled, can claim compensation before a tribunal.

If an employer dismisses an employee who tries to assert her rights in the two above suspension matters, the dismissal is automatically unfair whatever the employee's length of service.

Ante-natal care

Under the ERA, refusal of this right by the employer gives rise to a claim. A pregnant employee who has, on the advice of her doctor or midwife or health visitor, made an appointment to get ante-natal care must have time off to keep it and she must also be paid. Except for the first appointment, the employer can ask for proof of the appointment in the form, for example, of an appointment card. An employer who does not give the employee these rights can be taken to a tribunal by the employee, but this must normally be during the three months after the date of the appointment. Compensation may be given to the employee, both where the employer has failed to give time off and also where he has given time off but has failed to pay the employee. In either case the compensation will be the amount of pay to which she would have been entitled if time off with pay had been given as the law requires. The right to time off for ante-natal care is enjoyed by *all* female employees, except any who ordinarily work outside Great Britain. There is no service requirement.

Maternity leave and pay

This rather complex area of employment law can perhaps be best set out in table form.

The table takes into account the major changes made by the Maternity and Parental Leave etc. and the Paternity and Adoption Leave (Amendment) Regulations 2006 (SI 2006/2014), which are sanctioned by the Work and Families Act 2006.

The provision	The law
Ordinary Maternity Leave (OML)[1]	From 1 April 2007 an entitlement to 26 weeks Ordinary Maternity Leave
Additional Maternity Leave (AML)[1]	From 1 April 2007 an entitlement to a further period of 26 weeks end on to OML
Availability (OML)	Available to all female workers regardless of service
Availability (AML)	Available to female workers regardless of service
Statutory Maternity Pay	Available to female workers with 26 weeks' continuous service immediately preceding the 14th week before EWC
Notice required for entitlement	Notification to the employer in or before the 14th week before the EWC
Notice of what?	The pregnancy: the EWC and the date of starting OML
Employer's response to notice	The employer must write to the worker within 28 days of her notice stating the date of her return. *This fixes that date*
Notification of return	No notice is required but if the worker wants to return early she must give eight weeks' notice to the employer
Statutory Maternity Pay period[2]	39 weeks
Rate of SMP	90% of average earnings for the first eight weeks of leave and for the remaining weeks the *lesser* of £108.85 or 90% of average weekly earnings

Notes
(1) An employee can carry out a maximum of 10 days' work to 'keep in touch' during this period without bringing the leave to an end.
(2) The Work and Families Act 2006 allows the government to extend this period to 52 weeks.

SMP administration

Employers can recover 92 per cent of the amount paid out by way of SMP and small employers (broadly those whose National Insurance contributions payments for the qualifying tax year do not exceed £40,000) can recover 100 per cent plus an additional 4.5 per cent of each payment of SMP which is designed to recoup the NI contributions payable on such payments. All employers can recover SMP from tax and other payments due to the Revenue and not just NI contributions as before. Furthermore, under s 21 of the Employment Act 2002 advanced payments can be requested from the Revenue.

Section 21 is not yet in force.

Compulsory maternity leave

This leave is provided for by s 72 of the ERA 1996. The employer of a woman is prohibited from allowing her to return to work during the two weeks from the day on which the child is born. An employer who contravenes this requirement commits a criminal offence and is liable to a fine currently not exceeding £500. It is accepted that the woman will be most unlikely to want to return to work. The provision is basically designed to prevent the employer from pressurising her to do so.

Paternity leave

Male and female employees have a right to be away from work on paid paternity leave.

19

The qualifying conditions are set out below:

- the right is available to employees who:
  - have continuous service with the employer of 26 weeks by the end of the fifteenth week before the EWC;
  - have or expect to have responsibility for bringing up the child;
  - are either the biological father of the child or are married to or are the partner of the child's mother;
- leave is for two weeks and whether taken in single weeks or a block of two consecutive weeks it must be taken within a period of 56 days from the child's birth or the first day of the EWC. The second alternative is to deal with a very premature birth where the child might be kept in hospital for more than 56 days after the birth. The EWC will of course have been set to fit a normal term pregnancy and will obviously be later than in fact the birth was giving the opportunity to take leave after the child comes home;
- statutory paternity pay is at the weekly rate of the lesser of £108.85 or 90 per cent of normal earnings;
- as in the case of SMP employers can recover 92 per cent of the total payments from sums due to the Revenue and may ask for an advance payment. The small employers' provision is as for SMP;
- employees can take paternity leave in addition to unpaid parental leave of 13 weeks.

Additional paternity leave

There is now provision for up to 26 weeks of additional paternity leave (APL). The intention is for APL to apply in the second six months of the child's birth and for the father to start APL only when the mother returns to work before all her SMP entitlement expires. In practice, this means that APL cannot be taken if:

- in relation to births occurring on and after 1 April 2007 the mother has already exhausted her 39 weeks of SMP; or
- when the SMP has been increased to 52 weeks, the mother has also exhausted her full SMP or AML.

The government was not in favour of allowing APL to be taken during the first six months after the child's birth because the mother may feel pressurised to return to work. Therefore, APL will apply only where the mother has returned to work before all her SMP entitlement expires.

Adoption leave

Male and female employees are entitled to take adoption leave. There is provision for ordinary adoption leave (OAL) and additional adoption leave (AAL). Where there is a joint adoption by married couples they will be able to choose who takes the adoption leave. Where the adoption is by one of them only then that person will be entitled to the adoption leave though the other spouse will be entitled to paternity leave if the criteria are met. It should be noted that in current law couples in a long-term relationship but who are not married cannot adopt. Only married couples or one person in an unmarried relationship can adopt. As we have seen a married couple who adopt can choose which of them takes adoption leave and which takes paternity leave. The partner of a single person who adopts can take only paternity leave.

The following general points should be noted:

- an employee is entitled to OAL or AAL in regard to a child when he or she has been notified that he or she has been matched with a child by an adoption agency and he or she has been employed for 26 continuous weeks ending with the matching week;
- OAL is for 26 weeks of leave commencing either on the date the child is placed with the adopter or a date that is no more than 14 days before the expected date of placement, i.e. when the child comes to live permanently with the adopter;
- AAL is for a further period of 26 weeks end on to the OAL. No further service qualification is required;
- OAL is paid for by statutory adoption pay at the lesser of £108.85 or 90 per cent of normal earnings for 39 weeks;
- the provisions for employer recovery are the same as for SMP and SPP.

Notice provisions

Notice to the employer of 21 days is required of the intention to take leave. The employer must respond within 28 days stating when the leave ends under the employee's entitlement. This fixes the return date. The employee must give eight weeks' notice to the employer to change the intended start date and this is also the notice period for early return from leave.

Additional adoption leave

Provision is now made for an additional period of adoption leave of 26 weeks. This cannot be taken by the person who has taken adoption leave. Once again, this leave is intended to be taken by the partner who has not taken adoption leave and can commence only when the person taking the adoption leave has returned to work before exhausting that leave.

Unpaid parental leave

The new ss 76–78 of the ERA 1996 apply. These sections together with the Regulations provide for collective agreements to be made with trade unions and workforce agreements to be made with employees in regard to parental leave. Nevertheless, employees retain their rights under what is called the statutory fallback scheme unless the collective or workforce scheme is more generous, in which case such schemes can replace the fallback scheme. This book considers only the fallback scheme as follows.

The fallback scheme

An employee who has been continuously employed for a period of not less than one year has a right to 13 weeks of parental leave in respect of each child born on or after 15 December 1999 and each child under 18 who is adopted by the employee on or after that date (but see below). Women who qualify for parental leave can take it immediately after taking maternity leave. A week means seven days' absence from work, even though the employee would not have been required to work on every one of the working days. Leave must be taken in seven-day blocks up to maximum of four weeks' leave in respect of an individual child during a particular year calculated from the first time the employee became entitled to take parental leave. This was affirmed as a correct interpretation of the law in *Rodway* v *New Southern Railways Ltd* [2005] IRLR 583, where Mr Rodway, a train guard conductor, asked for a day off to look after his two-year-old son while the mother was away for the day. He was refused the time off but took it anyway, as he could not get anyone else. His employer later put him through a disciplinary procedure but his claim for detriment because he was trying to use the parental leave provisions was turned down by the Court of Appeal. Leave of one day was not within the leave provisions. Leave may be taken in blocks of one-day or multiples of one day where the child is disabled. The leave must be taken during the period of five years from the date of birth or adoption or until the child turns 18 years if disabled. As regards the adoption of older children, the leave period ends when they reach 18, even if five years from placement for adoption has not by then elapsed.

Notice

The employer must receive notice (not necessarily written notice) of 21 days specifying the dates on which leave is to begin and end. Where the leave is to be taken on birth, the notice must specify the EWC and the duration of leave to be taken and be given 21 days before the beginning of EWC. The same with adoption except that notice must be given 21 days before the expected week of placement.

Evidence

The employer is entitled to require evidence of the employee's legal responsibility for the child as well as evidence of the age of the child.

Postponement of leave

The employer may postpone a period of leave where he considers that the operation of the business would be affected in terms that it would be 'unduly disrupted'. He has only seven days to make his mind up about postponement which may be for a maximum period of six months. No postponement is allowed if leave is taken on the birth or adoption of a child.

The employment contract during leave

While on parental leave, employees remain bound by their obligation of good faith towards their employer and any express undertakings in the contract in regard to non-disclosure of confidential information and competition. The employer must continue to abide by the implied obligations of trust and confidence and offer the right to return to the same job but if that is not possible to another job which is suitable and appropriate in the circumstance. There is also protection in regard to salary, continuity of employment and pension rights on return.

Making a claim

The relevant provision is s 80 of the ERA 1996. It gives employees a right to complain to an employment tribunal within three months from the date when any of the rights under the parental leave arrangements are denied, in the sense that these have been unreasonably postponed or prevented. Any related dismissal is automatically unfair and there is no cap on the compensation that may be awarded.

Records

The Regulations do not require the keeping of records but it will be impossible for employers to avoid keeping them for accounting purposes to show that leave has been unpaid and that the rights are not being abused. Bearing in mind also that time off for domestic emergencies (also unpaid) exists (see below), employers must consider the need to set up systems and procedures to cope with the new rights and look at how they can run along with any existing contractual rights to be paid parental leave that employees already have within a particular organisation.

Time off for dependants

This is provided for by s 57A of the ERA 1996. It entitles every employee regardless of length of service to take a reasonable amount of time off work 'to take action that is necessary'

- to help when a dependant gives birth, falls ill or is assaulted;
- to make longer term arrangements for the care of a sick or injured dependant;
- as a result of a dependant's death;
- to cope when the arrangements for caring for a dependant break down unexpectedly; or
- to deal with an expected incident that involves a dependant child during school hours or on a school trip or in other situations when the school has responsibility for the child.

Dependants

This means a husband or wife or a child or parent of the employee whether they live with him or not or any member of the employee's household who is not employed by him or her and is not a tenant, lodger or boarder.

Amount of time off

There is no set limit. In every case the right is limited to the amount of time that is reasonable in the circumstances. Employment tribunals will be the ultimate arbitrators if a claim is brought by an employee.

Payment for time off

The employer is under no obligation to pay the employee for time taken off.

Notification

The right only applies if the employee 'as soon as is reasonably practicable' tells the employer why he or she is absent and unless the employee is already back at work for how long the absence is likely to last.

Enforcing the right

Section 57B of the ERA 1996 entitles an employee to complain to an employment tribunal that the employer has unreasonably refused to allow time off as required by s 57A. The period for application is three months of the employer's refusal and compensation may be an uncapped award such as is just and equitable.

Victimisation and dismissal

There is protection in terms of a tribunal complaint for any victimisation or dismissal resulting from the exercise or purported exercise of the right in a proper way and dismissal is automatically unfair. Selection for redundancy for the same reason will be automatically an unfair dismissal.

> *Qua* v *John Ford Morrison Solicitors*, 2003 – Guidance on dependants' leave (**255a**)

Maternity allowance

Those who do not qualify for statutory maternity pay because e.g. their earnings are below the lower earnings limit (currently £84 per week) may be able to get maternity allowance. The provisions are broadly as follows:

Amount of benefit

A successful claimant will receive weekly the lesser of £108.85 or 90 per cent of average earnings.

Payment period

Maternity allowance is paid for up to 39 weeks. The earliest the period can start is the eleventh week before the EWC unless the child is born before this and the latest is the Sunday after the child is born.

Service requirement

In order to qualify for maternity allowance, the claimant must have worked as an employee and/or been self-employed for at least 26 weeks in the 66 weeks immediately before the EWC. The weeks do not need to be consecutive or for the same employer and a part-week of work counts as a full week.

Earnings requirement

To qualify for maternity allowance the claimant's average weekly earnings must be at least equal to the maternity allowance threshold which is currently £30 per week. There are a number of ways of calculating average earnings but, for example, the highest earnings for 13 weeks out of the 66 weeks referred to above may be taken and divided by 13 to produce the average.

Flexible working

Under Part 8A of the Employment Rights Act 1996 (as inserted by s 47 of the Employment Act 2002) employers are under a duty to consider applications for flexible working from employees who are parents of children under age six or disabled children under 18. Changes in hours and times of work may be applied for.

Qualifying conditions for employees are:

- continuous employment with the employer for not less than 26 weeks. The purpose must be to care for a child.

   The employee must be:
   (i) the biological parent, guardian or foster carer of the child;
   (ii) married to a person within (i) above and lives with the child; or
   (iii) the partner of a person within (i) above and lives with the child.

   The employee must also have, or expect to have, responsibility for the upbringing of the child.
- The employee must apply before the fourteenth day before the child reaches six years of age or a disabled child reaches 18.
- The employer is then required to meet with the employee within 28 days of the application and the employer's decision must be notified to the employee within 14 days of the meeting. The employee must have a right of appeal. The employee also has the right to be accompanied by a fellow worker or a trade union representative at any meeting.
- The employee's application may be refused where the employer considers that one or more of the following grounds apply:
   (a) burden of additional costs;
   (b) detrimental effect on the ability to meet consumer demand;
   (c) inability to reorganise work among remaining staff;

(d) detrimental effect on quality;

(e) insufficiency of work during the periods the employee proposes to work, as where the employee proposes to be away at peak times and return at slack times when there might be a need for less staff;

(f) structural changes would be involved and require planning.

Where the employer fails to comply with his/her duties in regard to the application or bases his or her decision on incorrect facts, the employee may apply to an employment tribunal. If the employee's complaint is well-founded the tribunal may make an order to that effect and may order the employer to reconsider the matter and/or award compensation to the employee.

Additional rights inserted into the ERA 1996 by the Employment Relations Act 2004 make dismissal for trying to exercise the above rights automatically unfair and selection for redundancy also. The Work and Families Act 2006 extends the provision to the carers of adult persons.

Time off

There are circumstances in which employees may be entitled to paid time off work. Some of these rights, however, arise only if there is a trade union recognised for negotiating or collective bargaining purposes.

Trade union recognition

If a company has recognised a union and the union has appointed an employee as a safety representative, the employer must allow the employee paid leave to perform certain functions. These include investigating potential hazards and dangerous occurrences, investigating health and safety complaints; making representations to the company about these matters; and attending meetings of safety committees.

Branch officers and shop stewards of a recognised union are entitled to paid time off in order to carry out their duties as union officials. These include negotiation with the employer, informing and consulting the members about the negotiations and representing members in disciplinary matters as well as union courses of training.

In this connection, the decision in *Davies v Neath Port Talbot CBC* (1999) *The Times*, 26 October is of interest. Mrs Davies was employed by the Council's meals on wheels service on a part-time basis. She was elected as a GMB union health and safety representative. She attended courses arranged by the GMB. The time involved on these courses exceeded the normal 22 hours a week that she worked. The Council nevertheless paid her for 22 hours only. The EAT ruled that she was entitled to be paid for the hours actually worked on the courses and the Council was liable to pay the shortfall. The EAT followed directly applicable case law of the ECJ rather than the replacement of wages provision in s 169(2) of the ERA 1996 which was in conflict with Art 141 of the EC Treaty.

Members of a recognised union are also entitled to *unpaid* time off for certain union activities, such as attendance at an executive committee meeting or annual conference.

The above provisions in terms of union recognition have become more important because the proposals of the Employment Relations Act 1999 have been implemented. The Act stipulates that employers must recognise trade unions where a majority of those voting in a ballot and at least 40 per cent of those eligible to vote are in favour of recognition though firms with fewer than 21 workers will be exempt. However, in those companies where more than

19

50 per cent of the workers are union members, there will be automatic recognition on the ground that there is a manifest demonstration that employees wish to be represented by the union for the purposes of collective bargaining.

Trade union activities

An employee who is a member of an independent trade union which the employer recognises is entitled to reasonable unpaid time off for trade union activities such as relevant courses. ACAS has published a code of practice which gives guidance on the time off which the employer should allow for these activities and also for union learning representatives (see below). Paid time off for union officials for union duties is considered above.

Union learning representatives

These workers have a right to unpaid time off under s 168A of the Trade Union and Labour Relations (Consolidation) Act 1992 (inserted by s 43 of the Employment Act 2002). The learning representatives' function is to advise union members about their training and educational and development needs. The advice is usually given at the place of work often through face-to-face meetings with individuals. Union members are entitled to unpaid time off to consult their learning representatives.

Young persons – time off for study or training

Section 32 of the Teaching and Higher Education Act 1998 inserts s 63A into the Employment Rights Act 1996. It allows persons aged 16 to 18 to take reasonable paid time off work during working hours in order to undertake study or training leading to an external qualification: attainment of which would be likely to enhance the young person's prospects whether with his or her employer or otherwise. The young person is entitled to pay for the time off (see s 63B of the ERA 1996). These rights are enforceable by way of complaint to an employment tribunal. If an employee is dismissed for asserting these rights, the dismissal will be automatically unfair so that no period of service is required to assert the right. The Right to Time Off for Study or Training Regulations 1999 (SI 1999/986) set out the external qualifications referred to above. These include, e.g., the qualification awarded by the Association of Accounting Technicians.

Public duties

Employees have the right to take unpaid time off for certain public duties.

The public duties for which time off may be taken include the duties of a justice of the peace, a member of a local authority, a member of any statutory tribunal, a member of a health authority or NHS trust and a governor of a local authority school or member of a police authority.

The employer must allow as much time off as is reasonable in the circumstances.

Other cases

Other cases in which employees are entitled to paid time off are mentioned below. These are the cases of pregnant employees who require paid time off for ante-natal care, redundant employees who require paid time off to look for work or for training, and the Pensions Act 1995 introduces a new right for employees who are also pension fund trustees to be given paid time off work so that they may perform their duties and undergo relevant training. Like other statutory 'time off' rights, the right is to 'reasonable' time off taking into account all the circumstances. In addition, the Collective Redundancies and Transfer of Undertakings (Protection of Employment) (Amendment) Regulations 1999 (see further p 482) provide that in a redundancy situation an employer may consult elected workers' representatives instead of or as well as a recognised trade union. These representatives are entitled to reasonable time off with pay during normal working hours to carry out their duties as representatives. All of these rights to time off are now contained in Part VI of the ERA 1996. It is necessary to add now time off for dependant emergencies. Here the employer is under no obligation to pay those taking such leave (see further p 455).

The Health and Safety (Consultation with Employees) Regulations 1996 (SI 1996/1513) carry similar provisions for employee safety representatives.

Remedies

Refusal to allow an employee the time off to which he or she is entitled or a failure to pay for it where this is required can lead to an employment tribunal application which must be made within three months of failure to allow the time off or to pay the employee for that time (as the case may be). If the complaint is successful, the employment tribunal can award compensation.

Insolvency of employer

An employee whose employer becomes insolvent is entitled to obtain payment of certain debts owed to him from the National Insurance Fund. The legal rights and remedies in respect of the debts covered are transferred to the Secretary of State for Trade and Industry so that he can try to recover from the assets of the insolvent employer the cost of any payments made. Employees must apply for payment to the employer's representative, e.g. administrator or liquidator, who, if unable to pay the claim in the near future, will submit the application to the Secretary of State for payment from the National Insurance Fund which remains in existence for this purpose. Debts included are arrears of pay currently up to £310 per week for a period not exceeding eight weeks, holiday pay up to £310 per week with a limit of six weeks in the last 12 months of employment; payment in lieu of notice for the minimum statutory period relevant to the employee up to £310 per week; any outstanding payment in regard to an award by an employment tribunal of compensation for unfair dismissal; reimbursement of the fees of an apprentice or articled clerk.

It should be noted that the above amounts are reviewed annually by ministerial order.

There is no period of qualifying service before an employee becomes eligible and virtually all people in employment are entitled. The amount of £310 refers to the employee's gross pay.

Health and safety at work

The HASAWA (the Health and Safety at Work etc. Act 1974) lays down certain general duties of employers to their employees in the field of health and safety. There is a general duty on employers to ensure as far as is reasonably practicable the health, safety and welfare of all employees while at work.

However, particular, as distinct from general, health and safety duties are set out for most workplaces in the Management of Health and Safety at Work Regulations 1999

(SI 1999/2051). The Health and Safety Commission has issued an Approved Code of Practice to accompany these Regulations. Examples of some of the major duties of the employer are as follows. He must provide and maintain plant and equipment and safe systems of work; avoid risks to safety and health in handling, storing and transporting articles and substances; provide and maintain safe premises and safe means of entering and leaving them; provide and maintain adequate welfare facilities and arrangements; provide information, training and supervision as required in order to ensure the safety and health of employees; prepare and/or revise policy statements on the safety and health of employees and give proper publicity to these.

The statement of policy provisions does not apply to an employer with *fewer* than *five* employees.

An employer must also conduct his undertaking in such a way that so far as is reasonably practicable those who are not his employees are not exposed to risk. Additionally, an employer must ensure so far as is reasonably practicable that premises which are open to others not employed by him are safe. There is also a duty to use the best practical methods to prevent noxious or offensive substances going into the atmosphere.

Employees must take reasonable care of their own and other people's health and safety and co-operate with the employer in the carrying out of his duties. The Act also states that no person shall intentionally or recklessly interfere with or misuse anything which is provided in the interests of health, safety and welfare, e.g. safety equipment, and no employer may charge any employee for anything done or provided to comply with the employer's statutory duties. Finally, those who design, manufacture, import or supply equipment, machinery and plant must ensure that the design and construction is safe.

Also of interest are the Health and Safety (Display Screen Equipment) Regulations 1992 (SI 1992/2792). These Regulations, which are in force, deal with the risks involved with work on display screens, e.g. muscular problems, eye fatigue and mental stress.

The Regulations apply where there are one or more employees who habitually use display screen equipment as a significant part of daily work. The employer's duties are to:

(a) assess display screen equipment workstations and reduce any risks which are discovered;
(b) ensure that workstations satisfy minimum requirements in terms of the display screen itself, the keyboard, desk and chair, working environment, task design and software;
(c) plan work on display screen equipment so that the user has breaks or changes of activity;
(d) provide information and training for display equipment users.

Users are also entitled to eye and eyesight tests and to special spectacles where normal ones cannot be used.

Health and safety in the office

Offences and civil claims for accidents at work are more likely to arise in a factory than in an office. However, the following are examples of accidents which can occur and medical conditions which can arise in an office environment:

(a) injury in a fire caused by a discarded cigarette or by an overloaded or defective electrical system;
(b) a fall or other injury caused by a defect in the premises, such as a dangerous and badly-lit staircase;
(c) an electric shock caused by badly fitted or defective electrical equipment;
(d) injury caused by a defect in or careless use of equipment, such as a guillotine or stapler;
(e) a medical condition caused by defective or ill-designed chairs supplied to employees, particularly secretaries;
(f) eye strain and other conditions caused by exposure to VDU screens.

There has been a large number of claims for repetitive strain injury caused to workers using keyboards of one sort or another. The Court of Appeal has now decided that an employer is under a duty to instruct employees on the risks of repetitive strain injury and the need for taking breaks (see *Pickford* v *ICI plc* [1996] IRLR 622).

It is also necessary to note the case of *Walker* v *Northumberland County Council* [1994] NLJR 1659 where damages, eventually settled out of court at £175,000, were awarded to Mr Walker when he suffered psychiatric damage because he was overworked by his employer. The employer was in breach of his duty to provide a safe system of work for the employee and was, therefore, liable in negligence for not doing so.

However, these and other relevant cases are also considered in Chapter 21 (Negligence of employers) since these stress related cases can also be brought under the common law rule that an employer must provide a safe system of work. The Display Screen Regulations provide that information be given to employees regarding health and safety risks with VDUs and that risk assessments be made but claims for damages are brought at common law. Civil liability for breach of the relevant regulations is strict and the employer may be liable even though there is no negligence. Thus in *Stark* v *Post Office* [2000] IRC 1013 the Court of Appeal ruled that a postman was entitled to damages when the front wheel of his bicycle locked throwing him over the handlebars. The employer was liable even though there had been no negligence in terms of the bicycle's maintenance. The case was brought under the Provision and Use of Work Equipment Regulations 1992 which do not exclude civil claims.

Civil claims: reforming regulations

The Management of Health and Safety at Work and Fire Precautions (Workplace) (Amendment) Regulations 2003 (SI 2003/2457) give new rights to employees to bring civil law claims for damages from their employers if they have suffered injury or illness because of a breach by the employer of the Management of Health and Safety at Work Regulations 1999 and the Fire Precautions (Workplace) Regulations 1997. Employers are also able to make claims against employees for their breaches of duty under the above regulations.

Typically, health and safety regulations have excluded civil claims. Trade unions who often support workers in claims welcomed the Regulations and have become involved in claims.

The proceedings are brought in the county court or the High Court, not in employment tribunals. There is a general time limit of three years and damages can be reduced by a percentage on the grounds of the claimant's contributory negligence.

19

Smoking in the workplace

It is also arguable that at common law an employer is at fault in requiring employees to work in an atmosphere containing heavy concentrations of cigarette, pipe or cigar smoke, although it may be possible to call medical evidence to challenge the existence or degree of the risks involved in 'passive smoking'. In fact, in *Bland* v *Stockport Metropolitan Borough Council* [1993] CLY 1506, a woman who had been exposed to passive smoking from 1979 to 1990 when her employer implemented a no-smoking policy, received £15,000 damages for injury to her health, including, in particular, chronic bronchitis and sinusitis. There is, of course, a statutory duty now that the Health and Safety Regulations apply. Certainly there is no implied contractual right to smoke at work and if an employee leaves because he or she is not allowed to smoke, there is no constructive dismissal (see *Dryden* v *Greater Glasgow Health Board* [1992] IRLR 469, EAT), and it may well be that a dismissal for infringement of a no-smoking rule properly communicated and agreed with by the majority of staff would not be unfair.

More recently, the Employment Appeal Tribunal has decided that a secretary in a solicitor's office who left because of discomfort caused at the workplace by colleagues who smoked was constructively dismissed (see *Waltons and Morse* v *Dorrington* [1997] IRLR 488). In previous passive smoking cases the complainant has suffered physical injury. However, in this case, the EAT, after ruling that it is an implied term in all employment contracts that the employer will provide and continue to monitor, as far as is reasonably practicable, a working environment which is reasonably suitable for employees to carry out their duties, went on to comment that the right of an employee not to be required to sit in a smoky atmosphere affects the welfare of employees at work, even though employees who complain cannot necessarily prove that there has been any health and safety risk to them. It would appear that discomfort is enough.

The Health and Safety Commission has issued a code of practice on passive smoking. The code has no legal force as such but could lead to a successful claim for damages by an employee at common law if put in evidence to show that the employer was in breach of it.

A workplace smoking ban

The government has issued and consulted on the draft Smoke-free (General Provisions) Regulations. The Regulations will ban smoking in enclosed public places, including most workplaces by the summer of 2007. The Regulations give definitions of 'enclosed' and 'substantially enclosed' premises, together with requirements for displaying no-smoking signs in smoke-free premises and duties to prevent smoking in smoke-free vehicles, enforcement by local authorities and the form of penalty notices for offences.

As regards penalties, employees caught smoking in regulated areas after the Regulations are in force will face a fixed penalty of £50. Those who pay within 15 days will have the fine reduced to £30, but those who fail to pay could face a fine of up to £200 and a criminal record. Company cars must also be non-smoking if they are likely to be used by more than one person, unless the car is a convertible and the roof is open.

The consultation can be accessed at **www.dh.gov.uk/Consultations/fs/en**.

Drink and drugs in the workplace

Because of the duties of care placed upon them by statute and common law, employers must take reasonable steps to ensure that their workers are not under the influence of drink or drugs where it would create a risk to the health and safety of others if the workers' performance was impaired in this way. Employees who are under the influence of drink or drugs or who fail to report fellow workers who are may also be in breach of their own common law or statutory duties of care.

Except for these rather general duties there is little specific regulation with regard to drink and drugs in the workplace, though there is some regulation in regard to railways. The Transport and Works Act 1992 states that those who work on railways, tramways and other specified transport systems are guilty of a criminal offence if they are under the influence of drugs or alcohol while on duty.

Consultation

The Health and Safety (Consultation with Employees) Regulations 1996 (SI 1996/1513), impose duties on employers who do not have safety representatives appointed by a recognised trade union to consult their employees on certain specified health and safety matters. Employers have the choice of consulting employees directly or through representatives elected by the employees they are to represent. Employers must provide relevant information and give appropriate training, paid time off, and facilities in order that elected representatives can carry out their functions.

It should also be noted that under the ERA, s 100 designated or acknowledged health and safety representatives must not be subjected to detriments, e.g. loss of overtime, for carrying out health and safety activities in the workplace. Dismissal for these reasons is unfair, regardless of service. The provisions also apply to ordinary employees, regardless of service, who leave or refuse to return to the workplace because of a health hazard reasonably thought to exist.

The above Regulations work in tandem with the Safety Representatives and Safety Committee Regulations 1977 (SI 1977/500) which apply to consultations with safety representatives appointed where there is a recognised trade union and appointed by that trade union.

Enforcement

Enforcement is in the hands of the inspectorate of the Health and Safety Executive set up by the Act. Inspectors may issue a prohibition notice if there is a risk of serious personal injury. This operates to stop the activity concerned until remedial action specified in the notice has been taken. They may also issue an improvement notice if there is a contravention of any of the relevant statutory provisions, under which the employer must remedy the fault within a specified time. They may prosecute any person contravening the relevant statutory provision instead of or in addition to serving a notice. Failure to comply with a prohibition notice could lead to imprisonment, though there is an appeal to an employment tribunal. The right of appeal from the employment tribunal is not as might be expected to the Employment Appeal Tribunal but to the High Court, Queen's Bench Division.

> *R v Mara*, 1986 – Health and safety: the duty to non-employees (**256**)

Trade union membership and activities

19

Under the Trade Union and Labour Relations (Consolidation) Act 1992 employers have a duty not to take action against employees just because they are members of, or take part in at an appropriate time, the activities of a trade union which is independent of the employer. According to the decision in *Post Office* v *Union of Post Office Workers* [1974] 1 All ER 229 this includes activities on the employer's premises.

Under the provisions of the 1992 Act, dismissal for failing to join a trade union is always automatically unfair even if there is a closed shop situation within the industry concerned. This provision greatly weakens the maintenance by trade unions of closed shops.

Dismissal will also be automatically unfair if the employee is selected for redundancy on any of the above 'trade union' grounds. Furthermore, the Court of Appeal decided in *Fitzpatrick* v *British Railways Board* [1991] IRLR 376 that a dismissal for trade union activities in a *previous* employment was automatically unfair.

If action is taken against employees, they may complain to a tribunal within three months of the offending act, which can award money compensation of an unlimited amount or make an order saying what the trade union rights of the employee are so that the employer can grant them in the future. If the employee has been dismissed, the unfair dismissal remedies apply.

In addition, the 1992 Act gives job seekers a right not to be refused employment or the services of an employment agency on the ground that they are or are not trade union members. The Act also protects people who will not agree to become or cease to be union members or to make payments in lieu of membership subscriptions. This means that it is no longer lawful to operate any form of closed shop. Any individual who believes that he or she has been unlawfully refused employment or the service of an employment agency because of union or non-union membership can complain to an employment tribunal within three months of the refusal. If the case is made out, the tribunal can award compensation of unlimited amount.

The compensation will generally be paid by the employer or employment agency concerned, but in cases where a trade union is joined as a party and the tribunal decides that the unlawful refusal resulted from pressure applied by the union, it may order the union to pay some or all of the compensation.

The tribunal can also recommend that the prospective employer or employment agency take action to remedy the adverse effect of their unlawful action on the complainant.

Employer incentives not to join a union

The Employment Relations Act 2004 inserts additional provisions in the Trade Union and Labour Relations (Consolidation) Act 1992 so that a worker has a right not to have an offer made to him or her by the employer with the sole or principal purpose of inducing him or her to give up membership of an independent trade union or to refrain from joining or taking part in the activities or making use of the services of such a union. Further, a worker who is a member of an independent trade union has a right not to be made an offer by the employer where acceptance would result in the terms of the employment no longer being determined by collective bargaining where this is the sole or main purpose of the offer. Where offers made in contravention of the above provisions are accepted by the worker, the employer cannot enforce them as a change in the terms of employment. The provisions apply to those who provide services and do not work under a contract of employment.

If the employer goes further than the making of an offer and takes steps to prevent the above contacts with the union, the worker suffers a detriment for which a claim could be brought.

Union recognition – generally

Employers were formerly free to decide for themselves whether they wished to recognise trade unions regardless of the wishes of their employees, and irrespective of the level of union membership among their workers. Under the provisions of the Employment Relations Act 1999, which take effect as Sch A1 to the Trade Union and Labour Relations (Consolidation) Act 1992, employers will have to recognise trade unions where a majority of those voting in a ballot and at least 40 per cent of those eligible to vote are in favour of recognition. However, in those organisations where more than 50 per cent of the workers are members of the union, there will be automatic recognition on the ground that there is a manifest demonstration that the employees wish to be represented by the union for the purposes of collective bargaining. The Employment Relations Act 1999 will give protection against dismissal for those campaigning on behalf of recognition and unions will be allowed reasonable access to the workforce to seek their support and to inform employees about ballots. Those who employ less than 21 workers are exempt from the recognition procedures.

The areas for which compulsory recognition is required embrace negotiations relating to pay, hours of work, holidays and training.

Union recognition – disputes

Disputes are referred to the Central Arbitration Committee. An example of such a reference is to be found in *UNIFI* v *Bank of Ceylon* (2000) 652 IRLB 16. In that reference the CAC accepted a recognition application by the Union for the Investment Finance Industry in respect of workers, including managers, employed by the Bank of Ceylon under contracts based in the UK. The Bank employed at least 21 workers on the day the union lodged its recognition request with the Bank, even if employees based in Sri Lanka and in Britain on separate assignments were excluded. The CAC accepted the union's evidence that it had 14 members out of the 22 remaining staff in the proposed bargaining unit and statements from 13 staff that they wanted the union to seek recognition.

The CAC found that at least 10 per cent of the staff in the proposed bargaining unit were union members and that a majority of the relevant staff would be likely to favour collective bargaining and accepted UNIFI's recognition application.

Deduction from pay of union subscriptions

Employers may agree with a recognised union to deduct union subscriptions from pay and hand the relevant sum over to the trade union concerned. Employers must get the written authorisation of the relevant workers before starting what are known as check-off deductions and they must continue to give employees the usual itemised pay statement showing the amount of any check-off deduction. Furthermore, employees are free to withdraw from check-off at any time.

However, the Deregulation (Deduction from Pay of Union Subscriptions) Order 1998 (SI 1998/1529) removes from employers the requirement to:

- obtain repeat authorisations from employees at least every three years as confirmation that they wish to continue to pay their union subscriptions from wages; and
- notify employees at least one month in advance of any increase in the amount that will be deducted.

Citizen's right

Although not strictly speaking a matter of employment law, it is worth noting that under s 235 of the 1992 Act (as amended) any individual who is deprived, or likely to be deprived, of goods or services because of unlawfully organised industrial action, can bring proceedings before the High Court to restrain the unlawful act. Such an individual can apply to the Commissioner for Protection against Unlawful Industrial Action for assistance.

The first case to receive financial assistance concerned strike action threatened by members of a teaching union as a protest against the re-admission of a pupil to a secondary school after his parents' successful appeal against the decision of the head teacher and the school governors to exclude him.

Termination of the contract of employment

Unfair dismissal: generally

Before a person can ask an employment tribunal to consider a claim that another has unfairly dismissed him or her, it is once again essential to establish that the relationship of employer and employee exists between them. In this connection, the ERA provides that an employee is a person who works under a contract of service or apprenticeship, written or oral, express or implied.

> *Massey* v *Crown Life Insurance Co*, 1978 – Unfair dismissal claims and the
> self-employed (**257**)

In addition to showing that he is an employee, the claimant had to comply with an *age requirement*. The unfair dismissal provisions did not apply to the dismissal of an employee from any employment if the employee had on or before the effective date of termination attained the age which, in the undertaking in which he is employed, was the normal retiring age for an employee holding the position which he held, or for both men and women age 65. This exclusion is now repeated by the Age Discrimination Regulations 2006 and there is now no age limit.

As regards the period of employment, the unfair dismissal provisions do not apply to the dismissal of an employee from any employment if the employee, whether full or part-time, has not completed one year's continuous employment ending with the effective date of termination of employment unless the dismissal is automatically unfair.

Automatically unfair dismissals

Having noted some of these in various parts of the text, it may be useful to bring them together in a list, remembering that dismissals of this kind do not require any particular period of service with the employer.

The main reasons which make a dismissal automatically unfair can briefly be listed as follows:

- trade union membership or activities including dismissal during official strike action;
- not belonging to a trade union or particular union;
- pregnancy, maternity and dependant leave, adoption leave, paternity leave and parental leave;
- selection for redundancy on any of the above grounds;
- the transfer of the undertaking or a reason connected with it (unless there is an ETO (economic, technical or organisational reason)). It should, however, be noted at this point that the one-year qualifying period does not apply where the complaint is based on dismissal for one of the automatically unfair reasons, though if the dismissal related to the transfer of an undertaking the one-year qualifying period does apply;
- asserting a statutory employment right under ERA 1996, s 104 e.g. in regard to minimum notice;
- exercising rights as a part-time worker or fixed-term worker or in connection with flexible working;
- in health and safety cases involving union safety representatives and now including being an employee safety representative or putting up for election to be one;
- performing the duties of a member-nominated trustee under the Pensions Act 1995;
- being an employee representative in redundancy consultation or putting up for election to be one (ERA 1996, s 103);
- refusing (in certain circumstances) to do shop or betting work on a Sunday;
- exercising rights under the Working Time Regulations including rights as an employee representative in connection with the workforce agreements (s 101(A), ERA 1996, as inserted by the Regulations);
- asserting rights under the National Minimum Wage Act 1998 (s 104(A), ERA 1996, as inserted by the NMW Act 1998);
- asserting rights to time off for study and training under s 63A of the ERA 1996, as inserted by the Teaching and Higher Education Act 1998;
- protection of whistleblowers under the Public Interest Disclosure Act 1998.

Other exceptions

The following are ineligible and cannot claim.

(a) Any employee dismissed while taking unofficial strike or other industrial action is unable to complain of unfair dismissal (Trade Union and Labour Relations (Consolidation) Act 1992, s 237). Where the strike or other industrial action is official, the Employment Relations Act 1999 inserts additional provisions into the Trade Union and Labour Relations (Consolidation) Act 1992 so that it is automatically unfair to dismiss employees or select them for redundancy for the first 12 weeks of their participation in official and otherwise lawfully organised protected industrial action. Dismissal during unofficial action is not protected and action is also not protected if it involves unlawful secondary action.

Dismissals after the 12-week period are still unfair where the employer has not taken reasonable steps to resolve the dispute. Where the employer has not taken such steps or where the action was not lawfully organised, a worker who has been dismissed will normally be able to claim unfair dismissal where the employer has not dismissed all workers taking part in the action or has offered re-engagement to some but not all of the employees within a three-month time limit.

(b) Certain other categories are excluded by the ERA, e.g. members of the police force.

(c) It was once the case that a worker who under his or her contract of employment ordinarily worked mainly outside Great Britain could not claim unfair dismissal. The ERA 1999 abolished this exclusion but it remains for those who work *wholly* outside Great Britain, unless the employment contract is in Great Britain the worker having been merely posted abroad or the work is connected with Great Britain as where it is at a UK military base (*Lawson* v *Serco* [2006] 1 All ER 823).

(d) To claim unfair dismissal a worker must have been continuously employed for one year at the date of termination. There is no longer a requirement to have worked a specific number of hours in a week to qualify.

Under the ERA, s 192, members of the armed forces are now covered by the unfair dismissal provisions of that Act provided they have first availed themselves of service redress procedures.

It should also be noted that s 9 of the Employment Tribunals Act 1996 contains provisions to test the strength of the case of each party before a full hearing proceeds. Pre-hearing reviews are introduced at which the chairman of the tribunal may sit alone without the two lay assessors. The chairman may, at his discretion and following an application by one of the parties, or of his own motion, require a deposit of up to £500 from the other party as a condition of proceeding further if it is considered that his or her case has no reasonable prospect of success, or that to pursue it would be frivolous, vexatious or otherwise unreasonable.

Employment Tribunal Regulations also provide for pre-hearing assessments, and if a party to the proceedings before an employment tribunal considers that an application, or a particular contention, is unlikely to succeed or be accepted he can ask for a pre-hearing assessment to be made. A tribunal can make such an assessment of its own volition. Following the pre-hearing assessment, at which the parties may submit written representations and put forward oral argument but not evidence, the tribunal may indicate its opinion that if the party who is unlikely to succeed carries on with the application or persists in the contention an order for *costs* may be made against him. The opinion is placed before the tribunal which conducts the full hearing if it takes place. No member of the tribunal which gave the opinion may be a member of the tribunal which takes the full hearing.

A pre-trial review may therefore impose a *deposit* requirement and give a warning order as to *costs* if the case proceeds.

Dismissal – meaning of

An employee cannot claim unfair dismissal unless there has first been a dismissal recognised by law. We may consider the matter under the following headings.

Actual dismissal

This does not normally give rise to problems since most employees recognise the words of an actual dismissal, whether given orally or in writing.

A typical letter of dismissal appears below.

> Dear Mr Bloggs
> I am sorry that you do not have the necessary aptitude to deal with the work which we have allocated to you. I hope that you will be able to find other work elsewhere which is more in your line. As you will recall from your interview this morning, the company will not require your services after the 31st of this month.

Constructive dismissal

This occurs where it is the employee who leaves the job but is compelled to do so by the conduct of the employer. In general terms the employer's conduct must be a fundamental breach so that it can be regarded as a repudiation of the contract. Thus, if a male employer were to sexually assault his female secretary then this would be a fundamental breach entitling her to leave and sue for her loss on the basis of constructive dismissal.

It would also occur if the employer changed the terms of the contract without the employee's consent, e.g. by reducing wages payable under the contract – see *Rigby* v *Ferodo* [1987] IRLR 516. Furthermore, the EAT decided in *Whitbread plc (t/a Thresher)* v *Gullyes* (1994) 509 IRLB 14 that an employee who resigned from a management position because her employer did not give her proper support – since, among other things, the most experienced staff were transferred out of her branch without consultation with her – was constructively dismissed.

Fixed-term contracts

When a fixed-term contract expires and is not renewed, there is a dismissal.

Under the provisions of the Employment Rights Act, the ERA 1996 is amended so that an employee can no longer waive his right to claim unfair dismissal where a contract for one year or more is not renewed. It used to be possible to forgo the right to claim a redundancy payment at the end of a fixed-term contract that was of at least two years' duration. This is no longer possible by reason of the Fixed-Term Employees Regulations 2002 (see p 444).

Grounds for dismissal

If an employer is going to escape liability for unfair dismissal, he must show that he acted *reasonably* and, indeed, s 92 of the ERA requires the employer to give his reasons for dismissal to the employee in writing.

It should be remembered that the question of whether a dismissal is fair or not is a matter of *fact* for the particular tribunal hearing the case, precedents are not rigidly applied and one cannot predict with absolute accuracy what a particular tribunal will do on the facts of a particular case. Basically, when all is said and done, the ultimate question for a tribunal is – 'was the dismissal fair and reasonable' in fact.

Section 98 of the ERA includes in the test of reasonableness required in determining whether a dismissal was fair, the 'size and administrative resources of the employer's undertaking'. This was included as a result of fear that the unfair dismissal laws were placing undue burdens on small firms and causing them not to engage new workers. Earlier legislation also removed the burden of proof from the employer in showing reasonableness so that there is now no 'presumption of guilt' on the employer and the tribunal is left to decide whether or not the employer acted reasonably.

In this connection, the tribunal may think that the dismissal was severe but the question is was it within the band of reasonable responses open to the employer? (Within this band an employer might reasonably retain the employee, while another employer might dismiss him or her.) If so, there is no unfair dismissal even if the members of the tribunal would not have dismissed the claimant (see *British Leyland (UK)* v *Swift* [1981] IRLR 91 – a decision of the Court of Appeal). The EAT has challenged this approach as wrong and has decided that the view of the tribunal is the test (see *Haddon* v *Van den Berg Foods Ltd* [1999] IRLR 672). That decision was, however, questioned in *Midland Bank* v *Madden* (2000) 638 IRLB 2 where a differently constituted EAT said that the decision in *Swift* must stand and could not be overruled by the EAT. Thus, the rule of the possible reasonableness of the perverse employer goes on until the matter is resolved by the Court of Appeal.

The Court of Appeal heard an appeal in the *Madden* case in which the 'reasonable responses' test was affirmed, though the response of a perverse employer is excluded (see *HSBC Bank plc (formerly Midland Bank plc)* v *Madden* [2000] IRLR 827).

Reasons justifying dismissal

These are as follows.

(a) Lack of capability or qualifications. This would usually arise at the beginning of employment where it becomes clear at an early stage that the employee cannot do the job in terms of lack of skill or mental or physical health. It should be remembered that the longer a person is in employment, the more difficult it is to establish lack of capability.

By way of illustration, we can consider the case of *Alidair* v *Taylor* [1978] IRLR 82. The pilot of an aircraft had made a faulty landing which damaged the aircraft. There was a board of inquiry which found that the faulty landing was due to a lack of flying knowledge on the part of the pilot who was dismissed from his employment. It was decided that the employee had not been unfairly dismissed, the tribunal taking the view that where, as in this case, one failure to reach a high degree of skill could have serious consequences, an instant dismissal could be justified.

However, it was decided in *British Sulphur* v *Lawrie* [1987] IRB 338 that the dismissal of an employee who was alleged to be unwilling or incompetent to do a particular job could still be unfair if the employee was not provided with adequate training.

As regards qualifications, this could occur where a new employee does not have the qualifications claimed or fails to get a qualification which was a condition of employment, for example in the case of legal and accounting trainees who fail to complete their examinations.

It should also be noted that the Court of Appeal decided in *Nottingham County Council* v *P* (1992) *The Times*, 18 May, that even though an employee had become unsuitable it could still be unfair dismissal if the employer failed to make a reasonable investigation of possible alternative employment. P was an assistant groundsman at a girls' school and had pleaded guilty to a charge of indecent assault on his daughter. Obviously, he could not be allowed to continue to work at the school but the Council should have considered alternative employment within the authority. Failure to do so could amount to unfair dismissal. The case was sent back to the employment tribunal to see what efforts the Council had made, if any, in this regard.

19

(b) Conduct. This is always a difficult matter to deal with and much will depend upon the circumstances of the case. However, incompetence and neglect are relevant, as are disobedience and misconduct, e.g. by assaulting fellow employees. Immorality and habitual drunkenness could also be brought under this heading and, so it seems, can dress where this can be shown to affect adversely the way in which the contract of service is performed.

> *Boychuk v H J Symons (Holdings) Ltd*, 1977 – A dismissal for conduct (**258**)

Crime inside employment will normally justify a dismissal on the grounds of misconduct. For example, the EAT has decided that an employee was dismissed fairly on the ground of theft from the employer even though the employer could not specifically prove loss of stock but had only a reasonable belief in the employee's guilt. The employee had been seen at night by a security guard at the employer's warehouse loading boxes into his car (see *Francis* v *Boots the Chemist Ltd* (1998) 586 IRLB 11).

Dismissal on the ground of theft may also be fair even though what is stolen is of little value. Thus in *Tesco Stores Ltd* v *Khalid* [2001] All ER (D) 314 (Nov) the employee was dismissed for misappropriation of cigarettes from a petrol station where he worked. His dismissal was held to be fair even though the cigarettes were from damaged stock due for return to the manufacturer. Dismissal was within the range of reasonable responses of an employer.

Crime outside of employment raises more difficult issues and generally speaking the employer will have to show damage to his organisation. Thus in *Post Office* v *Liddiard* (2001) (unreported) a Post Office employee was involved in football violence in France. His dismissal for this was held to be unfair. It would be different of course where a company's accountant was convicted of dishonesty in terms of the funds of a local charity of which he or she was the honorary treasurer or where a teacher was convicted of offences involving violence or child-abuse in his or her non-work environment.

An employee's use of drugs or alcohol outside the workplace is unlikely to amount to a fair reason for dismissal nor will the mere fact that an employee did not reveal that he or she used drugs or alcohol when interviewed for the post. However, use of drugs and/or excessive drinking may constitute grounds for a fair dismissal where the employer believes on reasonable grounds that it makes the employee unsuitable for the position held. An employer who wishes to dismiss employees for drink or drug misconduct should have a drink and drugs policy and make it part of the employee's contract.

(c) Redundancy. Genuine redundancy is a defence. Where a person is redundant, his employer cannot be expected to continue the employment, although there are safeguards in the matter of *unfair selection for redundancy*.

Examples are selection because of pregnancy, or trade union membership or activities, or for asserting statutory rights or on health and safety matters as by selection for redundancy, without other reason, of health and safety representatives.

(d) Dismissals which are union related. These are known as the '*section 152 reasons*'. They are set out in the Trade Union and Labour Relations (Consolidation) Act 1992, s 152. An employee will be regarded as automatically unfairly dismissed if the principal reason for the dismissal was that he was, or proposed to become, a member of a trade union which was independent of the employer; that he had taken part or proposed to take part in the activities of such a union at an appropriate time, i.e. outside working hours or within working hours with the consent of the employer; that he was not a member of any trade union or of a particular one or had refused or proposed to refuse to become or remain a member. Under the relevant provisions of the Trade Union and Labour Relations (Consolidation) Act 1992 all dismissals to maintain a closed shop are now automatically unfair.

Dismissal will also be automatically unfair if the employee is selected for redundancy on any of the above s 152 grounds. Also the Court of Appeal ruled in *Fitzpatrick* v *British Railways Board* [1991] IRLR 376 that a dismissal for trade union activities in a *previous* employment was automatically unfair.

It is worth noting also that under s 146 of the 1992 Act an employee has a right not to have action taken against him or her short of dismissal such as victimisation in terms, e.g., of not being offered overtime where this is related to union membership and/or activities.

The position in regard to job applicants has already been considered.

(e) Statutory restriction placed on employer or employee. If, for example, the employer's business was found to be dangerous and was closed down under Act of Parliament or ministerial order, the employees would not be unfairly dismissed. Furthermore, a lorry driver who was banned from driving for 12 months could be dismissed fairly.

(f) Some other substantial reason. An employer may on a wide variety of grounds which are not specified by legislation satisfy an employment tribunal that a dismissal was fair and reasonable.

Crime and suspicion of crime may also be brought under this heading, though if dismissal is based on suspicion of crime, the suspicion must be reasonable and in all cases the employee must be told that dismissal is contemplated and in the light of this information be allowed to give explanations and make representations against dismissal.

Where an employee has been charged with theft from the employer and is awaiting trial, the best course of action is to suspend rather than dismiss him, pending the verdict. Investigations which the employer must make, as part of establishing a fair dismissal, could be regarded as an interference with the course of justice. It is best, therefore, not to make them, but to suspend the employee. The case of *Wadley* v *Eager Electrical* [1986] IRLR 93 should be noted. In that case husband and wife worked for the same company. The wife was convicted for stealing £2,000 from the company whilst employed as a shop assistant. The husband was a service engineer with the company. Husband and wife were dismissed and it was held that the husband's dismissal was unfair. He was a good employee of 17 years' standing and no misconduct had been made out against him.

The matter of fair or unfair dismissal depends also upon the terms of the contract. If the difficulty is that a particular employee is refusing to do work which involves him, say, spending nights away from home, then his dismissal is likely to be regarded as fair if there is an *express term* in his contract requiring this. Of course, the nature of the job may require it, as in the case of a long-distance lorry driver where such a term would be implied, if not expressed.

Employees who are in breach of contract are likely to be regarded as fairly dismissed. However, this is not an invariable rule. Thus a long-distance lorry driver who refused to take on a particular trip because his wife was ill and he had to look after the children would be unfairly dismissed (if dismissal took place) even though he was, strictly speaking, in breach of his contract.

Dismissal could also be for a substantial reason where a breakdown of relationships either within the office or with a customer have made an employee's position untenable. The following example illustrates the possibilities. In a small office there are two purchase ledger clerks working closely together. They were very good friends. One of them sets up home with the other's wife. The clerks are no longer on speaking terms and cannot work together. The employer has no other office to which one of them can be transferred.

There may be no alternative to dismissal. If no solution can be found in discussion with the clerks one should be dismissed on the basis of length of service and other factors that would be relevant if the one dismissed was being selected for redundancy.

19

In *Cobley* v *Forward Technology Industries plc* [2003] All ER (D) 175 the Court of Appeal ruled that the chief executive of a public listed company was not unfairly dismissed when the shareholders removed him from his office as a director by a resolution in general meeting. This effected his dismissal as CEO because his contract said that he could not continue as CEO unless he was also a director of the company. His dismissal was, ruled the court, for 'some other substantial reason' under the Employment Rights Act 1996 and that made the dismissal fair. The removal followed a successful hostile takeover of the company and the case shows that business reorganisations such as this can be brought under the heading of 'some other substantial reason'. The new owners clearly cannot be expected to retain the former board members.

Contractual grievance and disciplinary procedures

These are usually part of the contract. The employer must comply with them if he wishes to avoid liability. If a series of oral and written warnings is laid down, the procedure should be observed. However, reasonableness will always prevail.

No matter how good the employer's reason for dismissal may be, there may still be a claim by the employee for unfair dismissal if the dismissal was 'unfair in all the circumstances'.

In *Whitbread & Co plc* v *Mills* [1988] IRLR 43 the President of the Employment Appeal Tribunal (EAT), Mr Justice Wood, gave guidance on the issue of whether an employer had acted reasonably as the law requires. In applying the guidance let us assume that the main reason for dismissal is the acceptable one of incompetence as in the case of a senior member of a publisher's staff who commissions books without proper market research so that they do not sell and the publisher is caused loss.

Having reached the conclusion that the incompetence is established, the employer must according to Mr Justice Wood satisfy a tribunal on four other matters, otherwise the dismissal might still be unfair, though the employee's compensation might be reduced for contributory fault (see below). The four matters are:

(a) Can the employer satisfy a tribunal that he complied with the pre-dismissal procedures which a reasonable employer could and should have applied in the circumstances of the case? If the tribunal finds that the employer has not acted reasonably in this regard, at the date of dismissal, then according to the decision in *Polkey* v *A E Dayton Services Ltd* [1988] ICR 564 it is not open to the tribunal to say that the procedures do not matter since it is clear that the employee was incompetent. The unfairness of the dismissal could still give the employee a successful claim.

The decision of the House of Lords in *Polkey* makes clear the importance of consultation. There may be grounds for the dismissal but if there is no proper consultation the dismissal may still be unfair, though compensation may be reduced if there were grounds for the dismissal.

However, it is not always necessary to consult. Thus in *Eclipse Blinds* v *Wright* (1992) 444 IRLIB 12, Mrs Wright was dismissed because of poor health. The employer received a medical report with her consent. It revealed that she was more seriously ill than she thought. Rather than upset her, the employer wrote her a sympathetic letter ending her employment on the ground of incapacity. The court held she was not unfairly dismissed in spite of the lack of consultation.

(b) Where there is a contractual appeal process, the employer must have carried it out in its essentials. A minor departure may sometimes be ignored but a total or substantial failure entitles a tribunal to find that the dismissal was unfair. Even though no contractual appeal process exists, it may nevertheless be reasonable, as was decided in *West Midland Co-operative Society Ltd* v *Tipton* [1986] ICR 192, for some sort of appeal to be arranged since this is encouraged by the code of practice issued by ACAS.

(c) Where conduct is the main reason, the employer must show, on a balance of probabilities, that at the time of the dismissal he believed the employee was guilty of misconduct and that in all the circumstances of the case it was reasonable for him to do so.

(d) During the disciplinary hearings and the appeal process the employer must have been fair to the employee. In particular, the employee must have been heard and allowed to put his case properly or, if he was not at a certain stage of the procedures, this must have been corrected before dismissal.

Following parliamentary approval of a code of practice on disciplinary and grievance procedures issued by ACAS the government brought into force both the code and the new statutory right of a worker under ss 10–15 of the Employment Relations Act 1999 to be accompanied, if he or she so requests, by a fellow employee or a trade union representative at a disciplinary or grievance hearing. The code supplements the statutory provisions.

These rights allow a trade union official to enter the workplace to represent a trade union member if the member so requests, even though a trade union (or that particular union) is not recognised by the employer. Refusal to allow accompaniment will mean that a tribunal can make an award of up to two weeks' pay against the employer and a refusal of the right followed by a dismissal will result in the chances of a successful unfair dismissal claim being increased. The employer need not tell the worker of the right.

As regards the role of the companion at the hearing, the Employment Relations Act 2004 inserts provisions into the Employment Relations Act 1999 which deal with the rights of the companion.

The employer must permit the companion to put the worker's case on behalf of the worker, to sum up that case, respond on the worker's behalf to any view expressed at the hearing or meeting, and confer with the worker during the hearing.

The employer is not required to permit the companion to answer questions on behalf of the worker, address the hearing if the worker indicates that he or she does not wish the companion to do so, or use the powers given by the Act in any way that prevents the employer from explaining his or her case or prevents any other person at the hearing from making a contribution to it.

19

Statutory grievance and disciplinary procedures

The Employment Act 2002 in s 29 and Sch 2 provides statutory disciplinary and grievance procedures. These have already been considered earlier in this chapter. Section 30 of the Act of 2002 makes it an implied term of every contract of employment that the statutory procedures are to apply and employers and workers cannot contract out of them. Contractual procedures may continue so long as they are as protective as the statutory procedures and the latter are there anyway if the worker wishes to use them. Provided the statutory procedures are followed in a reasonable manner their fairness will not normally be challenged by the courts and the major case on the requirement for fair procedures – the House of Lords ruling in *Polkey* v *A E Dayton Services Ltd* [1988] ICR 564 – will not apply.

Employee's contributory fault

This can reduce the compensation payable to the employee by such percentage as the tribunal thinks fit. Suppose an employee is often late for work and one morning his employer, who can stand it no more, sacks him. The dismissal is likely to be unfair in view of the lack of warning but a tribunal would very probably reduce the worker's compensation to take account of the situation.

Principles of natural justice also apply; it is necessary to let the worker state his case before a decision to dismiss is taken. Furthermore, reasonable inquiry must be made to find the truth of the matter before reaching a decision. Failure to do this will tend to make the dismissal unfair.

Unacceptable reasons for dismissal

These are as follows.

(a) Dismissal in connection with trade unions. This has already been considered.

(b) Unfair selection for redundancy. An employee dismissed for redundancy may complain that he has been unfairly dismissed if he is of the opinion that he has been unfairly selected for redundancy, as where the employer has selected him because he is a member of a trade union or takes part in trade union activities, or where the employer has disregarded redundancy selection arrangements based, for example, on 'last in, first out'. Ideally, all employers should have proper redundancy agreements on the lines set out in the Department of Work and Pensions booklet, *Dealing with Redundancies*.

However, even though there is in existence an agreed redundancy procedure, the employer may defend himself by showing a 'special reason' for departing from that procedure, e.g. because the person selected for redundancy lacks the skill and versatility of a junior employee who is retained.

There is, since the decision of the EAT in *Williams* v *Compair Maxam* [1982] ICR 156, an overall standard of fairness also in redundancy arrangements. The standards laid down in the case require the giving of maximum notice; consultation with unions, if any; the taking of the views of more than one person as to who should be dismissed; a requirement to follow any laid down procedure, e.g. last in, first out; and finally, an effort to find the employees concerned alternative employment within the organisation. However, the EAT stated in *Meikle* v *McPhail* (*Charleston Arms*) (1983) (see Case **259**) that these guidelines would be applied less rigidly to the smaller business.

The statutory provisions relating to consultation on redundancy are considered later in this chapter.

(c) Industrial action. The position in this context has already been considered.

(d) Dismissals in connection with pregnancy, childbirth and parental and dependant leave. The relevant law has already been considered.

(c) Pressure on employer to dismiss unfairly. It is no defence for an employer to say that pressure was put upon him to dismiss an employee unfairly. So, if other workers put pressure on an employer to dismiss a non-union member so as, for example, to obtain a closed shop, the employer will have no defence to a claim for compensation for the dismissal if he gives in to that pressure. If an employer alleges that he was pressurised into dismissing an employee and that pressure was brought on him by a trade union or other person by the calling, organising, procuring or financing of industrial action, including a strike, or by the threat of such things, and the reason for the pressure was that the employee was not a member of the trade union, then the employer can join the trade union or other person as a party to the proceedings if he is sued by the dismissed worker for unfair dismissal. If the tribunal awards compensation, it can order that a person joined as a party to the proceedings pay such amount of it as is just and equitable, and if necessary this can be a complete indemnity so that the employer will recover all the damages awarded against him from the union.

(f) Transfer of business. The Transfer of Undertakings (Protection of Employment) Regulations 2006 (SI 2006/246) apply. Under the Regulations if a business or part of it is transferred and an employee is dismissed because of this, the dismissal will be treated as automatically unfair. In this case the one-year service limit with the transferor employer applies.

If the old employer dismissed before transfer, or the new employer dismissed after the transfer, either will have a defence if he can prove that the dismissal was for 'economic, technical or organisational' reasons requiring a change in the workforce and that the dismissal was reasonable in all the circumstances of the case.

Meikle v *McPhail (Charleston Arms)*, 1983 – A dismissal for economic reasons (**259**)

The Collective Redundancies and Transfer of Undertakings (Protection of Employment) (Amendment) Regulations 1995 (SI 1995/2587) as amended apply. These Regulations are dealt with more fully later in this chapter but they do require consultation on transfer of business. The provisions mirror those which relate to collective redundancies except that there is no limitation on the number of employees who have to be affected by the transfer before a duty to consult arises. The employer will have to consult relevant representatives as described later in this chapter even if only one person is to be transferred.

(g) Health and safety dismissals and detriments. Designated or acknowledged health and safety representatives must not be subjected to detriments, e.g. loss of overtime, for carrying out health and safety activities in the workplace. Dismissal for these reasons is automatically unfair and there is no service requirement. These provisions also apply to ordinary employees, regardless of service, who leave or refuse to return to the workplace because of a health hazard reasonably thought to exist.

The same is true under the Health and Safety (Consultation with Employees) Regulations 1996 (SI 1996/1513) where the dismissal is of a worker safety representative elected to take part in the health and safety consultation process where there is no recognised trade union.

(h) Dismissal for asserting statutory rights. This protects employees, regardless of service, against dismissal for trying to enforce employment rights under the ERA that can be brought before a tribunal, e.g. where the employee has asked for written particulars of the job. Dismissal will be unfair even if the worker does not in fact have the right, provided he has acted in good faith.

(i) Dismissal for performing the duties of a member-nominated trustee of an occupational pension scheme.

(j) Dismissal for performing the duties of an employee representative in redundancy consultation or putting up for election to be one.

Unfair dismissal and frustration of contract

In cases appearing before employment tribunals there is a certain interplay between the common-law rules of frustration of contract (see Chapter 17) and the statutory provisions relating to unfair dismissal. At common law a contract of service is frustrated by incapacity, e.g. sickness, if that incapacity makes the contract substantially impossible of performance at a particularly vital time, or by a term of imprisonment. If a contract has been so frustrated, a complaint of unfair dismissal is not available because the contract has been discharged on other grounds, i.e. by frustration. Thus, termination of a contract of service by frustration prevents a claim for unfair dismissal.

19

It is, of course, necessary now in terms of the sickness or incapacity of an employee for the employer to be alert to the rules about disability discrimination, particularly where an adjustment to working conditions might enable an employee to do the job satisfactorily.

Remedies for unfair dismissal

These are as follows.

Conciliation

An employment tribunal will not hear a complaint until a conciliation officer has had a chance to see whether he can help, provided that he or she has been *requested* so to do by a party to the potential complaint. A copy of the complaint made to the employment tribunal will in such a situation be sent to a conciliation officer of the Advisory, Conciliation and Arbitration Service (ACAS) and, if he is unable to settle the complaint, nothing said by the employer or employee during the process of conciliation will be admissible in evidence before the tribunal.

The reference of cases to a conciliation officer has led to the settlement of some one-third of them before the tribunal hearing, but the parties do not have to become involved in this procedure.

ACAS arbitration and compromise agreements

The following provisions of the Employment Rights (Dispute Resolution) Act 1998 should be noted.

Part II of the Act contains provisions to allow parties to opt for their dispute to be resolved by independent binding arbitration and gives ACAS powers to pay for and provide an arbitration service for claims of unfair dismissal and unlawful discrimination.

Part II also contains provisions making changes to the law relating to compromise agreements. The parties to an individual employment rights dispute may conclude that dispute by reaching, for example, a financial settlement. For such an agreement to be binding, the parties must have settled after an ACAS-appointed conciliation officer has taken action, or, alternatively, the terms of the settlement must be contained in a private compromise agreement. Formerly, a compromise agreement that had not involved ACAS had to be made in circumstances where the employee had received independent legal advice from a qualified lawyer. The 1998 Act changes this to advice from any independent adviser, provided that advice is covered by an insurance policy or an indemnity provision for members of a profession or professional body (ss 9 and 10). This will allow trade unions, advice agencies and others – in addition to lawyers – to give relevant advice.

Other provisions of Part II allow ACAS-appointed conciliation officers to conciliate in claims relating to statutory redundancy payments where before they had no duty to conciliate, as they have in almost all other individual employment rights disputes (s 11).

There are also provisions that clarify, streamline and make more flexible current legislation under which employers and employer-recognised trade unions can, by making a dismissal procedures agreement, opt out of the statutory rules on unfair dismissals (s 12).

Other remedies

An employee who has been dismissed may:

(*a*) seek reinstatement or re-engagement; or
(*b*) claim compensation.

The power to order (*a*) above is discretionary and in practice rarely exercised. However, reinstatement means taken back by the employer on exactly the same terms and seniority as before; re-engagement is being taken back but on different terms.

Calculation of compensation

Before proceeding further with a study of the calculations, it should be noted that the basic award is based on *gross* pay, but the compensatory award is based on *net* pay. A cap of £60,600 is placed on compensatory awards but this is removed for those who are unfairly dismissed for blowing the whistle on illegal practices or health and safety matters and who are protected against such dismissal by the Public Interest Disclosure Act 1998. There is no ceiling on such awards. This is because it was thought that some senior executives might have been deterred from whistle-blowing since they would have the most salary to lose. The basic award is calculated with reference to a week's pay that is currently £310, but is automatically increased annually to a figure that is index linked to the retail price index for September of each year. This is a maximum figure so gross pay is the starting point, but if this exceeds £310, the figure of £310 applies.

The compensation for unfair dismissal is in four parts as follows.

(a) The basic award (maximum: £8,700). This award is computed as a redundancy payment (see p 481 before reading on). There is a maximum of 20 years' employment counted (giving a maximum of 30 weeks' pay). Contributory misconduct or fault of the employee is taken into account.

Example

Fred, a 35-year-old lorry driver employed for 10 years earning £400 per week (take home £350) is unfairly dismissed. He did his best to get a comparable job but did not in fact obtain one until one week before the tribunal hearing to start two weeks after the tribunal hearing. Fred had a history of lateness for work and his contributory fault is assessed at 25 per cent.

Fred's basic award: Fred is in the category of 22 years of age or over but under 41 years of age for redundancy, which allows one week's gross pay for every year of service:

```
10 × £310   £3,100
Less: 25%   £  775
            £2,325 = basic award
```

There is a minimum basic award of £4,200 (currently) where the dismissal is due to trade union membership or activities, duties of a health and safety representative, trustee of an occupational pension scheme or employee representative. This may be reduced for contributory fault. The amount of the basic award is only *two weeks'* pay where the tribunal finds that the reason or principal reason for the dismissal was that the employee was redundant and then:

- he unreasonably refused or left suitable alternative employment; or
- his employment was renewed or he was re-engaged and he was, therefore, not considered dismissed (s 121, ERA 1996).

(b) Compensatory award (maximum: £60,600). This consists of:

(i)   estimated loss of wages, *net of tax and other deductions* to the date of the hearing less any money earned between date of dismissal and the hearing;
(ii) estimated future losses;
(iii) loss of any benefits such as pension rights and expenses;

19

(iv) loss of statutory rights. An award under this heading is given for loss of minimum notice entitlement. For example, Fred has been continuously employed for 10 years. He was entitled to 10 weeks' notice, which he did not get. He now has a new job but it will take him time to build up that entitlement again. A tribunal can award something for this. Once again, contributory fault is taken into account.

A compensatory award is not linked to a redundancy payment as a basic award is. The figure of one week's pay of £310 does not apply; the calculation is based on actual net pay and is designed to recompense the worker for the financial loss suffered as a result of being dismissed. The basic award is payable in all cases regardless of proved loss. The following example assumes that Fred had been out of work for 10 weeks before the tribunal hearing.

Fred's compensatory award:

		£
The loss up to the hearing	10 × £350	3,500
Loss up to time of getting new job	2 × £350	700
		4,200
Less: 25%		1,050
		3,150
	£	
Loss of statutory rights: a nominal figure of	100	
Less: 25%	25	75
		3,225

Fred's total award is therefore:

	£
Basic	2,325
Compensatory	3,225
	5,500

If Fred has lost anything else, e.g. use of firm's van at weekends and/or pension rights, these would be added to the compensatory award subject to 25 per cent discount for contributory fault.

Those on higher salaries may very well reach the maximum of £60,600. If the sum calculated in accordance with the above example exceeds the statutory ceiling, only £60,600 is awarded.

Additional award. This is payable in addition to the above where an employer fails to comply with an order for reinstatement or re-engagement unless it was not practicable for him to do so.

The amount of the additional award was varied by the Employment Relations Act 1999, s 33(2) and is now at one level, i.e. an amount not less than 26 weeks' nor more than 52 weeks' pay, subject to a weekly maximum of £310, i.e. £8,060 minimum and £16,120 maximum.

In all cases a deduction will be made for contributory fault, if any, of the employee.

Any unemployment or supplementary benefits received by the employee are deducted from any award made by a tribunal. However, the employer must pay the amount(s) in question direct to the DSS.

As regards *ex gratia* payments the general principle is that if the employer has made such a payment to the complainant in connection with the dismissal credit will be given for this in fixing the amount of compensation if and only if the dismissal is in the context of being unfairly chosen for redundancy. This results from the provisions of s 122 of the ERA as interpreted in *Boorman* v *Allmakes Ltd* (1995) *The Times*, 21 April. If the dismissal is not in that context, the employee keeps the *ex gratia* payment in addition to any compensation.

(c) Time limits. A claim for compensation against an employer must reach the tribunal within three months of the date of termination of employment. The period in regard to dismissal in connection with a strike or other industrial action is six months. A worker can claim while working out his notice but no award can be made until employment ends.

A tribunal can hear a claim after three months if the employee can prove that:

(i)   it was not reasonably practicable for him to claim within three months;
(ii) he did so as soon as he could in the circumstances.

Unfair dismissal: damages for injury to feelings not available

For many years the position regarding injury to feelings damages in unfair dismissal cases was clear. The judgment of the President of what was then the Industrial Relations Court in *Norton Tool Co* v *Tewson* [1972] IRLR 86 applied and was to the effect that no such damages were available. Loss in unfair dismissal claims was restricted to direct economic loss.

However, in *Johnson* v *Unisys Ltd* [2001] 2 All ER 801 Lord Hoffmann in remarks not essential to his judgment, i.e. *obiter* took the view that there was no reason why damages for injured feelings should not be awarded.

Since then some tribunals have gone along with Lord Hoffmann's remarks and made awards for injured feelings while others have refused to do so and have stood by the decision in *Norton Tool*.

The House of Lords has now ruled that damages for injury to feelings are not available in unfair dismissal claims. The legal position in these cases is thus clarified. The ruling was given in *Dunnachie* v *Kingston Upon Hull City Council* [2004] 3 All ER 1011.

Internal appeal procedures

The Employment Act 2002 procedures have already been considered earlier in this chapter along with the sanctions for failing to follow them.

19

Discriminatory dismissal

In addition to legislation relating to unfair dismissal generally, the various discrimination regulations deal with complaints to employment tribunals for dismissal on the grounds of discrimination. The nature and scope of these provisions have already been considered and it is only necessary to add here that there are provisions in the ERA which prevent double compensation being paid, once under discrimination legislation, and once under the general unfair dismissal provisions of the ERA.

Redundancy

The ERA gives an employee a right to compensation by way of a redundancy payment if he is dismissed because of a redundancy.

Meaning of redundancy

Under the ERA redundancy is *presumed* to occur where the services of employees are dispensed with because the employer ceases, or intends to cease carrying on business, or to cease to carry on business at the place where the employee was employed, or does not require so many employees to do work of a certain kind as where the number of staff is to be reduced because of a fall in work. Employees who have been laid off or kept on short time without pay for four consecutive weeks (or for six weeks in a period of 13 weeks) are entitled to end their employment and to seek a redundancy payment if there is no reasonable prospect that normal working will be resumed.

Managing redundancies

After a number of conflicting decisions on what could amount to redundancy the matter was largely resolved by the House of Lords in *Murray* v *Foyle Meats Ltd* [1999] 3 All ER 769. In that case their Lordships ruled that for employees to be regarded as redundant two things had to be shown:

- that there is a state of affairs in the employer's business which meets the statutory definition of redundancy, e.g. less work; and
- that the employee's dismissal is wholly or mainly *attributable* to that state of affairs.

Thus employer A makes widgets. There is a loss of orders and a diminution in the requirements of production. Therefore, anyone dismissed by reason of the general reduction in orders is to be regarded as redundant because the redundancy is *attributable* to the loss of orders. So if the employer applies a first-in first-out policy across the workforce, the dismissals will be regarded as redundancy and not the more costly ground of unfair dismissal.

In addition, a redundancy may be 'bumped'. Thus if Jones is to be dismissed because the employer no longer needs anyone to do his job the employer may, instead of dismissing Jones, give Jones Green's job and dismiss Green, e.g. on a first-in last-out basis Jones having been employed by the firm for longer than Green. Green may well be found to have been dismissed on the ground of redundancy although he has been 'bumped' out of his job by Jones. The decision in *Murray* sanctions this.

It should however be said that although the House of Lords in *Murray* put it in terms that Green's dismissal was *attributable to redundancy* it does seem that his dismissal arises not so much out of the redundancy situation but rather out of the way it was *managed*. The flexibility that the *Murray* decision allows saves the employer money in that he will not face a claim for unfair dismissal where the compensation can be much higher, e.g. where the tribunal proceeds to make a compensatory award.

Eligibility

In general terms, all those employed under a contract of service as employees are entitled to redundancy pay, including a person employed by his/her spouse. Furthermore, a volunteer for redundancy is not debarred from claiming. However, certain persons are excluded by statute or circumstances. The main categories are listed below.

(a) A domestic servant in a private household who is a close relative of the employer. The definition of 'close relative' for this purpose is father, mother, grandfather, grandmother, stepfather, stepmother, son, daughter, grandson, granddaughter, stepson, stepdaughter, brother, sister, half-brother, or half-sister.

(b) An employee who has not completed at least two years of continuous service. There is now no minimum age for starting continuous service under the Age Regulations. Alternate week working does not break continuity (*Colley* v *Corkindale t/a Corker's Lounge Bar* (1996) IRLB 8).

These continuous service provisions remain unchanged under amendments made by the Unfair Dismissal Statement of Reasons for Dismissal (Variation of Qualifying Period) Order 1999 that apply only to claims for unfair dismissal that can now be brought after one year's service.

(c) The right to claim a redundancy payment was lost by either sex at the age of 65 or the normal retiring age in the business for employees holding the position in question if earlier. Under the Age Regulations, employees who are dismissed for redundancy but who have attained the normal retiring age or 65 continue to be entitled to a redundancy payment.

(d) An employee who is *dismissed for misconduct* loses the right to a redundancy payment. In the circumstances of the *Boychuk* and *Kowalski* cases we can note that, although these cases were brought for unfair dismissal, they were also situations in which the employees concerned would have lost the right to a redundancy payment because the dismissal was not for redundancy. The only issue was whether there had been an unfair dismissal.

An employee who accepts an offer of suitable alternative employment with his employer is not entitled to a redundancy payment. Where a new offer is made, there is a trial period of four weeks following the making of the offer, during which the employer or the employee may end the contract while retaining all rights and liabilities under redundancy legislation.

> *Fuller* v *Stephanie Bowman*, 1977 – Unreasonable refusal of alternative employment (**260**)

Time limits

The employee must make a written claim to the employer or to an employment tribunal within six months from the end of the employment. An employment tribunal may extend the time for a further six months making 12 months in all, provided that it can be shown that it is just and equitable having regard to the reasons put forward by the employee for late application.

Amount of redundancy payment

Those aged 41 or over receive one-and-a-half weeks' pay (*up to a maximum of £310 per week*) for each year of service up to a maximum of 20 years. This period is *not* changed by the Age Regulations. In other age groups the above provisions apply, except that the week's pay changes: i.e. for those aged 22 but under 41, it is one week's gross pay; and for those under 22, it is a half week's pay. Service before the eighteenth birthday now counts under the Age Regulations and there is no maximum age.

For example, a man of 52 who is made redundant having been continuously employed for 18 years and earning £340 per week as gross salary at the time of his redundancy would be entitled to a redundancy payment as follows:

34 to 41 years = 7 years at one week's pay $\qquad$ = $\qquad$ 7 weeks
41 to 52 years = 11 years at one-and-a-half weeks' pay = $16^1/_2$ weeks
$\qquad\qquad\qquad\qquad\qquad\qquad\qquad\qquad\qquad\qquad$ $23^1/_2$ weeks

It follows, therefore, that the redundancy payment would be $23^1/_2$ weeks × £310 = £7,285.

19

Complaints by employees in respect of the right to a redundancy payment or questions as to its amount may, as we have seen, be made to an employment tribunal which will make a declaration as to the employee's rights which form the basis on which payment can be recovered from the employer.

Procedure for handling redundancies

Any agreed formula must be followed, e.g. last-in, first-out. Selection procedures may also be based on poor work performance or attendance record and there is no requirement on the employer to determine reasons for this (*Dooley* v *Leyland Vehicles Ltd* [1986] IRLR 36). In *Byrne* v *Castrol (UK) Ltd* (1997) 568 IRLB 12, the EAT decided that where selection for redundancy was based on absence records there was no need to go into the reasons for the absences since this failure to enquire made the selection more objective. If there is no agreed procedure the employer must decide after considering the pros and cons in each case.

It should be noted that the dismissal may well be unfair if some reasonable system of selection is not followed. In this connection the EAT decided in *Rogers* v *Vosper Thorneycroft (UK) Ltd* [1988] IRLR 22 that last-in, first-out is a relevant system but merely asking for volunteers is not. There must be some criteria, though calling for volunteers is acceptable as a preliminary step in the matter of eventual selection. The decision was affirmed by the Court of Appeal (see *The Times*, 27 October 1988). Everyone should, as far as possible, be allowed to express his or her views, e.g. through elected representatives, if any. An attempt to relocate a redundant worker should be considered. Failure to do so can result in a finding of unfair dismissal unless, of course, there was no chance of finding suitable alternative work. Fairness in the search for alternative work involves looking at other companies within a group (EAT decision in *Euroguard Ltd* v *Rycroft* (1993) 477 IRLB 5).

Selecting, say, a white single woman or a West Indian single man to go, rather than a married white man with two children and a mortgage, might appear to be humane. However, unless the decision is made on the basis of competence, experience, reliability and so on, the dismissal is likely to be unfair and also a breach of the SDA and/or the RRA. Selection on the grounds of gender reassignment, sexual orientation, religion or belief and disability would also be unfair.

Consultation on redundancies

The Collective Redundancies and Transfer of Undertakings (Protection of Employment) (Amendment) Regulations 1999 (SI 1999/1925) apply. The Regulations substantially amend s 188 of the Trade Union and Labour Relations (Consolidation) Act 1992 as follows:

- the obligation to consult about redundancies now arises where the employer is proposing to dismiss as redundant 20 or more employees at one establishment within a period of 90 days or less. This change will remove the need to consult from some 96 per cent of UK businesses;
- where consultation is required the employer must consult all those who are 'appropriate representatives';
- appropriate representatives of employees are:
  (1) employee representatives elected by them; or
  (2) if an independent trade union is recognised by the employer, representatives of the union.

Where the employees elect representatives and belong to a recognised union, the employer has a choice whether to consult the union or the elected representatives. It will be noted that the Regulations extend the requirement to consult to non-union workplaces. They further provide that:

■ Employee representatives may be elected by the employees for the specific purpose of consultation or while not having been specifically elected it is appropriate to consult them as where they are members of an existing works council or joint consultative committee. In all cases the employee representatives must be employed by the employer. No method is stipulated in the Regulations which means that *ad hoc* procedures as and when a redundancy situation will arise are acceptable.

■ Consultation must begin in good time as distinct from the earliest opportunity as was formerly required and before reaching final conclusions, and in any case.

■ Where the employer is proposing to dismiss 100 or more employees at one establishment within 90 days or less, consultation must begin, as before, 90 days *before any notice of dismissal is served*. In cases involving less than 100 but at least 20 employees, consultation must begin at least 30 days before that date. This means that the employer must wait the full 30- or 90-day period before serving notice and not, as before, when the first redundancies took effect. Thus the employee gets the full consultation period plus pay for the notice period plus any redundancy package (see the Collective Redundancies (Amendment) Regulations 2006).

■ Appropriate representatives must be given access to employees who are to be made redundant and facilities, e.g. an office and a telephone must be made available to them.

It should of course be borne in mind that fairness towards employees in a redundancy situation is always paramount if the matter goes to a tribunal asserting unfair dismissal. Therefore, individual consultation may be required even where the numbers involved are less than 20 and even though, the numbers being more, there has been consultation with representatives. Thus, in *Mugford* v *Midland Bank plc* [1997] IRLR 208 the EAT, in confirming that a particular employee had not in the circumstances been subject to unfairness, commented that if a person is selected for redundancy, individual consultation may become important in the circumstances of the case, even if the employer (as he had in this case) has conducted detailed consultation with what were in this case union representatives.

It should be noted:

■ that consultation must cover employees who have volunteered for redundancy; and

■ although consultation does not have to end in agreement, it must always be properly conducted.

It is, perhaps rather obviously, direct discrimination not to consult an employee about redundancy because she is on maternity leave (see *McGuigan* v *T&G Baynes* (1999) 622 IRLB 11), and employees who are on parental leave, paternity leave and adoption leave.

Notice

The employer must start the consultation process by giving written notice to the appropriate representatives stating:

(*a*) the reasons for the proposals;

(*b*) the numbers and descriptions of employees whom it proposes to dismiss as redundant;

(*c*) the total number of employees of that description. In *MSF* v *GEC Ferranti (Defence Systems) Ltd* (1994) 491 IRLB 12 the EAT held that the statutory period for consulting with a trade union over proposed redundancies did not begin when the employer gave the union a notice which contained only a 'best estimate' of the redundancies;

(*d*) the proposed method of selecting the employees to be dismissed;

(*e*) the proposed method of carrying out the dismissal, including the period over which the dismissals are to take effect;

(*f*) the method of calculating any non-statutory redundancy payments.

Consultation must also include consideration of ways to avoid redundancies, to reduce the number to be dismissed and to mitigate the consequences of dismissals. The employer must also, as part of the consultation process, consider any representations by the appropriate representatives.

The above obligations do not apply if the employees whom the employer proposes to dismiss fall into one of several specified categories. The most important of these categories, for practical purposes, are:

(*a*) employees who under their contract ordinarily work outside Great Britain;

(*b*) employees under a contract for a fixed term of three months or less or who have been engaged to carry out a specific task which is not expected to last for more than three months (unless in either case the employment has continued beyond the three months).

The employer must also be able to argue that there were special circumstances which made it not reasonably practicable for it to comply with the requirements. Even then it must do whatever is reasonably practicable. If, for example, the employer is proposing to dismiss 25 employees and cannot give the full 30 days' notice required, it must give as much notice as possible.

The main practical consequence, if the requirements are not complied with, is that the union or any employee representative or any of those made redundant can apply to an employment tribunal for what is known as a 'protective award'. The effect of the award is that a protected period of up to 90 days is specified and individual employees can then apply to have their remuneration paid for that period. The following example illustrates the position.

Example: A firm is proposing to dismiss 25 employees and fails to give notice to the appropriate representatives. The employment tribunal makes a protective award under which the protected period begins on the date when the first dismissal takes effect and runs for 30 days. Employees who are dismissed on that first date can claim remuneration for the whole of the 30-day period. Employees dismissed part-way through the protected period can claim remuneration for the balance of the period (subject in each case to the dismissal being for redundancy and not for some other reason).

Notifying the Secretary of State

The employer's other obligation is to notify the Department of Trade and Industry of proposed redundancies. The obligation is to give written notice to the Department:

(*a*) at least 90 days before the first dismissal notice is given, in the case of 100 or more redundancies;

(*b*) at least 30 days before the first dismissal notice is given, in the case of 20 or more redundancies.

The notice must be in a prescribed form available from local offices and the employer must give a copy to the relevant appropriate representatives.

If there are special circumstances which make it not reasonably practicable for the employer to comply with the requirements, it must do everything that is reasonably practicable. If the special circumstances prevent the full required notice being given, it must give as much notice as possible.

Failing to comply with the above requirements means that the employer can be prosecuted and fined.

Redundancy consultation and the Information and Consultation of Employees Regulations 2004

These Regulations (SI 2004/3426) require consultation and information to be undertaken or given to employees on an ongoing basis about issues affecting the business in which they work. From 6 April 2005 the Regulations have applied to employers with at least 150 employees. From 6 April 2007 they will apply to undertakings employing at least 100 employees and from 6 April 2008 to those with at least 50 employees.

The Department of Trade and Industry has issued guidance in terms of how these consultations fit in with the redundancy consultation provisions. The guidance states that the ICE Regulations are in addition to the redundancy consultation provisions and makes the following points:

- An employer who proposes to make collective redundancies must comply with the redundancy provisions even though it has established separate consultation arrangements as regards representatives under the ICE Regulations. Thus, if a trade union is recognised in regard to a collective redundancy situation, the employer must consult with the redundancy representatives even where there is a separate group of employees for consultation put in place as a result of ICE consultations.
- Where there is a separate group of employee representatives for ICE consultations, the employer will only be required to consult the ICE representative in a redundancy if the employer has agreed to do so under a 'negotiated agreement' under the ICE Regulations.
- Otherwise an employer need not consult on redundancy provisions with ICE representatives if it informs those representatives that the redundancy consultation provisions have been triggered and that consultation will take place under the redundancy provisions.

The guidance document is available at **http://www.dti.gov.uk/er**.

The role of ACAS

ACAS has now taken on redundancy pay entitlement as an issue on which it has a duty to conciliate. The Employment Rights (Dispute Resolution) Act 1998 confers a duty on ACAS to conciliate if a person puts an application to an employment tribunal concerning entitlement to redundancy pay.

Collective agreements on redundancy

The Secretary of State may, on the application of the employer and the unions involved, make an order modifying the requirements of redundancy pay legislation if he is satisfied that there is a collective agreement which makes satisfactory alternative arrangements for dealing with redundancy. The provisions of the agreement must be 'on the whole at least as favourable' as the statutory provisions, and must include, in particular, arrangements allowing an employee to go to an independent arbitration or to make a complaint to an employment tribunal.

Written statement of reasons for dismissal

At common law an employer is not required to give his employee any reasons for dismissal. However, s 92 of the ERA provides that where an employee is dismissed, with or without notice, or by failure to renew a contract for a fixed term, he must be provided by his employer on request, within 14 days of that request, with a written statement giving particulars of the reasons for his dismissal. This provision applies only to employees who have been continuously employed for a period of one year, though there is no service requirement in pregnancy dismissals. The written statement is admissible in evidence in any proceedings relating to the dismissal and if an employer refuses to give a written statement the employee may complain to an employment tribunal. If the tribunal upholds the complaint, it may make a declaration as to what it finds the employer's reasons were for dismissing the employee and must make an award of two weeks' pay without limit as to amount to the employee.

Other methods of terminating the contract of employment

These have already been considered in Chapter 17 and reference might usefully be made at this point to that chapter in terms of what is said about discharge of contract by notice, by agreement and by passage of time.

Employee's breach of contract

An employer may sue his employees for damages for breach of the contract of service by the employee. Such claims are potentially available, for example, for damage to the employer's property, as where machinery is damaged by negligent operation, as was the case in *Baster* v *London and County Printing Works* [1899] 1 QB 901, or for refusal to work resulting in damage by lost production, as was the case in *National Coal Board* v *Galley* [1958] 1 All ER 91. Such claims are rare and impractical because of the fact that the employee will not, in most cases, be able to meet the claim, and also, perhaps more importantly, because they lead to industrial unrest. In these circumstances we do not pursue the matter further here.

The employment contract and shop workers

The Sunday Trading Act 1994, which came into force on 26 August 1994, repeals previous restrictions on Sunday trading. Recognising the impact of this on shop workers, the ERA 1996, Part IV provides them with new and important rights. These rights are:

■ not to be dismissed or made redundant for refusing to work on Sunday; and
■ not to suffer a detriment for the same reason.

These rights extend to all shop workers in England and Wales if they are asked to do shop work on a Sunday. They are not available to Sunday-only workers.

The ERA 1996 defines a shop worker as an employee who is required or may be required by contract to work in or about a shop on a day when the shop is open to serve customers. However, the worker need not actually serve customers and the provisions extend beyond sales assistants and check-out operators to clerical workers doing work related to the shop, managers and supervisors, cleaners, storepersons, shelf fillers, lift attendants and security staff. Even those employed by outside contractors (but not self-employed) could be covered as also could van drivers based at the store who deliver goods to customers.

A shop is defined as including any premises where any retail or business is carried on. This does not include the sale of meals, refreshments or intoxicating liquor for consumption on the premises, e.g. public houses, cafés and restaurants, nor places preparing meals or refreshments to order for immediate consumption off the premises, e.g. take-aways.

The ERA 1996 defines two categories of shop workers:

- protected shop workers, i.e. those employed as such when the Act came into force, and those taking up employment afterwards whose contracts do not require Sunday working;
- opted-out workers, i.e. those who are employed after commencement of the Act under contracts which require them to work on Sundays but who opt out of this by giving three months' notice to the employer (see below).

Protected workers will have the right immediately regardless as to whether they have previously agreed to a contract requiring them to work on a Sunday. No procedures are involved. They can simply decide that they no longer wish to work on Sundays. Protected workers are able to give up their right to refuse to work on Sundays but only if:

- the employer is given a written 'opting-in notice' which must be signed and dated and state expressly that they do not object to Sunday working or actually wish to work on Sundays; and
- then enter into an express agreement with the employer to work on Sunday or on a particular Sunday.

Opted-out workers, i.e. those engaged after commencement of the Act or who have opted in to Sunday working, have the right to opt out. To do this they must give the employer a signed and dated written notice stating that they object to Sunday work. They then have to serve a three-month notice period. During this time they are still obliged to do Sunday work and if they refuse will lose statutory protection under the ERA 1996. However, they cannot be dismissed or made to suffer some other detriment merely because they have been given an opting-out notice. After the period of three months has expired, the worker has a right not to do Sunday work.

The ERA 1996 provides that dismissal or redundancy of protected and opted-out workers will be regarded as unfair dismissal if the reason or principal reason was that the worker(s) concerned have refused or proposed to refuse to work on Sundays.

The ERA 1996 gives protected and opted-out workers the right not to be subjected to any other detriment, e.g. non-payment of seniority bonuses, for refusing to work on a Sunday. These rights apply regardless of age, length of service or hours of work.

Employer's explanatory statement. The ERA 1996 provides that employers are required to give every shop worker who enters into a contractual agreement to work on Sundays after the new Act comes into force a written explanatory statement setting out their right to opt out. If an employer does not issue such a statement within two months of the worker entering into such a contractual agreement, the opt-out period is reduced from three months to one.

The ERA 1996 gives a prescribed form of statement to be given to employees.

19

STATUTORY RIGHTS IN RELATION TO SUNDAY SHOPWORK

You have become employed as a shop worker and are or can be required under your contract of employment to do the Sunday work your contract provides for.

However, if you wish, you can give a notice, as described in the next paragraph, to your employer and you will then have the right not to work in or about a shop which is open once three months have passed from the date on which you gave the notice.

Your notice must—

be in writing;
be signed and dated by you;
say that you object to Sunday working.

For three months after you give the notice, your employer can still require you to do all the Sunday work your contract provides for. After the three-month period has ended, you have the right to complain to an employment tribunal if, because of your refusal to work on Sundays on which the shop is open, your employer—

dismisses you, or
does something else detrimental to you, for example failing to promote you.

Once you have the rights described, you can surrender them only by giving your employer a further notice, signed and dated by you, saying that you wish to work on a Sunday or that you do not object to Sunday working and then agreeing with your employer to work on Sundays or on a particular Sunday.

Other important provisions are as follows:

- an employer is not obliged to compensate the employee for loss of Sunday work, either in terms of extra hours or remuneration;
- a provision in an agreement between a shop worker and his or her employer cannot generally exclude the provisions of the ERA 1996;
- the dismissal of an employee for asserting a statutory right contained in the ERA 1996 is to be regarded as being automatically unfair.

Betting offices

Betting offices and bookmaking establishments are allowed to do business on Sundays and the ERA protects workers against unfair dismissal or victimisation if they object to working on a Sunday. The provisions are largely the same as those in the case of shopworkers and appear in Part IV of the ERA 1996. They apply to workers regardless of age, hours of work or length of service.

Part 3

THE LAW OF TORTS

20

THE LAW OF TORTS: GENERAL PRINCIPLES

It is difficult to give a satisfactory definition of a tort. According to Professor Winfield (who was a distinguished author of a major text on the subject and whose definition has been accepted by our courts in many decided cases), 'tortious liability arises from a duty primarily fixed by law: this duty is towards persons generally and its breach is redressible by an action for unliquidated damages'.

The nature of a tort

It is a matter of dispute whether there should be a law of tort or a law of torts: there are two schools of thought. One maintains that there should be a law of tort, i.e. that all harm should be actionable in the absence of just cause or excuse. If there was merely a law of specific torts, then no new torts could be created by the courts and the categories of tortious liability would be closed. It is urged that under the flexibility of case law new torts have come into being, and in no case has an action been refused simply because it was novel. This is called the *general principle of liability theory*. The other view is that there should be a law of torts – that there should be only specific torts and unless the damage suffered can be brought under a known or recognised head of liability, there should be no remedy. This view is supported by modern cases where an attempt has been made, unsuccessfully, to establish a purported tort of eviction and a tort of perjury.

In *Khorasandjian* v *Bush* [1993] 3 All ER 669 the Court of Appeal granted an injunction to restrain the making of unwanted telephone calls and this might be regarded as a recognition of a new tort of harassment. However, the case is clearly founded on a breach of the rules of private nuisance and an expansion of that tort rather than the creation of a new one. Thus the courts have refused to create new torts even when given the opportunity. This is particularly unfortunate in the case of perjury. Perjury is not merely an offence against the state, as it has been traditionally regarded by the courts. It can cause an individual great loss or hardship and many feel that the victim should have a civil remedy in damages.

In addition, there is a danger in modern society of a serious invasion of privacy resulting from the increasing availability and use of electronic and other devices as a means of surreptitious surveillance and the accumulation of personal information about individuals in data banks, computers and credit registers. However, the common law of tort does now appear to be capable of extending to a remedy for invasion of privacy as such. This results from the ruling in *Douglas and Others* v *Hello! Ltd* (2005) (see below).

On the general issue of privacy we have, of course, to bear in mind the Human Rights Act 1998 which applies the European Convention on Human Rights in the UK. Article 8 provides that everyone has a right to respect for private, family and home life. Public bodies may only interfere with such rights for reasons of national security, public safety, economic wellbeing or as otherwise necessary in a democratic society. The Article was discussed in *R* v *Broadcasting Standards Commission, ex parte BBC* (1999) *The Times*, 14 September where the BBC had filmed secretly the sales transactions of Dixons for its 'watchdog' programme following the store's convictions for the sale of second-hand goods as new. No irregularities were uncovered. The High Court held that while the ECHR applied to human individuals, it did not apply to companies, so Dixons' complaint of infringement of its privacy to the Commission failed.

In addition, the Data Protection Act 1998 deals with information stored on computers. The details of the Act are beyond the scope of a book of this nature but the job of safeguarding the privacy of the individual in terms, e.g., of the information kept on him and the uses to which it is put falls under the Act to the Information Commissioner who is appointed by the Crown. The Commissioner supervises a central register on which all data users must enter details of data banks and their purposes. The Commissioner and 'data subjects', the latter through the courts, have access to records on computers. Following an EC Directive on the subject, the government obtained the enactment of the Data Protection Act 1998 which repeals the former legislation, i.e. the Data Protection Act 1984, and extends the controls in line with the Directive, e.g., by applying data control to certain types of manually produced data. The 1984 Act applied only to automatically processed data.

Hence, we may conclude that at the present there is no general principle of liability in tort. Nevertheless, if judges have not created new torts, privacy apart they have applied old cases to new situations. This has resulted in an extension of the old torts and there has been a tendency to expand the area of liability, particularly in the field of negligence (see Chapter 21). If this continues, the law may reach a stage approximating to a general liability for wrongful acts, for, as Lord Macmillan said in *Donoghue* v *Stevenson* (1932), 'the categories of negligence are never closed'.

Perera v *Vandiyar*, 1953 – No tort of eviction (**261**)

Hargreaves v *Bretherton*, 1958 – No tort of perjury (**262**)

Roy v *Prior*, 1969 – No tort of perjury reaffirmed (**263**)

Douglas and Others* v *Hello! Ltd, 2005 (**263a**) – Privacy and the law of confidence

Donoghue v *Stevenson*, 1932 – The categories of negligence can be expanded (**264**)

Damage and liability

The law distinguishes between two concepts – (1) *Damnum*, which means the damage suffered, and (2) *Injuria*, which is an injury having legal consequences. Sometimes, but not always, these two go together. For instance, if I negligently drive a car and injure a person, he suffers *damnum* (the hurt) and *injuria* (because he has a right of action to be compensated). There are, however, cases of *damnum sine injuria* (damage suffered without the violation of a legal right), and *injuria sine damno* (the violation of a legal right without damage).

The mere fact that a person has suffered damage does not entitle him to maintain an action in tort. Before an action can succeed, the harm suffered must be caused by an act which is a violation of a right which the law vests in the claimant or injured party. Damage suffered in the absence of the violation of such legal right is known as *damnum sine injuria*. Furthermore, a person who suffers *damnum* cannot receive compensation on the basis of *injuria* suffered by another. The concept of *damnum sine injuria* is not the same as that concerning whether there is a law of tort or a law of torts because under the concept of *damnum sine injuria* a person may suffer harm and have no claim even though the harm was suffered *as a result of a known tort*.

> *Best* v *Samuel Fox & Co Ltd*, 1952 – No proprietary right in a spouse (**265**)
>
> *Electrochrome Ltd* v *Welsh Plastics Ltd*, 1968 – Loss but no damage to the claimant's property (**266**)

Malice

The fact that the defendant acts with malice, i.e. with the intention of injuring his neighbour, does not give rise to a cause of action unless a legal right of the claimant is infringed (see 'Motive' below). On the other hand, whenever there is an invasion of a legal right, the person in whom the right is vested may bring an action and recover damages (though these may be nominal) or, what may be more important, obtain an injunction, although he has suffered no actual harm. For example, an action will lie for an unlawful entry on the land of another (trespass) although no actual damage is done. Furthermore, in *Ashby* v *White* (1703) 2 Ld Raym 938, it was held that an elector had a right of action, for a form of nuisance or disturbance of rights, when his vote was wrongly rejected by the returning officer although the candidate for whom he tried to vote was elected. This is known as *injuria sine damno*.

Motive

The law of torts is concerned more with the effects of injurious conduct than with the motives which inspired it. Hence, just as a bad intention will not necessarily make the infliction of damage actionable, so an innocent intention is usually no defence unless a bad intention can be imputed. However, there are circumstances in which malice is important. Thus where a person puts in motion the criminal law against another, this is actionable if malice is shown to be present and is known as the tort of malicious prosecution. Furthermore, the question of malice may be raised when certain *defences* are pleaded. Thus in the law of defamation the defences of qualified privilege and fair comment are allowed only where the defendant has not been malicious. Finally, in regard to the tort of nuisance, certain acts which would not necessarily be a nuisance may be regarded as such if they are exercised unreasonably. Malice is sometimes regarded as evidence of conduct which is unreasonable (see *Christie* v *Davey* (1893) Chapter 21).

20

> *Bradford Corporation* v *Pickles*, 1895 – Effect of bad intention (**267**)
>
> *Wilkinson* v *Downton*, 1897 – Effect of innocent intention and imputation of intention (**268**)

Parties in the law of torts

It is now necessary to consider certain categories of persons whose capacity in connection with tortious acts is limited.

Minors

A minor can sue in tort as a claimant in the ordinary way except that, as in contract, he must sue through an adult as litigation friend. He cannot compromise his action except by leave of the court, unlike an adult, who does not require such permission.

At common law there was a doubt as to whether a child had a cause of action for personal injuries caused before its birth. The matter is now covered by the Congenital Disabilities (Civil Liability) Act 1976. Section 1 establishes civil liability where a child is born disabled in consequence of the intentional act or the negligence or the breach of statutory duty of some person before the child's birth. There can be no liability unless the child is born alive. Section 44 of the Human Fertilisation and Embryology Act 1990 extends the 1976 Act to cover children conceived following infertility treatments.

It was held in *C v S* [1987] 1 All ER 123 that a foetus has no right of action unless it is subsequently born alive. If it is stillborn, the parents might have an action, e.g. for nervous shock. Causation must be proved which may be difficult in the case of pre-natal injuries. A mother cannot be liable under s 1 for causing injury to her child by her own negligence, except where the injury is caused by the mother's negligence in driving a motor vehicle when she knows, or ought reasonably to know, that she is pregnant. Barristers and judges, among others, have been strongly opposed to children being given a cause of action against their mothers, recognising the danger of inter-family disputes, and, subject to what has been said about motor vehicle liability where the action is in effect against an insurance company and not really against the mother, their view has prevailed in the Act. The liability of a father is not, however, excluded and he can be liable to his child for injuries caused by his own negligence.

The section also distinguishes between matters arising *before* conception (where the injury can be to *either* parent) and matters arising when the child's mother is pregnant or during the actual process of childbirth (where the injury can *only* be to the mother). Thus the injury could result, for example, from irradiation which damages the progenitive capacity of the father. It also covers physical damage to the child during childbirth as by the negligent handling of instruments by those attending the mother. The injuries must be caused during the pregnancy and there could be problems in dating the beginning of this in some cases. The defendant is presumed to take the mother as he finds her and thus cannot say that he did not know she was pregnant nor that the damage to her child was not foreseeable.

The common-law defence of *volenti non fit injuria* is applicable and in this sense if the mother is *volenti* so is the child. It is recognised that this may penalise the child but it was thought that any other solution would prejudice the position of women in society because organisations worried that a woman might be pregnant may refuse to enter into a wide variety of contracts with her. Incidentally, so far as the consent which the child is deemed to give results from an exemption clause in a contract made by the mother, then s 1 creates a new exception to the doctrine of privity of contract. Section 1 also provides that the child's damages awarded against the defendant are to be reduced by any contributory negligence of the mother. Finally, s 1 provides that professional persons, such as doctors, are under no liability for treatment or advice given according to prevailing professional standards of care. This codifies the common-law rule in *Roe v Minister of Health* (1954) (see Chapter 21).

Section 3 clarifies the compensation provisions of the Nuclear Installations Act 1965, where damage results from a nuclear incident and provides for compensation under the Act in the case of a child born subsequently with disabilities attributable to the incident.

A minor is liable as defendant for all his torts except in a limited number of instances. Where the tort alleged requires a mental ingredient, the age of the minor (in cases of extreme infancy) may show an inability to form the necessary intent. In cases of negligence, a very young child cannot be expected to show the same standard of care as an older person.

Basically children are liable for their own torts, but a father may be liable vicariously, if the relationship of employer and employee exists between him and the child or if there is the relationship of principal and agent. Simply as a father he is not liable unless the injury is caused by his negligent control of the child and so when he is liable, it is really for his own tort, i.e. negligence in looking after the child. Such a liability may extend to other persons (not being parents) who have control of children, e.g. teachers and education authorities, and, if such persons or authorities act negligently, they may be held responsible for the harm caused by children under their care or control. Nevertheless, the basis of the action is negligent control or supervision.

> *Williams* v *Humphrey*, 1975 – A minor is sued for negligence (**269**)
>
> *Donaldson* v *McNiven*, 1952 – Parental control: no negligence (**270**)
>
> *Bebee* v *Sales*, 1916 – Where a parent is negligent (**271**)
>
> *Carmarthenshire County Council* v *Lewis*, 1955 – Negligent control by a local authority (**272**)
>
> *Butt* v *Cambridgeshire and Ely County Council*, 1969 – A local authority is not negligent (**273**)

Persons suffering from mental disorder

In criminal law a person of unsound mind has considerable exemption from criminal liability (see Chapter 25), but these rules have never been applied to civil injuries. This is understandable if it is borne in mind that the aim of the law of torts is to compensate the injured party, not to punish the offender. In the light of this, any exemptions accorded to a person of unsound mind should be narrow, and he should be liable unless his state of mind prevents him having the necessary intent (where a mental ingredient is part of the tort) and in extreme cases where no voluntary act is possible.

> *Morriss* v *Marsden*, 1952 – Mental patients in tort (**274**)

Husband and wife

The rule used to be that a married woman was liable for her torts only to the extent of her separate property and that beyond this the husband was fully liable. Since the Law Reform (Married Women and Tortfeasors) Act 1935, the wife is fully liable for her torts and the husband as such is no longer held responsible, unless, as in the case of a minor, there is a relationship of employer and employee or principal and agent.

The old common-law rule whereby one spouse could not sue the other in tort has now been altered. The Law Reform (Husband and Wife) Act 1962 provides that each of the parties to a marriage shall have the like right of action in tort against the other as if they were not married, but where the action is brought by one of the parties to the marriage against the other during the subsistence of the marriage, the court may stay the action if it appears:

(*a*) that no substantial benefit would accrue to either party from the continuation of the proceedings; or

(*b*) that the question or questions in issue could more conveniently be disposed of on an application made under s 17 of the Married Women's Property Act 1882. (This provides for the determination of questions between husband and wife regarding title to or possession of property by a summary procedure.)

20

Those who have registered a civil partnership under the Civil Partnership Act 2004 are able to bring claims against each other.

It should also be noted that under s 2(a) of the Administration of Justice Act 1982 a husband has no right of action against a person who by a tortious act deprives him of the society and services of his wife, i.e. loss of consortium. A wife has no such right by reason of case law in respect of loss of consortium. (See *Best* v *Samuel Fox & Co Ltd* (1952), above.) The above rules apply also to civil partners.

The Crown and its servants

Prior to 1947 the Crown had considerable immunity in the law of tort and contract stemming from the common-law maxim: 'The King can do no wrong.' We have already seen that, by the Crown Proceedings Act 1947, the Crown is, in general, now liable in the same way as a subject (see further Chapter 8).

The Crown is not liable for torts committed by the police nor is the local authority which appoints and pays them. However, the Police Act 1996, s 88, provides that the chief officer of police for any police area is liable for the torts of police officers, e.g. wrongful arrest. The Act also provides that any damages and costs awarded against the chief officer shall be payable out of police funds.

Postal and telecommunications authorities

The Post Office is a public authority but is not an agent of the Crown. It is liable, subject to limitations set out in s 91 of the Postal Services Act 2000, for loss of or damage to inland registered postal packets. Apart from this, neither the Post Office nor any of its servants, officers or sub-postmasters is liable for anything done or omitted to be done in regard to anything in the post or for failure to collect the post (s 90 of the 2000 Act). Thus in *Harold Stephen & Co Ltd* v *Post Office* [1978] 1 All ER 939, the Court of Appeal refused under earlier legislation to grant an injunction against the Post Office to companies in the Cricklewood area of London whose businesses were in jeopardy because they were receiving no mail through the Post Office closing the local sorting office and suspending post office workers who refused to handle mail in support of workers employed in the private sector.

Persons engaged in the carriage of mail or their servants, agents or sub-contractors, are not liable for loss or damage in regard to the post (s 90 of the 2000 Act). Thus in *American Express Co* v *British Airways Board* [1983] 1 All ER 557, the claimants gave a postal packet containing travellers' cheques to the Post Office for delivery abroad. The Post Office gave it to the defendants and it was stolen by one of their employees. The claimants sought damages for breach of bailment. Lloyd, J held that the defendants were not liable; they were exempted by a similar provision in earlier legislation.

Since the enactment of the Telecommunications Act 1984 (see now Communications Act 2003) British Telecom provides its telecommunications service under standard service contracts and is liable in the ordinary way for breach. However, the contracts concerned have exclusion clauses, e.g. in the case of failure to repair equipment during an industrial dispute.

Judicial immunity

A judge has absolute immunity for acts in his judicial capacity. Section 51 of the Justices of the Peace Act 1997 extends this immunity to magistrates and their clerks, the intention being that they should be put in the same position as other judges. Counsel and witnesses have immunity in respect of all matters relating to the cases in which they are concerned. This is mainly of importance in connection with possible actions for slander.

Foreign sovereigns and ambassadorial staffs

These persons have immunity from actions in both contract and tort. However, it should be noted that if they remain in this country after finishing their duties, they may become liable even if the tort was committed before. They may, of course, voluntarily submit to the jurisdiction of our courts, since immunity is from suit and not from liability.

> *Dickinson* v *Del Solar*, 1930 – Ambassadorial staff are immune from suit not liability (**275**)

Aliens

Enemy aliens, including British subjects who voluntarily reside or carry on business in an enemy state, cannot bring an action in tort, although they themselves can be sued. Other aliens have neither disability nor immunity.

Corporations

A corporation can, as a claimant, sue for all torts committed against it. Obviously certain torts, such as assault, cannot by their nature be committed against corporations, but a corporation can maintain an action for injury to its business.

Section 32 of the Companies Act 2006 provides that unless a company's articles specifically restrict the objects of the company its objects are unrestricted. The *ultra vires* (beyond the powers) rule has no application to such a company. There will, however, be companies that wish to restrict the company's objects and will carry these in the articles. The ability of the directors to overcome lack of capacity in contract does not apply in tort and it is necessary therefor to examine the effect of the *ultra vires* rule here.

(a) *Intra vires* **activities.** Where an employee or agent of the corporation commits a tort while acting in the course of his employment in an *intra vires* activity, the corporation is liable. Although it has been said that any tort committed on behalf of a corporation must be *ultra vires* (since Parliament does not authorise corporations to commit torts), this view is fallacious since a corporation can have legal liability without legal capacity. A corporation is liable under the principles of vicarious liability for the torts of its employees or agents committed on *intra vires* activities.

(b) *Ultra vires* **activities.** Here we have to distinguish between express and non-express authority. A corporation will not be liable if an employee engages in an *ultra vires* activity without express authority. Thus, if a corporation has not got authority and has not given it, you cannot infer it. On the other hand, where a tortious action is *ultra vires* but has been expressly authorised, the courts have taken the view that the *ultra vires* doctrine is irrelevant, and the corporation is liable for it.

> *D & L Caterers Ltd and Jackson* v *D'Anjou*, 1945 – An action by a company (**276**)
>
> *Poulton* v *London and South Western Railway Co*, 1867 – An *ultra vires* act (**277**)
>
> *Campbell* v *Paddington Borough Council*, 1911 – Is *ultra vires* relevant if act authorised? (**278**)

20

Unincorporated associations and trade unions

These have already been considered in Chapter 8 and their position in tort is set out there.

Joint tortfeasors

Formerly there was no right of contribution between joint tortfeasors, but under the Law Reform (Married Women and Tortfeasors) Act 1935, it was laid down that, if one joint tortfeasor was sued and paid damages, he could claim a contribution from fellow wrongdoers. The relevant provisions are now contained in the Civil Liability (Contribution) Act 1978. However, there can be no contribution where the person claiming it is liable to *indemnify* the person from whom it is claimed. For example, an auctioneer is entitled to be indemnified by a client who has instructed him to sell goods to which, as it subsequently appears, the client does not have a title (*Adamson* v *Jarvis* (1827) 4 Bing 66). Therefore, if the true owner sues the client for wrongful interference and the client pays the damages, he has no right to a contribution against the auctioneer although the auctioneer is also liable for wrongful interference because the auctioneer is a person whom the client would have had to indemnify if the true owner had chosen to sue the auctioneer. The amount of the contribution is settled by the court on the basis of what is just and equitable given the responsibility of each party for the injury and may be the full amount of the damages originally awarded against the person claiming the contribution.

In connection with the right of contribution, the Law Reform (Husband and Wife) Act 1962 has an important effect. Where a spouse A is injured by the joint negligence of the other spouse B and of a third party C, e.g. in a car accident, if C is sued by A, he can now claim a contribution from the negligent spouse B, since B is now a person liable for the purposes of the Act of 1978.

Executors and administrators

General effect of death

Section 1(1) of the Law Reform (Miscellaneous Provisions) Act 1934 (as amended by the Law Reform (Miscellaneous Provisions) Act 1970) provides that all causes of action subsisting against or vested in a person at the time of his death shall survive against or, as the case may be, for the benefit of his estate.

This does not apply to actions for defamation. Furthermore, damages recoverable in an action by the representatives of the deceased shall not include exemplary damages (see further p 521). The right of a person to claim for bereavement under s 1A of the Fatal Accidents Act 1976 (see below) does not survive for the benefit of his estate (s 4(1) of the Administration of Justice Act 1982, amending s 1(2)(a) of the Act of 1934). No damages may be awarded for loss of income in respect of any period after the death of an injured person (s 4(2)(b) of the Administration of Justice Act 1982, amending s 1(2)(a) of the Act of 1934).

Under the Proceedings Against Estates Act 1970 all actions against the personal representatives of a deceased person, whether founded in contract or tort, are now subject to the normal three-year (personal injuries) or six-year (other injuries) limitation period.

Provisional damages which may be awarded where there is a recognised risk that the claimant may develop a further disease or deterioration (see further later in this chapter) are dealt with in the context of fatal accidents by s 3 of the Damages Act 1996. This provides that an award of provisional damages made during an injured person's lifetime does not prevent his dependants from claiming further damages if the injury results in death.

It was held by the Court of Appeal in *Hunger* v *Butler*, *The Independent*, 2 January 1996 that a widow could not claim as damages for dependency under the 1976 Act sums which her deceased husband would have earned by 'moonlighting' employments which he would not have declared because they would have affected his entitlement to social security benefits.

Fatal accidents

If, as a result, e.g., of negligence, a person is killed, there are two sorts of claim against the person responsible. The executors of the deceased may wish to go ahead with any claim *which the deceased would have had if he had lived*. There may also be relatives who wish to claim because they have suffered as a result of the death.

(a) Claims by the estate. As we have seen, under the Law Reform (Miscellaneous Provisions) Act 1934, most causes of action in tort subsisting at the time of a person's death survive for (or against) his estate.

As regards a fatal accident, the estate can claim damages for the period between the injury and death, e.g., for pain and suffering and loss of amenity, as where an arm is amputated before death. Damages may be awarded for earnings lost and medical expenses incurred up to the time of death.

There is no claim for loss of expectation of life (Administration of Justice Act 1982, s 1(1)(a)), nor is there a claim for lost earnings in respect of the period between the actual death and the cessation of notional working life (i.e. the lost years). Section 4(2) of the 1982 Act now states that no damages may be awarded for loss of income after death.

If the injured person died immediately the estate has no claim except for funeral expenses (s 1(2)(c) of the 1982 Act). If, e.g., a relative pays the funeral expenses but was not dependent on the deceased and so has no general claim under the Fatal Accidents Act 1976, the relative may claim those funeral expenses under the 1976 Act.

(b) Claims by dependants. These are brought under the Fatal Accidents Act 1976. The claim is independent of the one made by the estate under the 1934 Act (as amended). Two awards of damages may therefore be made, one for the executors on behalf of the estate, and the other to the executors collectively for the dependants.

Under the provisions of the Fatal Accidents Act 1976 a person whose negligence has caused the death of another may be liable to certain relatives of the deceased who have suffered financial loss because of the death. The following persons are entitled to claim *but only if they were dependent on the deceased* – husband, wife, children, grandchildren, parents, grandparents, brothers, sisters, aunts, and uncles, and their issue; the relationship may be traced through step-relatives, adoption, or illegitimacy, and relatives by marriage have the same rights as the deceased's own relatives. However, dependency ceases on adoption (*Watson* v *Willmott* [1990] 3 WLR 1103). Under s 1(3)(b) of the 1976 Act, as amended by the Administration of Justice Act 1982, any person who was living with the deceased in the same household for two years or more (including civil partners), immediately before the death and was living for all of the time as the husband or wife of the deceased may claim. This allows unmarried cohabitants to claim.

A single action must be brought on behalf of all eligible dependants and the total damages apportioned according to their dependency. The action may be brought by the personal representatives of the deceased, but if there are none, or they fail to bring the action within six months of the death, the dependants may bring it.

The Court of Appeal stated in *Gully* v *Dix* [2004] 1 WLR 1399 that the requirement of 'immediately before death' should not be construed literally. A woman who had lived with the deceased for 27 years and had been maintained by him was allowed to claim even though she had left him three months before his death. There was, it seemed, an intention to return, as she had always done when she had left in the past. Her right to make a claim was

20

challenged by the deceased's brother who would have received more from the estate if her claim had been turned down.

If the deceased was guilty of contributory negligence or was a volunteer (see later in this chapter), the damages awarded will be reduced or extinguished, according to the degree to which the deceased was at fault or was a volunteer. In addition, there can be no claim where the deceased made a full and final settlement with the potential defendant before the death: ruled by the House of Lords in *Jameson* v *Central Electricity Generating Board* [1999] 1 All ER 193. Ordinarily, also, if more than three years have elapsed between injury and death, no Fatal Accidents Act claim can be brought (Limitation Act 1980, s 11(1)). However, it is open to the personal representatives to ask the court to exercise the discretionary provisions of s 33 of the Limitation Act 1980 to override the limitation period (see further Chapter 18). Furthermore, if the claimant dies before the limitation period has expired, a new limitation period runs under s 11(5) of the Limitation Act 1980. This period is three years from either the date of death or the date of the personal representative's knowledge that there is a cause of action, whichever is the later.

The probability of pecuniary loss is a matter for the claimant to prove and the court to decide as a matter of fact. However, it should be noted that the object of the Fatal Accidents Act is to provide maintenance for relatives who have been deprived of maintenance by the death.

There is also now an award of £10,000 for bereavement (Fatal Accidents Act 1976, s 1A(3), as amended by the Administration of Justice Act 1982). This sum will be increased as appropriate by statutory instrument, the current figure being contained in SI 2002/644. It is in favour of a wife or husband or the parents of the deceased but in the case of parents only if he or she was under 18 at the time of death and unmarried, or the mother of a child under 18 at the time of death and unmarried who was illegitimate (Fatal Accidents Act 1976, s 1A(2)(b)). No proof of dependency is required.

Section 4 of the Fatal Accidents Act 1976, as amended by the Administration of Justice Act 1982, provides that in assessing damages any benefits which have arisen, or will arise, or may arise, to any person as a result of the death are to be disregarded. Thus, friendly society or trade union benefits, pensions or gratuities accruing to a relative would be ignored, even though the pecuniary loss was in a sense thereby reduced.

Finally, it is interesting to note that relatives have no right to sue for non-fatal accidents to relatives, even if they are a dependant. The action must be brought by the living relative who has been injured (see *Robertson* v *Turnbull* (1981) *The Times*, 6 October – a decision of the House of Lords).

Partners, principals and agents generally

Partners in ordinary and limited partnerships are jointly and severally liable for the torts of other partners committed in the ordinary course of business, or with the authority of co-partners. The position of members of a limited liability partnership is different and is considered at p 255. A principal is liable for the torts of his agent committed within the scope of his authority, whether by prior authority or subsequent ratification.

Vicarious liability

While the person who is actually responsible for the commission of a tort is always liable, sometimes another person may be liable although he has not actually committed it. In such a case both are liable as joint tortfeasors. This is the doctrine of vicarious liability, and the greatest area of this type of liability is that of master and servant. A master (employer) is liable for the torts of his servant (employee) committed in the course of his employment, and so wide is the risk that it is commonly insured against. Under the Employers' Liability (Compulsory Insurance) Act 1969, an employer *must* insure himself in respect of vicarious liability for injuries caused by his employees to their colleagues. Insurance is not compulsory in respect of injuries to persons other than employees.

There is a comparison to be made with contract because whether an employer is bound as a party to a contract made by the employee depends upon whether the employee has the *authority to make the contract* on behalf of the employer and not simply whether the employee was *acting within the course of employment* which is the basic tort test (*Director-General of Fair Trading* v *Smiths Concrete* (1991) *The Times*, 26 July).

Who is an employee?

According to *Salmond on Torts* (a leading text), an employee may be defined as 'any person employed by another to do work for him on the terms that he, the [employee], is to be subject to the control and direction of his employer in respect of the manner in which his work is to be done'. This definition was approved by the court in *Hewitt* v *Bonvin* [1940] 1 KB 188. In most cases the relationship is established by the existence of a *contract of service*, which may be express or implied and is usually evidenced by such matters as, for example, the power to appoint, the power of dismissal, the method of payment, the payment of national insurance by the employer, the deduction of tax under PAYE, and membership of pension schemes (if any).

It must be borne in mind that many of the defining principles, including those based on case law and statute, were laid down in a different day and age from our own. The words appearing in judgments and/or statutes cannot be altered because we must set out what the judge or Parliament actually said, and in some cases the expression 'servant' not 'employee' will be used.

The control test

However, in deciding whether the relationship of employer and employee exists, the courts have not restricted themselves to cases in which there is an ordinary contract of service but have often stated that the right of control is the ultimate test. In *Performing Right Society Ltd* v *Mitchel and Booker (Palais de Danse) Ltd* [1924] 1 KB 762 at p 767, McCardie, J said:

> The nature of the task undertaken, the freedom of action given, the magnitude of the contract amount, the manner in which it is paid, the powers of dismissal, and the circumstances under which payment of the reward may be withheld, all these bear on the solution of the question. But it seems clear that a more guiding test must be secured. . . . It seems . . . reasonably clear that the final test, if there be a final test, and certainly the test to be generally applied, lies in the nature and degree of detailed control over the person alleged to be a servant. This circumstance is, of course, one only of several to be considered but it is usually of vital importance.

The learned judge then went on to decide that the defendants, who employed a dance band under a written contract for one year, were liable for breaches of copyright, which occurred when members of the band played a piece of music without the consent of the holder of the copyright, because the agreement gave the defendants 'the right of continuous, dominant and detailed control on every point, including the nature of the music to be played'.

20

The existence of the control test means that where an employer (X) lends out his employee (Y) to another employer (Z), then Z may be liable for the wrongs of Y even though there is no contract of service between Y and Z, though such liability is rare.

An employer also owes certain duties to his employees, e.g. to provide proper plant, equipment and premises, and this is a further reason for deciding whether Z has become the master by virtue of the control test. There is a presumption that control remains with X and the onus is upon him to prove that control has passed to Z. The burden is a heavy one and the temporary employer will not often become liable. Nevertheless, transfer of control may be more readily inferred where an employee is lent on his own without equipment or where he is unskilled.

Transfer of control is often a convenient method of making the temporary employer liable to, and for, the employee and does not affect the contract of service. A contract of service is a highly personal one and it cannot be transferred from one employer to another without the consent of the employee. However, where there is a contract for hire of plant and the loan of an employee to operate it, the contract of hiring may provide that the hirer shall indemnify the owners for claims arising in connection with the operation of the plant by the employee.

> *Garrard v Southey*, 1952 – The control test: a transfer of employer (**279**)
>
> *Mersey Docks and Harbour Board v Coggins and Griffiths*, 1947 – A situation of no transfer (**280**)
>
> *Wright v Tyne Improvement Commissioners*, 1968 – Effect of contractual indemnity (**281**)

The control test was an appropriate one in the days when an employer could be expected to be superior to his employee in knowledge, skill and experience. However, in modern times it is unreal to say that all employers of skilled labour can tell employees *how* to do their work. Accordingly, the test has been modified in recent cases, the court tending to look for the power to control in incidental or collateral matters, e.g. hours of work and place of work. The existence of this sort of control enables the court to decide whether a person is part of the organisation of another, and it might be called a *'when and where'* test.

The control test also gives rise to difficulties in the case of the employees of companies. Subordinate employees are controlled by superior employees and some control is obviously present if the management is regarded as 'the company'. However, when one considers the position of directors and top management it is difficult to see how the company, being inanimate, can exercise control. In the case of 'one-man' companies, where the managing director is also virtually the sole shareholder, the reality of the situation is that the servant controls the company and not vice versa. Nevertheless, directors of companies, even 'one-man' companies, are regarded as employees, presumably because the usual incidents of a contract of service are present and despite the absence of genuine control.

However, as we have seen in Chapter 19, a controlling shareholder may not according to circumstances be an employee for the purposes of employment legislation in terms, e.g., of a claim for redundancy (see *Buchan* v *Secretary of State for Employment* (1997) 565 IRLB 2).

Although control is the ultimate test in establishing the relationship of employer and employee, it is also necessary to deal briefly with other circumstances which may be taken as evidence of the existence of the relationship. In *Short* v *J W Henderson Ltd* (1946) 62 TLR 427, Lord Thankerton regarded the power to select or appoint, the power to dismiss, and the payment of wages, as relevant in establishing the existence, or otherwise, of a contract of service.

Cassidy v *Ministry of Health*, 1951 – An organisation test (**282**)
Ferguson v *John Dawson & Partners*, 1976 – A 'when and where' test (**283**)
Lee v *Lee's Air Farming Ltd*, 1960 – Directors and senior employees (**284**)

Dual vicarious liability

The Court of Appeal has ruled that two parties can be jointly and individually liable for an employee's negligence where both have a degree of control over the employee concerned. Either can be sued for the full amount of the damage but the loss can be recovered only once.

Thus in *Viasystems (Tyneside) Ltd* v *Thermal Transfer (Northern) Ltd* [2005] 4 All ER 1181 a sub-contractor and a main contractor were held jointly and equally liable for the negligence of the sub-contractor's employee because his work had been supervised by both an employee of the main contractor and an employee of the sub-contractor.

Comment If one employer is sued, he or she would be able to join the other employer in the action and each would contribute 50 per cent to the loss.

The power to select or appoint

The absence of a power to select or appoint may prevent the relationship of employer and employee arising. Thus, in *Cassidy* v *Ministry of Health* [1951] 2 KB 343 Denning, LJ, as he then was, made it clear that a hospital authority is not liable for the negligence of a doctor or surgeon who is *selected* and *employed* by the patient himself. The employer need not make the appointment himself, and an appointee may be an employee even though the employer *delegated* the power of selection to another employee, or even an independent contractor, such as a firm of management consultants, or was *required by law to accept* the employee, e.g. Ministers of State often have power to appoint members of statutory bodies who become the employees of those bodies.

The power to dismiss

An express power of dismissal is strong evidence that the contract is one of service. Many public bodies have a restricted power of dismissal in the sense that rights of appeal are often provided for, but such rights do not prevent a contract of service from arising, nor does the fact that these authorities cannot dismiss certain of their employees without the approval of the Crown or a Minister.

Payment of wages or salary

A contract of service must be supported by consideration which usually consists of a promise to pay wages, or a salary. Where the amount of remuneration or the rate of pay is not fixed in advance, this suggests that the contract is not one of service, but is for services. The employer usually pays his employees directly, but in *Pauley* v *Kenaldo Ltd* [1953] 1 All ER 226 at p 228, Birkett, LJ said 'a person may be none the less a servant by reason of the fact that his remuneration consists solely of tips'.

An employee may be employed on terms that his remuneration is to consist wholly or partly of commission which the employer pays directly, the commission being a method of assessment of the amount of the remuneration.

20

Salaries are paid to people who are certainly not employees, e.g. Members of Parliament, whereas payment of wages generally indicates a contract of service. However, little, if anything, turns on the distinction between wages and salaries, and we may conclude that the terms used to describe the way in which a person is paid have little bearing on the relationship between himself and the person who pays him.

In addition to the above indications of a contract of service, the following matters have also been regarded as relevant in deciding difficult cases of relationship.

Delegation

In the normal contract of service the employee performs the work himself, and *power to delegate performance of the whole contract* to another is some indication that there is no contract of service. However, the fact that delegation is forbidden does not show *conclusively* that the contract is one of service, for agreements with independent contractors may forbid delegation.

Exclusive service

The fact that an employer can demand the *exclusive services of another* is a material factor leading to the inference of a contract of service and in some cases it has been the deciding factor. However, in the absence of an express contractual provision an employer cannot usually require the exclusive services of his employee, and cannot complain if the employee works for someone else in his spare time. This being so, an employee and an independent contractor are usually both able to work for more than one person, and the exclusive service test may not help in deciding difficult cases of relationship. However, it is true to say that the typical employee works for one person, and the typical independent contractor works for many.

Place of work

If the services are always rendered on the *employer's premises*, this is some evidence of the existence of a contract of service, though it is not conclusive. Similarly, the fact that a person works at his home or other premises is some evidence of a contract for services.

It may also be a material factor whether the services are rendered by a person having a *recognised trade or profession*, e.g. a surveyor or a consulting engineer, which he is exercising in a business because such persons tend to be independent contractors rather than employees and persons not exercising a particular calling may more easily be regarded as the employees of those who employ them.

Plant and equipment

Provision of large-scale plant and equipment by the employer is an indication of the existence of a contract of service and a person who supplies his own large-scale plant and equipment is often an independent contractor. However, provision of minor equipment, such as tools, carries little weight as a test of relationship, for many employees provide their own tools.

Obligation to work

A contract of service and one for services usually *impose an obligation to do the work concerned* and an obligation to work is not helpful in the matter of relationships. However, persons such as salesmen who are paid entirely by commission, and who are not obliged to work at all, are probably not working under a contract of service.

Hours of work and holidays

The right to control the *hours of work and the taking of holidays* (subject to the general provisions of the Working Time Regulations 1998) is also regarded as evidence of the existence of a contract of service. Further, an independent contractor is usually engaged for a specific job, whereas an employee is usually employed for an indefinite time. However, those on fixed-term contracts will usually be regarded as employees.

Employees and independent contractors

An employee is a person whose work is at least *integrated* into the employer's business organisation, whereas an independent contractor merely *works for* the business but is *not integrated* into it. Thus, firms of builders, architects, and estate agents are usually regarded as independent contractors, while factory and office workers are usually regarded as employees.

An employee works under a contract of service, whereas an independent contractor's contract is said to be one 'for services' under which he is to carry out a particular task or tasks. Although he may be sued for breach of contract if he fails to carry out his contract properly, the purchaser of his services has no other control over the manner of his work.

Rights of non-employees

Before leaving the topic of the relationship between employer and employee, it is worth noting that certain statutory rights are given to persons who are not employees. Rights in respect of discrimination are given to job applicants and contract workers. Job applicants also have the right not to be refused a job because they do not belong to a union. Thus a contract worker, such as a temporary secretary supplied by an agency to an organisation, could make a claim for sexual harassment against that organisation. In some cases, therefore, non-employees have the same rights as employees because the law has been widened to cover them.

Nature of vicarious liability

20

The doctrine seems at first sight unfair because it runs contrary to two major principles of liability in tort, viz:

(*a*) that a person should be liable only for loss or damage caused by his *own acts or omissions*; and

(*b*) that a person should only be liable where he was at *fault*.

The doctrine of vicarious liability is a convenient one in the sense that employers are, generally speaking, wealthier than their employees and are better able to pay damages, though the doctrine is often justified on the grounds that an employer *controls* his employee. However, it should be noted that control is not in itself a ground for imposing vicarious liability, e.g. parents are not vicariously liable for the torts of their children. It is also said that vicarious liability is a just concept because the employer profits from the employee's work and should therefore bear losses caused by the employee's torts. Again, the employer *chooses* his employee and there are those who say that if he chooses a careless employee he ought to compensate the victims of the careless employee's torts. Further, employer and employee are often identified in the sense that the act of the employee is regarded as the act of his employer and this theory that an employer and his employee are part of a *group* in much the same way as other associations of persons, e.g. companies, is expressed in the often quoted maxim *qui facit per alium facit per se* (he who does a thing through another does it himself). However, in practice the employer does not really suffer loss because he commonly insures against the possibility of vicarious liability and usually the cost of this insurance is put on to the goods or services which he sells. This has the effect of spreading the loss over a large section of the community in much the same way as welfare state benefits.

Course of employment

In order to establish vicarious liability, it is necessary to show that the relationship between the defendant and the wrongdoer is that of employer and employee, and that when the employee committed the wrong he was in the *course of his employment*. It is sometimes difficult to decide whether a particular act was done during the course of employment, but the following matters are relevant.

Acts personal to the employee

Some acts done by an employee while at work are so personal to him that they cannot be regarded as being within the scope of employment. Thus, in *Warren* v *Henlys Ltd* [1948] 2 All ER 935, the employer of a petrol pump attendant was held not liable for the latter's assault on a customer committed as a result of an argument over payment for petrol. However, where such authority exists, e.g. in the case of door-keepers at dance halls, the employer will be liable if the employee ejects a troublemaker but uses excessive force.

An example is provided by *Vasey* v *Surrey Free Inns plc* [1996] PIQR 373. The claimant went to a nightclub on New Year's Eve with his friends. He was refused entry and responded by kicking a glass door and breaking it. He was followed to a nearby car park by the club doormen. One of his friends offered an apology and said he would pay for the damage. The doormen asked who had broken the door and the claimant said it was him. Shortly after he got back into his car three of the doormen pulled him out and one hit him violently on the head with a weapon causing him grievous bodily harm. The Court of Appeal held the employer of the doormen to be liable. This was not just a personal attack. The doormen were intending to teach the claimant a lesson and protect the employer's property by deterrent means.

This area of the law is subject to continuing development and it appears that more and more the courts will decide, as a matter of fact from the circumstances, that acts which might have been regarded as personal to the employee will be regarded as the liability also of the employer who is normally carrying insurance against such risks.

Lister v *Hesley Hall Ltd*, 2001 – employer liable for employee's sex abuse (**284a**)

Improper performance of acts within scope of employment

The employer may be liable where the tort committed by the employee is not a personal or independent act but is merely an improper way of performing an act which is within the scope of employment.

The tortious acts for which an employer may be liable must arise out of the employee's employment, but the employer may be liable in such circumstances even if the act is one which he has expressly forbidden his employee to do. The point has arisen in cases in which employees have given lifts to third parties in the employer's vehicle. In *Twine* v *Bean's Express*

Ltd [1946] 1 All ER 202, a driver employed by the defendants gave a lift to a third person who was killed by reason of the employee's negligent driving. Instructions that employees were not to give lifts were displayed in the van. The court held that the employers were not liable because in giving a lift to the third person the driver went *beyond the scope of his employment*.

However, if the express prohibition only affects the way in which the employee is to perform his work and is not regarded as affecting the *scope* of his employment, the employer may be liable.

> *Century Insurance Co Ltd* v *Northern Ireland Road Transport Board*, 1942 – An improper act in course of employment (**285**)
> *Limpus* v *London General Omnibus Co*, 1862 – A race for passengers (**286**)
> *Rose* v *Plenty*, 1976 – Helping the milkman (**287**)

Emergencies

Where the employee takes emergency measures with the intention of benefiting his employer in cases where the latter's property appears to be in danger, the employer will tend to be liable even though the acts of the employee are excessive. Thus in *Poland* v *John Parr & Sons* [1927] 1 KB 236, a boy was injured by a carter who knocked the boy off the back of his cart to protect his employer's property from theft. It was held that the carter's action was within his implied authority and his employers were liable. If, however, the employee's act is not merely *excessive* but *outrageous* as in *Warren* v *Henlys Ltd* [1948] 2 All ER 935, the employer may not be liable, particularly where the act is not connected with the protection of the employer's property generally but, as in *Warren*, an argument about paying for goods (but see the developments considered at p 506).

Employee mixing employer's business with his own

The cases under this heading have arisen largely out of the use of motor vehicles, and since it is clear that there can be no vicarious liability if the employee's wrong is not the result of his carrying out his contract of service, the employer will not be liable if he lends his vehicle to his employee entirely for the employee's own purpose.

However, a more difficult situation arises where the activity is basically an authorised one but the employee deviates from it in order to execute some business of his own. The mere fact of deviation will not prevent the employer being liable and this was made clear in the judgment of Cockburn, CJ in *Storey* v *Ashton* (1869) LR 4 QB 476, when he said:

> I am very far from saying that, if the servant when going on his master's business took a somewhat longer road, that, owing to his deviation he would cease to be in the employment of the master so as to divest the latter of all liability; in such cases it is a question of degree as to how far the deviation could be considered a separate journey. Such a consideration is not applicable to the present case, because here the carman started on an entirely new and independent journey which had nothing to do with his employment.

However, if the journey is unauthorised, the employee does not render his employer liable merely by performing some small act for his employer's benefit during the course of it. Thus in *Rayner* v *Mitchell* (1877) 2 CPD 257, a brewer's vanman, without permission, took a van from his employer's stables for personal reasons, namely to deliver a coffin to a relative's house. On the way back he picked up some empty beer barrels and then was involved in an accident injuring the claimant. It was held that the brewer was not liable.

20

Britt v *Galmoye*, 1928 – An accident while not on the employer's business (288)

Employee using his own property on employer's business

The mere fact that an employee is using his own property in carrying out his employer's business will not prevent the employer from being liable for torts arising out of the use of the employee's property. The decided cases are largely concerned with methods of travel, and in *McKean* v *Rayner Bros Ltd (Nottingham)* [1942] 2 All ER 650, an employee who was told to deliver a message by using the firm's lorry was held to be in the course of his employment when he performed the task by driving his own car, contrary to his instructions. However, if the employee's act is unreasonable, as where an employee who is authorised to travel by car charters an aeroplane and flies it himself, then the act will be unauthorised and the employer will not be liable if the employee, or a third party, is injured.

Effect of contractual exceptions clauses

Cases may arise in which the employer has attempted to exempt himself from the wrongs of his employee by means of an exemption clause in a contract with a third person who is injured. Such clauses will be effective to exempt the employer from liability if they are properly communicated to the third person. However, they will not protect the employee against his personal liability at common law because he has not usually given any consideration to the third person and is not in privity of contract with him. Statute may extend the protection of an exemption clause in the employer's contract to his employees.

For example, the Carriage of Goods by Sea Act 1971 provides that an employee or agent of a carrier by sea, but not an independent contractor, shall be entitled to avail himself of the same defences and limits of liability as the carrier. As regards an independent contractor, note *New Zealand Shipping Co* v *A M Satterthwaite & Co* (1974) (see also Chapter 15) where stevedores, who were independent contractors, took the benefit of an exemption clause in a contract between the carrier and the owner of the goods. However, the principle of privity will apply in other situations, e.g. to an employee of a carrier of goods by road who would not be protected by an exclusion clause in the contract between his employer and the owner of the goods being carried.

Reference should now be made to the Contracts (Rights of Third Parties) Act 1999 where the parties to the original contract may, if they wish, extend exemption rights to third parties or the court may imply them under the Act unless, of course, the original parties expressly exclude third-party rights (see Chapter 10).

Fraudulent and criminal acts

In early law the courts would not accept the principle of vicarious liability in fraud but gradually the concept was extended, first to cases in which the employee's fraud was committed for his employer's benefit, and later even to cases where the fraud was committed by the employee entirely for his own ends. The leading case is *Lloyd* v *Grace, Smith & Co* [1912] AC 716. The defendants were solicitors and employed a clerk in their conveyancing department. The clerk fraudulently induced the claimant to transfer some property to him and later sold that property at a profit for his own purposes. Nevertheless, the defendants were held liable for the claimant's loss. The liability, however, still depends upon the employee having actual or apparent authority to undertake work or carry out duties of the sort which have enabled him to commit fraud, and obviously if the fraud is committed outside the course of employment then the employer will not be liable.

Scope of employment frauds were considered in *Balfron Trustees Ltd* v *Peterson* [2001] IRLR 758. The High Court ruled that a firm of solicitors that was not guilty of any dishonesty itself could be vicariously liable for the allegedly dishonest acts of a solicitor it employed. It was alleged that the solicitor in the course of employment knowingly assisted in the implementation of a scheme to misappropriate funds from a pension scheme existing for the former employees of the Balfron Group Ltd. The High Court concluded that the action against the firm in respect of the loss could not be struck out. There was an arguable case against the firm.

The House of Lords also found an innocent firm of solicitors liable in *Dubai Aluminium Ltd* v *Salaam* [2002] 3 WLR 1913. The proceedings arose out of a complex fraud under which Dubai paid out $50 million under bogus consultancy agreements. Dubai claimed against the recipients of money from the scheme and an innocent firm of solicitors. The latter were held vicariously liable for the acts of a solicitor/partner who had allegedly dishonestly assisted in setting up the scheme in the course of his work for the firm.

Criminal conduct on the part of an employee may be regarded as being in the course of his employment so that the employer will be liable at civil law for any loss or damage caused to a third person by the employee's criminal act.

> *Morris* v *C W Martin & Sons Ltd*, 1965 – Vicarious liability for civil aspects of crime (**289**)

Casual delegation

If Y lends his car to X for X's own purposes, then Y is not liable, even if in a general way X is his employee (see *Britt* v *Galmoye* (1928)). Nevertheless, if Y has a purpose and X also has a purpose, and X is driving a car of Y's partly for his own and partly for Y's purposes, then Y would apparently be liable if X committed a tort. This is known as a case of casual delegation of authority. In these cases of casual delegation, the courts are guided by the doctrine of the *de facto* employee, and by using this doctrine they have extended the vicarious liability of the employer into the area of principal and agent. In fact, the person actually committing the wrong is often called the agent. The result is to extend the area of operation of the doctrine of vicarious liability since it is easier to find the relationship of principal and agent than it is to establish the relationship of employer and employee.

However, merely giving permission to use the vehicle is not enough to make the owner liable, nor is he liable merely because he is the owner and there will, of course, be no vicarious liability in the owner where he did not consent to the taking of the vehicle.

> *Ormrod* v *Crosville Motor Services Ltd*, 1953 – A casual delegation (**290**)
> *Vandyke* v *Fender*, 1970 – Employer and employee or principal and agent? (**291**)
> *Nottingham* v *Aldridge*, 1971 – A trainee returning to work (**292**)
> *Morgans* v *Launchbury*, 1972 – Mere permission to drive is not enough (**293**)
> *Rambarran* v *Gurrucharran*, 1970 – Ownership alone does not produce liability (**294**)
> *Klein* v *Calnori*, 1971 – No liability if vehicle driven without owner's consent (**295**)

20

Liability for torts of independent contractors

An independent contractor is by definition a person whose methods and modes of work are not controlled by the person who employs him, and this being so it would be unfair to give an employer general liability for the torts of such a contractor. However, there are circumstances in which a person may be liable for the torts of an independent contractor employed by him and these are set out below. However, it should be borne in mind that the circumstances listed below are not truly examples of vicarious liability. Instead they are based on the idea that the employer himself is in breach of a primary duty which he owes the claimant, as where, e.g., he undertakes hazardous operations.

(a) Where the employer authorises or ratifies the torts of the contractor. If, for example, an employer authorises, or afterwards, with knowledge, approves the conduct of an independent contractor in tipping the employer's industrial waste material on another's land, both the employer and the contractor will be liable in trespass as joint tortfeasors.

(b) Where the employer is negligent himself, as where he selects an independent contractor without taking care to see, as far as he can, that he is competent to do the work required, or gives a competent contractor imperfect instructions or information, as where, for example, he knows that his land is liable to subsidence and fails to tell a contractor who erects something on the land which slips and causes damage to another.

(c) Where liability for the tort is strict, so that responsibility cannot be delegated. Thus, an employer is liable for injuries to workmen resulting from failure to fence dangerous machinery securely. This duty is laid down by safety legislation, and it is no defence that the employer has delegated the task of fencing to an independent contractor who has failed to do the job properly. Moreover, liability under the rule in *Rylands* v *Fletcher*, 1868 (see Chapter 21) cannot be avoided by employing an independent contractor. It seems also that liability is strict where there is interference with an easement of support.

(d) Finally there is **a miscellaneous group of cases** in which an employer has been held liable for the torts of an independent contractor and the principle which seems to run through them all is that the work which the employer has instructed the independent contractor to undertake is extra hazardous. Thus, work *on or under* the highway is attended with some risk if due precautions are not taken, though work *near* the highway is not for that reason alone regarded as extra hazardous. In *Pickard* v *Smith* (1861) 10 CB NS 470, the defendant who was the tenant of a refreshment room at a railway station was held liable when a coal merchant's servant left the coal cellar flap open while delivering coal to the defendant and a passenger on railway premises fell into the cellar and was injured. Again, in *Honeywill & Stein Ltd* v *Larkin Bros Ltd* [1934] 1 KB 191, the claimants had received permission from the theatre owner to take photographs in a theatre on which the claimants had recently done work. A firm of photographers was employed by the claimants and in order to take indoor photographs had, in those days, to use magnesium flares with the result that the theatre curtains caught fire and much damage was caused. The claimants paid for the damage, and sued the photographers for an indemnity to which the court said they were entitled. It also emerged that the claimants would have been liable if they had been sued by the theatre owner. Work on party walls would also appear to be an example of extra hazardous work.

Bower v *Peate*, 1876 – Where an independent contractor interferes with an easement of support (**296**)

Where an employer is held liable to a third person for the torts of an independent contractor he will, in most cases, be able to claim an indemnity from the contractor. It should also be noted that an employer is not liable for what are called the *collateral* wrongs of his contractor, but only for wrongs which necessarily arise in the course of the contractor's employment. Thus, if A employs B, an independent contractor, to do some excavation work on his land, A will be liable if, say, his neighbour's greenhouse is damaged by the excavations but A will not be liable for loss caused by B's servants making off with the plants.

Salsbury v *Woodland*, 1969 – Work on or near the highway (**297**)

General defences

Some torts have special defences which can be raised in a particular action, but there are certain general defences which can be raised in any action in tort if they seem to be appropriate.

Volenti non fit injuria

(To one who is willing no harm is done.) This is alternatively called the doctrine of the assumption of risk. There are two main aspects of this defence:

(*a*) deliberate harm;
(*b*) accidental harm.

In the first case the claimant's assent may prevent his complaining of some deliberate conduct of the defendant which would normally be actionable. If A takes part in a game of rugby football, he must be presumed to accept the rough tactics which are a characteristic and *normal* part of the game, and any damage caused would not give rise to an action, although if the same tactics were employed in the street, an action could be sustained. Similarly, although to stick a knife into a person would normally be actionable, if a surgeon does it with the consent of the patient it is not so.

In this connection, cases have come before the courts in recent times in which the issue of *informed consent* has been raised. For example, in *Sidaway* v *Bethlem Royal Hospital Governors* [1984] 1 All ER 1018, the claimant gave her consent for an operation to relieve pain in her neck. The surgeon did not tell her of the possibility of damage to the spinal cord, which was in any case remote. However, there was such damage to the claimant's spinal cord and she sued the surgeon regarding her consent as nullified because not all possible risks had been disclosed to her before she gave it. Her claim failed in the Court of Appeal. The risk of spinal cord injury was in any case too remote to found a claim in negligence. As regards the doctor's duty of disclosure prior to a valid consent, Sir John Donaldson, MR said it was 'giving or withholding information as is reasonable in all the circumstances . . . , including the patient's true wishes, with a view to placing the patient in a position to make a rational choice'. This test was satisfied here and the claimant's consent was valid.

Failure to obtain informed consent can result in liability even if the surgical procedures are carried out without negligence. Thus in *Chester* v *Afshar* [2004] 4 All ER 587 a neurosurgeon carried out a successful operation on the claimant's back. He was liable in negligence because he failed to warn the claimant before the operation of the risk of post-operative paralysis which was suffered by the claimant.

20

It is of interest to note that in *Chester* the claimant did not assert that if she had known about the post-operative paralysis *she would never have had the operation* but only that she would have asked for a second or third opinion. Nevertheless, the House of Lords ruled that it was only necessary for her to prove that she would not have proceeded with *the operation that was actually performed on her*, though she might have consented to others. This case seems to have changed the 'what if' concept: usually in the past claimants have asserted that they would not have gone ahead with the operation, but now it seems that even though the claimant says that he or she might have gone on with the operation at some stage, he or she will succeed. The issue of causation appears to have produced an area of strict liability. Will the ruling spread to other areas such as financial advice, as where a person says that he or she would still have bought the investment in spite of negligent advice from an adviser? The *Chester* case does raise issues of causation as well as consent.

It is worth noting that there has been a development in what might be called the 'vegetative state' cases. It was held by the House of Lords in *Airedale National Health Service Trust* v *Bland* [1993] 1 All ER 821 that life-sustaining artificial feeding and antibiotic drugs may be lawfully withheld from a patient who is in a persistent vegetative state with no hope of recovery, even though it is known that this will cause the patient to die. The court will make the necessary declaration on the application of relatives and/or the consultant but will normally require independent medical opinion, with the Official Solicitor (see Chapter 3) representing the interests of the patient, including the latter's own previously-expressed wishes, if any. A Practice Note issued by the Official Solicitor in 1994 requires at least two independent neurological reports. However, it was held by the Court of Appeal in *Frenchay Healthcare National Health Service Trust* v *S* (1994) *The Times*, 19 January, that a court would not refuse a health authority's urgent application for a declaration that it might stop life-saving emergency treatment solely on the ground that it had not been possible to obtain independent medical opinions in the pressurised timescale. The court can also give a declaration in other cases, as in *Re S* [1992] CLY para 2917 where a declaration was granted allowing a Caesarean section to be performed on a pregnant woman who had herself refused the operation on religious grounds. The operation was vital in her interests and those of the unborn child.

> *Simms* v *Leigh Rugby Football Club*, 1969 – Effect of consent in sports (**298**)

Implied consent

The claimant may *impliedly* consent to run the risk of accidental harm being inflicted upon him. Thus one of the risks incidental to watching an ice-hockey match is that the puck may strike and injure a spectator or, in attendance at a motor race, that cars may run off the track for various reasons, injuring spectators. These are possible hazards unless spectators are to be so fenced or walled in that they cannot see the sport and the maxim *volenti non fit injuria* would apply.

> *Murray* v *Harringay Arena*, 1951 – Watching ice-hockey (**299**)
> *Hall* v *Brooklands Auto-Racing Club*, 1933 – Watching motor sport (**300**)

While on the subject of implied consent, it is worth noting two cases in this area where the claim relates to accidents arising out of 'horseplay' between school pupils and accidents in the ordinary course of school activities that are beginning to show a trend away from the growing US-style compensation culture that has arrived on the UK legal scene since the introduction of conditional fee arrangements – the well known 'no-win, no-fee' contract.

In *Blake* v *Galloway* [2004] 3 All ER 315, a group of 15 boys went out to play at the lunchtime break. They began throwing bits of bark and twigs at each other. The claimant picked up a piece of bark and threw it towards the defendant's lower body. The defendant threw it back in the general direction of the claimant, striking him in the eye and causing significant injury. The claimant sued in negligence and battery.

The Court of Appeal turned down the claim. In doing so, the court laid down some principles to apply in these cases. They are:

- The accident must not be the result of a departure from the conventions of the activity. For example, in a snowball fight it is a convention that there are no stones in the snowballs. There will normally be no liability unless the conduct in question is regarded by the court as overstepping the mark. In this case there was no deliberate aiming at the claimant's eye, nor were the missiles selected as being inherently dangerous.
- Where the above principles were established the court would *imply consent*.

  An additional case in this area is *Babbings* v *Kirklees Council* (2004) *The Times*, 4 November, where the Court of Appeal refused a right of Appeal to Lauren Babbings when she broke her arm in a gym class. The Court of Appeal said that although such injuries were foreseeable, they were in the nature of the ordinary risks of school activity and Ms Babbings' claim failed. Brooke LJ said of the case: 'How boring things would be if there was no risk.'

When we come to consider the duty of care in negligence in Chapter 21, we shall see how the Compensation Act 2006 is also attacking the compensation culture which has caused problems in terms, for example, of school trips and holidays.

Notice

In addition, the claimant may be *expressly* put on notice that he undertakes a particular activity at his own risk. Thus in *Arthur* v *Anker* (1995) *The Times*, 1 December a motorist parked his car on private property despite having seen a warning notice. His car was clamped and a release fee of £40 charged. He sued for damages for tortious interference with his car. It was held by the Court of Appeal that his claim failed. By reading the sign he had impliedly consented to the clamping of his car. He had voluntarily accepted the risk that this would happen.

However, it is essential for the defendant to show as a matter of fact that the claimant agreed to *accept* the risk. This means, for one thing, that he must have had a choice and if a contract, e.g. of employment, forces him to accept the risk, there is no true assent.

Burnett v *British Waterways Board*, 1973 – No true consent (**301**)

Contractual consent

If a person's assent to harm being inflicted upon him is purely contractual, it can only operate within the limits allowed by the law of contract; the doctrine of privity of contract applies. Thus, if a carrier by road puts an exclusion clause in the contract with the customer excluding liability for damage to the goods, the customer could sue the driver if his negligence caused damage to the goods. The driver could not raise the exclusion clause in his defence because he was not a party to the contract in which it was contained. The above situation will only apply if the parties to the original contract have *not* granted third-party rights to the driver under the Contracts (Rights of Third Parties) Act 1999 or, if *not*, where the court does not in the circumstances *imply* the grant of rights. Sometimes a non-contractual agreement excluding liability for negligence has been upheld.

20

White v *Blackmore*, 1972 – A non-contractual assent (**302**)

Defendant's knowledge of risk

The defendant must show that the claimant knew of the risk (see *White* v *Blackmore*, 1972). He must then go on to show that the claimant agreed to accept the risk. It does not follow that because a person has knowledge of a potential danger he assents to it. The rule applies equally to cases of *implied volenti* and to cases of *express volenti* (see *Burnett* v *British Waterways Board*, 1973). This principle, i.e. that knowledge is not assent, is most often exemplified in the employer and employee cases and in rescue cases, and has restricted the application of the defence.

Baker v *James Bros*, 1921 – Knowledge is not assent: a defective motor car (**303**)
Dann v *Hamilton*, 1939 – A drunken driver (**304**)
Smith v *Baker*, 1891 – Stone which fell from a crane (**305**)

Inherent danger

Where the danger is inherent in the job, as in the case of a test pilot, the maxim applies; but where the danger is not inherent, the defence will rarely succeed (see *Smith* v *Baker*, 1891). In instances where an employee expressly assumes a risk, and is even paid extra for doing so, the harm resulting will hardly ever be laid at the door of the employer, unless there is evidence that the employer was negligent and created a risk which was not normally present even in a job inherently dangerous.

Statutory duties

The doctrine of *volenti non fit injuria* cannot be pleaded by an employer in an action for damages based on breach of a statutory duty, e.g., to fence machinery under safety legislation. The reason is that the object of the statute, to protect workers, cannot be defeated by a private agreement between employer and employee.

However, where an employee is in breach of a statutory duty and the employer is not, then if the party injured by the breach of statutory duty seeks to make the employer vicariously liable for the tort of the employee, the employer can plead the defence if the circumstances are appropriate.

ICI v *Shatwell*, 1964 – *Volenti* and breaches of statutory duty (**306**)

The rescue cases

A different situation arises in what are known as *rescue cases*. In these the claimant is injured while intervening to save life or property put in danger by the defendant's negligence. If the intervention is a reasonable thing to do for the saving of life or property, this does not constitute the assumption of risk, nor does the defence of contributory negligence apply, but if it is not reasonable then the defences of *volenti* and contributory negligence could apply.

A person may take greater risks in protecting or rescuing life than in the mere protection of property, though even in protecting property reasonable risks may be taken.

Baker v *Hopkins*, 1959 – An attempted rescue (**307**)
Cutler v *United Dairies*, 1933 – An unnecessary intervention (**308**)
Hyett v *Great Western Railway*, 1948 – Preserving property (**309**)

Duty to rescuers

The duty of care owed to a rescuer is an original one and is not derived from or secondary to any duty owed to the rescued person by another. Thus a rescuer may recover damages even though no duty was owed to the person rescued. In addition, the person rescued may be liable in negligence to the rescuer. In *Harrison* v *British Railways Board* [1981] 3 All ER 679, Mr Harrison, a guard, jumped off his train as it left the platform to rescue a fellow-employee, A, who was negligently trying to board the moving train, but had slipped and was hanging on to a carriage door. The driver, who was unaware of the incident, was not in any way negligent but A was held liable to Mr Harrison in negligence in regard to the injuries which Mr Harrison sustained when he jumped off the train in order to rescue A.

In *Frost* v *Chief Constable of South Yorkshire Police* (1996) 146 NLJ Rep 1651 police officers who suffered psychiatric illness as a result of their involvement as rescuers in the disaster at the Hillsborough football ground were held by the Court of Appeal to be owed a duty of care by the Chief Constable and entitled to damages. Rescuers were in a special category, it was said. People who witnessed the incident might not recover damages because they had to meet more stringent tests. Furthermore, the defendant could not successfully plead that the officers were volunteers.

This decision was reversed by the House of Lords on the basis that there was no duty of care to the police officers as rescuers for psychiatric injury because, although present, they were not relatives and to give them damages when bereaved relatives who had not seen the accident had been denied compensation would not fit easily or fairly with the general law on damages for nervous shock (see later in this chapter). A report of the case is to be found at [1998] 3 WLR 1509. The police officers were not regarded as volunteers, but the case illustrates that a rescuer even though not a volunteer will not be able to recover damages if there is in the circumstances no duty of care.

Moreover, it is important to remember that the question whether the claimant has assented to the possibility of harm being inflicted upon him does not arise until it has been shown that the defendant has committed a tort against the claimant. If the harm is not tortious, the defence is irrelevant.

Finally, Parliament has in s 149(3) of the Road Traffic Act 1988 legislated to prevent exclusion of liability to passengers in motor vehicles on the basis of *volenti*. This certainly covers cases of express *volenti* where a person is given a lift in a car in which there is a notice saying that passengers are at their own risk. Whether it covers cases of implied *volenti* such as *Dann* v *Hamilton* (1939) is more doubtful. A passenger who knows that a driver is under the influence of drink or drugs may, if he is injured, be barred from recovering damages on the grounds of *public policy* since he is aiding and abetting a criminal offence. For this reason there is doubt as to the correctness of the decision in *Dann* v *Hamilton* (1939) where the public policy principle was not considered.

Section 149 of the 1988 Act does not prevent the driver from pleading contributory negligence if this is appropriate.

20

> *Videan* v *British Transport Commission*, 1963 – Where no duty is owed to the person rescued (**310**)
>
> *Wooldridge* v *Sumner*, 1962 – Has the defendant committed a tort? (**311**)
>
> *Nettleship* v *Weston*, 1971 – Matters of public policy (**312**)

Inevitable accident

The mere fact that the damage caused is accidental cannot itself be a defence if there is a duty to avert the particular consequences, but there are occasions where the defence of inevitable accident can be raised. Such an accident would be one which was not avoidable by any precautions a reasonable person could have been expected to take. It should be noted, however, that most so-called accidents have a cause, and this defence is of comparatively rare occurrence.

> *Stanley* v *Powell*, 1891 – An inevitable accident (**313**)
>
> *National Coal Board* v *Evans*, 1951 – Cutting a cable (**314**)

Act of God

This is something which occurs in the course of nature, which was beyond human foresight, and against which human prudence could not have been expected to provide. It is something in the course of nature so unexpected in its consequences that the damage caused must be regarded as too remote to form a basis for legal liability. It arises always from the course of nature and has no human causation. This distinguishes it from inevitable accident.

> *Nichols* v *Marsland*, 1876 – An act of God (**315**)

Necessity

This defence is put forward when damage has been intentionally caused, either to prevent a greater evil or in defence of the realm. The latter is somewhat obsolete but there are some older cases which have allowed trespass by one person to the land of another to erect fortifications to defend the realm against an army. Such damage is justifiable if the act was reasonable. Thus where a whole area is threatened by fire, the destruction of property not yet alight with a view to stopping the spread of the flames would be damage intentionally done but reasonable in the circumstances. Furthermore, in *Leigh* v *Gladstone* (1909) 26 TLR 139 the forcible feeding of a suffragette in prison was held justified by the necessity of preserving her life. This decision, which has been much criticised, means that it is not an assault for prison officials to take reasonable steps to preserve the health and life of those in custody. The practice of force-feeding is no longer applied in the prison service.

However, duress does not appear to be a defence and in *Gilbert* v *Stone* (1647) Aleyn 35, the defendant was held liable for trespass although he entered the claimant's house only because 12 armed men had threatened to kill him if he did not do so.

> *Cresswell* v *Sirl*, 1948 – Necessity: when dogs worry sheep (**316**)
>
> *Cope* v *Sharpe*, 1912 – Necessity: a heath fire (**317**)

Mistake

It is normally no defence in tort to say that the wrongful act was done by mistake. Even if the consequences of an act were not fully appreciated, everyone is, at least in civil law, presumed to intend the probable consequences of his acts. A mistake of law is no excuse, and this is usually true of a mistake of fact, unless it is reasonable in the circumstances, e.g. in a case of wrongful arrest.

However, the defence of unintentional defamation under ss 2–4 of the Defamation Act 1996 is to some extent based on mistake (see Chapter 21).

> *Beckwith* v *Philby*, 1827 – A mistaken arrest (**318**)

Act of state

Sometimes the state finds it necessary to protect persons from actions in tort when they have caused damage whilst carrying out their duties. This defence cannot be raised in respect of damage done anywhere to British subjects or where the court holds that damage has been done to a friendly alien.

> *Buron* v *Denman*, 1848 – Act of State and a slave trader (**319**)
> *Nissan* v *Attorney-General*, 1967 – Defence not available against British subjects (**320**)
> *Johnstone* v *Pedlar*, 1921 – Damage to a friendly alien (**321**)

Statutory authority

The acts of public authorities, e.g., local authority councils, are often carried out under the provisions of a statute. This statutory authority to act may give the public authority concerned a good defence if an action in tort arises as a result. However, much depends upon the wording of the relevant statute. *Statutory authority may be absolute*, in which case the public authority concerned has a duty to act. Alternatively, *statutory authority may be conditional*, in which case the public authority concerned has the *power* to act but is not bound to do so.

If the authority given is *absolute*, the body concerned is not liable for damage resulting from the exercise of that authority, provided it has acted reasonably and there is no alternative way of performing the act.

On the other hand, if the authority given is *conditional*, the body concerned may carry out the relevant act only if there is no interference with the rights of others.

Whether statutory authority is *absolute* or *conditional* is a matter of construction of the statute concerned, though statutory powers are usually conferred in *conditional* or permissive form. The basic rules of construction in these cases appear to be as follows:

(*a*) Is the authorised act of such public importance as to override private interests?
(*b*) If it is not, statutory powers are probably conferred subject to common-law rights.

In addition, the matter of statutory compensation may be relevant. If the statute provides for compensation for loss resulting from an authorised act, there may be no other claim even though the maximum compensation allowed by the statute is less than the actual loss. On the other hand, if there is no provision for compensation in the statute, there is a presumption that private rights remain and that an action in respect of any infringement of these rights may be brought.

It should be noted that the above principles also apply where the act done is authorised by delegated legislation.

> *Vaughan* v *Taff Vale Railway*, 1860 – An absolute authority (**322**)
> *Penny* v *Wimbledon UDC*, 1899 – A conditional authority (**323**)
> *Marriage* v *East Norfolk Rivers Catchment Board*, 1950 – Statutory compensation (**324**)

Justification or self-defence

Where a person commits a tort in defence of himself or his property, he will not be liable, provided the act done in such defence is reasonable or proportionate to the harm threatened, though no provocation by words can justify a blow (*Lane* v *Holloway* [1967] 3 All ER 129). The defence extends to acts in defence of the members of one's family and probably to acts in defence of persons generally.

The matter of self-defence is most often raised in criminal cases and is an important part of the criminal law (see Chapter 25).

Illegality

It would appear that an action in tort may be defeated on the ground that the claimant was committing an illegal or immoral act when the tort occurred. Thus, in *Ashton* v *Turner* [1980] 3 All ER 870 three men committed a burglary after an evening's drinking and sought to escape in a car owned by one of them. The car crashed and a passenger was injured. He claimed damages alleging negligence against the driver and the car owner. It was held by Ewbank, J, dismissing the claim, that as a matter of public policy the law might not recognise a duty of care owed by one participant in a crime to another for acts done in the course of that commission, and in any case *volenti non fit injuria* was a defence open to the driver. Again, in the Irish case of *Hegarty* v *Shine* (1878) 4 LR Ir 288 the claimant, an unmarried woman, brought an action for trespass on the grounds that she had contracted venereal disease following her relationship with the defendant over a period of some two years. Palles, CB denied her a remedy, saying 'the cause of an action here is a *turpis causa* incapable of being made the foundation of an action. The cause of action is the very act of illicit sexual intercourse'. It would appear, therefore, that the maxim *ex turpi causa* is not confined solely to contract. (For the contractual application see Chapter 16.)

Remedies

The remedies available to a person who has suffered injury or loss by reason of the tort of another are *damages*, the granting of an *injunction*, and in some cases an order for *specific restitution* of land or chattels of which the claimant has been dispossessed.

Damages – generally

Usually the damages awarded are *compensatory* and the underlying principle is that of *restitutio in integrum*, i.e. the damages awarded are designed to put the claimant in the position he would have been in if he had not suffered the wrong.

In the case of *personal injury*, e.g. loss of a limb, damages obviously cannot restore the claimant to his previous position. However, damages for personal injuries may be awarded under the following heads:

(*a*) pain and suffering;
(*b*) loss of enjoyment of life, or of amenity, as where brain damage causes permanent unconsciousness;
(*c*) loss of earnings, both actual and prospective.

As regards pain and suffering, the House of Lords held in *Hicks* v *Chief Constable of the South Yorkshire Police* [1992] 2 All ER 65, a case arising from the Hillsborough disaster, that pain and suffering immediately prior to a rapid death was not recoverable.

As regards earnings, *Oliver* v *Ashman* [1962] 2 QB 210 decided that where a tortious act had reduced the life expectancy of the claimant, he could recover a sum representing loss of earnings for the reduced number of years for which he was likely to live but not for the lost years. In *Pickett* v *British Rail Engineering Ltd* [1979] 1 All ER 774, the House of Lords overruled *Oliver* and decided that earnings during the lost years should be taken into account, less, of course, taxation (see *Gourley* below) and the deduction of an estimated sum to represent the victim's probable living expenses during those years. Thus if A, aged 30, is injured by negligence and would have lived to 70 before but since the accident only to 50, then earnings from ages 30 to 50 and 50 to 65 (the lost years) must now be taken into account.

Although s 1(1)(a) of the Administration of Justice Act 1982 has abolished the claim for *damages* for loss of expectation of life, it leaves unchanged the right to claim *income* for the 'lost' years.

Personal injury – the amount

There had been concern in the judiciary following the Law Commission's Report, *Damages for Personal Injury Non-Pecuniary Loss* (1999 Law Com No 257), that the sums being awarded for pain, suffering and loss of amenity were too low and the matter was dealt with by the Court of Appeal in *Heil* v *Rankin* [2000] PIQR Q187. The general effect of the case is that where the court intends to award damages for pain, suffering and loss of amenity below £10,000 there is to be no increase. However, awards above that should be increased in accordance with a sliding scale which in the most serious cases is to be as high as an increase of one-third.

Deductions – tax

The House of Lords decided in *British Transport Commission* v *Gourley* [1955] 3 All ER 796 that the fact that the claimant would have paid tax on his earnings must be taken into account so as to reduce the damages awarded in regard to earnings. The money is not paid to the Revenue so it is a benefit either to the defendant or to his insurance company. However, the rule has some logic on the grounds that damages are *compensatory*, and gross salary must be reduced to net salary to achieve true compensation.

Reference should be made again to this case and the decision in *Shove* v *Downs Surgical plc* [1984] 1 All ER 7 which accompanies it to revise the precise nature of the tax deduction.

Deductions – collateral benefits

The Law Reform (Personal Injuries) Act 1948, s 2 (as amended) requires deduction of the value of certain Social Security benefits, e.g. benefits payable for sickness and/or disablement received by the claimant or likely to accrue to him for five years after the accident occurred, though if the claimant did not know that he had a right to a particular form of national insurance benefit, and had not acted unreasonably in failing to claim it, the sum which he might have received will not be deducted from the damages awarded (*Eley* v *Bedford* [1971] 3 All ER 285).

Many cases have come before the courts on the matter of deduction of a wide variety of collateral benefits. In general the policy is one of non-deduction and sums received from other forms of insurance are not taken into account, nor is a disability or state retirement pension (*Parry* v *Cleaver* [1969] 1 All ER 555 and *Hewson* v *Downes* [1969] 3 All ER 193).

Classification of damages

It is possible to classify damages under a number of headings, and this classification applies to both contract and tort.

Ordinary damages

These are damages assessed by the court for losses arising naturally from the breach of contract, and in tort for losses which cannot be positively proved or ascertained, and depend upon the court's view of the nature of the claimant's injury. For example, the court may have to decide what to award for the loss of an eye, there being no scale of payments, and this is so whether the action is in tort or for breach of contract.

Special damages

These are awarded in tort for losses which can be positively proved or ascertained, e.g. damage to clothing; garage bills, where a vehicle has been damaged; doctor's fees; and so on. However, where it is difficult to determine the exact proportions of a claim for special damages, e.g. loss of profit not supported by accurate figures, the court must do its best to arrive at a fair valuation (*Dixons Ltd* v *J L Cooper Ltd* (1970) 114 SJ 319). In contract, the term covers losses which do not arise naturally from the breach, so that they will not be recoverable unless within the contemplation of the parties as described in Chapter 18.

Exemplary and aggravated damages

The usual object of damages both in contract and tort is to compensate the claimant for loss which he has incurred arising from the defendant's conduct. The object of *exemplary (or punitive) damages* is to punish the defendant, and to deter him and others from similar conduct in the future. Thus, it was at one time thought that, if the court had arrived at a sum of money which would sufficiently compensate the claimant, it could award a further sum, not as compensation for the claimant, but as a punishment to the defendant, the exemplary damages being in the nature of a fine. An award of exemplary damages had always confused the functions of the civil and criminal law, and it would appear that since the judgment of Lord Devlin in *Rookes* v *Barnard* [1964] 1 All ER 367, an award of exemplary damages should only be made in certain special cases as follows:

(a) Where there is arbitrary or unconstitutional action by servants of the state, e.g. an unreasonable false imprisonment or detention by state authorities.

An example is to be found in *Kuddus* v *Chief Constable of Leicestershire Constabulary* (2001) *The Times*, 13 June, where the House of Lords ruled that exemplary damages could be awarded to the claimant based on the defendant chief constable's vicarious liability for the oppressive, arbitrary or unconstitutional action of a police constable who had forged the claimant's signature on a statement which withdrew a complaint about the theft from his home of goods worth some £6,000.

(b) Where the defendant's conduct has been calculated by him to make a profit for himself which may well exceed the compensation payable to the claimant. Thus a newspaper may decide that the increased sales of the paper containing a libel will more than compensate for any damages which may have to be paid to the person libelled. In such a case exemplary damages may be awarded to the claimant, though the intention to profit must be proved. It is not enough that the newspaper has been sold and some profit necessarily made. An example of the application of this head is to be seen in *Cassell & Co Ltd* v *Broome* [1972] 1 All ER 801 where the House of Lords upheld an award of £25,000 exemplary damages against defendants who published a book containing defamatory passages where the right circumstances appeared to exist and a defence, if raised, would have failed.

(c) Where exemplary damages are expressly authorised by statute. It was decided by the Court of Appeal in *AB* v *South West Water Services* [1993] 2 WLR 507 that exemplary (or punitive) damages are not available in those cases where they had not been awarded prior to the *Rookes* decision in 1964. This meant that they were not available in claims for negligence or public nuisance (see Chapter 21).

AB v *South West Water Services* was overruled in *Kuddus* as wrongly decided. However, Lord Scott observed *obiter* that exemplary damages should not be available in claims for negligence and nuisance or where the defendant was merely vicariously liable though this did not affect the *Kuddus* decision because it was justified by the *Rookes* case.

Exemplary or punitive damages were sometimes awarded in contract for breach of promise of marriage, particularly where a female claimant had allowed the defendant to have sexual intercourse with her on the promise of marriage. This action was abolished by the Law Reform (Miscellaneous Provisions) Act 1970, s 1 and examples of exemplary damages would seem in the main to be confined to actions in tort.

Aggravated damages, on the other hand, can be awarded (generally only in tort) where the defendant's conduct is such that the claimant requires more than the usual amount of damages to *compensate him* for the unpleasant method in which the tort was committed against him. However, an award of aggravated damages is still *compensatory*.

The state of the law may perhaps be illustrated by taking a hypothetical case. Suppose a tenant T is evicted from his flat by the landlord L before T's term has expired, and that in order to evict T the landlord uses excessive violence. The court may decide that in an ordinary case of trespass and assault T would be adequately compensated by an award of damages of, say, £750. However, if the court considers that L intentionally used particularly violent and unpleasant methods to achieve this eviction, it may increase the award by, say, £150 as the aggravated element because, on the facts of the case, this is necessary to compensate T. It would appear that the court cannot, since *Rookes'* case, go on and make a further award to T in order to punish and deter L.

The decision of the Court of Appeal in *Khodaparast* v *Shad* (1999) *The Times*, 1 December is to the effect that aggravated damages can be awarded for malicious falsehood. The defendant deliberately set out to injure the claimant by distributing throughout the Iranian community material suggesting that she provided services by way of telephone sex lines. She lost her job as a teacher in an Iranian school. She chose to claim malicious falsehood rather than libel because legal aid is available for such claims though not for libel. She received damages in a total award of £20,000. There is no split of the damages; the court simply makes a higher award. The Court of Appeal affirmed that aggravated damages are compensatory and will not be awarded unless the defendant acted deliberately. Thus, although they would seem to be

20

available for many intentional torts, e.g. trespass, they would not seem to be available in cases of negligence where there is no intentional conduct.

Nominal damages

Sometimes a small sum (say £2) is awarded where the claimant proves a breach of contract, or the infringement of a right, but has suffered no actual loss.

Contemptuous damages

A farthing was sometimes awarded to mark the court's disapproval of the claimant's conduct in bringing the action. Such damages may be awarded where the claimant has sued for defamation of character in spite of the fact that he has engaged in defamatory activities against the defendant. Since farthings are no longer legal tender, the decimal penny would now be used.

Liquidated damages

These are damages agreed upon by the parties to the contract, and only a breach of contract need be proved; no proof of loss is required. Damages in tort are not normally liquidated.

Unliquidated damages

Where no damages are fixed by the contract it is left to the court to decide their amount. In such a case the claimant must produce evidence of the loss he has suffered, as is normal in the case of tort.

Liquidated and unliquidated damages have already been considered in more detail (see Chapter 18).

Structured settlements

These are considered in more detail in Chapter 18.

Remoteness of damage

The consequences of a defendant's wrongful act or omission may be endless. Even so a claimant who has established that the defendant's wrong caused his loss may be unable to recover damages because his loss is not sufficiently connected with the defendant's wrong to make the latter liable. In other words, the loss is too remote a consequence to be recoverable. The decision of the Judicial Committee of the Privy Council in *Overseas Tankship (UK) Ltd* v *Morts Dock and Engineering Co Ltd* (1961) (see below) (generally referred to as *The Wagon Mound*) laid down the modern test for remoteness of damage in tort which is as follows:

(a) Regarding culpability or responsibility for the harm. The test is an objective test rather than a subjective one, because the law substitutes for the defendant a hypothetical reasonable man, and then proceeds to make the defendant only responsible for the damage which the reasonable man would have foreseen as a likely consequence of his act.

(b) Regarding liability to compensate the claimant. The law now requires the defendant to compensate the claimant only for the foreseeable result of his act. The defendant is not liable for all the direct consequences of his act, but only for those which, as a reasonable man, he should have foreseen. However, it appears from more recent decisions that the *precise* nature of the injury suffered need not be foreseeable: it is enough if the injury was of *a kind* that was foreseeable even though the form it took was unusual.

> *The Wagon Mound*, 1961 – The test for remoteness of damage (**325**)
> *Hughes* v *Lord Advocate*, 1963 – Precise chain of events need not be foreseen (**326**)

Status of **The Wagon Mound**

Certain problems were raised by the decision in *The Wagon Mound*.

(**a**) Being a decision of the Judicial Committee of the Privy Council, it was not binding on English courts but was persuasive only.

In the event the House of Lords in *Hughes* v *Lord Advocate* (1963) (see above) treated the decision in *The Wagon Mound* as a correct statement of the law, subject in *Hughes'* case to an additional principle that the precise chain of circumstances need not be envisaged if the consequence turns out to be within the general sphere of contemplation and not of an entirely different kind which no one can anticipate.

(**b**) Before *The Wagon Mound* there was a well-established principle called the 'unusual plaintiff [now "claimant"]' rule. For example, if X strikes Y a puny blow which might be expected merely to bruise him, but in fact Y has a thin skull and dies from the blow, the law has regarded X as liable for Y's death. The same rule has been applied where the claimant is a haemophiliac, i.e. a person with a constitutional tendency to severe bleeding.

The courts have held that this principle is not affected by *The Wagon Mound* and remains as an exception to it. However, the 'unusual [claimant]' rule seems to apply only to disabilities existing before the accident and not to disabilities arising afterwards.

The test of remoteness of damage in tort as laid down in *The Wagon Mound* relies upon the foreseeability of a reasonable person both in respect of culpability and liability to compensate. It appears, therefore, that the law of remoteness of damage is not the same as in the law of contract. In *The Heron II* (1967) (see Chapter 18) it will be recalled that the House of Lords decided that a party to a contract is not liable for all foreseeable damage but only for that which is 'in contemplation'.

Finally, it is perhaps worth noting that *damage which is intended* is never too remote and in this connection there is an inference that a person intends the natural consequences of his or her acts.

20

> *Smith* v *Leech Braine & Co Ltd*, 1962 – The thin skull rule survives (**327**)
> *Martindale* v *Duncan*, 1973 – Poverty is within the unusual claimant rule (**328**)
> *Morgan* v *T Wallis*, 1974 – There must be a prior disability (**329**)
> *Scott* v *Shepherd*, 1773 – Intended damage never too remote (**330**)

Novus actus interveniens: *a new act intervening*

A loss may be too remote a consequence to be recoverable if the chain of causation is broken by an extraneous act. The scope of this concept is as follows:

(**a**) When the act of a third person intervenes between the original act or omission and the damage, the original act or omission is still the direct cause of the damage if the act of the third person might have been expected in the circumstances (see *Scott* v *Shepherd* (1773)) or did not materially cause or contribute to the injury. There is a duty to guard against a *novus actus interveniens*.

> *Barnett* v *Chelsea and Kensington Hospital Management Committee*, 1968 – An immaterial *novus actus* (**331**)
> *Robinson* v *The Post Office*, 1973 – Complications from an injection (**332**)
> *Davies* v *Liverpool Corporation*, 1949 – Duty to prevent a *novus actus* (**333**)

(**b**) If the act of the third person is such as would not be anticipated by a reasonable person, the chain of causation is broken, and the third party's act and not the initial act or omission will be treated as the cause of the damage.

> *Cobb* v *Great Western Railway*, 1894 – Where a theft broke the chain of causation (**334**)

(**c**) The *novus actus* may be the act of the claimant and in these cases liability will turn on the precise facts.

> *Sayers* v *Harlow UDC*, 1958 – The new act may be that of the claimant (**335**)
> *McKew* v *Holland and Hannen and Cubitts*, 1969 – A fall down the stairs (**336**)

(**d**) In order to establish the liability of the intervenor, it is essential to show that he consciously intended to carry out the act.

> *Philco Radio Corporation* v *Spurling*, 1949 – The person who does the intervening act must intend it (**337**)

Nervous shock

Damages for illness brought on by nervous shock are not necessarily too remote and may be recoverable where the nervous shock causes physical illness and:

(**a**) the defendant *intended* the shock (see *Wilkinson* v *Downton*, 1897); or
(**b**) where the shock arises from *negligence*, the claimant was 'foreseeable'.

Nervous shock will be foreseeable:

(**a**) Where the defendant's negligent act puts the claimant in fear of his or her safety *as a primary victim*;

> *Dulieu* v *White*, 1901 – Nervous shock: fear for one's own life (**338**)

(**b**) Where the defendant's negligent act threatens or actually injures some person who has a relationship with the claimant, such as a family relationship. The relationship of rescuer and rescued is included. However, the fact that there is a relationship is not enough to allow a successful claim *by a secondary victim*. In addition such a claimant must have:

(i) had *actual* sight or hearing of the event or of its immediate aftermath; or

(ii) although not having seen it, suffered shock by a sensible imagining of it from observed surrounding circumstances; or

(iii) seen the victim afterwards.

There also is the requirement that the defendant must owe the claimant a duty of care, though such a duty can exist not merely in regard to personal injury but also to nervous shock following damage to property.

> *Chadwick* v *British Railways Board*, 1967 – Nervous shock: rescuer and rescued (**339**)
>
> *Hinz* v *Berry*, 1970 – Where the accident is seen (**340**)
>
> *Hambrook* v *Stokes*, 1925 – Where the accident is not seen but sensibly imagined (**341**)
>
> *McLoughlin* v *O'Brian*, 1982 – Where the victim is seen (**342**)
>
> *Bourhill* v *Young*, 1943 – There must be a duty of care (**343**)

Finally, it should be noted that damages for nervous shock may be recovered where the claimant has witnessed some awful spectacle even though neither his own life nor that of any third party was put in peril.

> *Owens* v *Liverpool Corporation*, 1939 – When a coffin was overturned (**344**)

The above rules were developed because of the following problems inherent in actions for nervous shock:

(a) the difficulty of proving the degree of suffering involved and the possibility of fraudulent claims; thus, only where a known physical or mental condition is manifest are damages awarded;

(b) the difficulty (in terms of endless claims which no insurer would take on) which might arise if the number of possible claims, e.g. from persons not present at the accident, was not limited.

20

Damage after successive accidents

If a second event, e.g., injury or illness, which is not connected with the tortious accident, comes on before the trial and makes the injury worse, damages are reduced to the extent caused by the further injury or illness. If the second event is a tortious accident, no deduction has traditionally been made.

This statement must now be taken in the light of the decision of the Court of Appeal in *Holtby* v *Brigham & Cowan (Hull) Ltd* (2000) 150 NLJ 544. In that case the claimant had been a marine fitter. During the course of that work he was exposed to asbestos dust. For some part of that period he was employed by the defendants and for the rest of the time of his employment he was employed by another firm in a similar capacity and exposed to asbestos. He contracted asbestosis and sued the defendants for damages representing the full period of exposure. The court made an award of damages less 25 per cent to represent the other employer's liability. The case presents a procedural problem in that a claimant must now ensure that all possible defendants are served process and brought before the court so that the balance of damages can be recovered in the same action. Otherwise separate proceedings will have to be taken against others who may be liable.

In *Fairchild* v *Glenhaven Funeral Services Ltd* [2003] 1 AC 32 the House of Lords ruled that a person who had contracted mesothelioma as a result of wrongful exposure to asbestos at different times by more than one negligent employer (or occupier of premises) could sue any of them, even though the claimant could not prove which exposure caused the disease because all the employers concerned had materially contributed to the risk of contracting the disease. However, the ruling in *Fairchild* did not say how liability would be apportioned. It was assumed by the parties that each employer would be liable for the whole damage and would then have a claim for a contribution from the others. In other words, liability would be joint and several and this approach was taken subsequently in practice.

However, in *Barker* v *Corus (UK) plc* [2006] 2 WLR 1027 the House of Lords decided on the question of apportionment and ruled that damages were to be apportioned among the employers responsible *according to their degree of contribution* to the chance of a person contracting the disease. This was unsatisfactory because a claimant would have to trace all relevant defendants as far as possible before liability could be apportioned and if any relevant organisation had become insolvent nothing would be recovered from that organisation, the loss falling on the claimant.

The matter is now resolved by the Compensation Act 2006, which in s 3 makes clear that liability is joint and several. Furthermore, it is the intention of the Act that all claimants affected by the judgment in *Barker* will receive full compensation and, to achieve that, the Act will apply to *Barker* and other cases since then retrospectively.

Similar problems arise where the claimant suffers a minor injury but cannot work again because the minor injury has aggravated an existing injury. Here the court may discount the claimant's damages. This happened in *Heil* v *Rankin* (2000) (see p 519) where a police officer, with a pre-disposition to post-traumatic stress disorder from a previous incident, had it revived by a later tortious act and could not work in the force again, had his damages reduced by 50 per cent. This would suggest that while you take your victim as you find him, for foresight, you do not necessarily do so for damages. *Liability* yes, but *damages* no.

Provisional damages

Under the Rules of the Supreme Court there can be an award of provisional damages. Suppose A loses the sight of one eye in an accident caused by B's negligence. There is a risk that he might lose the sight of the other eye. If an award of damages is increased because of this possibility and it does not occur, then the damages were too much. If the sight of the other eye is affected the damages might be too small because the *precise* nature of the injury was not before the court. The judge can now make an award of provisional damages on the basis that the risk will not develop and specify a period during which a 'further award' can be made if it does.

The effect of the Damages Act 1996 and the use of structured settlements was considered in Chapter 18 to which reference should be made.

Discounting damages

In the case of personal injury involving, e.g. inability to work again, the court, in assessing damages for future pecuniary loss, discounts the damages awarded on the basis that the lump sum will be invested and grow and so provide income as well for the claimant. In *Wells* v *Wells* [1998] 3 WLR 329 the Privy Council decided that the rate of growth of the fund should be linked to the average return from government securities over the three years preceding the award, giving a discount rate of 3 per cent. Interest rates and returns from investments have, of course, fallen and the Damages Act 1996 allows the Lord Chancellor to set the rate by statutory instrument. He did this most recently in the Damages (Personal Injury) Order 2001 (SI 2001/2301). This order sets the rate at 2.5 per cent per annum. The Lord Chancellor has announced that he does not propose 'to tinker with the rate frequently to take account of every transient shift in market conditions'. The courts have power, however, to adopt a different rate (see Damages Act 1996, s 1(2)) if there are exceptional circumstances justifying this. A reduction in the rate is, of course, not popular with defendants and their insurers.

Injunction

An injunction may be granted to prevent the commission, continuance or repetition of an injury, and there is a form of interlocutory injunction called *quia timet* (because he fears) which may be granted, though rarely, even though the injury has not taken place but is merely threatened. As we have seen, injunctions are discretionary remedies and cannot be obtained as of right. Furthermore, an injunction will not be granted where damages would be an adequate remedy. However, it is no defence to say that it will be costly to comply with the injunction, though the court may, as in *Pride of Derby and Derbyshire Angling Association Ltd* v *British Celanese Ltd* [1953] 1 All ER 179, where expensive alterations to sewage plant were required to prevent the pollution of a river, grant an injunction and suspend its operation for such time as may seem necessary to enable the defendant to comply with the order.

Other remedies

The court may order *specific restitution* of land or goods where the claimant has been deprived of possession and a claimant may be given an order for an *account* of profits received as a result of a wrongful act. Thus where a company or other business organisation carries on business under a name calculated to deceive the public by confusion with the name of an existing concern, it commits the tort of *passing off* and can be restrained by injunction from doing so. In addition, the existing concern may be given an order for an *account* of profits received by the offending concern as a result of the deception.

> *Jobling* v *Associated Dairies*, 1980 – Where there is a subsequent non-tortious act (**345**)
> *Baker* v *Willoughby*, 1969 – Where there is a subsequent tortious act (**346**)
> *Performance Cars Ltd* v *Abraham*, 1961 – Where a second accident occurred before the damage from the first was repaired (**347**)

20

Cessation of liability

Liability in tort may be terminated by *death*, and also by *judgment, waiver, accord and satisfaction and lapse of time.*

Judgment

Successive actions cannot be brought by the same person on the same facts and if a competent court gives a final judgment in respect of a right of action that right of action is *merged* into the judgment. Thus in *Fitter* v *Veal* (1701) 12 Mod Rep 542, the claimant sued the defendant for assault and battery and obtained a judgment for £11. After some years he discovered his injuries were worse than he had thought and he had to have part of his skull removed. It was held that he could not sue for further damages. This problem is now overcome in appropriate cases by an award of provisional damages. Here there is only *one award* which can be increased if further loss arises; the increase is part of the original award and not a second award.

There are certain exceptional cases, for example where two separate rights have been infringed. Thus in *Brunsden* v *Humphrey* (1884) 14 QBD 141, the Court of Appeal held that a cab driver who had brought a successful action for damage to his cab caused by the defendant's negligence was able to bring a further action for personal injuries. One action was for damage to *property*, the other for injury to the *person*.

Waiver

A person may waive a tort when he forgoes his right to bring an action upon the wrongful act. If, for example, S, a second-hand car dealer, buys a car from T, a thief, and sells it to B, then S will convert the vehicle. If the true owner agrees to settle the matter with S by accepting from S the sale price of the car which S received from B, then the true owner cannot sue S in the tort of conversion because he has waived his right.

Accord and satisfaction

A person may surrender a right of action in tort by deed or an agreement for consideration.

Lapse of time

In actions for damages for negligence, nuisance or breach of duty, e.g. the statutory duty of an employer to fence a dangerous machine, where damages consist of, or include, damages for personal injury, the limitation period is three years (Limitation Act 1980, s 11(1)). Under s 2 of the 1980 Act the period in all other actions in tort is six years. However, actions in respect of registered postal packets under s 91(3) of the Postal Services Act 2000 must be brought within 12 months.

The period of limitation generally begins from the date when the tort was committed, e.g. the date of a trespass to land. However, at one time an action in negligence arose only when the harm was suffered but not, apparently, when it was detected. Thus in *Pirelli General Cable Works Ltd* v *Oscar Faber & Partners Ltd* [1983] 1 All ER 65 the defendants designed a chimney for the claimant. It was in the event a negligent design. Cracks were discovered by the claimants in 1977 but evidence showed that they had appeared in 1970. When the claimants sued in 1978 for negligence the House of Lords held that their claim was statute-barred.

The Latent Damage Act 1986 (which inserted provisions into the Limitation Act 1980) now applies and the limitation period is either six years from the date on which the cause of action accrued or three years from the earliest date upon which the claimant had sufficient knowledge to sue. The Act imposes a 'long-stop' period of 15 years from the negligent act or omission or the occurrence of the damage whether or not the damage was discovered or even discoverable by then. No action can be brought after this time.

'Knowledge' for the above purposes is:

■ knowledge of such facts relating to the damage as to cause a reasonable person to consider it sufficiently serious to justify bringing a claim; and
■ knowledge that the damage was attributable in whole or in part to the act or omission which it is alleged constitutes negligence.

Knowledge that the act or omission was negligent as a matter of law is not relevant.

The claimant bears the burden of proving that he or she did not have the requisite knowledge during the primary period of six years and that, as regards the second three-year period, he or she first had knowledge no more than three years before he or she issued proceedings.

An example of the use of what is now s 14A of the Limitation Act 1980 is the ruling of the House of Lords in *Haward* v *Fawcetts (a firm)* [2006] 1 WLR 682. The defendants, a firm of chartered accountants, were retained by Mr Haward and relying on their advice he purchased a controlling interest in a company in 1994. The company did not succeed and further investments by Mr Haward in mid-1995, 1996, 1997 and 1998 failed to improve things. The allegation by Mr Haward was that the company had been insolvent. Mr Haward asked a specialist in corporate rescue to look into the ever-mounting losses and a claim for damages for professional negligence against Fawcetts was commenced on 6 December 2001. The claims for loss in regard to the 1996, 1997 and 1998 investments could proceed but under the primary period of six years, claims in respect of the 1994 and 1995 investments could not. However, Mr Haward relied on s 14A, saying that he had not acquired the requisite knowledge until December 1998, i.e. within three years of the start of his action.

The House of Lords ruled that he did have the requisite knowledge. The performance of the company had missed the original financial predictions by such a massive margin that Mr Haward must have known before December 1998 that something had gone wrong when those predictions were made in the first place and this was the 'essence' of his case, i.e. alleged negligent predictions. He knew he had made a bad investment. The key criterion, said their Lordships, is when a claiment first knows that *in essence* he has a case. The ruling on knowledge as being merely the essence of a case will make it harder for claimants to invoke extensions of time.

The above rules were also rather harsh in personal injury cases where, for example, the claimant did not know that he had a claim or the extent of that claim, as where he had contracted a dust disease and was not aware of its onset. Furthermore, if X had been run down by Y's negligent driving, and unknown to X the injuries inflicted on him at the time of the accident caused him to go blind, say, four years after the accident, then X's cause of action in respect of his blindness was barred before he knew it existed, since it was formerly held that once damage had occurred the cause of action accrued and that time began to run against the claimant even though he was unaware or mistaken as to the consequences of the damage.

The matter is now covered by the Limitation Act 1980. The Act applies only to claims for personal injury arising out of negligence, breach of contract, breach of statutory duty, or damage caused by intentional trespass to the person, as where, e.g., psychological damage follows sexual abuse. A claim form for damages can be served within three years of the claimant becoming aware that the damage was caused by the abuse, which may well be more than three years after the abuse took place (see *Stubbings* v *Webb* [1991] 3 All ER 949). The basic limitation period of three years is retained but time runs from the date of accrual of the cause of action or the 'date of the claimant's knowledge if later'. The 'date of the claimant's knowledge' is the date on which the claimant first had knowledge that his injury was significant and that it was attributable in whole or in part to the act or omission which constitutes the alleged negligence, or breach of duty.

The action may be brought by dependants or on behalf of the estate of a deceased person. Thus actions may be brought within three years of the date of death or of the date on which the personal representatives or dependants, as the case may be, acquired a knowledge of the relevant facts.

If the tort is of a continuing nature, as in the case of nuisance or possibly trespass, an independent cause of action arises on each day during which the tort is committed, and the aggrieved party can recover for such proportion of the injury as lies within the limitation period, even though the wrong was first committed outside the period.

20

When time does not run

Where the claimant is a minor or person suffering from mental disorder, the period of limitation does not run against him until his disability ends, i.e. on becoming 18 or on becoming sane or on death. But once time has started to run, any subsequent disability will not stop it running.

However, a minor was only regarded as being under a disability if he was not in the custody of a parent when the cause of action accrued. If he was in the custody of a parent the parent was expected to commence an action within the limitation period and if they did not the minor's action would be statute-barred. The Act of 1980, s 8, abolishes that rule so that periods of limitation do not run against a minor whether he is in the custody of a parent or not.

Contingencies

The House of Lords has ruled that the possibility of having to pay money in the future, i.e. a contingent liability, is not enough to start a period of limitation running. In *Law Society* v *Sephton & Co (a firm)* [2006] 3 All ER 401 the House of Lords dismissed an appeal by Sephton, an accountancy practice, which contended that damage to the Law Society which had to pay some £1.2 million from its compensation fund to clients of a Solihull solicitor, Andrew Payne, occurred more than six years before the Law Society issued its claim form on Sephton so that the Society's claim was statute-barred.

Over the period 1988–95, Andrew Payne misappropriated around £750,000 from his client account. He was later struck off and imprisoned. During that period the Law Society had relied on reports by Sephton that the books and accounts of Payne & Co had been examined and that they complied with the Solicitors' Accounts Rules. Lord Hoffmann said that the partner in Sephton was negligent in signing the relevant reports, since he could not have made a proper examination without discovering the misappropriations.

Sephton contended that the damage to the Law Society occurred when it supplied its reports for the years ending 31 October 1988 to 1995 and since the Law Society did not serve its claim form until 16 May 2002 the claim was statute-barred. The claim should not therefore proceed, having been brought more than six years after the damage (Limitation Act 1980, s 2).

The House of Lords did not agree. During the period 1988–95 the liability of the Law Society was only contingent in the sense that a client might make a claim on the compensation fund. In fact, the first claim by a client of Payne & Co was not made until July 1996, with payment being made in October 1996. Thus the Society's claim was made before the limitation period had expired. Sephton's appeal was dismissed.

Special periods of limitation

The periods of limitation in respect of actions against the estate of a deceased tortfeasor have already been considered. However, it should be noted that the Limitation Act 1980 does not operate to extend the time within which an action must be brought against a deceased tortfeasor's estate. So far as the death of an injured party is concerned, the ordinary six-year or three-year periods apply. They run from the accrual of the cause of action as if no death had occurred. As we have seen, personal representatives or dependants may ask for an extension of time under the provisions of the Limitation Act 1980.

Other special periods of limitation are as follows:

(*a*) actions arising out of collisions at sea: two years, subject to extension by the court (Maritime Conventions Act 1911, s 8);

(b) proceedings against air-carriers: two years (Carriage by Air Act 1961, s 1(1));

(c) a joint tortfeasor who wishes to recover a contribution must bring the action within two years from the date on which he admitted liability or judgment was entered against him (Limitation Act 1980, s 8);

(d) actions in respect of damage arising from nuclear incidents: 30 years (Nuclear Installations Act 1965, s 15).

Public authorities and their officers have no special position and actions against them are governed by the same rules as any other action in tort.

It should also be noted that by s 32 of the Limitation Act 1980, the defendant's *fraud* or *negligent concealment* may prevent his pleading that the claim is statute-barred.

> *Beaman v ARTS*, 1949 – Limitation of actions: fraudulent concealment of claim (**348**)

Reform

The current law on limitation periods is set for radical change following a government announcement in July 2002 that it accepts in principle the Law Commission's proposals for reform of the law on the limitation of actions for civil claims. The government will introduce legislation when the opportunity arises.

In broad terms a claim would have to be brought within a period of three years from knowledge of the cause of action with a long stop period of 10 years from the accrual of the cause of action after which a claim could not be brought even if a claimant only discovered its existence after that time. The court will have discretion to disapply the three-year period in personal injury claims and no long stop period would apply. The new regime would apply to most tort claims and contract claims and claims for breach of trust. Claims in relation to land would be subject to a limitation period equivalent to the long stop period. Claims on a statute would in general be covered by the primary three-year period and the 10-year long stop period.

At the time of writing there has been no legislation on these reforms.

Assignment

20

It is against the rules of public policy to allow the assignment of rights of action in tort, since actions for damages should not become a marketable commodity. However, rights may pass to others by operation of law in the following circumstances:

(a) Death. Rights and liabilities in tort survive for the benefit or otherwise of the estate, except actions for defamation unless damage to the deceased's estate has resulted.

(b) Bankruptcy. Rights of action in tort possessed by a debtor which relate to his *property* and which if brought will increase his assets will pass to his trustee in bankruptcy. Actions for *personal torts*, e.g. defamation, remain with the bankrupt.

(c) Subrogation. An insurance company which compensates an insured person under a policy of insurance can step into his shoes and sue in respect of the injury.

21

SPECIFIC TORTS

We shall next examine certain specific torts, beginning with those affecting the person.

Torts affecting the person

Trespass to the person

This has several aspects.

Assault

An assault is an attempt or offer to apply unlawful force to the person of another. There must be an apparent present ability to carry out the threat, the basis of the wrong being that a person is put in present fear of violence. On general principles, pointing even an unloaded weapon or a model gun at another, who does not know that it is unloaded or a model, would amount to an assault.

It is often said that mere words cannot constitute an assault but this is a doubtful proposition. In *Ansell* v *Thomas* [1974] Crim LR 31 the assault seems to have consisted in words threatening forcible ejectment of a director from the company's premises if he did not leave voluntarily. A threat to use force at some time in the future is not an assault, but it seems that it is enough if the threat is to use force if the person addressed does not immediately do some act. In *Read* v *Coker* (1853) 138 ER 1437, it was held that an assault was committed where the defendants threatened to break the claimant's neck if he did not leave the premises. Words, however, may prevent an assault coming into being.

As regards the unauthorised taking of a photograph the position is somewhat complicated. It may be that where a flash is used the simple taking of the photograph without more is unlawful, since it is probably a battery (see below) to project light on to another person in such a manner as to cause personal discomfort. Where no flash is used, it is hard to see how, by itself, the taking of a photograph can amount to a battery, an assault or any other trespass.

> *Turbervell* v *Savage*, 1669 – Words may prevent an assault (**349**)

Battery

Intentionally to bring any material object into contact with the person of another is enough application of force to give rise to a battery. Thus to throw water on a person (*Pursell* v *Horn*

(1838) 8 A & E 602), or to apply a 'tone-rinse' to the scalp of a customer which was not ordered and caused damage, i.e. a skin rash, is enough (*Nash* v *Sheen* (1953) *The Times*, 13 March). Substantial damages will be awarded when the battery is an affront to personal dignity, e.g. the wrongful taking of a fingerprint. It should, however, be noted that a person who has been detained and charged with or told he will be charged with a recordable offence, e.g. an offence punishable by imprisonment, can have his fingerprints taken without consent (s 61, Police and Criminal Evidence Act 1984 (referred to hereunder as PACE)). Persons who are convicted of a recordable offence but fined rather than imprisoned can be required to attend at a police station for prints to be taken. Failure to do so allows arrest without warrant (PACE, s 27). The mere jostling which occurs in a crowd does not constitute battery, because there is presumed consent and in any case there is normally no hostility which is also a requirement. Thus in *Wilson* v *Pringle* [1986] 2 All ER 440, one schoolboy had intentionally pulled a schoolbag off another boy's shoulder. However, this was only a form of horseplay and in the absence of a hostile intention there was no battery. It should be noted that there may be a battery without an assault, as where a person is attacked from behind.

There may be exeptional cases where there is a battery even though there is no physical contact with the victim. Thus, in *Haystead* v *DPP* (2000) *The Times*, 2 June a man hit a woman causing her to drop the child she was holding. The court ruled that in the circumstances there was a battery to both the woman and the child.

As regards strip searching of prison visitors, e.g. for drugs the case of *Secretary of State for the Home Department* v *Wainwright* [2002] QB 1334 is instructive. The Court of Appeal decided that the trial judge was wrong to award basic and aggravated damages to a mother and son who were strip searched without their consent while on a prison visit. The Court of Appeal made clear that an intention to do harm or recklessness as to the same must be present and here the prison officers did not intend harm nor were they reckless. This ruled out the common law rule of trespass and any privacy rights under the Human Rights Act 1998 though the events took place in 1997. As regards intention and recklessness, the Court of Appeal found it necessary to distinguish *Wilkinson* v *Downton* (1897) Case **268**.

This ruling was affirmed by the House of Lords (see *Secretary of State for the Home Department* v *Wainwright* [2003] 3 WLR 1137).

Was there consent?

In considering the defence of *volenti* there has already been some treatment of informed consent in an action for alleged negligence in medical cases (see *Sidaway* v *Bethlem Royal Hospital Governors* [1984] 1 All ER 1018 and the cases appearing with it in Chapter 20). A similar issue was raised in *Freeman* v *Home Office* [1984] 1 All ER 1036. The claimant was serving a sentence of life imprisonment. He was given drugs by a medical officer employed by the Home Office. He claimed that the drugs were given to discipline and control him and not, as he thought, as medical treatment. He claimed that the medical officer had committed battery upon him and that his consent was negatived because it was not informed. The Court of Appeal decided that since the doctrine of informed consent formed no part of English law, the sole issue was whether on the facts the claimant had consented to the administration of the drugs and on that issue the trial judge had found that the claimant had so consented. His claim therefore failed.

In *Re MB (Caesarian Section)* (1997) 147 NLJ 600 the Court of Appeal held that a woman with full capacity could consent to or refuse treatment even though refusal might result in harm to her or her baby. However, doctors were entitled to administer an anaesthetic to carry out birth by caesarian section where it was in the best interest of the woman and her child given that she had a temporary lack of capacity because of panic brought on by fear of injection by needle.

21

Those who suffer passively from the smoking of others are able to claim damages for battery. Since spitting at someone is a battery there seems no reason why blowing out poisonous smoke in the vicinity of other people should not also be. Thus in *Bland* v *Stockport Metropolitan Borough Council* [1993] CLY 1506 a woman who had been exposed to passive smoking for 11 years at her work received £15,000 damages for injury to her health including in particular bronchitis and sinusitis. The Smoke-free (General Provisions) Regulations 2006 will go some way to dealing with the problem but on the basis of criminal law. In addition, a claim for damages for mental illness allegedly caused by sexual abuse has been brought against an alleged abuser and has been allowed to proceed (*Stubbings* v *Webb* [1991] 3 All ER 949). Limitation of actions problems did exist in the case and the House of Lords eventually ruled that the claim was time-barred. But for this it seemed that the substance of the claim was acceptable (see *Stubbings* v *Webb* [1993] 2 WLR 120).

In general there will be some active conduct constituting the assault. However, the courts have accepted that a battery can arise from an omission.

> *Fagan* v *Metropolitan Police Commissioner*, 1968 – A battery from an omission (**350**)

Defences

There are certain defences to an action brought for assault or for battery:

(a) Self-defence. This is not merely the defence of oneself but also of those whom one has a legal or moral obligation to protect. It also applies to the protection of property, but no more than reasonable force must be used.

(b) Parental or similar authority. *As regards parents and those* in loco parentis, e.g. a step-father, s 1(7) of the Children and Young Persons Act 1933 provided a defence to the reasonable chastisement of a child on a charge of assault. This provision was removed by s 58 of the Children Act 2004. In addition, however, s 58(3) of the 2004 Act states that battery of a child causing actual bodily harm to the child cannot be justified in any civil proceedings on the ground that it constitutes reasonable punishment. This leaves problems as to what is 'actual bodily harm'. It is in fact a government compromise between retaining the defence and outlawing smacking. On the issue of the punishment of children in the home, the European Court ruled in *A* v *UK* [1998] CLY 3065 that UK law failed to protect a boy who had suffered repeated and severe beatings with a cane by his stepfather as contrary to Art 3 of the Human Rights Convention.

As regards schools, corporal punishment is outlawed in all schools under s 131 of the School Standards and Framework Act 1998 (see *Williamson* v *Secretary of State for Education and Employment* [2002] 1 FLR 493). In that case it was held that even religious belief in corporal punishment did not justify corporal punishment even where supported by a religious text and parental consent. The ruling was later affirmed by the House of Lords (see *R (on the application of Williamson)* v *Secretary of State for Education and Employment* [2005] 2 AC 246).

(c) *Volenti non fit injuria*. As in the case of the players in a rugby match (see *Simms* v *Leigh RFC* (1969)).

(d) Judicial authority. This includes the right to inflict proper punishment and to make lawful arrests.

(e) Necessity. This is not favoured as a defence but may be allowed if the defendant can prove that he committed the battery in order to prevent the happening of a greater harm. Thus in *Leigh* v *Gladstone* (1909) 26 TLR 139, the forcible feeding of a suffragette in prison was held justified by the necessity of preserving her life.

Although the forced feeding of prisoners is not in general practised in our penal institutions, the case of *Secretary of State for the Home Department* v *Robb* [1995] Fam 127 is of interest. The High Court held in that case that prison officials and medical attendants could lawfully abstain from providing food or drink to a prisoner who did not want it but only as long as he retained the capacity to refuse nutrition or hydration. After that presumably forced feeding could take place. Furthermore, in *B* v *Croydon Health Authority* [1995] Fam 133 the Court of Appeal held that where a patient was detained under the Mental Health Act 1983, feeding by tube without consent was lawful since it was treatment for the patient's disorder. The patient in this case was given to inflicting harm upon herself and her refusal to eat was another means of inflicting harm.

(f) Prosecution in a magistrates' court. Assault and battery is a crime as well as a civil wrong. If the wrongdoer is prosecuted, and *summary* proceedings are taken by the *victim* and not the *Crown* and the accused is convicted and punished, or the case is dismissed and the magistrates award a certificate of dismissal, no further action or civil proceedings may be taken in respect of the particular wrong (Offences against the Person Act 1861, ss 44–45).

It is now clear that trespass to the person is not actionable in itself; the claimant must prove intention or negligence, though he need not prove damage. It is also settled that where the interference is *unintentional* the claimant's only cause of action lies in negligence.

> *Fowler* v *Lanning*, 1959 – Trespass requires intention or negligence (**351**)

False imprisonment

This is the infliction of unauthorised bodily restraint without lawful justification. It is not necessarily a matter of bars and bolts, but any form of unlawful restraint might turn out to be false imprisonment. The imprisonment must be total, and if certain ways of exit are barred to a prisoner, but he is free to go off in another way, then there is no false imprisonment. If a person is on premises and is not given facilities to leave, this does constitute false imprisonment unless the refusal is merely the insistence on a reasonable condition. It is not even essential that the claimant should be aware of the fact of his imprisonment, provided it is a fact. *Volenti non fit injuria* is a defence to false imprisonment, as where a prison visitor agrees to be locked in a cell with the prisoner.

It should be noted that a defendant will not be liable for false imprisonment where he merely gives information to the prosecution which affects the claimant's arrest and detention. Thus a store detective who incorrectly informed police officers that the claimant had been shoplifting was not liable for false imprisonment where the police had at their discretion arrested and detained the claimant (see *Davidson* v *Chief Constable of the North Wales Police and Another* [1994] 2 All ER 597).

A further example is provided by *R* v *Governor of Brockhill Prison ex parte Evans (No 2)* [2000] 3 WLR 843 where the claimant was detained in prison for 59 days longer than she should have been following an error in the calculation of her sentence in terms of days spent in custody before sentence. The governor was held liable even though he had acted in good faith. The tort of false imprisonment is one of strict liability said the court.

> *Bird* v *Jones*, 1845 – Imprisonment must be total (**352**)
>
> *Herd* v *Weardale Steel, Coal and Coke Co Ltd*, 1915 – Where refusal to allow a person to leave is reasonable (**353**)
>
> *Meering* v *Grahame White Aviation Co Ltd*, 1919 – Knowledge of imprisonment is not required (**354**)

21

Arrest and the tort of trespass to the person

An arrest or other restraint of a person, as by stopping and searching him, will be unlawful and actionable as a trespass in civil law unless the following requirements are met.

Powers of arrest: the Serious Organised Crime and Police Act 2005

Any person may arrest without a warrant:

- anyone who is in the act of committing an indictable offence; or
- anyone whom he or she has reasonable grounds for suspecting to be committing such an offence;
- where an indictable offence has been committed a person other than a constable may arrest without warrant:
  - anyone who is guilty of the offence;
  - anyone whom he or she has reasonable grounds for suspecting to be guilty of it.

It is required in all of the above cases that the citizen has reasonable grounds to believe that it is necessary to make the arrest and the police are not available. The above material is in s 24A of PACE, having been inserted by the Serious Organised Crime and Police Act 2005.

In the above context, indictable offence includes each way offences.

The position regarding citizens arrest as it is called has always been unsatisfactory and still is because a citizen is unlikely to know what an indictable offence or each way offence is much less to identify them.

The police have a power to arrest for any offence subject only to a necessity requirement. This is to the effect that an arresting officer should believe, on reasonable grounds, that an arrest was necessary. The burden of proving this rests with the arresting officer.

The new powers significantly extend the police powers of arrest. The accompanying PACE Code which is useful to defence lawyers states that the power must be fully justified and officers exercising it should consider if the necessary objectives can be met by other and less intrusive means. It states: 'Arrest must never be used simply because it can be used.'

Section 28 of PACE requires that the person arrested should be told at the time of the arrest or as soon as practicable thereafter that he is under arrest and the grounds therefor, even if it is obvious, as where a thief is apprehended in the act of theft. However, an arrest made without these formalities is not unlawful if the arresting officer cannot comply with them because of the condition or behaviour of the person arrested, as where there is a struggle with police and it is impossible to inform him (see *DPP* v *Hawkins* [1988] 3 All ER 673).

Since arrest is a continuing act, an arrest which is made without reasons becomes lawful if reasons are given later, e.g. at the police station as in *Lewis* v *Chief Constable of the South Wales Constabulary* [1991] 1 All ER 206.

> *Christie* v *Leachinsky*, 1947 – An unlawful arrest (**355**)
> *Wheatley* v *Lodge*, 1971 – When arrest is lawful (**356**)

Under s 32 of PACE a person arrested may be searched for a weapon or evidence relating to the alleged offence. The power of search extends to any premises on which the arrest took place.

Powers to stop and search

In addition, s 1 of PACE gives the police power to stop and search persons. The Act gives the police the power to search any person or vehicle *found in a public place* for stolen or prohibited articles, e.g. a gun (and more recently fireworks) and to detain a person or vehicle for the purpose of such search. A person can be ordered to stop for the purpose of such a search and any stolen or prohibited article found in the course of the search may be seized. The statutory powers of stop and search are supported by a code of practice, a revised version of which took effect from 1 January 2006. Its provisions in terms of its details are unlikely to be the subject of an examination question and so are not considered further.

The matters of cautioning on arrest and procedure to be followed before the person arrested reaches court have already been considered (see Chapter 4).

Remedies available against false imprisonment

The *remedies* available against false imprisonment are self-help, i.e. breaking away, the writ of *habeas corpus* and an action for damages. This prerogative writ of *habeas corpus* is designed to provide a person, who is kept in confinement without legal justification, with a means of obtaining his release. If he can show a *prima facie* case that he might be unlawfully detained, he (or often a friend or relative) will apply to the Queen's Bench Division, though application may be made to any judge of the High Court during vacation times. The person detained applies, through counsel, for the writ to be issued, the facts alleging unlawful detention being set out on an affidavit supporting the application. If the writ is issued, the effect is to cause the alleged captor to 'bring the body' of the prisoner before the court which will then decide on the merits of the case whether there are any legal grounds for detention of the prisoner. If not, he is set free by the court. The civil procedure reforms introducing tracking arrangements have no relevance to these applications.

A person detained may also be able to make an application for release or damages (if released) as a result of the incorporation into UK law of the European Convention on Human Rights. Article 5(4) states: 'Everyone who is deprived of his liberty by arrest or detention shall be entitled to take proceedings by which the lawfulness of his detention shall be decided speedily by a court and his release ordered if the detention is not lawful'.

Torts affecting property

21

Trespass to land

Trespass to land is interference with the possession of land. It is not enough that the claimant is the owner; he must also have possession. So where land is leased for a term of years, the lessee is the person entitled to sue in trespass, though the lessor may bring an action if the damage is such as to affect his reversion when the lease ends. However, when a person signs a contract for the purchase of land, he becomes entitled to possession of it, and if a trespass takes place before he actually takes possession, then he can sue in respect of that trespass when he does. His right to sue relates back to the date on which he became entitled to the land under the contract.

In *Manchester Airport plc* v *Dutton* [1999] 3 WLR 524 the Court of Appeal appears to have rewritten the common law when it ruled that a mere licensee who was not in occupation was entitled to a possession order against a trespasser. There was no need, said the court, for the claimant to have a freehold or lease. It appeared that the claimant wanted another runway and that this involved felling or lopping trees in a wood owned by the National Trust. The Trust gave the airport a contractual licence to enter into the wood for that purpose. The defendants set up camps and tree houses to prevent this and the airport authority obtained a possession order against them. The House of Lords refused an appeal.

Interference with the possession of land may take many forms but it must be direct. For example, an unauthorised entry on land is a trespass. It is trespass to place things on land, e.g. leaving a dead cat in a neighbour's garden. To remain on land after one's authority is terminated constitutes a trespass. So, if a friend invites you into his house for a meal, tires of your company and asks you to leave, then if you refuse you are a trespasser. If you abuse the purpose for which you are allowed to be on land, you become a trespasser. In *Hickman* v *Maisey* [1900] 1 QB 752, where the highway was used for making notes of the form of racehorses being tried out on adjoining land, this constituted a trespass, since the proper use of a highway is for passing and re-passing.

While trespass usually takes place above the surface, it may be underneath by means of tunnelling or mining. With regard to trespass in the airspace above land, the position is doubtful, since there is no good authority. It is probably only a trespass if it is either within the area of ordinary user, or if it involves danger or inconvenience.

Section 76 of the Civil Aviation Act 1982 provides that, subject to the exception of aircraft belonging to, or exclusively employed in the service of Her Majesty, no action lies in respect of trespass or nuisance by reason only of the flight of an aircraft over any property at a height above the ground, which having regard to weather and the other circumstances of the case is reasonable.

> *Southport Corporation* v *Esso Petroleum Co*, 1954 – Trespass to land must be direct (**357**)
>
> *Kelson* v *Imperial Tobacco Co*, 1957 – A sign trespasses into airspace (**358**)
>
> *Woollerton and Wilson* v *Richard Costain (Midlands) Ltd*, 1969 – Crane invades airspace (**359**)
>
> *Bernstein* v *Skyviews & General*, 1977 – An aerial photograph (**360**)

Subject to the same exception in regard to aircraft in the service of Her Majesty, the owner of an aircraft is liable for all material loss or damage to persons or property caused by that aircraft, whether in flight, taking off, or landing, or by a person in it, or articles falling from it, without proof of negligence or intention, or other cause of action.

Trespass to land or goods will not be unlawful and actionable at civil law if it is by the police who follow the provisions laid down in PACE. Broadly speaking, s 17(1) of the Act gives the police power to enter premises without a warrant in certain circumstances, e.g. to make an arrest. The Court of Appeal ruled in *O'Loughlin* v *Chief Constable of Essex* [1998] 1 WLR 374 that when exercising power under s 17 a police officer should give reasons for the entry unless this is impossible, impractical or undesirable. The fact that this has not been done will assist the legal position of the occupier who resists the entry. Section 8 gives the police a power to enter premises to search under a warrant from a JP. Section 19 gives power to seize articles found on the premises unless they are exempt articles if the officer concerned reasonably believes that it is evidence in relation to an offence which he is investigating or any other offence, and that it is necessary to seize it in order to prevent its 'concealment, loss or destruction'. Section 19(6) states that items exempted from seizure are those subject to legal professional privilege.

Revocation of licences

Problems have arisen where a claimant has entered the premises by virtue of a licence, contractual or otherwise, because at one time it was not certain whether this licence could be revoked so as to make the claimant a trespasser and permit his ejection.

The common-law view was that, where a person paid for admission to premises, his licence to be on those premises could be revoked at any time, in spite of valuable consideration, so that he could then be ejected as a trespasser, the defendant being liable for breach of contract, but not for assault.

On the other hand, equity took the view that, if there was an enforceable contract not to revoke, express or implied, as where valuable consideration had been given, the licence could not be revoked so that if the claimant had been ejected he could sue for assault; he could not be made a trespasser by a mere attempt at revocation.

The equitable view gave rise to certain problems because it seemed to confuse rights over land with mere contracts, but the matter may now be regarded as settled. The position is that, although a licence for value is contractual in its nature and cannot create a right over land itself (or a right *in rem* which will run with the land and affect third parties), yet, as between the parties to the contract it may be implied, even if it is not expressed, that the licence cannot unreasonably be revoked during the period for which the parties intended it to continue.

Winter Garden Theatre (London) Ltd v *Millennium Productions Ltd*, 1948 – Revoking a licence (**361**)

Hounslow LBC v *Twickenham Garden Developments*, 1970 – Revoking a licence; a further example (**362**)

Extra-judicial remedies

There are certain extra-judicial remedies available to a person injured by a trespass. For example, *distress damage feasant* is the right to seize chattels which have done damage on land. There is no right to use or sell the chattels but merely to detain until the owner offers compensation. The remedy does not lie against Crown property, and the right to sue in trespass is postponed until the chattel is returned. Livestock may be detained (subject to notice to the owner and police) for compensation supported by a right of sale (Animals Act 1971, s 7). These provisions apply only to damage caused by straying animals; they do not give powers of detention in the case of other forms of damage by animals, e.g. damage caused by negligent control where the animal has not in fact strayed.

There is a further extra-judicial remedy, often referred to as *self-help*, whereby the person in possession of the land may eject the trespasser, using such force as is reasonably necessary. The trespasser must be asked to depart peacefully and given time in which to quit the land. A trespasser who enters by *force* may be removed immediately and without a previous request to depart.

Hemmings v *Stoke Poges Golf Club*, 1920 – Ejecting trespassers (**363**)

Other remedies

Trespass to land is actionable *per se* (in itself) and it is not necessary for the claimant to show actual damage in order to commence his action, although the damages would be nominal in the absence of real loss. Nevertheless, it is possible to obtain an injunction without proof of loss. Trespass upon property is not normally a criminal offence (but see below p 578). The law does penalise by statute a trespass on particular property, e.g. railway property, and also the law punishes trespass on property for the purpose of committing, e.g., theft or rape.

Access to Neighbouring Land Act 1992

Before this Act was passed the law did not provide any general right of access to neighbouring land in order to carry out work on one's own property, no matter how essential this might be. To do so without permission was trespass. The Act permits access under an access order obtainable from a county court or the High Court where the owner of the land concerned will not agree to entry. The applicant for the order must show that the work is reasonably necessary to preserve the whole or part of his land and buildings and that the work cannot be done at all, or it would be substantially more difficult to do it, if entry to the neighbouring land was not granted. The order is made against the person who could in other circumstances sue for trespass, so if the neighbouring land is let it will be made against the tenant.

The order may restrict entry to a specified area and provide for compensation to be paid to the neighbouring owner if this is appropriate. It may also require the person who is given access to make a payment to the neighbouring owner reflecting the financial benefit, if any, which the person given access has received. This does not apply where the land subject to the access order is residential property.

An order will not be granted where it would cause, e.g., unreasonable disturbance to the neighbouring land. The court may also make an order for inspection to see whether the works are necessary.

Finally, any provision in an agreement, whether made before or after the Act, which tries to prevent or restrict application for an access order is void.

Criminal Justice and Public Order Act 1994: criminal trespass

Section 61 of this Act enables a police officer to direct trespassers on land to leave that land where the occupier has taken steps to ask them to do so:

(a) if any of the trespassers has caused damage; or
(b) if they have been threatening, abusive or insulting; or
(c) if between them they have six or more vehicles on the land.

This part of the Act is aimed in large measure against hippies or travellers. Failure to obey such a direction, or returning to the land as a trespasser within three months, are criminal offences. The Act creates a number of other offences of what are, in effect, criminal trespass. These include a power to remove persons attending or preparing for a rave. There is also the new offence of aggravated trespass under which it becomes a crime to trespass on land in order to *disrupt or obstruct a lawful activity* which is *being carried out on it*. This is presumably aimed at groups such as hunt saboteurs and criminalises their activities. Of interest on the matter of aggravated trespass is the case of *DPP* v *Tilly* (2002) 166 JP 22. Ms Tilly appealed against her conviction for aggravated trespass under the 1994 Act. She had entered a field and damaged a crop forming part of a government sponsored trial of genetically modified organisms. The question for the Administrative Court on judicial review was whether in view of the requirement that an activity was being carried out it was necessary that someone was on the land at the time of the offence because neither the farmer concerned nor his employees was present on the land cultivating or doing anything else to the crop. Ms Tilly's appeal was allowed. A person could not commit aggravated trespass unless the individual(s) engaged in the relevant lawful activity was (were) physically present on the land at the time of the trespass. An individual could not be obstructed or disrupted from engaging in a lawful activity if that individual was absent from the land.

More seriously, it was held by the Divisional Court of Queen's Bench that under the Act there is no right to hold a peaceful non-obstructive assembly *on the public highway*. In *DPP* v *Jones* (1997) 147 NLJ Rep 162 the respondents took part in a peaceful non-obstructive assembly on the grass verge beside the perimeter fence of Stonehenge, demonstrating for the right to have access to the monument. The police had previously obtained a prohibiting order from the local authority under s 14A of the Public Order Act 1986 (as inserted by s 70 of the 1994 Act) and arrested the respondents whose criminal act was confirmed by the Divisional Court. They were rightly convicted by the Salisbury magistrates.

However, the House of Lords allowed an appeal by the demonstrators. A public highway, said their Lordships, was a public place where any activity that was reasonable, did not cause a public or private nuisance and did not obstruct the highway was not a trespass (see *DPP v Jones (Margaret)* [1999] 2 WLR 625).

Squatters

Apart from these statutory exceptions, the criminal law dealt with entering or remaining on property by means of the Statutes of Forcible Entry which were a confusing and archaic set of laws. The fact that trespass is not generally a crime has led to difficulties, particularly in times of acute housing shortage where the civil law is not adequate to deal with the growing activities of 'squatters'. The Criminal Law Act 1977, s 6 now creates the offence of using or threatening violence to secure entry to premises on which there is another person who opposes entry. The offence can be committed by a person notwithstanding he has some interest or right in the premises, as where he is a landlord, but the offence cannot be committed by a displaced residential occupier, i.e. a person whose residential occupation of the premises has been interrupted by the occupation of the premises by a trespasser, or someone acting for a displaced residential occupier. Section 7 makes it a summary offence for a trespasser to fail to leave premises when required to do so by a displaced residential occupier. Section 8 makes it an offence for a person who is a trespasser on any premises which he has entered as a trespasser to have with him a weapon of offence. Section 9 makes it an offence to enter or be upon as a trespasser diplomatic or consular premises or the premises or residence of any body or person having diplomatic immunity in respect of its or his premises or residence. Section 10 creates a summary offence of resisting or intentionally obstructing a court officer seeking to execute an order for possession of premises, while s 11 gives to a constable a power of entry and search for the purpose of exercising a power of arrest under that part of the Act which relates to offences of entering and remaining on property (i e Part II). Section 13 abolishes the common law offences of forcible entry and detainer and repeals related statutes.

The Criminal Justice and Public Order Act 1994 supplements the Criminal Law Act 1977 by making a change in the court procedure in relation to premises such as houses and shops as opposed to open land. The Act allows the court to make an 'interim order' for possession. If, following service of the interim order, the trespasser does not leave the premises within 24 hours or leaves and re-enters within a year, he is guilty of an offence and the police may arrest him. This is bringing the police even further into the civil law of trespass and the government announced that the police would be given a 'frontline role' to speed up evictions of squatters from houses and shops where they will usually have squatted in order to carry on a trade.

Countryside and Rights of Way Act 2000

The main provisions of this Act are as follows:

■ a proposed right of access on foot for open air recreation to mountain, moor, heath, down and registered common land (or open country);
■ land over 600 metres above sea level is automatically covered;
■ open land will be shown on maps that will be available to the public. There is an appeal to the Secretary of State where land is included by mistake;

21

- there are exceptions for land that is cultivated, land covered by buildings, parks and gardens, mineral workings, railway land and golf courses, aerodromes, race courses and development land where planning permission has been granted if development activities have commenced;
- landowners must not erect false or misleading signs likely to deter people from using their statutory right of access, though signs indicating boundaries are acceptable so long as they do not deter walkers by giving them false information;
- landowners may need to provide for new access to open country where public rights of way do not exist or are insufficient;
- open country access may be closed for up to 28 days each year, but not over bank holidays or weekends.

When the Act is in force it will mean that many former trespassers to land will have to be tolerated.

However, even where an access right is granted it is limited by Sch 2 so that no vehicle can be used (including bicycles), no craft can be sailed on waters and no organised games played – so no paintball games! Camping is also prohibited. If these activities are undertaken the persons concerned become trespassers. Countryside bodies also have power to restrict access during a specified period in the event for example of a fire risk and indefinitely for nature conservation, heritage preservation and national defence.

The liability of landowners is not increased by this statutory right of access. Those exercising the right will be in no better position than trespassers. Thus the owner has only a duty to warn of dangers known to him or which he reasonably believes to exist. There is no liability at all in regard to natural features such as ponds and ditches.

Wrongful interference with goods

We propose to discuss the tort of wrongful interference by outlining the basic features of it, i.e. the relationship between the claimant and the goods, the conduct of the defendant which the claimant must prove, and the principle of liability, bearing in mind that the Torts (Interference with Goods) Act 1977 defines, in s 1, wrongful interference with goods as including conversion of goods, trespass to goods, negligence or any other tort so far as it results in damage to goods or to an interest in goods.

Wrongful interference by trespass to goods

The relationship between the claimant and the goods

Wrongful interference by trespass to goods is a wrong against the possession of goods. Possession in English law is a difficult concept which is considered more fully in Chapter 22. For the moment it will suffice to say that a person possesses goods when he has some form of *control* over them and has the *intention to exclude* others from possession and to hold the goods on his own behalf.

Possession must exist at the moment when the wrongful interference is alleged to have been committed. Thus a bailee of goods can sue for a wrongful interference to them, but a bailor cannot because, although he is the owner of the goods, he does not possess them at the time. Where there is a *bailment at will*, i.e. one which can be determined at any time, both bailee and bailor have possession so that either can sue for a wrongful interference to the goods. Possession does not necessarily involve an actual grasp of the goods; often a lesser degree of control will suffice.

Difficulties have arisen over the requirement of the intention to exclude others as a necessary ingredient of possession, in regard to things found under or on land.

It has been held that where goods are not attached to land it is necessary to distinguish between a finding in a place over which the occupier has shown a clear intent to control exclusively, and finding in a place to which the finder has access as a matter of course. In the latter case, the finder's possessory title takes precedence over that of the occupier.

However, an occupier of land or a building has superior rights to those of a finder in regard to goods in or attached to the land or building.

The special rules relating to treasure are considered in Chapter 3.

> *The Tubantia*, 1924 – Possession and control (**364**)
> *Parker* v *British Airways Board*, 1982 – Finders of property (**365**)
> *South Staffordshire Water Co* v *Sharman*, 1896 – Goods which are on or attached to land (**366**)

Although the claimant relies on possession and not on ownership or title, the defendant can set up the *jus tertii* (right of a third party) under s 8(1) of the Torts (Interference with Goods) Act 1977. Under that section the defendant is entitled to show in accordance with rules of court that a third party has a better right than the claimant as regards all or any part of the interest sought by the claimant and any rule of law (sometimes and formerly called *jus tertii*) to the contrary is abolished. Under s 8(2) rules of court relating to proceedings for wrongful interference require the claimant to give particulars of his title; to identify any person who to his knowledge has or claims any interest in the goods; to authorise the defendant to apply for directions as to whether any person should be joined in the action with a view to establishing whether he has a better right than the claimant, or has a claim as a result of which the defendant might be doubly liable. If a party refuses to be joined the court may deprive him of any right of action against the defendant for the wrong, either unconditionally or subject to such terms or conditions as the court may specify.

The conduct of the defendant which the claimant must prove

In wrongful interference by trespass there must be a *direct* interference with the goods, and this may consist of moving a chattel or the throwing of something at it. A person who writes with his finger in the dust on the back of a car commits wrongful interference, as does a person who beats another's animals or administers poison to them.

In this connection, there have been problems where owners of land have introduced wheel-clamping to prevent the parking of vehicles on their land. The technique is also applied by public authorities to enforce parking restrictions. The legal position was stated definitively by the Court of Appeal in *Vine* v *Waltham Forest LBC* (2000) *The Times*, 12 April where it was ruled:

- that the act of wheel-clamping a car even when the car is on somebody else's land without authorisation is a trespass to goods unless it can be shown that the owner had consented to or willingly assumed the risk of his car being clamped;
- in order to show this, it has to be proved that the owner of the vehicle or its driver (on his behalf) was aware of the consequences of parking the car so that it trespassed on the land of another;
- this can be done by showing that the owner (or driver on his behalf) saw and understood the significance of a warning notice;
- if the notice is seen but not understood, there is nevertheless consent to clamping;

21

■ however, in *Vine*, where the notice was not seen, the clamping was a trespass and the clamper was liable in damages.

It is important to remember that in the *Vine* case the parking was on private land where implied consent following placing of a conspicuous notice is required. However this does not apply to all parking. In London, for example, there is local statute law in the shape of the Road Traffic Act 1991 together with subsidiary regulations made under it. Part II and regulations deal with parking in London. Wheel-clamping is permitted by s 69 of the 1991 Act in the case of a stationary vehicle illegally parked or in a parking place designated for another or other purposes. *Notice is not a requirement.* This gives a clamper the defence of statutory authority. The distinction in *Vine* is that Ms Vine parked her car in a parking bay on private land where the local authority's contractors clamped it. Here implied consent by notice was required. For those who are concerned about the 'cowboy' approach of some clampers reference should be made to the Private Security Industry Act 2001 which imposes and will raise professional standards in the clamping business.

The principle of liability

In wrongful interference by trespass to goods the liability would not now appear to be strict. The defence of inevitable accident would presumably be available to a defendant (*National Coal Board* v *Evans* (1951), see Chapter 20) and it is possible that, since *Letang* v *Cooper* (1964) (see Case **351**), the interference with the possession of goods must be intentional. Mere negligence may not suffice. This would follow a similar development in the tort of trespass to the person which began with the decision in *Fowler* v *Lanning* (1959) (see Case **351**).

Wrongful interference by conversion

The relationship between the claimant and the goods

It is often said that the right to sue for wrongful interference by conversion depends on ownership, but this is not really true. To be able to sue for wrongful interference the claimant must have had either possession or the immediate right to possess at the time the wrong was committed. Mere ownership without one of the above rights is not enough. Nor is the mere right to possess unless it is coupled with ownership.

As in wrongful interference by trespass to goods so in wrongful interference by conversion, the defendant can set up the right of a third party and s 8(1) and (2) of the 1977 Act apply.

The conduct of the defendant which the claimant must prove

In wrongful interference by conversion the defendant must do something which is a complete denial of, or is inconsistent with, the claimant's title to the goods; a mere interference with possession is not enough. Furthermore, wrongful interference by conversion need not be a trespass.

Generally the conduct of the defendant must be an act rather than a failure to act. Thus, although the claimant may base his case on a demand for the goods followed by a refusal, he must still show a denial of title in the defendant. If, therefore, the defendant can show that he was retaining the goods in the exercise of a lien for, say, repair charges unpaid, the claimant will fail in his action. A defendant may also refuse temporarily to give up the goods while he takes steps to check the title of the claimant.

The principle of liability

In general, liability in wrongful interference by conversion is strict and it is not necessary for the claimant to prove that the defendant had a wrong intention, though sometimes it may be a defence for the defendant to say that he acted honestly. Where the defendant had lost the goods by *negligence* there was no wrongful interference by conversion but the claimant may now sue under the provisions of the Torts (Interference with Goods) Act 1977 for damage to goods caused by negligence.

> *Jarvis* v *Williams*, 1955 – Conversion: there must be a right of property (**367**)
> *Fouldes* v *Willoughby*, 1841 – Mere interference with possession (**368**)
> *Oakley* v *Lyster*, 1931 – No need for trespass (**369**)
> *Elvin and Powell Ltd* v *Plummer Roddis Ltd*, 1933 – An honest defendant (**370**)

Detention of goods

Section 2(1) of the Torts (Interference with Goods) Act 1977 abolishes the old tort of detinue which was a tort relating to detention of goods. The Act substitutes statutory provisions. Under s 2(2) the tort of wrongful interference by conversion is substituted for the old action of detinue. Thus mere detention can now amount to conversion. In other words, detinue and conversion are merged.

As regards the form of judgment where goods are detained, s 3 provides that in proceedings for wrongful interference against a person who is in possession or in control of the goods relief may be given if appropriate in accordance with s 3(2). Under s 3(2) the relief is:

(*a*) an order for delivery of the goods, and for payment of any consequential damages; or
(*b*) an order for delivery of the goods, giving the defendant the alternative of paying damages by reference to the value of the goods, together in either alternative with payment of any consequential damages; or
(*c*) damages.

Section 3(2) provides that subject to rules of court relief should be given under only one of paragraphs (*a*), (*b*) and (*c*) above and relief under paragraph (*a*) is at the discretion of the court though the claimant may choose between the others. If it is shown to the satisfaction of the court that an order under (*a*) above has not been complied with, the court may revoke the order or the relevant part of it and make an order for payment of damages by reference to the value of the goods.

Where an order is made under (*b*) above the defendant may satisfy the order by returning the goods at any time before execution of judgment, but without prejudice to liability to pay any consequential damages.

Remedies

Reference has already been made to the form of judgment where goods are detained. So far as wrongful interference by trespass and by conversion are concerned, the remedy is damages. The value of the goods is usually determined at the date of conversion. When a claimant has a claim for conversion he cannot delay the issue of his claim form and the duty to mitigate loss operates. If the goods decrease in value between the date of the conversion and the time the court gives judgment, the claimant will normally still recover the value at the date of conversion (*Rhodes* v *Moules* [1895] 1 Ch 236).

Section 5 of the 1977 Act makes it clear that a claimant's title to the goods is not extinguished by a judgment for damages but only when the judgment has been paid. The judgment as such does not affect title.

21

Under s 6 an allowance is available for an improvement in the goods. For example, where a person in good faith buys a stolen car and improves it he is entitled to an allowance for that improvement, and where a person in good faith buys the car from the improver and is sued in conversion by the true owner, the damages may be reduced to reflect the improvement. Section 7 deals with double liability, providing in particular that where as the result of enforcement of a double liability the claimant is unjustly enriched to any extent he shall be liable to reimburse the wrongdoer to that extent. For example, if a converter of goods pays damages first to a finder of the goods and then to the true owner, the finder is unjustly enriched unless he accounts over to the true owner, which he is required to do, and then the true owner is unjustly enriched and becomes liable to reimburse the converter of the goods.

Special damage for conversion may be awarded. Thus a carpenter whose tools are converted can recover his loss of wages (*Bodley* v *Reynolds* (1846) 8 QB 779). Furthermore, in *Hillesden Securities Ltd* v *Ryjack Ltd* [1983] 2 All ER 184 the defendant converted a Rolls-Royce car which he had hired from the claimant. It was held that he remained liable for the hiring charge until he returned it. This was £13,000, although the value of the Rolls-Royce at the date of conversion was only £7,500.

Finally, s 2(3) of the Limitation Act 1980 provides that once the six-year period of limitation has expired the claimant's title to the goods is extinguished. The Act also provides that if there are successive conversions over the same goods, whether by the same person or not, the cause of action is extinguished six years from the first conversion (Limitation Act 1980, s 3(1)).

Recaption

A person who is entitled to the possession of goods of which he has been wrongfully deprived may retake them after a demand for their return but must not use more than reasonable force. It is not clear whether he may enter upon the land of an innocent third party in order to recover the goods. It would seem lawful only after explanation and permission.

Replevin

Goods which have been taken by what is alleged to be unlawful distress, e.g. by a landlord for unpaid rent which is alleged by the tenant to have been paid, may be recovered by the owner giving security to the Registrar of the county court that he will immediately bring an action to determine the legality of the distress. The Registrar issues a warrant for the restitution of the goods.

Nuisance

The tort of nuisance is of two types – public and private.

Public nuisance

This is some unlawful act or omission endangering or interfering with the lives, comfort, property or common rights of the public, e.g. the obstruction of a highway or the keeping of dangerous premises near a highway. A public nuisance is a crime for which the remedy is criminal proceedings. An example is provided by *R* v *Johnson (Anthony Thomas)* (1996) 160 JP 605 where the Court of Appeal held that obscene phone calls made on numerous occasions to 13 different women amounted to a public nuisance for which J was rightly sentenced to 240 hours of community service and ordered to pay £500 costs. It is actionable as a tort at the suit of a private individual if he has suffered peculiar damage over and above that suffered by the public as a whole.

Obstructions to the highway occur daily in our cities and towns, e.g. road repairs and scaffolding. However, these obstructions, being for reasonable purposes, are lawful unless they last for an excessive time. *Dangerous activities* carried on near to the highway may amount to a nuisance. With regard to *projections* on to the highway there is no liability for *things naturally on land*, e.g. trees, unless the person responsible for them knew, or ought to have known, that they were in a dangerous condition, as where a branch of a tree is rotten. However, liability appears to be strict in the case of *artificial projections*. However, where an action is brought for damages for personal injuries arising out of other forms of obstruction on the highway, it appears that fault is essential to liability. Thus, in this respect, the torts of nuisance and negligence are being drawn together.

Lack of actual knowledge of the nuisance is no defence. Thus in *R* v *Shorrock (Peter)* [1993] 3 All ER 917, S let a field on his farm to three people for the weekend and went away. S did not actually know that the field would be used for an 'acid house' party, which it was, and there were complaints from 275 people living up to four miles away. On prosecution for public nuisance S pleaded that he did not have actual knowledge of the event. It was held by the Court of Appeal that it was not necessary to prove actual knowledge of the nuisance; it was enough to show that S knew *or ought* to have known of it. The evidence seemed to establish that he at least knew there was some risk of creation of a nuisance and that constructive knowledge was enough. It is worth noting that judgments in the House of Lords in *Sedleigh-Denfield* v *O'Callaghan and Others* [1940] AC 880 suggest that constructive knowledge is also enough to found a claim in private nuisance.

> *Attorney-General* v *Gastonia Coaches*, 1976 – Public nuisance: obstruction of highways and public footpaths (**371**)
> *Castle* v *St Augustine's Links Ltd*, 1922 – A golf ball hits a car (**372**)
> *Tarry* v *Ashton*, 1876 – An artificial projection (**373**)
> *Dymond* v *Pearce*, 1972 – Other forms of highway obstruction (**374**)

21

Demise of public nuisance?

In the two following cases the House of Lords has almost passed a death sentence on the common law crime of public nuisance and has noted that the main areas which were once the province of public nuisance have to a large extent been taken over by statutory provisions, e.g. the Environment Protection Act 1990. Prosecutions said the House of Lords should be brought under the relevant statute because the statutory provisions were less vague than the common law concept of public nuisance and the penalties were known and the defences more clearly outlined.

The House of Lords looked again at the ingredients of the crime of public nuisance. Their Lordships affirmed that it requires an act or omission which the defendent knew or ought to have known would cause common injury to a section of the public at large. Thus a number of individual acts of private nuisance committed against several individuals was not an offence nor was an act or omission which had unintended or unforeseen consequences in causing a nuisance.

The above principles were applied in *R* v *Rimmington; R* v *Goldstein* [2006] 1 AC 459.

In *Rimmington* the defendant sent 538 postal packets containing racially offensive material to a number of individual members of the public based on their perceived ethnicity. The House of Lords ruled that these were acts of private nuisance and did not cause common injury to a substantial section of the public.

In *Goldstein* the defendant had owed his friend some money for a long time. When he finally sent his friend a cheque, he put some salt in the envelope as a joke, salt being used to preserve kosher food of which the defendant was a supplier. Unfortunately, the salt leaked out at a postal sorting office and went onto the hands of a postal worker who feared it might be anthrax. The building was evacuated causing disruption to the postal service.

The House of Lords ruled that the defendant could not possibly have intended or foreseen that the salt would leak out, since that would have ruined his joke. Both defendants were not guilty of public nuisance.

It is worth noting that the House of Lords did not rule out totally the existence of public nuisance and the relevant case law but clearly the courts will now require use of the many statutory provisions by prosecutors. (See further p 552.)

Private nuisance

This is an unlawful interference with people's use of their property or with their health, comfort or convenience, and such interference may vary according to the standard existing in the neighbourhood. It is a wrongful act causing material injury to property or sensible personal discomfort. In this connection injuries to *servitudes* may amount to private nuisance as where the defendant obstructs a right of way, or interferes with the claimant's water supply, access of air, light or support. It is worth noting that a local authority by granting planning permission for a development cannot prevent a claim for nuisance if that development causes one. Thus in *Wheeler* v *J J Saunders* [1995] 2 All ER 697 the Court of Appeal decided that the claimant was entitled to damages for nuisance caused by two pig units built on the defendant's land following the granting of planning permission for them by the local authority. Unlike Parliament, a local authority has no authority to authorise a nuisance.

In considering whether an act or omission is a nuisance, the following points are relevant:

(a) **There need be no direct injury to health.** It is enough that a person has been prevented to an appreciable extent from enjoying the ordinary comforts of life.

(b) **The standard of comfort must be expected to vary with the district.** There is no uniformity of standard between Park Lane and Poplar, although there may be common ground in some matters, e.g. light, since it requires the same amount of light to read in either place. However, where the alleged nuisance has caused *actual damage to property*, it is no defence to show that the district concerned is of any particular type.

In what may seem at first sight to be an unusual decision, the Court of Appeal ruled in *Murdoch* v *Glacier Metal Co Ltd* [1998] Env LR 732 that an action for nuisance by noise failed even though the noise was just above World Health Organisation levels for proper sleep. There was already a busy by-pass near to M's home and there were no other complaints from within the area. Thus, applying the standards of the district, M's claim failed.

(c) **A person cannot take advantage of his peculiar sensitivity to noise and smells.** There must be some give and take, and people cannot expect the same amenities in an industrial town as they might enjoy in the country.

(d) The utility of the alleged nuisance has no bearing on the question. Pigsties and breweries may be regarded by the community as very necessary, but if they infringe a person's right to the ordinary comforts of life, they are nuisances (see *Wheeler* above). Consent cannot be implied from the fact that the claimant came to the premises knowing that the nuisance was in existence. Nor is the fact that the nuisance arises out of the conferment of a public benefit a defence in the ordinary way.

Bliss v *Hall*, 1838 – Coming to the nuisance (**375**)

Adams v *Ursell*, 1913 – Public benefit (**376**)

Dunton v *Dover District Council*, 1977 – A noisy playground (**377**)

(e) The modes of annoyance are infinitely various. They may include such things as bell-ringing, circus performing, the excessive use of the radio, spreading tree roots, opening a sex shop in a residential area (*Laws* v *Florinplace* [1981] 1 All ER 659), low-flying aircraft and many others. It should also be noted that picketing a highway may be actionable as a nuisance and an injunction may be granted to prevent it. However, in *Hunter* v *Canary Wharf Ltd* [1997] 2 WLR 684 the House of Lords held that a nuisance action following the erection of a building on land could be brought in regard to interference by noise, dirt or smell but an action in regard to interference with a TV signal would fail.

Christie v *Davey*, 1893 – A versatile amateur musician (**378**)

Hubbard v *Pitt*, 1975 – Picketing the highway (**379**)

(f) A nuisance may result from the acts of several wrongdoers. Any one of them may be proceeded against, and he cannot plead in excuse that the nuisance was a joint effort, although he has a right of contribution against joint tortfeasors for the damages which might be assessed against him.

(g) Duration of the act. Although the acts complained of in nuisance are usually continuous, e.g. the constant emission of pungent smells from a factory, an act may constitute a nuisance even though it is temporary or instantaneous. The duration of the act complained of has a bearing upon the remedy which is appropriate and the court will not often grant an injunction in respect of a temporary nuisance because damages are an adequate remedy. Furthermore, a temporary nuisance may be too trivial to be actionable.

British Celanese Ltd v *A H Hunt (Capacitors) Ltd*, 1969 – A temporary nuisance (**380**)

21

(h) Sometimes malice or evil motive may become the gist of the offence. Malice or motive may be evidence that the defendant was not using his property in a lawful way.

Hollywood Silver Fox Farm v *Emmett*, 1936 – An evil motive (**381**)

(i) It is possible to acquire the right to create a private nuisance by prescription, that is, by 20 years' continuous operation since the act complained of first constituted a nuisance.

There is no corresponding right in respect of a public nuisance. Since a public nuisance is a crime, no length of time will make it legitimate.

Nuisance is primarily a wrong to property, but even where there is no physical damage the court can award compensation for annoyance and discomfort. A claim in private nuisance cannot be based solely upon personal injury, where an action would be in negligence. Claims for personal injuries can be made in public nuisance, though as we have seen in *Dymond* v *Pearce* (1972), *fault* in the defendant is generally required which makes the action in nuisance similar to that in negligence.

Bone v *Seale*, 1975 – No need for diminution in property values (**382**)

Furthermore, the tort of nuisance refers to the unreasonable use of property and is not a matter of reasonable care (compare negligence). Thus the defendant's use of his property may be offensive and constitute a nuisance no matter how careful he is.

Parties to sue or be sued

The occupant of the property affected by the nuisance is the person who should bring the action but a landlord may sue if the nuisance is effecting a permanent injury to his property, e.g. where the defendant is erecting a building which infringes the landlord's right to ancient lights.

Malone v *Laskey*, 1907 – Nuisance: occupier should sue (**383**)

Regarding liability, it is a general rule that the person who creates the nuisance is liable, and this will generally be the occupier. But a landlord may be liable, as a joint tortfeasor with his tenant: (*a*) if he created the nuisance and then leased the property; or (*b*) where the nuisance was due to the landlord's authorising the tenant expressly or impliedly to create or continue the nuisance; or (*c*) where the landlord knew or ought to have known of the nuisance before he let the premises.

Wilchick v *Marks*, 1934 – A landlord who had a right of entry (**384**)
Mint v *Good*, 1951 – A right of entry implied (**385**)
Harris v *James*, 1876 – A landlord authorised the nuisance (**386**)
Smith v *Scott*, 1972 – No authorisation by landlord (**387**)
Brew Bros v *Snax (Ross)*, 1969 – A landlord allowed a nuisance to continue (**388**)

An occupier must abate a nuisance which was on the premises before he took them over, or is placed there afterwards, even by trespassers, provided that the occupier knows or ought to have known of the nuisance. An occupier is also liable for nuisance arising out of the operations of an independent contractor engaged in work on the premises where there is a special danger of nuisance arising from the nature of the works being carried out, e.g. extensive tunnelling operations (and see *Bower* v *Peate* (1876) in Chapter 20).

Sedleigh-Denfield v *O'Callaghan*, 1940 – An occupier must abate a known nuisance (**389**)

Remedies

The remedies for nuisance are three in number:

(a) The injured party may abate the nuisance, that is, remove it, provided that no unnecessary damage is caused, that no injury arises to an innocent third party, e.g. a tenant, and that, where entry on the defendant's land is necessary, a notice requesting the removal of the nuisance has first been given. The remedies of abatement and self-help are limited to situations where lives or property are in danger, said the Court of Appeal in *Co-operative Wholesale Society Ltd* v *British Railways Board* (1995) *The Times*, 20 December. BRB appealed against an award to CWS of £6,056 which was the cost of pulling down and rebuilding BRB's wall which had bulged on to CWS's property. BRB did not agree that the wall was dangerous but agreed with CWS that the latter could rebuild it at their own expense. CWS did so and then claimed to recover the cost from BRB. The Court of Appeal allowed BRB's appeal. The right of abatement and self-help was only available where lives or property were in danger which was not the case here. The first instance order was varied by substituting £1,400, i.e. the cost of demolition only.

(b) He may sue for damages.

(c) He may seek an injunction if (i) damages would be an insufficient remedy; and (ii) the nuisance is a continuing nuisance, e.g. smoke frequently emitted from a chimney. Where a continuing actionable nuisance is proved, only in exceptional circumstances should the court award damages in lieu of an injunction.

> *Kennaway* v *Thompson*, 1980 – Noise from powerboats (**390**)

Defences

Certain defences are available to a person who is charged with committing the nuisance:

(a) The injury is trivial. The legal maxim is: *De minimis non curat lex* (the law does not concern itself with trifling matters). Such a case would be an extremely short exposure to fumes from road repairs.

(b) The so-called nuisance arose from the lawful use of the land (*Bradford Corporation* v *Pickles* (1895), see Chapter 20).

(c) The nuisance was covered by statutory authority, under the general principles elucidated under the defence of statutory authority.

(d) The person committing the alleged nuisance has acquired a prescriptive right through 20 years' use to do what is complained of.

(e) The character of the neighbourhood is such that the act, while it might be a nuisance elsewhere, cannot be regarded as such in that particular district.

(f) Consent of the claimant is a possible defence but consent will not be implied simply because the claimant came to the premises knowing that the nuisance was in existence (*Bliss* v *Hall*, 1838).

> *Sturges* v *Bridgman*, 1879 – Nuisance and prescription (**391**)

21

Remoteness of damage

For the purpose of deciding problems of remoteness of damage the Privy Council held in *The Wagon Mound (No 2)* [1966] 2 All ER 709 (see Chapter 20) that in a case of nuisance, as of negligence, it is not enough that the damage was a direct result of the nuisance if the injury was not *foreseeable*. Thus in *Lamb* v *Camden London Borough Council* [1981] 2 All ER 408 the claimants owned a house which had been let furnished but because of local council work a water main nearby was broken and escaping water severely damaged the house. The tenant left and the house was then unoccupied. While it was empty squatters entered and caused extensive damage before they were evicted. The defendants admitted liability in nuisance and on the issue of the squatters' damage the Court of Appeal held that it was too remote to form part of any damages. (See also *British Celanese* v *Hunt* (1969) and *Page Motors* v *Epsom and Ewell Borough Council* (1981).)

Statutory intervention

We have been discussing the civil law of nuisance. However, there is also the Environmental Protection Act 1990. Under s 80 of that Act an officer of a local authority who is satisfied that a nuisance exists can serve the person responsible for creating it with an abatement notice. Failure to comply is a criminal offence though there is a right of appeal. The section can be used for a wide variety of nuisances from noisy parties to dust from construction or demolition. A complaint is initiated through the environmental health department of the relevant local authority.

There is also the Noise and Statutory Nuisance Act 1993 (as amended by the Clean Neighbourhoods and Environment Act 2005). This makes noise in the street a statutory nuisance and includes provisions in regard to loudspeakers and their operation in the street and, most importantly, audible intruder alarms. Provision is also made for the charging by the enforcing local authority of expenses which have been incurred in abating or preventing the recurrence of the nuisance. Payment is by the person(s) responsible.

Of particular importance is the suppression of the 'rogue' car alarm. However, the procedures involved are complicated and this may put the relevant authorities off enforcement. The first complaint is to the local environmental health officer (EHO). The EHO must then locate the vehicle and affix an 'abatement notice' to it. He must then wait one hour and only then can he act by breaking into the car to switch off the alarm. The Act also states that the EHO must do as little damage to the vehicle as possible and leave it as secure as when he found it. This may mean that other experts such as locksmiths will have to travel with the EHO, which will make enforcement more difficult.

There has been other statutory intervention as follows:

- the Noise Act 1996 (as amended by the Clean Neighbourhoods and Environment Act 2005) gives the local authority a duty to investigate any complaint that excessive noise is coming from another house. If the local authority officer is satisfied that there is such noise and that it exceeds permitted limits and is being emitted between 11 pm and 7 am he may serve a warning notice. If the person responsible continues to create noise during the period specified in the notice and in excess of the permitted level, he is guilty of an offence;
- the Protection from Harassment Act 1997 may also be of help. It is a very wide-ranging Act and covers noisy and nuisance neighbours. These activities could be the subject of criminal or civil proceedings under the Act.

However, the High Court ruled in *Huntingdon Life Sciences Ltd* v *Curtin* (1997) *The Times*, 11 December that Parliament had clearly not intended the Act to be used to prevent individuals from exercising their right to protest and demonstrate about issues of public interest, and the courts would resist any attempts to interpret the statute widely. The claimants were refused an injunction against the British Union for the Abolition of Vivisection which was demonstrating by a non-threatening campaign against the company which used animals for research purposes.

With regard to nuisance caused by the spread of weeds, it is uncertain whether the common law has any rules controlling this (see *Giles* v *Walker* (1890)), and reference should be made to the Weeds Act 1959. Where any one of five specified weeds is out of control the Minister of Agriculture can call on the occupier of the land concerned to take action to stop them from spreading. The Minister can get the work done himself if the occupier defaults, and prosecute the occupier.

Negligence – generally

In ordinary language negligence may simply mean not done intentionally, e.g. the negligent publication of a libel. But while negligence may be one factor or ingredient in another tort, it is also a specific and independent tort with which we are now concerned.

The tort of negligence has three ingredients and to succeed in an action the claimant must show (i) the existence of a duty to take care which was owed to him by the defendant, (ii) breach of such duty by the defendant, and (iii) resulting damage to the claimant.

The duty of care – generally

Whether a duty of care exists or not is a question of law for the judge to decide, and it is necessary to know how this is done. The law of contract dominated the legal scene in the nineteenth century and this affected the law of torts. The judges, influenced by the doctrine of privity of contract, used it to establish the existence of a duty of care in negligence in those cases where a contract existed by laying down the principle that, if A is contractually liable to B, he cannot simultaneously be liable to C in tort for the same act or omission.

The House of Lords in *Donoghue* v *Stevenson* (1932) (see Chapter 20) dispelled the confusion caused by the application of the doctrine of privity of contract where physical injury is caused to the claimant by the defendant's negligent act. As we have seen from the *Donoghue* case, the fact that the maker of the ginger beer was liable for its defects in *contract* to the café owner did not prevent him being liable also to *Donoghue* in the *tort of negligence*. There is, of course, now the possibility of giving third parties rights in contract so that the privity rule is avoided, although the tort claim would still be available, and where the rule of privity applies, the tort remedy is the only one available. This results from the Contracts (Rights of Third Parties) Act 1999 (see further Chapter 10). In this case Lord Atkin also formulated what has now become the classic test for establishing a duty of care when he said:

21

> You must take reasonable care to avoid acts or omissions which you can reasonably foresee would be likely to injure your neighbour. Who then is my neighbour? The answer seems to be persons who are so closely and directly affected by my act that I ought reasonably to have them in contemplation as being affected when I am directing my mind to the acts or omissions which are called in question.

It will be seen, therefore, that the duty of care is established by putting in the defendant's place a hypothetical 'reasonable man' and deciding whether the reasonable man would have foreseen the likelihood or probability of injury, not its mere possibility. The test is objective not subjective, and the effect of its application is that a person is not liable for every injury which results from his carelessness. There must be a duty of care (see *Bourhill* v *Young* (1943) (see Chapter 20)).

Nevertheless, new duties are established from time to time by case law. As we have seen, Lord Macmillan stated in *Donoghue* v *Stevenson* (1932) 'the categories of negligence are never closed'. However, there is always the requirement of foresight, i.e. the claimant must be within the area of foreseeable danger (see *Bourhill* v *Young* (1943), in Chapter 20).

Furthermore, there is, in general terms, no liability for failure to act, i.e. for omissions.

Argy Trading v *Lapid Developments*, 1977 – No liability for omissions (**392**)

Creation of new duties

For a period of time the tendency of the courts was to widen liability in negligence to the point where it was more a matter of public policy whether a particular defendant was liable. The view has been, in some cases, that the court can assume objective foresight and then see whether there is anything to prevent the defendant from being liable, e.g. a very wide liability which is currently not insured against may not be imposed as contrary to public policy.

One major development in this direction was the judgment of Lord Reid in *Home Office* v *Dorset Yacht Club Co Ltd* [1970] 2 All ER 294. This was an action by the owner of a yacht which was damaged by runaway Borstal boys who escaped while the three officers in charge of them were, contrary to instructions, in bed. In holding that the Home Office owed a duty of care to the owner of the yacht, Lord Reid made the following general comment regarding duty of care. '*Donoghue* v *Stevenson* may be regarded as a milestone . . . It will require qualification in new circumstances. But I think that the time has come when we can and should say that it ought to apply unless there is some justification or valid explanation for its exclusion.' In other words, Lord Reid is saying that the court should lean in favour of finding a duty of care. The House of Lords seems also in this case to have found liability for the officers' failure to act, i.e. an omission but this seems to be confined to negligent failure to exercise statutory powers, in this case powers of control over the boys.

Further moves along these lines came in *Anns* v *London Borough of Merton* [1977] 2 All ER 492. In that case, the claimants held a lease of a block of flats built in 1962. Later, considerable settlement caused cracks and the tilting of floors. The claimants blamed the builders and also the local council because, it was alleged, the council had not inspected the flats during building as the by-laws required, so their shallow foundations were not detected. Their Lordships found that the local authority had a duty of care to the claimants and made general comments on the duty of care. Once again, liability arose from a failure to act.

Lord Wilberforce, in particular, took the remarks of Lord Reid (as mentioned) a stage further when he said:

> The position has now been reached that in order to establish that a duty of care arises in a particular situation, it is not necessary to bring the facts of that situation within those of previous situations in which a duty of care has been held to exist. Rather the question has to be approached in two stages.

First, one has to ask whether, as between the alleged wrongdoer and the person who has suffered damage there is a sufficient relationship of proximity or neighbourhood such that, in the reasonable contemplation of the former, carelessness on his part may be likely to cause damage to the latter, in which case a *prima facie* duty of care arises.

Second, if the first question is answered affirmatively, it is necessary to consider whether there are any considerations which ought to negate, or reduce or limit the scope of the duty or the class of person to whom it is owed or the damages to which any breach of it may give rise.

The retreat from *Anns*

However, the Privy Council in *Yuen Kun Yeu* v *Attorney-General of Hong Kong* [1987] 2 All ER 705 and the House of Lords in *Curran* v *Northern Ireland Co-Ownership Housing Association* [1987] 2 WLR 1043 pointed out the danger of assuming that the comments of Lord Wilberforce in *Anns* lead to a rule that objective foreseeability of itself automatically leads to a duty of care and that a defendant with objective foresight is therefore liable unless there are reasons, e.g. public policy, why he should not be so.

The movement towards a position where virtually any event can be foreseen leaving the only bar to liability to rest on public policy came to an end in *Murphy* v *Brentwood District Council* [1990] 2 All ER 908 when the House of Lords overruled its own decision in *Anns* as the 1966 declaration gives it power to do.

The facts of *Murphy* are similar to those of *Anns*, i.e. a house built on inadequate foundations followed by a claim against the local authority for negligent failure to ensure that the house was built in accordance with the relevant regulations. The House of Lords decided that the local authority was not liable and overruled *Anns*. The judgments of the House of Lords indicate that the problem with *Anns* was not so much what it decided in terms of the liability of the local authority but the broad statements as to the duty of care made by Lord Wilberforce in the case. Their Lordships felt that if the case was left as good law, its principles could not be confined to the local authority situation. In fact, it had already started to expand professional liability to the point where accountants, in particular, were unable to get adequate indemnity insurance. In this connection, the retreat from *Anns* is to be seen in the *Caparo* case (see later in this chapter) which some think has gone too far the other way.

It would seem that since *Murphy* we are back to a tighter test of liability. A duty of care will be based upon the need for proximity enshrined in Lord Atkin's neighbour test in *Donoghue*.

Nevertheless, given sufficient proximity new duties can arise in new fact situations. For example, in *Swinney* v *Chief Constable of Northumbria Police* [1996] 3 All ER 449 the Court of Appeal held that the police had a duty of care not to let information supplied to them regarding criminal activities get into the hands of a suspect. A statement by the claimant was allowed, because of police negligence, to get into the hands of a suspect who subjected the claimant to violence and arson of his premises, a public house. He suffered mental injury and had to give up the tenancy of the pub. The Court of Appeal held that he was entitled to damages and no rule of public policy prevented this.

In *Vowles* v *Evans* [2003] 1 WLR 1607 the Court of Appeal ruled that a rugby referee owed a duty of care to his players. The claimant was injured and became confined to a wheelchair when two front rows failed to engage cleanly in the final set scrum of the match. The incident occurred because the referee allowed the substitution of an inexperienced and untrained player to play in the front row without making any inquiry of his captain or the player as to his suitability for the front row.

21

The duty of care – economic loss

An area of some difficulty, and in which there has been much development, is in the field of economic loss. Is there a duty to avoid causing foreseeable economic loss? The position is as follows:

(a) Careless misstatements. These are considered in greater depth later in this chapter. However, broadly speaking, a person who makes a careless statement which causes economic loss to a claimant within the area of his *foresight* may be liable to compensate that claimant for economic loss.

(b) Physical injury – parasitical damages. Damages for economic loss may be awarded if there is foreseeable physical injury to the claimant or his property, though issues of public policy still govern where the line is to be drawn.

> *Weller & Co* v *Foot and Mouth Disease Research Institute*, 1965 – Where economic loss is irrecoverable (**393**)
>
> *SCM (UK) Ltd* v *W J Whittall & Son Ltd*, 1970 – Where economic loss is not a consequence of physical damage (**394**)
>
> *Spartan Steel and Alloys Ltd* v *Martin & Co Ltd*, 1972 – Economic loss following from physical damage (**395**)

(c) The *Junior Books* case. In *Junior Books Ltd* v *Veitchi Co Ltd* [1982] 3 All ER 201 the House of Lords decided that the claimants could recover economic loss which was not parasitical because in that case there was no physical injury to the claimant or his property, but merely faulty work.

However, it would be unwise to assume that injury to person or property is now never necessary. There was a very close proximity in terms of foresight of injury between the parties in *Junior Books* and as a matter of public policy it may still be necessary to restrict liability in cases such as *Weller* where liability was potentially endless. There have, in more recent times, been a considerable number of restrictions placed on *Junior Books* almost confining it to its own facts (see below).

> *Junior Books Ltd* v *Veitchi Co Ltd*, 1982 – A rare recovery of economic loss (**396**)

Breach of the duty

If a duty of care is established as a matter of law, whether or not the defendant was in breach of that duty is a matter to be decided by the judge on the facts of the case, though the standard required, i.e. that of acting as a reasonable man, is a *legal standard*.

Here we are concerned with how much care the defendant must take. It is obvious that if motorists did not take out their cars many lives would be saved, and yet it is not negligent to drive a car. Once again, the test is to place the 'reasonable man' in the defendant's position. It is an objective test and was thus stated by Baron Alderson in *Blyth* v *Birmingham Waterworks Co* (1856) 11 Ex 781:

> Negligence is the omission to do something which a reasonable man guided upon those considerations which ordinarily regulate the conduct of human affairs would do, or doing something which a prudent and reasonable man would not do.

The standard required is not that of a particularly conscientious person but that of the average prudent person in the eyes of the court. It has been said that the reasonable person is to be found on the Clapham omnibus, but it should not be thought that the average prudent person has a low standard of care. Most of us behave unreasonably from time to time, and if during one of these lapses a person suffers injury, it will be no good our pleading that we are usually reasonable people.

> *Daniels* v *R White and Sons Ltd*, 1938 – Duty to take reasonable care (**397**)
>
> *Hill* v *J Crowe*, 1977 – A packing case collapses (**398**)

Causation

It is also necessary for the claimant to prove causation, i.e. that the negligent act in breach of duty actually caused the situation for which he claims.

Thus in *Gregg* v *Scott* [2005] 2 AC 176 the claimant, Mr Gregg, developed a lump under his arm. He went to see Dr Scott, who told him that it was a collection of fatty tissues. One year later another doctor discovered it was cancer of a lymph gland. By this time the claimant's chances of surviving for 10 years or more if treated promptly had fallen, it was said, from 42 per cent to 27 per cent. The tumour had spread to his chest. The treatment temporarily destroyed the tumour but the claimant had a relapse and was left with a poor prospect of survival.

He claimed against Dr Scott in negligence for the loss of a chance of medium term recovery. The House of Lords ruled against him. The reason was, basically, that the court will not move on damages unless the claimant can prove causation. Nobody could say that the claimant's chances of recovery had been reduced. Nobody had actual knowledge of that. When a court is faced with lack of knowledge of the facts of a case it deals with it by burden of proof. The claimant must prove causation. Sadly, neither Mr Gregg nor anyone else could. Even medical science cannot prove a result in cases such as this. Many treatments work, but not all do on all persons. In such a situation the rule of proof of causation will defeat the claim.

Objective standards – professionals

When a person has undertaken a duty which requires extraordinary skill, a higher standard of care will be expected. For example, one would expect from a builder the degree of skill appropriate to a reasonably competent member of his trade and from an accountant or solicitor also an objective standard of competence. Such persons may, therefore, be negligent even though they do their best.

> *Greaves* v *Baynham Meikle*, 1974 – An objective standard (**399**)

Medical practitioners

In the case of medical practitioners, it seems that because allegations of negligence in the medical context are more frequent and serious, a high standard of proof of negligence is required so that an error of clinical judgement does not of itself amount to negligence. Thus in *Whitehouse* v *Jordan* [1981] 1 All ER 267 the claimant was born with severe brain damage following a difficult birth and sued the defendant, a senior hospital registrar, for damages. The defendant had used forceps to assist delivery of the claimant and it was alleged that he pulled too hard and too long. It was held by the Court of Appeal and later by the House of Lords that if the damage had indeed been caused by the defendant's use of forceps the most that could be said with the benefit of hindsight was that he had made an error of clinical judgement which did not of itself amount to negligence, so that the claimant's claim failed.

However, the standard of care in cases of medical negligence is changing. The necessary standard of care required of a doctor towards his patient was laid down in *Bolam* v *Friern Hospital Management Committee* [1957] 2 All ER 118. It was to the effect that a doctor is not liable in negligence if he has acted in accordance with a practice accepted as proper by a responsible body of medical men and women skilled in the particular procedure. This meant that doctors could between them set their own standards of care. In more recent times the *Bolam* case has not been followed. An example is provided by *Newell* v *Goldenberg* [1995] 6 Med LR 371. The claimant complained that he had not been warned of the small risk (1 in 2,300) of a possible failure of his vasectomy. The defendant produced evidence to show that at the relevant time it was not usual for surgeons to give such warning. However, Mantel J held that there was liability and that doctors who did not warn could not be regarded as acting responsibly.

Of even greater importance is the decision of the House of Lords in *Bolitho* v *City and Hackney Health Authority* [1997] 4 All ER 771 where their Lordships qualified the long-established principle outlined in *Bolam*. A court was not bound they said 'to hold that a defendant doctor escapes liability for negligent treatment or diagnosis just because he leads evidence from a number of medical experts who are generally of the opinion that the defendant's treatment or diagnosis accorded with sound medical practice . . . The court has to be satisfied that the exponents of the body of opinion relied on can demonstrate that such an opinion has a logical basis'. The ruling goes wider than medical practitioners in that accountants may not be able to rebut a charge of negligence merely by showing that they have followed standards, e.g. Financial Reporting Standards, issued by the profession. In fact, the Court of Appeal of British Columbia in *Kripps* v *Touche Ross* (1992) 94 DLR (4th) 284 held against Touche Ross on the ground that the accountants had known that a simple application of a Canadian accounting standard would omit material information in the particular case. However, the courts, which lack expertise in these matters, will not often depart from good professional practice, but since *Bolitho* may do so in an appropriate case.

Advocates

Advocates provided an exception to the above rule because no action lay against them for negligence in conducting a case (see *Rondel* v *Worsley* (1967), in Chapter 3) though it did (and does) in respect of preparatory work or advice unless it was pre-trial work intimately connected with the trial itself.

This immunity was removed by the House of Lords in *Hall* v *Simons* (2000) *The Times*, 2 July. The immunity in civil disputes and criminal cases has gone and claims may now be made against barristers and solicitor advocates even in regard to the way in which the trial was conducted in court. In the view of the House of Lords, it was not in the public interest nor in the interest of members of other professions that the advocate's immunity should continue.

Standard set by public policy

In other cases public policy may also require a higher standard of care than the defendant possesses so that again he may be negligent even though he does his best (see *Nettleship* v *Weston* (1971), in Chapter 20).

Other special cases

It should be noted that if precautions are taken which would have been reasonable in the case of persons possessed of the usual faculties of sight and hearing, this will be sufficient to absolve a person who does injury to those not possessed of such faculties, so long as he was not aware of their infirmity. However, persons engaged on operations on the *highway* must act reasonably so as not to cause damage to those who are using the highway, including blind people. Furthermore, the court will take into account the importance of the object which the defendant was trying to achieve and whether it was practicable and necessary for the defendant to have taken the precautions which the claimant alleged should have been taken.

> *Paris* v *Stepney Borough Council*, 1951 – Those with infirmities (**400**)
>
> *Haley* v *LEB*, 1964 – Works on the highway (**401**)
>
> *Watt* v *Hertfordshire County Council*, 1954 – The importance of the objective (**402**)
>
> *Latimer* v *AEC Ltd*, 1953 – What could the defendant reasonably do? (**403**)

Resulting damage to the claimant

It is necessary for the claimant to show that he has suffered some loss, since negligence is not actionable *per se* (in itself). A breach of contract with no loss will at least give an action for nominal damages but not so in tort. The major problem arising here is the question of remoteness of damage which was dealt with earlier in the chapter. The judge decides the measure of general damages.

Res ipsa loquitur

Although the burden of proof in negligence normally lies on the claimant, there is a principle known as *res ipsa loquitur* (the thing speaks for itself), and where the principle applies the court is prepared to lighten his burden. The principle applies wherever it is so unlikely that such an accident would have happened without the negligence of the defendant that the court could find, without further evidence, that it was so caused. It seems also to be a commonsense rule in that there is no point in asking the claimant to prove negligence because he has no view of what happened. If two cars collide on a public road, at least the drivers have a view of what happened prior to the crash but when, for example, a barrel falls out of a warehouse on to A he has no view at all of the happenings leading to the impact.

   However, two conditions must be satisfied:

(*a*) the thing or activity causing the harm must be wholly under the control of the defendant or his servants; and

(*b*) the accident must be one which would not have happened if proper care had been exercised.

> *Easson* v *LNE Railway*, 1944 – No exclusive control (**404**)
>
> *Roe* v *Minister of Health*, 1954 – A defective ampoule (**405**)
>
> *Byrne* v *Boadle*, 1863 – A falling barrel (**406**)
>
> *Scott* v *London and St Katherine Docks*, 1865 – Falling bags of sugar (**407**)

21

It should be noted that just because the principle *res ipsa loquitur* applies, it is not certain that the claimant will succeed; the court is not bound to find the defendant negligent. The defendant may be able to prove how the accident happened and that he was not negligent. He may not know how the accident happened but he may be able to prove that it could not have arisen from his negligence. Finally, he may suggest ways in which the accident could have happened without his negligence, and the court may find his explanations convincing. If a tile falls off Y's roof and injures X who is lawfully on the highway below, this would probably be a situation in which *res ipsa loquitur* would apply. But if Y can show that at the time an explosion had occurred nearby and this had probably dislodged the tile, and the court is impressed by this explanation of the event, the burden of proof reverts to X. However, it is not enough to offer purely hypothetical explanations (*Moore* v *R Fox and Sons* [1956] 1 All ER 182), nor is it sufficient to explain how the accident happened unless the explanation also shows that the defendant was not negligent (*Colvilles* v *Devine* [1969] 2 All ER 53).

> *Pearson* v *North-Western Gas Board*, 1968 – Rebutting a presumption of negligence (**408**)

If the defendant successfully rebuts the presumption of *res ipsa loquitur* the claimant has to establish his case by positive evidence. He will probably be unable to do this by the very nature and cause of the accident and the chances are that he may lose his claim. If he had had such positive evidence he would probably have adduced it in the first place and not relied on the maxim at all.

Contributory negligence

Sometimes when an accident occurs, both parties have been negligent and this raises the doctrine of *contributory negligence*. At one time a claimant guilty of contributory negligence could not recover any damages unless the defendant could, with reasonable care, have avoided the consequences of the claimant's contributory want of care. Thus the courts were often concerned to find out who had the last chance of avoiding the accident, and this led to some unsatisfactory decisions.

Now, however, under the Law Reform (Contributory Negligence) Act 1945, liability is apportionable between claimant and defendant. The claim is not defeated but damages may be reduced according to the degree of fault of the claimant. A person may contribute to the *damage* he suffers although he is not to *blame* for the accident. Thus failure by a claimant to wear a crash helmet on a motor cycle or moped may reduce the damages he obtains on the ground of contributory negligence (*O'Connell* v *Jackson* [1971] 3 All ER 129). Similarly, failure by a claimant to wear a seat belt in a motor car *may* also reduce damages on the grounds of contributory negligence (*Froom* v *Butcher* [1975] 3 All ER 520 (see below)). The defence of contributory negligence also applies to an action brought under the Fatal Accidents Act. Thus a wife whose husband failed to wear a seat belt and was thrown out of the van he was driving and killed had her damages reduced by one-fifth (*Purnell* v *Shields* [1973] RTR 414).

Where a defendant is insured against the injury he has caused, which is often the case, the effect of a finding of contributory negligence is in a sense to punish the claimant. There have been suggestions in case law that the rule should be abolished where the defendant is insured since the doctrine merely saves the insurance company money. However, in *Froom* v *Butcher* [1975] 3 All ER 520, Lord Denning disapproved of these cases and held that where injuries resulting from a road accident would have been prevented or lessened if a fitted seat belt had been worn, the failure to wear a seat belt amounted to contributory negligence on the part of the claimant and damages awarded should therefore be reduced. In consequence, Lord Denning has produced an additional definition of contributory negligence so that there are two:

(*a*) to contribute to the accident, which is the old view of contributory negligence; and
(*b*) to contribute to the resulting damage, which is a new concept.

Furthermore, in *Froom* Lord Denning laid down a rather precise formula for contributory negligence in order to introduce as much certainty as possible in road traffic cases and reduce the number of trials, by saying that if failure to wear a seat belt by a front-seat passenger or driver would have made no difference, then nothing should be taken off the damages. If it would have prevented the accident altogether the damages should be reduced by 25 per cent, and if the accident would have been less severe the damages should be reduced by 15 per cent, though exemptions would be made, said Lord Denning, for pregnant women and those who were very fat.

Since 1983 it has been a criminal offence for the driver and front-seat passenger not to wear seat belts. The courts may therefore reduce still further the damages where a seat belt is not worn. It is thought unlikely that they will refuse to give damages altogether because the claimant is breaking the law, i.e. the defence will probably not be able to raise *ex turpi causa* (see Chapter 16) as a complete defence.

Since the rules relating to the wearing of seat belts are now extended in many cases to rear seat passengers no doubt their damages will be reduced if they are injured while not wearing a belt.

It should be noted that the rules laid down by Lord Denning do not prevent the courts from looking at all the circumstances of the case. For example, in *Jones* v *Morgan* (1994) Current Law, Week No 26, the damages awarded to a taxi-driver as a result of the injuries caused by the negligent driving of the defendant were not reduced because he was not wearing a seat belt. The court took into account the fact that a taxi-driver may be attacked by a passenger and a seat belt if attached would inhibit his ability to defend himself.

It should be mentioned that a young child will not normally be guilty of contributory negligence but it is a matter of fact in each case. Furthermore, the contributory negligence of an adult who happened to be with the child is no defence to an action brought by the child.

> *Jones* v *Lawrence*, 1969 – Contributory negligence and children (**409**)
> *Oliver* v *Birmingham Bus Co*, 1932 – A grandfather's negligence (**410**)

21

Furthermore, it was held in *Yianni* v *Edwin Evans & Sons* [1981] 3 All ER 592 that a house buyer who relies on a valuation of the property he is buying prepared by a building society surveyor is not contributorily negligent because he has not had the property surveyed by another independent surveyor employed by himself.

The victim's contributory negligence is no defence where the victim's claim is for deceit (fraud). Thus if an employer, A, is made vicariously liable for damage caused by an employee's fraud in overvaluing properties in order to obtain higher mortgages, it is no defence for A to say that C, the victim, did not use usual procedures to check on the fraudulent valuations (*Alliance & Leicester Building Society* v *Edgetop Ltd* [1994] 2 All ER 38). (For other non-fraudulent situations, see below.)

It was also held in *Corporation Nacional del Cobre de Chile* v *Sogemin Metals Ltd* [1997] 2 All ER 917 that the defence of contributory negligence was not available to the defendant where he had bribed the claimant's employee to act contrary to its interests in making futures contracts, i.e. contracts made for the future delivery of goods at a price fixed at the time of the contract which price may rise or fall by the time of delivery.

Contributory negligence in property valuation

One of the most difficult areas in terms of contributory negligence in business has been the use of the concept where a lender, such as a building society, bank or other mortgage lender, lends money on a property that valuers have in the event and by negligence overvalued. If the borrower cannot repay the loan and the lender repossesses the property and sells it, but because of the negligent valuation (and not because of a falling market) fails to recover what was lent and sues the valuer, what happens if the valuer puts in a defence of contributory negligence on the basis that the lender is partly to blame in that the inability of the borrower to repay is in part due to the lender's failure to properly vet his financial circumstances? If this is a cause of the sale, then a defence of contributory negligence is relevant.

In these cases the first step is to establish what is the basic loss of the lender. This will be the difference betwen the amount of the loan and the sale price. This must be reduced by a percentage for contributory negligence by the lender (see *Platform Home Loans Ltd* v *Oyston Shipways Ltd* [2000] 2 AC 190).

The second step is to see whether the basic loss now exceeds the amount of the overvaluation (see *Banque Bruxelles Lambert SA* v *Eagle Star Insurance* [1997] 1 WLR 1627). If it does, the lender's right of recovery from the valuer is limited to the extent of the overvaluation.

Thus, if the overvaluation was £3,000 and the lender's loss on re-sale was after deduction of contributory negligence £2,000, the lender would recover £2,000. If, however, the lender's loss was £4,000 after deduction for contributory negligence, he would recover only £3,000. In the absence of contributory negligence, he would recover the actual loss.

Contributory negligence and deceit

In *Standard Chartered Bank* v *Pakistan National Shipping Corp (Reduction of Damages)* [2001] QB 167 the Court of Appeal affirmed that a defendant who has been found liable for deceit, as in a fraudulent misrepresentation, cannot successfully establish a defence based upon the contributory fault of the claimant. The defendants had fraudulently issued a bill of lading to the bank giving a false shipping date for goods which they knew would cause the bank to make payment of a letter of credit. The defendants tried to defend the claim against them by alleging the bank's contributory negligence in failing to notice certain discrepancies in the bill of lading. This defence failed.

Contributory negligence – warning the victim

The fact that the victim of negligence received a warning of possible harm will not mean that the damages will be totally eliminated. In *Brannan* v *Airtours plc* (1999) *The Times*, 1 February the defendants put on a party with unlimited free wine, as part of a package holiday. Guests were told not to stand on tables because of danger from overhead fans. The claimant climbed on to a table and was injured by a fan. The trial judge reduced his damages by 75 per cent, but the Court of Appeal said the defendants could have avoided the damage by ensuring that tables were not under fans, and so assessed contributory negligence at 50 per cent.

The effect of warnings was also raised in one of the first reported cases on the subject of whether the smoking of tobacco constituted contributory negligence in terms of a death from cancer of the lung.

The matter was raised in *Badger* v *Ministry of Defence* [2005] 3 All ER 173. The claimant's husband died of lung cancer. The primary responsibility for this rested with, and was admitted by, his employer because he had been exposed to asbestos dust and fibres in his work as a boiler maker. However, his employer asked for a reduction in the damages because he had smoked from 1955 onwards and this was a cause also of lung cancer.

The High Court did not regard the early years of his smoking as contributory negligence because the connection between smoking and ill-health was not widely accepted. However, he continued to smoke after 1971 when warnings were put on cigarette packets and this began the process of contributory negligence. The damages were reduced by 20 per cent.

The doctrine of alternative danger or the 'dilemma principle'

It sometimes happens that a person is injured in anticipating negligence. If a passenger jumps off a bus which he believes to be out of control, and breaks his leg in so doing, he is not prejudiced by the fact that the driver later regains control and the anticipated accident is averted. He is not deprived of his remedy. This is sometimes referred to as the *doctrine of alternative danger*, and an act done in the agony of the moment cannot be treated as contributory negligence. Thus in *Jones* v *Boyce* (1816) 1 Starkie 493, in a coach accident, the claimant was placed by the negligence of the defendant in a perilous alternative either to jump or not to jump. He jumped off the coach and was injured and it transpired that had he kept his seat he would have escaped. However, he was able to recover from the defendant because he had acted reasonably and in the apprehension of danger.

Statutory duties

Sometimes a particular duty of care is laid upon a person by statute, e.g. the duty laid on an employer as to guarding machinery under safety legislation. Such duties are high and very often absolute, though the employer can plead contributory negligence as a defence. In addition, where there is a breach of a statutory duty, it must be shown that the duty is owed to the claimant personally and not to the public as a whole.

Atkinson v *Newcastle Waterworks Co*, 1877 – Where the duty is owed to the public (**411**)

A conditional statutory power saying that the person upon whom it is conferred may act cannot be converted into a statutory duty which says he must act. Thus in *East Suffolk Rivers Catchment Board* v *Kent* [1940] 4 All ER 527, a river catchment board, which had a power to repair river banks, could not be sued successfully for failing to do so on the grounds that a statutory duty had been breached.

However, where a statute prescribes provision to prevent damage, if an action is brought, the harm resulting from the breach of duty must be of the type contemplated by the statute.

Gorris v *Scott*, 1874 – Is the damage of the type contemplated? (**412**)

Compensation Act 2006

Before leaving negligence generally, note should be taken of the Compensation Act 2006. This Act is designed to overcome some of the problems created by claims management companies encouraging persons who have suffered injury where there might be negligence to 'have a go' under the 'no-win, no-fee' arrangements. The problems are that desirable activities such as school trips and school camps etc. abroad have been reduced and stifled by fear of litigation if anything goes wrong. The Act deals with this as follows:

21

- the court should consider whether the usual standards of care should apply where if they are so applied it may prevent a desirable activity from being undertaken; or
- discourage persons from organising and taking part in them;
- an apology or offer of treatment or other redress shall not in itself amount to an admission of negligence.

The Act also sets up the office of regulator of claims management services. These must be authorised by the regulator who will then supervise their conduct.

It has already been noted that the Act deals with the decision in *Barker* v *Corus (UK) plc* [2006] 2 WLR 1027 by restoring the joint and several liability ruling in *Fairchild* v *Glenhaven Funeral Services Ltd* [2003] 1 AC 32.

Negligence – product liability

Here we shall consider the liability of a manufacturer for defective goods where in the absence of a contract between the parties liability is based on the common law of negligence and to some extent now on statute law.

Physical injury

Where the goods are purchased from a retailer, no action can be brought under the Sale of Goods Act by the purchaser against the manufacturer. The doctrine of privity of contract applies (see Chapter 10) with the result that there is no contract between them into which the warranties and conditions set out in the Act can be implied. However, the purchaser may have an action in negligence against the manufacturer in respect of *physical* injury caused by defects in the goods (see *Donoghue* v *Stevenson* (1932)). The rule arrived at in *Donoghue* v *Stevenson* has been widened since 1932, and now applies to defective chattels generally which cause injuries to purchasers (see *Grant* v *Australian Knitting Mills Ltd* (1936), in Chapter 14). However, although the *Donoghue* case shows that the manufacturer has a duty to take care, evidence may show that he was not in breach of that duty because he took proper precautions.

In addition, liability in negligence is not strict as it is under the Sale of Goods Act. The claimant must prove negligence in the process of manufacture. However, assistance is given by the plea of *res ipsa loquitur* (the thing speaks for itself). If this plea is accepted by the court the defendant must as we have seen show he was not negligent or explain how the matter could have come about without his negligence. If he fails to do this the claimant wins the case.

In this regard, the decision of the Court of Appeal in *Carroll* v *Fearon* [1998] PIQR P416 is of interest. In that case one of the tyres on a car suffered a sudden and complete failure resulting in tread strip while on a motorway, and causing a collision with one fatality and a number of serious injuries. The makers of the tyre defended a claim for negligence by saying that the claimants must prove what act(s) of theirs made the tyre defective. However, the court ruled that the manufacturers were negligent and liable and it was not necessary to identify specific acts of negligence in the process of manufacture of the tyre. The facts themselves spoke of negligence by the maker, which was enough.

In certain of the cases mentioned above the question of inspection of the goods was raised. It was an important fact in the decision in *Donoghue* v *Stevenson* (1932) that the bottle was made of dark glass, so that the snail could not be seen on external inspection of the bottle, and that normally no inspection of goods would take place until they reached the consumer. It is not thought that in the developing law of negligence a manufacturer can rely on an inspection revealing the defects in his product, except perhaps in a special case where it is known that an expert inspection normally takes place. If such an inspection does not take place, or fails to find the defect which it should have found, the manufacturer may regard this as a *novus actus interveniens* (a new act intervening) breaking the chain of causation between his negligence and the injury so that the claimant's claim will fail.

The purchaser of goods from a retailer may have a right to sue in contract under the Sale of Goods Act conditions and warranties if third-party rights have been conferred on him (or implied) under the Contracts (Rights of Third Parties) Act 1999.

Economic loss

Product liability in negligence has, up to recent times, been confined to defective chattels which cause *physical* injury to purchasers as in *Donoghue* and *Grant*. The law seemed to have taken a step forward in the *Junior Books* case by extending product liability in negligence to complaints relating to defects in goods which had caused economic loss rather than physical injury. This seems unlikely to develop at the present time for the reasons given in the comment to the case.

Contributory negligence

Even though the claimant has managed to prove negligence in the manufacturer the latter may still be able to obtain a reduction in the damages or even defeat the claim by proving that the claimant was guilty of contributory negligence as where he contributed to the damage or was even entirely responsible for it by, for example, failing to observe operating instructions or using the product after knowledge that it was defective. As we have seen, the Law Reform (Contributory Negligence) Act 1945 applies. Under it the court may, for example, assess damages at £20,000 but decide that the claimant was 50 per cent to blame and reduce the damages to £10,000. In an extreme case the court may decide that the claimant was 100 per cent to blame so that he recovers nothing.

Third-party proceedings

Strict liability under the Act of 1979 can, in effect, be imposed on a manufacturer by means of third- (or fourth-)party proceedings. Thus, if the seller is sued by the buyer for breach of an implied condition under the Act, the seller may claim an indemnity from his own supplier which may be the manufacturer. If the retailer has purchased from a wholesaler, the retailer may claim an indemnity from the wholesaler who may in turn claim an indemnity from the manufacturer who supplied the goods. In this way the manufacturer can be made to pay for defects affecting the quality or fitness of the goods. *Godley* v *Perry* (1960) (see Chapter 14) provides an example of joinder of parties in a civil action. In connection with third-party proceedings, it should be borne in mind that the retailer may be unable to make a successful claim because of a 'reasonable' exclusion clause in the contract between him and his previous suppliers. In addition, the retailer's claim will be ineffective if one or more of the previous suppliers is insolvent.

Collateral contracts with the manufacturer

The manufacturer may also be liable for defects in quality or fitness under a collateral contract. Thus in *Shanklin Pier Ltd* v *Detel Products Ltd* [1951] 2 All ER 471 Shanklin entered into a contract with A to paint the pier and asked A to use paint made by Detel, the suitability of which had been communicated to Shanklin by Detel's agent. The paint was not suitable and Shanklin recovered damages against Detel for breach of a contract which the court held was collateral to the main contract with A. This applies, however, only where a specific and express undertaking has been given by the manufacturer to the seller, and it is doubtful whether such a claim could be based on statements made in a manufacturer's public advertisements. There are no firm illustrations of this in English law, though *Carlill* v *Carbolic Smoke Ball Co* (1893) (see Chapter 9) could perhaps be developed. The court did not in fact go for the collateral contract solution in *Lambert* v *Lewis* (1981) (see Chapter 14). The action against the manufacturer in that case was framed in negligence.

The Law Commission has recognised the need to provide some *general* form of action against the manufacturer but has determined that this cannot be done by a simple amendment to the Sale of Goods Act 1979. The Commission, therefore, recommends that a wider study of the problem be made before embarking upon legislative measures (*Exemption Clauses, First Report*, para 63).

Manufacturers' guarantees

A manufacturer's guarantee (or warranty, as it is sometimes called) normally amounts to a warranty to repair or replace during a specified time with the addition in the case of vehicles of a mileage limit. Such guarantees are presumably enforceable by the buyer as a collateral contract as in *Carlill* v *Carbolic Smoke Ball Co* (1893) (see Chapter 9 and also Chapter 14 in connection with guarantees under the provisions of the Sale and Supply of Goods to Consumers Regulations 2002).

They cannot affect the purchaser's right to sue upon the implied conditions and warranties set out in the Sale of Goods Act 1979 or at common law for negligence because under s 5 of the Unfair Contract Terms Act 1977 a clause in a manufacturer's or distributor's guarantee cannot operate to exclude or restrict the manufacturer's or distributor's liability to the customer, provided the goods are of a type ordinarily supplied for private use or consumption and prove defective while in consumer use, i.e. not used exclusively for the purposes of a business.

It should be noted, of course, that in addition to the above three procedures which overcome the privity rule, there is also now the possibility that third-party rights have been conferred on the claimant (or implied) by the Contracts (Rights of Third Parties) Act 1999.

This Act does not confer a *general* right on a purchaser against the manufacturer. It will only do so if the parties to the original contract (say, between the manufacturer and the retailer) confers such a right or if it can be implied that such rights exist in the circumstances of the case.

Statutory product liability – claims against the manufacturer

The Consumer Protection Act 1987 now provides a statutory basis for a claim against the manufacturer.

Part I of the Consumer Protection Act 1987

This brings into law strict product liability so that the consumer will no longer have to prove negligence when claiming compensation for damage or injury caused by products which are defective or unsafe. Civil liability will arise if damage is caused by a defective product. The

Act is by no means a 'cure-all' because the claimant will still have to prove that the product *caused* the injury – not always an easy matter.

Damage is described as death, personal injury, or loss of or damage to *private* property. Thus, damage to business property is not included. Furthermore, damage to property cannot be recovered unless it exceeds £275. If it does then the whole amount is recoverable, including the first £275. This is to prevent trivial claims for damage to property.

In assessing whether the product is unsafe, the court must have regard to any warnings as to its use in advertising and marketing in general, instructions for use, how long ago the goods were supplied, and whether the product was put to what might be described as a reasonable use.

The following may be liable under the Act: the manufacturer of the product; a person who puts his name on the product thus holding himself out to be the manufacturer, i.e. a supermarket 'own brand' which is made for it by another manufacturer; an importer and a supplier if that supplier will not respond to a request to identify the person who supplied the product to him.

It is a defence to show that: (*a*) the product was not supplied in the course of a business; (*b*) the defect did not exist when the product was supplied; (*c*) technical knowledge was such that the defect could not have been known (called the 'development risk defence'). Hence, the manufacturers of the drug Thalidomide may well have had a defence under the Act. However, manufacturers pressed for the retention of the development risk defence so as not to inhibit the development of new products.

The Act provides that any attempt to exclude liability by a term of a contract or notice will be ineffective. An injured party has three years in which to commence an action after the injury and discovery of the producer. There is a time bar on claims in any event 10 years from when the product was supplied.

The Act did not impose liability on the producer of game or agricultural produce provided it has not undergone an industrial process. SI 2000/2771 now extends Part I to do so.

> *Abouzaid* v *Mothercare* (*UK*) *Ltd*, 2000 – Older products (**412a**)
> *Bogle* v *McDonald's Restaurants Ltd*, 2002 – The hot drinks (**412b**)

Part II of the Consumer Protection Act 1987

21

This repeals the Consumer Safety Act 1978 and the Consumer Safety (Amendment) Act 1986 and provides a better legal framework to give the public protection from unsafe goods. The main provisions are as follows:

(a) A person is guilty of an offence if he supplies any *consumer* goods which fail to comply with the general safety requirement. Section 10 of the 1987 Act which contained the general safety requirements is disapplied by the General Product Safety Regulations 1994 (SI 1994/2328). The Regulations now contain the general safety requirements for goods and these are expanded so that producers of consumer goods and those involved in the supply chain, e.g. distributors, will have to ensure among other things that their internal systems are equipped to supply the consumer with information required by the Regulations, e.g. warning of any risks in use and precautions to be taken, and that product recall procedures are adequate. The goods must be ordinarily intended for private use or consumption.

(b) The government may make safety regulations for the purpose of defining the general safety requirement set out in (*a*) above.

(c) The Department of Trade and Industry may serve upon a supplier a 'prohibition notice' prohibiting him from supplying goods which are considered unsafe or a 'notice to warn' requiring him to publish a warning about the goods at his own expense.

(d) A suspension notice may also be served by enforcement authorities, e.g. weights and measures authorities, prohibiting a supplier from supplying specified goods where the authority has reasonable grounds for suspecting that there has been a contravention of the general safety requirement, any safety regulations or any prohibition notice.

Part II is primarily enforced by criminal sanctions. However, the duties laid down in Part II can assist a claimant in a civil claim which is why reference has been made to them. A claimant injured by goods which infringe the safety requirements of the Act will be able to bring a claim for damages in negligence on the basis that the manufacturer is in breach of his statutory duty under the Act. This will make the claimant's suit much easier since he or she will not have to show a duty of care at common law. In this respect the Act is available to those who have no contractual claim against the seller as where they have received the goods as a gift.

Part III of the Act is concerned with misleading price indications but here again the sanctions are criminal not civil, and since they do not have relevance to civil claims Part III is not considered further.

Negligence – professional liability

We have considered the scope of a manufacturer's liability for defective products which he puts into circulation and the way in which a consumer can take direct action against a manufacturer in negligence. The law of negligence also applies to the provision of services. In particular, we are concerned with the position of those whose work involves giving professional business advice. The law has developed mainly in cases against accountants but the principles apply also to e.g. lawyers and valuers and surveyors.

The background and development

Liability for negligent statements is an important area of the law, and the number of claims continues to increase. Negligent *statements* are now a more potent cause of actions at law than negligent *acts*. This state of affairs has had, and will continue to have, a major influence on the cost of indemnity insurance arrangements.

It was not always so. For example, in *Candler v Crane, Christmas* [1951] 2 KB 164 Mr Ogilvie, the owner of a number of companies, was anxious to obtain an investment in them from Mr Candler. The defendants, a firm of accountants, prepared financial statements for Mr Ogilvie, *knowing* that they were to be shown to Mr Candler as a basis for his investment decision. Mr Candler did invest some money but a liquidation followed and he lost it.

He sued the defendants for damages, alleging negligent preparation of the financial statements. It was claimed that the defendants included freehold cottages and leasehold buildings as corporate assets without obtaining ownership evidence.

It was further claimed that the cottages were, in fact, owned by Mr Ogilvie, and that the title deeds were deposited with his bank to secure a personal overdraft. The leasehold buildings, it was alleged, did not belong to the company, but to Mr Ogilvie, and in any case, they had been forfeited, it was said, for non-payment of rent.

To succeed Mr Candler had first to establish, *as a matter of law*, that the defendants owed him a duty of care. If they had indeed been negligent in the preparation of the accounts this could then give rise to liability. The majority of the Court of Appeal decided that there was no duty of care in such circumstances, and so the accountants were not liable to Mr Candler, and would not have been, even if it had been proved that the financial statements were prepared negligently. There was no further appeal.

However, Lord Denning dissented from the majority view, being of the opinion that the accountants did owe a duty to Mr Candler, even though he was not a client. In his judgment, he said:

> I think the law would fail to serve the best interests of the community if it should hold that accountants and auditors owe a duty to no one but their client. There is a great difference between the lawyer and the accountant. The lawyer is never called on to express his personal belief in the truth of his client's case, whereas the accountant, who certifies the accounts of his client, is always called on to express his personal opinion whether the accounts exhibit a true and correct view of his client's affairs, and he is required to do this not so much for the satisfaction of his own client, but more for the guidance of share-holders, investors, revenue authorities and others who may have to rely on the accounts in serious matters of business. In my opinion, accountants owe a duty of care not only to their own clients, but also to all those whom they know will rely on their accounts in the transactions for which those accounts are prepared.

However, although Lord Denning was prepared to widen the liability of accountants to encompass a person who was not a client, he does appear to have restricted that liability to persons who it is *known* will rely on the accounts, as the last sentence of the above extract from his judgment clearly reveals. But he was alone in his view of the case, and the expansion of the liability of accountants (and others) for negligent statements had to wait for more than a decade.

In *Hedley Byrne & Co Ltd* v *Heller & Partners* (1963) (see Chapter 13), the House of Lords overruled the majority judgment of the Court of Appeal in *Candler*, and approved the dissenting judgment of Lord Denning.

The decision in *Hedley Byrne* widened the liability of all professionals (including, of course, accountants), but the House of Lords refrained, as a matter of public policy, from imposing the even wider test of *foresight* formulated by Lord Atkin in *Donoghue* v *Stevenson* (1932). That case, as we have seen, related to negligence actions for *physical injury* arising from negligent *acts*, e.g. liability for a negligently manufactured product which causes physical injury to a consumer. Liability under that test extended to anyone who might reasonably be foreseen as suffering injury.

The need for a special relationship – knowledge of victim

Instead the House of Lords decided that in the negligent *statement* cases, there had to be a 'special relationship' between the maker of the statement and the person injured by it. Obviously, this need not be a contractual client relationship. Although their Lordships did not draw up a list of special relationships, comments made by them in their judgments suggest that the duty in regard to a negligent statement would be owed only to those persons whom the maker of the statement *knows* will rely on it, and not beyond that to those whom he might *foresee* relying on it. Thus, the test for negligent statements causing monetary loss (knowledge) was narrower than that for negligent acts causing physical injury (foresight), though, in all honesty, it was difficult to see why liability as such should depend upon the nature of the damage.

21

Indeed, during the decade following *Hedley Byrne* there were a number of judicial decisions which suggested that the foresight test propounded in *Donoghue* v *Stevenson* could be appropriate in the negligent statement situation thus potentially widening liability (see below). This development was of course encouraged by the judgment of Lord Wilberforce in *Anns* v *London Borough of Merton* (1977), already referred to.

From knowledge to foresight

Lord Wilberforce's view that judges should consider broad principle rather than slavishly follow relevant previous decisions enabled Mr Justice Woolf to break out of the *Hedley Byrne* strait-jacket of 'special relationships' in *JEB Fasteners Ltd* v *Marks, Bloom & Co* [1981] 3 All ER 289. In April 1975, the defendants, a firm of accountants, prepared an audited set of accounts for a company called BG Fasteners Ltd for the year ended 31 October 1974. The company's stock, which had been bought for some £11,000, was shown as being worth £23,080, that figure being based on the company's own valuation of the net realisable value of the stock.

The accountants nevertheless described the stock in the accounts as being 'valued at lower of cost and net realisable value'. On the basis of the inflated stock figure, the accounts showed a profit of £11.25. If the stock had been shown at cost, with a discount for possible errors, the accounts would have shown a loss of more than £13,000.

The defendant auditors were aware when they prepared the accounts that the company faced liquidity problems, and was looking for outside financial support from, amongst other people, the claimants, JEB Fasteners, who manufactured similar products and were anxious to expand their business. The accounts which the defendants had prepared were made available by the directors of BG to the claimants, who, although they had some reservations about the stock valuation, decided that they would take the company over in June 1975 for a nominal amount, because they would in so doing obtain the services of the company's two directors who had considerable experience in the type of manufacturing which the claimants, JEB, carried on.

There were discussions between the claimants and the defendant auditors during the takeover, but the auditors did not inform the claimants that the stock had been put into the accounts at an inflated figure. The merger of the companies was not a financial success, and the claimants brought an action for damages against the defendants.

The claimants alleged that the defendants had prepared the company's accounts negligently, and that they relied on the accounts when buying BG Fasteners, and would not have bought the company had they been aware of its true financial position. It was contended on behalf of JEB that an auditor when preparing a set of accounts owes a duty to all persons whom he ought reasonably to have foreseen would rely on the accounts. The defendant auditors argued that if a duty of care existed, it could only be to persons who had made a specific request for information.

Woolf, J decided that the defendant auditors did owe a duty of care to the claimants, but that they were not liable in damages, since their alleged negligence was not the cause of the loss. The overriding reason for the takeover had been to obtain the services of two of BG's directors. On the balance of probabilities, the takeover would have gone ahead even if the accounts had shown the true position.

The judge said that, but for the statement of Lord Wilberforce in *Anns* (as mentioned), Marks, Bloom would not have owed a duty of care to those who took over BG because the foresight test could not have been applied, and a 'special relationship' would not have existed (it was admitted that at the time the accounts in question were audited, Marks, Bloom did not know that they would be relied on by the claimants, or even that any takeover was contemplated).

Furthermore, Woolf, J, having found a duty of care, said that following the Wilberforce test in *Anns*, he could find no considerations which he felt ought to exclude it in the circumstances of the *JEB* case.

As regards the foreseeability issue, the judge said:

As Mr Marks was aware of the financial difficulties of BG Fasteners Ltd, and the fact that they were going to need financial support from outside of some sort, I am satisfied that Mr Marks, whom I can treat as being synonymous with the defendants, ought to have realized the accounts could be relied on until the time that a further audit was carried out by the commercial concerns to whom BG Fasteners were bound to look for financial assistance. When he audited the accounts, Mr Marks would not know precisely who would provide the financial support, or what form the financial support would take, and he certainly had no reason to know that it would be by way of takeover by the [claimants].

However, this was certainly one foreseeable method, and it does not seem to me that it would be right to exclude the duty of care merely because it was not possible to say with precision what machinery would be used to achieve the necessary financial support. Clearly, any form of loan would have been foreseeable, including the raising of money by way of debenture and, while some methods of raising money were more obvious than others, and a takeover was not the most obvious method, it was certainly one method which was within the contemplation of Mr Marks.

The judge went on to decide that the events leading to the takeover of BG were therefore foreseeable.

There was an appeal by JEB to the Court of Appeal, which upheld Woolf, J's finding that there was a lack of causal connection between JEB's loss and the auditors' alleged negligence. Thus they were not liable.

However, the Court of Appeal went on to say that it was not necessary in order to decide the appeal to determine the scope of an auditor's liability for professional negligence.

From foresight back to knowledge

In more recent times the courts have made it clear that mere foresight is not enough. There must be some 'relationship' or 'proximity' or 'neighbourhood' between the parties. This is likely to restrict liability to within reasonable bounds and close the floodgates to a wide variety of claims by claimants *unless they are known to be the users of professional statements and, further, that the professional concerned knows of the use to which they will be put.* Given such a situation a duty of care will exist.

This development was taking place before the *Anns* case was overruled by the decision of the House of Lords in *Murphy* v *Brentwood District Council* (1990) as the case law below shows.

Caparo Industries plc v *Dickman*, 1990 – Accountants' liability (**413**)
Morgan Crucible Co plc v *Hill Samuel*, 1990 – Accountants' liability in a takeover (**414**)

Current trends in liability

A case which appears to widen the liability of auditors beyond statements to mere omissions is *Coulthard* v *Neville Russell* (1997) *The Times*, 18 December, where the Court of Appeal held that, as a matter of principle, auditors have a duty of care to advise that a transaction which the

21

company and its directors intend to carry out might be a breach of the financial assistance provisions of the Companies Act 1985. The High Court has also ruled that two companies which invested venture capital in a shopfitting company that later went into receivership were entitled to damages from the shopfitters' auditors on the basis of negligent misstatements by the auditors in the company's accounts and in letters sent by the auditors to the investing companies. The auditors owed those companies a duty of care. (See *Yorkshire Enterprise Ltd* v *Robson Rhodes, New Law Online*, 17 June 1998, Transcript Case No 2980610103, approved judgment.) A main problem had been that the provision for bad debts was inadequate. The court was saying, in summary, that had the auditors carried out the audit work thoroughly, they would have found certain bookkeeping errors and would have made a greater and more appropriate provision for bad debts. In consequence, the auditors were liable in damages. The facts of the case showed that the auditors were aware of the user of their statements and the use to which they would be put.

In *Abbot* v *Strong* (1998) *The Times*, 9 July, the High Court decided that a circular issued by a company to its shareholders in connection with a rights issue – allegedly containing misleading profit forecasts by the directors – together with an allegedly negligent letter from the company's accountants and management consultants confirming that the forecast statement was properly compiled and in accordance with the company's accounting policies did not lead to the accountants having a duty of care in negligence to the shareholders who acquired shares in the rights issue. Their attempt to claim against the accountants failed. Once again, the court has decided that those advising companies owe no duty of care to the individual shareholders of those companies. This maintains the *Caparo* line. Notably, there were 200 potential claimants in this case, so the court may also have been concerned not to open the floodgates of liability in the public interest, bearing in mind that it is already difficult for professionals to get adequate indemnity insurance.

Also of interest is the decision of the High Court in *Sayers* v *Clarke-Walker (a Firm)* [2002] 2 BCLC 16. It was decided that where a piece of professional work carried out by accounting practitioners can be regarded as within the competence of general practitioners they cannot absolve themselves from liability in negligence by advising the client that he/she should consult also a higher specialist. In the case the issue was the tax consequences of a contract of purchase of a company on which negligent advice was given with the advice also that the client should consult tax counsel. The firm was liable. It should have done the work competently and not required the client to spend more money on a further adviser.

An illustration of professional negligence liability in terms of solicitors and barristers is to be found in *Griffin* v *Kingsmill* [2001] Lloyd's Rep PN 716. The claimant's claim, following personal injury in a road accident, was settled on the basis of written advice from a barrister to her solicitors which resulted in the conclusion that she had no real prospects of success. The settlement was for £50,000 whereas the claim would have been worth at least £500,000. The essence of the claimant's case was that both her former lawyers had been negligent in taking it that her prospects were so poor. There was an acute conflict of evidence as to fault but the claimant alleged that her lawyers had wrongly evaluated it. The barrister had failed to give logical and sensible reasons for his view of the conflict of evidence. The solicitor did not try to hide behind counsel's opinion, rightly so in the view of the Court of Appeal. Notwithstanding that opinion she ought to have weighed up the evidence and formed an independent view. The claimant's action succeeded.

Avoiding and excluding liability

The most practical suggestion that can be made in terms of avoiding liability is for professionals to follow strictly the recommendations of their professional bodies, e.g. the many financial reporting standards and other published material. If this is done the professional will at least have the advantage of the judgment of McNair, J in *Bolam* v *Friern Hospital Management Committee* [1957] 2 All ER 118. He said in connection with doctors: 'A doctor is not guilty of negligence if he has acted in accordance with a practice accepted as proper by a responsible body of medical men skilled in that particular art . . . merely because there is a body of opinion who would take a contrary view.' The statement is, of course, equally applicable to other professions.

On the other hand, as we have seen in discussing medical negligence, the above case does rather suggest that accountants and lawyers and other professionals can set their own standards. Doubt was thrown on the applicability of *Bolam* in *Newell* v *Goldenberg* [1995] 6 Med LR 371 which is considered earlier in this chapter.

However, it is worth noting that the view taken in *Bolam* was reinforced so far as accountants are concerned in *Lloyd Cheyham & Co* v *Littlejohn & Co* [1987] BCLC 303 where the judge said SSAPs (i.e. Statements of Standard Accounting Practice, more recent ones known as Financial Reporting Standards) 'are very strong evidence as to what is the proper standard which should be adopted and unless there is some justification a departure . . . will be regarded as constituting a breach of duty.' Nevertheless, these statements are also put in some doubt by the *Newell* case.

There is also the case of *Bolitho* v *City and Hackney Health Authority* (1997) to consider, that continues the development of the theme that professional persons cannot be the sole judges of their own liability. The case was considered in that context earlier in this chapter.

As regards ability to exclude liability by notice under s 2(2) of the Unfair Contract Terms Act 1977 (see Chapter 15), this will work only if the clause is reasonable. It would seem that there are two factors of major importance in deciding the reasonableness or otherwise of limitations or exclusion of liability for professional negligence and these are: (*a*) insurance, and (*b*) the operation of a two-tier service.

As regards insurance, it would seem unreasonable for a professional person to try to exclude total liability for negligence because that can hardly be regarded as best professional practice. On the other hand, it would probably be reasonable for him to limit his liability to a specified sum. In fact s 11(4) of the 1977 Act states that if a person seeks to restrict his liability in this way the court must have regard to the resources which he would expect to be available to him for the purposes of meeting the liability and also how far it was possible for him to cover himself by insurance. It is thought, therefore, that a firm which takes out the maximum insurance cover which is reasonable in the circumstances, being one where the cover is not so great that the effect could be greatly to inflate the fees charged by the firm, then to limit liability to that sum would satisfy the requirement of reasonableness. There is judicial support for this argument in a number of cases, particularly *George Mitchell* v *Finney Lock Seeds* (1983) (see Chapter 15).

As regards a two-tier service, a professional person could offer a full service at a full price and a reduced service at a lower price. Again, it would seem so long as the user of the service is aware that the two-tier service is available and that he is accepting a reduced service at a reduced price without full liability, then the exclusion clause in a lower-tier service ought to be regarded as reasonable.

It is, of course, worth bearing in mind in all of this that a limitation of liability for professional negligence is much more likely to be regarded as reasonable in a contract with a non-consumer, i.e. a business, than it is in a consumer contract. In fact we have already seen in *Smith* v *Eric S Bush* (1987) that a disclaimer used by a professional person in a consumer situation was not effective. However, as we have seen in *McCullagh* v *Lane Fox* (1995) a more sophisticated consumer of a high-priced property may have to accept a disclaimer.

21

This theme was followed in *Omega Trust Co Ltd* v *Wright Son and Pepper* (1997) 73 P & CR D39 where the Court of Appeal ruled that an exclusion clause under the Unfair Contract Terms Act 1977 applied to exclude the liability of valuers to a lending bank for a negligent valuation of three leases of small supermarkets. This, said the court, was a commercial transaction in which the parties where able to look after themselves. The identity of the bank was not disclosed to the valuers when they made the valuation for the owners, so there is an element of 'unknown user' in the case which, as we have seen, can prevent a duty of care arising even in the absence of an exclusion clause.

It is also worth noting that as regards auditors engaged by a company to carry out a Companies Act audit, s 310 of the Companies Act 1985 makes void any provision in a contract of engagement of the auditors which purports to exclude them from liability for negligence or breach of duty to the company, though the company can now pay the premiums on an insurance policy both for auditors and directors.

Accountants: developments in exclusion of liability

The case of *Royal Bank of Scotland plc* v *Bannerman Johnstone Maclay (a firm)* 2003 SLT 181 has raised issues in regard to accountants' liability and also their ability to exclude that liability. The bank lent money to a company APC Ltd on the strength of accounts audited by the defendants. It was alleged by the claimant that the audited accounts were less than adequately informative in terms, e.g., of the going concern factor. The bank had later to appoint a receiver to the company which was insolvent.

The auditors had notice that under overdraft facility letters the bank was entitled to see management accounts and annual audited accounts. However, they contended that the claimant had to prove that as auditors they *intended* the bank to rely on the accounts to make further loans or advances. The auditors said in effect 'when auditing the accounts our only intention was to carry out Companies Act duties to audit the accounts'. The Scottish Court of Session (Outer House) in this case, equally applicable in England and Wales, ruled that the case law did not support a requirement of intention. The compelling effect of the authorities was that knowledge of user and use formed the basis of a duty of care for those making information or advice available. The auditors had the requisite knowledge and therefore owed a duty of care.

The bank had yet to prove that the accounts were prepared negligently. These duty of care cases are decided without proof of the allegations of negligence. A major matter relating to this case was that *the auditors had not disclaimed liability to third parties such as the bank*. In this connection, the Institute of Chartered Accountants in England and Wales has stated that it is clear that auditors assume reponsibility for the contents of the audit report to shareholders as a body under s 235 of the Companies Act 1985 (now s 509 of the Companies Act 2006). It also states that the absence of a disclaimer may in some cases enable a court to draw an inference that the auditors have assumed responsibility for the audit report to a third party such as the bank in this case. *The ICAEW recommends* that auditors include the following wording in audit reports to clarify their duty of care to third parties by indicating that no such duty is owed.

This report is made solely to the company's members as a body, in accordance with s 235 of the Companies Act 1985 (now s 509 of the Companies Act 2006). Our audit work has been undertaken so that we might state to the company's members those matters we are required to state to them in an auditor's report and for no other purpose. To the fullest extent permitted by law, we do not accept or assume responsibility to anyone other than the company and the company's members as a body, for our audit work, for this report, or for the opinions we have formed.

Professional negligence insurance

Professional indemnity policies are available for a whole range of professional persons and experts, e.g. accountants, solicitors, company directors and insurance brokers. These policies carry an excess clause under which the insured bears the first part of the claim up to a fixed amount. The risk covered is variously described but there is now a tendency to cover 'full civil liability' followed by exclusions from cover of things such as libel. The policies usually cover loss caused to a client (i.e. by breach of contract), and to a non-client (i.e. in the tort of negligence).

Companies Act 2006

Insofar as a number of the illustrations of professional liability concern auditors of companies, the provisions of the Companies Act 2006 are worth noting. Section 548 allows the company and its auditors to enter into a liability limitation agreement to limit the liability of the auditor in regard to damage caused to the company and occurring in the course of auditing the accounts. The agreement must be approved by the members and can only limit liability in terms of what is fair and reasonable in regard to the responsibilities of an auditor. Disclosure of the existence of the agreement must be made in a note to the company's accounts or in the directors' report.

Reform

The rule of joint and several liability of partners in a number of areas including professional negligence has produced what might be regarded as unfairness, particularly with accountants in the audit situation. Suppose that there is a major fraud by an employee of a company which the auditors fail negligently to detect. The person primarily liable to replace the funds fraudulently abstracted is the employee but even if he is caught the funds may have been used up or impossible to find. Others responsible may be the directors who have not put in place internal controls to prevent fraud. However, the directors will not in all cases have insurance or at least not much and the best defendant will be the auditors (as by their having the larger 'pocket') and the loss may well rest with them. Obviously the auditors will have a contribution against other wrongdoers but they may not be able to contribute much or may be insolvent and not contribute anything.

New limited liability partnerships

Parliament has passed the Limited Liability Partnerships Act 2000, which means that a new limited liability partnership is available as a business organisation. These partnerships are registered with the Registrar of Companies and, so far as liability is concerned, the liability of the firm is limited to the capital provided by the partners, and the personal liability of the partners individually is limited in the sense that if in a firm Bloggs, Snooks and Co, Snooks prepares a set of accounts in a negligent fashion knowing that an outsider, say, a takeover bidder, will rely on them, the firm is then liable up to the total of its assets and so are the private assets of Snooks. Bloggs' personal assets are not liable. They would be if the negligent accounts were jointly prepared.

However, the private assets of persons such as Snooks should not often be at risk because it will normally be made clear that he acts for the firm as its agent on all documents and letters issued in connection with the preparation of the accounts. The assets of the firm will be at risk but not the private assets of the partners. Where agency is not made clear there may be liability in Snooks.

21

The present position regarding duty of care – a summary

As we have seen, the duty of care in regard to negligent misstatements by auditors has been considered in a number of cases since the early 1950s. However, the present position has been the subject of comprehensive analysis by the House of Lords in *Caparo Industries* v *Dickman* [1990] 1 All ER 568.

From this decision and two important later ones the position would appear to be as follows:

(a) Auditors do not owe a duty of care to potential investors in the company, e.g. those who reply on the audited accounts when contemplating a takeover bid. The fact that the accounts and auditors' report might foreseeably come into their hands and be relied on is not enough to create a duty of care. In addition, it was decided in *James McNaughton Paper Group* v *Hicks Anderson* [1991] 1 All ER 134 that even if an auditor knew that the audited accounts would be used by a bidder as the basis of a bid, he would not be liable if he reasonably believed and was entitled to assume that the bidder would also seek the advice of his own accountant.

(b) Auditors do not owe a duty of care to potential investors even if they already hold shares in the company since, although they are shareholders and auditors are under a statutory duty to report to shareholders, the duty of the auditors is to the shareholders as a whole and not to shareholders as individuals.

(c) Even where the auditors are aware of the person or persons who will rely upon the accounts, they are not liable unless they also know what the person or persons concerned will use them for, e.g. as the basis for a takeover.

(d) Where there is knowledge of user and use, then in that restricted situation the Court of Appeal held in *Morgan Crucible Co plc* v *Hill Samuel Bank Ltd* [1991] 1 All ER 142 that a duty of care would exist in regard to the user. However, even in such a situation the auditor will not be liable if, in the circumstances, he was entitled to assume that the user would also seek the advice of his own accountant and not rely solely on the audited accounts (see the *McNaughton* case, above). It is not necessary to prove *intention* in the auditors that a third-party should rely on the audit report provided there is knowledge in the auditors of user and use (*Royal Bank of Scotland plc* v *Bannerman Johnstone Maclay (a firm)* 2003 SLT 181).

(e) *Coulthard* v *Neville Russell* (1997) would seem to extend liability to mere omissions.

Negligence – occupiers' liability

The question of the liability of occupiers of premises to persons suffering injury thereon may be regarded as a further aspect of negligence. The occupier is the person who has *de facto* control of the premises or the possession of them; it is a question of fact in each case and does not depend entirely on title. It should also be noted that occupation may be *shared* between two or more persons, and that an employer may be vicariously liable for the torts of an employee who is acting within the scope of his employment. Thus in *Stone* v *Taffe* [1974] 3 All ER 1016, the owner of a hotel was liable when the manager failed to ensure that there was adequate lighting on the premises so that a guest fell and was killed.

Wheat v Lacon & Co Ltd, 1966 – When two persons occupy (**415**)

The Occupiers' Liability Act 1957

A common duty of care is owed to all lawful visitors to premises, 'visitor' being a term which includes anyone to whom the occupier has given, or is deemed to have given, an invitation or permission to use the premises. It includes some persons who enter the premises by right of law, such as inspectors, but not those who cross land in pursuance of a public or private right of way. A person using a public or private right of way (the latter as an easement, see Chapter 22) does so by right and cannot therefore be the visitor of the owner of the land over which the way passes (*McGeown* v *Northern Ireland Housing Executive* [1994] 3 WLR 187) and see now the Occupiers' Liability Act 1984 where rights other than those of a visitor were created (see below).

Implied permission to enter premises is a matter of fact to be decided in the circumstances of each case, and the burden of proof is upon the person who claims implied permission. However, persons who enter upon premises for purposes of business which they believe will be of interest to the occupier, as where they wish to sell him a product, have implied permission to enter even though their presence is distasteful to the occupier.

Under the Act, an occupier of premises owes to all visitors the duty to take such care as, in the circumstances of the case, is necessary to see that the visitor will be reasonably safe in using the premises for the purpose for which he is invited or permitted to be there. If the visitor uses the premises for some other purpose, the occupier does not owe him the same duty; such a person is in effect a trespasser, and liability to him falls to be decided on that basis (see below).

Under s 2(1) of the 1957 Act the occupier may restrict or exclude his liability, by giving adequate warning or by contract. However, this section must be looked at in the light of the Unfair Contract Terms Act 1977, which states that the common-law duty of care in regard to liability for death or personal injury cannot be excluded in relation to business premises. In addition, liability for other loss or damage occurring on such premises can only be excluded where it is reasonable to do so. However, the owner of a path adjacent to self-evidently dangerous cliffs is not under a duty to put up a notice giving warning that the cliffs are dangerous (Court of Appeal in *Cotton* v *Derbyshire Dales District Council* (1994) *The Times*, 20 June). Furthermore, the Court of Appeal ruled in *Darby* v *National Trust* (2002) 3 LGLR 29 that there was no need to warn against swimming in a pond in the grounds of a stately home which was under the control of the trust. The relevant pond was no more hazardous than any other. The claim that there should have been a warning notice relating to the possibility of contracting Weil's disease from swimming in the pond was also turned down because the claim was for causing death by negligence and there was therefore no causative loss in regard to Weil's disease.

Where the accident has arisen through the defective work of an independent contractor, the occupier can avoid liability by showing that he behaved reasonably in the selection of the contractor.

The defence of *volenti non fit injuria* is available to the occupier, though he must show that the entrant assented to the risk, not that he merely knew of it: the entrant's knowledge is no longer a defence.

The occupier may also raise the defence of *contributory negligence* by the entrant which, though not defeating his claim, may reduce damages.

> *Cook* v *Broderip*, 1968 – Faulty work of an independent contractor (**416**)
> *Bunker* v *Charles Brand*, 1969 – Knowledge is not assent (**417**)

21

Trespassers

The main case on an occupier's liability to a trespasser was *British Railways Board* v *Herrington* [1972] 1 All ER 749 in which the House of Lords was unanimous in deciding that there could be liability to a trespasser. Unfortunately the five judges concerned reached that decision in different ways and the matter was referred to the Law Commission. Eventually Parliament passed the Occupiers' Liability Act 1984 which now governs the position of trespassers and certain other non-visitors.

Section 1 deals with the duty of an occupier to persons other than his visitors – this includes trespassers and persons entering land without the consent of the owner, but in exercise of a private right of way or public access. In these cases the occupier owes a duty, if he is aware of the danger which exists, or has reasonable grounds to believe that it exists. He must also know, or have reasonable grounds to believe, that the non-visitor concerned is in the vicinity of the danger – whether he has lawful authority for being in that vicinity or not. Furthermore, the risk must be one which in all the circumstances of the case it is reasonable to expect the occupier to offer the non-visitor some protection against. It was held, for example, in *Proffit* v *British Railways Board* (1984) *The Times*, 4 February that British Rail had no *general* duty to erect or maintain fences sufficient to keep trespassers out.

The duty is to take such care as is reasonable in all the circumstances of the case to see that the non-visitor does not suffer injury because of the danger concerned. The duty may be discharged by giving warning of the danger or taking steps to discourage persons from incurring risk. Thus the defence of *volenti* is preserved.

A case in point is *Ratcliff* v *McConnell* [1999] 1 WLR 670 where the claimant sued for tetraplegic injuries sustained by diving into the shallow end of a college swimming pool when the pool was closed for the winter. He had climbed over a locked gate in the early hours of the morning. There were warning notices and notices prohibiting use. The claimant, who was an adult, did not recover any damages against the college (represented by a defendant governor). He willingly accepted the risk, said the Court of Appeal.

The Court of Appeal reached a similar conclusion in *Donoghue* v *Folkestone Properties* [2003] All ER (D) 382 where the claimant was rendered tetraplegic when after an evening drinking with friends the claimant trespassed on to a slipway in Folkestone harbour, dived into the water and struck his head on an underwater obstruction. The defendants had no duty of care towards him. They would only have been liable if they knew that someone was likely to swim from the slipway in the middle of the night in the depth of winter.

Again, in *Tomlinson* v *Congleton BC* [2003] 3 All ER 1122 the Court of Appeal refused the claim of an 18-year-old who ignored a notice at a country park lake which said 'Dangerous Water: No Swimming'. He waded into the water and dived from a standing position striking his head on the bottom of the lake. Once again, he became tetraplegic. The House of Lords affirmed the decision of the Court of Appeal (see the above reference).

While these injuries are tragic the cases do seem to provide an injection of balance into liability in tort at a time when there is a prevailing compensation culture. The decisions indicate that there is a place for personal responsibility in these matters: something that can be overlooked in an increasingly litigious society encouraged by the 'no-win, no-fee' litigation arrangements.

Access to the countryside

Section 2 of the Occupiers' Liability Act 1984 is designed to encourage access to the countryside. The Unfair Contract Terms Act 1977 had discouraged landowners with, say, a mountain crag, or potholes on their land, from admitting the public thereto because of the difficulty of excluding liability which might result. Under the 1984 Act they can exclude liability, e.g. by notice, for the dangerous state of the land provided they are prepared to allow the public to come on to it for nothing. So long as the actual letting in of the public is not part of a business, as where access for recreational or educational purposes is charged for, the letting in of the public for nothing will not constitute running a business for the purposes of the 1977 Act.

The provisions of the Countryside and Rights of Way Act 2000 are considered in Chapter 21 but the 'right to roam', as it is called, created under certain conditions does not increase the liability of landowners.

Children on premises

Dealings with children always demand a high degree of care, whether a person is sued in the capacity of an occupier of premises or not. However, in the case of an occupier of premises, the duty towards children was rather different from the corresponding duty to adults. If, with knowledge of the trespass of children on his land, the occupier made no reasonable attempt to prevent such trespass, e.g. by repairing fences, and a child was injured by something on the land which was especially alluring to children, e.g. turntables, escalators, bright and poisonous berries, then the occupier in general was liable, even though the child was on the face of it a trespasser. The difference owed to child trespassers is no longer so great in view of the broader rules laid down in the Occupiers' Liability Act 1984. However, it should be noted that what is adequate warning to an adult might not be so to a child. These rules will presumably apply to the warnings which the 1984 Act allows the occupier to give.

> *Yachuk* v *Oliver Blais & Co Ltd*, 1949 – Negligence liability and children (**418**)
> *Gough* v *National Coal Board*, 1954 – Occupiers' liability and children (**419**)
> *Mourton* v *Poulter*, 1930 – Warning children (**420**)
> *Pannett* v *McGuinness & Co*, 1972 – An alluring bonfire (**421**)

Landlord and tenant

As regards landlord and tenant, s 4 of the Occupiers' Liability Act 1957 provided that a landlord would be liable to his tenants' visitors who were injured or whose goods were damaged on the leased premises because of some defect which resulted from his failure to repair. However, s 4 only applied where the landlord was under an obligation express, implied or statutory to repair, but the Defective Premises Act 1972 repeals s 4 and places liability on a landlord who has merely reserved a right to enter and repair. A landlord who does not repair where he has no obligation to do so, nor a power of entry, has no liability, under the Act or at common law.

Thus, now that s 4 of the 1957 Act is repealed, the landlord's liability is similar to his liability in nuisance. Of course, only an occupier can sue in nuisance, but under the Defective Premises Act 1972 the landlord is liable to all persons who might reasonably be expected to be affected by defects in the state of the premises. This covers not only the tenant, his family and his visitors, but also neighbours, passers-by and trespassers.

Furthermore, under the 1957 Act it became established that a landlord was only liable to his tenants' visitors if he had been notified of the defect by the tenant. However, s 4(2) of the 1972 Act provides that the duty is owed where the landlord knew or ought to have known of the relevant defect, so notice given by the tenant is no longer essential. Where the lease or tenancy expressly imposes on the tenant a duty to inform the lessor of defects but the tenant fails to do so with the consequence that a third party is injured, then the landlord can still be sued provided it can be shown that he ought to have known of the defect but in this case he will have a right of indemnity against the tenant for what that may be worth.

21

However, there are still gaps in the law because the duties imposed upon a landlord by s 4 relate only to the *maintenance* of a property which was satisfactory when let. If an owner knows of a defect – not created by him – in the premises *before he either sells or lets the premises* but does not repair it or warn about it the 1972 Act imposes no liability on him for harm caused after the property is let or sold. Furthermore there is no liability at common law (*Cavalier* v *Pope* [1906] AC 428, affirmed in *McNerny* v *Lambeth Borough Council* (1989) 139 NLJ 114).

Where the person injured is the tenant himself the 1972 Act allows a tenant to sue his landlord for breach of his statutory duty but then the lessor would be able to allege contributory negligence in that the tenant failed to notify him of the defect. Where, however, the defect was due to a tenant failing to carry out an obligation expressly imposed on him by the lease or tenancy, the landlord does not owe the tenant any duty, although he would still owe a duty to third parties if they were injured, but in these circumstances could recover an indemnity or contribution from the tenant who would be a joint tortfeasor. There is little a landlord can do to exclude or restrict his liability. Section 6(3) of the 1972 Act renders void any exclusion clause in a lease or tenancy agreement.

Highway authorities

A highway authority is liable for damage which is caused by its *active misfeasance* and, under the Highways Act 1980, for damage which arises from its failure to repair.

In an action for damages against a highway authority based upon its *failure to repair*, it is a defence to prove that the authority has in all the circumstances taken reasonable care to ensure that the highway was not dangerous by reason of its failure to *repair*.

Griffiths v *Liverpool Corporation*, 1966 – Failure to repair a flagstone (**422**)

Defective Premises Act 1972

This Act brought about three major changes. In the first place a landlord's liability for defects in leased premises was increased. This has already been dealt with in occupiers' liability. Second, much of the common-law immunity of a vendor or landlord for negligence was abolished. Third, there is a statutory duty on those concerned with providing dwellings to do the work properly. Section 1 places a duty on builders and developers, sub-contractors, architects and local authorities to see that building contracts are carried out in a workmanlike, or where appropriate, professional manner with proper materials so that the dwelling is fit for habitation. It should be noted that this statutory duty is owed not merely to the immediate client but to everyone who acquires a legal or equitable interest in the dwelling. The liability does not, of course, last for ever. It is subject to the Limitation Act, though s 1(5) of the 1972 Act provides that a cause of action accrues at the time when the dwelling was completed, but where further work has to be done to put right a fault then the cause of action accrues only when the further work is completed. This means that from that date a claimant has six years to start an action or three years where the defect has caused death or personal injury. Section 6(3) of the 1972 Act renders void any term of an agreement which purports to exclude or restrict this statutory duty.

Under s 1(3) a mere agreement by a client to a particular design or specification being used does not discharge the builder or other persons involved from this statutory duty. Section 2 offers an alternative by providing that no action can be brought where a state-approved scheme has conferred rights on the first sale or letting to those who have or will have an interest in the property in respect of defects in the state of the dwelling. Such schemes can be approved or withdrawn by the Secretary of State by statutory instrument.

The National Housebuilders Registration Council scheme is approved under these arrangements and where an NHRC scheme is in operation it applies rather than the Act. The advantage of an NHRC scheme over the Act is that if the builder becomes bankrupt the Council compensates the claimant. Section 3 of the Act sweeps away most of the old common-law immunity from liability for negligence which was formerly enjoyed by sellers of property and lessors of property; they are now liable within the wider rule of *Donoghue* v *Stevenson* (1932). Thus, under the 1972 Act, the maxim *caveat emptor* no longer provides a defence to a claim of negligence against a vendor or lessor in respect of defects in the premises sold or let and this liability extends beyond the immediate purchaser or lessee and can be brought by others who buy or rent the property within the constraints of the Limitation Act 1980 and s 1(5) of the 1972 Act. Thus, there is now a law against building or letting tumbledown properties.

It should be carefully noted, however, that s 3 has gaps. The defects have to be caused by *works* of construction, repair, maintenance or demolition or other works. The section does not apply at all to negligent *omissions to repair* and the common law provides in general no redress (see *McNerny* v *Lambeth Borough Council* (1989) above).

Negligence – of employers

Where an employee's case is based on his employer's negligence at *common law*, he will have to prove that his injury was the result of the employer's breach of a duty of care. The employee is assisted in this task because certain specific duties of an employer were laid down by the House of Lords in the leading case of *Wilsons and Clyde Coal Co* v *English* [1938] AC 57, and an employer must take reasonable care to provide:

(a) *proper and safe plant and appliances* for the work;
(b) *a safe system of work* with adequate supervision and instruction;
(c) *safe premises*; and
(d) *a competent staff* of fellow employees.

The employer's duty is a personal one so that he remains liable even though he has delegated the performance of the duty to a competent independent contractor. Thus in *Paine* v *Colne Valley Electricity Supply Co Ltd* [1938] 4 All ER 803, an employer was held liable for injuries to his employee caused by the failure of contractors to install sufficient insulation in an electrical kiosk.

However, in *Davie* v *New Merton Board Mills* [1958] 1 All ER 67, the House of Lords decided that an employer was not liable for damage caused by a defective implement purchased from a reputable manufacturer. The employee was thus left to sue the manufacturer and this could prove difficult where the manufacturer had left the country or gone out of business or could not for any other reason be identified. Now the Employers' Liability (Defective Equipment) Act 1969, provides that an employee who is injured because of a defect in his employer's equipment can recover damages from the employer if he can show that the defect is due to the fault of some person, e.g. the manufacturer, but if no one is at fault damages are not

21

recoverable. Agreements by employees to contract out are void, and rights under the Act are *in addition* to common-law rights. Thus, an injured employee can sue a third party such as a manufacturer if he wishes, e.g. as where the employer is insolvent, though the Employer's Liability (Compulsory Insurance) Act 1969, requires employers to insure against their liability for personal injury to their employees. The injury must result from equipment provided for the employer's *business*. Thus, domestic servants injured by household equipment would not be covered.

As regards a safe system of work, there is no duty on the employer to set up a system for a 'one-off' operation where the employee uses his own initiative. The Court of Appeal so ruled in *Chalk* v *Devises Reclamation Co Ltd* (1999) *The Times*, 2 April, where a large piece of lead fell from a wagon during unloading and, on his own initiative, Mr Chalk picked it up causing himself back injuries. His claim for damages failed. An employee's claim may also fail under what is known as the 'nursemaid' school of negligence. In *Makepeace* v *Evans Bros (Reading)* (2000) *The Times*, 13 June a painter and decorator was using a tower scaffold which fell over while he was working on it. The Court of Appeal dismissed his claim because on the facts it appeared that a tower scaffold was an ordinary piece of equipment used frequently by painters on building sites, so that the claimant should have known that it might be danger-ous to use such equipment in certain situations instead of, e.g., ladders. The employer had no duty to ask him whether he knew how to use the scaffold safely.

Liability for stress-related injury

Over the years the employer's duty to provide a safe system of work has almost exclusively involved cases of physical injury. However, in *Walker* v *Northumberland County Council* (1994) *The Times*, 24 November the High Court decided that psychiatric damage caused by over-work, in this case as a social worker, was also included.

Another modern example of safe system requirements is in the field of repetitive strain injury caused amongst other things by the operation of keyboards of one sort or another. The Court of Appeal has held that an employer has a duty to instruct employees on the risk of repetitive strain injury and the need to take breaks (see *Pickford* v *ICI plc* [1996] IRLR 622). Breach of this duty by the employer can result in a successful action for damages by the employee. Ann Pickford's injury was caused by long periods of typing without adequate rest breaks, on the need for which she had received no instruction, though typists in other departments of the business had been given such instructions.

Employers have been facing an ever increasing number of claims for psychiatric damage caused by stress at work. High awards of damages have been made but the Court of Appeal in *Hatton* v *Sutherland and Other Appeals* [2002] 2 All ER 1 gave a ruling that gives some relief to employers in terms of claims for occupational stress. The ruling was given in regard to four test cases where the Court of Appeal gave a single unanimous judgment. The claimants were two teachers, a local authority administrative assistant and a factory worker. The court overturned awards of damages totalling £208,000 but upheld an award of £150,000 to the administrative worker but 'not without some hesitation'.

The Court of Appeal also gave important guidance on this type of claim as follows:

■ there are no special controls that an employer must put into place in regard to stress;
■ the ordinary principles of employers' liability apply;
■ stress must like other harm be foreseeable and attributable to stress at work as distinct from other factors;
■ an employer is normally entitled to assume that the employee can stand the normal pressures of the job unless he or she knows of some particular vulnerability or problem;

- the test is the same whatever the employment;
- there are no occupations that should be regarded as intrinsically dangerous to mental health;
- finally where dismissal or demotion is the only reasonable and effective procedure open to an employer but the employee wishes to work on and the employer lets him or her do so he or she will not normally be liable if injury results.

It is worth noting that a differently constituted Court of Appeal threw some doubt on this last statement at least so far as physical injury is concerned. In *Coxall* v *Goodyear GB Ltd* [2003] 1 WLR 536 the danger arose from a new paint put into use by the employer, the claimant was allergic to it and in spite of using protective equipment provided by the employer he still suffered from asthma. The employee wanted to go on working and the employer allowed him to do so. The claimant became too ill to work and left his employment. He then claimed damages for his employer's negligence. The Court of Appeal ruled that his claim succeeded. If there was no alternative to the claimant working with the paint the employer should have dismissed him (even though the employee wanted to go on working) and could be in breach of his duty as an employer if he did not. The only sensible resolution of these decisions is to dismiss in mental and physical injury cases. The employer should have a good defence in either case if there is no alternative employment. If the claim is for disability discrimination as it might be the defence would apply with the difference that the employer is required to consider and make if possible adjustments to the workplace to enable the disabled person to do the job. There would appear to have been no such adjustments that could have been made in the *Coxall* scenario.

Stress-related injury: the House of Lords rules

The House of Lords has now ruled on the liability of an employer for the occupational stress injury of an employee. While the House of Lords finds *Hatton* to be a valuable contribution, their Lordships depart in a significant way from certain parts of the *Hatton* judgment.

In *Barber* v *Somerset County Council* [2004] 2 All ER 385, it appeared that Mr Barber was an experienced teacher. He had two jobs: one as head of maths and the other to market his school. Between 1995 and 1996 he was working between 61 and 70 hours per week. This workload caught up with him and he had three weeks off sick during the summer term. His medical certificates referred to 'stress' and 'depression'. He subsequently returned to work but nothing was done to deal with his workload. The headmistress and senior staff were unsympathetic and eventually he left work. The only advice from the deputy headmaster was to prioritise his workload. The House of Lords found this to be a totally inadequate response and affirmed the trial judge's award of damages against the employer.

Their Lordships considered in particular the ruling of the Court of Appeal in *Hatton*, which was to the effect that an employer is normally entitled to assume that an employee can stand the pressures of the job unless he or she knows of some particular vulnerability or problem. This carries the suggestion that the onus is on the employee to complain about stress problems. The House of Lords rejected this ruling and stated that employers must be proactive by giving positive thought to the safety of the workforce in the light of what they know or ought to know. The senior management team should have made enquiries about the claimant's problems and have discovered what they could have done to ease them in both Mr Barber's case and throughout the school. Their Lordships placed the onus on the employer to develop a knowledge of occupational stress and to keep up to date with effective precautions that can be taken to alleviate it. **This is a significant change of emphasis.**

21

Health and safety statutes

There are numerous statutes which are designed to protect the health, and provide for the welfare and safety, of employees. The relevance of such statutes for our present purposes is that where the breach of a statutory duty, e.g. failure to fence a dangerous machine, has caused injury to a worker, he may be able to sue his employer for damages by using the breach of statutory duty to establish the duty of care under the principles already discussed.

> *Millard* v *Serck Tubes Ltd*, 1969 – A statutory duty of care (**423**)

Torts against business interests

It is a tort knowingly to induce a person to *break his contract* with a third party whereby that party suffers damage. It is also an actionable wrong for two or more persons to combine together (*or conspire*) for the purpose of wilfully causing damage to the claimant. There is also an action for *passing off* which occurs where A represents his goods or services to be those of B.

Inducement of breach of contract

If A induces B to break his contract with C, C can sue A.

Trade union activity often involves interference with contract and the position as regards the immunity or otherwise of trade unions in this context has already been considered in Chapter 8.

> *Lumley* v *Gye*, 1853 – Inducing a breach of contract (**424**)
> *Daily Mirror Newspapers* v *Gardner*, 1968 – Boycotting a newspaper (**425**)

Conspiracy

Where two or more persons act without lawful justification for the purpose of wilfully causing damage to the claimant and actual damage results, they commit the tort of conspiracy. The tort was fully considered in *Crofter Hand Woven Harris Tweed Co Ltd* v *Veitch* (1942) (see below), where the following principles were laid down:

(*a*) the tort covers acts which would be *lawful if done by one person*;
(*b*) the combination will be justified if the predominant motive is self-interest or protection of one's trade rather than injury to the claimant;
(*c*) damage to the claimant must be proved.

> *Crofter Hand Woven Harris Tweed Co Ltd* v *Veitch*, 1942 – The principles of conspiracy (**426**)

Passing off – generally

Any person, company or other organisation which carries on or proposes to carry on business under a name calculated to deceive the public by confusion with the name of an existing concern, commits the civil wrong of *passing off*. Other examples of passing off are the use of similar wrappings, identification marks, and descriptions. Thus in *Bollinger* v *Costa Brava Wine Co Ltd* [1959] 3 All ER 800, the champagne producers of France objected to the use of the name 'Spanish Champagne' to describe a sparkling wine which was made in Spain and they were granted an injunction to prevent the use of that term.

However, passing-off claims have become more frequent in recent times in the areas of marking, style of trading and appearance of goods. For example, the House of Lords accepted in *Reckitt & Coleman Products Ltd* v *Borden* [1990] 1 All ER 873 that lemon juice sold by the defendants in lemon-shaped, lemon-coloured containers misled the public into thinking they were buying 'Jif' lemon juice – the product of Reckitt and Coleman. In the leading case of *Erven Warnink BV* v *J Townend & Sons* (*Hull*) *Ltd* [1979] AC 731 (the *Advocaat* Case) the House of Lords decided that four characteristics must be present in order to create a valid action for passing off:

(*a*) That there has been a misrepresentation. (To engage in the same line of business as the claimant and use the same or a similar name may be passing off.)

(*b*) The misrepresentation was made by a trader in the course of trade, which includes a profession such as lawyer or accountant. Thus in *Kean* v *McGivan* [1982] FSR 119 a claimant who claimed that the defendant was wrongly calling a political party the Social Democratic Party could not successfully sue in passing off.

(*c*) It was calculated to injure the business or goodwill of another trader (in the sense that it is a foreseeable consequence). It is a matter for the judge to decide on the evidence whether the defendant's misrepresentation was calculated to deceive.

(*d*) It has caused actual damage to the business or goodwill of the other trader or will probably do so.

It will be seen from the above characteristics that mere confusion is not enough. An illustration is provided by the decision of the High Court in *HFC Bank plc* v *Midland Bank plc* (1999) *The Times*, 22 September. The Midland Bank and many other companies within the Hong Kong and Shanghai Banking corporation group rebranded their business, branches and services as HSBC. HFC Bank plc brought an action to restrain Midland Bank from passing off its business as HFC business by using the name HSBC which it claimed was confusingly similar.

The High Court ruled that the fact that customers might be confused by similar competing brand names was not enough for a passing off action to succeed; there had to be a misrepresentation causing damage to goodwill. HFC had not proved this and its claim failed. The judge seems to have taken the view that, although there had been some confusion, this could be dealt with by managing it in terms of marketing. The solution should be commercial not legal.

It is also necessary that the users of a name be in the same line of business. Thus, the High Court held in *Safeway Stores plc* v *Hachette Filipacchi Presse*, 13 December 1999 (unreported) that the defendant magazine owner could not prevent the name of its magazine 'Elle' from being registered as a trade mark for the claimant's sanitary products, as there was no real tangible danger of a substantial number of members of the public being made to wonder whether the sanitary products were connected with the magazine or its owner.

However, in *Pfizer Ltd* v *Eurofood Link (UK) Ltd*, 10 December 1999 (unreported) the High Court held that naming a beverage that was to be marketed as an aphrodisiac 'Viagrene' was an infringement of UK and Community trade marks protecting the well-known drug 'Viagra' and constituted passing off.

As regards remedies:

(*a*) An injunction is on general principles available to prevent the continuance of the wrong but, being an equitable remedy, it is up to the court's discretion whether to grant it.

21

(*b*) The claimant may also recover damages for loss of profits incurred because business is diverted away from him to the defendant and for loss of business reputation and goodwill.

(*c*) As an alternative to an assessment of damages at common law, a court may direct the equitable remedy of an account of profit actually made by the defendant because of the passing off.

In connection with passing off, the effect of the Trade Marks Act 1994 should be noted. It is now possible to register a business name as a trade mark as where Mr Ahmed trades as 'Ahmed's Barbican Tandoori'. Such geographical marks are registrable under the 1994 Act and once the mark is registered any infringement is automatically illegal and the court can give redress by means of damages, injunction, or an account and payment over of profits made from illegal use of the trade mark.

As we have seen, passing off is a more difficult matter to prove. For example, proof of deception is essential (*Hodgkinson & Corby* v *Wards Mobility Services* (1994) *The Times*, 3 August). Since the Act also applies to the registration of the shape of goods, things such as the shape of a Coca-Cola bottle can also be protected in this easier way.

Passing-off: use of own name

It does not follow that because a person trades in his or her own name they will be able to mount a successful defence against passing off. Thus in *Asprey & Garrard Ltd* v *WRA (Guns) Ltd* [2001] All ER (D) 163 (Oct) the claimants for a passing off and infringement of trade mark rights were a well known and established trader in luxury goods. The defendant company traded in the same line of business in London, i.e. the same location as the claimants *in the business name* of William R Asprey Esq. William Asprey who was a former employee of the claimants effectively controlled the defendant company. The High Court granted an injunction against passing off and infringement of the claimant's trade mark. The court dismissed the defence of own name on the ground that it must not as here be used to cause deception.

Passing off – on the Internet

The High Court has shown itself willing to issue an injunction, to prevent the use of an Internet domain name, in a passing-off claim (see *Pitman Training Ltd* v *Nominet UK* [1997] Current Law 4875). An additional problem that has arisen because of the rapid growth of the Internet and its use by business organisations for e-mail and commerce generally is the parallel growth of a breed of speculators who register domain names that form a crucial part of a particular business website and e-mail address in the hope for example of offering it for sale to the business concerned with the possibility of receiving a high price for exclusivity. In *BT* v *One in a Million* [1998] 4 All ER 476 the Court of Appeal affirmed the High Court's granting of injunctions to restrain the defendants who had registered company names and/or trade marks, e.g. Marks and Spencer and J Sainsbury as domain names on the Internet on the basis of passing off and trade-mark infringement. The decision means that, at least in the UK, it should be easier to protect Internet domain names.

Defamation

Defamation is the publication of a statement which tends to lower a person in the estimation of right-thinking members of society generally, or which tends to make them shun or avoid that person.

Byrne v *Deane*, 1937 – What is defamation? (**427**)

In order to constitute a tort the statement must be false and capable of bearing a defamatory meaning. Lord Reid in *Lewis* v *Daily Telegraph Ltd* [1964] AC 234 at p 258 indicated how a trial judge might proceed in deciding whether words in their ordinary and natural meaning are capable of bearing a defamatory meaning.

> What the ordinary person would infer without special knowledge has generally been called the natural and ordinary meaning of the words. But the expression is rather misleading in that it conceals the fact that there are two elements in it. Sometimes it is not necessary to go beyond the words themselves, as where the [claimant] has been called a thief or a murderer. But more often the sting is not so much in the words themselves as in what the ordinary person will infer from them, and that is also regarded as part of their natural and ordinary meaning . . . In this case it is, I think, sufficient to put the test in this way. Ordinary men and women have different temperaments and outlooks. Some are unusually suspicious, and some are unusually naive. One must try to envisage people between these two extremes and see what is the most damaging meaning they would put on the words in question.

In consequence, the ordinary and natural meaning of words is to be gathered not only by considering a strictly literal interpretation but also from the inference which would be drawn by the ordinary person who heard or read the words. Statements of *opinion* may be defamatory; defamation is not confined to statements of fact. Thus in *Slazengers Ltd* v *Gibbs (C) & Co* (1916) 33 TLR 35 the defendants stated during the First World War with Germany that the claimants were a German company and would, in their opinion, be closed down. This statement of opinion was held to be defamatory of the claimants.

It was held in *Berkoff* v *Burchill* [1996] 4 All ER 1008, by the Court of Appeal that derogatory references to an actor's physical appearance were capable of being defamatory and the matter should go to trial. The actor was described as 'hideously ugly'. The defendant's appeal on the basis that to be defamatory words had to cause injury to a person's *reputation* was rejected by the court. The words were capable of lowering the claimant's standing in the estimation of the public and of making him the object of ridicule.

Publication

21

The essence of the tort is the publication or communication of the falsehood to at least one person other than the person defamed, and other than the author's own husband or wife. Obviously publication to the claimant's spouse is defamatory (*Wenman* v *Ash* (1853) 13 CB 836). Every successive repetition of the statement is a fresh commission of the tort. Hence, a defamatory statement written upon a postcard is published by the sender not only to the ultimate recipient but also to the postal officials through whose hands it may pass, and to every individual who legitimately handles the message, e.g. the secretary of the sender or the receiver. Similarly a libel contained in a newspaper is published by the reporter or author, and by the editor, the printer, the publisher, the proprietor, the wholesaler and the retail seller of that newspaper.

However, at common law mere *mechanical distributors*, e.g. news vendors, booksellers, libraries and the like, were not liable for their acts if they were unaware of the libel. However, if, as in *Viztelly* v *Mudie's Select Library Ltd* [1900] 2 QB 170, the library had overlooked a publisher's circular requesting return of copies of a libellous book, then there was and is a liability. Persons lending books gratuitously or making gifts of them and tape and record dealers were also protected if unaware of the defamation. There is, of course, no need to consider the liability of the Post Office because it is exempt from any liability in tort in regard to postal packets. Nor is there any need to consider the liability of British Telecommunications because, although the telecommunications service is run under contract, there are excluding terms.

Section 1 of the Defamation Act 1996 now deals with the defence of innocent dissemination and has constricted its ingredients in some respects. At common law the defence was available to a distributor who did not *know* that the publication was a libel. Now the defence will only apply where the distributor or other secondary publisher did not know *or have reason to believe* that he was causing or contributing to the publication of a libel. This means that secondary publishers will have difficulty in setting up the defence where the main publisher has a track record of publishing defamatory material. However, under the Act Internet service providers are protected from liability for defamation as are broadcasters of live programmes in respect of statements made by persons over whom they have no control.

Under s 1(3) of the 1996 Act Internet service providers are not publishers under the Act, i.e. in a statutory sense. However, it was held in *Godfrey* v *Demon Internet Ltd* [1999] 4 All ER 342 that they can nevertheless be publishers at common law in appropriate circumstances. The High Court ruled in the case that an Internet service provider that was notified that it was carrying a libellous statement on a Usenet newsgroup but took no action could face defamation proceedings. It could not rely on the defence of innocent defamation under s 1 of the 1996 Act because, although it was not an author, editor or publisher under s 1(3), it had published the statement at common law without taking reasonable care as required by s 1(1)(b) of the 1996 Act. The posting in this case was made by an unknown person in the USA and was said to be obscene and defamatory of the claimant, a lecturer resident in England.

However, in *Bunt* v *Tilley* [2006] 3 All ER 336 the High Court ruled that as a matter of law an Internet service provider that performed no more than a passive role in facilitating postings on the Internet could not be regarded as a publisher at common law.

While on the subject of Internet defamation an Australian landmark case relating to the liability of online publishers is worth considering. The case is entitled *Dow Jones & Co Inc* v *Gutnick* [2002] HCA 56. Dow Jones published an article called 'Unholy Gains' in its publication *Barron's* magazine. It carried the imputation that G, who was a well-known Australian business man, was purporting to be a reputable citizen but was in fact money laundering and evading tax. Dow Jones also placed the article on its website which was a subscriber website called Barrons. Dow Jones had 550,000 subscribers to the site: 1,700 of these paid by Australian credit cards. G refuted the allegations and sued Dow Jones for defamation in Victoria, Australia for damage caused to his reputation by the Victoria publications. The defendants contended that the case should be heard in New Jersey, USA where Barron's online server was located and the law there applied. G argued that the claim was validly brought in Victoria where the article was viewed. The Australian High Court agreed with G. The case was rightly brought in Victoria and Australian law would be applied. Under both English and Australian law every communication creates a separate cause of action which arises in every place where the defamatory matter is read or heard. It was near certain that UK courts would have reached the same conclusion since English and Australian law on defamation is largely the same.

In fact, a UK court did take that line in *King* v *Lewis and Others* [2004] All ER (D) 234 (Oct) where the Court of Appeal affirmed the High Court's ruling that the common law of England and Wales takes the view that the act of defamation, i.e. publication of the defamatory material, takes place when the information is downloaded and if downloaded in England and Wales by Internet users the proceedings in respect of it may be brought here even though the statement was not originally made in the UK.

The case followed New York attorney Judd Berstein's allegedly defamatory statements in the US about the boxing promoter Don King. The court rejected Mr Berstein's contention that UK courts had no jurisdiction to try the matter, the statements having been made in the US though downloaded in the UK. The court said it had jurisdiction. There was a real potential loss to Mr King in the UK because he had a substantial reputation to protect. US law is more liberal.

The situation for online publishers could hardly be worse. They are potentially liable for publication anywhere on their website and will be judged by local law. Where defamatory material is published within the EU the position is the same and is reinforced by the provisions of the Brussels Convention on Jurisdiction and Enforcement of Judgments in Civil and Commercial Matters of 1968.

So far as defamation arising from a US online publisher is concerned a major difficulty will be enforcing say a damages judgment in the USA. The US court may very well refuse to enforce a foreign judgment on the grounds that it infringes the defendant's right to free speech.

As to what precautions can be taken the best approach for UK online publishers would seem to be to have a material defamation reading by a UK specialist lawyer. UK defamation law is amongst the most strict and conservative of any in the world and if the material is cleared under UK law it should not be regarded as defamatory in other more liberal jurisdictions.

A defendant is not liable when a father opens his son's letter (*Powell* v *Gelstone* [1916] 2 KB 615), or the butler opens the unsealed letter of his employer (*Huth* v *Huth* [1915] 3 KB 32). However, a correspondent should expect that clerks of the claimant, if a business person, might in the ordinary course of business open letters addressed to him at his place of business and not marked 'personal' or 'private', etc., and such a correspondent is responsible for publication of a libel. It should also be noted that marking the communication 'private', 'personal', etc. may not prevent publication in the case of a very busy public figure such as the Prime Minister.

The third person who receives the defamatory statement must be capable of appreciating its significance. A written defamatory statement cannot be published to a blind person except in Braille. It is not publication to repeat a defamatory statement in a foreign language in the presence only of persons who cannot understand the tongue. But if X writes a defamatory statement to Y in, say, German, knowing that Y cannot understand it, X will be responsible for the publication which results from Y's showing it to a linguist for the purpose of translation. In addition, to constitute publication, the person to whom the statement is communicated must understand that it refers to the claimant.

Republication

Problems can occur where the main damage emanating from defamatory material is caused by reason of its republication. Can the republications be regarded as independent acts or where the claimant is suing the maker of the defamatory statement can that person be made liable for the damage resulting from republication? The matter was raised in *McManus* v *Beckham* [2002] 4 All ER 497. It appeared that the defendant, a well-known singer, visited the claimant's shop which sold autographed memorabilia. It was alleged that while in the shop she advised other customers that the signature on a photograph of her husband, a well-known footballer, was a fake. The incident was widely reported in the tabloid press. The claimants' case was that they had suffered loss to their business because of the negative press coverage and that the defendant's remarks suggested that they habitually sold memorabilia with fake autographs. They said they bought their goods from reputable sources and had offered to have this particular signature checked by Mr Beckham. The defendant asked the court to strike out the claim for damages in respect of republication. The claimants were not claiming against the media but seeking recovery of the wider media publication losses from the defendant.

The matter reached the Court of Appeal which refused to strike out the claim for republication damage. The whole matter rested, as in many tort situations, on foreseeability. Republication was reasonably foreseeable here said the Court of Appeal. However, it must be said that in these defamation republication cases the maker of the statement is only likely to be held liable for republication damage where republication is, as in this case, a *significant risk*, arising as it did here from the known interest of the media in the Beckhams.

Who may be defamed?

No action lies at civil law for defaming a dead person, no matter how much it may annoy or upset his relatives. Although from time to time there have been discussions as to reform, the same is currently true where either the victim of the defamation or the defamer dies after publication of the defamation but before judgment has been obtained. There may possibly be a prosecution for criminal libel if the necessary or natural effect of the words used is to render a breach of the peace imminent or probable.

As regards criticism of a trader, it is not defamatory merely to criticise his goods so long as the trader himself is not attacked. To say that a trader is bankrupt or insolvent is defamatory, but to say that he has ceased to be in business is not, for it does not reflect on his reputation (*Ratcliffe* v *Evans* [1892] 2 QB 254) nor as in *Berkoff* is it capable of lowering the claimant's standing in the estimation of the public or of making him the object of ridicule. As we have seen, the law of defamation applies to corporations as it does to private individuals (*D & L Caterers Ltd* v *D'Anjou* (1945) – see Chapter 20).

However, the House of Lords held in *Derbyshire County Council* v *Times Newspapers* (1993) 91 LGR 179 that a local authority could not sue for defamation. It was, said their Lordships, in the highest interest of the public that a council should be subject to scrutiny and criticism and it would be against such interest for such authorities to have any right under the common law to bring a claim for defamation.

It should also be noted that in *Goldsmith* v *Bhoyrul* [1998] QB 459, it was held that it was contrary to the public interest for a political party to have a right at common law to sustain an action for defamation. In a free and democratic society parties which put up for office should always be open to criticism. The public interest in freedom of speech should not be fettered. Candidates could bring claims but to extend this to political parties was not in the public interest.

Libel and slander

The form of publication determines whether the tort committed is libel or slander. *Libel* is defamation in some permanent form; *slander* is a statement of a like kind in transient form. Pictures, effigies, writing and print are clearly libel. Speech is slander, and probably gestures and facial mimicry also. It has been held that a defamatory sound film was a libel, and legislation states that the broadcasting of defamatory matter is libel, whether sound or visual images are transmitted (Defamation Act 1952, s 1). (See also Theatres Act 1968.) Publication on the Internet is libel (see *Godfrey* v *Demon Internet Ltd* (1999) (above)).

Youssoupoff v *Metro-Goldwyn-Mayer*, 1934 – A film is libel (**428**)

It is necessary to determine whether a tort is libel or slander for two reasons:

(a) libel may be a crime as well as a tort;

(b) libel is actionable without the claimant having to prove special damage, i.e. pecuniary loss, whereas the claimant in an action for slander must as a general rule prove such special damage.

Slander is actionable *per se*, i.e. without proof of special damage, in the following cases:

(a) Where there is an imputation that the claimant has been guilty of a criminal offence punishable with imprisonment, e.g. a statement such as 'I have enough information to put John in gaol'.

(b) Where there is an imputation of unchastity to any woman or girl (Slander of Women Act 1891). This probably includes the case where a woman is alleged to have been the victim of rape and seems to include a false allegation of lesbianism (*Kerr* v *Kennedy* [1942] 1 KB 409).

(c) Where there is an imputation that the claimant is suffering from venereal disease and possibly other contagious diseases, e.g. leprosy or plague, which might cause him to be shunned and avoided. To say that a person *has suffered* from these diseases is not actionable *per se*.

(d) Where there have been words calculated to disparage the claimant in any office, profession, business or calling, by imputing dishonesty, unfitness or incompetence (Defamation Act 1952, s 2). However, it is not necessary for the claimant to show, e.g., that he has lost his job as a result, but the remark must be one likely to lower his standing in his trade or profession. Presumably, therefore, the old case of *Lumbe* v *Allday* (1831) 1 Cr & J 301 is still good law. In that case the court decided that a statement that a clerk employed by a gas company associated with whores was not actionable *per se* because his quality as a clerk would be in no way diminished by his association with prostitutes.

A suggestion, therefore, that a clergyman has been found guilty of immoral conduct, or that a solicitor knows no law, is actionable without proof of special damage. Spoken words in a broadcast are actionable *per se* since they are regarded as libel (Defamation Act 1952, s 1).

It is not enough that the words are abusive. Thus to say of A, a bricklayer, that he is a legal ignoramus is not defamatory, though the same words would be defamatory if said of B, a solicitor. Difficulties might arise if the words were said of a chartered accountant who is required to have a knowledge of certain branches of the law.

To resolve problems such as these, two questions must be answered:

(i) Are the alleged words capable of bearing a meaning which is defamatory of the claimant? (This is a matter of law and is decided by the judge.)

(ii) If so, in this particular case are the words in fact defamatory of the claimant? (This is a matter of fact to be decided by the jury.)

What is special damage?

Some material loss is required, e.g. refusal of persons to enter into contracts with the claimant, or the loss of hospitality from friends who have provided food or drink on former occasions (*Storey* v *Challands* (1837) 8 C & P 234). Illness resulting from mental suffering is probably special damage. There were some early cases which said that it was not, but the better view is that these would not be followed now.

21

Innuendo

Cases may arise where the words are not at first sight defamatory, and only appear as such when the surrounding circumstances have been explained. Again a statement may be ironical, or accompanied by a wink or a gesture, or it may be ambiguous, e.g. the statement that 'X drinks'. In such a case the claimant must show that the words contain an innuendo or hidden meaning and that reasonable persons could, and in fact would, interpret the *words* used in a defamatory sense. However, a newspaper article may be defamatory of a person whom readers only identify from their own knowledge of extrinsic facts. The defamation need not arise from words themselves. Evidence is admissible to show that innocent words have a defamatory meaning. The judge decides as a matter of law whether the words are capable of bearing the innuendo alleged by the claimant, and the jury decides whether in fact the words do bear that meaning. The meaning sought to be placed upon the words by the innuendo pleaded must be reasonable, and the court will not read into a statement a defamatory sense which is not there on a reasonable interpretation. Furthermore, a claimant who claims that the innuendo to be drawn by those with special knowledge of the facts from a publication is libellous is bound to particularise those readers of the publication whom he alleges to have such special knowledge.

> *Cassidy* v *Daily Mirror Newspapers*, 1929 – Innuendo: at the racecourse (**429**)
>
> *Morgan* v *Odhams Press*, 1971 – Innocent words may have a defamatory meaning (**430**)
>
> *Tolley* v *Fry*, 1931 – An amateur golfer defamed (**431**)
>
> *Sim* v *Stretch*, 1936 – Defamation must appear on a reasonable interpretation (**432**)
>
> *Fulham* v *Newcastle Chronicle and Journal*, 1977 – Who has special knowledge? (**433**)

Where a claimant relies on an innuendo he must prove that the words were published to a specific person who knew *at the time of the publication* of specific facts enabling that person or persons to understand the words in the innuendo sense. Facts which come into existence afterwards do not make a statement defamatory.

> *Grappelli* v *Derek Block (Holdings) Ltd*, 1981 – Innuendo must arise at the time of publication (**434**)

Reference to the claimant

If the judge decides that the words are capable of bearing a defamatory meaning, he must then consider whether the words are capable of referring to the claimant. This again is a question of law. If he finds the answer to be yes, he must leave to the jury the question: 'Do the words in fact refer to the claimant?' This is a simple matter where the claimant has been referred to by name, and until recently the rule was that an author used a name at his peril if it turned out that it could reasonably be taken to refer to the claimant. Indeed the more obscure the name selected, the greater the chance of success of a claimant who bore that name should he sue for libel. It is not uncommon to attach a disclaimer at the beginning of a work of fiction: 'The persons and events described in this book are wholly imaginary', but it is doubtful whether this affects the author's liability.

> *Hulton* v *Jones*, 1910 – Do the words refer to the claimant? (**435**)

The practical restriction on so-called 'gold-digging' actions was the power of the jury to award contemptuous damages of a farthing (when that coin was in existence), but the costs involved in defending an action might well lead a defendant to settle out of court for a substantial sum. The position has been modified by the Defamation Act 1996, ss 2–4, which provide for an offer of amends.

It sometimes happens that a whole class of persons is the subject of a defamatory statement. Here a member of the class may only sue if he can show that he himself is the person pointed out by the defamatory statement.

> *Knupffer* v *London Express Newspaper Ltd*, 1944 – A class libel fails (**436**)
>
> *Schloimovitz* v *Clarendon Press*, 1973 – How 'Jew' was defined (**437**)

Words may, of course, be defamatory of the claimant without his being mentioned by name, if the statement can be shown to apply to him (see *Youssoupoff* v *M-G-M* (1934)).

The defendant's motives are generally immaterial. The most laudable motives will not by themselves prevent a defamatory statement from being actionable. But where the defendant puts his motives in issue, as where he pleads fair comment or qualified privilege, or relies on ss 2–4 of the Defamation Act 1996 (unintentional defamation), the claimant may then prove the malice of the defendant, or improper motive, to rebut the defence.

Defences

There are certain special defences which are peculiar to an action for defamation, but these defences do not preclude a defendant from denying in addition that the words are defamatory, or asserting that they do not refer to the claimant, or that they were not published.

Justification

There is no burden of proof on the claimant to establish that the defendant's statement is untrue; all the claimant has to do is to prove publication plus the defamatory nature of the statement. However, as the essence of defamation is a false statement, a defendant may always plead the truth of the statement as a defence in civil proceedings (but not in an action for criminal libel, where the rule is: 'The greater the truth, the greater the libel', since true libels are more likely to influence passions). If the statement is true, no injury is done to the claimant's reputation; it is simply reduced to its true level. It does not matter that the statement was made maliciously or even that the defendant did not believe it to be true; so long as it is true the defence of justification is complete.

In the defence of justification the defendant asserts that the statements are 'true both in substance and in fact'. He must show not merely that the words are literally true, but also that there are no significant omissions which would affect the truth of the statement taken as a whole. If, however, the statement is essentially true, an incidental inaccuracy will not deprive the defendant of his right to justify.

> *Alexander* v *The North Eastern Railway Co*, 1865 – The defence of justification (**438**)

However, that which is proved to be true must tally with that which the defendant's statement is interpreted to mean. Thus in *Wakley* v *Cooke* (1849) 4 Exch 511 the defendant called the claimant 'a libellous journalist'. The defendant proved that the claimant had had

21

one judgment against him for libel but the court held that the statement meant that the journalist habitually libelled people and so the defendant had not justified it.

The defence of justification really amounts to a positive charge against the claimant, and if it fails the damages may be increased, since the original wrong has been aggravated. The defendant's honest belief that the statement is true is no justification, though it may reduce damages. Nor is it a justification to prove that a quoted statement was made, if the quotation cannot be proved to be true. Suppose a statement is made: 'Mrs A tells me that Dr B has been committing adultery with a woman patient.' It is no justification to show that Mrs A made the statement to the defendant; he must show that Dr B is actually guilty of the conduct alleged.

In connection with this defence, it is important to note s 5 of the Defamation Act 1952, which provides that in an action for libel and slander in respect of words containing two or more distinct charges against a claimant, a defence of justification shall not fail by reason only that the truth of every charge is not proved if the words not proved to be true do not materially injure the claimant's reputation having regard to the truth of the remaining charges.

In connection with justification it should be noted that under s 8 of the Rehabilitation of Offenders Act 1974 (see further Chapter 4) a claimant who proves that the defendant has maliciously published details of a spent conviction may recover damages. However, the section does not affect the defences of absolute or qualified privilege and fair comment. Thus an employer will, in the absence of malice, still be protected if he writes a reference which mentions a spent conviction. It was decided in *Herbage* v *Pressdram* [1984] 2 All ER 769 by the Court of Appeal that a rehabilitated offender who seeks an interlocutory injunction to prevent publication of his conviction is in the same position as a person against whom a defence of qualified privilege is raised. An injunction will only be granted if there is overwhelming evidence of malice in the publication or some irrelevant, spiteful or improper motive.

Fair comment on a matter of public interest

Here the defendant must show that the statement alleged to be defamatory is in fact legitimate comment. The defence is designed to cover criticism of matters of public interest in the form of comment upon true, or privileged, statements of fact, such comment being made honestly by a person who did not believe the statements to be untrue and who was not otherwise actuated by malice. The malice element makes the defence similar to that of qualified privilege (see below). The statement must be comment, i.e. the speaker's opinion of a true state of affairs; it must not be an assertion of facts, but a comment on known facts.

> *London Artists* v *Littler*, 1969 – A comment on the wrong facts (**439**)

Comment is the individual reaction to facts, and the court and the jury require to be satisfied only of the defendant's honesty. The test is: 'Would any honest person, however prejudiced he may be, however exaggerated or obstinate his views, have said that which this criticism has said of what is criticised?' If the answer is 'yes', the comment is fair for the purposes of raising this defence.

The matter upon which the comment is made must be one of legitimate public interest such as the conduct of Parliament, the government, local authorities and other public authorities, or the behaviour of a trade union whose actions affect supplies and services to the public. Further, a matter may become the subject of public interest because the claimant has voluntarily submitted himself and his affairs to public criticism. A person who makes a public speech or publishes a book or presents a play thereby submits the subject matter of such thing for public comment, and cannot complain if the comment is adverse.

It should also be noted that the facts relied on to support a plea of fair comment must be facts existing at the time of the comment and not facts which have occurred some time before the comment was made (*Cohen* v *Daily Telegraph* [1968] 2 All ER 407).

It is important to distinguish fair comment from the defence of justification. In fair comment it is not necessary to prove the truth of the comment but merely that the opinion was honestly held; if justification is pleaded in regard to matters of opinion, the defendant must prove not merely that he honestly held the views expressed but that they were correct views. Thus, if we take the following statement – 'X's speech last night was inconsistent with his profession of Liberalism', in a plea of justification the defendant must prove that it was inconsistent, but in a plea of fair comment the defendant need only show that he honestly held this opinion of X's speech.

Privilege

This defence protects statements made in circumstances where the public interest in securing a free expression of facts or opinion outweighs the private interests of the person about whom the statements are made. Privilege may be absolute – such a statement is never actionable – or qualified, when privilege may be defeated by proof of the defendant's malice.

Absolute privilege

The Bill of Rights 1689 protects statements in both Houses of Parliament. The Parliamentary Papers Act 1840 affords a similar protection to reports, papers, etc., published by order of either House, e.g. *Hansard* and government White Papers. The Defamation Act 1952, s 9 protects verbatim broadcasts and newspaper reports of parliamentary proceedings but Parliament itself can fine or imprison those who abuse this privilege. Members of the European Parliament also have immunity for statements made during sessions of the European Parliament *even if it is not actually sitting* (*Wybot* v *Faure* Case 149/85 [1986] ECR 2391).

Section 13 of the Defamation Act 1996 allows waiver of parliamentary privilege. The matter was raised in *Hamilton* v *Al Fayed* (2000) 26 Sol Jo LB 157. The claimant, a former Member of Parliament, had waived his parliamentary privilege under s 13 and commenced libel proceedings after the defendant had alleged that he had accepted payments as a reward for asking questions in Parliament. The defendant asked for the action to be struck out on the basis that the Committee on Standards and Privileges and the Parliamentary Commissioner for Standards had already investigated the allegations and s 13 did not extend to waive Parliament's exclusive jurisdiction over its internal affairs. The House of Lords ruled that the waiver applied and Mr Hamilton's claim could proceed. The claimant's waiver of his parliamentary protection overrode any privilege belonging to Parliament as a whole and thus allowed the parties to challenge the truthfulness of evidence given to the parliamentary bodies without breaching parliamentary privilege. If that challenge could not have been made by reason of privilege, the trial would have been impossible to pursue.

With regard to the courts, statements by the judge, members of the jury, counsel, and the parties or witnesses are absolutely privileged, as are orders of court. Thus an order of court for divorce, including a finding of adultery against a woman, is not actionable even though reversed on appeal. A statement made by a witness is not actionable even though the judge finds it untrue and malicious. The abuse of the above privilege is checked by (*a*) the law of perjury (in the case of untrue statements by witnesses), (*b*) the power of the judge to report improper behaviour on the part of counsel to the Benchers of his Inn, and (*c*) the judge's power to commit persons to prison for contempt of court.

21

Communications between senior and responsible public officers in the course of their duty are absolutely privileged. However, the defence of absolute privilege does not apply to information given to a social security adjudication officer by a person applying for benefit, and so allegations made by an employee against a former employer as to the manner of a dismissal could be the subject of an action for libel (see *Purdew* v *Seress-Smith* [1993] IRLR 77).

Where in the course of legal proceedings (as distinct from the giving of legal advice), the solicitor for one party requests the solicitor for the other party for information regarding the case which his client will advance, the answer given is subject to absolute privilege (see *Waple* v *Surrey County Council* [1997] 2 All ER 836).

It was held by the Court of Appeal in *Mahon* v *Rahn (No 2)* [2000] 2 All ER (Comm) 1 that a letter from an informant to a financial services regulator, the Securities Association (a predecessor to the Financial Services Authority), during an investigation into a person's fitness to carry out investment business attracted absolute privilege.

Absolute privilege and human rights

The European Court of Human Rights has ruled that absolute privilege does not infringe Art 6 (right to a fair trial) of the Convention. In *A* v *United Kingdom* (2002) *The Times*, 28 December a young black woman tried to challenge the rule of absolute privilege in circumstances where her MP had named her in a parliamentary debate, gave her full address and made adverse comments concerning her behaviour and that of her children. The court ruled that absolute privilege of parliamentary proceedings did not infringe Art 6. It was very limited and did not impose a disproportionate restriction on an individual's right of access to the courts. The MP was protected by the Bill of Rights Act 1689, Art 9 of the Convention (freedom of thought, conscience and religion) and press reports of the proceedings were protected by qualified privilege.

Qualified privilege

Where such privilege exists, a person is entitled to communicate a defamatory statement so long as he does so honestly and reasonably with regard to the words used and the means of publication, and without malice. Qualified privilege has been held to arise in the following cases:

(a) Common interest, i.e. where a statement is made by a person who is under a legal or moral duty to communicate it to a person who has a similarly legitimate interest in receiving it. This covers testimonials or references to prospective employers, or to trade protection societies whose function it is to investigate the creditworthiness of persons who are the objects of their enquiry.

> *London Association for the Protection of Trade* v *Greenlands*, 1916 – A bad report from a trade association (**440**)

(b) Statements in protection of one's private interests are privileged.

> *Osborn* v *Thos Boulter*, 1930 – An allegation of watering the beer (**441**)

(c) Statements by way of complaint to a proper authority, e.g. petitions to Parliament and complaints to officials of local authorities and professional bodies. It was decided in *Graff* v *Panel on Take-Overs and Mergers* (1980) *Financial Times*, 11 October that the Panel had a moral duty to investigate alleged breaches of the code and that it followed from this that if the

Panel had learned of an alleged breach of the code and had circularised copies of an article – which was the subject of this libel action – in order to establish or to demolish the allegations, the Panel was protected by the defence of qualified privilege.

Beach v *Freeson*, 1971 – An MP's duty (**442**)

(**d**) Professional confidential communications between solicitor and client on legal advice. As we have seen, correspondence during the course of legal proceedings between solicitors is subject to absolute privilege (*Waple* v *Surrey County Council* [1997] 2 All ER 836).

(**e**) Newspaper reports on various public matters. The Defamation Act 1996, in s 15 and Sch 1, confers qualified privilege upon fair and accurate newspaper reports of various matters of public interest and importance. The Defamation Act 1996 extends this to fair and accurate reports in *all* publications, provided the publisher has, if asked, published a reasonable letter or statement by way of explanation or contradiction. Failure to do so rules out the defence. These reports are of two classes:

(i)   Those which are privileged without any explanation or contradiction being issued, e.g. reports of public proceedings of colonial or dominion legislatures, reports of public proceedings of the United Nations Organisation, of the International Court of Justice, or of British courts martial, and fair and accurate copies of and extracts from British public registers and notices.

(ii) Those which are privileged only if the newspaper concerned is prepared, on the claimant's request, to publish a reasonable letter or statement in explanation or contradiction of the original report, e.g. semi-judicial findings of the governing bodies of learned societies, professional and trade associations, or authorities controlling games and sports. This also applies to fair and accurate reports of public meetings, meetings of local and public authorities, and the meetings of public companies. In this context a press conference can be regarded as within the expression 'public meeting' so that press reports emanating from it can be subject to the defence of qualified privilege (see *McCarten Turkington Breen (a firm)* v *Times Newspapers Ltd* [2000] 4 All ER 913: a ruling of the House of Lords).

(**f**) Fair and accurate reports of parliamentary proceedings are the subject of qualified privilege whether contained in a newspaper or not.

21

Cook v *Alexander*, 1973 – Privilege and a parliamentary sketch (**443**)

(**g**) Fair and accurate reports of public judicial proceedings are privileged. This does not protect reports of proceedings in domestic tribunals, e.g. the Law Society, unless the report is in a newspaper. Such reports will not be privileged if the court has forbidden publication, as is often done in cases affecting children, or if the matter reported is obscene or scandalous. It is also a criminal offence to report indecent matter relating to judicial proceedings (Judicial Proceedings (Regulation of Reports) Act 1926; Domestic and Appellate Proceedings (Restriction of Publicity) Act 1968).

(**h**) An apology published in connection with defamation is not subject to qualified privilege and if it contains further defamatory material this can be sued upon without the need for proof of malice in the author and publisher (see *Watts* v *Times Newspapers Ltd* [1996] 2 WLR 427).

Qualified privilege may be rebutted by proof of malice or some improper motive, and proof of actual spite or ill will in the publication will defeat it. An improper motive may be inferred from the tone of the statement or from the circumstances attending its publication, and malice may also be inferred from abuse of the privilege, such as the giving of excessive publicity to statements protected by qualified privilege. However, the gross and unreasoning prejudice of the defendant will not defeat the defence of privilege if the defendant honestly believed that what he published was true. But where a person without malice joins with a malicious person in publishing a libel in circumstances of qualified privilege, the person without malice is not liable to the person defamed.

> *Horrocks* v *Low*, 1972 – Malice cannot be inferred (**444**)
> *Egger* v *Viscount Chelmsford*, 1964 – A judge of Alsatian dogs (**445**)

Where there is a pressing obligation to communicate defamatory matter, a person may communicate it, although he does not believe it to be true, and still claim qualified privilege. Thus an accountant who, on going through the books of a firm, finds evidence that the cashier has embezzled money, may communicate that view to authority and still claim qualified privilege, even though the accountant does not believe that the cashier has, in fact, embezzled the money.

The media: qualified privilege: developments

The categories of situations where the defence of qualified privilege is available have tended to expand over the years. In this connection, the Lord Chancellor has power under the Defamation Act 1996 to create new situations of qualified privilege (see Sch 1, para 15 to the Act), though there has as yet been no extension under this power. However, journalists have tried to get the courts to extend the defence to matters of 'political importance'. This trend has been brought to a halt by the decision of the House of Lords in *Reynolds* v *Times Newspapers Ltd* [1999] 3 WLR 1010. The claimant was the former Taoiseach of Ireland. He complained of an article appearing in the *Sunday Times* that gave the impression that he had deliberately and dishonestly misled the Irish Dail. The defence that the article was subject to qualified privilege by reason of being 'political information' was rejected.

An important aspect of the *Reynolds* case is the guidelines laid down by the House of Lords in connection with the acceptance of the defence of qualified privilege when put forward by newspapers and other media. Matters to be taken into account by a court are:

- the seriousness of the allegation;
- the nature of the information and the extent to which the subject matter was a matter of public concern;
- the source of the information;
- the steps taken to verify the information;
- the status of the information;
- the urgency of the matter;
- whether comment had been sought from the claimant;
- whether the article contained the gist of the claimant's side of the story;
- the tone of the article;
- the circumstances of the publication including the timing.

> *Loutchansky* v *Times Newspapers Ltd*, 2002 – The *Reynolds* guidelines applied: limitation and the Internet (**445a**)

Reynolds liberalised

The tests in *Reynolds* were still difficult to pass but in *Jameel* v *Wall Street Journal Europe* [2006] 3 WLR 642 the House of Lords has liberalised the *Reynolds* guidance and heralded a new era for British investigative journalism. The *Jameel* ruling is to the following effect:

■ The publishers of an article of undoubted public concern are not to be denied the protection of qualified privilege where, having taken detailed steps to verify its contents, they fail to obtain the claimant's comments before publication.

■ The key test is whether a media organisation or newspaper acted fairly and responsibly in gathering and publishing the information. If the reporter and editor did so and the information was of public importance then the fact that it contained relevant but defamatory allegations against prominent people would not allow them to recover libel damages.

The story published by the *Wall Street Journal Europe* said that bank accounts associated with a number of prominent Saudi citizens, including Mr Jameel's family, had been monitored by the Saudi government at the request of the US authorities to ensure that no money was provided intentionally or knowingly to support terrorists. The High Court and the Court of Appeal had not found that the *Reynolds* public interest test applied because, among other things, no comment had been sought from the claimant. The House of Lords, however, allowed the journal's appeal and in doing so further liberalised the public interest test. What the journal had published was clearly in the public interest.

Offer of amends

The Defamation Act 1996 sets out in ss 2–4 a new offer of amends defence. It is described as a 'qualified offer' and is an offer of amends which is limited to a specific defamatory meaning which the defendant who makes the offer accepts that the statement which is complained of conveys. A qualified offer is appropriate:

■ where the defendant accepts that his defamatory statement is partially untrue; or
■ where the defendant maintains that although the statement is defamatory it is not so in the sense argued by the claimant.

If, for example, an accountant complained that an article in a newspaper relating to a financial scandal in which he was involved accused him of fraud but the newspaper said that in its view the article merely made an allegation of incompetence, the newspaper could make a qualified offer of amends in regard to the less serious meaning and this would be a defence if the offer was refused and the jury accepted that an allegation of incompetence was the true meaning.

It was held in *Watts* v *Times Newspapers Ltd* [1996] 2 WLR 427 that the publication of an apology is not protected by qualified privilege so that if the apology contains further accusations regarding the claimant *or a third party* a claim may be made without the need to prove malice.

The offer may be made before proceedings or after proceedings commence but before submission of defence. Thus, the publisher has under the 1996 Act rather longer than before to investigate and assess his position before deciding whether to run an offer to make amends. The offer is to make a suitable correction and sufficient apology in a reasonable and practicable way and to pay compensation equivalent to defamation damages. However, the major costs of proceeding to trial may be saved. Making such an offer is a defence and, if used must be the *only* defence relied on. It is essential to the defence that the publisher did not know and had no reason to believe that the statement complained of was likely to be understood as referring to the aggrieved party and that it was false and defamatory of him.

21

Under s 3(5) of the 1996 Act it is up to the court to quantify an unresolved issue as to the amount of the offer. In this connection the defendant who is making the offer may rely on evidence relevant to the claimant's character such as previous convictions for violent offences where the libel related to the claimant's alleged violence on a woman in order to obtain possession of certain tape recordings and recording equipment in her possession (see *Abu* v *MGN Ltd* [2003] 2 All ER 864).

It is well worth a defendant's while to use the offer of amends procedure because a prompt acknowledgement of the defamation together with an unqualified offer of amends and published apologies can reduce the damages significantly as for example in *Nail* v *News Group Newspapers Ltd* [2005] 1 All ER 1040, where they were reduced by 50 per cent.

Consent of the claimant to publication

If the claimant has agreed to publication, he cannot subsequently sue in respect of that statement. Consent may be given in respect of a particular publication or it may be general.

> *Chapman* v *Lord Ellesmere*, 1932 – Where the claimant is a volunteer (446)

Theatres Act 1968

Section 4 of the Theatres Act 1968 amends the law of defamation (including the law relating to criminal libel) by providing that the publication of words (including pictures, visual images, gestures, and the like) in the public performance of a play shall be treated as publication in permanent form, i.e. libel. Performances given on a domestic occasion in a private dwelling house are exempt (s 7(1)) and so are rehearsals and performances for broadcast or recording purposes (s 7(2)) provided such rehearsals and performances are attended only by the persons *directly* connected with the giving of them.

Section 5 of the Act creates an offence of incitement to racial hatred by presenting or directing the public performance of a play though, again, rehearsals and performances attended only by persons directly concerned are exempt. Prosecution under s 5 is with the consent of the Attorney-General (s 8).

It is of interest to note also that s 1 of the Act abolishes the power of the Lord Chamberlain to censor plays.

Summary procedure

Summary proceedings are already available under the Civil Procedure Rules 1998 where the claim has no prospect of succeeding or there is no reasonable prospect of defending, though the summary proceedings may reveal that this is not so and a trial will ensue. However, the new machinery under the 1996 Act is now in force. The new machinery is available where the claimant applies for all or any of the following reliefs:

- a declaration (of liability or no liability);
- an order for publication of an apology, or correction;
- damages not exceeding £10,000; and
- an order restraining repetition.

The court is entitled to dismiss the claim if it has no real prospect of success and there is no reason why it should be tried. Additionally, the court may give judgment for the claimant if there is no defence that has a reasonable prospect of success and there is no reason for a trial. A trial may be required where there is a conflict of evidence and the seriousness of the wrong in terms, e.g., of its extensive publication.

Trial may be in the county court if the parties consent.

An example of the use of the summary procedure arose in *Oryx Group* v *BBC* (2002) High Court, 17 July. The Oryx Group is an international corporation with investments and business interests across a range of industries including banking, hotels, automotive, natural resources, food production, construction and marketing. Oryx's claim arose from a BBC broadcast on the 10 o'clock news on 31 October 2001. It was a special report entitled 'The diamonds that pay for Bin Laden's terror'. In the report Oryx was falsely accused of funding Bin Laden and the Al Qaeda network. On 19 November 2001 the BBC broadcast an apology. The BBC did not put forward the defence of justification using instead the defences of qualified privilege and no defamatory meaning. On 10 May 2002 four days before the BBC was required to serve its evidence it abandoned the defence of qualified privilege. Oryx then applied for summary judgment on the basis that the BBC had no credible defence. This was granted and on 17 July 2002 the High Court awarded judgment and costs to Oryx. A fairly speedy conclusion in the circumstances of the case.

It is important to note that the fact that a judge has agreed to a request for summary proceedings does not mean that the defendant is denied a jury trial. There may be an appeal to the Court of Appeal on the issue and the Court of Appeal may require a jury trial where it is of opinion, e.g. that the defendant has a reasonable prospect of success with the defence (see *Safeway Stores plc* v *Tate* [2001] QB 1120).

Limitation period

Section 5 of the Defamation Act 1996 reduces the limitation period from three years to one in actions for libel, slander or malicious falsehood, the reason being that one year is the time within which most actions should be brought if the action is to minimise damage to the claimant's reputation. The court may allow a late claim if it is equitable to do so having regard to prejudice to either party and taking into account, e.g., situations where the claimant was not aware that he had a claim on the first anniversary of the publication of the offending material and provided he has acted reasonably and promptly when he did find out, and the availability of evidence which would have been available during the primary 12-month period – or in other words, is vital evidence still available?

The court has a jurisdiction to extend the one year period but will not normally do so unless there is a satisfactory explanation of the delay (see *Steedman* v *BBC* [2001] Entertainment and Media Law Reports 17: Court of Appeal). The position with regard to online continuous libels has already been considered (see *Dow Jones & Co Inc* v *Gutnick* [2002] HCA 56 at p 588).

Criminal convictions

As regards criminal convictions, such a conviction of the claimant is regarded as conclusive in defamation proceedings so that the possibility of a defamation action being used by a convicted criminal to challenge his conviction is removed. However, a criminal conviction is not conclusive where the defendant is not the criminal concerned. This will enable investigative journalists to defend libellous statements about police irregularities connected with a criminal's case by means of evidence to show that the criminal concerned might not have been guilty (see s 12 of the Defamation Act 1996).

Pre-trial interpretation of relevant material

It should also be noted that following changes to the Rules of Supreme Court judges are now allowed, even before a case has been regarded as suitable for trial, to rule on the interpretation of words and phrases which are ambiguous before the start of full proceedings. 'Are the words capable of being defamatory?' is the question. This will save time and money where, subject to recommendation by the claimant's advisers, the case does not proceed to full trial where the preliminary ruling is that the words or phrases are not defamatory.

Damages

Although many slanders are actionable only on proof of special damage to the claimant, actual damages awarded by the court will not be confined to the special damage so proved. For example, if as a result of defamation a person loses his or her employment, he or she can prove special damage in this connection, but the actual damages awarded may take in much more than this particular loss. Damages for defamation tend to be high. Juries are often used in such cases, and they are concerned with the quantum of damages. The damages awarded for loss of reputation may often be higher than damages awarded for the loss of life. In this connection, the case of *John* v *Mirror Group Newspapers Ltd* (1995) *The Times*, 14 December is of interest. MGN appealed against a total libel award of £350,000 comprising £75,000 compensatory damages and £275,000 exemplary damages awarded to Elton John in a libel action in respect of an article in the *Daily Mirror*. The Court of Appeal reduced the damages to £75,000 and stated that it was offensive to public opinion that awards for defamation should often well exceed sums awarded for injury cases. There was no reason why counsel or the judge should not indicate to the jury what might be a reasonable sum in a particular case. However, damages should be compensatory and not punitive though they may be *aggravated* by mental suffering arising from the defamation, or *mitigated* by a full apology, provocation by the claimant, or the claimant's bad reputation.

> *Davis* v *Rubin*, 1967 – Where libel damages are excessive (**447**)

Injunctions

Apart from damages, a defamed person may seek an injunction restraining further publication. Such injunctions are of two kinds:

(*a*) **a perpetual injunction**, which is usually granted at the trial; and
(*b*) **an interim injunction** (or interlocutory injunction), which is granted pending the trial, and may be *quia timet*, that is before the wrong is actually done.

However, publication of an article will not be restrained merely because it is defamatory where the defendant says he intends to justify it or make fair comment on a matter of public interest, or claim privilege and the claimant cannot show that the defence(s) concerned will be likely to fail (*Harakas* v *Baltic Mercantile and Shipping Exchange Ltd* [1982] 2 All ER 701).

Before concluding the tort of defamation we should notice also the separate tort of *injurious falsehood*. Just as defamation is an attack on a person's reputation, so injurious falsehood is an attack on his or her goods. To say that A's goods are inferior in quality to B's may be an injurious falsehood. To say that A sells inferior goods as goods of superior quality may, on the other hand, be a defamatory statement.

Reform

The Law Commission has recommended that there should be an urgent review of Internet libel laws. There is evidence that Internet service providers are increasingly shutting down sites because of defamation allegations even where the information is true or in the public interest. These difficulties are exposed by the cases considered in this chapter.

At the time of writing, no legislation was forthcoming.

The rule in *Rylands* v *Fletcher*

This celebrated rule was stated in the case of *Rylands* v *Fletcher* (1868):

> Where a person for his own purposes brings and keeps on land in his occupation anything likely to do mischief if it escapes, he must keep it in at his peril, and if he fails to do so he is liable for all damage naturally accruing from the escape.

The rule has been held to apply whether the things brought on the land be 'beasts, water, filth or stenches'. The rule also applies to fire. It does not apply to the pollution of beaches by oil because, *inter alia*, the oil does not escape from *land* but from the sea (see *Southport Corporation* v *Esso Petroleum Co* (1954)).

In more recent times an element of foresight of consequences has been imported into the rule so that, although liability does not require negligence and is strict in that sense, it does require foresight of consequences, as where the defendant knew or ought to have known of them, before there can be a liability (see *Cambridge Water Co Ltd* v *Eastern Counties Leather plc* (1994) below).

This decision should be borne in mind when considering earlier case law appearing in this text. It may be that in some of the older cases the defendants escaped liability by showing that they had no foresight of consequences either subjectively (themselves) or objectively (through the rule of the reasonable person). Development along these lines may convert the rule in *Rylands* to an aspect of negligence.

Emanuel v *Greater London Council*, 1970 – An escape of fire (**448**)

In the case which gave rise to the rule, the defendant had constructed a reservoir on his land, employing competent workmen for the purpose. Water escaped from the reservoir and percolated through certain old mine shafts, which had been filled with marl and earth, and eventually flooded the claimant's mine. The defendant was held liable in that he had collected water on his land, the water not being naturally there, and it had escaped and done damage. Since the defendant employed competent workmen, it follows that the liability was absolute and did not depend on negligence, and in any case, the defendant's action was quite innocent as there was no reason why he should know of, or even suspect the existence of, the disused shafts. Thus, even in the leading case, *there was no foresight of consequences*.

In order for the rule to apply, there must be an escape of the thing which inflicts the injury from a place over which the defendant has occupation or control to a place which is outside his occupation or control. It is doubtful to what extent the rule covers personal injury.

Read v *Lyons*, 1947 – There must be an escape (**449**)

The rule is not confined to wrongs between owners of adjacent land and does not depend on ownership of land but the claimant must have some interest in the land. Thus in *McKenna* v *British Aluminium Ltd* (2002) *The Times*, 25 April the High Court dismissed an application to strike out (or bring to an end) claims in strict liability under *Rylands* v *Fletcher* and nuisance.

21

The judge stated that the 30 or so claimants who were alleging harm caused by emissions could not succeed in an action in nuisance or *Rylands* because they did not have an interest in the land affected by it. The judge concluded, however, that the claimants had an arguable case because of the Human Rights Act 1998 and that this Act may well have extended the common law (and see also *Weller* v *Foot and Mouth Disease Research Institute* (1965)). Neither is it confined to the escape of water, but may cover the escape of any offensive or dangerous matter arising out of abnormal use of land provided the defendant has control of it.

> *Charing Cross Electricity Supply Co* v *Hydraulic Power Co*, 1914 – No need for ownership of land (**450**)
> *Attorney-General* v *Corke*, 1933 – An abnormal use of land (**451**)

In general, there is no liability under the rule for damage caused by the escape of things naturally on the land, though there may be an action in nuisance or in negligence.

> *Giles* v *Walker*, 1890 – Escaping thistles (**452**)
> *Davey* v *Harrow Corporation*, 1957 – Escaping tree roots (**453**)

Although *Rylands* v *Fletcher* imposes strict liability, the following defences are still open to the defendant:

(a) That the escape was the claimant's fault. It should also be noted that there is no reason why the Law Reform (Contributory Negligence) Act 1945 should not apply where the claimant is partly to blame.

(b) That it was an act of God (see *Nichols* v *Marsland* (1876)), though the defence is not often successfully pleaded.

> *Greenock Corporation* v *Caledonian Railway Co*, 1917 – The defence of an act of God fails (**454**)

(c) That the escape was due to the wrongful act of a stranger.

> *Rickards* v *Lothian*, 1913 – An act of a stranger (**455**)

(d) That the damage was caused by artificial works done for the common benefit of the claimant and the defendant.

> *Peters* v *Prince of Wales Theatre (Birmingham) Ltd*, 1943 – Property installed for common benefit (**456**)

(e) That there was statutory authority for the act of the defendant, provided that the defendant was not negligent. It should be noted that the defence of statutory authority is not available in respect of reservoirs (Reservoirs Act 1975, s 28 and Sch 2).

The rule is liberalised – foresight required?

In more recent times the rule has been liberalised. In *Cambridge Water Co Ltd* v *Eastern Counties Leather plc* (1991) *The Times*, 23 October, the High Court held that the storage of organochlorines by businesses involved in the tanning industry and based at Sawston, an industrial village, was a natural use of land for the purposes of the rule in *Rylands* v *Fletcher*. Sawston was properly described as an industrial village, said Mr Justice Ian Kennedy, and the creation of employment was clearly for the benefit of that community. Storage in that place was therefore natural use of land. He rejected a claim from the water company in regard to the pollution of a nearby public water supply borehole.

The decision of Mr Justice Ian Kennedy was reversed by the Court of Appeal, which held that the accidental spillage of chemicals gave rise to strict liability (see *Cambridge Water* v *Eastern Counties Leather plc* [1994] 2 AC 664), so that Eastern Counties was liable. However, the House of Lords reversed the Court of Appeal and found that Eastern Counties was not liable (also reported at [1994] 2 AC 664). It based its decision on the need for foreseeability of consequences and not non-natural user. In fact, Lord Goff stated that the storage of chemicals in substantial quantities on industrial land '. . . should be regarded as an almost classic case of non-natural use'. It follows, therefore, that the element of foresight was built into *Rylands* and, since Eastern Counties had not foreseen the consequences of the spillage, it was not liable.

It may therefore be said that strict liability (i.e. non-negligent liability) for the escape from land of things likely to do damage only arises under *Cambridge Water* if the defendant knew or ought reasonably to have foreseen that those things might, if they escaped, cause damage. Incidentally, the House of Lords doubted whether the fact that Eastern Counties' activities gave employment could lead to the conclusion that keeping chemicals on land was natural use.

The House of Lords rules

The latest position derives from *Transco plc* v *Stockport Metropolitan Borough Council* [2004] 1 All ER 589. The facts can be stated briefly. The claimants' gas main was left without support by the collapse of an embankment on which it stood. The collapse was caused by a leak of water supplied by the defendants to a block of flats which they owned. The pipe carrying the water was of correct size but failed and leaked water. This was undiscovered for a prolonged period and a considerable quantity of water built up and escaped, causing the embankment to collapse. The House of Lords found for the defendants, mainly because the supply of water to the flats was nothing other than natural or ordinary user. However, since in all of the above events it was accepted that the defendants had not been negligent, and in case *Rylands* liability might succeed, the defendants asked the House of Lords to follow Australian authority and absorb *Rylands* into the principles of ordinary negligence.

The House of Lords quite firmly refused to do this. *Rylands*, they said, was an aspect of the law of private nuisance and would remain so. The main reasons given were:

- The age of the case the principles of which had been relied on for many years. To remove it might cause some future claimant to lose a right which *Rylands* gave, i.e. strict liability in the defendant where perhaps negligence could not be proved.
- The concern that the interpretation of statutes which do sometimes create strict liability might be taken as requiring negligence once *Rylands* had been absorbed.
- Although to absorb *Rylands* into the law of negligence would unify the law of England and Wales on this point with that of Australia it would effect disunity with Europe where some states, e.g. Germany and France, do have not dissimilar forms of strict liability.

Their Lordships' comments on the requirements of *Rylands* leave things much as they always have been.

21

Part 4

THE LAW OF PROPERTY

22

THE LAW OF PROPERTY

English law divides property into real property and personal property. Real property includes only freehold interests in land, and personal property comprises all other proprietary rights, whether in land or chattels. This classification is not identical with the obvious distinction between immoveables and moveables, and this is the result of the attitude of early law to the nature of a lease.

The nature of property

Actions in respect of property fall into two kinds: actions *in rem* or real actions, and actions *in personam* or personal actions. An action *in rem* in English law is an action in which a specific thing is recovered; an action *in personam* gives damages only.

It so happened that in early days the courts would allow a real action or *actio realis* only for the specific recovery of land. If an owner was dispossessed of other forms of property, the person who had taken the property had a choice; he could either restore the property taken or pay damages to the rightful owner. Hence, land became known as real property or *realty*, and all other forms of property were called personal property or *personalty*. So far the distinction corresponds to that between moveables and immoveables, but this convenient classification was disturbed by the lease for a term of years.

Although a lease of land was an interest in immoveable property, the real action was not available to the dispossessed tenant. Leases did not fit into the feudal system of landholding by tenure but were regarded as personal business arrangements whereby one person allowed another the use of the land for a period in return for a rent.

These transactions were personal contracts and created rights *in personam* between the parties, and not rights *in rem* which could affect feudal status. It was not an uncommon form of investment to buy land and let it out on lease to obtain an income on capital invested, and such transactions were more akin to commercial dealings than to landholding as it was understood in early days. Moreover, the system had its advantages, since a lease was immune from feudal burdens and could be left by will at a time when dispositions by will of other land were still not permitted.

Leaseholds, therefore, come under the heading of personal property or chattels, but because they partake so strongly of the character of land, they are often referred to as *chattels real* to distinguish them from pure personalty, e.g. a watch or a fountain pen. Since the property legislation of 1925 this distinction has lost much of its importance, but it is still true that if in his will a testator says, 'All my personalty to P and all my realty to R', P would get the leaseholds.

Pure personalty itself comprises two different kinds of property known as *choses in possession* and *choses in action*. *Choses in possession* denote chattels, such as jewellery and furniture, which are tangible objects and can be physically possessed and enjoyed by their owner. *Choses in action* are intangible forms of property which are incapable of physical possession, and their owner is usually compelled to bring an action if he wishes to enforce his rights over property of this kind. Examples of *choses in action* are debts, patents, copyrights, trade marks, shares, and negotiable instruments.

Up to now we have been considering the main rights which one has in one's own things. However, it is possible to have rights over the things of another. We have already mentioned the lease, which is the right to possess another's land for a term in return for a rent, but in addition it is possible to become the owner of a *servitude* over the land of another, e.g. a right of way, a right of light, or a right to the support of buildings. A servitude may also be a right to take something from the land of another, e.g. the right to fish or collect firewood. Rights of the first class are called *easements*, and of the second profits *à prendre*. Further, a person may raise a loan on the security of his property either real or personal, and the lender has certain rights over the property so used as a security if the loan is not repaid.

Ownership

Ownership is a term used to express the relationship which exists between a person and certain rights which are vested in him. Ownership is the greatest right or collection of rights – the ultimate right – which a person can have over or in a thing.

For example, X may own a fee simple (freehold) in Blackacre and may lease the land to Y, so giving up possession. But however long the lease, the ultimate right of ownership is in X, and eventually the right to possess, which he has for the moment forfeited, will return to him or to his estate if he is dead. Z may have a right of way over Blackacre. This is not ownership of Blackacre, but is ownership of a right over it which limits X's enjoyment of the land. B may have lent money to X on the security of the land, so that B is a mortgagee and, therefore, the owner of a right in Blackacre, but this does not constitute ownership of the land; it is a mere encumbrance attached to it, limiting X's enjoyment to the extent of the rights given to B as mortgagee. Nevertheless, the supreme right is vested in X, and this right is called ownership of Blackacre.

Ownership is a *de jure* (i.e. legal) relationship; there is no need to possess the thing. Possession tends to be *de facto* (i.e. factual), that is evidenced by physical possession, although, as we shall see, physical possession is not necessary in order to have legal possession.

It may be said that in a general sense all rights are capable of ownership, which is of many kinds:

(a) Corporeal. That is, the ownership of a thing or *chose in possession* such as a watch or a fountain pen.

(b) Incorporeal. That is, the ownership of a right only, e.g. the right to recover a debt of £20 from X by an action at law, or the ownership of a *chose in action*. A share certificate is a *chose in action*, and ownership of it is incorporeal, for it is ownership of certain rights: the right to dividends as and when declared, the right to vote at meetings, and so on.

(c) Sole ownership. That is, as where X is the sole owner of Blackacre.

(d) Co-ownership. That is, as where X and Y are simultaneously owners of Blackacre, as joint tenants or tenants in common.

(e) Legal or equitable ownership. A grant (by conveyance (transfer) or will) giving X the fee simple absolute in possession of Blackacre constitutes him the legal owner. But a grant giving X a life interest only constitutes him as equitable owner, whose interest can exist only behind a trust, the legal estate being held by trustees.

(f) Trust or beneficial ownership. In the grant set out above giving X a life interest, the trustees hold the legal estate but not beneficially; the beneficial interest is in X and equity will protect it.

(g) Vested (completed) or contingent ownership. In a grant to X for life with remainder to Y, X and Y have equitable interests and both are vested. Admittedly Y will not become entitled in enjoyment until X dies, but his interest is, nevertheless, vested, and if Y were to die before X, the property would descend through Y's estate on X's death.

In a grant to X for life, with remainder to Y if he attains the age of 18 years, X's interest is equitable and vested, Y's interest is equitable and contingent since he must satisfy the requirement of majority before his interest vests. If Y does not reach 18 years the interest is held by the trustees on what is known as a 'resulting trust' for the settlor (if alive). If he is dead, the interest will go into his estate (or intestacy if there is no will), and in the case where there is a will, the gift will go to the residuary beneficiary, i.e. the one who gets the balance of the estate after particular gifts have been made.

Possession

The physical control of a thing by a person is what is normally known as possession, and if the idea of possession had remained wedded to physical control, the position would have been simple enough. But the widening sphere of legal activity made it necessary to attribute to persons who were not actually in physical control some or all of the advantages enjoyed by persons who were.

There are three possible situations at law:

(*a*) A person can have physical control without legal possession, as in the case of a porter carrying a traveller's suitcase in a station.
(*b*) A person can have possession and its advantages without actual physical control, e.g. a person may have books at home which are still in his possession even when he is away on holiday.
(*c*) A person can have both physical control and possession, e.g. a watch in his pocket or a pen in his hand.

Possession, therefore, has acquired a technical legal meaning, and the separation of possession from physical control has given the concept a high degree of flexibility.

The old theory of possession, derived from the Roman Law, relies upon (*a*) *corpus*, i.e. physical control, and (*b*) *animus*, i.e. the intention to exclude others. But although these concepts help in deciding possession, they do not provide the complete answer. In fact, English law has never worked out a completely logical and exhaustive definition of possession. The handing over of a key may be sufficient by itself to pass the possession of the contents of a room or box if it provides the effective means of control over the goods.

Wrongful interference

In the law of torts, wrongful interference to property is an invasion of possession. The policy of this branch of the law is to compensate the party whose interests have been affected, and

22

in order to enable such persons to recover, the court has contrived to attribute possession to them.

A bailee is a person who gets possession of a chattel from another with his consent. A bailment may be at will, i.e. revocable by the bailor at any time, or it may be for a term, i.e. for a fixed period of time, as by hiring a television set for six months. Where a bailment is at will, the bailee, who by definition has possession, can sue a third party for wrongful interference. Since the bailment is revocable at will, the bailor also has an interest worth protecting, and in order that he too may bring an action for wrongful interference, his right to possess is treated as possession itself. Where, on the other hand, the bailment is for a term, only the bailee can bring an action for wrongful interference and not the bailor, although, where the bailee brings the action, he will have to account to the bailor for any damages obtained. If a third person destroys or permanently injures the chattel while it is in the bailee's possession, the bailor may have an action against the third party for injury to his reversionary interest (*Mears v LSW Railway* [1862] 11 CB (NS) 850).

Where an employer has temporarily handed a thing to his employee, possession remains with the employer and the employee takes only custody. Thus an employer can sue for wrongful interference for an injury to the goods by a third party.

A person who loses a thing retains his ownership in it, and for the purpose of suing for wrongful interference someone who has taken it, his right to regain possession will suffice. But for the purpose of claiming from an insurance company for loss, he will be regarded as having lost possession, within the terms of the contract, if the thing cannot in fact be found.

Trespass to land by relation is another example of the artificial manipulation of the concept of possession to provide a remedy in trespass to one who needs to be compensated. When a person, with a right to possess, enters because of that right, he is regarded as having been in possession from the time when his right originally accrued, e.g. from the time when he made the original contract for a purchase or a lease. He can, therefore, sue for any trespass that has been committed between the accrual of the right and the actual entry.

As we have seen, difficulties have arisen over the requirement of the intention to exclude others as a necessary ingredient of possession where property of one sort or another has been found on the land of a person who was not its owner (see *Parker v British Airways Board* (1982) and *South Staffordshire Water Co v Sharman* (1896) and the cases noted with it).

However, it should be noted that *unless an owner* of chattels can be shown to have *abandoned* or *sold* them he remains their owner and has a better title than a finder or a person on whose property they are found.

> *Moffat v Kazana*, 1968 – The rights of an owner (**457**)

Adverse possession

A person may sometimes acquire the ownership of land by adverse possession. This arises from the occupation and use of land without the permission of, or any interference from, the true owner, as where a stranger encloses and cultivates a portion of a neighbour's land or occupies another's house. Under s 15 of the Limitation Act 1980 adverse possession for a period of 12 years will give the possessor a title, but such adverse possession must take the form of open and visible acts which are inconsistent with the title of the owner, and in this case possession is viewed much more strictly than in the others we have been considering above.

Hayward v *Challoner*, 1967 – The period required (**458**)

Littledale v *Liverpool College*, 1900 – Acts must be inconsistent with owner's rights (**459**)

Whether adverse possession necessarily involves inconvenience to the true owner is not clear. In *Wallis's Caton Bay Holiday Camp* v *Shell-Mex & BP* [1974] 3 All ER 575, the defendants had purchased land for development, though they had no immediate use for it. The claimants used it for 12 years for the purposes of grazing cattle on it and cultivating it. The Court of Appeal held that the claimants had not established a good possessory title because what they had done was of no inconvenience to the defendants who had no immediate use for the land. However, in *Treloar* v *Nute* [1977] 1 All ER 230, the claimant owned freehold land for which he had no immediate use and which was left derelict. The defendants bought land adjacent and occupied part of the derelict land for a period of 12 years. In holding that the defendants had a good possessory title to that land the Court of Appeal said it was not necessary to import into the definition of adverse possession a requirement that the owner must be inconvenienced or affected by that possession.

This line of reasoning was adopted also in *Buckinghamshire County Council* v *Moran* [1989] 2 All ER 225 where the council had acquired a plot of land adjacent to some houses for future use as a road diversion. They had no immediate use for it. Mr Moran (and previous owners) treated it as part of the garden of the Moran residence. It was fenced in and the grass was cut regularly and bulbs planted. This went on for more than 12 years and the Court of Appeal eventually held that Mr Moran had a possessory title to the plot although the council having no immediate use for the plot were not inconvenienced by what had been done.

Where a tenant, during the currency of his tenancy, takes possession of other land belonging to the landlord, the land is presumed to have been taken as part of the holding comprised in the tenancy, and the tenant cannot acquire a good possessory title unless he communicates to his landlord some disclaimer of the landlord's title.

It should be noted that periods of successive trespass (for that is what it is) may be added together. A trespasser who has occupied for, say, five years may add to that a period of seven years enjoyed by the immediate previous trespasser in order to bar the claim of the true owner provided there was no gap in adverse possession. However, each occupier must have had exclusive possession. Thus where the landlord of a property adjoining the disputed strip of land claimed adverse possession of it on the basis that his tenants had enjoyed exclusive possession for the necessary time his claim failed because the tenants had from time to time given the keys to others and that showed a lack of intention to exclude others which is a requirement of the law of adverse possession (see *Battersea Freehold and Leasehold Property Co Ltd* v *Wandsworth LBC* [2001] 20 LS Gaz R 41).

Rather than wait for a legal claim to be brought, a claim to legalise adverse possession can be made to the Land Registry in London. It will then be up to the Registry to determine the claim.

It should be noted that there are a few limited exceptions where the 12-year period is increased, e.g. to 30 years in the case of acquisition of title by the Crown (Limitation Act 1980, s 15(1)).

Smirk v *Lyndale Developments Ltd*, 1974 – Taking possession of a landlord's land (**460**)

22

Adverse possession: effect of Land Registration Act 2002

Landowners including business landowners will welcome restrictions on the acquisition of squatters' rights over registered land. There was some concern over the apparent ease with which land could be acquired in this way – in some cases land belonging to companies. *Squatters' rights remain as stated above where the land is unregistered land.*

The Act abolishes a squatter's automatic right to register title after 12 years' adverse possession. Instead the squatter will be entitled to apply for registration after 10 years but the Land Registry will serve a notice of the application on the registered owner or proprietor. The registered proprietor has three months to object. If there is no objection the squatter will be registered. If there is an objection the squatter has to establish certain conditions before he or she can be registered. The main condition on which a squatter may succeed in a claim for registration is that the property over which adverse possession has been exercised is adjacent to his or her own and the boundaries have never been properly and acceptably defined. More importantly in order to obtain registration given no objection by the owner, the squatter will have to establish that for at least 10 years of the period of adverse possession ending on the date of the application for registration he or she reasonably believed that the land belonged to him or her. This will defeat many claims by squatters.

If the squatter fails to establish one of the conditions for registration the proprietor has two years in which to take action to remove the squatter or regularise his or her position, e.g. by a lease. If the registered proprietor fails to remove the squatter or institute proceedings to effect removal within the two years then the squatter can apply for registration of his or her possessory interest. This time no one will be entitled to object. Section 96 and Sch 6 of the Act apply to the above law.

The fact that the Act does not apply to unregistered land does not provide a long-term difficulty since unregistered land is being converted to registered land as registrable events occur over it at the Land Registry, e.g. a sale or mortgage. Consequently, little if any unregistered land will remain in the medium or longer term.

Bailment

Bailments are concerned with pure personalty and not with real property. The bailment may or may not originate in a contract. As to the source of the expression 'bailment', it derives from the adoption by English law of an old French word to describe the handing over of goods without passing the title and property, i.e. *bailler* – to deliver.

Possession

An essential feature of a bailment is the transfer of possession to the bailee. There is no precise definition of possession, but the basic features are *control* and *an intention to exclude others*. However, a person can have possession of chattels which he does not know exist (see *South Staffordshire Water Co* v *Sharman* (1896)). An employee who receives goods from his employer to take to a third party has mere *custody*; possession remains with the employer and the employee is not a bailee. If a third party hands goods to an employee for his employer, the employee obtains possession and is the bailee.

In a bailment for a fixed term the bailee has possession to the exclusion of the bailor, and is, therefore, the only person who can sue a third party for wrongful interference. In a bailment at will, i.e. one which the bailor can terminate at will, the bailor retains either possession or an immediate right to possess and an action for wrongful interference is available to him as well as to the bailee. A bailee can sue a third party in tort for loss of or damage to the goods even though the bailee is not liable to the bailor for the loss or damage.

The Winkfield, 1902 – Recovery of damages, bailee in possession (**461**)

Bailment and licence

The problem of distinguishing between bailment and licence has arisen mainly in connection with the parking of vehicles. If a vehicle is parked on land, either gratuitously or even on payment of a charge, the transaction may amount to a mere licence and not a bailment which gives rise to duties of care.

Ashby v *Tolhurst*, 1937 – Is it a bailment or a licence? (**462**)
Ultzen v *Nicols*, 1894 – A stolen coat (**463**)
Deyong v *Shenburn*, 1946 – An actor's clothes (**464**)

Finders and involuntary recipients

For an act to constitute a bailment, the person who is given possession of goods must be entrusted with them for a particular purpose, e.g., to use and return as in the case of loan or hire, or to take from one place to another as in carriage. A banker is not a bailee of money paid into a customer's account, for his obligation is to return an equivalent sum and not the identical notes and coins. However, a banker is a bailee of property (e.g. jewellery) deposited with him for safe custody.

A finder is not a true bailee because he is not entrusted with the goods for a particular purpose. However, if he takes them into his possession he will be liable for loss or damage resulting from his negligence.

Newman v *Bourne & Hollingsworth*, 1915 – A finder and bailment (**465**)

A person cannot be made a bailee against his will. Where the receipt of the goods is involuntary it is unlikely that the recipient is under any higher duty than to refrain from intentional damage. However, he must not convert the goods, but although liability for conversion is usually strict, an involuntary recipient will only be liable if he acts intentionally or negligently.

Neuwirth v *Over Darwen Industrial Co-operative Society*, 1894 – An involuntary bailee (**466**)

The Unsolicited Goods and Services Acts 1971 and 1975 are relevant in this connection. The Acts are designed to deal with selling techniques involving the sending of unsolicited goods, thus rendering the recipient an involuntary bailee. The Acts provide for fines to be made on persons making demands for payment for goods they know to be unsolicited. If the demand is accompanied by threats a higher scale of fines applies. Furthermore, unsolicited goods may be kept by the recipient without payment *after a period of 30 days* provided the recipient gives notice to the sender asking that they be collected, or *after six months* even if no notice has been given. The legislation applies to private, not business, recipients.

Obligations of the bailor

Where the bailment is gratuitous it has been said that the limit of the liability of the bailor is to communicate to the bailee defects in the article lent of *which he is aware*. However, the principle in *Donoghue* v *Stevenson* (1932) may apply to gratuitous bailments so that the bailor would be liable if he had not taken reasonable care to ensure that the goods bailed were not dangerous, even though he had no actual knowledge of a defect in the chattels lent.

When the bailment is for reward there is an implied warranty on the part of the bailor that he has a title to the goods so that the bailee's possession will not be disturbed, and that the goods are fit and suitable for the bailee's purpose. This does not mean that the bailee is liable for all defects but only for those which skill and care can guard against. However, the warranty as to fitness and suitability does not apply where the defect is apparent to the bailee and he does not rely on the skill or judgement of the bailor.

> *Hyman* v *Nye*, 1881 – A defective carriage (**467**)
> *Reed* v *Dean*, 1949 – A fire on a motor launch (**468**)

Obligations of the bailee

When Lord Holt, in *Coggs* v *Bernard* (1703), established the liability of the bailee in negligence he laid down different duties of care for different kinds of bailments. Thus, in a bailment for the sole benefit of the bailee, such as a gratuitous loan, the bailee's duty of care was much higher than in a bailment for the benefit of both parties such as a hiring. However, in more recent times there has been disapproval of Lord Holt's different standards of care, and it is now the better view that the standard of care required of a bailee is to take reasonable care in all the circumstances of the case, which equates his duty with that owed by any person in the law relating to negligence, though the burden of disproving negligence is on the bailee.

> *Houghland* v *R Low (Luxury Coaches) Ltd*, 1962 – An old folks' outing (**469**)
> *Global Dress Co* v *W H Boase & Co*, 1966 – Goods stolen from the docks (**470**)

The *main* circumstances which the court is likely to consider when deciding the question of negligence in a bailee are as follows.

The type of bailment

Although some current legal opinion is against a legal distinction between bailment for reward and gratuitous bailment, reward or lack of reward will continue to be an *important circumstance* in the matter of the bailee's negligence. A gratuitous bailee must take the same care of the property bailed as a reasonable man would take of his own property. It is no defence for a bailee to show that he kept the goods with as much care as his own because the test of reasonableness is objective. In a bailment for reward the duty of care tends to be somewhat higher.

> *Doorman* v *Jenkins*, 1843 – Negligence leading to theft (**471**)
> *Brabant* v *King*, 1895 – Damage to explosives (**472**)

The expertise of the bailee

If the bailee's profession or situation implies a certain expertise he will be liable if he fails to show it.

> *Wilson* v *Brett*, 1843 – A horse and slippery turf (**473**)

The property bailed

If the goods bailed are, to the knowledge of the bailee, fragile or valuable, a high standard of care will be expected. In addition a bailee may be liable in negligence if he does not give notice to the bailor of a loss or try to recover lost or stolen property.

> *Saunders (Mayfair) Furs* v *Davies*, 1965 – Valuable fur coat: the care required (**474**)
>
> *Coldman* v *Hill*, 1919 – Giving notice of loss of cows (**475**)

Bailor's negligence

In some cases the court may regard the negligent or dilatory conduct of the bailor as negating the liability of the bailee. Thus in *Jerry Juhan Developments SA* v *Avon Tyres Ltd* [1999] CLC 702 the claimants allowed the defendants to make and distribute tyres made from the claimants' moulds. AT later terminated the contract and for two years thereafter made enquiries of the claimants as to the disposal of the moulds but received no instructions. Some five years after termination of the contract the claimants demanded the moulds which by that time had been lost. The court implied a term into the contract that the owner would collect within six months of their being available. The claimants being in breach of that term had relieved AT of their obligations as bailees. The claimants' case failed.

A bailee is vicariously liable for the torts of his employees, but an employee who becomes a thief may not be regarded as acting within the scope of his employment. However, in *Morris* v *C W Martin & Sons Ltd* (1965) it was held that a bailee for reward cannot necessarily escape liability for loss of goods stolen by his employee because theft is not necessarily beyond the scope of employment (see Chapter 20). The decision in *Morris* represents the better view.

A bailee may attempt to exclude his liability by an exemption clause in the contract of bailment. This matter must now be considered in the light of the rules of construction of contracts and the Unfair Contract Terms Act 1977 (see Chapter 15).

22

Delegation by bailee

Whether a bailee can delegate performance of the contract to another depends upon the nature of the bailment and the particular contract which may authorise delegation. Contracts involving the carriage, storage, repair or cleaning of goods often assume personal performance by the bailee. Where there is a delegation, even though unknown to the bailor, the delegate is a bailee and owes a duty of care directly to the bailor.

> *Davies* v *Collins*, 1945 – Delegation by a bailee (**476**)
>
> *Edwards* v *Newland*, 1950 – Where a bailee sub-contracts (**477**)
>
> *Learoyd Bros* v *Pope*, 1966 – Duty of care following delegation (**478**)

Estoppel and interpleader

A bailee is estopped at common law from denying the title of his bailor and if the bailor demands the return of the goods it is no defence for the bailee to plead that the bailor is not the owner. However, a bailee may defend an action for non-delivery of the goods:

(*a*) by showing that he has delivered them to another under an authorisation by the bailor;

(*b*) by showing that he has not got the goods because he has been dispossessed by a person with a better title, as in a bailment of stolen goods which are reclaimed by the owner;

(*c*) if he still retains possession he may allege that a third party has a better title but he must defend the action on behalf of, and with the authority of, the true owner.

> *Rogers, Sons & Co v Lambert & Co*, 1891 – Defence of superior title (**479**)

Where adverse claims are made against the bailee by the bailor and a third party, the bailee should take interpleader proceedings under the rules of the Supreme Court. The effect of this will be to bring the bailor and the third party together in an action which will decide the validity of their claims. The bailee can then hand over the goods to whichever party has established his claims and will not risk liability for wrongful interference.

Lien

A bailee may, in certain circumstances, have a lien on the goods. The general nature of a lien is described later in this chapter.

Land law

Since the Norman Conquest, absolute ownership of land has been impossible. William the Conqueror considered himself owner of all land in England and parcelled it out to his barons who became his tenants. In return for this 'honour', the barons had to render to the Crown certain services, of either a military or other public nature, but an exception was made in the case of land held by the Church. The ecclesiastics were not able to provide military services, and special spiritual tenures were introduced.

In order to assist themselves in supplying the services required by the King, the barons began to subgrant part of the land, and a series of tenures sprang up, all persons holding as tenants of the Crown in the last analysis.

It is outside our scope to pursue the rise and fall of the system of tenures, but all land is now held on a single tenure called 'common socage', and all obligations to the Crown have disappeared, except for certain ceremonials preserved because of their antiquity. Even today, however, a person does not own land; he holds an estate in land. The *tenure* answers the question 'How is the land held?' The term *estate* answers the question 'For how long is the land held?'

The term 'estate' arises because in legal theory the Queen is still the owner of all land and we can only have a part of what the Queen owns. This is called an 'estate'. The matter is purely traditional and theoretical since the Queen has no rights over our 'estates'.

The legislation of 1925

Before this legislation, which is described below, there were many different ways of holding land, referred to as estates in land. The existence of so many estates in land made the transfer of land most complicated. There might be a large number of legal owners of the same piece of land, and before the land could be conveyed to a purchaser all the interests had to be got in. Other problems arose on intestacy, which occurs where the deceased does not leave a will or an effective will, because the rules for intestate succession were not the same for realty and personalty. In 1925 a thorough reform of land law was undertaken and was eventually achieved by the following statutes: the Law of Property Act 1925, the Settled Land Act 1925, the Administration of Estates Act 1925, the Land Charges Act 1925 and the Land Registration Act 1925.

Legal estates – generally

The Law of Property Act 1925 reduced the number of legal estates which can exist over land to two, and the number of legal interests or charges in or over land to five. All other estates, interests and charges in or over land take effect as equitable interests, and can exist only behind a trust, the trustees having the legal fee simple estate.

The difference between a legal estate and a legal interest is that the owner of the legal estate is entitled to the enjoyment of the whole of the property, either in possession or receiving rents, whereas the owner of a legal interest has a limited right in or over the land of another.

The three legal estates possible today are:

(a) *a fee simple absolute in possession* (or a freehold); and
(b) *a term of years absolute* (or a lease);
(c) *a commonhold.*

The word *fee* implies that the estate is an estate of inheritance, and the word *simple* shows that the fee is capable of descending to the general class of heirs, and is not restricted to heirs of a particular class. The word *absolute* distinguishes a fee simple which will continue for ever, from a fee which may be determinable. The fee simple must be *in possession*, although this does not imply only physical possession but also the right to receive rents and profits. Even if a landlord has granted a lease he may still have a fee simple in possession because he is entitled to the rent reserved by the lease.

The *term of years absolute* is what is normally understood by a lease. But a term of years includes a term for less than a year, or for a year or years and a fraction of a year, or even a tenancy from year to year. The essential characteristic is that a term of years has a minimum period of certain duration. It seems, therefore, that a lease for life is no longer a legal estate; nor is a tenancy at will or sufferance since there is no certainty as to the period of their continuance. A term of years may be absolute notwithstanding that it may be determined by notice, re-entry, forfeiture or operation of law or other event.

Legal estates – the commonhold

The Commonhold and Leasehold Reform Act 2002 created a new form of landholding called the 'commonhold'.

Commonhold generally

A commonhold is defined as a freehold with special characteristics – mainly that it is not necessary for the property to have foundations in the land, which is a requirement for the ordinary freehold. This is why it is often referred to colloquially as a 'flying freehold'.

The owners of commonhold units such a commonhold flats will be members automatically of the commonhold association that will own the common parts such as lifts, entrance halls, stairs, refuse areas, gardens and driveways. The association will be a company limited by guarantee governed by the Companies Act 1985. The use and maintenance of the units will

22

be governed by the commonhold community statement (CCS): the CCS is the constitution of the commonhold land and must be registered at HM Land Registry, and a commonhold assessment will fix the percentage payable for each unit. This in other situations, e.g. leasehold flats, would be a service charge.

Most commonholds will be a block of flats but they could be shop units in an arcade or units on a business park. Therefore, property capable of becoming a commonhold unit is residential or commercial property. A unit holder will have a registered freehold title to it.

The usual provisions for company winding-up will apply where a commonhold association becomes insolvent and it will be necessary to dissolve an association where the unit holders wish to sell the block for redevelopment.

Three major points about commonhold from a commercial aspect are:

(a) Although it is possible to convert from leasehold to commonhold it is necessary to obtain the consent of all the existing leaseholders, which indicates that the legislation is aimed mainly at new developments.

(b) In the case of a residential commonhold there is a restriction on the commonholder letting the premises. A maximum of only seven years is permitted. This provision is most unattractive to the property industry because it means in effect that investors will not want to invest in commonhold property. The object of the restriction is to develop a community and not encourage the absentee landlord syndrome which has often blighted leasehold developments. Business leases, e.g. shops within the development, are subject to the terms of the commonhold statement that is filed at the Land Registry when the commonhold arrangement is set up, e.g. by the developer.

(c) It is anticipated that commonhold residential developments will become, in time, more desirable than leasehold properties and will trade at a premium compared with such properties.

Commonhold should not be confused with leasehold enfranchisement under which flat owners in blocks of flats collectively buy out the freehold owner of the property and so obtain control of the freehold of the block but not their individual flats in the sense that they are still tenants. Implementation of commonhold will necessitate the passing of detailed legislation much of it highly technical.

This subordinate legislation is clearly beyond the scope of this text and would not normally be required by examinations at this level.

Comment It is the responsibility of the association to enforce any breaches of the CCS. In effect this gives the association a role similar to that of a landlord in a landlord and tenant relationship. In common with most leases the CCS will restrict the granting of leases in the commonhold unit. In general a unit holder will not be able to grant a leasehold interest of the unit unless the commonhold association is a party to the lease or gives its consent (CLRA 2002, s 20(3)).

Advantages over leaseholds

The commonhold legislation is concerned to overcome certain weaknesses in leasehold arrangements as follows:

- A lease is granted for a fixed term and admittedly the term may sometimes be lengthy. However, the issue of renewal will arise and this may require troublesome negotiation that can also be costly. A commonhold is a type of freehold and therefore permanent.
- Leasehold properties have no standard management structure as the commonhold has and the structures offered can vary greatly in their quality.

- Mistakes may occur in the documentation so that the terms of the various leases in, say, a block do not match. This can cause difficulty in enforcing conditions that do not occur in a commonhold development where one document, i.e. the CCS sets out the obligations and terms of ownership for all units. There is thus no chance of mismatching provisions.
- Premature termination of a leasehold development can cause problems in terms of dividing assets. However, commonhold arrangements have documentation laying down the terms in advance of termination but the court has a power to vary these in a termination situation.
- A leasehold is a wasting asset. A leasehold is a term of years absolute that will eventually come to an end even where there is a long term, e.g. 99 years. A freehold is a *perpetual estate*.
- A lease is subject to forfeiture if there is a breach of covenant, e.g. assigning or sub-letting by the tenant.

A main business application is, therefore, that a freehold title in commonhold land is a better security than a lease in terms of lending and borrowing.

Disadvantages over leaseholds

These are, first, that the commonhold association in spending money on the commonhold property is not restricted by the 'reasonableness' of the expenditure requirement on the landlord of a lease. Secondly, the Commonhold and Leasehold Reform Act 2002 relies on alternative dispute resolution through an Ombudsman, so that there is no redress through the courts. Therefore, commonhold developments will not offer the rights and protections available to leaseholders.

Setting up a commonhold

A commonhold may be established in two ways:

- It can be registered at the Land Registry *with unit-holders* where the identity of the unit-holders is known. The freehold of the units vests in them and the commonhold arrangements come into force on registration; this will occur where there is a conversion from a leasehold arrangement but will otherwise be uncommon.
- A person developing by building afresh or converting an empty building with the intention of selling off the units will register a commonhold *without unit-holders*. The developer retains ownership after registration for an interim period until the first unit is sold. The developer has complete control during the interim period and can, if he wishes, abandon the development and cancel the registration. Even after the initial sale the developer's business is protected in the sense that the CCS can give him rights to prevent early purchasers from interfering with the process of marketing the units.

Comment The cost of establishing commonhold arrangements will not always justify conversion of an existing leasehold arrangement unless the leases are near to termination. However, since commonhold arrangements will put a premium on sale of the units, this might prove an incentive to conversion from leasehold.

The nature of the property

Agricultural land cannot be registered as commonhold but an existing freehold or leasehold can be converted. An existing freehold can be divided into parcels or plots and held under commonhold arrangements.

Termination of commonhold

A commonhold arrangement is brought to an end by winding-up the commonhold association. Since the units are not owned by the association they are not available to pay its debts.

However, the court may make what is called a 'succession order' under which a new common-hold association is substituted, the members being those who have met their liabilities to the full. This has been called a 'Phoenix association' that takes over the management so that the unit-holders can continue to hold and enjoy their properties. If no succession order is made the commonhold arrangement ceases to exist and the properties will be dealt with in accordance with the directions of the liquidator.

Joint owners

A commonhold unit can be held by joint owners.

Legal interests and charges

We have seen that there are only three possible legal estates: a fee simple absolute in posses-sion, a term of years absolute and a commonhold but the Law of Property Act 1925 also lays down a number of legal interests in land. The most important are:

(a) an easement, right or privilege for an interest equivalent to either of the above estates. Thus, an easement for life would not be a legal interest;

(b) a charge by way of legal mortgage.

Equitable interests

All estates, interests or charges over land except those outlined above take effect as equitable interests only and must exist behind a trust. Life interests, for example, are equitable.

The two major trust arrangements over land are called settled land and trusts of land.

Settled land

Settlements created after 1925 other than by will require, under the Settled Land Act 1925, two deeds to be executed – the vesting deed and the trust instrument. The vesting deed must contain a description of the settled land, a statement that the settled land is vested in the tenant for life upon the trusts for the time being affecting the settled land, the names of the trustees of the settlement, and a statement of any larger powers granted to the tenant for life in addition to his statutory powers.

The trust instrument must contain the appointment of the trustees, the names of the persons entitled to appoint new trustees, a statement of any additional powers conferred by the settlement in extension of the statutory powers, and the trusts of the settlement. Where a settlement is created by will, the will is regarded as the trust instrument, and the personal representatives must execute a vesting instrument, vesting the legal estate in the tenant for life. Thus, a purchaser of settled land is only concerned with the vesting deed or assent, since it is from such documents that he derives his title. The trusts can remain secret since the trust instrument need not be produced on sale.

Under the settlement the person obtaining the benefit from the estate is usually an adult with a life interest and he is called the *tenant for life*. It is his function to manage the estate and he has power to sell or exchange the settled land or any part of it with an adjustment of any difference in value in the case of exchange. He may grant leases subject to certain restric-tions, but in the absence of a contrary provision in the settlement, he has no power to mortgage or charge the legal estate for his own benefit, although he can mortgage or assign his own beneficial life interest.

He has other powers which he can only exercise with the consent of the settlement trustees or the court, e.g. the power to sell or otherwise dispose of the principal mansion house, the power to cut and sell timber, the power to compromise claims and sell settled chattels. He has the power to make improvements at his own expense, or the cost may be borne by the capital money if he complies with the provisions of the Act. He has also power to select investments for capital money.

The tenant for life is in a strong position, for he is subject to no control in the exercise of his powers except that he must give notice to the trustees of his intention to exercise the most important ones, he must obtain the consent of the trustees or leave of the court in certain cases, and he is in fact himself a trustee for the other beneficiaries. There may be joint tenants for life under a settlement and, where this is so, they must usually agree as to the exercise of their joint powers. The court will exercise a power, e.g. by ordering a sale of property, but only if the joint tenant who does not agree to sell is acting in bad faith (*Barker* v *Addiscott* [1969] 3 All ER 685).

It is clear that under a settlement a proper balance must be preserved between the tenant for life and the persons who will be entitled to the land or the proceeds of the land after his death. He is not allowed, therefore, to run down the estate during his lifetime in order to increase his own income, but is only allowed to take from the land the current income and must pass on the estate substantially unimpaired.

Trusts of Land and Appointment of Trustees Act 1996

The above Act has effect upon strict settlements as described above.

The first effect is to prevent the creation of strict settlements over land. Formerly, if successive interests were created over land, as where land was left 'to A for life with remainder to B', then unless a trust for sale (now a trust for land) (see below) was specified in the instrument setting up the trust, e.g. a will, the land became settled land and subject to the Settled Land Act 1925, the trust being managed by the life tenant A as described above. The scheme of the Act is to stop the Settled Land Act applying even where no trust for land is specified in the creating instrument but to allow it to apply to existing settled land arrangements. Therefore these will exist for some time and so it is worth acquiring some knowledge of them (see above).

Where successive interests are created now they will be regarded as trusts of land and operate under the management of the trustees as a trust of personal property, e.g. as shares would.

The second effect is to give trustees of trusts of land all the powers of an absolute owner in regard to the land. There is now no need for the trust instrument to specifically confer such powers on the trustees. The new arrangements do not apply to the power of trustees to invest the trust property, e.g. rents, received as they wish. They were still subject to control in regard to investment in, e.g., equity (or ordinary) shares in companies unless the trust instrument gave them power to do so. However, the Trustee Act 2000 gives a full power of investment of the trust property to trustees as if it were their own, subject to liability in negligence for investing trust property in a risky investment. The power given in s 3 of the Act covers acquisition of freehold and leasehold land (s 8) and may be extended or restricted by the particular trust instrument, i.e. the instrument setting up the trust. The rule of conversion formerly applied to land in a trust is abolished. Thus, if a beneficiary under a trust leaves 'all my realty to R and all my personalty to P', then P no longer gets the land but R does. The land is no longer converted into personal property merely because it is held under a trust for land. This does not affect what has been said in the chapter about the nature of a lease which remains personal property.

22

Trusts of land

A trust of land is an immediate binding trust for sale whether or not exercisable at the request or with the consent of any person, and with or without a power of discretion to postpone the sale. Such a trust may be either express or by operation of law. Trusts for sale are governed by the Law of Property Act 1925, and not by the Settled Land Act 1925.

An express trust of land is almost always created by two documents – a conveyance to trustees on an express trust of land (see the Trusts of Land and Appointment of Trustees Act 1996, above) and a trust instrument. But even where a trust of land is embodied in a single document, a purchaser of the legal estate is not concerned with the trusts affecting the rents and profits of the land until sale, or with the proceeds of the sale, provided he obtains a receipt for the purchase money signed by at least two trustees or a trust corporation.

There are cases where a trust of land is imposed by statute. These are:

(*a*) where a person dies intestate, i.e. without leaving a will (or valid will);
(*b*) where two or more persons are entitled to land as joint tenants or tenants in common;
(*c*) where trustees lend money on mortgage and the property becomes vested in them free from the right of redemption. Mortgages and the right of redemption are considered later in this chapter.

Co-ownership

Two persons may own land simultaneously. In such a case they are either joint tenants or tenants in common. Where they are joint tenants, there is no question of a share of the property – each is the owner of the whole. Where there is a tenancy in common, each is regarded as owning an individual share in the property, but that share has not positively been marked out. Tenants in common hold property in undivided shares.

A joint tenancy arises where land is conveyed to two or more persons and no words of severance are used. A tenancy in common arises when there are words of severance. Thus a conveyance 'to A and B' would create a joint tenancy, whilst a conveyance 'to A and B equally' would create a tenancy in common. The right of survivorship or *jus accrescendi* is a distinguishing feature of joint tenancies, and upon the death of one joint tenant, his share in the property passes to the survivors until there is only one person left and he becomes the sole owner of the property. The *jus accrescendi* does not apply to tenancies in common and such a tenant may dispose of his share by will. It will be appreciated also that the conveyance (or a will) may, and usually does, actually state the type of co-ownership, e.g. 'to A and B as joint tenants'.

Both types of co-ownership have advantages and disadvantages. The *jus accrescendi* as applied to joint tenancies prevents too many interests being created in the land, because a joint tenant cannot leave any part of the property by will and so the number of interests decreases. When the land is sold the number of signatures on the conveyance will not be excessive. On the other hand, joint tenancies are unfair in that eventual sole ownership depends merely on survival. Where there is a tenancy in common, each tenant can leave his interest by will possibly by dividing it between two or more persons; thus the number of interests increases and on sale many interests must be got in.

The common law preferred the joint tenancy. But equity preferred the tenancy in common and would in certain circumstances treat persons as tenants in common rather than joint tenants regardless of words of severance. For instance, where two persons lend money on mortgage, equity regards them as tenants in common of the interest in the land subject to the mortgage; also where joint purchasers of land put up the purchase money in unequal shares; and in the case of partnership land, the partners are treated as tenants in common in equity.

The Law of Property Act 1925 has combined the best features of both types of co-ownership by providing that where land is owned by two or more persons they, or the first four of them if there are more than four, should be treated as holding the legal estate as trustees and joint tenants, for the benefit of themselves and other co-owners (if any) in equity. Thus a purchaser of the property is never required to get more than four signatures on the conveyance, and the trusts attach to the purchase money for the benefit of the co-owners. However, the Act does not state what shares the co-owners are to have and this should be dealt with specifically in the conveyance or will, otherwise the court may have to decide in a case of dispute. It does not follow from the provisions of the Act that the co-owners share in equity equally. The statutory trusts on which the property is held are: to sell the property with power to postpone the sale; and to hold the proceeds of sale, and the rents and profits until sale, for those beneficially entitled under the trust. Thus, where there is a trust for sale of land (now a trust for land), it does not mean that the land must be sold straightaway. There is a power to postpone sale.

It should be noted that although the provisions set out in the above paragraph deal with the problems which formerly arose in conveying land which was in joint ownership, it is still possible to create a joint tenancy in both the land and the proceeds of sale. Where such a joint tenancy exists, the *jus accrescendi* will apply to the equitable interests of the joint tenants in the proceeds of sale, unless there has been a severance of the joint tenancy since the creation of the estate. Severance is possible under s 36(2) of the Law of Property Act 1925, which provides that:

> where a legal estate (not being settled land) is vested in joint tenants beneficially, and any tenant desires to sever the joint tenancy in Equity, he shall give to the other joint tenants a notice in writing of such desire or do such other acts or things as would, in the case of personal estate, have been effective to sever the tenancy in Equity, and thereupon under the trust for sale affecting the land [now a trust for land] the net proceeds of sale, and the net rents and profits until sale, shall be held upon the trusts which would have been requisite for giving effect to the beneficial interest if there had been an actual severance.

A notice of severance may be regarded as properly served if sent by post even if it is not received by the addressee (*Re 88 Berkeley Road, London NW9; Rickwood v Turnsek* [1971] 1 All ER 254). Furthermore, the sending of a notice of severance operates to create a tenancy in common, even where the sender of the notice has changed his or her mind and does not desire severance (*Kinch v Bullard* [1998] 4 All ER 650).

The better view is that severance of a joint tenancy may be effected unilaterally by one party other than by giving notice.

Re Draper's Conveyance, 1967 – Unilateral severance (**480**)

It should be noted that one tenant in common is not entitled to rent from another tenant in common, even though that other occupies the whole of the property (*Jones (A E) v Jones (F W)* [1977] 2 All ER 231).

Co-ownership and the law of trusts: Trustee Delegation Act 1999

An essential difficulty presented to co-owners has been that each of them is a trustee for themselves and the others. Trustees have in the past had somewhat limited powers of delegation of their duty to act and so if, for example, it is thought necessary to sell the co-owned land, each co-owner/trustee must sign the contract and the conveyance and any other documents essential in law to the sale. This created particular difficulties in the case of the matrimonial home where, if as is usual, husband and wife are joint tenants of the property they are also and inevitably trustees. It is difficult where, say, the husband is going away for a business trip of a few weeks for steps to be taken by the wife in regard, for example, to the sale of the matrimonial home which has been put in train. Under previous law the husband could not delegate to his wife because the law did not allow delegation to a sole trustee. However, this situation is changed by the Trustee Delegation Act 1999 which received the Royal Assent on 15 July 1999. Section 1 of the Act provides for the drafting of a power of attorney under which one of the two trustees can deal to some extent with, e.g. the sale of property on his or her own, including agreeing to the contract of sale. *However*, the sole trustee cannot complete the sale on his or her own. The statutory rules that require the proceeds of sale to be paid to and receipted by at least two trustees remain, as does the need for at least two trustees to sign the conveyance to convey title (see s 7 of the 1999 Act). Section 8 provides for the appointment of other trustees by the attorney and so, if a wife or husband wishes to complete the sale, another trustee must be appointed, e.g. the couple's accountant. This provides some safeguard in terms of an unwise sale.

Party Wall, etc. Act 1996

Another form of joint ownership arises in connection with party walls dividing properties. London has been covered by protective legislation for many years, the last Act in a line of legislation being the London Building Act (Amendment) Act 1939.

The 1996 Act extends the London provisions to the rest of England and Wales. The Act was inspired by the case of a woman in West Sussex who suffered considerable renovation work by her neighbours who refused to tell her anything about the nature of the alterations. She owned the wall to its mid-point and her neighbours owned the other half and they were, at that time, entitled to do what they liked with it.

The basic principles of the 1996 Act are:

- if the 'building owner', as he is called, wants to carry out work to a party wall, he must serve on the 'adjoining owner' notice of what is proposed;
- the adjoining owner then has the right to appoint a surveyor at the expense of the building owner, and in the case of dispute a further surveyor may be called in to adjudicate.

The procedure has been used regularly in London and has worked well. The legislation applies also to walls which form boundary fences.

A leasehold or a term of years

The major characteristics of a term of years are that the lessee is given exclusive possession of the land and that the period for which the term is to endure is fixed and definite. It is open to the parties to decide whether their agreement shall be a lease or a licence, though the words used by the parties are not conclusive. If there is no right to exclusive possession, then there is a mere licence and not a lease. For example, a guest in a hotel does not normally have a lease, because the proprietor retains general control over the room.

Shell-Mex and BP Ltd v *Manchester Garages Ltd*, 1971 – Is it a lease or a licence? (**481**)

Contractual licences

The parties may put the matter beyond doubt by a properly drafted and signed contract of licence. These have a number of commercial uses as follows:

- for short-term trading, for example, during the Christmas period or during the summer holiday period, either for retailing or storage purposes;
- where a prospective tenant wants early access to premises before a formal lease can be drafted and granted or an existing tenant wishes to remain in occupation for a short period after the lease expires (here the landlord will be anxious to retain rental income but will not want the tenant to acquire security of tenure under, e.g. the Landlord and Tenant Act 1954).

The duration of leases

Leases must be for a fixed period of time, and in this case the commencement and termination of the lease must be ascertainable before the lease takes effect. Thus a lease 'for the life of X' would not come under this heading. A lease may be for an indefinite period in the sense that it is to end when the lessor or lessee gives notice. Even so such an arrangement would operate as a valid lease, since the duration of the term can be made certain by the parties giving notice.

In the absence of agreement, the period of a lease may be determined by reference to the payment of rent. Thus, if a person takes possession of the premises with the owner's consent for an indefinite period, but the owner accepts rent paid, say, weekly, monthly, quarterly or annually, the term may be based on that period, though from early times there has been a presumption that the payment and acceptance of rent shows an intention to create a yearly tenancy. A yearly tenancy requires half a year's notice to terminate it if there has been no agreement on the matter. Other periodical tenancies, in the absence of agreement, are determined by notice for the full period. Even where there has been a definite term, a periodical tenancy can arise. Where X is granted a lease of 21 years and stays on after the expiration of that term with the owner's consent, there is a new implied term based on the period of payment of rent.

However, where the tenant is permitted to stay in possession on the understanding that there are to be negotiations for a new lease, there is a tenancy at will.

A *tenancy at will* may also arise *by agreement* where a person takes possession of property with the owner's consent, the arrangement being that the term can be brought to an end by either party giving notice. However, the court will look at the transaction in order to ascertain its true nature and will not be put off by ambiguous or wrong terminology.

Binions v *Evans*, 1972 – What is the true nature of the transaction? (**482**)

If there is no agreement as to rent, the tenancy can become a periodical tenancy if the tenant pays and the owner accepts rent paid at given periods of time. A tenancy at will may also arise *by implication* from the conduct of the parties. For example, a prospective purchaser of land who is allowed to take possession before completion occupies the property as a tenant at will until completion.

22

Where a tenant stays on after the expiration of his term without the consent of the owner, there is a *tenancy by sufferance*. No rent is payable under such a tenancy, but the tenant must compensate the owner by a payment in respect of the use and occupation of the land. This compensation is referred to as *mesne profits*. Such a tenancy can be brought to an end at any time, though it may become a periodical tenancy if the owner accepts a payment of rent at given intervals of time.

It should be noted that the law bases the duration of a periodical tenancy on the intervals of time at which the rent has been paid and accepted, on the ground that this is evidence of the parties' intention. If there is other evidence of intention, then the court will also take this into account, e.g. there may be a prior lease which negatives the intention to create the sort of periodical tenancy which the payment of rent suggests.

Special protection for residential and business tenants

The material set out above is amended in certain situations by statutory provisions as follows:

Public-sector tenancies

Here there is a public-sector landlord, such as a local council. These tenancies are governed by the Housing Act 1985. There is security of tenure in that the landlord must prove grounds for possession, e.g. non-payment of rent, and requires a court order. There is no rent control.

Housing association tenancies

These are now generally assured tenancies with security of tenure in that the landlord must prove grounds for possession, e.g. non-payment of rent, but rents are normally market rents. They may also be assured shorthold tenancies with no security of tenure but some rent control. Where a housing association has taken over council tenants, there is security of tenure but no rent control.

Residential tenancies protected by the Rent Act 1977 (private sector)

Many residential tenancies granted before 15 January 1989 remain protected by the Rent Act 1977. The main ingredients of the protection are security of tenure and rent control.

Rent control prevented the landlord from recovering more than a 'fair rent' as decided by the Rent Officer disregarding scarcity value. The position now is that for the first application to a Rent Officer for an increase in rent the increase is capped at the rate of inflation since the previous rent was registered plus 7.5 per cent. For all subsequent applications the limit is inflation plus 5 per cent.

Security of tenure prevents a landlord from evicting a tenant even after the tenancy has expired without a court order which may only be granted on specified narrow grounds. The parties may not contract out of protection unless, e.g., they use the machinery for shorthold tenancies introduced by the Housing Act 1980 (see now the Housing Acts 1988 and 1996).

The Housing Act 1988 provides for new tenancies, but is concerned also to protect existing Rent Act tenants. Therefore, a tenancy granted to a person with a subsisting Rent Act tenancy by a person's landlord or joint landlord will still be protected by the Rent Act, even if granted on or after 15 January 1989. There must, however, be no gap between the Rent Act tenancy and the new tenancy.

Assured residential tenancies under the Housing Act 1988 (private sector)

This is a new regime introduced for residential tenancies granted on or after 15 January 1989.

The security provisions are similar but not identical to those of the Rent Act 1977. However, they are subject only to minimum control of rent and by and large the overriding rule about rent is freedom of contract, i.e. payment of market rent.

Assured shorthold tenancies (private sector)

The Housing Act 1988 permits contracting out of security of tenure by granting an assured shorthold tenancy. If the formalities are correctly followed the landlord has a mandatory ground for possession at the end of the tenancy. The requirements included an initial fixed term certain of not less than six months preceded by service of a shorthold notice in the form prescribed. Unlike the assured residential tenancy, excessive rents may be referred to a Rent Assessment Committee. The shorthold status continues for renewals but the power to refer rents ceases.

Changes effected by the Housing Act 1996

From 28 February 1997 all tenancies which are assured tenancies are automatically to be regarded as assured shorthold tenancies which will be able to run for less than six months unless the parties specifically state otherwise. In addition landlords will be able to seek repossession through the courts after:

(i)   rent is in arrears for eight weeks where rent is payable weekly or fortnightly; or
(ii) rent is in arrears for two months where the rent is payable monthly.

The previous provisions were 13 weeks and three months respectively. The 1996 provisions make eviction easier and are designed to encourage the letting of premises. There are also provisions making the eviction of anti-social tenants quicker and easier.

Protection of business tenants by the Landlord and Tenant Act 1954

The 1954 Act is substantially amended by the Regulatory Reform (Business Tenancies) (England and Wales) Order 2003 (SI 2003/3096). The position as regards protection in business leases is as follows:

(a) The tenancy continues. Unless the parties agree otherwise before the lease is entered into, then the tenancy will continue automatically after the term agreed by the parties expires.

(b) Ending by the landlord and renewal. The landlord can only end the tenancy by following the strict notice procedures laid down in the Act. Even then, provided the tenant acts in time, he or she is entitled to apply to the court for a new tenancy. The landlord can oppose the application only on one of the grounds set out in the Act, e.g. his or her intention to reconstruct or demolish the premises or the landlord's intention to occupy the premises himself or herself either for the purposes of a business or as a residence.

(c) Request for a new tenancy. There is a procedure for a tenant or landlord to take the initiative and request a new lease.

(d) What are the terms of the new tenancy? The length of the new lease is as a maximum 15 years. This reflects the fact that rent reviews are now every five years and not seven years as before.

(e) Compensation on quitting. If the landlord is successful in opposing renewal, the tenant may be entitled to compensation.

(f) Contracting out. There is a procedure by which a business tenancy may be excluded from the protection of the Act.

22

Creation of leases

Leases are normally created by deed. However, where the lease is not to exceed three years, a written or oral lease will suffice, so long as the lease takes effect in possession at once at the best rent obtainable without a premium or capital payment. It is usual to draw up an arrangement such as a tenancy agreement, rather than execute a deed. Where a tenancy is in excess of three years then, if the agreement is not by deed, it will operate at common law as a yearly tenancy if the tenant enters into possession and pays rent on a yearly basis, i.e. by reference to a year, even if the rent is paid in quarterly instalments.

The position in equity is rather different. In equity, if a person has entered into an agreement for a lease but has no deed, then, if he has entered and paid rent or carried out repairs, i.e. if there is a sufficient act of part performance, equity will insist that the owner of the property execute a formal lease by deed. The equitable maxim, 'Equity looks upon that as done which ought to be done', applies. The contract must be in writing and comply with the formalities of the Law of Property (Miscellaneous Provisions) Act 1989 (see further Chapter 11). It should be noted that the above exceptions apply only to the creation of a lease. Subsequent assignment or transfer requires a deed even for a short lease which could be created orally or in writing.

> *Walsh* v *Lonsdale*, 1882 – Effect of an agreement for a lease (**483**)

It may seem that the above rule makes an agreement for a lease as effective as a lease by deed, and certainly, as between the parties to the agreement, absence of a deed is not vital.

However, the rights of the tenant under the rule are equitable and not legal rights, and the tenant can be turned out by a third party to whom the landlord sells the legal estate, if the third party purchases the property for value with or without notice of the existence of the lease.

Nevertheless, since the property legislation of 1925, the tenant can register the agreement as an *estate contract*, and, once the agreement is so registered, all subsequent purchasers of the legal estate are deemed to have notice of the lease and are bound to honour it.

A lease which is to commence from the date of the lease is called a lease *in possession*. However, a *reversionary lease* may be created under which the term is to commence at some future date. A restriction is imposed by s 149(3) of the Law of Property Act 1925 which provides that the creation of a reversionary lease which is to take effect more than 21 years from the execution of the lease, e.g. a lease signed in 1997 for a term of 10 years to run from 2033, is void. This does not affect the granting of a lease with an option to renew in the future.

In considering the words 'writing', 'signature' and 'deed' in the above material the passing of the Electronic Communications Act 2000 should be noted. Section 7, which is already in force, allows electronic signatures to be adduced and acceptable as evidence of a signature. However, delegated legislation will be required to make changes in statutes, such as the Law of Property Act 1925, to eliminate the 'paper' requirements. The relevant areas are being identified for change.

Rights and liabilities of landlord and tenant

The rights and liabilities of the parties depend largely upon the lease though a landlord has a special right at common law to distrain for rent, i.e. to move in on the tenant's personal property and remove it for sale to satisfy the amount owing for rent. Where the lease is by deed, the deed will usually fix the rights and liabilities by express clauses which are called covenants. Certain covenants are also implied by law where there is no provision in the lease. The most usual express covenants are covenants to pay rent, covenants regarding repairs and renewals, and a covenant that the tenant will not assign or sub-let without the landlord's consent. In this connection, s 1 of the Landlord and Tenant Act 1988 imposes a duty upon a landlord to give consent unless he has good reason to withhold it and within a reasonable period of a written application for consent. An action for damages arises if consent is not given or is unreasonably withheld.

The Landlord and Tenant (Covenants) Act 1995 (see later in this chapter) provides that in respect of leases entered into on or after 1 January 1996 (other than wholly residential leases or farm leases) the landlord can agree with the tenant the terms on which an assignment will be permitted, e.g. that the assignee satisfies certain prescribed conditions, as where he is not a dealer in scrap metal. The landlord will not be taken as withholding consent unreasonably if the conditions are not fulfilled. This is a major concession to landlords.

The main implied covenants are as follows:

Implied obligations of the landlord

(a) Quiet enjoyment. This means that the tenant shall be allowed to take possession and will be able to recover damages if his enjoyment of the property is disturbed by acts of the landlord, as in one case where the landlord removed the doors and windows of the property (see *Lavender* v *Betts* [1942] 2 All ER 72).

This implied covenant does not extend to requiring the landlord to have sufficient sound-proofing to protect the tenant from the sounds of ordinary domestic life in neighbouring flats, said the House of Lords in *Southwark LBC* v *Mills* [1999] 4 All ER 449. A covenant for quiet enjoyment cannot be converted into a covenant to improve the premises. Thus:

- rent a terraced house where you can hear your neighbours through the walls – no liability in the landlord to correct this;
- rent a flat with a large overhanging balcony above affecting privacy – no obligation on the landlord here;
- rent a bed-sit with no double glazing overlooking a busy and noisy main road – no concern of the landlord.

(b) Landlord and Tenant Act 1985. A provision in this Act implies a condition that a house let for human habitation is fit for human habitation at the beginning of the tenancy and will be kept fit during the tenancy. This Act applies to fewer and fewer properties because the premises concerned must be let at a very low rent, i.e. £80 a year in Greater London and £52 elsewhere (s 8 of the 1985 Act). Inflation and its effect on rents over the years has made the Act almost obsolete.

(c) Landlord and Tenant Act 1985. Under ss 11–16 of the Act landlords have implied repairing obligations when premises are let wholly or mainly as a dwelling house under a lease for a term of less than seven years. This includes a longer term which the landlord can bring to an end within seven years. The implied obligations are:

(i) to repair the structure and exterior including drains, gutters and external pipes;
(ii) to repair and keep in working order the services and sanitary installations;
(iii) to repair and keep working the installations for room heating and heating water.

There is no liability to remedy a latent defect until the landlord knows of it.

It should not be assumed that the above provisions of the 1985 Act work well. There is no obligation to keep the premises fit for human habitation. In particular, condensation has been regarded as a design fault and not a matter of disrepair although it can do untold harm, e.g. to furniture. The Law Commission has recommended reform (see *Landlord and Tenant: Responsibility for State and Condition of Property* (Law Com No 238)).

(d) Defective Premises Act 1972. As we have seen, there is under this Act a duty to build dwellings properly and a duty to take reasonable care to keep the premises reasonably safe (see further Chapter 21). This Act relates, of course, to injuries as a result of defective premises which result in a claim for compensation in the civil courts. It does not provide a direct method of getting defects put right.

(e) Non-derogation from the grant. This means that the landlord must not take action to prevent the use for which the premises were let, e.g. by letting a substantial part of a residential block for business purposes.

Implied obligations of the tenant

(a) General. There is a general obligation to keep and deliver up the premises in a tenant-like manner. This means that the tenant must take proper care of the premises, e.g. by doing small jobs such as replacing fuses and cleaning windows. There may be a duty to keep the premises wind tight and water tight but this was doubted in *Warren v Keen* [1954] 1 QB 15 by the Court of Appeal. If it does exist, it does not require the tenant to do anything of a substantial nature.

(b) Waste. A tenant must not commit waste, i.e. he must not do deliberate damage to the premises.

> *O'Brien v Robinson*, 1973 – Latent defects (**484**)

Breach of covenant by the tenant can result in forfeiture of the lease. A landlord's covenant to repair can be enforced by specific performance (*Jeune v Queens Cross Properties Ltd* [1973] 3 All ER 97). However, since specific performance is a discretionary remedy, it is advisable for tenants to rely on doing their own repairs and recouping from the rent for relatively trivial breaches rather than to approach the courts for specific performance.

Privity of contract

Liability of original parties: leases granted before 1 January 1996

It sometimes comes as a surprise to a tenant that the original landlord and the original tenant remain liable on the lease throughout its term. Thus, if A leases property to B and B with A's consent assigns the remainder of the lease to C, if C then defaults on the covenants in the lease, e.g. payment of rent, the landlord A can sue B for the amount due.

The problem is particularly acute where C becomes insolvent and cannot pay rent. In *W H Smith Ltd v Wyndram Investments Ltd* [1994] 2 BCLC 571 the insolvency of an assignee and a disclaimer of liability by the insolvency practitioner dealing with the insolvency left W H Smith, the original tenant, liable to the landlord on the substantial part of a 25-year lease.

The Landlord and Tenant (Covenants) Act 1995: leases granted on or after 1 January 1996

The above rules deriving from privity changed when the above Act came into force on 1 January 1996. The key elements of reform are as follows:

Abolition of privity

The Act abolishes liability arising under the privity law in respect of leases granted on or after 1 January 1996 so that a landlord will only be able to pursue the tenant for the time being unless there is an authorised guarantee agreement in force.

Authorised guarantee agreement

A landlord may require an assigning tenant to enter into a guarantee with the landlord as a condition of the landlord giving his consent to the assignment. Under such an agreement the outgoing tenant guarantees the performance of the lease *by his immediate (but not subsequent) assignee.*

Landlord's release

Landlords are allowed to apply for a release from liability when they dispose of their interest in the premises. This would occur when the landlord sold the freehold reversion in the property to another. Release is obtained by serving a statutory notice on the current tenant.

Notice requirement

In both existing and new leases a landlord must notify a former tenant (or guarantor, e.g. of rent) within six months of a breach of a covenant in order to be able to take action against him in respect of the breach.

Limitation on increase in liability

A former tenant will be liable only for rent increases due to rent review clauses in the original lease and not for increases due to changes in the terms of the lease since he assigned it.

Overriding leases

In both existing and new leases a former tenant (or his guarantor) who is called upon to remedy the default of the current tenant is given a right to call for an 'overriding lease' thus enabling him to reacquire the premises. This means that a former tenant will have the right to re-enter the premises if he is paying for them. This was not the case in previous law.

Main commercial effects of tenant release from liability

The 1995 Act has the following main commercial effects:

- Landlords will impose stricter criteria before consenting to the assignment of a lease. This affects the 'consent will not be unreasonably withheld' principle. Consequently, a business entering into a new lease as a tenant will need to take advice as to the covenants relating to assignment.
- Those involved in property investment will be concerned about the effect on investment values resulting from loss of privity. An investor will tend to choose an older lease since the original tenant and subsequent assignees will remain liable for the whole term since the 1995 Act is not retrospective.
- Difficulties in relation to assignment may result in businesses going for shorter term leases.

Landlord selling freehold: release from covenants

Where a landlord disposes of his reversion as by selling the freehold so that the tenant has a new landlord the selling landlord may under ss 7 and 8 of the 1995 Act seek release from his covenants so that the incoming landlord alone is liable on them. The outgoing landlord must serve notice on the tenant within four weeks of the transfer of his interest and the tenant has four weeks thereafter to serve an objection. If there is no tenant objection the former landlord is released. If the tenant serves an objection the landlord must make application to the court for a ruling that it is reasonable for the covenants to be released.

In *BHP Petroleum Great Britain Ltd* v *Chesterfield Properties Ltd* [2001] 2 All ER 914 the High Court ruled that only covenants appearing in the lease could be released under the 1995 Act. Thus where a landlord had, as in this case, given a personal covenant to repair defective glass cladding on office premises this liability could not be released. It was a personal covenant. This ruling was affirmed by the Court of Appeal in *BHP Petroleum Great Britain Ltd* v *Chesterfield Properties* [2002] 1 All ER 821.

So far as those in business are concerned, there is no reason why both parties to a lease should not state in it that personal covenants also end on assignment.

Contracts (Rights of Third Parties) Act 1999

This Act is given a more detailed consideration in Chapter 10. Briefly the Act enables a third party to enforce a term of a contract where the contract expressly gives him that right. In addition, a third party is able to enforce a term of a contract where that term purports to confer a benefit on him and on a proper construction of the contract it appears that the parties to the contract intended to give him that right, even if there is no express provision in the contract to that effect.

As regards the law of landlord and tenant, the Act could apply where the tenant has sublet enabling the subtenant to enforce a provision against the head or main landlord, e.g. an obligation in the head lease to decorate. This could be done without the involvement of the intermediate landlord. No doubt lawyers will bear this in mind when drafting leases to make sure that the rights, if any are to be given, are made clear in the lease.

Tenants' rights to acquire the freehold of houses and blocks of flats

The Leasehold Reform Act 1967, the Leasehold Reform, Housing and Urban Development Act 1993 and the Commonhold and Leasehold Reform Act 2002 together contain the relevant rights. Although as we have seen it is possible to convert from leasehold to commonhold it is necessary for such a conversion to get the consent of 100 per cent of the existing leaseholders and/or other owners of what would become units in the commonhold. Thus many leaseholders are unlikely to convert to commonhold so that there is a need to address the rights of leaseholders under the above legislation. The main rights and requirements appear below. The chapters referred to are chapters in the 2002 Act and the relationship of that Act and the 1967 and 1993 Acts are explained under the headings set out below to give the current legal regime.

Chapter 1. Right to manage

This introduces a new right for leaseholders of flats to manage their building. The qualifying conditions are that they must hold a 'long lease' of a flat in the building, which is principally any lease granted originally for a term exceeding 21 years. Eligible leaseholders must set up a company known as a RTM (Right to Manage) company in order to exercise the right. The Act, combined with a power to make regulations, specifies the constitution of the company. In outline an RTM company must be a private company limited by guarantee and must include the acquisition and exercise of the right to manage as one of its objects. A company that is also a commonhold association cannot be a RTM company. Any person who is a qualifying tenant of a flat in the premises is entitled to be a member of the RTM company at any time. A landlord is entitled to be a member but only after the RTM takes over the management of the premises.

Chapter 1 also provides for the service on all qualifying tenants of a notice of invitation to participate. There are also provisions relating to the service upon the landlord of a claim notice and of counter notices by the landlord. Where a counter notice contends that the RTM company is not entitled to manage the dispute will be settled by an application to the Leasehold Valuation Tribunal (LVT). The Act provides that a RTM company may apply to an LVT to acquire the right to manage where the landlord cannot be traced. The chapter also provides for the termination of the right to manage where the company wishes to cease the right and the landlord agrees or where the company becomes insolvent.

Chapter 2. Collective enfranchisement by tenants of flats

This chapter amends the Leasehold Reform, Housing and Urban Development Act 1993 that deals with the right of leaseholders to buy collectively the freehold of their building. The eligibility criteria are simplified. In particular the requirement that at least two-thirds of the leaseholders in the block must participate and that at least half of the participating group must have lived in their flats for the previous 12 months (or periods totalling three years in the last ten) are removed. The proportion of participating leaseholders who must participate is reduced to one half. The low rent test is abolished in the few situations where it applied (i.e. leases of less than 35 years). Formerly, the rent had not to exceed £250 pa (£1,000 pa in London). The chapter also increases the proportion of the building that can be occupied for non-residential purposes from 10 per cent to 25 per cent and reduces the scope of the exemption for certain resident landlords. Currently, premises converted into four or fewer flats where the landlord or an adult family member has occupied one of the flats as their only or principal home for at least 12 months are exempt. Under the CLRA 2002 the exemption will apply only if the landlord has owned the freehold since before the conversion and carried out the conversion.

The business application. Enfranchisement claims will increase. For example, in the case of a block of flats that contains 12 flats, it was necessary under previous provisions for at least eight leaseholders to participate and at least four had to be resident. Under the CLRA 2002 only six have to participate and none will have to be resident. Also, more leaseholders with flats over shop premises will be able to claim.

Formerly the freehold of the building was acquired by a 'nominee purchaser', but there were no provisions as to the nature and constitution of this purchaser. The 2002 Act amends the 1993 Act so that the freehold is acquired under the tenants' *right to exercise* the purchase by a RTE company of which the participating leaseholders are members. The RTE company must be a private company limited by guarantee and its memorandum must include as one of its objects the exercise of the right to collective enfranchisement. A company that is a commonhold association cannot be a RTE company. All qualifying leaseholders have a right to participate in the purchase by joining the company.

The price of the freehold should also be cheaper under the 2002 Act. This chapter amends the valuation principles of the 1993 Act. It provides that where marriage value exists it should be divided equally between the landlord and the leaseholders in all cases. It also provides that where the unexpired term of the leases held by qualifying leaseholders exceeds

22

80 years no marriage value is payable. The marriage value relates to the fact that on acquisition the tenant has, in effect, merged the freehold and leasehold interest having a lease and also controlling the landlord function by a collective ownership of the freehold. This obviously increases the value payable to the old landlord but the above rules reduce or eliminate this extra value.

It is not necessary for all the leases to have at least 80 years unexpired. Those that have will have the marriage value ignored.

Chapter 3. New leases for tenants of flats

This chapter amends the provisions of the 1993 Act covering the right of individual leaseholders to buy a new lease. The low rent test is abolished and the same provisions apply to marriage values as those set out above. The former requirement that the leaseholder must have lived in the flat for the last three years (or periods totalling three years in the last 10) is replaced by the requirement to have held the lease for at least two years. Where deceased leaseholders would have been eligible to buy a new lease immediately before death their personal representatives will qualify for a period of two years after the date of granting probate of the will or letters of administration as for example where there is an intestacy.

The business application. Personal representatives can increase the value of the estate by extending a lease that might otherwise be difficult to sell or mortgage.

Chapter 4. Leasehold house

The chapter amends the provisions of the Leasehold Reform Act 1967 that covers the right of leaseholders of houses to buy their freeholds or extend their lease. Qualifying leaseholders have the right to an extended lease 90 years longer than the original terms. The provisions of Chapter 4 reflect those of Chapters 2 and 3 as follows:

- the low rent test is abolished;
- the marriage value provisions are the same as those set out above;
- under the new provisions a leaseholder is required only to have held the lease for at least two years;
- acquisition by the personal representatives of a deceased leaseholder are the same as those set out above.

This chapter also provides new rights for leaseholders who have extended their leases under the 1967 Act. They will be able to buy their freehold *after* the extended lease has commenced. The price will be determined by s 9(1A) of the 1967 Act. Where they do not buy the freehold they will become entitled to an assured tenancy under the Housing Act 1988 Part I when the extended lease expires.

The chapter also amends the 1967 Act in order to simplify the procedure where the landlord cannot be found. Leaseholders can apply to the county court (rather than the High Court) for a vesting order and the price payable will be determined by an LVT rather than a surveyor appointed by the President of the Lands Tribunal. The relevant procedures are the same as those applying to flats under the 1993 Act.

Chapter 5. Other provisions about leases

- The definition of 'service charge' is extended to cover improvement costs. This means that improvement costs must be reasonable and that unreasonableness can be challenged at an LVT.

The business application. Tenants will find that this provision deals with a number of notorious landlord scams particularly where all manner of works have been bundled into 'improvement works' because this head of charge was unchallengeable under previous law.

■ LVTs are given jurisdiction to decide whether leaseholders are liable to pay service charges as well as whether these are reasonable. Formerly LVTs had no jurisdiction to consider the reasonableness of service charges once they had been paid. They now have that right (CLRA 2002, s 155).

■ The chapter introduces new accounting and inspection provisions to tighten up the Landlord and Tenant Act 1985. Leaseholders get a new right to withhold payment of service charges if accounts are not provided by the landlord. In future the landlord must hold service charge money, that is subject to a trust to defray the relevant costs, in a separate bank account and it will not be permissible to run a number of properties through one general account. However, the Secretary of State is given power to exempt certain payees from this requirement (CLRA 2002, s 151). This could be used to exempt managing agents whose general client accounts are audited in accordance with statutory requirements.

■ Charges that are to be paid under leases for approvals, for the provision of information as a result of a failure to pay rent or other charges on time or as a result of a breach of a covenant or condition of a lease are contained in a new concept called 'administration charges'. These must be reasonable and can be challenged in terms of liability to pay or reasonableness before an LVT.

■ Section 20 of the Landlord and Tenant Act 1985 under which landlords must consult tenants before carrying out works above a prescribed sum recoverable through service charges is replaced. The consultation requirements are extended to cover contracts for works or other services of more than 12 months' duration. LVTs (rather than county courts) can grant dispensation if they think that it is reasonable to do so.

■ The chapter also introduces a requirement that ground rent is not payable unless it has been demanded by giving the tenant prescribed notice. Application of any provisions in the lease relating to late or non-payment is prevented if the rent is paid within 30 days of the demand being issued.

■ Forfeiture procedures for non-payment of service or administration charges are prohibited unless the charge has be agreed or admitted by the tenant or a court or LVT has determined that it is reasonable. Forfeiture proceedings for other breaches cannot be commenced unless a court or LVT has determined that the breach has occurred.

■ As regards insurance of long leasehold houses, e.g. those exceeding 21 years, leaseholders can insure wherever they choose provided that the policy is issued by an authorised insurer, i.e. authorised under the Financial Services and Markets Act 2000. The policy must cover the landlord and the leaseholder and provide the cover required by the lease. This provision overrules covenants under which the insurer must be nominated by the landlord, the use of which often gave him large commissions. Owners of other dwellings, e.g. maisonettes, must continue to rely on the Landlord and Tenant Act 1985 and apply to the county court or the LVT for an order requiring the landlord to nominate another insurer but only on the grounds that the cover is inadequate or the premiums excessive. The CLRA 2002 however makes it clear that this ability to apply to the county court or the LVT applies where the insurer has to be *approved* by the landlord as well as cases where the insurer must be *nominated* by him.

Chapter 6. Leasehold Valuation Tribunals

There are important new powers here to make regulations to exclude the case of a party before an LVT, in whole or in part, where the party fails to comply with the directions of the

LVT. Costs can be awarded of up to £500 or any higher amount that regulations might prescribe against frivolous, vexatious or disruptive parties and those who act unreasonably.

Effect of Human Rights Act 1998 (HRA)

This legislation came into force in October 2000. In terms of its effect upon the law of landlord and tenant, the following material should be noted.

Forfeiture and distraint

These self-help remedies of landlords may be subject to challenge under the HRA.

Forfeiture. It is the better view so far that forfeiture will survive a challenge under the HRA. This is based upon the fact that both landlord and tenant have agreed in the lease that forfeiture will be the consequence of breach of covenant, e.g. non-payment of rent. Also the state has provided a method of relief through the courts.

Distraint. This remedy, widely known as distress for rent, is seen as unfair in terms of the fact that the tenant's goods can be taken and sold at cheap prices by the landlord because of problems of title in sheriffs' sales. There is statutory intervention by the state, and the state sanctions the mechanism for distraint by certifying bailiffs. Third parties' goods on the premises may also be taken. For these reasons, exercise of this remedy appears threatened by the HRA.

The Competition Act 1998

This Act came into force on 1 March 2000. Property transactions are subject to the competition rules.

Penalties for infringing the Act

Those who infringe the Act with their property documents will find that these documents, i.e. leases, will be void and there may be exposure to significant fines or litigation brought by a third party claiming to have suffered loss through the anti-competitive behaviour. Fines can be up to 10 per cent of annual turnover for the previous three years.

Exclusions

The Competition Act 1998 (Land and Vertical Agreements Exclusion) Order 2000 (SI 2000/310) applies, and gives a specific exclusion for 'land agreements' covering transfers of freeholds, leases, assignments of leasehold interests, easements, licences and agreements to enter into any of these. The exemption will apply if the restriction is concerned to protect the interest in land, but not if it is intended to protect trading interests.

Examples

- *A landlord is an insurance company.* The lease requires the tenant to insure the premises with the landlord's company. *This restriction would not benefit from the exclusion because the landlord is protecting his business, which is insurance, and not his interest in the land.*
- *A landlord is the owner of the only retail park outside a particular town.* He proposes to increase the rents under his business leases by 200 per cent. *This increase is not within the exception. The landlord is abusing a dominant position within the market.*

There will, of course, be many fine distinctions made, but until we have case law, it is difficult to be precise in marginal cases.

Servitudes

Servitudes are rights over the property of another and may be either *easements* or profits *à prendre*.

Easements

An easement may be defined as a right to use or restrict the use of the land of another person in some way. There are various classes of easement and these include:

(*a*) rights of way;
(*b*) rights of light;
(*c*) rights to abstract water;
(*d*) rights to the support of buildings.

To be valid an easement must satisfy the following conditions.

There must be a dominant and servient tenement

The land in respect of which, and for the benefit of which, the easement exists is called the dominant tenement, and the land over which the right is exercised is called the servient tenement. A valid easement cannot exist *in gross*, i.e. without reference to the holding of land. A right of way enjoyed by members of the public generally is a public right of way but not an easement.

> *Hill* v *Tupper*, 1863 – No easement 'in gross' (**485**)

The grant of a right of way over his land by a landowner to be exercised by the grantee personally, and without reference to any land capable of deriving benefit from the right of way, is merely a licence and not an easement.

The easement must accommodate the dominant tenement

The easement must confer some benefit on the land itself so as to make it a better and more convenient property; it is not enough that the owner obtains some personal advantage. A right of way over contiguous (adjoining) land generally benefits the dominant tenement, and an easement can exist even where two tenements do not actually adjoin, provided it is clear that the easement benefits the dominant tenement.

Thus it is not possible to have a right of way over land in Kent as the result of owning land in Northumberland. There is no connection between the two. Equally the sole and exclusive right given to the leaseholder of land on a canal bank to let out pleasure boats on the canal does not constitute an easement; it is not beneficial to the land on the canal bank as such (see *Hill* v *Tupper* (1863), above).

The dominant tenement and the servient tenement must not be both owned and occupied by the same person

Thus, if P owns both Blackacre and Whiteacre and habitually walks over Blackacre to reach Whiteacre, he is not exercising a right of way in respect of Blackacre, but merely walking from one part of his land to another. For this rule to apply, P must have simultaneously both ownership and possession of the two properties concerned. It is not enough that he owns the two if they are leased to different tenants, or that he is the tenant of both if they are owned by different owners.

22

The easement must be capable of forming the subject of a grant

This means that the right must be sufficiently definite. There must be a capable grantor and a capable grantee, and the right must be within the general nature of the rights capable of existing as easements.

> *Bass* v *Gregory*, 1890 – Is the easement definite enough? (**486**)

An easement is a right to use or restrict the use of a neighbour's land which should not normally involve him in doing any work or spending any money, though the Court of Appeal has recognised an easement of fencing.

> *Crow* v *Wood*, 1970 – An easement of fencing (**487**)

The categories of easements are not closed and new rights have from time to time been recognised as easements, though in general the courts are still reluctant to extend the categories.

> *Re Ellenborough Park*, 1956 – Expansion of easements (**488**)
> *Phipps* v *Pears*, 1964 – No easement of property protection (**489**)
> *Grigsby* v *Melville*, 1972 – No easement giving exclusive right of user (**490**)

Profits à *prendre*

A profit à *prendre* is the right to take something of legal value from the land of another, e.g. shooting, fishing and grazing rights; the right to cut turf or take wood for fuel. The exception is a right to take water from a stream which is treated as an easement because running water cannot be privately owned and is not therefore a thing of legal value.

A profit necessarily involves a servient tenement but there may or may not be a dominant tenement, for a profit can exist *in gross*. A profit may be a several profit, where enjoyment is granted to an individual as is often the case with shooting and fishing rights; or a profit may be in common which may be enjoyed by more than one person, as is often the case with grazing rights and the right to take various materials for use as fuel.

The expression is legal French for 'profit to take'. An acceptable legal pronunciation of the third word is 'prawn-dra'.

Acquisition of servitudes

Servitudes may be acquired (*a*) by statute, (*b*) by express or implied grant, (*c*) by prescription, (*d*) by equitable estoppel (see *Crabb* v *Arun District Council* (1975) (Chapter 10)).

Easements created by statute are usually in connection with local Acts of Parliament.

When land is sold, a servitude may be expressly reserved in favour of another tenement of the seller, or may be expressly granted in similar circumstances by deed; and under the Law of Property Act 1925, s 62, a conveyance, if there is no contrary express intention, operates to convey servitudes appertaining to the land conveyed (see *Crow* v *Wood* (1970)).

Under the rule in *Wheeldon* v *Burrows* (1879) 12 Ch D 31 where a vendor sells part of his land, the purchaser will have rights over the vendor's retained land if:

- such rights were previously used by the vendor for the benefit of the land conveyed and either;
- they were reasonably necessary for the land conveyed; or
- were continuous and apparent.

Section 62 has, therefore, a similar effect to the rule in *Wheeldon* but, whereas s 62 applies only where the property is transferred by conveyance, *Wheeldon* applies to other transfers, e.g. where property is left by a will.

Where an owner of two plots conveys one of them, then certain easements are implied. These are *easements of necessity*, as where the piece of land would be completely surrounded and inaccessible without a right of way; *intended easements*, which would be necessary to carry out the common intentions of the parties; *ancillary easements*, which would be necessary in view of the right granted, as the grant of the use of water implies the right of way to reach the water. Where part of a tenement is granted, then the grantee acquires easements over the land which are continuous and apparent, are necessary to the reasonable enjoyment of the land granted, and have been and are used by the grantor for the benefit of the part granted. An example of this is a window enjoying light.

Ward v *Kirkland*, 1966 – An easement for reasonable enjoyment (**491**)

It will be appreciated therefore that easements do not always show up in the title deeds. Although the Law Society's National Conditions of Sale put the seller under a duty to disclose latent easements, this only applies if they are known to him. The purchaser must take the risk of unknown easements such as an underground sewer the existence of which was unknown to the seller (*William Sindall plc* v *Cambridge County Council* [1993] NPC 82).

Even where there is no easement, access to adjacent land may in certain circumstances be obtained under the Access to Neighbouring Land Act 1992 which is further considered in Chapter 21.

Prescription

Prescription may be based on a presumed grant or alternatively may be established by use as of right.

Prescription at common law depended on use since time immemorial, which at law means since 1189. Clearly in most cases it is out of the question to show continuous use for this period, and so the courts were prepared to accept 20 years' continuous use as raising the presumption of a grant. This presumption may be rebutted by showing that at some time since 1189 the right could not have existed, and it follows that an easement of light cannot be claimed by prescription at common law in a building erected since 1189. This serious difficulty was met in part by the presumption of a lost modern grant, and juries (when they were in use in civil matters) were told that if there had been use during living memory or even for 20 years, they might presume a lost grant or deed, and this ultimately became mandatory, even though neither judge nor jury had any belief that such instrument had ever existed.

The position is now clear under the Prescription Act 1832, which was passed to deal with the difficulties arising under the common law. Under this Act, which supplements the common law, we must distinguish easements other than light from easements of light and easements from profits.

Tehidy Minerals v *Norman*, 1971 – Lost modern grant (**492**)

Easements other than light

Twenty years' uninterrupted use as of right will establish an easement. Use as of right means *nec vi, nec clam, nec precario*, i.e. without force, stealth or permission. The law of prescription rests upon the acquiescence of the owner of the servient tenement. Thus he must have knowledge of the exercise of the right claimed. If the owner of the so-called servient tenement can prove that he has given verbal permission, i.e. that the easement is *precario*, then it cannot be claimed. Nevertheless 40 years' similar use will establish the easement, and in this case, if the owner of the servient tenement wishes to prove that the right was exercised by permission, he must produce a written agreement to that effect. To establish a right of way by prescription, periods of use of an original and a substituted way may be added together.

> *Diment* v *Foot*, 1974 – Where there is no knowledge (**493**)
> *Davis* v *Whitby*, 1974 – Original and substituted ways (**494**)

Easements of light

These can be established by 20 years' use, the defences being that the owner of the servient tenement gave permission and that there is a deed or written agreement to this effect, or that the owner of the servient tenement interrupted the enjoyment of the right for a continuous period of a year by erecting something which blocked the light. Under the Rights of Light Act 1959 (as amended by the Local Land Charges Act 1975), it is no longer necessary to erect something of this nature; the owner of the servient land may now register on the local land charges register a statutory notice indicating where he would have put up a screen, and this operates as if the access of light had been restricted for one year. Use as of right is not necessary, and oral consent will not bar the claim even if the claimant has made regular money payments for the use of the right.

The right can only be claimed having regard to the type of room affected. A bedroom does not require the amount of light that other rooms do, and if the claimant has used the bedroom to repair watches for 20 years, he will still only be able to claim that amount of light appropriate to a bedroom. There is no right to receive unlimited light but in *Ough* v *King* [1967] 3 All ER 859, the Court of Appeal held that in determining whether there was an infringement of a right to light regard must be had to the nature of the locality and to the higher standard of lighting required in modern times.

However, in *Allen* v *Greenwood* [1979] 2 WLR 187, the Court of Appeal held that the measure of light which can be acquired by prescription can, so far as a greenhouse used for its normal purposes is concerned, include the right to an extraordinary amount of light, and also to the benefits of that light, including the rays of the sun. Nevertheless, there is no claim to a view or a prospect which can be seen from a window.

The right to light is not limited to a freeholder and may be claimed by a tenant.

Artificial light

In *Midtown Ltd* v *City of London Real Property Co Ltd*; *Joseph* v *City of London Real Property Ltd* [2005] 1 EGLR 65 the High Court appears to have dealt a severe blow to those trying to protect the right of light to their properties. On the facts of the case it was accepted by the parties that the activities of a developer would have a significant effect on the claimant's right to light to its property. Nevertheless, the court refused an injunction to prevent the development on the basis of the presence of artificial light which the claimant could use. The court did not rule that the existence of artificial light would prevent *all* claims for infringement of a right to light, but the case will no doubt be raised by defendants in future cases.

The ruling suggests that there is no absolute right to natural light as some previous cases have suggested.

Distinction between presumption of grant and Prescription Act 1832

It is worth noting that the period of user under the 1832 Act is a period of enjoyment *immediately before a claim* to establish the right is made by bringing an action. However, the period under prescription by lost modern grant is *not limited to the period next before the claim is made*.

For example A uses a track over B's land giving access to a wood from A's house. A uses the vehicular access for 20 years. It is then interrupted by B who orders A to stop using the track. A acquiesces in this for 14 months while he tries to negotiate a compromise with B. This fails and A goes back to using the track. It was held in these circumstances in *Smith* v *Brudenell-Bruce* [2002] 2 P & CR 51 that A succeeded under the rules of lost modern grant but failed under the Act of 1832.

Profits à *prendre*

The general period for prescription here is 30 years under the Act of 1832, though 20 years is enough if the court is presuming a lost modern grant (see *Tehidy Minerals* v *Norman* (1971)).

If an easement is denied or threatened, it would be necessary to ask the court for an injunction to prevent the owner of the servient tenement from acting contrary to the easement, and its existence would have to be proved under one of the headings given above. The court may then:

(*a*) find the easement not proved; or
(*b*) grant an injunction to restrain the owner of the servient tenement from acting contrary to it; or
(*c*) if the infringement is not serious, award damages once and for all, in which case the servient owner will have bought his right to act contrary to the easement.

Reduction of easements

The court has power to reduce the scope of an easement when insistence on full use of it is unreasonable. Thus in *B & Q plc* v *Liverpool and Lancashire Properties Ltd* [2000] 39 LS Gaz R 41 the defendants wished to extend their premises over part of an easement of access possessed by B & Q. The easement of way would not be extinguished but reduced. B & Q asked for an injunction to prevent the extension and the court granted it. B & Q had shown that they would be placed in a difficult access situation otherwise and it was not unreasonable of them to resist a reduction in their easement of way. The High Court made clear however that where the holder of an easement would not be placed in difficulty by its reduction and was unreasonably resisting a reduction the court would not grant relief.

22

Termination or extinguishment of servitudes

Servitudes may be extinguished by statute, as where the property concerned is compulsorily purchased under statutory powers, or by express or implied release. At law a deed is necessary for express release, but in equity an informal release will be effective if it would be inequitable for the dominant owner to claim that the right still exists.

An example of an easement being extinguished under statutory authority is provided by *Jones* v *Cleanthi* [2006] 1 All ER 1029.

The claimant had a leasehold interest in a flat. The lease gave her access down the hall of the block to a place from which refuse was collected by the local authority. She sub-let the flat and while she was away the local authority, acting under Part XI of the Housing Act 1985, and in connection with the fact that the property was in multi-occupation, served a notice on the landlord to carry out works on the premises. These included building a fire wall across the hall so that that form of access to the refuse are was denied to the claimant. When she returned to the flat she raised before the High Court her right to an easement of way down the hall. The High Court ruled that, since the work had been done under statutory power and in compliance with a statutory duty, the easement of way had been extinguished. The landlord had no alternative but to carry out the instructions of the local authority. The claimant would have to reach the refuse area by a longer route.

If the dominant owner shows by his conduct an intention to release an easement, it will be extinguished. The demolition of a house to which an easement of light attaches may amount to an implied release, but not if it is intended to replace the house by another building. Mere non-use is not enough (see *Tehidy Minerals* v *Norman* (1971)).

We have already seen that an easement is extinguished when the dominant and servient tenements come into simultaneous ownership and possession of the same person, since a person cannot have an easement over his or her own land.

Indemnity insurance. If the existence of an easement is crucial to the purchase of land and its existence is not crystal clear, it will generally be advisable to obtain indemnity insurance from a company specialising in such business, compensating the landowner if the 'easement' is successfully challenged.

Declarations by the court. Although no question of extinguishing the easement arises, it is possible to ask the court for a judgment declaring that the dominant owner will not be able to prevent a particular development on the servient land before the development goes ahead. Thus, in *Greenwich Healthcare NHS Trust* v *London Quadrant Housing Trust* (1998) *The Times*, 11 June the court made such a declaration where the proposed development was the realignment of a dangerous road in the public interest.

Restrictive covenants

A restrictive covenant is essentially a contract between two owners of land whereby one agrees to restrict the use of his land for the benefit of the other. We are not concerned here with covenants in leases, which are governed by separate rules already outlined.

Such covenants were not adequately enforced by the common law because the doctrine of privity of contract applied, and as soon as one of the parties to the covenant transferred his land, the covenant was not enforceable by the transferee because he had not been a party to the original contract. However, the common law realised that this was rather too rigid and went so far as to allow a transferee to enforce the benefit of the covenant against the original party to it. Thus, if A, the owner of Blackacre, agreed with B, the owner of Whiteacre, that he would not use Blackacre for the purposes of trade, if B then sold Whiteacre to C, C could enforce the covenant against A. However, if A sold Blackacre to D, C could not enforce the covenant against D, because the common law would not allow D to bear the burden of a covenant he did not make.

Equity takes a different view, and allows C to enforce the sort of covenant outlined above by injunction, if the following conditions are fulfilled.

(a) The covenant must be substantially negative. Much depends upon the words used in the covenant, and an undertaking which seems *prima facie* to be positive may imply a negative undertaking and this may then be enforced (see *Tulk* v *Moxhay* (1848), Chapter 10). A covenant to use a house as a dwelling house implies that it will not be used for other purposes, and would be enforceable in the negative sense. If the covenant requires the covenantor to spend money, it is not a negative covenant. Thus in *Rhone* v *Stephens* [1994] 2 WLR 429 it was held by the House of Lords that a positive covenant to repair the roof of an adjacent property did not run with the land, i.e. it did not pass the repairing duty to a subsequent owner.

(b) The covenant must benefit the land. It is often said that the covenant must 'touch and concern' the land and must not be merely for the personal benefit of the claimant. Restrictive covenants usually endeavour to keep up the residential character of the district and benefit the land by preserving value and amenities as a residential property.

(c) The person claiming the benefit must retain land which can benefit from the covenant taken. If X owns a piece of land which he splits up into two plots, selling one plot to Y and taking a restrictive covenant in favour of the plot he has retained, then he can enforce the covenant so long as he retains the land to be benefited. If X now sells the plot he had retained, he will not be able to enforce the covenant for the future, although the purchaser from X will be able to do so.

> *Kelly* v *Barrett*, 1924 – Restrictive covenants: land must benefit (**495**)

There is an exception to this rule in the case of *building schemes* involving an estate of houses. Here the covenants are taken by the owner of the land from each person purchasing a house, and although the owner does not retain any of the land, the covenants may be enforced by the purchasers as between themselves. However, a building scheme will not be implied simply because there is a common vendor and the existence of common covenants. It was at one time thought that there must be a defined area and evidence of laying out in lots (*Re Wembley Park Estate Co Ltd's Transfer* [1968] 1 All ER 457). However, in *Re Dolphin's Conveyance* [1970] 2 All ER 664, Stamp, J held that so long as the covenants held in the conveyances were, as a matter of construction, intended to give the purchasers of the parcels mutual rights, this was sufficient to make them enforceable and there was no need, in particular, to consider lotting.

Since restrictive covenants are in general enforceable only in equity, the question of notice arises. In fact, restrictive covenants created after 1925 are void against a purchaser of the legal estate, even one who has notice of them, unless they are registered as land charges. There is an exception as regards covenants between lessor and lessee. These cannot be registered and will be binding only if known to an assignee of the lease. In practice, it is usual for an assignee to inspect the lease. As regards covenants created before 1 January 1926, they bind all persons who acquire the land which is subject to them with the exception of a purchaser for value of the legal estate in the land without notice, actual or constructive, of the covenants.

The general position regarding assignment of leases and the enforcement of covenants against the assignee is also dealt with by the Landlord and Tenant (Covenants) Act 1995, which has already been considered.

Under s 84 of the Law of Property Act 1925 (as amended by the Law of Property Act 1969, s 28(1) and Sch 3), the Lands Tribunal has power, on the application of any person interested, to discharge or modify a restrictive covenant. However, a developer may try to obtain indemnity insurance against restrictions on development caused by possible restrictive covenants. The time and expense factors involved in a Lands Tribunal application often mean that the developer will choose the insurance route, and get his compensation for his loss that way if the covenant is enforceable against him.

Whether a covenant runs with the land depends upon the words. In *Roake* v *Chadha* [1983] 3 All ER 503 the covenant between plots of land was that no more than one house should be built on each plot. The covenants were expressed to pass *only if specifically assigned*. A plot was sold to the defendant but the covenant was not assigned. He proposed to build more than one house on the plot and the claimant, who owned an adjacent plot, tried to enforce the 'one house' covenant. It was held that he could not do so because the covenant had not been specifically assigned as the agreement required.

Restrictive covenants and competition law

Situations have occurred where the owner of a building has sold it to a purchaser subject to an anti-competitive covenant. For example, suppose a cinema company sells one of its art deco listed cinemas to a purchaser with a covenant that it cannot be used as a cinema again and this is to support an out-of-town multiplex that the cinema company has set up. The purchaser may find that since the building is listed he or she cannot get permission for a change of use to other activities e.g. a health club, and since it cannot be used as a cinema the purchaser is in difficulties in regard to the purchase. The government may have to consider a change in the law otherwise properties may be left unsold or unused which is undesirable. Problems relating to land agreements are not really resolved by the Competition Act 1998 and the Enterprise Act 2002 which are considered in Chapter 16.

Enforcing restrictive covenants

Restrictive covenants may be enforced by an action for damages or a claim for an injunction prohibiting breach. As we have seen, an action for an injunction may be lost by delay and/or acquiescence leaving a claim for damages only (see further Chapter 18).

In *Gifford* v *Graham* (1998) *The Times*, 1 May a landowner had the benefit of a restrictive covenant over adjoining land. With full knowledge of his legal rights he failed to seek relief to restrain the unlawful erection of an indoor riding school and to prevent the unlawful use of the covenanted land by its owner. It was held that he could not be granted an injunction for the demolition of the building and to prevent the use of the land for the riding school business. The landowner was only entitled to damages for the injury to his legal rights. Acquiescence had barred his right to injunctive relief.

There is a presumption that restrictive covenants are intended to bind subsequent owners but this presumption is rebutted (does not apply) if the conveyance states that the relevant covenants are not binding. In any case, the conveyance should refer to successors in title otherwise the covenant might be regarded as operative only between the parties to the conveyance and not beyond. This is particularly likely where some covenants are stated to apply to successors and others remain silent as to this. In such a case, the presumption in s 79 of the Law of Property Act 1925 will not apply. The silence indicates a contrary intention as in *Morrells of Oxford Ltd* v *Oxford United Football Club Ltd* [2001] Ch 459, a ruling by the Court of Appeal.

The transfer of land

The material in this section will be changed in parts under the provisions of the Electronic Communications Act 2000 that received the Royal Assent on 25 May 2000. The Cabinet Office has identified some of the departmental priorities for using the Act to update legislation to allow for the electronic option in conveyancing which could cut the time for buying property from months to weeks, at least so far as the legal process is concerned. The ambitious proposals include the setting up of nationwide databases allowing the buying, selling and mortgaging of homes online. Without this updating, electronic conveyancing would not be possible since the contract of sale of the land and the deed required to convey the title to it must be in writing and signed. The Law of Property Act 1925 and related statutes passed in that year, together with the Law of Property (Miscellaneous Provisions) Act 1989, are the main measures requiring change. However, since the change to electronic methods may take some time, the following materials should be studied since they represent current procedures.

As regards developments, the paper conveyancing process is speeded up by the Land Registration Act 2002 which came into force on 13 October 2003 in terms of electronic searching of title at the Land Registry. The Registry began piloting e-conveyancing as such in 2006.

The latest position is as follows:

- e-conveyancing will be set up in five tranches between 2006 and 2010.
- *Tranche one* began in the autumn of 2006 and was placed before a small and controlled number of pilot users in Portsmouth, Fareham and Bristol. The pilot had only limited features for users. It ran for six months and was not extended beyond the pilot areas.
- *Tranche 2* will take place as a pilot in 2007. Features will be expanded to include, for example, electronic signatures.
- *Tranches 3, 4 and 5* will come in in 2008, 2009 and 2010, each adding more electronic facilities, including electronic transfer of funds, until a complete e-conveyancing service exists. Relevant changes in the text will be incorporated as the service moves to completion. The issue is mainly one for solicitors in practice and there seems little point in going into depth here about the changes while they are merely at a limited pilot stage.

It is usual, when a disposition of land is contemplated, to draw up a contract. For a contract of sale to be valid both parties must have contractual capacity, the contract must be legal, there must be clear agreement on all the essential terms, and acceptance of the offer must be unconditional. As we have seen, contracts for the sale or other disposition of land are invalid unless they are in writing (Law of Property (Miscellaneous Provisions) Act 1989 (see further Chapter 11)).

When a valid contract for sale exists, the purchaser acquires an equitable interest in the property and the vendor is in effect a qualified trustee for him. Thus, if the property increases in value between contract and completion, the purchaser is entitled to the increase and similarly he must bear any loss. This is particularly important in cases where property is destroyed by fire between contract and completion, since the purchaser would still have to pay the purchase money, even though he only received a conveyance of the land with the useless buildings on it. It is now provided by s 47 of the Law of Property Act 1925 that in such a case the purchaser may become entitled to money payable on an insurance policy maintained by the vendor. However, it is prudent for the purchaser to take out his own insurance in case the vendor has none or his policy is defective. If, as is usual, the Law Society's Standard Conditions of Sale are used, they expressly state that the risk of damage to the property stays with the seller until completion. Thus they impose an obligation on the seller to transfer the property in the same physical state as it was at the date of the contract (subject to fair wear and tear). If between contract and completion there is a change in the physical state of the property which makes it unusable for the contract purpose, the buyer is given an unlimited right to rescind.

On a sale of business property it is fair to say that the above provisions have been resisted, e.g. by modifying the Standard Conditions. For business property, therefore, the buyer will usually need to insure from exchange.

22

The vendor has a lien on the property sold to the extent of the unpaid purchase money and may enforce this by an order for sale; this lien may be registered as a general equitable charge. The purchaser has a similar lien in respect of money paid under the contract prior to conveyance.

On a sale of land it is usual to use a standard form of contract prepared by the Law Society since this saves much trouble in drafting. In what is called an open contract for the sale of land, the vendor must under s 23 of the Law of Property Act 1969 show a title for at least 15 years, beginning with a good 'root of title', i.e. a document dealing with the whole legal and equitable interests in the land. It may be necessary to go back more than 15 years in order to find such a document. The vendor prepares an abstract of title, listing all the relevant documents in connection with its establishment, and he must produce these documents in order to justify the abstract of title he has prepared. It should be noted that all the above matters are attended to by the parties' solicitors.

The Administration of Justice Act 1985 and the Courts and Legal Services Act 1990 have removed the monopoly on conveyancing which has been possessed by solicitors for many years (see Chapter 3).

A contract for the sale of land will normally contain a completion date which is the time by which the transaction must be concluded. The transfer of land involves the following stages:

(a) The preparation of the contract by the seller's solicitor.

(b) The exchange of contracts between the vendor's and purchaser's solicitors, when the purchaser pays a deposit, usually 10 per cent of the purchase money though the matter is one for negotiation and deposits of only 5 per cent are sometimes taken. It should be noted that a high deposit which is not returnable if the contract does not go through can be set aside by the court as a penalty (see Chapter 18). In *Workers Trust and Merchant Bank* v *Dojap Investments* [1993] 2 WLR 702 a non-returnable deposit of 25 per cent was set aside.

The Standard Conditions of Sale provide that the deposit is to be held by the seller's solicitors as stakeholders and paid to the seller on completion together with accrued interest. This keeps it safe in the remote event of the buyer being entitled to rescind the contract and claim return of the deposit. Where there is a related purchase by the seller the Standard Conditions allow the seller to use the deposit in the related purchase. If there was to be a rescission by the buyer the buyer's claim for a return of deposit would then shift from the seller's solicitor to the seller personally. Except at auction the Standard Conditions require a deposit to be paid by a banker's draft or cheque drawn on the solicitor's bank account. Consequently, the solicitor will ask a buyer for the deposit funds, made payable to the solictor's firm, some days before exchange of contracts is expected.

(c) The delivery by the vendor's solicitors of an abstract of title, or as is more usual today, copies of the documents, e.g. previous conveyances, upon which the vendor bases his title.

(d) The examination of this title by the purchaser's solicitors and the checking of the abstract against the actual deeds to see that it is correct.

In any case, the Law of Property (Miscellaneous Provisions) Act 1994 provides for title guarantees which apply on a transfer of land whether for consideration or not. The Act applies to leases and property other than land such as intellectual property, e.g. copyright. Transferors of the relevant property will give implied guarantees.

If the property is sold with a 'full title guarantee' or with a 'limited title guarantee', there will be implied the following covenants:

■ that the person making the disposition has the right (with the agreement of any other person conveying the property) to dispose of the property as he purports to; and

■ that that person will, at his own cost, do all he reasonably can to give the person to whom he disposes of the property the title he purports to give.

The full guarantee, in addition, warrants freedom from encumbrances, e.g., mortgages, while the limited guarantee gives freedom from encumbrances limited to matters occurring since the last disposition for value. The limited title guarantee is intended for lenders and receivers not ordinary purchasers. Furthermore, the title warranties are only implied in full in the absence of contrary specific provisions.

(e) After all outstanding queries have been solved, a conveyance is prepared by the purchaser's solicitors which is sent to the vendor's solicitors for approval. The draft conveyance may be exchanged a number of times before agreement is reached. Where the land is registered, a simpler form of transfer deed is used.

(f) Just before completion, the purchaser's solicitors will make the necessary searches in the Land Charges Register and in the register maintained by the appropriate local authority to see what encumbrances are registered in respect of the property.

(g) An appointment is then arranged for completion and the purchaser hands over the money, the vendor handing over the conveyance, which he has signed, together with the title deeds. This brings the transaction to a conclusion. However, today there need not be attendance at an office. Completion is very often carried out by post and payment is by bank telegraphic transfer.

The above procedure refers to unregistered land where the need to examine title is to some extent cumbersome and expensive. The Land Registration Act 1925 provides that the title to land can be examined by and registered with the state and that this is followed by the issue of a certificate guaranteeing ownership. Where there is a sale of registered land, the certificate is handed over and the name of the new owner registered. A transfer, rather than a conveyance, is prepared. This is a more simple procedure than the one outlined above for unregistered land and the legal fees for the transaction are less.

Entry of price paid or value declared

The Land Registration (No 3) Rules 1999 (SI 1999/3462) provide that from first registration of land and on subsequent changes of proprietorship the Land Registry will, whenever practicable, enter on the register the price paid or the value declared. The entry will be removed when the next transfer is registered. The information should be helpful to creditors and former spouses seeking settlements. The Land Registry has announced that house price information is available in regard to any property sold in England and Wales since 1 April 2000 on the Land Registry website at www.landreg.gov.uk. There is a charge (currently £2) for each search.

Home Information Packs

The Housing Act 2004 introduces, among other things, the Home Information Pack (HIP), scheduled to come into force in June 2007 as an essential ingredient of the sale of domestic property. It must be prepared by or on behalf of the seller. Its contents were originally to be quite extensive and its cost high, estimated at £800 for a semi-detached house and £1,000 for a detached house. After much protest and lobbying of Parliament, the HIP will come into force as planned in June 2007 but will no longer be required to contain home condition reports. Instead, it will contain only energy performance certificates (introduced by EU law) and local planning searches.

Personal property

We have already mentioned that personal property is divided into two classes – *choses in action* and *choses in possession*, the latter being divided into *chattels real* (i.e. leaseholds) and *chattels personal*. We have already dealt with leaseholds, and the sale of chattels personal has been codified by the Sale of Goods Act 1979, a full study of which would not be appropriate to a book of this nature. The assignment of choses in action is considered later in this chapter.

Mortgages of land

The following types of mortgage are relevant.

Legal mortgage of freeholds

Under the 1925 legislation the mortgagor (the borrower) does not divest himself of his legal estate, but grants to the mortgagee (the lender) a *demise* (i.e. a lease) for a term of years absolute. Thus, if X owns Blackacre and borrows money on mortgage from Y, he will grant Y a term of usually 3,000 years in Blackacre, both agreeing that the term of years will end when the loan is repaid. X will also agree to pay interest on the loan at a stipulated rate.

Alternatively, under the provisions of s 87 of the Law of Property Act 1925 it is possible to create a legal mortgage of freeholds by means of a short deed stating that a charge on the land is created. Such a charge does not give a term of years, but the mortgagee has the same rights and powers as if he had received a term of years under a mortgage by demise.

Before 1926 mortgages were created by conveying the freehold to the mortgagee. Since 1925 an attempt to create a mortgage by this method operates as a grant of a mortgage lease of 3,000 years, subject to cesser on redemption (Law of Property Act 1925, s 85). This is how solicitors arrived at the enormously long period of lease in a mortgage by demise. There is no need to use such a long term.

Legal mortgage of leaseholds

If X, the owner of a 99-year lease of Blackacre, borrows money on mortgage from Y, he may grant Y a sub-lease of, say, 99 years less 10 days, both agreeing that when the loan is repaid the term shall cease. X also agrees to pay interest. Such a term is known as a *mortgage by demise*.

Alternatively, a legal mortgage of leaseholds may be created by a charge by way of legal mortgage under s 87 of the Law of Property Act 1925, if made by deed. No sub-lease is created but the remedies of the mortgagee are the same as if it had been.

When a person has borrowed money by mortgaging property, he may still be able to borrow further sums, if the amount of the charge is not equal to the full value of the property and there seems to be adequate security for further loans. The owner of freehold land may grant a term of 3,000 years plus one day to another mortgagee, whilst the owner of a lease may grant a second sub-lease of, say, 99 years less nine days. Alternatively, a second charge by way of legal mortgage may be created by a further deed.

The only limit to further borrowing on second and subsequent mortgages is that of finding a lender who is prepared to become a second, third or fourth mortgagee.

Equitable mortgage

A mortgagee who receives a mere equitable interest in the land is said to have an equitable mortgage. Thus, if the borrower's interest is equitable, e.g. a life interest, then any mortgage of it is necessarily equitable. Such an interest may be mortgaged by lease or charge, as in legal mortgages, or by a deposit of title deeds with the lender, usually accompanied by a memorandum explaining the transaction. Such mortgages must be in writing and signed by the borrower or his agent (Law of Property Act 1925, s 53). The requirement of writing is reinforced by s 2 of the Law of Property (Miscellaneous Provisions) Act 1989 (see Chapter 11). So writing is required to accompany the deposit of title deeds. A mere deposit of the deeds is not enough (see *United Bank of Kuwait* v *Sahib* (1996) *The Times*, 13 February; Court of Appeal).

An informal mortgage of a legal estate or interest creates an equitable mortgage, e.g. an attempt to create a legal mortgage otherwise than by deed.

Where there is a binding agreement to create a legal mortgage, but the formalities necessary to do so have not been carried out, equity regards the agreement as an equitable mortgage. The agreement can be enforced by specific performance so that the mortgagee can obtain a legal mortgage from the borrower under the rule in *Walsh* v *Lonsdale* (1882). Bexfore there is a binding agreement there must be either written evidence of the agreement, signed by the borrower or his agent, or a sufficient act of part performance by the lender. Given the above requirements the parties can be required to execute a legal mortgage by suing in equity for specific performance.

Joint borrowers: liability

Where for example a business partnership obtains a joint facility for the business secured on property jointly owned by the partners who are joint borrowers and if the lender has to sell the mortgaged property to recoup the loan and there is a shortfall between what is owed and the sale price then where, as is usual, the mortgage contains a joint and several liability clause each borrower is liable under the provision for several liability to pay off the whole balance to the lender with a right to seek a contribution against the other joint borrower(s) (see *AIB Group (UK) plc* v *Martin* [2002] 1 All ER 353). The same would be true of a non-business mortgage that carried a joint and several liability clause.

Rights of the mortgagor or borrower

The borrower has a *right to occupy* the land, unless the lender has taken possession as where the borrower has defaulted on the repayments. There is also a *statutory right in s 99 of the Law of Property Act 1925 to grant leases* which bind the lender and the borrower for up to 50 years or a building lease for 999 years. In practice, however, *the mortgage invariably excludes the right* except with the consent of the lender as s 99(13) allows. *The business application* can arise where a borrower who cannot currently sell the property wishes to rent it but the lender refuses to allow this. The borrower may challenge this decision in court. For example in *Citibank International plc* v *Kessler* [1999] 2 CMLR 603 the borrower challenged the right of the lender to exclude the letting power on the basis that it was contrary to what is now Art 39 of the Treaty of Rome. Mr Kessler had bought a house in England with a view to assisting with BMW's operations here. He moved back to Germany and wished to let it since structural defects and a boundary dispute made it impossible to sell. Article 39 deals with restriction on movement of workers within the EU. The Court of Appeal ruled that his case failed. It was not the object of Art 39 to hinder a bank's financial judgements in this way when it was protecting its security.

22

A major right of the mortgagor is the right to redeem (or recover) the land. Originally at common law the land became the property of the lender as soon as the date decided upon for repayment had passed, unless during that time the loan had been repaid. However, equity regarded a mortgage as essentially a security, and gave the mortgagor the right to redeem the land at any time on payment of the principal sum, plus interest due to the date of payment. What is more important, this rule applied even though the common-law date for repayment had passed. This right, which still exists, is called the *equity of redemption*, and there are two important rules connected with it:

(a) Once a mortgage always a mortgage. This means that equity looks at the real purpose of the transaction and does not always have regard to its form. If equity considers that the transaction is a mortgage, the rules appertaining to mortgages will apply, particularly the right to redeem the property even though the contractual date for repayment has passed, or has not yet arrived. In the latter case, however, the mortgagor must generally give six months' notice of his intention to redeem, or pay six months' interest in lieu, so that the mortgagee may find another investment. However, if the parties contract at arm's length, and there is no evidence of oppression by the mortgagee, the court will endeavour to uphold the principle of sanctity of contract and will enforce any reasonable restriction on the right to redeem.

> *Knightsbridge Estates Trust Ltd* v *Byrne*, 1939 – Right of redemption postponed (**496**)

(b) There must be no clog on the equity of redemption. This means that:

(i)   the court will not allow postponement of the repayment period for an unreasonable time; and
(ii) the property mortgaged must, when the loan is repaid, be returned to the borrower in the same condition as when it was pledged.

> *Noakes* v *Rice*, 1902 – No clog on the equity of redemption (**497**)

Nevertheless, particularly in modern times, so long as the parties are at arm's length when the loan is negotiated, equity will allow a collateral transaction.

It is worth noting that the mortgagor may, where he is in possession of the land, grant leases to third parties subject to any special agreement to the contrary.

In practice, the right in the borrower to lease the property is excluded in accordance with the lender's wishes and the terms of the mortgage require his consent, as s 99(13) of the Law of Property Act 1925 allows. The validity of this exclusion has been challenged in the courts when properties subject to a mortgage cannot be sold in a flat market and the borrower wishes to move to other premises and lease the old one. These challenges have failed (see e.g. *Citibank International plc* v *Kessler* [1999] 2 CMLR 603 where the challenge that failed was based on infringement of the Treaty of Rome, Art 48 (now 39) (free movement of workers)). The Court of Appeal ruled that the Article was not intended to hinder the financial judgement of lenders.

> *Kreglinger* v *New Patagonia Meat*, 1914 – Collateral transaction (**498**)
> *Cityland and Property* v *Dabrah*, 1967 – An unreasonable collateral advantage (**499**)

(c) Sections 140A and 140B of the Consumer Credit Act 1974 (as inserted by the Consumer Credit Act 2006) allow the court to make orders in regard to *unfair relationships* between creditors and debtors where a term or terms of an agreement are taken to be unfair to the debtor. The court can make a variety of orders to redress the situation, including altering the terms of the agreement and reducing or discharging any sum payable under the agreement by the debtor.

Companies and partnerships of more than four partners are excluded from the unfair relationship test.

(d) A term must not be in restraint of trade. This has already been considered in Chapter 16 where the case of *Esso* v *Harper's Garage* (1967) was discussed.

(e) Undue influence. A mortgage may be set aside for undue influence by the lender or his agent (see Chapter 13).

Powers and remedies of the legal mortgagee

A legal mortgagee (the lender) has the following concurrent powers and remedies.

To take possession

This right does not depend upon default by the mortgagor, but the mortgagee will normally only enter into possession of the property under the term of years granted to him, or under the charge by way of legal mortgage, when he is not being paid the sum due, and when he wishes to pay himself from the proceeds of the property. In addition, the court will grant a possession order where an insurance policy which is the security has been allowed to lapse by the borrower (*Western Bank* v *Schindler* [1976] 2 All ER 393). This is not a desirable remedy, however, because when the mortgagee takes possession he is strictly accountable to the mortgagor, not only for what he has received but for what he might have received with the exercise of due diligence and proper management.

> *White* v *City of London Brewery Co*, 1889 – When a mortgagee takes possession (500)

In recent times mortgage lenders have been extracting from the courts at the sale time not only an order for possession but also a money judgment. If during a period of negative equity the sale of the property does not cover the loan, the money judgment can be used to attack other property of the borrower and there is no need to go back to court. This approach was approved by the Court of Appeal in *Cheltenham & Gloucester Building Society* v *Grattidge* (1993) 25 HLR 454.

If the mortgagee is simply concerned to intercept rents, where the mortgaged property is let and the mortgagor is a landlord, he will do better to appoint a receiver under the Law of Property Act 1925, s 109. Most mortgagees who ask for a possession order do so in order to sell with vacant possession. The Administration of Justice Act 1970, which is concerned, amongst other things, with mortgage possession actions, reinstates the old practice of the Chancery masters by allowing the court to make an order adjourning the proceedings, or suspending or postponing a possession order provided it appears that the mortgagor is likely to be able to pay within a reasonable time any sums due under the mortgage (s 36). However, the court cannot suspend the execution of an order for possession indefinitely and must specify the period of suspension (*Royal Trust Co of Canada* v *Markham* [1975] 3 All ER 433).

The Act applies wherever a mortgage includes a dwelling house even though part may be used for business purposes. Unfortunately, it was held in *Halifax Building Society* v *Clark* [1973] 2 All ER 33 that where, as is often the case, the mortgage provided that the whole sum

22

should become payable on default by the mortgagor, the court's power to adjourn or stay execution under s 36 could only be exercised if it appeared likely that the mortgagor could pay the *whole* sum within a reasonable period. This plainly defeated the intention of the 1970 Act in most cases as the period of the stay envisaged is short, and the likelihood of the mortgagor being able to repay the entire redemption figure remote. Accordingly, s 8 of the Administration of Justice Act 1973 now provides that a court may treat as due under the mortgage only those instalments actually in arrear, but shall not exercise the power to postpone the order for possession unless the mortgagor will be able to catch up within a reasonable period. This means that not only must he be able to pay the instalments due month by month but also the arrears within a reasonable time.

It should be noted that where a house is owned by a husband and is mortgaged to secure the loan, the interest of the wife occupying the home overrides the lender's claim under the mortgage and the court may refuse a possession order (*Williams & Glyn's Bank Ltd* v *Boland* (1980) (see later in this chapter)).

It is worth noting that the discretion of the court to refuse an order for possession has been widened by the Trusts of Land and Appointment of Trustees Act 1996, s 15. In general terms, before this Act the primacy of the lender seeking the order was indicated by the case law. However, now where, say, the matrimonial home is charged as security for a mortgage and is held on trust by husband and wife as joint tenants, the court may consider to a greater degree than before, e.g., the potential homelessness of children of the family and the general welfare of the family in residence. Having used this wider discretion in *Mortgage Corporation* v *Shaire* [2001] Ch 743 the court refused to grant a possession order to the claimants for mortgage arrears.

However, there is nothing to stop the lender from suing the borrower on his personal undertaking to pay the debt, even though if he or she cannot pay the judgment there may be a bankruptcy and the trustee in bankruptcy may seek an order to sell the property. A claim on the borrower's covenant to repay is not an abuse of process said the Court of Appeal in *Alliance and Leicester plc* v *Slayford* [2000] NLJR 1590.

Taking possession without a court order

In *Ropaigealach* v *Barclays Bank plc* [2000] 1 QB 263 the Court of Appeal ruled that a lender could take possession at common law without a court order. In the case the lender served a valid demand for payment to which the borrower did not respond and then wrote to him telling him that the house was up for sale. The sale was later declared by the court to be valid. The borrower was not living in the house at the time and although this undoubtedly facilitated the sale it does not seem essential to the possession ruling.

Possession order and money judgment

Lenders have been extracting from the courts in the same proceedings an order for possession and also a money judgment. If the sale of the property does not cover the loan then the money judgment can be used to attack other property of the borrower to get in the shortfall and there is no need to go to court again. This approach was sanctioned by the Court of Appeal in *Cheltenham and Gloucester Building Society* v *Grattidge* (1993) 25 HLR 454. It is a particularly useful approach in times of negative equity.

Foreclosure

The mortgagee may obtain a foreclosure order from the court if the mortgagor fails to pay for an unreasonable time. The first order is a *foreclosure order nisi* providing that the debt must be paid within a stated time. If it is not so paid, the order is made *absolute* and the property becomes that of the mortgagee, the mortgagor's equity of redemption being barred, and the property vesting in the mortgagee, free from any right of redemption either in law or equity. Such orders are seldom used, for it is still open to the court to reopen the foreclosure, i.e. to give the mortgagor a further opportunity to redeem. In addition, the court has power to order a sale instead of foreclosure on the application of any interested party. An order for sale is likely to be made, e.g., if the value of the property exceeds the mortgage debt. Section 36 of the Administration of Justice Act 1970 excluded the power to postpone a foreclosure order because it was considered that the court's power to give the mortgagor time to redeem when granting the decree *nisi* was an adequate remedy. The Payne Committee recommended including actions for foreclosure, and they are now included by the Administration of Justice Act 1973, s 8(3). Thus the courts now have power to postpone an order for foreclosure.

Right of sale

Normally this is the most valuable right of the mortgagee. Subject to certain conditions he can, on the default of the mortgagor, sell and convey to a purchaser the whole of the mortgaged property, and recoup himself out of the proceeds. Unless the mortgagee is a building society (Building Societies Act 1986, Sch 4), he is not a trustee of the power of sale for the benefit of the mortgagor. However, he must not fraudulently, wilfully or recklessly sacrifice the property of the mortgagor (*Kennedy* v *De Trafford* [1897] AC 180) and in addition owes a duty to the mortgagor to take reasonable care to obtain the best price that can be had in the circumstances (*Cuckmere Brick Co Ltd* v *Mutual Finance* [1971] 2 All ER 633).

Strictly speaking, the power of sale only arises when the money lent on mortgage has become due and the fixed date for redemption is past. However, most mortgages are drafted to provide that the mortgage money is due immediately on the signing of the mortgage deed, though the lender will not try to recover it at once if the terms of the mortgage are complied with.

The general rule is that a mortgagee cannot sell to himself or to his nominee. Although a mortgagee is not a trustee of the power of sale and need not get the best possible price (though a building society must), the conflict of interest where he sells to himself is one which equity generally forbids. However, it is thought that the mortgagee could purchase the property, subject to the mortgage, if he had leave from the court, which is the general rule for trustees who wish to buy the trust property, and provided the mortgagor did not object and possibly also if no other purchaser at an adequate price could be found. It is also probable that a mortgagee could buy the property at an auction since in that event the sale is not directly to himself but through an intermediary, i.e. the auctioneer, and given that there is no collusion between the mortgagee and the auctioneer there would seem to be no good reason why the mortgagee should not buy the property in.

In *Tsi Kwong Lam* v *Wong Chit Sen* [1983] 3 All ER 54, the Privy Council decided that a sale by a mortgagee exercising his power of sale to a company in which he had an interest would not necessarily be banned by the law provided the sale was made in good faith and that the mortgagee had taken reasonable precautions to obtain the best price reasonably obtainable at the time, namely by taking expert advice as to the methods of sale and the steps which ought reasonably to be taken to make the sale a success.

It should be noted that the court may, at its discretion, under s 91 of the Law of Property Act 1925, order the sale of a mortgaged property at a value insufficient to repay the mortgage (see *Palk* v *Mortgage Services Funding* [1993] Ch 330). This at least enables the borrower to clear a large amount of his borrowing so that interest accruing on the balance is reduced to manageable proportions.

22

The *Palk* case was applied in *Polonski* v *Lloyds Bank Mortgages Ltd* [1998] 1 FCR 282, where the High Court held that in addition to financial matters relating to the clearing of the mortgage it could also take into account social considerations. The claimant was a single parent living in a run-down area who wished to sell her property to move to an area where she would have a better chance of employment and her children would have better schooling.

Sale price and guarantors

Failure to obtain the current market value is a breach of duty certainly in the case of a building society, but it does not release a guarantor of the loan from all liability but rather reduces to that extent the amount for which the guarantor is liable (see *Skipton Building Society* v *Bratley* (2000) *The Times*, 12 January and *Stott* v *Skipton Building Society* [1999] All ER (D) 1408).

To sue for the money owing

The mortgage is a pledge for the repayment of the money, but mortgagors almost invariably give a personal covenant to repay. This is of value should the property be destroyed or lose its value. When the date fixed for redemption is passed, the mortgage money is due and the mortgagee can sue for it. He will rarely do so, for in most cases the other remedies will be more satisfactory. (But see above possession orders and money judgments which may be asked for.)

An action to recover the sum lent is barred unless it is brought within 12 years from the date when the right to receive the money accrues which is the date fixed by the mortgage deed for repayment. However, on each occasion that some part of the sum lent or interest on it is paid or the borrower gives a written acknowledgement of his liability to pay the period of 12 years begins to run again so far as what is left to pay is concerned. In the case of interest, only arrears for six years are recoverable (Limitation Act 1980).

The right to appoint a receiver

The Law of Property Act 1925, s 109 gives the mortgagee the right to appoint a receiver to receive the rents and profits on the mortgagee's behalf in order to pay the money due. However, since the powers under the Law of Property Act 1925 are limited, the mortgage deed frequently contains a power to appoint a receiver with wide powers given in the deed. The receiver is deemed to be the agent of the mortgagor, who is liable for his acts and defaults unless otherwise provided by the mortgage. The mortgagee thus avoids the disadvantage of strict accountability to which he would be subject if he entered himself because it is the borrower not the lender who is responsible for the acts and defaults of the receiver.

Remedies of equitable mortgagees

Where the mortgage is equitable and is created by deed, then the mortgagee has virtually the same remedies as have been set out above. Otherwise, if the mortgage is by a deposit of title deeds and a written mortgage instrument, then the mortgagee must ask the court:

(*a*) for an order to sell; or
(*b*) for an order appointing a receiver.

Other rights of mortgagees

A mortgagee has other rights and he may, where the mortgage is created by deed, insure the mortgaged property against loss by fire up to two-thirds of its value, and charge the premiums on the property in the same way as the mortgage money.

A mortgagee has a right to the title deeds of the property, and if the mortgage is redeemed by the mortgagor, the mortgagee must return the deeds to him in the absence of notice of a second or subsequent mortgage, in which case the deeds should be handed to the next mortgagee.

There are other important rights which a mortgagee may exercise in appropriate circumstances as follows.

Consolidation

Where a person has two or more mortgages, he may refuse to allow one mortgage to be redeemed unless the other or others are also redeemed. This right is particularly valuable where property might fluctuate in value, and where a mortgagor might redeem one mortgage where the security was more than adequate, leaving the mortgagee with a debt on the other property not properly secured.

Consolidation is only possible if the right to consolidate was reserved in one of the mortgage deeds. The contractual date for redemption must have passed on all mortgages and they must have been created by the same mortgagor, though not necessarily in favour of the same mortgagee. Nevertheless, in such cases where it is proposed to consolidate two mortgages, both the mortgages must have been vested in one person at the same time, as both the equities of redemption were vested in another.

Tacking

The right to tack may bring about a modification of the priority of mortgages. It is now confined to the tacking of further advances. Thus, where a person has lent money on a first mortgage and there are second and third mortgages, if the first mortgagee agrees to advance a further sum, he may tack this to his first mortgage and thus get priority over the second and third, which would normally rank before the tacked mortgage. This can now only be done if the intervening mortgagees agree, or if the further advance is made without notice of an intervening mortgage, or if the prior mortgage imposed an obligation to make further advances.

Attornment clause

A mortgage may contain an attornment clause by which the borrower attorns or acknowledges himself as a tenant at will, or from year to year, of the lender at a nominal rent such as a peppercorn. The advantage of such a clause was that it entitled the lender to evict the borrower for failure to pay the mortgage instalments and so obtain possession more speedily. However, changes in the rules of court from 1933 to 1937 made a speedy procedure available to mortgagees as such, and there is now no substantial advantage in an attornment clause.

Solicitor disclosure

Legal action by mortgage lenders against solicitors has prompted the Law Society and the Council of Mortgage Lenders to agree a standard set of conveyancing instructions under which solicitors are obliged to disclose relevant information on borrowers as part of the conveyancing service they offer to lenders. This will involve disclosure by solicitors of information in their possession to the effect that the borrower has, e.g., existing mortgage arrears. This will mean that borrowers with a record of bad debts will find it harder to get a mortgage. Solicitors have been successfully sued, and on an increasing scale, for failing to make these disclosures to mortgage lenders on the grounds of confidentiality which will now no longer apply, at least in this context.

22

Priority of mortgages

The Land Charges Act 1925 introduced the principle of registering charges on land. The object of searching the Land Charges Register is to discover the rights, if any, of third parties which are enforceable against the land. It is a general principle that a purchaser or mortgagee of land is deemed to have actual notice of all third-party rights capable of registration and actually registered, whereas he acquires his interest in the land free from third-party rights capable of registration and not registered. There are five separate registers kept in the Land Charges Department of the Land Registry. Search is usually done by filling in an appropriate form and sending it to the Land Charges Superintendent. This results in an *official search certificate*.

Where there is a mortgage of a legal estate with deposit of title deeds, the mortgage ranks from the date of its creation and such a mortgage cannot be registered.

Where there is a mortgage of a legal estate without deposit of title deeds, the mortgage ranks from its date of registration as a land charge.

Regarding mortgages of equitable interests, the question of priority is based on the rule in *Dearle* v *Hall* (1828) 3 Russ 1, and such mortgages rank from the date on which the mortgagee gave notice of his mortgage to the trustees of the equitable interest, though such notice will not postpone a previous mortgage of which the mortgagee giving notice was aware. Equitable mortgages of interests other than equitable interests rank in priority according to the date of creation. Thus, an equitable mortgage created in January 1996, would take priority over one created in May 1998. Legal mortgages take precedence over equitable mortgages, but an equitable mortgagee who obtains a legal interest does not thereby gain priority over an equitable interest of which he has constructive notice. Thus, if A obtains an equitable interest in property, e.g. a contract to purchase land, in January 1996, and fails to register it as an estate contract until May 1998, and B, in February 1998, obtains an equitable mortgage over the land which is converted into a legal mortgage in April 1998, at a time when B knows or ought to know that A has an interest, as where A is on the land and carrying out works, then B's mortgage, although legal, will not rank over A's equitable interest (*McCarthy and Stone* v *Julian S Hodge & Co* [1971] 2 All ER 973).

Where there are two or more lenders with a mortgage on the same property, they can alter the priority of their mortgages without the consent of the borrower, who is not affected since he must pay both mortgages off in order to recover his property loan-free (see *Cheah* v *Equiticorp Finance Group Ltd* [1991] 4 All ER 989).

The Leasehold Reform Act 1967

Where, under the provisions of this Act, a leaseholder buys the freehold, the conveyance automatically discharges the premises from any mortgage even though the lender is not a party to the conveyance (s 12(1)). However, the leaseholder must apply the money which he is using to buy the freehold, in the first instance, in or towards the payment (or redemption) of the mortgage (s 12(2)). If the lender raises difficulties, the tenant may, in order to protect his interest, pay the money into court (s 13). The lender (or mortgagee) must accept not less than three months' notice to pay off the whole or part of the principal secured by the mortgage, together with interest to the date of payment regardless of any provisions to the contrary in the mortgage (s 12(4)).

The court is also given power, under s 36, to alter the rights of the parties to a mortgage in order to mitigate any financial hardship which may arise as a result of the purchase of a freehold under the provisions of the Act.

If it is desired that a mortgage of the former leasehold interest should be extended to cover the freehold, this may be done by requesting the borrower to execute a deed of substituted security. If a tenant acquires an extended lease a lender is entitled to possession of the documents of title relating to the new lease (s 14(6)) and should ask for them when the borrower obtains an extended lease. The borrower should also be required to execute a mortgage of the extended lease.

Leasehold Reform, Housing and Urban Development Act 1993

Similar provisions relating to discharge of mortgages on interests acquired under this Act apply as in the acquisition of the freehold in the 1967 Act. Mortgage interests are discharged and payment of the mortgage is governed by similar rules to those in the 1967 Act. The 1993 Act references are s 35 and Sch 8. In the case of both Acts, failure to observe the mortgage pay-off procedures means that the mortgage *is not discharged*.

Registration of land charges

The object of searching the Land Charges Register is to discover the rights, if any, of third parties which are enforceable against the land.

The present system of registration of land charges is governed by the Land Charges Act 1972 in the case of unregistered land, and by the Land Registration Act 2002 in the case of registered land.

Registration of rights affecting unregistered land

Registration at the Land Registry constitutes notice to buyers, lenders or other interested persons, whether they search the relevant register or not. Failure to register means that a buyer in good faith takes free of the charges or right, i.e. is not affected by it.

The most usual types of rights to be registered are:

(*a*) pending actions, including a petition in bankruptcy;
(*b*) claim forms and orders affecting land, including a bankruptcy order;
(*c*) deeds of arrangement affecting land, as where a creditor has used the land as an asset in reaching a compromise for his debts to creditors, e.g. to pay over a period up to 75p in the pound;
(*d*) land charges, such as mortgages, estate contracts, restrictive covenants and equitable easements (an estate contract could be a contract to buy freehold land but as yet there is no completion);
(*e*) Class F rights of occupation of a dwelling house given, e.g. to a spouse or civil partner under the Family Law Act 1996 (as amended).

Compulsory registration of title

Titles which are not yet registered must become so. Freehold sales or leases granted for seven years or more must be registered within two months of the transaction at HM Land Registry, the title then becoming registered. This rule applies to the whole of England and Wales.

The Land Registration Act 2002 (LRA 2002) extended compulsory registration to leases on creation where the term is for seven years or more. Formerly only leases with terms of 21 years or more were compulsorily registrable. The effect for business is that most office leases will now be registrable. Section 4 of the LRA 2002 applies. In addition, under that section

22

compulsory registration applies on the assignment of leases with more than seven years left to run. The above provisions apply to leases entered into after the LRA 2002 came into force, i.e. 13 October 2003. However, it is possible to register voluntarily as distinct from compulsorily an existing lease that has more than seven years to run. Voluntary first registration also applies now to franchises and profits à prendre such a fishing and shooting rights.

Land Registration Act 2002

The major aim of s 4 of this Act is to increase the rate at which unregistered land is brought on to the register of title kept by the Land Registry. This will simplify the transfer of the property. Unregistered land must be registered on sale and purchase, but under the Land Registration Act 1997 transfers by way of gift trigger registration, as does the creation of a first mortgage which is protected by deposit of the documents of title with written memorandum. There is also a fairer provision for those who suffer loss by reason of some error or omission in the register. This covers losses that continue even after an error is rectified, as where a restrictive covenant in a conveyance is omitted from the register which is later rectified but the covenant is ineffective against a lease granted *before* rectification. Section 3 LRA 2002 gives a more flexible regime for charges for voluntary registration as a basis for doing a 'deal' with the Land Registry on charges.

Registered land

Registration is under the Land Registration Act 2002 and provides a record at HM Land Registry of the owners of registered land and of rights affecting it.

It is not, however, a complete record of all rights. In particular, rights known as 'overriding interests' affect land whether or not they are mentioned in the Land Registry entries.

The Register

This is in three parts:

(a) The property register. This gives a short description of the land and a reference to a filed map, together with rights which may benefit the land or affect it such as rights of access. However, there may be overriding interests which are not mentioned.

(b) The proprietorship register. This indicates whether the land is freehold or leasehold, and shows the registered proprietor and whether there are any restrictions on dealings with the land.

(c) The charges register. This gives details of third party rights, such as those of lenders who have taken a mortgage on the land, and, e.g., restrictive covenants.

Classes of title

The main ones are as follows:

(a) Absolute freehold or leasehold title. This gives an effective guarantee that the registered proprietor owns the land subject to any matters shown on the register and to 'overriding interests'.

(b) Good leasehold title. This is similar to the absolute title except that it does not guarantee that the lease was validly granted.

(c) Possessory freehold or leasehold title. This deals with titles under the Limitation Act 1980. A squatter can register a possessory title when he has successfully barred the rights of the true owner and subsequently. Sections 96–98 of the Land Registration Act 2002 now deal with adverse possession registration. The provisions are considered at p 614.

The squatter is subject to all the terms of a lease over which he has acquired rights by adverse possession. An example of acquisition by adverse possession is provided by *Central London Commercial Estates Ltd* v *Kato Kagaku Ltd* [1998] 4 All ER 948 where Kato acquired a title to the west courtyard of Bush House in London in this way. The adverse possession consisted of use as a car park.

Inspection by public

The Land Registration Act 1988 allows any person to apply to the Land Registry or a District Registry for an office copy of entries. This can be of use to creditors in establishing whether a particular piece of land is owned by a debtor and whether there are any charges over it. This facility is not available for unregistered land.

Overriding interests

These may not be mentioned on the register and yet para 3 of Sch 3 of the Land Registration Act 2002 states that all registered land is subject to overriding interests listed in the section. Easements and profits are or may be overriding interests because they can be created without the use of documents, as by implication or long user. However, an easement or profit will be an overriding interest only if it is within the actual knowledge of the person acquiring the land or would have been obvious on a reasonable and careful inspection of the land subject to the easement or profit (para 3 Sch 3, LRA 2002). The position where an express grant of an easement or profit is made is that it should now be registered since these express grants are no longer overriding interests. If not registered, these interests take effect only in equity. Specific grants were regarded as overriding interests before the LRA 2002 and for that reason were often not registered. They should now be registered to obtain legal status. Most important, however, are 'rights of occupation'.

Overriding interests and the Land Registration Act 2002

The LRA 2002 deals in Schs 1 and 3 with overriding interests. The Act adds profits such as shooting and fishing rights to the list of registrable rights. Leasehold interests of not more than seven years are now overriding on first registration. Leases of more than seven years must be registered. The rights of persons in actual occupation are preserved. However, the overriding rights of an individual who receives rents and profits of registered land but is not in actual possession remain overriding only while that individual continues to receive the rents and profits.

The matrimonial home

The Family Law Act 1996 contains a type of land charge referred to as Class F. It restores the legal position to what it was before the decision of the House of Lords in *National Provincial Bank Ltd* v *Ainsworth* [1965] 2 All ER 472. In that case it was decided that a deserted wife had no special right or 'equity' to continue to occupy the matrimonial home though there had formerly been such a right. The effect of the decision in *Ainsworth*'s case was that a husband who was the owner of the matrimonial home could, having deserted his wife and children, sell or mortgage the house to a third party who would in most cases be able to get an order for possession in order to enforce his rights. In these circumstances the deserted wife and children would have to give up occupation of the matrimonial home and find other accommodation.

The 1996 Act provides that where one spouse owns or is the tenant of the matrimonial home, the other spouse has certain 'rights of occupation' (s 30) and cannot be evicted without

22

an order of the court. Where a spouse is not in occupation of the matrimonial home he or she has a right, with the leave of the court, to enter and occupy the house. However, the court may order a spouse who is occupying the matrimonial home by reason of the Act to make periodical payments to the other spouse in respect of that occupation. It should be noted that the Act protects husbands as well as wives.

It should be noted that s 1 of the Act 1996 provides that either of the spouses may apply to the court for an order prohibiting, suspending, or restricting the exercise by either spouse of the right to occupy the dwelling house or requiring either spouse to permit the exercise by the other of that right.

The Family Law Act 1996 provides that the rights of occupation provided for in s 30 are a charge on the estate or interest of the other spouse (s 31), registrable as a type of land charge (Class F) under the Land Charges Act 1972. Where the land is registered land, a notice or caution must be registered under the LRA 2002. A purchaser or mortgagee is deemed to have notice of rights of occupation which have been properly registered. Rights of occupation may be registered on marriage though in most cases registration will not take place unless and until the marriage breaks down.

Where a spouse registers rights of occupation, the house is unlikely subsequently to be an acceptable security for a loan because the rights of occupation represent a prior charge on the property which cannot be sold with vacant possession. However, a spouse who is entitled to rights of occupation may, under Sch 4 of the 1996 Act, agree in writing that any other charge shall rank in priority to his or her charge.

However, even if the spouse's right of occupation is not registered, it may still be recognised by the court.

Williams & Glyn's Bank Ltd v *Boland*, 1980 – An overriding interest (**501**)

The Land Registration Act 2002 and boundaries

Under ss 60 and 61 of the LRA 2002 provision is made for a registered owner to have a boundary determined. Boundary disputes between neighbours may become a thing of the past under the new rules. Prior to the enactment of the new rules general boundary lines were drawn and loosely marked on Ordnance Survey maps held with the title deeds of the relevant property. The procedure requires the submission of the relevant form accompanied by a plan or a plan with a verbal description identifying the exact line of the boundary. The procedures to be followed on receipt of these documents by the Registrar are set out in rules. However, any ensuing dispute will be settled by the Registrar at the expense of those who want a boundary exactly fixed. The procedure could be time consuming and costly and the Registrar is likely to try to dissuade people from the boundary fixing exercise and agree a boundary. The existence of the procedure may encourage agreement. A previous procedure under the Land Registration Rules 1925 was used from time to time.

Land certificates and charge certificates

Instead of issuing a certificate to the registered proprietor of land or a charge over it the Registry will issue an official copy of the register showing all the entries that exist on the register on completion of the application for registration together with an official copy of the title plan and a Title Information Document giving the title number, property description and names of registered proprietors. Existing certificates will cease to have any legal significance.

Land Registry Adjudicator

The Land Registration Act 2002, Part 11 (ss 107–114), which is now in force, sets up the judicial office of Adjudicator to HM Land Registry. The office provides an independent dispute resolution procedure for land registration matters, both in regard to paper conveyancing and the e-conveyancing network. Unfortunately, it does not deal with disputes between applicants and the Land Registry but only with disputes between applicants to the Registry. Disputes with the Registry, e.g. whether a title satisfies the requirements for registration as an absolute title, are still matters for the ordinary courts and the method of proceeding is by judicial review of a Registry decision. The Registry procedure will deal with applicants' disputes regarding such matters as boundaries, squatters and claims to ownership of or rights to land.

Local land charges

Search on a transfer of property will also be made in the local land charges register kept by the local authority. A common example of a local land charge is road charges, i.e. charges against land which the local authority incurs in regard to the cost of making up a road which adjoins that land.

Planning matters also appear, though it should be emphasised that the standard enquiries ask questions which concern the property and not the neighbourhood. They will not, e.g., disclose planning permissions granted on adjoining property. A buyer who needs information outside the standard search should make special enquiries of the planning office or instruct his solicitor to do so.

Mortgages of personal chattels

Just as land can be used as a means of securing debts, so also can personal chattels. There are two principal ways in which this can be done.

(a) By mortgage. In this case the borrower retains possession of his goods but transfers their ownership to the lender to secure the loan.

This raises a problem because, since the borrower retains the chattels, he also retains an appearance of wealth, and this may mislead others into giving him credit. Accordingly the Bills of Sale Acts 1878–82 were passed, and under the statutory provisions, where chattels are retained by the mortgagor, a bill of sale must be made out. Where ownership of the chattel passes to the mortgagee conditionally upon its being reconveyed to the mortgagor on repayment of the loan, the bill of sale is called a 'conditional bill'. An absolute bill of sale is one which transfers completely the ownership in chattels by way of sale, gift or settlement.

All bills of sale must be attested and registered within seven days of execution. Registration is currently in the Central Office of the Supreme Court. Conditional bills of sale must be reregistered every five years if they are still operative.

A conditional bill of sale is totally void if it is not registered, whilst an unregistered absolute bill of sale is void against the trustee in bankruptcy and judgment creditors of the grantor so that the chattels represented by the bill are available to pay the grantor's debts. However, an absolute bill of sale will not be void for want of registration unless the chattels remain in the sole possession, or apparent possession, of the transferor (or grantor) of the bill.

Koppel v *Koppel*, 1966 – What is apparent possession? (**502**)

(b) By pledge, or 'pawn'. In this case the lender obtains possession of the goods, the borrower retaining ownership. Thus there is no danger that the borrower will obtain credit on the strength of his possession of the chattels, and the law relating to pledges is mainly concerned to protect the interests of the borrower (or pledger) against dishonest pawnbrokers.

Mortgages of choses in action

It is possible to use a chose in action as security for a loan, and mortgagees frequently take life assurance policies as security, e.g. a bank in the case of an overdraft. However, shares in companies are perhaps the commonest chose in action to be used as security.

Shares may be made subject to a legal mortgage, but here the shares must actually be transferred to the mortgagee so that his name is in fact on the company's share register. An agreement is made out in which the mortgagee agrees to retransfer the shares to the mortgagor when the loan is repaid.

It is also possible to have an equitable mortgage of company shares, and this is in fact the usual method adopted. The share certificate is deposited with the mortgagee, together with a blank transfer signed by the registered holder, the name of the transferee being left blank. The shares are not actually transferred, but the agreement accompanying the transaction allows the mortgagee to sell the shares by completing the form of transfer and registering himself as the legal owner or selling the shares to a third party if the mortgagor fails to repay the loan.

Other forms of security

A security is some right or interest in property given to a creditor so that, if the debt is not paid, the creditor can obtain the amount of the debt by exercising certain remedies against the property, rather than by suing the debtor by means of a personal action on his promise to pay. Securities, therefore, create rights over the property of another and since we have already discussed mortgages of land, chattels and choses in action it remains only to consider the lien.

Lien

A lien is a right over the property of another which arises by operation of law and independently of any agreement. It gives a creditor the right (*a*) to retain possession of the debtor's property until he has paid or settled the debt, or (*b*) to sell the property in satisfaction of the debt in those cases where the lien is not possessory. Where the parties agree that a lien shall be created, such agreement will effectively create one.

Possessory or common-law lien

To exercise this type of lien the creditor must have actual possession of the debtor's property, in which case he can retain it until the debt is paid or settled. It should be noted that the creditor cannot ask for possession of the debtor's goods in order to exercise a lien.

A common-law lien may be particular or general:

(a) Particular lien. This gives the possessor the right to retain goods until a debt arising in connection with those goods is paid.

(b) General lien. This gives the possessor the right to retain goods not only for debts specifically connected with them, but also for all debts due from the owner of the goods however arising.

The law favours particular rather than general liens.

If X sends a clock to R to be repaired at a cost of £5, R may retain the clock under a particular lien until the £5 is paid. If, however, X owed R £10 for the earlier repair of a watch, R cannot retain the clock to enforce payment of £15 unless, as is unlikely, he can claim a general lien.

The following are cases of *particular lien*:

(i)   A carrier can retain goods entrusted to him for carriage until his charges are paid.

(ii) An innkeeper has a lien over the property brought into the inn by a guest and also over property sent to him while there, even if it does not belong to him. The lien does not extend to motor cars or other vehicles, or to horses or other animals.

> *Robins v Gray*, 1895 – An innkeeper's lien (**503**)

(iii) A shipowner has a lien on the cargo for freight due.

(iv) In a sale of goods, the unpaid seller has a lien on the goods, if still in his possession, to recover the price.

(v)   Where a chattel is bailed in order that work may be done on it or labour and skill expended in connection with it, it may be retained until the charge is paid. Such liens may arise, e.g., in favour of a car repairer over the car repaired, by an arbitrator on an award and by an architect over plans he has prepared.

A *general lien* may arise out of contract or custom, and the following classes of persons have a general lien over the property of their customers or clients – factors, bankers, solicitors, stockbrokers, and in some cases insurance brokers.

> *Caldwell v Sumpters*, 1971 – A solicitor's lien (**504**)

In the course of their professional work accountants have at least a particular lien for unpaid fees over any books, files and papers delivered to them by clients and also over any other documents which come into their possession while acting for clients. The documents must be the client's property (see *Woodworth v Conroy* [1976] 1 All ER 107), but not the statutory books of a registered company since these are in many cases open to inspection by members and in some cases by the public. This rule derives from the decision of the High Court in *DTC (CNC) Ltd v Gary Sargeant & Co* [1996] 2 All ER 369, where it was held that an accountant could not exercise a lien over the accounting records of a company for unpaid fees since the records were required by statute (i.e. the Companies Act 1985) to be kept in specific places, e.g. the registered office, for certain periods for inspection.

Again, in *Harrison v Festus* [1998] CLY 4 the High Court doubted whether an accountant's lien could extend to a client's VAT records as they were statutory records to be preserved at the taxpayer's principal place of business.

Although a common-law lien normally gives no power of sale, there are some exceptional cases in which a right of sale is given by statute. Such a right is given to innkeepers (Innkeepers Act 1878), unpaid sellers of goods (Sale of Goods Act 1979) and bailees who accept goods for repair or other treatment for reward (Torts (Interference with Goods) Act 1977). Briefly, the

22

latter Act provides for the sale of goods accepted for repair or other treatment or for valuation or appraisal or for storage and warehousing provided the bailee gives notice to the bailor specifying the date on or after which he proposes to sell the goods. The period between the notice and the date specifying sale must be such as will afford the bailor a reasonable opportunity of taking delivery of the goods. However, if he does not do so, the bailee may sell them but must account to the bailor for the balance of the proceeds of sale after deduction of charges and expenses.

It should also be noted that the High Court has a discretion to order the sale of goods if it is just to do so, e.g. where the goods are perishable.

> *Larner* v *Fawcett*, 1950 – Power of court to order a sale (**505**)　　

A common law lien is discharged:

(*a*) by payment of the sum owing;

(*b*) by parting with the possession of the goods or other property upon which the lien is being exercised (but see *Caldwell* v *Sumpters* (1971), above);

(*c*) by an agreement to give credit for the amount due;

(*d*) by accepting an alternative security for the debt owing.

Maritime lien

A maritime lien does not depend on possession. It is a right which attaches to a ship in connection with a maritime liability. It travels with the ship and may be enforced by the arrest and the sale of the ship through the medium of a court having Admiralty jurisdiction. Examples of such liens are:

(*a*) liens of salvors;

(*b*) the lien of a master for his outgoings;

(*c*) liens which arise from damage due to collision;

(*d*) liens of bottomry bond holders. A bottomry bond is a form of security under which a ship and/or its cargo is pledged for the repayment of money borrowed for the purposes of a voyage.

The order of attachment is important and depends on circumstances.

Successive salvage liens attach in inverse order, later ones being preferred to earlier ones, since the earlier lien would be useless if the later salvage had not preserved the ship from loss. Claims for collision damage are treated as of equal rank. Liens for wages, in the absence of salvage liens, have priority over other liens; however, liens for wages earned before a salvage operation are postponed to the lien for salvage, since the value of such a lien has been preserved by the salvage operation.

If a ship which is subject to lien is sold, the purchaser takes it subject to the lien and is responsible for discharging it.

Equitable lien

An equitable lien is an equitable right, conferred by law, whereby one person acquires a charge on the property of another until certain claims have been met. It differs from a common-law lien which is founded on possession and does not confer a power of sale. An equitable lien is independent of possession and may be enforced by a judicial sale.

An equitable lien may arise out of an express provision in a contract or from the relationship between parties. Thus a partner has an equitable lien upon the partnership assets for the purpose of ensuring that they are applied, on dissolution, to paying partnership debts. Furthermore, an *unpaid* vendor of land has an equitable lien on the property even after conveyance of ownership to the purchaser, or a third party who has taken it with notice of the lien, under which he may ask the court for an order to sell the property so that he may obtain the purchase money owing to him.

An equitable lien can, like all equitable rights, be extinguished by the owner selling the property to a *bona fide* purchaser for value who has no notice of the lien.

An equitable lien differs from a mortgage. A mortgage, as we have seen, is always created by the act of parties, and an equitable lien may arise by operation of law.

Banker's lien

At common law a banker has a general possessory lien on all securities, and, e.g., bills of exchange, promissory notes and bonds, deposited with him by customers in the ordinary course of business unless there is an agreement, express or implied, to the contrary. The lien does not extend to property or securities deposited for safe custody. However, a customer may deposit a security as collateral for a loan, in which case the banker has rights over it, but the transaction is an equitable mortgage rather than a lien.

A banker's lien gives a right of sale, at least of negotiable securities subject to the lien, because s 27 of the Bills of Exchange Act 1882 provides that a person having a possessory lien over a bill is deemed a holder for value to the extent of the lien, and can, therefore, sell and transfer the bill.

Assignments of choses in action

The common law does not recognise assignments of choses in action, but equity does and so does statute.

Assignment by act of parties

There are four possible categories.

A legal assignment of a legal chose under s 136 of the Law of Property Act 1925

To be effective such an assignment, e.g. to the debtors of a business, must be absolute and not partial; must be in writing signed by the assignor; and must be notified in writing to the debtor, generally by the assignee. If the above requirements are complied with, the assignee can sue the debtor without making the assignor a party to the action. Failure to give notice to the debtor means that there is no legal assignment; the debtor can validly pay the assignor, and the assignee is liable to be postponed to a later assignee for value who notifies the debtor. However, it is not necessary for the date of the assignment to be given in the notice of assignment as long as the letter, or other form of written notice, states clearly that there has been an assignment and identifies the assignee (*Van Lynn Developments Ltd* v *Pelias Construction Co Ltd* [1968] 3 All ER 824).

22

Equitable assignments of legal choses

Equitable assignments of equitable choses

The difference between a legal and an equitable chose is historical in that an equitable chose is a right which, before 1875, could only be enforced in the Court of Chancery, e.g. the interest of a beneficiary under a trust fund.

In equitable assignments of legal choses the assignor must be made a party in any action against the debtor, but if the chose is equitable this is not necessary. No particular form is required; all that is necessary is evidence of intention to assign. Notice should be given to the debtor or the trustees, as the case may be, in order to preserve priority as outlined above.

Thus the transfer of a debt by word of mouth, although invalid under statute, may nevertheless be good and enforceable in equity.

Equitable assignments of mere expectancies

These are mere hopes of future entitlement, e.g. a legacy under the will of a living testator. The rules regarding such assignments are the same as those set out under the previous two sub-headings, but no notice to the debtor can be given because there is none. Value is not needed for assignments within s 136 of the Law of Property Act 1925, or for equitable assignments of equitable choses in action. It is probably not needed for an equitable assignment of a legal chose, though the position is not clear. Value is needed for the assignment of mere expectancies; a document by deed is not enough. Value is also needed to support an agreement to assign an equitable chose, but if the assignee lawfully takes delivery of the property assigned, the assignor cannot recover it.

Assignments are said to be 'subject to equities'; the person to whom the right is assigned takes it subject to any right of set off which was available against the original assignor. So if X assigns to Z a debt of £10 due from Y, and X also owes Y £5, then in any action brought by Z for the money, Y can set off the debt of £5. But the assignee is not subject to purely personal claims which would have been available against the assignor, e.g. damages for fraud, though the remedy of rescission is available against the assignee where the assignor obtained the contract by fraud.

Assignments of certain choses in action are governed by special statutes so that the rules outlined above do not apply. In such cases the special statute must be complied with. Examples are:

(*a*) *bills of exchange, cheques and promissory notes* – Bills of Exchange Act 1882;
(*b*) *shares in companies* registered under the Companies Act 2006 and previous Acts – Companies Act 2006;
(*c*) *policies of life assurance* – Policies of Assurance Act 1867.

Rights of a personal nature under a contract cannot be assigned. If X contracts to write newspaper articles for a certain newspaper, it cannot assign its rights under the contract to another. The right to recover damages in litigation cannot be assigned, for reasons of public policy. Liabilities under a contract cannot be assigned; the party to benefit cannot be compelled by mere notice to accept the performance of another, though a liability can be transferred by a novation (a new contract), if the party to benefit agrees.

Assignment by operation of law

The involuntary assignment of rights and liabilities arises in the case of death and bankruptcy.

Death

The personal representatives of the deceased acquire his rights and liabilities, the latter to the extent of the estate. Contracts of personal service are discharged.

Bankruptcy

The trustee in bankruptcy has vested in him all the rights of the bankrupt, except for actions of a purely personal nature which in no way affect the value of the estate, e.g. actions for defamation. The trustee is liable to the extent of the estate for the bankrupt's liabilities, though the trustee has a right to disclaim onerous or unprofitable contracts.

Part 5

CRIMINAL LAW

23

CRIMINAL LAW: GENERAL PRINCIPLES

Crime and civil wrongs distinguished

As we have indicated in Chapter 1 the distinction does not lie in the *nature of the act* itself. For example, if a railway porter is offered a reward to carry A's case and runs off with it, then the porter has committed one crime, that of theft, and two civil wrongs, i.e. the tort of wrongful interference and a breach of his contract with A. Again, a signalman who carelessly fails to operate signals so that a fatal accident occurs will have committed one crime, i.e. manslaughter, because persons are killed, and two civil wrongs, the tort of negligence in respect of those who died and those who are merely injured, and a breach of his contract of service with the employing rail company in which there is an implied term to take due care. It should also be noted that in this case the right of action in tort and the right of action in contract are vested in different persons.

The distinction does depend on the *legal consequences* which follow the act. If the wrongful act is capable of being followed by what are called criminal proceedings, that means that it is regarded as a crime. If it is capable of being followed by civil proceedings, that means that it is regarded as a civil wrong. If it is capable of being followed by both, it is both a crime and a civil wrong. Criminal and civil proceedings are usually easily distinguishable, they are generally brought in different courts, the procedure is different, the outcome is different and the terminology is different. A major consequence of classifying proceedings as criminal is that the burden of proof is on the Crown.

Terminology and outcome of criminal and civil proceedings

In criminal proceedings a prosecutor prosecutes a defendant. If the prosecution is successful, it results in the conviction of the defendant. After the conviction the court may deal with the defendant by giving him a custodial sentence, e.g. prison or some other form of detention (see Chapter 4) or a non-custodial sentence, e.g. a supervision order under a probation officer or a community order imposing e.g. an unpaid work requirement. In rare cases the court may discharge the defendant without sentence.

As regards *civil proceedings*, a claimant *sues* (brings an action against) a defendant. If the claimant is successful, this leads to the court entering judgment ordering, for example, that the defendant pay a debt owed to the claimant or damages. Alternatively, it may require the defendant to transfer property to the claimant or to do or not to do something (injunction) or to perform a contract (specific performance). Some of these remedies are legal, others equitable. The matter of remedies for breach of contract and for torts has already been dealt with in detail in the chapters on those topics.

Nulla poena sine lege – no punishment unless by law

This important maxim means that a person should not be made to suffer criminal penalties except for a clear breach of *existing* criminal law, that law being precise and well defined.

The maxim thus prohibits:

(*a*) the introduction of new crimes which operate retrospectively under which a person might be found guilty of a crime for doing an act which was not criminal when he did it;

(*b*) wide interpretation of precedents to include by analogy crimes which do not directly fall within it. Thus the extension of the criminal law in the way, for example, in which the civil law of negligence has been extended (see Chapter 21) is undesirable;

(*c*) the formulation of criminal laws in wide and vague terms.

The last rule has in general terms been observed in England, with perhaps the major exception of the law of conspiracy under which there has been a tendency to charge persons with criminal conspiracy rather than with specific criminal offences. Thus a conviction might be obtained for conspiracy to do an act even though there were doubts as to whether the act was or ought to be criminal.

Under ss 1–5 of the Criminal Law Act 1977, the offence of conspiracy at common law is abolished and the new statutory offence of conspiracy is restricted to agreements to commit criminal offences, though the common-law offences of conspiracy to defraud and conspiracy to corrupt public morals or outrage public decency are retained. The consent of the Director of Public Prosecutions to mount a prosecution is required.

The purpose in retaining conspiracy to defraud at common law is that it enables the courts to keep up with the increasing methods of fraud which may outpace legislation such as the Theft Act 1968 which may not cover them. Acts outraging public decency are offences in themselves as the Court of Appeal decided in *R* v *Gibson* [1991] 1 All ER 439, where the defendant exhibited earrings made from freeze-dried human foetuses of three to four months' gestation. In view of the fact that acts outraging public decency are crimes in themselves a conspiracy to outrage public decency would also be covered by s 1 of the 1977 Act as a conspiracy to commit a criminal offence.

> *Woolmington* v *DPP*, 1935 – Burden of proof in crime (**506**)
> *Shaw* v *DPP*, 1961 – No punishment except for breach of existing law (**507**)

Constituent elements of a criminal offence

The commission of a crime necessarily involves two elements:

(*a*) the *actus reus* (guilty act); and

(*b*) the *mens rea* (guilty mind).

Therefore, a guilty act does not make a person guilty of crime unless the mind is guilty and vice versa. The essential key to proving criminal charges generally is to show that the defendant had the necessary state of mind at the required time. The coincidence of the state of mind with the criminal act is crucial. The exception to this rule of mental attitude is a group of offences referred to as crimes of strict liability.

The *actus reus*

The defendant's conduct must in general be *voluntary*. If a person is made to act, there is no *actus reus*. Sir Matthew Hale says in his treatise on the criminal law entitled *Pleas of the Crown* written in 1682: 'If A takes the hand of B in which is a weapon and therewith kills C, A is guilty of murder but B is excused.' Duress as by threats which cause a person to act is not in fact regarded as involuntary conduct, but may be a defence for some crimes (see further Chapter 25).

In addition, if a person acts instinctively in response to some stimulus and in so doing commits a criminal offence, he will not be liable. A famous example was given in *Hill v Baxter* [1958] 1 All ER 193 in connection with a prosecution for dangerous driving where the court said that a person would not be guilty of such an offence if 'the car was temporarily out of control by his being attacked by a swarm of bees'. It will be found, however, that in the case of some statutory offences no voluntary act is required.

The act must be causative

In order to convict a person of a crime, it is necessary to show that the act which he did was the *substantive cause of the crime*. In this connection, it should be noted that the accused takes his victim as he finds him so that the abnormal state of the victim's health or his or her age will not normally excuse a person who by his acts has accelerated the death of such a victim.

However, the Court of Appeal ruled in *R v Bollom* [2004] 2 Cr App R 50 that, in considering whether injuries amounted to grievous bodily harm and not actual bodily harm, the age and health of the victim should be brought into account. Thus, injuries to a baby or young child or an old person might well constitute grievous bodily harm whereas they would not in the case of a young adult in the fulness of health. (See further Chapter 24.)

> *R v Towers*, 1874 – Need to prove causation (**508**)
>
> *R v Hayward*, 1908 – Accused cannot successfully plead the victim's state of health (**509**)

23

Intervening acts and events

It may be that between the initial act of the defendant and the criminal event with which he is charged a new act or event occurred and contributed to the criminal event. The defendant will nevertheless be liable unless the intervening event was unforeseeable and would have brought about the consequence on its own.

Sometimes the intervening act is that of the victim but the accused will still be guilty if it was reasonably foreseeable that the victim would act in the way he did as a result of the behaviour of the accused. Finally, the intervening act may be the improper medical treatment of an injury inflicted upon the victim by the accused. Here the general rule is that the court will be reluctant to blame doctors and other medical personnel for a death where the condition which they were called upon to treat was brought about by the unlawful act of the accused.

> *R v Curley*, 1909 – Intervening act of victim (**510**)
> *R v Smith*, 1959 – Improper medical treatment (**511**)

It should be noted that it is not necesary for the Crown to establish which of the accused's actions caused the death. Thus in *Attorney-General's Reference (No 4 of 1980)* [1981] 1 WLR 705 the accused pushed his girlfriend downstairs and, believing her to be dead, dragged her upstairs by a rope around her neck, cut her throat, and dismembered and disposed of the body. He was charged with manslaughter and it was held by the Court of Appeal that he could be convicted, provided the jury was satisfied that one of the actions did cause the death, notwithstanding that it was impossible to say which of the culpable acts did so.

Omissions or failure to act

In general terms, a mere failure to act cannot lead to criminal liability. However, there may be liability for an omission in the following situations.

Moral obligations arising from particular relationships

Sometimes where a person is in a particular relationship with another which is either imposed by law such as parent or child or voluntarily assumed as where A is looking after an old aunt, the relationship may give rise to an obligation to act. Failure to discharge the responsibilities arising from the relationship may result in criminal liability at common law.

> *R v Instan*, 1893 – Liability for omissions at common law (**512**)

While *R v Instan* (1893) and the cases set out in the comment to it illustrate the position at common law, the statutory position should also be noted. The Domestic Violence, Crime and Victims Act 2004 closes a loophole in the law that could allow those jointly accused of the murder of a child or vulnerable adult to escape liability by remaining silent and blaming each other. This has occurred where husband and wife or partners have adopted this approach where a child or vulnerable person has been the victim. The Act now puts legal responsibility on adult household members who have frequent contact with a child or vulnerable adult *to take reasonable steps* to protect that person if they knew, or ought to have known, they were at significant risk of serious physical harm. Persons can be guilty *for not doing so*.

Contractual duties

A person may incur criminal liability because a contract, e.g. of employment, places upon him a duty to act. The duty is not confined to the other party to the contract but may extend also to third parties.

> *R v Pittwood*, 1902 – A crossing gate is left open (**513**)

Previous conduct creating a dangerous situation

Where the defendant has by his previous acts created a potentially dangerous situation and later comes to realise this, he has a duty to act to prevent the danger.

> *R v Miller*, 1983 – A smoking mattress (**514**)

Duty to act under statute

Some modern statutes make failure to act a crime. For example, s 170 of the Road Traffic Act 1988 makes it an offence if those involved in road accidents fail to report the accident to the police within 24 hours or give relevant details to any other person who being at the scene of the accident reasonably requests them. It is necessary, however, that personal injury is caused to a person other than the driver of the vehicle or to an animal other than one in the driver's vehicle or in a trailer being pulled by him or her.

A further example is provided by the decision of the Queen's Bench Divisional Court in *Greener* v *DPP* (1996) *The Times*, 15 February. G's Staffordshire bull terrier was chained up in his garden. It escaped into a nearby garden and attacked a child. Section 3(3) of the Dangerous Dogs Act 1991 states that an offence is committed if the owner 'allows' a dog to enter a private place where it is not permitted and it then injures some person. G submitted that the section required a mental element and, since he had not taken any positive step to release the dog, he was not guilty. It was held that since the section did not require intention, negligence or knowledge, but was a strict liability offence the offence could have and had been committed by an omission to take adequate precautions to keep the dog in.

The *mens rea* – generally

The *actus reus* must be accompanied by an appropriate state of mind which is referred to as *mens rea*. The *mens rea* and the *actus reus* must coincide in order to constitute a crime. Before looking at the different states of mind involved it should be noted that as in the law of torts *motive*, i.e. the reason why the defendant did the act, is irrelevant in regard to his guilt or innocence if his direct intention was to commit the offence.

> *Chandler* v *DPP*, 1962 – Impeding the operation of an airfield (**515**)

The following states of mind are relevant.

23

Direct intent

This occurs where there exists in the mind of the defendant *a desire* to commit the crime, as where A shoots at B foreseeing and desiring and wishing that B will be killed, or as where A deliberately fails to feed an aged parent in the hope and expectation of bringing about that parent's death.

Oblique intent

Here *the consequence is not desired* as such. The defendant may even hope that what happened would not happen but has nevertheless gone ahead with the harmful activity, in what one is tempted to say is a reckless fashion. Indeed, the concepts of oblique intent and recklessness as states of mind are at times quite close and not readily distinguishable. In homicide cases an oblique intent will normally result in a conviction for manslaughter and not murder, and the major change brought about by modern case law is that intent is no longer established by a kind of objective foresight of consequences as is liability in tort, although the mental element of recklessness may be.

> *R v Maloney*, 1985 – Larking with guns (**516**)

Recklessness: *Cunningham* and *Caldwell*

In some crimes it is necessary to find a direct intent. Included here would be murder and wounding with intent under s 18 of the Offences Against the Person Act 1861 (causing grievous bodily harm). The House of Lords has reaffirmed that to establish an offence under s 20 (malicious wounding) it is necessary for the prosecution to prove either that the appellant intended to or that he actually foresaw his act might cause physical harm, even if only of a minor character. This is oblique intent (see *R v Savage* [1991] 2 All ER 220).

In other cases, e.g. criminal damage and rape, intention or recklessness is enough. So far as manslaughter is concerned, either an oblique intent or recklessness would seem to suffice. The line between oblique intent and recklessness in the decided cases is, as we have seen, often very difficult to draw. Recklessness, so far as the earlier cases were concerned, was to be decided *subjectively*, i.e. the defendant must have appreciated the risk which is close to oblique intent. *Objective* tests, i.e. the defendant *ought* to have appreciated the risk, were to be reserved for the civil law. However, in more recent times the courts have developed an objective test for recklessness though at the moment this test seems to be applied largely in cases involving criminal damage, though a fairly recent case applied it to manslaughter.

> *R v Cunningham*, 1957 – Recklessness: the subjective test (**517**)
> *R v Caldwell*, 1981 – Recklessness: the objective test (**518**)

The two tests are therefore available and it seems that the *Cunningham* test survives in cases of rape (see Chapter 24) while the *Caldwell* test is to be found in statutory crimes such as criminal damage and in motor manslaughter now referred to as causing death by dangerous driving (see Chapter 24).

However, in the crime of rape the recklessness required is as to the victim's non-consent to the act of sexual intercourse, which places such recklessness virtually in a category of its own.

Gross negligence

In modern law the objective test of recklessness has not progressed beyond the *mens rea* for causing death by dangerous driving (see Chapter 24) and criminal damage. It was rejected in *R v Adomako* (1994), a case of involuntary manslaughter, in favour of a 'gross negligence' test (see Chapter 24), in a crime now referred to as gross negligence manslaughter.

The Road Safety Act 2006 creates a new offence of causing death by careless driving, with a penalty of up to five years' imprisonment. The definition of careless driving in the Act puts it beyond doubt that causing death by reckless or careless driving (the bad driving offences), can be used by the courts as an alternative to manslaughter.

Negligence

It is extremely rare to find that negligence is a state of mind for a criminal offence. However, the fact that a person has not been negligent can be a defence in some statutory crimes. For example, where foreign matter has got into food it is a defence for a person involved in its sale to show that he acted *with due diligence* to prevent the commission of the offence (Food Safety Act 1990, s 21). Thus only persons who are negligent will be successfully prosecuted.

Where intent is transferred

Provided the defendant has the necessary *mens rea* and commits the intended *actus reus* it does not matter that the victim is not the person he intended to harm. However, the *mens rea* for one offence cannot be transferred to another.

> *R v Latimer*, 1886 – A different victim (**519**)
> *R v Pembliton*, 1874 – A different crime (**520**)

The rule of transferred malice can also be relevant in regard to the liability of accessories or secondary parties to crime. Thus, if A incites B to attack C, A will be liable for the attack along with B. If, however, B decides to attack someone else instead, A will not be liable for that attack. If in trying to attack as by throwing a stone or chair at him B injures D, A will be liable for the attack on D.

Mens rea and *actus reus* must coincide

There must be a coincidence of these two elements. However, it may be that although at the outset the act did not carry with it the necessary *mens rea* this came later during what the court regards as a continuing act or one transaction.

It is not necessary that the requisite state of mind should remain unaltered throughout. A later change of mind will not prevent the commission of an offence. Thus, if A steals B's goods with the intention to deprive him permanently of them, A will still commit the offence of theft even if he later changes his mind and gives the goods back to B.

In regard to the concept of the continuing act, in *Fagan* (see below) the *actus reus* preceded the *mens rea*, whereas in *Thabo Meli* (see below) the *mens rea* preceded the *actus reus*.

> *Fagan* v *Metropolitan Police Commissioner*, 1968 – A car on a policeman's foot (**350**)
> *Thabo Meli* v *R*, 1954 – A killing in one transaction (**521**)

23

Mens rea in statutory offences

The principles applied in regard to *mens rea* where the offence is set out in a statute are somewhat different from those applied in common-law offences. Some statutory criminal offences are said to be offences of *strict liability* which means that there may be a need only to prove the commission of the offence, the state of mind of the defendant being immaterial. They are usually regulatory offences where no major moral issue is involved, but where there is some social danger or concern involved in the regulated conduct.

The topic may be considered under the headings which follow.

Mens rea implied

As Lord Reid said in *Sweet* v *Parsley* (1969) (see below), 'There has for centuries been a presumption that Parliament did not intend to make criminals of persons who were in no way blameworthy in what they did. This means that whenever a section of an Act is silent as to the requirement of *mens rea* there is a presumption that, in order to give effect to the will of Parliament, we must read in words appropriate to require *mens rea*.'

> *Sweet* v *Parsley*, 1969 – Statutory offences: presumption of requirement of *mens rea* (**522**)
>
> *R* v *Tolson*, 1889 – A bigamous wife (**523**)

However, as we have seen, statutes which regulate public conduct and which cannot be enforced effectively if *mens rea* is required, e.g. pollution of the environment, are sometimes excepted from the rule that statutory crimes require *mens rea* by implication.

> *Alphacell* v *Woodward*, 1972 – Strict liability for pollution (**524**)
>
> *Cundy* v *Le Cocq*, 1884 – Selling liquor to a drunk (**525**)

Particular words connoting *mens rea*

The use of words such as 'maliciously', 'knowingly', 'wilfully', 'permitting' and 'suffering' in a statute is usually an indication that *mens rea* is required to establish the offence. However, the absence of such words does not necessarily mean that no *mens rea* is required, as we have seen from cases such as *Sweet* v *Parsley* (1969), above.

> *Gaumont British Distributors Ltd* v *Henry*, 1939 – Where a record was not knowingly made (**526**)
>
> *R* v *Lowe*, 1973 – A charge of wilful neglect (**527**)
>
> *Somerset* v *Wade*, 1894 – Permitting drunkenness (**528**)

Vicarious liability

If the offence is one which does not require *mens rea* so that it is an *absolute offence*, an employer may be liable where an employee commits the offence in the course of his employment. It is no defence for the employer to say that he had no *mens rea* because none is required.

However, if the offence requires *mens rea* as where, for example, it is one involving 'permitting', an employer will not be liable vicariously if it is the employee who does the permitting.

> *Griffiths* v *Studebakers Ltd*, 1924 – Vicarious liability: an absolute offence (**529**)
>
> *James* v *Smee*, 1955 – Vicarious liability: where *mens rea* is required (**530**)

If a person carries on a business which requires a licence which is issued subject to the observance of certain conditions, he cannot escape liability by delegating the duty of seeing that those conditions are observed to either an employee or a stranger. However, where the offence requires *knowledge*, i.e. *mens rea*, the holder of the licence will not be liable for the acts of his delegate unless the delegation is of the whole function of the licensee as where he leaves the premises to take a holiday so that the management of the business is in the hands of the delegate.

An employer cannot, it would appear, be liable vicariously for *aiding and abetting* an offence unless he has knowledge of the offence. The knowledge of an employee in regard to such a charge is not imputed to the employer in order to make him liable.

> *Vane* v *Yiannopoullos*, 1965 – Delegation of duties (**531**)
> *Ferguson* v *Weaving*, 1951 – Aiding and abetting (**532**)

Finally, there is no vicarious liability for an offence which is merely attempted but not completed (*Gardner* v *Ackroyd* [1952] 2 QB 743).

The mental element – corporations

In October 1987 an application was made for leave to apply for judicial review against the decision of the coroner for East Kent made on 18 and 19 September 1987 in the course of an inquest into the deaths of 188 people arising out of the capsize on 6 March 1987 of the *Herald of Free Enterprise* off Zeebrugge (see *ex parte Spooner and Others*; *ex parte de Rohan and Another* (1987) The Times, 10 October).

As we have seen, application can be made to the Queen's Bench Division for judicial review to correct an alleged defect in a proceeding in a lower court, tribunal or public body. The coroner had decided as a matter of law that:

(*a*) A corporate body could not be guilty of manslaughter.
(*b*) Where the individual acts or omissions of individuals employed by a corporate body or engaged in its management were insufficient to render them guilty of manslaughter, those acts or omissions could not be aggregated in order to make the corporate body guilty.
(*c*) The acts and omissions of the company, Townsend Car Ferries Ltd, were not the direct cause of the deaths.

The applicants, who were seeking to have the coroner's decisions reviewed, relied on three points made against the company in the Sheen Report published in July 1987 following an inquiry under Mr Justice Sheen. These were that:

(*a*) the company had failed to consider seriously a proposal to fit a warning light system on the ferry;
(*b*) five or six previous incidents of ferry doors being left open had not been properly reported and collated by the company; and
(*c*) it lacked any proper system to ensure that the highest standards of safety were observed.

In hearing the application for judicial review, Lord Justice Bingham said that he was prepared tentatively to accept that a corporate body was capable of being found guilty of manslaughter and Mr Justice Mann and Mr Justice Kennedy agreed.

23

However, the court refused leave to apply for judicial review. No substantial case had been made against named directors of the company and in any case the court was always reluctant to intervene in inquests.

So far the proceedings may seem to have been rather ordinary and straightforward but in fact the tentative acceptance of corporate liability for serious crime is far from innocuous. Up to now corporations have been convicted of crimes as follows:

(a) Those for which no guilty mind (*mens rea*) or even recklessness as to consequences is necessary. Some Acts of Parliament which regulate public conduct cannot be enforced effectively if an intentional or reckless state of mind is required, either in an individual or a corporation, e.g. statutory crimes relating to the pollution of the environment are sometimes excepted from the rule that even statutory crimes require *mens rea*, either expressly or by implication even though no state of mind is mentioned in the statute. An example is provided by *Alphacell* v *Woodward* (1972).

(b) Crimes which require a state of mind. Here, if the appropriate human decision-making organ within the company has the necessary state of mind the company may be found guilty. Examples are to be found in *Director of Public Prosecutions* v *Kent & Sussex Contractors Ltd* [1944] 1 All ER 119 where a company was convicted under statutory defence regulations for using a document with *intent* to deceive and for making a false statement, since those managing the company had the necessary state of mind.

Again, in *R* v *ICR Haulage Ltd* [1944] KB 551 the company was successfully prosecuted for a *common-law* conspiracy to defraud because of the state of mind of its managing director.

Finally, in *Moore* v *Bresler Ltd* [1944] 2 All ER 515 a company was successfully prosecuted for using a document with *intent* to defraud when the acts and state of mind were those of the company secretary and a branch manager, not those of the directors.

The requirements were clearly laid down by Lord Denning in *H L Bolton (Engineering) Ltd* v *T J Graham & Sons Ltd* [1956] 3 All ER 624 where he said:

> A company may in many ways be likened to a human body. It has a brain and nerve centre which controls what it does. It also has hands which hold the tools and act in accordance with directions from the centre. Some of the people in the company are mere servants and agents who are nothing more than hands to do the work and cannot be said to represent the mind or will. Others are directors and managers who represent the directing mind and will of the company and control what it does. The state of mind of these managers is the state of mind of the company and is treated by the law as such.

The above material represents what is called the *attribution rule* which means that the court must be able to indentify a guilty directing mind and will so that the crime can be attributed to the corporation. The rule was retained by the Court of Appeal in *Attorney-General's Reference (No 2 of 1999)* (2000) *The Times*, 29 February following a failed attempt to convict Great Western Trains of manslaughter after a major rail disaster at Paddington. The court felt unable to move to *personal liability* as a basis for corporate manslaughter.

(c) If there is to be a third category of corporate liability it would be based upon the fact that although no single individual is criminally culpable, he or she is nevertheless part of a complex and collective corporate mind which, when aggregated, gives the necessary culpability. These non-culpable people may be regarded by the courts in the future as part of a group lacking, say, a proper system of control and supervision to ensure observance of safety elements which, in a particular case, could lead to a conviction of the organisation involved – the company – for a crime as serious as manslaughter where death of a person or persons has ensued. Since manslaughter can be punishable by a fine, which is at the discretion of the court and has no limit, there would be no problem in punishing the corporation (see now the Corporate Manslaughter and Corporate Homicide Act 2007 below).

If such a prosecution were successful, it would bring *Salomon v Salomon* (1897) (see Chapter 8) full circle. Since that case, people have accepted gradually that it is *companies that do things*, such as make contracts, obtain licences and so on. The last frontier is the corporate doing of a crime where the necessary state of mind is not derived from any particular individual but from all those individuals involved in the failure of the system in general. The admission by the court in *ex parte Spooner and Others* (above) that a corporate body is capable of being guilty of manslaughter suggests that if appropriate circumstances arise the law will take the final leap in the personification of corporate entities.

It has to be said, however, that the great leap forward did not take place in the *Spooner* case. The Director of Public Prosecutions decided in 1989 to prosecute in regard to the Zeebrugge disaster. The prosecution collapsed because the Crown was unable to prove that the senior officers involved had any specific duties and responsibilities for certain areas of safety which they had failed to carry out.

However, the development of the law relating to corporate manslaughter took a step forward in the case of *R v OLL* (1994) *The Times*, 9 December where the managing director of an activity centre was sentenced to three years' imprisonment for manslaughter following the deaths of four teenagers in the Lyme Bay canoe disaster on 22 March 1994. In a landmark decision, the judge (Ornall, J) also decided that Mr Kite's company OLL, formerly Activity Leasing and Leisure, was guilty of manslaughter and was fined £60,000. Mr Kite's sentence was later reduced to one year by the Court of Appeal. It should be borne in mind that it was fairly easy to regard Mr Kite as the company's *alter ego* because he was a majority shareholder and a director. OLL was virtually a 'one-person company'.

Following the above successful conviction, a jury at Bradford Crown Court returned a verdict in *Jackson Transport (Ossett) Ltd* (1994) (unreported) that the company and the company's former director, Alan Jackson, were guilty of manslaughter. James Hodgson, one of the company's former employees, was unlawfully killed by his employer in 1994 (so found the jury). He died after being sprayed in the face with chemicals which had solidified inside a tanker which he had been cleaning under steam pressure. There were no first aid facilities available and he was not given any protective clothing. Three months before Mr Hodgson had been hospitalised for three days following a similar incident, except on that occasion he had become exposed to dangerous fumes. This evidence demonstrated that the company, through its former managing director, Mr Jackson, was aware of the dangers but failed to do anything about them. The company was fined and Mr Jackson received a prison sentence of one year.

It will have been noted that a company can be liable for an offence of strict liability because no menetal element is required (see *Alphacell* v *Woodward* (1972) at p 650).

23

Reform

The Corporate Manslaughter and Corporate Homicide Act 2007

The above material shows the background to this legislation. The 2007 Act makes provision for a new offence of corporate manslaughter (to be called corporate homicide in Scotland). The Act was introduced in the Commons on 20 July 2006.

Under common law, a company can, as we have seen, only be convicted of corporate manslaughter if there is enough evidence to find a senior individual within the company guilty. This does not reflect the reality of modern corporate life, certainly in larger companies, and to date only small organisations have been convicted, as in *R v OLL* (1994) *The Times*,

9 December, where the company and its managing director were found guilty of manslaughter following the deaths of four teenagers in the Lyme Bay canoe disaster. Significantly, the managing director was also the sole shareholder in the one-man company and it was easy to impute his conduct also to that of the company. He was imprisoned for one year and the company was fined.

The new criminal offence addresses this situation by allowing the courts to consider the overall picture of how an organisation's activities were managed by its senior managers, rather than focusing on the actions of one individual. Section 2 defines a senior manager as an individual who plays a significant role in the making of decisions about how the whole or a substantial part of those activities are to be managed or organised or actually managed. Failings at junior management level will not lead to the prosecution of the company.

An organisation will be guilty of the new offence where the gross failure of senior management has led to the death of an employee or a member of the public. It will include failure to ensure safe working practices for employees and failure to maintain the safety of premises. It will cover the provision of goods and services to members of the public and the construction, use and maintenance of the infrastructure or vehicles when operating commercially. Crown organisations are included.

Companies found guilty of corporate manslaughter will be subject to an unlimited fine. The court will also be able to impose a remedial order to take specified steps to remedy the breach within a specified period.

The Act does not include a directors' offence carrying with it the possibility of imprisonment, as has been proposed in the past.

24

SPECIFIC OFFENCES

The intention here is to include only specific offences against the person. These are set out below.

Homicide

Homicide is the unlawful killing of a human being. There are three main homicides, i.e. murder, voluntary manslaughter and involuntary manslaughter, which includes causing death by dangerous driving.

Murder

This is basically a common-law offence and to constitute it there must be an unlawful killing of another human being under the Queen's peace with malice aforethought. Formerly, the victim had to die within a year and a day of the defendant's criminal conduct.

The year and a day rule prevented the prosecution of defendants for murder as medical science developed techniques for keeping seriously injured persons alive for long periods.

The Law Reform (Year and a Day Rule) Act 1996 abolished the year and a day rule, i.e. the irrebuttable presumption that applied for the purposes of offences causing death where more than a year and a day had elapsed. The Act abolishes the rule in regard to murder, manslaughter, abetting suicides, infanticides, causing death by dangerous driving when under the influence of drink, and aggravated vehicle taking causing death (s 1). It does not affect the application of the rule to acts or omissions occurring before the relevant part of the Act came into force, i.e. 17 June 1996 (s 3).

Section 2 restricts the bringing of proceedings in that the consent of the Attorney-General is required before a prosecution can be brought in cases where the injury alleged to have caused the death did in fact occur more than three years before the death and also where the person to be prosecuted for a fatal offence has already been convicted of an offence, e.g. grievous bodily harm, connected to the circumstances of the death.

The *actus reus*

Since the killing must be of a human being, the unlawful killing of an unborn child is not murder. However, such killings are covered and made criminal in appropriate circumstances by s 58 of the Offences Against the Person Act 1861, s 1 of the Infant Life (Preservation) Act 1929 and the Abortion Act 1967. The detail of these offences is not considered here. The expression 'another human being' includes a child that has been born alive and has an existence independent of the mother. Where a person injures a child while it is in its mother's womb and it dies later from those injuries *after being born*, it may be appropriate to bring a charge of murder. The fact that the victim must be 'under the Queen's peace' prevents the killing of the enemy in wartime from being murder. This refers to killing in action. It is murder to kill prisoners of war. Under the Offences Against the Person Act 1861 any British citizen who commits murder anywhere in the world may be tried in England or Wales. In addition, a killing in self-defence may be lawful and so not murder (see further Chapter 25).

> *R v Dyson*, 1908 – Death within a year and a day; Attorney-General's consent now required (**533**)

The *mens rea*

Some consideration has already been given to this. However, the *mens rea* for murder is defined as 'malice aforethought'. According to the House of Lords in *Maloney* (1985), murder is a crime which requires a specific intent, either direct as where the defendant *desired* the consequences, or oblique as where he foresaw the consequences as *near certain*. Recklessness is not enough. The court must be satisfied of the presence of such an intent either to kill or cause grievous bodily harm.

In this connection, it should be noted that the decision in *Maloney* (1985) confirms that it is enough malice if the intention is not to kill but to cause grievous bodily harm.

Maloney thus decides that intent to kill and intention to cause grievous bodily harm are the only forms of *mens rea* for murder.

In so far as the expression 'malice aforethought' suggests evidence of premeditation or plot, it is misleading since this is not necessary, provided the specific intent to kill is present.

Manslaughter

Manslaughter is divided into voluntary manslaughter and involuntary manslaughter.

Voluntary manslaughter

This is murder reduced to manslaughter by the presence under the Homicide Act 1957 of provocation, diminished responsibility or suicide pact. Once it is shown that one of these partial defences exists, the crime ceases to be murder and the fixed penalty of life imprisonment goes, giving the judge a discretion as to sentence.

The *mens rea* is, therefore, the *mens rea* for murder, but with the mitigating factors of provocation, diminished responsibility or suicide pact.

Provocation generally

Section 3 of the Homicide Act 1957 applies. It provides as follows.

> Where on a charge of murder there is evidence on which the jury can find that the person charged was provoked (whether by things done or by things said or by both together) to lose his self control, the question whether the provocation was enough to make a reasonable man do as he did shall be left to be determined by the jury; and in determining that question the jury shall take into account everything both done and said according to the effect which, in their opinion, it would have on a reasonable man.

The questions to consider

There are two questions to consider, as follows:

- Was the defendant actually provoked? This is a matter for the jury, as the Homicide Act 1957 states. If the jury decides that the defendant was not provoked, the second question does not arise and the defence of provocation will fail.
- If the jury does decide that the defendant was provoked, then that provocation must be such that it would have caused a reasonable person to be provoked. The problem here has been whether any particular characteristics of the defendant are to be taken into account so that, although a reasonable person would not have been provoked, the defence must be allowed because of the particular characteristics of the defendant. Bad temper is clearly not a characteristic that counts because it is a character defect not an excuse.

The problems have arisen in regard to what characteristics apart from the above should be taken into account and what should not or whether they should be taken into account at all being regarded as defects which would not be possessed by the reasonable man which the 1957 Act uses as the yardstick.

The relevant case law is given in the Comment to *R* v *Camplin* (1978), see Case **534** on p 904.

Was there provocation?

Although the issue of provocation is normally raised by the defence, the burden of proving that there was *no* provocation is on the prosecution once it is raised. Where, therefore, the jury has a reasonable doubt about the matter, it must be taken that the defendant was provoked. The judge can put the matter to the jury if it is not raised by the defence. In fact it was decided by the Court of Appeal in *R* v *Cambridge* (1994) *The Times*, 15 February that in a murder trial a judge is *obliged* to leave the matter of provocation to the jury if he decides that there is evidence of it, even if provocation has not been put forward by the defence and is contrary to it. The test here is subjective, i.e. was the particular defendant provoked? If the jury finds that he was not, then it is not relevant that a reasonable man would have been.

In *Franco* v *The Queen* (2001) *The Times*, 11 October the Privy Council added a further point which is that a court cannot *infer* what a jury might have decided in terms of provocation. In *Franco* the conviction of the defendant for murder was quashed and a conviction of manslaughter substituted on the ground that there was evidence of provocation that was not put to the jury. It should have been even though the defendant had relied on self-defence.

However, it is the role of the judge to determine whether there is enough evidence for a jury to find that there was a reasonable possibility of specific provoking words or conduct which caused the defendant to lose self-control. If so, the judge must leave the question of provocation to the jury, no matter whether the source of the evidence came from the defence or the prosecution. If in the view of the trial judge, taken on reasonable grounds that there was no such evidence, he had no need to put the defence to the jury, an appeal on the grounds that he should will normally fail (see *R* v *Acott (Brian Gordon)* [1997] 1 WLR 306 where the defendant had killed his mother in a violent attack and the prosecution had referred in cross-examination to the fact that he had lost his self-control).

It was decided by the Court of Appeal in *R* v *Stewart* [1995] 4 All ER 999 that if the defence of provocation is not raised but the judge nevertheless decides to refer it to the jury, he should give the jury some assistance as to what evidence they have to consider in relation to provocation, i.e. did the defendant lose his self-control as a result of things done or said, and whether a reasonable man would have been provoked by such things.

How would a reasonable person react?

The next stage in the test is objective. If the jury decides that the defendant was provoked, then it must go on to decide how a *reasonable person* would have responded to that provocation and whether any particular characteristics of the defendant should be brought into account, if at all, having received the judge's summing up. The reasonable person test means in effect that the defendant's reaction will normally have to bear some proportion to the provocation.

> *R* v *Camplin*, 1978 – Taunting a 15-year-old (**534**)

Other matters

A relevant provocation can be induced by the defendant himself. This covers the case where the defendant started the trouble and caused his victim to provoke him. In addition, there must be a 'sudden and temporary loss of self-control', which means that there must not be a significant 'cooling-off' period between the provocation and the killing.

> *R* v *Johnson*, 1989 – Where provocation is self-induced (**535**)
> *R* v *Thornton*, 1991 – A slow wearing down of control (**536**)

As regards domestic homicides, the government has considered proposals for change in regard to the defence of provocation which is raised by women who have killed their male partners but claim to have been provoked. The defence by no means always succeeds. It is often raised by men who kill their partners and the stance taken by government ministers is that in these cases the crime is too often reduced to manslaughter. Crown prosecutors would be issued with guidance that domestic homicides should carry a charge of murder not manslaughter together with a new category of self-defence for women who kill their partners after years of abuse. There is currently no legislation on these proposals.

Diminished responsibility

By reason of s 2(1) of the Homicide Act 1957 this defence is available in respect of a murder charge only. The *burden of proof is on the defence* which must show that the defendant 'was suffering from such abnormality of mind (whether arising from a condition of arrested or retarded development of mind or any inherent causes or induced by disease or injury) as substantially impaired his mental responsibility for his acts and omissions in doing or being a party to the killing'.

The question whether the requirement that the defence must prove diminished responsibility in terms of Art 6 of the Human Rights Convention (right to a fair hearing) was raised in *R v Lambert* [2001] 1 All ER 1014. The Court of Appeal ruled that this burden of proof was not contrary to Art 6. The presumption of innocence still applied. This was a special defence and did not interfere with the general rule that the burden of proof is on the prosecution.

The defence is wider than that of insanity (see Chapter 25) and covers other mental conditions. In fact the defendant may *know* what he is doing and that it is *wrong*. His alleged problem is that he finds it *substantially more difficult to control* his actions than would a normal person, and this difficulty is caused by some *abnormality of his mind*.

It is not correct for a judge to direct the jury that only partial or borderline insanity amounts to diminished responsibility (*R v Seers* [1984] 79 Cr App R 261).

A killing arising from drink or drugs is not covered because these conditions do not come within 'disease or injury'. However, where the taking of excessive drink or drugs over a period have, in effect, caused mental disease then the defence has been applied.

> *R v Tandy*, 1987 – Use of alcohol not involuntary (**537**)
> *R v Gittins*, 1984 – Where the taking of drink and drugs is a disease (**538**)

It was held in *R v Hobson (Kathleen)* (1997) *The Times*, 25 June that since battered woman's syndrome was added to the British classification of mental diseases in 1994, it could now be raised as forming the basis of the defence of diminished responsibility.

A person who is unfit to plead cannot raise the diminished responsibility defence because he is not liable to be convicted of murder (see *R v Antoine* [2000] 2 WLR 703, which is considered more fully in Chapter 25).

Suicide pact

The Homicide Act 1957 states in s 4(1) that:

> It shall be manslaughter and not murder, for a person acting in pursuance of a suicide pact between him and another to kill the other or be a party to the other being killed by a third person.

The defendant must show:

- that a suicide pact was made; and
- that he or she intended to die at the time the killing took place.

A suicide pact is defined by the Homicide Act 1957 in s 4(3) as:

> A common agreement between two or more persons having for its object the death of all of them, whether or not each is to take his own life, but nothing being done by a person who enters into a suicide pact shall be treated as done by him in pursuance of the pact unless it is done while he has a settled intention of dying in pursuance of the pact.

It is relevant to mention here the offence of aiding suicide. In this connection, s 2 of the Suicide Act 1961 states that a person who aids, abets, counsels or procures the suicide of another or an attempt by another to commit suicide shall be liable to a maximum of 14 years' imprisonment. The crime is triable on indictment and is an arrestable offence. It is an alternative verdict on a charge of murder or manslaughter. It was formerly an offence for a person to commit suicide but this was repealed by s 1 of the above Act. The House of Lords has ruled that the 1961 Act is not incompatible with the Convention on Human Rights.

24

In the same case their Lordships upheld the decision of the Director of Public Prosecutions to prosecute in a case where a woman suffering from motor neurone disease wanted her husband to help her die. The DPP had no power to give an undertaking that he would not prosecute in advance of the offence being committed. Even if the power existed using it for that purpose would be an abuse of due process because the circumstances of the offence would not be known before it took place (see *R (on the application of Pretty)* v *DPP* (2001) *The Times*, 23 October). Mrs Pretty was also unsuccessful in her attempt to have the Lords' ruling overturned by the European Court of Human Rights.

Involuntary manslaughter

It is apparent from the case law that involuntary manslaughter is based upon either an unlawful act resulting in death, sometimes called constructive manslaughter, or death resulting from gross (or criminal) negligence.

Manslaughter from an unlawful act (constructive manslaughter)

Constructive manslaughter has three ingredients as follows:

■ *An unlawful act committed by the defendant that results in the death of another person*: as in the law of tort, the chain of causation can be broken and, in particular, this has resulted in drug dealers being regarded as not liable for the deaths of those supplied, as in *R* v *Dalby* [1982] 1 All ER 916. However, there may be liability where there is, in fact, little if any break in the chain of causation. Thus, in *R* v *Kennedy* [1999] Crim LR 739 the victim asked the defendant to get him something that would make him sleep. The defendant prepared a syringe filled with heroin and handed it to the victim. The victim paid the defendant and injected himself and left. He died less than an hour later and the defendant was convicted of manslaughter.

   The ruling in *Kennedy* was doubted but not overruled by the Court of Appeal in *R* v *Rogers (Stephen)* (2003) *The Times*, 20 March. Rogers held a tourniquet around the arm of a drug abuser so that the abuser could inject himself. This was regarded by the Court of Appeal as sufficient involvement in the activity of injection as to make Rogers guilty of manslaughter when the abuser died following cardiac arrest. The Court of Appeal doubted whether there was sufficient participation by the defendant in the mechanics of the injection to have found Kennedy guilty of manslaughter. There is no question of aiding and abetting in such a situation because self-injection is not a crime other than being in possession of the relevant drug. Much turns therefore on the circumstances of the case. Those involved in, say, handing drugs to the abuser in this sort of case are not parties to his or her obtaining them. Rogers was not a party but the dealer in *Kennedy* was and the death quickly followed. It could be said therefore that the issue of whether the dealer caused the death of the user by the unlawful act of supplying the drug should have been left to the jury but it was not. There are cases stating that drug dealers cannot, in general, be held liable for the *ultimate* as distinct from *proximate* death of their user victims (see *R* v *Dalby* [1982] 1 All ER 916).

   Nevertheless, when Kennedy appealed to the Court of Appeal, that court affirmed his conviction, saying that there was no error in the trial judge's judgment. Those involved were acting in concert in administering the heroin (see *R* v *Kennedy* [2005] 1 WLR 2159).

- *The act must have involved a risk that someone would be harmed*: the risk is judged objectively i.e. would a reasonable and sober person observing the act see an apparent risk. The harm must be physical. The risk of psychological or emotional harm is not enough.
- *The defendant must have had the* mens rea *for the unlawful act, such as an assault, that led to the victim's death*: thus, in *R v Lamb* [1967] 2 QB 981 the defendant pointed a gun at his friend believing, as was the case, that the two rounds in the gun were not in the firing chamber. The defendant pulled the trigger, but with no intention of harming his friend. However, the barrel rotated so that a bullet moved into the firing chamber and the friend was shot and killed. The defendant did not know how the gun worked and saw the incident as a joke. *He lacked the* mens rea *for assault and, therefore, was not guilty of manslaughter.*

> *R v Church*, 1966 – The unlawful act must create the risk of physical harm (**539**)
>
> *R v Lowe*, 1973 – Unlawful omission not generally enough (**527**)

Manslaughter by gross negligence

To cause death by *any* lack of due care will not amount to manslaughter. A very high degree of negligence is necessary for the establishment of a crime. Whether the appropriate degree of negligence exists is a matter for the jury, following direction by the judge. The test according to the House of Lords in *R v Adomako* [1994] 3 All ER 79 is that a defendant is properly convicted of involuntary manslaughter by breach of duty if the jury is directed and finds that the defendant was in breach of a duty of care towards the victim who died, that the breach of duty caused the death of the victim and that the breach of duty was such as to be characterised as gross negligence and, therefore, a crime. Lord Mackay LC said, giving an analysis of the law:

> . . . in my opinion the ordinary principles of the law of negligence apply to ascertain whether or not the defendant has been in breach of a duty of care towards the victim who has died. If such breach of duty is established the next question is whether that breach of duty should be characterised as gross negligence and therefore as a crime. This will depend on the seriousness of the breach of duty committed by the defendant in all the circumstances in which the defendant was placed when it occurred. The jury will have to consider whether the extent to which the defendant's conduct departed from the proper standard of care incumbent upon him, involving as it must have done a risk of death to the patient, was such that it should be judged criminal.

The circumstances to which a charge of involuntary manslaughter may apply are so various that it is unwise to attempt to categorise or detail specimen directions, but certainly civil liability, although sufficient to establish the duty of care, is not sufficient to amount to 'gross negligence', nor is *Caldwell* recklessness. The test as stated in *Adomako* is enough. In the case the defendant was an anaesthetist during an eye operation on a patient. A tube supplying oxygen to the patient became disconnected but the defendant failed to notice this for some six minutes. The patient suffered cardiac arrest and died. The defendant was convicted of manslaughter and his appeal to the House of Lords was dismissed. There would, of course, have been an action in negligence as a fatal accident (see Chapter 20) but it is interesting to note that, because the negligence here is gross, criminal liability can also result.

24

Manslaughter by gross negligence and human rights

The definition of manslaughter by gross negligence continues to produce cases mainly in the field of medical treatment and care. Counsel for the defence in this sort of case have challenged the House of Lords' definition in *Adomako* as being circular and uncertain. The *Adomako* ruling is, as we have seen, to the effect that the jury are to be directed that in order to find gross negligence they must find that there has been a departure from the expected standard of professional practice so serious as to amount to a criminal act. Some lawyers say this direction is circular, in that, in order to find the defendant guilty of a crime, you must find that he or she is guilty of a crime.

This direction to the jury was challenged in *R v Misra* [2005] Crim App Rep 328 on the grounds that it contravened the Convention on Human Rights, Art 6 (right to a fair trial) and Art 7 (creation of criminal offences after the event). In other words, it is impossible to obey an uncertain law.

The defendants in the case were doctors. The patient had toxic shock syndrome. The defendants failed to appreciate how ill the patient was, so that he did not get the proper treatment and died. The jury convicted both doctors of gross negligence manslaughter on the basis of the *Adomako* direction. The doctors appealed to the Court of Appeal which dismissed the appeal, ruling that:

- The requirement for legal certainty of an offence was not *absolute* certainty but *sufficient* certainty. This common law principle had not been changed by the Convention.
- The offence of manslaughter by gross negligence was based on well-established principles, i.e. death resulting from a negligent breach of a duty of care owed by the defendant to the deceased; that in the negligent breach of that duty the victim was exposed to the risk of death; and that the circumstances were so reprehensible as to amount to gross negligence (*Adomako* applied).
- Gross negligence manslaughter should not be replaced by or confined to cases of reckless negligence.
- On the issue that a criminal offence normally requires *mens rea*, the court said that the requirement for gross negligence provided the necessary element of culpability.

Gross negligence manslaughter was not incompatible with the Convention.

Causing death by dangerous or careless driving

Under s 1 of the Road Traffic Act 1988 as substituted by s 1 of the Road Traffic Act 1991 the offence of causing death by dangerous driving replaces the offence of causing death by reckless driving in earlier legislation. It was thought that while the general remarks about criminal recklessness in case law had relevance in regard to manslaughter generally, they were not entirely suitable in the road traffic situation. In particular, it was felt to be *too subjective* so that there was a need to move to an *objective assessment of the standard of driving of the defendant*. The offence of causing death by dangerous driving has two elements as follows:

(a) there must be a standard of driving which falls far below that to be expected of a competent and careful driver; and
(b) the driving must carry a potential or actual danger of physical injury or serious damage to property.

The standard of driving will be judged objectively taking no account, e.g., of inexperience, age or disability – though these will be reflected in the sentence. The requirements of the section would be met where the state of the vehicle was such that a competent and careful driver would not drive it at all. If a driver was in an unfit condition to drive, e.g. by reason of drink or drugs, this would not be a defence if he drove dangerously as defined above.

In addition to the cases of dangerous *driving*, it should be noted that successful prosecutions have been brought on the basis of the *state of the vehicle and the state of the driver*. Thus in *R* v *Skelton* [1995] Crim LR 635 the defendant was a lorry driver who drove his lorry on a motorway after receiving a warning from another driver that the air pressure gauges were low. While on the motorway the pressure problem activated the handbrake which is an effect of such a problem and another lorry driver was killed when he ran into the back of the defendant's lorry. Although the crash was not immediate but some 10 minutes after the defendant's lorry stopped blocking the lane the Court of Appeal ruled that the chain of causation had not been broken and the defendant was rightly convicted. In *R* v *Marison* [1996] Crim LR 909 a diabetic was successfully charged with causing death by dangerous driving. He had suffered periods of unconsciousness in the previous six months. As regards this prosecution, he went into an unconscious state and veered on to the wrong side of the road hitting an oncoming vehicle and killing its driver. He was convicted of causing death by dangerous driving.

Section 3A of the Road Traffic Act 1988 contains an offence of causing death by careless driving *under the influence of drink or drugs*. It creates an objective test of negligence that requires merely that the defendant's driving has fallen below the reasonable standard of care and that drink or drugs were involved.

Violent offences which are not fatal

Under this heading we must consider the following crimes.

Assault and battery

It has already been pointed out in Chapter 21 on the law of specific torts that assault is a threat to apply force immediately to the person of the victim and a battery is the actual application of that force. This distinction also exists in the criminal law. Assault and battery are summary offences under s 39 of the Criminal Justice Act 1988.

Assault

The *actus reus* of assault consists of an act which gives the victim reasonable cause to believe that there will be an immediate infliction of violence. Assault requires basic intent and so actual intention or *Cunningham* recklessness is enough.

Battery

The *actus reus* consists in the actual application of force however slight to another without that other's consent. As we have seen, a battery can consist of an omission (see *Fagan* v *Metropolitan Police Commissioner* (1968) in Chapter 21).

The *mens rea* is a basic intent and so once again actual intention or *Cunningham* recklessness will suffice.

Defences

The following defences are available.

24

Chastisement

Chastisement of children, which is the main scenario, is considered in Chapter 21 (trespass to the person).

Self-defence

This is also called the 'private defence'. Where an attack which is, e.g., of a violent or indecent nature, is made against a person who is put in fear of his life or the safety of his person, then that person is entitled to protect himself and repel the attack but must not use more force than is necessary or reasonable in the circumstances. If the defence is accepted, it is a complete and not a partial defence because it negates the unlawful nature of the assault carried out in self-defence – in fact, there is no *actus reus* and *mens rea* (see further Chapter 25).

Statutory offences against the person

Assault and battery are common-law offences, but the more serious offences against the person are contained in the Offences Against the Person Act 1861 as follows.

Assault occasioning actual bodily harm

Under s 47 of the Offences Against the Person Act 1861 it is an offence punishable with imprisonment for a term not exceeding five years for a person to assault another thereby 'occasioning actual bodily harm'. Actual bodily harm merely means that the victim has suffered some injury. Bruising or abrasions are enough. Psychiatric injury can amount to actual bodily harm as where, e.g., this results from harassment of a woman by obscene phone calls, but there must be properly-qualified expert evidence before it can be left to the jury, since it must be something more than mere emotion such as fear, distress or panic (see Court of Appeal decision in *R* v *Chan-Fook* [1994] 2 All ER 552).

The mental state of the defendant is set out in the judgment of the House of Lords in *Parmenter* (see p 907).

The Queen's Bench Divisional Court has concluded that the lopping of hair without consent can constitute an offence under s 47 (see *DPP* v *Smith (Michael Ross)* [2006] 2 All ER 16 (Chapter 21)).

> *DPP* v *K*, 1990 – Acid in the hand washer (**540**)

Malicious wounding

Section 20 of the Offences Against the Person Act 1861 provides as follows:

> Whosoever shall unlawfully and maliciously wound or inflict any grievous bodily harm upon any person either with or without any weapon or instrument shall be guilty of an offence and being convicted thereof shall be liable to imprisonment for five years.

The word 'unlawfully' indicates that acts of genuine self-defence are excluded. As regards the *actus reus*, there are two possibilities, i.e. (*a*) wounding and (*b*) inflicting grievous bodily harm. Wounding is fairly straightforward and requires a breaking of the skin, though a graze would be enough. Grievous bodily harm must be some serious harm and where only slight harm is inflicted a prosecution under s 47 would be more appropriate.

As regards inflicting grievous bodily harm, while one normally thinks of the application of force to the person of the victim the concept does not necessarily require an assault.

> *R v Martin*, 1881 – Inflicting grievous bodily harm: no assault (**541**)

As regards the *mens rea*, this is set out in the judgment of the House of Lords in *Parmenter* (below).

> *R v Parmenter*, 1991 – Injury to a child (**542**)

Sexually transmitted diseases and ss 20 and 47

The growth of sexually transmitted diseases including HIV in society may well lead to an alteration in the criminal law landscape and in civil claims. The Victorian legal contribution to this problem was unhelpful to persons who had been infected with disease following sexual intercourse with a person who knowingly had the disease but did not inform the other person who consented to sexual intercourse without the relevant knowledge. The doctrine of informed consent that has been brought into civil cases has now it would appear been introduced into the criminal law of offences against the person. The Victorian case is *R v Clarence* (1888) 22 QBD 23. Clarence knew he had gonorrhoea. He had consensual intercourse with his unknowing wife. She contracted the disease and Clarence was prosecuted under ss 20 and 47 of the Offences Against the Person Act 1861. He was convicted at his trial because the jury did not believe that his wife who did not know about his condition had truly consented. His conviction was quashed by the appeal court. The wife had consented to sexual intercourse and that was enough.

More recently in *R v Dica (Mohammed)* (2003) (unreported) D was convicted of causing grievous bodily harm to two women he infected with HIV. He knew he was HIV-positive and appreciated the risk of unprotected sex. The women consented to unprotected sexual intercourse but said that they would not have done so if they had known of D's infection. The jury at the Inner London Crown Court seems to have bypassed *Clarence* and accepted that there may be a *biological offence* under ss 47 or 20 of the 1861 Act. This would seem to cover a person who knows he or she is infected or possibly is reckless regarding whether or not there is an infection that has caused the actual or grievous bodily harm of the disease.

Dica appealed against his conviction (see *R v Dica* [2004] QB 1257) and that appeal succeeded because the trial judge withdrew from the jury the issue of whether the female complainants in the case consented to sexual intercourse *knowing of his condition*, as he alleged they did. He was granted a re-trial where the issue of consent was turned down. It is a general rule of law that, unless the activity is lawful, the consent of the victim does not provide a defence to grievous bodily harm and the trial judge felt bound by this. Dica was convicted at his re-trial. He again appealed against this conviction but his appeal to the Court of Appeal failed and he was refused permission to appeal to the Lords (see *R v Dica* (2005) *The Times*, 7 September). While the case impacts mainly on sexual behaviour, it could affect the liability of practitioners in the medical and dental professions. Certainly it is a new development for these old statutory provisions.

24

Causing grievous bodily harm

Section 18 of the Offences Against the Person Act 1861 provides as follows:

> Whosoever shall unlawfully and maliciously by any means whatsoever wound or cause grievous bodily harm to any person with intent . . . to do some grievous bodily harm to any person or with intent to resist or prevent the lawful apprehension or detainer of any person shall be guilty of an offence and being convicted thereof shall be liable to imprisonment for life.

The expressions 'wounding' and 'grievous bodily harm' (GBH) carry the same meanings as they do for the purposes of s 20. The expression 'cause grievous bodily harm' is used in s 18 whereas the expression 'inflict grievous bodily harm' is used in s 20. It might have been assumed that s 18 applied to cases of grievous bodily harm caused by any means, whereas the expression 'inflict' in s 20 meant that it had to be as the result of an assault. However, since it seems that a s 20 offence can be committed without an assault the distinction between s 20 and s 18 is not really clear. The judgment of the House of Lords in *R v Mandair* [1994] 2 All ER 715 considered the two sections. D was tried under s 18 for 'causing grievous bodily harm with intent'. Counsel and the judge agreed that the jury could convict on the lesser charge of 'inflicting grievous bodily harm'. The judge in referring to the s 20 offence in his direction to the jury said it consisted of 'causing' GBH. The jury acquitted the defendant on the s 18 charge but convicted him on the s 20 count of 'causing' GBH. The Court of Appeal quashed the conviction on the ground that the defendant had been convicted of an offence not known to law.

The prosecution appealed to the House of Lords which held that it was open to a jury trying a charge of causing GBH with intent contrary to s 18 of the Offences Against the Person Act 1861 to convict of the lesser s 20 charge even where this had been expressed to be 'causing' (rather than 'inflicting') GBH contrary to s 20. 'Causing' GBH was wide enough to include 'inflicting' GBH.

Since a conviction under s 18 carries a maximum sentence of imprisonment for life, it is reserved for the more serious assaults. There are two forms of intent, as follows:

(*a*) an intent to do some grievous bodily harm; or
(*b*) an intent to resist or prevent a lawful detention or arrest.

In both cases the intent must be accompanied by an intention to cause really serious bodily harm as distinct from slight harm. Recklessness even of the *Cunningham* variety is not sufficient *mens rea*. The wounding must be deliberate and without justification and committed with intent; foresight is not enough. The test of intent is subjective.

> *R v Belfon*, 1976 – Causing grievous bodily harm: recklessness not enough (**543**)

Statutory offences against the person and stalking: case law

Stalking, particularly of women, has become an increasing problem in our society and, although Parliament has responded in terms of remedial measures, there has been a significant response by the courts which has resulted from the development of the statutory offences discussed above into the field of psychological injury. As we have seen, a start had been made in *R v Chan-Fook* (1993) *The Times*, 19 November. This case was applied again in *R v Burstow* [1996] Crim LR 331, where it was held that a stalker could be convicted of the offence of unlawfully and maliciously inflicting grievous bodily harm contrary to s 20 of the Offences

Against the Person Act 1861, even though he had not applied physical violence directly or indirectly to the body of the victim. B had become obsessed with a woman who worked with him and after she ended the relationship he made telephone calls and sent letters and photographs and visited the victim's home; all of this had a profound psychological effect on her. There is no doubt that this decision of the Court of Appeal has made a major breakthrough in anti-stalking law.

In *R v Ireland* [1997] 1 All ER 112 the defendant made unwanted telephone calls to three women on a number of occasions and remained silent when the telephone was answered. He was convicted of an offence under s 47 of the 1861 Act and the Court of Appeal later dismissed his appeal holding that psychological injury could amount to actual bodily harm.

As regards the possibility of a prosecution for public nuisance, we have already noted the decision in *R v Johnson (Anthony Thomas)* (1996) (see Chapter 21).

In *R v Constanza* [1997] 2 Cr App Rep 492 the defendant wrote more than 800 letters to a 23-year-old computer operator and also engaged in many telephone calls and the daubing of paint. The Court of Appeal held that his conviction at Luton Crown Court was correct. The offence of causing actual bodily harm by psychological assault could be sustained and words alone were enough. Once again this is an important conviction.

Where a custodial sentence is to be imposed, the judge should take into account any report from a psychiatrist stating that the defendant will not if at liberty represent a continuing threat to the victim (see *R v Smith (Leonard)* [1998] 1 Cr App Rep (S) 138).

Before leaving the case law it is important to note that it is necessary to prove psychological injury resulting from the defendant's activities. Fear, distress or panic is not enough to found a criminal conviction.

Stalking and harassment: statute law

Two Acts of Parliament are relevant as follows.

Section 4A of the Public Order Act 1986

This creates the offence of intentional harassment. The penalty on conviction by magistrates is imprisonment for up to six months and/or a fine of up to £5,000.

It covers harassment on the grounds of race, sex, disability, age and sexual orientation.

The present conviction rate against stalkers under this Act is poor. Very few defendants have been convicted for intentional harassment under s 4A of the Act.

The Protection from Harassment Act 1997

This Act makes it an offence to pursue a course of conduct which the person pursuing it *knows or ought to know* amounts to the harassment of another. There is thus an element of objectivity in the offence, i.e. 'knows or ought to know'. The course of conduct must involve conduct on at least two occasions and conduct is defined as including speech, e.g. nuisance telephone calls. The penalty on conviction by magistrates is the same as that under the 1986 Act (see above).

A civil tort is also created under which an order restraining harassment may be sought. Criminal courts are also given power to make an order preventing further harassment, breach of which will constitute a criminal offence.

The problem with the 1986 Act has been defining harassment, a word which everybody understands but nobody can define. The 1997 Act also avoids a definition stating only that references to harassment include alarming a person or causing them distress, and that conduct can include speech. However, the 1997 Act states that the test of whether

24

conduct amounts to harassment is that of the reasonable man, which should make the test more objective.

In connection with the requirement of harassing conduct on two occasions the following cases provide illustrations. In *Pratt* v *DPP* (2001) 165 JP 800 Pratt engaged in two incidents of offensive conduct towards his wife in their home. In one he threw water at her and in the second chased her threateningly around the house. The incidents were three months apart and different in detail. The High Court upheld P's conviction under the 1997 Act on his appeal from a magistrates' court, ruling that incidents of harassment did not need to exceed two incidents but the fewer and wider apart the incidents were the less likely it would be that harassment could be proved. In this case the second incident was sufficiently similar to the first to amount to a course of conduct but it was a borderline case. In *R* v *Hills* [2001] Crim LR 318 H & W lived together. H assaulted W on two occasions at their home. The first was in the nature of an indecent assault and the second was a fight. Between the incidents the pair appeared to have been reconciled at least for a while. The Court of Appeal quashed H's conviction. The incidents were too far apart and the claimed similarity of the events, i.e. pulling W's hair on both occasions was tenuous. The Court of Appeal pointed out that by charging harassment under the 1997 Act the prosecution had lost its case. It should have charged the incidents as two separate assaults since conviction on those charges could not have been challenged.

In two further cases the fact of harassment was not in question but the method was. In *R (a child)* v *DPP* [2001] 3 Current Law 127 the High Court held that a person can be harassed by threats to her dog. In *Kellett* v *DPP* [2001] All ER (D) 124 (Feb) the High Court held on judicial review that a person can be harassed by malicious telephone calls to her employer.

Sexual offences

We shall be concerned here only with the offences of rape and assault by penetration. There are, of course, other sexual offences, but because of the developments in both the *actus reus* and the *mens rea* of rape, it provides a further opportunity to consider in yet another context these ingredients of crime.

Rape

Section 1 of the Sexual Offences Act 2003 defines rape. It provides that a person (A) commits an offence if:

■ he intentionally penetrates the vagina, anus or mouth of another person (B) with his penis where;
■ B does not consent to the penetration; and
■ A does not reasonably believe that B consents.

Whether a belief is reasonable is to be determined having regard to all the circumstances including any steps A has taken to ascertain whether B consents.

Thus, where the defendant asserts an honest belief, the jury will have to assess all the surrounding circumstances of a case before deciding whether or not the belief was reasonable. So, for the first time, the common law defence of honest but mistaken belief appears in a statute but will not in itself entitle the defendant to an acquittal.

It remains unclear as to whether the personal characteristics of the defendant should be taken into account by the jury, e.g. mental impairment.

The situation is further complicated by rebuttable and irrebuttable presumptions that rape has been committed set out in ss 75 and 76. These are concerned with the victim's consent.

Section 75 presumptions

These can be *rebutted by evidence* to the contrary. They are:

- use of violence by the defendant or fear of the defendant's violence, either towards the victim or another person, e.g. the child of the victim;
- where the complainant was unlawfully detained;
- where the victim was asleep or otherwise unconscious at the time of the relevant act;
- where the victim's physical disability prevented communication to the defendant, whether or not there was consent;
- where the defendant or another person had administered or caused to be administered a substance enabling the victim to be stupified or overpowered at the time of the relevant act.

Section 76 presumptions

These are *conclusive* presumptions and cannot be rebutted. They are:

- where the defendent intentionally deceived the victim as to the nature or purpose of the relevant act;
- where the defendant impersonated someone personally known to the victim.

These presumptions will cover intercourse by deception and intercourse with a married woman by impersonating her husband. This can occur where, for example, the woman has gone to bed and the defendant has intercourse with her when she is in a drowsy state by pretending to be her husband just returned from work.

A husband can now be guilty of raping his wife and would commit rape by aiding or assisting others to rape her.

It will be noted that the s 1 offence can only be committed by a man and covers anal rape of women or men and oral sex with a woman or a man.

It should also be noted that the ruling of the House of Lords in *DPP v Morgan* (1975) (see below), where a defendant believed that there was consent and that belief need not be based on reasonable grounds, is replaced by the requirements of the 2003 Act.

No degrees of penetration

It is not necessary to constitute the crime of rape that sexual intercourse should be completed by male ejaculation of semen. In fact, the slightest penetration by the penis of the vagina (or vulva), anus or mouth of another person will suffice.

R v R, 1991 – A husband can rape his wife (**544**)

R v Williams, 1923 – Intercourse by deception (**545**)

DPP v Morgan, 1975 – Rape: a subjective test (**546**)

24

Assault by penetration

Section 2 of the Sexual Offences Act 2003 creates a new offence of assault by penetration. Previously this was a form of indecent assault.

Section 2 provides that a person (A) commits this offence if:

- he or she intentionally penetrates the vagina or anus of another person (B) with a part of his or her body or anything else;
- the penetration is sexual;

- B does not consent to the penetration; and
- A does not believe that B consents.

Whether a belief is reasonable is to be determined having regard to all the circumstances, including any steps A has taken to ascertain whether B consents. The ss 75 and 76 presumptions apply.

This offence can be committed by a man or woman and in fact penile penetration may be charged as assault under this section, so there is some duplication with the s 1 offence. However, this section is intended for penile penetration where the victim is not certain that the penis was used, as where the victim is blindfolded. Note also that the penetration must be sexual, which excludes intimate searching and medical procedures.

25

AGE AND RESPONSIBILITY
– GENERAL DEFENCES

In this chapter we shall consider the liability of minors in the criminal law, together with the general defences which are available in regard to all prosecutions for crime.

Liability of minors

For the purposes of criminal liability minors are divided into three classes as follows:

(a) Those under 10 years of age. It is presumed that minors under 10 years of age are incapable of any crime and the presumption is irrebuttable (Children and Young Persons Act 1963, s 16). Consequently, no evidence to the contrary will be accepted by a court so that children under 10 cannot be convicted of a criminal offence. Their actions may, however, result in a parenting order being made under the Crime and Disorder Act 1998.

(b) Those between 10 and 14 years of age. The presumption here was wholly dependent on the common law and is that the minor was incapable of forming a guilty intent, but this could be rebutted by proving 'mischievous discretion', i.e. knowledge that what was done was morally or seriously wrong.

This rebuttable presumption was abolished by s 34 of the Crime and Disorder Act 1998 *so that children aged 10 or over have full criminal responsibility*, though this is mitigated by a number of factors as follows:

- the general requirement that a defendant should, in a subjective sense, be aware of circumstances;
- the special provisions for dealing with youth crime; and
- the part played by the Crown in deciding whether or not to bring prosecutions.

The child's age may be a relevant factor in deciding on the reasonableness of his or her actions where such a factor is relevant.

(c) There is a special provision in relation to sexual offences. The Sexual Offences Act 1993 abolishes the previous presumption that a boy under the age of 14 is incapable of sexual intercourse. This means that it is now possible for rape cases to be brought against boys under the age of 14, since they are no longer presumed incapable of vaginal or anal penile intercourse. However, young boys can still seek the protection of the general rules relating to minors set out above.

Insanity

The leading case is *R* v *M'Naghten* (1843) 10 Cl & Fin 200. M'Naghten was charged with murder and acquitted on the grounds of insanity. The acquittal became the subject of debate in the House of Lords and it was decided to ask the opinion of the judges on the law governing insanity. The following rules arose.

(a) Every defendant is presumed to be sane until the contrary is proved.

(b) To establish a defence on the ground of insanity, it must be clearly proved that, at the time of the committing of the act, the party accused was labouring under such a defect of reason, from disease of mind, as not to know the nature and quality of the acts he was doing; or, if he did know it, that he did not know he was doing what was wrong. It is a question of the party's knowledge of right and wrong in respect of the act with which he is charged.

The defence is required to show on a balance of probabilities that the defendant is insane. The right to raise the issue of insanity at a trial is generally a matter for the defence and not the prosecution. However, it was held in *R* v *Dickie* [1984] 3 All ER 173 that exceptionally the trial judge may raise it and leave the decision to the jury if the evidence suggests that the accused was insane. Furthermore, the prosecution can raise the matter if the defendant has pleaded diminished responsibility (see Chapter 24) and where he has brought in evidence of mental incapacity.

In *DPP* v *H* [1997] 1 WLR 1406 it was held by a Queen's Bench Divisional Court that insanity can only be a defence where *mens rea* is required. Because driving with excess alcohol is an offence of strict liability the defence of insanity is not available on a prosecution for that offence.

If the defence of insanity is successful, the verdict is 'Not guilty by reason of insanity' as provided for by s 2(1) of the Trial of Lunatics Act 1883. The judge was then required to order the defendant to be detained in a special hospital, e.g. Broadmoor. This was often a worse form of sentence than might be given for a finding of guilty. For this reason persons who might have pleaded insanity did not do so, pleading guilty instead, and the defence became confined in practical terms to cases of murder. Now the Criminal Procedure (Insanity and Unfitness to Plead) Act 1991 inserts a new s 5 into the Criminal Procedure (Insanity) Act 1964, under which the court can make guardianship or supervision or treatment orders or an order for absolute discharge. However, in the case of murder, the court is still bound to make an admission order as before.

Before returning to the defence of insanity, it should be noted that the defendant's sanity or mental state is also relevant:

(a) When he is put up for trial. Although there may be no doubt that the accused was sane when he did the act with which he is charged, he may be too insane to stand trial or as it is usually put – 'unfit to plead'. If this is found to be so by the judge (not now the jury: s 22, Domestic Violence, Crime and Victims Act 2004), the court's options on a finding of unfitness to plead are:

- to make a hospital order under s 37 of the Mental Health Act 1983, which can also be accompanied by a restriction order under s 41 of the same Act;
- to make a supervision order;
- to order the defendant's absolute discharge.

If the court wishes the defendant to be detained in hospital, the appropriate order will be a hospital order.

The above options are inserted into the Criminal Procedure (Insanity) Act 1964 by the Domestic Violence, Crime and Victims Act 2004. The main differences under the new system are that the Secretary of State no longer has a role in deciding whether or not the defendant is admitted to hospital, and a court can no longer order the defendant's admission to a psychiatric hospital without medical evidence.

It is not possible to avoid the above orders where the defendant raised diminished responsibility as a defence but the judge found unfitness to plead (see *R v Antoine (Pierre Harrison)* [2000] 2 WLR 703).

A further example is provided by *R v Grant (Heather)* [2002] QB 1030. Heather Grant had been found unfit to stand trial for the murder of her boyfriend. She appealed against the finding of the jury (now the judge) that she had committed the act as charged. She said she should have been allowed to raise the defences of lack of intent (i.e. appropriate *mens rea*) and provocation. The Court of Appeal dismissed her appeal. It was clear from the Criminal Procedure (Insanity) Act 1964 (as amended) that the jury, in reaching conclusions as to unfitness to plead, was not required to consider the defendant's state of mind at the time of commission of the criminal act. Thus the defences of lack of intent and provocation could not be raised at a fitness to plead hearing (*R v Antoine* (2000) above applied).

(b) On conviction. Here the accused's mental condition is relevant to punishment. Under the Mental Health Act 1983, the court can make a variety of hospital and guardianship orders, though not in the case of murder.

(c) After sentence. If the accused is found to be suffering from mental disorder after receiving a sentence of imprisonment, he may be transferred to a mental hospital under the Mental Health Act 1983.

We can now look at the essential ingredients of the defence of insanity.

Disease of the mind

The judiciary has never been entirely swayed by the evidence of practitioners in this field of medicine. The matter is, the judiciary says, basically one of *responsibility for the act*. In other words, a person may be suffering from a defect of reason due to a disease of the mind and yet be *responsible*, in the view of the court, for what has been done or not according to the circumstances of the case. The test is thus legal not medical.

It may be for this reason that the courts have considered as part of the issue of responsibility a variety of mental states which do not truly come within the normal definition of insanity.

> *R v Kemp*, 1956 – A sufferer from arteriosclerosis (**547**)
> *R v Hennessy*, 1989 – A sufferer from diabetes (**548**)

Defect of reason

The disease of the mind must cause a defect of reason so that the defendant (*a*) did not know the nature and quality of his act or (*b*) did not know that what he was doing was wrong. This means essentially that to establish the *M'Naghten* defence the defendant must be deprived of reason. The defence does not, therefore, apply to those who have retained the powers of reasoning but who in a moment of forgetfulness, confusion or absent-mindedness have failed to use those powers properly or to the full.

> *R v Clarke*, 1972 – A shoplifter (**549**)

25

Knowing that the act is wrong

It is this branch of the *M'Naghten* defence which has produced difficulty, not the rarely pleaded branch which relates to not knowing what was being done, i.e. failure to understand the physical nature of the act. The problems have arisen in regard to whether, if the act is contrary to law, there might be a successful plea of insanity because the defendant thought the act to be morally right. It would appear that knowledge that the act is *legally* wrong means the defence fails.

> *R v Windle*, 1952 – A fatal dose of aspirin (**550**)

Automatism

As we have seen, it is a general rule of the common law that a *voluntary act* is required before liability for a crime can be established in terms of the *actus reus*. In addition, it is necessary that the defendant be *conscious of his acts*, otherwise there is no *mens rea*.

Sometimes a defendant will plead automatism as a defence which, if established, will negative the essential ingredients of the crime and result in an acquittal. The defence of automatism is difficult to establish but seeks to prove that the crime was committed by an *involuntary act* caused by an external factor.

> *Hill* v *Baxter*, 1958 – A sudden illness while driving (**551**)

Distinguished from insanity

Where automatism is induced by a disease of the mind, this is insanity and the judge may withdraw the defence of automatism from the jury (*Bratty* v *Attorney-General for Northern Ireland* [1963] AC 386).

However, an overdose of insulin in diabetes leading to hypoglycaemia (a medical state with side-effects, e.g. double vision, and leading eventually to coma) is not a malfunction of the mind and may be put to a jury as automatism.

> *R v Quick*, 1973 – Defence of automatism admissible (**552**)

Where automatism is self-induced

A court will not accept the defence of automatism if it is self-induced as by drink or drugs. This is clearly based upon public policy and is considered further below.

In other cases self-induced automatism may be put to the jury as a defence, as where a diabetic does not take sufficient precautions to prevent reduction of blood sugar (see *Moses* v *Winder* (1980)).

> *R v Lipman*, 1969 – Automatism induced by drugs (**553**)

Drunkenness and drugs

Automatism induced voluntarily by drink or drugs could well prevent the defendant from committing a voluntary act or from being conscious of what he was doing. Nevertheless, on grounds of public policy it is not normally a complete defence to allege automatism by drink or drugs (see *Finegan* v *Heywood* (2000) *The Times*, 10 May where the defence of drink-induced automatism failed on a charge of drink driving). It can be partially successful where the crime requires a specific intent which the drink or drugs can negative. However, in offences against the person where the drink/drugs defence is most usually raised this does not result in an acquittal because these crimes are often bolstered up by a similar crime which does not require a specific intent. Thus, drink or drugs may reduce murder to manslaughter and wounding with intent to unlawful wounding under ss 18 and 20 of the Offences Against the Person Act 1861 respectively, but there will still be a conviction for the lesser crime which does not require a specific intent. The jury can be asked to consider drink or drugs as a defence where recklessness is involved.

The reason why drunkenness is not and never will be a *general* defence in crime is a matter of public policy because so many crimes are committed under the influence of alcohol that a high proportion of crimes would go unpunished. The same is true, on an increasing scale, of drugs.

> *DPP* v *Majewski*, 1976 – Where no specific intent is required (554)
> *R* v *Hardie*, 1984 – Drugs and recklessness (555)

The drink/drugs defence is certainly not applicable to rape where the issue before the court is the defendant's intent or the issue of the victim's consent nor in situations where the defence of mistake is raised.

> *R* v *O'Grady*, 1987 – A mistaken self-defence (556)

In addition, where the defendant takes drink or drugs in order to pluck up courage to commit the offence, the drink/drugs defence will not be accepted by the court even as nullifying a specific intent. Thus murder remains murder and is not reduced to manslaughter.

> *Attorney-General for Northern Ireland* v *Gallagher*, 1963 – Drinking to get 'Dutch courage' (557)

Drink/drugs states not self-induced

Here the court will consider the defence of automatism by drink or drugs where the defendant has lost control by drink or drugs administered to him without his knowledge.

> *Ross* v *HM Advocate*, 1991 – Drugs in a can of lager (558)

25

Effect of drink on defence of diminished responsibility

The House of Lords ruled in *R* v *Dietschmann* [2003] 1 All ER 897 that a defendant is entitled to be convicted of manslaughter rather than murder on the grounds of diminished responsibility even though he has been drinking if he can satisfy the jury that despite the heavy alcohol consumption his mental abnormality substantially impaired his responsibility for his acts. It would appear from the ruling of the House of Lords that the defence of diminished responsibility *operates as a separate defence* even in circumstances of drunkenness. The defence of diminished responsibility can be established even though the defendant has failed to prove that he would not have killed if he had not taken drink. The drunken state is no defence but the underlying mental state can still be. The Homicide Act 1957, said the House of Lords, does not require the abnormality of mind *to be the sole cause* of the defendant's acts. Drink may be an unacceptable contributory cause but the mental state defence remains.

Duress

Duress when raised as a defence may be said to amount to a defence of no voluntary *actus reus*. It may also negative *mens rea* because a person who is made to do an act by threats of a serious nature, e.g. death or serious personal injury, can hardly be said to intend to do the criminal act.

Duress by threats

Duress is not available as a defence to murder (*R v Howe* [1987] 1 All ER 771) or attempted murder. It is, however, available in offences of strict liability as in *Eden DC v Braid* [1998] Crown Office Digest (now Administrative Court Digest) 259 where a taxi driver was forced by threats to carry an excessive number of persons in breach of the licensing conditions. The defence of duress applied.

> *R v Gotts*, 1991 – Attempted murder under duress (**559**)

The essential ingredients of duress by threats are as follows:

(a) The threats must be serious such as threats of death or serious personal injury. Threats to property are probably not enough. The threat of serious *psychological injury* is not it seems included. Thus in *R v Baker* [1997] Crim LR 497, the father of a child refused to return her after a contact visit. Her mother and her husband went to the father's house and hearing a child crying and fearing for her psychological health banged on the door and caused criminal damage. They were convicted of criminal damage and the defence of duress of circumstances was rejected.

(b) The response of the defendant to those threats must be reasonable. He must have acted as a sober person of reasonable firmness (*R v Graham* [1982] 1 All ER 801).

(c) Where the defence of duress is applicable it must also be shown that the overpowering of the defendant's will was operative at the time when the crime was actually committed by him, though this general rule is not always applied.

> *R v Hudson*, 1971 – Duress and perjury (**560**)

(d) There is also a duty to neutralise the threat as by informing the police where this is possible, having regard to the age of the defendant and the circumstances and risks involved.

It should be noted that the defence of duress does not apply where the defendant *voluntarily entered a situation likely to end in duress.* (See also Membership of a gang, below.) Thus, if A owes his drug dealer money, he can expect that pressure might be brought to bear upon him by the dealer to clear the debt by helping him to supply drugs to others on the basis of threats of violence (see *R* v *Heath (Patrick Nicholas)* [2000] Crim LR 109). The House of Lords gave a similar ruling in *R* v *Hasan (Aytach)* [2005] 2 AC 467, where the defendant alleged duress in that a drug dealer with a reputation for violence had threatened him and his family unless he carried out the burglary with which he was charged. The dealer was the boyfriend of his employer, who ran an escort agency, and was involved in prostitution. The House of Lords ruled that the defence of duress was excluded because of his voluntary association with criminals who he foresaw or ought to have forseen might make threats of violence.

It is not, however, necessary for the defendant to prove that a perceived threat is real. Thus, in *R* v *Cairns (John)* [1999] 2 Cr App R 137 the victim climbed on the bonnet of C's car. As he drove away, he saw a group of the victim's friends following in what he took to be a hostile way. He braked and threw the victim off the bonnet and ran over him inflicting serious injuries. The defence of duress was accepted by the Court of Appeal. It appeared that the victim's friends meant no harm, they said, to C but merely wished to prevent the victim from acting as he was; nevertheless, the perceived threat was enough to make C's conviction unsafe.

Duress and low intelligence

In *R* v *Bowen (Cecil)* [1996] 4 All ER 837 the Court of Appeal dealt with the defence of duress in the case of persons of low intelligence. The defendant had obtained electrical goods on credit by deception as to his intention to pay for them in due course. He was charged with obtaining goods by deception and claimed that he had been under duress because of threats to petrol bomb his home by the two men for whom he obtained the goods. The Court of Appeal held that although the defendant was a person of low intelligence, this was not a relevant factor in duress since it would not necessarily make an accused person more timid or suggestible to threatening behaviour. The defence of duress failed.

Membership of a gang – an aspect of voluntary exposure to threats

In some recent cases the court has had to consider whether the voluntary joining of a gang of persons by the defendant affects his ability to raise the defence of duress when he is caused to become involved in gang crime by threats from other members of the gang. It would appear that the defence is not available to a person who knows when he voluntarily joins a gang that he might be put under some pressure to commit an offence. It can be available if at the time of joining the defendant failed to appreciate the risk of violence.

> *R* v *Sharp (David)*, 1987 – The risk of violence was known (**561**)
> *R* v *Shepherd*, 1988 – Risk of violence not appreciated (**562**)

Duress of circumstances

In some recent cases there has been a blurring of the so-called defence of necessity (see below) with that of duress. This form of duress has been referred to as 'duress of circumstances'.

This is probably a more accurate analysis of certain necessity cases. Thus, if A who is disqualified from driving drives his son to work because he will otherwise be late and might lose his job because his wife becomes hysterical and threatens to kill herself unless he does so, this situation of 'threat' is called 'duress of circumstances' and can operate as a defence.

> *R v Martin*, 1989 – A threat of suicide (**563**)

Duress – the special case of a wife

Duress is clearly a defence for a wife. Section 47 of the Criminal Justice Act 1925, which abolished the presumption that a wife who committed a crime in her husband's presence did so under such compulsion as entitled her to an acquittal provides as follows:

> Any presumption of law that an offence committed by a wife in the presence of her husband is committed under the coercion of the husband is hereby abolished, but on a charge against a wife for any offence other than treason or murder it shall be a good defence to prove that the offence was committed in the presence of and under the coercion of the husband.

It was decided in *R v Shortland* [1995] Crim LR 893 that in applying s 47 of the 1925 Act and to invoke a defence of marital coercion it was necessary for a defendant to prove on a balance of probabilities (as distinct from beyond a reasonable doubt) that the offence was committed because her will had been overborne by the wishes of her husband and that she was therefore forced unwillingly to take part in the offence. However (and importantly), the defence did not necessarily require proof of physical force or the threat of physical force.

The Court of Appeal allowed an appeal by Malena Iris Shortland against a conviction for two offences of making a false statement to procure a passport. It appeared that she had applied for a visitor's passport and a 10-year passport, the latter in the name of Valerie Lopez, a dead child. All of this was done under the coercion and in the presence of her husband.

Necessity

English law does in extreme circumstances recognise a defence of necessity, but when it does so it arises from some pressure on the defendant's will from the wrongful threats or violence of another. Equally, however, it can arise from other objective dangers threatening the defendant or others when it is called by the judiciary 'duress of circumstances' (see *R v Martin* (1989), above and *A (Children)* (2000) *The Times*, 10 October: necessity to separate conjoined twins – court consents to inevitable death of one twin).

In the absence of the elements of threat or objective danger where the defence is probably better regarded as duress, there is no general defence of necessity in English law.

It is, therefore, murder to take another's life to save one's own unless it is a case of self-defence (see below).

> *R v Dudley and Stephens*, 1884 – Killing a member of the crew (**564**)

However, situations of genuine necessity not set in a background of duress can be taken into account by the court in the sentence imposed and at an earlier stage, where there is discretion, by the authorities in not bringing a prosecution.

Mistake

It will be appreciated that a normal sane and sober person may make a mistake and it is the effect of such mistakes on criminal liability with which we must now deal.

Suppose that a defendant X saw A apparently attacking B. X believed that A was mugging B and fought A off. It then turned out that A was trying to arrest B who had just mugged an old lady. Can X raise the defence of mistake, i.e. that he believed he was acting to prevent crime (see below)?

The only major problem arising in the case law from attempts to establish the defence of mistake have been as to whether it is enough that the defendant had an honest belief that the facts were as he mistakenly thought them to be or whether that belief must be not only *honest* but also *reasonable*. The defence of mistake should therefore be put to the jury in the trial of our defendant X. Indeed, his mistake may be both honest and reasonable – not that the latter is relevant in *law* rape apart.

However, although the courts do not require as a matter of law that an honest mistake be at the same time reasonable, it is unlikely that a jury will accept that the defendant made an honest mistake in circumstances where an ordinary person would not or could not reasonably have made the mistake. So whatever the test, it can be said with some confidence that a defendant is unlikely to be acquitted following a pleading of 'honest' mistake in 'unreasonable' circumstances. Finally, and as would be expected, a mistake as to law is no defence.

> *R v Kimber*, 1983 – An indecent assault (**565**)
> *R v Bailey*, 1800 – A mistake as to law (**566**)

In *R v Lee (Dennis Percival)* [2001] 1 Cr App R 19 the Court of Appeal reviewed the law in this area. The defendant was convicted of assault on police with intent to resist arrest. He mistakenly believed he had passed a roadside breath test and punched one of the police officers during the course of an arrest. His appeal on the grounds of mistake was dismissed. The Court of Appeal ruled:

- that persons under arrest are not entitled to form their own view as to the lawfulness of an arrest; they have a duty to comply with the police and hear the details of the charge;
- a belief that one is innocent however honestly or genuinely held cannot afford a defence to a charge of assault with intent to resist arrest.

Consent

Genuine consent of the victim may negate liability for offences such as assault (properly called battery) and rape, though consent must be genuine (see *R v Williams* (1923) in Chapter 24). However, even where consent is genuine there may be a successful prosecution for reasons of public policy. Thus in *R v Brown* [1993] 2 All ER 75 the House of Lords held that, in the absence of good reason, the consent of the victim was no defence to a charge under ss 20 and 47 of the Offences Against the Person Act 1861 (see Chapter 24). In that case the appellants belonged to a group of sado-masochistic homosexuals who over a period of 10 years willingly participated in acts of violence against each other including genital torture for the sexual pleasure which it induced by reason of the giving and receiving of pain. The acts were committed in private. However, video tapes were made and the case was largely

25

conducted on these. The House of Lords held that the above activities constituted offences contrary to ss 20 and 47 of the 1861 Act regardless of the consent of the victims. Public policy required that society be protected against cults of violence.

However, in *R v Wilson* (1996) *The Times*, 5 March, the Court of Appeal decided that consensual activity between husband and wife in the privacy of their home was not a proper matter for criminal investigation or prosecution.

In that case the wife had undergone a medical examination which revealed that there was a scar on both her buttocks. On her right buttock, as photographs before the court showed, there was the capital letter W and the left buttock the capital letter A. It appeared that her husband had burnt these initials into her buttocks by using a hot knife. She had consented and even instigated the branding because she wanted his initials on her body. A prosecution under s 47 of the 1861 Act failed. The Court of Appeal distinguished *R v Brown* (above) on the basis that the facts in that case were truly extreme.

Consent of the victim is raised in the civil law by way of the defence of *volenti non fit injuria* (or the rule of assumption of risk) and more rarely in the criminal law, where the courts are more reluctant to allow consent as a defence at least where there is infliction of bodily harm the ground being public policy (see *R v Brown* [1993] 2 All ER 75) (above). However, the Court of Appeal has now ruled and set out guidance in relation to the criminal prosecution of alleged offences resulting from sporting injuries.

In *R v Barnes* [2005] 2 All ER 113, the Court of Appeal quashed the conviction of the defendant, who had been found guilty of causing a serious injury to the leg of an opponent following a tackle during an amateur soccer match. The prosecution had contended that the tackle was late, unnecessary, reckless and high up on the legs. The defence contended unsuccessfully at the trial that the tackle, while 'hard', was a fair sliding tackle in the course of play, resulting in an unintended accidental injury. The defendant was convicted of inflicting grievous bodily harm under s 20 of the Offences against the Person Act 1861.

In quashing that conviction, the Court of Appeal ruled that criminal proceedings should be reserved for grave cases; sufficiently grave to be classified as criminal. Those who take part in sports said the court consented to physical injury that was an inevitable risk and an instinctive error, reaction or misjudgement in the heat of the game was not to be classed or categorised as criminal activity.

This judgment will go a long way to stopping the growing practice of disgruntled players using the criminal law to compensate for defeat or humiliation on the field of play.

Self-defence

A person may use such force as is reasonable in all the circumstances in his own defence. What is reasonable force is a matter of fact for the jury, but there must be some reciprocity or mutuality between the force being offered and the force used in defence. If A kissed B against her will, she may not succeed with self-defence if she stabbed A in the chest with her hatpin! There is no duty to retreat or run away in the face of force. Failure to do so before providing countervailing force is merely a factor to be taken into account when deciding whether (*a*) force was necessary at all and (*b*) if so, whether it was reasonable or whether backing off might have solved the problem.

If excessive force is used and death results, the defence fails. Murder is not reduced to manslaughter unless the defendant is regarded as having acted reasonably on the spur of the moment and under stress.

The test of whether the force used was reasonable or not is, however, *objective*. So if the prosecution shows that *in fact* excessive force was used, the defence fails. The use of excessive force is *not* at present decided in terms of *the defendant's perception of events*, which would be a *subjective test*.

> *R v McInnes*, 1971 – Greasers and skinheads: an affray (**567**)

Apprehended imminent attack

There is no need for an attack to be taking place. A person can make preparations for self-defence where there is an apprehension of imminent attack.

> *Attorney-General's Reference (No 2 of 1983)*, 1984 – Fear of a riot (**568**)

Self-defence and mental states

In dealing with the defence of provocation the court may take into account the mental state of the defendant. In *R v Martin (Anthony Edward)* [2002] 2 WLR 1, Mr Martin appealed against his conviction for murder. He shot two people who were engaged in burglary at his home. He killed one and wounded the other. When tried he pleaded unsuccessfully self-defence. After conviction he was found to be suffering from a longstanding paranoid personality disorder. Mr Martin said that this had affected the risk he perceived to his safety from the burglars. This he said was relevant in deciding whether the force he used against the burglars was reasonable. The Court of Appeal ruled that the defences of provocation and self-defence were distinguishable. A mental condition that affected the degree of self-control could not except in exceptional circumstances be relied upon when dealing with reasonable force in self-defence. However, Mr Martin's mental state had resulted in diminished responsibility and his conviction for murder was quashed and a conviction of manslaughter substituted with a sentence of imprisonment for five years. It is also worth noting that as regards protection of property, Art 2(2) of the European Convention on Human Rights does not permit the taking of life in order to protect property.

Preventing crime

Section 3 of the Criminal Law Act 1967 provides that: 'A person may use such force as is reasonable in the circumstances in the prevention of crime or in effecting or assisting in the lawful arrest of offenders or suspected offenders or of persons unlawfully at large.' This provision would, given reasonable force, cover acts in defence of other persons whether relatives or not. It would also cover defence of property as where reasonable force is used by A against B to prevent B from stealing A's briefcase.

25

> *R v Rose*, 1884 – A son shoots his father (**569**)

Genuine religious belief

Finally, it should be noted that the defendant's genuine belief that he is carrying out God's instructions will not provide a defence. Thus, in *Blake* v *DPP* (1993) *The Times*, 19 January Blake (who was a vicar) had, during a protest at the use of military force in the Gulf, written words from the Bible on a concrete pillar. He was charged with criminal damage and said that he had been carrying out God's instructions to him. A Divisional Court held that this could not provide a defence of lawful excuse.

Part 6

CASES AND MATERIALS

THE NATURE AND DEVELOPMENT OF ENGLISH LAW

Where common law and equity are in conflict equity prevails

 1 *The Earl of Oxford's Case* (1615) 1 Rep Ch 1

Merton College, Oxford, had been granted a lease of Covent Garden for 72 years at £9 a year, and some 50 years later sold the lease to the Earl for £15 a year. Later the college retook possession of part of it, on the ground that a statute of Elizabeth prevented the sale of ecclesiastical and college lands so that the conveyance to the Earl was void. The Earl brought a claim to eject the college from the land, and the common law judges found in favour of the college, saying that they were bound by the statute. The Earl filed a Bill in Equity for relief, and Lord Ellesmere granted it, stating that the claim of the college was against all good conscience. This brought law and equity into open conflict and resulted in the ruling of James I that, where common law and equity are in conflict, equity should prevail. (See now s 49 of the Supreme Court Act 1981.)

The court must apply an Act of Parliament and cannot declare it illegal

2 *Cheney v Conn* [1968] 1 All ER 779

Cheney objected to his tax assessments under the Finance Act 1964, on the ground that the government was applying part of the tax collected to the making of nuclear weapons. Cheney alleged that this was contrary to the Geneva Conventions – which had been incorporated into the Geneva Conventions Act 1957 – and conflicted with international law.

Held – even if there was a conflict between the 1964 and 1957 Acts, the 1964 Act gave clear authority to collect the taxes in question and being later in time prevailed. 'It is not for the court to say that a parliamentary enactment, the highest law in this country, is illegal,' said the judge.

A statute remains law until repealed by Parliament

 3 *Prince of Hanover v Attorney-General* [1957] 1 All ER 49

A statute of Anne in 1705 provided for the naturalisation of Princess Sophia, Electress of Hanover, and the issue of her body. The statute was repealed by the British Nationality Act 1948, s 34(3), but by s 12 a person who was a British subject immediately before the commencement of the Act (1 January 1949) became a citizen of the United Kingdom and Colonies. The claimant was born in 1914 in Hanover and was lineally descended from the Electress. He now claimed a declaration that he was a British subject immediately before the commencement of the British Nationality Act. It was necessary for him to establish this in order to make a claim on a fund, put up by the Polish government, to compensate Britons who had lost property in Poland because of nationalisation. It was held at first instance that the statute had not lost its force merely because of its age, but nevertheless, although the statute was unqualified and plain in its meaning, its words taken alone produced an absurd result, since, under the statute, the Kaiser, who led Germany in the 1914–18 world war, would have been a British subject. Parliament must, therefore, have intended some limitation on the operation of the words used. By referring to the preamble it seemed possible to draw the conclusion that the purpose of the Act was to be effected in the lifetime of Anne, and that after that time its purpose was spent and the claimant was not entitled to his declaration. On reaching the Court of Appeal, *it was held* that the appellant was a British subject under the statute of Anne which had remained law until repealed by the 1948 Act, the statute being so clear in its meaning that it was unnecessary to apply rules of interpretation to it. Rules of interpretation were to be used only in case of ambiguity or doubts as to meaning. The decision of the Court of Appeal was affirmed by the House of Lords.

Parliament may specifically abolish or alter statute law by a later enactment. This will take place by implication if the later enactment is wholly inconsistent with the former

4 *Vauxhall Estates Ltd v Liverpool Corporation* [1932] 1 KB 733

In 1928 the Minister of Health made a street improvement scheme order for a certain area of Liverpool. The order required the compulsory purchase of property, and the question of compensation payable to owners arose. Under s 2 of the Acquisition of Land (Assessment of Compensation) Act 1919, the claimants would receive £2,370, but if s 46 of the Housing Act 1925 applied, the claimants would receive £1,133. A provision of the Act of 1919 stated that other statutes inconsistent with the 1919 Act were not to have effect.

Held – the 1925 Act impliedly repealed the 1919 Act. It was inconsistent with it. Compensation was to be assessed under the latest enactment.

Comment (i) It was held in *Re Berry* [1936] 1 Ch 274 that the court will not construe a later Act as repealing an earlier Act by implication unless it is *impossible* to make the two Acts, or certain sections of them, stand together, i.e. if a section of the later Act can only be given a sensible meaning, as in *Vauxhall*, if it is treated as impliedly repealing the relevant section of the earlier Act.

(ii) The matter of repeal by implication was raised in *A v DPP* [2002] 4 Current Law 124. As noted in Chapter 4, the Powers of Criminal Courts (Sentencing) Act 2000 allows a youth court to subject an offender to a period of detention and training in a Young Offenders Institution that is followed by a period of supervision. The 2000 Act limits the making of such orders to persons under 18. The Children and Young Persons Act 1963 allows a youth court to sentence a person as if they were of the age at which they committed the offence even if because of delays in proceedings they are over 18 at the time of conviction. The issue in the above case was whether these statutes could be reconciled or whether the 1963 Act was repealed by implication by the 2000 Act.

A appealed to the Queen's Bench Divisional Court in regard to the imposition of a detention and training order on him even though at the time of sentence he was over 18. He had, however, been under 18 at the time he committed the offence of wounding with intent and common assault. He claimed that sentence was invalid since the 1963 Act had been repealed by implication.

The Divisional Court dismissed the appeal. The 1963 Act was concerned mainly with procedure in the youth court, whereas the 2000 Act was purely concerned with sentencing. It was not irrational to apply the 1963 Act where a young person reached the age of 18 before conviction, and Parliament's intention was to be construed so as to allow the 2000 Act to be interpreted subject to the 1963 Act.

Modern texts as a point of reference

5   *Boys v Blenkinsop* [1968] Crim LR 513

Mrs Nellie Blenkinsop was charged at Lewes with having 'permitted' her son Donald to drive a car without third-party insurance. The registered owner of the car was the driver's father whose insurance policy did not cover driving by his son. However, it appeared that the son had asked his mother's permission to drive and she had given it and had said she was the owner when asked by a constable. The defence submitted that there was no case to answer because only the registered owner could permit use of the vehicle. The prosecution submitted that this was wrong because Mrs Blenkinsop might have been, if not joint owner, at any rate responsible for care, management or control of the car within *Lloyd v Singleton* [1953] 1 All ER 291. The prosecuting inspector had asked the justices to refer to *Wilkinson's Road Traffic Offences* (5th edn,

1965, p 202) which in relation to that case stated: 'A person may "permit" though he is not the owner.' Counsel for the defence objected that unless the justices were referred to the case itself they were not allowed to look at the textbook. The inspector did not have a report of the case with him. The justices dismissed the case and the prosecution appealed to the Divisional Court. The court allowed the appeal and remitted the case to the justices to continue the hearing of it. Parker, LCJ said: 'They are entitled to and should look at the textbook; and if they then feel in doubt they should, of their own motion, send for the authority, and if necessary, adjourn for it to be obtained.'

Comment Modern texts are not books of authority as the older texts are because in modern times we have statutes and law reports to give that authority but they are a useful source of reference in the case of the major practitioners' titles.

ADR rejected by a party: no award of costs

5A   *Dunnett v Railtrack plc* [2002] 2 All ER 850

The claimant Susan Dunnett had lost a claim in negligence against the defendants in connection with the death of three of her horses when they were struck by an express train near Bridgend in terms of failure to restrict access to the line. She was given permission to appeal to the Court of Appeal but in giving permission the judge said she should explore the possibility of ADR. She approached Railtrack concerning this but they rejected it, though they did offer to settle the claim prior to the appeal being heard. Ms Dunnett lost her appeal and in the ordinary course of events Railtrack would have recovered its costs from Ms Dunnett but the Court of Appeal refused to make an order as to costs which meant that each party paid their own costs. This said the Court of Appeal was because Railtrack had refused to even contemplate ADR. In the circumstances it was not appropriate to take into account the fact that Railtrack had made offers to settle the claim.

Comment (i) A firm decision from an appeal court that the Civil Procedure Rules 1998 must be followed in regard to ADR, otherwise the party concerned will be punished by the refusal to award costs even though they succeed with a claim or a defence.

(ii) More recent cases show that the courts are prepared to use their powers under procedural rules to penalise parties to litigation who do not consider ADR where appropriate or who unreasonably refuse an offer from a party to mediate or who, having agreed to mediate withdraw without proper excuse (see *Leicester Circuits Ltd v Coates Brothers plc* [2003] EWCA Civ 333). This was a contract dispute as to the suitability of goods supplied by Coates. The parties had agreed to mediate but before the commencement of this procedure Coates withdrew. The trial proceeded and Coates was successful. Normally Coates would have obtained the usual costs against Leicester but because of Coates' withdrawal from the agreed mediation Leicester was ordered to pay the costs up to the time when Coates withdrew from mediation. Thereafter each party paid its own costs thus penalising Coates.

However, in *Wyatt Co (UK) Ltd* v *Maxwell Batley (a firm)* Ch D, Lawtel, 15 November 2002 a successful party who refused several offers to mediate was not penalised in costs because in particular the offer to mediate was made too late for the party to whom it was made to prepare for it. To do so would have provided a distraction from the main proceedings that were well advanced. Also the motives of the party making the offer were questionable. It seemed that the motive of the party making the offer of mediation was to extract a more substantial settlement in their favour than the court might award.

Again, in *Corenso (UK)* v *Burden Group plc* [2003] EWHC 1805 (QB) a successful party that had refused to mediate was not penalised by having to pay the costs because it had entered into another form of ADR i.e. Part 36 of the Civil Procedure Rules 1998 offers had been made. This means they had paid sums of money into court to try to settle the dispute without trial.

In *Halsey* v *Milton Keynes General NHS Trust; Steel* v *Joy* [2004] 4 All ER 920, the Court of Appeal gave guidance as to when it is reasonable to refuse ADR. In *Halsey* the claim was for clinical negligence involving an elderly patient. The claimant made invitations to mediate, but the trust refused on the grounds that the claim had no prospects of success before a court and the low value of the claim which meant that the costs of mediation would be disproportionate. The claim was brought before the court and failed. The judge refused to penalise the trust in costs because of its failure to mediate. The Court of Appeal agreed and found that the trust's position was not unreasonable.

The *Steel* case, which was a conjoined appeal, was a personal injury claim where the defendant felt he had a strong defence and refused to compromise. The Court of Appeal found that the defendant's stance was a reasonable one and, the claim having failed, the defendant was entitled to recover the defence costs from the claimant.

The Court of Appeal then offered some general guidelines on the matter of ADR, as follows:

- the court has no power to order litigants to mediate: to do so would be a violation of their human rights;
- the court does, however, have a role to encourage ADR;
- all parties should consider as a matter of routine whether their claims are suitable for ADR;

- where a successful party has acted unreasonably in refusing ADR then the court can displace the normal costs rule and require the successful party to pay the costs;
- the burden of showing 'reasonableness' lies with the successful party;
- while most cases are suitable for ADR, there should not be a presumption in favour of mediation.

Comment The Court of Appeal did, however, recognise that some disputes are 'intrinsically unsuitable' for ADR. These include cases which involve allegations of fraud, cases where an injunction may be required as a remedy, cases where it would be useful to have a judicial precedent, and cases where the parties wish the court to determine an issue of law or construction.

OTHER COURTS AND TRIBUNALS AND LEGAL SERVICES

The courts can control the defective jurisdiction of a tribunal or administrative authority by the doctrine of *ultra vires*

6 | ***Attorney-General* v *Fulham Corporation*** [1921] 1 Ch 440

The local authority was authorised by the Baths and Wash-houses Acts 1846–78 to establish a wash-house where people could come and wash their own clothes. The Corporation decided to run a municipal laundry where people could bring their clothes to be washed by employees of the Corporation.

Held – the statutory powers did not cover running a laundry. The action of the authority was, therefore, *ultra vires* and an injunction was granted to prevent the Corporation from running the laundry.

Comment (i) The *ultra vires* principle was used in *Bromley London Borough Council* v *Greater London Council* [1982] All ER 153, where the House of Lords decided that the Labour-controlled GLC had no power under the Transport (London) Act 1969 to pass resolutions to enforce a 25 per cent cut in London's bus and tube fares. It was also decided that a public authority is under a *fiduciary duty* to hold the balance fairly between the various interests of those who are within its care, i.e. in this case between the ratepayers and the transport users. The effect of the resolutions was to pass on the cost of the reduction to ratepayers. The Labour Party's manifesto, which had advocated a reduction in fares, was no justification. It could not be assumed that all who voted Labour agreed with the whole of the manifesto. A manifesto is not a binding contract between a party and its supporters.

(ii) In *R* v *Lewisham BC, ex parte Shell UK* [1988] 1 All ER 938 the Council passed a resolution to boycott all Shell products where suitable alternatives were available as part of the Council's anti-apartheid policy and on the basis of alleged activities by Shell in South Africa. The court granted Shell a declaration that the resolution was *ultra vires*. The Council had no power to put pressure on Shell in this way no matter how reasonable its desire to promote good race relations might be.

(iii) In *R v Lord Chancellor, ex parte Witham* [1997] 2 All ER 779 the Lord Chancellor made an order repealing previous provisions so that those on income support and who were litigants in person were no longer excused from paying court fees. W wished to bring a claim in defamation for which there is no legal aid and he claimed that the further requirement for him to pay court fees, even though he was on income support, was a violation of his right to access to the courts and, therefore, *ultra vires* as being beyond the order-making powers vested in the Lord Chancellor under s 130 of the Supreme Court Act 1981. The court allowed W's application. The order was *ultra vires*. There was nothing in s 130 to suggest that court fees might be imposed in a manner that could deny absolutely a person's access to the courts and thus the relevant Article of the Supreme Court Fees (Amendment) Order 1996 was *ultra vires*.

The supervisory jurisdiction of the High Court cannot normally be invoked if other and more appropriate procedures for appeal exist

Note. The order of *mandamus* is, since July 2000, referred to as a mandatory order, an order of prohibition is called a prohibitory order and *certiorari* becomes a quashing order. This should be borne in mind when referring to cases heard before the above date.

7   *R v Brighton Justices, ex parte Robinson* [1973] 1 WLR 69

The defendant was convicted and ordered to pay a fine in her absence for failing to give information about a driver's identity. She applied for *certiorari* on the grounds that she had not received the summons.

Held – by the Queen's Bench Divisional Court – the application would be granted but the court would not be minded to grant *certiorari* in such cases in the future since a statutory procedure existed under s 24(3) of the Criminal Justice Act 1967 (see now, Magistrates' Courts Act 1980 s 14(1)).

Comment (i) Section 14(1) provides that the defendant may make a statutory declaration that he did not know of any summons or proceedings until after the trial commenced. The statutory declaration must be served on the clerk to the justices within 14 days of the date when the defendant came to know of the proceedings whereupon the summons and subsequent proceedings are void.

(ii) Judicial review may be granted in exceptional cases. Thus in *R v Inspector of Taxes, ex parte Kissane* [1986] 2 All ER 37 taxpayers were granted leave to apply for judicial review against the decision of a tax inspector, even though they could have appealed to the Special Commissioners, because they could not recover costs on an appeal to the Commissioners (and see *R v Wiltshire CC, ex parte Lazard Bros* [1998] CLY 95).

An application for judicial review will not be granted unless the applicant has a sufficient interest in the matter to which the application relates

8   *Inland Revenue Commissioners v National Federation of Self-Employed and Small Businesses Ltd* [1981] 2 All ER 93

The Federation asked for an order of *mandamus* on the Commissioners of Inland Revenue to assess and collect arrears of income tax said to be due from casual employees on national newspapers. The long-standing practice of Fleet Street employers had been to pay the casuals without deduction of tax and for the casuals to supply fake names and addresses when drawing their pay in order to avoid tax. Their true identities were known only to their union which operated a closed shop and controlled all casual employment on the newspapers.

Held – by the House of Lords – the Federation could not be granted the order of *mandamus*. The Federation had no *locus standi*. 'The total confidentiality of assessments and of negotiations between individuals and the Revenue is a vital "element in the working of the system". As a matter of general principle I would hold that one taxpayer has no sufficient interest in asking the court to investigate the tax affairs of another taxpayer or to complain that the latter has been underassessed or overassessed; indeed there is a strong public interest that he should not. And this principle applies equally to groups of taxpayers: an aggregate of individuals each of whom has no interest cannot of itself have any interest.' (*Per* Lord Wilberforce)

A quashing order is also available to control tribunals which have acted beyond their powers

9   *R v London County Council, ex parte Entertainment Protection Association Ltd* [1931] 2 KB 215

The Council granted a new licence, under s 2 of the Cinematograph Act 1909, in respect of a cinema called the Streatham Astoria. One of the conditions contained in the Act was that the premises were not to be opened on Sundays, Christmas Day or Good Friday. Subsequent to the grant of the licence, a committee of the Council considered an application that the Streatham Astoria be allowed to open on the above-mentioned days. The committee resolved that 'no action be taken for the present in the event of the premises being opened . . . on Sundays, Christmas Day and Good Friday', subject to the applicants paying a sum of money to a selected charity. The Association challenged the ruling of the committee by *certiorari*.

Held – the Council was usurping its jurisdiction in breaking a condition of the licence, and that this was prohibited by the Act of 1909. *Certiorari* lay to quash the committee's ruling.

A court or other authority must not act if there is bias in the sense of any substantial pecuniary, personal or proprietary interest in the dispute before it. Natural justice also embraces the right to be heard

10   *Dimes* v *Grand Junction Canal* (1852) 3 HLC 759

Dimes was the Lord of a manor through which the canal passed, and he had been concerned in a case with the proprietors of the canal in which he disputed their title to certain land. Dimes had obtained an order of ejectment, but the canal company approached the Lord Chancellor (Lord Cottenham) to prevent Dimes enforcing the order and to confirm the company's title. The Lord Chancellor granted the relief sought. Dimes now appealed to the House of Lords on the ground that the Lord Chancellor was a shareholder in the company and was therefore biased.

Held – the Lord Chancellor's order granting the relief must be quashed because, although there was no evidence that his pecuniary interest had influenced him, yet it should not appear that any court had laboured under influences of this nature.

Comment (i) This case was distinguished in *R* v *Mulvihill* [1990] 1 All ER 436 which was an appeal from a conviction in connection with bank robberies. It appeared that the trial judge had 1,650 shares in one of them – National Westminster Bank plc. The Court of Appeal would not accept a plea of bias. This was a criminal trial with a jury, which had found M guilty so that the judge was bound to give effect to the verdict of the jury whether he personally agreed with it or not. *Dimes* was a civil matter without a jury, the decision being a matter for the judge alone.

(ii) The Court of Appeal ruled in *AT & T Corp* v *Saudi Cable Co* [2000] 2 All ER (Comm) 625 that the common law test of bias applies to an arbitrator conducting arbitration proceedings.

11   *R* v *Bingham Justices, ex parte Jowitt*, *The Times*, 3 July 1974

In announcing the conviction of the defendant for speeding, the chairman of the justices said: 'Quite the most unpleasant cases that we have to decide are those where the evidence is a direct conflict between a police officer and a member of the public. My principle in such cases has always been to believe the evidence of the police officer, and therefore we find the case proved.' Mr Jowitt applied to the Divisional Court for *certiorari* and it was *held* that the attitude of the chairman clearly amounted to bias and the conviction was quashed.

Comment (i) More recently, in *R* v *Liverpool City Justices, ex parte Topping* [1983] 1 All ER 490, a conviction by magistrates was quashed by *certiorari* on the basis of bias where it was shown that they had gone on to try a case of criminal damage after becoming aware from court computer sheets of T's previous convictions.

(ii) A famous case of non-pecuniary bias is *R* v *Bow Street Metropolitan Stipendiary Magistrate, ex parte Pinochet Ugarte (No 2)* [1999] 1 WLR 272. Following a House of Lords decision that PU as former head of the state of Chile did not have immunity from arrest and extradition, PU discovered that one of the judges, Lord Hoffmann, had been an unpaid director and chairman of the Amnesty International charity since 1990. The charity was a party to the proceedings and in favour of PU's extradition. In a subsequent decision recorded above, PU's application to a differently constituted House of Lords to set the decision aside was granted on the basis of Lord Hoffmann's possible bias.

(iii) As regards the right to be heard, see *R* v *Wear Valley District Council, ex parte Binks* [1985] 2 All ER 699 where B operated a hot-food take-away caravan at a market under an informal arrangement with the Council. She was given notice to quit without reasons or warning. Taylor, J quashed the Council's decision on the grounds of denial of natural justice. B had a right to be heard and to prior notification and reasons.

(iv) Again, in *R* v *Board of Governors of London Oratory School, ex parte R*, *The Times*, 17 February 1988 the rules of natural justice were applied to an expulsion of a child from school. The child must have an opportunity to state his case and know the nature of the accusations.

(v) The right to be heard was also raised in *R* v *Secretary of State for the Environment, ex parte Slot* [1998] CLY 2873. A landowner asked the county council to divert a bridleway on her land. There was an objection to this. The matter was resolved by written submissions but Ms Slot was not allowed to make representations nor to see the objector's submissions. The decision not to divert the bridleway was quashed by the Court of Appeal because a rule of natural justice had been infringed.

Rules of natural justice need not be applied where matters of national security are involved

12 *R v Secretary of State for Home Department, ex parte Hosenball* [1977] 3 All ER 452

Mr Hosenball was an American journalist working in London. He received a letter from the Home Department saying that the Home Secretary had decided to deport him in the interests of national security. The statement said that Mr Hosenball had tried to obtain and, indeed, had obtained, information harmful to the United Kingdom and relating to security arrangements and that that information was prejudicial to the safety of servants of the Crown. Mr Hosenball was given no further particulars and was told that he could not appeal but might make representations and appear before an independent advisory panel. Mr Hosenball did so but he did not see the panel's report, though the Home Secretary gave it his personal consideration. A deportation order was made under the Immigration Act 1971, s 5, and Mr Hosenball applied for an order of *certiorari* to quash the Home Secretary's decision. The Court of Appeal *held* unanimously that the application would be refused. Mr Hosenball had not been given enough information to enable him to meet the charge made against him. However, this was a case in which national security was involved, and where the state was in danger, even the rules of natural justice must take second place.

In addition, there was no infringement of Art 6 of the Convention for the Protection of Human Rights and Fundamental Freedoms. The European Commission of Human Rights in the case of Mr Philip Agee, whose deportation had been ordered by the Home Secretary at the same time as Mr Hosenball, had considered his application against the United Kingdom under the Convention as manifestly ill-founded. The Commission considered that where the public authorities of a state decided to deport an alien on grounds of security that constituted an Act of State falling within the public sphere this did not constitute a determination of his civil rights or obligations within the meaning of Art 6.

Comment In *R v Secretary of State for the Foreign and Commonwealth Office, ex parte The Council of Civil Service Unions, The Times*, 23 November 1984 (and [1984] 3 All ER 935) the House of Lords decided that the government, in preventing its employees at Government Communication Headquarters (GCHQ) from joining trade unions, was acting in the interests of national security, and was entitled to act irregularly as regards procedure by not consulting its employees. Procedural propriety must give way to national security, when personal rights taken away by the action of the executive conflict with that security.

The decision of a tribunal acting in breach of the rules of natural justice (or *ultra vires*) is void

13 *Ridge v Baldwin* [1963] 2 All ER 66

Mr Ridge, who was the Chief Constable of Brighton, had been acquitted on a charge of conspiring with other police officers to obstruct the course of justice, though the trial judge, Donovan, J said that Mr Ridge had not given the necessary professional or moral leadership to the Brighton Police Force. The Brighton Watch Committee subsequently dismissed Mr Ridge from his post as Chief Constable under a power in the Municipal Corporations Act 1882, giving them a right to dismiss 'any constable whom they think negligent in the discharge of his duty or otherwise unfit for the same'. Ridge was not given a chance to answer the charges or appear before the Watch Committee.

Held – by the House of Lords – the action taken, i.e. the dismissal, was void; Mr Ridge should have been heard.

A mandatory order lies to compel the exercise of a discretionary power but not in any particular way

14 *R v Commissioner of Police of the Metropolis, ex parte Blackburn* [1973] 1 All ER 324

Blackburn sought what was then an order of *mandamus* requiring the Commissioner of Police to secure the enforcement of the law against pornography upon various publishers and booksellers, and to reverse his decision that no prosecution should be undertaken without the prior consent of the Director of Public Prosecutions.

Held – by the Queen's Bench Divisional Court – although the evidence showed that pornography was widely available, the Commissioner, because of an under-manned force, had to decide an order of priorities to deal with various offences. In these circumstances it was perfectly proper for the Commissioner to seek the Director's advice before embarking on a prosecution, so long as he did not consider himself bound to follow his advice, and, accordingly, the situation in London was not attributable to any breach of legal duty by the Commissioner and the court would not interfere with the legitimate exercise of his discretion in the matter of police powers.

A mandatory order is not available against the Crown itself but it can issue against a Minister

15   *R v Secretary of State for Social Services, ex parte Grabaskey*, *The Times*, 15 December 1972

A dentist treating a patient with a broken tooth claimed payment not only for crowning the tooth but also for an amalgam filling. The latter claim was disallowed by the Dental Estimates Board and the Minister dismissed the appeal as unarguable under the proviso to reg 18 of the National Health Service (Service Committees and Tribunals) Regulations 1956.

Held – by the Queen's Bench Divisional Court – the dentist's case was reasonably arguable and accordingly the Minister had no jurisdiction to dismiss the appeal and *mandamus* would be granted requiring him to refer the matter to two dental referees.

Comment In *Padfield v Minister of Agriculture, Fisheries and Food* [1968] 1 All ER 694 the House of Lords decided that an order of *mandamus* should issue to the Minister of Agriculture, requiring him to refer a complaint by milk producers against the working of a Milk Marketing Board Scheme to a committee of investigation in the exercise of a discretionary power conferred on him by s 19 of the Agricultural Marketing Act 1958.

A simple declaration of what the law on a particular matter is may sometimes be an appropriate remedy against an administrative authority or a Minister

16   *Laker Airways v Department of Trade* [1977] 2 All ER 182

The Civil Aviation Authority granted Laker Airways a licence for 10 years from 1973 for a cheap passenger service between the UK and the USA called 'Skytrain'. Laker Airways was then designated as an airline under the Bermuda Agreement of 1946 made between the UK and the USA. Such designation was essential to get 'Skytrain' across the Atlantic. The Civil Aviation Act 1971, gave the Secretary of State for Trade wide powers to revoke licences without reference to anyone and subject only to questions being asked in Parliament. However, these powers were restricted to time of war or great national emergency or where international relations might be affected. This part of the Act could not, therefore, have been applicable in regard to the revocation of the licence granted to Laker

Airways. The Act also gave the Secretary of State power to give policy guidance in regard to civil aviation and it was under this power that the Secretary of State announced in 1976 by a White Paper that future policy would be to license only one UK airline on any given long route. Paragraphs 7 and 8 of the White Paper contained an instruction to the Civil Aviation Authority to revoke the licence for 'Skytrain'. Laker Airways now claimed a declaratory judgment that paras 7 and 8 were *ultra vires* and that the Secretary of State was not entitled to withdraw their licence. Mocatta, J granted the declaration sought, holding among other things that the power given to the Secretary of State to issue policy guidance did not extend to the revocation of licences in this way. On appeal to the Court of Appeal by the Department of Trade it was held, dismissing the appeal, that Laker Airways were entitled to the declaration sought. The Secretary of State could not lawfully use the procedure of 'guidance' for the revocation of licences.

Comment (i) An example of the use of a declaratory judgment against a Minister is to be found in *Congreve v Home Office* [1976] 1 All ER 697. Mr Congreve, on discovering that the price of a TV licence was to be increased shortly, bought a new one at the old rate before his old one expired thereby saving about £6. Some 25,000 others did the same. The Home Secretary claimed to revoke the licences under s 1(4) of the Wireless Telegraphy Act 1949, under which he had power. Mr C asked for a declaratory judgment that he could not do so. This was granted by the Court of Appeal. Mr C had done nothing unlawful and the revocation was a misuse by the Home Secretary of the powers in the 1949 Act.

(ii) Note the use of the declaratory judgment in *R v Secretary of State for Employment, ex parte Equal Opportunities Commission* (1994) in Chapter 19.

Where discretionary powers are entrusted to the executive by statute, the courts may examine the exercise of those powers in order to ensure that they have not been exercised mistakenly or improperly

17   *Secretary of State for Education and Science v Tameside Metropolitan Borough Council* [1976] 3 All ER 665

Tameside, a local education authority, submitted proposals for a comprehensive system of education to the Secretary of State in March 1975. These proposals were approved and Tameside planned to implement them by September 1976. In May 1976, local elections were held and the membership of Tameside changed from a Labour to a Conservative authority. The Conservative council decided not to implement the scheme for comprehensive education fully and on

7 June 1976 notified the Secretary of State of that intention. The Secretary of State was given a supervisory role by s 68 of the Education Act 1944. The section provides: 'If the Secretary of State is satisfied, either on complaint by any person or otherwise, that any local education authority or the managers or the governors of any county or voluntary school have acted or are proposing to act unreasonably with respect to the exercise of any power conferred or the performance of any duty imposed by or under this Act, he may, notwithstanding any enactment rendering the exercise of the power or the performance of the duty contingent upon the opinion of the authority or of the managers or governors of the authority, give such directions as to the exercise of the power or the performance of the duty as appear to him to be expedient.' On 11 June the Secretary of State replied to Tameside saying that it had acted, or was proposing to act, unreasonably within s 68 of the 1944 Act and accordingly directed Tameside to implement the 1975 scheme. Tameside refused, so the Secretary of State applied for *mandamus*. The Divisional Court of Queen's Bench granted the order but the Court of Appeal and the House of Lords reversed that decision. Before giving directions under s 68, the Secretary of State had to be satisfied that Tameside was acting unreasonably, i.e. that its conduct was such that no authority could reasonably engage in it. It had been alleged that there was insufficient time to carry out the necessary selection procedure for entry into grammar school. However, the House of Lords said that there were no grounds for concluding that the authority was acting unreasonably in taking the view that there was sufficient time available to carry out the necessary selection procedure. Although the Secretary of State might legitimately take the view that the authority's proposal to retain the grammar schools and to implement the selection procedure for the two schools where places were available was misguided or wrong, there were no grounds which could justify a conclusion that the proposal was such that no education authority, acting reasonably, would carry it out. It followed that the Secretary of State's direction was *ultra vires* and of no effect.

Advocates and litigators are now liable in contract or tort for negligence in connection with litigation

18 *Arthur J. S. Hall & Co (a firm) v Simons* [2000] 3 WLR 543

As regards the facts, three clients sued their solicitors for negligence. In the first case, Mr Simons claimed his solicitors negligently allowed him to become involved in lengthy and expensive litigation when they should have advised him to settle. In the second case, Mr Barrett claimed his solicitors, involved in matrimonial proceedings out of court, negligently advised him to settle his divorced wife's claim for a share of the matrimonial home on disadvantageous terms. In the third case, Mrs Harris complained about the terms on which her solicitors, involved in matrimonial proceedings out of court, advised her to settle her maintenance claim against her ex-husband. The solicitors applied for the claims to be struck out, relying on the advocates' immunity from suit in negligence. The Court of Appeal heard the cases together and ruled that in none of them were the solicitors immune from suit and ordered that the claims be reinstated. The solicitors appealed to the House of Lords. The main issue for the House of Lords to decide was whether the current immunity of both solicitors and barristers in relation to the conduct of legal proceedings as set out in *Rondel* should continue.

The judges stated that the issue was relevant to both barristers and solicitor advocates. The Court of Appeal had decided that in all three cases the alleged negligence of the solicitors was not within the scope of the immunity as extended to out-of-court work. The solicitors' advice was not closely connected with the way in which the cases would have been conducted in court if not settled. However, in the House of Lords, counsel on behalf of the three clients made a basic attack on the immunity in general and argued that it should be abolished.

The judges considered the changes in society and in the law that have taken place since the decision in *Rondel* and decided that it was appropriate to review the whole matter of advocates' immunity from liability for the negligent conduct of a case in court. Maintaining such immunity depended on the balance between, on the one hand, the normal right of the individual to be compensated for a legal wrong done to him and, on the other, the advantages which accrued to the public interest from such an immunity.

As regards the decision, the public interest in the administration of justice no longer required that advocates enjoy immunity from suit for alleged negligence in the conduct of litigation. The appeal was dismissed.

Comment (i) Advocates therefore no longer enjoy immunity from suit in respect of their conduct of civil and criminal proceedings, although three of the seven judges dissented on the conduct of criminal proceedings, thinking that the immunity should be preserved in such proceedings. It will not be easy to sue advocates successfully since Lord Hoffmann, in particular, suggested that the collateral attack principle would be applied, certainly in criminal proceedings and to some extent in civil matters. This means that the court may strike out claims that involve the same issues being tried again as part of proving an advocate's negligence. It is also unclear as to whether the immunity is retrospective, as case law can be. Lord Hope expressed the view (without reasons) that the abolition of immunity would only apply to future cases.

(ii) In *Moy v Pettman Smith (a firm) and another* [2005] 1 All ER 903 the House of Lords ruled that when giving clients advice as to whether to accept a settlement offer at the door of the court and given that the advice was not negligent barristers need not spell out all the factors and reasons behind their advice. The claimant builder sustained fractures of the left leg. The surgical treatment was he alleged carried out negligently. He brought a claim against the relevant health authority. In this claim a necessary report by a consultant orthopaedic surgeon was not obtained by the claimant's solicitors in time. Eventually a report was made and the claimant's barrister, Ms Perry, asked for an adjournment of the proceedings to adduce further evidence. A county court judge turned her request down and the proceedings went on. The health authority had made an offer to settle out of court in the sum of £150,000. However Ms Perry advised her client, the claimant, to refuse it, as he would get more by proceeding to trial. The offer was made by the health authority on the day of the trial. Ms Perry had in mind that the claimant would have a separate action against the solicitors which would make up any shortfall. This was the claimant's safety net but this did not form part of Ms Perry's advice to continue to trial. The offer of £150,000 was turned down by the claimant. When the health authority realised that the report would not be available in this trial, they dropped their offer to £120,000, which the claimant accepted contrary to advice. He then claimed against Ms Perry for negligent advice and made a separate claim against the solicitors for alleged negligence in failing to obtain the report in time to comply with the timetable set for the proceedings. Their Lordships ruled that Ms Perry was not in breach of her duty to the claimant. She was not obliged to spell out all the factors and reasons behind her advice.

Criminal conduct cannot be prevented by injunction unless the Attorney-General is prepared to take or agree to the taking of proceedings

19   *Gouriet v Union of Post Office Workers* [1977] 3 All ER 70

Under ss 58 and 68 of the Post Office Act 1953, it is an offence punishable by fine and imprisonment for persons employed by the Post Office wilfully to delay or omit to deliver packets and messages in the course of transmission and for any person to solicit or endeavour to procure another to commit such an offence. The Council of the Union of Post Office Workers called on its members not to handle mail to South Africa for a week because they disapproved of South Africa's policies. The claimant, who was the Secretary of the National Association for Freedom, asked the Attorney-General for his consent to act as claimant in relator proceedings for an injunction to restrain the Union from soliciting or endeavouring to procure any person wilfully to detain or delay a postal packet in the course of transmission to South Africa. The Attorney-General refused. The claimant took the matter to court and eventually the House of Lords decided that proceedings to prevent the infringement of public rights can only be instituted by the consent of the Attorney-General unless an individual has a special interest as where his private rights are threatened. Mr Gouriet had no such interest and was not entitled to the relief sought. Presumably, a company which dealt on a regular basis with South Africa by mail would have had the necessary *locus standi*.

CRIMINAL PROCEDURE

Excessive reporting of criminal proceedings: no need to show prejudice to accused

20   *The Eastbourne Herald Case*, *The Times*, 12 June 1973

The *Eastbourne Herald* published an article upon the committal proceedings of a case in which a man was charged with unlawful sexual intercourse. The prosecution of the editor and proprietors which followed was based on the following matters which appeared in the articles:

(*a*) a headline reading 'New Year's day Bridegroom Bailed';

(*b*) a description of the offence charged as being 'serious';

(*c*) a description of the alleged offender as 'bespectacled and dressed in a dark suit';

(*d*) a note to the effect that he had been 'married at St Michael's Church on New Year's Day';

(*e*) a reference to the way in which the prosecuting solicitor had handled the case.

The editor and proprietors were each found guilty by the Eastbourne magistrates on the five counts relating to these different passages and were each fined a total of £2,000 and ordered to pay £37.50 costs. This strange decision stems initially from the fact that liability may be incurred under what is now s 8(4) of the Magistrates' Courts Act 1980 where a report of committal proceedings contains any details other than those permitted by s 8(4) and quite irrespective of whether or not the details are potentially prejudicial in nature. All that the prosecution is required to show is:

(a) that the defendant published a report of committal proceedings to which the restrictions apply; and
(b) that the report contained matters for which no specific provision is made in s 8(4).

Thus, in this case it was an offence under the Act to describe unlawful sexual intercourse as a 'serious' offence for s 8(4) permits of no such qualifying adjective. Equally, it was an offence to describe the defendant as 'bespectacled and dressed in a dark suit' for s 8(4) only provides for reference to his name, address and occupation. Furthermore, it is not necessary for the prosecution to show that the offending item purported to be an account of what transpired in court, provided only that it is contained within a report of committal proceedings. Thus, in this case the magistrates held that it was an offence under the Act to refer to the fact that the defendant had been married at St Michael's Church on New Year's Day although this piece of background information does not appear to have been adduced as evidence in court.

THE LAW-MAKING PROCESS I: THE UK PARLIAMENT

The courts cannot examine the proceedings of Parliament to see whether an act or delegated legislation can be regarded as invalid on the ground that it was obtained by some irregularity or fraud

21 *British Railways Board v Pickin* [1974] 1 All ER 609

Section 259 of the Bristol and Exeter Railways Act 1836 provides that if the railway, which it set up, should at any time be abandoned, the land acquired for the track should vest in the adjoining landowners; the same provision was contained in the Act setting up the Yatton to Clevedon line. The British Railways Board, in whom the railways had become vested, closed the line in the early 1960s and took up the tracks in 1969. A private Act of Parliament, the British Railways Act, was passed in 1968 cancelling the effect of s 259 and vesting the track in the Board; the Act's

preamble recited that plans and books of reference had been deposited with Somerset County Council. Pickin, who objected to the closing of the line, purchased a few feet of land adjoining the track in 1969 and sought a declaration that he owned the land as far as the middle of the track, the railway having been abandoned within s 259. In reply to the Board's defence that the land was vested in it by virtue of s 18 of the Act of 1968, Pickin pleaded that that Act had contained a false recital in that the requisite documents had not been deposited, that the Board had misled Parliament in obtaining the Act *ex parte* (in effect, without hearing other views) and that it was ineffective to deprive him of his land.

Held – by the House of Lords – the courts had no power to examine proceedings in Parliament in order to determine whether the passing of an Act was obtained by means of any irregularity or fraud; Mr Pickin failed.

Comment (i) As regards delegated legislation, in *R v Immigration Appeal Tribunal, ex parte Joyles* [1972] 3 All ER 213 it was alleged that some regulations made under the Immigration Appeals Act 1969 had not been properly laid before Parliament as required by s 24(2) of the 1969 Act. A Divisional Court of the Queen's Bench relied on letters from the Clerks of the Journal to the Commons and Lords stating that the rules had been duly presented and laid. The court was not prepared to go further and examine the internal proceedings of Parliament.

(ii) Of course, if it is argued that the legislation conflicts with EC law, the court is obliged to give interim relief and suspend the operation of the legislation until a final ruling is obtained (see *Factortame Ltd v Secretary of State for Transport* (*No 2*) [1991] 1 All ER 70).

Delegated legislation – judicial control; the application of the doctrine of *ultra vires*

22 *Hotel and Catering Industry Training Board v Automobile Proprietary Ltd* [1969] 2 All ER 582

This was a test case brought by the Board to decide whether the Industrial Training (Hotel and Catering Board) Order 1966 made by the Minister of Labour pursuant to powers conferred upon him by the Industrial Training Act 1964, was *ultra vires* in so far as it purported to extend to any members' clubs. If the order was *ultra vires*, the RAC club in Pall Mall was not liable to pay a levy to the Board by reason of its activities in providing midday and evening meals and board and lodging for reward. The relevant order was made under s 1(1) of the Act of 1964, which provides that the Minister may 'for the purpose of making better provision for . . . training . . . for employment in any activities of industry or commerce' make an order specifying 'those activities', and establishing a board to exercise the functions of an industrial training board. The 1966 order specified 'the activities' as including the supply of main meals and lodgings for reward by a members' club. Nevertheless, this provision was only valid if the activities of members' clubs were activities of 'industry or commerce'.

Held – by the House of Lords – the general object of the Act of 1964 was to provide employers in industry and commerce with trained personnel and to finance the training by a levy on employers in the industry, and that it was not intended to allow a levy to be made on private institutions like members' clubs. Although such institutions might pursue activities not unlike those of a hotel keeper, they could not be regarded as within the phrase 'activities of industry or commerce'.

Comment The question of *ultra vires* was raised in *R v Secretary of State for the Environment, ex parte Spath Holme Ltd* [2000] 1 All ER 884 where Spath Holme, the landlord of flats, challenged the validity of the Rent Acts (Maximum Fair Rent) Order 1999 made under the Landlord and Tenant Act 1985, s 31. The 1985 Act gave power to cap rent increases to tenants to combat inflation, but the 1999 Order, which was made at a time of very low inflation, was intended purely to cap rent increases. The Court of Appeal, dealing with judicial review asked for by Spath Holme, ruled that the 1999 Order was *ultra vires* and of no effect.

This decision was subsequently affirmed by the House of Lords (see *R v Secretary of State for the Environment ex parte Spath Holme Ltd* [2001] 1 All ER 195).

Local authority by-laws can be challenged in the courts as being unreasonable

23   **Burnley Borough Council v England**, *The Times*, 15 July 1978

In this case it was *held* that a by-law of the Council prohibiting any person from causing any dog belonging to him or in his charge to enter or remain in specified pleasure grounds other than a guide dog in the charge of a blind person was not unreasonable. The Council was concerned about the fouling of pleasure grounds by dogs. The court went on to say that a by-law could be unreasonable if so unjust and oppressive that no reasonable council could have made it – for example, a by-law directed against dog owners with red hair.

Interpretation Act 1978: application to statutory interpretation

24   **Hutton v Esher Urban District Council** [1973] 2 All ER 1123

The Council proposed to construct a sewer to drain surface water from houses and roads and also to take flood water from a river. The most economical line of the sewer would take it straight through the claimant's bungalow, which would have to be demolished but might be rebuilt after the sewer had been constructed. The Public Health Act 1936 empowered the Council to construct a public sewer 'in, on, or over any land not forming part of a street'. The claimant argued that the expression 'land' did not include buildings and, therefore, the Council had no power to demolish his bungalow. However, s 3 of the Interpretation Act of 1889 (see now the Interpretation Act 1978, s 5 and Sch 1) provided that unless a contrary intention appears, the expression 'land' includes buildings. It was *held* – by the Court of Appeal – that the Interpretation Act was applicable and 'land', therefore, included buildings. In consequence, the Council had the power to demolish the claimant's bungalow.

Judicial interpretation of statutes: the mischief rule: a statute is to be construed so as to suppress the mischief in the common law and advance the remedy

25   **Gardiner v Sevenoaks RDC** (1950) 66 TLR 1091

The local authority served a notice under the Celluloid and Cinematograph Film Act 1922 on the occupier of a cave where film was stored, requiring him to comply with certain safety regulations. Obviously, the common law had no such rules. The cave was described in the notice as 'premises'. Gardiner, who was the occupier, appealed against the notice on the ground that a cave could not be considered 'premises' for the purposes of the Act.

Held – whilst it was not possible to lay down that every cave would be 'premises' for all purposes, the Act was a safety Act and was designed to protect persons in the neighbourhood and those working in the place of storage. Therefore, under the 'mischief rule', this cave was 'premises' for the purposes of the Act.

Comment The mischief rule is very close to the more recent recommendation of the Law Commission for a purposive interpretation of statutes.

The golden rule of interpretation: extends the literal rule where the application of that rule leads to an absurd result

26 *Keene* v *Muncaster* [1980] RTR 377

Regulation 115 of the Motor Vehicles (Construction and Use) Regulations 1973 provides that a motorist may only park a motor vehicle on the road during the hours of darkness with the nearside of the vehicle to the kerb. There is an exception to this if he has the permission of a police officer in uniform to do otherwise. The defendant, a police officer in uniform, parked his vehicle with the offside to the kerb during the hours of darkness. When he was charged with an offence under reg 115, he claimed that he had given himself permission to park that way. He was convicted by the magistrates and appealed to the Divisional Court of Queen's Bench.

Held – dismissing the appeal – under the golden rule of interpretation the word 'permission' meant permission had to be requested by one person from another. The permission could not be given by the person whose vehicle was parked with the offside to the kerb.

Comment The golden rule of interpretation was considered in *Prince of Hanover* v *Attorney-General* (1957) to which reference could usefully be made again at this point.

The *ejusdem generis* rule

27 *Lane* v *London Electricity Board* [1955] 1 All ER 324

The claimant was an electrician employed by the defendant to install additional lighting in one of its sub-stations. While inspecting the sub-station, he tripped on the edge of an open duct and fell, sustaining injuries. The claimant claimed that the defendant was in breach of its statutory duty under the Electricity (Factories Act) Special Regulations in that the part of the premises where the accident occurred was not adequately lighted to prevent 'danger'.

Held – it appeared that the word 'danger' in the regulations meant 'danger from shock, burn or other injury'. Danger from tripping was not *ejusdem generis*, since the specific words related to forms of danger resulting from contact with electricity.

Comment This summary is concerned only with the claimant's claim under the Regulations. The failure of this claim did not prevent a claim for damages for negligence at common law.

The *expressio unius est exclusio alterius* rule of statutory interpretation: the expression of one thing implies the exclusion of another

28 *R* v *Immigration Appeals Adjudicator, ex parte Crew*, *The Times*, 26 November 1982

An Immigration Appeals Tribunal had, in interpreting the Immigration Act 1971, ruled that a woman who was born in Hong Kong of a Chinese mother and putative English father was not entitled to a certificate of patriality (a certificate allowing immigration). There was an appeal to the Court of Appeal where the sole question was whether the word 'parent' used in the 1971 Act included the father of an illegitimate child. The father in this case was unknown. It was held that since the definition section in the 1971 Act specifically mentioned the mother alone in the context of an illegitimate child, the rule *expressio unius est exclusio alterius* served to exclude the father of an illegitimate child for these purposes as a 'parent'. The appeal was dismissed. The Act required patriality to be decided on the basis of the mother alone. The daughter of a Chinese mother was not a patrial.

The *noscitur a sociis* rule of statutory interpretation: the meaning of a word may be gathered from its context

29 *Muir* v *Keay* (1875) LR 10 QB 594

Section 6 of the Refreshment Houses Act 1860 stated that all houses, rooms, shops or buildings, kept open for public refreshment, resort and entertainment during certain hours of the night, must be licensed. The defendant had premises called 'The Café', and certain persons were found there during the night when the café was open. They were being supplied with cigars, coffee and ginger beer which they were seen to consume. The justices convicted the defendant because the premises were not licensed. He appealed to the Divisional Court by case stated, suggesting that a licence was required only if 'entertainment' in terms, e.g., of music or dancing was going on. The Divisional Court, applying the *noscitur a sociis* rule, *held* – that 'entertainment', because of the context in which it appeared in the Act of 1860, meant matters of bodily comfort and not matters of mental enjoyment such as theatrical or musical performances with which the word 'entertainment' is so often associated in other contexts. The justices were, therefore, right to convict.

THE LAW-MAKING PROCESS II: CASE LAW AND THE LEGISLATIVE ORGANS OF THE EUROPEAN UNION

Since its declaration of 1966 the House of Lords is not bound by its own decisions: application of the declaration

30 *Schorsch Meier Gmbh v Hennin* [1975] 1 All ER 152

The claimant, which carried on business in West Germany, had sold goods to the defendants in England. They had not been paid in full for the goods and DM 3,756 remained owing. At the date of the invoice the sterling equivalent of this sum was £452, but between the invoice date and the date of the county court summons sterling had been devalued so that the value of £452 was only £266. Consequently, the claimant asked for judgment in deutschmarks. The difficulty facing the claimant was that the House of Lords had decided in *Re United Railways of Havana* [1960] 2 All ER 332 that an English court could not give judgment for an amount in foreign currency. The claimant challenged this on the ground that the *Havana* case ran contrary to Art 106 (now 107) of the EEC Treaty (now EC Treaty). The county court judge held that he was bound by the *Havana* case and could only give judgment in sterling. On appeal, however, the Court of Appeal with Lord Denning, MR came to a different decision and found for the claimant on two grounds – (i) as an English court had since *Beswick v Beswick* (1967) the power to order specific performance of a contract to make a money payment, there was no longer a justification for the rule in *Havana* that judgment could only be given for a sum of money in sterling; (ii) the effect of Art 106 (now 107) of the EEC Treaty (now EC Treaty) was to require the English courts to give judgment in favour of a creditor of a member state in the currency of that state.

31 *Miliangos v George Frank (Textiles) Ltd* [1975] 3 All ER 801

This case was concerned with a contract for the sale of polyester yarn and, in particular, the money of payment and the money of account in the contract were in Swiss francs. The Swiss seller, who was unpaid, was allowed in view of the decision in *Schorsch Meier* to claim payment in Swiss francs. Sterling had fallen in value against the Swiss franc and if the new rule in *Schorsch* were to be applied, the claimant stood to gain £60,000 as opposed to £42,000 under the *Havana*

principle. At first instance Bristow, J *held* that the decision in *Schorsch* had been decided *per incuriam*, the Court of Appeal having been bound by the *Havana* case. Consequently, he felt able to give a judgment only in sterling. From his judgment an appeal was made to the Court of Appeal and his decision was reversed by a court presided over by Lord Denning, who had been in the majority in the Court of Appeal when *Schorsch* was decided. From the judgment of the Court of Appeal a further appeal was made to the House of Lords. Their Lordships quickly reached the conclusion that the *Havana* case had not been overruled, since the only means by which that could have been done was by the House of Lords itself under the declaration of 1966 and, accordingly, the Court of Appeal should have felt bound by the case. It was, however, now open for the House of Lords to re-examine its previous decision in *Havana*. The House of Lords concluded that as the situation regarding currency stability had substantially changed since 1961 when the *Havana* case was decided, there was justification for a departure from that decision under the 1966 declaration. Accordingly, the House refused to follow the *Havana* case and held that an English court may give judgment in a foreign currency. However, the majority of their Lordships were highly critical of the wide interpretation of Art 106 (now 107) adopted by the Court of Appeal, Switzerland not being a member of the Common Market, and it remains to be seen when the matter comes before the courts again whether that Article is adequate to sustain the view taken in this case.

Comment (i) In *Fitzleet Estates Ltd v Cherry (Inspector of Taxes)* [1977] 3 All ER 996, a case concerned with the tax treatment of interest paid on a loan used to buy property, the House of Lords refused to depart from its previous decision in *Chancery Lane Safe Deposit and Offices Co Ltd* [1966] 1 All ER 1 and stated that, in the absence of a change of circumstances, it would not normally depart from a previous decision unless there were serious doubts as to its correctness. So change of circumstances would seem to be the major factor. It will be noted that in the *Miliangos* case the circumstances were very different from those which applied when the *Havana* case was decided. The situation regarding currency stability had changed. Currency values were much more volatile and this justified a departure from the *Havana* case.

(ii) A further example of the use of the 1966 declaration can be seen in *Murphy v Brentwood District Council* (1990) (see Chapter 21) where the House of Lords departed from a previous decision because there were serious doubts as to its correctness.

Precedent: Court of Appeal Criminal Division: considerations applying on a criminal appeal

32 R v Gould [1968] 1 All ER 849

The appellant was convicted of bigamy although when he remarried he believed on reasonable grounds that a decree *nisi* of divorce in respect of his previous marriage had been made absolute which it had not, so that he was still married at the time of the second ceremony. The Court of Criminal Appeal in *R v Wheat and Stocks* [1921] 2 KB 119 had decided on similar facts that a reasonable belief in the dissolution of a previous marriage was no defence. In this appeal to the Court of Appeal (Criminal Division) the court quashed the conviction *holding* that in spite of the decision in *R v Wheat and Stocks*, a defendant's honest belief on reasonable grounds that at the time of his second marriage his former marriage had been dissolved was a good defence to a charge of bigamy. Diplock, LJ, giving the judgment of the court, said that in its criminal jurisdiction the Court of Appeal does not apply the doctrine of *stare decisis* as rigidly as in its civil jurisdiction, and if it is of the opinion that the law has been misapplied or misunderstood it will depart from a previous decision.

Comment In this case a three-judge court expressly overruled *Wheat and Stocks* which was itself a decision of a five-judge Court of Criminal Appeal.

Cause of action and issue estoppel distinguished

33 Arnold v National Westminster Bank plc [1990] 1 All ER 529

The bank leased premises to the claimants for a term of years. The lease had rent review clauses in it. The reviews were to take place every five years. The review was to give the bank as landlords a 'fair market rent' according to a formula in the lease. At the first review in 1983 the judge who was called upon to interpret the review clause decided that upon its wording he had to give a rent on the basis that there were no review clauses in the lease. This meant a rent which would last until the end of the lease and such a rent would have to be some 20 per cent more than if the fair rent was based on a lease with regular reviews of rent.

The parties went to court again on the 1988 review and that litigation produced this decision. It appeared that following the judge's decision on the 1983 review other cases interpreting similar review clauses decided that the wording meant a fair rent based on a lease with regular rent reviews. The claimants wanted such a decision in regard to the 1988 review. The bank said the court could not give such a decision because the matter had been decided in 1983 and must stand for the whole of the lease in terms of the interpretation of the rent review clause. The Court of Appeal said that the issue could be looked at again in regard to the 1988 review. This was not cause of action estoppel but only issue estoppel and the issue could be litigated again.

Comment It is worth noting that cause of action estoppel would prevent the overruling of the 1983 decision but at least the *issue* which was at the root of the 1983 decision could be looked at again for the future.

Supremacy of EC law

34 Factortame Ltd v Secretary of State for Transport (No 2) [1991] 1 All ER 70

The problem in this case was the Merchant Shipping Act 1988. This required 75 per cent of directors and shareholders in companies operating fishing vessels in UK waters to be British. This effectively barred certain ships owned by UK companies controlled by Spanish nationals from fishing in British waters. This was alleged to be in conflict with the Treaty of Rome because it deprived Spanish-controlled companies and, by implication, their Spanish directors and members, of their EC rights under the common fishing policy. The matter was going to take up to two years to sort out. The Spanish would suffer financial loss during that time. They asked the court for a suspension of the operation of the 1988 Act until the final issue had been determined. The House of Lords eventually decided to refer the matter to the European Court which gave an unequivocal answer. It laid down that Community law must be fully and uniformly applied in all the member states and that a relevant Community law rendered automatically inapplicable any conflicting provision of national law. It followed that the courts were obliged to grant interim relief in cases of alleged conflict, where as in this case the only obstacle was a rule of national law. Accordingly, the House of Lords granted interim relief by suspending the relevant provision of the 1988 Act until a final ruling on the issue of conflict could be obtained.

Comment (i) The supremacy of EC law has been upheld, not only where there is a conflict, but even where there might be. The decision makes a big dent in parliamentary supremacy, to say the least.

(ii) It is worth noting that the UK Parliament repealed the relevant sections of the 1988 Act in 1993.

(iii) In 1999 the House of Lords held that Factortame Ltd and 96 other companies or shareholders or directors which had been operating British-registered fishing vessels that were barred when the 1988 Act was implemented were entitled to damages from the UK government for breach of the EC common fisheries policy (see *R v Secretary of State for Transport, ex parte Factortame Ltd and Others* [1999] 4 All ER 906).

PERSONS AND THE CROWN

Domicile of origin and choice: effect on taxation

35 *IRC v Bullock* [1976] 3 All ER 353

Mr Bullock was born in Nova Scotia in 1910 and had his domicile of origin there. In 1932 he came to England to join the RAF, intending to go back to Canada when his service was completed. In 1946 he married an Englishwoman and they went on a number of visits to Mr Bullock's father in Canada. In 1959 Mr Bullock retired from the RAF and took up civilian employment in England. In 1961 he was able to retire fully, having become entitled to money from his father's estate on the latter's death. Mr Bullock had always tried to persuade his wife to live in Canada but she would not do so. Even so, Mr Bullock always hoped she would change her mind. In 1966 he made a will subject to Nova Scotian law under which he said that his domicile was Nova Scotia and that he intended to return and remain there if his wife died before him. The Crown claimed that he had acquired a domicile of choice in England and that all his income from Canada was chargeable to income tax. If Mr Bullock was not domiciled in England, tax would be chargeable only on that part of the income from his father's estate which was actually sent to him in England. This was less than all the income. It was *held* – by the Court of Appeal – that the fact that Mr Bullock had established a matrimonial home in England was evidence of his intention, but was not conclusive. On the evidence of his retention of Canadian citizenship and of the terms of a declaration as to domicile in his will, it was impossible not to hold that Mr Bullock had always maintained a firm intention to return to Canada in the event of his surviving his wife, and there was a sufficiently substantial possibility of his surviving his wife to justify regarding the intention to return as a real determination to do so, in that event, rather than a vague hope or aspiration. Accordingly, Mr Bullock could not be said to have formed the intention to acquire an English domicile of choice. Thus, he could be taxed only on that part of the Canadian estate which was remitted to England.

Domicile: a person who abandons a domicile of choice without acquiring another reverts to the domicile of origin

36 *Tee v Tee* [1973] 3 All ER 1105

The parties were married in England in November 1946 when the husband was a domiciled Englishman and the wife was an American citizen. In 1951 they went to the United States and in 1953 the husband became an American citizen and acquired a domicile of choice in that country. In 1960 the husband was posted to Germany by his employer, and in 1965 he left his wife and set up home with a German woman by whom he had two children. Some time during 1966/7 the husband decided to make his permanent home in England, but it was not until November 1972 that the husband with his mistress and children actually took up residence in the house he had bought in England in May 1972. The husband had been granted a permit to work in England in 1969. In July 1972, he presented a petition for divorce. The wife challenged the jurisdiction of the English court to hear this petition, and the question for the court was whether the husband was domiciled in England in July 1972.

Held – by the Court of Appeal – the husband was domiciled in England. He had left the United States in 1960 and the intention not to return there was formed over the period 1966/7. In consequence, the two elements necessary to establish the abandonment of a domicile of choice had been proved. When a domicile of choice was lost, the domicile of origin revives; the fact that the husband did not actually take up permanent residence in England until 1972 was immaterial since it is not necessary for the revival of a domicile of origin that residence should also be taken up in that country.

Domicile: evidence of change: naturalisation: purchase of business

37 *Steiner v Inland Revenue Commissioners* [1973] STC 547

Steiner was born in the former Austro-Hungarian Empire. He lived in Berlin from 1906 but was driven out of Germany by the Nazis in 1939 and came to England. He acquired a flat in London in 1941 and by the end of 1948 had established a business in England and was naturalised in 1948. From 1948 to 1963 he spent six months of each year in Berlin where he had a property. He was assessed to income tax for the years 1960/61 to 1966/7 on rents on properties in West Berlin, the Special Commissioners holding that he had acquired an English domicile of choice. He appealed.

Held – by the Court of Appeal – the appeal would be dismissed; there were no grounds for holding the Special Commissioners' decision to be wrong in law. The court refused to grant leave to appeal to the House of Lords.

Comment (i) If a person is domiciled or resident in England and Wales, tax is charged on the full amount of income arising within a given year wherever made or received (Income and Corporation Taxes Act (1988), ss 334–336).

(ii) See also *IRC* v *Bullock* (1976) for other examples of evidence of change of domicile, e.g. by a will.

Racial discrimination: inducement to discrimination on racial grounds

38 *The Commission for Racial Equality* v *Imperial Society of Teachers of Dancing* [1983] ICR 473

The Society wished to employ a filing clerk. A telephone call was made to a local girls' school to find a suitable applicant. During the course of the phone call it was made clear that a 'coloured girl' would be out of place because there were no coloured employees. It was *held* by the Employment Appeal Tribunal that the words 'to induce' in s 31 of the Race Relations Act 1976 meant to persuade or to prevail upon or to bring about, and the words used did constitute an attempt to induce the head of careers at the girls' school not to send a coloured girl. In consequence, the Society had contravened s 31.

Sex discrimination: facilities and services

39 *Gill* v *El Vino Co Ltd* [1983] 1 All ER 398

The claimants, both women, entered a wine bar and stood at the bar and ordered wine. They were refused service under house rules but were told that if they would sit at a table their drinks would be brought to them. The claimants brought an action alleging breach of the 1975 Act. It was *held* – by the Court of Appeal – that applying the simple words of the Act the defendants had failed to provide the claimants with facilities afforded to men and by doing so they had treated women less favourably than men contrary to the 1975 Act.

Comment (i) In *James* v *Eastleigh Borough Council* [1990] 2 All ER 607 the claimant and his wife, who were both retired and aged 61, went to a leisure centre run by the Council. The wife was admitted to the swimming pool free because she was of pensionable age. The claimant had to pay because he was not. He brought proceedings alleging discrimination. Eventually the House of Lords ruled that the distinction operated by the Council was unlawful direct discrimination on the grounds of sex.

(ii) In *McConomy* v *Croft Inns* [1992] IRLR 561 the complainant was refused a drink in a public house because he wore two earrings in his left ear. He was awarded £250 damages for sex discrimination since clearly there would have been no question of not serving a woman because she was wearing earrings.

(iii) The Race Relations Act 1976, s 25 prohibits racial discrimination in relation to membership of political and social clubs with a membership of more than 25. The Sex Discrimination Act 1975 does not carry such a prohibition. Sex discrimination by private clubs is not outlawed under the provisions of the SDA 1975 relating to provision of services or facilities to the public or a section of it since private membership clubs cannot be said to provide such facilities or services. As the *Gill* case shows the position is different in relation to pubs or clubs open to the public.

Sex discrimination: credit: a requirement that a woman must have her husband's guarantee is unlawful

40 *Quinn* v *Williams Furniture Ltd* [1981] ICR 328

Mrs Quinn wanted to buy certain goods from a shop on hire-purchase terms. She was told by the shop assistant that if she took out a hire-purchase agreement her husband would have to give a guarantee for the credit allowed, but if he took out the agreement she would not be required to give a guarantee of his liability. She bought the goods and took out the agreement herself, her husband acting as guarantor. She then complained that the shop's refusal to give her credit facilities on the same basis as they would to a man in her position was a breach of the Sex Discrimination Act 1975. The Court of Appeal held that it was. On the facts Mrs Quinn had not been allowed credit facilities in the same way as they would normally be offered to men. Even a suggestion or advice such as this to get her husband's guarantee was unlawful. There did not have to be an outright refusal of credit.

Comment The case shows that credit restrictions based on sex, at one time usual in business, may now infringe the 1975 Act.

A registered company has a separate legal entity

41 *Salomon* v *Salomon & Co* [1897] AC 22

Salomon carried on business as a leather merchant and boot manufacturer. In 1892 he formed a limited company to take over the business. The memorandum of association was signed by Salomon, his wife, daughter and four sons. Each subscribed for one share. The company paid £38,782 to Salomon for the business and the mode of payment was to give Salomon £10,000 in debentures, secured by a floating charge, 20,000 shares of £1 each and £8,782 in cash. The company fell on hard times and a liquidator was appointed. The debts of the unsecured creditors amounted to nearly £8,000, and the company's assets were approximately £6,000. The unsecured creditors claimed all the remaining assets on the ground that the company was a mere alias or agent for Salomon.

Held – the company was a separate and distinct person. The debentures were perfectly valid and, therefore, Salomon was entitled to the remaining assets in part payment of the secured debentures held by him.

Comment In a company winding-up such as this, secured creditors such as Mr Salomon must be paid before the unsecured (or trade) creditors.

Looking behind the corporate mask

42 *Gilford Motor Company v Horne* [1933] Ch 935

Mr Horne had been employed by Gilford. He had agreed to a restraint of trade in his contract under which he would not approach the company's customers to try to get them to transfer their custom to any similar business which Mr Horne might run himself. Mr Horne left his job with Gilford and set up a similar business using a registered company structure. He then began to send out circulars to the customers of Gilford inviting them to do business with his company. Gilford asked the court for an injunction to stop Mr Horne's activities and he said he was not competing but his company was and that the company had not agreed to a restraint of trade. However, an injunction was granted against both Mr Horne and his company to stop the circularisation of Gilford's customers. The corporate structure could not be used to evade legal responsibilities.

A member may obtain an injunction to restrain a company from acting in a manner inconsistent with its constitution

43 *Jenkin v Pharmaceutical Society* [1921] 1 Ch 392

The defendant society was incorporated by Royal Charter in 1843 for the purpose of advancing chemistry and pharmacy and promoting a uniform system of education of those who should practise the same, and for the protection of those who carried on the business of chemists or druggists.

Held – the expenditure of the funds of the society in the formation of an industrial committee, to attempt to regulate hours of work and wages and conditions of work between employers and employee members of the society, was *ultra vires* the charter, because it was a trade union activity which was not contemplated by the Charter of 1843. Further, the expenditure of money on an insurance scheme for members was also not within the powers given in the charter, for it amounted to converting the defendant society into an insurance company. The claimant, a member of the society, was entitled to an injunction to restrain the society from implementing the above schemes.

Disclosure of documents: Crown or public interest privilege

44 *Norwich Pharmacal Co v Commissioners of Customs and Excise* [1973] 2 All ER 943

The claimants held the patent of a chemical compound used in animal foods, which they discovered was being infringed by unknown importers. The Commissioners of Customs and Excise were allowing the importation and charging duty thereon, and consequently knew the identity of the importers concerned. The claimants brought proceedings against the Commissioners for infringement of their patent, and for an order that they disclose the identity of the importers. The order was granted by the judge but reversed by the Court of Appeal. On appeal to the House of Lords by the claimants it was *held* – allowing the appeal – that the interests of justice outweighed any public interest in the confidential nature of such information. The Commissioners were under a duty to assist a person wronged by disclosing the identity of the wrongdoer.

45 *Alfred Crompton Amusement Machines v Customs and Excise Commissioners (No 2)* [1973] 2 All ER 1169

The appellants had paid purchase tax on the wholesale value of amusement machines for some years on the basis of a formula negotiated with the Commissioners of Customs and Excise. The appellants claimed that the assessments were too high and thereupon the Commissioners investigated the appellants' books and obtained from customers and other sources information bearing on the ascertainment of the wholesale value of the machines. The appellants did not agree with the opinion of the Commissioners as to the way in which the tax should be computed and in subsequent arbitration proceedings Crown privilege was claimed in respect of documents received by the Commissioners from third parties. It was *held* – by the House of Lords – that the considerations for and against disclosure were evenly balanced. In these circumstances it was held that the court ought to uphold the claim to privilege and trust the Executive to mitigate the ill-effects of non-disclosure.

Comment It seems that where there is a doubt in regard to disclosure, the benefit of the doubt is unfortunately to be allowed in favour of the Executive and against disclosure. On considering the issue of Crown privilege, their Lordships indicated by way of preface that the title is a misnomer; a more accurate term would be privilege on the ground of 'public interest', since privilege extends beyond cases against the Crown.

MAKING THE CONTRACT I

Offer and unilateral agreements

46 *Carlill v Carbolic Smoke Ball Co* [1893] 1 QB 256

The defendants were proprietors of a medical preparation called 'The Carbolic Smoke Ball'. They inserted advertisements in various newspapers in which they offered to pay £100 to any person who contracted influenza after using the ball three times a day for two weeks. They added that they had deposited £1,000 at the Alliance Bank, Regent Street, 'to show our sincerity in the matter'. The claimant, a lady, used the ball as advertised, and was attacked by influenza during the course of treatment, which in her case extended from 20 November 1891 to 17 January 1892. She now sued for £100 and the following matters arose out of the various defences raised by the company: (*a*) It was suggested that the offer was too vague since no time limit was stipulated in which the user was to contract influenza. The court said that it must surely have been the intention that the ball would protect its user during the period of its use, and since this covered the present case it was not necessary to go further. (*b*) The suggestion was made that the matter was an advertising 'puff' and that there was no intention to create legal relations. Here the court took the view that the deposit of £1,000 at the bank was clear evidence of an intention to pay claims. (*c*) It was further suggested that this was an attempt to contract with the whole world and that this was impossible in English law. The court took the view that the advertisement was an offer to the whole world and that, by analogy with the reward cases, it was possible to make an offer of this kind. (*d*) The company also claimed that the claimant had not supplied any consideration, but the court took the view that using this inhalant three times a day for two weeks or more was sufficient consideration. It was not necessary to consider its

adequacy. (*e*) Finally, the defendants suggested that there had been no communication of acceptance but here the court, looking at the reward cases, stated that in contracts of this kind acceptance may be by conduct.

Comment (i) An offer to the public at large can only be made where the contract which eventually comes into being is a unilateral one, i.e. where there is a promise on one side for an act on the other. An offer to the public at large would be made, for example, where there was an advertisement offering a reward for services to be rendered such as finding a lost dog. It is interesting to note that an invitation to treat may be put to the world at large, as where A advertises his car for sale in the local press, inviting offers which may eventually lead to a bilateral contract, but an offer cannot be unless designed to produce a unilateral contract.

(ii) Most business contracts are bilateral. They are made by an exchange of promises and not, as here, by the exchange of a promise for an act. Nevertheless, *Carlill's* case has occasionally provided a useful legal principle in the field of business law (see, e.g., *New Zealand Shipping Co Ltd v AM Satterthwaite & Co Ltd* [1974] 1 All ER 1015 (Case **181**)). *As regards motive*, presumably Mrs Carlill used the ball to prevent influenza and not to recover £100. However, she had seen the offer and her motive was immaterial.

(iii) A deposit of money from which to pay is not essential. In *Wood v Lectrik Ltd*, *The Times*, 13 January 1932 the defendants who were makers of an electric comb had advertised: 'What is your trouble? Is it grey hair? In ten days not a grey hair left. £500 Guarantee.' Mr Wood used the comb as directed but his hair remained grey at the end of ten days of use. All the comb had done was to scratch his scalp. There was no bank deposit by the company but Rowlatt, J held that there was a contract and awarded Mr Wood the £500.

(iv) Where the offer is made to a particular person it may only be accepted by that person. Thus in *Boulton v Jones* (1857) 2 H & N 564 the defendant ordered (offered to buy) 50 feet of leather hose from Brocklehurst (a business). Boulton had earlier on the same day bought the Brocklehurst business of which he had been the manager. Boulton 'accepted' the offer and supplied the hose. It was held that there was no contract since the offer was made to Brocklehurst personally. It was important to Jones that he was dealing with Brocklehurst because he was owed money by him and was intending to deduct that sum from the price of the goods (called a set-off). Since Jones had used the hose before he received Boulton's invoice, he could not be required to return it and Boulton failed in his claim for the purchase price.

(v) In *Boulton v Jones* the problem would not have arisen if the Brocklehurst business had been a company in which Boulton had acquired, by way of its purchase, a controlling interest in its shares. Why?

Offer and invitation to treat – auction sales

47 Harris v Nickerson (1873) LR 8 QB 286

The defendant, an auctioneer, advertised in London newspapers that a sale of office furniture would be held at Bury St Edmunds. A broker with a commission to buy furniture came from London to attend the sale. Several conditions were set out in the advertisement, one being: 'The highest bidder to be the buyer.' The lots described as office furniture were not put up for sale but were withdrawn, though the auction itself was held. The broker sued for loss of time in attending the sale.

Held – he could not recover from the auctioneer. There was no offer since the lots were never put up for sale, and the advertisement was simply an invitation to treat.

Comment (i) A sensible decision, really. The statement, 'I *intend* to auction some office furniture' is not the same as an offer for sale, and in any case there seems to be no way of accepting the 'offer' in advance of the event.

(ii) In *British Car Auctions* v *Wright* [1972] 3 All ER 462 the auctioneers sold an unroadworthy vehicle. An attempt to charge them with the offence of 'offering' the car for sale contrary to road traffic legislation failed. The bidder made the offer and not the auctioneer (and see *Partridge* v *Crittenden* (1968)).

Invitation to treat: price indications, circulars, etc.

48 Pharmaceutical Society of Great Britain v Boots Cash Chemists (Southern) Ltd [1953] 1 QB 401

The defendants' branch at Edgware was adapted to the 'self-service' system. Customers selected their purchases from shelves on which the goods were displayed and put them into a wire basket supplied by the defendants. They then took them to the cash desk where they paid the price. One section of shelves was set out with drugs which were included in the Poisons List referred to in s 17 of the Pharmacy and Poisons Act 1933, though they were not dangerous drugs and did not require a doctor's prescription. Section 18 of the Act requires that the sale of such drugs shall take place in the presence of a qualified pharmacist. Every sale of the drugs on the Poisons List was supervised at the cash desk by a qualified pharmacist, who had authority to prevent customers from taking goods out of the shop if he thought fit. One of the duties of the Society was to enforce the provisions of the Act, and the action was brought because the claimants alleged that the defendants were infringing s 18.

Held – the display of goods in this way did not constitute an offer. The contract of sale was not made when a customer selected goods from the shelves, but when the company's employee at the cash desk accepted the offer to buy what had been chosen. There was, therefore, supervision in the sense required by the Act at the appropriate moment of time.

Comment (i) The fact that a price ticket is not regarded as an offer is somewhat archaic, being based, perhaps, on a traditional commercial view that a shop is a place for bargaining and not a place for compulsory sales. However, because currently there is a return to bargaining in some areas of purchase, e.g. cars, white goods and electrical goods, the price ticket is perhaps rightly regarded in those areas as an invitation to treat; a starting point for the bargaining.

(ii) Although a trader can *refuse to sell* at his wrongly advertised price, he commits a criminal offence under ss 20 and 21 of the Consumer Protection Act 1987 for giving a misleading price indication where the price ticket shows a *lower* price than that at which he is prepared to sell.

(iii) The relevant provisions of the 1933 Act are now in ss 2 and 3 of the Poisons Act 1972.

(iv) See also *Esso Petroleum Ltd* v *Customs and Excise Commissioners* [1976] 1 All ER 117 where the House of Lords decided that price indications at a petrol filling station were invitations to treat.

(v) The concept of invitation to treat also applies to goods displayed with a price ticket in a shop window (*Fisher* v *Bell* [1960] 3 All ER 731).

49 Partridge v Crittenden [1968] 2 All ER 421

Mr Partridge inserted an advertisement in a publication called *Cage and Aviary Birds* containing the words 'Bramblefinch cocks, bramblefinch hens, 25s each'. The advertisements appeared under the general heading 'Classified Advertisements' and in no place was there any direct use of the words 'offer for sale'. A Mr Thompson answered the advertisement enclosing a cheque for 25s, and asking that a 'bramblefinch hen' be sent to him. Mr Partridge sent one in a box, the bird wearing a closed ring.

Mr Thompson opened the box in the presence of an RSPCA inspector, Mr Crittenden, and removed the ring without injury to the bird. Mr Crittenden brought a prosecution against Mr Partridge before the Chester magistrates alleging that Mr Partridge had offered for sale a brambling contrary to s 6(1) of the Protection of Birds Act 1954 (see now s 6(1) of the Wildlife and Countryside Act 1981), the bird being other than a close-ringed specimen bred in captivity and being of a species which was resident in or visited the British Isles in a wild state.

The justices were satisfied that the bird had not been bred in captivity but had been caught and ringed. A close-ring meant a ring that was completely closed and incapable of being forced or broken except with the intention of damaging it; such a ring was forced over the claws of a bird when it was between three and 10 days old, and at that time it was not possible to determine what the eventual girth of the leg would be so that the close-ring soon became difficult to remove. The ease with which the ring was removed in this case indicated that it had been put on at a much later stage and this, together with the fact that the bird had no perching sense, led the justices to convict Mr Partridge.

He appealed to the Divisional Court of the Queen's Bench Division where the conviction was quashed. The court accepted that the bird was a wild bird, but since Mr Partridge had been charged with 'offering for sale' the conviction could not stand. The advertisement constituted in law an invitation to treat, not an offer for sale, and the offence was not, therefore, established. There was of course a completed sale for which Mr Partridge could have been successfully prosecuted but the prosecution in this case had relied on the offence of 'offering for sale' and failed to establish such an offer.

Comment (i) The case shows how concepts of the civil law are sometimes at the root of criminal cases (and see *British Car Auctions* v *Wright* (1972)).

(ii) In *Spencer* v *Harding* (1870) LR 5 CP 561 the defendants were selling off a business and issued a circular inviting submission of tenders to buy the goods listed. It was held that the circular was merely an invitation to submit offers and not an offer. The defendants need not accept any tender, even the highest.

Offer and invitation to treat – alleged contracts for the sale of land

50 *Harvey* v *Facey* [1893] AC 552

The claimants sent the following telegram to the defendant: 'Will you sell us Bumper Hall Pen? Telegraph lowest cash price.' The defendant telegraphed in reply: 'Lowest price for Bumper Hall Pen £900.' The claimants then telegraphed: 'We agree to buy Bumper Hall Pen for £900 asked by you. Please send us your title deeds in order that we may get early possession.' The defendant made no reply. The Supreme Court of Jamaica granted the claimants a decree of specific performance of the contract. On appeal the Judicial Committee of the Privy Council *held* that there was no contract. The second telegram was not an offer, but was in the nature of an invitation

to treat at a minimum price of £900. The third telegram could not, therefore, be an acceptance resulting in a contract.

Comment (i) The point was also raised in *Clifton* v *Palumbo* [1944] 2 All ER 497 where the owner of a very large estate wrote to the other party to the case as follows: 'I am prepared to offer you or your nominee my Lytham estate for £600,000.' The letter was regarded as an invitation to treat and not an offer. The Court of Appeal said of the letter: 'It is quite possible for persons on a half sheet of notepaper, in the most informal and unorthodox language, to contract to sell the most extensive and most complicated estate that can be imagined. This is quite possible, but, having regard to the habits of the people in this country, it is very unlikely.'

(ii) The matter of invitation to treat and offer in the context of the alleged sale of land produced the most interesting case of *Gibson* v *Manchester City Council* [1979] 1 All ER 972. The City Treasurer wrote to Mr Gibson saying that the Council 'may be prepared' to sell the freehold of his council house to him at £2,725 less 20 per cent, i.e. £2,180. The letter said that Mr G should make a formal application, which he did. Following local government elections three months later the policy of selling council houses was reversed. The Council did not proceed with the sale to Mr Gibson. He claimed that a binding contract existed. The House of Lords said that it did not. The Treasurer's letter was only an invitation to treat. Mr G's application was the offer, but the Council had not accepted it. In the Court of Appeal Lord Denning said that there was an 'agreement in fact' which was enforceable. It was not always necessary, he said, to stick to the strict rules of offer and acceptance in order to produce a binding agreement. The House of Lords would not accept this and Lord Denning's view has not, as yet, found a place in the law.

(iii) The above cases are unlikely to occur on their own facts, at least in modern law. Under s 2 of the Law of Property (Miscellaneous Provisions) Act 1989 a contract for the sale of land has to be in writing and must contain all the terms expressly agreed by the parties and each of those terms must be set out in the written agreement, although the Act does allow terms of the agreement to be incorporated in the document where it refers to some other document or documents containing the terms. So, because people now have to go through that procedure to get a valid contract for the sale of land, they are surely not going to be able to say that they did not intend to offer (or accept) and plead invitation to treat. Nevertheless, the cases do provide examples of invitations to treat in other areas, as where A says to B, 'The lowest price for my BMW is £20,000' and B tries to 'accept' or where A says to B, 'I may be prepared to sell you my BMW for £20,000' and B tries to 'accept'. Examination questions may well be set involving these principles in regard to sales other than land.

Acceptance of no effect until communicated to the offeror: agreement may be inferred from conduct

51 *Brogden* v *Metropolitan Railway* (1877) 2 App Cas 666

The claimant had been a supplier of coal to the railway company for a number of years, though there was no formal agreement between them. Eventually the claimant suggested that there ought to be one, and the agents of the parties met and a draft agreement was drawn up by the railway company's agent and sent to the claimant. The claimant inserted several new clauses into the draft, and in particular filled in the name of an arbitrator to settle the parties' differences under the agreement should any arise. He then wrote the word 'Approved' on the draft and returned it to the railway company's agent. There was no formal execution, the draft remaining in the agent's desk. However, coal was supplied according to the prices mentioned in the draft, though these were not the market prices, and prices were reviewed from time to time in accordance with the draft. The parties then had a disagreement and the claimant refused to supply coal to the railway company on the ground that, since the railway company had not accepted the offer contained in the amended draft, there was no binding contract.

Held –

(a) The draft was not an *express* binding contract because the claimant had inserted new terms which the railway company had not accepted; but

(b) the parties had indicated by their conduct that they had waived the execution of the formal document and agreed to act on the basis of the draft. There was, therefore, an *implied or inferred* binding contract arising out of conduct, and its terms were the terms of the draft.

The effect of lock-out agreements

52 *Pitt* v *PHH Asset Management Ltd*, *The Times*, 30 July 1993

In September 1991 Tim Pitt made an offer to buy a cottage in a Suffolk village. The vendor was PHH Asset Management. The offer was initially accepted subject to contract but rejected when another prospective purchaser made a higher offer.

Mr Pitt made a second offer which was initially accepted by PHH's estate agent but the acceptance was withdrawn when the other contender again made a higher offer. After further communications between Mr Pitt and the estate agent it was agreed that PHH would stay with Mr Pitt's offer subject to contract and would not consider any further offers on the basis that contracts would be exchanged within two weeks of the receipt of draft contracts.

However, after sending the contract to Mr Pitt PHH sold at a higher price to the other contender before the end of the two-week period. Mr Pitt sued PHH for breach of contract.

The matter eventually reached the Court of Appeal which decided that there was no contract for the sale of land nor any option for the sale of land but there was a lock-out agreement which was enforceable in law. The effect of the agreement was that PHH could not negotiate with other prospective purchasers for a short stipulated period. PHH was liable to pay damages to Mr Pitt.

Comment It will be appreciated that at the end of the lock-out period the vendor can sell elsewhere if he wishes. The agreement only stops him from dealing with anyone else during that period. It is also worth noting that the lock-out agreement which was made orally was not unenforceable under s 2 of the Law of Property (Miscellaneous Provisions) Act 1989. It was not a sale or other disposition of land. As Bingham, LJ said, 'The vendor does not agree to sell to that purchaser – such an agreement would be covered by s 2 of the 1989 Act – but he does give a negative undertaking that he will not for the given period deal with anyone else.' So writing was not required.

Counter-offer: if an offeree makes a counter-offer he cannot then effectively accept the original offer: what constitutes a counter-offer: the offeror can accept a counter-offer

53 *Hyde* v *Wrench* (1840) 3 Beav 334

The defendant offered to sell his farm for £1,000. The claimant's agent made an offer of £950 and the defendant asked for a few days for consideration, after which the defendant wrote saying he could not accept it, whereupon the claimant wrote purporting to accept the offer of £1,000. The defendant did not consider himself bound, and the claimant sued for specific performance.

Held – the claimant could not enforce this 'acceptance' because his counter-offer of £950 was an implied rejection of the original offer to sell at £1,000.

54 *Stevenson* v *McLean* (1880) 5 QBD 346

On Saturday the defendant offered to sell to the claimants a quantity of iron at 40s nett cash per ton open till Monday (close of business). On Monday the claimants telegraphed asking whether the defendant would accept 40s for delivery over two months, or if not what was the longest limit the defendant would give. The claimants did not necessarily want to take delivery of the goods at once and pay for them. They would have liked to have been able to ask for delivery and pay from time to time over two months as they themselves found buyers for quantities of the iron. The defendant received the telegram at 10.01 am but did not reply, so the claimants, by telegram sent at 1.34 pm, accepted the defendant's original offer. The defendant had already sold the iron to a third party, and informed the claimants of this by a telegram despatched at 1.25 pm arriving at 1.46 pm. The claimants had therefore accepted the offer before the defendant's revocation had been communicated to them. If, however, the claimants' first telegram constituted a counter-offer, then it would amount to a rejection of the defendant's original offer.

Held – the claimants' first telegram was not a counter-offer, but a mere inquiry for different terms which did not amount to a rejection of the defendant's original offer, so that the offer was still open when the claimants accepted it. The defendant's offer was not revoked merely by the sale of the iron to another person.

Comment The case shows that a distinction must be drawn between a rejection by counter-offer and a request for information. A common example of this distinction occurs in business when an offer to sell at a stated price is not regarded as rejected, where, as here, the seller is asked whether he is prepared to give credit or even whether he is prepared to reduce the price.

55 *Butler Machine Tool Co Ltd v Ex-Cell-O Corporation (England) Ltd* [1979] 1 All ER 965

In this case it appeared that on 23 May 1969 Butler quoted a price for a machine tool of £75,535, delivery to be within 10 months of order. The quotation gave terms and conditions which were stated expressly to prevail over any terms and conditions contained in the buyer's order.

One of the terms was a price variation clause which operated if costs increased before delivery. Ex-Cell-O ordered the machine on 27 May 1969, its order stating that the contract was to be on the basis of Ex-Cell-O's terms and conditions as set out in the order. These terms and conditions did not include a price variation clause but did contain additional items to the Butler quotation, including the fact that Ex-Cell-O wanted installation of the machine for £3,100 and the date of delivery of 10 months was changed to 10–11 months.

Ex-Cell-O's order form contained a tear-off slip which said: 'Acknowledgment: please sign and return to Ex-Cell-O. We accept your order on the terms and conditions stated therein – and undertake to deliver by . . . date . . . signed.' This slip was completed and signed on behalf of Butler and returned with a covering letter to Ex-Cell-O on 5 June 1969.

The machine was ready by September 1970, but Ex-Cell-O could not take delivery until November 1970 because it had to rearrange its production schedule. By the time Ex-Cell-O took delivery, costs had increased and Butler claimed £2,892 as due under the price variation clause. Ex-Cell-O refused to regard the variation clause as a term of the contract.

The Court of Appeal, following a traditional analysis, decided that Butler's quotation of 23 May 1969 was an offer and that Ex-Cell-O's order of 27 May 1969 was a counter-offer introducing new terms and that Butler's communication of 5 June 1969 returning the slip was an acceptance of the counter-offer: so the contract was on Ex-Cell-O's terms and not Butler's, in spite of the statement in Butler's original quotation.

Thus, there was no price variation clause in the contract, and Ex-Cell-O did not need to pay the £2,892.

Comment (i) Most commonly the parties will exchange terms relating to delivery dates, rights of cancellation, the liability of the supplier for defects, fluctuations in price (as here), and arbitration clauses to settle differences.

(ii) Title retention clauses (where goods are delivered to a buyer with a clause stating that he does not own the goods until he has paid for them) may also be exchanged in this way. For example, in *Sauter Automation* v *Goodman (HC) (Mechanical Services)* [1987] CLY, para 451, Sauter tendered to supply the control panel of a boiler. The tender contained a title retention clause. Goodman accepted on the basis of their standard contract which did not contain retention arrangements. Sauter did not formally accept what was in effect a counter-offer by Goodman but they did deliver the panel which was deemed acceptance. Goodman went into liquidation but the court held that Sauter could not recover the panel or the proceeds of its sale. The contract was on Goodman's terms. Goodman's terms did not contain a retention arrangement. Sauter were left to prove in the liquidation of Goodman with little, if any, prospect of getting paid.

(iii) It is not uncommon in business to find price variation and fluctuation clauses in longer-term contracts, as where the contract involves the manufacture or delivery of goods over, say, a period in excess of one year. These allow for changes in wages and/or the cost of materials. The alternative would be to try to get a variation to the original contract but this may be more difficult since a business may not be willing to pay more and the change cannot be made unilaterally by the supplier. This way the variation arrangements are in the original contract following what is acceptance of a qualified offer, i.e. 'I will supply these goods for £X but they might cost more before the contract ends'. An offer, unlike an acceptance, may be conditional.

Effect of accepting a tender for the supply of goods of an indefinite amount: the standing offer

56 *Great Northern Railway* v *Witham* (1873) LR 9 CP 16

The company advertised for tenders for the supply for one year of such stores as they might think fit to order. The defendant submitted a tender in these words: 'I undertake to supply the company for 12 months with such quantities of [certain specified goods] as the company may order from time to time.' The company accepted the tender, and gave orders under it which the defendant carried out. Eventually the defendant refused to carry out an order made by the company under the tender, and this action was brought.

Held – the defendant was in breach of contract. A tender of this type was a standing offer which was converted into a series of contracts as the company made an order. The defendant might revoke his offer for the remainder of the period covered by the tender, but must supply the goods already ordered by the company.

Comment (i) Tendering by referential bid is invalid. In *Harvela Investments Ltd* v *Royal Trust Co of Canada Ltd* [1985] 2 All ER 966 the claimants submitted a tender for the purchase of shares in the following form: '2,100,000 dollars or 100,000 dollars in excess of any other offer'. The House of Lords held that such a bid was invalid. The decision is obviously a sensible one since, if all tenderers had bid in this way, there would not have been an ascertainable offer to accept.

(ii) If a person submits a tender which conforms in all respects with the rules laid down for submission of tenders, i.e. as to date, time, form and so on, this may give rise to an obligation on those asking for the tenders at least to consider all those that are properly submitted. It was held in *Blackpool and Fylde Aero Club Ltd* v *Blackpool BC* [1990] 3 All ER 25 that failure to do so could lead to a successful action for damages for what is, in effect, a breach of a contract to consider all tenders, at least if properly submitted.

Vague or incomplete agreements: treatment by the courts

57 *Hillas & Co Ltd* v *Arcos Ltd* [1932] All ER 494

The claimants had entered into a contract with the defendants under which the defendants were to supply the claimants with '22,000 standards of soft wood (Russian) of fair specification over the season 1930'.

The contract also contained an option allowing the claimants to take up 100,000 standards as above during the season 1931. The parties managed to perform the contract throughout the 1930 season without any argument or serious difficulty, in spite of the vague words used in connection with the specification of the wood. However, when the claimants exercised their option for 100,000 standards during the season 1931, the defendants refused to supply the wood, saying that the specification was too vague to bind the parties, and the agreement was therefore inchoate as requiring a further agreement as to the precise specification.

Held – by the House of Lords – the option to supply 100,000 standards during the 1931 season was valid. There was a certain vagueness about the specification, but there was also a course of dealing between the parties which operated as a guide to the court regarding the difficulties which this vagueness might produce. Since the parties had not experienced serious difficulty in carrying out the 1930 agreement, there was no reason to suppose that the option could not have been carried out without difficulty had the defendants been prepared to go on with it. Judgment was given for the claimants.

Comment (i) In these cases the defendant is trying to avoid damages for failing to perform the contract by saying: 'I would like to perform the contract but I don't know what to do.' If there are, e.g., previous dealings then he does know what to do and the defence fails.

(ii) The case of *Baird Textile Holdings Ltd* v *Marks and Spencer plc* [2001] All ER (D) 352, provides a good illustration of the law relating to vague and inchoate contracts, the requirement of certainty of terms in the context of intention to create legal relations and promissory estoppel. It also provides a timely reminder to those in business of the need to ensure that contracts are made in writing even though this may not be a legal requirement.

Baird had been a major supplier of garments to M & S for some 30 years. There had never been a written contract between them. M & S terminated the agreement at short notice costing Baird some £50 million. Baird claimed that it was entitled to reasonable notice which it suggested should be three years at least. M & S declined and Baird sued for breach of contract. But what were the terms of the contract? Baird contended from the way the contract had been performed M & S were obliged to place orders 'in quantities and at prices which in all the circumstances were reasonable'. Baird also claimed that if an enforceable contract did not exist at common law equitable principles should be applied, i.e. promissory estoppel where the court will prevent a person from going back on his or her word. The Court of Appeal ruled that there was no enforceable contract at common law. There were no objective criteria to enable the court to assess what was reasonable in terms of quantity, quality or price. Furthermore, the lack of certainty showed that the parties did not intend to create legal relations. This was not said the court an appropriate case in which to apply promissory estoppel. The rule was essentially a defence and could not be used to create an enforceable right in the circumstances of this case. Of course, in *Hillas* the court did imply a contract where only the quality of the timber was vague. Here the quantity, quality and price were not ascertained by the agreement and to have filled in all these matters would have brought the court into a position where it was making the contract for the parties – a power the courts do not possess.

58 *Foley* v *Classique Coaches Ltd* [1934] 2 KB 1

F owned certain land, part of which he used for the business of supplying petrol. He also owned the adjoining land. The company wished to purchase the adjoining land for use as the headquarters of their charabanc business. F agreed to sell the land to the company on condition that the company would buy all their petrol from him. An agreement was made under which the company agreed to buy its petrol from F 'at a price to be agreed by the parties in writing and from time to time'. It was further agreed that any dispute arising under the agreement should be submitted 'to arbitration in the usual way'. The agreement was acted upon at an agreed price for three years. At this time the company felt it could get petrol at a better price, and the company's solicitor wrote to F repudiating the petrol contract.

Held – although the parties had not agreed upon a price beyond three years, there was a contract to supply petrol at a reasonable price and of reasonable quality, and although the agreement did not stipulate the future price, but left this to the further agreement of the parties, a method was provided by which the price could be ascertained without such agreement, i.e. by arbitration.

Comment (i) The court awarded the claimant damages, a declaration that the agreement was binding, and an injunction restraining the company from buying petrol elsewhere, thus giving the company an enormous incentive to agree a price or go to arbitration as the contract provided. Generally speaking, of course, if the contract is silent as to price, the court is prepared to use s 8(2) of the Sale of Goods Act 1979 and imply and ascertain 'a reasonable price'. It would not have been appropriate in *Foley* to use this provision of sale of goods legislation (which in those days was in the 1893 Act) because the contract in *Foley* was not in fact silent as to price.

(ii) A similar problem arose in *F & S Sykes (Wessex)* v *Fine-Fare* [1967] 1 Lloyd's Rep 53. In that case producers of broiler chickens agreed with certain retailers to supply between 30,000 and 80,000 chickens a week during the first year of the agreement and afterwards 'such other figures as might be agreed'. The agreement was to last for not less than five years, and it was agreed that any differences between the parties should be referred to arbitration. Eventually the retailers contended that the agreement was void for uncertainty.

Held – by the Court of Appeal – that it was not, because in default of the further agreement envisaged, the number of chickens should be such reasonable number as might be decided by the arbitrator.

(iii) In *Rafsanjan Pistachio Producers Co-operative* v *Kauffmanns Ltd*, *The Independent*, 12 January 1998 the High Court decided that a contract which specified that the price was to be 'agreed before each delivery' was an agreement to agree and unenforceable. There was no provision for arbitration.

(iv) A price fluctuation or variation clause in the original contract could be used in this situation. The parties could agree in the original contract that the price from time to time of the goods as the contract proceeds shall be increased (or exceptionally decreased) on the basis of relevant indices of labour and materials costs. This is less expensive than reference to arbitration.

59 *Scammell (G) and Nephew Ltd* v *Ouston* [1941] AC 251

Ouston wished to acquire a new motor van for use in his furniture business. Discussions took place with the company's sales manager as a result of which the company sent a quotation for the supply of a suitable van. Eventually Ouston sent an official order making the following stipulation, 'This order is given on the understanding that the balance of the purchase price can be had on hire-purchase terms over a period of two years.' This was in accordance with the discussions between the sales manager and Ouston, which had taken place on the understanding that hire purchase would be available. The company seemed to be content with the arrangement and completed the van. Arrangements were made with a finance company to give hire-purchase facilities, but the actual terms were not agreed at that stage. The appellants also agreed to take Ouston's present van in part exchange, but later stated that they were not satisfied with its condition and asked him to sell it locally. He refused and after much correspondence he issued a writ against the appellants for damages for non-delivery of the van. The appellants' defence was that there was no contract until the hire-purchase terms had been ascertained.

Held – the defence succeeded; it was not possible to construe a contract from the vague language used by the parties.

Comment (i) If there is evidence of a trade custom, business procedure or previous dealings between the parties, which assists the court in construing the vague parts of an agreement, then the agreement may be enforced. Here there was no such evidence. It should also be noted that the hire-purchase term was essential to the contract which could not be enforced without it.

(ii) It is worth noting the quite common use in business contracts of the expressions 'best endeavours' and 'reasonable endeavours'. It would be too easy to fall into the *Scammell* trap and assume that these expressions made the contract in which they were used inchoate or uncertain but this is not the case. The courts have in a number of cases held that the use of these expressions does not have that effect. These are useful rulings because it is not possible in many business situations to necessarily achieve performance. For example, suppose an agent makes a contract to find a publisher to publish an author's book. The agent cannot say that he will find such a publisher, but he can, and often will, use the 'best endeavours' or 'reasonable endeavours' formula. If the agent has, on the facts, used best or reasonable endeavours and not obtained a publisher, he will be entitled to his contractual fee. If the agent, on the facts, has not done so, any claim by him will fail. Clearly, best endeavours also requires more effort than reasonable endeavours (see *Lambert* v *HTV Cymru (Wales) Ltd, The Times,* 17 March 1998 where an all reasonable endeavours contract in connection with book publishing was held to be enforceable).

60 *Nicolene Ltd v Simmonds* [1953] 1 All ER 882

The claimants alleged that there was a contract for the sale to them of 3,000 tons of steel reinforcing bars and that the defendant seller had broken his contract. When the claimants sought damages, the seller set up the defence that, owing to one of the sentences in the letters which constituted the contract, there was no contract at all. The material words were: 'We are in agreement that the usual conditions of acceptance apply.' In fact, there were no usual conditions of acceptance so that the words were meaningless, but the seller nevertheless suggested that the contract was unenforceable since it was not complete.

Held – by the Court of Appeal – the contract was enforceable and that the meaningless clause could be ignored:

In my opinion a distinction must be drawn between a clause which is meaningless and a clause which is yet to be agreed. A clause which is meaningless can often be ignored, whilst still leaving the contract good; whereas a clause which has yet to be agreed may mean that there is no contract at all, because the parties have not agreed on all the essential terms. . . . In the present case there was nothing

yet to be agreed. There was nothing left to further negotiation. All that happened was that the parties agreed that 'the usual conditions of acceptance apply'. That clause was so vague and uncertain as to be incapable of any precise meaning. It is clearly severable from the rest of the contract. It can be rejected without impairing the sense or reasonableness of the contract as a whole, and it should be so rejected. The contract should be held good and the clause ignored. The parties themselves treated the contract as subsisting. They regarded it as creating binding obligations between them; and it would be most unfortunate if the law should say otherwise. You would find defaulters all scanning their contracts to find some meaningless clause on which to ride free. (*Per* Denning, LJ)

Comment (i) In this case there was no evidence of any usual conditions either in the trade or between the parties as a result of previous dealings. Therefore, the expression 'the usual conditions of acceptance apply' had to be regarded as meaningless.

It should also be noted that it was possible to enforce the contract without the meaningless term. (Compare *Scammell* above.)

(ii) In view of the general policy to reduce litigation in court, clauses in contracts providing for alternative dispute resolution may more readily be found to be binding even where the form of ADR to be used is left vague (see *Cable & Wireless plc* v *IBM (United Kingdom) Ltd* [2002] 2 All ER (Comm) 1041). In that case where the ADR clause did not specify the type of ADR to be followed Mr Justice Coleman ruled that for the court not to enforce contractual references to ADR would 'fly in the face' of public policy. There were, he said, clearly recognised and well-developed processes of ADR. As such, a reference to ADR in a contract was certain enough to enforce. His judgment seems to suggest, though not specifically stated, that mediation in accordance with the Centre for Effective Dispute Resolution's Model Mediation procedure would be regarded as the method to adopt. In practical terms, of course, an ADR clause should state whether ADR is optional or not and the form of ADR should be spelled out.

Communication of acceptance

61 *Felthouse* v *Bindley* (1862) 11 CB (NS) 869

The claimant had been engaged in negotiations with his nephew John regarding the purchase of John's horse, and there had been some misunderstanding as to the price. Eventually the claimant wrote to his nephew as follows: 'If I hear no more about him I consider the horse is mine at £30.15s.' The nephew did not reply but, wishing to sell the horse to his uncle, he told the defendant, an auctioneer who was selling farm stock for him, not to sell the horse as it had already been sold. The auctioneer inadvertently put the horse up with the rest of the stock and sold it. The claimant now sued the auctioneer in conversion, the basis of the claim being that he had made a contract with his nephew and the property in the animal was vested in him (the uncle) at the time of the sale.

Held – that the claimant's action failed. Although the nephew intended to sell the horse to his uncle, he had not communicated that intention. There was, therefore, no contract between the parties, and the property in the horse was not vested in the claimant at the time of the auction sale.

Comment (i) The rule that silence cannot amount to acceptance does not necessarily mean that words of acceptance have to be spoken or written to the offeror. In a unilateral contract situation such as *Carlill's* case (see Chapter 9), an acceptance may be inferred from the way in which the offeree behaves and communication of acceptance may be dispensed with. However, in this case the contract was bilateral so that the conduct of John Felthouse in removing the horse from the sale was not relevant, as it might have been in a unilateral situation. In a bilateral situation the rule against acceptance by silence means only that the offeror is unable to impose on the offeree a stipulation that the offeree will be bound if he merely ignores the offer.

Nevertheless, while the general principle laid down in this case, i.e. that an offeree who does not wish to accept an offer should not be put to the trouble of actively refusing it, is quite acceptable the decision is difficult to support on its own facts. John wanted to accept the offer and intended to accept it and his uncle had waived his right to receive an acceptance in his letter – so why no contract?

It should be noted, however, that although the approach in *Felthouse* appears unfair, it does run fairly consistently through English law in regard to positive obligations involving the payment of money for goods and services. Thus, if A asks B to clean his (A's) car but B by mistake cleans A's neighbour's car, the neighbour cannot be required to pay B even though the neighbour is not prejudiced because, as it happens, he did want his car cleaned.

(ii) It should also be noted that the communication of acceptance must be authorised. In *Powell* v *Lee* (1908) 99 LT 284 P offered his services to the managers of a school as headmaster. The secretary to the managers told P that he had been appointed which was true. The secretary had no authority actual or otherwise to do this. The managers later decided to offer the post to another candidate. P's action for breach of contract failed.

(iii) In a not dissimilar case a deputy headteacher's verbal assurance that a member of staff's temporary promotion

would be made permanent had no contractual effect because, among other things, the deputy head had no authority to make a contract that would bind the school governors (see *Pantis* v *Governing Body of Isambard Brunel School* [1997] 573 IRLB 15).

Where the mode of acceptance is prescribed: must the offeree comply?

62 *Yates Building Co v R J Pulleyn & Sons (York)* (1975) 119 SJ 370

An option to purchase a certain plot of land was expressed to be exercisable by notice in writing by or on behalf of the intending purchaser to the intending vendor 'such notice to be sent by registered or Recorded Delivery post'. It was *held* – by the Court of Appeal – that the form of posting prescribed was directory rather than mandatory, or alternatively permissive rather than obligatory, and the option was validly exercised by a letter from the purchaser's solicitors to the vendor's solicitors sent by ordinary post and received within the option period.

Comment The fact that the letter arrived within the option period shows that there was no prejudice to the offeror.

Use of telephone and telex as a means of communicating acceptance

63 *Entores Ltd* v *Miles Far East Corporation* [1955] 2 QB 327

The claimants, who conducted a business in London, made an offer to the defendants' agent in Amsterdam by means of a teleprinter service. The offer was accepted by a message received on the claimants' teleprinter in London. Later the defendants were in breach of contract and the claimants wished to sue them. The defendants had their place of business in New York and in order to commence an action the claimants had to serve notice of writ on the defendants in New York. The Rules of Supreme Court allow service out of the jurisdiction when the contract was made within the jurisdiction. On this point the defendants argued that the contract was made in Holland when it was typed into the teleprinter there, stressing the rule relating to posting.

Held – where communication is instantaneous, as where the parties are face to face or speaking on the telephone, acceptance must be received by the offeror. The same rule applied to communications of this kind. Therefore, the contract was made in London where the acceptance was received.

Comment (i) The suggestion was made that the doctrine of estoppel may operate in this sort of case so as to bind the offeror, e.g. suppose X telephones his acceptance to Y, and Y does not hear X's voice at the moment of acceptance, as where there is a break in the line or Y simply puts the phone down on his desk for a while without telling X, then Y may be estopped from denying that he heard X's acceptance and may be bound in contract. It is thought that the conversation prior to the acceptance which is not heard must suggest the possibility of an impending acceptance. It should be noted that this estoppel theory amounts to an exception to the rule that silence cannot amount to acceptance.

(ii) The House of Lords approved the *Entores* decision in *Brinkibon v Stahag Stahl* [1982] 1 All ER 293. The claimant wanted leave to serve a writ out of the jurisdiction, as in *Entores*. The message accepting an offer had been sent by telex from London to Vienna. The House of Lords *held* that the writ could not be served because the contract was made in Vienna and not London.

(iii) These decisions presumably apply to acceptances by fax and e-mail.

Use of the post in offer and acceptance

64   *Household Fire Insurance Company v Grant* (1879) 4 ExD 216

The defendant handed a written application for shares in the company to the company's agent in Glamorgan. The application stated that the defendant had paid to the company's bankers the sum of £5, being a deposit of 1s per share on an application for 100 shares, and also agreed to pay 19s per share within 12 months of the allotment. The agent sent the application to the company in London. The company secretary made out a letter of allotment in favour of the defendant and posted it to him in Swansea. The letter never arrived. Nevertheless, the company entered the defendant's name on the share register and credited him with dividends amounting to five shillings. The company then went into liquidation and the liquidator sued for £94 15s, the balance due on the shares allotted. It was *held* by the Court of Appeal that the defendant was liable. Acceptance was complete when the letter of allotment was posted on the ground that, in this sort of case, the Post Office must be deemed the common agent of the parties, and that delivery to the agent constituted acceptance. Bramwell, LJ, in a dissenting judgment, regarded actual communication as essential. If the letter of acceptance does not arrive, an unknown liability is imposed on the offeror. If actual communication is required the status quo is preserved, i.e. the parties have not made a contract.

Comment (i) Not all lawyers would accept the point that the Post Office is the common agent of the parties. Those who do not accept this point would say that the Post

Office cannot be an agent for communication since the Post Office and its servants do not know what is in the letter.

(ii) In *Re London and Northern Bank* [1900] 1 Ch 220 the court decided that the letter of acceptance must be properly stamped and addressed. If not, there is no communication until the letter arrives. The case also decides that the letter must be actually posted and not given to a person to post, even a postman. If this happens, the acceptance takes place when the person concerned actually posts the letter. This is a matter of evidence. As regards handing a letter of acceptance to a postman, this may operate as an acceptance in a country district where the custom of postmen taking letters in this way is better established.

(iii) Bramwell LJ's point is well taken since the post rule places the risk of accidents in the post on the offeror, as can be seen from *Grant*'s case. Furthermore, it was decided in *Dunlop v Higgins* (1848) 1 HL Cas 381 that there was a good contract on posting even where a correctly addressed, stamped and posted acceptance was not delivered in due course of post because of an accident in the post office.

(iv) The case has some unusual features. First the initial deposit on application for the shares was not, in fact, paid. Instead the defendant was credited with an equivalent sum due to him from the company. Second, the dividends declared by the company were not actually paid to the defendant but merely credited to his account with the company, but for the above circumstances, the defendant would have known long before the end of three years that he was being regarded as a shareholder.

65   *Holwell Securities Ltd v Hughes* [1974] 1 All ER 161

By an agreement of 19 October 1971 Dr Hughes, a medical practitioner of Wembley, had granted to the claimants an option to purchase his premises in Wembley for £45,000. The agreement provided that the option should be exercisable 'by notice in writing' to Dr Hughes at any time within six months of the date of the agreement. On 14 April 1972, the claimants' solicitors sent to Dr Hughes by ordinary post a written notice exercising the option. That notice was never delivered to Dr Hughes nor left at his address.

Held – by the Court of Appeal – on a construction of the agreement – notice in writing had to be given to Dr Hughes in the sense that he had either to have actually received it or to be deemed to have received it under s 196 of the Law of Property Act 1925 which provides for service of notices by registered post, or within the Recorded Delivery Service Act 1962, which applies a similar rule to Recorded Delivery. This was not the case, said Russell, LJ, where the basic principle of the need for communication to the offeror was displaced by the artificial concept of communication by the act of posting: the language of the agreement 'notice . . . to' was inconsistent with the theory that acceptance could be constituted by posting and s 196 of the Law of Property Act 1925 also impliedly excluded such a mode of acceptance.

Comment (i) The case illustrates that the rule of acceptance by post does not apply in all situations to which it might logically be applied. As the court said in this case the rule would not be applied where it led to 'manifest inconvenience and absurdity'. In each case, therefore, it is a matter of fact for the court to decide whether the rule should be applied, the test being whether it produces, on balance, a convenient and reasonable result.

(ii) This agreement for an option over land was governed by the Law of Property Act 1925 and s 196 deals with the method of serving 'notices' under the Act. It implies that they must be received. So here both the agreement and statute law required actual delivery.

(iii) On a related point it was held in *Miss Sam (Sales) Ltd v River Island Clothing Co Ltd* [1994] NLJR 419 that a cheque sent through the post is not payment unless it arrives and there can be no extension of the postal rule to this situation unless by express agreement between the parties.

66   *Adams v Lindsell* (1818) 1 B & A 681

The defendants were wool dealers in business at St Ives, Huntingdon. By letter dated 2 September they offered to sell wool to the claimants who were wool manufacturers at Bromsgrove, Worcestershire. The defendants' letter asked for a reply 'in course of post' but was misdirected, being addressed to Bromsgrove, Leicestershire. The offer did not reach the claimants until 7 pm on 5 September. The same evening the claimants accepted the offer. This letter reached the defendants on 9 September. If the offer had not been misdirected, the defendants could have expected a reply on 7 September, and accordingly they sold the wool to a third party on 8 September. The claimants now sued for breach of contract.

Held – where there is a misdirection of the offer, as in this case, the offer is made when it actually reaches the offeree, and not when it would have reached him in the ordinary course of post. The defendants' mistake must be taken against them and for the purposes of this contract the claimants' letter was received 'in course of post'.

Comment The position may be different if the fact of delay is obvious to the offeree so that he is put on notice that the offer has lapsed, e.g. A writes to B offering to sell him certain goods and saying that the offer is open until 30 June. If A misdirects the offer so that it

does not reach B until 2 July, it is doubtful whether B could accept it.

Revocation of offer: the effect of an option

67   *Routledge v Grant* (1828) 4 Bing 653

The defendant made an offer to take a lease of the claimant's premises: 'a definitive answer to be given within six weeks from 18 March 1825'. On 9 April the defendant withdrew his offer and on 29 April the claimant purported to accept it. The Court of Common Pleas *held* that there was no contract. Best, CJ *held* that the defendant could withdraw at any moment before acceptance, even though the time limit had expired. The claimant could only have held the defendant to his offer throughout the period, if he had bought the option, i.e. given consideration for it.

Comment (i) The consideration need not be adequate. For example, let us suppose that on Monday Fred offers to sell Joe his house for £30,000 and Joe says 'Give me until Friday to think it over and I will buy you a pint.' The purchase of the pint for Fred or the promise to buy him a pint is enough to give Joe an enforceable option on the house. Again, in *Mountford v Scott* [1974] 1 All ER 248 the Court of Appeal held that a West Indian who signed an agreement in consideration of £1 giving the claimant an option to purchase his house for £10,000 within six months, was bound by the option in spite of the fact that only £1 was given for it.

(ii) The option is really a separate contract to allow time to decide whether to accept the original offer or not. It was thought at one time that, where the option to buy property was not supported by consideration, the offer could be revoked by its sale to another, but in modern law it is necessary for the offeror to communicate the revocation to the offeree either himself, or by means of some reliable person. (See *Stevenson v McLean* (1880) where the defendant's offer was not revoked merely by the sale of the iron to another.)

(iii) Before leaving the topic of options, it should be noted that the Law Commission in Working Paper No 60 entitled *Firm Offers* and published in 1975 criticised the present position under which a promise to keep an offer open will not be binding on the offeror unless consideration for the promise is given by the offeree (though of course this is not necessary where the option is made in a deed), on the grounds that it is contrary to business practice and also contrary to the law of most foreign countries. The Law Commission makes a provisional recommendation that 'an offeror who has promised that he will not revoke his offer for a definite time should be bound by the terms of that promise provided that the promise has been made in the course of business'. No action has so far been taken on this recommendation.

Revocation of an offer must be communicated. It is not effective on posting

68 *Byrne v Van Tienhoven* (1880) 5 CPD 344

On 1 October the defendants in Cardiff posted a letter to the claimants in New York offering to sell them tin plate. On 8 October the defendants wrote revoking their offer. On 11 October the claimants received the defendants' offer and immediately telegraphed their acceptance. On 15 October the claimants confirmed their acceptance by letter. On 20 October the defendants' letter of revocation reached the claimants who had by this time entered into a contract to resell the tin plate.

Held – (*a*) revocation of an offer is not effective until it is communicated to the offeree, (*b*) the mere posting of a letter of revocation is no communication to the person to whom it is sent. The rule is not, therefore, the same as that for acceptance of an offer. Thus, the defendants were bound by a contract which came into being on 11 October.

Revocation of offer: may be by a third party if a reasonable person would rely on that party's knowledge of the facts

69 *Dickinson v Dodds* (1876) 2 Ch D 463

The defendant offered to sell certain houses by letter, stating, 'This offer to be left over until Friday 9 am'. On Thursday afternoon the claimant was informed by a Mr Berry that the defendant had been negotiating a sale of the property with one Allan. On Thursday evening the claimant left a letter of acceptance at the house where the defendant was staying. This letter was never delivered to the defendant. On Friday morning at 7 am Berry, acting as the claimant's agent, handed the defendant a duplicate letter of acceptance explaining it to him. However, on the Thursday the defendant had entered into a contract to sell the property to Allan.

Held – since there was no consideration for the promise to keep the offer open, the defendant was free to revoke his offer at any time. Further, Berry's communication of the dealings with Allan indicated that Dodds was no longer minded to sell the property to the claimant and was in effect a communication of Dodds' revocation. There was, therefore, no binding contract between the parties.

Comment (i) The question of whether the person who communicates the revocation is a reliable source and should be relied on is a matter of fact for the court, but it could, e.g., be a mutual friend of the offeror and offeree. There is in fact no general statement in this case as to what is reliability or even that it is necessarily required.

(ii) This decision as it stands could cause hardship because it may mean that the offeree will have to accept as revocation all kinds of rumour from people who may not necessarily appear to be reliable and well informed. It would be nice to think that in modern law the third party would have to be apparently reliable and likely to know the true state of affairs, as where he is the offeror's agent, but as we have seen there is no actual clear statement in this case that this is so.

Lapse of offer after a reasonable time

70 *Ramsgate Victoria Hotel Co v Montefiore* (1866) LR 1 Exch 109

The defendant offered by letter dated 8 June 1864 to take shares in the company sending part-payment of 1 shilling (5p) a share. No reply was made by the company, but on 23 November 1864, they allotted shares to the defendant. The defendant refused to take up the shares.

Held – his refusal was justified because his offer had lapsed by reason of the company's delay in notifying their acceptance. He also recovered his part-payment.

Comment The question of 'reasonable time' is a matter of fact to be decided by the court on the basis of the subject matter of the contract and the conditions of the market in which the offer is made. Offers to take shares in companies are normally accepted quickly because the price fluctuates in the market. The same would be true of an offer to sell perishable goods. An offer to sell a farm might well not lapse so soon. The form in which the offer is made is also relevant so that an offer by mobile phone could well lapse quickly.

Conditional offer: termination on failure of condition

71 *Financings Ltd v Stimson* [1962] 3 All ER 386

On 16 March 1961, the defendant saw a motor car on the premises of a dealer and signed a hire-purchase form provided by the claimant (a finance company), this form being supplied by the dealer. The form was to the effect that the agreement was to become binding only when the finance company signed the form. It also carried a statement to the effect that the hirer (the defendant) acknowledged that before he signed the agreement he had examined the goods and had satisfied himself that they were in good order and condition, and that the goods were at the risk of the hirer from the time of purchase by the owner. On 18 March the defendant paid the first instalment and took possession of the car. However, on 20 March, the defendant, being dissatisfied with the car, returned it to the dealer, though the finance company was not informed of this. On the night of 24–25 March the car was stolen from the dealer's premises and was recovered badly damaged. On 25 March the finance company signed the agreement accepting the defendant's offer to hire the car. The defendant did not regard himself as bound and refused to pay the instalments. The finance company sold the car, and now sued for damages for the defendant's breach of the hire-purchase agreement.

Held – the hire-purchase agreement was not binding on the defendant because:

(a) he had revoked his offer by returning the car, and the dealer was the agent of the finance company to receive notice;

(b) there was an *implied* condition in the offer that the goods were in substantially the same condition when the offer was accepted as when it was made.

Death of offeror before acceptance

72 *Bradbury v Morgan* (1862) 1 H & C 249

The defendants were the executors of J M Leigh who had entered into a guarantee of his brother's account with the claimants for credit up to £100. The claimants, not knowing of the death of J M Leigh, continued to supply goods on credit to the brother, H J Leigh. The defendants now refused to pay the claimants in respect of such credit after the death of J M Leigh.

Held – the claimants succeeded, the offer remaining open until the claimants had *knowledge* of the death of J M Leigh.

Comment This was a continuing guarantee which is in the nature of a standing offer accepted piecemeal whenever further goods are advanced on credit. Where the guarantee is not of this nature, it may be irrevocable. Thus, in *Lloyds v Harper* (1880) 16 Ch D 290, the defendant, while living, guaranteed his son's dealings as a Lloyds underwriter in consideration of Lloyds admitting the son. It was *held* that, as Lloyds had admitted the son on the strength of the guarantee, the defendant's executors were still liable under it, because it was irrevocable and was not affected by the defendant's death. It continued to apply to defaults committed by the son after the father's death.

Death of offeree before acceptance

73 *Re Cheshire Banking Co, Duff's Executors'* Case (1886) 32 Ch D 301

In 1882 the Cheshire and Staffordshire Union Banking Companies amalgamated, and Duff received a circular asking whether he would exchange his shares in the S Bank for shares in the C Bank which

took the S Bank over. Duff held 100 £20 shares on which £5 had been paid, but he did not reply to the circular and died shortly afterwards. The option was exercised on behalf of his executors, Muttlebury, Bridges and Watts, and a certificate was made out in their names and an entry made in the register in which they were entered as shareholders, described as 'executors of William Duff, deceased'. The executors objected to having the share certificates in their names, so the directors of the Cheshire Banking Co cancelled the certificate and issued a fresh one in the name of William Duff. On 23 October 1884, the company went into liquidation.

Held – the liquidator acted rightly when he restored the executors' names to the register. The executors wished to enter into a new contract which had not previously existed. They could not make a dead man liable and so could only make themselves personally liable. Their names were improperly removed and must be restored. Although they had a right of indemnity against the estate, they were personally liable for the full amount outstanding on the shares, regardless as to whether the estate was adequate to indemnify them.

Comment This case probably has more to do with the liability of personal representatives in the law of succession than the law of contract. Personal representatives, like receivers, can be personally liable on contracts which they make, subject to a right of indemnity from the estate. The benefit of the contract is held on trust for the estate. This personal liability rule is essential in order to ensure that personal representatives cannot subject the estate to further debt without risk to themselves. There seems to be no direct contract law authority as to the effect of the death of the offeree. In *Reynolds* v *Atherton* (1922) 127 LT 189, Warrington, LJ said: 'The offer having been made to a living person who ceases to be a living person before the offer is accepted, there is no longer an offer at all. The offer is not intended to be made to a dead person, nor to his executors, and the offer ceases to be an offer capable of acceptance.' There is, however, some Canadian authority. In *Re Irvine* [1928] 3 DLR 268 an offeree gave his son a letter of acceptance to post. The son did not post it until after the offeree's death. The Supreme Court of Ontario held that the acceptance was invalid.

Offer and acceptance not essential: the collateral contract

74 *Rayfield v Hands* [1958] 2 All ER 194

The articles of a private company provided by Art 11 that: 'Every member who intends to transfer his shares shall inform the directors who will take the said shares . . . at a fair price.' The claimant held 725 full-paid shares of £1 each, and he asked the directors to buy them but they refused.

Held – the directors were bound to take the shares. Having regard to what is now s 14(1) of the Companies Act 1985, Art 11 constituted a binding contract between the directors, as members, and the claimant, as a member, in respect of his rights as a member. The word 'will' in the Article did not import an option in the directors. Vaisey, J did say that the conclusion he had reached in this case may not apply to all companies, but it did apply to a private company, because such a company was an intimate concern closely analogous with a partnership.

Comment (i) Although the articles placed the obligation to take shares of members on the directors, Vaisey, J construed this as an obligation falling upon the directors in their capacity as members. Otherwise, the contractual aspect of the provision in the articles would not have applied, since the articles are not a contract between the company and the directors.

(ii) The leading case is *Clarke v Dunraven* [1897] AC 59 where it was held that competitors in a regatta had made a contract not only with the club which organised the race but also with each other so that one competitor was able to sue another for damages when his boat was fouled and sank under a rule which said that each competitor was liable 'to pay all damages' that he might cause.

(iii) Section 14(1) of the Companies Act 1985 provides that the provisions in the company's articles and memorandum form a contract between the company and its members, which the parties are bound to observe. Incidentally, the Contracts (Rights of Third Parties) Act 1999, which is further considered in Chapter 10, clearly excludes the operation of s 14(1) from its provisions so that third parties cannot acquire rights under the contract. Thus, the appointment of a person as solicitor or accountant to the company would not operate as a contract enforceable against the company.

MAKING THE CONTRACT II

Consideration need not be adequate so long as it has some economic value

75　*Thomas v Thomas* (1842) 2 QB 851

The claimant's husband had expressed the wish that the claimant, if she survived him, should have use of his house. He left a will of which his brothers were executors. The will made no mention of the testator's wish that his wife should be given the house. The executors knew of the testator's wish and agreed to allow the widow to occupy the house on payment of £1 per year for so long as she remained unmarried. The claimant remained in possession of the house until the death of one of the executors, Samuel Thomas. The other executor then turned her out. She sued him for breach of contract. It was *held* that the claimant's promise to pay £1 per year was consideration and need not be adequate. The action for breach of contract succeeded.

Comment The rule that consideration need not be adequate allows virtually gratuitous promises to be binding even though not made by deed (and see *Mountford v Scott*, above).

76　*Chappell & Co Ltd v Nestlé Co Ltd* [1959] 2 All ER 701

The claimants owned the copyright in a dance tune called 'Rockin' Shoes', and the defendants were using records of this tune as part of an advertising scheme. A record company made the records for Nestlés which advertised them to the public for 1s 6d each but required in addition three wrappers from their 6d bars of chocolate. When Nestlé received the wrappers, they were thrown away. The claimants sued the defendants for infringement of copyright. It appeared that under s 8 of the Copyright Act of 1956 a person recording musical works for retail sale need not get the permission of the holder of the copyright, but had merely to serve him with notice and pay 6¼ per cent of the retail selling price as royalty. The claimants asserted that the defendants were not retailing the goods in the sense of the Act and must therefore get permission to use the musical work. The basis of the claimants' case was that retailing meant selling entirely for money, and that as the defendants were selling for money plus wrappers, they needed the claimants' consent. The defence was that the sale was for cash because the wrappers were not part of the consideration. The House of Lords by a majority gave judgment for the claimants. The wrappers were part of the consideration since the offer was to supply a record in return, not simply for money, but for the wrappers as well. On the question of adequacy, Lord Somervell said: 'It is said that, when received, the wrappers are of no value to the respondents, the Nestlé Co Ltd. This I would have thought irrelevant. A contracting party can stipulate for what consideration he chooses. A peppercorn does not cease to be good consideration if it is established that the promisee does not like pepper and will throw away the corn.'

Comment (i) There seems to be no doubt that the wrappers could, on their own, have formed the consideration.

(ii) The statutory licence to copy records sold by retail under s 8 of the Copyright Act 1956 was repealed by the Copyright, Designs and Patents Act 1988, Sch 1, para 21. Permission to reproduce is now required even by those retailing the records. However, the case remains a classic example of an adequacy of consideration ruling by the House of Lords.

77 *White* v *Bluett* (1853) 23 LJ Ex 36

This action was brought by White who was the executor of Bluett's father's estate. The claimant White, alleged that Bluett had not paid a promissory note given to his father during his lifetime. Bluett admitted that he had given the note to his father, but said that his father had released him from it in return for a promise not to keep on complaining about the fact that he had been disinherited.

Held – the defence failed and the defendant was liable on the note. The promise not to complain was not sufficient consideration to support his release from the note.

Comment This case illustrates the general point that on formation of contract consideration must be capable of expression in terms of value. On its facts, of course, the case is concerned with consideration on discharge of contract, i.e. the promissory note, where the rule is the same. In addition, the decision seems to be based upon the fact that the son had no right to complain of his disinheritance, so he was not giving up anything which he had a right to do. 'The son had no right to complain, for the father might make what distribution of his property he liked; and the son's abstaining from doing what he had no right to do can be of no consideration', said the judge, Chief Baron Pollock, in the old Exchequer Division of the High Court.

Adequacy of consideration: implied forbearance to sue can support a promise

78 *Horton* v *Horton* [1961] 1 QB 215

The parties were husband and wife. In March 1954, by a separation agreement by deed the husband agreed to pay the wife £30 a month. On the true construction of the deed, the husband should have deducted income tax before payment but for nine months he paid the money without deductions. In January 1955, he signed a document, not by deed, agreeing that instead of 'the monthly sum of £30' he would pay such a monthly sum as 'after deduction of income tax should amount to the clear sum of £30'. For over three years he paid this clear sum but then stopped payment. To an action by his wife he pleaded

that the later agreement was unsupported by consideration and that the wife could sue only on the earlier deed. The Court of Appeal *held* that there was consideration to support the later agreement. It was clear that the original deed did not implement the intention of the parties. The wife, therefore, might have sued to rectify the deed and the later agreement represented a compromise of this possible action. Whether such an action would have succeeded was irrelevant; it sufficed that it had some prospect of success and that the wife believed in it.

Comment It will be seen from the facts of this case that although the person who forbears to sue may actually promise not to do so, there may be implied forbearance on the facts. A promise is not essential, provided there is evidence to show that there was some causal connection between the forbearance and the way in which the parties acted.

Adequacy of consideration: the position in bailment

79 *Gilchrist Watt and Sanderson Pty* v *York Products Pty* [1970] 1 WLR 1262

Two cases of German clocks were bought by the respondents and shipped to Sydney. The shipowners arranged for the appellant stevedores to unload the ship. The goods were put in the appellants' shed but when the respondents came to collect them one case of clocks was missing. It was admitted that this was due to the appellants' negligence.

Held – by the Privy Council – that the appellants were liable. Although there was no contract between the parties an obligation to take due care of the goods was created by delivery and voluntary assumption of possession under the sub-bailment.

Comment (i) The matter of consideration and bailment was first raised in *Coggs* v *Bernard* (1703) 2 Ld Ray 909 where the defendant had agreed to take several hogsheads of brandy, belonging to the claimant, from the cellar of one inn to another. One of the casks was broken and the brandy lost and the claimant alleged that this was due to the defendant's carelessness. The defendant denied liability on the ground that there was no consideration to support the agreement to move the casks.

Held – the claimant's suit succeeded. The case seems to have been decided on the ground that once the relationship of bailor and bailee is established certain duties fall upon the bailee independently of any contract.

(ii) It should be borne in mind, of course, that if a person agrees to take charge of goods gratuitously he could not be sued if he fails to take them into his custody. The duty seen in this case arises only when the goods are in the custody of the gratuitous bailee.

Sufficiency of consideration: promise to perform or performance of an existing public or contractural duty will not support a further promise: acts in excess of the duty may

80 *Collins v Godefroy* (1831) 1 B & Ad 950

The claimant received a witness summons (previously a subpoena) to give evidence for the defendant in an action to which the defendant was a party. The claimant now sued for the sum of six guineas which he said the defendant had promised him for his attendance.

Held – the claimant's action failed because there was no consideration for the promise. Lord Tenterden said: 'If it be a duty imposed by law upon a party regularly subpoenaed to attend from time to time to give his evidence, then a promise to give him any remuneration for loss of time incurred in such attendance is a promise without consideration.'

81 *Stilk v Myrick* (1809) 2 Camp 317

A sea-captain, being unable to find any substitutes for two sailors who had deserted, promised to divide the wages of the deserters among the rest of the crew if they would work the ship home shorthanded.

Held – the promise was not enforceable because of absence of consideration. In sailing the ship home the crew had done no more than they were already bound to do. Their original contract obliged them to meet the normal emergencies of the voyage of which minor desertions were one. Compare *Hartley v Ponsonby* (1857) 7 E & B 872, where a greater remuneration was promised to a seaman to work the ship home when the number of deserters was so great as to render the ship unseaworthy.

Held – this was a binding promise because the sailor had gone beyond his duty in agreeing to sail an unseaworthy ship. In fact, the number of desertions was so great as to discharge the remaining seamen from their original contract, leaving them free to enter into a new bargain.

Comment (i) It must be said that the decision in *Stilk* took a nasty knock in *Williams v Roffey Bros and Nicholls (Contractors) Ltd* [1990] 1 All ER 512. The defendants in that case were building contractors. They made a contract to refurbish a block of 27 flats and engaged Mr Williams to carry out carpentry work for £20,000. This turned out to be too low to enable Mr Williams to operate at a profit and after completing some of the flats and receiving interim payments of £16,000 he got into financial difficulties. The defendants, concerned that the job might not be finished on time and that they would in that event have to pay money under a penalty clause in the main contract, made an oral promise to pay Mr Williams a further sum of £10,300 to be paid at the rate of £575 for each flat on which work was completed. Mr Williams was not paid in full for this work and later brought this claim for the additional sum promised. The Court of Appeal *held* that he was entitled to it because where a party to a contract agrees to make an additional payment to secure its performance on time this may provide sufficient consideration contractually to support the extra payment, if the agreement to pay is obtained without economic duress or fraud (see further Chapter 13) and where it ensures the completion of the contract to the paying party's satisfaction and benefit as by avoiding a penalty which was the position here. Apparently, *Stilk* survives only where the person making the promise receives no benefit for it. It would seem to have been possible to find benefit in *Stilk* so that it may well be overruled on its own facts though the Court of Appeal would only say that the principle had been 'refined'.

(ii) The Court of Appeal took a more traditional approach and did not apply the decision in *Williams* in a case entitled *Re Selectmove*, *The Times*, 13 January 1994, where a company was having difficulty paying its taxes and agreed with the Revenue, through one of its officers, to pay by instalments. Some instalments were paid but then, while sums were still owing, the Revenue demanded the balance at once and on failing to get it started proceedings to wind up the company. The Court of Appeal held that the agreement to take instalments was not binding because it was not supported by consideration. The *Williams* case was distinguished because it was concerned with an obligation to supply goods and services, whereas the *Selectmove* case was an obligation to pay money. It was well established by the House of Lords in *Foakes v Beer* (1884) (see Case **92**) that an agreement to pay an existing debt by instalments was not enforceable in the absence of either consideration or a deed.

(iii) The facts of *Selectmove* were virtually the same as those in *Foakes*, i.e. payment of debt by instalments without consideration or a deed. Therefore, the Court of Appeal could hardly have decided differently. Nevertheless, it seems a pity that a promise to pay by instalments made in good faith and accepted, initially, by both parties should be ineffective on the technicality of the absence of consideration or a deed.

(iv) The company in *Selectmove* could, of course, have protected itself by agreeing to pay the Revenue a slightly higher rate of interest on the money owed by way of diminishing balance which would have amounted to good consideration for the agreement to pay by instalments.

82 *Glasbrook Bros Ltd v Glamorgan County Council* [1925] AC 270

In 1921 the Glamorgan police were asked to provide 100 police officers to be billeted on the premises of Glasbrook's colliery near Swansea because it was feared that striking miners were going to prevent safety men going into the mine with the consequence that it would be flooded. The owners of the mine signed a document saying that they would pay not only for the services of the officers but also their travelling expenses. Glasbrook's also undertook to provide them with food and sleeping accommodation. Eventually a bill amounting to £2,200 11s 10d was rendered to the claimants by the Glamorgan County Council, for the above services. Glasbrook's refused to pay the bill, alleging that the police were doing no more than was their duty and therefore there was no consideration for Glasbrook's written promise to pay for the protection which they had had.

Held – by the House of Lords – Glasbrook's promise was binding on them on the ground that the number of constables provided was in excess of what the local police superintendent thought was necessary and, therefore, provided consideration over and above the obligation resting on the police to take all steps necessary for protecting property from criminal injury. In the course of his judgment Viscount Cave, LC said:

> No doubt there is an absolute unconditional obligation binding the police authorities to take all steps which appear to them to be necessary for keeping the peace, preventing crime, or for protecting property from criminal injury; and the public, who pay for this protection through the rates and taxes, cannot lawfully be called upon to make a further payment for that which is their right. . . . But it has always been recognized that, where individuals desire that services of a special kind which, though not within the obligations of a police authority, can most effectively be rendered by them, should be performed by members of the police force, the police authorities may . . . 'lend' the services of constables for that purpose in consideration of payment. Instances are the lending of constables on the occasions of large gatherings in and outside private premises, as on the occasions of weddings, athletic or boxing contests or race meetings, and the provision of constables at large railway stations.

Comment (i) This case was applied in *Harris* v *Sheffield United Football Club* [1987] 2 All ER 838, where Boreham, J held that the provision of policemen at a football ground to keep law and order was the provision of special services by the police. The police authority is under a duty to protect persons and property against crime or threatened crime for which no payment is due. However, the police have no public duty to protect persons and property against the mere fear of possible future crime. The claim of the police authority for some £70,000 for police services provided at the defendants'

football ground over 15 months was allowed. The Court of Appeal later affirmed this ruling.

(ii) The issue of exceeding a statutory duty was also raised in *Ward* v *Byham* [1956] 2 All ER 318. In that case an unmarried mother sued to recover a maintenance allowance by the father of the child. The defence was that, under s 42 of the National Assistance Act 1948, the mother of an illegitimate child was bound to maintain it. However, it appeared that in return for the promise of an allowance the mother had promised:

(*a*) to look after the child well and ensure that it was happy; and

(*b*) to allow it to decide whether it should live with her or the father.

Held – there was sufficient consideration to support the promise of an allowance because the promises given in (*a*) and (*b*) above were in excess of the statutory duty, which was merely to care for the child.

(iii) 'Is a promise to make a child happy adequate consideration?' (Compare *White* v *Bluett* (1853).) This point is not taken in the case and shows the considerable power which judges have to find or not to find contractual obligations.

(iv) Cases such as *Ward* v *Byham* (1956) show that the concepts of the law of contract are not confined to business arrangements and so students should have a knowledge of adequacy and sufficiency rulings. However, the concepts are not likely to be met with in business or at least not often. The reason is simple: those in business seldom if ever (perhaps never) enter into commercial transactions for nothing or for inadequate prices or fees. The problem for those in business (and the consumer) is to prevent other businesses charging customers too much!

Sufficiency of consideration: performance of a contractual duty owed by X to Y can support a promise made by Z to X

83 *Shadwell* v *Shadwell* (1860) 9 CB (NS) 159

The claimant was engaged to marry a woman named Ellen Nicholl. In 1838 he received a letter from his uncle, Charles Shadwell, in the following terms: 'I am glad to hear of your intended marriage with Ellen Nicholl and, as I promised to assist you at starting, I am happy to tell you that I will pay you one hundred and fifty pounds yearly during my life and until your income derived from your profession of Chancery barrister shall amount to six hundred guineas, of which your own admission will be the only evidence that I shall receive or require.' The claimant duly married Ellen Nicholl and his income never exceeded six hundred guineas during the 18 years his uncle lived after the marriage. The uncle paid 12 annual sums and part of the thirteenth but no more. On his death, the claimant sued his uncle's executors for the balance of the 18 instalments to which he suggested he was entitled.

Held – the claimant succeeded even though he was already engaged to Ellen Nicholl when the promise was made. His marriage was sufficient consideration to support his uncle's promise, for, by marrying, the claimant had incurred responsibilities and changed his position in life. Further, the uncle probably derived some benefit in that his desire to see his nephew settled had been satisfied.

Comment (i) In this case the consideration is a little dubious in that it is in part a sentimental benefit to the uncle. This type of consideration, e.g. the 'love and affection' variety, has often been regarded as ineffective to support a contract. Nevertheless, the principle of the case is a good one and makes more sense in a business context. (See *New Zealand Shipping Co Ltd* v *Satterthwaite* (1974), Chapter 15.)

(ii) An engagement to marry is no longer binding as a contract: see s 1 of the Law Reform (Miscellaneous Provisions) Act 1970.

Past consideration: where a particular activity is undertaken without any promise of payment, a subsequent promise to pay is not actionable. If there is a request to carry out the act in a commercial situation where a promise to pay can be implied, the subsequent promise may be enforceable

84 *Re McArdle* [1951] Ch 669

Certain children were entitled under their father's will to a house. However, their mother had a life interest in the property and during her lifetime one of the children and his wife came to live in the house with the mother. The wife carried out certain improvements to the property, and, after she had done so, the children signed a document addressed to her stating: 'In consideration of your carrying out certain alterations and improvements to the property . . . at present occupied by you, the beneficiaries under the Will of William Edward McArdle hereby agree that the executors, the National Provincial Bank Ltd, . . . shall repay to you from the said estate when so distributed the sum of £488 in settlement of the amount spent on such improvements . . .'. On the death of the testator's widow the children refused to authorise payment of the sum of £488, and this action was brought to decide the validity of the claim.

Held – since the improvements had been carried out before the document was executed, the consideration was past and the promise could not be enforced.

Comment (i) The rule applied also in *Roscorla* v *Thomas* (1842) 3 QB 234 where a horse was sold and the seller after the sale gave a warranty as to its quality, i.e. that it was not vicious whereas it was. There was no action on the warranty by the buyer.

(ii) If Mrs McArdle had actually been paid by a cheque, she would not have been able to sue upon it under s 27 of the Bills of Exchange Act 1882 because her acts were gratuitous and did not create an antecedent (or previous) debt or liability, for which she could have claimed to be paid in legal tender or otherwise.

85 *Re Casey's Patents, Stewart* v *Casey* [1892] 1 Ch 104

Patents were granted to Stewart and another in respect of an invention concerning appliances and vessels for transporting and storing inflammable liquids. Stewart entered into an arrangement with Casey, whereby Casey was to introduce the patents. Casey spent two years 'pushing' the invention and then the joint owners of the patent rights wrote to him as follows: 'In consideration of your services as the practical manager in working both patents we hereby agree to give you one-third share of the patents.' Casey also received the letters patent. Some time later Stewart died and his executors claimed the recovery of the letters patent from Casey, suggesting that he had no interest in them because the consideration for the promise to give him a one-third share was past.

Held – the previous request to render the services raised an implied promise to pay. The subsequent promise could be regarded as fixing the value of the services so that Casey was entitled to a one-third share of the patent rights.

Privity of contract: effect of the rule: remedies (if any) available to a person not in privity

86 *Tweddle* v *Atkinson* (1861) 1 B & S 393

William Tweddle, the claimant, was married to the daughter of William Guy. In order to provide for the couple, Guy promised the claimant's father to pay the claimant £200 if the claimant's father would pay the claimant £100. An agreement was accordingly drawn up containing the above-mentioned promise, and giving William Tweddle the right to sue either promisor for the sums promised. Guy did not make the promised payment during his lifetime and the claimant now sued Guy's executor.

Held – the claimant's action failed because he had not given any consideration to Guy in return for the promise to pay £200. The provision in the agreement allowing William Tweddle to sue was of no effect without consideration.

87 *Dunlop v Selfridge* [1915] AC 847

The appellants were motor tyre manufacturers and sold tyres to Messrs Dew & Co who were motor accessory dealers. Under the terms of the contract, Dew & Co agreed not to sell the tyres below Dunlop's list price, i.e. £4.05 per tyre, and as Dunlop's agents, to obtain from other traders a similar undertaking. In return for this undertaking Dew & Co were to receive special discounts, some of which they could, if they wished, pass on to retailers who bought tyres. Selfridge & Co accepted two orders from customers for Dunlop covers at a lower price. They obtained the covers through Dew & Co and signed an agreement not to sell or offer the tyres below the list price. For giving this undertaking, Dew & Co gave them part of the discount received by Dew & Co from Dunlop. It was further agreed that £5 per tyre sold should be paid to Dunlop by way of liquidated damages. Selfridge supplied one of the two tyres ordered below list prices, i.e. at £3.65 per tyre. They did not actually supply the other, but informed the customer that they could only supply it at list price. The appellants claimed an injunction and damages against the respondents for breach of the agreement made with Dew & Co, claiming that Dew & Co were their agents in the matter.

Held – there was no contract between the parties. Dunlop could not enforce the contract made between the respondents and Dew & Co because they had not supplied consideration. Even if Dunlop were undisclosed principals, there was no consideration moving between them and the respondents. The discount received by Selfridge was part of that given by Dunlop to Dew & Co. Since Dew & Co were not bound to give any part of their discount to retailers, the discount received by Selfridge operated only as consideration between themselves and Dew & Co and could not be claimed by Dunlop as consideration to support a promise not to sell below list price.

Comment (i) It was in this case that the House of Lords adopted the definition of consideration given by Sir Frederick Pollock, i.e.: 'An act or forbearance of one party, *or the promise thereof*, is the price for which *the promise* of the other is bought and *the promise* thus given for value is enforceable.'

(ii) The case would now be dealt with under the Competition Act 1998. A resale price agreement is outlawed by s 2(2)(a) of the Act as an agreement preventing, restricting or distorting competition. The automatic result of breaching the 1998 Act is to make the offending parts of the agreement null and void so that the resale price aspect would not be enforceable. If it is possible to sever other legal provisions in the contract, these may be enforced and it may well be that the court would allow a claim by a buyer who has taken goods under the contract for breach of condition or warranty in regard to the quality of the goods. The Act does not specifically set out a right of private action as was seen in the *Dunlop* case. However, s 60(6)(b) says, in effect, that there is a private right of action under the Act (which mirrors EU law) if, and only if, there is a similar right under EU competition law. Most of those who have commented on the Act believe that EU law provides a right to damages and as appropriate an injunction. So damages and injunctions are clearly available to those who have suffered as a result of infringements of the 1998 Act. These individual claims are further considered in Chapter 16.

(iii) The case will live on because of the definition of consideration given in it. It is not such a good example of privity on its own facts because in the modern context the contract is unenforceable *because it is void* under competition law.

88 *Jackson v Horizon Holidays* [1975] 3 All ER 92

Mr Jackson had booked a four-week holiday in a hotel in Ceylon for himself and his family, everything to be 'of the highest standard'. The brochure issued by the defendants described the hotel as enjoying many facilities including a mini golf course, a swimming pool, and beauty and hairdressing salons. None of these in fact materialised and the food was distasteful. It was *held* that Mr Jackson could sue on the contract not only for his own loss and disappointment but also for that of his family. The decision was based on the fact that Mr Jackson had entered into the contract partly for the benefit of his family. On that basis an award of damages of £1,100 was not excessive. In the course of his judgment Lord Denning, MR said: 'The case comes within the principle stated by Lush, LJ in *Lloyd's v Harper* [1880] 16 Ch D 290 at p. 321: "... I consider it to be an established rule of law that where a contract is made with A for the benefit of B, A can sue on the contract for the benefit of B and recover all that B could have recovered if the contract had been made with B himself."' Speaking of these words, Lord Denning said: 'I think they should be accepted as correct, at any rate so long as the law forbids the third persons themselves to sue for damages. It is the only way in which a just result can be achieved.'

Comment (i) This judgment of Lord Denning has been much criticised since it infringes a very old rule of English contract law which states that if A contracts with B in return for B's promise to do something for C, if B then repudiates the contract, C has no enforceable claim, and A is restricted to an action for nominal damages by reason of his having suffered no loss. The judgment in *Jackson* was criticised by the Lords in *Woodar v Wimpey*

[1980] 1 All ER 571 and they assumed that only nominal damages were available in *Beswick* (see below) so that it must be regarded with caution.

The House of Lords said that the *Jackson* case could be justified on the basis that Mr Jackson *actually saw* his family suffering discomfort and disappointment. Their Lordships would not, however, accept that there was a general rule in contract that A could recover damages from B in respect of loss suffered by C.

(ii) If damages are recovered under the ruling given by Lord Denning in *Jackson*, the recipient must hand over the relevant shares to the other members of the family, and if he does not they can sue him in quasi-contract (see Chapter 18).

(iii) The House of Lords ruling in *Linden Gardens Trust Ltd v Lenesta Sludge Disposals Ltd* [1993] 3 All ER 417 is worth nothing. The owner of a site made a building contract with a contractor to erect offices, shops and flats. The site when developed was transferred to a third party who suffered loss because of the contractor's bad workmanship. The site owner sued for damages and was awarded full damages even though he had parted with the site but only because their Lordships found on the facts that the parties had envisaged that the site would be transferred to the third party and the contractor had impliedly taken on liability to him. The damages were held by the site owner *for the benefit of the third party* who had suffered the loss. The case provides an exception to the general rule that a claimant can only recover damages for his own loss and that a claimant who sues on behalf of others will only recover nominal damages. The implication of liability to the third party made the difference.

(iv) The solution is now clear: make sure that your third-party beneficiaries (here the family) are named in the contract and then they will be able to sue in their own right under the Contracts (Rights of Third Parties) Act 1999. In fact, the 1999 Act may well have applied here without naming the third parties specifically since the 1999 Act allows identification to be by description, e.g. 'Mr J Bloggs and family'. That expression in a contract could well cover those members of Mr Bloggs' family accompanying him.

89 *Beswick* v *Beswick* [1967] 2 All ER 1197

A coal merchant agreed to sell the business to his nephew in return for a weekly consultancy fee of £6 10s payable during his liftime, and after his death an annuity of £5 per week was to be payable to his widow for her lifetime. After the agreement was signed, the nephew took over the business and paid his uncle the sum of £6 10s as agreed. The uncle died on 3 November 1963, and the nephew paid the widow one sum of £5 and then refused to pay her any

more. On 30 June 1964, the widow became the administratrix of her husband's estate, and on 15 July 1964, she brought an action against the nephew for arrears of the weekly sums and for specific performance of the agreement for the future. She sued in her capacity as administratrix of the estate and also in her personal capacity. Her action failed at first instance and on appeal to the Court of Appeal, [1966] 3 All ER 1, it was decided amongst other things that:

(a) specific performance could in a proper case be ordered of a contract to pay money;

(b) 'property' in s 56(1) of the Law of Property Act 1925 included a contractual claim not concerned with realty and that, therefore, a third party could sue on a contract to which he was a stranger. The widow's claim in her personal capacity was, therefore, good (*per* Denning, MR and Danckwerts, LJ);

(c) the widow's claim as administratrix was good because she was not suing in her personal capacity but on behalf of her deceased husband, who had been a party to the agreement;

(d) that no trust in her favour could be inferred.

There was a further appeal to the House of Lords, though not on the creation of a trust, and there it was *held* that the widow's claim as administratrix succeeded, and that specific performance of a contract to pay money could be granted in a proper case. However, having decided the appeal on these grounds, their Lordships went on to say that the widow's personal claim would have failed because s 56 of the Law of Property Act 1925 was limited to cases involving realty. The 1925 Act was a consolidating not a codifying measure, so that if it contained words which were capable of more than one construction, effect should be given to the construction which did not alter the law. It was accepted that when the present provision was contained in the Real Property Act 1845, it had applied only to realty. Although s 205(1) of the 1925 Act appeared to have extended the provision to personal property, including things in action, it was expressly qualified by the words 'unless the context otherwise requires', and it was felt that Parliament had not intended to sweep away the rule of privity by what was in effect a sidewind.

Comment (i) Here the problem of whether or not to award nominal damages to the claimant referred to in *Jackson*'s case was overcome because the court awarded specific performance. However, four Law Lords said that if damages had been awarded they would have been nominal only, though Lord Pearce would have awarded substantial damages. Furthermore, it is unlikely that s 56 does have a very wide application. The sub-section says that a person may take the benefit of an agreement although he is not 'named as a party'. The legislation does not say that he need not *be a party*. There are those who take the view, therefore, that s 56(1) is designed to cover the situation where there is a covenant over land in favour of, say, 'the owner of Whiteacre', so that the owner of Whiteacre could benefit from the covenant, provided he could be ascertained, even though he was not named in the instrument creating the covenant. If this interpretation is correct, then s 56(1) of the 1925 Act has little effect on the law of contract generally.

(ii) The circumstances of this case are ideal for the application of the Contracts (Rights of Third Parties) Act 1999. If the contract between the coal merchant and his nephew had expressly provided that the widow could sue, she would have succeeded in her personal capacity and the case would probably have never come to court. In any case, s 1(1)(b) of the Act applies in that the contract conferred a benefit on her, which in itself would have allowed her to claim in a personal capacity on the assumption that her rights had not been excluded, as the 1999 Act allows.

Privity of contract: exceptions in the case of benefits and burdens attaching to land

90 *Smith and Snipes Hall Farm Ltd v River Douglas Catchment Board* [1949] 2 KB 500

In 1938 the defendants entered into an agreement with 11 persons owning land adjoining a certain stream, that, on the landowners paying some part of the cost, the defendants would improve the banks of the stream and maintain the said banks for all time. In 1940 one landowner sold her land to Smith, and in 1944 Smith leased the land to Snipes Hall Farm Ltd. In 1946, because of the defendant's negligence, the banks burst and the adjoining land was flooded.

Held – the claimants could enforce the covenant given in the agreement of 1938 even though they were strangers to it. The covenants were for the benefit of the land and affected its use and value and could therefore be transferred with it.

91 *Tulk v Moxhay* (1848) 2 Ph 774

The claimant was the owner of several plots of land in Leicester Square and in 1808 he sold one of them to a person called Elms. Elms agreed, for himself, his heirs and assigns, 'to keep the Square Garden open as a pleasure ground and uncovered with buildings'. After a number of conveyances, the land was sold to the defendant who claimed a right to build on it. The claimant sued for an injunction preventing the development of the land. The defendant, whilst admitting that he purchased the land with notice of the covenant,

claimed that he was not bound by it because he had not himself entered into it.

Held – an injunction to restrain building would be granted because there was a jurisdiction in equity to prevent, by way of injunction, acts inconsistent with a restrictive covenant on land, so long as the land was acquired with notice of the covenant, and the claimant retains land which can benefit from the covenant.

Comment (i) Such notice may now be constructive where the covenant is registered under land charges legislation. Knowledge need not be actual. It is assumed everyone knows, whether they have seen the register or not.

(ii) It was held in *Roake v Chadha* [1983] 3 All ER 503 that whether a covenant runs with the land depends upon its wording. If the words used in it prevent the benefit of the covenant, in this case that the plot holder of land would not build more than one house on it, passing to a subsequent owner of the land unless specifically assigned to him by the present owner, then the covenant would not run with the land as such but would depend upon assignment.

The common law rule of accord and satisfaction: agreed variations in contractual obligations are generally unenforceable without consideration

92 *Foakes v Beer* (1884) 9 App Cas 605

Mrs Beer had obtained a judgment against Dr Foakes for debt and costs. Dr Foakes agreed to settle the judgment debt by paying £500 down and £150 per half-year until the whole was paid, and Mrs Beer agreed not to take further action on the judgment. Dr Foakes duly paid the amount of the judgment plus costs. However, judgment debts carry interest by statute, and while Dr Foakes had been paying off the debt, interest amounting to £360 had been accruing on the diminishing balance. In this action Mrs Beer claimed the £360.

Held – she could do so. Her promise not to take further action on the judgment was not supported by any consideration moving from Dr Foakes. *Pinnel's* Case applied.

Comment (i) In view of the possible development of equity envisaged by Lord Denning in the *D & C Builders* case, see below, it might be better to restrict the application of this case to situations where the promise has been extorted and not freely given. If this were so, *Foakes v Beer* would be reconcilable with any development of the equitable rule of promissory estoppel on the lines envisaged by Lord Denning in *D & C Builders v Rees*.

(ii) However, in *Re Selectmove* (1994) the Court of Appeal followed *Foakes* by deciding that a promise to allow payment by instalments was invalid because it was not supported by consideration and even though the promise to accept instalments had in no way been extorted.

Accord and satisfaction: payment by cheque is not substituted performance: promissory estoppel may, in appropriate circumstances, extinguish as distinct from suspend contractual rights

93　*D & C Builders Ltd* v *Rees* [1965] 3 All ER 837

D & C Builders, a small company, did work for Rees for which he owed £482 13s 1d. There was at first no dispute as to the work done but Rees did not pay. In August and October 1964, the claimants wrote for the money and received no reply. On 13 November 1964, the wife of Rees (who was then ill) telephoned the claimants, complained about the work, and said, 'My husband will offer you £300 in settlement. That is all you will get. It is to be in satisfaction.' D & C Builders, being in desperate straits and faced with bankruptcy without the money, offered to take the £300 and allow a year to Rees to find the balance. Mrs Rees replied: 'No, we will never have enough money to pay the balance. £300 is better than nothing.' The claimants then said: 'We have no choice but to accept.' Mrs Rees gave the claimants a cheque and insisted on a receipt 'in completion of the account'. The claimants, being worried about their financial position, took legal advice and later brought an action for the balance. The defence was bad workmanship and that there was a binding settlement. The question of settlement was tried as a preliminary issue and the judge, following *Goddard* v *O'Brien* [1880] 9 QBD 33, decided that a cheque for a smaller amount was a good discharge of the debt, this being the generally accepted view of the law since that date. On appeal it was *held* (by the Master of the Rolls, Lord Denning) that *Goddard* v *O'Brien* was wrongly decided. A smaller sum in cash could be no settlement of a larger sum and 'no sensible distinction could be drawn between the payment of a lesser sum by cash and the payment of it by cheque'.

In the course of his judgment Lord Denning said of *High Trees*:

> It is worth noting that the principle may be applied, not only so as to suspend strict legal rights, but also so as to preclude the enforcement of them.
>
> This principle has been applied to cases where a creditor agrees to accept a lesser sum in discharge of a greater. So much so that we can now say that, when a creditor and a debtor enter on a course of negotiation, which leads the debtor to suppose

that, on payment of the lesser sum, the creditor will not enforce payment of the balance, and on the faith thereof the debtor pays the lesser sum and the creditor accepts it as satisfaction: then the creditor will not be allowed to enforce payment of the balance when it would be inequitable to do so. . . . But he is not bound unless there has been truly an accord between them.

In the present case there was no true accord. The debtor's wife had held the creditors to ransom, and there was no reason in law or equity why the claimants should not enforce the full amount of debt.

Comment (i) The case also illustrates the requirements of equality of bargaining power and the absence of economic duress in the negotiation (or as here, the re-negotiation) of a contract. (See also *Lloyds Bank* v *Bundy* (1974), Chapter 13.)

(ii) It was held in *Stour Valley Builders (a Firm)* v *Stuart, The Times*, 22 February 1993 that the fact that a cheque for a lesser sum, said to be given in full satisfaction but without consideration, was cashed by the recipient did not prevent him from suing for the balance, even though the cashing of the cheque might indicate agreement to take a lesser sum. The decision serves to confirm that, at common law, an *agreement*, express or implied, to change existing obligations is ineffective unless it is a *contract*.

(iii) The same rule was applied in *Inland Revenue Commissioners* v *Fry* [2001] STC 1715 where a cheque in payment of only half the tax bill was sent to the Revenue 'in full and final settlement'. The Revenue was able to sue for the balance even though the cheque had been cashed.

Accord and satisfaction: compromises between creditors

94　*Good* v *Cheesman* (1831) 2 B & Ad 328

The defendant had accepted two bills of exchange of which the claimant was the drawer. After the bills became due and before this action was brought, the claimant suggested that the defendant meet his creditors with a view perhaps to an agreement. The meeting was duly held and the defendant entered into an agreement with his creditors whereby the defendant was to pay one-third of his income to a trustee to be named by the creditors, and that this was to be the method by which the defendant's debts were to be paid. It was not clear from the evidence whether the claimant attended the meeting, though he certainly did not sign the agreement. There was, however, evidence that the agreement had been in his possession for some time and it was duly stamped before the trial. No trustee was in fact appointed, though the defendant was willing to go on with the agreement.

Held – the agreement bound the claimant and the action on the bills could not be sustained. The consideration, though not supplied to the claimant direct, existed in the forbearance of the other creditors. Each was bound in consequence of the agreement of the rest.

Comment (i) The better view is that the basis of this decision is to be found not in the law of contract but in tort, in the sense that once an agreement of this kind has been made it would be a *fraud* on the other creditors for one of their number to sue the debtor separately.

This also applies to joint debtors. A payment from one debtor of part of the sum owing with the agreement of the creditor and 'in full and final settlement' of the debt operates to release other joint debtors, such as partners, from liability and although such joint debtors are jointly and severally liable, a compromise with one in regard to the total sum owing prevents a claim against other joint debtors under the Civil Liability (Contribution) Act 1978 (see *Morris* v *Wentworth-Stanley*, *The Times*, 2 October 1998). Both the joint and several aspects of liability are released.

(ii) The *Good* v *Cheesman* arrangements would more usually be made today under the Insolvency Act 1986. Section 260 of that Act states that such an arrangement binds every creditor if it is approved by a meeting of creditors at which three-quarters in value vote in favour of the arrangement. Therefore, s 260 really provides an exception to the rule of accord and satisfaction.

Accord and satisfaction: payments by third parties

95 | *Welby* v *Drake* (1825) 1 C & P 557

The claimant sued the defendant for the sum of £9 on a debt which had originally been for £18. The defendant's father had paid the claimant £9 and the claimant had agreed to take that sum in full discharge of the debt.

Held – the payment of £9 by the defendant's father operated to discharge the debt of £18.

Comment (i) Here again, the basis of the decision is that it would be a fraud on the third party to sue the original debtor. 'If the father did pay the smaller sum in satisfaction of this debt, it is a bar to the [claimant's] now recovering against the son; because by suing the son, he commits a fraud on the father, whom he induced to advance his money on the faith of such advance being a discharge of his son from further liability.' (*Per* Lord Tenterden, CJ)

(ii) Also, of course, the creditor breaks his contract with the third party.

(iii) Where there is a payment by a third party, the acceptance of, say, a cheque by the creditor will be regarded as an acceptance of the payment in discharge of the debtor's liability. This is not the case where the creditor accepts a smaller payment by cheque from the debtor as distinct from a third party. (See *Stour Valley Builders (a firm)* (1993).)

Promissory estoppel: variation of contractual rights without consideration: the approach of equity: suspension of rights

96 | *Central London Property Trust Ltd* v *High Trees House Ltd* [1947] KB 130

In 1937 the claimant company granted to the defendants a lease of 99 years of a new block of flats at a rent of £2,500 per annum. The lease was by deed. During the period of the war the flats were by no means fully let owing to the absence of people from the London area. The defendant company, which was a subsidiary of the claimant company, realised that it could not meet the rent out of the profits then being made on the flats, and in 1940 the parties entered into an agreement which reduced the rent to £1,250 per annum, this agreement being put into writing but not by deed. The defendants continued to pay the reduced rent from 1941 to the beginning of 1945, by which time the flats were fully let, and they continued to pay the reduced rent thereafter. In September 1945, the receiver of the claimant company investigated the matter and asked for arrears of £7,916, suggesting that the liability created by the lease still existed, and that the agreement of 1940 was not supported by any consideration. The receiver then brought this action to establish the legal position. He claimed £625, being the difference in rent for the two quarters ending 29 September and 25 December 1945.

Held – (*a*) a simple contract can in equity vary a deed (i.e. the lease), though it had not done so here because the simple contract was not supported by consideration; (*b*) as the agreement for the reduction of rent had been acted upon by the defendants, the claimant was estopped in equity from claiming the full rent from 1941 until early 1945 when the flats were fully let. After that time it was entitled to do so because the second agreement was only operative during the continuance of the conditions which gave rise to it. To this extent the limited claim of the receiver succeeded. If the receiver had sued for the balance of rent from 1941, he would have failed.

97 | *Tool Metal Manufacturing Co Ltd* v *Tungsten Electric Co Ltd* [1955] 2 All ER 657

The appellants were the registered proprietors of British letters patent. In April 1938, they made a contract with the respondents whereby they gave the latter a licence to manufacture 'hard metal alloys' in accordance with the inventions which were the subject of patent. By the contract the respondents agreed to pay 'compensation' to the appellants if in any one month they sold more than a stated quantity of metal alloys.

Compensation was duly paid by the respondents until the outbreak of war in 1939 but thereafter none was paid. It was found as a fact that in 1942 the appellants agreed to suspend the enforcement of compensation payments pending the making of a new contract. In 1944 negotiations for such new contracts were begun but broke down. In 1945 the respondents sued the appellants for breach of contract and the appellants counterclaimed for payment of compensation as from 1 June 1945. As regards the arguments on the counterclaim, it was eventually *held* by the Court of Appeal that the agreement of 1942 operated in equity to prevent the appellants demanding compensation until they had given reasonable notice to the respondents of their intention to resume their strict legal rights and that such notice had not been given.

In September 1950, the appellants themselves issued a writ (now claim form) against the respondents claiming compensation as from 1 January 1947. The respondents pleaded the equity raised by the agreement of 1942 and argued that reasonable notice of its termination had not been given. When this action reached the House of Lords it was *held* – affirming *Hughes* v *Metropolitan Railway Co* and the *High Trees* case – that the agreement of 1942 operated in equity to suspend the appellants' legal rights to compensation until reasonable notice to resume them had been given. However, the counterclaim in the first action in 1945 amounted to such notice and since the appellants were not now claiming any compensation as due to them before 1 January 1947, the appellants succeeded in this second action and were awarded £84,000 under the compensation claim.

Promissory estoppel: the meaning of reliance upon the promise

98 **W J Alan & Co v El Nasr Export and Import Co** [1972] 2 All ER 127

A contract for the sale of coffee provided for the price expressed in Kenyan shillings to be paid by irrevocable letter of credit. The buyers procured a confirmed letter expressed in sterling and the sellers obtained part payment thereunder. While shipment was in progress sterling was devalued and the sellers claimed such additional sum as would bring the price up to the sterling equivalent of Kenyan shillings at the current rate. Orr, J *held* that the buyers were liable to pay the additional sum as the currency of account was Kenyan shillings. On appeal by the buyers it was *held* – allowing the appeal – that the sellers by accepting payment in sterling had irrevocably waived their right to be paid in Kenyan currency or had accepted a variation of the sale contract, and that a party who has waived his rights cannot afterwards insist on them if the other party has acted on that belief differently from the way in which he would otherwise have acted; and the other party need not show that he has acted to his detriment. In the course of his judgment Lord Denning, MR said:

> If one party, by his conduct, leads another to believe that the strict rights arising under the contract will not be insisted on, intending that the other should act on that belief, and he does act on it, then the first party will not afterwards be allowed to insist on the strict legal rights when it would be inequitable for him to do so. . . . There may be no consideration moving from him who benefits by the waiver. There may be no detriment to him acting on it. There may be nothing in writing. Nevertheless, the one who waives his strict rights cannot afterwards insist on them. His strict rights are at any rate suspended so long as the waiver lasts. He may on occasion be able to revert to his strict legal rights for the future by giving reasonable notice in that behalf, or otherwise making it plain by his conduct that he will thereafter insist on them. . . . I know that it has been suggested in some quarters that there must be a detriment. But I can find no support for it in the authorities cited by the judge. The nearest approach to it is the statement by Viscount Simonds in the *Tool Metal* case that the other must have been led 'to alter his position' which was adopted by Lord Hodson in *Emmanuel Ayodeji Ajayi* v *RT Briscoe (Nigeria) Ltd* [1964] 3 All ER 556. But that only means that he must have been led to act differently from what he otherwise would have done. And, if you study the cases in which the doctrine has been applied, you will see that all that is required is that one should have 'acted on the belief induced by the other party'. That is how Lord Cohen put it in the *Tool Metal* case and it is how I would put it myself.

Comment Since, as in *High Trees*, a tenant who only pays one-half of the rent cannot be said to be 'acting to his detriment', 'detriment' cannot be a requirement of equitable estoppel. It is a requirement of estoppel at common law.

Promissory estoppel: does not operate to create new contractual rights but merely to suspend existing ones

99 **Combe v Combe** [1951] 2 KB 215

The parties were married in 1915 and separated in 1939. In February 1943, the wife obtained a decree *nisi* of divorce, and a few days later the husband entered into an agreement under which he was to pay his wife £100 per annum, free of income tax. The decree was made absolute in August 1943. The husband did not make the agreed payments and the wife did not apply to the court for maintenance but chose to rely on the alleged contract. She brought this action for arrears under that contract. Evidence showed that her income was between £700 and £800 per annum and the defendant's was £650 per annum. Byrne, J, at first instance, *held* that, although the wife had not supplied consideration, the agreement was nevertheless enforceable, following the decision in the *High Trees* case, as a promise made to be acted upon and in fact acted upon.

Held – (*a*) the *High Trees* decision was not intended to create new actions where none existed before, and it had not abolished the requirement of consideration in the formation of simple contracts. In such cases consideration was a cardinal necessity; (*b*) in the words of Birkett, LJ, the doctrine was 'a shield not a sword', i.e. a defence to an action, not a cause of action; (*c*) the doctrine applied to the modification of existing agreements by subsequent promises and had no relevance to the formation of a contract; (*d*) it was not possible to find consideration in the fact that the wife forbore to claim maintenance from the court, since no such contractual undertaking by her could have been binding even if she had given it. Therefore, this action by the wife must fail because the agreement was not supported by consideration.

Promissory estoppel: other applications

100 *Durham Fancy Goods Ltd v Michael Jackson (Fancy Goods) Ltd* [1968] 2 All ER 987

On 18 September 1967, the claimants drew a bill of exchange on the first defendants in the following form, 'M. Jackson (Fancy Goods) Co'. The bill was signed by Mr Jackson who was the director and company secretary. The bill was dishonoured and the claimants brought an action against Mr Jackson contending that by signing the form of acceptance he had committed a criminal offence under s 108 of the Companies Act 1948 and had made himself personally liable on the bill because he should either have returned the bill with a request that it be re-addressed to Michael Jackson (Fancy Goods) Ltd, or he should have accepted it 'M. Jackson (Fancy Goods) Ltd p.p. Michael Jackson (Fancy Goods) Ltd, Michael Jackson'. It was *held* – by Donaldson, J – that the misdescription was in breach of s 108 of the Companies Act 1948, and that Mr Jackson was personally liable, under the section, to pay the bill. However, since the error was really that of the claimants, they were estopped from

enforcing Mr Jackson's personal liability. The principle of equity upon which the promissory estoppel cases were based was applicable and barred the claimants' claim. That principle was formulated by Lord Cairns in *Hughes* v *Metropolitan Railway Co* (1877) 2 App Cas 439 at p 448, and although in his enunciation Lord Cairns assumed a pre-existing contractual relationship between the parties, that was not essential provided that there was a pre-existing legal relationship which could in certain circumstances give rise to liabilities and penalties. Such a relationship was created by s 108.

Comment (i) A holder other than the claimants might have been able to bring an action against Mr Jackson under s 108 since such a holder would not have been affected by the equity in that he would not have drawn the bill in an incorrect name. The provisions are now in the Companies Act 1985, s 349.

(*Note*: s 108 provided: '(1) every company . . . (c) shall have its name mentioned in legible characters . . . in all bills of exchange . . . purporting to be signed by or on behalf of the company . . . (4) If an officer of the company or any person on his behalf . . . (b) signs . . . on behalf of the company any bill of exchange . . . wherein its name is not mentioned in manner aforesaid . . . he shall be liable to a fine not exceeding £50, and shall further be personally liable to the holder of the bill of exchange . . . for the amount thereof unless it is duly paid by the company.')

(ii) A further application of the doctrine occurred in *Crabb* v *Arun District Council* [1975] 3 All ER 865 where Arun represented to Mr Crabb that he had a right of way across Arun's land which gave access to the public highway. It was *held* – by the Court of Appeal – that Arun could not go back on that promise after Mr Crabb had sold some of his land and had left himself without access to the public highway except by the right of way across Arun's land. He was granted an injunction to enforce the right. When promissory estoppel is used in this situation, a claimant can raise it and indeed base his action upon it. Thus, the expression of Birkett, LJ in *Combe* v *Combe* (1951) that the doctrine is 'a shield not a sword' is not always applicable where estoppel is used in situations other than the variation of contractual rights.

Contractual intention: domestic agreements between husband and wife are in general terms unenforceable

101 *Balfour* v *Balfour* [1919] 2 KB 571

The defendant was a civil servant stationed in Ceylon. In November 1915, he came to England on leave with his wife, the claimant in the present action. In August

1916, the defendant returned alone to Ceylon because his wife's doctor had advised her that her health would not stand up to a further period of service abroad. Later the husband wrote to his wife suggesting that they remain apart, and in 1918 the claimant obtained a decree *nisi*. In this case the claimant alleged that before her husband sailed for Ceylon he had agreed, in consultation with her, that he would give her £30 per month as maintenance, and she now sued because of his failure to abide by the said agreement. The Court of Appeal *held* that there was no enforceable contract because in this sort of situation it must be assumed that the parties did not intend to create legal relations. The provision for a flat payment of £30 per month for an indefinite period with no attempt to take into account changes in the circumstances of the parties did not suggest a binding agreement. Duke, LJ seems to have based his decision on the fact that the wife had not supplied any consideration.

Contractual intention: agreements between husband and wife designed to regulate the terms of their separation are usually regarded as binding contracts

102 *Merritt* v *Merritt* [1970] 2 All ER 760

After a husband had formed an attachment for another woman and had left his wife, a meeting was held between the parties on 25 May 1966, in the husband's car. The husband agreed to pay the wife £40 per month maintenance and also wrote out and signed a document stating that in consideration of the wife paying all charges in connection with the matrimonial home until the mortgage repayments had been completed, he would agree to transfer the property to her sole ownership. The wife took the document away with her and had herself paid off the mortgage. The husband did not subsequently transfer the property to his wife and she claimed a declaration that she was the sole beneficial owner and asked for an order that her husband should transfer the property to her forthwith. The husband's defence was that the agreement was a family arrangement not intended to create legal relations.

Held – by the Court of Appeal:

(*a*) the agreement, having been made when the parties were not living together in amity, was enforceable (*Balfour* v *Balfour* (1919) distinguished);

(*b*) the contention that there was no consideration to support the husband's promise could not be sustained. The payment of the balance of the mortgage was a detriment to the wife and the husband had received the benefit of being relieved of liability to the building society.

Accordingly, the wife was entitled to the relief she claimed.

Contractual intention: family agreements other than those between husband and wife

103 *Simpkins* v *Pays* [1955] 3 All ER 10

The defendant and the defendant's granddaughter made an agreement with the claimant, who was a paying boarder, that they should submit in the defendant's name a weekly coupon, containing a forecast by each of them, to a Sunday newspaper fashion competition. On one occasion a forecast by the granddaughter was correct and the defendant received a prize of £750. The claimant sued for her share of that sum. The defence was that there was no intention to create legal relations but that the transaction was a friendly arrangement binding in honour only.

Held – there was an intention to create legal relations. Far from being a friendly domestic arrangement, the evidence showed that it was a joint enterprise and that the parties expected to share any prize that was won.

Comment A family agreement which went the other way was *Julian* v *Furby* (1982) 132 NLJ 64. J was an experienced plasterer who helped F, his son-in-law, and his wife (J's favourite daughter) to buy, alter and furnish a house for them. They later quarrelled and J sued for £4,440. This included materials supplied and F was prepared to pay for these but not for J's labour which, it was understood, would be free. It was held by the Court of Appeal that there was never an intention to create a legal relationship between the parties in regard to the labour which J and F jointly provided in refurbishing the house.

Contractual intention: family agreements: effect of vagueness

104 *Jones* v *Padavatton* [1969] 2 All ER 616

In 1962 the claimant, Mrs Jones, who lived in Trinidad, made an offer to the defendant Mrs Padavatton, her daughter, to provide maintenance for her at the rate of £42 a month if she would leave her job in Washington in the United States and go to England and read for the Bar. Mrs Padavatton was at that time divorced from her husband having the custody of the child of that marriage. The agreement was an informal one and there was uncertainty as to its exact terms. Nevertheless, the daughter came to England in November 1962, bringing the child with her, and began to read for the Bar, her fees and maintenance being paid for by Mrs Jones. In 1964 it appeared that the daughter was experiencing some discomfort in England occupying one room in Acton for which she had to pay £6 17s 6d per week. At this stage Mrs Jones offered to buy a large house in London to be occupied partly by the daughter and partly by tenants, the income from rents to go to the daughter in lieu of maintenance. Again, there was no written agreement but the house was purchased for £6,000 and conveyed to Mrs Jones. The daughter moved into the house in January 1965, and tenants arrived, it still being uncertain what precisely was to happen to the surplus rent income (if any) and what rooms the daughter was to occupy. No money from the rents was received by Mrs Jones and no accounts were submitted to her. In 1967 Mrs Jones claimed possession of the house from her daughter, who had by that time married again, and the daughter counterclaimed for £1,655 18s 9d said to have been paid in connection with running the house. At the hearing the daughter still had, as the examinations were then structured, one subject to pass in Part I of the Bar examinations and the whole of Part II remained to be taken.

Held – by the Court of Appeal:

(*a*) the arrangements were throughout family agreements depending upon the good faith of the parties in keeping the promises made and not intended to be rigid binding agreements. Furthermore, the arrangements were far too vague and uncertain to be enforceable as contracts (*Per* Danckwerts and Fenton Atkinson, LJJ);

(*b*) although the agreement to maintain while reading for the Bar might have been regarded as creating a legal obligation in the mother to pay (the terms being sufficiently stated and duration for a reasonable time being implied), the daughter could not claim anything in respect of that agreement which must be regarded as having terminated in 1967, five years being a reasonable time in which to complete studies for the Bar. The arrangements in relation to the home were very vague and must be regarded as made without contractual intent. (*Per* Salmon, LJ)

The mother was, therefore, entitled to possession of the house and had no liability under the maintenance agreement. The counterclaim by the daughter was left to be settled by the parties.

Comment In this case there was an inference of contractual intent in the mother's promise because it caused Mrs Padavatton to leave one job to study for another,

but the vagueness of the arrangement negatived that intent as in *Gould* v *Gould* [1969] 3 All ER 728.

Contractual intent: generally but not always assumed in business agreements unless excluded by the parties

105 *Kleinwort Benson Ltd* v *Malaysia Mining Corporation, Berhad* [1989] 1 All ER 785

In this case the High Court had decided that a letter of comfort (as they are called) stating that it was the policy of Malaysia Mining to ensure that its subsidiary MMC Metals Ltd was 'at all times in a position to meet its liabilities' in regard to a loan made by Kleinwort to MMC had contractual effect. This meant that Kleinwort was entitled to recover from Malaysia the amount owed to it by the insolvent MMC which went into liquidation after the tin market collapsed in 1985. Malaysia appealed to the Court of Appeal which reversed the High Court ruling. The problem has always been to decide whether a letter of comfort of the usual kind contains a legal obligation or only a moral one. In the High Court Mr Justice Hirst decided that there was a legal obligation: the Court of Appeal decided that it was only a moral one. The letter, said the Court of Appeal, stated the policy of Malaysia. It gave no contractual warranty as to the company's future conduct. In these circumstances there was no need to apply the presumption of an intention to create legal relations just because the transaction was in the course of business as laid down in *Edwards* v *Skyways* (1964).

Comment The wording of the letter of comfort must be looked at and if it appears to create a moral obligation only, then it has no contractual force. It is of course no bad thing for those in business to honour moral obligations but as Lord Justice Ralph Gibson said, moral responsibilities are not a matter for the courts.

106 *Jones* v *Vernon's Pools Ltd* [1938] 2 All ER 626

The claimant said that he had sent to the defendants a football coupon on which the penny points pool was all correct. The defendants denied having received it and relied on a clause printed on every coupon. The said clause provided that the transaction should not 'give rise to any legal relationship . . . or be legally enforceable . . . but . . . binding in honour only'. The court *held* that this clause was a bar to any action in a court of law.

Comment This case was followed by the Court of Appeal in *Appleson* v *Littlewood Ltd* [1939] 1 All ER 464, where the contract contained a similar clause.

107 *Rose and Frank Co v Crompton (J R) & Brothers Ltd* [1925] AC 445

In 1913 the claimant, an American company, entered into an agreement with the defendant, an English company, whereby the claimant was appointed sole agent for the sale in the USA of paper tissues supplied by the defendant. The contract was for a period of three years with an option to extend that time. The agreement was extended to March 1920, but in 1919 the defendant terminated it without notice. The defendant had received a number of orders for tissues before the termination of the contract, and it refused to execute them. The claimant sued for breach of contract and for non-delivery of the goods actually ordered. The agreement of 1913 contained an 'Honourable Pledge Clause' drafted as follows: 'This arrangement is not entered into nor is this memorandum written as a formal or legal agreement and shall not be subject to legal jurisdiction in the courts of the United States of America or England . . .'. It was *held* by the House of Lords that the 1913 agreement was not binding on the parties, but that in so far as the agreement had been acted upon by the defendant's acceptance of orders, the said orders were binding contracts of sale. Nevertheless, the agreement was not binding for the future.

Comment Those in business have only rarely to address themselves to the concept of intention to create legal relations, and this is why the law, as dispensed in the courts, has created a presumption that business agreements are to be regarded as binding in the absence of something such as an 'honourable pledge clause', as in this case. It is also worth noting that even these clauses are comparatively rare in the business world.

MAKING THE CONTRACT III

Formalities: contracts which must be evidenced in writing: guarantee and indemnity: s 4, Statute of Frauds 1677 and its effect

108 *Mountstephen v Lakeman* (1871) LR 7 QB 196

The defendant was chairman of the Brixham Local Board of Health. The claimant, who was a builder and contractor, was employed in 1866 by the Board to construct certain main sewage works in the town. On 19 March 1866, notice was given by the Board to owners of certain homes to connect their house drains with the main sewer within 21 days. Before the expiration of the 21 days Robert Adams, the surveyor of the Board, suggested to the claimant that he make the connections. The claimant said he was willing to do the work if the Board would see him paid. On 5 April 1866, i.e. before the expiration of the 21 days, the claimant commenced work on the connections. However, before work commenced, it appeared that the claimant had had an interview with the defendant at which the following conversation took place:

Defendant: 'What objection have you to making the connections?'
Claimant: 'I have none, if you or the Board will order the work or become responsible for the payment.'
Defendant: 'Go on Mountstephen and do the work and I will see you paid.'

The claimant completed the connections in April and May 1866, and sent an account to the Board on 5 December 1866. The Board disclaimed responsibility on the ground that it had never entered into any agreement with the claimant nor authorised any officer of the Board to agree with him for the performance of the work in question. It was *held* – that Lakeman had undertaken a personal liability to pay the claimant and had not given a guarantee of the liability of a third party, i.e. the Board. In consequence, Lakeman had given an indemnity which did not need to be in writing under s 4 of the Statute of Frauds 1677. The claimant was, therefore, entitled to enforce the oral undertaking given by the defendant.

Comment (i) Section 4 of the Statute of Frauds 1677 provides that: 'No action shall be brought . . . whereby to charge the defendant upon any special promise to answer for the debt default or miscarriage of another person . . . unless the agreement upon which such action shall be brought or some memorandum or note thereof shall be in writing and signed by the party to be charged therewith or some other person thereunto by him lawfully authorized.' It was held in *Birkmyr* v *Darnell* (1704) 1 Salk 27 that the words 'debt default or miscarriage of another person' meant that the section applied only where there was some person other than the surety who was primarily liable.

(ii) It should be noted that the absence of writing makes a contract of guarantee unenforceable and not void. This is because s 4 of the 1677 Act states in effect that 'No action shall be brought . . .' unless the guarantee is in writing. So if a person is *defending* an action and not *bringing* one and the existence of a guarantee would provide a defence, the guarantee can be proved orally and the judge will not require a written memorandum of it.

In *Deutsche Bank AG* v *Ibrahim and Others, Financial Times*, 15 January 1992, Mr Ibrahim's two daughters were the tenants of two leases. The leases were deposited with the bank to secure Mr Ibrahim's overdraft. The daughters later regretted having done this and tried to get the leases back from the bank. If this were done the bank would lose a good security since it would not be able to sell the leases to a third party in order to repay Mr Ibrahim's overdraft. The bank brought this action to establish that it had a right to the leases. The daughters counterclaimed against the bank for the return of the leases. They were thus, in effect, *bringing an action* against the bank, which *the bank was defending* by trying to establish its right to the leases. Part of the counter-claim was that by depositing the leases the daughters were guaranteeing their father's overdraft and yet there was no memorandum in writing signed by the daughters. The court accepted that they had given a guarantee but allowed the bank to prove the contract, i.e. overdraft for leases, *orally* because the bank was *defending* its right to retain the leases as security under the guarantee. The bank succeeded and was allowed to retain the leases.

(iii) The Act of 1677 continues to be of relevance in modern commercial cases, and *Actionstrength Ltd* v *International Glass Engineering* [2002] 1 WLR 566 shows it can still make an important commercial agreement unenforceable. The defendants were contracted to build a glass factory. The defendants sub-contracted Actionstrength to provide the workforce. The defendants were late making payments to Actionstrength and so Actionstrength threatened to remove the workforce from the site. The owners of the factory agreed orally with Actionstrength to pay them amounts due from the defendants if the defendants did not do so, if they would keep the workforce on site. This they did but later the defendants failed to pay Actionstrength and this claim was brought against the owners of the factory who were the second defendants for payment of the guarantee. The claim failed, the Court of Appeal ruling that the oral contract was a guarantee not an indemnity and there being no evidence in writing the claim failed.

Minors: necessaries: the general test

109 *Nash* v *Inman* [1908] 2 KB 1

The claimant was a Savile Row tailor and the defend-ant was a minor undergraduate at Trinity College, Cambridge. The claimant sent his agent to Cambridge because he had heard that the defendant was spend-ing money freely, and might be the sort of person who would be interested in high-class clothing. As a result of the agent's visit, the claimant supplied the defendant with various articles of clothing to the value of £145 0s 3d during the period October 1902 to June 1903. The clothes included 11 fancy waistcoats. The claimant now sued the minor for the price of the clothes. Evidence showed that the defendant's father was in a good position, being an architect with a town house and a country house, and it could be said

that the clothes supplied were suitable to the defendant's position in life. However, his father proved that the defendant was amply supplied with such clothes when the claimant delivered the clothing now in question.

Held – the claimant's claim failed because he had not established that the goods supplied were necessaries.

Minors: beneficial contracts

110 *Roberts* v *Gray* [1913] 1 KB 520

The defendant wished to become a professional billiards player and entered into an agreement with the claimant, a leading professional, to go on a joint tour. The claimant went to some trouble in order to organise the tour, but a dispute arose between the parties and the defendant refused to go. The claimant now sued for damages of £6,000.

Held – the contract was for the minor's benefit, being in effect for his instruction as a billiards player. There-fore, the claimant could sustain an action for damages for breach of contract, and damages of £1,500 were awarded.

Comment (i) In *Chaplin* v *Leslie Frewin (Publishers)* [1965] 3 All ER 764 the claimant, the minor son of a famous father, made a contract with the defendants under which they were to publish a book written for him, telling his life story and entitled *I Couldn't Smoke the Grass on my Father's Lawn*. The claimant sought to avoid the contract on the ground that the book gave an inaccurate picture of his approach to life.

Held – amongst other things – the contract was binding if it was for the minor's benefit. The time to determine that question was when the contract was made and at that time it was for the minor's benefit and could not be avoided.

(ii) Although this was not a contract of service, it could be regarded as analogous to one, and was for the claimant's benefit because although he had a ghost writer the publishing contract could have helped him to make a start as an author. So the court still thought it necessary to use the contract of service analogy and not merely say that the contract was beneficial because it made Mr Chaplin money.

(iii) In *Denmark Productions* v *Boscobel Productions* (1967) 111 Sol J 715 Widgery, J held that a contract by which a minor appoints managers and agents to look after his business affairs is, in modern conditions, necessary if he is to earn his living and rise to fame, and if it is for his benefit it will be upheld by analogy with a contract of service.

(iv) The case of *De Francesco* v *Barnum* (1890) 45 Ch D 430 shows that so far as beneficial contracts are con-cerned the subject matter of the contract is not decisive. Two minors bound themselves in contract to the claimant for seven years to be taught stage dancing. The minors agreed that they would not accept any engagements without his consent. They later accepted an engagement with Barnum, and the claimant sued Barnum for interfering with the contractual relationship between himself and the minors, to enforce the apprenticeship deed against the minors and to obtain damages for its breach. The contract was, of course, for the minors' benefit and was *prima facie* binding on them. However, when the court considered the deed in greater detail, it emerged that there were certain onerous terms in it. For example, the minors bound themselves not to marry during the apprenticeship; the payment was hardly generous, the claimant agreeing to pay them 9d per night and 6d for matinee appearances for the first three years, and 1s per night and 6d for matinee performances during the remainder of the apprenticeship. The claimant did not undertake to maintain them whilst they were unemployed and did not undertake to find them engagements. The minors could also be engaged in performances abroad at a fee of 5s per week. Further the claimant could terminate the contract if he felt that the minors were not suitable for the career of dancer. It appeared from the contract that the minors were at the absolute disposal of the claimant.

Held – the deed was an unreasonable one and was, therefore, unenforceable against the minors. Barnum could not, therefore, be held liable, since the tort of interference with a contractual relationship presupposes the existence of an enforceable contract.

Minors: trading contracts are not binding on a minor unless exceptionally they are analogous to a contract of service

111   *Mercantile Union Guarantee Corporation v Ball* [1937] 2 KB 498

The purchase on hire-purchase terms of a motor lorry by a minor carrying on a business as a haulage contractor was *held* not to be a contract for necessaries, but a trading contract by which the minor could not be bound.

Comment It would be possible for the owner to recover the lorry without the assistance of s 3 of the Minors' Contracts Act 1987 because a hire-purchase contract is a contract of bailment not a sale. Thus, ownership does not pass when the goods are delivered.

Minors: contracts binding unless repudiated: consequences of defective contracts

112   *Steinberg v Scala (Leeds) Ltd* [1923] 2 Ch 452

The claimant, Miss Steinberg, purchased shares in the defendant company and paid certain sums of money on application, on allotment and on one call. Being unable to meet future calls, she repudiated the contract whilst still a minor and claimed:

(*a*) rectification of the Register of Members to remove her name therefrom, thus relieving her from liability on future calls; and

(*b*) the recovery of the money already paid.

The company agreed to rectify the register but was not prepared to return the money paid.

Held – the claim under (*b*) above failed because there had been total failure of consideration. The shares had some value and gave some rights, even though the claimant had not received any dividends and the shares had always stood at a discount on the market.

Comment In *Davies* v *Beynon-Harris* (1931) 47 TLR 424 a minor was allowed to avoid a lease of a flat without liability for future rent or damages but was not allowed to recover rent paid. However, in *Goode* v *Harrison* (1821) 5 B & Ald 147 a partner who was a minor took no steps to avoid the partnership contract while a minor or afterwards. He was held liable for the debts of the firm incurred after he came of age.

113   *Pearce v Brain* [1929] 2 KB 310

Pearce, a minor, exchanged his motor cycle for a motor car belonging to Brain. The minor had little use out of the car, and had in fact driven it only 70 miles in all when it broke down because of serious defects in the back axle. Pearce now sued to recover his motor cycle, claiming that the consideration had wholly failed.

Held – (*a*) a contract for the exchange of goods, whilst not a sale of goods, is a contract for the supply of goods, and that if the goods are not necessaries, the contract was void if with a minor (now not binding unless ratified); (*b*) the car was not a necessary good, so the contract was void; (*c*) even so, the minor could only recover money paid under a void contract if the consideration had wholly failed. The court considered that the minor had received a benefit under the contract, albeit small, and that he could not recover the motor cycle.

Comment In *Corpe* v *Overton* (1833) 10 Bing 252 a minor agreed to enter into a partnership and deposited £100 with the defendant as security for performance of the contract. The minor rescinded the contract before the partnership came into existence.

Held – he could recover the £100 because he had received no benefit having never been a partner. There had been total failure of consideration.

Contracting with persons of unsound mind and drunkards

114 *Imperial Loan Co v Stone* [1892] QB 599

This was an action on a promissory note. The defendant pleaded that at the time of making the note he was insane and that the claimant knew he was. The jury found that he was, in fact, insane but could not agree on the question of whether the claimant knew it. The judge entered judgment for the defendant.

Held – he was wrong. The defendant in order to succeed must convince the court on both issues.

Comment (i) In *Hart v O'Connor* [1985] 2 All ER 880 the Privy Council refused to set aside an agreement to sell farmland in New Zealand because although the seller was of unsound mind, his affliction was not apparent. The price paid was not unreasonable. If it had been, the Privy Council said that the contract could have been set aside for equitable fraud as an unconscionable bargain.

(ii) This case is retained to show the changes effected by the Mental Capacity Act 2005. The question of whether the other party knew of the mental incapacity does not arise. There is a presumption of capacity unless and until the person claiming not to have capacity (or his or her representatives) can show otherwise. The knowledge requirement still applies in cases of drunkenness (see below).

115 *Matthews v Baxter* [1873] LR 8 Exch 132

Matthews agreed to buy houses from Baxter. He was so drunk as not to know what he was doing. Afterwards, when sober, he ratified and confirmed the contract. It was *held* that both parties were bound by it.

Comment A contract with a drunken person must in effect always be voidable by him because presumably the fact that he is drunk will be known to the other party. This is not so in regard to unsoundness of mind which might not be known to the other party.

Registered companies: the *ultra vires* rule: position at common law

116 *Ashbury Railway Carriage & Iron Co v Riche* (1875) LR 7 HL 653

The company was formed for the purposes (stated in the memorandum of association) of making and selling railway wagons and other railway plant and carrying on the business of mechanical engineers and general contractors. The company bought a concession for the construction of a railway system in Belgium from Antwerp to Tournai and entered into an agreement whereby Messrs Riche were to construct the railway line. Messrs Riche commenced the work and the company paid over certain sums of money in connection with the contract. The Ashbury company later ran into difficulties, and the shareholders wished the directors to take over the contract in a personal capacity and indemnify the shareholders. The directors thereupon repudiated the contract on behalf of the company and Messrs Riche sued for breach of contract.

Held – the directors were able to repudiate because the contract to construct a railway system was *ultra vires* and void. On a proper construction of the objects, the company had power to supply materials for the construction of railways but had no power to engage in the actual construction of them. Further, the subsequent assent of all the shareholders could not, in those days, make the contract binding, for, at common law, a principal cannot ratify the *ultra vires* contracts of his agent.

REALITY OF CONSENT I

Mistake: documents mistakenly signed: relevance of signer's negligence

117 *Saunders v Anglia Building Society* [1970] 3 All ER 961

Mrs Gallie, a widow aged 78 years, signed a document which Lee, her nephew's friend, told her was a deed of gift of her house to her nephew. She did not read the document but believed what Lee had told her. In fact, the document was an assignment of her leasehold interest in the house to Lee, and Lee later mortgaged that interest to a building society. In an action by Mrs Gallie against Lee and the building society, it was *held* at first instance – (*a*) that the assignment was void and did not confer a title on Lee; (*b*) that although Mrs Gallie had been negligent, she was not estopped from denying the validity of the deed against the building society for she owed it no duty. The Court of Appeal, in allowing an appeal by the building society, *held* that the plea of *non est factum* was not available to Mrs Gallie. The transaction intended and carried out was the same, i.e. an assignment.

The appeal to the House of Lords was brought by Saunders, the executrix of Mrs Gallie's estate. The House of Lords affirmed the decision of the Court of Appeal but took the opportunity to restate the law relating to the avoidance of documents on the ground of mistake as follows.

(*a*) The plea of *non est factum* will rarely be available to a person of full capacity who signs a document apparently having legal effect without troubling to read it, i.e. negligently.

(*b*) A mistake as to the identity of the person in whose favour the document is executed will not normally support a plea of *non est factum* though it may do if the court regards the mistake as fundamental (Lord Reid and Lord Hodson). Neither judge felt that the personality error made by Mrs Gallie was sufficient to support the plea.

(c) The distinction taken in *Howatson* v *Webb* [1908] 1 Ch 1 that the mistake must be as to the class or character of the document and not merely as to its contents was regarded as illogical. Under the *Howatson* test, if X signed a guarantee for £1,000 believing it to be an insurance policy he escaped all liability on the guarantee, but if he signed a guarantee for £10,000 believing it to be a guarantee for £100 he was fully liable for £10,000. Under *Saunders* the document which was in fact signed must be 'fundamentally different', 'radically different', or 'totally different'. The test is more flexible than the character/contents one and yet still restricts the operation of the plea of *non est factum*.

Comment (i) The charge of negligence might be avoided where a person was told he was witnessing a confidential document and had no reason to doubt that he was. Many such documents are witnessed each day and the witnesses would never dream of asking to read them nor would they think themselves negligent because they had not done so. Surely the *Saunders* decision is not intended to turn witnesses into snoopers. Thus the decision in the old case of *Lewis* v *Clay* (1898) 77 LT 653 would probably be the same under modern law. In that case Clay was asked by Lord William Neville to witness a confidential document and signed in holes in blotting paper placed over the document by Neville. In fact, he was signing two promissory notes and two letters authorising Lewis to pay the amount of the notes to Lord William Neville. The court *held* that the signature of Clay in the circumstances had no more effect than if it had been written for an autograph collector or in an album and he was not bound by the bills of exchange.

In fact, the survival of the plea of *non est factum* in cases such as *Lewis* is recognised in certain of the judgments in the House of Lords in *Saunders* (see Lord Pearson at p 979 where, because of the cunning deception of a friend and the supposedly confidential nature of the documents in *Lewis*, he would have allowed the plea in *Lewis's* case to succeed, as indeed it did).

(ii) As between the immediate parties to what is always in effect a fraud, there is, of course, no difficulty in avoiding the contract or transaction mistakenly entered into. The rules set out above are relevant only where the contract or transaction mistakenly entered into has affected a third party, as where he has taken a bill of exchange bona fide and for value on which the defendant's signature was obtained under circumstances of mistake (*Foster* v *Mackinnon* (1869) LR 4 CP 704) or has lent money on an interest in land obtained by a fraudulent assignment under circumstances of mistake (*Saunders* v *Anglia Building Society* (1970) – see above).

The principles set out in *Saunders'* case apply also to those who sign blank forms as well as to those who sign completed documents without reading them (*United Dominions Trust Ltd* v *Western* [1975] 3 All ER 1017).

Unilateral mistake: ingredients: A is mistaken and B the other party to the contract knows or ought to know he is

118 | *Higgins (W) Ltd* v *Northampton Corporation* [1927] 1 Ch 128

The claimant entered into a contract with the corporation for the erection of dwelling houses. The claimant made an arithmetical error in arriving at his price, having deducted a certain rather small sum twice over. The corporation sealed the contract, assuming that the price arrived at by the claimant was correct.

Held – the contract was binding on the parties. Rectification of such a contract was not possible because the power of the court to rectify agreements made under mistake is confined to common not unilateral mistake. Here, rectification would only have been granted if fraud or misrepresentation had been present.

Comment (i) Since this case was decided the courts have moved away from the idea that rectification of a contract for unilateral mistake is permissible only if there is some form of sharp practice (*Thomas Bates & Sons Ltd* v *Wyndham's (Lingerie) Ltd* (1981) – see Chapter 12, Rectification). Even so, rectification would not have been granted in this case because Northampton Corporation was not aware of the claimant's error, which is still a requirement for rectification.

(ii) The rule of unilateral mistake does not seem to apply to mistakes as to the value of the contract. If you go into a junk shop and recognise a genuine Georgian silver teapot marked at £10, your contract of purchase, if made, would be good in law, although it would be obvious that the seller had made a mistake and that the buyer was aware of it. This is the rule of *caveat venditor* (let the seller beware) and applies provided the seller intends to offer the goods at his marked price.

119 | *Cundy* v *Lindsay* (1878) 3 App Cas 459

The respondents were linen manufacturers in Belfast. A fraudulent person named Blenkarn wrote to the respondents from 37 Wood Street, Cheapside, ordering a quantity of handkerchiefs but signed his letter in such a way that it appeared to come from Messrs Blenkiron, a well-known and solvent house doing business at 123 Wood Street. The respondents knew of the existence of Blenkiron but did not know the address. Accordingly, the handkerchiefs were sent to 37 Wood Street. Blenkarn then sold them to the appellants, and was later convicted and sentenced for the fraud. The respondents sued the appellants in conversion claiming that the contract they had made with Blenkarn was void for mistake, and that the property had not passed to Blenkarn or to the appellants.

Held – the respondents succeeded; there was an operative mistake as to the party with whom they were contracting.

Comment (i) It is, however, essential that at the time of making the apparent contract the mistaken party regarded the identity of the other party as vital and that he intended to deal with some person other than the actual person to whom in fact he addressed the offer, as in *Cundy v Lindsay* (1878) (see above). The mistake must be as to *identity*, not *attributes*, e.g. creditworthiness. As between the parties, the result is much the same since a mistake as to attributes may make the contract *voidable*, but the difference may vitally affect the interests of third parties. Thus, in *King's Norton Metal Co Ltd v Edridge, Merrett and Co Ltd* (1897) 14 TLR 98, where the facts were similar to *Cundy*, a fraudulent person called Wallis ordered goods from the claimants using notepaper headed Hallam & Co. The notepaper said that Hallam & Co had agencies abroad and generally represented the company as creditworthy. The claimants sold Hallam & Co some brass rivet wire on credit. The goods were never paid for but Wallis sold the goods on to Edridge Merrett who paid for them and were innocent of the way in which Wallis had obtained them. The claimants sued Edridge Merrett in conversion saying that the contract between them and Hallam/Wallis was void for mistake so that Edridge Merrett did not become owners of the wire because Hallam/Wallis had not. The Court of Appeal *held* that the contract between King's Norton and Edridge was voidable for fraud but not void for mistake. The claimants could not show a confusion of entities. There was no other Hallam or Wallis in their business lives with whom they could have been confused.

(ii) The difference between *Cundy* and *King's Norton* is that in *Cundy* there was another entity to get mixed up with. In *King's Norton* there was no one else to get mixed up with.

Unilateral mistake: where the parties are face to face

120 *Lewis v Averay* [1971] 3 All ER 907

Mr Lewis agreed to sell his car to a rogue who called on him after seeing an advertisement. Before the sale took place the rogue talked knowledgeably about the film world giving the impression that he was the actor Richard Green in the 'Robin Hood' serial which was running on TV at the time. He signed a dud cheque for £450 in the name of 'RA Green' and was allowed to have the log book and drive the car away late the same night, when he produced a film studio pass in the name of 'Green'.

Held – by the Court of Appeal – Mr Lewis had effectively contracted to sell the car to the rogue and could not recover it or damages from Mr Averay, a student, who had bought it from the rogue for £200. The contract between Mr Lewis and the rogue was voidable for fraud but not void for unilateral mistake.

Comment (i) It is thought that the contract would be void for mistake in a case such as this if the dishonest person assumed a disguise so that he appeared physically to be the person he said he was.

(ii) It should not be assumed that this case is of general application. It does depend on the parties being face to face. Therefore, if as in *Shogun Finance Ltd v Hudson* [2000] CLY 2600 A buys a car on hire-purchase through a dealer and claims to be someone else producing that person's driving licence A forging his signature on the HP documents sent to the finance company in order to satisfy credit investigation, then the contract with the finance company is void for mistake as to the person contracted with and the impersonator does not get a title to the car nor can he give a title to a purchaser from him. The finance company therefore can recover the vehicle. Although the purchaser was not a trade purchaser, he could not rely on Part III of the Hire Purchase Act 1964 to get a good title because this applies only to sales by persons who have cars on a hire-purchase agreement and since the contract was void there never was an agreement.

(iii) Part III of the Hire Purchase Act 1964 is designed to protect bona fide purchasers for value of motor vehicles where the seller is a mere bailee under a hire-purchase agreement and where he sells the vehicle before he has become the owner as where he has not paid all the instalments. A good title can be obtained by a private purchaser but not a trade purchaser. However, the seller must have a valid agreement and therefore be what the 1964 Act describes as the 'debtor'.

121 *Ingram and Others v Little* [1961] 1 QB 31

The claimants, three ladies, were the joint owners of a car. They wished to sell the car and advertised it for sale. A fraudulent person, introducing himself as Hutchinson, offered to buy it. He was taken for a drive in it and during conversation said that his home was at Caterham. Later the rogue offered £700 for the car but this was refused, though a subsequent offer of £717 was one which the claimants were prepared to accept. At this point the rogue produced a cheque book and one of the claimants, who was conducting the negotiations, said that the deal was off and that they would not accept a cheque. The rogue then said that he was PGM Hutchinson, that he had business interests in Guildford, and that he lived at Stanstead House, Stanstead Road, Caterham. One of the claimants checked this information in a telephone directory and, on finding it to be accurate, allowed him to take the car in return for a cheque. The cheque was dishonoured, and in the meantime the rogue had sold the car to the defendants and had disappeared without a trace. The claimants sued for the return of the car, or for its value as damages in conversion, claiming that the contract between themselves and the rogue was void for mistake, and that the property (or ownership) had not passed. At the trial judgment was given for the claimants, Slade, J finding the contract void. His judgment was *affirmed* by the Court of Appeal, though Devlin, LJ dissented, saying that the mistake made was as to the creditworthiness of the rogue, not as to his identity, since he was before the claimants when the contract was made. A mistake as to the substance of the rogue would be a mistake as to quality and would not avoid the contract. Devlin, LJ also suggested that legislation should provide for an apportionment of the loss incurred by two innocent parties who suffer as a result of the fraud of a third.

Comment (i) The distinction drawn in some of these cases are fine ones. It is difficult to distinguish *Ingram* from *Lewis*. As we have seen, the question for the court to answer in these cases is whether or not the offeror at the time of making the offer regarded the identity of the offeree as a matter of vital importance. The general rule seems to be that where the parties are face to face when the contract is made identity will not be vital and the contract voidable only. *Ingram* would appear to be the exceptional case.

(ii) The reader may wonder why the cheque did not give the rogue away in the sense that it would carry his name and not that of PGM Hutchinson. The reason is that cheques were not personalised in those days in the sense of carrying the name of the account holder. The rogue wrote the Hutchinson name and address on the back of the cheque, whereas today, if a seller requests this, it is only necessary to write the address of the account holder, as the name appears on the front.

Unilateral mistake: effect in equity: refusal of specific performance and rescission

122 *Webster* v *Cecil* (1861) 30 Beav 62

The parties had been negotiating for the sale of certain property. Later Cecil offered by letter to sell the property for £1,250. Webster was aware that his offer was probably a slip because he knew that Cecil had already refused an offer of £2,000, and in fact Cecil wished to offer the property at £2,250. Webster accepted the offer and sued for specific performance of the contract. The court refused to grant the decree.

Comment This is not merely a case of mistake as to the value of the contract because here Webster knew that Cecil did not intend to offer the property at £1,250. The rule of 'let the seller beware' applies where the seller is mistaken as to the value but at least intends to offer the goods at his marked price.

Common mistake: the rules of *res extincta* and *res sua*

123 *Couturier* v *Hastie* (1856) 5 HLC 673

Messrs Hastie dispatched a cargo of corn from Salonica and sent the charterparty and bill of lading to their London agents so that the corn might be sold. The London agents employed Couturier to sell the corn and a person named Callander bought it. Unknown to the parties, the cargo had become overheated and had been landed at the nearest port and sold, so that when the contract was made the corn was not really in existence. Callander repudiated the contract and Couturier was sued because he was a *del credere* agent, i.e. an agent who, for an extra commission, undertakes to indemnify his principal against losses arising out of the repudiation of the contract by any third party introduced by him.

Held – the claim against Couturier failed because the contract presupposed that the goods were in existence when they were sold to Callander.

124 *Cochrane* v *Willis* (1865) LR 1 Ch App 58

Cochrane was the trustee in bankruptcy of Joseph Willis who was the tenant for life of certain estates in Lancaster. Joseph Willis had been adjudicated bankrupt in Calcutta where he resided. The remainder of the estate was to go to Daniel Willis, the brother of Joseph, on the latter's death, with eventual remainder to Henry Willis, the son of Daniel. Joseph Willis had the right to cut the timber on the estates during his life interest, and the representative of Cochrane in England threatened to cut and sell it for the benefit of Joseph's creditors. Daniel and Henry wished to preserve the timber and so they agreed with Cochrane through his representatives to pay the value of the timber to Cochrane if he would refrain from cutting it. News then reached England that when the above agreement was made Joseph was dead, and, therefore, the life interest had vested in (i.e. become owned by)

Daniel. In this action by the trustee to enforce the agreement it was *held* that Daniel was making a contract to preserve something which was already his and the court found, applying the doctrine of *res sua*, that the agreement was void for an identical or common mistake.

Common mistakes as to quality: no effect at common law

125 *Bell v Lever Bros Ltd* [1932] AC 161

Lever Bros had a controlling interest in the Niger Company. Bell was the chairman, and a person called Snelling was the vice-chairman of the Niger Company's Board. Both directors had service contracts which had some time to run. They became redundant as a result of amalgamations and Lever Bros contracted to pay Bell £30,000 and Snelling £20,000 as compensation. These sums were paid over and then it was discovered that Bell and Snelling had committed breaches of duty against the Niger Company during their term of office by making secret profits of £1,360 on a cocoa pooling scheme. As directors of the Niger Company, Bell and Snelling attended meetings at which the selling price of cocoa was fixed in advance. Both of them bought and sold on their own account before the prices were made public. They could, therefore, have been dismissed without compensation. Lever Bros sought to set aside the payments on the ground of mistake.

Held – the contract was not void because Lever Bros had got what they bargained for, i.e. the cancellation of two service contracts which, though they might have been terminated, were actually in existence when the cancellation agreement was made. The mistake was as to the quality of the two directors and such mistakes did not avoid the contracts. The case is one of common mistake because although Bell and Snelling admitted that they were liable to account to the company for the profit made from office, they convinced the court that they had forgotten their misdemeanour of insider dealing when they made the contract for compensation. They thought they were good directors who were entitled to that compensation.

Comment The case also decided that an employee was not under a duty to disclose to his employer his own misconduct or breaches of duty towards his employer. However, employee/directors do have a duty to disclose their *own* breaches of contract to their companies. This is because their fiduciary position as directors overrides the ordinary employer/employee relationship. However, in the *Bell* case the directors concerned kept the compensation and were not required to disclose their wrongdoings

to Lever Bros because they were not directors of Lever Bros but only of Niger. However, a director of, say, company A is under a duty to disclose his wrongdoing, if any, towards company A where he receives his compensation from company A itself. Failure so to disclose will allow the company to claim back a golden handshake of the kind given to Bell and Snelling.

It is worth mentioning that an employee is under a duty to disclose breaches of duty/misconduct of subordinate employees, even though he is not under a duty to disclose to his employer his own misconduct or breaches of duty. This follows from the decision of the Court of Appeal in *Sybron Corporation v Rochem Ltd* [1983] 2 All ER 707.

126 *Leaf v International Galleries* [1950] 1 All ER 693

In 1944 the claimant bought from the defendants an oil painting of Salisbury Cathedral for £85. A label on the back said that the painting had been exhibited as by Constable. Five years later the claimant tried to sell the drawing at Christie's and was told that this was not so. He now sued for rescission of the contract, no claim for damages being made. The following points of interest emerged from the decision of the Court of Appeal. (*a*) It was possible to restore the status quo by the mere exchange of the drawing and the purchase money so that rescission was not prevented by inability to restore the previous position. (*b*) The mistake made by the parties in assuming the drawing to be a Constable was a mistake as to quality and did not avoid the contract. (*c*) The statement that the drawing was by Constable could have been treated as a warranty giving rise to a claim for damages, but it was not possible to award damages because the appeal was based on the claimant's right to rescind. (*d*) The court, therefore, treated the statement as a representation and, finding it to be innocent, refused to rescind the contract because of the passage of time since the purchase.

Comment Mr Leaf might well have recovered damages if he had sued for these under what is now s 13 of the Sale of Goods Act 1979 (sale by description – goods described as by Constable). Mr Leaf asked for leave to amend his claim to include this when the case was in the county court but leave was refused.

Common mistake: the equitable approach

127 *Cooper v Phibbs* (1867) LR 2 HL 149

Cooper agreed to take a lease of a fishery from Phibbs, his uncle's daughter who became apparent owner of it on her father's death. Unknown to either party, the fishery already belonged to Cooper. This arose from a mistake by Cooper's uncle as to how the family land was held. The uncle innocently thought he owned the fishery and before he died told Cooper so, but in fact it was owned by Cooper himself. Cooper now brought this action to set aside the lease and for delivery up of the lease.

Held – the lease must be set aside on the grounds of common or identical bilateral mistake. However, since equity has the power to give ancillary relief, Phibbs was given a lien on the fishery for the improvements she had made to it during the time she believed it to be hers. This lien could be discharged by Cooper giving Phibbs the value of the improvements.

Equity has no power to rescind a contract on the ground of mistake as to quality

128 *Great Peace Shipping Ltd* v *Tsavliris Salvage (International) Ltd* (2002) 152 New Law Journal 1616

A ship suffered damage in the Indian Ocean. Its owners engaged the defendant salvors to assist in the recovery. The salvors found a tug through a firm of London brokers. However, it was five or six days away from the scene. Fearing the ship would be lost the salvors approached the brokers again. The brokers asked a third party. They suggested the claimant's vessel *Great Peace* which the third party thought on the basis of false information was nearby. A contract of hire was made for *Great Peace* for a minimum of five days. In fact, *Great Peace* was several hundred miles from the damaged ship. The defendant cancelled the contract and refused to pay the hire. There was a minimum five-day hire clause in the contract (called a charterparty). This claim for the hire was then brought.

All parties to the arrangement were genuinely mistaken as to the actual position of *Great Peace*. No warranties were given or representations made as to the actual position of *Great Peace*. A common mistake as to quality therefore. Was she near or far? The defendant's case for rescission of the contract in equity based on *Solle* v *Butcher* (1950) was refused by the Court of Appeal. The court ruled that the contract was enforceable and the claimant's case succeeded. The court concluded that it was impossible to reconcile *Solle* v *Butcher* (1950) with the decision of the House of Lords in *Bell* v *Lever Bros* (1932). *Solle* had not been developed. It had been a fertile source of academic debate but in practice had given rise to very few cases and caused confusion in the law. If coherence was to be restored, it could only be done by declaring that there could be no rescission of a contract on the ground of common mistake where

that contract was valid and enforceable on ordinary principles of contract law.

Comment (i) The better answer for the claimant in this case would have been to make the statement about the suitability of *Great Peace* a condition precedent of the contract. It would not then have come into being given the distance of the *Great Peace* from the damaged ship.

(ii) In spite of putting an end to rescission for common mistake, other equitable approaches survive. Thus in *Grist* v *Bailey* [1966] 2 All ER 875 a house was sold cheaply because the parties thought that vacant possession could not be obtained as there was a tenant in it who was protected by rent legislation. This was not the case and the tenant gave up possession. The claimant asked for the equitable remedy of specific performance but this was refused. The fact that the court did offer rescission to the defendant is perhaps now more dubious.

Rectification: equity can rectify mistakes made by the parties in recording their agreement

129 *Joscelyne* v *Nissen* [1970] 1 All ER 1213

The claimant, Mr Joscelyne, sought rectification of a written contract made on 18 June 1964, under which he had made over his car hire business to his daughter, Mrs Margaret Nissen. It had been expressly agreed during negotiations that in return for the car hire business Mrs Nissen would pay certain expenses including gas, electricity and coal bills but the agreement on these matters was not expressly incorporated in the written contract. Furthermore, the parties had agreed that no concluded contract was to be regarded as having been made until the signing of a formal written document.

Mrs Nissen failed to pay the bills and the claimant brought an action in the Edmonton County Court claiming amongst other things a declaration that Mrs Nissen should pay the gas, electricity and coal bills and alternatively that the written agreement of 18 June 1964 should be rectified to include a provision to that effect. The county court judge allowed the claim for rectification although there was no binding antecedent contract between the parties on the issue of payment of the expenses. The Court of Appeal, after considering different expressions of judicial views upon what was required before a contractual instrument might be rectified by the court, *held* that the law did not require a binding antecedent contract, provided there was some outward expression of agreement between the contracting parties. Rectification could be made even though there was no binding contract until the written agreement which was to be rectified was entered into.

130 Frederick Rose (London) Ltd v William Pim & Co Ltd [1953] 2 All ER 739

The claimants received an order from an Egyptian client for feveroles (a type of horsebean). The claimants did not know what was meant by feveroles and asked the defendants what they were and whether they could supply them. The defendants said that feveroles were horsebeans and that they could supply them, so the claimants entered into a written agreement to buy horsebeans from the defendants which were then supplied to the Egyptian client under the order. In fact, there were three types of horsebeans: feves, feveroles and fevettes, and the claimants had been supplied with feves, which were less valuable than feveroles. The claimants were sued by the Egyptian client and now wished to recover the damages they had had to pay from the defendants. In order to do so, they had to obtain rectification of the written contract with the defendants in which the goods were described as 'horsebeans'. The word 'horsebeans' had to be rectified to 'feveroles', otherwise the defendants were not in breach.

Held –

(*a*) Rectification was not possible because the contract expressed what the parties had agreed to, i.e. to buy and sell horsebeans. Thus, the supply of any of the three varieties would have amounted to fulfilment of the contract.

(*b*) The claimants might have rescinded for misrepresentation but they could not restore the status quo, having sold the beans.

(*c*) The claimants might have recovered damages for breach of warranty, but the statement that 'feveroles are horsebeans and we can supply them' was oral, and warranties in a contract for the sale of goods of £10 and upwards had in 1953 to be evidenced in writing. This is not the case today.

(*d*) The defence of mistake was also raised, i.e. both buyer and seller thought that all horsebeans were feveroles. This was an identical bilateral or common mistake, but since it was not a case of *res extincta* or *res sua*, it had no effect on the contract.

Comment This case is quite complex on its facts but, to put the rule in a simpler context, if A and B orally agreed on the sale of A's drawing of Salisbury cathedral, thought by A and B to be by John Constable, but in fact by Fred Constable, an unknown Victorian artist, and then put that agreement into a written contract, the contract could not be rectified simply because A and B thought that the drawing was by John Constable, because the written contract would be the same as the oral one, as in the above case. The approach is, after all, logical enough. You cannot sensibly ask the court to make the written agreement conform with the one actually made when it already does. The agreement is for the sale of A's drawing of Salisbury cathedral, not 'a drawing of Salisbury cathedral by John Constable'.

131 Thomas Bates & Sons Ltd v Wyndham's (Lingerie) Ltd [1981] 1 All ER 1077

The claimant granted in 1956 a lease to the defendants with an option for renewal. This lease had a clause under which the rent on renewal was to be agreed by the parties or by arbitration. The option was exercised in 1963 for a seven-year lease, and again in 1970 for a 14-year lease at a rent of £2,350 per annum for the first five years and thereafter subject to rent review every five years. This lease, which was drafted by the claimants' managing director, did not contain an arbitration clause. The defendants knew that it did not. At the end of the first five-year period the claimants suggested that a new rent should be agreed. The defendants would not agree and took the view that the rent of £2,350 should continue for the whole 14 years unless there was an agreement between the parties to the contrary. Deputy Judge Michael Wheeler QC, sitting in the High Court, ordered rectification and the Court of Appeal affirmed that decision. The clause inserted by the court allowed the rent to be settled by arbitration if the parties did not agree.

Comment At one time it was thought that rectification was available only for a common mistake by both parties. However, as appears from this case, rectification can be given for unilateral mistake. The principles on which it is granted appear in the judgment of Buckley, LJ who said: 'First, that one party, A, erroneously believed that the document sought to be rectified contained a particular term or provision, or possibly did not contain a particular term or provision, which, mistakenly, it did contain; second that the other party, B, was aware of the omission or the inclusion and that it was due to a mistake on the part of A; third that B has omitted to draw the mistake to the notice of A. And I think there must be a fourth element involved, namely that the mistake must be calculated to benefit B.' The general principle upon which the judgment is based would appear to be one of equitable estoppel.

Mutual mistake: effect at common law and in equity: the sense of the promise

132 Wood v Scarth (1858) 1 F & F 293

The claimant was suing for damages for breach of contract alleging that the defendant had entered into an agreement to grant the claimant a lease of a public house, but had refused to convey the property. It was shown in evidence that the defendant intended to offer the lease at a rent, and also to include a premium on taking up the lease of £500. The defendant had told his agent to make this clear to the claimant, but the agent had not mentioned it. After discussions with the agent, the claimant wrote to the defendant proposing to take the lease 'on the terms already agreed upon', to which the defendant replied accepting the proposal. There was a mutual or non-identical bilateral mistake. The defendant thought that he was agreeing to lease the premises for a rent plus a premium, and the claimant thought he was taking a lease for rental only because he did not know of the premium. The claimant had sued for specific performance in 1855, and the court in the exercise of its equitable jurisdiction had decided that specific performance could not be granted in view of the mistake, as to grant it would be unduly hard on the defendant. However, in this action the claimant sued at common law for damages, and damages were granted to him on the ground that in mutual or non-identical mistake the court may find the sense of the promise and regard a contract as having been made on these terms. Here it was quite reasonable for the claimant to suppose that there was no premium to be paid. Thus, a contract came into being on the terms as understood by the claimant, and he was entitled to damages for breach of it. The contract clearly identified the agreement made.

Comment This case shows that equitable remedies are discretionary and not available as of right as damages at common law are. Also note the benefits of the Judicature Acts, 1873–75. In this case, which pre-dates those Acts, the action for specific performance was brought in Chancery in 1855 and the action at common law for damages in 1858. Common law and equitable remedies could not be granted in one and the same action until the Judicature Acts were passed.

133 *Raffles v Wichelhaus* (1864) 2 HC 906

The defendants agreed to buy from the claimants 125 bales of cotton to arrive 'ex *Peerless* from Bombay'. There were two ships called *Peerless* sailing from Bombay, one in October and one in December. The defendants thought they were buying the cotton on the ship sailing in October, and the claimants meant to sell the cotton on the ship sailing in December. In fact, the claimants had no cotton on the ship sailing in October. The defendants refused to take delivery of the cotton when the second ship arrived and were now sued for breach of contract.

Held – since there was a mistake as to the subject matter of the contract, there was, in effect, no contract between the parties, or at least no contract

which clearly identified the agreement made. The claimants' action failed.

REALITY OF CONSENT II

Misrepresentation: effect of change of circumstances making a statement untrue

134 *With v O'Flanagan* [1936] 1 All ER 727

The defendant was a medical practitioner who wished to sell his practice. The claimant was interested and in January 1934 the defendant represented to the claimant that the income from the practice was £2,000 a year. The contract was not signed until May 1934, and in the meantime the defendant had been ill and the practice had been run by various other doctors who substituted for the defendant while he was ill. In consequence, the receipts fell to £5 per week, and no mention of this fact was made when the contract was entered into. The claimant now claimed rescission of the contract.

Held – he could do so. The representation made in January was of a continuing nature and induced the contract made in May. The claimant had a right to be informed of a change of circumstances, and the defendant's silence amounted to a misrepresentation.

Comment An interesting modern example is provided by *Spice Girls Ltd v Aprilia World Service BV, The Times*, 5 April 2000, where the company agreed to a contract for the Spice Girls to make a video promoting its goods on the basis that there were five Spice Girls, and logos and other material showed the five members of the band. In fact, Geri Halliwell had already disclosed her intention to leave the band, but this was not mentioned. The company was awarded damages under s 2(1) of the Misrepresentation Act 1967. The Spice Girls had no reasonable grounds to believe that there would be five of them to perform the contract.

Misrepresentation: statements of intention, opinion or belief as actionable statements of fact

135 *Edgington v Fitzmaurice* (1885) 29 Ch D 459

The claimant was induced to lend money to a company by a representation made by its directors that the money would be used to improve the company's buildings and generally expand the business. In fact, the directors intended to use the money to pay off the company's existing debts as the creditors were pressing hard for payment. When the claimant discovered that he had been misled, he sued the directors for damages for fraud. The defence was that the statement that they had made was not a statement of a past or present fact but a mere statement of intention which could not be the basis of an action for fraud.

Held – the directors were liable in deceit. Bowen, LJ said: 'There must be a misstatement of an existing fact: but the state of a man's mind is as much a fact as the state of his digestion. It is true that it is very difficult to prove what the state of a man's mind at a particular time is, but if it can be ascertained, it is as much a fact as anything else. A misrepresentation as to the state of a man's mind is, therefore, a misstatement of fact.'

136 *Smith v Land and House Property Corporation* (1884) 28 Ch D 7

The claimants put up for sale on 4 August 1882 the Marine Hotel, Walton-on-the-Naze, stating in the particulars that it was let to 'Mr Frederick Fleck (a most desirable tenant) at a rental of £400 for an unexpired term of $27^1/_2$ years'. The directors of the defendant company sent the Secretary, Mr Lewin, to inspect the property and he reported that Fleck was not doing much business and that the town seemed to be in the last stages of decay. The directors, on receiving this report, directed Mr Lewin to bid up to £5,000, and in fact he bought the hotel for £4,700. Before completion, Fleck became bankrupt and the defendant company refused to complete the purchase, whereupon the claimants sued for specific performance. It was proved that on 1 May 1882 the March quarter's rent was wholly unpaid, that a distress was then threatened, i.e. the landlord was threatening to remove property from the hotel for sale to pay the rent, and that Fleck paid £30 on 6 May, £40 on 13 June, and the remaining £30 shortly before the sale. No part of the June's quarter rent had been paid. The chairman of the defendant company said that the hotel would not have been purchased but for the statement in the particulars that Fleck was a most desirable tenant.

Held – specific performance would not be granted. The description of Fleck as a most desirable tenant was not a mere expression of opinion, but contained an implied assertion that the vendors knew of no facts leading to the conclusion that he was not. The circumstances relating to the unpaid rent showed that Fleck was not a desirable tenant and there was a misrepresentation. Bowen, LJ said:

> It is material to observe that it is often fallaciously assumed that a statement of opinion cannot involve the statement of a fact. In a case where the facts are equally well known to both parties, what one of them says to the other is frequently nothing but an expression of opinion. The statement of such opinion is in a sense a statement of a fact about the condition of the man's own mind, but only of an irrelevant fact, for it is of no consequence what the opinion is. But if the facts are not equally known to both sides, then a statement of opinion by the one who knows the facts best involves very often a statement of a material fact, for he impliedly states that he knows facts which justify his opinion.

Comment These principles are followed in claims for negligent misrepresentation under the Misrepresentation Act 1967. Thus in *BG plc* v *Nelson Group Services (Maintenance) Ltd* [2002] EWCA Civ 547 the Court of Appeal in dealing with statements of opinion as actionable under s 2(1) stated: 'When an opinion was expressed where the person who expressed it did not know of facts that justified that opinion he is misrepresenting his state of knowledge sufficient to bring the case within s 2(1)'.

Misrepresentation: must induce the contract: materiality

137 *Peek v Gurney* [1873] LR 6 HL 377

Peek purchased shares in a company on the faith of statements appearing in a prospectus issued by the respondents who were directors of the company. Certain statements were false and Peek sued the directors. It appeared that Peek was not an original allottee, but had purchased the shares on what is now called the 'after-market', though he had relied on the prospectus.

Held – Peek's action failed because the statements in the prospectus were only intended to mislead the original allottees. Once the statements had induced the public to be original subscribers, their force was spent.

Comment (i) The decision has a somewhat unfortunate effect because at those times when public issues are oversubscribed it is most likely that persons who did not receive an allotment or an adequate allotment as subscribers will try to purchase further shares within a short time on the Stock Exchange (i.e. the 'after-market'). These people will clearly be relying on the prospectus, but under this decision would have no claim in respect of false statements in it.

(ii) This decision, and the one in *Re Northumberland* (see p 319), would appear to be seriously affected, at least on its own facts, by more recent legislation in the Financial Services and Markets Act 2000. As regards who can sue under an inaccurate prospectus, s 87(1) states: 'any person who has acquired securities to which the particulars apply and suffered loss in respect of them . . .'. This would seem to include all subscribers whether they have relied on the prospectus (or listing particulars) or not. It seems, therefore, that a subscriber need not be aware of the error or even have seen the listing particulars. The sub-section would also seem to cover subsequent purchasers after the first issue thus affecting *Peek* v *Gurney* (above), at least on its own facts.

(iii) It should be noted, however, that s 87(1) is a statutory remedy in company law. So far as the law of contract is concerned, the purpose of the statements in the listing particulars (or prospectus) is to invite persons to apply for shares in the company, i.e. to induce the contract with the company, and in contract law the statement must have been relied on and be material. So far as remedies for contractual misrepresentation (including remedies under the Misrepresentation Act 1967) are concerned, the particulars cannot be relied upon by those who purchase shares from some source other than the company or by persons who have not seen them. In contract law, therefore, *Peek* and *Re Northumberland* survive. However, most claimants will sue successfully under the statutory remedy in s 87(1). There are, none the less, some special defences to a claim under s 87(1) (see p 295) and where a particular defendant, e.g. a director of the company, can claim one or more of these, the claimant may have to revert to a remedy under the Misrepresentation Act 1967. Under this Act these special defences, apart from reasonable grounds for believing the statement to be true, do not apply. Such a claimant would be faced with the rulings in *Peek* and *Re Northumberland*, though he would seem to be able to sue under the *Hedley Byrne* case (see below) where, once again, the statutory defences do not apply. The claim there is in tort (negligence) and not contract. Section 87(1) of the 2000 Act expressly reserves the right of claimants to sue under the Misrepresentation Act 1967 and/or tort under *Hedley Byrne*.

(iv) A claim in tort for damages for negligent misstatement should also be available under *Hedley Byrne* (see p 773) in that those who publicly advertise a prospectus must surely in the modern context foresee that it will be relied upon by subscribers *and* by those who purchase from subscribers on the stock market for a reasonable time after the issue of the prospectus.

(v) In fact, in the most recent decision *Possfund Custodian Trustee Ltd* v *Victor Derek Diamond, Financial Times*, 13 April 1996 Mr Justice Lightman in the High Court stated that nowadays it is at least arguable that those who are responsible for issuing prospectuses owe a duty of care to those who purchase the shares in what can be described as the after-market in reliance on the prospectus. This could place liability on the company's directors, the company itself and its financial advisers if they are negligent. The matter did not come to a full trial,

Lightman, J's statement being made in preliminary proceedings. It should be noted that purchasers on the after-market following an issue with a listing are already protected by the Financial Services and Markets Act 2000. The only advantage of suing under *Possfund* is that not all of the 2000 Act defences are available at common law.

138 *Redgrave v Hurd* (1881) 20 Ch D 1

The claimant was a solicitor who wished to take a partner into the business. During negotiations between the claimant and Hurd the claimant stated that the income of the business was £300 a year. The papers which the claimant produced showed that the income was not quite £200 a year, and Hurd asked about the balance. Redgrave then produced further papers which he said showed how the balance was made up, but which only showed a very small amount of income making the total up to about £200. Hurd did not examine these papers in any detail, but agreed to become a partner. Later Hurd discovered the true position and refused to complete the contract. The claimant sued for breach, and Hurd raised the misrepresentation as a defence and counterclaimed for rescission of the contract.

Held – Hurd had relied on Redgrave's statements regarding the income and the contract could be rescinded. It did not matter that Hurd had the means of discovering their untruth; he was entitled to rely on Redgrave's statement.

Comment Relief is not barred simply because there is an unsuccessful attempt by the person misled to discover the truth where the misrepresentation is fraudulent.

139 *Smith v Chadwick* (1884) 9 App Cas 187

This action was brought by the claimant, who was a steel manufacturer, against Messrs Chadwick, Adamson and Collier, who were accountants and promoters of a company called the Blochairn Iron Co Ltd. The claimant claimed £5,750 as damages sustained through taking shares in the company which were not worth the price he had paid for them because of certain misrepresentations in the prospectus issued by the defendants. The action was for fraud. Among the misrepresentations alleged by Smith was that the prospectus stated that a Mr J J Grieves MP was a director of the company, whereas he had withdrawn his consent the day before the prospectus was issued.

Held – the statement regarding Mr Grieves was untrue but was not material to the claimant, because the evidence showed that he had never heard of Mr Grieves. His action for damages failed.

Misrepresentation: negligent misrepresentation: principal but not agent liable to third party for agent's negligence

140 *Gosling v Anderson*, The Times, 8 February 1972

Miss Gosling, a retired schoolmistress, entered into negotiations for the purchase of one of three flats in a house at Minehead owned by Mrs Anderson. Mr Tidbury, who was Mrs Anderson's agent in the negotiations, represented to Miss Gosling by letter that planning permission for a garage to go with the flat had been given. Mrs Anderson knew that this was not so. The purchase of the flat went through on the basis of a contract and a conveyance showing a parking area but not referring to planning permission which was later refused. Miss Gosling now sought damages for misrepresentation under s 2(1) of the Misrepresentation Act 1967.

Held – the facts revealed a negligent representation by Mr Tidbury made without reasonable grounds for believing it to be true. Mrs Anderson was liable for the acts of her agent and must pay damages under the Act of 1967.

Comment (i) This action was against Mrs Anderson who was the other party to the contract. It was decided in *Resolute Maritime Inc and Another* v *Nippon Kaiji Kyokai and Others* [1983] 2 All ER 1 that no action is available against an agent such as Mr Tidbury under s 2(1) of the Misrepresentation Act 1967. Section 2(1) of the 1967 Act begins: 'Where a person has entered into a contract after a misrepresentation has been made to him by another party thereto . . .'. Thus, the sub-section only applies when the representee has entered into a contract after a misrepresentation has been made to him by another party to the contract. Where an agent acting within the scope of his authority makes a representation under s 2(1), the principal is liable to the third party misled, but not the agent. The agent will be liable to the third party only if he is guilty of fraud or, under the rule in *Hedley Byrne* v *Heller* (1963) (see below), for negligence at common law. Here the principal will be liable vicariously *along with the agent* for the latter's fraud or negligence if the agent is acting within the scope of his authority.

(ii) As regards proving reasonable grounds, an expert will be expected to verify his statements in a professional way. However, those without relevant technical knowledge will often find that the court will accept a statement as made innocently if the maker of the statement had been induced to purchase the goods himself by the same statement.

Thus in *Humming Bird Motors* v *Hobbs* [1986] RTR 276 H was a young man whom the judge found to be an amateur doing a bit of 'wheeling and dealing' in the motor trade. He bought a car from a dealer who told him that the mileage recorded, 34,900 miles, was correct. H sold the car on to the claimants making the same statement, i.e. that the recorded mileage was, to the best of his knowledge and belief, correct. The claimants discovered that the vehicle had done 80,000 miles and tried to claim damages for negligent misrepresentation. The Court of Appeal decided that H was not negligent; he was an amateur and was merely repeating what he himself believed.

Misrepresentation: fraud: definition and burden of proof

141 *Derry v Peek* (1889) 14 App Cas 337

The Plymouth, Devonport and District Tramways Company had power under a special Act of Parliament to run trams by animal power, and with the consent of the Board of Trade (now the Department of Trade and Industry) by mechanical or steam power. Derry and the other appellants were directors of the company and issued a prospectus, inviting the public to apply for shares in it, stating that they had power to run trams by steam power, and claiming that considerable economies would result. The directors had assumed that the permission of the Board of Trade would be granted as a matter of course, but in the event the Board of Trade refused permission except for certain parts of the tramway. As a result, the company was wound up and the directors were sued for fraud. The court decided that the directors were not fraudulent but honestly believed the statement in the prospectus to be true. As Lord Herschell said: 'Fraud is proved when it is shown that a false representation had been made (*a*) knowingly, or (*b*) without belief in its truth, or (*c*) recklessly, careless whether it be true or false.'

Comment (i) This case gave rise to the Directors' Liability Act 1890 which made directors of companies liable to pay compensation for negligent misrepresentation in a prospectus, subject to a number of defences. The latest provisions are in the Financial Services and Markets Act 2000.

(ii) It will be noticed from this case that the mere fact that no grounds exist for believing a false statement does not of itself constitute fraud. There must also be an element of dishonesty which was not present in this case.

(iii) Fraud is the most difficult of all the forms of misrepresentation to prove. It must be proved beyond a reasonable doubt which is the criminal standard. The civil standard is proof on a balance of probabilities.

(iv) There is something of a problem with the meaning of the word 'recklessly' since it envisages a state of mind short of actual knowledge. It seems that the maker of the statement must be *almost sure* that it is false, but is nevertheless reckless and goes on to make it anyway.

Misrepresentation: the contribution of the tort of negligence

142 *Hedley Byrne & Co Ltd* v *Heller & Partners Ltd*
[1963] 2 All ER 575

The appellants were advertising agents and the respondents were merchant bankers. The appellants had a client called Easipower Ltd who was a customer of the respondents. The appellants had contracted to place orders for advertising Easipower's products on television and in newspapers, and since this involved giving Easipower credit, they asked the respondents, who were Easipower's bankers, for a reference as to the creditworthiness of Easipower. The respondents said that Easipower Ltd was respectably constituted and considered good, although they said in regard to the credit: 'These are bigger figures than we have seen' and also that the reference was 'given in confidence and without responsibility on our part'. Relying on this reply, the appellants placed orders for advertising time and space for Easipower Ltd, and the appellants assumed personal responsibility for payment to the television and newspaper companies concerned. Easipower Ltd went into liquidation and the appellants lost over £17,000 on the advertising contracts. The appellants sued the respondents for the amount of the loss, alleging that the respondents had not informed themselves sufficiently about Easipower Ltd before writing the statement, and were therefore liable in negligence.

Held – in the present case the respondents' disclaimer was adequate to exclude the assumption by them of the legal duty of care, but, in the absence of the disclaimer, the circumstances would have given rise to a duty of care in spite of the absence of a contract or fiduciary relationship.

Comment (i) The House of Lords stated that the duty of care arose where there was 'a special relationship' requiring care.

The boundaries of the *Hedley* case are still not entirely clear but the requirement of a 'special relationship' between the maker of the statement and the recipient is an attempt to mark some boundaries. Can one complain, for example, if casual advice given on a train journey by a solicitor turns out to be erroneous? An extract from the judgment of Lord Devlin in the *Hedley* case is helpful. He said:

. . . Payment for information or advice is very good evidence that it is being relied upon and that the informer or adviser knows that it is. Where there is no consideration, it will be necessary to exercise greater care in distinguishing between social and professional relationships and between those which are of a contractual character and those which are not. It may often be material to consider whether the adviser is acting purely out of good nature or whether he is getting his reward in some direct form. The service that a bank performs in giving a reference is not done simply out of a desire to assist commerce. It would discourage the customers of the bank if their deals fell through because the bank had refused to testify to their credit when it was good . . .

Thus, the solicitor's advice should not be actionable because there was no consideration to found contract liability and equally no 'special relationship' to found the tort claim. Of course, the absence of consideration and a contract prevents s 2(1) of the Misrepresentation Act 1967 from applying. However, the requirement of a 'special relationship' as a substitute for consideration brings the *Hedley* tort of negligence much closer to contract than the general law of negligence – a casual statement is not actionable, but there is obviously a claim by persons knocked over by a casual bad driver, who is, of course, the worst kind! (For further developments in professional liability see Chapter 21.)

(ii) The ease with which the duty to take care placed upon the bank was excluded in this case by the disclaimer was disappointing. However, such a disclaimer of negligence liability would, these days, have to satisfy the test of 'reasonableness' under the Unfair Contract Terms Act 1977 (see Chapter 15). It would seem that such a disclaimer would fall short of the reasonable expectations of those in business who naturally and reasonably expect that a bank will have taken proper care before giving a reference of this kind.

(iii) In this connection it was held in *Smith* v *Eric S Bush* [1987] 3 All ER 179 that it was unreasonable to allow a surveyor to rely on a general disclaimer of negligence where he had been asked by a building society to carry out a reasonably careful visual inspection of the property for valuation purposes (paid for by the would-be purchaser) when the valuer knew that the purchaser would be likely to rely on his report and not get another one. The house was purchased but, because of defects, turned out to be unfit for habitation. The surveyors when sued could not escape liability for damages on the basis of disclaimer.

The case suggests that in so far as such disclaimers are still used by professional persons they may not be effective, at least as regards ordinary consumers of professional services.

(iv) However, much would seem to depend on the sophistication of the person misled. In *McCullagh* v *Lane Fox* and *Partners*, *The Times*, 22 December 1995 the Court of Appeal heard a claim against an estate agent for negligently misrepresenting the size of a plot of land to a purchaser. The purchaser's claims failed because the agents had included a disclaimer in the sales particulars which negated the element of proximity and assumption of responsibility required if negligence was to be established. In addition, it was not unfair under s 11 of the Unfair Contract Terms Act 1977 to allow the agents to rely on the disclaimer. The distinction between this case and *Bush* would appear to be the cost of the property (some £800,000) compared with the property in *Bush* (some £17,000) and the normally worldly wise nature of people who buy such expensive properties. Lord Justice Hobhouse said: 'Here the transaction involved a sophisticated member of the public who had had ample opportunity to regulate his conduct having regard to the disclaimer and who would have been assumed by all concerned to have had the benefit of legal advice before exchanging contracts.' The judge went on to say that since disclaimers are usually inserted by estate agents into their contracts it would have been unfair not to allow the defendants to rely on theirs.

Misrepresentation: loss of the right to rescind

143 *Long v Lloyd* [1958] 2 All ER 402

The claimant and the defendant were haulage contractors. The claimant was induced to buy the defendant's lorry by the defendant's misrepresentation as to condition and performance. The defendant advertised a lorry for sale at £850, the advertisement describing the vehicle as being in 'exceptional condition'. The claimant telephoned the defendant the same evening when the defendant agreed that his advertisement was a little ambiguous and said that the lorry was 'in first-class condition'. The claimant saw the lorry at the defendant's premises at Hampton Court on a Saturday. During a trial run on the following Monday the claimant found that the speedometer was not working, a spring was missing from the accelerator pedal, and it was difficult to engage top gear. The defendant said there was nothing wrong with the vehicle except what the claimant had found. He also said at this stage that the lorry would do 11 miles to the gallon.

The claimant purchased the lorry for £750, paying £375 down and agreeing to pay the balance at a later date. He then drove the lorry from Hampton Court to his place of business at Sevenoaks. On the following Wednesday, the claimant drove from Sevenoaks to Rochester to pick up a load, and during that journey the dynamo ceased to function, an oil seal was leaking badly, there was a crack in one of the road wheels,

and he used eight gallons of petrol on a journey of 40 miles. That evening the claimant told the defendant of the defects, and the defendant offered to pay half the cost of a reconstructed dynamo, but denied any knowledge of the other defects. The claimant accepted the offer and the dynamo was fitted straightaway. On Thursday the lorry was driven by the claimant's brother to Middlesbrough, and it broke down on the Friday night. The claimant, on learning of this, asked the defendant for his money back, but the defendant would not give it to him. The lorry was subsequently examined and an expert said that it was not roadworthy. The claimant sued for rescission.

Held – at first instance, by Glyn-Jones, J – the defendant's statements about the lorry were innocent and not fraudulent because the evidence showed that the lorry had been laid up for a month and it might have deteriorated without the defendant's precise knowledge. The Court of Appeal affirmed this finding of fact and made the following additional points.

(*a*) The journey to Rochester was not affirmation because the claimant was merely testing the vehicle in a working capacity.

(*b*) However, the acceptance by the claimant of the defendant's offer to pay half the cost of the reconstructed dynamo, and the subsequent journey to Middlesbrough, did amount to affirmation, and rescission could not be granted to the claimant.

Comment (i) Damages could now be obtained for negligent misrepresentation under the Misrepresentation Act 1967, s 2(1), for how could the seller say he had reasonable grounds for believing that the lorry was in exceptional condition or first-class condition?

(ii) It seems remarkable that Glyn-Jones, J did not find fraud. However, fraud must be proved according to the criminal standard, i.e. beyond a reasonable doubt, and not according to the civil standard which is on balance of probabilities. Fraud is, therefore, difficult to prove and in this case there was presumably a reasonable doubt in the mind of the judge on the issue of fraud.

(iii) The Court of Appeal would not accept that the statement that the lorry was in first-class condition was a term of the contract (see Chapter 14) but decided that it was only a misrepresentation.

144 *Clarke v Dickson* (1858) 27 LJQB 223

In 1853 the claimant was induced by the misrepresentation of the three defendants, Dickson, Williams and Gibbs, to invest money in what was in effect a partnership to work lead mines in Wales. In 1857 the partnership was in financial difficulty and with the claimant's assent it was converted into a limited company and the partnership capital was converted into shares. Shortly afterwards the company commenced winding-up proceedings and the claimant, on discovery of the falsity of the representations, asked for rescission of the contract.

Held – rescission could not be granted because capital in a partnership is not the same as shares in a company. The firm was no longer in existence, having been replaced by the company, and it was not possible to restore the parties to their original positions.

Comment (i) It should be noted that in addition to the problem of restoration, third-party rights, i.e. creditors, had accrued on the winding-up of the company and this is a further bar to rescission.

(ii) However, the court still retains its power to rescind 'on terms' where the problem is only one of deterioration of the subject matter. In *Erlanger* v *New Sombrero Phosphate Co* (1878) 3 App Cas 1218 rescission was granted of a contract to purchase a phosphate mine even though some phosphate had been extracted from it since sale. The House of Lords granted rescission on terms that the purchaser must account to the seller for profits made from the sale of the phosphate extracted since purchase.

Contracts of utmost good faith: insurance: effect of contractual clauses

145 *Dawsons Ltd* v *Bonnin* [1922] 2 AC 413

Dawsons Ltd insured its motor lorry against loss by fire with Bonnin and others, and signed a proposal form which contained the following as Condition 4: 'Material misstatement or concealment of any circumstances by the insured material to assessing the premium herein, or in connection with any claim shall render the policy void.' The policy also contained a clause saying that the 'proposal shall be the basis of the contract and shall be held as incorporated therein'. Actually the proposal form was filled up by an insurance agent, and although he stated the proposer's address correctly as 46 Cadogan Street, Glasgow, he also stated that the vehicle would usually be garaged there, although there was no garage accommodation at the Cadogan Street address and the lorry was garaged elsewhere. Dawsons' secretary, who signed the proposal, overlooked this slip made by the agent. The lorry was destroyed by fire and Dawsons claimed under the policy.

Held – on appeal, by the House of Lords – the statement was not material within the meaning of Condition 4. However, the basis clause was an independent provision, and since the statement, though not material, was untrue, the policy was void for breach of condition.

Viscount Cave said: 'The meaning and effect of the basis clause, taken by itself, is that any untrue statement in the proposal, or any breach of its promissory clauses, shall avoid the policy, and if that be the contract of the parties, the question of materiality has not to be considered.'

Comment (i) The Unfair Contract Terms Act 1977 does not apply to contracts of insurance. This resulted from a deal between the insurance companies and the government under which the insurance companies agreed to abide by voluntary statements of practice. These have no legal effect but some moral force. If the insurance company follows these statements of practice, then certainly in consumer, i.e. non-business, insurance the worst effect of the basis clause (which is what they are called) should be eliminated.

(ii) However, even if we get rid of the basis clause problem, the rules of disclosure of material matters by the person seeking insurance remains a difficulty. It is based upon s 18(2) of the Marine Insurance Act 1906. This should not have been used as a basis for *all* insurances. Those seeking marine insurance are well aware of the risks they seek to insure. Those seeking, for example, domestic fire insurance are not. The Law Commission Report entitled *Non-Disclosure and Breach of Warranty* places a heavy burden on insurance companies to phrase their questions so as to elicit the kind and amount of information they want and not to leave it, as at present, to the person seeking insurance to make uninformed guesses as to what might be material to the insurers. The common law has already taken steps in this direction in *Hair* v *Prudential Assurance* [1983] 2 Lloyd's Rep 667, the court deciding in that case that if a person seeking insurance answered honestly all the questions put to him by the proposal for insurance, he should not be required to disclose any other matters. The questions should reveal all material issues.

(iii) The courts continue to try to assist the insured in terms of the utmost good faith rule, which has for so long been the insurer's best friend. In *Pan Atlantic Insurance Co Ltd* v *Pine Top Insurance Co Ltd* [1994] 3 All ER 581 the House of Lords decided that whereas in the past a mere innocent non-disclosure had enabled insurers to avoid the contract, it was now necessary to show that the insurer had actually been induced by the non-disclosure to enter into a policy on its terms.

Their Lordships did decide, however, that there was a presumption that an insurer would have been influenced by a non-disclosure of a material fact. This means that the person insured will have the burden of proving that the insurer was not influenced by the non-disclosure. This rather weakens the decision so far as the insured is concerned.

(iv) Further progress by the courts in defending the rights of the consumer against the harsher application of the utmost good faith rule is to be seen in *Economides* v *Commercial Union Insurance Co plc* [1997] 3 All ER 636 where the Court of Appeal ruled, at least so far as the private consumer buying insurance cover is concerned, that the insured's duty to the insurance company is primarily one of honesty and he need only disclose those material facts which are known to him. Mr E's flat was burgled and £31,000 worth of valuables stolen, mainly those belonging to his parents. His contents insurance had been valued by Mr E, with his father's consent, at £16,000 and the maximum cover for valuables was £5,333. The defendants repudiated liability on the grounds of misrepresentation as to value and failure to disclose material facts. Mr E was, of course, under-insured and could only cover part of his loss, but the defendants did not want to pay at all. The Court of Appeal ruled in favour of Mr E for recovery of the reduced sum.

Fiduciary relationships: the duty to disclose

146 *Gordon* v *Gordon* (1819) 3 Swan 400

Two brothers made an agreement for division of the family estates. The elder supposed he was born before the marriage of his parents and was, therefore, illegitimate. The younger knew that their parents had been married before the birth of the elder brother and the elder brother was, therefore, legitimate and his father's heir. He did not communicate this information to his elder brother. Nineteen years afterwards the elder brother discovered that he was legitimate and the agreement was set aside following this action brought by him. He would have had no case if at the time of the agreement both brothers had been in honest error as to the date of their parents' marriage.

Duress: effect upon contracts

147 *Welch* v *Cheesman* (1973) 229 EG 99

Mrs Welch lived with the defendant, C, for many years in a house which she owned. C was a man given to violence, and after he threatened her Mrs Welch sold the house to him for £300. C died and his widow claimed the house which was worth about £3,000. Mrs Welch brought this action to set aside the sale of the house to C on the grounds of duress and she succeeded.

Undue influence: situations in which presumed: special relationships

148 *Lancashire Loans Ltd* v *Black* [1934] 1 KB 380

A daughter married at 18 and went to live with her husband. Her mother was an extravagant woman and was in debt to a firm of moneylenders. When the daughter became of age, her mother persuaded her to raise £2,000 on a property in which the daughter had an interest, and this was used to pay off the mother's debts. Twelve months later the mother and daughter signed a joint and several promissory note of £775 at 85 per cent interest in favour of the moneylenders, and the daughter created a further charge on her property in order that the mother might borrow more money. The daughter did not understand the nature of the transaction, and the only advice she received was from a solicitor acting for the mother and the moneylenders. The moneylenders brought this action against the mother and daughter on the note.

Held – the daughter's defence that she was under the undue influence of her mother succeeded, in spite of the fact that she was of full age and married with her own home.

149 *Allcard* v *Skinner* (1887) 36 Ch D 145

In 1868 the claimant joined a Protestant institution called the sisterhood of St Mary at the Cross, promising to devote her property to the service of the poor. The defendant, Miss Skinner, was the Lady Superior of the Sisterhood. In 1871 the claimant ceased to be a novice and became a sister in the order, taking her vows of poverty, chastity and obedience. By this time she had left her home and was residing with the sisterhood. The claimant remained a sister until 1878 and, in compliance with the vow of poverty, she had by then given property to the value of £7,000 to the defendant. The claimant left the order in 1879 and became a Roman Catholic. Of the property she had transferred, £1,671 remained in 1885 and the claimant sought to recover this sum, claiming that it had been transferred in circumstances of undue influence.

Held – that the gifts had been made under pressure of an unusually persuasive nature, particularly since the claimant was prevented from seeking outside advice under a rule of the sisterhood which said, 'Let no sister seek the advice of any extern without the superior's leave.' However, the claimant's suit was barred by her delay because, although the influence was removed in 1879, she did not bring her action until 1885.

Presumption of undue influence: other categories

150 *Hodgson* v *Marks* [1970] 3 All ER 513

Mrs Hodgson, who was a widow of 83, owned a freehold house in which she lived. In 1959 she took in a Mr Evans as a lodger. She soon came to trust

Evans and allowed him to manage her financial affairs. In June 1960, she transferred the house to Evans, her sole reason for so doing being to prevent her nephew from turning Evans out of the house. It was orally agreed between Mrs Hodgson and Evans that the house was to remain hers, although held in the name of Evans. Evans later made arrangements to sell the house without the knowledge or consent of Mrs Hodgson. The house was bought by Mr Marks and Mrs Hodgson now asked for a declaration that he was bound to transfer the property back to her. The following questions arose:

(*a*) whether Evans held the house in trust for Mrs Hodgson. It was *held* – by Ungoed-Thomas, J – that he did. The absence of written evidence of trust as required by s 53 of the Law of Property Act 1925 was not a bar to Mrs Hodgson's claim. The section does not apply to implied trusts of this kind;

(*b*) whether Evans had exercised undue influence. It was *held* that he had and that a presumption of undue influence was raised. Although the parties were not in the established categories, Evans had a relationship of trust and confidence with Mrs Hodgson of a kind which raised a presumption of undue influence.

However, Mrs Hodgson lost the case because Mr Marks was protected by s 70 of the Land Registration Act 1925, which gives rights to a purchaser of property for value in respect of interests in that property of which the purchaser is not aware. In this case Mr Marks bought the house from Mr Evans, the house being in the name of Evans and he had no reason to suppose that Mrs Hodgson had any interest in it.

Comment (i) Mrs Hodgson's appeal to the Court of Appeal in 1971 succeeded and she got her house back, the court holding that in spite of s 70, a purchaser must pay heed to the possibility of rights in all *occupiers*. Mrs Hodgson was obviously in occupation with Mr Evans and inquiries should have been made by the purchaser as to her rights in the property.

(ii) The application of the presumption in a relationship which was not one of the established ones is also illustrated by *Goldsworthy* v *Brickell* [1987] 1 All ER 853, where a contract to grant a tenancy of a farm advantageous to the defendant in that, for example, it did not allow the landlord, G, to make any rent increases, was set aside. The defendant, B, who had become the tenant, was a neighbour of G. G was 85 and had come to rely implicitly on the advice of B. Undue influence was presumed although neighbours are not within the established categories where undue influence is generally presumed.

Unconscionable bargains: protection against improper pressure and inequality of bargaining power

151 *Lloyds Bank* v *Bundy* [1974] 3 All ER 757

The defendant and his son's company both banked with the claimants, the defendant having been a customer for many years. The company's affairs deteriorated over a period of years and at the son's suggestion the bank's assistant manager visited the defendant and said that the bank could not continue to support an overdraft for the company unless the defendant entered into a guarantee of the account. The defendant received no independent advice, nor did the bank's assistant manager suggest that he should do so. The defendant charged his house as security for the overdraft and shortly afterwards the company went into receivership. The bank obtained possession of the house from the defendant in the county court, where the assistant branch manager in evidence said that he thought that the defendant had relied upon him implicitly to advise him about the charge.

The defendant appealed to the Court of Appeal in an attempt to set aside the guarantee and the security and it was *held* – allowing the defendant's appeal – that in the particular circumstances a special relationship existed between the defendant and the bank's assistant manager, as agent for the bank, and the bank was in breach of its duty of fiduciary care in procuring the charge which would be set aside for undue influence. The defendant, without any benefit to himself, had signed away his sole remaining asset without taking independent advice.

Comment (i) While the majority of the Court of Appeal (Cairns, LJ and Sir Eric Sachs) were content to decide that appeal on the conventional ground that a fiduciary relationship existed between the bank and its customer, which is to suggest that a new fiduciary relationship has come into being, Lord Denning took the opportunity to break new ground by deciding that in addition to avoiding the contract on the grounds of fiduciary relationship, Mr Bundy could also have done so on the basis of 'inequality of bargaining power'. Although inequality of bargaining power obviously includes undue influence, Lord Denning made it clear that the principle does not depend on the will of one party being dominated or overcome by the other. This is clear from that part of the judgment where he says: 'One who is in extreme need may knowingly consent to a most improvident bargain, solely to relieve the straits in which he finds himself.' This approach is, of course, at variance with the traditional view of undue influence which was that it was based on dominance resulting in an inferior party being unable to exercise independent judgment or on a relationship of trust and confidence.

(ii) It should be noted that cases such as this which introduce into the law a requirement that a contract must be fair may eventually develop to the point where adequacy of consideration is required in contract. This is not the case at the present time.

(iii) In *National Westminster Bank plc v Morgan* [1983] 3 All ER 85 the Court of Appeal set aside a charge over a wife's share in the matrimonial home after she executed it without legal advice, in order to secure a loan from the bank to clear a building society mortgage, and after the bank manager had assured her that the charge would not be used to secure her husband's business advances, whereas it did in fact extend to such advances. However, the bank had no intention of using the charge other than to secure the advance to clear the building society mortgage, nor did it.

The above decision, which moved in the direction of saying that banks would have to ensure that all their customers had independent legal advice before taking out a bank mortgage was reversed by the House of Lords in *National Westminster Bank plc v Morgan* [1985] 1 All ER 821. Undue influence, the House of Lords said, was the use by one person of a power over another person to take a certain course of action generally to his or her disadvantage. A bank manager need not advise independent legal advice in a situation such as this. The manager in this case had stuck to explaining the legal effect of the charge which, though erroneous as to the terms of the charge, correctly represented his intention and that of the bank. The security represented no disadvantage to Mrs Morgan. It was exactly what she wanted, to clear the building society loan on her home. The House of Lords also rejected the view that a court would grant relief where there was merely an inequality of bargaining power. Their Lordships rejected that view which was expressed by Lord Denning in *Bundy*. The courts will not, said the House of Lords, protect persons against what they regard as a mistake merely because of inequality of bargaining power. This is a much harder line.

(iv) In *Bundy*, therefore, the Court of Appeal *held* that the bank in not advising the person giving the security to get independent advice exercised undue influence and for this reason set the security aside. In *Morgan* the House of Lords *held* that no presumption of undue influence existed. In *Cornish v Midland Bank* [1985] 3 All ER 513 the Court of Appeal decided that the proper way to deal with these cases was not through undue influence but by using the law of negligence, though only where the bank had actually given wrong advice.

In *Cornish* the claimant had signed a second mortgage on a farmhouse jointly owned with her husband in order to secure £2,000 which her husband had borrowed from the bank. She did so because the bank clerk involved said that the mortgage was like a building society mortgage.

It was not because unlike a building society mortgage it covered all future borrowing by the husband. The bank later tried to enforce the security. Eventually the Court of Appeal *held* that the bank was liable in negligence for the wrong advice of its clerk who made a negligent misstatement causing damage, i.e. that £2,000 was the borrowing limit when it was not. The mortgage was not set aside for undue influence so that the bank was entitled to the proceeds of the sale of the farmhouse but had to pay the claimant £11,231 damages plus interest for negligence. Thus, although it would be good practice for a bank to advise independent advice, it is not necessary for it to do so. The security will be good and there is no presumption of undue influence. However, if an employee of the bank *actually* gives negligent advice or fails to explain the consequences of the charge and/or fails to advise the taking of independent advice (see *Midland Bank plc v Perry*, *The Times*, 28 May 1987), the bank will be able to enforce the security but will be liable in damages under the ruling in *Hedley Byrne v Heller & Partners* (1963).

(v) This may in some cases make the security of little use to the bank because it will have to set off the damages it is required to pay against the money it receives from the sale of the security. Much depends, of course, on the amount of damages awarded. Nevertheless, cases such as *Morgan, Cornish* and *Perry* do seek to remove these security situations from the realm of undue influence, and it seems that the courts which decided them were moving away from the old rules previously provided by equity for married women who provided security for their husbands' debts. A security is a business transaction and those giving securities must look after themselves as others in business must. However, the older rules seem to have survived and were stated in definitive form by the House of Lords in *Barclays Bank plc v O'Brien* [1993] 4 All ER 417. Their Lordships decided that a married woman (or cohabitee) must be treated as a special protected class of guarantor when guaranteeing her husband's (or cohabitee's) debts because of the emotional involvement of which the bank is on constructive notice. Unless the transaction is fully explained and understood by the protected guarantor, it will be void.

(vi) What then is new about *O'Brien*? First and most importantly is the fact that the bank was fixed with *constructive notice* of the possibility that the wife may not have fully understood the transaction, either because she had been misled by the husband or cohabitee, or had not been fully informed. It was not necessary for the branch manager to have *actual knowledge* of this.

What this means, in effect, is that when taking a security on a property which is jointly owned, as in the *O'Brien* case, by persons with an emotional involvement, the person taking the security must *assume* that there may be deceit or undue influence upon the wife or cohabitee, though the security will be good if the bank official ensures that the wife or cohabitee fully understands the transaction and its risks, either by means of its own explanations or as a result of the receipt of independent advice. If following explanation or advice the wife or cohabitee signs a document to the effect that the transaction and its risks are understood, the court is likely to accept this as good evidence of the wife or cohabitee's liability.

This 'counselling' aspect is also new. At a time when counselling is regarded as a cure for all kinds of ills, it is perhaps not surprising that the House of Lords should have put this forward as an answer to the problems of lenders. Finally, there is a recognition by the court that any variety of relationships comprised in the term 'cohabitees' can give rise to the constructive notice of emotional involvement.

(vii) It is worth noting that in a similar case entitled *CIBC Mortgages plc v Pitt* [1994] 4 All ER 433, handed down on the same day as *O'Brien* by the House of Lords, the decision was that a wife who had been pressurised into giving security over the jointly-owned family home was bound by it. The distinction was made in *Pitt* that the loan was made *jointly* to the husband and wife, and not to the husband alone, so that the wife derived some benefit from it. In such cases, said the House of Lords, the rule of constructive notice does not arise and in the absence of actual knowledge of pressure, which was not present in *Pitt*, the bank has not the same need to follow the 'counselling' approach.

(viii) More recently the Court of Appeal gave guidance including the extent of the *O'Brien* advice to be given by solicitors (see *Royal Bank of Scotland plc v Etridge (No 2)* [1998] 4 All ER 705). The court made the assumption that the claimant is the wife (or cohabitee) and the person using the influence is the husband (or cohabitee), although similar principles would apply to a situation where the wife or cohabitee used the undue influence. The guidance appears below:

- the client must be told that she is not under any obligation to enter into the transaction;
- the solicitor must be satisfied that the client is not subject to any improper influence and then consider whether the transaction is one which she ought to be allowed to make, even if she was not subject to influence. If it is not, she should be advised not to enter into it;
- if the lender is asking for an 'all monies' guarantee or charge, the solicitor should make clear to the client that she is being asked to undertake liability for any existing indebtedness, new debts and future debts and not merely the amount contemplated in the current arrangements and that the client may be unable to control the amount of future indebtedness;
- if a wife is being asked to give an unlimited guarantee, she should be told of the option of giving a limited guarantee or charge and the solicitor should offer to

negotiate for her. It is not acceptable practice to assume that the arrangements are not negotiable.

(ix) The amount of litigation involving occupiers who try to avoid eviction by relying on *O'Brien* shows no sign of abating, despite the clear statement of principles both in *O'Brien* and *Etridge*. There is little point in proliferating authorities. The rules to be applied lie mainly in the two cases mentioned above. It is, however, worth mentioning that the mere presence of the family solicitor during the transaction of loan is not enough. The lender must be satisfied that proper advice has been given. This cannot be assumed from the mere presence of a lawyer (see *Lloyds TSB Bank plc v Holdgate* [2002] EWCA Civ 1543).

CONTRACTUAL TERMS

Representations and terms distinguished

152   *Bannerman v White* (1861) 10 CB (NS) 844

The defendant was intending to buy hops from the claimant and he asked the claimant whether sulphur had been used in the cultivation of the hops, adding that if it had he would not even bother to ask the price, by which he meant he would not make the contract. The claimant said that no sulphur had been used, though in fact it had. It was *held* that the claimant's assurance that sulphur had not been used was a term of the contract and the defendant was justified in raising the matter as a successful defence to an action for the price.

153   *Oscar Chess Ltd v Williams* [1957] 1 All ER 325

In May 1955, Williams bought a car from the claimants on hire-purchase terms. The claimants took Williams' Morris car in part exchange. Williams described the car as a 1948 model and produced the registration book, which showed that the car was first registered in April 1948, and that there had been several owners since that time. Williams was allowed £290 on the Morris. Eight months later the claimants discovered that the Morris car was a 1939 model there being no change in appearance in the model between 1939 and 1948. The allowance for a 1939 model was £175 and the claimants sued for £115 damages for breach of warranty that the car was a 1948 model. Evidence showed that some fraudulent person had altered the registration book but he could not be traced, and that Williams honestly believed that the car was a 1948 model.

Held – the contract might have been set aside in equity for misrepresentation but the delay of eight months defeated this remedy. This mistake was a mistake of quality which did not avoid the contract at common law and in order to obtain damages the claimants must prove a breach of warranty. The court was unable to find that Williams was in a position to give such a warranty, and suggested that the claimants should have taken the engine and chassis number and written to the manufacturers, so using their superior knowledge to protect themselves in the matter. The claimants were not entitled to any redress. Morris, LJ dissented, holding that the statement that the car was a 1948 model was a fundamental condition.

Comment (i) No doubt Mr Williams would have been liable for innocent and not negligent misrepresentation under the Misrepresentation Act 1967 for he had reasonable grounds to believe that the car was a 1948 Morris. He was merely repeating an earlier deception made when he bought the vehicle.

(ii) Since the remedy of rescission had been lost by reason of delay, the court would not even now grant that remedy or damages at the court's discretion, which the court can do even if the remedy of rescission is not available. The reluctance of the court to say that statements by non-dealers are contractual terms for breach of which damages can be recovered leads to an unfair result as in this case. After all, Mr Williams obtained £115 more for his Morris than it was worth.

(iii) The case is not without its difficulties because it seems to be based on the fault of the agents of Oscar Chess in not discovering the date of the vehicle. In most cases the courts do not concern themselves with fault when dealing with the terms of a contract. If, as in Oscar Chess, A warrants to B that goods have certain characteristics, it is no defence if they have not that the giver of the warranty honestly and reasonably believed that they had. (Compare the law relating to misrepresentation.) Nor is B normally expected to check up on the statement. What this case shows is that it is much harder for a private individual to give a warranty to a dealer, and that the dealer may be regarded as at fault in terms of the contract he made because he should have known better!

(iv) A contrast to Oscar Chess is provided by Dick Bentley Productions Ltd v Harold Smith (Motors) Ltd [1965] 2 All ER 65 where a dealer sold a Bentley to a customer, the instruments showing that it had done only 30,000 miles since a replacement engine was fitted when, in fact, it had done 100,000 miles since that time. The seller was held liable for breach of condition, whereas in Oscar Chess the seller – who was not a dealer – was not.

Conditions and warranties distinguished

154 *Poussard* v *Spiers and Pond* (1876) 1 QBD 410

Madame Poussard had entered into an agreement to play a part in an opera, the first performance to take place on 28 November 1874. On 23 November Madame Poussard was taken ill and was unable to appear until 4 December. The defendants had hired a substitute, and discovered that the only way in which they could secure a substitute to take Madame Poussard's place was to offer that person the complete engagement. This they had done, and they refused the services of Madame Poussard when she presented herself on 4 December. The claimant now sued for breach of contract.

Held – the failure of Madame Poussard to perform the contract as from the first night was a breach of condition, and the defendants were within their rights in regarding the contract as discharged.

Comment This case merely illustrates the availability of repudiation for serious breach of contract. Madame Poussard was not liable to pay damages for breach because unlike the defendants in *Gill & Duffus SA* she could not help the breach, the contract being also frustrated (see Chapter 17).

155 *Bettini* v *Gye* (1876) 1 QBD 183

The claimant was an opera singer. The defendant was the director of the Royal Italian Opera in London. The claimant had agreed to sing in Great Britain in theatres, halls and drawing rooms for a period of time commencing on 30 March 1875, and to be in London for rehearsals six days before the engagement began. The claimant was taken ill and arrived on 28 March 1875, but the defendant would not accept the claimant's services, treating the contract as discharged.

Held – the rehearsal clause was subsidiary to the main purpose of the contract, and its breach constituted a breach of warranty only. The defendant had no right to treat the contract as discharged and must compensate the claimant, but he had a counterclaim for any damage he had suffered by the claimant's late arrival.

Comment This case is also concerned with the availability of repudiation and the court decided that the breach was not sufficiently serious. The court suggested that if Gye wanted redress he should cross-claim for damages against Bettini. If and when he did, and there is no report suggesting that he did, the matter of Bettini's illness excusing his breach would have had to be raised. Presumably, it would have been a defence even though in this case the contract was not discharged by frustration.

Intermediate or innominate terms

156 Cehave NV v Bremer Handelsgesellschaft mbH (The Hansa Nord) [1975] 3 All ER 739

The defendants sold citrus pulp pellets to the claimants. A term of the contract was 'shipment to be made in good condition'. The goods were not delivered all at once but in consignments, and when a particular consignment arrived at Rotterdam, the market price of the goods had fallen and it was found that 1,260 tons of the goods out of a total consignment of 3,293 tons was damaged. The claimants rejected the whole cargo on the ground that the shipment was not made in good condition. The claimants then sought the recovery of the price, which amounted to £100,000. In the event, a middle man bought the goods at the price of £33,720 and resold them to the claimants at the same price. The claimants then used the pellets for making cattle food as was the original intention. The total result of the transaction, if it had been left that way, was that the claimants had received goods which they had bought for £100,000 for the reduced price of £33,720. The Court of Appeal decided in favour of the sellers. The court *held* that the contractual term 'shipment to be made in good condition' was not a contractual condition but was an intermediate or innominate term. As Lord Denning, MR said: 'If a small portion of the whole cargo was not in good condition and arrived a little unsound, it should be met by a price allowance. The buyers should not have the right to reject the whole cargo unless it was serious or substantial.'

Lord Denning also rejected the view that the goods were not of merchantable (now satisfactory) quality simply because they were not perfect in every way. He said that the definition now contained in s 14(2) of the Sale of Goods Act 1979 (as amended) was to be preferred because it was more flexible than some of the earlier judicial decisions on previous legislation. In fact, the definition delegates to the court the task of deciding what is satisfactory quality in the circumstances of each particular case.

Comment (i) This intermediate or innominate term approach was endorsed by the House of Lords in *Reardon Smith Line v Hansen-Tangen* [1976] 3 All ER 570.

(ii) The breach did not seem to have affected the use of the goods and looks like a business ploy to get them more cheaply. The views of Lord Denning in this case are now contained in s 15A of the Sale of Goods Act 1979 (inserted by the Sale and Supply of Goods Act 1994) under which the right to reject the goods for slight breaches is retained in consumer contracts, but in non-consumer contracts such as this, a buyer will, where the breach is slight, have to take delivery and sue for any loss.

Contractual terms: terms implied by custom

157 Hutton v Warren (1836) 150 ER 517

The claimant was the tenant of a farm and the defendant the landlord. At Michaelmas 1833, the defendant gave the claimant notice to quit on the Lady Day following. The defendant insisted that the claimant cultivate the land during the period of notice, which he did. The claimant now asked for a fair allowance for seeds and labour, of which he had had no benefit, having left the farm before harvest. It was proved that by custom a tenant was bound to farm for the whole of his tenancy and on quitting was entitled to a fair allowance for seeds and labour.

Held – the claimant succeeded.

> We are of opinion that this custom was, by implication, imported into the lease. It has long been settled, that in commercial transactions, extrinsic evidence of custom and usage is admissible to annex incidents to written contracts in matters with respect to which they are silent. The same rule has also been applied to contracts in other transactions of life, in which known usages have been established and prevailed; and this has been done upon the principle of presumption that, in such transactions, the parties did not mean to express in writing the whole of the contract by which they intended to be bound, but to contract with reference to those known usages. (*Per* Parke B)

Comment (i) Michaelmas Day is 29 September and is a quarter day for payment of rent as well as a Christian feast. Lady Day is 25 March. It is also a quarter day for the payment of rent and is so called because it is a Christian feast.

(ii) The case also provides an example of an exception to the parol evidence rule which has already been considered. Outside evidence was admitted, though there was a written agreement as Parke B explains.

(iii) A comparison is provided by the ruling in *Lancaster v Bird, The Times*, 9 March 1999 where it was held that although there was some evidence of a custom in the building trade that prices were quoted exclusive of VAT, this customary term could not be applied to a contract between a small builder and a part-time farmer for work and materials in connection with the erection of a farm shed. The builder's price had been quoted exclusive of VAT but, of course, the account rendered added 17$\frac{1}{2}$ per cent to that figure to cover VAT, the builder being registered for VAT. This increased the bill by a percentage which the farmer could not recover since he was not registered for VAT, his turnover being presumably below the then VAT threshold.

The non-VAT price was payable by the farmer with the builder accounting for VAT on the reduced price. A bad deal for him!

Judicial implied terms

158 *The Moorcock* (1889) 14 PD 64

The appellants in this case were in possession of a wharf and a jetty extending into the River Thames, and the respondent was the owner of the steamship *Moorcock*. In November 1887, the appellants and the respondents agreed that the ship should be discharged and loaded at the wharf and for that purpose should be moored alongside the jetty. Both parties realised that when the tide was out the ship would rest on the river bed. In the event the *Moorcock* sustained damage when she ceased to be waterborne owing to the centre of the vessel settling on a ridge of hard ground beneath the mud. There was no evidence that the appellants had given any warranty that the place was safe for the ship to lie in, but it was *held* – by the Court of Appeal – that there was an implied warranty by the appellants to this effect, for breach of which they were liable in damages. *Per* Bowen, LJ:

> Now, an implied warranty, or as it is called, a covenant in law, as distinguished from an express contract or express warranty, really is in all cases founded on the presumed intention of the parties, and upon reason. The implication which the law draws from what must obviously have been the intention of the parties, the law draws with the object of giving efficacy to the transaction and preventing such a failure of consideration as cannot have been within the contemplation of either side; and I believe if one were to take all cases, and they are many, of implied warranties or covenants in law, it will be found that in all of them the law is raising an implication from the presumed intention of the parties with the object of giving to the transaction such efficacy as both parties must have intended that at all events it should have. In business transactions such as this, what the law desires to effect by the implication is to give such business efficacy to the transaction as must have been intended at all events by both parties who are business men; not to impose on one side all the perils of the transaction, or to emancipate one side from all chances of failure, but to make each party promise in law as much, at all events, as it must have been in the contemplation of both parties that he should be responsible for in respect of those perils or chances.

Comment (i) This statement of the law is to the effect that the court cannot imply a term because it is reasonable to do so but only when it is commercially necessary to do so. Lord Denning, particularly, in *Liverpool City Council v Irwin* [1977] put forward the view that the court could imply a term whenever it was reasonable to do so, even if it was not necessary to do so to make the contract work in a commercial sense. This view is still not entirely accepted by the judiciary in general.

(ii) Although the court most often implies covenants or terms which are positive, i.e. the party concerned *has to do something, negative* covenants can be implied. Thus, in *Fraser v Thames Television Ltd* [1983] 2 All ER 101 the members of a group called Rock Bottom brought an action alleging that Thames had broken an agreement with them about a TV series, an implied term of which was that Thames would not use the idea for the series, which was based on the history of the group and its subsequent struggles, unless the members of the group were employed as actresses in the series. Hirst, J implied this negative term on the ground that it was necessary to give business efficacy to the agreement between the parties.

Statutory implied terms: seller's right to sell

159 *Rowland v Divall* [1923] 2 KB 500

In April 1922, the defendant bought an 'Albert' motor car from a man who had stolen it from the true owner. One month later the claimant, a dealer, purchased the car from the defendant for £334, repainted it, and sold it for £400 to Colonel Railsdon. In September 1922, the police seized the car from Colonel Railsdon and the claimant repaid him the £400. The claimant now sued the defendant for £334 on the ground that there had been a total failure of consideration since the claimant had not obtained a title to the car.

Held – the defendant was in breach of s 12 of the Sale of Goods Act, which implies conditions and warranties into a sale of goods relating to the seller's right to sell, and there had been a total failure of consideration in spite of the fact that the car had been used by the claimant and his purchaser. The claimant contracted for the property in the car and not the mere right to possess it. Since he had not obtained the property, he was entitled to recover the sum of £334 and no deductions should be made for the period of use.

Comment (i) Although the court purported to deal with this case as a breach of s 12(1) of the Act, it would appear that in fact it operated on common-law principles and gave complete restitution of the purchase price because of total failure of consideration arising out of the seller's lack of title. The condition under s 12(1) had by reason of the claimant's use of the car and the passage of time become a warranty when the action was brought, and if the court had been awarding damages for breach of warranty it would have had to reduce the sum of £334 by a sum representing the value to the claimant of the use of the vehicle which he had had.

(ii) The drawback to making an allowance to the seller for use is that he gets an allowance for a car which is not his and the owner might sue the buyer in damages for conversion so that he would have to pay an allowance and damages to the true owner in conversion. In other words, pay for use twice.

(iii) It is also relevant to say that the court felt an allowance for use should not be made because the claimant had paid the price for the car to become its *owner*, and not merely to have *use* of it. So why should he be subject to an allowance for use when that is not what he wanted or bargained for? As Bankes, LJ said: 'He did not get what he paid for – namely a car to which he would have title.'

160 *Niblett Ltd v Confectioners' Materials Co Ltd* [1921] 3 KB 387

The defendants agreed to sell to the claimants 3,000 cases of condensed milk to be shipped from New York to London. Of these, 1,000 cases bore labels with the word 'Nissly' on them. This came to the notice of the Nestlé Company and it suggested that this was an infringement of its registered trade mark. The claimants admitted this and gave an undertaking not to sell the milk under the title of 'Nissly'. They tried to dispose of the goods in various ways but eventually discovered that the only way to deal with the goods was to take off the labels and sell the milk without mark or label, thus incurring loss.

Held – by the Court of Appeal – the sellers were in breach of the implied condition set out in s 12(1) of the Sale of Goods Act. A person who can sell goods only by infringing a trade mark has no right to sell, even though he may be the owner of the goods. Atkin, LJ also found the sellers to be in breach of the warranty under s 12(2) because the buyer had not enjoyed quiet possession of the goods.

Sale by description: Sale of Goods Act 1979, s 13 applied

161 *Beale v Taylor* [1967] 3 All ER 253

The defendant advertised a car for sale as being a 1961 Triumph Herald 1200 and he believed this description to be correct. The claimant answered the advertisement and later visited the defendant to inspect the car. During his inspection he noticed, on the rear of the car, a metal disc with the figure 1200 on it. The claimant purchased the car, paying the agreed price. However, he later discovered that the car was made up of the rear of a 1961 Triumph Herald 1200 welded to the front of an earlier Triumph Herald 948. The welding was unsatisfactory and the car was unroadworthy.

Held – by the Court of Appeal – the claimant's case for damages for breach of the condition implied in the contract by s 13 of the Sale of Goods Act succeeded. The claimant had relied on the advertisement and on the metal disc on the rear and the sale was one by description, even though the claimant had seen and inspected the vehicle.

Comment It is, however, necessary for the buyer to show that it was the intention of the parties that the description should be relied upon by the buyer. In *Harlingdon Ltd v Hull Fine Art Ltd* [1990] 1 All ER 737 Hull was a firm of art dealers controlled by Mr Christopher Hull. It was asked to sell two oil paintings described as being by Münter, a German artist of the Impressionist School. Mr Hull had no knowledge of the German Impressionist School. He contacted Harlingdon: art dealers specialising in that field. Mr Hull told Harlingdon that the paintings were by Münter. Harlingdon sent an expert to examine the paintings and at this stage Mr Hull made it clear that he was not an expert in the field. Following the inspection, Harlingdon bought one of the paintings which turned out to be a forgery. Harlingdon sued for breach of s 13. It was held by the Court of Appeal that the claim failed. Harlingdon had not relied on the description of the painting, but had bought it after a proper and expert examination. The 'description' had not, therefore, become an essential term or condition of the contract.

It should be noted that this matter was not raised in *Leaf v International Galleries* (1950) (see Chapter 12) because Mr Leaf did not claim a breach of s 13. Presumably, if he had done so, he would have been required to show that it was the intention of the parties that he should rely on the description that the painting was by John Constable. This will normally be fairly easy to prove where the purchaser is an inexpert consumer. However, it was held in *Cavendish-Woodhouse v Manley* (1984) 82 LGR 376 that a seller could show that the sale was not by description by using such phrases as 'Sold as seen' or 'Bought as seen'. Such phrases do not, however, avoid the conditions of fitness and satisfactory quality because the phrases are not regarded as general exclusion clauses.

Section 13 applies to packaging

162 *Moore & Co v Landauer & Co* [1921] 2 KB 519

The claimants entered into a contract to sell the defendants a certain quantity of Australian canned fruit, the goods to be packed in cases containing 30 tins each. The goods were to be shipped 'per SS *Toromeo*'. The ship was delayed by strikes at Melbourne and in South Africa, and was very late in arriving at London. When the goods were discharged about one-half of the consignment was packed in cases containing 24 tins only, instead of 30, and the buyers refused to accept them.

Held – although the method of packing made no difference to the market value of the goods, the sale was by description under s 13 of the Sale of Goods Act, and the description had not been complied with. Consequently, the buyers were entitled to reject the whole consignment.

Comment (i) The court seems to have adopted a somewhat purist approach to s 13 in this case and had no real regard to the effect which the breach of description had on the contract, i.e. substantially none. Decisions such as this were described by Lord Wilberforce in the *Reardon Smith* case as 'excessively technical'.

(ii) Under s 15A of the Sale of Goods Act 1979 (as inserted by the Sale and Supply of Goods Act 1994) the right of rejection in the above circumstances is retained but a business buyer will, where (as in this case) the breach is of slight or no effect, have to take delivery and sue for loss if any.

Fitness for the purpose: no need to reveal a usual purpose but a special purpose must be disclosed

163 *Priest v Last* [1903] 2 KB 148

The claimant, a draper who had no special knowledge of hot-water bottles, bought such a bottle from the defendant who was a chemist. It was in the ordinary course of the defendant's business to sell hot-water bottles and the claimant asked him whether the india-rubber bottle he was shown would stand boiling water. He was told that it would not, but it would stand hot water. The claimant did not state the purpose for which the bottle was required. In the event the bottle was filled with hot water and used by the claimant's wife for bodily application to relieve cramp. On the fifth time of using, the bottle burst and the wife was severely scalded. Evidence showed that the bottle was not fit for use as a hot-water bottle.

Held – the claimant was entitled to recover the expenses he had incurred in the treatment of his wife's injuries for the defendant's breach of s 14(3) of the Sale of Goods Act. The circumstances showed that the claimant had relied on the defendant's skill and judgement, and although he had not mentioned the purpose for which he required the bottle, he had in fact used it for the usual and obvious purpose.

Comment There was no question of the wife suing the chemist under Sale of Goods legislation because she was not a party to the contract. She could today have sued the manufacturer or the chemist in negligence (see *Donoghue v Stevenson* (1932)) if she could have proved negligence in either of them. A claim against the manufacturers could now be brought under the Consumer Protection Act 1987, even where negligence cannot be proved (see further Chapter 21).

164 *Griffiths v Peter Conway Ltd* [1939] 1 All ER 685

The defendants, who were retail tailors, supplied the claimant with a Harris tweed coat which was made to order for her. The claimant wore the coat for a short time and then developed dermatitis. She brought this action for damages alleging that the defendants were in breach of s 14(3) of the Sale of Goods Act because the coat was not fit for the purpose for which it was bought. Evidence showed that the claimant had an abnormally sensitive skin and that the coat would not have affected the skin of a normal person.

Held – the claimant failed because s 14(3) did not apply. The defendants did not know of the claimant's abnormality and could not be expected to assume that it existed.

Comment A claim against the manufacturer of the tweed under the Consumer Protection Act 1987 is not appropriate here. Although the Act does not require negligence to be proved, it is necessary to prove causation, and the effective cause here was the claimant's sensitive skin, not the coat.

Fitness for the purpose: reliance on the seller's skill and judgement readily inferred unless the seller is known to sell only one brand of goods

165 *Grant v Australian Knitting Mills Ltd* [1936] AC 85

This was an appeal from the High Court of Australia to the Privy Council in England by a Dr Grant of Adelaide, South Australia. He bought a pair of long woollen underpants from a retailer, the respondents being the manufacturers. The underpants contained an excess of sulphite, a chemical used in their manufacture. This chemical should have been eliminated before the product was finished, but a quantity was left in the underpants purchased by Dr Grant. After wearing the pants for a day or two, a rash, which turned out to be dermatitis, appeared on the appellant's ankles and soon became generalised, compelling the appellant to spend many months in hospital. He sued the retailers and the manufacturers for damages.

Held – (a) the retailers were in breach of the South Australian Sale of Goods Act 1895 (which is in the same terms as the English Act of 1979). They were liable under s 14(3) because the article was not fit for the purpose; they were liable under s 14(2) because the article was not of merchantable (now satisfactory) quality; (b) the manufacturers were liable in negligence, following *Donoghue* v *Stevenson*. This was a latent defect which could not have been discovered by a reasonable examination. It should also be noted that the appellant had a perfectly normal skin. (Compare *Griffiths* v *Peter Conway Ltd* (1939) above.)

Comment (I) Section 13 (sale by description) also applied even though this was a sale of a specific object which was seen by the purchaser. On the issue of reliance, Lord Wright said: 'The reliance will be in general inferred from the fact that a buyer goes to the shop in confidence that the tradesman has selected his stock with skill and judgement.'

(ii) This case provides an interesting contrast between the liability of the supplier who was liable although not negligent, Sale of Goods Act liability being strict, and the liability of the manufacturer where the claimant was put to the extra burden of proving the manufacturer negligent (but see now Consumer Protection Act 1987 in Chapter 21).

166 *Wren v Holt* [1903] 1 KB 610

The claimant was a builder's labourer at Blackburn, and the defendant was the tenant of a beerhouse in the same town. The beerhouse was a tied house so that the defendant was obliged to sell beer brewed by a company called Richard Holden Limited. The claimant was a regular customer and knew that the beerhouse was a tied house, and that only one type of beer was supplied. The claimant became ill and it was established that his illness was caused by arsenical poisoning due to the beer supplied to him. He now sued the tenant.

Held – there was no claim under s 14(3) because the claimant could not have relied on the defendant's skill and judgement in selecting his stock, because he was bound to supply Holden's beer. However, s 14(2) applied, and since the beer was not of merchantable (now satisfactory) quality, the claimant was entitled to recover damages.

Fitness: second-hand goods: where defects occur fairly quickly after sale

167 *Crowther v Shannon Motor Company* [1975] 1 All ER 139

The claimant, relying on the skill and judgement of the defendants, bought a second-hand car from them. After being driven for over 2,000 miles in the three weeks after the sale, the engine seized and had to be replaced. In his evidence, the previous owner said that the engine was not fit for use on the road when he sold it to the defendants, and on that basis the Court of Appeal *held* that there was a breach of s 14(3) at the time of resale. The fact that a car does not go for a reasonable time after sale is evidence that the car was not fit for the purpose at the time of sale.

Comment This case makes clear that there is an obligation of reasonable durability on the seller of goods.

Fitness and satisfactory quality: s 14(3) can operate independently

168 *Baldry v Marshall* [1925] 1 KB 260

The claimant was the owner of a Talbot racing car and was anxious to change it for a touring car because his wife refused to ride in the Talbot. The claimant wrote to the defendants asking for details of the Bugatti car for which they were agents. The claimant knew nothing of the Bugatti range, but asked for a car that would be comfortable and suitable for touring purposes. The defendants' manager said that a Bugatti would be suitable. The claimant later inspected a Bugatti chassis and agreed to buy it when a body had been put on it. When the car was delivered it was to all intents and purposes a racing car and not suitable for touring. The claimant returned the car, but he had paid £1,000 under the contract and now sued for its return on the ground that the defendants were in breach of s 14(3) of the Sale of Goods Act, the car not being fit for the purpose.

Held – the claimant had relied on the skill and judgement of the defendants and it was in the course of their business to supply cars. Therefore, there was a breach of s 14(3).

Comment It will be appreciated that the Bugatti was of merchantable (now satisfactory) quality.

Resale price has some bearing upon satisfactory quality

169 BS Brown & Son Ltd v Craiks Ltd [1970] 1 All ER 823

Brown and Son ordered a quantity of cloth from Craiks who were manufacturers. Brown's wanted it for making dresses but did not make this purpose known to Craiks who thought the cloth was wanted for industrial use. The price paid by Brown's was 36.25p per yard, which was higher than the normal price for industrial cloth but not substantially so. The cloth was not suitable for making dresses and Brown's cancelled the contract and claimed damages. Both parties were left with substantial quantities of cloth but Craiks had managed to sell some of their stock for 30p per yard. Having failed in the lower court to establish a claim under s 14(3), since they had not made the purpose known to Craiks, Brown's now sued for damages under s 14(2).

Held – by the House of Lords – the claim failed. The cloth was still commercially saleable for industrial purposes though at a slightly lower price. It was not a necessary requirement of merchantable (now satisfactory) quality that there should be no difference between purchase and resale price. If the difference was substantial, however, it might indicate that the goods were not of merchantable (now satisfactory) quality. The difference in this case was not so material as to justify any such inference.

Comment (i) Even where the goods are not purchased for resale the purchase price may be relevant. Thus, the sale of a car with a defective clutch would be sale of unsatisfactory goods, but if the seller makes an allowance in the price to cover the defect, it may not be (*Bartlett* v *Sydney Marcus Ltd* [1965] 2 All ER 753).

(ii) The case also decides that goods may be satisfactory if they are fit for one of the purposes for which they might be used even though they are unfit when used for another purpose.

Implied terms relating to fitness and satisfactory quality: items supplied with the goods

170 Geddling v Marsh [1920] 1 KB 668

The defendants were manufacturers of mineral waters and they supplied the same to the claimant who kept a small general store. The bottles were returnable when empty. One of the bottles was defective, and whilst the claimant was putting it back into a crate, it burst and injured her.

Held – even though the bottles were returnable, they were supplied under a contract of sale within s 14 of the Sale of Goods Act. The fact that the bottles were only bailed to the claimant was immaterial. There was an implied warranty of fitness for the purpose for which they were supplied, and the defendant was liable in damages.

Comment Bray, J was careful to point out that his decision was an interpretation of s 14 of the Sale of Goods Act only. It does not decide that the liability of a bailor is the same as that of a vendor.

171 Wilson v Rickett, Cockerell & Co Ltd [1954] 1 QB 598

The claimant, a housewife, ordered from the defendants, who were coal merchants, a ton of 'Coalite'. The Coalite was delivered and when part of it was put on a fire in an open grate, it exploded causing damage to the claimant's house. In this action the claimant sought damages for breach of s 14 of the Sale of Goods Act. The county court judge found that the explosion was not due to the Coalite but to something else, possibly a piece of coal with explosive embedded in it, which had got mixed with the Coalite in transit and had not come from the manufacturers of the Coalite. Therefore, he *held* that s 14(3) applied only to the Coalite and dismissed the action since the Coalite itself was fit for the purpose. The Court of Appeal, however, in allowing the appeal, pointed out that fuel of this kind is not sold by the lump but by the bag, and a bag containing explosive materials is, as a unit, not fit for burning. The explosive matter was 'goods supplied under the contract' for the purposes of s 14 and clearly s 14(2) applied, because the goods supplied were not of merchantable (now satisfactory) quality. Damages were awarded to the claimant. Regarding the applicability of what is now s 14(3), the Court of Appeal did not think this applied since the sale was under a trade name, and the claimant had not relied on the defendant's skill and judgement in selecting a fuel.

Comment The assumption of no reliance where goods are purchased under a trade name no longer applies under the 1979 Act.

172 Wormell v RHM Agriculture (East) Ltd [1986] 1 All ER 769

Mr Wormell, an experienced arable farmer, was unable by reason of cold, wet weather to spray his winter wheat crop to kill wild oats until much later than usual in the spring of 1983. He asked the defendants to recommend the best wild-oat killer which could be used later than normal. The agricultural chemical manager recommended a particular herbicide and Mr Wormell bought £6,438 worth of it.

The instructions on the cans stated that it ought not to be applied beyond the recommended stage of crop growth. It was said that damage could occur to crops sprayed after that stage and the herbicide would give the best level of wild-oat control at the latest stage of application consistent with the growth of the crop.

Mr Wormell felt that the need to kill the wild oats was so important that he would risk some damage to the crops by applying the herbicide quite late. From his understanding of the instructions the risk was not that the herbicide would not be effective on the wild oats, but if the spray was used after the recommended time then the crop might be damaged. The herbicide was applied but proved to be largely ineffective.

Mr Wormell claimed damages for breach of contract in respect of the sale of the herbicide. He alleged that it was not of merchantable (now satisfactory) quality contrary to s 14(2) of the Sale of Goods Act, nor was it fit for the purpose for which it was supplied, namely to control weeds, and in particular, wild oats, contrary to s 14(3) of the same Act.

RHM argued that since the herbicide would kill the wild oats, the fact that the instructions caused it to be applied at a time when it was not effective did not make the herbicide itself unmerchantable (now unsatisfactory) or unfit for the purpose.

Piers Ashworth QC sitting as a Deputy Judge of the High Court, said that one had to look at how Mr Wormell understood the instructions and how a reasonable user would understand them. Mr Wormell understood the instructions to mean that the herbicide would be effective if it was sprayed at any time, but if sprayed late there was a risk of crop damage. The judge concluded that a reasonable farmer would have understood the instructions in the same way. He thought that the instructions were consequently misleading.

For the purposes of the Sale of Goods Act, 'goods' included the container and packaging for the goods and any instructions supplied with them. If the instructions were wrong or misleading the goods would not be of merchantable (now satisfactory) quality or fit for the purpose for which they were supplied under s 14(2) and (3). This statement was approved in a 1987 appeal to the Court of Appeal, though on the facts the court reversed the decision of the High Court, having found the instructions adequate.

Comment The decision was reversed by the Court of Appeal because the instructions were adequate but merely misunderstood. However, the Court of Appeal agreed that there is a legal obligation to give adequate guidance as to how the product is to be used.

Retailer does not warrant safety of goods used by the buyer after buyer knows of their defects

173 *Lambert v Lewis* [1981] 1 All ER 1185

Mr Lewis owned a Land Rover and a trailer. His employee, Mr Larkin, was driving it when the trailer broke away. It collided with a car coming from the opposite direction. Mr Lambert, who was driving that car, was killed and so was his son. His wife and daughter, who were also passengers, survived and then sued Mr Lewis for damages in negligence. He joined the retailer who sold him the towing hitch which had become detached from the trailer and was basically the cause of the collision. The retailer was sued under s 14 (goods not fit for the purpose nor of merchantable (now satisfactory) quality). The court found that the towing hitch was badly designed and a securing brass spindle and handle had come off it so that only dirt was keeping the towing pin in position. It had been like that for some months and Mr Lewis had coupled and uncoupled the trailer once or twice a week during that time and knew of the problem.

The claimants succeeded in their action against Mr Lewis. He failed in his claim against the retailer. The House of Lords decided that when a person first buys goods he can rely on s 14. However, once he discovers that they are defective but continues to use them and so causes injury, he is personally liable for the loss caused. He cannot claim an indemnity under s 14 from the retailer. The chain of causation is broken by the buyer's continued use of the goods while knowing that they are faulty and may cause injury.

Comment The above summary does not concern itself with the possible liability of the manfacturers in terms of the design problem. However, a point of interest arises in connection with it. The issue of the manufacturers' liability was taken by an action in negligence. The court refused to construe a collateral contract between Mr Lewis and the manufacturers although he bought the hitch on the strength of the manufacturers' advertising. (Compare *Carlill* (Chapter 9), where such a contract was rather exceptionally construed.)

Sale by sample: what is a reasonable examination?

174 *Godley v Perry* [1960] 1 All ER 36

The first defendant, Perry, was a newsagent who also sold toys, and, in particular, displayed plastic toy catapults in his window. The claimant, who was a boy aged six, bought one for 6d. While using it to fire a stone, the catapult broke and the claimant was struck in the eye, either by a piece of the catapult or the stone, and as a result he lost his left eye. The chemist's report given in evidence was that the catapults were made from cheap material unsuitable for the purpose and likely to fracture, and that the moulding of the plastic was poor, the catapults containing internal voids. Perry had purchased the catapults from a wholesaler with whom he had dealt for some time, and this sale was by sample, the defendant's wife examining the sample catapult by pulling the elastic. The wholesaler's supplier was another wholesaler who had imported the catapults from Hong Kong. This sale was also by sample and the sample catapult was again tested by pulling the elastic. In this action the claimant alleged that the first defendant was in breach of the conditions implied by s 14(2) and (3) of the Sale of Goods Act.

The first defendant brought in his supplier as third party, alleging against him a breach of the conditions implied by s 15(2)(c), and the third party brought in his supplier as fourth party, alleging breach of s 15(2)(c) against him.

Held –

(*a*) the first defendant was in breach of s 14(2) and (3) because:
  (i) the catapult was not reasonably fit for the purpose for which it was required. The claimant relied on the seller's skill or judgement, this being readily inferred where the customer was of tender years (s 14(3));
  (ii) the catapult was not merchantable (now of satisfactory quality) (s 14(2));

(*b*) the third and fourth parties were both in breach of s 15(2)(c) because the catapult had a defect which rendered it unmerchantable (now unsatisfactory) and this defect was not apparent on reasonable examination of the sample. The test applied, i.e. the pulling of the elastic, was all that could be expected of a potential purchaser. The third and fourth parties had done business before, and the third party was entitled to regard without suspicion any sample shown to him and to rely on the fourth party's skill in selecting his goods.

EXCLUSION CLAUSES

Exclusion clauses: the effect of signing a document containing such a clause: effect of misrepresentation as to contents

175 *L'Estrange v Graucob (F)* [1934] 2 KB 394

The defendant sold to the claimant, Miss L'Estrange, who owned a café in Llandudno, a cigarette slot machine, inserting in the sales agreement the following

clause: 'Any express or implied condition, statement or warranty, statutory or otherwise, is hereby excluded.' The claimant signed the agreement but did not read the relevant clause, apparently because she thought it was merely an order form, and she now sued for breach of what is now s 14(3) of the Sale of Goods Act 1979 (goods not fit for the purpose) in respect of the unsatisfactory nature of the machine supplied which often jammed and soon became unusable.

Held – the clause was binding on her, although the defendants made no attempt to read the document to her nor call her attention to the clause. 'Where a document containing contractual terms is signed, then in the absence of fraud, or I will add, misrepresentation, the party signing it is bound, and it is wholly immaterial whether he had read the document or not.' (*Per* Scrutton, LJ)

Comment (i) The ruling in this case would appear to apply even where the party signing cannot understand the document as where the signer cannot read or does not understand the language in which the document is written (*The Luna* [1920] P 22). This would not, of course, apply if the person relying on the clause *knew* that the other party could not read (*Geir v Kujawa* [1970] 1 Lloyd's Rep 364). It will, of course, be realised that s 6(3) of the Unfair Contract Terms Act 1977 would now apply so that the clause could only be effective if reasonable. In addition, s 3 of the 1977 Act would require reasonableness because the contract was on the supplier's standard terms which were applicable to everyone and could not be varied.

(ii) The ruling in the *Geir* case has assumed more importance now that business within Europe has expanded and indeed because of the increase in international trade generally. Where such trade is with a country in which English is not the first language, exclusion clauses and other terms should be translated as appropriate. In a case involving Allianz, a German company, the court decided that an exclusion clause in an insurance policy issued by Allianz in France but without a translation into French did not apply. However, illiteracy or failure to understand English in the UK business scene is still no defence and an English clause will apply (see *Thompson v LMS Railway* (1930) below).

176 *Curtis v Chemical Cleaning and Dyeing Co* [1951] 1 All ER 631

The claimant took a wedding dress, with beads and sequins, to the defendant's shop for cleaning. She was asked to sign a receipt which contained the following clause: 'This article is accepted on condition that the company is not liable for any damage howsoever arising.' The claimant said in evidence: 'When I was asked to sign the document I asked why? The assistant said I was to accept any responsibility for damage to beads and sequins. I did not read it all before I signed it.' The dress was returned stained, and the claimant sued for damages. The company relied on the clause.

Held – the company could not rely on the clause because the assistant had misrepresented the effect of the document so that the claimant was merely running the risk of damage to the beads and sequins.

Comment It will be appreciated that the assistant's statement was true as far as it went. As we have seen, half-truths such as this can amount to misrepresentation (see Chapter 13).

Communication of exclusion clauses: in contractual and non-contractual documents

177 *Thompson v LMS Railway* [1930] 1 KB 41

Thompson, who could not read, asked her niece to buy her an excursion ticket to Manchester from Darwin and back, on the front of which was printed the words, 'Excursion. For conditions see back.' On the back was a notice that the ticket was issued subject to the conditions in the company's timetables, which excluded liability for injury however caused. Thompson was injured and claimed damages.

Held – her action failed. She had constructive notice of the conditions which had, in the court's view, been properly communicated to the ordinary passenger.

Comment (i) The railway ticket was regarded as a contractual document. (Contrast *Chapelton* below.)

(ii) The injuries, which were caused when the train on returning to Darwin at 10 pm did not draw all the way into the station so that the claimant fell down a ramp, would have been the subject of a successful action at law today because the Unfair Contract Terms Act 1977 outlaws exclusion clauses relating to death and personal injury. Thus, on its own facts, this case is of historical interest only, though still relevant on the question of constructive notice.

178 *Chapelton v Barry Urban District Council* [1940] 1 All ER 356

The claimant Chapelton wished to hire deck-chairs and went to a pile owned by the defendants, behind which was a notice stating: 'Hire of chairs 2d per session of three hours.' The claimant took two chairs, paid for them, and received two tickets which he put into his pocket after merely glancing at them. One of the chairs collapsed and he was injured. A notice on the back of the ticket provided that: 'The council will not be liable for any accident or damage arising from hire of chairs.' The claimant sued for damages and the Council sought to rely on the clause in the ticket.

Held – the clause was not binding on Chapelton. The board by the chairs made no attempt to limit the liability, and it was unreasonable to communicate conditions by means of a mere receipt.

Comment The defendants would now have an additional problem, i.e. the 1977 Act outlaws such clauses.

Exclusion clause: communication at or before the contract essential

179 *Olley v Marlborough Court Ltd* [1949] 1 All ER 127

A husband and wife arrived at a hotel as guests and paid for a room in advance. They went up to the room allotted to them; on one of the walls was the following notice: 'The proprietors will not hold themselves responsible for articles lost or stolen unless handed to the manageress for safe custody.' The wife closed the self-locking door of the bedroom and took the key downstairs to the reception desk. There was inadequate and, therefore, negligent staff supervision of the keyboard. A third party took the key and stole certain of the wife's furs. In the ensuing action the defendants sought to rely on the notice as a term of the contract.

Held – the contract was completed at the reception desk and no subsequent notices could affect the claimant's rights.

Comment (i) It was said in *Spurling v Bradshaw* [1956] 1 WLR 461 that if the husband and wife had seen the notice on a previous visit to the hotel it would have been binding on them, though this is by no means certain in view of cases such as *Hollier v Rambler Motors* [1972] 1 All ER 399, which suggest that in consumer transactions previous dealings are not necessarily incorporated unless perhaps the dealings have been frequent.

(ii) A further illustration is provided by *Thornton v Shoe Lane Parking Ltd* [1971] 1 All ER 686 where the Court of Appeal decided that the conditions exempting the company from certain liabilities on a ticket issued by an automatic barrier at the entrance to a car park were communicated too late. The contract was made when the claimant put his car on the place which activated the barrier. This was before the ticket was issued.

Exclusion clause: ineffective where there is an express undertaking running contrary to the clause

180 *J Evans & Son (Portsmouth) Ltd v Andrea Merzario Ltd* [1976] 2 All ER 930

The claimants imported machines from Italy. They had contracted with the defendants since about 1959 for the transport of these machines. Before the defendants went over to the use of containers the claimants' machines had always been crated and carried under deck. When the defendants went over to containers they orally agreed with the claimants that the claimants' goods would still be carried under deck. However, on a particular occasion a machine being transported for the claimants was carried in a container on deck. At the start of the voyage the ship met a swell which caused the container to fall off the deck and the machine was lost. The contract was expressed to be subject to the printed standard conditions of the forwarding trade which contained an exemption clause excusing the defendants from liability for loss or damage to the goods unless the damage occurred whilst the goods were in their actual custody and by reason of their wilful neglect or default, and even in those circumstances, the clause limited the defendants' liability for loss or damage to a fixed amount. The claimants sued for damages against the defendants for the loss of the machine, alleging that the exemption clause did not apply. It was *held* by the Court of Appeal that it did not apply. The printed conditions were repugnant to the oral promise for, if they were applicable, they would render that promise illusory. Accordingly, the oral promise was to be treated as overriding the printed conditions and the claimants' suit succeeded, the exemption clause being inapplicable.

Comment The court may also regard these oral promises as collateral contracts (see also Chapter 9), i.e. in this case a collateral contract to carry the machine under deck, that collateral contract not having an exclusion clause in it.

Exclusion clause: overcoming the privity rule

181 *The New Zealand Shipping Co Ltd v A M Satterthwaite & Co Ltd* [1974] 1 All ER 1015

In this case the makers of an expensive drilling machine entered into a contract for the carriage of the machine by sea to New Zealand. The contract of carriage (the bill of lading) exempted the carriers from full liability for any loss or damage to the machine during carriage and also purported to exempt any servant or agent of the carrier, including independent contractors employed from time to time by the carrier. The machine was damaged by the defendants, who were stevedores, in the course of unloading, and the question to be decided was whether the defendant stevedores, who had been employed by the carrier to unload the machine, could take advantage of the exemption clause in the bill of lading since they were not parties to the contract. It was decided by the Privy Council that they could. The stevedores provided

consideration and so became parties to the contract when they unloaded the machine (*Carlill* v *Carbolic Smoke Ball Co* (1893) (see Chapter 9) applied). The performance of services by the stevedores in discharging the cargo was sufficient consideration to constitute a contract, even though they were already under an obligation to the carrier to perform those services because the actual performance of an outstanding contractual obligation was sufficient to support the promise of an exemption from liability given by the makers of the drill to the shippers, who were in effect third parties to the contract between the carrier and the stevedores (*Shadwell* v *Shadwell* (1860) in Chapter 10 applied).

Comment (i) It is not easy to see when and where the relevant offers and acceptances were made in this case but, as we have already noted, a court can construe a contract from the circumstances without a precise application of the offer and acceptance formula (see *Rayfield* v *Hands* (1958) in Chapter 9).

(ii) The case is and will remain an example of the ingenuity of the common law to reach conclusions which are thought to be fair in the circumstances of the case. The Contracts (Rights of Third Parties) Act 1999 now provides the answer by allowing the contracting parties to confer third-party rights as required in terms at least of exclusion clauses in these contracts. The rights of persons involved in the performance of the contract may be implied by the court unless it appears that the main parties did not intend them to apply or they had specifically excluded the operation of the Act.

An ambiguous exclusion clause is construed against the party who put it in the contract

182 *Alexander v Railway Executive* [1951] 2 All ER 442

Alexander was a magician who had been on a tour together with an assistant. He left three trunks at the parcels office at Launceston station, the trunks containing various properties which were used in an 'escape illusion'. The claimant paid 5d for each trunk deposited and received a ticket for each one. He then left saying that he would send instructions for their dispatch. Some weeks after the deposit and before the claimant had sent instructions for the dispatch of the trunks, the claimant's assistant persuaded the clerk in the parcels office to give him access to the trunks, though he was not in possession of the ticket. The assistant took away several of the properties and was later convicted of larceny (now theft). The claimant sued the defendants for damages for breach of contract, and the defendants pleaded the following term which was contained in the ticket and which stated that the Railway Executive was 'not liable for loss mis-delivery or damage to any articles where the value was in excess of £5 unless at the time of the deposit the true value and nature of the goods was declared by the depositor and an extra charge paid'. No such declaration or payment had been made.

Held – the claimant succeeded because, although sufficient notice had been given constructively to the claimant of the term, the term did not protect the defendants because they were guilty of a breach of a fundamental obligation in allowing the trunks to be opened and things to be removed from them by an unauthorised person.

Comment (i) Devlin, J said that a deliberate delivery to the wrong person did not fall within the meaning of 'mis-delivery', and this may be regarded as the real reason for the decision, as it involved the application of the *contra proferentem* rule.

(ii) Note also that the receipt or ticket for the goods deposited was held to be a contractual document. (Contrast the *Chapelton* case.)

(iii) A further example of the use of the *contra proferentem* rule is to be found in *Williams v Travel Promotions Ltd (T/A Voyages Jules Verne), The Times*, 9 March 2000, where the claimant spent part of the last day of his holiday in Zimbabwe travelling to a different hotel nearer to the airport to save an early start. The contract allowed changes to be made in hotels 'if necessary'. This change, said the court, while it might be 'sensible' was not 'necessary'. A wider expression should have been used to cover the change in this case. The claimant succeeded.

Rules of construction: repugnancy and the four corners rule

183 *Pollock* v *Macrae* [1922] SC (HL) 192

The defendants entered into a contract to build and supply marine engines. The contract had an exclusion clause which was designed to protect them from liability for defective materials and workmanship. The engines supplied under the contract had so many defects that they could not be used. The House of Lords struck out the exclusion clause as repugnant to the main purpose of the contract, which was to build and supply workable engines. The claimant's action for damages was allowed to proceed.

184 *Thomas National Transport (Melbourne) Pty Ltd and Pay v May and Baker (Australia) Pty Ltd* [1966] 2 Lloyd's Rep 347

The owners of certain packages containing drugs and chemicals made a contract with carriers under which the packages were to be carried from Melbourne to various places in Australia. The carriers employed a subcontractor to collect the parcels and take them to the carriers' depot in Melbourne. When the subcontractor arrived late at the Melbourne depot it was locked and so he drove the lorry full of packages to his own house and left it in a garage there. This was in accordance with the carriers' instructions to their subcontractors in the event of late arrival at the depot. There was a fire and some of the packages were destroyed. The cause of the fire was unknown. However, the alleged negligence of the carriers consisted in their instruction to the subcontractors to take the goods home. The court said it was unthinkable that valuable goods worth many thousands of pounds should be kept overnight at a driver's house, regardless of any provision for their safety. The owners sued the carriers who pleaded an exemption clause in the contract of carriage.

Held – by the High Court of Australia – the claimants succeeded. There had been a fundamental breach of contract. The intention of the parties was that the goods would be taken to the carriers' depot and not to the subcontractor's house, in which case the carriers could not rely on the clause.

Comment (i) The decision, which was partly based on fundamental breach of contract (see below), is perhaps better founded on the four corners rule, i.e. the exclusion clause is available only so long as the contract is being performed in accordance with its terms.

(ii) For the avoidance of doubt, Australian courts' decisions are of persuasive authority in UK courts.

Exclusion clauses: no rule of fundamental breach

185 *Photo Production Ltd* v *Securicor Transport Ltd* [1980] 1 All ER 556

The claimant company had contracted with the defendant security company for the defendant to provide security services at the claimant's factory. A person employed by the defendant lit a fire in the claimant's premises while he was carrying out a night patrol. The fire got out of control and burned down the factory. The trial judge was unable to establish from the evidence precisely what the motive was for lighting the fire – it may have been deliberate or merely careless. The defendant relied on an exclusion clause in the contract which read:

Under no circumstances shall the company (Securicor) be responsible for any injurious act or default by any employee of the company unless such act or default could have been foreseen and avoided by the exercise of due diligence on the part of the company as his employer . . .

It was accepted that Securicor was not negligent in employing the person who lit the fire. He came with good references and there was no reason for Securicor to suppose that he would act as he did. It was *held* by the House of Lords that the exclusion clause applied so that Securicor was not liable. All the judges in the House of Lords were unanimous in the view that there was no rule of law by which exclusion clauses became inapplicable to fundamental breach of contract, which this admittedly was. Although the Unfair Contract Terms Act 1977 was not in force at the time this action was brought and so could not be applied to the facts of this case, the existence of the Act and its relevance was referred to by Lord Wilberforce who said that the doctrine of fundamental breach had been useful in its time as a device for avoiding injustice. He then went on to say:

But . . . Parliament has taken a hand; it has passed the Unfair Contract Terms Act 1977. This Act applies to consumer contracts and those based on standard terms and enables exception clauses to be applied with regard to what is just and reasonable. It is significant that Parliament refrained from legislating over the whole field of contract. After this Act, in commercial matters generally, when the parties are not of unequal bargaining power, and when risks are normally borne by insurance . . . there is everything to be said. . . . for leaving the parties free to apportion the risks as they think fit. . . .

Comment (i) In *Harbutt's Plasticine Ltd* v *Wayne Tank & Pump Co Ltd* [1970] 1 All ER 225 Lord Denning accepted that the principle which said that no exclusion clause could excuse a fundamental breach was not a rule of law when the injured party carried on with (or affirmed) the contract. Where this was so rules of construction must be used and the exclusion clause might have to be applied. However, if the injured party elected to repudiate the contract for fundamental breach and, as it were, pushed the contract away, the exclusion clause went with it and could never apply to prevent the injured party from suing for the breach. The same, he said, was true where the consequences were so disastrous (as they were in *Photo Production*) that one could assume that the injured party had elected to repudiate. The *Photo Production* case overrules *Harbutt*, as does s 9(1) of the Unfair Contract Terms Act 1977. This provides that if a clause, as a matter of construction, is found to cover the breach and if it satisfies the reasonableness test, it can apply and be relied on by the party in breach, even though the contract has been terminated by express election or assumed election following the disastrous results of the breach.

(ii) The House of Lords also allowed a Securicor exemption clause to apply in circumstances of fundamental breach

in *Ailsa Craig Fishing Co Ltd* v *Malvern Fishing Co Ltd* [1983] 1 All ER 101. In that case the appellants' ship sank while berthed in Aberdeen harbour. It fouled the vessel next to it which was owned by Malvern. The appellants sued Malvern. Securicor was the second defendant. Securicor had a contract with the appellants to protect the ship. The accident happened as a result of a rising tide. At the time, the Securicor patrolman had left his post to become involved in New Year celebrations. Although there were arguments by counsel to the contrary, the House of Lords *held* that the exclusion clause covered the circumstances of the case, provided the words were given their natural and plain meaning. It, therefore, applied to limit the liability of Securicor, and the appellants failed to recover all their loss.

(iii) The Unfair Contract Terms Act 1977 gives its strongest protection to those who deal as consumers. The contracts in *Photo Productions* and *Ailsa Craig* were non-consumer contracts where both parties were in business. It by no means follows that in a consumer transaction (see below) the court would have allowed a defendant to rely on a 'Securicor' type of clause. It might well be regarded as unreasonable in that context.

(iv) The apportionment of loss referred to by Lord Wilberforce and as applied in the *Photo Production* case and the *Ailsa Craig* case will result in the claimant's insurance company bearing the loss. Many cases, particularly in business and personal injury, are, in effect, battles between insurance companies in regard to liability. They always sue or defend through their clients since the loss is not directly that of the insurance company but if the loss is the fault of the individual or organisation insured the insurance contract requires the insurance company to indemnify the client. That is the nature of the insurance company's interest in the case. An insurance contract will commonly contain an express condition that the insured can be required by the insurer to bring a claim before or after the insurer has paid the insured.

Exclusion of inducement liability: reasonableness

186 *Walker* v *Boyle* [1982] 1 All ER 634

The vendor of a house was asked in a pre-contract enquiry whether the boundaries of the land were the subject of any dispute. The vendor asked her husband to deal with the enquiries. He said that there were no disputes. There were, in fact, disputes but the husband did not regard them as valid because he believed that he was in the right and his view could not be contradicted. His answers were nevertheless wrong and misleading. Contracts were later exchanged. These contracts were on the National Conditions of Sale (19th Edition) produced under the aegis of the Law Society. Condition 17(1) excluded liability for misleading replies to preliminary enquiries. The purchaser later heard of the boundary disputes and claimed in the High Court for rescission of the contract and the return of his deposit. Dillon, J held that condition 17(1) did not satisfy the requirements of reasonableness as set out in s 3 of the Misrepresentation Act 1967 (as substituted by s 8(1) of the Unfair Contract Terms Act 1977). The claimant, therefore, succeeded.

Comment (i) The National Conditions of Sale have been revised and, as regards misrepresentation, the contract now only attempts a total exclusion of the purchaser's remedies if the misrepresentation is not material or substantial in terms of its effect and is not made recklessly or fraudulently.

(ii) The provisions relating to inducement liability were also applied in *South Western General Property Co Ltd* v *Marton, The Times*, 11 May 1982; the court *held* that conditions of sale in an auction catalogue which tried to exclude liability for any representations made, if these were incorrect, were not fair and reasonable. The defendant had relied upon a false statement that some building would be allowed on land which he bought at an auction, even though the facts were that the local authority would be most unlikely to allow any building on the land. The clauses excluding liability for misrepresentation did not apply and the contract could be rescinded.

Exclusion clauses and reasonableness

187 *Mitchell (George) (Chesterhall) Ltd* v *Finney Lock Seeds Ltd* [1983] 1 All ER 108

This case is a landmark. It was the last case heard by Lord Denning, one of the foremost opponents of exclusion clauses that could operate unfairly, in the Court of Appeal. In it he gave a review of the development of the law relating to exclusion clauses in his usual clear and concise way. The report is well worth reading in full. Only a summary of the main points can be given here.

George Mitchell ordered 30 lb of cabbage seed and Finney supplied it. The seed was defective. The cabbages had no heart; their leaves turned in. The seed cost £192 but Mitchell's loss was some £61,000, i.e. a year's production from the 63 acres planted. Mitchell carried no insurance. When sued Finney defended the claim on the basis of an exclusion clause limiting their liability to the cost of the seed or its replacement. In the High Court Parker, J found for Mitchell. Finney appealed to the Court of Appeal. The major steps in Lord Denning's judgment appear below:

(a) *The issue of communication – was the clause part of the contract?* Lord Denning said that it was. The conditions were usual in the trade. They were in the back of Finney's catalogue. They were on the back of the invoice. 'The inference from the course of dealing would be that the farmers had accepted the conditions as printed – even though they had never read them and did not realize that they contained a limitation on liability . . .'.

(b) *The wording of the clause.* The relevant part of the clause read as follows: 'In the event of any seeds or plants sold or agreed to be sold by us not complying with the express terms of the contract of sale or with any representation made by us or by any duly authorized agent or representative on our behalf prior to, at the time of, or in any such contract, or any seeds, or plants proving defective in varietal purity we will, at our option, replace the defective seeds or plants, free of charge to the buyer or will refund all payments made to us by the buyer in respect of the defective seeds or plants and this shall be the limit of our obligation. We hereby exclude all liability for any loss or damage arising from the use of any seeds or plants supplied by us and for any consequential loss or damage arising out of such use or any failure in the performance of or any defect in any seeds or plants supplied by us for any other loss or damage whatsoever save for, at our option, liability for any such replacement or refund as aforesaid.'

Lord Denning said that the words of the clause did effectively limit Finney's liability. Since the Securicor cases (see *Photo Production* and *Ailsa Craig*), words were to be given their natural meaning and not strained. A judge must not proceed in a hostile way towards the wording of exclusion clauses as was, for example, the case with the word 'mis-delivery' in *Alexander* v *Railway Executive* (1951).

(c) *The test of reasonableness.* Lord Denning then turned to the new test of reasonableness which could be used to strike down an exclusion clause, even though it had been communicated, and in spite of the fact that its wording was appropriate to cover the circumstances. On this he said: 'What is the result of all this? To my mind it heralds a revolution in our approach to exemption clauses; not only where they exclude liability altogether and also where they limit liability; not only in the specific categories in the Unfair Contract Terms Act 1977, but in other contracts too. . . . We should do away with the multitude of cases on exemption clauses. We should no longer have to harass our students with the study of them. We should set about meeting a new challenge. It is presented by the test of reasonableness.'

(d) *Was the particular clause fair and reasonable?* On this Lord Denning said: 'Our present case is very much on the borderline. There is this to be said in favour of the seed merchant. The price of this cabbage seed was small: £192. The damages claimed are high: £61,000. But there is this to be said on the other side. The clause was not negotiated between persons of equal bargaining power. It was inserted by the seed merchants in their invoices without any negotiation with the farmers. To this I would add that the seed merchants rarely, if ever, invoked the clause. . . . Next, I would point out that the buyers had no opportunity at all of knowing or discovering that the seed was not cabbage seed: whereas the sellers could and should have known that it was the wrong seed altogether. The buyers were not covered by insurance against the risk. Nor could they insure. But as to the seed merchants the judge said [Lord Denning here refers to Parker, J at first instance]: "I am entirely satisfied that it is possible for seedsmen to insure against this risk . . .". To that I would add this further point. Such a mistake as this could not have happened without serious negligence on the part of the seed merchants themselves or their Dutch suppliers. So serious that it would not be fair to enable them to escape responsibility for it. In all the circumstances I am of the opinion that it would not be fair or reasonable to allow the seed merchants to rely on the clause to limit their liability.'

Oliver and Kerr, LJJ also dismissed the appeal.

The suppliers asked for leave to appeal to the House of Lords but the Court of Appeal refused. However, the House of Lords granted leave and affirmed the decision of the Court of Appeal in 1983 (see [1983] 2 All ER 737).

Comment This is in effect an application of s 6(3) of the Unfair Contract Terms Act 1977. It was actually brought under the Sale of Goods Act 1979 which contained transitional provisions and s 55(3) of the 1979 Act plus para 11 of Sch 1 applied to this contract. For contracts made after 31 January 1978 the Unfair Contract Terms Act 1977, s 6(3) would apply.

ILLEGALITY AND PUBLIC POLICY

Public policy: judiciary: illegal contracts

188 *Dann v Curzon* (1911) 104 LT 66

An agreement was made for advertising a play by means of collusive criminal proceedings brought as a result of a prearranged disturbance at the theatre. The claimants, who agreed to create the disturbance and did in fact do so, sued for the remuneration due to them under the agreement.

Held – the action failed because it was an agreement to commit a criminal offence and was, therefore, against public policy.

189 *Pearce v Brooks* (1866) LR I Exch 213

The claimants hired a carriage to the defendant for a period of 12 months during which time the defendant was to pay the purchase price by instalments. The defendant was a prostitute and the carriage, which was of attractive design, was intended to assist her in obtaining clients. One of the claimants knew that the defendant was a prostitute but he said that he did not know that she intended to use the carriage for purposes of prostitution. The evidence showed to the contrary. The jury found that the claimant knew the purpose for which the carriage was to be used and thereupon the court *held* that the claimant's action for the sum due under the contract failed for illegality.

Comment (i) The contract would, of course, have been valid if the claimants had not *known* of the intended use of the carriage.

(ii) It was decided by the Court of Appeal in *Armhouse Lee Ltd v Chappell* [1996] 1 CLY 1208, that contracts to advertise telephone sex lines for pre-recorded erotic one-to-one conversations did not amount to prostitution and were not unenforceable as a matter of public policy. The whole matter of these advertisements was the subject of regulation by the Independent Committee for the Supervision of Standards of Telephone Information, and judges sitting as part of the civil jurisdiction should not restrict the freedom of contract on the grounds of their own moral attitudes (*Fender v St John Mildmay* [1937] 3 All ER 402 followed).

190 *Regazzoni v KC Sethia Ltd* [1958] AC 301

The defendants agreed to sell and deliver jute bags to the claimant, both parties knowing and intending that the goods would be shipped from India to Genoa so that the claimant might then send them to South Africa. Both parties knew that the law of India prohibited the direct or indirect export of goods from India to South Africa, this law being directed at the policy of apartheid adopted at the time by South Africa. The defendants did not deliver the jute bags as agreed and the claimant brought this action in an English court, the contract being governed by English law.

Held – although the contract was not illegal in English law, it could not be enforced because it had as its object the violation of the law of a foreign and friendly country in which part of the contract was to be carried out.

Comment In an earlier case, *Foster* v *Driscoll* [1929] 1 KB 470, decided on this ground, the court held that a contract to smuggle whisky to the USA during the period of prohibition was illegal and void. Again, in *Soleimany* v *Soleimany* [1999] 3 All ER 847 the Court of Appeal refused to deal with a dispute between father and son, who were Iranians, in regard to the shares of the proceeds of a business under which the son, in contravention of Iranian revenue and export laws, arranged for the export from Iran of carpets that were subsequently sold by his father in England and other countries.

191 *John* v *Mendoza* [1939] 1 KB 141

The defendant owed the claimant some £852. The defendant was made bankrupt and the claimant was intending to prove for his debt in the bankruptcy. The defendant asked him not to do so, but to say that the £852 was a gift whereupon the defendant would pay the claimant in full regardless of the sum received by other creditors. In view of the defendant's promise the claimant withdrew his proof, but in the event all the other creditors were paid in full and the bankruptcy was annulled. The claimant now sued for the debt.

Held – there was no claim, for the claimant abandoned all right to recover on failure to prove in the bankruptcy, and the defendant's promise to pay in full was unenforceable, being an agreement designed to defeat the bankruptcy laws.

192 *Parkinson* v *The College of Ambulance Ltd and Harrison* [1925] 2 KB 1

The first defendants were a charitable institution and the second defendant was the secretary, who fraudulently represented to the claimant, Colonel Parkinson, that the charity was in a position to obtain some honour (probably a knighthood) for him if he would make a suitable donation to the funds of the charity. The claimant paid over the sum of £3,000 and said he would pay more if the honour was granted. No honour of any kind was received by the claimant and he brought this action to recover the money he had donated to the College.

Held – the agreement was contrary to public policy and illegal. No relief could be granted to the claimant.

193 *Napier* v *National Business Agency Ltd* [1951] 2 All ER 264

The defendants engaged the claimant to act as their secretary and accountant at a salary of £13 per week plus £6 per week for expenses. Both parties were aware that the claimant's expenses could never amount to £6 a week and in fact they never exceeded £1 per week. Income tax was deducted on £13 per week, and £6 per week was paid without deduction of tax as reimbursement of expenses. The claimant, having been summarily dismissed, claimed payment of £13 as wages in lieu of notice.

Held – the agreement was contrary to public policy and illegal. The claimant's action failed.

Comment (i) In an earlier case on this point (*Alexander* v *Rayson* [1936] 1 KB 169), Mrs Rayson took a lease of a service flat. The rent was £1,200 per annum and she signed two forms: under one she agreed to pay £450 for the lease, under the other £750 for services provided by the claimant landlord. His purpose in splitting the transaction was to defraud the rating authorities who assessed the flat for rates on the basis of a rent of £450 pa which was all the claimant disclosed. This was unknown to the defendant. It was held that the contract was illegal. Mrs Rayson could not be sued for the rent. The service contract was also void.

(ii) In *Salvesen* v *Simons* [1994] 490 IRLB 3 the Employment Appeal Tribunal decided that an arrangement whereby part of an employee's pay was paid to a partnership that provided no services to the employer amounted to a fraud on the Inland Revenue and made the employment contract illegal and unenforceable so that the employee had no right to bring a complaint of unfair dismissal. The arrangement resulted at the least in a deferral of payment of tax and a potential evasion of tax lawfully due under Schedule E (PAYE) because the partnership could offset legitimate business expenses under Schedule D, whereas this was not possible under Schedule E.

(iii) The public policy rules do not prevent genuine tax planning. Thus, in *Lightfoot* v *D & J Sporting Ltd* [1996] IRLR 64 L was assisted in his duties as an employed gamekeeper by his wife who initially received no remuneration from L's employer, the defendant. Eventually L made an agreement with his employer under which over a third of his income was paid to his wife. The object of this arrangement was to reduce L's liability for income tax and national insurance. He was later dismissed and both he and his wife received P45s. He claimed unfair dismissal but his employer said that his claim must fail because his contract was illegal as a result of the agreement regarding his wife. The Employment Appeal Tribunal decided that the arrangement in regard to the wife was not illegal merely because its sole purpose was to reduce L's tax and national insurance liabilities. The scheme had been entered into in good faith and was a proper method of reducing tax which had been or would be disclosed to the Revenue. The claim for unfair dismissal could proceed.

Illegal contracts: consequences: is performance necessarily unlawful or not? The *in pari delicto* rule: the matter of repentance

194 *Bowmakers Ltd v Barnet Instruments Ltd* [1944] 2 All ER 579

Bowmakers bought machine tools from a person named Smith. This contract was illegal because it contravened an order made by the Minister of Supply under the Defence Regulations, Smith having no licence to sell machine tools. Bowmakers hired the machine tools to Barnet Instruments under hire-purchase agreements which were also illegal because Bowmaker did not have a licence to sell machine tools. Barnet Instruments failed to keep up the instalments, sold some of the machine tools and refused to give up the others. Bowmakers sued, not on the illegal hire-purchase contracts, but in conversion, and judgment was given for Bowmakers. The Court of Appeal declared the contracts illegal but, since Bowmakers were not suing under the contracts but as owner, their action succeeded. The wrongful sales by Barnet Instruments terminated the hire-purchase contracts.

Comment Although the contract between Smith and Bowmakers was illegal, ownership passed to Bowmakers by reason of delivery. When goods are delivered, the person receiving them has some evidence of title by reason of possession and need not necessarily plead a contract. Where, in an illegal situation, the goods have not been delivered, there may be difficulty in establishing ownership without relying on the illegal contract. Nevertheless, ownership was established without delivery in *Belvoir Finance Co Ltd v Stapleton* [1970] 3 WLR 530. In this case A (a dealer) sold certain cars to B (a finance company) which let them on hire-purchase to C (a car-hire company). C did not pay the minimum deposit required by regulation to B, thus the hire-purchase contract was illegal. Later, C's manager, S, sold the cars to innocent purchasers. C did not pay the hire-purchase instalments and B sued S in conversion, the company C having gone into liquidation. It was *held* by the Court of Appeal that B succeeded. It was the owner of the cars and S had converted its property. The decision is of interest since B (the finance company) had never taken delivery of the cars; they were sent direct from A to C, as is usual in these transactions. Nevertheless, B was accepted as owner, although the only means of proving ownership open to B seems to have been the illegal hire-purchase contract with C. This was the only document which showed how B came to acquire ownership of the cars. On the assumption that this case means what it says, the rule that there can be no enforcement of illegal contracts loses much of its practical value since the major remedy of claiming the goods back appears to be available equally against a hirer in default, whether the contract is legal or illegal.

195 *Edler v Auerbach* [1950] 1 KB 359

The defendant leased premises to the claimant for use as offices. The lease was contrary to the provisions of the Defence Regulations of 1939, since the premises had previously been used as residential accommodation and should have been let as such. The local authority discovered the illegal use and would not allow it to continue. The claimant now sued for rescission of the lease together with rent paid under it. The defendant counterclaimed for rent due and for damage done to the premises, including the removal of a bath.

Held – the landlord could not enforce the illegal lease but was entitled to damages for the claimant's failure to replace the bath.

196 *Hughes v Liverpool Victoria Legal Friendly Society* [1916] 2 KB 482

John Henry Thomas, a grocer, had orginally taken out five policies on customers who owed him money. It was agreed that Thomas had an insurable interest in the customers because they were his debtors. Thomas let the policies drop and an agent of the defendant company persuaded a Mrs Hughes to take them up, assuring her that she had an insurable interest which she had not. She now brought this action to recover the premiums paid.

Held – the contract was illegal but the claimant could recover the premiums. She had been induced to take up the policies by the fraud of the defendant's agent.

Comment In an earlier case on this point (*Atkinson v Denby* (1862) 7 H & N 934), the claimant was insolvent and wished to compromise with his creditors by paying 25p in the £1. One creditor would not agree unless the claimant paid him £50. This sum was paid and was later recovered by the claimant who had been forced to defraud his creditors. The money was then available for distribution to creditors generally.

197 *Bigos v Bousted* [1951] 1 All ER 92

The defendant was anxious to send his wife and daughter abroad for the sake of the daughter's health, but restrictions on currency were in force so that a long stay abroad was impossible. In August 1947, the defendant, in contravention of the Exchange Control Act 1947, made an agreement under which the claimant was to supply £150 of Italian money to be made available at Rapallo, the defendant undertaking to repay the claimant with English money in England. As security, the defendant deposited with the claimant a share certificate for 140 shares in a company. The wife and daughter went to Italy but were not supplied with currency, and had to return sooner than they would have done. The defendant, thereupon, asked for the return of his share certificate but the claimant refused to give it up. This action was brought by the claimant to recover the sum of £150 which she insisted she had lent to the defendant. He denied the loan, and counterclaimed for the return of his certificate. In the course of the action the claimant abandoned her claim, but the defendant proceeded with his counterclaim saying that, although the contract was illegal, it was still executory so that he might repent and ask the court's assistance.

Held – the court would not assist him because the fact that the contract had not been carried out was due to frustration by the claimant and not the repentance of the defendant. In fact, his repentance was really want of power to sin.

198   *Taylor v Bowers* (1876) 1 QBD 291

The claimant was under pressure from his creditors and in order to place some of his property out of their reach, he assigned certain machinery to a person named Adcock. The claimant then called a meeting of his creditors and tried to get them to settle for less than the amount of their debts, representing his assets as not including the machinery. The creditors would not and did not agree to a settlement. The claimant now sued to recover his machinery from the defendants who had obtained it from Adcock.

Held – the claimant succeeded because the illegal fraud on the creditors had not been carried out.

199   *Kearley v Thomson* (1890) 24 QBD 742

The claimant had a friend who was bankrupt and wished to obtain his discharge. The defendant was likely to oppose the discharge and accordingly the claimant paid the defendant £40 in return for which the defendant promised to stay away from the public examination and not to oppose the discharge. The defendant did stay away from the public examination but before an application for discharge had been made the claimant brought his action claiming the £40.

Held – the claim failed because the illegal scheme had been partially effected.

Illegal contracts: consequences: lawful on the face of it

200   *Fielding and Platt Ltd v Najjar* [1969] 2 All ER 150

The claimants entered into an agreement with a Lebanese company to make and deliver an aluminium press. Payment was to be made by six promissory notes given at stated intervals by the defendant personally. The defendant, who was the managing director of the Lebanese company, told the claimants that they ought to invoice the goods as part of a rolling mill, his intention being to deceive the Lebanese import authorities into believing that the import of the press was authorised whereas in fact it was not. The first promissory note was dishonoured and the claimants stopped work on the press and cabled a message to the Lebanese company to that effect. The second promissory note was then dishonoured and the claimants sued upon the notes. The case eventually reached the Court of Appeal where it was *held* that:

(a) since the first note covered work in progress there was no defence based on failure of consideration;

(b) any illegality in connection with the importing of the press was not part of the contract or agreed to by the claimants;

(c) the claimants' claim was not, therefore, affected by illegality;

(d) since the claimants had repudiated the contract before the second note was dishonoured they had no claim for the amount of the note as such but could only sue for damages; the defendant was not liable on the second note.

Comment In an earlier case on this point (*Clay v Yates* (1856) 1 H & B 73) it was *held* that a printer who had, without knowledge, printed a book containing libels could recover his charges.

201   *Cowan v Milbourn* (1867) LR 2 Ex 230

A person hired a hall to deliver blasphemous lectures and then was refused possession of it. His action claiming possession was refused on the ground that no relief could be granted by the court where the purpose of the contract was illegal.

202   *Berg v Sadler and Moore* [1937] 1 All ER 637

The claimant was a hairdresser and sold tobacco and cigarettes. He was a member of the Tobacco Trade

Association, the Association having as its object the prevention of price cutting. Manufacturers would supply tobacco to traders who agreed not to sell at less than the fixed retail price. The claimant sold tobacco at cut prices and was put on the manufacturers' stop list which meant that he could not obtain supplies. The claimant made contact with a person named Reece who was a member of the Association and Reece agreed to obtain goods from manfacturers and hand them over to the claimant, in return for which Reece was to receive a commission from the claimant. One such transaction was carried out. On a later occasion the claimant's assistant and a representative of Reece went to the defendant's premises to obtain a supply of cigarettes. The claimant's assistant handed over some £72 to Moore, who had some doubt about the matter and said he would send the goods direct to Reece's shop. Thereupon the claimant's assistant demanded the return of the money. Moore refused to give it back, and this action was brought to recover it.

Held – this was an attempt by the claimant to obtain goods by false pretences and, since no action arises out of a base cause, the claimant's action failed.

Public policy: contracts to oust the jurisdiction of the courts; severance

203 *Goodinson* v *Goodinson* [1954] 2 All ER 255

A contract made between husband and wife, who had already separated, provided that the husband would pay his wife a weekly sum by way of maintenance in consideration that she would indemnify him against all debts incurred by her, would not pledge his credit, and would not take matrimonial proceedings against him in respect of maintenance. The wife now sued for arrears of maintenance under this agreement. The last promise was admittedly void since its object was to oust the jurisdiction of the courts, but it was *held* that this did not vitiate the rest of the contract; it was not the sole or even the main consideration, and the wife's action for arrears succeeded, this promise being severable.

Comment In a later case on this point (*Re Davstone Estates Ltd* [1969] 2 All ER 849) it was decided that a clause in a lease providing that, as regards certain payments to be made by tenants for services to common parts, e.g. staircases, in a block of flats, the certificate of the landlord's surveyor was to be final and conclusive, could be regarded as void.

Restraint of trade and the public interest

204 *Wyatt* v *Kreglinger and Fernau* [1933] 1 KB 793

In June 1923, the defendants wrote to the claimant, who had been in their service for many years, intimating that upon his retirement they proposed to give him an annual pension of £200, subject to the condition that he did not compete against them in the wool trade. The claimant's reply was lost and he did not appear ever to have agreed for his part not to engage in the wool trade, but he retired the following September and received the pension until June 1932 when the defendants refused to make any further payments. The claimant sued them for breach of contract. The defendants denied any contract existed and also pleaded that if a contract did exist, it was void as being in restraint of trade. The Court of Appeal gave a judgment for the defendants and although there was no unanimity with regard to the *ratio decidendi*, it appeared to two judges that the contract was injurious to the interests of the public, since to restrain the claimant from engaging in the wool trade was to deprive the community of services from which it might derive advantage.

Comment The basis of this decision seems to be that if a contract did exist it was supported only by an illegal consideration moving from Wyatt, i.e. an agreement not to engage in the wool trade. If he had been entitled to a pension as part of his original contract of service, then no doubt the pension arrangements would have been severed and enforced.

Restraints on employees: trade secrets

205 *Forster & Sons Ltd* v *Suggett* (1918) 35 TLR 87

The works manager of the claimants, who were mainly engaged in making glass and glass bottles, was instructed in certain confidential methods concerning, amongst other things, the correct mixture of gas and air in the furnaces. He agreed that during the five years following the termination of his employment he would not carry on in the United Kingdom, or be interested in, glass-bottle manufacture or any other business connected with glass-making as conducted by the claimants. It was *held* that the claimants were entitled to protection in this respect and that the restraint was reasonable.

Comment (i) The Court of Appeal decided in *PSM International and McKechnie* v *Whitehouse and Willenhall Automation* [1992] IRLR 279 that the court has power to prevent a contract made following an abuse of trade secrets from being carried out. Thus, if A is employed by B and goes to work for C and, by using trade secrets obtained while working for B, helps C to obtain a contract with D, then the court can grant B an injunction to restrain C from fulfilling its contract with D where there is evidence that B has lost the contract with D because of the misuse of its trade secrets, even though the effect on D appears unfair. C is not liable to D for breach of contract because it is frustrated (see further Chapter 17) since it could not be carried out without C being in contempt of court.

(ii) A more recent example involving a famous name can be found in *Dyson Technology Ltd v Strutt* [2005] All ER (D) 355 (Nov). Mr Strutt is an engineer who had been employed by Dyson and possessed confidential knowledge of a technical nature belonging to Dyson and relating to vacuum cleaners. Because of this, he was contractually restrained from being involved in a competing business for 12 months from leaving his employment with Dyson. He left Dyson and joined Black & Decker, known mainly for power tools but having a small business in vacuum cleaners. The High Court granted Dyson an injunction which prevented Mr Strutt from working for any business that competed with Dyson for the 12-month period. The judge took the view that Black & Decker could realistically be regarded as a competitor, in spite of the small business presence, and the 12-month term was reasonable in the circumstances.

Restraints on employees: solicitation of customers and clients

206 ***Home Counties Dairies v Skilton*** **[1970] 1 All ER 1227**

Skilton, a milk roundsman employed by the claimants, agreed, amongst other things, not for one year after leaving his job 'to serve or sell milk or dairy produce' to persons who within six months before leaving his employment were customers of his employers. Skilton left his employment with the claimants in order to work as a roundsman for Westcott Dairies. He then took the same milk round as he had worked when he was with the claimants.

Held – by the Court of Appeal – this was a flagrant breach of agreement. The words 'dairy produce' were not too wide. On a proper construction they must be restricted to things normally dealt in by a milkman on his round. 'A further point was taken that the customer restriction would apply to anyone who had been a customer within the last six months of the employment and had during that period ceased so to be, and it was said that the employer could have no legitimate interest in such persons. I think this point is met in the judgment in *GW Plowman & Sons Ltd v Ash* [1964] 2 All ER 10 where it was said that a customer might have left temporarily and that his return was not beyond hope and was therefore a matter of legitimate interest to the employer'. (*Per* Harman LJ)

Comment (i) It was held by the Court of Appeal in *John Michael Design v Cooke* [1987] 2 All ER 332 after referring to *Plowman v Ash* that a restraint in a contract of employment preventing an employee (A) from competing with his former employer (B) could be enforced by an injunction even to prevent the former employee from doing business with a customer (C) of his former employer who had made it clear that he would not do business with (B) again. There was always the possibility that (C) would change his mind.

(ii) It is better in these customer/client restraints to restrict the restraint to not soliciting. If in addition the restraint prevents the employee from working in a given area, it may fail. Thus, in *Office Angels Ltd v Rainer-Thomas and O'Connor* [1991] IRLR 214 the defendants were employed by the claimants at their employment agency in Bow Lane in the City of London. Janette Rainer-Thomas and Elizabeth Ann O'Connor were employed as the manager of the branch and temporaries consultant respectively. The defendants' contracts of employment included a clause which provided that, in order to protect Office Angels' goodwill, for a six-month period following the termination of employment, office managers and temporaries consultants should not solicit custom from people or companies which had been a client of the company at any time during the period for which the employee was employed by the claimants. In addition, during those six months the relevant employees agreed not to engage in the trade or business of any employment agency within a radius of 3,000 metres of the branch or branches of the company at which they had been employed for a period of not less than four weeks during the six months prior to the date of termination of employment, or in the case of a branch or branches in the Greater London area, then within a radius of 1,000 metres.

The defendants gave notice and left the claimants' employment on 23 October 1990. On 1 November they became directors and shareholders of a company called Pertemps City Network (London) Ltd which operated an employment agency from Fenchurch Street.

Injunctions preventing the defendants from so operating were granted by the High Court. The defendants appealed to the Court of Appeal. The Court of Appeal allowed the appeal and discharged the injunctions, dismissing all the claimants' claims for relief in the action. While the court would have been prepared to accept the restraint on the poaching of clients for a period of six months, it was not prepared to accept the area restraint, and for this reason the whole of the clause setting out the restraints failed.

In the main judgment, Sir Christopher Slade said: 'Looking at the matter broadly, a restriction which precludes the defendants, albeit only for a period of six months, from opening an office of an employment agency anywhere in an area of about 1.2 square miles, including most of the City of London, is not an appropriate form of covenant for the protection of the [claimants'] connection with its clients and is, in any event, wider than is necessary for such protection. The City of London, where there are some 400 employment agencies, is clearly a particularly fertile area for persons carrying on this class of business in view of the many thousands of potential clients and job-seekers who operate in that area. I fully understand the desire of the [claimants] to preclude the defendants from seeking unfair advantage of the contacts with the 100 or so of the [claimants'] clients which the defendants had made during their employment by the [claimants]. In my judgment, however, the restriction imposed by [the clause] placed a disproportionately severe restriction on the defendants' right to compete with the [claimants] after leaving [their] employment and went further than was reasonable in the interest of the parties.'

(iii) The case represents the modern approach to restraints of trade on ex-employees in regard to the poaching of customers and clients. If the employees agree not to poach clients then it surely does not matter whether they set up in business next door or not. The area restraint does little to protect a customer/client connection and can lead to the unenforceability of the whole restraint clause, as in this case.

(iv) Other cases of interest in this area are *Morris Angel and Son Ltd v Hollande and Lee* [1993] IRLR 169 where the Court of Appeal *held* that a covenant restraining an employee from dealing with his employer's business contacts for a year after his employment could be enforced by the company to which the business was transferred, but only in regard to the contracts of the original employer who took the covenant and not to those of the transferee, who had no such covenant with the employee. *Briggs v Oates* [1991] 1 All ER 411 is also of interest in that it decided that if a contract containing an employee restraint is repudiated by the employer all contractual obligations are discharged with the contract and the restraint cannot be enforced. Thus if an employer were unilaterally to reduce the restrained employee's pay so that he left under a constructive dismissal (see further Chapter 19) the employer could not subsequently legally enforce the restraint in the former employee's contract.

(v) The decision in *Briggs* will not apply if the employee resigns and is not dismissed. In *Rock Refrigeration Ltd v Jones* [1997] 1 All ER 1 J was employed under a contract which imposed restrictions on future employment for 12 months following termination of the contract 'howsoever occasioned'. He resigned and went to work for a competitor and the restraint was held enforceable. The Court of Appeal said that if he had been dismissed, constructively or otherwise, the clause would not have applied though it seemed to cover such a situation. A dismissal by the employer would mean that he had repudiated the contract and the restraint would then be unenforceable under the rules of the House of Lords in *General Billposting v Atkinson* [1909] AC 118. But where there was a resignation, the restraint could be applied.

(vi) Many covenants are drafted to apply on termination of the contract 'for whatever reason'. It is clear from the decision in *Rock* that (*a*) such words do not prevent the application of the rule in *General Billposting*, but (*b*) they do not make the whole covenant unreasonable.

(vii) Of particular interest because it relates to a restraint placed upon an employee/partner of a professional firm is *Taylor Stuart v Croft* [1998] 606 IRLB 15. The High Court had to deal with a contractual restraint of trade on an accountant/salaried partner which placed a three-year restraint on him in terms of working for clients of the firm after his employment terminated. This restraint was regarded by the High Court as unreasonable and unenforceable. Other restraints, namely soliciting, canvassing and enticing away clients, were enforceable. A liquidated damages clause in the contract payable by the salaried partner for breach of the restraints was regarded as penal and unenforceable being two-and-a-half times the salaried partner's gross annual income. However, since the salaried partner had after leaving the firm taken some steps to canvass his former clients, e.g. by telephoning them, and some had taken their work to him, a claim for unliquidated damages would seemingly have succeeded. The claimants had, however, relied on enforcing the penal liquidated damages clause and, therefore, their action failed.

Restraints on employees: exceptionally for life

207 *Fitch v Dewes* [1921] 2 AC 158

A solicitor at Tamworth employed a person who was successively his articled clerk and managing clerk. In his contract of service, the clerk agreed, if he left the solicitor's employment, never to practise as a solicitor within seven miles of Tamworth Town Hall.

Held – the agreement was good because during his service the clerk had become acquainted with the details of his employer's clients, and could be restrained even for life from using that knowledge to the detriment of his employer.

Comment (i) Although the restraint was for life, it did cover a rather small area in which at the time there were comparatively few people. It is unlikely that such a restraint would be regarded as valid today, particularly in a more densely populated area.

(ii) The Privy Council stated quite clearly in *Deacons v Bridge* [1984] 2 All ER 19 that a restraint such as this would only be applied in unusual circumstances. The decision seems confined to its own facts, though the statements of principle in the case by the House of Lords are more enduring.

(iii) Ignoring *Fitch v Dewes* (1921) which is a one-off decision, restraints of trade have not always found favour with the smaller business, such as a small to medium firm of accountants or lawyers, or with small traders such as the owners of hair-styling salons. The canvassing of clients after leaving service can be damaging and does go on. However, the advice generally received by such business organisations is that a six-month restraint is all that a court is likely to accept under the 'reasonableness' principles and since injunctive relief would be the best remedy to stop canvassing on pain of contempt of court and possible fine or imprisonment (the latter being rather unlikely) in this context, by the time the lawyers have got a case in motion and to the court, the acceptable period of six months is likely to be up anyway, though a claim for damages is available if clients and customers have been lost, the question being, of course, can the ex-employee pay them? The three-year period allowed in *Taylor Stuart* is, therefore, of value. It is longer than what has in general been allowed and would give time to seek injunctive relief for a large part of the time.

In large concerns, and in respect of higher management, restraint clauses may well be worthwhile to protect the business and retain skilled employees (see Restraint in the City at p 376).

Restraints on employees: taken in a contract between their employers

208 *Kores Manufacturing Co Ltd v Kolok Manufacturing Co Ltd* [1958] 2 All ER 65

The two companies occupied adjoining premises in Tottenham and both manufactured carbon papers, typewriter ribbons and the like. They made an agreement in which each company agreed that it would not, without the written consent of the other, 'at any time employ any person who during the past five years shall have been a servant of yours'. The claimant's chief chemist sought employment with the defendant, and the claimant was not prepared to consent to this and asked for an injunction to enforce the agreement.

Held – by the Court of Appeal:

(a) a contract in restraint of trade cannot be enforced unless:
 (i) it is reasonable as between the parties; and
 (ii) it is consistent with the interest of the public;
(b) the mere fact that the parties are dealing on equal terms does not prevent the court from holding that the restraint is unreasonable in the interests of those parties;
(c) the restraint in this case was grossly in excess of what was required to protect the parties and accordingly was unreasonable in the interests of the parties;
(d) the agreement therefore failed to satisfy the first of the two conditions set out in (a) above and was void and unenforceable.

Comment The restrictive agreement which was at the root of *Kores Manufacturing Co Ltd v Kolok Manufacturing Co Ltd* is not covered by the Competition Act 1998 which is not concerned with agreements between traders in regard to their employees and was decided on common-law principles. These principles are that the agreement must be reasonable between the parties and reasonable in the public interest. Both of these points arose in *Kores*, the Court of Appeal holding that the agreement was unreasonable as between the parties and also that it was contrary to the public interest, though the *ratio* is based on the fact that the agreement was unreasonable as between the parties.

Restraints on vendors of businesses

209 *British Reinforced Concrete Co v Schelff* [1921] 2 Ch 563

The claimant carried on a large business for the manufacture and sale of BRC Road Reinforcements. The defendant carried on a small business for the sale of 'Loop Road Reinforcements'. The defendant sold his business to the claimant and agreed not to compete with the defendant in the manufacture or sale of road reinforcements in any part of the UK. It was *held* that the covenant was void. All that the defendant transferred was the business of selling the reinforcements called 'Loop'. It was, therefore, only with regard to that particular variety that it was justifiable to curb his future activities.

Comment It would have been possible to sever the restraint by deleting the part relating to manufacture, but the court said that even if this were done it would still be too wide. Not to 'sell any road reinforcement in any part of the UK' was much too wide for what was a very small business.

210 *Nordenfelt v Maxim Nordenfelt Guns and Ammunition Co* [1894] AC 535

Nordenfelt was a manufacturer of machine guns and other military weapons. He sold the business to a company, giving certain undertakings which restricted his business activities. This company was amalgamated with another company and Nordenfelt was employed by the new concern as managing director. In his contract Nordenfelt agreed that for 25 years he would not manufacture guns or ammunition in any part of the world, and would not compete with the company in any way.

Held – the covenant regarding the business sold was valid and enforceable, even though it was worldwide, because the business connection was worldwide and it was possible in the circumstances to sever this undertaking from the rest of the agreement (see further p 365). However, the further undertaking not to compete in any way with the company was unreasonable and void.

Restraints on employee/shareholders: what is the test?

211 Systems Reliability Holdings plc v Smith [1990] IRLR 377

In 1986 Mr Smith commenced work with a company called Enterprise Computer Systems (ECS). He was a computer engineer engaged upon the reconfiguration of IBM mainframe computers. He became highly skilled in the modification and rebuilding of the latest generation of IBM's 3090 computer. His skill was instrumental in making ECS a leading company providing computer services. He was dismissed on 1 February 1990.

While he was employed by ECS Mr Smith had purchased shares totalling 1.6 per cent of the holding in the company. After his dismissal Systems Reliability Holdings plc acquired all the shares in ECS and Mr Smith received £247,000 for his 1.6 per cent holding. The share sale agreement had a restrictive covenant. Mr Smith had seen and initialled the agreement in final draft form. The covenant said: 'None of the specifically restricted vendors will during the restricted period directly or indirectly carry on or be engaged or interested . . . in any business which competes with any business carried on at the date of this agreement . . . by the company or any of its subsidiaries.'

Mr Smith was one of the specifically restricted vendors and the restricted period was in effect one of 17 months from the date of the sale. There was a further covenant which provided that: 'None of the vendors will at any time after the date of this agreement disclose or use for his own benefit or that of any other person any confidential information which he now possesses concerning the business or affairs or products of or services supplied by the company or any of the subsidiaries or of any person having dealings with the company or any of its subsidiaries.'

Soon after his dismissal and the share sale, Mr Smith set up in business supplying computer services. Systems Reliability asked for an injunction to enforce the restrictive covenant in the share sale agreement.

The High Court *held* that a restrictive covenant imposed upon the defendant as part of the claimant's acquisition of the shares in the company in which he was formerly employed was entirely reasonable and would be enforced against him notwithstanding that his shareholding in the company had amounted to only 1.6 per cent of the total. The present case was a true vendor and purchaser situation in which the defendant had received £247,000 for his 1.6 per cent shareholding. There was no public policy to prevent the defendant taking himself out of competition for what was a comparatively short period of 17 months as required under the agreement which on the evidence was entirely reasonable, or to prevent the imposition

of a worldwide restriction which was also reasonable given that the business was completely international. The covenant would, therefore, be enforced.

Comment As we have seen, the courts have traditionally allowed wider restraints on competition to be placed on the vendors of businesses than on employees. In Mr Smith we have a mix of the two and the court applied the wider vendor/purchaser approach.

It must, of course, be significant that Mr Smith got £247,000 for a comparatively small shareholding and it must remain doubtful whether the court would apply the vendor/purchaser test to an employee whose shareholding was merely nominal. Presumably, here the tighter employer/employee test of reasonableness would apply.

The matter is one of some importance because the number of employee/shareholders has increased rapidly over the past few years.

Restraints on distributors or merchandise

212 Esso Petroleum Co Ltd v Harper's Garage (Stourport) Ltd [1967] 1 All ER 699

The defendant company owned two garages with attached filling stations, the Mustow Green Garage, Mustow Green, near Kidderminster, and the Corner Garage at Stourport-on-Severn. Each garage was tied to the claimant oil company, the one at Mustow Green by a solus supply agreement only with a tie clause binding the dealer to take the products of the claimant company at its scheduled prices from time to time. There was also a price-maintenance clause which was no longer enforceable and a 'continuity clause' under which the defendant, if it sold the garage, had to persuade the buyer to enter into another solus agreement with Esso. The defendant also agreed to keep the garage open at all reasonable hours and to give preference to the claimant company's oils. The agreement was to remain in force for four years and five months from 1 July 1963, being the unexpired residue of the 10-year tie of a previous owner. At the Corner Garage there was a similar solus agreement for 21 years and a mortgage under which the claimant lent Harper's £7,000 to assist it in buying the garage and improving it. The mortgage contained a tie covenant and forbade redemption for 21 years. In August 1964, Harper's offered to pay off the loan but Esso refused to accept it. Harper's then turned over all four pumps at the Corner Garage to VIP, and later sold VIP at Mustow Green. The claimant company now asked for an injunction to restrain the defendant from buying or selling fuels other than Esso at the two garages during the subsistence of the agreements.

Held – by the House of Lords – the rule of public policy against unreasonable restraints of trade applied to the solus agreements and the mortgage. The shorter period of four years and five months was reasonable so that the tie was valid but the other tie for 21 years in the solus agreement and the mortgage was invalid, so that the injunction asked for by the claimant could not be granted.

Comment The House of Lords appears to have been influenced by the report of the Monopolies Commission on the Supply of Petrol to Retailers in the United Kingdom (Cmnd 1965, No 264) which recommended the period of five years.

213 *Cleveland Petroleum Co Ltd* v *Dartstone Ltd* [1969] 1 All ER 201

The owner of a garage and filling station at Crawley in Sussex leased the property to Cleveland and it in turn granted an underlease to the County Oak Service Station Ltd. The underlease contained a covenant under which all motor fuels sold were to be those of Cleveland. There was power to assign in the underlease and a number of assignments took place so that eventually Dartstone Ltd became the lessee, having agreed to observe the covenants in the underlease, but then challenged the covenant regarding motor fuels, and Cleveland asked for an injunction to enforce it. The injunction was granted. Dealing in the Court of Appeal with *Harper*'s case Lord Denning, MR said:

> It seems plain to me that in three at least of the speeches of their Lordships a distinction is taken between a man who is already in possession of the land before he ties himself to an oil company and a man who is out of possession and is let into it by an oil company. If an owner in possession ties himself for more than five years to take all his supplies from one company, that is an unreasonable restraint of trade and is invalid. But if a man, who is out of possession, is let into possession by the oil company on the terms that he is to tie himself to that company, such a tie is good.

Comment (i) The essential distinction is, as we have seen, that where the restraint on the use of the land is contained in a conveyance or lease the common law rules of restraint of trade do not apply. The person who takes over the property under a conveyance or lease has given nothing up. In fact, he has acquired rights which he never had before even though subject to some limitations.

(ii) In *Alec Lobb (Garages) Ltd* v *Total Oil GB Ltd* [1985] 1 All ER 303 the claimant company borrowed from the defendant to develop a site. As part of the loan arrangements, the claimant agreed to buy the defendant's petrol for 21 years. Since the company was already in occupation of the garage and filling station when the agreement was made, it was subject to the doctrine of restraint of trade, being a *contract* and not a *lease*. The High Court said that 21 years was too long and that the restraint was

unenforceable. The Court of Appeal rejected that view and with it the opinion of the Monopolies Commission that it was not in the public interest that a petrol company should tie a petrol filling station for more than five years in the circumstances of this case.

Therefore, the *Lobb* case seems to show that the courts may not be prepared to help the so-called weaker party, i.e. the garage owner, as they were in the past. In the *Lobb* case the Court of Appeal said that each case must depend on its own facts. In fact, the longer restriction in this case seems to have been justified. The loan by Total was a rescue operation greatly benefiting Lobb and enabling it to continue in business. There were also break clauses in the arrangement at the end of seven and 14 years if Lobb wished to use them. In view of the ample consideration offered by Total, the restraint of 21 years was not, according to the Court of Appeal, unreasonable and was, therefore, valid and enforceable.

(iii) These agreements would in any case appear to be contrary to the prohibition contained in the Competition Act 1998. Section 2(2)(e) of the Act prohibits agreements which require the acceptance of supplementary trading conditions which have no connection with the subject matter of the contract. This would cover cases in which a manufacturer or a supplier insisted that a retailer did not stock the products of a rival manufacturer. This is at the root of solus agreements and yet has nothing essentially to do with the supply and sale of petrol and other products such as oil normally sold by a garage.

Involuntary restraints on members of trade associations and the professions

214 *Pharmaceutical Society of Great Britain* v *Dickson* [1968] 2 All ER 686

The Society passed a resolution to the effect that the opening of new pharmacies should be restricted and be limited to certain specified services, and that the range of services in existing pharmacies should not be extended except as approved by the Society's council. The purpose of the resolution was clearly to stop the development of new fields of trading in conjunction with pharmacy. Mr Dickson, who was a member of the Society and retail director of Boots Pure Drug Company Ltd, brought this action on the ground that the proposed new rule was *ultra vires* as an unreasonable restraint of trade. A declaration that the resolution was *ultra vires* was made and the Society appealed to the House of Lords where the appeal was dismissed, the following points emerging from the judgment.

(*a*) Where a professional association passes a resolution regarding the conduct of its members the validity of the resolution is a matter for the courts even if binding in honour only, since failure to observe it is likely to be construed as misconduct and thus become a ground for disciplinary action.

(*b*) A resolution by a professional association regulating the conduct of its members is *ultra vires* if not sufficiently related to the main objects of the association. The objects of the society in this case did not cover the resolution, being 'to maintain the honour and safeguard and promote the interests of the members in the exercise of the profession of pharmacy'.

(*c*) A resolution by a professional association regulating the conduct of its members will be void if it is an unreasonable restraint of trade.

Comment (i) Once again, the court is concerned with business efficiency and an arrangement under which retail chemists are prevented from selling general merchandise is not likely to lead to greater efficiency and competition. It was, therefore, struck down as too restrictive.

(ii) Agreements which involve the rules relating to the regulation of professional bodies are excluded from the operation of the Competition Act 1998 (see s 3 and Sch 4) but their activities are subject to common-law principles of restraint of trade.

(iii) Without the benefit of exclusion, the exclusive right of barristers and solicitors to practise law could be found to be illegal. Nevertheless, the exclusion depends for its continuance upon the Secretary of State for Trade and Industry 'designating' the profession concerned. In this connection the Director-General of Fair Trading may carry out an investigation to see whether a particular profession should continue to be designated. An early investigation was of the legal and accountancy professions, which could lead to multi-disciplinary practices.

DISCHARGE OF CONTRACT

Discharge by performance: entire contracts

215 *Bolton* v *Mahadeva* [1972] 2 All ER 1322

Bolton installed a central heating system in the defendant's house. The price agreed was a lump sum of £560. The work was not done properly and it was estimated that it would cost £179 to put the system right. The Court of Appeal decided that the lump-sum payment suggested that the contract was entire, and since Bolton had not performed his part of it properly and in full, he could not recover anything for what he had done.

Comment The case of *Cutter* v *Powell* (1795) 6 Term Rep 320 is sometimes used to illustrate the point about entire contracts. The facts of the case were that a seaman agreed to serve on a ship from Jamaica to Liverpool for the sum of 30 guineas (£31.50 today) to be paid on completion of the voyage. He died when the ship was 19 days short of Liverpool. The court *held* that the contract was entire and his widow was not entitled to anything on behalf of his estate. While the case is valid as an illustration, it has been overtaken on its own facts by more recent law. The Merchant Shipping Act 1995 now provides for the payment of wages for partial performance in such cases and the Law Reform (Frustrated Contracts) Act 1943 would also have assisted the widow to recover because the seaman had conferred a benefit on the master of the ship prior to his death (which would now frustrate the contract) giving the widow the right to sue the master of the ship for the benefit of the seaman's work up to the time of his death.

Discharge by performance: effect of substantial performance

216 *Hoenig* v *Isaacs* [1952] 2 All ER 176

The defendant employed the claimant, an interior decorator and furniture designer, to decorate a one-room flat owned by the defendant. The claimant was also to provide furniture, including a fitted bookcase, a wardrobe and a bedstead, for the total sum of £750. The terms of the contract regarding payment were as follows: 'Net cash as the work proceeds and the balance on completion'. The defendant made two payments to the claimant of £150 each, one payment on 12 April and the other on 19 April. The claimant alleged that he had completed the work on 28 August, and asked for the balance, i.e. £450. The defendant asserted that the work done was bad and faulty, but sent the claimant a sum of £100 and moved into the flat and used the furniture. The claimant now sued for the balance of £350, the defence being that the claimant had not performed his contract, or in the alternative that he had done so negligently, unskilfully and in an unworkmanlike manner.

The court assessed the work that had been done, and found that generally it was properly done except that the wardrobe required replacing and that a bookshelf was too short and this meant that the bookcase would have to be remade. The defendant claimed that the contract was entire and that it must be completely performed before the claimant could recover. The court was of the opinion that there had been substantial performance, and that the defendant was liable for £750 less the cost of putting right the above-mentioned defects, the cost of this being assessed at £55 18s 2d. The court accordingly gave the claimant judgment for the sum of £294 1s 10d.

Comment The case illustrates that while full performance is essential to the right to be paid in *full*, perfect performance is not required in order to obtain a *part-payment*. This contract had been performed but badly. Nevertheless, a claim could be made for the price of the work less a deduction, like damages, for the defendant's breach of contract by bad work.

Discharge by performance: partial performance

217 *Sumpter v Hedges* [1898] 1 QB 673

The claimant entered into a contract with the defendant under the terms of which the claimant was to erect some buildings for the defendant on the defendant's land for a price of £565. The claimant did partially erect the buildings up to the value of £333, and the defendant paid him that figure. The claimant then told the defendant that he could not finish the job because he had run out of funds. The defendant then completed the work by using materials belonging to the claimant which had been left on the site. The claimant now sued for work done and materials supplied, and the court gave him judgment for materials supplied, but would not grant him a sum of money by way of a *quantum meruit* (an action for reasonable payment for work done), for the value of the work done prior to his abandonment of the job. The reason given was that, before the claimant could sue successfully on a *quantum meruit*, he would have to show that the defendant had voluntarily accepted the work done, and this implied that the defendant must be in a position to refuse the benefit of the work as where a buyer of goods refuses to take delivery. This was not the case here; the defendant had no option but to accept the work done, so his acceptance could not be presumed from conduct. There being no other evidence of the defendant's acceptance of the work, the claimant's legal action for the work failed.

Comment In practice, this form of injustice to the builder is avoided because a building contract normally provides for progress payments as various stages of construction are completed, thus making it a divisible agreement.

Discharge by performance: performance prevented

218 *De Barnardy v Harding* (1853) 8 Exch 822

The claimant agreed to act as the defendant's agent for the purpose of preparing and issuing certain advertisements and notices designed to encourage the sale of tickets to see the funeral procession of the Duke of Wellington. The claimant was to be paid a commission of 10 per cent upon the proceeds of the tickets actually sold. The claimant duly issued the advertisements and notices, but before he began to sell the tickets the defendant withdrew the claimant's authority to sell them and in consequence the claimant did not sell any tickets and was prevented from earning his commission. The claimant now sued upon a *quantum meruit* and his action succeeded.

Discharge by performance: time of performance; waiver

219 *Bowes v Shand* (1877) 2 App Cas 455

The action was brought for damages for non-acceptance of 600 tons (or 8,200 bags) of Madras rice. The sold note stated that the rice was to be shipped during 'the months of March and/or April 1874'. In fact, 8,150 bags were put on board ship on or before 28 February 1874, and the remaining 50 bags on 2 March 1874. The defendants refused to take delivery because the rice was not shipped in accordance with the terms of the contract.

Held – the bulk of the cargo was shipped in February and therefore the rice did not answer the description in the contract and the defendants were not bound to accept it.

Comment (i) A buyer can reject in these circumstances even though there is nothing wrong with the goods and he merely wants to reject because the market price has fallen.

(ii) It is of interest to note that the rules about delivery apply to early delivery as well as late delivery. Incidentally, the defendants refused to take delivery early because they were not ready with their finance at that time.

220 *Chas Rickards Ltd v Oppenhaim* [1950] 1 KB 616

The defendant ordered a Rolls-Royce chassis from the claimants, the chassis being delivered in July 1947. The claimants found a coachbuilder prepared to make a body within six or at the most seven months. The specification for the body was agreed in August 1947, so that the work should have been completed in March 1948. The work was not completed by then but the defendant still pressed for delivery. On 29 June 1948, the defendant wrote to the coachbuilder saying that he would not accept delivery after 25 July 1948. The body was not ready by then and the defendant bought another car. The body was completed in October 1948, but the defendant refused to accept delivery and counterclaimed for the value of the chassis which he had purchased.

Held – time was of the essence of the original contract, but the defendant had waived the question of time by continuing to press for delivery after the due date. However, by his letter of 29 June he had again made time of the essence, and had given reasonable notice in the matter. Judgment was given for the defendant on the claim and counterclaim.

Comment (i) That a waiver of a date of delivery without consideration is binding can be based on promissory estoppel (as in *High Trees* – see Chapter 10) said Denning, LJ in *Rickards*, or on s 11(2) of the Sale of Goods Act 1979 which states: 'Where a contract of sale is subject to any condition to be fulfilled by the seller, the buyer may waive that condition.' This section was used to justify a waiver without consideration by McCardie, J in *Hartley v Hymans* [1920] 3 KB 475.

(ii) This is an example of the doctrine of promissory estoppel being used by a claimant, i.e. as a sword not a shield, because a seller may tender delivery after the originally agreed date relying on the buyer's promise to accept such delivery by reason of his waiver. If the buyer then refuses to accept the delivery the seller can claim damages and is in essence suing upon the waiver which is unsupported by consideration.

(iii) Those in business often find it unsatisfactory to rely on the willingness of the courts to imply that time is of the essence of the contract, in terms of delivery dates and other matters. An express provision in the contract is the solution of which the following is an example:

> Time shall be of the essence of this agreement as regards times, dates or periods specified in this agreement and as to times, dates or periods that may by agreement between the parties be substituted for them.

Discharge by performance: appropriation of payments

221 *Deeley v Lloyds Bank Ltd* [1912] AC 756

A customer of the bank had mortgaged his property to the bank to secure an overdraft limited to £2,500. He then mortgaged the same property to the appellant for £3,500, subject to the bank's mortgage. It is the normal practice of bankers, on receiving notice of a second mortgage, to rule off the customer's account, and not to allow any further withdrawals since these will rank after the second mortgage. In this case the bank did not open a new account but continued the old current account. The customer thereafter paid in sums of money which at a particular date, if they had been appropriated in accordance with the rule in *Clayton*'s Case, would have extinguished the bank's mortgage. Even so the customer still owed the bank money, and they sold the property for a price which was enough to satisfy the bank's debt but not that of the appellant.

Held – the evidence did not exclude the rule in *Clayton*'s Case, which applied, so that the bank's mortgage had been paid off and the appellant, as second mortgagee, was entitled to the proceeds of the sale.

Comment The operation of *Clayton*'s Case is normally prevented by the bank stating in the mortgage that it is a continuing security given on a running account varying from day to day and excluding the repayment of the borrower's liability, which would otherwise take place as credits are paid in.

Discharge by frustration: contracts of personal service

222 *Storey v Fulham Steel Works* (1907) 24 TLR 89

The claimant was employed by the defendant as manager for a period of five years. After he had been working for two years he became ill, and had to have special treatment and a period of convalescence. Six months later he was recovered, but in the meantime the defendant had terminated his employment. The claimant now sued for breach of contract, and the defendant pleaded that the claimant's period of ill-health operated to discharge the contract.

Held – the claimant's illness and absence from duty did not go to the root of the contract, and was not so serious as to allow the termination of the agreement.

223 *Norris v Southampton City Council* [1982] IRCR 141

Mr Norris was employed as a cleaner. He was convicted of assault and reckless driving and was sentenced to a term of imprisonment. His employer wrote dismissing him and Mr Norris complained to an employment tribunal that his dismissal was unfair. The tribunal held that the contract of employment was frustrated and that the employee was not dismissed and, therefore, not entitled to compensation. The Employment Appeal Tribunal to which Mr Norris appealed laid down that frustration could only arise where there was no fault by either party. Where there was a fault, such as deliberate conduct leading to an inability to perform the contract, there was not frustration but a repudiatory breach of contract. The employer had the option of whether or not to treat the contract as repudiated and if he chose to dismiss the employee, he could do so, regarding the breach as repudiatory. The question then to be decided was whether the dismissal was fair. The case was remitted to the employment tribunal for further consideration of whether there was unfair dismissal on the facts of the case.

Discharge by frustration: government intervention

224 Re Shipton, Anderson & Co and Harrison Bros' Arbitration [1915] 3 KB 676

A contract was made for the sale of wheat lying in a warehouse in Liverpool. Before the seller could deliver the wheat, and before the property in it had passed to the buyer, the government requisitioned the wheat under certain emergency powers available in time of war.

Held – delivery being impossible by reason of lawful requisition by the government, the seller was excused from performance of the contract.

Discharge by frustration: destruction of subject matter

225 Taylor v Caldwell (1863) 3 B & S 826

The defendant agreed to let the claimant have the use of a music hall for the purpose of holding four concerts. Before the first concert was due to be held the hall was destroyed by fire without negligence by any party, and the claimant now sued for damages for wasted advertising expenses.

Held – the contract was impossible of performance and the defendant was not liable.

Comment A more modern example of the rule is to be found in *Vitol SA v Esso Australia, The Times*, 1 February 1988, where the buyers of petroleum were discharged from the contract by frustration when the vessel and cargo were destroyed by a missile attack during the Gulf War.

Discharge by frustration: non-occurrence of an event

226 Krell v Henry [1903] 2 KB 740

The claimant owned a room overlooking the proposed route of the Coronation procession of Edward VII, and had let it to the defendant for the purpose of viewing the procession. The procession did not take place because of the King's illness and the claimant now sued for the agreed fee.

Held – the fact that the procession had been cancelled discharged the parties from their obligations, since it was no longer possible to achieve the real purpose of the agreement.

Comment This type of decision is rare since the court will in general assume that the parties to a contract are not concerned with the motive for which it was made (see *Herne Bay Steamboat Co v Hutton* (1903) below). However, this seems to be an exceptional situation where

the motive and contract were fused and could not be separated: '. . . it is the coronation procession and the relative position of the rooms which is the basis for the contract as much for the lessor as the hirer . . .', said Vaughan-Williams, LJ.

Also a contract will remain binding even if it turns out to be more expensive or difficult to perform than was thought. Thus a contract to ship ground nuts from the Mediterranean to India was not frustrated by the closure of the Suez Canal so that the goods would have to go around the Cape of Good Hope, which was twice as far. (See *Tsakiroglou v Noblee Thorl GmbH* [1961] 2 All ER 179.)

227 Herne Bay Steamboat Co v Hutton [1903] 2 KB 683

The claimant company agreed to hire a steamboat to the defendant for two days, in order that the defendant might take paying passengers to see the naval review at Spithead on the occasion of Edward VII's Coronation. An official announcement was made cancelling the review, but the fleet was assembled and the boat might have been used for the intended cruise. The defendant did not use the boat, and the claimant employed her on ordinary business. The action was brought to recover the fee of £200 which the defendant had promised to pay for the hire of the boat.

Held – the contract was not discharged, as the review of the fleet by the Sovereign was not the foundation of the contract. The claimant was awarded the difference between £200 and the profits derived from the use of the boat for ordinary business on the two days in question.

Comment (i) It may be thought that it is difficult to reconcile this case with *Krell* (see above). However, whatever the legal niceties may or may not be, there is clearly a difference in fact. To cruise round the fleet assembled at Spithead, even though the figure of the Sovereign (minuscule to the viewer, anyway) would not be present, is clearly more satisfying as the subject matter of a contract than looking through the window at ordinary London traffic.

(ii) In addition, Vaughan-Williams, LJ and the Court of Appeal thought that motive was less relevant here. The judge said, 'I see nothing that makes this case differ from a case where, for instance, a person has engaged a brake (the judge refers to a form of carriage) to take himself and a party to Epsom to see the races there, but for some reason or other, such as the spread of an infectious disease, the races are postponed. In such a case it could not be said that he could be relieved of his bargain.' Romer, LJ added, 'The ship (as a ship) had nothing particular to do with the review of the fleet except as a convenient carrier of passengers to see it; and other ships suitable for carrying passengers would have done equally as well.'

Discharge by frustration: commercial purpose defeated

228 *Jackson* v *Union Marine Insurance Co* (1874) LR 10 CP 125

The claimant was the owner of a ship called *Spirit of the Dawn* which had been chartered to go with all possible dispatch from Liverpool to Newport, and there load a cargo of iron rails for San Francisco. The claimant had entered into a contract of insurance with the defendant insurance company, in order that he might protect himself against the failure of the ship to carry out the charter. The vessel was stranded in Caernarfon Bay whilst on its way to Newport. It was not refloated for over a month, and could not be fully repaired for some time. The charterer hired another ship and the claimant now claimed on the policy of insurance. The insurance company suggested that since the claimant might claim against the charterer for breach of contract, there was no loss, and the court had to decide whether such a claim was possible.

Held – the delay consequent upon the stranding of the vessel put an end, in the commercial sense, to the venture, so that the charterer was released from his obligations and was free to hire another ship. Therefore, the claimant had no claim against the charterer and could claim the loss of the charter from the defendants.

Discharge by frustration: where frustration is self-induced

229 *Maritime National Fish Ltd* v *Ocean Trawlers Ltd* [1935] AC 524

The respondents were the owners and the appellants the charterers of a steam trawler, the *St Cuthbert*. The *St Cuthbert* was fitted with, and could only operate with an otter trawl. When the charterparty was renewed on 25 October 1932, both parties knew it was illegal to operate with an otter trawl without a licence from the Minister. The appellants operated five trawlers and applied for five licences. The Minister granted only three and said that the appellants could choose the names of three trawlers for the licences. The appellants chose three but deliberately excluded the *St Cuthbert* though they could have included it. They were now sued by the owners for the charter fee, and their defence was that the charterparty was frustrated because it would have been illegal to fish with the *St Cuthbert*. It was *held* that the contract was not frustrated, in the sense that the

frustrating event was self-induced by the appellants and that therefore they were liable for the hire.

Comment An otter trawl is a type of net which can, because of its narrow mesh, pick up small immature fish. Its use is restricted for environmental reasons.

Discharge by frustration: contracts concerning land

230 *Cricklewood Property and Investment Trust Ltd* v *Leighton's Investment Trust Ltd* [1945] AC 221

In May 1936, a building lease was granted between the parties for 99 years, but before any building had been erected war broke out in 1939 and government restrictions on building materials and labour meant that the lessees could not erect the buildings as they intended, these buildings being in fact shops. Leighton's sued originally for rent due under the lease and Cricklewood, the builders, said the lease was frustrated. The House of Lords *held* that the doctrine of frustration did not apply because the interruption from 1939 to 1945 was not sufficient in duration to frustrate the lease, and so they did not deal specifically with the general position regarding frustration of leases, basing their judgment on the question of the degree of interruption. In so far as they did deal with the general position, this was *obiter*, but Lord Simon thought that there could be cases in which a lease would be frustrated, and the example that he quoted was a building lease where the land was declared a permanent open space before building took place; here he thought that the fundamental purpose of the transaction would be defeated. Lord Wright took much the same view on the same example. Lord Russell thought frustration could not apply to a lease of real property, and Lord Goddard, CJ took the same view. Lord Porter expressed no opinion with regard to leases generally and so this case does not finally solve the problem.

Comment (i) Even if the courts were prepared to apply the doctrine of frustration, it would not often apply to leases, particularly long leases. In a lease for 99 years a tenant temporarily deprived of possession as by requisition of the property would hardly ever be put out of possession long enough to satisfy the test of frustration (see below).

(ii) In *National Carriers* v *Panalpina (Northern)* [1981] 1 All ER 161 the House of Lords was of the opinion that a lease could be frustrated. The claimants leased a warehouse to the defendants for 10 years. The Hull City Council closed the only access road to it because a listed building nearby was in a dangerous condition. The access road was closed for 20 months. The defendants refused to pay the rent for this period. The House of Lords said that they must. A lease could be frustrated, they said, but 20 months out of 10 years was not enough to frustrate it in the particular circumstances of this case. Once again, therefore, the decision of the House of Lords on the matter of frustration of leases was *obiter*.

(iii) In *Amalgamated Investment and Property Co Ltd v John Walker & Sons Ltd* [1976] 3 All ER 509 Buckley, LJ was prepared to presume that the doctrine of frustration could be applied to contracts for the sale of land, though once again this decision was *obiter* because he did not have to apply the doctrine in this case. Walker sold a warehouse to Amalgamated, both parties believing that the property was suitable and capable of being redeveloped. After the contract was made the Department of the Environment included it in a list of buildings of architectural and historic interest so that the development became more difficult. The Court of Appeal *held* that the contract was not frustrated. The listing merely affected the value of the property and the purchaser always took the risk of this in terms of a listing order or, indeed, compulsory purchase. The contract could be completed according to its terms and specific performance was granted to Walkers. Nor was the contract voidable under *Solle* v *Butcher* (1950) (but see now Chapter 12) because the mistake did not exist at the date of the contract.

Discharge by frustration: effect at common law

231 *Chandler v Webster* [1904] 1 KB 493

The defendant agreed to let the claimant have a room for the purpose of viewing the Coronation procession on 26 June 1902 for £141 15s. The contract provided that the money be payable immediately. The procession did not take place because of the illness of the King and the claimant, who had paid £100 on account, left the balance unpaid. The claimant sued to recover the £100 and the defendant counterclaimed for £41 15s. It was *held* by the Court of Appeal that the claimant's action failed and the defendant's counterclaim succeeded because the obligation to pay rent had fallen due before the frustrating event.

Comment This case is included only to show how important the Law Reform (Frustrated Contracts) Act 1943 really is!

Discharge by breach: anticipatory breach

232 *Hochster v De la Tour* (1853) 2 E & B 678

The defendant agreed in April 1852 to engage the claimant as a courier for European travel, his duties to commence on 1 June 1852. On 11 May 1852, the defendant wrote to the claimant saying that he no longer required his services. The claimant commenced an action for breach of contract on 22 May 1852, and the defence was that there was no cause of action until the date due for performance, i.e. 1 June 1852.

Held – the defendant's express repudiation constituted an actionable breach of contract.

Comment (i) This decision should not be accepted as entirely logical. It is odd in a way to say that a person who has stated that he will not perform a contract when the time comes to perform it is for that reason *in breach of contract now* and can be sued. This is particularly so where, as in this case, the defendant might still at the commencement of the proceedings have performed the contract when the time came. Of course, by the time the case came to court it was obvious that the defendant had not performed his part of the contract and the device of anticipatory breach at least prevented the claimant's action from being defeated on the technicality that when he served his writ (now claim form) there was in fact no breach of contract as such. A case in which A was obliged to commence performance of a contract in December and said in the previous January that he would not do so, and which came before the court in September, might be decided differently because A would still have time to change his mind.

(ii) A more modern example of the application of the rule in *Hochster* is to be found in *Sarker v South Tees Acute Hospitals NHS Trust* [1997] ICR 673. The Trust sent a letter of appointment to a post within the Trust to S. It stated that her employment was to begin on 1 October, but on 6 September the offer was withdrawn. The Employment Appeal Tribunal ruled that S was an employee and could bring a claim for wrongful dismissal based on breach of contract. A claim for unfair dismissal could be brought in similar circumstances, but it would have to be a case not requiring one year's service as where dismissal was connected with pregnancy as where the offer was withdrawn because the employer found out that the employee was pregnant (see further Chapter 19).

233 *Omnium D'Enterprises and Others v Sutherland* [1919] 1 KB 618

The defendant was the owner of a steamship and agreed to let her under a charter to the claimant for a period of time and to pay the second claimants a commission on the hire payable under the agreement. The defendant later sold the ship to a purchaser, free of all liability under his agreement with the claimants.

Held – the sale by the defendant was a repudiation of the agreement and the claimants were entitled to damages for breach of the contract.

Comment (i) The charterer would have no claim against the purchaser of the vessel because restrictive covenants do not pass with chattels (which a ship is) but only with land. Compare *Dunlop* v *Selfridge* (1915) (see Case **87**) and *Tulk* v *Moxhay* (1848) (Case **91**) (see Chapter 10).

(ii) This decision is more logical because by selling the ship the defendant had clearly put it beyond his power to perform the charter.

234 *White and Carter (Councils) Ltd* v *McGregor*
[1961] 3 All ER 1178

The respondent was a garage proprietor on Clydebank and on 26 June 1957, his sales manager, without specific authority, entered into a contract with the appellants whereby the appellants agreed to advertise the respondent's business on litter bins which they supplied to local authorities. The contract was to last for three years from the date of the first advertisement display. Payment was to be by instalments annually in advance, the first instalment being due seven days after the first display. The contract contained a clause that, on failure to pay an instalment or other breach of contract, the whole sum of £196 4s became due. The respondent was quick to repudiate the contract for on 26 June 1957, he wrote to the appellants asking them to cancel the agreement, and at this stage the appellants had not taken any steps towards carrying it out. The appellants refused to cancel the agreement and prepared the advertisement plates which they exhibited on litter bins in November 1957, and continued to display them during the following three years. Eventually the appellants demanded payment, the respondent refused to pay, and the appellants brought an action against him for the sum due under the contract.

Held – the appellants were entitled to recover the contract price since, although the respondents had repudiated the contract, the appellants were not obliged to accept the repudiation. The contract survived and the appellants had not completed it. The House of Lords said that there was no duty to mitigate loss until there was a breach which the appellants had accepted and they had not accepted this one.

Comment (i) Although the respondent's agent had no actual authority, he had made a similar contract with the appellants in 1954, and it was not disputed that he had apparent authority to bind his principal.

(ii) It is worth pointing out that there was in this case no evidence that the appellants could have mitigated their loss. No evidence was produced to show that the demand for advertising space exceeded the supply so it may be that the appellants could not have obtained a new customer for the space on the litter bins intended for the respondent. Thus, White and Carter may have had a 'legitimate interest' in continuing with the contract. Perhaps if evidence that mitigation was possible had been produced, the House of Lords would have applied the principles of mitigation to the case, or held that White and Carter had no 'legitimate interest' in continuing the agreement. This view is supported by a decision of the Court of Appeal in *Attica Sea Carriers Corporation* v *Ferrostaal Poseidon Bulk Reederei GmbH* [1976] 1 Lloyd's Rep 250 where the charterer of a ship agreed to execute certain repairs before he redelivered it to the owner and to pay the agreed hire until that time. He did not carry out the repairs but the owner would not take redelivery of the ship until they had been done and later sued for the agreed hire. It was *held* that the owner was not entitled to refuse to accept redelivery and to sue for the agreed hire. The cost of the repairs far exceeded the value which the ship would have if they were done and the owner had therefore no legal interest in insisting on their execution and the payment of the hire. The court held that he should have mitigated his loss by accepting redelivery of the unrepaired ship so that his only remedy was damages and not for the agreed hire.

(iii) This line was followed also in the case of *Clea Shipping Corporation* v *Bulk Oil International, The Alaskan Trader* [1984] 1 All ER 129. A vessel had been chartered by the claimant owners to the defendants, the hire charge having been paid in advance. However, the ship broke down and required expensive repairs. The charterers thereupon gave notice that they intended to end the contract. However, the claimants decided to keep the agreement open and undertook the repairs and then informed the defendants that the vessel was at their disposal. The claimants said they were exercising their right of election conferred upon the innocent party in such circumstances to keep the contract open, thus entitling them to keep the hire money instead of suing for damages. Lloyd, J denied the existence of an unfettered right of election for an innocent party to keep the contract running in such circumstances. He found that, in the absence of a 'legitimate interest' in the contract's perpetuation by the party faced with repudiation, the party concerned could, though innocent, be forced to accept damages in lieu of sums falling due under the contract subsequent to the actionable event. This restraint is founded on general equitable principles, to be based on what is reasonable on the facts of each case.

235 *Avery* v *Bowden* (1855) 5 E & B 714

The defendants chartered the claimant's ship *Lebanon* and agreed to load her with a cargo at Odessa within 45 days. The ship went to Odessa and remained there for most of the 45-day period. The defendant told the captain of the ship that he did not propose to load a cargo and that he would do well to leave, but the captain stayed on at Odessa, hoping that the defendant would change his mind. Before the end of the 45-day period the Crimean War broke out so that performance of the contract would have been illegal as a trading with the enemy.

Held – the claimant might have treated the defendant's refusal to load a cargo as an anticipatory breach of contract but his agent, the captain, had waived that right by staying on at Odessa, and now the contract had been discharged by something which was beyond the control of either party.

Comment A more modern application of the above rule can be seen in *Fercometal Sarl* v *Mediterranean Shipping Co Ltd* [1988] 2 All ER 742. The claimants chartered a ship to the defendants. The charterparty (i.e. the contract) provided that if the ship was not ready to load during the period 3–9 July the defendants could cancel the contract. On 2 July the defendants said that they were not going on with the contract anyway but the claimants did not accept that breach and provided the ship, but this was not ready to load until 12 July and the defendants said again that they would not go on with the contract. The claimants sued for damages and failed. They could have based an action on the first breach but had not done so. Their action on the second 'breach' failed because the ship was not ready to load.

REMEDIES AND LIMITATION OF ACTIONS

Damages: must be a genuine pre-estimate of loss

236 *Ford Motor Co (England) Ltd* v *Armstrong* (1915) 31 TLR 267

The defendant was a retailer who received supplies from the claimant company. As part of his agreement with the claimant the defendant had undertaken:

(*a*) not to sell any of the claimant's cars or spares below list price;

(*b*) not to sell Ford cars to other dealers in the motor trade;

(*c*) not to exhibit any car supplied by the company without its permission.

The defendant also agreed to pay £250 for every breach of the agreement as being the agreed damage which the manufacturer will 'sustain'. The defendant was in breach of the agreement and the claimant sued. It was *held* by the Court of Appeal that the sum of £250 was in the nature of a penalty and not liquidated damages. The same sum was payable for different kinds of breach which were not likely to produce the same loss. Furthermore, its size suggested that it was not a genuine pre-estimate of loss.

Comment (i) A contrast is provided by *Dunlop* v *New Garage & Motor Co Ltd* [1915] AC 79 where the contract provided that the defendants would have to pay £5 for every tyre sold below the list price. The House of Lords *held* that this was an honest attempt to provide for a breach and was recoverable as liquidated damages. Privity problems did not arise here (even though the Contracts (Rights of Third Parties) Act 1999 was not in force, obviously) because the wholesalers were Dunlop's agents. (See further Chapter 10.)

(ii) In *Jeancharm Ltd (t/a Beaver International)* v *Barnet Football Club Ltd* [2003] All ER (D) (Jan) the Court of Appeal ruled that a clause providing for a rate of interest of 260 per cent a year on late payments was unenforceable as a penalty. Jeancharm contracted to supply football kit to Barnet. The contract provided that any late payments by Barnet would be subject to interest of 5 per cent per week (or some 260 per cent a year). Both of the parties had accepted this as a late payment penalty. Disputes arose regarding delivery and payment. The High Court applied the penalty rate set out in the contract on the late payments. Barnet appealed to the Court of Appeal. The Court of Appeal allowed Barnet's appeal ruling that while equality of bargaining power, as in this case, was always a relevant factor it did not in every case mean that a penalty clause could not be regarded as unenforceable. The rate of interest here was an 'extraordinarily large amount' and far exceeded a genuine pre-estimate of loss. The interest clause had only a deterrent function and was unenforceable. This meant that there was no enforceable rate of interest based on the contract.

237 *Cellulose Acetate Silk Co Ltd* v *Widnes Foundry Ltd* [1933] AC 20

The Widnes Foundry entered into a contract to erect a plant for the Silk Co by a certain date. It was also agreed that the Widnes Foundry would pay the Silk Co £20 per week for every week it took in erecting the plant beyond the agreed date. In the event, the plant was completed 30 weeks late, and the Silk Co claimed for its actual loss, which was £5,850.

Held – the Widnes Foundry was only liable to pay £20 per week as agreed.

Damages: the object is to put the claimant in the same position financially as if the contract had been properly performed

238 *Beach* v *Reed Corrugated Cases Ltd* [1956] 2 All ER 652

This was an action brought by the claimant for wrongful dismissal by the defendant. The claimant was the managing director of the company and he had a 15-year contract from 21 December 1950 at a salary of £5,000 per annum. His contract was terminated in August 1954 when he was 54 years old and the sum of money that he might have earned would have been £55,000, but the general damages awarded to him were £18,000 after the court had taken into account income tax, including tax on his private investments.

Comment (i) In a later case and on similar reasoning it was *held* that what the claimant would have paid by way of national insurance contributions must also be deducted (see *Cooper* v *Firth Brown Ltd* [1963] 2 All ER 31).

(ii) It must be said that some of the 'tax must be deducted' cases are far from clear in terms of how the court reaches its final conclusion. The clearest of all is *Shove* v *Downs Surgical plc* [1984] 1 All ER 7, where the claimant had been wrongfully dismissed 30 months before the end of a fixed-term contract of employment as managing director. The figures involved as set out in the judgment are as follows:

	£
Gross pay for the 30 months	90,000
Court's estimate of net pay	53,000*
Initial award	53,000
Of this £30,000 is tax free (see Income Tax (Earnings and Pensions) Act 2003)	30,000
	23,000

This sum is taxable in Mr Shove's hands (see IT(E and P)A 2003). The tax is estimated to be £6,000 on the £23,000
*Mr Shove's highest tax rate used.

Therefore, the court's *final award* to Mr Shove is	59,000
to give	£53,000 net

(iii) In *C & P Haulage* v *Middleton* [1983] 3 All ER 94, C & P let Mr Middleton have a licence for six months renewable of premises from which he conducted a business as a self-employed engineer. He lived in a council house and would have used his own garage there, but the Council objected. There was a quarrel between the parties and M was evicted from the premises before the licence term expired. This was a breach of contract by C & P. M stopped a cheque which was payable to C & P because of his grievance. They sued him on it. He counterclaimed for damages because of his eviction. In fact the Council had let him use his own garage for the remainder of the six months' term.

Held – by the Court of Appeal – since he had paid no rent for the premises in which he had worked following his eviction, he was no worse off than if the contract had been properly carried out. It was not the function of the court to put a claimant in a better position than he would have been if the contract had not been broken. Only nominal damages were awarded.

(iv) Damages have been awarded for the loss of a chance. This is not prevented by the rule that the claimant must not be better off. Thus in *Chaplin* v *Hicks* [1911] 2 KB 786 the claimant who had won earlier stages of a beauty contest was, by error of the defendant organiser, not invited to the final. Although it was by no means certain that she would have won, the claimant was awarded £100 damages. In a similar case, though in tort, the Court of Appeal affirmed an award of a sum of money for the loss of a chance where, because of personal injury suffered in a road accident caused by the negligence of the defendant, the claimant was unable to qualify and obtain employment as a drama teacher. Once again, a percentage of the damages was awarded for loss of a chance (see *Doyle* v *Wallace* [1998] Current Law para 1447).

Damages: for mental distress

239 *Jarvis* v *Swans Tours Ltd* [1973] 1 All ER 71

Swans promised the claimant a 'Houseparty' holiday in Switzerland. Some of the more important things promised were a welcome party on arrival, afternoon tea and cake, Swiss dinner by candlelight, fondue party, yodeller evening and farewell party. Also the hotel owner was said to speak English.

Among the matters which the claimant complained about were that the hotel owner could not speak English. This meant he had no one to talk to since, although there were 13 people present during the first week, he was on his own for the second week. The cake for tea was potato crisps and dry nutcake. The yodeller evening consisted of a local man who came in his overalls and sang a few songs very quickly. The Court of Appeal *held* that the claimant was entitled to an award of £125 damages. (Incidentally, the holiday had cost £63.)

Comment (i) Damages for disappointment, inconvenience or loss of enjoyment are not awarded except in contracts such as the above which are for the provision of pleasure. Such damage may be foreseeable in other contracts but is not awarded as a matter of public policy. Thus, in *Alexander* v *Rolls-Royce Motor Cars, The Times*, 4 May 1996 the Court of Appeal held that the owner of a Rolls-Royce car could not claim damages for disappointment, loss of enjoyment or distress as part of an award of damages for breach of a contract to repair. It was accepted by the court that the car had been bought for pleasure, prestige and enjoyment but that was not enough to bring the case outside the general rule that damages for disappointment are not awarded for breach of a commercial contract.

(ii) Another case where the matter of damages for non-pecuniary loss was raised is *Farley* v *Skinner* [2001] 3 WLR 899. The claimant bought a house that was surveyed by the defendant. It was 15 miles from Gatwick airport. The claimant asked the defendant surveyor to deal with the possibility of aircraft noise. The defendant reported that the property was unlikely to suffer to any great extent from aircraft noise. After moving in, the claimant found that there was substantial interference from aircraft noise. A claim for breach of contract was made. Damages for disappointment at the loss of a pleasurable amenity and disappointment at the loss of pleasure, relaxation and peace of mind were asked for. The Court of Appeal refused the claim because the contract was not for the supply of a pleasurable amenity but for a property survey.

On appeal the House of Lords ruled that a sum of £10,000 was recoverable in the circumstances of the case even though the contract did not have the provision of pleasure as its object.

Damages: remoteness; loss must be proximate and not too remote

240 *Hadley v Baxendale* (1845) 9 Exch 341

The claimant was a miller at Gloucester. The driving shaft of the mill being broken, the claimant engaged the defendant, a carrier, to take it to the makers at Greenwich so that they might use it in making a new one. The defendant delayed delivery of the shaft beyond a reasonable time, so that the mill was idle for much longer than should have been necessary. The claimant now sued in respect of loss of profits during the period of additional delay. The court decided that there were only two possible grounds on which the claimant could succeed.

(*a*) That in the usual course of things the work of the mill would cease altogether for the want of the shaft. This the court rejected because, to take only one reasonable possibility, the claimant might have had a spare.

(*b*) That the special circumstances were fully explained, so that the defendant was made aware of the possible loss. The evidence showed that there had been no such explanation. In fact, the only information given to the defendant was that the article to be carried was the broken shaft of a mill, and that the claimant was the miller of that mill.

Held – the claimant's case failed, the damage being too remote.

Comment (i) The loss here did not arise *naturally* from the breach because there might have been a spare. The fact that there was no spare was not within the contemplation of the defendant and he had not even been told about it, much less accepted the risk. The defendant did not know that there was no spare nor

as a reasonable man ought he to have known there was not.

(ii) Damage caused by a supervening event may also be too remote. In *Beoco v Alfa Laval Co, The Times*, 12 January 1994, Alfa installed a heat exchanger at Beoco's works. It developed a crack and a third party, S, was brought in to repair it. The work was done negligently and shortly afterwards the exchanger exploded, causing damage to property and economic loss of profit until it was put right. It was held that Alfa was liable in damages for the costs of replacing the heat exchanger and for loss of profit up to the time of the repair but not subsequently. Although the matter is not raised in the report, presumably S would be liable for the subsequent loss. The position in regard to supervening events is, therefore, the same in contract as in tort. For the latter see *Jobling v Associated Dairies* (1980) in Chapter 20.

241 *The Heron II (Koufos v Czarnikow)* [1967] 3 All ER 686

Shipowners carrying sugar from Constanza to Basra delayed delivery at Basra for nine days during which time the market in sugar there fell and the charterers lost more than £4,000. It was *held* that they could recover that sum from the shipowners because the very existence of a 'market' for goods implied that prices might fluctuate and a fall in sugar prices was likely or in contemplation.

Comment (i) The existence of a major sugar market at Basra made it within the *contemplation* of the defendants that the claimant might sell the sugar and not merely use it in a business.

(ii) As Lord Hodson said in his judgment: 'Goods may be intended for the purpose of stocking or consumption at the port of destination and the contemplation of the parties that the goods may be resold is not necessarily to be inferred.' He went on to decide, however, that resale must be inferred as in contemplation because Basra was a well-known sugar market. Damages of £4,183 were awarded, this being the fall in price of sugar between the date when the ship did arrive and the date when it should have arrived.

(iii) The contemplation test was, of course, set out in *Hadley* as the comment at (i) to the summary of the case shows. So what is new about the ruling of the House of Lords in *The Heron II*? *The Heron II* deals with a problem that had arisen following the interpretation by subsequent courts in subsequent cases that the test in *Hadley* was foreseeability of damage. *The Heron II* merely restores in an authoritative way the *Hadley* rule of contemplation. This is a tighter test for loss. A person may *foresee* all sorts of things in terms of damage but not actually *contemplate* them. This makes the ruling in, say, negligent personal injury, where the claim is in tort and the foreseeability test applies, different from contract, where the test for breach of contract damages is in contemplation.

242 Horne v Midland Railway Co (1873) LR 8 CP 131

The claimant had entered into a contract to sell 4,595 pairs of boots to the French Army at a price above the market price. The defendant railway company was responsible for a delay in the delivery of the boots, and the purchasers refused to accept delivery, regarding time as the essence of the contract. The claimant's claim for damages was based on the contract price, namely 4s per pair, but it was *held* that he could only recover the market price of 2s 9d per pair unless he could show the defendant was aware of the exceptional profit involved, and that it had undertaken to be liable for the loss of that profit.

Comment In *Simpson v London & North Western Rail Co* (1876) 1 QBD 274 the claimant entrusted samples of his products to the defendant for it to deliver them to Newcastle for an agricultural exhibition. The goods were marked 'Must be at Newcastle on Monday certain'. The defendant did not get them to Newcastle on time and was *held* liable for the claimant's prospective loss of profit arising because he could not exhibit at Newcastle. The railway company had agreed to carry the goods knowing of the special instructions of the customer.

243 Victoria Laundry Ltd v Newman Industries Ltd [1949] 2 KB 528

The defendants agreed to deliver a new boiler to the claimants by a certain date but failed to do so, being 22 weeks late, with the result that the claimants lost (*a*) normal business profits during the period of delay, and (*b*) profits from dyeing contracts which were offered to them during the period. It was *held* that (*a*) but not (*b*) were recoverable as damages.

Comment The general loss of profit in this case arises naturally from the breach and no further 'contemplation' or 'notice' test need be applied. The loss of profit on the dyeing contracts was not *known* to the defendants nor as reasonable men *ought* they to have had it in *contemplation*.

Damages: the injured party must mitigate his loss

244 Brace v Calder [1895] 2 QB 253

The defendant partnership, consisting of four members, agreed to employ the claimant as manager of a branch of the business for two years. Five months later the partnership was dissolved by the retirement of two of the members and the business was transferred to the other two who offered to employ the claimant on the same terms as before but he refused the offer. The dissolution of the partnership constituted a wrongful dimissal of the claimant and he brought an action for breach of contract seeking to recover the salary that he would have received had he served the whole period of two years. It was *held* that he was entitled only to nominal damages since it was unreasonable to have rejected the offer of continued employment.

Injunction: of a negative stipulation

245 Warner Brothers Pictures Incorporated v Nelson [1937] 1 KB 209

The defendant, the film actress Bette Davis, had entered into a contract in which she agreed to act exclusively for the claimant corporation for 12 months. She was anxious to obtain more money and so she left America, and entered into a contract with a person in England. The claimant now asked for an injunction restraining the defendant from carrying out the English contract.

Held – an injunction would be granted. The contract contained a negative stipulation not to work for anyone else, and this could be enforced. However, since the contract was an American one, the court limited the operation of the injunction to the area of the court's jurisdiction, and although the contract stipulated that the defendant would not work in any other occupation, the injunction was confined to work on stage or screen.

Comment (i) Even where, as here, there is a negative stipulation, the court will not grant an injunction if the pressure to work for the claimant is so severe as to be for all practical purposes irresistible. In this case it was said that Bette Davis could still earn her living by doing other work.

(ii) The idea that persons such as Bette Davis or others subjected to injunctions of negative stipulations would take other work was challenged by the Court of Appeal in *Warren v Mendy* [1989] 3 All ER 103 on the grounds of 'realism and practicality'. The Court of Appeal said that it was unrealistic to suppose that such persons would take up other work, i.e. that boxers would become clerks and actresses secretaries. Thus, the making of an injunction of a negative stipulation in this sort of case was, in general terms, likely to operate as a decree of specific performance. This means that it is in modern law less likely that such injunctions will be granted or that the *Warner Brothers* case will be followed, though it is not overruled.

246 **Whitwood Chemical Co v Hardman** [1891] 2 Ch 416

The defendant entered into a contract of service with the claimant company and agreed to give the whole of his time to them. In fact, he occasionally worked for others, and the claimant tried to enforce the undertaking in the service contract by injunction.

Held – an injunction could not be granted because there was no express negative stipulation. The defendant had merely stated what he would do, and not what he would not do, and to read into the undertaking an agreement not to work for anyone else required the court to imply a negative stipulation from a positive one. No such implication could be made.

Comment It is because of the fact that the granting of an injunction of a negative stipulation is so close to specific performance that it is restricted to cases where the negative stipulation is express.

Quantum meruit: as a quasi-contractual remedy

247 **Craven-Ellis v Canons Ltd** [1936] 2 All ER 1066

The claimant was employed as managing director by the company under a deed which provided for remuneration. The articles provided that directors must have qualification shares, and must obtain these within two months of appointment. The claimant and other directors who appointed him never obtained the required number of shares so that the deed was invalid. However, the claimant had rendered services, and he now sued on a *quantum meruit* for a reasonable sum by way of remuneration.

Held – he succeeded on a *quantum meruit*, there being no valid contract.

Limitation of actions: effect of fraud, concealment and mistake

248 **Lynn v Bamber** [1930] 2 KB 72

In 1921 the claimant purchased some plum trees from the defendant and was given a warranty that the trees were 'Purple Pershores'. In 1928 the claimant discovered that the trees were not 'Purple Pershores' and sued for damages. The defendant pleaded that the claim was barred by the current Limitation Act.

Held – the defendant's fraudulent misrepresentation and fraudulent concealment of the breach of warranty provided a good answer to this plea, so that the claimant could recover.

Comment (i) The present jurisdiction is s 32 of the Limitation Act 1980.

(ii) In *Peco Arts Inc* v *Hazlitt Gallery Ltd* [1983] 3 All ER 193 the claimants bought from the defendants in November 1970 what purported to be an original drawing in black chalk on paper, *Etude pour le Bain Turc* by JAD Ingres, for the price of $18,000. In 1976 it was revalued by an expert for insurance purposes. No doubts were cast upon its authenticity. However, on a valuation in 1981 it was discovered that the drawing was a reproduction. The claimants sought rescission and recovery of the purchase price plus interest on the grounds of mutual, common or unilateral mistake of fact. The trial was adjourned on the first day because the parties wished to simplify the issues. After this the only defence was the Limitation Act 1980, i.e. that the claimants' claim was statute-barred. It was *held* that it was not and judgment was given for the claimants. Webster, J decided that a prudent buyer in the position of the claimants would not normally have obtained an independent authentication but would have relied on the defendant's reputation, as the claimants had done. Further, the claimants were entitled to conclude that the drawing was an original as the valuers who had examined it in 1976 had not questioned its authenticity. There was no lack of diligence on the part of the claimants. Accordingly, the action was not time barred and there would be judgment for the claimants.

(iii) The *Peco* case does not decide what the effect of the mistake was, and to that extent does not go contrary to *Leaf* and *Bell* (see Chapter 12). These matters were not contested by the defendants. In *Leaf* the court was deciding how soon an action must be brought for rescission for *innocent misrepresentation*. The issue here was how soon must an action be brought where the claimant sought relief for the consequences of an operative mistake.

(iv) More recently the House of Lords has decided that the normal period under the Limitation Act 1980 of six years governing the start of legal claims can be extended where information relevant to the possible claim is deliberately concealed *after* the period of six years has started to run. (See *Sheldon & Others* v *RHM Outhwaite (Underwriting Agencies) Ltd and Others* [1995] 2 All ER 558.)

The claimants, being Lloyds names on Syndicates 317 and 661, brought an action against the first defendant and other members' agents. They claimed damages for alleged breach of contract, breach of fiduciary duty, and negligence. The central allegation was that the managers of the syndicates had failed properly to perform their responsibilities in regard to writing and re-insuring a number of contracts in 1981 and 1982. Ordinarily, the claims should have been made within six years of the alleged default. However, the claimants issued their writ (now claim form) in 1992, well outside the normal six-year period.

As regards this, the claimants said that the defendants had, in 1984, deliberately concealed facts relevant to the claimants' action. They had not discovered these facts until a time, less than six years, prior to the issue of the writ (now claim form), so that s 32 of the 1980 Act applied and their action was not statute-barred and could proceed. Section 32 provides:

> (1) . . . where in the case of any action for which a period of limitation is prescribed by this Act, either – (a) the action is based upon the fraud of the defendant; or (b) any fact relevant to the [claimant's] right of action has been deliberately concealed from him by the defendant; or (c) the action is for relief from the consequences of a mistake; the period of limitation shall not begin to run until the [claimant] has discovered the fraud, concealment or mistake . . . or could with reasonable diligence have discovered it . . .

The previous applications of s 32 were typically in situations where deliberate concealment has taken place at the time of the default and it was held, perhaps straightforwardly, that time did not begin to run until the claimant discovered the facts.

A typical case under earlier identical legislation and one referred to in the *Sheldon* judgment is *Beaman* v *ARTS* (1949) (see Chapter 20) where, in 1935, the claimant left some packages containing goods in store with the defendant. In 1940 the defendants disposed of them without the claimant's consent or knowledge, thus committing the tort of conversion. She was allowed to bring a claim against the defendants more than six years later when she discovered the facts.

Despite the wording of s 32 in terms of the phrase 'begin to run', the House of Lords decided that concealment *after time started to run* was within the section. As Lord Browne-Wilkinson said:

> There is no commonsense reason why Parliament should have wished to distinguish between cases where the concealment takes place at the time of commission of the wrong and concealment at a later date. In both cases the mischief aimed at would be the same – to ensure that the Act does not operate to bar the claim of a [claimant] whose ignorance of the relevant facts is due to the improper actions of the defendant.

Therefore, time now begins to run only when the claimant has discovered the facts or could, with reasonable diligence, have discovered them.

Two of the Law Lords dissented, taking the view that the words 'shall not begin to run' were inapt to cover a case where time had already started to run.

The case has major significance in regard to actions by clients of, e.g., accountants and solicitors for breach of contract and negligence where a potential dispute may take a long time to arise and where material facts might well be concealed until after the six-year period has elapsed.

EMPLOYMENT RIGHTS

Discrimination: direct discrimination: less favourable treatment of a person on grounds of race

249 *Johnson* v *Timber Tailors (Midlands)* [1978] IRLR 146

When the claimant, a black Jamaican, applied for a job with the defendants as a wood machinist, the defendants' works manager told him that he would be contacted in a couple of days to let him know whether or not he had been successful. Mr Johnson was not contacted and after a number of unsuccessful attempts to get in touch with the works manager, was told that the vacancy had been filled. Another advertisement for wood machinists appeared in the paper on the same night as Mr Johnson was told that the vacancy had been filled. Nevertheless, Mr Johnson applied again for the job and was told that the vacancy had been filled. About a week later he applied again and was again told that the job had been filled although a further advertisement had appeared for the job on that day. It was held by an employment tribunal that the evidence established that Mr Johnson had been discriminated against on the grounds of race.

Comment The other side of the coin is illustrated by *Panesar* v *Nestlé & Co Ltd* [1980] ICR 144 where an orthodox Sikh who naturally wore a beard, which was required by his religion, applied for a job in the defendant's chocolate factory. He was refused employment because the defendant company applied a strict rule under which no beards or excessively long hair were allowed for reasons of hygiene. The claimant made a complaint of indirect discrimination but the defendant said that the rule was justified. The Court of Appeal *held* that as the defendant had supported the rule with scientific evidence there was in fact no discrimination. There would seem to be no reason to doubt this decision even if the Religion and Belief Regulations were applied. These regulations do protect Sikhs in terms of requirements to wear helmets but provide, at any rate, no specific protection, in the circumstances of this case.

Sex discrimination: genuine occupational qualification: requirement of decency

250 *Sisley* v *Britannia Security Systems* [1983] ICR 628

The defendant employed women to work in a security control station. The claimant (a man) applied for a vacant job but was refused employment. It appeared that the women worked 12-hour shifts with rest periods and that beds were provided for their use during such breaks. The women undressed to their underwear during these rest breaks. The claimant complained that by advertising for women the defendant was contravening the Sex Discrimination Act 1975. The defendant pleaded genuine occupational qualification, i.e. that women were required because the removal of uniform during rest periods was incidental to the employment. The Employment Appeal Tribunal accepted that defence. The defence of preservation of decency was, in the circumstances, a good one. It was reasonably incidental to the women's work that they should remove their clothing during rest periods.

Comment It should be noted that the SDA imposes a duty on employers to take reasonable steps to avoid relying on GOQ exceptions. Thus in *Wylie* v *Dee & Co (Menswear) Ltd* [1978] IRLR 103 a woman was refused employment in a men's tailoring establishment in which the remainder of the staff were men because it was inappropriate for her to measure the inside legs of male customers. She complained to an employment tribunal and succeeded on the basis that this particular task could have been carried out by one of the male employees.

There is no presumption that a contract of employment contains an implied term that sick pay will be provided

251 *Mears* v *Safecar Security* [1982] 2 All ER 865

Mr Mears was absent from his employment through sickness for six months out of some 14 months' employment. He then resigned because of ill-health. During the period of his sickness he made no claim for wages, and the written statement of his terms of employment under the EPCA, s 1 (see now s 1 of the ERA 1996) made no mention of sick pay. Indeed, he was told by other employees who visited him while he was sick that the employer did not pay wages during periods when employees were off work through sickness. After resigning Mr Mears applied to an employment tribunal to determine what particulars regarding sick pay should have been included in the s 1 statement. The tribunal *held* that the contract of employment included an implied term under which the employer would pay wages during sickness, subject to deducting any sickness benefit. There was an appeal against that decision by both parties. However, it is the employer's appeal which is of concern here. The employer alleged that the term relating to sick pay should not be implied at all. The Employment Appeal Tribunal upheld the employer's contention.

The employment tribunal was not right in assuming that a contract of employment must contain an implied term about sick pay. All the facts must be considered and here the implied term was that wages were not paid during sickness.

Comment The Employment Appeal Tribunal did not follow an earlier decision, i.e. *Orman* v *Saville Sportswear Ltd* [1960] 3 All ER 105, under which it was said that the court could imply a term relating to sick pay and that, indeed, in modern law there seemed to be a presumption in favour of the employee being entitled to sick pay unless an employer could bring evidence to show that this was not the case.

A man and a woman will be regarded as engaged in 'like work' even though there may be some differences between the jobs, but not if these differences are 'material'

252 *Capper Pass* v *Lawton* [1976] IRLR 366

A female cook who worked a 40-hour week preparing lunches for the directors of Capper was paid a lower rate than two male assistant chefs who worked a 45-hour week preparing some 350 meals a day in Capper's works canteen. The female cook claimed that by reason of the EPA (as amended) she should be paid at the same rate as the assistant chefs since she was employed on work of a broadly similar nature.

It was held by the EAT that if the work done by a female applicant was of a broadly similar nature to that done by a male colleague, it should be regarded as being like work for the purposes of the EPA unless there were some practical differences of detail between the two types of job. In this case the EAT decided that the work done by the female cook was broadly similar to the work of the assistant chefs and that the differences of detail were not of practical importance in relation to the terms and conditions of employment. Consequently, the female cook was entitled to be paid at the same rate as her male colleagues.

253 *Navy, Army and Air Force Institutes* v *Varley* [1977] 1 All ER 840

Miss Varley worked as a Grade E clerical worker in the accounts office of NAAFI in Nottingham. NAAFI conceded that her work was like that of Grade E male clerical workers employed in NAAFI's London Office. However, the Grade E workers in Nottingham worked a 37-hour week, while the male Grade E clerical workers in the London office worked a 36½-hour week. Miss Varley applied to an employment tribunal under the EPA for a declaration that she was less favourably treated as regards hours worked than the male clerical workers in London and that her contract term as to hours be modified so as to reduce it to 36$\frac{1}{2}$ hours a week. The employment tribunal granted that declaration and NAAFI appealed.

It was *held* by the EAT that the variation in hours was genuinely due to a material difference other than the difference of sex. It was due to a real difference in that the male employees worked in London where there was a custom to work shorter hours. Accordingly NAAFI's appeal was allowed and Miss Varley was *held* not to be entitled to the declaration.

> There is a geographical distinction between the conditions operated by NAAFI in respect of their employees in London and those outside London. That is by no means a unique situation; it is common to the Civil Service and to all sorts of other employment. . . . In other words, the variation between her contract and a man's contract is due really to the fact that she works in Nottingham and he works in London. It seems to us that it is quite plain that that is the difference between her case and his case, namely that she works in Nottingham where this old custom operates and he works in London where the custom of a shorter working week operates. (*Per* Phillips, J)

Comment (i) Another common example of a sensible material difference occurs where, for example, employee A is a new entrant of, say, 21 and employee B is a long-serving employee of, say, 50 and there is a system of service increments; then it is reasonable to pay B more than A though both are employed on like work. Obviously, it is not enough to say that because at the present time men are on average paid more than women this is a material difference justifying paying a woman less in a particular job. This was decided in *Clay Cross (Quarry Services) Ltd* v *Fletcher* [1979] 1 All ER 474.

(ii) It was decided in *Rainey* v *Greater Glasgow Health Board* [1987] 1 All ER 65 that it is in order to pay more to a man if this is necessary to meet skill shortages. In that case a man skilled at fitting artificial limbs was brought in from the private sector because of skill shortage and paid more than a female doing the same job who went straight into the public sector after training.

(iii) Experience can be rewarded by giving a man with greater experience higher pay (*McGregor* v *General Municipal Boilermakers and Allied Trade Unions* [1987] ICR 505) and an employer may also pay a man more for doing the same job if the man works nights and the women do not (*Thomas* v *National Coal Board* [1987] IRLR 451).

(iv) The fact that there is no sex discrimination is not relevant in turning down an equal pay claim. There must be a 'material difference'. Thus, if in a collective agreement made with a trade union, but with no element of sex discrimination, group A (mainly men) receives a higher hourly rate than group B (mainly women), the employer cannot successfully defend an equal pay claim by the women merely because there is no sex discrimination. There must be 'material difference'. This was decided in *Barber* v *NCR (Manufacturing) Ltd* [1993] IRLR 95.

(v) In *Ratcliffe* v *North Yorkshire County Council* [1995] 526 IRLB 12 the House of Lords decided that a local authority was not justified in cutting women school catering assistants' pay in order to tender for work at a commercially competitive rate. 'Market forces' do not necessarily amount to a genuine material factor other than sex. The result of this case is likely to have ramifications for public-sector competitive tendering exercises by council agencies. If these agencies cannot reduce wages in this way, the chances of a private-sector employer who is paying staff less are greatly enhanced.

Part-time firefighters: less favourable treatment

253a **Matthews v Kent and Medway Towns Fire Authority** (2006) 2 All ER 171

The House of Lords has considered the right of part-time workers to equal treatment with full-time workers in terms of pension and sick pay rights. The Part-Time Workers (Prevention of Less Favourable Treatment) Regulations 2000 (SI 2000/1551) provide in essence that a part-time worker must not be treated less favourably than a comparable full-time worker who at the time of the alleged less favourable treatment is employed by the same employer under the same type of contract and engaged in the same or broadly similar work. Very often in the past, part-timers have been unable to satisfy the comparison requirements because, among other things, full-timers undertake extra tasks and there may be differences in qualifications and skills. However, while accepting this, the House of Lords has ruled that a tribunal should concentrate on the similarities in the work rather than merely the differences in concluding whether part-timers are engaged in the same or broadly similar work.

Part-time firefighters represented by the Fire Brigades Union contended that they were suffering discrimination in comparison with their full-time colleagues in terms of the right to join the Firefighters Pension Scheme and in terms of sick pay conditions. The claim failed before a tribunal and the

Employment Appeal Tribunal and the Court of Appeal, all of these ruling that the part-time retained firefighters were not engaged in the same or broadly similar work. However, the House of Lords allowed their appeal, though two out of the five Law Lords dissented. In broad terms, the judgment of the House of Lords had two main planks. The first was that in the lower court and tribunals there had been an over-concentration on differences instead of similarities. It had been accepted by the original tribunal that both sets of firefighters' work at the site of a blaze was in effect the same and that work was central to the work of a firefighter and to the enterprise of the Fire Brigade as a whole. Secondly, while accepting that the full-timers carried out measurably additional job functions and that there could be material differences in qualifications and skills, this did not prevent the work of the part-timers in terms of *the core function of a firefighter*, being the same or broadly similar. The case was remitted to the tribunal for reconsideration at a second hearing, which should also decide how to remedy the situation.

Comment The conditions on which, for example, the part-timers should be admitted to the pension scheme in terms of back-dating remained to be looked at. In general terms, however, the ruling gives a green light to many other part-time workers in other employments to bring discrimination claims on the basis of the 'core function' ruling.

Sex discrimination: direct discrimination; less favourable treatment of a person on grounds of sex or race

254 *Coleman v Skyrail Oceanic Ltd* (1981) 131 NLJ 880

The claimant, who was a female booking clerk for Skyrail, a travel agency, was dismissed after she married an employee of a rival agency. Skyrail feared that there might be leaks of information about charter flights and had assumed that her dismissal was not unreasonable since the husband was the breadwinner. The Employment Appeal Tribunal decided that the dimissal was reasonable on the basis that the husband was the breadwinner. However, there was an appeal to the Court of Appeal which decided that those provisions of the Sex Discrimination Act 1975 which dealt with direct discrimination and dismissal on grounds of sex had been infringed. The assumption that husbands were breadwinners and wives were not, was based on sex and was discriminatory. The claimant's injury to her feelings was compensated by an award of £100 damages.

Comment The claimant was also held to be unfairly dismissed, having received no warning that she would be dismissed on marriage. The additional and discriminatory reason regarding the breadwinner cost the employer a further £100. It was not the totality of the claimant's award.

Sexual and racial discrimination: indirect discrimination; requirements or conditions applied to all workers but the ability of some persons to comply because of sex or race is considerably smaller and cannot be justified

255 *Price v The Civil Service Commission* [1977] IRLR 291

The Civil Service required candidates for the position of executive officer to be between $17^1/_2$ and 28 years. Belinda Price complained that this age bar constituted indirect sex discrimination against women because women between those ages were more likely than men to be temporarily out of the labour market having children or caring for children at home. It was *held* by the Employment Appeal Tribunal that that age bar was indirect discrimination against women. The court *held* that the words 'can comply' must not be construed narrowly. It could be said that any female applicant could comply with the condition in the sense that she was not obliged to marry or to have children or to look after them – indeed she may find someone else to look after them or, as a last resort, put them into care. If the legislation was construed in that way it was no doubt right to say that any female applicant could comply with the condition. However, in the view of the court to construe the legislation in that way appeared to be wholly out of sympathy with the spirit and intention of the Act. A person should not be deemed to be able to do something merely because it was theoretically possible, it was necessary to decide whether it was possible for the person to do so in practice, as distinct from theory.

Guidance on dependants' leave

255a *Qua v John Ford Morrison Solicitors* (2003) 153 New Law Journal 95

The claimant began work as a legal secretary in January 2000. She was dismissed in October 2000. She then complained to an employment tribunal that her dismissal was because she had taken time off to deal with her son's medical problems. It was agreed that the reason for her dismissal was her high level of absence. The employer contended that many absences had been unauthorised. She maintained that the majority of the absences were concerned with her son and that on each occasion she had informed the employer and that the time taken off was reasonable so that there had been no unauthorised absences. The tribunal ruled that she had not informed her employer as soon as was reasonably practicable and so dismissed her claim. The tribunal went on to hold that the time taken off was unreasonable. The claimant appealed to the Employment Appeal Tribunal.

The EAT allowed the appeal and remitted it for a rehearing. In doing so it pointed to errors made by the tribunal in construing the relevant legislation. The EAT first laid down that it was not possible to specify maximum periods of time that were reasonable and that it all depended on a study of the circumstances of the case. The EAT then stated that although the tribunal had found that the claimant had been absent for a total of 17 days it had wrongly regarded it as unnecessary to further identify those occasions and the extent to which the claimant had over that period complied with the notice requirements. The tribunal had also suggested that there was a duty on the employee to report to her employer 'on a daily basis' while off work. The EAT noted that there was no such duty under the relevant legislation.

Perhaps most importantly as leading to an understanding as to the purpose of the leave the EAT said that it was to find a carer in the emergency and then return to work. The leave was not intended to be used over a period so that the employee could provide the care. It is to deal with an emergency and then put in place arrangements that will obviate absence for an extended period. If this is not possible obviously time off will have to be taken but it will not qualify as dependants' leave.

The Health and Safety at Work Act 1974 Section 3 provides that it shall be the duty of every employer to conduct his undertaking in such a way as to ensure, so far as reasonably practicable, that persons not in his employment who may be affected thereby are not thereby exposed to risks to their health and safety

256 *R v Mara*, The Times, 13 November 1986

In this case it was alleged that the director of a company was in breach of his duty under the Health and Safety at Work Act where machinery belonging to his cleaning and maintenance company was left at a store which the company was under contract to clean, and the cleaning company agreed that employees of the store could use the machinery for part of the cleaning

and one of the employees of the store was electrocuted because of a fault in the cable of one of the machines. The Court of Appeal *held* that the director concerned was in breach of his duty and dismissed his appeal from the Warwick Crown Court where he had been fined £200. Mr Mara was the director of a small company, Cleaning & Maintenance Ltd (CMS). In December 1983 CMS made a contract with International Stores plc (IS) to clean its premises. The work required the use of certain electrical cleaning machines provided by CMS and these were left on the IS premises when CMS employees were not there. The machines included a polisher/scrubber.

The cleaning of the loading bay for the store in the morning was inconvenient and it was agreed that its cleaning should be removed from the ambit of the contract and at that time CMS agreed at the request of IS that its cleaning machines could be used by IS employees for cleaning the loading bay, and to Mr Mara's knowledge they were so used.

On 10 November 1984 an employee of IS was using a CMS polisher/scrubber for cleaning the loading bay when he was electrocuted because of the defective condition of the machine's cable.

The legal point was one of construction of the relevant section of the Health and Safety at Work Act which is set out in the headnote to this case. Mr Mara claimed that when the electrocution took place his company, CMS, was not conducting its undertaking at all; the only undertaking being conducted was that of IS whose employees were using the machine to clean the IS premises. The Court of Appeal did not accept this. The undertaking of CMS was the provision of cleaning services. So far as IS was concerned, the way in which CMS conducted its undertaking was to do the cleaning and to leave its machines and other equipment on the premises with permission for IS employees to use the same, with the knowledge that they would use the same. The equipment included an unsafe cable. The failure to remove or replace that cable was clearly a breach by CMS of its duty both to its own employees as well as under the Health and Safety at Work Act to the workers of IS.

Comment (i) This case shows the wide ambit of the Health and Safety at Work Act 1974. The liability of a director for offences by the company is set out in the 1974 Act which provides that where an offence under any of the provisions of the Act is committed by a body corporate, then should it be proved to be committed with the consent or connivance of, or to have been attributable to any neglect on the part of any director, manager, secretary, or similar officer of the body corporate, or a person who is purporting to act in such capacity, he as well as the body corporate shall be guilty of that offence and shall be liable to be proceeded against and punished accordingly. It should also be remembered that there is a civil claim for damages for this kind of breach. This case is concerned solely with the criminal offence.

(ii) It should be noted that fines are now much higher than the one in this case, both on the company and its directors. Six-figure sums are not uncommon.

(iii) There is a particular difficulty for the proprietor of a business in cases under s 3 of the 1974 Act in that the Court of Appeal ruled in *Davies* v *Health and Safety Executive* [2003] IRLR 170 that where an offence has been committed under the section there is a reverse burden of proof on the employer. This means that a prosecution will succeed under the section unless the proprietor can show, on a balance of probabilities, that it would not have been reasonably practicable for him or her to have done more to ensure safety. If he or she cannot produce such evidence the conviction stands. The allegation by Mr Davies that this reversed burden of proof was contrary to the Human Rights Convention (Art 6 (fair trial)) failed because, among other things, the proprietor was likely to have a unique knowledge of the risk and the special measures needed to avoid it. Mr Davies's conviction resulted from the death of a self-employed sub-contractor who was crushed by a JCB being reversed by an employee after Mr Davies had instructed him to put it into a garage and had then gone away to get on with his own work leaving the employee unsupervised. The rear arm of the JCB was retracted thus obscuring the driver's visibility. Mr Davies was fined £15,000 and had to pay £22,500 prosecution costs.

Unfair dismissal: is the court or tribunal dealing with an employee?

257 *Massey* v *Crown Life Insurance Co* [1978] 2 All ER 576

Mr Massey was employed by Crown Life as the manager of its Ilford branch from 1971 to 1973, the company paying him wages and deducting tax. In 1973, on the advice of his accountant, Mr Massey registered a business name of J R Massey & Associates and with that new name entered into an agreement with Crown Life under which he carried out the same duties as before but as a self-employed person. The Inland Revenue was content that he should change to be taxed under Schedule D as a self-employed person. His employment was terminated and he claimed to have been unfairly dismissed. The Court of Appeal decided that, being self-employed, he could not be unfairly dismissed.

Comment (i) It should also be noted that the EAT has held that a director, even with a service contract, who controls the votes in general meeting cannot be an employee for the purposes of employment legislation. The EAT distinguished the case of *Lee* v *Lee's Air Farming*

Ltd [1960] 3 All ER 420 where the director/controlling shareholder's widow was claiming, in effect, against an insurance company which had insured the company in respect of the death of its employees in the course of employment. Employment claims are met by the state and not by a company backed by insurers (see *Buchan* v *Secretary of State for Employment* [1997] IRLB 2).

(ii) In addition to the public policy point, i.e. who is the paymaster, there is also the legal point that the relationship of employer and employee requires an element of control by the employer over the employee and there is no way an employee who is the controlling shareholder can be dismissed except by his agreement.

(iii) Nevertheless, the Court of Appeal in *Secretary of State for Trade and Industry* v *Bottrill* (1999) 615 IRLB 12 ruled that while a controlling shareholding is likely to be a significant factor in all situations and in some may be decisive, it is only one of the relevant facts and is not to be taken as determining the relationship without taking into account all the relevant circumstances. Even so, in most cases it is likely that a controlling shareholder will not be regarded as an employee.

Conduct justifying dismissal may be the way in which an employee dresses

258 *Boychuk* v *H J Symons (Holdings) Ltd* [1977] IRLR 395

Miss B was employed by S Ltd as an accounts audit clerk but her duties involved contact with the public from time to time. Miss B insisted on wearing badges which proclaimed the fact that she was a lesbian, and from May 1976 she wore one or other of the following: (*a*) a lesbian symbol consisting of two circles with crosses (indicating women) joined together; (*b*) badges with the legends 'Gays against fascism', and 'Gay power'; (*c*) a badge with the legend 'Gay switchboard' with a telephone number on it and the words 'Information service for homosexual men and women'; (*d*) a badge with the word 'Dyke', indicating to the initiated that she was a lesbian.

These were eventually superseded by a white badge with the words 'Lesbians ignite' written in large letters on it. Nothing much had happened in regard to the wearing of the earlier badges, but when she began wearing the 'Lesbians ignite' badge there were discussions about it between her and her employer. She was told that she must remove it – which she was not willing to do – and that if she did not she would be dismissed. She would not remove the badge and was dismissed on 16 August 1976 and then made a claim for compensation for unfair dismissal.

No complaint was made regarding the manner of her dismissal in terms, e.g., of proper warning. The straight question was whether her employer was entitled to dismiss her because she insisted on wearing the badge. An employment tribunal had decided that in all the circumstances the dismissal was fair because it was within an employer's discretion to instruct an employee not to wear a particular badge or symbol which could cause offence to customers and fellow employees. Miss B appealed to the Employment Appeal Tribunal which dismissed her appeal and said that her dismissal was fair. The EAT said that there was no question of Miss B having been dismissed because she was a lesbian or because of anything to do with her private life or private behaviour. Such a case would be entirely different and raise different questions. This was only a case where she had been dismissed because of her conduct at work. That, the EAT said, must be clearly understood.

Comment (i) The decision does not mean that an employer by a foolish or unreasonable judgement of what could be expected to be offensive could impose some unreasonable restriction on an employee. However, the decision does mean that a reasonable employer, who is, after all, ultimately responsible for the interests of the business, is allowed to decide what, upon reflection or mature consideration, could be offensive to customers and fellow employees, and he need not wait to see whether the business would in fact be damaged before he takes steps in the matter.

(ii) In *Kowalski* v *The Berkeley Hotel* [1985] IRLR 40 the EAT decided that the dismissal of a pastrycook for fighting at work was fair though it was the first time he had done it.

(iii) On the issue of conduct, it was decided in *Dryden* v *Greater Glasgow Health Board* (1992) 447 IRLIB 11 that employees had no implied right under their contracts of employment to smoke at work. If, as in Ms Dryden's case, the employee leaves because he or she is not allowed to smoke there is no constructive dismissal. The employer had in this case offered counselling but without success.

Dismissal on a transfer of business

259 *Meikle* v *McPhail (Charleston Arms)* [1983] IRLR 351

After contracting to take over a public house and its employees, the new management decided that economies were essential and dismissed the barmaid. She complained to an employment tribunal on the grounds of unfair dismissal. Her case was based upon the fact that the 1981 Regulations state that a dismissal is to be treated as unfair if the transfer of a business or a reason connected with it is the reason or principal reason for the dismissal. The pub's new management defended the claim under another provision in the 1981 Regulations which states that a dismissal following a transfer of business is not to be regarded as automatically unfair where there was, as in this case, an economic reason for making changes in the workforce. If there is such a reason, unfairness must be established on grounds other than the mere transfer of the business.

The Employment Appeal Tribunal decided that the reason for dismissal was an economic one under the Regulations and that the management had acted reasonably in the circumstances so that the barmaid's claim failed.

Comment It should be noted that in *Gateway Hotels Ltd* v *Stewart* [1988] IRLR 287 the Employment Appeal Tribunal decided that on a transfer of business dismissal of employees of the business transferred prior to the transfer at the insistence of the purchaser of the business is not an 'economic' reason within the Regulations so that the dismissals are unfair.

An employee who unreasonably refused an offer of alternative employment is not entitled to a redundancy payment

260 *Fuller* v *Stephanie Bowman* [1977] IRLR 7

F was employed as a secretary at SB's premises which were situated in Mayfair. These premises attracted a very high rent and rates so SB moved its offices to Soho. These premises were situated over a sex shop and F refused the offer of renewed employment at the same salary and she later brought a claim before an employment tribunal for a redundancy payment. The tribunal decided that the question of unreasonableness was a matter of fact for the tribunal and F's refusal to work over the sex shop was unreasonable so that she was not entitled to a redundancy payment.

Comment (i) It should be noted that in *North East Coast Ship Repairers* v *Secretary of State for Employment* [1978] IRLR 149 the Employment Appeal Tribunal decided that an apprentice who, having completed the period of his apprenticeship, finds that the employer cannot provide him with work, is not entitled to redundancy payment. This case has relevance for trainees and others completing contracts in order to obtain relevant practical experience.

(ii) In *Elliot* v *Richard Stump Ltd* [1987] IRLR 215 the EAT decided that a redundant employee who is offered alternative employment by an employer who refuses to accept a trial period is unfairly dismissed.

(iii) In *Cambridge and District Co-operative Society Ltd* v *Ruse* [1993] IRLR 156 the EAT held that it was reasonable for an employee to refuse alternative work if the new job involved what he reasonably believed to be a loss of status. In that case the manager of a Co-op mobile butcher's shop was offered a post in the butcher's section of a Co-op supermarket which he refused to accept because he was under another manager; quite reasonably, he felt it involved a loss of status. He was successful in his claim for a redundancy payment.

LAW OF TORTS: GENERAL PRINCIPLES

Nature of tort: not all harm is actionable

261 *Perera* v *Vandiyar* [1953] 1 All ER 1109

The claimant was the tenant of a flat in Tooting, and the defendant was the landlord. On 8 October 1952, the landlord cut off the supply of gas and electricity to the flat in order to induce the claimant to leave. As a result, the claimant was forced to move out of the flat and lived elsewhere until the services were restored on 15 October 1952. The claimant sought damages for breach of implied covenant for quiet enjoyment, and for eviction.

Held – the claimant was entitled to damages for breach of the implied covenant, but punitive damages on the purported tort of eviction were not recoverable because the defendant had not committed a tort. It had not been necessary for the defendant to trespass on any part of the demised premises in order to cut off the services, and mere intention to evict was not a tort.

Comment This kind of conduct by a landlord is now a criminal offence under s 1 of the Protection from Eviction Act 1977. However, there is no civil action for breach of the statutory duty (*McCall* v *Abelesz* [1976] 1 All ER 727).

262 *Hargreaves* v *Bretherton* [1958] 3 WLR 463

The claimant pleaded that the defendant had falsely and maliciously and without just cause or excuse committed perjury as a witness at the claimant's trial for certain criminal offences, and that as a result the claimant had been convicted and sentenced to eight years' imprisonment. A point of law arose because the claimant's case was, in effect, based on the purported tort of perjury.

Held – no action lay on this cause, since there was no tort of perjury, and, therefore, the claimant's claim must be struck out.

263 *Roy* v *Prior* [1969] 3 All ER 1153

The claimant, a doctor, sued the defendant, a solicitor, for damages alleging, amongst other things, that the defendant had caused his arrest and forcible attendance at court to give evidence in a criminal case by saying falsely in court that the claimant was evading a witness summons. The action failed, Lord Denning, MR saying in the course of his judgment:

> It is settled law that, if a witness knowingly and maliciously tells untruths in the witness box, and as a result an innocent person is imprisoned, nevertheless no action lies against that witness. . . . The reason lies in public policy. Witnesses must be able to give their evidence without fear of the consequences. They might be deterred from doing so if they were at risk of being sued for what they said. So the law gives a witness the cloak of absolute immunity from suit. This applies not only to statements made by a witness in the box, but also to statements made whilst he is giving his proof to his solicitor beforehand. The reason is because the protection given to the witness in the box would be useless to him if it could be got round by an action against him in respect of his proof. . . .

Comment The Criminal Justice Act 1988 gives prisoners whose convictions are quashed or pardoned a *right* to monetary compensation from the government. The matter of compensation was formerly a matter for the discretion of the Home Secretary.

Nature of tort: no tort of invasion of privacy: effect of the law of confidence

263a *Douglas and Others* v *Hello! Ltd* [2005] 4 All ER 128

The first two claimants are well-known film stars. They married in November 2000. Before the ceremony they made a contract with the third claimant, *OK!* magazine, under which that magazine acquired exclusive photographic rights to the event. Unauthorised photographs were taken at the event and sold to *OK!*'s rival magazine *Hello!* which published them on the same day as *OK!* magazine. The claimants asked for damages for breach of confidence and the film stars claimed additionally for breach of the law of privacy.

The High Court ruled in 2003 that there was no existing tort of breach of privacy and refused to extend the common law into this area. There was furthermore no need to introduce Art 8 of the Convention on Human Rights (right to respect for private and family life) because English law was not inadequate in regard to the circumstances of this case. It could be dealt with as a breach of commercial confidence which was a recognised head of law. The judge also awarded the Douglases compensation for damage and distress under the Data Protection Act 1998. The unauthorised pictures were to be regarded as personal data and *Hello!* magazine was a data controller. Thus publication of the pictures was 'processing' by *Hello!* which was bound by the requirements of the Act. The judge said however that damages for the data infringement would be nominal. The amount of the other damages was left to be dealt with on the basis of submissions by the parties at a later date.

Comment (i) The High Court was of the opinion that if a general law of invasion of privacy was to be created it should be done by Parliamentary legislation and not by the judiciary since the latter did not have adequate consultation powers with interests that might be affected.

On appeal to the Court of Appeal in 2005 that court, in a landmark privacy ruling, found that *Hello!* had breached the privacy rights of Michael Douglas and Catherine Zeta-Jones by taking unauthorised pictures of their wedding but had not tried to cause commercial damage to rival *OK!* by publishing the photos. Overruling the 2003 High Court judgment, the Court of Appeal ruled that *Hello!* need not pay *OK!* £1 million compensation for commercial damage and a similar amount for legal costs. However, the court upheld the Douglases' award of £14,750 but refused to increase it, as they had received £1 million from *OK!* for the authorised shots. As regards the position between the magazines, the economic tort relied upn by *OK!* had to be done with the intention of injuring the claimant, whereas *Hello!* merely intended to boost its own sales.

It appears from this judgment that an individual has a right to protect his or her privacy.

(ii) In *A v B plc* [2001] 1 WLR 2341 the claimant was a married professional footballer. He claimed an injunction against the first defendant newspaper to restrain it from publishing or disclosing any information concerning the sexual relationship he had had with the second defendant and another woman and to restrain any disclosure by the women to anyone with a view to such information being published in the media.

The High Court granted the injunction. Having said that the claimant succeeded on the basis of confidentiality there being no matter of public interest (in the legal sense) in the circumstances as there might be in revelations of commercial fraud, the judge went on to say that the claimant's Convention right to privacy under Art 8 of the Convention prevailed over the defendant newspaper's right to freedom of expression under Art 10 of the Convention.

Nature of tort: expanding role of negligence from the Atkinian neighbour test

264 *Donoghue (or M'Alister)* v *Stevenson* [1932] AC 562

The appellant's friend purchased a bottle of ginger beer from a retailer in Paisley and gave it to her. The respondents were the manufacturers of the ginger beer. The appellant consumed some of the ginger beer and her friend was replenishing the glass, when, according to the appellant, the decomposed remains of a snail came out of the bottle. The bottle was made of dark glass so that the snail could not be seen until most of the contents had been consumed. The appellant became ill and served a writ (now claim form) on the manufacturers claiming damages. The question before the House of Lords was whether the facts outlined above constituted a cause of action in negligence. The House of Lords *held* by a majority of three to two that they did. It was stated that a manufacturer of products, which are sold in such a form that they are likely to reach the ultimate consumer in the form in which they left the manufacturer with no possibility of intermediate examination, owes a duty to the consumer to take reasonable care to prevent injury. This rule has been broadened in subsequent cases so that the manufacturer is liable more often where defective chattels cause injury. The following important points also arise out of the case.

(*a*) It was in this case that the House of Lords formulated the test that the duty of care in negligence is based on the foresight of the reasonable man. As Lord Atkin said:

The liability for negligence, whether you style it such or treat it as in other systems as a species of 'culpa' [fault] is no doubt based upon a general public sentiment of moral wrongdoing for which the offender must pay. But acts or omissions which any moral code would censure cannot in a practical world be treated so as to give a right to every person injured by them to demand relief. In this way rules of law arise which limit the range of complainants and the extent of their remedy. The rule that you are to love your neighbour becomes in law, you must not injure your neighbour; and the lawyer's question, Who is my neighbour? receives a restricted reply. You must take reasonable care to avoid acts or omissions which you can reasonably foresee would be likely to injure your neighbour. Who, then, in law, is my neighbour? The answer seems to be – persons who are so closely and directly affected by my act that I ought reasonably to have them in contemplation as being so affected when I am directing my mind to the acts or omissions which are called in question.

(b) Lord Macmillan's remark in his judgment that the categories of negligence are never closed suggests that the tort of negligence is capable of further expansion. That this has been so is revealed by the discussion of later cases in Chapter 21. There are still some difficulties in regard to the extension of the principle where physical damage to *property* causes a money loss, e.g. a loss of profit.

(c) The duty of care with regard to chattels as laid down in the case relates to chattels not dangerous in themselves. The duty of care in respect of chattels dangerous in themselves, e.g. explosives, is much higher.

(d) The appellant had no cause of action against the retailer in contract because her friend bought the bottle, so that there was no privity of contract between the retailer and the appellant. Therefore, terms relating to fitness for purpose and merchantable (now satisfactory) quality, now implied into such contracts by the Sale of Goods Act 1979, did not apply here.

Comment (i) A remedy under the Sale of Goods Act could have been given to the appellant if the reasoning of Tucker, J in *Lockett v A & M Charles Ltd* [1938] 4 All ER 170 had been applied in *Donoghue*. In *Lockett*, husband and wife went into a hotel for lunch. The wife ordered whitebait which was not fit for human consumption. She only ate a small amount of the whitebait and was then taken ill. In the subsequent action against the hotel, Tucker, J *held* that although the husband ordered the meal there was an assumption in these cases that each party would be, if necessary, personally liable for what he or she consumed. There was, therefore, a contract between the hotel and the wife into which Sale of Goods Act terms could be implied and she was awarded damages because the whitebait was not fit for the purpose or of merchantable (now satisfactory) quality. This approach is surprisingly modern in spite of the fact that the case was decided in 1938.

(ii) The general statement of principles in this case is at the root of the tort of negligence. However, it should be noted that the Consumer Protection Act 1987 provides a statutory basis for claims against a manufacturer for product liability and without the need to prove negligence (see further Chapter 21).

Damage and liability: *damnum sine injuria*; effect of malice and relevance of motive

265   **Best v Samuel Fox & Co Ltd** [1952] 2 All ER 394

Best was a workman at the defendant's factory and because of an accident caused by the defendant's negligence he was emasculated and thus rendered incapable of sexual intercourse. Best's claim for damages was successful but his wife also claimed damages for loss of her husband's *consortium* through the defendant's negligence. The House of Lords *held* that her claim failed because the *damnum* was not of a kind recognised by law. 'It is true that a husband is entitled to recover damages for loss of *consortium* against a person who negligently injures his wife, but this exceptional right is an anomaly at the present day. A wife . . . was never regarded as having any proprietary right in her husband. . . .' (*per* Lord Morton of Henryton).

Comment Some American jurisdictions allow such a claim. The *Best* case is in no sense anti-female. The House of Lords simply took the view that the right of *consortium* in both parties was an anachronism and took the opportunity to deny the right of *consortium* in the wife. The Law Commissioners recommended giving equal rights to husband and wife by abolishing the husband's right to compensation for loss of his wife's *consortium*. (See Report No 56 on *Personal Injury Litigation – Assessment of Damages* (1973).) This has been achieved by s 2(a) of the Administration of Justice Act 1982.

266   **Electrochrome Ltd v Welsh Plastics Ltd** [1968] 2 All ER 205

A lorry driver employed by the defendants drove the defendants' vehicle into a fire hydrant near to the claimant's factory. Water escaped from the damaged hydrant and the supply had to be cut off while repairs were carried out. The claimant lost a day's work at its factory and sued for this loss. However, since it was not the owner of the hydrant, it was *held* that no action lay. The claimant had suffered loss, but there had been no infringement of its legal rights.

Comment (i) The case is a good example of the reluctance of a court to allow the law of tort to be used to compensate for economic loss, i.e. the mere loss of an opportunity to make a profit, perhaps on the ground that the law of contract is more concerned with the loss of expectations. Furthermore, the decision in this case can be reached by way of *damnum sine injuria* or by saying that there was no duty of care or, if there was, that the damage was too remote.

(ii) In *Junior Books Ltd v Veitchi Co Ltd* (1982) (see Chapter 21) the House of Lords decided that if a claimant was in sufficiently close proximity to the defendant, he could recover foreseeable economic loss, even though there was no physical damage either to a person or to property. It would, however, be unwise to assume that *Junior Books* covers all cases of economic loss, particularly where, as in the *Electrochrome* case, proximity of the claimant and defendant does not exist in the *Junior Books* way. Anyway, the effect of the decision has been largely whittled away in more recent cases (see Chapter 21).

267 *Bradford Corporation* v *Pickles* [1895] AC 587

The Corporation had statutory power to take water from certain springs. Water reached the springs by percolating (but not in a defined channel) through neighbouring land belonging to Pickles. In order to induce the Corporation to buy his land at a high price, Pickles sank a shaft on it, with the result that the water reaching the Corporation's reservoir was discoloured and its flow diminished. The Corporation asked for an injunction to restrain Pickles from collecting the subterranean water.

Held – an injunction could not be granted. Pickles had a right to drain from his land subterranean water not running in a defined channel. (This right of a landowner was established by the House of Lords in *Chasemore* v *Richards* (1859) 7 HL Cas 349.) Any malice which he might have had in doing it did not affect that right, since English law knows no doctrine of abuse of rights. No use of property which would be legal if due to a proper motive can become illegal because it is prompted by an improper or malicious motive.

268 *Wilkinson* v *Downton* [1897] 2 QB 57

The defendant as a 'practical joke', called on Mrs Wilkinson and told her that her husband had been seriously injured in an accident while returning home from the races and had had both his legs broken. Mrs Wilkinson travelled to see her husband at Leytonstone and, believing the message to be true, sustained nervous shock and in consequence was seriously ill. This action was brought for damages for false and malicious representation. Damages were awarded. The court *held* that intentional physical harm is a tort even though it does not consist of a trespass to the person. Further, whether the act is malicious or by way of a joke is irrelevant.

Comment (i) Although it is often stated that trespass lies only for direct damage, trespass is felt to be the basis of this action and it clearly suggests that the tort of trespass is available for indirect physical damage caused wilfully.

(ii) The *Wilkinson* case was the sole basis of liability in the defendant in *C* v *D* [2006] All ER (D) 329 (Feb). The case concerned the alleged sexual abuse of the claimant while a school pupil. The first incident involved showing a video of the claimant and others in the school showers and the second concerned an incident in the school infirmary where the defendant had allegedly pulled down the claimant's trousers and underwear and had stared at his genitals. The claim was for psychiatric injury and the mental intention of the defendant to cause it. The judge found that the video was not a cause of psychiatric injury but the infirmary incident was. The question was 'did the defendant mean it?' Was it possible to impute a bad motive under in the *Wilkinson* situation? The judge ruled that a less than innocent motive could be imputed and was imputed as regards the infirmary incident on the basis that the defendant was at least reckless as to whether he caused psychiatric harm.

There was little discussion of the vicarious liability of D's employer, a local authority, but the authority was held vicariously liable, since sexual abuse had been regarded as within the course of employment in the sense that D's employment gave him the opportunity to carry out the abuse (see *Lister* v *Hesley Hall Ltd* [2001] 1 AC 215 (Case **284a**)).

Minors: liability as defendant

269 *Williams* v *Humphrey*, *The Times*, 20 February 1975

The defendant, a youth of nearly 16, accompanied his friend and the friend's parents to a swimming pool. As part of the general fun, the defendant pushed the friend's father, the claimant, a middle-aged man, into the shallow end of the pool, merely intending to cause a big splash. The claimant's left foot struck the edge of the pool and he sustained severe injuries to his foot and ankle. He underwent five operations and ended up disabled. It was *held* – by Talbot, J – the claimant had not taken such part in the pool activities that he could be said to have willingly accepted the risk of personal injury and the defendant was guilty of both negligence and trespass to the person. The claimant succeeded.

Comment (i) It may be puzzling to the reader why this action was worthwhile in terms of the fact that the defendant would not have had a lot of money in his personal capacity. However, there was a household insurance policy available. Most modern household insurance policies have a public liability clause which provides cover, sometimes up to £1 million or more for accidents caused by the householder or his family.

(ii) In *Mullin* v *Richards* [1998] 1 WLR 1304 the defendant was a 15-year-old schoolgirl, as was the claimant. A play fight between the two with plastic rulers ended with the claimant getting a piece of plastic in her eye and losing the sight in it. The matter of the defendant's liability in negligence arose. The Court of Appeal ruled that she was not liable. There was not sufficient evidence to show that the accident was readily foreseeable by a ordinarily prudent and reasonable 15-year-old schoolgirl. There was no dangerous force used over and above that which was inherent in play fencing of this kind that the school had not prohibited.

Minors: liability of parents and others in charge of minors; negligent control

270 *Donaldson* v *McNiven* [1952] 1 All ER 1213

The defendant lived in a densely populated area of Liverpool and allowed his 13-year-old son to have an air rifle on condition that he did not use it outside the house. The defendant's house had a large cellar and the boy was told to use the rifle there. Without the defendant's knowledge, the boy fired the air rifle at some children playing near to the house, injuring the claimant, a child of five.

Held – in the circumstances the precautions taken by the defendant were reasonable and would have been adequate but for his son's disobedience, which could not have been foreseen because the boy was usually obedient. The defendant was not guilty of negligence.

271 *Bebee* v *Sales* (1916) 32 TLR 413

A father allowed his 15-year-old son to retain a shotgun with which he knew he had already caused damage. The father was *held* liable for an injury to another boy's eye.

Comment Cases **270** and **271** were decided on the ordinary principles of negligence at common law. However, since the Air Guns and Shot Guns Act 1962 (see now the Firearms Act 1968 and amending legislation), an action may lie against the parent for breach of statutory duty. The Act makes it a criminal offence to give an air weapon to a person under 14 years, and restricts the use or possession of air weapons by young persons in public places except under supervision. In any case, breaches of these statutory duties could be relied upon as evidence of negligence. Furthermore, a person injured might now claim compensation from the Criminal Injuries Compensation Board. The age of the child causing the injury is not a bar to a claim against the Board because payments will be made even though the child inflicting the injury is below the age of criminal responsibility. In *Gorely* v *Codd* [1966] 3 All ER 891, the claimant was injured by a pellet from Codd's air rifle when they were larking about in a field in open country. Codd was 16½ years of age, and when the claimant sued Codd's father, the court found that he had given proper instruction to his son and was not liable at common law. Since the shooting did not occur in a public place, there was no breach of the Air Guns and Shot Guns Act 1962 (see now the Firearms Act 1968 and amending legislation).

272 *Carmarthenshire County Council* v *Lewis* [1955] 1 All ER 565

A boy aged four years was a pupil at a nursery school run by the appellants who were the local education authority. The boy and another were made ready to go out for a walk with the mistress in charge who left them for a moment in order to get ready herself. She did not return for 10 minutes, having treated another child who had cut himself. During her absence, the boy got out of the classroom and made his way through an unlocked gate, down a lane, and into a busy highway. He caused the driver of a lorry to swerve into a telegraph pole, as a result of which the driver was killed. His widow brought an action for damages for negligence.

Held – in the circumstances of the case the mistress was not negligent so the liability of the local authority was not vicarious. However, the local authority was negligent itself because it had not taken reasonable precautions to keep young children who used the premises from getting out into the highway.

273 *Butt* v *Cambridgeshire and Isle of Ely County Council* (1969) 119 NLJ 118

The claimant was a pupil in a class of 37 girls of nine and 10 years of age. She lost an eye when another girl in her class waved pointed scissors which the children were using to cut out illustrations. The teacher was giving individual attention to another child.

Held – by the Court of Appeal – her claim for damages failed. The teacher was not under a duty to require all work to stop while she was giving individual attention to members of the class. She was not negligent so that there was no vicarious liability in the local authority. The local authority was not liable for its own negligence in that evidence of experienced teachers showed that there was no fault in the system of using pointed scissors.

Mental patients: liability in tort

274 *Morriss* v *Marsden* [1952] 1 All ER 925

The defendant took a room at a hotel in Brighton, and whilst there he violently attacked the claimant, who was the manager of the hotel. Evidence showed that at the time of the attack the defendant was suffering from a disease of the mind. He knew the nature and quality of his act, but did not know that what he was doing was wrong. The claimant sued for damages for assault and battery.

Held – since the defendant knew the nature and quality of his tortious act, it did not matter that he did not know what he was doing was wrong, and he was liable in tort.

Diplomatic immunity in tort: nature of

275 *Dickinson v Del Solar* [1930] 1 KB 376

The claimant had been knocked down by a car driven by the defendant's servant. The defendant was the First Secretary of the Peruvian Legation in London. The Head of the Legation directed the defendant not to plead diplomatic privilege, and the defendant entered an appearance in the action. The claimant succeeded and the defendant's insurance company refused to indemnify its client, saying, in effect, that his diplomatic immunity was immunity from liability.

Held – the insurer was liable to indemnify the defendant. Diplomatic agents are not immune from liability for wrongful acts, but are merely immune from suit. This immunity can be waived with the sanction of the sovereign of the state in question, or an official superior of the person concerned. The defendant's act in entering an appearance operated as a waiver of diplomatic privilege, and judgment was properly entered against him.

Corporations: as claimants in tort

276 *D & L Caterers and Jackson v D'Anjou* [1945] 1 All ER 563

The claimant owned a West End restaurant called the 'Bagatelle'. The defendant made certain statements alleging that the restaurant was operated illegally and obtained its supplies on the black market.

Held – the statements were defamatory and a limited liability company could sue for slander without proof of special damage. Where the slander related to its trade or business, the law implied the existence of damage to found the action.

Corporations: as defendants in tort

277 *Poulton v London and South Western Railway Co* (1867) LR 2 QB 534

The claimant was arrested by a stationmaster for non-payment of carriage in respect of his horse. The defendant (the employer of the stationmaster) had power to detain passengers for non-payment of their own fare, but for no other reason.

Held – since there was no express authorisation of the arrest by the defendant, the stationmaster was acting outside the scope of his employment and the defendant was not liable.

278 *Campbell v Paddington Borough Council* [1911] 1 KB 869

The defendant Council, in accordance with a resolution duly passed, erected a stand in Burwood Place in order that members of the Council might view the funeral procession of King Edward VII passing along the Edgware Road. The claimant, who occupied certain premises in Burwood Place, often let the premises for the purpose of viewing public processions passing along the Edgware Road. The stand obstructed the view of the funeral procession from the claimant's house and she was unable to let the premises for that purpose.

Held – as the stand constituted a public nuisance, the claimant could maintain an action for the special damage which she had sustained through the loss of view. The Council was properly sued, and the fact that the erection of the stand was probably *ultra vires* did not matter.

Comment The damages in this case must be regarded as parasitical because the law does not recognise a right to a view or prospect and it must be accepted therefore that a claimant may recover as part of his damages for injury to a recognised interest a financial loss related to another interest which would not in itself be protected by the law. (See also *Spartan Steel and Alloys Ltd v Martin & Co Ltd* (1972) in Chapter 21.)

Vicarious liability: who is a servant? Control and other tests; transfer of employees

279 *Garrard v Southey (A E) and Co and Standard Telephones and Cables Ltd* [1952] 2 QB 174

Two persons employed by electrical contractors were sent to work in a factory on electrical installations. The electrical contractors continued to employ the men, paying their wages, stamping their insurance cards, and retaining the sole right to dismiss them. The electricians worked exclusively at the factory and used the factory canteen. The occupiers of the factory supplied them with all materials, tools and plant, except for certain special tools belonging to the electricians themselves. They were supervised by a foreman employed by the occupiers and they followed the system laid down in the factory. One of the electricians was injured when he fell from a defective trestle owned by some building contractors who were also working in the factory.

Held – the occupiers of the factory, and not the electrical contractors, owed the injured electrician the common-law duty of a master to his servant (to provide proper plant and equipment) and they were liable to him for breach of that duty.

Comment It is worth noting that the *Garrard* decision is an extremely rare one. There is a very strong presumption that the general or permanent employer remains liable. Thus in *Morris* v *Breaveglen (t/a Anzac Construction Co), The Times*, 29 December 1993, the Court of Appeal held that an employer was liable to his employee sent to work under a labour-only sub-contract, which was under the direction and control of the main contractor, if the system of work was unsafe.

280 Mersey Docks and Harbour Board v Coggins and Griffiths (Liverpool) Ltd and McFarlane [1947] AC 1

A company of stevedores had hired from the Harbour Board the use of a crane together with its driver, Mr Newall, to assist in loading a ship lying in the Liverpool docks. The contract of hire was subject to the Board's regulations, one of which contained the clause: 'The driver provided shall be the servant of the applicants.' The driver of the crane was a skilled man appointed and paid by the Board, and the Board alone had power to dismiss him. The stevedores told the driver what they wanted the crane to lift but had no authority to tell him how to work the crane. McFarlane, who was a checker employed by the forwarding agents, was noting the number and marks on a case which the crane had picked up when he was trapped because of the negligence of the crane driver in failing to keep the crane still.

The question to be determined was whether in applying the doctrine of vicarious liability the general employer of the crane driver or the hirer was liable for his negligence. The Board contended that, under the terms of the contract between the Board and the stevedores, the stevedores were liable.

Held – by the House of Lords:

(*a*) The question of liability was not to be determined by any agreement between the general employer and the hirer, but depended on the circumstances of the case. The test to apply was that of control.

(*b*) The Board, as the general employer of the crane driver, had not established that the hirer had such control of the crane driver at the time of the accident as to become liable as employer for his negligence. Although the hirer could tell the crane driver where to go and what to carry, the hiring company had no authority to tell him how to operate the crane. The Board was, therefore, liable for his negligence.

Comment The answers given by Mr Newall to counsel's questions in this case were highly important. At one point he said: 'I take no orders from anybody.' Commenting on this, Lord Simonds said that it was 'a sturdy answer which meant that he was a skilled man and knew his job and would carry it out in his own way. Yet ultimately he would decline to carry it out in the appellants' way at his peril, for in their hands lay the only sanction the power of dismissal.'

281 Wright v Tyne Improvement Commissioners (Osbeck & Co Ltd, Third Party) [1968] 1 All ER 807

Tyne Improvement Commissioners hired a crane to Osbeck & Co Ltd, under a written contract whereby the hirer agreed 'to bear the risk of and be responsible for all damage, injury or loss whatsoever, howsoever and whensoever caused arising directly or indirectly out of or in connection with the hiring or use of the said crane'. The claimant, who was a docker employed by Osbeck & Co, was injured when a wagon, in which he was standing to receive timber, was negligently moved forward by the capstan driver causing the claimant to collide with timber being lowered into the wagon by the crane. The claimant and the crane driver did all they could to avoid the accident but failed to do so and it was accepted that the capstan driver, who was employed by the Commissioners, was wholly to blame. Under the doctrine of vicarious liability, the Commissioners were also to blame. When the action was tried at Newcastle-upon-Tyne Assizes, Waller, J awarded the claimant damages of some £2,985 against the Commissioners, but dismissed a claim by the Commissioners against Osbeck & Co, as the hirer of the crane, for an indemnity against the claimant's claim by virtue of the clause quoted above. The Commissioners now appealed against the dismissal of the claim for indemnity.

Held – by the Court of Appeal – as the accident arose directly, or at least indirectly, out of or in connection with the use of the crane, the indemnity clause entitled the Commissioners to an indemnity against Osbeck & Co even though the use to which the crane was being put was not a blameworthy cause of the accident.

282 Cassidy v Ministry of Health [1951] 2 KB 343

The claimant's left hand was operated on at the defendant's hospital by a whole-time assistant medical officer of the hospital. After the operation the claimant's hand and forearm were put in a splint for 14 days. During this time the claimant complained of pain but was merely given sedatives by the doctors who attended him. When the splint was removed, it was found that all four fingers of the claimant's hand were stiff, and that his hand was virtually useless. Someone – either the doctor, the surgeon, or a nurse

– had been negligent, but the claimant could not in fact point to which of these it was. The claimant sued the defendant for negligence.

Held – the defendant was liable, in spite of its absence of real control over the type of work done by the doctors it employed. Denning, LJ stated that only where the patient himself selects and employs the doctor will the hospital authorities escape liability for that doctor's negligence. If the person causing the harm is part of the organisation, the employer is liable.

Comment In this case Lord Denning used the doctrine *res ipsa loquitur* (see Chapter 21) in order to help the claimant to establish his case. In other words, he presumed negligence, thus relieving the claimant of the burden of actually having to point to a particular employee of the negligent Ministry.

283 Ferguson v John Dawson & Partners (Contractors) [1976] 3 All ER 817

The claimant who was working 'on the lump' was injured whilst working for the defendants who were contractors. No deductions were made by the defendants for income tax or national insurance contributions and the claimant had been told that he was working 'purely as a lump labour force'. The defendants' site agent was responsible for hiring and dismissing the workmen, including the claimant; he told them what to do and moved them from site to site. If tools were required for the work, the defendants provided them. The claimant was injured when he fell off a roof which had no guard rail and he brought this action against the defendants on the basis that they were liable as his employers for failing to provide a guard rail on the flat roof which was required by construction regulations. It was *held* – by the Court of Appeal – that whatever label was put on the parties' relationship, other factors should be considered, such as the fact that the defendants could dismiss the workmen, including the claimant, and tell them what to do and where to do it. Accordingly, the claimant was the employee of the defendants who were, therefore, liable under the construction regulations and must pay the claimant damages for breach of that statutory duty.

284 Lee (Catherine) v Lee's Air Farming Ltd [1960] 3 All ER 420

In 1954 the appellant's husband formed the respondent company which carried on the business of crop spraying from the air. In March 1956, Mr Lee was killed while piloting an aircraft during the course of topsoil dressing, and Mrs Lee claimed compensation from the company, as the employer of her husband, under the New Zealand Workers' Compensation Act 1922. Since Mr Lee owned 2,999 of the company's 3,000 £1 shares and since he was its governing director, the question arose as to whether the relationship of master and servant could exist between the company and him. He was employed as the company's chief pilot under a provision in the articles at a salary to be arranged by himself.

Held – Mrs Lee was entitled to compensation because her husband was employed by the company in the sense required by the Act of 1922, and the decision in *Salomon* v *Salomon & Co* was applied.

Comment The Employment Appeal Tribunal distinguished *Lee's* case in *Buchan* v *Secretary of State for Employment* (1997) 565 IRLB 2 (see Chapter 19). Policy considerations were involved. Employment protection claims are met by the state and not, as in *Lee's* case, by a company backed up by an insurance company.

Acts personal to the employee: a move towards greater employer liability

284a Lister v Hesley Hall Ltd [2001] 2 All ER 769

The claimants were boys at a school for children with emotional difficulties. It was owned and managed by the defendant company. The company employed a warden and housekeeper to look after the claimants. He systematically abused them. They brought claims for personal injury against the company as vicariously liable for the acts of the warden. The case reached the House of Lords on appeal. Their Lordships were faced by a defence that in essence stated that the warden in abusing the claimants was not acting in the course of his employment but was in abusing the claimants doing acts personal to himself. The abuse was no part of his employment. The employment merely gave him the *opportunity* to abuse the claimants. The House of Lords did not accept this defence. Whatever may be the grounds for this *fact* decision, it must be regarded as an essential background to the case that the employers were better able to pay any damages awarded to the claimants. Nevertheless, it would now seem to be the law that even though the act is not within the ordinary course of employment and where the employment merely gives the employee an *opportunity to commit the tortious act* the employer may nevertheless be held liable for it. A previous decision by the Court of Appeal in *Trotman* v *North Yorkshire CC* [1998] 1 CLY 2243 that acts of sexual abuse were beyond the scope of employment so that the employer was not liable was overruled by the House of Lords in the *Lister* case.

Comment The decision of the Court of Appeal in *Fennelly* v *Connex South Eastern Ltd* (2001) 675 IRLB 11 further liberalises the attitude of the courts to what can be regarded as within the scope of employment.

The facts of the case occurred at Bromley South railway station. Mr Fennelly had already shown his ticket to an inspector and refused to show it again to another inspector, a Mr Sparrow. There was an altercation that ended with Mr Sparrow assaulting Mr Fennelly by putting a headlock on him and dragging him down a a few steps on the station stairway. On being sued as vicariously liable for the assault, Mr Sparrow's employer Connex was held not liable because the trial judge said that Mr Sparrow had become angry and 'was pursuing his own ends'. The Court of Appeal did not agree and found Connex liable. The judgment says that the High Court from which the appeal was made had taken too narrow a view of the facts. What had occurred would not have done so without Mr Sparrow's power given by his employers to inspect tickets while he was on his employer's premises. The downside of decisions like this is that the business employer, who is normally insured against these risks has to pay higher insurance premiums. They are not helpful to the consumer either since the employer's insurance costs are normally passed on to the consumer by way of increased prices for the goods and/or services. The third party benefits, of course, but ultimately at the consumer's expense.

A further and later example is to be found in the ruling of the Court of Appeal in *Mattis* v *Pollock (t/a Flamingo's Nightclub), The Times*, 16 July 2003. In that case the defendant ran a nightclub and employed a doorman. The defendant knew that the doorman was prepared to use physical force when carrying out his duties. The claimant became involved in an altercation with the doorman. Afterwards the doorman went home and armed himself with a knife. He returned to the vicinity of the nightclub intending to take revenge for the injuries he had received earlier. He attacked the claimant with the knife. The claimant's spinal cord was severed and he was rendered a paraplegic. The claimant sued the defendant as owner of the nightclub and so vicariously liable for the damage caused by the injuries.

The Court of Appeal ruled that the defendant was vicariously liable because:

- the doorman had been encouraged by the defendant to carry out his duties in an aggressive and intimidatory manner. This had included man-handling the customers;
- the stabbing represented the end of an incident that had started in the club. It could not in any fair or just sense be treated in isolation from the earlier events. It was not a separate and distinct incident;
- at the moment of the stabbing, the responsibility for the acts of the aggressive doorman that rested with the defendant had not been extinguished and so the defendant was vicariously liable.

Vicarious liability: improper performance of acts within scope of employment

285 *Century Insurance Co Ltd* v *Northern Ireland Road Transport Board* [1942] AC 509

A tanker belonging to the respondent, and driven by one of its employees, was delivering petrol to a garage in Belfast. While the tanker was discharging petrol at the garage, the driver lit a cigarette and threw away the lighted match. The resulting explosion caused considerable damage. The contract under which the petrol was being delivered said that the respondent's employees were to take their orders from a petrol company to which the tankers were hired, a company named Holmes, Mullin and Dunn, though they were not by virtue of this to be deemed the hirer's employees. The appellant had insured the defendant against liability to third parties, and pleaded that no claim could be made on it because, although the driver was admittedly negligent, he was at the time the servant of the hirer.

Held – the appellant must pay the third-party claim because the terms of the contract as a whole did not involve a transfer of the employees to Holmes, Mullin and Dunn, therefore, the respondent was liable for the negligence of the driver and was entitled to claim under its insurance.

Comment (i) It would seem that, however improper the manner in which an employee is doing his work, whether negligently or fraudulently, or contrary to express orders, his employer is liable.

(ii) This case was followed in *Harrison* v *Michelin Tyre Company* [1985] 1 All ER 918 where the claimant, a tool grinder employed by the defendant, was injured at work when standing on a duckboard of his machine talking to a fellow employee. Another employee was pushing a truck along a passage in front of the claimant and decided as a joke to suddenly turn it two inches outside the chalk lines of the passageway and push the edge under the claimant's duckboard. The duckboard tipped. The claimant fell off and suffered injury. In an action against the defendant he claimed that the employee had acted in the course of his employment and that the defendant was vicariously liable. The defendant denied liability saying that the employee had embarked on a frolic of his own. It was held by Comyn, J that the employer was liable. The test for determining vicarious liability was whether a reasonable man would say either that the employee's act was part and parcel of his employment, even though unauthorised or prohibited, or that it was so divergent as to be plainly alien to it. In this case the employee's act was part and parcel of the employment.

(iii) There will always be a tendency to make the employer liable because of his greater wealth and insurance. However, a contrast to *Harrison* is provided by *McCready* v *Securicor Ltd* (1992) 460 IRLIB 12 where it was held that the employer (Securicor) was not vicariously liable for the negligence of its employee in playing a prank. The employee concerned, as a prank, started to close the door of a secure vault, knowing Mr McCready was inside. Mr McCready rushed to get out and caught his hand in the door, suffering serious injury. The employee alone was held liable. Unlike *Harrison*, the act was totally unauthorised.

286 *Limpus v London General Omnibus Co* (1862) 1 H & C 526

The claimant's omnibus was overturned when the driver of the defendant's omnibus drove across it so as to be first at a bus stop to take all the passengers who were waiting. The defendant's driver admitted that the act was intentional, and arose out of bad feeling between the two drivers. The defendant had issued strict instructions to its drivers that they were not to obstruct other omnibuses.

Held – the defendant was liable. Its driver was acting within the scope of his employment at the time of the collision, and it did not matter that the defendant had expressly forbidden him to act as he did.

Comment As we have seen, the matter to be decided in these cases is whether the employee was doing what he was employed to do. If he is not, then the employer is not liable. Thus, in *Beard* v *London General Omnibus Co* [1900] 2 QB 530 a bus conductor, who turned the bus round when the driver was absent and injured the claimant whilst he was doing this, was held by the Court of Appeal to have been acting outside the course of his employment so that his employer was not liable.

287 *Rose v Plenty* [1976] 1 All ER 97

Leslie Rose, aged 13, was given to helping Mr Plenty, a milkman, to deliver milk. Co-operative Retail Services Ltd, who employed Mr Plenty, expressly forbade its milkmen to take boys on their floats or to get boys to help them deliver the milk. On one occasion, while helping Mr Plenty, Leslie was sitting in the front of the float when his leg caught under the wheel. The accident was caused partly by Mr Plenty's negligence. It was *held* – by the Court of Appeal (Lord Denning, MR and Scarman, LJ) – that Mr Plenty had been acting in the course of his employment so that his employer was liable to compensate Leslie Rose for his injuries. Lawton, LJ (dissenting) said that the case of *Twine* v *Bean's Express* (1946) and similar cases were indistinguishable and that, in giving Leslie a lift, Mr Plenty had acted outside the *scope* of his employment.

Comment There is really very little difference in the facts of *Rose* v *Plenty* and *Twine* other than the fact that Leslie Rose was more than a mere hitchhiker. His presence on the milk-float was connected with the delivery of the milk, which was the reason connected with the *scope* of employment, and this is why Lord Denning and Scarman, LJ felt able to distinguish *Twine* and other similar cases.

Vicarious liability: employee mixing employer's business with his own

288 *Britt v Galmoye and Nevill* (1928) 44 TLR 294

The first defendant, who had the second defendant in his employment as a van-driver, lent him his private motor car, after the day's work was finished, to take a friend to a theatre. The second defendant by his negligence injured the claimant.

Held – as the journey was not on the master's business and the master was not in control, he was not liable for his servant's act.

Vicarious liability at civil law for criminal conduct of employee

289 *Morris v C W Martin & Sons Ltd* [1965] 2 All ER 725

The claimant sent a mink stole to a furrier for the purpose of cleaning. The furrier later told the claimant by telephone that he did not clean furs himself but intended to send the stole to the defendants, one of the biggest cleaners of fur in the country. The claimant knew of Martin & Sons and agreed that the stole be sent to them. Martin & Sons did work only for the fur trade and had issued to the furrier printed conditions which provided that goods belonging to customers were at customer's risk when on the premises of Martin & Sons, and that they should not be responsible for loss or damage however caused, though they would compensate for loss or damage to the goods during the cleaning process by reason of their negligence, but not by reason of any other cause. The furrier knew of these conditions when he handed the stole to the defendants and the defendants knew that it belonged to a customer of the furrier, but they did not know that it was Morris. While in the possession of Martin & Sons, the fur was stolen by a youth named Morrisey, who had been employed by them for a few weeks only, though they had no grounds to suspect that he was dishonest. The claimant sued the defendants for conversion or negligence but the county court judge felt bound by *Cheshire* v *Bailey* [1905] 1 KB 237 and *held* that the act of Morrisey, who had removed the stole by wrapping it round his body, was beyond the scope of his employment. In the Court of Appeal it was *held* that *Cheshire* v *Bailey* (1905) had been impliedly overruled by *Lloyd* v *Grace, Smith & Co* [1912] AC 716 (where it was held that a solicitor was liable for the criminal frauds of his managing clerk so long as the clerk was acting in the apparent scope of his authority). The defendants, as sub-bailees, were liable to the claimant, and on the matter of the exemption clause the Court of Appeal said that the terms of such a clause must be strictly construed, and since they referred only to goods 'belonging to customers' this could be taken to mean goods belonging to the furrier and not to the furrier's customer, and because of this ambiguity the clause was inapplicable.

Comment (i) The above decision applies only to bailees for reward and only in circumstances where the servant is entrusted with, or put in charge of, the bailor's goods by his master. The mere fact that the servant's employment gave him the opportunity to steal the bailor's goods is not enough. Thus, in *Leesh River Tea Co* v *British India Steam Navigation Co* [1966] 3 All ER 593 a stevedore stole a brass cover plate from the hold of a ship when he was unloading tea and the Court of Appeal held that he was not acting in the course of his employment on the ground that his job had nothing to do with the cover plate. Perhaps if the plate had been stolen by someone who was sent to clean it, that person would have been acting within the course of his employment.

(ii) The tortious or criminal act must be committed as part of the employment, i.e. as an act within the scope of the employment. In *Heasmans* v *Clarity Cleaning* [1987] IRLR 286 the Court of Appeal decided that the defendant was not liable when its employee, who was sent to the claimants' premises to clean telephones, made unauthorised telephone calls on them to the value of £1,400. He was employed to clean telephones, not to use them.

Vicarious liability: casual delegation to 'agents'; liability of 'principal'

290 ***Ormrod* v *Crosville Motor Services Ltd* [1953] 2 All ER 753**

By an arrangement between the owner of a motor car and his friend, the friend was to drive the car from Birkenhead to Monte Carlo in order that the owner, the friend and the friend's wife might use the car during their holiday in Monte Carlo. The owner of the car was travelling to Monte Carlo in another car as a competitor in the Monte Carlo Rally. Owing to the friend's negligent driving, the car was involved in a collision in which a motor bus was damaged. The question of the liability of the owner of the car for the damage arose.

Held – the friend was acting as the owner's agent in the matter. The owner had an interest in the arrival of

the car at Monte Carlo, and the driving was done for his benefit. Accordingly, the owner was vicariously liable for his friend's negligence.

291 ***Vandyke* v *Fender* [1970] 2 All ER 335**

Mr Vandyke and Mr Fender were employed by the same company and lived 30 miles from the business premises. The employer agreed to supply a car to Mr Fender and to pay him 50p a day for petrol for the journey. The journey could have been made by train but was more convenient by car. Two other employees who lived in the same area were also carried. On one occasion the car loaned to Mr Fender was not available and he was allowed to use a car belonging to the company secretary. While driving this car, an accident occurred resulting in an injury to Mr Vandyke, who claimed damages from the company. It was *held* that the company was liable because Mr Fender, though not a paid driver, *was driving the car as the company's agent* and it was liable for his negligence. The question then arose as to which of the insurance companies involved should indemnify the company. If the risk was to be borne by the employer's liability insurance, it was necessary to show that the accident occurred during and in the course of Mr Vandyke's employment, otherwise the risk would be borne by a road traffic insurance policy of Mr Fender, which covered him while driving someone else's car. It was *held* – by the Court of Appeal – that a person going to or from work as a passenger in a vehicle provided by his or her employer for that purpose is not in the course of employment unless he or she is obliged by the terms of his employment to travel in that vehicle. If not, then, as here, the liability must be borne by the road traffic insurer and not by the employer's liability insurer.

292 ***Nottingham* v *Aldridge; Prudential Assurance Co* [1971] 2 All ER 751**

In this case a Post Office trainee was returning to his normal work in his father's van after spending the weekend at his home having attended a training course the previous week. He was carrying another trainee, Nottingham, as a passenger and was entitled to a mileage allowance from the Post Office for himself and his passenger. Nottingham was injured as a result of an accident caused by the defendant's negligent driving.

Held – by Eveleigh, J – the Post Office was not liable because the two trainees were not in the course of employment while travelling to work, *nor was Aldridge the agent of the Post Office for the purposes of the journey.*

The vehicle did not belong to the Post Office, nor was it provided by it. The Post Office had not prescribed the method of travel; admittedly a mileage allowance was payable, but travelling expenses of any other kind would have been paid, e.g. bus or train fare. The question of agency was one of fact and on the facts of this case Aldridge was not an agent. The company which had insured the van was, therefore, liable to indemnify Aldridge in respect of his own liability to Nottingham.

293 *Morgans v Launchbury* [1972] 2 All ER 606

In this case the family car was registered in the name of the wife, though it was used mainly by the husband who worked seven miles from home. The wife had asked her husband not to drive the car home himself if he had been drinking. On one occasion the husband had been drinking heavily and asked a friend, C, to drive him home together with three other passengers. There was an accident caused by the negligent driving of C and the husband and he were killed. The three passengers were injured and sued the wife claiming that she was liable vicariously for the negligence of C, who had been appointed to drive on her behalf by her husband. If the wife was held liable, her insurance company would be liable to the claimants. The House of Lords held that she was not liable. The concept of agency required more than mere permission to use. Use must be at the owner's request or on his instructions.

Comment Before 1971 it was not compulsory for road traffic insurance to cover passengers. In fact, Mrs Launchbury had an insurance policy which covered passengers, but only in respect of accidents which occurred while she or her agent was driving. The claimants would have preferred to get their money from the insurance company than to sue the estate of C.

294 *Rambarran v Gurrucharran* [1970] 1 All ER 749

In this case Rambarran, a chicken farmer in Guyana, owned a car which was used by several of his sons, Rambarran himself being unable to drive. One of his sons, Leslie, damaged Gurrucharran's car by negligently driving the family car. The Privy Council found that Rambarran was not liable for Leslie's negligence because he did not know that Leslie had taken the car since he was away from home at his chicken farm at the time in question. Furthermore, there was no evidence to show what the purpose of Leslie's journey was, but it was clearly not for any business or family purpose. Ownership of the vehicle was not enough in itself to establish liability.

295 *Klein v Calnori* [1971] 2 All ER 701

The defendant, Calnori, was the manager of a public house at Sunbury-on-Thames. While he was busy at the bar, a Mr Freshwater, who knew Calnori, took his car and drove it away without his permission. Later Freshwater telephoned Calnori and told him he had taken his car. Calnori told him to bring it back. On the way back to Sunbury, Freshwater collided with Klein's stationary car severely damaging it. Klein alleged that Calnori was liable for this damage because Freshwater was his agent. By asking Freshwater to bring the car back, Freshwater was driving it partly for Calnori's purposes.

Held – by Lyell, J – Calnori was not liable. If Freshwater had borrowed the car with Calnori's consent, then the loan to Freshwater, for his own purposes, would have involved returning it. In these circumstances Calnori would not have been liable for an accident on the return journey. Therefore, Calnori's liability could not be greater in circumstances in which the car had been taken without his consent and had been used solely for the taker's purpose.

Comment A similar result was obtained in *Topp v London Country Bus (South West)* [1993] 1 WLR 976 where a bus belonging to the defendant company was stolen from a public car park, the keys being in the ignition, and was then involved in a collision in which a woman was killed. Her husband sued the bus company in negligence. The Court of Appeal *held* that, although the bus company may have been negligent to leave the bus with the keys in it in an accessible place, it could not be held responsible for the accident as it had occurred through the voluntary act of a third party over whom the company had no control.

Liability for the torts of independent contractors

296 *Bower v Peate* (1876) 1 QBD 321

The claimant and defendant were the respective owners of two adjoining houses, the claimant being entitled to the support for his house of the defendant's land. The defendant employed a contractor to pull down his house and to rebuild it after excavating the foundations. The contractor undertook the risk of supporting the claimant's house during the work and to make good any damage caused. The claimant's house was damaged in the progress of the work because the contractor did not take appropriate steps to support it.

Held – the defendant was liable. The fact that the injury would have been prevented if the contractor had provided proper support did not take away the defendant's liability. A person employing a contractor to perform a duty cast upon himself, in this case a duty of support, is responsible for the contractor's negligence in performing it.

Comment It would appear that any work on a party wall is regarded as giving rise to a special risk of damage for which there may be liability for the negligent work of an independent contractor. The matter was raised again in *Johnson v BJW Property Developments Ltd* [2002] 3 All ER 574. The defendants used an independent contractor to replace a fireplace in a party wall between them and the claimant's premises. The work was done negligently in that the existing firebrick lining was removed and not replaced with fire retardant material. The defendants lit a fire in the new fireplace and it caused a fire and damage to the claimant's premises. The defendants were held liable vicariously for the negligence of the contractor. This was not based on the rule in *Rylands v Fletcher* (see p 603) because that does not apply to the escape of a fire from a domestic fireplace but rather on a rule of the common law relating to work giving rise to a special risk of damage. *Bower v Peate* (above) was quoted in *Johnson* as an example of this rule in connection with work on party walls.

297 *Salsbury v Woodland* [1969] 3 All ER 863

The defendant employed, as an independent contractor, an experienced tree-feller to fell a large tree in his front garden. The contractor was negligent and the tree fell towards the highway bringing down telephone wires on to the highway. A car came along too fast, and the claimant, who was a bystander watching the whole operation, was injured when he dived out of the way of the inevitable collision between the car and the wire.

Held – by the Court of Appeal – the defendant was not liable though the contractor was. There was no special liability in the defendant merely because the contractor was employed to work near, as distinct from on, the highway.

Comment (i) In *Tarry v Ashton* (1876) 1 QBD 314 the defendant employed an independent contractor to carry out repairs to a lamp which, though attached to his house, overhung the highway. The contractor failed to secure the lamp properly and it fell, injuring the claimant. It was held that the defendant was liable because it was his duty to make the lamp safe and he was in breach of that duty because the contractor had not secured the lamp properly.

(ii) The liability of occupiers for hazards on the highway was considered in *Rowe v Herman, The Times*, 9 June 1997. H engaged independent contractors to build a garage at his home. The contractors laid metal plates on the paving stones outside the house to protect them against heavy lorries delivering materials to the site. The contractors failed to remove them after the completion of the job. R, while walking home at night, tripped over the plates and suffered injury. His action against H failed because H had no control over how the contractor did his work or how he cleared up afterwards. H was not under any special duty merely because his premises abutted the highway.

General defences: *volenti non fit injuria*

298 *Simms v Leigh Rugby Football Club* [1969] 2 All ER 923

The claimant was a member of a visiting team playing rugby football on the defendant club's ground when his leg was broken as he was tackled and thrown towards a concrete wall which ran at a distance of 7ft 3ins from the touch line. The League's by-laws prescribed that the distance had to be at least 7ft.

Held – by Wrangham, J – the claimant must be taken willingly to have accepted the risks involved in playing on that field. The ground complied with the by-laws of the Rugby Football League and the defendants were not, therefore, liable under the Occupiers' Liability Act 1957, or in general negligence by reason of the claimant's consent.

Comment (i) In this connection, the decision of the Court of Appeal in *Condon v Basi* [1985] 2 All ER 453 is of interest. In that case the defendant, a non-professional player, made a late and reckless slide tackle upon the claimant resulting in the claimant sustaining a broken right leg and the defendant being sent from the field of play. The county court judge awarded the claimant £4,900 for damages for the injuries sustained and the Court of Appeal dismissed an appeal against that decision. It was decided by the Court of Appeal that participants in competitive sport owe a duty of care to each other to take all reasonable care having regard to the particular circumstances in which the participants are placed. If one participant injures another, he will be liable in negligence for damages at the suit of the injured participant if it is shown that he failed to exercise the degree of care appropriate in all the circumstances or that he acted in a manner to which the injured participant could not have been expected to consent. The law is clearly having to respond to the increasing amount of unnecessary violence in certain sports.

(ii) The rule in *Condon* also applies to professional footballers. Thus, in *Watson v Gray, The Times*, 26 November 1998 the claimant, a professional footballer, suffered injury in terms of a double fracture to his right lower leg following a high tackle on him after the ball had moved on. The defence of *volenti* did not apply and the claimant succeeded in a damages claim.

(iii) Again, in *Smolden v Whitworth, The Times*, 18 December 1996, the defence of *volenti* did not apply where S was seriously injured in an under-19 colts rugby match in the course of which his neck was broken after a scrum collapsed. The referee was held liable as having a duty of care. His conduct had fallen below an acceptable standard in terms of observing rules designed to prevent scrum collapse.

(iv) And, of course, there may be a criminal prosecution as in *R v Lloyd* [1989] Crim LR 513 where L was sentenced to 18 months' imprisonment for kicking an opposing rugby player in the face while he was down, fracturing a cheekbone.

299 *Murray v Harringay Arena Ltd* [1951] 2 KB 529

David Charles Murray, aged six, was taken by his parents to the defendant's ice rink to watch a hockey match. They occupied front seats at the rink, and during the game the boy was hit in the eye by the puck. This action was brought against the defendant for negligence.

Held – the risk was voluntarily undertaken by the claimants. The defendant had provided protection by means of netting and a wooden barrier which, in the circumstances, was adequate, since further protection would have seriously interfered with the view of the spectators.

Comment As the above case shows, it is possible to plead *volenti* against a minor. It is not, however, possible to do so against a person who is mentally disturbed. In *Kirkham v Anderton* [1990] 2 WLR 987 a prisoner was remanded in custody. He had suicidal tendencies known to the police which they failed to pass on to the prison authorities. The prisoner killed himself and a claim for negligence was brought against the police authority. The police authority was held liable and the defence of *volenti* failed.

300 *Hall v Brooklands Auto-Racing Club* [1933] 1 KB 205

The claimant paid for admission to the defendants' premises to watch motor-car races. During one of the races a car left the track, as a result of a collison with another car, and crashed through the railings injuring the claimant. It was the first time that a car had gone through the railings, and in view of that the precautions taken by the defendants were adequate. In this action by the claimant for personal injury, it was *held* that the danger was not one which the defendants ought to have anticipated, and that the claimant must be taken to have agreed to assume the risk of such an accident.

Exclusion clauses: contractual assent and *volenti non fit injuria*: the relationship

301 *Burnett v British Waterways Board* [1973] 1 WLR 700

Burnett was a lighterman working on his employer's barge. Due to the defendant Board's negligence a capstan rope parted while the barge was docking, injuring Burnett. At the dock office was a notice stating that persons availed themselves of the dock facilities at their own risk. Burnett had read the notice when he was a young apprentice. The defendant admitted negligence but claimed that Burnett had voluntarily undertaken the risk of injury.

Held – by the Court of Appeal – Burnett was an employee sent by his employer and it could not be said that he had freely and voluntarily incurred the risk of negligence on the part of the defendant. In the course of his judgment Lord Denning, MR said: 'If there was a contract with Mr Burnett, of course, the Board could rely upon it. But there was no contract with him. He was just one of the men working on the barges. The contract was with the barge owners . . .'.

Comment If the defence of *volenti* succeeds then, of course, the claimant's suit fails.

General defences: *volenti* – the claimant must know of the risk, though knowledge is not necessarily assent

302 *White v Blackmore* [1972] 3 All ER 158

The husband of the claimant widow was a member of a 'jalopy' racing club. He went to a meeting organised by the defendants as a competitor but stood outside the spectators' ropes close to a stake. The wheel of a car caught on one of the ropes some distance away so that the stake was pulled up sharply and the husband was killed when he was catapulted some 20 feet. The defendants displayed notices warning the public of the danger and stating as a condition of admission that they were absolved from all liabilities for accidents howsoever caused. The widow claimed damages for breach of s 2 of the Occupiers' Liability Act 1957 and/or general negligence.

Held – by the Court of Appeal – (*a*) even though the deceased had been negligent in standing where he did, the defence of *volenti* would not succeed as the deceased did not know of the risk that had caused his death; (*b*) however, the claim would fail as the defendants were at that time entitled to exclude their liability and this they had done by warning notices.

Comment The case is still an example of the point that for *volenti* to succeed the claimant must know of the risk. However, it has been overtaken on its own facts by the Unfair Contract Terms Act 1977. Where liability for breach of obligations or duties arises from occupation of premises which are used, as here, for business purposes, a person cannot by reference to any contract term or notice exclude or restrict his liability for death or personal injury resulting from negligence (1977 Act, s 1). In the case of other loss or damage, there can be no exclusion or restriction of liability for negligence unless the term or notice is 'reasonable' (1977 Act, s 2). Finally, the 1977 Act cannot be avoided by raising the defence of *volenti* even if the risk is known (1977 Act, s 3). The above applies to occupiers and to actions in general negligence.

303 *Baker* v *James Bros* [1921] 2 KB 674

The defendants were wholesale grocers and they employed the claimant as a traveller. He was supplied by the defendants with a motor car, the starting gear of which was defective. The claimant repeatedly complained about this to the defendants, but nothing was done to remedy the defect. While the claimant was on his rounds, the car stopped, and he was injured whilst trying to restart.

Held – notwithstanding the claimant's knowledge of the defect, he had never consented to take upon himself the risk of injury from the continued use of the car. He was not guilty of any contributory negligence and was entitled to recover damages.

304 *Dann* v *Hamilton* [1939] 1 KB 509

The claimant had been with a party to see the Coronation decorations in London. They made the journey in the defendant's car. During the day and evening the defendant had consumed a quantity of intoxicating liquor, but he drove the party back to Staines where they all got out. The claimant was at this point a 2d bus ride from her home but she accepted the defendant's invitation to take her there. During this part of the journey there was an accident caused by the defendant's negligence, and the claimant was injured. She now sued in respect of these injuries and the defendant pleaded *volenti non fit injuria*.

Held – the defence did not apply and the claimant succeeded. She had knowledge of a potential danger, but that did not mean that she assented to it.

Comment (i) The court left open the question whether the driver was 'dead drunk' or 'very drunk'. In such a case the maxim might have applied.

(ii) It should be noted that the defence of contributory negligence was not pleaded in *Dann*, although Asquith, J encouraged counsel for the defence to raise it, but he would not be drawn. However, it is now accepted that although *volenti* may not apply in a situation such as *Dann*, a claimant may be guilty of contributory negligence if he travels as a passenger when he knows the driver has consumed enough alcohol to impair his ability to drive safely, or if he goes drinking with the driver knowing he will be a passenger later when the drink deprives him of his own capacity to appreciate the danger (so decided in *Owens* v *Brimmell* [1976] 3 All ER 765).

(iii) In *Pitts* v *Hunt, The Times*, 13 April 1990 it was held that a passenger on a motor cycle could not sue the rider whom he had aided and abetted in illegally driving a motor cycle dangerously after they both got drunk together. Further, in *Morris* v *Murray, The Times*, 18 September 1990 a claimant who knowingly and willingly flew with a pilot who was drunk was not entitled to damages for personal injury. The defence of *volenti* applied in both cases.

305 *Smith* v *Baker and Sons* [1891] AC 325

Smith was employed by Baker and Sons to drill holes in some rock in a railway cutting. A crane, operated by fellow employees, often swung heavy stones over Smith's head while he was working on the rock face. Both Smith and his employers realised that there was a risk the stones might fall, but the crane was nevertheless operated without any warning being given at the moment of jibbing or swinging. Smith was injured by a stone which fell from the crane because of negligent strapping of the load. The House of Lords *held* that Smith had not voluntarily undertaken the risk of his employers' negligence, and that his knowledge of the danger did not prevent his recovering damages.

General defences: *volenti* – actions against employers based on breach of statutory duty

306 *Imperial Chemical Industries Ltd* v *Shatwell* [1964] 2 All ER 999

George and James Shatwell were certificated and experienced shot-firers employed by ICI. Statutory rules imposed an obligation on them personally (not on their employer) to ensure that certain operations connected with shot-firing should not be done unless all persons in the vicinity had taken cover. They knew of the risks of premature explosion which had been explained to them; they knew of the prohibition; but on one occasion because a cable they had was too short to reach the shelter, they decided to test without taking cover rather than wait 10 minutes for their companion Beswick who had gone to fetch a longer cable. James gave George two wires, and George applied them to the galvanometer terminals. An explosion occurred and both men were injured. At the trial it was found that James was guilty of negligence and breach of statutory duty for which the employer was held vicariously liable, damages being assessed at £1,500 on a basis of 50 per cent contributory negligence. The Court of Appeal affirmed, but the House of Lords *reversed*, the decision and *held* that, although James's acts were a contributory cause of the accident to George, the employer was not liable.

(*a*) The employer was not itself in breach of a statutory duty.

(*b*) It could plead *volenti non fit injuria* to a claim of vicarious liability.

(*c*) It had shown no negligence. It had instilled the need for caution, made proper provision, and even arranged a scale of remuneration in a way which removed a temptation to take short cuts.

(*d*) The Shatwell brothers were trained men well aware of the risk involved so the principle of *volenti non fit injuria* applied. Lord Pearce said: 'The defence [of *volenti non fit injuria*] should be available where the employer was not in himself in breach of a statutory duty and was not vicariously in breach of a statutory duty through the neglect of some person of superior rank to the [claimant] and whose commands the [claimant] was bound to obey or who has some special and different duty of care.'

Comment (i) If the employer had been compelled to rely on the defence of contributory negligence, it might have escaped liability if only one man were involved and treated as solely responsible, but where two men were involved, as here, it would have been vicariously liable for James's contribution to George's injury and for George's contribution to James's injury so it would have been compelled partially to compensate each man.

(ii) Deliberate disobedience to regulations and the employer's own orders is not to be excused by impatience to get on with the work. Anyone who does so must be regarded as a volunteer in regard to any resulting injury. That is the gist of this case.

General defences: *volenti* – the rescue cases; generally

307 *Baker v T E Hopkins and Son Ltd* [1959] 3 All ER 966

The defendants were building contractors and were engaged to clean out a well. Various methods had been used in order to pump out the water, including hand-operated pumps, but eventually a petrol-driven pump was employed. The exhaust from the engine on the pump resulted in a lethal concentration of carbon monoxide forming inside the well. Two of the defendants' employees went down the well to carry on the work of cleaning it and were overcome by the fumes. Baker was a local doctor and, on being told what had happened, he went along to give what assistance he could. He was lowered down the well on a rope, and on reaching the two men, he realised that they were beyond help. He then gave a prearranged signal to those at the top of the well and started his journey to the surface. Unfortunately, the rope became caught on a projection and Dr Baker was himself overcome by fumes and died. His executors claimed damages in respect of Dr Baker's death.

Held – the defendants were negligent towards their employees in using the petrol-driven pump and the maxim *volenti non fit injuria* did not bar the claim of Dr Baker's executors. Although Dr Baker may have had knowledge of the risk he was running, he did not freely and voluntarily undertake it, but acted under the compulsion of his instincts as a brave man and a doctor.

Comment In an earlier case, *Haynes v Harwood* [1935] 1 KB 146, a policeman was injured while stopping a runaway horse and van in a crowded street. It was held that he could recover damages. *Volenti* and contributory negligence did not apply.

308 *Cutler v United Dairies (London) Ltd* [1933] 2 KB 297

The defendant's carman left the defendant's horse and van, two wheels being properly chained, while he delivered milk. The horse, being startled by the noise coming from a river steamer, bolted down the road and into a meadow. It stopped in the meadow and was followed there by the carman who, being in an excited state, began to shout for help. The claimant, a spectator, went to the carman's assistance and tried to hold the horse's head. The horse lunged and the claimant was injured. In this action by the claimant against the defendant for negligence it was *held* that in the circumstances the claimant voluntarily and freely assumed the risk. This was not an attempt to stop a runaway horse so that there was no sense of urgency to impel the claimant. He, therefore, knew of the risk and had had time to consider it, and by implication must have agreed to incur it.

Comment Evidence showed negligence in that the horse had bolted before and should not have been used on the milk round at all.

309 *Hyett v Great Western Railway Co* [1948] 1 KB 345

The claimant was employed by a firm of wagon repairers and he was on the defendant's premises with its authority to carry out his duties. While repairing a wagon he saw smoke rising from one of the defendant's wagons in the same siding and went to investigate. The floor of the wagon, which contained paraffin oil, was in flames. The claimant was trying to get the drums of paraffin oil out, when one of them exploded and injured him. Evidence showed that the defendant railway company knew that there was a paraffin leakage in the wagon, but had nevertheless allowed it to remain in the siding.

Held – the claimant was entitled to recover damages from the defendant, and the maxim *volenti non fit injuria* did not apply. A man may take reasonable risks in trying to preserve property put in danger by another's negligence.

General defences: *volenti* – duty to a rescuer

310 *Videan v British Transport Commission* [1963] 2 All ER 860

A child managed to get on to a railway line and was injured by a trolley. The Court of Appeal *held* that the child's presence was not in the circumstances foreseeable and the defendant did not owe him a duty of care. However, a duty was owed to his father who was injured trying to rescue him.

Comment (i) It is difficult to follow the reasoning by which the Court of Appeal held that the defendant ought to have foreseen that a stationmaster would try to rescue a minor on the line (the minor being the son of the stationmaster) yet need not have foreseen the presence of that minor himself.

(ii) The situation where no duty of care is owed to the rescuer is dealt with by *Frost v Chief Constable of South Yorkshire* [1998] 3 WLR 1509.

General defences: *volenti* – defence irrelevant unless the defendant has committed a tort

311 *Wooldridge v Sumner* [1962] 2 All ER 978

A competitor of great skill and experience was riding a horse at a horse show when it ran wide at a corner and injured a cameraman who was unfamiliar with horses and who had ignored a steward's request to move outside the competition area. The rider was thrown, but later rode the horse again and it was adjudged supreme champion of its class. The cameraman brought an action for damages, and at the trial was awarded damages on the ground of negligence.

Held – on appeal, no negligence had been established because (*a*) any excessive speed at the corner was not the cause of the accident, and was not negligence but merely an error of judgement; and (*b*) the judge's finding that the horse would have gone on to a cinder track without harm to the claimant if the rider had allowed it to, was an inference from primary facts and unjustified, and in any event an attempt to control the horse did not amount to negligence.

If, in the course of a game or competition, at a moment when he has not time to think, a participant by mistake takes a wrong measure, he is not to be held guilty of any negligence. . . . A person attending a game or competition takes the risk of any damage caused to him by any act of a participant done in the course of and for the purpose of the game or competition, notwithstanding that such act may involve error of judgement or a lapse of skill, unless the participant's conduct is such as to evince a reckless disregard of the spectator's safety. The spectator takes the risk because such an act involves *no breach of the duty of care* owed by the participant to him. He does not take the risk by virtue of the doctrine expressed or obscured by the maxim *volenti non fit injuria*. . . . The maxim in English law *presupposes a tortious act* by the defendant. The consent that is relevant is not consent to the risk of injury but consent to the lack of reasonable care that may produce that risk. (*Per* Diplock, LJ)

General defences: *volenti* – public policy; duty of care

312 *Nettleship v Weston* [1971] 3 All ER 581

The claimant, a non-professional driving instructor, gave the defendant driving lessons after having first satisfied himself that the car was insured to cover injury to passengers. The defendant was a careful driver but on the third lesson she failed to straighten out after turning left and struck a lamp standard breaking the claimant's kneecap. The defendant was convicted of driving without due care and attention.

Held – by the Court of Appeal – since the claimant had checked on the insurance position, he had expressly not consented to run the risk and there was no question of *volenti*. Furthermore, the duty of care owed by a learner-driver was the same as that owed by every driver and the defendant was liable for the damages. A learner-driver owes a duty to his instructor to drive with proper skill and care, the test being the objective one of the careful driver and it is no defence that he was doing his best.

Comment (i) Nobody would suggest that a learner-driver can do any more than his best. However, the mere fact of learning to drive a motor car is dangerous, at least in its initial stages, and the risk of injury has to be upon the driver. This facilitates an insurance claim by the injured party. In addition, the application of an objective standard of care facilitates a speedier and cheaper settlement of the many road accident cases. These two points mean that in essence the learner-driver's standard is a matter of public policy.

(ii) A passenger who knows that a driver is under the influence of drink or drugs may, if he is injured, be barred from recovering damages on the grounds of *public policy* since he is aiding and abetting a criminal offence. As Megaw, LJ said in this case: 'There may in such cases sometimes be an element of aiding and abetting a criminal offence; or, if the facts fall short of aiding and abetting, the passenger's mere assent to benefit from the commission of a criminal offence may involve questions of *turpis causa*.' The phrase '*turpis causa*' denotes something dishonourable or immoral about the claim.

General defences: inevitable accident

313 *Stanley v Powell* [1891] 1 QB 86

The defendant was a member of a shooting party, and the claimant was employed to carry cartridges and also any game which was shot. The defendant fired at a pheasant, but a shot glanced off an oak tree and injured the claimant.

Held – the claimant's claim failed. The defendant's action was neither intentional nor negligent.

Comment The defence will not apply where the court finds intention or negligence in the defendant. In *Pearson v Lightning, The Times*, 30 April 1998 the eighth and ninth holes of a golf course ran parallel to each other. The defendant was on the eighth fairway and being in the rough had to hit the ball over a coppice of trees. His shot hit a tree and was deflected on to the ninth fairway where it struck the claimant who was injured in the eye. When the defendant saw the ball heading for the claimant he shouted, 'Fore'. The Court of Appeal ruled that the claimant was entitled to damages. Being aware of the position of the fairways, the defendant should have asked the party *before* he made his shot whether he should wait until the party had gone. He did not do so and was liable in negligence, particularly since he knew that he was making a difficult shot.

314 *National Coal Board v Evans (J E) & Co (Cardiff) Ltd and Another* [1951] 2 KB 861

Evans & Co Ltd was engaged by Glamorgan County Council to carry out certain work on land belonging to the Council. It was necessary to excavate a trench across the land, and Evans & Co sub-contracted with the second defendants to do this work. An electric cable passed under the land, but the Council, Evans & Co, and the sub-contractors had no knowledge of this and it was not marked on any available map. During the course of the excavation a mechanical digger damaged the cable so that water seeped into it causing an explosion. The electricity supply to the claimant's colliery was cut off, and it sued the defendants in trespass and negligence. Donovan, J, at first instance, found that the defendants were not negligent, but were liable in trespass. The Court of Appeal *held* that the defendants were entirely free from fault and there was no trespass by them.

General defences: act of God

315 *Nichols v Marsland* (1876) 2 Ex D 1

For many years there had existed certain artificial ornamental lakes on the defendant's land, formed by damming up of a natural stream the source of which was at a point higher up. An extraordinary rainfall 'greater and more violent than any within the memory of witnesses' caused the stream and the lakes to swell to such an extent that the artificial banks burst, and the escaping water carried away four bridges belonging to the county council. Nichols, the county surveyor, sued under the rule in *Rylands v Fletcher* (see Chapter 21).

Held – the defendant was not liable for this extra-ordinary act of nature which she could not reasonably have anticipated. The escape of water was owing to the act of God, and while one is bound to provide against the ordinary operations of nature, one is not bound to provide against miracles.

Comment If the claim had been in negligence, the defendant would not have been liable because she was not negligent. However, the claim was brought under the rule in *Rylands v Fletcher* (see Chapter 21) where liability is strict and negligence is not required, though foresight of consequences may be. Nevertheless, the defendant was not liable because an act of God is a defence to *Rylands* liability.

General defences: necessity

316 *Cresswell v Sirl* [1948] 1 KB 241

The defendant, a farmer's son, was awakened during the night by dogs barking, and on going out found certain ewe sheep in lamb, penned up by the dogs in a corner of a field. The dogs seemed about to attack the sheep and had been chasing them for an hour. A light was turned on the dogs, who then left the sheep and started for the defendant. When they were about 40 yards away, the defendant fired and killed one of the dogs. The owner of the dog sued the defendant for damages. In the county court, judgment was given for the owner of the dog on the ground that such a killing could be justified only if it took place while the dog was actually attacking the sheep. In the view of the Court of Appeal, however, the defendant could justify his act by showing that it was necessary to avert immediate danger to property. It was not necessary that the dog actually be attacking the sheep. This decision is affirmed by s 9 of the Animals Act 1971, which now covers the situation. However, the section requires that the person shooting the dog must have had reasonable grounds to believe that there were no other reasonable means of dealing with the problem or ascertaining the owner. Under s 9 the defendant must notify the police within 48 hours of the killing or injury. Section 9 does not specifically repeal the common law defence in the *Cresswell* case and so the common-law defence may be available instead of s 9 where the police have not been notified.

317 *Cope* v *Sharpe (No 2)* [1912] 1 KB 486

The claimant was a landowner and he let the shooting rights over part of his land to a tenant. A heath fire broke out on part of the claimant's land and the defendant, who was the head gamekeeper of the tenant, set fire to patches of heather between the main fire and a covert in which his master's pheasants were sitting. His object was to prevent the fire spreading. In fact, the fire was extinguished independently of what the defendant had done, and the claimant now sued the defendant for damages for trespass.

Held – the defendant was not liable because when he carried out the act it seemed reasonably necessary, and it did not matter that in the event it turned out to be unnecessary.

Comment (i) In *Rigby* v *Chief Constable of Northampton* [1985] 2 All ER 985, R's shop was burnt out when the police fired a canister of CS gas into the building to force out a dangerous psychopath. R's claim in trespass failed on the ground of the defence of necessity. His claim in negligence succeeded because there was, to the knowledge of the police, no fire-fighting equipment available.

(ii) In *Monsanto plc* v *Tilly* [1999] EGCS 143 the Court of Appeal ruled that the defence of necessity did not apply to the uprooting of genetically modified crops growing under government licence. There was no immediate danger as in *Cresswell* and *Cope* and emergency trespass was not justified where a public authority was responsible for public protection.

(iii) In *Re A (Children) (Conjoined Twins: Medical Treatment) (No 1)* [2001] Fam 147 the Court of Appeal considered an application by the parents of six-week-old Siamese twins appealing against a ruling granting medical staff authority to proceed with surgical separation. One of the twins had a good chance of developing normally. The other had severe brain abnormalities, no lung tissue and no properly functioning heart. The blood supply of this twin emanated from the other and she would inevitably die on separation. The Court of Appeal ruled that the wishes of the parents which were against the separation could not be overriden on the basis of benefit to the children because it was clear that separation would not be beneficial to them both and both interests had to be considered equally. However, permission to go ahead with the separation was granted since the death of one of the twins was inevitable and the operation that would result in the death of one of the twins would not be a crime or actionable at civil law because the defence of necessity would apply. The three constituents of that defence were present, i.e. (a) the act was required to avoid inevitable and irreparable evil; (b) no more would be done than was reasonably necessary for the purpose to be achieved, and (c) the evil to be inflicted was not disproportionate to the evil avoided.

General defences: mistake

318 *Beckwith* v *Philby* (1827) 6 B & C 635

In this case it was *held* that the mistaken arrest of an innocent man on suspicion of an arrestable offence by an ordinary citizen is not actionable as false imprisonment, if the offence has been committed, and if there are reasonable grounds for believing that the person arrested is guilty of it.

General defences: Act of State

319 *Buron* v *Denman* (1848) 2 Exch 167

The captain of a British warship was *held* not liable for trespass when he set fire to the barracoon of a Spaniard slave trader on the West Coast of Africa and released the slaves. The captain had general instructions to suppress the slave trade, and in any case his conduct in this matter was afterwards approved by the Admiralty and the Foreign and Colonial Secretaries. It seems, therefore, that neither the official responsible nor the Crown can be sued for injury inflicted upon others outside the territorial jurisdiction of the Crown, if this is authorised or subsequently ratified by the Crown.

320 *Nissan v Attorney-General* [1967] 2 All ER 1238

The claimant, a British subject, was the tenant of a hotel in Cyprus. In December 1963, the government of Cyprus accepted an offer that British Forces stationed in Cyprus should give assistance in restoring peace to the island. The British troops occupied the claimant's hotel for some months and the claimant now sued the Crown for compensation. It was *held* – *inter alia* that the Crown was obliged to pay compensation and that a plea by the Crown of an 'Act of State' was no defence as against a Britsh subject.

321 *Johnstone v Pedlar* [1921] 2 AC 262

Johnstone was the Chief Commissioner of the Dublin Metropolitan Police. He was the defendant in an action in which Pedlar sued for the detention of £124 in cash and a cheque for £4 15s 6d. Pedlar was convicted of being engaged in the illegal drilling of troops in Ireland, and the above property was found on him at the time of his arrest. Pedlar, who was a naturalised citizen of the United States of America, sued for the return of his property, and the defence was 'Act of State'. A certificate given by the Chief Secretary for Ireland was put in at the trial, certifying that the detention of the property was formally ratified as an Act of State.

Held – Pedlar was entitled to claim his property, because the defence of 'Act of State' cannot be raised against an alien who is a subject of a friendly nation.

General defences: statutory authority

322 *Vaughan v Taff Vale Railway* (1860) 5 H & N 679

The defendants were *held* not liable for fires caused by sparks from engines which they were bound by statute to run and which were constructed with proper care.

Comment (i) By s 1 of the Railway Fires Acts 1905 as amended by s 38 of the Transport Act 1981, railway companies are under a liability of up to £3,000 for damage to crops caused by fire by engines run under statutory authority, though the advent of diesel and electric trains makes the statute somewhat out of date.

(ii) Even if the authority to act is absolute, the damage will not be excused unless it is necessarily incidental. Thus, it is not necessary to the processing of sewage that rivers be polluted. (*Pride of Derby and Derbyshire Angling Association v British Celanese Ltd* [1952] 1 All ER 1326.)

323 *Penny v Wimbledon Urban District Council* [1899] 2 QB 72

The defendant Council, acting under conditional powers conferred upon it by s 150 of the Public Health Act 1875, employed a contractor to make up a road in its district. The contractor removed the surface soil and placed it in heaps on the road. The claimant, while passing along the road in the dark, fell over one of the heaps, which had been left unlighted and unguarded, and was injured. She now sued for damages.

Held – she succeeded. Although the Council was operating under statutory powers it must, if it does acts likely to cause danger to the public, see that the work is properly carried out, and take reasonable measures to guard against danger. The Council did not discharge this duty by delegating it to a contractor, and the local authority was liable for negligence.

324 *Marriage v East Norfolk Rivers Catchment Board* [1950] 1 KB 284

In pursuance of their powers under s 34 of the Land Drainage Act 1930, the Catchment Board deposited dredgings taken from the river on the south bank of that river, so raising its height by one to two feet. When the river next flooded, the flood waters instead of escaping over the south bank, as they had always done, ran over the north bank and swept away a bridge leading to a mill owned by the claimant. Section 34(3) of the Land Drainage Act 1930 provided that, in the event of injury to any person by reason of the exercise by a drainage board of any of its powers, the board concerned should make full compensation, disputes being settled by a system of arbitration. The claimant had issued a writ (now claim form) for nuisance against the board.

Held – no action in nuisance lay; the claimant's only remedy was to claim compensation under s 34(3).

Remoteness of damage: the foresight test

325 *Overseas Tankship (UK) Ltd v Morts Dock and Engineering Co Ltd (The Wagon Mound)* [1961] AC 388

The appellant was the charterer of a ship called the *Wagon Mound*. While the ship was taking on furnace oil in Sydney harbour, the appellant's servants negligently allowed oil to spill into the water. The action of the wind and tide carried this oil some 200 yards and over to the respondent's wharf where the business of shipbuilding and repairing was carried on. The servants of the respondent were at this time engaged in repairing a vessel, the *Corrimal*, which was moored alongside the wharf, and for this purpose they were using welding equipment. The manager of the respondent, seeing the oil on the water, suspended welding operations and consulted the wharf manager who told him it was safe to continue work – a decision which was justified, because previous knowledge showed that sparks were not likely to set fire to oil floating on water. Work, therefore, proceeded with safety precautions being taken. However, a piece of molten metal fell from the wharf and set on fire a piece of cotton waste which was floating on the oil. This set the oil alight and the respondent's wharf was badly damaged. The case eventually came before the Judicial Committee of the Privy Council on appeal.

Held – the appellant was successful in its appeal, the Judicial Committee holding that foreseeability of the actual harm resulting was the proper tort test. On this principle, the Privy Council *held* that the damage caused by the fire was too remote, though it would have awarded damages for the fouling of the respondent's slipways by oil, if such a claim had been made, since this was foreseeable.

Comment In *Overseas Tankship (UK) Ltd v Miller Steamship Property Ltd (The Wagon Mound (No 2))* [1966] 2 All ER 709, the same blaze had caused damage to the respondent's ship (it was the owner of the *Corrimal*). However, the members of the Privy Council had by this time the decision of the House of Lords in *Hughes v Lord Advocate* (1963) (see below) before them. It said that the precise nature of the particular injury suffered need not be foreseeable so long as it was one of a kind that was foreseeable, i.e. within the *band* of reasonable foreseeability. Therefore, the respondent recovered damages in negligence and also nuisance. The Privy Council held that in the case of nuisance, as of negligence, it is not enough that the damage was a direct result of the nuisance if the injury was not foreseeable.

326 *Hughes v Lord Advocate* [1963] 1 All ER 705

Workmen opened a manhole in the street and later left it unattended having placed a tent above it and warning paraffin lamps around it. The claimant and another boy, who were aged eight and 10 respectively, took one of the lamps and went down the manhole. As they came out, the lamp was knocked into the hole and an explosion took place injuring the claimant. The explosion was caused in a unique fashion because the paraffin had vaporised (which was unusual) and been ignited by the naked flame of the wick. The defendants argued that although some injury by burning was foreseeable, burning by explosion was not.

Held – by the House of Lords – the defendants were liable. 'The cause of this accident was a known source of danger, the lamp, but it behaved in an unpredictable way. . . . This accident was caused by a known source of danger but caused in a way which could not have been foreseen and in my judgment that affords no defence.' (*Per* Lord Reid) 'The accident was but a variant of the foreseeable. It was, to quote the words of Denning, LJ in *Roe v Minister of Health* [see Chapter 21], "within the risk created by the negligence". . . . The children's entry into the tent with the ladder, the descent into the hole, the mishandling of the lamp, were all foreseeable. The greater part of the path to injury had thus been trodden, and the mishandled lamp was quite likely at this stage to spill and cause a conflagration. Instead, by some curious chance of combustion, it exploded and no conflagration occurred, it would seem, until after the explosion. There was thus an unexpected manifestation of the apprehended physical dangers. But it would be, I think, too narrow a view to hold that those who created the risk of fire are excused from the liability for the damage by fire because it came by way of explosive combustion. The resulting damage, though severe, was not greater than or different in kind from that which might have been produced had the lamp spilled and caused a more normal conflagration in the hole.' (*Per* Lord Pearce)

Comment (i) A good illustration of the rule in *Hughes* that the *precise* mechanics of the way in which harm occurs need not be foreseen if it is within the risk caused by the negligence appears in *Draper v Hodder* [1972] 2 All ER 210. The defendant owned 30 Jack Russell terriers which he kept on his ungated premises. The dogs could run into a nearby house which was owned by the claimant's parents. That house was also ungated. On one occasion the dogs ran into the yard of the nearby house and one or more of them attacked the claimant, a three-year-old boy and bit him. His action for damages succeeded. It was foreseeable immediately that the dogs would bowl over and scratch the child. Nevertheless, the fact that one or more of them bit him was within the risk created by the negligence.

(ii) In spite of the more liberal attitude taken to foresight in *Hughes*, some things are still too remote as consequences. For example, in *Meah v McCreamer (No 2)* [1986] 1 All ER 943 the claimant had been injured in a car accident by reason of the defendant's negligence. The claimant alleged that he had suffered a personality change leading to him attacking women. He raped one and indecently assaulted another. The women recovered damages against him and he tried to recover them from the defendant. It was held that the alleged damage was too remote.

(iii) As regards damages for rape, it was held in *Meah* that these should be similar to those awarded in general personal injury cases. However, in *Griffiths v Williams, The Times*, 24 November 1995 the Court of Appeal decided that since attitudes to rape had changed, it was now in a different category to ordinary personal injury and higher awards could be made. The claimant's appeal against an award of £50,000 to his victim failed.

(iv) The decision of the House of Lords in *Jolley v Sutton LBC* [2000] 1 WLR 1082 should be noted. The case was brought under the Occupiers' Liability Act 1957 (see Chapter 21). The Council allowed a derelict abandoned boat to remain on its land outside a block of flats which it owned. J and another boy jacked the boat up and went underneath it to effect repairs. The boat fell on J and rendered him paraplegic. The Council contended that it was only foreseeable that children would *play* in the boat and not attempt to *repair* it. The House of Lords held that what the boys had done was, after a consideration of *The Wagon Mound* and *Hughes*, within the band of foreseeability so that the Council was liable to J.

Remoteness of damage: the unusual claimant rule

327 *Smith* v *Leech Braine & Co Ltd* [1962] 2 WLR 148

The claimant was the widow of a person employed by the defendant. Mr Smith's work consisted of lowering articles into a galvanising tank containing molten zinc. On one occasion he was struck on the lip by a piece of molten metal which caused a burn. This resulted in a cancer from which he died three years later. Mr Smith's work had given him a predisposition to cancer and the question arose whether, since *The Wagon Mound*, the so-called 'thin skull rule' had disappeared, so that the claimant had to show that the cancer was foreseeable. The Lord Chief Justice, Lord Parker, finding for the claimant, said in the course of his judgment: 'I am satisfied that the Judicial Committee of the Privy Council did not have what are called "thin skull" cases in mind. It has always been the common law that a tortfeasor must take his victim as he finds him.'

328 *Martindale* v *Duncan* [1973] 1 WLR 674

The claimant's car was damaged in a collision with the defendant's car because of the negligence of the defendant. The claimant delayed repairs to his car pending the approval of the defendant's insurer and also of his own. The defendant's insurer wished to seek the advice of independent engineers and did so.

About nine weeks after the accident, the defendant's insurer approved the estimate. A few days later the claimant's insurer did so and the repairs were started one week afterwards. The District Registrar awarded the claimant damages including £220 for loss of use of his vehicle for 10 weeks at the rate of £22 per week for hire of a substitute vehicle to cover the period during which he had delayed repairs pending approval of the estimate by the insurers. The defendant had argued that the repairs were not commenced as early as they could have been since the claimant was not himself able to pay for the repairs but had to wait to see what the position was as regards payment from an insurance company. On appeal by the defendant it was *held* – by the Court of Appeal, dismissing the appeal – that the claimant was not in breach of his duty to mitigate his loss and had acted reasonably in the circumstances.

329 *Morgan* v *T Wallis* [1974] 1 Lloyd's Rep 165

Mr Morgan, a lighterman on the River Thames, sustained back injuries in trying to avoid a wire rope thrown by a stevedore on to a barge where Mr Morgan was working. Liability for his injuries was admitted by the defendants, his employers, because they should have had a better system of working, but the amount of damages was disputed because Mr Morgan unreasonably refused to undergo tests and an operation because he genuinely feared both of these things. The highest estimate by a surgeon of the chances of success of such an operation was 90 per cent. It was *held* – by Browne, J – that the defendants had proved that Mr Morgan's refusal was unreasonable as to the investigations and that the operation would have been successful on a balance of probabilities. Where there was no prior disability, physical, mental or psychological, a defendant did not have to take a claimant as he found him.

Remoteness of damage: intended damage never too remote: *novus actus interveniens*: act of a third party expected

330 *Scott* v *Shepherd* (1773) 2 Wm Bl 892

On the evening of a fair-day at Milborne Port, Shepherd threw a lighted squib on to the market stall of one Yates, who sold gingerbread. Then one Willis, in order to protect the wares of Yates, threw it away and it landed on the stall of one Ryal. He threw it to another part of the market house where it struck the claimant in the face, exploded and put out his eye.

Held – Shepherd was liable for the injuries to Scott because he intended the initial act and there was no break in the chain of causation. Shepherd should have anticipated that Willis and Ryal would act as they did.

Comment The decision in this case is initially difficult to understand because Shepherd did not injure the claimant. It would seem that since battery is also a crime the maxim of the criminal law that a person intends the natural consequences of his acts was applied to produce the 'transferred intent' of the type seen in criminal cases.

Remoteness of damage: *novus actus* not materially causing or contributing to injury

331 *Barnett* v *Chelsea and Kensington Hospital Management Committee* [1968] 1 All ER 1068

Mr Barnett drank tea which had, unknown to him, been contaminated with arsenic. He attended at the casualty department of a hospital saying that he had been vomiting for some three hours after drinking the tea. The casualty doctor failed to examine him but sent a message that he should report to his own doctor. Some five hours later Mr Barnett died and on his widow's action for damages, it was *held* that the hospital authority owed a duty of care and that the doctor was negligent in failing to examine and admit Mr Barnett and accordingly there had been a breach of that duty. However, on the facts the deceased's condition was such that he must have died despite any medical attention which the hospital could have given so that causation was not established and the widow's claim failed.

332 *Robinson* v *The Post Office*, *The Times*, 26 October 1973

The claimant suffered a minor injury for which the defendant, his employer, admitted liability. As a result, the claimant received an anti-tetanus injection which produced a rare complication of encephalitis, with grave consequences. Ashworth, J *held* that the doctor had acted negligently in administering the injection in that he had failed to administer a test dose. However, it appeared that even if such a test had been made the claimant would have shown no reaction to it. Thus, the doctor's negligence had had no causative effect, since even with the proper precautions the encephalitis would not have been prevented. The defendant appealed and it was *held* – by the Court of Appeal – that the judge's conclusions on the question of the medical negligence were correct and that accordingly the defendant could not rely on

that negligence as a *novus actus interveniens*. It was, therefore, liable for all the claimant's disabilities, and the contention that these were too remote was to be rejected.

Remoteness of damage: duty to guard against *novus actus*

333 *Davies* v *Liverpool Corporation* [1949] 2 All ER 175

The claimant was trying to board a tramcar belonging to the defendant Corporation at a request stopping place. An unauthorised person (a passenger) rang the bell, whereupon the car started, throwing the claimant off the platform and causing her injury. The conductor was on the upper deck collecting fares. Evidence showed that the car had been standing at the request stop for an appreciable time, and that the conductor had been upstairs for the whole of that time, though it was not a particularly busy period. In this action for negligence brought by the claimant, it was *held* that the defendant was liable for the negligent act of the conductor. He should have foreseen that if he was absent from the platform of the car for an appreciable time, some passenger might ring the bell. The act of the passenger did not, therefore, break the chain of causation because it was just that sort of act which the conductor was employed to prevent.

Remoteness of damage: *novus actus* not anticipated by defendant

334 *Cobb* v *Great Western Railway* [1894] AC 419

The railway company allowed a railway carriage to become overcrowded, and because of this the claimant was hustled and robbed of £89. He now sued the company in respect of his loss.

Held – this was too remote a consequence of the defendant's negligence. The robbery was a *novus actus interveniens* breaking the chain of causation.

Comment In *Stansbie* v *Troman* [1948] 2 KB 48 the owner of a house was obliged to leave a painter working alone on the premises. The owner told the painter to shut the front door when he left the house, but in fact the painter left the house empty for about two hours in order to obtain some wallpaper and left the door unlocked. It was held that the painter was liable for the loss of jewellery stolen by a third party who entered the house in his absence because this was foreseeable as being just the kind of thing which might happen in the situation. It is difficult to reconcile *Stansbie* with *Cobb* and this leads to the suggestion that *Cobb* may no longer be good law, though it has never been overruled.

Remoteness of damage: *novus actus* may be that of the claimant

335 *Sayers* v *Harlow UDC* [1958] 2 All ER 342

The defendant Council owned and operated a public lavatory. The claimant having paid for admission entered a cubicle. Finding that there was no handle on the inside of the door, and no means of opening the cubicle, the claimant had tried for some 10 to 15 minutes to attract attention. Having failed to do so, and wishing to catch a bus to London in the next few minutes, she tried to see if there was a way of climbing out. She placed one foot on the seat of the lavatory and rested her other foot on the toilet roll and fixture, holding the pipe from the cistern with one hand and resting the other hand on the top of the door. She then realised it would be impossible to climb out, and she proceeded to come down, but as she was doing so, the toilet roll rotated owing to her weight on it and she slipped and injured herself. She sued the defendant for negligence. In the county court the defendant was found negligent, but, as the claimant was in no danger on that account, and as she chose to embark on a dangerous act, she must bear the consequences. It was *held* – by the Court of Appeal – that her act was not a *novus actus interveniens*, and the damage was not too remote a consequence of the defendant's negligence. She was 36 years of age, and in her predicament her act was not unreasonable, though if she had been an old lady it might have been. However, the damages recoverable by the claimant would be reduced by one-quarter in respect of her share of the responsibility for the damage.

336 *McKew* v *Holland and Hannen and Cubitts (Scotland) Ltd* [1969] 2 All ER 1621

McKew sustained an injury during the course of his employment for which his employer was liable. The injury caused him occasionally and unexpectedly to lose the use of his left leg. On one occasion he left a flat and started to descend some stairs which had no handrail. His leg gave way and he sustained further injury.

Held – by the House of Lords – his conduct in trying to descend the stairs was unreasonable and thus broke the chain of causation. The subsequent injury was, therefore, too remote and the employer was not liable.

Remoteness of damage: *novus actus* – the intervener must intend the act

337 *Philco Radio Corporation* v *Spurling* [1949] 2 All ER 882

Certain packing cases containing inflammable film scrap were delivered in error by the defendants to the claimant's premises. No warning as to their contents was given on the cases. The cases were opened by the claimant's servants, and a foreman recognised the contents as inflammable, and gave instructions that the scrap was to be replaced, and that there was to be no smoking in the vicinity. He telephoned the defendants and arranged to have the cases delivered to their proper destination, 150 yards away. Before the cases had been moved, a typist employed by the claimant negligently set light to the scrap with a cigarette, and it exploded causing damage. The defendants pleaded that the proximate cause of the damage was the typist's act and that the chain of causation was broken.

Held – the defendants were negligent in not ensuring that such dangerous material was properly delivered. The act of the typist did not break the chain of causation; she did not intend to injure her employer, and when she approached the scrap with a cigarette she did so as a joke. Her act was not such a conscious act of violation as to relieve the defendants from liability, and in any case the act formed part of the very risk that was envisaged.

Remoteness of damage: nervous shock

338 *Dulieu* v *White* [1901] 2 KB 669

The defendant who was driving a van negligently, ran into a public house. The claimant, who was pregnant, was in the public house and because of the shock became ill and gave birth to a premature and mentally deficient child. It was *held* that she could recover damages.

339 *Chadwick* v *British Railways Board* [1967] 1 WLR 912

A serious railway accident was caused by negligence for which the Board was liable. A volunteer rescue worker suffered nervous shock and became psychoneurotic as a result. The claimant, as administratrix of his estate, claimed damages for nervous shock. It was *held* that:

(a) damages were recoverable for nervous shock even though the shock was not caused by fear for one's own safety or that of one's children;

(b) in the circumstances injury by shock was foreseeable;

(c) the defendant ought to have foreseen that volunteers might attempt rescue and accordingly owed a duty of care to those who did.

Comment (i) If the deceased had merely read of this accident to strangers in his newspaper, there would have been no claim for nervous shock if this had resulted.

(ii) It should be noted that in *Chadwick* and the other cases of nervous shock there was an illness following upon the shock. A contrast is provided by the decision of the Court of Appeal in *Nicholls* v *Rushton, The Times*, 19 June 1992, where the claimant had been in a road traffic accident but suffered no physical injury. He experienced a nervous reaction which fell short of a psychological illness. He was not entitled to damages. The Court of Appeal said there were no damages for 'shock and shaking up' without more.

(iii) *Chadwick* v *British Railways Board* (1967) was held to be correctly decided but distinguished in *White* v *Chief Constable of South Yorkshire* [1999] 1 All ER 1. The case involved claims by police officers for nervous shock following their involvement as rescuers in the Hillsborough football stadium disaster. There was, said the House of Lords, no liability to the officers. A rescuer, it said, is not placed in any special position as regards liability for nervous shock merely by reason of the fact that he was a rescuer unless, as in *Chadwick*, he had exposed himself to danger or reasonably believed that he was doing so. In *Chadwick* the claimant was exposed to danger by trying to rescue passengers in a train which might have caught fire or toppled over on him and so on. The police officers at Hillsborough were not in danger as such. The danger was past. It follows that a person who suffers nervous shock or psychiatric injury caused by witnessing or participating in the aftermath of an accident that has caused death or injury to others cannot recover damages unless he was himself in danger or fear of it.

340 *Hinz v Berry* [1970] 1 All ER 1074

Mrs Hinz witnessed a car accident in which her husband was killed and her children injured. The accident was caused by the negligent driving of the defendant. As a result of seeing the accident Mrs Hinz, who had been a vigorous and lively woman, became morbid and depressed for years afterwards.

Held – by the Court of Appeal – she was entitled to damages of £4,000 for nervous shock. She was a woman of robust character who would probably have stood up to the strain if she had not *seen* the accident.

Somehow or other the court has to draw a line between sorrow and grief for which damages are not recoverable, and nervous shock and psychiatric illness for which damages are recoverable. The way to do this is to estimate how much the claimant would have suffered if, for instance, her husband had been killed in an accident when she was 50 miles away, and compare it with what she is now, having suffered all the shock due to being present at the accident. The evidence shows that she suffered much more by being present. (*Per* Lord Denning, MR)

341 *Hambrook v Stokes* [1925] 1 KB 141

The defendant left his lorry unattended on a sloping street and, because of his negligence in failing to brake the vehicle properly, it began to run away. The claimant's wife had just left her children further down the street though they were in fact round a bend and not within her view. However, she saw the lorry moving and suffered shock, which resulted in her death, because she feared for the safety of her children. Her husband brought this action for loss of her services and was *held* entitled to recover damages provided that the shock was brought about by his wife's own experience and not by the accounts of bystanders.

342 *McLoughlin v O'Brian* [1982] 2 All ER 278

The claimant's husband and three children were involved in a road accident caused by the negligence of the defendant. One child was killed and the husband and the other two children were badly injured. At the time of the accident the claimant was at home two miles away and was told of the accident by a neighbour and taken to hospital where she saw the injured members of her family and the extent of their injuries and shock, and heard that her daughter had been killed. As a result of hearing and seeing the results of the accident, the claimant suffered severe and persisting nervous shock and brought this action against the defendant for negligence. It was *held* by the Court of Appeal that the claim failed. Even though the claimant's nervous shock was a reasonably foreseeable consequence of the defendant's negligence, in accordance with precedent and social policy the duty of care owed by a driver of a motor vehicle was limited to persons and owners of property on the road or near it who might be directly affected by the driver's negligent driving and accordingly the defendant did not owe a duty of care to the claimant because she had not been in the physical proximity of the accident when it occurred.

The House of Lords reversed the Court of Appeal and upheld the claimant's claim, even though she was two miles from the accident. The argument that this would open the floodgates to many claims by people who had not actually seen the accident, which was a former restriction on claims of this sort, did not deter their Lordships. They all agreed that the claimant's nervous shock was a foreseeable event producing an identifiable mental illness. However, that part of the decision in *Hinz v Berry* (above) which says that nervous shock does not cover sorrow or grief was upheld.

Comment (i) If the floodgates ever did open, they were closed by the Court of Appeal in *Alcock v Chief Constable of South Yorkshire, The Times*, 6 May 1991. The case was brought following the disaster at Hillsborough football ground at Sheffield where it was alleged that the police let too many people get into the ground causing those in front of them to be crushed against railings and barricades. It was held that only the parents and spouses of the victims could recover damages for nervous shock and then only if they had actually seen the accident by being at the ground or identified bodies afterwards. Parents and spouses who had only seen the disaster by viewing it on a simultaneous TV broadcast could not get damages. The decision was affirmed by the House of Lords. (See *Alcock v Chief Constable of South Yorkshire, The Times*, 29 November 1991.) The decisions in *Frost v Chief Constable of South Yorkshire Police* (1996) and *White v Chief Constable of South Yorkshire* (1999) have already been noted as *not* putting police rescuers who were not related to the Hillsborough victims in a special category as rescuers and, therefore, unable to recover damages for nervous shock.

(ii) However, it was held in *Attia v British Gas plc* [1987] 3 All ER 456 that damages for nervous shock could be recovered where it was caused by damage to property. It need not result from the death or injury of a person. The claimant's shock in this case arose when, on returning home, she saw the whole of her house on fire as a result of the defendant's negligence.

(iii) There have been further developments as follows. It was held in *Vernon v Bosley, The Times*, 4 April 1996 by the Court of Appeal that a father (V) who witnessed the aftermath of an accident caused by B's negligent driving in which V's two children died could recover for nervous shock and obtain further damages for grief and bereavement of a normal kind. V was clearly suffering from mental illness as a result of what he had seen and it was not necessary, if indeed it was possible, to say that one part of his mental state was due to what he had seen and some other part was due to normal grief and bereavement.

(iv) The above ruling was not applied in *Greatorex v Greatorex, The Times*, 6 June 2000. In that case the claimant was a fire officer who went to the scene of a car accident in which the defendant, his son, was trapped following an accident *caused by the son's negligent driving while under the influence of alcohol*. The father suffered severe post-traumatic stress disorder, though his son was later released from the car and recovered. The High Court ruled that the claimant failed. There was no duty of care owed by the *victim of a self-inflicted injury* to a secondary party in these circumstances. In effect, the son's insurer was not liable because the son was not.

(v) In *Robertson v Forth Road Bridge Joint Board*, 1996 SLT 263 it was held that two friends of a worker whom they saw blown off the Forth Bridge to his death could not recover for nervous shock. They were not within the *Alcock* categories of secondary victims.

(vi) More importantly, perhaps, the House of Lords has decided that where the claimant is *not a witness but the primary victim*, if the accident is foreseeable, so is that element of damage from it which can be put down to nervous shock; see *Page v Smith* [1995] 2 WLR 644 where the claimant was involved in an accident with a car driven negligently by the defendant. Page suffered no physical injury but the accident worsened his previous nervous state. As the House of Lords said, if it was reasonably foreseeable that the claimant might suffer personal injury as a result of the defendant's negligence, it was not necessary to ask a separate question as to whether the defendant should have foreseen injury by shock. The House of Lords ruling in no way changes the rules relating to *witnesses who are secondary victims*.

(vii) The control mechanisms set out in *Alcock* continue to be applied in these cases. Thus in *Keen v Tayside Contracts* 2003 SLT 500 Mr Keen was a roadworker. He was instructed by his employers to set up a road diversion at the scene of a road accident. While doing this he became aware that there were four crushed and burned bodies in a car. He developed post-traumatic stress disorder and claimed damages against the employer for exposing him to the accident scenario and failing to provide debriefing to enable him to come to terms with what he had seen. His case failed largely because he had no close ties of love and affection with the victims, which is one of the *Alcock* control mechanisms.

Remoteness of damage: nervous shock – there must be a duty of care

343 *Hay (or Bourhill)* **v** *Young* [1943] AC 92

The claimant, a pregnant Edinburgh fishwife, alighted from a tramcar. While she was removing her fish-basket from the tram, Young, a motor cyclist, driving carelessly but unseen by her, passed the tram and collided with a motor car some 15 yards away. Young was killed. The claimant heard the collision, and after Young's body had been removed, she approached the scene of the accident and saw a pool of blood on the road. She suffered a nervous shock and later gave birth to a stillborn child. The House of Lords *held* that her action against Young's personal representative failed, because Young owed no duty of care to persons whom he could not reasonably anticipate would suffer injury as a result of his conduct on the highway.

344 *Owens* v *Liverpool Corporation* [1939] 2 KB 394

A funeral procession was making its way to the cemetery when a negligently driven tram owned by the defendant collided with the hearse and overturned the coffin. Several mourners who were following in a carriage suffered shock and it was *held* by the Court of Appeal that they were entitled to damages.

Remoteness of damage: successive accidents and supervening events

345 *Jobling* v *Associated Dairies* [1980] 3 All ER 769

The claimant, an employee in a butcher's shop, suffered a partially disabling accident at work in 1973. In 1976 before the trial in regard to that accident came on, the claimant was found to be suffering from a totally disabling but unconnected condition. At the trial in 1979 the judge took no account of the supervening disability. On appeal on amount of damages it was *held* – allowing the appeal – that where a claimant was subsequently injured by a non-tortious act, the tortfeaser's damages were to be reduced by the extent of the claimant's further injuries and consequent loss. *Baker* v *Willoughby* (1969) (below) should not be extended further.

346 *Baker* v *Willoughby* [1969] 3 All ER 1528

In September 1964, the claimant was involved in an accident on the highway caused by the negligent driving of the defendant, but attributable as to one-quarter to the claimant's contributory negligence. The claimant received serious injuries to his left leg, but after long hospital treatment he took up employment with a scrap metal merchant. On 29 November 1967, while in the course of his employment, the claimant was the innocent victim of an armed robbery receiving gunshot wounds necessitating the immediate amputation of his left leg, which was already defective because of the previous accident. The question of the amount of damages for the claimant's injuries in the road accident of September 1964 came before the court for assessment in February 1968.

Held – by the Court of Appeal – no consequence of the accident of September 1964 survived the amputation

of the claimant's left leg and the defendant was liable only for loss suffered by the claimant up to 29 November 1967. Damages are compensation for loss arising from a tortious act and cease when by reason of recovery, supervening disease, or further injury there is no continuing loss attributable to that act.

The House of Lords, [1969] 3 All ER 1528, reversed the Court of Appeal decision holding that damages are not merely compensation for physical injury but for the loss which the injured person suffers. This loss was not diminished by the supervening event and the second injury was irrelevant. 'The supervening event has not made the appellant less lame nor less disabled nor less deprived of amenities. It has not shortened the period over which he will be suffering. It has made him more lame, more disabled, more deprived of amenities. He should not have less damages through being worse off than he might have expected . . .' (*Per* Lord Pearson, LJ)

Comment *Holtby* v *Brigham & Cowan (Hull) Ltd* (2000) (see p 525) may perhaps be distinguished. In that case the existing injury was merely *aggravated* by the continuing employment – it was not a *different* injury.

347 *Performance Cars Ltd* v *Abraham* [1961] 3 All ER 413

The claimant owned a motor car which was damaged in a collision with a car driven by the defendant. The damage to the claimant's car was such that it would necessitate respraying the whole of the lower body. Two weeks before the accident the claimant's car had been involved in another collision which had also made respraying of the lower body of the car necessary. The claimant obtained judgment against the driver responsible for the first collision, but that judgment was not satisfied and the car had not been resprayed at the time when the second collision took place. The court was asked to decide whether the claimant was entitled to recover as damages from the defendant the cost of respraying the lower body of its car.

Held – by the Court of Appeal – the claimant was not entitled to recover the cost of respraying from the defendant because that damage was not the result of his wrongful act.

Limitation of actions: fraudulent or negligent concealment of claim

348 *Beaman* v *ARTS* [1949] 1 All ER 465

In November 1935, Mrs Beaman, before leaving for Istanbul, deposited with the defendant company several packages to be sent to her as soon as she gave notice requesting it. In May 1936, the defendant at her request dispatched one of the packages, but afterwards regulations made by the Turkish authorities prevented dispatch of the other packages and Mrs Beaman asked the defendant to keep them in store pending further instructions. Three years later the defendant, not having received instructions, wrote and asked the claimant to insure the contents of the packages. She did not do so but replied saying that she was hoping to return to England. However, the outbreak of war while she was still in Turkey prevented this.

On the entry of Italy into the war in 1940 the defendant, being a company controlled by Italian nationals, had its business taken over by the Custodian of Enemy Property. Wishing to wind up the business as soon as possible, the manager of ARTS Ltd examined the packages, reported that they were of no value, and gave them to the Salvation Army. No steps were taken to obtain the claimant's consent. The claimant returned to England in 1946 and commenced proceedings more than six years after the packages were disposed of, claiming damages for conversion. The defendant set up the defence that the action was barred by the Limitation Act. The claimant relied on what is now s 32 of the Limitation Act 1980, which provides that where '(*a*) the action is based on fraud of the defendant . . . or (*b*) the right of action is concealed by the fraud of any such person . . . the period of limitation shall not begin to run until the [claimant] has discovered the fraud . . .'.

Held:

(*a*) The action for conversion was not 'based on fraud', so that what is now s 32(1)(a) had no application.

(*b*) The conduct of the defendant constituted a reckless 'concealment by fraud' of the right of action within what is now s 32(1)(b). Therefore, the claimant's action was not barred.

Comment (i) It appears that it is not necessary to prove a degree of moral turpitude to establish fraud for the purposes of s 32. Thus, in *Kitchen v Royal Air Force Association* [1958] 1 WLR 563, solicitors negligently concealed a payment of money on behalf of the claimant and this conduct was held to amount to 'fraud' for the purposes of what is now s 32, even though the court accepted that the solicitors were not dishonest.

(ii) Reference should also be made at this point to *Sheldon v HM Outhwaite* [1995] 2 All ER 558 where the House of Lords decided that the normal period of six years governing the start of legal claims can be extended where information relevant to the possible claim is deliberately concealed *after* the period of six years has started to run.

SPECIFIC TORTS

Trespass to the person: words may prevent an assault

349 *Turbervell v Savage* (1669) 2 Keb 545

In this old case a man laid his hand menacingly on his sword, but at the same time said, 'If it were not assize time I would not take such language from you.'

Held – this was not an assault because it was assize time, and there was no reason to fear violence.

Trespass to the person: battery may arise from a failure to act

350 *Fagan v Metropolitan Police Commissioner* [1968] 3 All ER 442

Fagan was driving his car when he was told by a constable to draw into the kerb. He stopped his car with one wheel on the constable's foot and was slow in restarting the engine and moving the vehicle off. He was convicted of assault on the constable and Quarter Sessions dismissed his appeal. He then appealed to the Queen's Bench Divisional Court where it was *held* – dismissing his appeal – that whether or not the mounting of the wheel on the constable's foot had been intentional, the defendant had deliberately allowed it to remain there when asked to move it, and that constituted an assault. The decision seems to extend the law because there was no act but merely an omission. Furthermore, there was no intentional application of force but only a failure to withdraw it. A more appropriate charge might have been false imprisonment because the constable could not presumably have moved while the wheel remained on his foot.

Comment This was a criminal prosecution for assault, an expression which is commonly used to mean battery also. In strict civil law terms, the trespass to the policeman was a battery.

Trespass to the person: is not actionable in itself: the claimant must prove intention or negligence

351 *Fowler v Lanning* [1959] 1 All ER 290

By a writ (now claim form) the claimant claimed damages for trespass to the person. In his statement of claim (now statement of case) he alleged that on 19 November 1957, at Vineyard Farm, Corfe Castle, in the County of Dorset, the defendant shot the claimant. By reason of the premises, the claimant sustained personal injury and suffered loss and damage;

particulars of the claimant's injuries were then set out. The defendant denied the allegations of fact and objected that the statement of claim disclosed no cause of action, because the claimant had not alleged that the shooting was either intentional or negligent.

Held – in an action for trespass to the person, onus of proof of the defendant's intention or negligence lay on the claimant and the claimant must allege that the shooting was intentional or that the defendant was negligent, stating the facts alleged to constitute the negligence. The claimant's statement of claim, therefore, disclosed no cause of action.

Comment If the interference is *unintentional* it was held in *Letang* v *Cooper* [1964] 2 All ER 929 that an action must be brought in negligence.

Trespass to the person: false imprisonment

352 *Bird* v *Jones* (1845) 7 QB 742

A bridge company enclosed part of the public footway on Hammersmith Bridge, put seats on it for the use of spectators at a regatta on the river, and charged admission. The claimant insisted on passing along this part of the footpath, and climbed over the fence without paying the charge. The defendant, who was the clerk of the Bridge Company, stationed two policemen to prevent, and they did prevent, the claimant from proceeding forwards along the footway in the direction he wished to go. The claimant was at the same time told that he might go back into the carriage way and proceed to the other side of the bridge if he wished. He declined to do so and remained in the enclosure for about half an hour.

Held – there was no false imprisonment, for the claimant was free to go off another way.

353 *Herd* v *Weardale Steel, Coal and Coke Co Ltd* [1915] AC 67

The claimant was an employee of the defendant company and at 9.30 am on 30 May 1911, he descended the defendant's mine. In the ordinary way he would have been entitled to be raised at the end of his shift at 4 pm. The claimant and two other men were given certain work to do which they believed to be unsafe, and they refused to do it. At about 11 am they, and 29 men acting in sympathy with them, asked the foreman to allow them to ascend the shaft. The foreman, acting on instructions from the management, refused this request. At about 1 pm the cage came down carrying men, and emptied at the bottom of the shaft. The 29 men were refused permission to enter, but some got in and refused to leave the cage,

which was left stationary for some 20 minutes. At 1.30 pm permission was given for the men to leave and the claimant was brought to the top. He now sued for false imprisonment.

Held – there was no false imprisonment. There was a collective agreement regarding the use of the cage, and the claimant's right to be taken to the surface did not arise under the agreement until 4 pm. The defendant was perfectly willing to let the claimant ascend, but was not required, in the absence of any emergency, to provide him with the means of doing so except in accordance with the agreement.

354 *Meering* v *Grahame White Aviation Co Ltd* (1919) 122 LT 44

The claimant, being suspected of stealing a keg of varnish from the defendant, his employer, was asked by two works policemen to accompany them to the works office to answer questions. The claimant, not realising that he was suspected, assented to the suggestion and even suggested a short cut. He remained in the office for some time during which the works policemen stayed outside the room without his knowledge. The claimant later sued for false imprisonment and the question arose as to whether the claimant must know that the defendant is restraining his freedom.

Held – the claimant was imprisoned and his knowledge was irrelevant, though knowledge of imprisonment might increase the damages.

Trespass to the person: unlawful arrest

355 *Christie* v *Leachinsky* [1947] AC 573

The appellants, without the necessary warrant, arrested the respondent for unlawful possession of a number of bales of cloth. They had reasonable grounds for thinking that the bales were stolen but did not disclose this until later.

Held – by the House of Lords – the arrest was unlawful.

356 *Wheatley* v *Lodge* [1971] 1 All ER 173

The defendant's car collided with a parked vehicle. A constable saw him about an hour later and smelling alcohol on his breath, cautioned him and said that he was arrested for driving under the influence of drink contrary to what is now the Road Traffic Act 1988. The defendant was deaf and could not lip read, though the constable did not know this. Nevertheless, the defendant got into a police car, which the constable pointed to, and was taken to the police station where he indicated his deafness. From then on the charge and all relevant matters were made clear to him by written and printed matter. On the question of the lawfulness of his arrest, it was *held* by the Queen's Bench Divisional Court that the original arrest was valid. A police officer arresting a deaf person had to do what a reasonable person would do in the circumstances and the magistrates were clearly of the opinion that the constable had done so.

Comment (i) Presumably, on the basis of this decision, if a person is arresting someone who cannot speak English, he is not obliged to find an interpreter.

(ii) The Police and Criminal Evidence Act 1984 confirms the common-law rule that where an arrest is made by seizure of a person, words indicating that the person is under arrest should accompany the seizure (s 28(1)). However, the common-law rule is modified by requiring that where an arrest is made by a policeman, the person arrested must be informed that he is under arrest, even though that fact is obvious. The common law also requires that the person arrested be told the reason(s) for the arrest, and s 28(3) confirms this rule but modifies it where there is an arrest by a constable, requiring that in such a case information regarding the ground for the arrest be furnished, regardless of whether it is obvious (s 28(4)). The section confirms the common-law rule that there is no requirement to tell a person that he is under arrest or of the ground for arrest if it is not reasonably practicable to do so, as where he has escaped from arrest before the information can be given (s 28(5)). The grounds for the arrest may be given subsequently, e.g. at the police station as in *Lewis* v *Chief Constable of the South Wales Constabulary* [1991] 1 All ER 206.

Trespass to land

357 *Southport Corporation* v *Esso Petroleum Co* [1954] 2 QB 182

The Esso company's tanker became stranded in the estuary of the River Ribble. The master of the tanker discharged oil in order to refloat the ship. The action of the wind and tide took the oil on to the Corporation's foreshore and caused damage. The Corporation sued in trespass and negligence. Devlin, J, at first instance, thought that trespass would lie, but on appeal to the Court of Appeal, Denning, LJ contended that there could be no trespass because the injury was not direct, but was caused by the tides and prevailing winds; in trespass, the injury must be direct and not consequential. In the House of Lords, [1956] AC 218, Lord Tucker agreed with Denning, LJ, though in the House of Lords trespass was not pursued. The appeal was based on negligence and the defendant was *held* not liable.

Comment This case illustrates the difficulties of trying to recover at common law for oil pollution damage in negligence or trespass. The action for nuisance has similar difficulties. *Rylands* v *Fletcher* does not apply because, among other things, the oil does not escape from the land but from the sea and the sea is the equivalent of a public highway. Oil pollution is now dealt with by the Merchant Shipping (Oil Pollution) Act 1971, which provides a more straightforward method of making claims.

358 *Kelson* v *Imperial Tobacco Co* [1957] 2 All ER 343

The claimant was the lessee of a one-storey tobacconist's shop and brought this action against the defendant, seeking an injunction requiring it to remove from the wall above the shop a large advertising sign for cigarettes showing the words 'Players Please'. The sign projected into the airspace above the claimant's shop by a distance of some eight inches. The claimant alleged that the defendant, by fixing the sign in that position, had trespassed on his airspace.

Held – the invasion of an airspace by a sign of this nature constituted a trespass and, although the claimant's injury was small, it was an appropriate case in which to grant an injunction for the removal of the sign.

Comment The claimant seemed prepared for the sign to remain until he became involved in a dispute with the defendant regarding the quota of cigarettes supplied to him. It was after the dispute that he brought this action, but the court found that the claimant's case was not affected by his acts.

359 *Woollerton and Wilson* v *Richard Costain (Midlands) Ltd* (1969) 119 NLJ 1093

In this case the court granted to the owners of a factory and warehouse in Leicester an injunction restraining the defendants from trespassing on and invading airspace over their premises by means of a swinging crane. The injunction was suspended for 12 months to enable the defendants to finish their work, the defendants having offered to pay for the right to continue to trespass and to provide insurance cover for neighbouring properties. It was also *held* that it was no answer to a claim for an injunction for trespass that the trespass did no harm to the claimants.

Comment There has not been full support from the judiciary on the issue of postponing the injunction. In *John Trenbart Ltd* v *National Westminster Bank Ltd* (1979) 123 SJ 38, Walton, J would not postpone the operation of an injunction in similar circumstances and refused to follow *Woollerton* saying it was wrongly decided.

360   *Bernstein v Skyviews & General* [1977] 2 All ER 902

The claimant sued for damages for trespass against Skyviews, which had taken an aerial photograph of his home from about 630 feet, crossing his land in order to do so. It was *held* – by Griffiths, J – that an owner of land at common law had rights above his land to such height as was necessary for the ordinary use and enjoyment of the land and the structures upon it. The plane was, therefore, too high to be trespassing. In any case, s 40(1) of the Civil Aviation Act 1949 (see now Civil Aviation Act 1982, s 76) provides a defence to such a claim where the height was reasonable. However, the judge did say that constant surveillance from the air with photographing might well be actionable nuisance.

Trespass to land: effect of revocation of licences

361   *Winter Garden Theatre (London) Ltd v Millennium Productions Ltd* [1948] AC 173

The respondents were permitted by a contractual licence to use the Winter Garden Theatre, Drury Lane, which belonged to the appellants, for the purpose of producing plays, concerts or ballets in return for a weekly payment of £300. There was no express term in the licence providing that the appellants could revoke it. However, the appellants did revoke it, giving the respondents one month in which to quit the premises, but stating that they were prepared to give fresh notice for a later date if the respondents required further time in which to make other arrangements. The respondents contended that the licence could not be revoked so long as the weekly payments were continued. The appellants claimed that it was revocable on giving reasonable notice.

Held – on a proper construction of the contract, the licence was not intended to be perpetual, but nevertheless could only be determined by reasonable notice. What was reasonable notice depended on the commitments of the licensees and the circumstances of the parties. In this case the notice given by the appellants was reasonable and valid to determine the licence.

Comment This case also has a bearing on the ejection of hooligans from soccer and other sports grounds. They may have paid and have a contractual right to enter, but as Viscount Simon said in this case: 'The ticket entitles the purchaser to enter and, if he behaves himself, to remain on the premises until the end of the event which he has paid to witness.' This clearly implies that those who do not behave in a reasonable way cease to be licensees and become trespassers and can be evicted.

362   *Hounslow London Borough Council v Twickenham Garden Developments* [1970] 3 WLR 538

A building owner granted a licence under a building contract to a builder to enter on his land and do work there. The procedure for terminating the building contract involved an architect giving notice that the work was not being carried out properly. Such a notice was given but the building contractor refused to leave the land and carried on his work. The owner claimed an injunction and damages for trespass.

Held – by Megarry, J – in view of the fact that it was not certain whether the architect's notice had been given as a result of following proper procedures, the contract had not necessarily been terminated and the builder was not, unless and until that was done, a trespasser. The owner's action failed.

Trespass to land: self-help

363   *Hemmings v Stoke Poges Golf Club* [1920] 1 KB 720

The claimant was employed by the defendants and occupied a cottage belonging to them. Later he left the defendants' service and was called upon to give up possession. On refusal, he and his property were ejected with no more force than was necessary.

Held – the defendants were not liable for assault or trespass.

Comment (i) Since this case concerns the eviction of an employee/occupier, it would seem to be overruled on its facts by s 8(2) of the Protection from Eviction Act 1977. Hemmings could now claim damages for breach of that Act. However, the principle behind the decision on the *Hemmings* facts is still relevant in that the occupier of property could eject a person not covered by the 1977 Act, e.g. a squatter, from his property by the use of reasonable force.

(ii) It will, of course, *not* be regarded as reasonable to fire a shotgun at a trespasser to effect his removal and such a trespasser may be awarded damages (see *Revill v Newberry*, *The Times*, 3 November 1995).

Wrongful interference with goods: what is possession?

364   *The Tubantia* [1924] P 78

The claimant, who was a marine salvor, was trying to salvage the cargo of the SS *Tubantia* which had been sunk in the North Sea. He had discovered the wreck and marked it with a marker buoy, and his divers were already working in the hold, when the defendant, a rival salvor, appeared on the scene and started to send divers down to salvage the cargo from the wreck.

Held – whoever was the owner of the property salvaged, the claimant was sufficiently in possession of the wreck to found an action in trespass.

Conversion: may be based on a possessory title: finders of property

365 *Parker v British Airways Board* [1982] 1 All ER 834

The claimant was in BA's first class lounge at Heathrow waiting for a flight. He found a gold bracelet on the floor and gave it to an employee of BA together with his name and address asking that it be returned to him if not claimed. It was not claimed but BA sold it. The claimant sued in conversion and the Court of Appeal *held* that the claimant was entitled to the proceeds of sale.

Comment This principle was applied in two earlier cases, i.e. *Bridges v Hawkesworth* (1851) 21 LJ QB 75 where the finder of some banknotes which were lying on the floor in the public part of a shop was held entitled to them as against the shopkeeper; and *Hannah v Peel* [1945] KB 509, where a soldier billeted in a house found a brooch lying loose in an upstairs room, and he was held entitled to it as against the freeholder of the property who had no knowledge of the brooch until the claimant found it.

Conversion: possessory title: goods on or attached to land or buildings

366 *South Staffordshire Water Co v Sharman* [1896] 2 QB 44

The claimant company sued the defendant in detinue (now wrongful interference by conversion), claiming possession of two gold rings found by the defendant in the Minster Pool at Lichfield. The claimant was the owner of the pool and the defendant was a labourer it employed to clean the pool. It was in the course of cleaning the pool that the defendant came across the rings. He refused to hand them to his employer, but gave them to the police for enquiries to be made to find the true owners. No owner was found and the police returned the rings to the defendant who retained them.

Held – the rings must be given over to the claimant. The claimant was the freeholder of the pool, and had the right to forbid anyone coming on the land; it had a right to clean the pool out in any way it chose. The claimant possessed and exercised a practical control over the pool and had a right to its contents.

Comment It is also worth noting *Elwes v Brigg Gas Co* (1886) 33 Ch D 562 where it was held that a prehistoric boat found some six feet below the surface of the land belonged to the landowner and not to the finders. Similarly, in *Corporation of London v Appleyard* [1963] 2 All ER 834, the owner of a building site was held entitled against workers of a demolition contractor to banknotes found in a wall safe in an old cellar.

Conversion: the relationship between the claimant and the goods

367 *Jarvis v Williams* [1955] 1 All ER 108

Jarvis agreed to sell some bathroom fittings to Peterson and at Peterson's request delivered them to Williams. Peterson refused to pay the price and Jarvis agreed to take them back if Peterson would pay for collection. Peterson accepted this offer and Jarvis sent his lorryman, with a letter of authority, to collect the fittings but he was told that he could not take them, so he returned empty-handed. Jarvis claimed against Williams in conversion for the return of the goods.

Held – on the delivery to Williams the property in the goods passed to Peterson, and the arrangement for re-collection did not re-vest the property in Jarvis. It follows that at the time of collection, Jarvis had no right of property in the goods to sustain an action in conversion.

Conversion: the defendant's conduct

368 *Fouldes v Willoughby* (1841) 8 M & W 540

The claimant had put his horses on the defendant's ferry boat and, a dispute having arisen, the defendant asked the claimant to take them off. The claimant refused so the defendant did so, and since the claimant refused to leave the boat, the defendant ferried him across the river. The claimant sued in conversion. Maule, J directed the jury that the putting of the horses ashore was a conversion, but on appeal, the Court of Exchequer *reversed* the decision and found there was no conversion. Lord Abinger, CB said:

> In order to constitute a conversion it is necessary either that the party taking the goods should intend some use to be made of them by himself or by those for whom he acts, or that owing to his act, the goods are destroyed or consumed to the prejudice of the lawful owner. The removal of the horses involved not the least denial of the right of the [claimant] to enjoyment or possession of them and was thus no conversion.

369 *Oakley* v *Lyster* [1931] 1 KB 148

Oakley, a demolition contractor, agreed to pull down an aerodrome on Salisbury Plain and reinstate the land, a process which involved disposing of 8,000 tons of hard core and tar macadam. He thereupon rented three and a half acres of a farm on the opposite side of the road on which to dump it. He sold 4,000 tons, but in January 1929, there was still 4,000 tons undisposed of when Lyster bought the freehold of the farm. Shortly afterwards Oakley found that some of the hard core was being removed on Lyster's instructions, and Oakley saw him and was told that Lyster had bought the land and all that was on it, and on 9 July 1929, his solicitors wrote to Oakley to this effect and forbade Oakley to remove the hard core otherwise he would become a trespasser on Lyster's land. Correspondence followed but at the trial it was admitted that Oakley was a lawful tenant and owner of the hard core. While the correspondence was continuing, Oakley agreed to sell that 4,000 tons to Mr Edney, but in view of Lyster's claim, Edney withdrew and the stuff was undisposed of. The conversion alleged was the removal by Lyster of some of the hard core and the denial of title in the correspondence.

Held – the defendant was liable in damages for conversion. In the correspondence Lyster was asserting and exercising dominion over the goods inconsistent with the rights of the true owner, Oakley. Nor was it sufficient to allow Oakley to resume dominion over the hard core and remove it. He was entitled to damages of £300 for the loss of the sale to Edney.

Conversion: principle of liability; where the defendant has acted honestly

370 *Elvin and Powell Ltd* v *Plummer Roddis Ltd* (1933) 50 TLR 158

A fraudulent person ordered a consignment of goods from the claimants in the name of the defendants. He then telephoned the defendants in the claimants' name, saying that the goods had been dispatched to them in error and that they would be collected. The fraudulent person then himself collected the goods from the defendants and absconded with them. The claimants now sued the defendants for conversion.

Held – as involuntary bailees of goods, the defendants had acted reasonably in returning them, as they believed, to the claimants, by a trustworthy messenger. They had not committed conversion.

Comment An honest defendant was also held not liable in conversion in *Marcq* v *Christie Manson & Woods Ltd*

(*t/a Christies*) [2002] EWHC 2148. In that case an innocent buyer of a stolen painting sent it for sale by auction to the defendants. It did not meet the reserve price and the defendants returned it to the innocent purchaser who eventually sold it. The defendants acted in good faith and without notice that the innocent purchaser did not own the painting. The defendants checked the painting on the stolen art register but received a negative reply. The true owner later sued the defendants in conversion but failed. The mere receipt by an auctioneer of stolen goods does not make him liable in conversion. There was no delivery by the auctioneer to a purchaser. If there had been the High Court said that the defendants would have been liable. The innocent purchaser who delivered the goods to the auctioneer would have been liable because he denied the owner's title by delivering for sale. He was also clearly liable when he later sold the painting.

Public nuisance: obstruction of the highway; dangerous activities near the highway

371 *Attorney-General* v *Gastonia Coaches*, *The Times*, 12 November 1976

G, a coach operator, owned 22 coaches of which 16 were parked in residential roads adjoining the Gastonia offices. No matter how carefully these coaches were parked, they inevitably interfered with the free passage of other traffic. It was *held* – on a public relator action by the Attorney-General – that Gastonia was guilty of a public nuisance and would be restrained from parking the vehicles on the highway. Damages would also be awarded to private litigants who had suffered from the emissions of exhaust gases, excessive noise and obstruction of drives.

Comment (i) Reference should also be made to *Campbell* v *Paddington BC* (1911) (see Chapter 20) which is an example of an action by a private person for a public nuisance.

(ii) Public nuisance in terms of interference with a public path arose in *Wandsworth LBC* v *Railtrack plc* [2001] 1 WLR 368. The claimant sought to recover from the defendant its costs in regard to rectifying problems caused by pigeons congregating under the defendant's railway bridge. The pigeon droppings were causing substantial discomfort and inconvenience to members of the public using a footpath. The High Court ruled that the defendant was liable in public nuisance. The defendant had control of the bridge and the means to prevent pigeons from roosting under the bridge. The claimant was entitled to recover its reasonable costs in putting things right but in the absence of damage to its property it had no right to a claim in private nuisance.

372 Castle v St Augustine's Links Ltd and Another (1922) 38 TLR 615

On 18 August 1919, the claimant was driving a taxicab from Deal to Ramsgate when a ball played by the second defendant, a Mr Chapman, from the thirteenth tee on the golf course, which was parallel with the Sandwich Road, struck the windscreen of the taxicab. In consequence, a piece of glass from the screen injured the claimant's eye and a few days later he had to have it removed. He then brought this action.

Held – the claimant succeeded. Judgment for £450 damages was given by Sankey, J. The proximity of the hole to the road constituted a public nuisance. Compare *Bolton v Stone* [1951] AC 650, where cricket balls had been hit out of the ground and into the highway six to 10 times in 35 years but had injured nobody.

Held – no nuisance. See also *Miller v Jackson* [1977] 3 WLR 20, where the Court of Appeal held that the public interest, which requires young people to have the benefit of outdoor games, may be held to outweigh the private interest of neighbouring house-holders who are the victims of sixes landing in their gardens so that it would be impossible to use the garden when cricket was being played. Thus, no injunction was granted, even though the sportsmen were *held* to be guilty of both nuisance and negligence.

Comment In *Kennaway v Thompson* (1980) the Court of Appeal refused to follow this approach on the matter of an injunction and said in effect that a court ought not to refuse an injunction if the tort is established merely because there is benefit to a section of the public.

373 Tarry v Ashton (1876) 1 QBD 314

A lamp projected from the defendant's premises over the highway. It fell and injured the claimant, who then sued the defendant in respect of his injuries.

The defendant had previously employed an independent contractor, who was not alleged to be incompetent, to repair the lamp and it was because of the negligence of that contractor that the lamp fell. Even so, the defendant was *held* liable and the decision suggests that there is strict liability in respect of injuries caused by artificial projections over the highway.

374 Dymond v Pearce [1972] 1 All ER 1142

A lorry was left parked on a road subject to a 30 mph speed limit with its lights on beneath a street lamp. The claimant collided with the vehicle and suffered injury. He sued the defendants alleging negligence and nuisance. It was *held* – by the Court of Appeal

– that the claim in negligence failed as there was no evidence to show that the driver had not acted reasonably in the circumstances. The claim in nuisance also failed, for although a nuisance had been created, the injury suffered resulted solely from the negligence of the motorcyclist himself. Of more importance than the actual decision are the comments made in the Court of Appeal regarding the relationship between negligence and nuisance in terms of fault. See in particular Edmund Davies, LJ, who said: 'But if an obstruction be created, here too, in my judgment, fault is essential to liability in the sense that it must appear that a reasonable man would be bound to realize the likelihood of risk to highway users resulting from the presence of the obstructing vehicle on the road.'

Nuisance: utility or benefit of activity no defence: nor is coming to the nuisance

375 Bliss v Hall (1838) LJ CP 122

The defendant carried on the trade of a candle-maker in certain premises near to the dwelling house of the claimant and his family. Certain 'noxious and foul smells' issued from the defendant's premises and the claimant sued him for nuisance. The defence was that, for three years before the claimant occupied the dwelling house in question, the defendant had exercised the trade complained of in this present establishment.

Held – this was no answer to the complaint and judgment was given for the claimant.

Comment In *Miller v Jackson* [1977] 3 WLR 20 the Court of Appeal decided that it was no defence to the claim in nuisance that the cricket ground only became a nuisance when the claimant built a house close by it.

376 Adams v Ursell [1913] 1 Ch 269

The claimant was a veterinary surgeon and he purchased a house in 1907 for £2,370. In November 1912, the defendant opened a fried fish shop at premises adjoining the claimant's house. Very soon after the commencement of the business, the claimant's house was permeated with the odour of fried fish, and the vapour from the stoves filled the rooms 'like fog or steam'.

Held – an injunction would be granted because the defendant's activities materially interfered with the ordinary comfort of the claimant and his family; and it did not matter that the shop was in a large working-class district and, therefore, supplied a public need.

377 *Dunton* v *Dover District Council*, *The Times*,
31 March 1977

The Council provided a play area for children of a housing estate on grazing land at the rear of the claimant's hotel. The playground was not fenced and there was no restriction on the age of the children using it. The claimant suffered noise and inconvenience and was awarded £200 damages and a continuing injunction against the Council that the playground should only be open between 10 am and 6.30 pm to children under 12 years of age.

Nuisance: modes of annoyance

378 *Christie* v *Davey* [1893] 1 Ch 316

The claimant was the occupier of a semi-detached house, and she and her daughter gave pianoforte, violin and singing lessons in the house, four days a week for 17 hours in all. There was also practice of music and singing at other times, and occasional musical evenings. The defendant, a woodcarver and a versatile amateur musician, occupied the adjoining portion of the house, and he found the activities of the claimant and her family annoying. In addition to writing abusive letters, he retaliated by playing concertinas, horns, flutes, pianos and other musical instruments, blowing whistles, knocking on trays or boards, hammering, shrieking or shouting, so as to annoy the claimant and injure her household's activities.

Held – what the claimant and her family were doing was not an unreasonable use of the house, and could not be restrained by the adjoining tenant. However, the adjoining tenant was himself restrained from making noises to annoy the claimant, the court being satisfied that such noises had been made wilfully for the purpose of annoyance.

Comment (i) It was held in *Khorasandjian* v *Bush* [1993] 3 WLR 476 by the Court of Appeal that harassment by unwanted telephone calls was actionable as a private nuisance. The claimant alleged that the defendant's unwanted telephone calls were causing her great distress. A court order restraining the defendant from 'using violence or harassing, pestering or communicating with' the claimant was affirmed by the Court of Appeal.

The decision is founded in private nuisance and does not involve the creation of a new tort, i.e. harassment. For a situation where there was public nuisance, see *R* v *Johnson (Anthony Thomas)* (1996).

(ii) In *Paterson* v *Humberside County Council*, *The Times*, 19 April 1995 the claimant successfully claimed damages

for nuisance and negligence for cracks in his house resulting from trees planted by the Council in soil which to the Council's knowledge was of medium shrinkability.

(iii) Nuisance emanating from low flying aircraft was the source of a case entitled *Dennis* v *Ministry of Defence*, *The Times*, 6 May 2003. Harrier squadrons trained at RAF Wittering. The claimant's property was adjacent to the base. Aircraft flew at low altitudes and frequently over the claimant's property when landing. The claimant alleged that this constituted a nuisance at common law and an infringement of his human rights under Art 8 of the Convention (right to respect for private and family life). The High Court found for the claimant on both grounds but would not grant an injunction to stop the flying because this was in the public interest. Furthermore, the Harrier training was scheduled to end some nine years after the date of the proceedings. However, an award of damages would be made and this would satisfy the infringements in terms of nuisance at common law and breach of human rights. The award was for capital loss, loss of amenity and loss of commercial opportunities. Damages of £950,000 were awarded. The court stated that the defendant had not acquired the right to commit any nuisance by prescription because the claimant had neither consented to nor acquiesced in the nuisance.

379 *Hubbard* v *Pitt* [1975] 3 All ER 1

The defendants picketed in the road outside the offices of the claimant estate agents to protest against a particular property development. An interlocutory injunction was granted to restrain them from doing so. The Court of Appeal *held* – dismissing their appeal – (*a*) that the original ground for granting the injunction, namely, that street picketing other than in furtherance of a trade dispute was unlawful, was correct; (*b*) that the balance of convenience required an injunction to be issued there being a serious issue to be tried.

Comment As regards what is lawful picketing in a trade dispute, s 15(1) of the Trade Union and Labour Relations Act 1974 (see now s 220 of the Trade Union and Labour Relations (Consolidation) Act 1992) provides: 'It shall be lawful for a person in contemplation or furtherance of a trade dispute to attend – (*a*) at or near his own place of work, or (*b*) if he is an official of a trade union, at or near the place of work of a member of that union whom he is accompanying and whom he represents, for the purpose only of peacefully obtaining or communicating information, or peacefully persuading any person to work or abstain from working.' This provision would not appear to provide a defence if pickets approached and stopped vehicles.

Nuisance: duration of offending acts

380 *British Celanese Ltd v A H Hunt (Capacitors) Ltd* [1969] 2 All ER 1252

The defendants allowed metal foil to escape from their land and foul the bus bars of overhead electric cables. The claimants lost power and their machines were clogged up and time and material wasted.

Held, by Lawton, J:

(a) the defendants were not liable under *Rylands* v *Fletcher*, because there was no non-natural use of land;

(b) the defendants owed a duty of care to the claimants and could be liable in negligence – the claimants had a proprietary interest in the machines which were damaged and could recover loss flowing from that – pure economic loss was not involved;

(c) the defendants were liable in nuisance – an isolated happening such as this could create an actionable nuisance and the claimants were directly and foreseeably affected.

Nuisance: effect of malice or evil motive

381 *Hollywood Silver Fox Farm Ltd v Emmett* [1936] 2 KB 468

The claimants were breeders of silver foxes and erected a notice board on their land inscribed: 'Hollywood Silver Fox Farm'. The defendant owned a neighbouring field, which he was about to develop as a building estate, and he regarded the notice board as detrimental to such development. He asked the claimants to remove it, and when this request was refused, he sent his son to discharge a 12-bore gun close to the claimants' land, with the object of frightening the vixens during breeding. The result of this activity was that certain of the vixens did not mate at all, and others, having whelped, devoured their young. The claimant brought this action alleging nuisance, and the defence was that Emmett had a right to shoot as he pleased on his own land.

Held – an injunction would be granted to restrain Emmett. His evil motive made an otherwise innocent use of land a nuisance.

Comment (i) It seems at first sight difficult to reconcile the above case with *Bradford Corporation* v *Pickles* (1895), see Chapter 20. The difference probably is in the fact that *Hollywood Silver Fox Farm* v *Emmett* was an action for nuisance by noise, so that the defendant's motive was relevant in establishing the tort. In *Bradford Corporation* v *Pickles*, the action was really one for interference with a servitude or right over land, and motive was not relevant in establishing the rights of the parties.

(ii) In *Christie* v *Davey* (1893) (see Case **378**) also, North, J took into account the malice of the defendant by saying that the noise was 'made deliberately and maliciously for the purpose of annoying the [claimant]'.

Nuisance: act need not cause ill-health or diminish the value of property

382 *Bone v Seale* [1975] 1 All ER 787

Over a period of $12^1/_2$ years smells coming from a neighbouring pig farm owned by the defendant had caused a nuisance to properties owned by the claimant who sought an injunction restraining the nuisance and damages. The judge found that no diminution in the value of the properties had resulted but granted an injunction and awarded over £6,000 damages. The defendants appealed, saying, amongst other things, that the award was too high. It was *held* – by the Court of Appeal allowing the appeal against the award – that by drawing a parallel with loss of sense of smell as a result of personal injury the award was erroneous and £1,000 for the claimant would be substituted.

Nuisance: who can sue? who can be sued?

383 *Malone v Laskey* [1907] 2 KB 141

The defendants owned a house which they leased to Witherby & Co, which sublet it to the Script Shorthand Company. The claimant's husband was employed by the latter company, and was allowed to occupy the house as an emolument of his employment. A flush cistern in the lavatory of the house was unsafe, the wall brackets having been loosened by the vibration of the defendants' electric generator next door. The claimant told Witherby & Co of the situation, and it communicated with the defendants who sent two of their plumbers to repair the cistern gratuitously. The work was carried out in an improper and negligent manner, and four months later the claimant was injured when the cistern came loose. The claimant sued the defendants (a) in nuisance, and (b) in negligence.

Held – there was no claim in nuisance against the defendants. The claimant was not their tenant, and in nuisance the tenant is the person to sue, not other persons present on the premises, though such persons may have a claim where the nuisance is a public nuisance. Further, there was no claim in negligence, because the defendants owed no duty of care: first, because there was no contractual relationship; second, because the defendants did not undertake any duty towards the claimant. They were under no obligation to carry out repairs but sent their plumbers merely as a matter of grace. This was a voluntary act and was not in any sense the discharge of a duty. The defendants were not in occupation of the premises and had not invited the claimant to occupy them.

Comment (i) The case still represents the law regarding nuisance. Regarding the claim for negligence it was overruled in *Billings v Riden* [1958] AC 240, where it was held that there may be liability in negligence, where premises are left in a dangerous condition by workmen so that injury results, even though the injured person is not the occupier but is a visitor to the premises.

(ii) The *Khorasandjian* case (see p 491) should be noted here. The claimant, aged 18, received the calls at her mother's home in which the claimant had no proprietary interest. Nevertheless, the Court of Appeal said she could sue for private nuisance. Dillon, LJ said it would be ridiculous to regard the law of private nuisance by harassing telephone calls to be actionable only where the recipient has a freehold or leasehold interest in the premises at which they were received.

384 *Wilchick v Marks and Silverstone* [1934] 2 KB 56

Landlords who had let premises with a defective shutter, and had expressly reserved the right to enter the premises to do repairs, were *held* liable along with their tenant, to a passer-by injured by the shutter.

385 *Mint v Good* [1951] 1 KB 517

Landlords were *held* liable to the minor claimant who was injured when a wall on the premises, which they had let, collapsed on to the highway. They had not reserved the right to enter to do repairs, but the Court of Appeal stated that such a right must be implied, because the premises were let on weekly tenancies and it was usual to imply a right to enter to do repairs in such tenancies.

386 *Harris v James* (1876) 45 LJQB 545

A landlord was *held* liable for the nuisance created by his tenant's blasting operations at a quarry because he had let the property for that purpose. The tenant, therefore, inevitably created a nuisance.

Comment In *Tetley v Chitty* [1986] 1 All ER 663, a local authority granted a seven-year lease to a go-kart club. T and others, who were ratepayers living near the track, obtained an injunction against the Council to prevent the continuance of the nuisance by noise. Damages were an inadequate remedy.

387 *Smith v Scott* [1972] 3 All ER 645

The local authority had placed in an adjoining house to the claimant's a family which it knew was likely to cause a nuisance, but on conditions of tenancy which expressly prohibited the commission of such. These tenants had a large and unruly family and their conduct was, in the words of Pennycuick, V-C, 'altogether intolerable both in respect of physical damage and noise'. The claimant and his wife, an elderly couple, found it impossible to live next door and moved away. Notwithstanding protests on the part of the claimant, the local authority took no effective steps to control the unruly family or to evict them. It was *held* by Pennycuick, V-C, that, whatever the precise tests might be, it was impossible to apply the exception rendering a landlord liable for his tenants' acts in the present case. The exception was not based on cause and probable result apart from express or implied authority. The property had been let on conditions of tenancy which expressly forbade the commission of a nuisance, and it would not be legitimate to say that the local authority had authorised the nuisance.

It should also be noted that the court *held* that the rule in *Rylands* v *Fletcher* could not be applied and that the rights and liabilities of landowners had already been determined by the law and it was not open to the court to reshape those rights and liabilities by reference to the concept of duty of care. Thus the defendant was not liable in negligence. On the matter of *Rylands* v *Fletcher* liability, Pennycuick, V-C said:

> The rule in *Rylands* v *Fletcher* was applied in *Attorney-General* v *Corke* against a defendant who brought caravan dwellers on to his land as licensees but so far as counsel has been able to ascertain the rule has never been sought to be applied against a landlord who lets his property to undesirable tenants and I do not think it can be properly applied in such a case. The person liable under the rule in *Rylands* v *Fletcher* is the owner or controller of the dangerous 'thing', and this is normally the occupier and not the owner of the land. . . . A landlord parts with possession of the demised property in favour of his tenant and could not in any sense known to the law be regarded as controlling the tenant on property still occupied by himself. I should respectfully have thought that *Attorney-General* v *Corke* could equally well have been decided on the basis that the landowner there was in possession of the property and was himself liable in nuisance for the acts of his licensees.

Comment It should be noted that in *O'Leary* v *Islington London Borough Council, The Times*, 5 May 1983 it was decided by the Court of Appeal that there was no implied term in a tenancy agreement obliging landlords to enforce a tenant's agreement not to cause nuisance to neighbours who were also their tenants, and the appropriate remedy for aggrieved tenants was to bring an action in tort against the tenant causing the nuisance.

388 *Brew Brothers v Snax (Ross)* [1969] 3 WLR 657

In June 1965, the freehold owners of premises leased them for a term of 14 years. The lease contained covenants by the tenants regarding repairs, payment of maintenance expenses and viewing by the landlords. In November 1966, one of the walls of the premises tilted towards the neighbouring premises which belonged to the claimant. It was shored up but caused an obstruction for 18 months. It appeared that the reason why the wall had tilted was the seeping of water from certain drains and the removal of a tree by the tenants. The claimant sued the landlords and the tenants, and the landlords contended that the responsibility fell entirely on the tenants under the lease.

Held – by the Court of Appeal:

(a) the tenants were responsible for repairing defects pointed out by the landlords but that the work required on the wall was not within the terms of the lease;

(b) the landlords must be presumed to know the state of the premises and were liable for nuisance in that they allowed the state of affairs to continue;

(c) the tenants were jointly liable in nuisance in that they failed to put the matter right – this liability was quite independent of their duties under the lease.

Nuisance: abatement

389 *Sedleigh-Denfield v O'Callaghan and Others* [1940] AC 880

One of the respondents (a college for training foreign missioners) was the owner of property adjoining the appellant's premises in Mill Hill. On the boundary of the property owned by the college there was a ditch and it was admitted that the ditch also belonged to the college. About 1934, when a block of flats was erected on the western side of the appellant's premises, the county council had laid a pipe and grating in the ditch but no permission was obtained and no steps were taken to inform the college authorities of the laying of the pipe. However, the presence of the pipe became known to a member of the college who was responsible for cleaning out the ditch twice a year. The Council had not put a guard at the entrance to the pipe to prevent its being blocked by debris. The

pipe became blocked and the appellant's garden was flooded. He claimed damages from the college on the ground that the pipe was a nuisance.

Held – by the House of Lords – that the college was liable because it appeared that the college should have known about the pipe and realised the risk. Furthermore, it had adopted the nuisance by using the pipe to drain its land.

Comment (i) This case was applied in *Page Motors v Epsom and Ewell Borough Council* (1981) 80 LGR 337 where a site on an industrial estate was leased to a firm for the sale and repair of motor vehicles but was occupied by gypsies who caused a nuisance. The firm claimed damages against the Council for the nuisance in the years 1973 until 1978, by which time the authorised gypsy caravans had all left the site. It was held by the Court of Appeal that the Council was liable because it had adopted the nuisance by failing to take steps to move the gypsies on. Furthermore, the claimant could recover damages for loss of business. This was a foreseeable result of having a gypsy site nearby.

(ii) In this case Lord Wright said, '. . . it has been rightly established in the Court of Appeal that an occupier is not *prima facie* responsible for a nuisance created without his knowledge and consent. If he is to be liable a further condition is necessary, namely, that he had knowledge or means of knowledge, that he knew or *should have known* of the nuisance in time to correct it and obviate its mischievous effects.' The words in italics indicate that knowledge in private nuisance may be constructive, as it can also be in public nuisance (see *R v Shorrock (Peter)* [1993] 3 All ER 917).

Nuisance: the remedy of injunction

390 *Kennaway v Thompson* [1980] 3 All ER 329

The defendants represented a club at which motor-boat racing and water-skiing were carried on. In 1972 the claimant moved into a house which she had had built near to the lake on which the above activities were carried out, as they had been since the early 1960s. After the claimant moved in the nature of the club's activities increased in frequency and noise because large powerboats took part in international meetings which were preceded by periods of noisy practice. The claimant sought damages for nuisance and an injunction but Mais, J awarded her damages only – £1,000 for the past nuisance and £15,000 in respect of future nuisance, since he regarded it as oppressive to issue an injunction to prevent the club from continuing its activities on the ground that this was contrary to public interest. The Court of Appeal allowed the claimant's appeal and awarded an injunction stating that the public interest should not prevail over the private interest of a person affected by a continuing nuisance, and accordingly the claimant was entitled to an injunction under which the club was ordered to curtail its activities, restricting noisy meetings to a limited number of occasions.

Nuisance: defences: prescription

391 *Sturges v Bridgman* (1879) 11 Ch D 852

For more than 20 years the defendant, a confectioner, had used large pestles and mortars in his premises in Wigmore Street. Then the claimant, a physician in Wimpole Street, built a consulting room in his garden abutting on the confectioner's premises. The noise and vibration made by the confectioner's activities interfered materially with the claimant's practice. He sued for an injunction to prevent the offensive activities and the defence was that the defendant had acquired a prescriptive right to commit the nuisance.

Held – though it was possible to acquire a right, the defendant had not done so, because the nuisance only arose when the consulting room was built.

Negligence: liability for omissions

392 *Argy Trading Development Co Ltd v Lapid Developments Ltd* [1977] 1 WLR 444

In an under-lease for six years from 19 October 1971 the tenant agreed to insure against fire for the full value of the premises, including two years' rent, and in the event of loss or damage by fire to reinstate the premises. In fact, the landlords insured the premises under a block policy covering other property as well and the tenant paid the landlords the appropriate proportion of the premium. In 1973 there was a change in the control of the landlords and the landlords did not renew the block policy but failed to notify the tenant of its cancellation. In 1973, some months after the policy had lapsed, the premises were gutted by fire. Neither party wanted the premises, which were scheduled for redevelopment, to be reinstated. The landlords undertook not to enforce the covenant to reinstate but the tenant wished to recover damages from the landlords on the ground that it had been deprived of the insurance moneys, which it would otherwise have received, by the landlords' failure to continue the insurance or to notify the tenant of its cancellation so that it had no opportunity to take out the policy. It was *held* – by Croom-Johnson, J – that there was no implied term that the landlords would maintain their block policy or not cancel it without notifying the tenant. Nor was there any equitable estoppel such as was applied in

the *High Trees* case (see Chapter 10), since there was no representation by the landlords intended to affect the legal relations of the parties. There was a special relationship between the parties which might have created a duty of care under the principle of *Hedley Byrne* (see Case **142**) but that duty was not to *give* negligent information. The *failure* to give information which amounted to an omission was not within the principle of *Hedley Byrne*.

Comment A further example, this time of liability by omission, occurred in *John D Wood & Co v Knatchbull* [2003] 08 EG 131. The claimants sued for their commission on a sale of the defendant's property. He counterclaimed for damages for the fact that the claimants had not, before sale, advised him of an increase in the selling prices of properties near to his in Notting Hill, London. The claimants advised an asking price of £1.5 million and the property was bought for that price 'subject to contract'. Before contracts were signed another property close to the defendant's was put on the market at £1.95 million. Sign boards were not allowed in the area so that the defendant was not aware of this attempt to sell. The claimants did, however, become aware of it but allowed the defendant to enter into a binding contract at £1.5 million. Damages for loss of a chance to sell at a higher price were awarded to the the defendant, i.e. £120,000 on the basis of a 66 per cent chance of finding a buyer at £1.7 million. Allowances were made and deducted for interim use by the defendant and the increased commission he would have had to pay. The judge said that it was an implied term of the of agency contract with a concurrent duty of care in tort that an estate agent should exercise the skill and care of a reasonably competent member of his or her profession. There was a continuing duty so long as the agency lasted to make relevant disclosures.

Negligence: economic loss recoverable by way of parasitical damages

393 *Weller & Co v Foot and Mouth Disease Research Institute* [1965] 3 All ER 560

The defendants carried out experiments on their land concerning foot and mouth disease. They imported an African virus which escaped and infected cattle in the vicinity. As a consequence, two cattle markets in the area had to be closed and the claimants, who were auctioneers, sued for damages for loss of business.

Held – by Widgery, J – so far as negligence was concerned, the defendants owed no duty of care to the claimants who were not cattle owners, and had no proprietary interest in anything which could be damaged by the virus. Furthermore, the defendants owed no absolute duty to the claimants under *Rylands v Fletcher* (1868) because the claimants had no interest in any land to which the virus could have escaped.

Comment Had a duty of care been found, the liability in this case would have been endless. The closing of the market no doubt affected also the takings of cafés, car parks, shops, and public houses, amongst others. It would not seem likely that the courts are yet ready to extend liability in this way.

394 SCM (United Kingdom) Ltd v W J Whittall & Son Ltd [1970] 3 All ER 245

A workman employed by the defendants carrying out construction work near the claimants' factory, cut into an underground electric cable so that the power to the claimants' factory failed. The claimants made typewriters and the lack of power caused molten materials to solidify in their machines which were *physically* damaged. The machines had to be stripped down and reassembled and production was brought to a halt for seven-and-a-half hours. In the Court of Appeal the claimants limited their claim to damages in respect of the physical damage to the machines and the financial loss *directly* resulting from that damage. This enabled the court to decide that the claimants' property had foreseeably been damaged by the defendants' act so that the claimants could recover for damage to the machines and the consequential financial loss flowing from it. Nevertheless, the court went on to consider economic loss in the context of negligence and dealt in effect with the position as it might have been if the power cut had stopped production without damaging the machines. The following aspects of the judgments are important: *Per* Lord Denning, MR:

> In actions of negligence, when the [claimant] has suffered no damage to his person or property, but has only sustained economic loss, the law does not usually permit him to recover that loss. Although the defendants owed the [claimants] a duty of care, that did not mean that additional economic loss which was not consequent on the material damage suffered by the plaintiffs [claimants] would also be recoverable; in cases such as *Weller & Co v Foot and Mouth Disease Research Institute* (1965) [see above], and *Electrochrome Ltd v Welsh Plastics Ltd* (1968) [see above] the [claimants] did not recover for economic loss because it was too remote to be a head of damage, not because there was no duty owed to the [claimants] or because the loss suffered in each case was not caused by the negligence of the defendants.

Per Winn, LJ:

> Apart from the special case of imposition of liability for negligently uttered false statements, there is no liability for unintentional negligent infliction of any form of economic loss which is not itself consequential on foreseeable physical injury or damage to property.

Comment The power shut-off lasted for some time and during that time the claimants would normally have processed four more 'melts'; because they had been unable to do so, they had lost the profits they would have made on them. However, this was regarded as economic loss not consequent upon the physical damage and, therefore, what was recoverable was only the loss of profit on the melt which was actually interrupted by the failure of electrical supplies.

395 Spartan Steel and Alloys Ltd v Martin & Co Ltd [1972] 3 All ER 557

While digging up a road, the defendants' employees damaged a cable which the defendants knew supplied the claimants' factory. The cable belonged to the local electricity board and the resulting electrical power failure meant that the claimants' factory was deprived of electricity. The temperature of their furnace dropped and so metal that was in melt had to be poured away. Furthermore, while the cable was being repaired the factory received no electricity so it was unable to function for some 14 hours. The Court of Appeal, however, allowed only the claimants' damages for the spoilt metal and the loss of profit on one 'melt'. They refused to allow the claimants to recover their loss of profit which resulted from the factory being unable to function during the period when there was no electricity. Lord Denning, MR chose to base his decision on remoteness of damage rather than the absence of any duty of care to avoid causing economic loss. However, he did make it clear that public policy was involved. In the course of his judgment he said:

> At bottom I think the question of recovering economic loss is one of policy. Whenever the courts draw a line to mark out the bounds of duty, they do so as a matter of policy so as to limit the responsibility of the defendant. Whenever the courts set bounds to the damages recoverable – saying that they are, or are not, too remote – they do it as a matter of policy so as to limit the liability of the defendant.

Negligence: economic loss: injury to person or property not always essential

396 Junior Books Ltd v Veitchi Co Ltd [1982] 3 All ER 201

Junior Books (J) owned a building. Veitchi (V) were flooring contractors working under a contract for the main contractor who was doing work on the building. There was no privity of contract between J and V. It was alleged by J that faulty work by V left J with an unserviceable building and high maintenance costs so that J's business became unprofitable. The House of Lords decided in favour of J on the basis that there was a duty of care. V were in breach of a duty owed to J to take reasonable care to avoid acts or omissions, including laying an allegedly defective floor, which they ought to have known would be likely to cause the owners economic loss of profits caused by the high cost of maintaining the allegedly defective floor and, so far as J were required to mitigate the loss by replacing the floor itself, the cost of replacement was the appropriate measure of liability so far as this loss was concerned. The standard of care required is apparently the contractual duty, and so long as the work is up to contract standard, the defendant in a case such as this cannot be in breach of his duty. Lord Fraser of Tullybelton said:

> Where a building is erected under a contract with a purchaser, then provided the building, or part of it, is not dangerous to persons or to other property and subject to the law against misrepresentation, I can see no reason why the builder should not be free to make with the purchaser whatever contractual arrangements about the quality of the product the purchaser wishes. However jerry-built the product, the purchaser would not be entitled to damages from the builder if it came up to the contractual standards.

Comment (i) The effect of the decision in *Junior Books* was whittled away in *Simaan General Contracting Co v Pilkington Glass Ltd* [1988] 1 All ER 345. The claimant (S Ltd) was the main contractor to construct a building in Abu Dhabi for a sheikh. The erection of glass walling together with supplying the glass was subcontracted to an Italian company (Feal). Feal bought the glass from the defendant (P Ltd). The glass units should have been a uniform shade of green but some were various shades of green and some were red. The sheikh did not pay S Ltd. It chose to sue P Ltd in tort rather than Feal in contract for its loss, i.e. the money the sheikh was withholding.

Held – by the Court of Appeal – since there was no physical damage, this was purely a claim for economic loss and P Ltd had no duty of care. S Ltd's claim failed. Feal would have been liable under the Supply of Goods and Services Act 1982 (see Chapter 14) but for some reason was not sued. Economic loss can be recovered in contract.

Dillon, LJ said of *Junior Books* that it had 'been the subject of so much analysis and discussion that it cannot now be regarded as a useful pointer to any development of the law. It is difficult to see that future citation from *Junior Books* can ever serve any useful purpose.'

(ii) It is now possible to use the law of contract to deal with third-party claims under the Contracts (Rights of Third Parties) Act 1999. There is no problem about recovering economic loss in contract claims. A great many of them are precisely for that (see further Chapter 10).

Negligence: breach of duty; behaviour as a reasonable man

397   *Daniels v R White and Sons Ltd* [1938] 4 All ER 258

The claimants, who were husband and wife, sued the first defendants, who were manufacturers of mineral waters, in negligence. The claimants had been injured because a bottle of the first defendants' lemonade, which they had purchased from a public house in Battersea, contained carbolic acid, presumably from the bottle-washing plant. Evidence showed that the manufacturers took all possible care to see that no injurious matter got into the lemonade. It was *held* that the manufacturers were not liable in negligence because the duty was not one to ensure that the goods were in perfect condition but only to take reasonable care to see that no injury was caused to the eventual consumer. This duty had been fulfilled.

398   *Hill v J Crowe (Cases)*, *The Times*, 19 May 1977

The claimant was injured when he stood on a packing case whose boards collapsed causing him to fall. It was *held* – by MacKenna, J – that the case had been badly made and the manufacturers owed a duty of care to the claimant. They could not escape liability by showing that they had a good system of work and proper supervision. *Daniels v White and Sons* (1938), above, was not followed.

399   *Greaves & Co (Contractors) v Baynham Meikle & Partners* [1974] 3 All ER 666

The claimant, a builder, was instructed to build a warehouse and sub-contracted its structural design to the defendant firm of consultant structural engineers. B knew or, by reason of the relevant British Standard Code of Practice, ought to have known, that as the warehouse was to carry loaded trucks there was a danger of vibration. The design was competent but inadequate for the purpose of carrying the trucks and it was *held* – by Kilner Brown, J, allowing the claimant's claim for breach of duty of care and breach of an implied term of the contract – that the duty of the defendant firm was not simply to exercise the care and skill of a competent engineer which it had done, but to design a building fit for its purpose in the light of the knowledge which the firm had as to its proposed use.

400 Paris v Stepney Borough Council [1951] AC 367

The claimant was employed by the defendant on vehicle maintenance. He had the use of only one eye and the defendant was aware of this. The claimant was endeavouring to remove a bolt from the chassis of a vehicle, and was using a hammer for the purpose, when a chip of metal flew into his good eye so that he became totally blind. The claimant sued for damages from his employer for negligence in that he had not been supplied with goggles. The defendant showed in evidence that it was not the usual practice in trades of this nature to supply goggles, at least where the employees were men with two good eyes. The trial judge found for the claimant, but the Court of Appeal reversed the decision on the ground that the claimant's disability could be relevant only if it increased the risk, i.e. if a one-eyed man was more likely to get a splinter in his eye than a two-eyed man. Having found that the risk was not increased, it allowed the appeal. The House of Lords reversed the judgment of the Court of Appeal, holding that the gravity of the harm likely to be caused would influence a reasonable employer, so that the duty of care to a one-eyed employee required the supply of goggles, and Paris, therefore, succeeded.

401 Haley v London Electricity Board [1964] 3 All ER 185

The appellant, Haley, a blind man who was on his way to his work as a telephonist, tripped over an obstacle placed by servants of the London Electricity Board near the end of a trench excavated in the pavement of a street in Woolwich. He fell and suffered an injury which rendered him deaf, and brought about his premature retirement from his employment. The guard was sufficient warning for sighted people but was by its nature inadequate to protect or warn the blind. It consisted of a hammer hooked in the railings and resting on the pavement at an angle of 30 degrees, and Haley's white stick, which he was properly using as a guide, did not encounter the obstacle with the result that instead of being warned by it he fell over it. Evidence was given that about one in 500 people were blind and there were 258 registered blind people in Woolwich, many of whom were capable of walking in the streets alone, taking the normal precautions that such blind persons were accustomed to take. The House of Lords held, reversing the decision of the Court of Appeal, that the London Electricity Board was liable in negligence. Those engaged in operations on the pavement or a highway must act reasonably to prevent danger to passers-by including blind people who must, however, also take reasonable

care of themselves. The Board had not fulfilled this duty and was liable in damages for negligence which were assessed at £3,000 general damages, and £2,250 special damages, Haley's retirement being accelerated by four years.

402 Watt v Hertfordshire County Council [1954] 2 All ER 368

A fireman was injured by a heavy jack which slipped while being carried in a lorry which was going to the scene of an accident. The lorry was not equipped to carry such a heavy jack but it was required to free a woman who had been trapped in the wreckage. No proper vehicle was available and it was *held* that the fire authority was not liable.

403 Latimer v AEC Ltd [1953] 2 All ER 449

A heavy rainstorm flooded a factory and made the floor slippery. The occupiers of the factory did all they could to get rid of the water and make the factory safe, but the claimant fell and was injured. He alleged negligence in that the occupiers did not close down the factory.

Held – the occupiers of the factory were not liable. The risk of injury did not justify the closing down of the factory.

Negligence: *res ipsa loquitur*

404 Easson v LNE Railway Co [1944] 1 All ER 246

The claimant, a boy aged four years, fell through the open door of a corridor train seven miles from its last stopping place. It was *held* that the defendants did not have sufficient control over the doors for *res ipsa loquitur* to apply. In the course of his judgment, Goddard, LJ said:

> It is impossible to say that the doors of an express corridor train travelling from Edinburgh to London are continuously under the sole control of the railway company . . . passengers are walking up and down the corridors during the journey and get in and out at stopping places. The fact that the door came open could as well have been due to interference by a passenger as to the negligence of the defendants' servants.

405 Roe v Minister of Health [1954] 2 QB 66

Two patients in a hospital had operations on the same day. Both operations were of a minor character and in each case nupercaine, a spinal anaesthetic, was injected by means of a lumbar puncture. The injections were given by a specialist anaesthetist, assisted by the theatre staff of the hospital. The nupercaine had been contained in sealed glass ampoules, stored in a solution of phenol. After the operations both patients developed symptoms of spastic paraplegia caused by the phenol, which had contaminated the nupercaine by penetrating almost invisible cracks in the ampoules. In the event, both patients became permanently paralysed from the waist down, and they now sued the defendants for negligence.

Held – the defendants were vicariously liable for the negligence (if any) of those concerned with the operations, but on the standard of medical knowledge in 1947, when the operations took place, those concerned were not negligent. The cracks in the ampoules were not visible on ordinary examination, and could not be reproduced even by deliberate experiment. It was true that in 1954, when the case was brought, phenol used for disinfectant purposes was tinted so that it might be seen on examination, but the case must be decided on medical knowledge at the time when the operations were carried out. It was also suggested that once the accident has been explained, there is no question of *res ipsa loquitur* applying. Nor does the maxim apply when many persons might have been negligent. Denning, LJ suggested that every surgical operation is attended by risks. Doctors, like the rest of us, have to learn by experience. Further, one must not condemn as negligence that which is only misadventure.

Comment Although it is not certain what effect it would have had on the above case, it is worth noting the more modern standard of care put forward in *Newell* v *Goldenberg* (1995) and *Bolitho* (1997) (see p 558).

406 *Byrne v Boadle* (1863) 2 H & C 722

The claimant brought an action in negligence alleging that, as he was walking past the defendant's shop, a barrel of flour fell from a window above the shop and injured him. The defendant was a dealer in flour, but there was no evidence that the defendant or any of his servants were engaged in lowering the barrel of flour at the time. The defendant submitted that there was no evidence of negligence to go to the jury, but it was *held* that the occurrence was of itself evidence of negligence sufficient to entitle the jury to find for the claimant in the absence of an explanation by the defendant.

407 *Scott v London and St Katherine Docks Co* (1865) 3 H & C 596

The claimant, a Customs officer, proved that when he was passing in front of the defendant's warehouse six bags of sugar fell upon him. It was *held* that the

maxim *res ipsa loquitur* applied. In the course of his judgment, Erle, CJ said: 'Where the thing is shown to be under the management of the defendant, or his servants, and the accident is such as, in the ordinary course of things, does not happen if those who have the management use proper care, it affords reasonable evidence, in the absence of explanation by the defendant, that the accident arose from want of care.'

Comment This case was followed in *Ward* v *Tesco Stores* [1976] 1 All ER 219, where the Court of Appeal held that an accident which had occurred due to a spillage of yoghurt on a shop floor put an evidential burden upon the defendant shopowner to show that the accident did not occur through any want of care on its part. The defendant was not able to satisfy that burden and the claimant succeeded.

408 *Pearson v North Western Gas Board* [1968] 2 All ER 669

The claimant's husband was killed by an explosion of gas which also destroyed her house. It appeared from the evidence that a gas main had fractured due to a movement of earth caused by a severe frost. When the weather was very cold the defendants had men standing by ready to deal with reports of gas leaks, but unless they received reports there was no way of predicting or preventing a leak which might lead to an explosion.

Held – by Rees, J – assuming the principle of *res ipsa loquitur* applied, the defendants had rebutted the presumption of negligence and the claimant's case failed.

Contributory negligence

409 *Jones v Lawrence* [1969] 3 All ER 267

A boy aged seven years and three months ran out from behind a parked van across a road apparently without looking in order to get to a fun-fair. He was knocked down by Lawrence who was travelling on his motor cycle at 50 miles per hour in a built-up area. The boy's injuries adversely affected his school work and he subsequently failed his eleven-plus examination. In an action on his behalf for damages it was *held* – by Cumming-Bruce, J – that:

(a) his conduct was only that to be expected of a seven-year-old child and could not amount to contributory negligence;

(b) the failure to obtain a grammar-school place and the permanent impairing of his powers of concentration affected his job attainment potential and were factors to be taken into account in assessing damages.

Comment The matter is, however, one of fact in each case. Thus, in *Minter v D & H Contractors (Cambridge) Ltd, The Times*, 30 June 1983, the defendants had been negligent in leaving a pile of hard core in the road, into which the claimant, aged nine, rode his cycle. He was found to be guilty of contributory negligence to the extent of 20 per cent. The judge said that this claimant, who on the evidence was a 'good rider', could not be said to come into the category of minors who were incapable of any contributory negligence.

410 *Oliver v Birmingham Bus Co* [1932] 1 KB 35

A grandfather was walking with his grandchild aged four, when a bus approached quickly and without warning. The grandfather, being startled, let go of the child's hand and the bus struck the child. It was *held* that the damages awarded to the child should not be reduced to take account of the grandfather's negligence.

Negligence: actions based on breach of statutory duty

411 *Atkinson v Newcastle and Gateshead Waterworks Co* (1877) LR 2 Ex D 441

The claimant's timber yard caught fire and was destroyed, there being insufficient water in the mains to put it out. The defendant was required by the Waterworks Clauses Act 1874, to maintain a certain pressure of water in its water pipes, and the Act provided a penalty of £10 for failure to keep the required pressure and 40s for each day during which the neglect continued, the sums being payable to aggrieved ratepayers. The claimant sued the defendant for loss caused by the fire on the ground that it was in breach of a statutory duty regarding the pressure in the pipes.

Held – that the defendant was not liable. The statute did not disclose a cause of action by individuals for damage of this kind. It was most improbable that the legislature intended the company to be a gratuitous insurer against fire of all the buildings in Newcastle.

412 *Gorris v Scott* (1874) LR 9 Exch 125

A statutory order placed a duty on the defendant to supply pens of a specified size in those parts of a ship's deck occupied by animals. The defendant did not supply the pens, and sheep belonging to the claimant were swept overboard. The claimant sued for damages from the defendant for breach of statutory duty.

Held – the claimant could not recover for his loss under breach of statutory duty, because the object of the statutory order was to prevent the spread of disease, not to prevent animals from being drowned.

Comment A similar point is raised in *Lane v London Electricity Board* (1955) (see Chapter 6).

Product liability: illustrative case law

412a *Abouzaid v Mothercare (UK) Ltd* [2000] All ER (D) 2436

This case is of interest because it deals with product liability for older products. The claim related to a fleecy-lined sleeping bag for a child's pushchair sold by the defendant company in 1990. While helping to fix the bag on to his brother's pushchair, one of the elasticated straps flew out of the claimant's hand and caught the claimant in the eye so that he ended up with no central vision. The claimant was 12 years old at the time. When the matter eventually reached the Court of Appeal it was decided that the defendant was not negligent at common law. There was no knowledge of the defect at the time of sale. Nevertheless, the product was defective under s 3 of the Consumer Protection Act 1987 in that it did not provide the level of safety that persons are generally entitled to expect in all the circumstances. This liability is strict and does not depend on negligence. There is, however, the possibility of raising the development risk defence. This was done by the defendant in this case. It stated in particular that there had been no accidents reported to the relevant government agencies on the use of the straps. This certainly went to showing it was not negligent. However, the s 3 defence being strict was not affected by this. In addition, the Court of Appeal did not accept the development risk defence. There had been no developments between 1990 and the present day in regard to tests and the defendant could have tested the product in 1990 in exactly the same way as currently. In the view of the court, the defendant had not used the available methods in 1990 to test the product and so was not able to plead the defence successfully. The claimant succeeded.

412b *Bogle and Others v McDonald's Restaurants Ltd* [2002] unreported

A group of claimants sued for personal injury caused by the spillage of hot drinks served to them by the defendant. The claim was by way of a group litigation order. The majority of claimants were children. The issues before the High Court were whether the defendant was negligent in dispensing and serving hot drinks at the temperature it did and whether the defendant was in breach of the Consumer Protection Act 1987. The most significant part of the claimants' case was that the thermal cups in which the drinks were served masked the actual temperature of the drink so that it was not allowed to cool and the drink container had to be opened to add sugar and creamer before it could be consumed. There was also the contention that the drinks being served at between 75°C and 95°C were served too hot and that a temperature of 70°C would have been more appropriate. The High Court did not find the defendant negligent. There was no evidence to show that serving the drinks at a lower temperature of 70°C would have caused less injury. The range of temperatures used by the defendant was normal in the catering industry. Customers would be assumed by the defendant to know that drinks would be served hot and the cups and lids were adequately designed and made.

On the matter of liability under the 1987 Act, the judge ruled that the safety of the hot drinks involved met the public's legitimate expectations as to safety generally. The public would expect the drinks to be served hot. The public would expect scalding to result if there was a spillage. Therefore, serving the drinks in the way the defendant had did not constitute a breach of the 1987 Act.

Negligence: professional liability

413 *Caparo Industries plc v Dickman and Others*
[1990] 2 WLR 358

The facts were, briefly, that Caparo, which already held shares in Fidelity plc, eventually acquired the controlling interest in the company. The group later alleged that certain purchases of Fidelity shares and the final bid were made after relying on Fidelity's accounts, which had been prepared by Touche Ross & Co, the third defendants.

The accounts, Caparo alleged, were inaccurate and misleading in that an apparent pre-tax profit of some £1.3 million should in fact have been shown as a loss of £400,000. It was also alleged that, if the supposed true facts had been known, Caparo would not have made a bid at the price it did and might not have made a bid at all.

The Court of Appeal decided that while Touche Ross did not have a duty of care towards members of the public in regard to the Fidelity accounts, it did owe a duty of care to Caparo because Caparo was already a shareholder in Fidelity when it made the final purchase of shares and the bid.

The two main judgments in the House of Lords provide an interesting contrast: Lord Bridge concentrates more on the case law and in particular on the dissenting judgment of Lord Denning in *Candler v Crane, Christmas* [1951] 1 All ER 426, where Lord Denning thought that the defendant accountants should have

a duty of care to Candler because they had prepared allegedly negligent financial statements on the basis of which they knew Mr Candler might invest in the company concerned; and the judgment of the House of Lords in *Hedley Byrne & Co Ltd v Heller & Partners Ltd* [1963] 2 All ER 575, where a bank supplied an allegedly negligent reference as to the creditworthiness of a company called Easipower which it knew would be used by Hedley Byrne as a basis for extending credit to the company, which then went into liquidation.

A salient feature of both those cases, said Lord Bridge, was that the defendant giving advice on information was fully aware of the nature of the transaction the claimant was contemplating, knew that the advice or information would be communicated to him, and knew that it was likely that the claimant would rely on that advice or information in deciding whether or not to engage in the transaction in contemplation.

The situation was quite different where the statement was put into more or less general circulation and might foreseeably be relied on by strangers for any one of a variety of different purposes which the maker of the statement had no specific reason to anticipate.

Lord Bridge felt that it was one thing to owe a possibly wider duty of care to avoid causing injury to the person or property of others, but quite another to owe a similar duty to avoid causing others to suffer purely economic loss.

His Lordship concluded that auditors of a public company's accounts owed no duty of care to members of the public at large who relied on the accounts in deciding to buy shares in the company. And as a purchaser of additional shares in reliance on the auditors' report, the shareholder stood in no different position from any other investing member of the public to whom the auditor owed no duty.

Lord Oliver was concerned with establishing the purpose of an audit under the Companies Act 1985. He went on to say that in enacting the statutory provisions Parliament did not have in mind the provision of information for the assistance of purchasers of shares in the market, whether they were already the holders of shares or other securities or people with no previous proprietary interest in the company.

The purpose for which the auditors' certificate was made and published was that of providing those entitled to receive the report with information to enable them to exercise the powers which their respective proprietary rights in the company conferred on them and not for the purposes of individual speculation with a view to profit.

The duty of care was one owed to the shareholders as a body and not to individual shareholders.

Comment (i) The decision represents a further retreat from the judgment of Lord Wilberforce in *Anns* v *Merton London Borough Council* [1977] 2 All ER 492. There was a view taken of that judgment that a person should owe a duty of care in negligence to anyone allegedly injured by his conduct, including those suffering economic loss, unless there was any good reason or ground of public policy to prevent the duty being imposed. More recently, and particularly in this case, the courts have shown that there is a real need for proximity and so have gone a long way to reducing the fear of ever increasing potential professional liability.

It now seems that knowledge as to the user of the statement concerned and, seemingly, also as to the purpose or probable purpose for which it will be used, is required to establish the necessary proximity in these cases where allegedly careless misstatements result in economic loss. It seems unlikely that there will now be any further movement towards foresight of the user and use which had begun to show itself in *JEB Fasteners* v *Marks Bloom & Co* [1983] 1 All ER 583.

(ii) Problems of causation continue to arise. In *Galoo Ltd and Others* v *Bright Grahame Murray*, *The Times*, 14 January 1994, there were unproved allegations of negligence by the auditors in terms of the accounts of two companies. These accounts, it was alleged, gave too optimistic a view of the companies' financial position, thus allowing them to trade on to insolvency, causing loss to various parties. The Court of Appeal held that even if it were to be assumed that the unproven allegations were true the claim against the auditors would fail. The accounts may have allowed the companies to exist and trade but a company's existence is not the cause of its trading losses nor, for that matter, its profits. These depend upon many things including market forces for which the auditors are obviously not responsible.

(iii) The *Caparo* judgment has angered some in the business world because investors have, in a sense, lost their right to make investment judgments on the basis of the annual audited accounts. This is not really surprising because the annual accounts are in essence stewardship statements, i.e. how the directors have conducted the company's business during the year covered by the accounts. They are, by their nature, backward-looking and not a suitable vehicle to help speculators to predict a future which is uncertain, nor are they intended to be. 'Decision-usefulness' is not the primary purpose of annual accounts. The accounting statements in *Morgan* (see below) went much further.

414 *Morgan Crucible Co plc* v *Hill Samuel Bank Ltd and Others*, *Financial Times Law Reports*, 30 October 1990

The crucial events in the case were as follows. On 6 December 1985, Morgan Crucible (MC) announced a proposed unsolicited offer to acquire the entire share capital of First Castle Electronics plc (FC). When the announcement was made, FC's most recent published financial statements were the reports and audited accounts for the years ended 31 January 1984 and 1985.

On 17 December 1985, MC published a formal offer document which was addressed to FC shareholders. Morgan Grenfell advised MC and Hill Samuel advised FC. The directors of FC, acting on its behalf, sent their shareholders a number of circulars. They were also issued as press releases by Hill Samuel and copies were supplied to MC's advisers.

Two days later, a circular was sent out by the directors of FC, comparing MC's profit record unfavourably with FC's and recommending refusal of the bid. In subsequent circulars reference was made to the published financial statements, and one circular of 31 December 1985 stated that they could be inspected.

An FC circular to its shareholders, issued on 24 January 1986, forecast an increase in profits before tax in the year to 31 January 1986 of 38 per cent. A letter from the auditors, Judkins, was included, saying that the profit forecast had been properly compiled. Included also was a letter from Hill Samuel stating that in its opinion the profit forecast had been prepared after due and careful inquiry.

On 29 January, MC increased its bid; on 31 January, FC's board sent another letter to shareholders recommending acceptance of that increased bid; on 14 February, the bid was declared unconditional; and on 27 February, a further recommendation to accept the bid was sent by FC to its shareholders.

Later, MC alleged that the financial statements (audited and unaudited) issued prior to the bid, the profit forecast of 24 January, and the financial material contained in the circulars and recommendation documents were prepared negligently and were misleading. MC asserted that if the true facts had been known the bid would not have been made or completed. MC issued a writ (now claim form) on 6 May 1987 joining as defendants Hill Samuel, Judkins, and FC's chairman and board. It alleged that the board and the auditors were responsible for circulating the financial statements; that they and Hill Samuel were responsible for the profit forecast; that all of them owed a duty of care to MC as a person who could foreseeably rely on them; that the statements and forecasts were negligently prepared; and that MC relied on them in making and increasing its offer and thereby suffered heavy loss.

In dealing with the allegations and the House of Lords judgment in *Caparo*, Lord Justice Slade said, first, that in *Caparo* all of the representations relied on had been made before an identified bidder had come forward, whereas in this case some of the representations had been made after a bidder had emerged and indeed because a bid had been made. They were clearly made with an identified bidder in mind, i.e. MC. MC had, therefore, applied for leave to amend its statement of claim (now statement of case) to representations made after the bid and as part of the takeover battle. This could then distinguish MC's case from the situation in *Caparo*.

The issue before the court was whether MC's allegations disclosed a reasonable cause of action. On the assumption that the allegations were true, was there a duty of care to MC? The judge went on to say, on the assumed facts, that the defendants could have foreseen that MC would or might suffer financial loss if the representations were incorrect; but that foreseeability in itself was not enough for liability to arise – there had to be a sufficient relationship of proximity between the claimant and defendant. In addition, it must be just and reasonable to impose liability on the defendant.

The fatal weakness in the *Caparo* case, the judge said, was that the auditors' statement, i.e. the annual accounts, had not been prepared for the purpose for which the claimant relied on it. It was, therefore, arguable that this case could be distinguished from *Caparo*.

On the assumed facts, the directors of FC, when making the relevant representations, were aware that MC would rely on them for the purpose of deciding to make an increased bid and, indeed, intended that they should. MC did rely on them for that purpose. It was, therefore, arguable that there was a sufficient proximity between the directors of FC and MC to give rise to a duty of care.

For the same reasons, it could be argued that Hill Samuel and Judkins owed MC a duty of care in terms of their representations involving the profit forecast and the audited accounts.

Leave was given to amend the statement of claim (now statement of case). MC's amended case should be permitted to go forward to trial.

Comment (i) So, some reliance can be placed on financial statements and other representations in a takeover after all. If, during the conduct of a contested takeover and after an identified bidder has emerged, the directors and financial advisers of the target company make express representations with a view to influencing the conduct of the bidder, then they owe him a duty of care not to mislead him negligently as was alleged.

(ii) Liability in negligence can extend to a wide variety of professionals, e.g. those who value property and, of course, solicitors. In regard to the latter it was held in

White v *Jones* [1993] 3 All ER 481 by the Court of Appeal that a solicitor who was instructed to prepare a will but failed to do so was liable to a disappointed beneficiary because the testator died before a will in the new form was signed. There was sufficient proximity between the solicitor and the beneficiary, and financial loss was reasonably foreseeable.

(iii) The *White* case was distinguished in *Carr-Glynn* v *Freasons (a firm)* [1997] 2 All ER 614 where Lloyd, J held that where a solicitor's breach of his duty of care to a testator in preparing his will resulted in loss to the estate – in this case failure to sever a joint tenancy in land – so that on death the whole interest passed to the other joint owner (see Chapter 22), the solicitor owed no duty of care to an intended beneficiary under the will whose gift of the testatrix's part was lost since it was unacceptable that the solicitor should be at risk of two separate claims for identical loss, one by the personal representatives on behalf of loss to the estate and one by the disappointed beneficiary. Since there was only one claim in *White*, i.e. that of the beneficiary, it probably survived. It seems that in any case there was no breach of any duty. The solicitors warned that there might be a joint tenancy but the testatrix did not pursue the matter by providing the solicitors with the relevant deeds. This decision was reversed by the Court of Appeal (see [1998] 4 All ER 225). The court stated that it was consistent with the reasoning in *White* that the assumption of responsibility by a solicitor towards a client be extended in favour of a beneficiary who as a result of the negligence of the testatrix's solicitors in carrying out the testamentary instructions suffered a loss of expectation.

Occupiers' liability: two or more occupiers

415 *Wheat v E Lacon & Co Ltd* [1966] 1 All ER 582

The manager of a public house was permitted by the owners, Lacon & Co, to take paying visitors who were accommodated in a part of the premises labelled 'Private'. The claimant's husband, while a paying visitor, was killed by a fall from a staircase in the private part of the premises. Lacon & Co denied liability on the ground that they were not occupiers of the private part of the premises.

Held – by the House of Lords – that:

(a) the defendants retained occupation and control together with the manager;
(b) the deceased was a visitor to whom the defendants owed a common duty of care;
(c) on the facts the staircase, though not lit, was not dangerous if used with proper care.

Wheat's claim, therefore, failed because there was no breach of the duty of care.

Comment A not dissimilar case is *Manning v Hope (t/a Priory), The Times*, 18 February 2000. M fell down some steps and injured her ankle whilst on property belonging to H. She recovered damages on the basis that a hand rail should have been fitted. The Court of Appeal reversed this decision. There was no finding that the steps were unsafe without a hand rail and H had no duty to fit one.

Occupiers' liability: defective work of an independent contractor

416 *Cook v Broderip* (1968) 112 SJ 193

The owner of a flat employed an apparently competent contractor to put in a new socket. Mrs Cook, who was a cleaner, received an electric shock caused because the socket was faulty. It appeared that the contractor had negligently failed to test the socket for reversed polarity.

Held – by O'Connor, J – Major Broderip, the owner of the flat, was not vicariously liable for the contractor's negligence and was not in breach of duty under the Occupiers' Liability Act 1957. Damages of £3,081 were awarded against the contractor who was the second defendant.

Comment (i) On the issue of inspection of the work done, the House of Lords stated in *Ferguson v Welsh, The Times*, 30 October 1987 that it would not ordinarily be reasonable to expect an occupier, having engaged a contractor, whom he believed on reasonable grounds to be competent, to supervise the contractor's activities. If he knew, however, that an unsafe system was being used it might be reasonable for the occupier to take steps to see that things were made safe. If not, he might be liable.

(ii) The occupier may be liable where although work on the premises is done by an independent contractor the occupier does not check to see whether the contractor has adequate insurance to meet a claim for injury caused by his negligent work. This will be particularly likely where the work consists of something involving some risk, e.g. the setting up of a ride at a fête (see *Gwilliam v West Hertfordshire Hospital NHS Trust, The Times*, 7 August 2000).

Occupiers' liability: effect of claimant's knowledge of danger

417 *Bunker v Charles Brand & Sons* [1969] 2 All ER 59

The claimant's employers were engaged as subcontractors by the defendants who were the main contractors for tunnelling in connection with the Victoria Line. The claimant was required to carry out modifications to a digging machine. He had seen the machine *in situ* and was taken to have appreciated the danger in crossing its rollers when in operation. He was injured while attempting to cross the rollers in the course of his work and sued for damages.

Held – by O'Connor, J – the defendants having retained control of the tunnel and the machine were the occupiers. They were not absolved from liability under the Act of 1957 merely because of the claimant's knowledge of the danger. Knowledge was not assent. However, the claimant's damages were reduced by 50 per cent on the ground of his contributory negligence.

Comment It was held in *Salmon v Seafarer Restaurants Ltd* [1983] 3 All ER 729 that an occupier owes a duty to firemen attending his premises to put out a fire. A fire occurred in the defendants' fish and chip shop because of the negligence of an employee. The employee failed to turn off a gas heater prior to closing the shop. The claimant fireman was injured when attending the fire. The court said that the defendants were vicariously liable. It was foreseeable that a fireman might be injured following the employee's negligence.

Occupiers' liability and negligence liability: the special case of children

418 *Yachuk v Oliver Blais & Co Ltd* [1949] AC 386

In this appeal from the Supreme Court of Canada to the Judicial Committee of the Privy Council the facts were as follows: a servant of Oliver Blais & Co Ltd had supplied five cents' worth of gasoline in an open lard pail to certain boys, aged nine and seven, who told him that they needed it for their mother's car, which had run out of petrol down the road. In fact, they wanted it for a game of Red Indians. The boys dipped a bullrush into the pail and lit it. This set fire to the petrol in the pail and the boy Yachuk was seriously injured. The Judicial Committee *held* that the company was liable for the negligence of its servant in allowing the boys to take away the gasoline. The question of contributory negligence did not arise, because there was no evidence that the minors appreciated the dangerous quality of gasoline. The company was fully responsible even though the boys had resorted to deceit to overcome the supplier's scruples.

419 *Gough v National Coal Board* [1954] 1 QB 191

The defendant Board was the owner of a colliery which included a small railway which was constantly in use. The railway lines were not fenced or guarded, although there were houses on both sides. The public had for a long time been permitted to cross the lines, and children often played on the wagons, although the defendant's servants had been told to keep children off. The claimant, a boy aged six-and-a-half, was seriously injured when he jumped off a wagon on which he had been riding. At the trial the boy admitted that he knew he was not supposed to ride on the wagons, and that his father had threatened to punish him if he did. Nevertheless, it was *held* that the defendant was liable. The fact that children had for many years played near the railway made them licensees, and although the boy was, strictly speaking, a trespasser as regards the wagon, he was allured by the slow-moving wagons which the defendants knew were an attraction to children.

Comment Although the reference in these cases is to 'children', the rules extend also to young persons. Thus, in *Adams v Southern Electricity Board*, *The Times*, 21 October 1993, the Court of Appeal decided that the electricity board owed a duty of care to a boy of 15 who was electrocuted and injured by being able to climb on to apparatus consisting of a pole-mounted transformer because of a defective anti-climbing device. The boy had climbed the pole before and had become insensitive to the danger. His damages were reduced by two-thirds for contributory negligence. Nevertheless, the Court of Appeal held that the Board was in breach of its common law duty to take reasonable care for the safety of the boy.

420 *Mourton v Poulter* [1930] 2 KB 183

The owner of certain land wished to carry out building operations on it, but before he could so do, it was necessary to fell a large elm tree. The land was unfenced, and children of the locality were in the habit of using it as a playground. During the process of felling, a large number of children gathered near the tree and Poulter, who had been employed to fell the tree, warned the children of the danger likely to arise when the tree came down. He failed to repeat the warning when the tree was about to fall, and the claimant, a boy of 10, was crushed by the falling tree.

Held – the defendant was liable. Even though the children were trespassers, he owed them a duty to give adequate warning.

421 *Pannett v McGuinness & Co* [1972] 3 All ER 137

The defendants were demolishing a warehouse in a heavily populated area near a park where children played. Three workmen were specially appointed to make a bonfire of rubbish and to keep a look-out for children and to see that they came to no harm. The claimant, a boy of five, got in while the three men were away and was severely burned. The men had frequently chased children away in the past and in particular the claimant on a number of occasions. The contractors contended that the claimant was a trespasser, that he had been warned off and that they were under no duty.

Held – the contractors were in breach of the duty of care owed to the child; their workmen had failed to keep a proper look-out.

Comment *Penny v Northampton Borough Council* (1974) 72 LGR 733 provides a contrast. In that case a child trespasser was not successful in recovering damages following injury from an aerosol can which exploded when it was thrown into a fire by another child. The accident took place in a discarded rubbish tip some 50 acres in an area which resembled a rough field. The children had often been warned off the land by the Council's workmen. The court considered the authority had behaved with common sense and humanity and could not have known of the danger on the land so that it had discharged its duty of care. However, in *Harris v Birkenhead Corporation* [1975] 1 All ER 1001, a local authority was not successful in showing that it had discharged its duty of care to a child trespasser who had entered a derelict house which the Corporation had purchased under a compulsory purchase order. The child fell from an upstairs window and the authority was held to be the occupier since the previous owner had got out of the premises in view of the order. The authority was fixed with knowledge of the relevant facts and Kilner Brown, J found for the claimant.

Highways Act, 1980: no defence unless authority has done what was reasonably required

422 *Griffiths v Liverpool Corporation* [1966] 2 All ER 1015

The claimant tripped and fell on a flagstone which rocked on its centre. In this action against the highway authority for breach of s 1(1) of the Highways (Miscellaneous Provisions) Act 1961 (see now Highways Act 1980), it appeared that a regular system of inspection was desirable but was not carried out because the authority could not get tradesmen to put right faults discovered. The present fault could, however, have been put right by a labourer and no shortage of labourers was alleged.

Held – by the Court of Appeal – the authority had not brought itself within the statutory defence in s 1(2) and damages should be awarded.

Comment (i) In *Pridham v Hemel Hempstead Corporation* (1970) 69 LGR 525, the authority proved that it had inspected the footpath of a minor residential road every three months and had kept a complaints book. The Court of Appeal held that this excluded the authority from liability for injury caused by a defect in the footpath.

(ii) Highway authorities which cause accidents by their failure to remove ice and snow from the carriageway are not liable for accidents caused. The House of Lords so ruled in *Goodes* v *East Sussex County Council, The Times*, 16 June 2000. Such removal is not within their duty to repair. The claimant who suffered injuries which left him almost entirely paralysed when his car skidded on black ice and crashed into the parapet of a bridge recovered no damages. There was no suggestion that there was a duty at common law, although the case was based upon the Highways Act 1980.

It is to be hoped that our injuries, if we must have them, are caused by potholes!

(iii) In *Goodes* v *East Sussex CC* [2000] 1 WLR 1356 the House of Lords ruled that *highway legislation* did not require a local authority to spread salt and thus neutralise icy road conditions. The claimant had sustained serious injuries when he skidded on ice on an untreated road. Lord Hoffmann in his judgment said that the statutory duty of a highway authority was to repair and although in modern road conditions it might be reasonable to expect that a local authority should compensate a person who suffered serious injuries after skidding on ice which could have been removed by the local authority it was clear from *the legislation* that such a remedy was not yet available under that legislation.

However, in *Sandhar* v *Department of the Environment, Transport and the Regions* [2001] All ER (D) 245 a claim at common law for negligence was allowed to proceed.

(iv) In *Calderdale MBC* v *Gorringe* [2002] RTR 27 the Court of Appeal ruled that there was no statutory duty to paint warning signs such as 'slow' on the surface of the road arising under highways legislation. The claimant claimed damages for an accident that occurred on the crest of a hill of a road. The statutory duty did not cover the erection of warning signs either. However, there could be liability at common law for not painting road signs and erecting signs at an accident blackspot. That was not the case here, however, and the claimant's case failed.

Employers' negligence: effect of statutory duties of care

423 *Millard* v *Serck Tubes Ltd* [1969] 1 All ER 598

The claimant operated a power drill during the course of his employment. The drill was fenced, but the guard was not complete in that there was a gap in it through which the operator's hand could be drawn. While the claimant's hand was resting on the guard a piece of swarf thrown out from the drill wound itself around the claimant's hand and drew it into the drill causing injury to the claimant. The defendant employers conceded that the drill had not been properly fenced but contended that they were not liable

because the accident itself was unforeseeable. This defence was rejected by the Court of Appeal and the claimant succeeded in his pursuit of damages. Where a defendant has failed to fence dangerous machinery, as here, in breach of s 14 of the Factories Act 1961, he cannot escape liability for injury on the ground that such injury occurred in a way that was not reasonably foreseeable. Thus, a claimant might succeed when suing on a statutory duty and fail if suing on a common-law one.

Comment Of course, an employer will not breach his statutory duties where an employee makes equipment unsafe by deliberately misusing it. Thus in *Horton* v *Taplin Contracts Ltd, The Times*, 25 November 2003 the claimant was injured when working on a scaffolding tower that was deliberately toppled by another employee. The claimant alleged that the employer had failed to stabilise the tower as required by health and safety regulations. The case reached the Court of Appeal which ruled that it was only necessary to stabilise equipment where the behaviour to be guarded against was reasonably foreseeable. This did not include the 'extraneous, deliberate, unpredictable and violent act of a third party'. The claimant's action failed.

Torts against business interests: inducing a breach of contract

424 *Lumley* v *Gye* (1853) 2 E & Bl 216

The claimant, who was the manager of an opera house, made a contract with a *prima donna* Johanna Wagner for her exclusive services for a period of time. Gye induced Johanna Wagner to break her operatic engagement with the claimant and sing for him. It was *held* that whatever might have been the origin of the right to sue in such cases as this, it was not now confined to actions by masters for the enticement of their servants but extended to wrongful interference with any contract of personal service.

425 *Daily Mirror Newspapers* v *Gardner* [1968] 2 All ER 163

The executive committee of the retailers' federation recommended their members to boycott the *Daily Mirror* for one week after that newspaper had announced that the retailers' discount rate was to be reduced when the price of the newspaper was increased. The newspaper asked for interlocutory injunctions requiring the committee to communicate with their members and withdraw the recommendation on the grounds that:

(a) it was an unlawful interference with the newspaper's contracts with the wholesalers because the wholesalers would not want to take copies of the *Daily Mirror* if the retailers would not take it; and

(b) it was equivalent to an agreement contrary to the public interest within s 21(1) of the Restrictive Trade Practices Act 1956 (see now the Competition Act 1998).

Held – by the Court of Appeal – a sufficient *prima facie* case had been made out on both grounds and the injunctions would be granted.

Comment The essential difference between the *Lumley* and *Gardner* cases is that the interference in *Lumley* was aimed at the other party to the contract, i.e. *direct* interference, whereas in *Gardner* the interference was indirect, i.e. the retailers were not trying directly to persuade the wholesalers not to take the *Daily Mirror* but the inevitable result would be that they would not. If in indirect interference it is unclear from the evidence what effect the interference will have, the court may refuse to grant a remedy.

Thus, in *Middlebrook Mushrooms Ltd* v *TGWU* [1993] IRLR 232, women who were sacked from a mushroom farm, after refusing new contracts that they said had made cuts in their pay, proposed to carry out a leaflet campaign to persuade customers at supermarkets not to buy the farm's produce. The Court of Appeal refused to grant an injunction to prevent this because it was indirect interference and it was not clear from the evidence what effect it would have. Customers might ignore it; they were not like the wholesalers in the *Gardner* case who clearly could not ignore the retailers' ban. Also, to grant an injunction would be contrary to Art 10 of the European Convention on Human Rights and Fundamental Freedoms because it would affect the right of free speech (see now also the UK Human Rights Act 1998).

Civil conspiracy: the principles illustrated

426 *Crofter Hand Woven Harris Tweed Co Ltd* v *Veitch* [1942] AC 435

Veitch and the other defendants were officials of the Transport and General Workers Union. The dockers at Stornoway on the island of Lewis were all members of the union and so were most of the employees in the spinning mills on the island. The yarn when spun in the mills was woven into tweed cloth by crofters working at home, the woven cloth being finished in the mills. The tweed thus produced was sold by the owners of the mill as Harris Tweed. The Crofter Company also produced tweed cloth but its yarn was not spun on the island but instead was obtained more cheaply on the mainland. This cloth was sold as Harris Tweed but did not bear the trade mark in the form of a special stamp. The mill owners making the genuine Harris Tweed were being pressed by the

union to increase wages but they said that they could not accede to union requests because of the damaging competition of the Crofter Company. Consequently, Veitch and others acting in combination placed an embargo on the Crofter Company's imported yarn and exported tweed by instructing dockers at Stornoway to refuse to handle these goods. The dockers obeyed these instructions but were not on strike or in breach of contract. The Crofter Company sought an interdict (or injunction) against the embargo. The House of Lords *held* that the union officials were not liable in conspiracy because their purpose was to benefit the members of the union and the means employed were not unlawful.

Defamation: what is?

427 *Byrne* v *Deane* [1937] 1 KB 818

The claimant was a member of a golf club in which there had been some gaming machines. The defendants, Mr and Mrs Deane, were proprietors of the club. As a result of a complaint being made to the police, the machines were removed. Shortly afterwards, the following typewritten lampoon was placed on the wall of the clubhouse near to the place where the machines had stood:

> For many years upon this spot
> You heard the sound of the merry bell
> Those who were rash and those who were not,
> Lost and made a spot of cash
> But he who gave the game away,
> May he Byrne in hell and rue the day.
>
>   Diddleramus

The claimant brought this action for libel alleging that the defendants were responsible for exhibiting the lampoon, and that the lampoon was defamatory in that it suggested that he was disloyal to his fellow club members.

Held – the words were not defamatory because the standard was the view which would be taken by right-thinking members of society, and, in the view of the court, right-thinking persons would not think less of a person who put the law into motion against wrongdoers.

Defamation: libel or slander: form of publication

428 *Youssoupoff* v *Metro-Goldwyn-Mayer Pictures Ltd* (1934) 50 TLR 571

The claimant was a member of the Russian royal house. The defendants produced in England a film dealing with the life of Rasputin who had been the adviser of the Tsarina of Russia. The film also dealt with the murder of Rasputin. In the course of the film, a lady (Princess Natasha), who was affectionate towards the murderer of Rasputin, was also represented as having been raped by Rasputin, a man of the worst possible character. The claimant was married to a man who was undoubtedly one of the persons concerned in the killing of Rasputin. The claimant alleged that because of her marriage reasonable people would think that she was the person who was so raped. The action was for libel.

Held – the action was properly framed in libel and the claimant succeeded.

Comment This case is generally accepted as authority for the view that a defamatory talking film is always libel. However, the rape of Princess Natasha was in the pictorial part of the film and not on the sound track. It is also uncertain whether a claimant can sue for a slanderous imputation of rape without proving special damage. The Slander of Women Act 1891 provides that the 'words spoken and published . . . which impute unchastity or adultery to any woman or girl shall not require special damage to render them actionable'. However, lack of consent, which is essential in rape, may mean that there is no imputation of unchastity.

Defamation: innuendo: illustrations from case law

429 *Cassidy v Daily Mirror Newspapers Ltd* [1929] 2 KB 331

A man named Cassidy or Corrigan who was well known for his indiscriminate relations with women, allowed a racing photographer to take a photograph of himself and a lady, and said that she was his fiancée and that the photographer might announce his engagement. The photograph was published in the *Daily Mirror* with the following caption: 'Mr M Corrigan, the race-horse owner, and Miss X whose engagement has been announced.' The claimant, Cassidy's lawful wife, who was also known as Mrs Corrigan, sued the newspaper for libel alleging as an innuendo that if Mr Corrigan was unmarried and able to become engaged, she must have been cohabiting with him in circumstances of immorality.

Held – since there was evidence that certain of her friends thought this to be so, she was entitled to damages.

Comment The case is authority for the view that a person may be liable for a statement which he does not actually know to be defamatory. It does not decide, nor does any other relevant case, that a person who has taken all possible steps to ensure the accuracy of his statement and could not, by reasonable enquiries, have discovered that his statement was defamatory is or is not liable in defamation.

430 *Morgan v Odhams Press* [1971] 2 All ER 1156

In 1965 the *Sun* reported that a kennel girl had been kidnapped by a dog-doping gang. In or about the relevant period various witnesses had seen her in the company of Mr Morgan whose friend she was. The newspaper article made no mention of Mr Morgan's name. Nevertheless, he began an action against the newspaper pleading that he had been libelled by innuendo in that persons would think he was involved either in the kidnapping or the dog-doping, or both.

Held – by the House of Lords – the article was potentially libellous:

(a) the newspaper article was not, by itself, capable of being so understood, but;

(b) an article to be defamatory of a person need not contain a 'key or pointer' showing it refers to him. Evidence is admissible to import a defamatory meaning to otherwise innocent words.

431 *Tolley v J S Fry & Sons Ltd* [1931] AC 333

The claimant was a well-known golfer. The defendants published an advertisement without the claimant's consent containing his picture and underneath the following words:

The caddy to Tolley said, 'Oh Sir,
Good shot, Sir! That ball, see it go, Sir.
My word, how it flies,
Like a cartet of Fry's,
They're handy, they're good, and priced low, Sir.'

The claimant brought an action for libel, alleging an innuendo. It was said that a person reading the advertisement would assume that the claimant had been paid for allowing the use of his name in it, and that in consequence he had prostituted his amateur status as a golfer.

Held – the evidence showed that the advertisement was capable of this construction and the claimant was awarded damages.

432 *Sim v Stretch* (1936) 52 TLR 669

The defendant had encouraged the claimant's housemaid to leave the claimant's employ and re-enter the defendant's. The defendant later sent the following telegram to the claimant: 'Edith has resumed her services with us to-day. Please send her possessions and the money you borrowed, also her wages.' The telegram was said to impute that the claimant was in financial difficulties and had in consequence borrowed from his housemaid, and that he had been unable to pay her wages, and was a person of no credit. The claimant succeeded at first instance and in the Court of Appeal, but the House of Lords reversed the judgment, *holding* that the telegram was incapable of bearing a defamatory meaning. In the words of Lord Atkin: 'It seems to me unreasonable that, when there are a number of good interpretations, the only bad one should be seized upon to give a defamatory sense to the statement.' It was also in this case that Lord Atkin suggested the following test of a 'defamatory' statement: 'Would the words tend to lower the [claimant] in the estimation of right-thinking members of society generally?'

433 *Fulham v Newcastle Chronicle and Journal* [1977] 1 WLR 651

In 1962 the claimant left the Catholic priesthood. He married in 1964, a child being born 14 months later. In 1973 he was appointed as deputy headmaster of a school in Teesside having previously lived in South Yorkshire. A Newcastle newspaper published by the defendants commented upon his appointment stating that he 'went off very suddenly' from Salford where he had been a priest 'about seven years ago' and had subsequently married. The claimant alleged that such statements contained a libellous imputation that he had married while still a priest and had fathered an illegitimate child. The particulars supplied by the claimant simply stated his date of marriage and the date of birth of his eldest child. The defendants sought to strike out his claim. It was *held* – by the Court of Appeal – that only those knowing of the dates of the claimant's marriage and/or the birth of his child could draw the imputation alleged and that since the defendants' newspaper did not circulate in the area where the claimant had been a priest or subsequently lived it was necessary for him to plead particulars of persons receiving the publication having the requisite knowledge and that unless he was able to do so his allegation of innuendo would be struck out.

434 *Grappelli v Derek Block (Holdings) Ltd* [1981] 2 All ER 272

The claimants, Mr Grappelli and Mr Disley, were jazz musicians with an international reputation. The defendants were their managers and agents. The defendants had, so the claimants alleged, purported to book contracts for them without authority. Then it was said that one of these concerts had been cancelled because Mr Grappelli was seriously ill which was an entirely untrue story. It was said that that was defamatory, not as it stood, but because of an innuendo that people finding out that the claimants were appearing at other concerts on the same dates as those cancelled would think that the claimants had given a false story. It was *held* by the Court of Appeal that where a claimant relies on an innuendo, he must prove that the words were published to a specific person who knew *at the time* of the publication of specific facts enabling him to understand the words in the innuendo meaning. Facts which came into existence afterwards did not make the statement defamatory. As Lord Denning said, the statement was not defamatory as it stood, since it is not defamatory of a person to say that he is seriously ill. At the time the statement was made those becoming aware of it would not have access to facts to suggest that it was wrong. Obviously, later on, when concerts were advertised in the *Sunday Times* on the same dates as those which had been cancelled it might have been possible to construe that Mr Grappelli and Mr Disley were not really ill and that the whole story was a put-up job. However, this information had to be available at the time of publication of the defamatory words since, according to Lord Denning, the cause of action arises in defamation when the words are published and they must be seen to be defamatory then, and not later.

Defamation: the words must refer to the claimant

435 *E Hulton & Co v Jones* [1910] AC 20

A newspaper published an article descriptive of life in Dieppe in which one Artemus Jones, described as a churchwarden at Peckham, was accused of living with a mistress in France. All persons concerned contended that they were ignorant of the existence of any person of that name, and the writer of the article said that he had invented it. Unfortunately, the name so chosen was that of a Welsh barrister and journalist, and the evidence showed that those who knew him thought that the article referred to him.

Held – the newspaper was responsible for the libel and the claimant was awarded damages.

Comment (i) In cases of this kind the defence of offer of amends may be available under ss 2–4 of the Defamation Act 1996. However, it is by no means certain that it would have been available on the actual facts of this case, because ss 2–4 apply only where the defendant did not know or have reasonable grounds to believe that the statement complained of referred to the claimant or was likely to be understood as referring to him, and was both false and defamatory of the claimant. On the facts of *Hulton v Jones* it seems that the publication was attended by some carelessness. It should be noted that the 1996 Act offer of amends is, unlike previous provisions, only available to a defendant who is willing to pay such compensation as is agreed or assessed by a judge and to publish a correction and an apology.

(ii) In *Hayward* v *Thompson* [1981] 3 All ER 450 the defendants were the editor, a journalist on, and the proprietors and publishers of, a Sunday paper. In one article it was alleged that a wealthy benefactor of the Liberal Party was connected with an alleged murder plot but no name was given. In a later article the paper named the claimant reporting that the police wished to interview him in connection with the alleged murder plot which was not, of course, a defamatory allegation that he was involved in it as the first article had been. It was *held* – by the Court of Appeal – that the two articles could be connected. Thus, the libel in the first article was of the claimant by reason of connection with the second one.

436 *Knupffer* v *London Express Newspaper Ltd* [1944] AC 116

The claimant was head in the United Kingdom of a Russian refugee organisation, active in France and the United States of America, but having only 24 members in England. An article in the newspaper ascribed Fascism to this 'minute body established in France and the United States of America', but without mentioning the English branch.

Held – the article was not defamatory of the claimant since he was not marked out by it, even assuming that it was defamatory to call someone a Fascist.

437 *Schloimovitz* v *Clarendon Press*, *The Times*, 6 July 1973

The claimant by statement of claim (now statement of case) alleged that the definitions of the word 'Jew' contained in three dictionaries published by the defendant were derogatory, defamatory and deplorable and sought an injunction restraining the defendant from publishing such definitions, at least without qualification, in any future editions of such dictionaries.

Held – by Goff, J – what was before the court was not whether the definitions were right or wrong or whether they were justly applied to any Jews, but whether in law the claimant had a cause of action to restrain the conduct of the defendant. No individual could maintain an action in respect of defamatory matter published about a body of persons unless in its terms, or by reason of the circumstances, it should and must be construed as a reference to him as an individual. There were two questions: (*a*) were the words defamatory? (*b*) did they in fact apply to the claimant or were they capable in law of being so regarded? The claimant failed to satisfy the latter test and accordingly the defendant was entitled to have

the writ (claim form) and statement of claim struck out. (*Knupffer* applied.)

Comment It was decided in *Farringdon* v *Leigh*, *The Times*, 10 December 1987, that it was at least arguable that where defamatory words in a publication referred to an unidentified member or members of a group of persons, each of those persons had a cause of action in libel. In these circumstances an action by members of a team of seven police officers was allowed to proceed to trial where they alleged that certain articles in the *Observer* were defamatory of them in alleging that at least two of them, who were unnamed, had passed confidential information to journalists.

Defamation: defences: justification

438 *Alexander* v *The North Eastern Railway Co* (1865) 6 B & S 340

The defendant published the following notice:

> North Eastern Railway. Caution. J Alexander, manufacturer and general merchant, Trafalgar Street, Leeds, was charged before the magistrates of Darlington on 28th September, for riding on a train from Leeds, for which his ticket was not available, and refusing to pay the proper fare. He was convicted in the penalty of £9 1s, including costs, or three weeks' imprisonment.

In this action for libel, the claimant contended that the defence of justification could not lie because, although he had been convicted as stated, the alternative prison sentence was 14 days not three weeks.

Held – the substitution of three weeks for a fortnight did not make the statement libellous. It could be justified, since the rest of it was true.

Defamation: defences: fair comment

439 *London Artists* v *Littler* [1969] 2 All ER 193

In 1965 four of the principal actors and actresses in a play called *The Right Honourable Gentleman* simultaneously wrote to the defendant, who was the producer of the play, terminating their engagement by four weeks' formal notice. This was, of course, highly unusual and the defendant wrote to the actors and actresses concerned wrongly accusing the claimants, who were their agents, of conspiracy to close down the play. The defendant also communicated the letter to the press. The defendant was now sued for libel. It was *held* – by the Court of Appeal – that he had libelled the claimants because although the subject matter of the allegations was of public interest, i.e. the fate of the play, the defence of fair comment did not apply to the allegation of a plot which was an allegation of fact. The allegation of a plot was defamatory and had not been justified. In fact, it seemed that all the actors and actresses involved had their own good and different reasons for leaving the play. There was no evidence of combination.

Defamation: defences: qualified privilege

440 *London Association for the Protection of Trade v Greenlands* [1916] 2 AC 15

The respondent was a limited company carrying on business as drapers and general furnishers in Hereford. The appellants were members of an unincorporated association consisting of about 6,300 traders and had, as one of their objects, the making of private inquiries as to the means, respectability and trustworthiness of individuals and firms. A member of the association was about to sell goods to the respondent and he asked the association to report on the company, and particularly to say whether the respondent was a good risk for credit of between £20 and £30. In the report submitted, the association declared that the respondent was a fair trade risk for the sum mentioned, but said that it had heavy mortgages charged on its assets, and that the assets barely covered the loans. In fact, the mortgages were secured by a charge upon the real and leasehold property only, and all other assets were entirely free from any mortgage whatever, and constituted a large and valuable fund. The respondent company was originally the claimant in an action for libel contained in the statement about the mortgages, and the statement that it was only good for credit of between £20 and £30.

Held – the occasion was privileged and thus the respondent had no claim in the absence of malice which it had not proved. Judgment was, therefore, given for the appellants.

Comment A further example of qualified privilege arising out of common interest is *Kearns v General Council of the Bar* [2002] 4 All ER 1075. In that case the head of the Bar Council's Professional Standards and Legal Services Department sent a letter to all heads of chambers, senior clerks and practice managers stating that the claimants (who were an agency) were not solicitors and that it would, in consequence, be improper to accept work from them unless certain specified conditions were satisfied, e.g. that the instructions came from a solicitor. This statement was not in fact true. Within two days a letter correcting the error and apologising was sent to all the recipients of the original letter. Nevertheless, the claimants brought defamation proceedings. The Bar Council put forward the defence of qualified privilege based on common interest. The claimants did not plead malice and the defendants applied for the case to be summarily dismissed. The High Court allowed the application taking the view that in this sort of case the defence of qualified privilege should apply in the absence of malice.

441 *Osborn v Thomas Boulter & Son* [1930] 2 KB 226

The claimant, a publican, wrote a letter to the defendants, his brewers, complaining of the quality of the beer. The defendants sent one of their employees to investigate and report. After receiving the report, Mr Boulter dictated a letter to his typist in which he suggested that the claimant had been adding water to the beer, and pointing out the penalties attaching to this if the claimant was caught. The claimant sued, alleging publication to the typist and certain clerks.

Held – the occasion was privileged, and since the claimant could not prove malice in the defendants, his action failed.

442 *Beach v Freeson* [1971] 2 WLR 805

A Member of Parliament wrote to the Law Society complaining of the conduct of a firm of solicitors reported to him by his constituents. He also sent a copy of the letter to the Lord Chancellor.

Held – by Geoffrey Lane, J – both publications were protected by qualified privilege. The privilege arose out of a Member of Parliament's duty to his constituents and the responsibilities of the Law Society and the Lord Chancellor.

443 *Cook v Alexander* [1973] 3 WLR 617

The claimant sued the defendant for libel in respect of an account of a House of Lords debate which he had written for the *Daily Telegraph*. The debate had been about an approved school where the claimant had been a teacher and which had been closed partly because of the claimant's revelations as to the system of punishment there. The newspaper had published a précis of each speech on one of the inside pages, but the claimant objected to a report written by the defendant which appeared on the back page. In this report, known as 'Parliamentary Sketch', the writer gave his impression of the debate and emphasised the salient aspects of it, but there was a reference to the more detailed account on another page. The claimant alleged that the sketch was defamatory of him because it gave great prominence to a speech that was very critical of him and his conduct, while it dismissed in uncomplimentary terms a speech which defended his action. It was *held* – by the Court of Appeal – that such a Parliamentary sketch was protected by qualified privilege. A reporter was entitled to select from a debate those parts which seemed to him to be of public interest and provided that the account as a whole was fair and honest, such a Parliamentary sketch was protected by qualified privilege.

444 *Horrocks v Low* [1972] 1 WLR 1625

At a local authority council meeting Low made a speech defamatory of Horrocks who in answer to Low's defence of justification, fair comment and qualified privilege, alleged that Low had been actuated by express malice.

Held – by the Court of Appeal – malice could not be inferred. Low held an honest and positive belief in the truth of his statement and had not abused the privileged occasion. '[The defendant] is not to be held malicious merely because he was angry or prejudiced even unreasonably prejudiced, against the [claimant], so long as he honestly believed what he said to be true. Such is the law as I have always understood it to be.' (*Per* Lord Denning, MR)

'What has to be proved is that the defendant was activated by malice in the popular meaning of the word: that is to say, in speaking as he did, he must have been actuated by spite or ill-will against the person defamed or by some indirect or improper motive.' (*Per* Edmund Davis, LJ)

'When there is . . . [gross and unreasoning] prejudice there will often, perhaps usually, be reckless indifference whether what is said is true or false. But if there is honest belief that it is true, there cannot in any judgment be recklessness whether it be true or false.' (*Per* Stephenson, LJ)

445 *Egger v Viscount Chelmsford* [1964] 3 All ER 406

Mrs Egger, a judge of Alsatian dogs, was on the list of judges of the Kennel Club, and Miss Ross, the secretary of a dog club in Northern Ireland, wrote to the Kennel Club asking it to approve of Mrs Egger as a judge of Alsatians at a show. The assistant secretary of the Kennel Club, C A Burney, wrote to Miss Ross to say that the committee could not approve the appointment. Mrs Egger brought an action for libel against the 10 members of the committee and the assistant secretary on the ground that the letter reflected on her competence and integrity. There were two long trials at both of which the judge ruled that the occasion was privileged. The jury disagreed the first time, but at the second trial the jury found that the letter was defamatory and that five members of

the committee were actuated by malice but three were not. The other two had meanwhile died. The judge gave judgment against all the defendants including the assistant secretary.

Held – on appeal – the defence of qualified privilege is a defence for the individual who is sued, and not a defence for the publication. It is quite erroneous to say that it is attached to the publication. The three committee members innocent of malice were entitled to protection and were not liable. The assistant secretary also had an independent and individual privilege, and was not responsible or liable for the tort of those members of the committee who had acted with malice. Even in a joint tort, the tort is the separate act of each individual; each is severally answerable for it; and each is severally entitled to his own defence.

Defamation: media developments in qualified privilege

445a *Loutchansky v Times Newspapers Ltd (No 2)* [2002] 1 All ER 652

The Times newspaper published articles alleging that Dr Grigori Loutchansky was in charge of a major Russian criminal organisation involved in money laundering and the smuggling of nuclear weapons. The defence was qualified privilege based on public interest. *The Times* was found liable by reason of having failed to apply the House of Lords guidelines in *Reynolds v Times Newspapers Ltd* [1999] 3 WLR 1010. *The Times* appealed to the Court of Appeal.

The Court of Appeal dealing with *Reynolds* said that the House of Lords had established in that case that when deciding whether to publish defamatory material to the public the relevant interest was that of the public in a modern democracy, to free expression and the promotion of a free and vigorous press to keep the public informed. However, there was a corresponding duty on the journalist and his or her editor to behave responsibly and if they did not do so privilege could not arise. In regard to responsible behaviour, the House of Lords in *Reynolds* laid down a number of matters to be considered. In the *Loutchansky* case the court considered that *The Times* failed a number of these tests as follows:

- reliability and motivation of its sources of information;
- urgency (the judge had found that there was none);
- did the articles contain the gist of the claimant's side of the story? (it did not said the judge);
- was comment sought from the claimant? (apparently not).

Up to that point the Court of Appeal would have dismissed the appeal but the High Court judge had introduced an additional test, i.e. would *The Times* have been subject to legitimate criticism if it had failed to publish the information? This the Court of Appeal felt was too strict from the newspaper's point of view. The case was remitted to the High Court and the judge for him to examine his findings on the *Reynolds* principles but without the more stringent test identified in his judgment.

Comment (i) Courts dealing with this type of case will now have to use the more liberal approach to media publication set out in *Jameel v Wall Street Journal Europe* [2006] 3 WLR 642 (see p 599).

(ii) A further item of interest arose in this case from the posting of the article on *The Times* website. Section 5 of the Defamation Act 1996 reduces the limitation period for bringing claims for defamation from three years to one year. But how is this period to be applied where a libel is published on an Internet website and remains there for some time? The claimant in *Loutchansky* brought his action more than one year after the libel was first published on *The Times* website that contained news items and remained on the website for some time receiving a number of visits every month. *The Times* contended that the time should run from first publication which is the rule applied in the USA. The claimant contended that taking the number of visits each month since first publication his claim was within the one year period. On this point the Court of Appeal ruled that there had been a continuing publication so that the claimant's case was not barred by the one year limitation rule. The first or single publication rule could not be adapted to an English law context. Time does not begin to run until the material is removed from the website.

Defamation: consent of the claimant to publication

446 *Chapman v Lord Ellesmere and Others* [1932] 2 KB 431

The claimant was a trainer and one of his horses, after winning a race, was found to be doped. An inquiry was held by the Stewards of the Jockey Club, as a result of which they decided to disqualify the horse for future racing, and to warn the claimant off Newmarket Heath. The decision was published in the *Racing Calendar*. The claimant contended that the words were defamatory because they implied that he had doped the horse. The defendants, who were the proprietors of the *Racing Calendar*, contended that the words were not defamatory, and meant simply that the claimant had been warned off for not protecting the horse against doping. Evidence showed that it was a condition of a trainer's licence that the

withdrawal of that licence should appear in the *Racing Calendar*, which was also to be the recognised vehicle of communication for all matters concerning infringement of rules.

Held – the claimant being bound by the terms of his licence, the doctrine of *volenti non fit injuria* applied as regards publication in the *Racing Calendar*, so that the claimant had no cause of action.

Defamation: damages: compensatory not punitive

447 *Davis v Rubin* [1967] 112 Sol J 51

The claimants were chartered accountants of good reputation and they wished to buy the lease of business premises. The defendants, who were the landlords, wrote to the holder of the lease saying that they would not accept the claimants if the lease was assigned and referred in a defamatory fashion to the claimants' business and references. The claimants sued for damages in respect of the libel published in the letter, and were awarded £4,000 each. The Court of Appeal, allowing the defendants' appeal, said that the damages were 'excessive, extravagant and exorbitant'. There had been publication to one person only and there was no evidence that the claimants' reputation had been diminished in the minds of other persons. A reasonable sum would not have exceeded £1,000 each and a new trial was ordered on the issue of damages.

Comment Over the past few years damages awarded by juries in defamation cases have generally been regarded as excessive, often exceeding those granted for serious physical injuries. Section 8 of the Courts and Legal Services Act 1990 allows the Court of Appeal to substitute its own award of damages for those of the jury at first instance instead of ordering a new trial. As regards defamation, this power was used in *Rantzen v Mirror Group Newspapers* [1993] 3 WLR 953.

The defendants had alleged that Esther Rantzen had kept secret the fact that a particular person was a child abuser and that this had put children at risk. They were found guilty of libel and the jury in the High Court awarded Ms Rantzen £250,000.

On appeal the Court of Appeal reduced the award to £110,000, using the s 8 power and also because of the European Convention for the Protection of Human Rights and Fundamental Freedoms. The Convention is designed, among other things, to prevent the restriction of free speech, which excessive libel damages obviously do (see also *John v Mirror Group Newspapers* (1995)).

The matter of an excessive award of damages arose in *Grobbelaar v News Group Newspapers Ltd* [2002] 4 All ER 732. The Court of Appeal had regarded a verdict of libel and an award of damages of £85,000 by a jury to G as perverse in terms of the evidence. It was alleged that G had conspired to fix and had actually fixed football matches. The Court of Appeal said that the decision and the award were perverse because they could only have been based on the fact that G was innocent in terms of the allegations whereas he had admitted taking money to fix matches. It therefore quashed the decision. The House of Lords restored the verdict in terms of the libel but reduced G's damages to £1.

Rylands v *Fletcher*: strict liability: escape of fire

448 ***Emanuel* v *Greater London Council*** (1970) 114 Sol J 653

A contractor employed by the Ministry of Public Building and Works removed prefabricated bungalows from the Council's land. The contractor lit a fire and negligently allowed sparks to spread to the claimant's land where buildings and goods were damaged. The claimant sued the GLC and it was *held* – by James, J – that:

(*a*) on the facts the Council remained in occupation of the site;

(*b*) the contractor was not a 'stranger' to the Council since it retained a power of control over his activities; and

(*c*) although the Council had not been negligent and was not vicariously liable for the contractor's negligence since it did not employ him, it was strictly liable under *Rylands* v *Fletcher* for the escape of fire.

Rylands v *Fletcher*: there must be an escape: whether the rule applies to personal injuries

449 ***Read* v *J Lyons & Co Ltd*** [1947] AC 156

The appellant was employed by the Ministry of Supply as an Inspector of Munitions in the respondents' munitions factory. In the course of her employment there she was injured by the explosion of a shell which was in course of manufacture. She did not allege negligence on the part of the defendants, but based her claim on *Rylands* v *Fletcher*. The trial judge found that there was liability under the rule, but the Court of Appeal and the House of Lords reversed this decision, *holding* that the rule did not apply since there had been no escape of the thing that inflicted the injury. In the words of Viscount Simon, LC, 'Escape for the purpose of applying the proposition in *Rylands* v *Fletcher* means escape from a place which the defendant has occupation of, or control over, to a place which is outside his occupation or control.' It was also suggested *obiter* in this case that the rule in *Rylands* v *Fletcher* does not extend to personal injury, but only to injury to property.

Comment The *ratio* of the Court of Appeal in *Hale* v *Jennings Bros* [1938] 1 All ER 579 suggests that there may be liability for personal injury. In that case a stallholder at a fair suffered personal injury because of the escape of the defendants' chair-o-plane. It was held that she had a good claim under *Rylands* v *Fletcher*.

Rylands v *Fletcher*: does not depend on ownership of land: covers escapes of a variety of offensive and dangerous substances

450 ***Charing Cross Electricity Supply Co* v *Hydraulic Power Co*** [1914] 3 KB 772

The defendant's water mains under a public street burst and damaged the claimant's cables which were also laid under the street.

Held – the defendant was liable under the rule in *Rylands* v *Fletcher*, because the rule was not confined to wrongs between owners of adjacent land and did not depend on ownership of land. Here it could be applied to owners of adjacent chattels.

451 ***Attorney-General* v *Corke*** [1933] Ch 89

The defendant was the owner of disused brickfields, and he permitted a number of gypsies to occupy them and live in caravans and tents. The gypsies threw slop water about in the neighbourhood of the fields and accumulated all sorts of filth thereabouts. The court *held* that *Rylands* v *Fletcher* applied, and an injunction was granted against the defendant. While it was not unlawful to license caravan dwellers, it was abnormal use of land, since such persons often have habits of life which are offensive to those persons with fixed homes.

Comment Reference should also be made to *Smith* v *Scott* (1972).

Rylands v *Fletcher*: not applicable to escape of things naturally on land: other claims

452 ***Giles* v *Walker*** (1890) 24 QBD 656

The defendant wished to redeem certain forest land and ploughed it up. Thistles grew up on the land and thistle-seed was blown in large quantities by the wind from the defendant's land to that of the claimant.

Held – there was no duty as between adjoining occupiers to cut things such as thistles which are the natural growth of the soil, therefore, the defendant was not liable. Presumably if a person deliberately set thistles on his land, he would be liable under the rule in *Rylands* v *Fletcher*, for it is not usual to cultivate weeds on one's land.

Comment An action for nuisance would probably have succeeded here, because a person is liable for a nuisance on his land (even if he has not caused it) if he lets it continue (but note Weeds Act 1959).

453 *Davey* v *Harrow Corporation* [1957] 2 All ER 305

The roots of the defendant's elm trees spread to the claimant's land and caused damage to the claimant's property.

Held – the defendant was liable in nuisance, whether the trees were self-sown or not. It was no defence to an action for nuisance that the thing causing the nuisance was naturally on the defendant's land, though it might be a defence to liability under the rule in *Rylands* v *Fletcher*.

Rylands v *Fletcher*: defence of act of God

454 *Greenock Corporation* v *Caledonian Railway Co* [1917] AC 556

The Corporation, in laying out a park, constructed a concrete paddling pool for children in the bed of a stream, thereby altering its course and natural flow. Owing to rainfall of extraordinary violence, the stream overflowed and poured down the street, flooding the railway company's premises. The House of Lords *held* that this was not an act of God and the Corporation was liable. The House of Lords indicated the restricted range of the defence of act of God and of the decision in *Nichols* v *Marsland* (1876), distinguishing that case on the ground that whereas in *Nichols* v *Marsland* the point at issue was the liability for storing water in artificial lakes, the point here was interference with the natural course of a stream, and anyone so interfering must provide even against exceptional rainfall.

Rylands v *Fletcher*: defence: wrongful act of stranger

455 *Rickards* v *Lothian* [1913] AC 263

The defendant was the occupier of business premises and leased part of the second floor to the claimant. On the fourth floor was a men's cloakroom with a wash basin. The cloakroom was provided for the use of tenants and persons in their employ. The claimant's stock in trade was found one morning seriously damaged by water which had seeped through the ceiling from the wash basin on the fourth floor. Examination showed that the waste pipe had been plugged with various articles such as nails, penholders, string and soap, and the water tap had been turned full on. The defendant's caretaker had found the cloakroom in proper order at 10.20 pm the previous evening.

Held – the defendant was not liable under the rule in *Rylands* v *Fletcher* because the damage had been caused by the act of a stranger.

Rylands v *Fletcher*: defence: common benefit

456 *Peters* v *Prince of Wales Theatre (Birmingham) Ltd* [1943] KB 73

The defendants leased to the claimant a shop in a building which contained a theatre. In the latter there was, to the claimant's knowledge, a sprinkler system installed as a precaution against fire and the system extended to the claimant's shop. In a thaw, following a severe frost, water poured from the sprinklers in the defendants' rehearsal room into the claimant's shop and damaged his stock. The claimant sued for damages for negligence, and under *Rylands* v *Fletcher*.

Held – there was no negligence on the part of the defendants and there was no liability under *Rylands* v *Fletcher*, because the sprinkler had been installed for the common benefit of the claimant and defendants.

THE LAW OF PROPERTY

Ownership and possession: rights of owner paramount

457 *Moffat* v *Kazana* [1968] 3 All ER 271

The claimant hid banknotes in a biscuit tin in the roof of his house. He sold the house to the defendant, one of whose workmen discovered the money. In this action by the claimant to recover the money it was *held* – by Wrangham, J – that the claimant succeeded. He had never shown any intention to pass the title in the money to anyone. Therefore, his title was good, not only against the finder, but also against the new owner of the house.

Adverse possession or squatters' rights

458 *Hayward* v *Challoner* [1967] 3 All ER 122

The predecessors in title of the claimant landowner let land to the rector of a parish at a rent of 10s (50p) a year. The rent was not collected after 1942 and the claimant now sued for possession.

Held – by the Court of Appeal – a right of action in respect of rent or possession must be held to have accrued when the rent due was first unpaid, and therefore was barred by what is now the Limitation

Act 1980. The rector as a corporation sole had acquired a good squatter's title.

459 *Littledale* v *Liverpool College* [1900] 1 Ch 19

The claimants had a right of way for agricultural purposes over a strip of grass land belonging to the defendants. The claimants put up gates which they kept locked at each end of the strip, and used the grass for grazing, keeping the hedges of the strip clipped. They now claimed ownership of the land by virtue of adverse possession.

Held – the claimants' acts could be construed as protecting the right of way, rather than excluding the owner, and were insufficient to establish the claimants' title to the land.

460 *Smirk* v *Lyndale Developments Ltd* [1974] 2 All ER 8

The claimant had a service tenancy of a house owned by the British Railways Board. In 1960 he took effective possession of an adjacent plot of land owned by the Board, though the Board was unaware of his action. The claimant did not communicate to the Board at any time that he disclaimed the Board's title. The Board sold the house and the plot to the defendants who granted a new tenancy of the house to Smirk on different terms not including the adjacent plot. The claimant asserted a possessory title to that plot. It was *held* – by Pennycuick, V-C – that the claimant did not have a good possessory title to the plot.

Bailment: damage to goods; action by bailee

461 *The Winkfield* [1902] P 42

This was an Admiralty action arising because a ship called the *Mexican* was negligently struck and sunk by a ship called the *Winkfield*. The *Mexican* was carrying mail from South Africa to England during the Boer War. The Postmaster-General made, among other things, a claim for damages in respect of the estimated value of parcels and letters for which no claim had been made or instructions received from the senders. The Postmaster-General undertook to distribute the amount recovered when the senders were found. An objection was made that the Postmaster-General represented the Crown and was not liable to the senders (see now Crown Proceedings Act 1947).

Held – as a bailee in possession the Postmaster-General could recover damages for the loss of the goods irrespective of whether or not he was liable to the bailors.

Comment It should be noted that a bailee cannot sue for loss or damage to the bailed goods if the bailor has already brought a successful claim for that loss or damage. Thus, in *O'Sullivan* v *Williams* [1992] 3 All ER 385, A allowed B to use his car while he was on holiday. While it was parked outside B's home it was written off when an excavator fell off a tractor on to it. A sued for damages and that action was settled by the payment of an appropriate sum. B sued for damages for nervous shock and inconvenience due to the loss of the car. It was held by the Court of Appeal that B's claim for nervous shock succeeded but that she could not recover damages for inconvenience since this arose from damage to the bailed chattel.

Bailment and licence distinguished

462 *Ashby* v *Tolhurst* [1937] 2 All ER 837

The claimant drove his car on to a piece of land at Southend owned by the defendants. He paid one shilling to an attendant who was the defendants' servant and was given a ticket. He left the car with the doors locked. When he returned his car had gone, the attendant having allowed a thief, who said he was a friend of the claimant, to drive it away. The ticket was called a 'car-park ticket' and contained the words: 'The proprietors do not take any responsibility for the safe custody of any cars or articles therein, nor for any damage to the cars or articles however caused nor for any injuries to any persons, all cars being left in all respects entirely at their owner's risk. Owners are requested to show a ticket when required.'

Held that:

(a) the relationship between the parties was that of licensor and licensee, not that of bailor and bailee because there was in no sense a transfer of possession. There was, therefore, no obligation upon the defendants towards the claimant in respect of the car;

(b) if there was a contract of bailment, the servant delivered possession of the car quite honestly under a mistake and the conditions on the tickets were wide enough to protect the defendants;

(c) there could not be implied into the contract a term that the car should not be handed over without production of the ticket.

Comment (i) Where the claimant hands over the key, the court may find a transfer of possession and a bailment, but the delivery of the key is not conclusive.

Thus, in *Sadler* v *Brittania Country House Hotel* (1993) CLW 40, S left his car by agreement with the hotel in one of the hotel's two car parks for two weeks while he went abroad. He paid £75 for this service. He took the keys with him but nevertheless the car was stolen in his absence. The system of guarding the cars was negligent. Only one guard checked both car parks on only five days per week, with no cover for breaks. S recovered damages for the loss of the car and inconvenience for loss of use. This was not, the judge said, a car park of 'general invitation' such as a public car park. It was not a temporary parking arrangement and the defendants owed him a duty of care as bailees. They were not mere licensees with no duty of care.

(ii) It was held in *Chappell (Fred) v National Car Parks, The Times*, 22 May 1987, that where a vehicle was parked on NCP land for a fee but there was no barrier, the land was open and no keys to the vehicle were handed over, as the owner locked the vehicle and retained the keys, no bailment of the vehicle took place and NCP were not liable for its theft.

(iii) It should not be assumed that because in the *Chappell* case there was no bailment that this result will be arrived at in all such public car parks. A modern multi-storey car park with its careful checks on incoming and outgoing cars and a fee in return for a parking space and tickets to be presented before allowing departure will almost invariably constitute a bailment.

The position may be different where the car park is on open land albeit fenced since in such a case it is difficult to show the essential ingredient of bailment, i.e. that the owner gives the bailee the ability to exclude all others except the owner.

463 *Ultzen v Nicols* [1894] 1 QB 92

A waiter took a customer's overcoat, without being asked to do so, and hung it on a peg behind the customer. The coat was stolen and it was *held* that the restaurant keeper was a bailee of the coat and that there was negligence in supervision on the part of the bailee.

Comment In this case the servant seems to have been regarded as taking possession, but it is unlikely that a bailment will arise if a customer merely hangs his coat on a stand or other device provided by the establishment.

464 *Deyong v Shenburn* [1946] 1 All ER 226

An allegation that an actor who left his clothes in a dressing room had constituted the theatre owners bailees of the clothes was not sustained.

Bailment: finders and involuntary recipients

465 *Newman v Bourne & Hollingsworth* (1915) 31 TLR 209

The claimant went into the defendant's shop on a Saturday in order to buy a coat. While trying on coats she took off a diamond brooch and put it on a show

case. She left the shop having forgotten the brooch; an assistant found it and handed it to the shopwalker who put it in his desk. By the firm's rules the brooch ought to have been taken to its lost property office. The brooch could not be found on the following Monday.

Held – there was evidence to support the trial judge's finding that the firm had become a bailee and had not exercised proper care.

466 *Neuwirth v Over Darwen Industrial Co-operative Society* (1894) 70 TLR 374

A concert hall was hired for an evening performance. No mention was made of rehearsal but the orchestra rehearsed in the hall during the afternoon without opposition from the proprietors or the keeper of the hall. After the rehearsal Neuwirth left his double-bass fiddle in an ante-room in such a position that when the hall keeper came to turn on the gas in the ante-room he could not do so without first moving the instrument. The fiddle fell and was badly damaged.

Held – there was no contract of bailment between the parties. The care of musical instruments was outside the scope of the hall keeper's authority and there was no evidence that he had been guilty of negligence in the course of his employment.

Comment Reference should also be made to *Elvin and Powell Ltd v Plummer Roddis Ltd* (1933).

Bailment: obligations of bailor

467 *Hyman v Nye* (1881) 6 QBD 685

The claimant hired a landau with a pair of horses and a driver for a drive from Brighton to Shoreham and back. The claimant was involved in an accident owing to a broken bolt which caused the carriage to upset so that the claimant was thrown out of it.

Held – the trial judge's direction to the jury that the claimant must prove negligence was wrong. There was an implied warranty that the carriage was as fit for the purpose for which it was hired as skill and care could make it.

468 *Reed v Dean* [1949] 1 KB 188

The claimants hired a motor launch called the *Golden Age* from the defendant for a family holiday on the Thames. The claimants set sail at about 7 pm on 22 June 1946, and at about 9 pm, when they were near Sonning, they discovered that a liquid in the bilge by the engine was on fire. They attempted to extinguish the fire but were unable to do so, the fire-fighting equipment with which the launch was supplied being out of order. The claimants had to abandon the launch and suffered personal injury and loss of belongings. The claimants admitted to a fireman after the accident that they might have spilt some petrol when the tank was refilled.

Held – the claimants succeeded because there was an implied undertaking by the defendant that the launch was fit for the purpose for which it was hired as reasonable care and skill could make it. Further, as the launch had caught fire due to an unexplained cause, there was a presumption that it was not fit for this purpose. The defendant's failure to provide proper fire-fighting equipment was a breach of the implied warranty of fitness.

Bailment: obligations of bailee

469 *Houghland v R Low (Luxury Coaches) Ltd* [1962] 2 All ER 159

The defendant company supplied a coach for the purposes of an old people's outing to Southampton. On returning the passengers put their luggage into the boot of the coach. During a stop for tea the coach was found to be defective and another one was sent for and the luggage was transferred from the first coach to the relief coach. The removal of the luggage from the first coach was not supervised, but the restacking of the luggage into the new coach was supervised by one of the defendant's employees. When the passengers arrived home a suitcase belonging to the claimant was missing and he brought an action against the defendant for its loss. It was *held*, by the Court of Appeal, that whether the action was for negligence or in detinue, the defendant was liable unless it could show that it had not been negligent. On the facts it had failed to prove this and was, therefore, liable. It was in this case that Ormerod, LJ made some observations on bailments in general. The county court judge had found that the bailment was gratuitous and that the defendant was liable only for gross negligence. Dealing with this question, Ormerod, LJ said:

> For my part I have always found some difficulty in understanding just what was gross negligence, because it appears to me that the standard of care required in a case of bailment or any other type of case is the standard demanded by the circumstances of the particular case. It seems to me to try and put bailment, for instance, into a watertight compartment, such as gratuitous bailment on the one hand and bailment for reward on the other, is to overlook the fact that there might well be an infinite variety of cases which might come into one or other category.

470 *Global Dress Co v W H Boase & Co* [1966] 2 Lloyd's Rep 72

B & Co were master porters and had custody of 30 cases of goods belonging to G & Co at a Liverpool dock shed. One case was stolen and G & Co brought an action for damages against B & Co. B & Co offered evidence of their system of safeguarding the goods and the county court judge at first instance found the system to be as good as any other in the Liverpool Docks, but notwithstanding this he found B & Co liable. On appeal to the Court of Appeal it was *held* that if B & Co could not affirmatively prove that their watchman was not negligent it was of no avail to show that they had an impeccable system, and the appeal should be dismissed. Thus, the onus of proving that their servant was not negligent lay upon B & Co.

471 *Doorman v Jenkins* (1843) 2 Ad & El 256

The claimant left the sum of £32 10s with the defendant, who was a coffee-house keeper, for safe custody and without any reward. The defendant put the money in with his own in a cash box which he kept in the taproom. The taproom was open to the public on a Sunday but the rest of the house was not and the cash was, in fact, stolen on a Sunday. Lord Denman *held* that the loss of the defendant's own money was not enough to prove reasonable care and the court found for the claimant.

472 *Brabant v King* [1895] AC 632

This action was brought against the government of Queensland for damage to certain explosives belonging to the claimant which the government, as bailee for reward, had stored in sheds situated near the water's edge on Brisbane River. The water rose to an exceptional height and the store was flooded. The question of inevitable accident was raised and also the degree of negligence required. The Privy Council *held* that, because of the nature of the site, the bailee was required to place the goods at such a level as would in all probability ensure their absolute immunity from flood water, and the defendant was held liable. The Privy Council went on to say, in case of deposit for reward, that bailees were 'under a level of obligation to exercise the same degree of care, towards the preservation of the goods entrusted to them from injury, which might reasonably be expected from a skilled storekeeper, acquainted with the risks to be apprehended from the character either of the storehouse or of its locality; and the obligations included, not only the duty of taking all reasonable precautions to obviate these risks but the duty of taking all proper measures for the protection of the goods when such risks were imminent or had actually occurred'. Counsel for the government suggested that a bailee was not liable for damage caused by the defects in his warehouse where these defects were known to the bailor, in this case the proximity of the warehouse to the Brisbane River. The Privy Council dismissed this argument on the ground that it was a dangerous one, not supported by any authority. It said that the bailor could rely on the skill of the bailee in this matter. It will be seen from this decision that a bailee for reward is liable even in the case of uncommon or unexpected danger, unless he uses efforts which are in proportion to the emergency to ward off that danger.

473 *Wilson v Brett* (1843) 11 M & W 113

Wilson was in process of selling his horse and Brett volunteered to ride the horse in order to show it off to a likely purchaser. Brett rode the horse on to wet and slippery turf and the horse fell and was injured. Brett pleaded that he was not negligent but the court *held* that he had not used the skill he professed to possess when he volunteered to ride the horse and that he was liable.

474 *Saunders (Mayfair) Furs v Davies* (1965) 109 SJ 922

The claimants delivered a valuable fur coat to a shop belonging to the defendants, on sale-or-return terms. The defendants displayed it in their shop window and at 2.30 am one morning the coat was stolen in a smash-and-grab raid.

Held – in all the circumstances and because of the valuable nature of the property, the defendants had taken an unreasonable risk and were negligent in leaving the coat on display in the window all night.

475 *Coldman v Hill* [1919] 1 KB 443

The defendant was a bailee of cows belonging to the claimant. Two of these cows were stolen through no fault of the defendant, though he failed to notify the claimant and did not inform the police or take any steps to find the cows. The claimant now sued him for negligence and it was *held* – by the Court of Appeal – that it was up to the defendant to prove that, even if notice had been given, the cows would not have been recovered. In the circumstances of this case that burden had not been discharged and the defendant was liable.

Bailment: delegation by bailee

476 *Davies v Collins* [1945] 1 All ER 247

An American Army officer sent his uniform to the defendants to be cleaned. It was accepted on the following conditions: 'Whilst every care is exercised in cleaning and dyeing garments, all orders are accepted at owner's risk entirely and we are unable to hold ourselves responsible for damage.' The defendants did not clean the uniform but sub-contracted the work to another firm of cleaners. In the event, the uniform was lost and the defendants were *held* liable in damages. The Court of Appeal took the view that the limitation clause operated to exclude the right to sub-contract because it used the words 'every care is exercised', which postulated personal service.

477 *Edwards v Newland* [1950] 2 All ER 1072

The defendant agreed to store the claimant's furniture for reward. Later, without the claimant's knowledge, the defendant made arrangements with another company to store the claimant's furniture. The third party's warehouse was damaged by a bomb and they asked the defendant to remove the furniture but this was not done immediately because there was a dispute about charges. Eventually the claimant removed his furniture but some pieces were missing.

Held – the claimant could recover from the defendant because he had departed from the terms of the contract of bailment by sub-contracting. However, the defendant was not entitled to damages against the third party because the latter, though a bailee, had not, in the circumstances, been negligent.

478 *Learoyd Bros & Co v Pope & Sons* [1966] 2 Lloyd's Rep 142

The claimants entered into an agreement with a carrier for the transport of their goods. The carrier sub-contracted the work to the defendants, who were also a firm of carriers, though the claimants had no notice of this arrangement. The lorry was stolen while the defendants' driver was in the wharf office upon arrival at London Docks, and the carrier with whom the claimants had contracted paid some of the claimants' loss and the claimants now sued the defendants for the balance.

Held – the defendants were bailees to the claimants, notwithstanding the absence of any contract between them, and that the defendants' driver was negligent in leaving the lorry unattended and, therefore, the defendants were liable for the claimants' loss.

Bailment: actions against bailees for non-delivery: defence of superior title

479 Rogers, Sons & Co v Lambert & Co [1891] 1 QB 318

The claimants had purchased copper from the defendants but did not take delivery of it and left it with the defendants as warehousemen. The claimants then resold the copper to a third person. Some time later the claimants asked for delivery of the copper from the defendants, but the defendants refused to deliver on the ground that the claimants no longer had a title to it.

Held – this was no defence to an action of detinue. The defendants must show that they were defending the action on behalf and with the authority of the true owner.

Co-ownership: severance of joint tenancy

480 Re Draper's Conveyance [1967] 3 All ER 853

In 1951 a house was conveyed to a husband and wife in fee simple as joint tenants at law and of the proceeds of the trust for sale. In November 1965, the wife was granted a decree *nisi* of divorce and this was made absolute in March 1966. In February 1966, she applied by summons under s 17 of the Married Women's Property Act 1882, for an order that the house be sold and in her affidavit asked that the proceeds of sale be distributed equally between her husband and herself. The court made such an order in May 1966, and in August 1966 a further order was made under the Act of 1882 that the former husband give up possession of the house. In spite of the order, the former husband remained in possession until January 1967, when a writ of possession was executed. Four days later he died without having made a will. The former wife now applied to the court to determine whether she held the proceeds of any sale absolutely (which would have been the case if she and her former husband had been joint tenants at his death) or for herself and the deceased's estate as tenants in common in equal shares (which would have been the case if there had been severance).

Held – severance of a joint tenancy in a matrimonial home may be effected by the wife's issue of a summons under s 17 of the Married Women's Property Act 1882, and her affidavit in support. The affidavit had stated the former wife's wish for severance and had operated accordingly. Therefore, she held any proceeds of sale as trustee for herself and the estate of her former husband as tenants in common in equal shares.

Leasehold: leases and licences distinguished

481 Shell-Mex and BP Ltd v Manchester Garages Ltd [1971] 1 All ER 841

The claimants by an agreement contained in a document called a licence let the defendants into occupation of a petrol filling station for one year. The parties had some disagreements during this time and at the end of the year the claimants asked the defendants to leave. The defendants refused claiming that the agreement gave them a business tenancy protected by the Landlord and Tenant Act 1954, Part II, which deals with the method of terminating business tenancies. This method had not been followed by the claimants.

Held – by the Court of Appeal – it was open to parties to an agreement to decide whether that agreement should constitute a lease or a licence, but the fact that it was called a licence was not conclusive. However, in this case it was a licence because the claimants retained, under the agreement, the right to visit the premises whenever they liked and to exercise general control over the layout, decoration and equipment of the filling station. These rights were inconsistent with the grant of a tenancy.

Comment In *Westminster City Council* v *Clarke* [1992] 2 WLR 229 the House of Lords decided that Mr Clarke, who was an occupant of a council hostel for single homeless persons, was a licensee and not a tenant under a lease. He had no exclusive rights of occupation and his licence could be terminated on seven days' notice or forthwith if in breach of the rules. The claimants gave him notice because of complaints about him and were entitled to possession of his room.

Leasehold: exclusive possession of land not necessarily a tenancy in spite of agreement

482 Binions v Evans [1972] 2 All ER 70

Mr Evans was employed as a chauffeur by the Tredegar Estate which owned a number of houses. His father and grandfather had also worked for the estate. Mr Evans died in 1965 and the trustees of the estate allowed Mrs Evans to continue to reside in a cottage which belonged to the estate, free of rent and rates. In 1968 the trustees made a formal agreement with Mrs Evans, the defendant in this case, who was then aged 76. The agreement purported to create a tenancy at will in order to provide her with a temporary home for the rest of her life free of rent without any rights to assign, sub-let or part with possession. Two years later the trustees sold the cottage and other properties to Mr and Mrs Binions, the claimants, expressly subject to the tenancy of Mrs Evans and because of that tenancy the trustees accepted a lower price. A copy of the trustees' agreement with Mrs Evans was given to the purchasers. Shortly afterwards the purchasers tried to evict Mrs Evans on the ground that her tenancy, being at will, was liable to determination at any time. She refused to vacate and the court was asked to decide whether her occupation was in the nature of a tenancy at will or a mere licence.

Held – by the Court of Appeal – the interest of the defendant was not a tenancy at will, although it had been so described in the agreement. When the trustees created a right in her favour to live in the cottage for the rest of her life, it could not be a tenancy at will liable to be terminated at any time. It was, therefore, a mere licence, though equity would not permit the claimants to revoke it as long as the defendant was not in breach of the licence. The claimants held on a constructive trust to give effect to the agreement with Mrs Evans.

Comment In *Prudential Assurance Co v London Residuary Body* [1992] 3 WLR 279 the House of Lords held that an agreement which stated that certain land was leased until it was required for road widening was void as a lease for uncertainty as all leases of land must be for a term of certain duration.

Leaseholds: effect in equity of agreement for a lease other than by deed; part performance; liability of landlord for latent defects

483 *Walsh v Lonsdale* (1882) 21 Ch D 9

The defendant agreed in writing to grant a seven years' lease of a mill to the claimant at a rent payable one year in advance. The claimant entered into possession without any formal lease having been granted, and he paid his rent quarterly and not in advance. Subsequently the defendant demanded a year's rent in advance, and as the claimant refused to pay, the defendant distrained on his property. At common law the claimant was a tenant from year to year because no formal lease had been granted, and as such his rent was not payable in advance. The claimant argued that the legal remedy of distress was not available to the defendant.

Held – as the agreement was one of which the court could grant specific performance, and as equity regarded as done that which ought to be done, the claimant held on the same terms as if a lease had been granted. Therefore, the distress was valid.

Leaseholds: implied covenants: inapplicable to latent defects

484 *O'Brien v Robinson* [1973] 1 All ER 583

The claimant was the tenant of a flat to which s 32 of the Housing Act 1961 (giving an implied covenant to repair) applied (see now Landlord and Tenant Act 1985). In 1965 the claimant had complained about stamping on the ceiling above, but it was found that the landlord was not given notice that the ceiling was defective. In 1968 the ceiling fell and the claimant was injured.

Held – by the House of Lords – the defendant landlord was not liable for breach of covenant.

Comment (i) In *Sheldon v West Bromwich Corporation* (1973) 25 P & CR 360, the Court of Appeal held the defendant landlord liable where a water tank in a council house had remained discoloured for some considerable time to the knowledge of the Council. The tank burst and the Council was in breach of its implied covenant, under what was then s 32 of the Housing Act 1961, to keep the installation for the supply of water in repair. The discolouration of the tank, which the Council knew about, meant that this was not a latent defect.

(ii) The relevant provisions of the 1961 Act are now to be found in ss 11–16 of the Landlord and Tenant 1985.

Easements: cannot exist 'in gross' but only with reference to the holding of land

485 *Hill v Tupper* (1863) H & C 121

Hill was the lessee of land on the bank of a canal. The land and the canal were owned by the lessor, and Hill was granted the sole and exclusive right of putting pleasure boats on the canal. Later Tupper, without authority, put rival pleasure boats on the canal. Hill now sued Tupper for the breach of a so-called easement granted by the owner of the canal.

Held – the right to put pleasure boats on the canal was not an interest in property which the law could recognise as attaching to the land. It was in the nature of a contractual licence which could not be enforced against the whole world. Tupper could have been sued by the owner of the canal, or by Hill, as lessee, if he had also been granted a lease of the canal.

Easements: right must be definite enough to form subject of grant

486 *Bass v Gregory* (1890) 25 QBD 481

The claimants were the owners of a public house in Nottingham, and the defendant was the owner of some cottages and a yard adjoining the claimants' premises. The claimants claimed to be entitled, by user as of right, to have the cellar of their public house ventilated by means of a hole or shaft cut from the cellar to an old well situated in the yard occupied by the defendant. The claimants sought an injunction to prevent the defendant from continuing to block the passage of air from the well.

Held – the right having been established, an injunction would be granted because the access of air to the premises came through a strictly defined channel, and it was possible to establish it as an easement.

Comment In *Bryant* v *Lefever* (1879) 4 CPD 172, the claimant and defendant occupied adjoining premises, and the claimant's complaint was that the defendant, in rebuilding his house, carried up the building beyond its former height and so checked the access of the draught of air to the claimant's chimneys. The Court of Appeal held that the right claimed could not exist at law, because it was an attempt to claim special rights over the general current of air which is common to all mankind.

Easements: not necessarily negative

487 *Crow* v *Wood* [1970] 3 All ER 425

This case arose out of damage done on a farm in Yorkshire by sheep which strayed on to it from an adjoining moor. The owner of the sheep, who was the owner of another farm adjoining the moor, raised, as a defence against an action for trespass, an obligation on the claimant to fence her own property to keep the sheep out. It was *held* – by the Court of Appeal – that a duty to fence existed as an easement and that it had passed under s 62 of the Law of Property Act 1925, when the defendant purchased his farm, even though his conveyance and previous ones had made no reference to the obligation of other farmers to keep up their fences. However, the right was appurtenant to the land sold and, therefore, became an easement in favour of the defendant and his successors in title.

Easements: categories capable of limited expansion

488 *Re Ellenborough Park* [1956] Ch 131

Ellenborough Park was a piece of open land near the seafront at Weston-super-Mare. The park and the surrounding land was jointly owned by two persons. The surrounding land was sold for building purposes, and the conveyances granted an easement over the park in favour of the owners of the houses. The owners of the houses undertook to be responsible for some of the maintenance, and the owners of the park agreed not to erect dwelling houses or buildings, other than ornamental buildings, on the park. The park was later sold, and the question of the rights of the owners or occupiers of the houses fronting on to the park to enforce their rights over the park arose. It was contended that the rights created by the conveyances were not enforceable, because they did not conform to the essential qualities of an easement, and that they gave a right of perambulation which was not a right legally capable of creation.

Held – the rights granted to the owners of the houses were enforceable as a legal easement.

Comment As regards the categories of easements, there have been a number of cases concerning car parking as an easement. From these case rulings it can be said that although parking can exist as an easement, parking that monopolises the use of the land will be regarded as too great an interference with the land to exist as an easement as in *Batchelor* v *Marlow* (2001) 82 P & CR 459. In that case the claimant claimed a right to an easement to park six cars in a space only large enough for six cars. The same problem arose in *Central Midland Estates Ltd* v *Leicester Dyers Ltd* [2003] 4 CL 404 where the court conceded that the right to park could exist in law. However, since the claim was to park an unlimited number of vehicles anywhere on the piece of land concerned being restricted only by the space available, there could be no easement on the facts because this would make the actual owner's right to the land illusory as in the *Batchelor* case. The only way to achieve such wide rights is to ask for a lease of the relevant land. In this connection, it is worth noting that in *Stonebridge* v *Bygrave* [2001] All ER (D) 376 (Oct) the High Court ruled that where a tenant has an exclusive right in a lease to park in a specified parking place the problems described above did not arise because the owner of the land must be taken to have retained sufficient use of his own land.

489 *Phipps* v *Pears* [1964] 2 All ER 35

A Mr Field owned two houses, Nos 14 and 16 Market Street, Warwick, and in 1930 he demolished No 16 and built a new house with a wall adjacent to the existing wall of No 14. In 1962, No 14 was demolished under an order of Warwick Corporation, leaving exposed the wall of No 16. This wall had never been pointed; indeed it could not have been because it was built hard up against the wall of No 14. It was not, therefore, weatherproof and the rain got in and froze during the winter causing cracks in the wall. The claimant sued for the damage done, claiming an *easement of protection*. It was *held* by the Court of Appeal that there is no such easement. There is a right of support in appropriate cases. No 16 did not depend on No 14 for support; the walls, though adjoining, were independent. Lord Denning, MR said in the course of his judgment:

> A right to protection from the weather (if it exists) is entirely negative. It is a right to stop your neighbour pulling down his house. Seeing that it is a negative easement, it must be looked at with caution because the law has been very chary of creating any new negative easements. . . . If we were to stop a man pulling down his house, we would put a brake on desirable improvement. If it exposes your house to the weather, that is your misfortune. It is not wrong on his part. . . . The only way for an owner to protect himself is by getting a covenant from his neighbour that he will not pull down his house. . . . Such a covenant would be binding in contract; and it would be enforceable on any successor who took with notice of it, but it would not be binding on one who took without notice.

Comment These walls would not appear to be party walls as where two properties are semi-detached. Thus, the newer Party Wall, etc. Act 1996 may not have applied.

490 *Grigsby v Melville* [1972] 1 WLR 1355

A Mr Holroyd owned two adjoining properties, consisting of a cottage and a shop which had recently been occupied in single occupation by a butcher. Beneath the drawing room of the cottage there was a cellar, the only practical means of access to which was by way of steps from the shop which the butcher had used for storing brine in connection with the business of the shop. In 1962, Holroyd conveyed the cottage to Natinvil Builders Ltd, the predecessor in title of the claimant in this case. The conveyance accepted 'such rights and easements or quasi-rights and quasi-easements as may be enjoyed in connection with the . . . adjoining property'. A month later Holroyd conveyed the shop to a Mrs Melville. Mrs Melville, who was a veterinary surgeon, began to use the cellar for storage. The claimant acquired the cottage in 1969 but did not realise the situation until 1971 when she heard hammering beneath her drawing room floor. She sought an injunction to prevent Mrs Melville from trespassing there. The defendants claimed that the cellar was excluded from the property conveyed, or alternatively that they enjoyed an easement of storage there equivalent to an estate in fee simple.

Held – by Brightman, J – (*a*) that the cellar, though not the steps leading to it, formed part of the property conveyed to Natinvil Builders Ltd; (*b*) that the exclusive

right of use claimed was so extensive as probably to be incapable of constituting an easement at law; (*c*) that in any event on the facts use of the cellar for the purposes of the shop had ceased when the properties were divided, it had never been contemplated that such would be the case in the future and the defendants' claim to an easement failed. This decision was confirmed by the Court of Appeal [1973] 3 All ER 455.

Easements: acquisition; effect of Law of Property Act 1925, s 62

491 *Ward v Kirkland* [1966] 1 All ER 609

The wall of a cottage could be repaired only from the yard of the adjoining farm. Before 1928 both properties belonged to a rector and the tenant of the cottage repaired the wall without seeking the permission of the tenant of the farm. In that year the cottage was conveyed to a predecessor in the title of Ward and in 1942 Mrs Kirkland became the tenant of the farm. From 1942 to 1954 work to the wall was done with her permission as tenant and in 1958 she bought the farm. In October 1958, Ward did not make entry on to the farmyard to maintain the wall because Mrs Kirkland would not let him enter as of right. In this action, which was brought to determine, amongst other things, whether Ward was entitled to enter the farmyard to maintain the wall and for an injunction to prevent interference with drains running from the cottage through the farmyard, it was *held* – by Ungoed Thomas, J that:

(*a*) assuming such a right could exist as an easement it would not be defeated on the ground that it would amount to possession or joint possession of the defendant's property;

(*b*) although such a right was not created by implication because it was not 'continuous and apparent', yet the advantage having in fact been enjoyed, it was transformed into an easement by s 62 of the Law of Property Act 1925;

(*c*) no easement had arisen by prescription because permission had been given between 1942 and 1958;

(*d*) permission having been granted by the rector to Ward to lay drains from the cottage through the farmyard and Ward having incurred expense in so doing it was assumed that the permission was of indefinite duration and an injunction would be granted to prevent interference with the drains by Mrs Kirkland.

Comment (i) Even in the absence of an easement, advantage may now be taken of the provisions of the Access to Neighbouring Land Act 1992 (see Chapter 21).

(ii) A further illustration is provided by *Bratts Ltd* v *Habboush*, High Court, 1 July 1999 (unreported). The claimant was a tenant of a nightclub in part of a building. The landlord removed emergency lighting and exit signs from the common parts of the building. The claimant submitted that the right to use and maintain the lighting and exit signs was an easement under s 62 of the 1925 Act. The High Court so held and decided also that the claimant was entitled to damages to replace the signs and lights.

Easements: acquisition: by prescription

492 *Tehidy Minerals* v *Norman* [1971] 2 WLR 711

The owners of a number of farms adjoining a down claimed to be entitled to grazing rights over it. The facts of the case were as follows:

(*a*) the farms and the downs had been owned by one person until 19 January 1920;

(*b*) the down had been requisitioned by the government on 6 October 1941;

(*c*) during the period of requisition the owners of surrounding farms had grazed cattle on the down by arrangement with the Ministry concerned;

(*d*) on 31 December 1960, the down was derequisitioned and the association of farmers which had made the arrangements with the Ministry entered into a further arrangement with the owner of the down for the maintenance of certain fences erected by the Ministry and grazing continued but under the control of the association of farmers.

On appeal from a decision of the county court judge that the farmers were entitled to grazing rights over the down it was *held* by the Court of Appeal that:

(*a*) as there had been no enjoyment of the grazing rights between October 1941 and 31 December 1960, except by permission of the Ministry, the farmers could not claim 30 years' prescription which the Act of 1832 required for a profit to be established by user as of right;

(*b*) despite the extreme unreality of such a presumption, it must be presumed that a modern grant, since lost, had been made of grazing rights at some time between 19 January 1920 and 6 October 1921, i.e. 20 years before the requisition; this presumption could not be rebutted by evidence that no such grant had been made but only by evidence – of which there was none – that it could not have been made;

(*c*) the period of 20 years applied to profits as well as to easements for the purposes of the law of lost modern grant although the Act of 1832 provided for different periods in the two cases;

(*d*) only the demonstration of a fixed intention never at any time to assert the right or to attempt to transmit it to anyone else could amount to an abandonment of an easement or profit, thus the acquiescence by the farmers in the arrangement under which the association controlled the grazing for a period of time did not amount to abandonment.

Comment It was held by the Court of Appeal in *Benn* v *Hardinge*, *The Times*, 13 October 1992, that non-user for 175 years of a grant of a right of way made in 1818 did not of itself indicate an intention of the owner (or his predecessors) of the right to abandon it, so that it still existed in the absence of any evidence of intention to abandon it. Comment in a leading text that 20 years' non-user was enough was not approved.

493 *Diment* v *N H Foot* [1974] 2 All ER 785

A vehicular way across the claimant's field was claimed and had been used by the defendant from time to time without dispute between 1936 and 1967. The claimant, although the registered owner of the field throughout that period, had never farmed the land herself but had had tenants and during much of the time had lived far away or abroad. Until 1967 the claimant knew nothing of the way claimed.

Held – by Pennycuick, V-C – (*a*) the law of prescription rested upon acquiescence for which knowledge was essential; (*b*) the claimant had no actual knowledge and knowledge was not to be imputed to her either (i) because there was a gateway from the field to a parcel of the defendant's land to which there was no vehicular access; there were a number of possible explanations for it; or (ii) because the claimant had not shown that her agents did not have knowledge of the use of the way or the means of knowledge. The presumption that long use was known to the owner was rebuttable and in the present case had been rebutted. It did not extend to the knowledge of agents. The burden of proving such knowledge or means of knowledge lay on the defendant and there was no evidence of either in the present case.

Comment Even if the owner of the servient tenement (A) knows of the use the right will not arise if A *permits* the use. Thus, in *Goldsmith* v *Burrow Construction Co Ltd*, *The Times*, 31 July 1987, the claimants had used a path over the defendants' land for over 20 years. However, the defendants had a gate across the path and locked it from time to time. The Court of Appeal held that no easement had come into being. The claimants' use depended on the permission of the defendants. They had shown this by locking the gate from time to time.

494 *Davis v Whitby* [1974] 1 All ER 806

The claimant and his predecessors in title had enjoyed a right of way over the defendant's land by a certain route for 15 years and then by another route, substituted by agreement, for a further 18 years. On appeal by the defendant to the Court of Appeal against the decision that a right of way over the substituted route had been established by prescription, it was *held* – by the court – that the appeal should be dismissed. 'When you have a way used for some time and then afterwards a substituted way is used for the same purpose, both uses being as of right, with the apparent consent or acquiescence of those concerned, then the original way and the substituted way should be considered as one.' (*Per* Lord Denning, MR)

Restrictive covenants: there must be land which can benefit

495 *Kelly v Barrett* [1924] 2 Ch 379

The owner of an estate in Hampstead developed it for building purposes. He made a new road through it, and sold plots of land along the road to a building firm who erected dwelling houses on the land. The purchasers undertook that the houses built should be used as private dwelling houses only. The owner of the estate did not retain any land except the road, which was afterwards taken over and vested in the local authority. A subsequent purchaser of two adjoining houses carried on a nursing and maternity home in them. The tenant for life under the former estate owner's will and one of the original purchasers claimed an injunction to restrain the defendant's activities.

Held – no injunction could be granted because the agreement was not a valid building scheme, and the vendor's successor did not retain any interest capable of being affected by the restrictions.

Mortgages: equity of redemption; restraint on redemption enforced if parties at arm's length; collective transactions

496 *Knightsbridge Estates Trust Ltd v Byrne* [1939] Ch 441

The claimant company was the owner of a large freehold estate close to Knightsbridge. This estate was mortgaged to a friendly society for a sum of money, which, together with interest, was to be repaid over a period of 40 years in 80 half-yearly instalments. The company wished to redeem the mortgage before the expiration of the term, because it was possible for it to borrow elsewhere at a lower rate of interest.

Held – the company was not entitled to redeem the mortgage before the end of the 40 years because, in the circumstances, the postponement of the right was not unreasonable, since the parties were men of business and equal in bargaining power. A postponement of the right of redemption is not by itself a clog on the equity of redemption; much depends upon the circumstances. Further, the postponement did not offend the rule against perpetuities, which did not apply to mortgages.

497 *Noakes v Rice* [1902] AC 24

The appellant was a brewery company and the respondent wished to become the purchaser of a public house owned by the company. The respondent borrowed money from the company in order to effect the purchase, and agreed that the company should have the exclusive right to supply the premises with malt liquors during the period of the mortgage and afterwards, whether any money was or was not owed. The respondent subsequently gave notice to the company that he was prepared to pay off the money secured by the mortgage, if the company would release him from the above-mentioned contract. This was refused and the respondent asked the court for relief.

Held – the covenant was invalid as a clog on the equity of redemption in so far as it purported to tie the public house after payment of the principal money and interest due on the security.

498 *Kreglinger v New Patagonia Meat and Cold Storage Co* [1914] AC 25

The appellants were a firm of merchants and wool brokers. The respondents carried on the business of preserving and canning meat, and of boiling down carcasses of sheep and other animals. The appellants advanced money to the respondents, the loan being secured by a charge over all the respondents' property. The appellants agreed not to demand repayment for five years, but the respondents could repay the debt at an earlier period on giving notice. The agreement also contained a provision that the respondents should not sell sheepskins to anyone but the appellants for five years from the date of the agreement, so long as the appellants were willing to purchase the same at an agreed price. The loan was paid off before the expiration of the five years.

Held – the option of purchasing the sheepskins was not terminated on repayment, but continued for the period of five years. The option was a collateral contract which was not a mortgage and in no way affected the right to redeem the property.

499 *Cityland and Property (Holdings) Ltd v Dabrah* [1967] 2 All ER 639

A first mortgage of £2,900 was granted by the seller of property to a purchaser and was expressed to be repayable in the sum of £4,553 for which the property was charged. The £4,553 was to be repaid over six years by equal monthly instalments and there was no mention in the mortgage of any interest. The whole of the balance of the £4,553 became payable if the borrower defaulted and for this reason Goff, J *held* that the premium amounting to £1,653 was an unreasonable collateral advantage and, therefore, void under the principle in *Kreglinger*'s case (1914) (above). The judge having disallowed the premium was prepared to allow interest at 7 per cent on a day-to-day basis which he thought to be somewhat more than market rates, but in fact it was below market rates. The premium was an interest computation of $9^1/2$ per cent, non-reducing over six years, and if it had been expressed as such in the mortgage it would appear that the court could not have set it aside since the court can only set aside unreasonable collateral advantages. However, in regard to interest rates, it appears that 'equity does not reform mortgage transactions because they are unreasonable' (Greene, MR in *Knightsbridge Estates Trust Ltd v Byrne* (1939) (see above)). But this case was not cited to Goff, J. It would seem that for the future interest in mortgages should be expressed as such and not disguised as a premium.

Remedies of legal mortgagee: taking possession; duty of mortgagee

500 *White v City of London Brewery Co* (1889) 42 Ch D 237

The claimant had a lease of a public house in Canning Town, and he mortgaged it to the defendants to secure a loan of £900 with interest. One year later, no interest having been paid since the date of the mortgage, the defendants entered into possession of the public house. They later let the premises on a tenancy determinable at three months' notice under which the tenant was to take all his beer from the defendants. Eventually the lease was sold by the defendants, and the claimant asked the defendants to account and pay him what should be found due.

Held – the defendants must account to the claimant for the increased rent they might have received if they had let the public house without the restrictive condition regarding the sale of the defendants' beer, since a 'free house' would produce more rent than a 'tied house'.

Charges and encumbrances over land: spouse's right of occupation

501 *Williams & Glyn's Bank Ltd v Boland* [1980] 3 WLR 138

A husband and wife lived together in the matrimonial home which was owned by the husband and subject to a mortgage with the bank. The husband was registered as the owner for the purposes of the Land Registration Act 1925. It appeared that his wife had made a substantial contribution of money towards buying the house and that she had, accordingly, equitable rights in it. The husband failed to keep up the mortgage repayments and the bank asked the court for a possession order over the house with a view to selling it. The wife raised objection to the possession order, claiming that her rights and occupation gave her an 'overriding interest' in the home which overrode the bank's claim to possession under s 70(1) of the Land Registration Act 1925. Section 70 includes as an overriding interest: 'The rights of every person in actual occupation . . .'. The bank argued that the wife was not in actual occupation and also relied on s 3 of the 1925 Act which provides that equitable rights, such as the wife had, were not an overriding interest but a 'minor interest' and it was admitted that these would not have defeated the bank's claim. However, the House of Lords *held* that the wife's objection must be sustained and refused the bank an order for possession. The wife was in actual possession just as much as her husband and the fact that he was in occupation did not prejudice her right to be regarded as in occupation also. If she had not been in occupation, apparently her equitable rights would have been a minor interest, but since she was also in occupation this fact converted them into an overriding interest.

Comment (i) This decision has caused considerable concern to banks and building societies since the occupation of most houses is shared either with a spouse or a cohabitee or relatives who have made some financial contribution towards the purchase.

(ii) The response of lending institutions has been to ask a spouse (or other relatives who may have rights of occupation) to sign a Deed of Postponement as s 6(3) of the Matrimonial Homes Act 1983 allows. This postpones the interest of an occupier to that of the lender.

(iii) Following the decision of the House of Lords in *Abbey National v Cann* [1990] 2 WLR 832 the person claiming an overriding interest must occupy the property from the time of purchase. Persons who take up occupation later are excluded. For example John buys a house with some help from his mother in terms of finance. Some time after the purchase John's mother comes to live with John. John's mother cannot claim an overriding interest against a person who, e.g., lent John money on mortgage to complete the purchase.

(iv) A contrast is provided by the decision of the House of Lords in *City of London Building Society* v *Flegg* [1987] All ER 435. In this case the property was owned by a husband and wife, Mr and Mrs Maxwell-Brown, as joint tenants. They were, therefore, trustees of land of the property and could give a good receipt for purchase money so as to override all beneficial interests of themselves and others. The building society had advanced capital money to them by way of mortgage and their receipt for that money had overriden all equitable interests including their own and that of Mr & Mrs Flegg, parents of the wife, who lived there. The building society could sell the property without regard to those interests if the loans were not repaid.

(v) See also *Hodgson* v *Marks* (1970) in Chapter 13.

(vi) In *Hypo-Mortgage Services Ltd* v *Robinson* [1997] 2 FCR 422, the Court of Appeal held that children who lived with a parent who was the legal owner of a property could not have an overriding interest protected under the LRA 1925, s 70(1)(g) by reason of actual occupation because they had no rights of their own to occupy and were present only because their parents were the occupiers.

(vii) The decision of the Court of Appeal in *Ferrishurst Ltd* v *Wallcite Ltd*, *The Times*, 8 December 1998 makes it clear that in order to rely on s 70 a person does not have to be in occupation of the whole of the land. In that case, Ferrishurst had a lease of office premises and a third party had a lease of a garage contained within the same premises. Ferrishurst had an option to acquire a lease of the whole premises when its lease of the office premises expired. Wallcite bought the freehold of the whole of the premises, there being no entry on the title register regarding the right of Ferrishurst to ask for a lease of the whole of the premises. Nevertheless, the Court of Appeal said that Ferrishurst had the right and that Wallcite must grant it the lease. So instead of becoming an unfettered freeholder, Wallcite became a landlord.

The case demonstrates how important it is to ascertain the fact of a person's occupation of land (or now part of it) when acquiring a property or dealing with the land in terms, e.g. of a security. Full and stringent enquiries should be made, and it is also desirable (if not essential) to inspect the property to ascertain all the facts.

(viii) Overriding interests may themselves be overridden. The court has a discretion under s 14 of the Trusts of Land and Appointment of Trustees Act 1996. This discretion was used by the Court of Appeal where the property was jointly owned by a husband and wife and the husband became bankrupt and the wife was in occupation. The court ordered a sale of the property where otherwise there was no prospect of the claimant being paid and the wife having a resource which would enable her to reaccommodate herself (see *Bank of Baroda* v *Dhillon* [1998] 1 FCR 489).

Mortgages of chattels: bills of sale

502 *Koppel* v *Koppel* [1966] 2 All ER 187

Mr Koppel, who was estranged from his wife, invited a Mrs Wide to come to his house and look after his children on a permanent basis. Mrs Wide agreed to do so provided that Mr Koppel transferred the contents of his house to her to compensate for giving up her own home and disposing of her furniture. The transfer was recorded in writing. Later Mrs Koppel sought to levy execution on the contents of the house for her unpaid maintenance which amounted to £114. In proceedings resulting from Mrs Wide's claim to the property, a county court registrar held that the written transfer of the property to Mrs Wide was void as an unregistered bill of sale.

Held – by the Court of Appeal – the contents of the house were not in Mr Koppel's 'possession or apparent possession' within s 8 of the Bills of Sale Act 1878, because:

(*a*) Mr Koppel had transferred possession to Mrs Wide under the document which was an absolute bill of sale;

(*b*) the grantor of the bill, Mr Koppel, had, therefore, neither possession nor apparent possession. He did not have apparent possession because Mrs Wide was living in the house with him and both had apparent possession of the property, not merely Mr Koppel;

(*c*) Mrs Wide was, therefore, entitled to the property.

Lien: innkeepers

503 *Robins & Co* v *Gray* [1895] 2 QB 501

The claimants dealt in sewing machines and employed a traveller to sell the machines on commission. The claimants' traveller put up at the defendant's inn in April 1894, and stayed there until the end of July 1894. During this time the claimants sent the traveller machines to sell in the neighbourhood. At the end of July, the traveller owed the defendant £4 for board and lodgings, and he failed to pay. The defendant detained certain of the goods sent by the claimants to their traveller, asserting that he had a lien on them for the amount of the debt due to him, although the defendant knew that the goods were the property of the claimants.

Held – the defendant was entitled to a lien on the claimants' property for the traveller's debt.

Lien: solicitors

504 *Caldwell* v *Sumpters* [1971] 3 All ER 892

The defendants, a firm of solicitors, were holding the title deeds to property recently sold by a former client, Mrs Caldwell, who had not paid their charges. They voluntarily released the deeds to another firm which had been instructed to take their place to complete the sale, stating that they did so on the understanding that the deeds would be held to their order until Mrs Caldwell had paid. The second firm of solicitors kept the deeds and refused to accept that understanding.

Held – by Megarry, J – Sumpters' lien was lost when they voluntarily parted with possession of the deeds and could not be retained by a one-sided reservation of the kind made. If the agreement of the second firm of solicitors had been obtained, the lien would have been preserved, as it would also if Sumpters had lost possession by trickery or other wrongdoing. The second firm was under no obligation to accept the reservation or to return the deeds.

Comment The decision of Megarry, J was reversed by the Court of Appeal (*Caldwell* v *Sumpters* [1972] 1 All ER 567), the court holding that Sumpters' lien was not lost when they parted with the deeds since:

(a) possession was given up on the clear and express understanding that the deeds were to be held to Sumpters' order; and

(b) solicitors as officers of the court could not be allowed to take advantage of this sort of situation even out of regard for any duty owed to a client.

Lien: power of court to order sale

505 *Larner* v *Fawcett* [1950] 2 All ER 727

The defendant owned a racehorse and made an agreement with a Mr Davis under which it was agreed that Davis would train and race the filly and receive half of any prize money she might win. Davis, unknown to the defendant, agreed to let Larner have the animal to train. Larner did so, and when his charges had reached £125, he discoverd that Fawcett was the true owner. Larner, being unable to recover the cost of training and feeding the filly from Davis, who had no funds, now applied to the court for an order for sale. Fawcett was brought in as defendant.

Held – by the Court of Appeal – Larner had a common-law lien for his charges, and although such a lien does not carry with it a power of sale, the power given in the Rules of the Supreme Court to make an order for

sale was appropriate here, particularly since the filly was eating a great quantity of food. Fawcett had not made any attempt to get his property back but had clothed Davis with all the indicia of ownership. An order for sale would therefore be made unless Fawcett paid into court the amount of Larner's charges by a given date.

CRIMINAL LAW: GENERAL PRINCIPLES

Crime and civil wrongs distinguished: the burden of proof in crime

506 *Woolmington* v *Director of Public Prosecutions* [1935] AC 462

W had been charged with the murder of his wife. He had, on his own admission, shot her but said in his defence that the gun had gone off accidentally. The judge told the jury that so long as the prosecution had shown that the accused had caused the death malice was presumed and that the accused must prove that the killing was an accident. The jury convicted W who appealed to what was then the Court of Criminal Appeal where his conviction was upheld. However, on appeal to the House of Lords his conviction was quashed.

> Throughout the web of English Criminal Law one golden thread is always to be seen that it is the duty of the prosecution to prove the prisoner's guilt subject to what I have already said as to the defence of insanity and subject also to any statutory exceptions. If, at the end of and on the whole of the case, there is a reasonable doubt created by the evidence given by either the prosecution or the prisoner, as to whether the prisoner killed the deceased with a malicious intention, the prosecution has not made out the case and the prisoner is entitled to an acquittal. (*Per* Viscount Sankey, LC)

Nulla poena sine lege: the common law offence of conspiracy

507 *Shaw* v *Director of Public Prosecutions* [1961] 2 All ER 446

S published a booklet called *The Ladies Directory* which contained names and addresses of prostitutes. The entries gave telephone numbers and indicated that they were offering their services for sexual intercourse and some of them for the practice of sexual perversions. S was convicted of conspiracy to corrupt public morals and his appeal eventually reached the House of Lords. His appeal was dismissed and his conviction affirmed. However, Lord Reid, in a strong dissenting judgment, said that in his view there was no such general offence known to the law as conspiracy to corrupt public morals and the court in convicting S of it was creating a new crime on the basis of public mischief which is the criminal law equivalent of public policy. He thought that if the courts had stopped creating new heads of public policy in, for example, the civil law of contract, then they certainly should refrain from doing so in criminal law.

The requirement of causation

508 *R v Towers* (1874) 12 Cox 530

T had attacked a woman by hitting her and pulling her hair. She was holding a baby of four-and-a-half months. The woman screamed loudly and the baby went black in the face. From then on it had convulsions and died some six months later. Prior to the attack the child had been healthy. T was charged with the murder of the child. He was found not guilty. There was doubt whether a child of such an age could be frightened in the way suggested. The jury took the view that the act of the accused in assaulting the woman was unconnected with the child's death.

Comment A not dissimilar situation occurred in *Haystead* v *DPP* (2000) 164 JP 396 where a woman was holding a child and the defendant punched her, causing her to drop the child so that it hit its head. He was charged with assault (effectively battery here) and was held by the High Court to have been guilty of assault. Although the assault would normally require the use of direct force against the person of the child, the defendant was guilty of an assault upon its mother and no distinction could be drawn between using the mother or a weapon to assault the child. The child's fall had resulted directly from the assault on the mother and the defendant was guilty of assault by beating. In any case, battery did not necessarily require the direct application of force at least in criminal matters. Force can be applied indirectly.

Cases that support the concept of indirect battery are few and thought by some to be wrongly decided. The concept of indirect battery is, however, supported by the decision in *DPP* v *K* (1990, Case No 540 below).

509 *R v Hayward* (1908) 21 Cox 692

H came home one night in a violent state of excitement. He had said previously that he was going to 'give his wife something' when she returned home. When she arrived there were sounds of quarrelling and soon afterwards the wife ran out of the house followed by H. The wife fell on to the road and H kicked her on her left arm. She died and the medical examination showed that the kick was not the cause of her death. She was in good health apart from thymus gland trouble, on which the medical evidence was that a person with such a condition might die from the combined effects of fright, strong emotion and physical exertion. H was charged with manslaughter at Maidstone Assizes and found guilty. Ridley, J said that the abnormal state of the deceased's health did not affect the question whether the prisoner knew or did not know of it, if it were proved to the satisfaction of the jury that the death was accelerated by the prisoner's illegal act.

510 *R v Curley* (1909) 2 Cr App R 109

C had been indicted for murder but convicted of manslaughter. He had been heard quarrelling with the woman he lived with. She had been heard shouting in her bedroom. She had said: 'Let me out', 'murder' and 'police'. C was heard to go into her room and the window was opened. The woman later jumped from it. C told a police officer: 'I ran at her to hit her. I didn't quite touch her. Out she jumped.' The court *held* the accused to be guilty. The jumping out of the window was contributed to by C's unlawful act.

511 *R v Smith* [1959] 2 All ER 193

The facts were that the victim of a barrack-room brawl who was stabbed twice with a bayonet was dropped twice by those trying to get him to hospital and given artificial respiration when he got there although he was wounded in the lungs so that this was not advisable. Nevertheless, these events were *held* not to break the chain of causation. However, it must be said that the events in this case, including the death of Private Creed who was the victim, all occurred within a period of some two hours.

> A man is stabbed in the back, his lung is pierced and haemorrhage results; two hours later he dies of haemorrhage from that wound; in the interval there is no time for a careful examination, and the treatment given turns in the light of subsequent knowledge to have been inappropriate and, indeed, harmful. In those circumstances no reasonable jury or court could, properly directed, in our view possibly come to any other conclusion than that the death resulted from the original wound. Accordingly the court dismisses this appeal. (*Per* Lord Parker, CJ)

Comment (i) This case seems to illustrate the usual approach of the court to these causation problems. The case of *R v Jordan* (1956) 40 Cr App R 152 seems to be the odd man out. In that case J had stabbed the victim but it was established that the wound was healing satisfactorily. The victim died after being given an anti-biotic to which he was allergic and over-large quantities of liquid intravenously. J's conviction for murder was quashed on appeal.

(ii) In *R v Malcherek* [1981] 2 All ER 422 two victims of assault were placed on life-support machines and in both cases doctors having diagnosed brain death discontinued treatment and disconnected the life-support system. It was held by the Court of Appeal that the original injuries were the continuing operating cause of death. The discontinuance of the treatment did not break the chain of causation between the initial injury and the death.

(iii) More recently in *R v Cheshire* [1991] 3 All ER 670, following an argument in a fish and chip shop C shot his victim in the leg and stomach, seriously wounding him. The victim died two months later following complications after surgery to assist his breathing. C was convicted of murder even though there was evidence that the leg and stomach wounds were no longer life threatening at the time of his death. The Court of Appeal in dismissing an appeal said that the acts of the accused need not be the sole or even the main cause of the death, it being sufficient that his acts contributed significantly to the death.

(iv) Again, in *R v Mellor (Gavin Thomas)*, *The Times*, 29 February 1996 M appealed against conviction of the murder of a 71-year-old man who had died two days after he had been admitted to hospital with facial and chest injuries caused by M. The appeal was dismissed by the Court of Appeal, the court holding that in the supervening event cases the prosecution had only to establish that the injuries inflicted by the defendant were a significant, if not the only, cause of death. It was not necessary, e.g., for the prosecution to establish that there had been no medical negligence in the treatment of the victim.

Actus reus: liability for failing to act

512 *R v Instan* [1893] 1 QB 450

Instan lived with her 73-year-old aunt. The aunt seemed to be in reasonable health until shortly before her death. During the 12 days prior to her death she had gangrene in her leg and could not look after herself or summon help. That she was in this condition was a matter known only to Instan. It appeared that she had not given her aunt any food nor had she tried to obtain medical or nursing aid. Following the death of her aunt she was accused of manslaughter and convicted. The Court for Crown Cases Reserved (as it then was) affirmed the conviction.

> The prisoner was under a moral obligation to the deceased from which arose a legal duty towards her; that legal duty the prisoner has wilfully and deliberately left unperformed, with the consequence that there has been an acceleration of the death of the deceased owing to the non-performance of that legal duty. It is unnecessary to say more than that upon the evidence this conviction was most properly arrived at. (*Per* Lord Coleridge, CJ)

Comment (i) An example of liability arising from an omission in a special relationship situation of parent and child is provided by *R v Gibbins and Procter* (1918) 13 Cr App R 134. In that case G was the father of a child and he was living, together with the child, with P the female second defendant. They failed to feed the child and she died. The convictions of G and P for murder were upheld by the appeal court. Of course, in the case of P it was necessary to show that she had *assumed a duty* towards G's child. It was held that she had by living with him and receiving money from him for food.

(ii) An additional illustration is provided by *R v Hood* [2004] 1 Cr App R (S) 431, where the accused was found guilty of the manslaughter of his wife. He was her sole carer. She suffered from diabetes and osteoporosis causing brittle bones. She broke several bones in a fall and the accused failed to summon medical assistance for some weeks. The wife died shortly after being admitted to hospital in a debilitated state. The accused's sentence was reduced from four years to 30 months on the basis of the wife's reluctance to go to hospital.

(iii) Problems can arise where persons suffering injury have, because of irreversible brain damage, gone into a persistent vegetative state. To avoid liability for failing to sustain life or bringing about death by turning off life-support apparatus, the family and health trust concerned should ask the court for a declaratory judgment of no liability at criminal or civil law. They are then protected against criminal and/or civil proceedings. This approach was used in *Airedale National Health Service Trust v Bland* where it was upheld by the House of Lords (see [1993] AC 789).

Euthanasia is still illegal in the UK and can result in a conviction for murder, even though there may be the most compelling compassionate grounds.

Actus reus: contractual duties

513 *R v Pittwood* (1902) 19 TLR 37

Pittwood was a gatekeeper employed by a railway company. It was his duty to keep the gate shut whenever a train was passing between 7 am and 7 pm. The gate was left open on one afternoon and a hay cart which was crossing the line was struck by a train. A man was killed and another seriously injured. The defendant was charged with manslaughter and was found guilty. Wright, J said there was gross and criminal negligence as the man was paid to keep the gate shut and protect the public. He added that a man might incur criminal liability from a duty arising out of contract.

Actus reus: previous conduct

514 *R v Miller* [1983] 1 All ER 978

The defendant, who was a vagrant squatter, fell asleep after lighting a cigarette. He woke to find his mattress smouldering. He left it as it was and went to sleep in another room. There was a fire and the defendant was charged with arson. He was found guilty and his appeal was dismissed by the House of Lords. His conviction was justified either on the basis that there was a continuous act or on the basis that the defendant owed a responsibility to try to undo the harm which he had unwittingly done. The House of Lords felt that this latter basis which is really an omission would be easier to explain to juries.

Mens rea: motive: irrelevant to guilt or innocence

515 *Chandler v Director of Public Prosecutions* [1962] 3 All ER 142

In this case the defendants impeded the operation of an airfield at Wethersfield, Essex. Their object was to demonstrate against nuclear armament.

> In the result, I am of opinion that if a person's direct purpose in approaching or entering is to cause obstruction or interference, and such obstruction or interference is found to be a prejudice to the defence dispositions of the State, an offence is thereby committed, and his indirect purposes or his motives in bringing about the obstruction or interference do not alter the nature or content of his offence. . . . Is a man guilty of an offence, it was asked, if he rushed on to an airfield intending to stop an airplane taking off because he knows that a time-bomb has been concealed on board? I should say that he is not, for the reason that his direct purpose is not to bring about an obstruction but to prevent a disaster, the obstruction that he causes being merely a means of securing that end. (*Per* Lord Radcliffe)

Mens rea: states of mind

516 *R v Maloney* [1985] 1 All ER 1025

The defendant and his stepfather had been drinking heavily at a family party. They were part of a united and happy family. In the early hours of the morning they began larking about with shotguns. There was a challenge as to who could load fastest. The defendant was able to load faster and pointed his gun at the stepfather, saying: 'You've lost'. The stepfather said: 'You wouldn't dare pull the trigger'. The defendant

did just that and killed the stepfather. It appeared that he did not aim the gun but just pulled the trigger. He was later charged with murder but that was reduced to manslaughter by the House of Lords. The House of Lords felt that the circumstances did not show that the defendant had the intent to kill or cause really serious injury and nothing else would do for the crime of murder. Lord Bridge said:

> I do not believe it is necessary for the judge to do more than invite the jury to consider two questions. First, was death or really serious injury . . . a natural consequence of the defendant's voluntary act? Second, did the defendant *foresee* that consequence as being a natural consequence of his act? The jury should then be told that if they answer Yes to both questions it is a proper inference for them to draw that he intended that consequence.

Comment (i) The matter came before the House of Lords again in *R v Hancock* [1986] 1 All ER 641. The defendant, Hancock, and another defendant, Shankland, had thrown items including lumps of concrete from a road-bridge in order to block the road so that a taxi carrying a working miner would not be able to get through and so to some extent break the miners' strike. A lump of concrete hit the windscreen of the taxi and the driver was killed. The defendants were charged with murder and eventually appealed to the House of Lords from their conviction for that offence. Lord Scarman and the other Law Lords were critical of Lord Bridge's approach. His *Maloney* guidelines required a reference to *probability*. Lord Scarman said: 'They also require an explanation that the greater the probability of a consequence the more likely it is that the consequence was foreseen and that if that consequence was foreseen the greater the probability is that the consequence was also intended.' But he went on to stress that the jury should not be told more except that any inference of intent was for them to make on all the evidence and circumstances of the case and not merely on the judge's directions.

(ii) The matter came before the Court of Appeal again in *R v Nedrick* [1986] 3 All ER 1 where the defendant poured paraffin through the letter box of the house of a woman against whom he had a grudge. He set light to it and the woman's child died in the resulting fire. He was convicted of murder, the judge bringing in the *Hancock* approach, i.e. that if the defendant knew that it was *highly probable* that his act would result in serious bodily injury to someone inside the house he was guilty of murder. The defendant had admitted starting the fire but said he wanted just to frighten the woman and not to kill anyone. The Court of Appeal substituted a verdict of manslaughter and the Lord Chief Justice had to lay down guidelines as to the direction of juries in this sort of case. He said that the jury should be told that they are not entitled to infer the necessary intent for murder unless they feel sure that death or serious bodily harm was a virtually certain result of the defendant's action (barring some unforeseen intervention) and that the defendant appreciated that fact. This is where the matter currently lies. To equate foresight with intention is now ruled out unless intent can be construed from evidence surrounding the act (see below).

(iii) In *R v Woollin (Stephen Leslie)*, *The Times*, 12 August 1996 W appealed to the Court of Appeal against his conviction for the murder of his three-month-old son whom he had thrown towards a pram which was against the wall. The child seemed to have hit the wall and died from injuries sustained. When summing up the judge directed the jury that they could find the necessary intent for murder if they felt that W appreciated that there was 'a substantial risk' that serious bodily harm would result to the child. W claimed that the judge should have used the expression 'virtual certainty' of serious bodily harm. The former expression related to recklessness for manslaughter and the latter to an intent for murder. Whilst the Court of Appeal agreed that, taking *only* the act of throwing the child at the pram, the direction might have been faulty, if there were surrounding circumstances and evidence of intent other than the act, a conviction for murder could be sustained. Here the defendant had admitted that he 'lost his cool' when the child started to choke upon his food and that he had shaken him in a fit of rage or frustration before throwing him at the pram.

(iv) The *Woollin* case came before the House of Lords (see *R v Woollin (Stephen Leslie)* [1998] 3 WLR 382). Their Lordships accepted that the trial judge, in using the expression 'a substantial risk', had blurred the distinction between intention and recklessness, and thus murder and manslaughter. Accordingly, Woollin's conviction for murder could not stand. A conviction for manslaughter was substituted.

(v) The problem the trial judge has in getting the right direction to the jury in these cases on the border of intention or criminal negligence was again illustrated in *R v Matthews (Darren John)*; *R v Alleyne (Brian Dean)*, *The Times*, 18 February 2003. The defendants had assaulted and robbed the victim. In the assault the victim lost his glasses and having left the scene of the assault, a nightclub, he was going home and was flagging down cars when the defendants' car came up. They stopped and forced him into the car and took him to a river bridge. They threw him over the bridge into the river, although he had told them he could not swim. The victim drowned. The charge was murder and the trial judge directed the jury to find the necessary intent provided that they were satisfied that the defendants had an appreciation of the 'virtual certainty of death'. The Court of Appeal found this to be the wrong direction which should have been that the jury were 'not entitled to find

the necessary intention unless they felt sure that death or serious bodily harm was a virtual certainty as a result of the defendants' actions and that the defendants appreciated that this was the case'. Nevertheless, the Court of Appeal dismissed the appeal. The judge had repeatedly made the point about the need for intent and, although the main direction was a misdirection, that misdirection was immaterial.

Recklessness: a subjective test

517 *R v Cunningham* [1957] 2 All ER 412

C was convicted of unlawfully and maliciously causing to be taken by Sarah Wade a certain noxious thing, namely, coal gas, so as to endanger her life contrary to s 23 of the Offences Against the Person Act 1861. The crime is unlawfully and maliciously administering to or causing to be administered to or taken by any person any poison or other destructive or noxious thing so as to endanger the life of such person or so as thereby to inflict upon such person any grievous bodily harm. C had gone into an empty house and torn away the gas meter in the cellar in order to take the money it contained with the intention of stealing that money. However, coal gas poured out of the pipe he had fractured and percolated into the house next door where it almost asphyxiated the occupant, Sarah Wade. C appealed and his appeal was allowed.

> We think it is incorrect to say that the word 'malicious' in a statutory offence merely means wicked. We think the judge was, in effect, telling the jury that if they were satisfied that the appellant acted wickedly – and he had clearly acted wickedly in stealing the gas meter and its contents – they ought to find that he had acted maliciously in causing the gas to be taken by Mrs Wade so as thereby to endanger her life.
>
> In our view it should have been left to the jury to decide whether, even if the appellant did not intend to injure Mrs Wade, he foresaw that the removal of the gas meter might cause injury to someone but nevertheless removed it. We are unable to say that a reasonable jury, properly directed as to the meaning of the word 'maliciously' in the context of s 23, would without doubt have convicted.
>
> In these circumstances this court has no alternative but to allow the appeal and quash the conviction. (*Per* Byrne, J)

Comment The fact that the judge is applying a subjective standard is indicated by the fact that he says, 'he (i.e. the defendant) foresaw'. This is what the jury must find if the test is to be subjective. Of course, no jury can really know what a particular defendant may or may not have foreseen.

They can only do their best in the light of answers which the defendant or other witnesses may have given to questions posed by counsel in examination-in-chief and cross-examination. It is by no means an exact science!

Recklessness: an objective test

518 *R v Caldwell* [1981] 1 All ER 961

Caldwell had done some work for the owner of a hotel and had a quarrel with the owner about this. He got drunk and set fire to the hotel in revenge. The fire was discovered and put out before any serious damage was done and none of the guests was injured. He was charged with criminal damage under the Criminal Damage Act 1971. It was *held* incidentally that his self-induced intoxication was no defence but on the issue of recklessness which was part of the charge, i.e. intentionally or recklessly destroying or damaging property, the House of Lords eventually dismissed his appeal. A person is reckless they said if (*a*) he does an act which in fact creates an obvious risk that property will be destroyed or damaged; and (*b*) when he does the act he either has not given any thought to the possibility of there being any such risk or has recognised that there was some risk involved and has nonetheless gone on to do it. The test is objective because a person is guilty if he has given no thought at all to the risk when in effect a reasonable person would have done so.

Comment (i) Although the above words were spoken in regard to recklessness for the statutory offence of criminal damage, it seems from the general tenor of the judgments in *Caldwell* and another decision of the House of Lords, *R v Lawrence* [1981] 1 All ER 974 (a case of reckless driving), that they might apply to the construction of criminal statutes generally and to recklessness at common law.

(ii) The principles laid down in *Caldwell* and *Lawrence* were applied in another case of criminal damage, i.e. *Elliott v C* [1983] 2 All ER 1005. C was a 14-year-old schoolgirl who was charged with criminal damage under s 1(1) of the Criminal Damage Act 1971 (destroying or damaging property without danger to life). She spent one entire night awake and wandering around. She had entered a toolshed and there poured white spirit on to a carpet and set light to it, destroying the shed. The magistrates found that she did not appreciate just how inflammable the spirit was, and having regard to her extreme state of tiredness, that she did not in fact give any real thought to the risk of fire. In consequence, the magistrate acquitted her. It was held by a Divisional Court of Queen's Bench, allowing the prosecutor's appeal, that the correct test was whether a reasonably prudent man would realise the dangers of fire in the circumstances, even though the particular accused might

not appreciate them. In other words, it would appear that the test at criminal law has become an objective test of recklessness, at least where criminal damage is concerned.

(iii) The objective standard approach to recklessness was followed in *R v Sangha*, *The Times*, 2 February 1988 where the Court of Appeal said that the test was 'would an ordinary prudent bystander have perceived an obvious risk that property of value and life would be endangered?' Sangha was convicted of arson under s 1(2) of the Criminal Damage Act 1971 because life was endangered.

Transferred malice

519 *R v Latimer* (1886) 17 QBD 359

Latimer was quarrelling with A in a pub. He struck out at A with his belt. The blow glanced off A and severely injured another person, B. Latimer was found guilty of unlawful and malicious wounding. Lord Coleridge, CJ said:

> We are of opinion that this conviction must be sustained. It is common knowledge that a man who has an unlawful and malicious intent against another, and, in attempting to carry it out, injures a third person, is guilty of what the law deems malice against the person injured, because the offender is doing an unlawful act, and has what the judges call general malice, and that is enough. . . .

520 *R v Pembliton* (1874) LR 2 CCR 119

Pembliton was fighting outside a pub. He picked up a stone and threw it at the persons he had been fighting. It missed them but broke a window in the pub. It was held that the evidence did not support a conviction for unlawful and malicious damage under the Malicious Damage Act 1861. There was no intention to break the window.

Comment (i) He might now have been successfully charged with criminal damage if he was in fact reckless within the *Caldwell* test, or of an *attempt to cause* actual or grievous bodily harm. Nevertheless, in the terms in which he was charged the case makes its point that *mens rea* is not transferable from crime to crime.

(ii) The rule is somewhat arbitrary and appears generous to the defendant. This was admitted by the House of Lords in *Attorney-General's Reference (No 3 of 1994)* [1998] AC 245 but their Lordships nevertheless applied it ruling that the defendant's malice towards his girlfriend in stabbing her did not extend to the crime of murder of a child which, to his knowledge, she was carrying. The House of Lords acknowledged that the rule is an exception to the general principles of law.

Mens rea: must coincide with actus reus

521 Thabo Meli v R [1954] 1 All ER 373

In this case the accused persons planned to kill the victim in a hut and thereafter to roll his body over a cliff so that it would appear that he had died an accidental death. The victim was made unconscious in the hut by the attack and thinking him to be dead, the accused persons rolled him over a cliff. There was evidence that the victim was not in fact killed in the hut but that he died on account of exposure at the bottom of the cliff.

> The point of law which was raised in this case can be simply stated. It is said that two acts were necessary and were separable; first, the attack in the hut; and, secondly, the placing of the body outside afterwards. It is said that, while the first act was accompanied by *mens rea*, it was not the cause of death; but that the second act, while it was the cause of death, was not accompanied by *mens rea*; and on that ground it is said that the accused are not guilty of any crime, except perhaps culpable homicide.
>
> It appears to their Lordships impossible to divide up what was really one transaction in this way. There is no doubt that the accused set out to do all these acts in order to achieve their plan and as part of their plan; and it is much too refined a ground of judgment to say that, because they were under a misapprehension at one stage and thought that their guilty purpose had been achieved before in fact it was achieved, therefore they are to escape the penalties of the law. . . . (*Per* Lord Reid)

The appeal of the accused persons was, therefore, dismissed.

Comment It is not necessary for the acts to be part of a preconceived plan which went wrong. In *R v Le Brun* [1991] 3 WLR 653 a husband had an argument with his wife in the street and hit her without intending serious harm. She fell unconscious on the highway and he then tried to move her on to the pavement. Her head hit the pavement and she fractured her skull and died. He was acquitted of murder and convicted of manslaughter and his appeal against that conviction was dismissed. The unlawful application of force and the eventual act causing death were part of the same sequence of events. They did not have to be part of a preconceived plan as in *Thabo Meli*.

Mens rea: statutory offences

522 Sweet v Parsley [1969] 1 All ER 347

The magistrates had convicted Sweet of being concerned in the management of premises which were used for the purpose of smoking cannabis or cannabis resin, contrary to s 5(b) of the Dangerous Drugs Act 1965. The evidence showed that she had no knowledge whatever that the house was being used for the purpose of smoking cannabis or cannabis resin. She visited the premises only occasionally to collect letters and rent and though sometimes she stayed overnight, generally she did not. Section 5 of the 1965 Act provides 'if a person (*a*) being the occupier of any premises, permits those premises to be used for the purpose of smoking cannabis or cannabis resin or of dealing in cannabis or cannabis resin (whether by sale or otherwise); or (*b*) is concerned in the management of any premises used for any purposes aforesaid; he shall be guilty of an offence under the Act'. The House of Lords, after holding that in spite of the wording of the Act in terms of the 'management' offence *mens rea* must be implied, found that there was no *mens rea* in the accused in this case and that, therefore, her appeal should be allowed and her conviction quashed.

Comment (i) The offence of 'permitting' would normally require *mens rea* but the 'management' offence was regarded in this case by the magistrates as not requiring *mens rea* and they convicted Ms Sweet. However, the House of Lords decided *mens rea* must be implied. The *mens rea* may, however, be little more than 'wilful blindness' to what is going on in the premises. There was no finding that Ms Sweet had this.

(ii) The presumption of a requirement of *mens rea* in statutory offences has become stronger in more recent cases. An example is *B v DPP* [2000] 2 Cr App R 65. The defendant a 15-year-old boy sat next to a 13-year-old girl on a bus and requested her to give him a 'shiner'. As the judge remarked, 'This in the language of today's gilded youth apparently means not a black eye but an act of oral sex'. The girl refused. He was charged with having incited a girl under the age of 14 to commit an act of gross indecency with him contrary to s 1(1) of the Indecency with Children Act 1960. This is a strict offence and both the trial judge and the Court of Appeal ruled that it was no defence that the boy believed that the girl was over 14. However, the House of Lords followed the approach in *Sweet v Parsley* (above) and applied a presumption in favour of a requirement for *mens rea*. The prosecution had to prove, said their Lordships, an absence of genuine belief by the defendant that the victim was aged 14 or over. This belief which does not have to be on reasonable grounds will if genuinely held result in an acquittal.

(iii) The ruling in *B v DPP* (above) was applied in *R v K* [2001] Crim LR 993 again by the House of Lords. The defendant in this case was charged with indecent assault on a girl under 16 contrary to s 14 of the Sexual Offences Act 1956. The girl had consented. However, by reason of s 14(2) a girl under 16 cannot give a legally valid consent although in this case she had also told the defendant that she was over 16. The House of Lords allowed the defendant's appeal and held that the defendant's mistaken belief that the girl was over 16 was a valid defence. Such a belief need not be based on 'reasonable grounds' but the more unreasonable it is the less likely it is that it will be taken as genuine. Obviously, the reasons the defendant gives for the belief will be a crucial piece of evidence for the police to establish when dealing with this type of offence.

(iv) The Sexual Offences Act 2003 has relevant provisions which should be noted (see p 698).

523 *R v Tolson* (1889) 23 QBD 168

Martha Ann Tolson, who married in September 1880, was deserted by her husband in December 1881. She made enquiries and learned from his elder brother that he had been lost at sea in a ship bound for America which sank with all hands. Believing herself to be a widow, she went quite openly through a ceremony of marriage on 10 January 1887, with Y who was fully aware of the circumstances. It was held that she could not be convicted of bigamy under s 57 of the Offences Against the Person Act 1861, even though the opening part of that section says: 'Whosoever, being married, shall marry any other person during the life of the former husband or wife . . . shall be guilty of a felony . . .'. She had no *mens rea*. The object of Parliament was not to treat the marriage of widows as an act to be if possible prevented as presumably immoral. Mrs Tolson's conduct was not immoral but perfectly natural and legitimate. A statute may relate to such subject matter and may be so framed as to make an act criminal whether there has been any intention to break the law or not. In other cases a more reasonable construction requires the implication into the statute that a guilty mind is required.

524 *Alphacell v Woodward* [1972] 2 All ER 475

A Ltd was the owner of paper-making mills. In the course of manufacture effluent passed into two tanks on the banks of a river. Pumps were used to remove the effluent from the tanks but it was inevitable that if the pumps failed, the effluent would enter the river and pollute it. As a result of foliage blocking the pump inlets, such an overflow occurred and A Ltd was charged with 'causing' polluting matter to enter the river under s 2(1) of the Rivers (Prevention of Pollution) Act 1951. It was *held* – by the House of Lords – that A Ltd was guilty of that offence even though it had not been negligent. The intervening

act of a trespass or act of God would have been a defence, but there was no such trespass or act of God in this case.

Comment (i) 'Causing' is a word which does not require *mens rea*. The statute did not say 'knowingly causing'. That would have required *mens rea*.

(ii) It was *held* in *R v CPC (UK)*, *The Times*, 4 August 1994 that 'causing' polluting matter to enter a river contrary to s 85(1) of the Water Resources Act 1991 and s 4(1) of the Freshwater Fisheries Act 1975 was a question of fact and did not require fault or knowledge on the part of the defendant. It does however, require some *active* participation: *Attorney-General's Reference (No 1 of 1994)* [1995] 2 CLY 5135.

(iii) There is a tendency in more recent statutes to use expressions that do not require *mens rea* but contain a 'due diligence' defence, which allows the defendant to escape conviction by showing that all reasonable precautions were taken.

525 *Cundy v Le Cocq* (1884) 13 QBD 207

C, who was a licensed victualler, sold liquor to a person who was drunk though C did not know this. He was, however, convicted of unlawfully selling liquor to a drunken person contrary to s 13 of the Licensing Act 1872, which provided that: 'If any licensed person . . . sells any intoxicating liquor to a drunken person he shall be liable to a penalty . . .'. It was *held* – by Stephen, J – that knowledge of the condition of the person to whom the liquor was sold was not necessary to constitute the offence.

> Against this view we have had quoted the maxim that in every criminal offence there must be a guilty mind; but I do not think that maxim has so wide an application as it is sometimes considered to have. In old time, and as applicable to the common law or to earlier statutes, the maxim may have been of general application; but a difference has arisen owing to the greater precision of modern statutes. It is impossible now, . . . to apply the maxim generally to all statutes, and the substance of all the reported cases is that it is necessary to look at the object of each Act that is under consideration to see whether and how far knowledge is of the essence of the offence created. Here, as I have already pointed out, the object of this part of the Act is to prevent the sale of intoxicating liquor to drunken persons, and it is perfectly natural to carry that out by throwing on the publican the responsibility of determining whether the person supplied comes within that category. I think, therefore, the conviction was right and must be affirmed.

Comment Is it perhaps simply that a landlord is supposed to know when a customer is drunk? Contrast *Sherras* v *De Rutzen* [1895] 1 QB 918 where a publican was convicted of serving a constable while on duty. He thought he was off-duty and anyway had no way of knowing whether he was or not. His conviction was quashed by a Divisional Court.

526 *Gaumont British Distributors Ltd* v *Henry* [1939] 2 KB 717

Gaumont British was charged under s 1(a) of the Dramatic and Musical Performers' Protection Act 1925, with knowingly making a record of a musical work without the written consent of the performers. No consent had actually been given but GB said, and it was accepted, that it had never thought about the question of consent. Nevertheless GB was convicted and appealed. The appeal was allowed.

> I desire to add emphatically that no colour can be obtained from this case, or from the argument, or from any opinion which is present to my mind, that the wholesome and fundamental principle *ignorantia juris neminem excusat* (ignorance of the law is no excuse) is in any degree to be modified or departed from. . . . I should be very sorry, directly or indirectly, even to appear to add any colour to the suggestion, if it were made – as I do not think it is – that in circumstances of this kind ignorance of the law might excuse. The way in which the topic of the appellants' knowledge came in was solely with reference to the words 'knowingly makes any record without the consent in writing of the performers', and the contention was a contention of fact. According to a true view of the evidence of fact in this case it was incorrect to say that the appellants did knowingly without the consent in writing of the performers that which was done. (*Per* Lord Hewart, CJ)

527 *R* v *Lowe* [1973] 1 All ER 805

Lowe was charged under s 1 of the Children and Young Persons Act 1933 as being a person who had the charge of a child and wilfully neglected it in a manner likely to cause it unnecessary suffering or injury to health. L's case was that the child's critical condition arose after he had told the woman he was living with, who was the child's mother, to take the child to a doctor and that she later falsely told him that she had done so. He was convicted and appealed.

> It did not matter what he ought to have realised as the possible consequences of his failure to call a doctor; the sole question was whether his failure to do so was deliberate and thereby occasioned

the results referred to in s 1(1) of the Act of 1933. We are quite satisfied that the conviction on count 2 was justified both on the law and the facts . . .'. (*Per* Phillimore, LJ)

Comment There was another count on the indictment for manslaughter but this was allowed on appeal.

528 *Somerset* v *Wade* [1894] 1 QB 574

Wade was charged with permitting drunkenness under s 13 of the Licensing Act 1872 which provides that if any licensed person permits drunkenness, or any violence, quarrelsome or riotous conduct to take place on his premises or sells any intoxicating liquor to any drunken person, he commits an offence. A drunken woman was actually found on Wade's premises but it was accepted that Wade did not know that she was drunk. The charge having been dismissed the prosecutor appealed. The appeal of the prosecutor failed and Wade was not convicted.

> But the word 'suffers' is not distinguishable from 'permits', which is the word used in s 13, the section now before us. In a case where the defendant does not know that the person who was on his premises was in fact drunk, he cannot be said to permit drunkenness. In the present case the justices have found that the respondent did not know that the person was drunk and there was evidence to support that finding. (*Per* Mathew, J)

Comment (i) As regards the word 'malicious', it will be recalled that in *R* v *Cunningham* (1957), *mens rea* was required for an offence which had to be committed 'maliciously'.

(ii) In the *Somerset* case Mathew, J was prepared to say that the word 'suffers' was the same as 'permits', i.e. a word requiring *mens rea* in the accused.

(iii) The distinction between this case and *Cundy* appears to be that Wade did not serve or sell liquor to the woman while she was in a drunken state and did not know she was on the premises.

Vicarious liability in crime

529 *Griffiths* v *Studebakers Ltd* [1924] 1 KB 102

Studebakers were holders of a limited trade licence and were charged with having used on a public road a motor car carrying more than two persons in addition to the driver, which was an offence under the Road Vehicles (Trade Licences) Regulations 1922. At the time of the alleged offence, the car was being driven by a servant of the respondents. He was in the course of his employment because he was giving a trial run to prospective purchasers of the car but, by carrying more than two passengers, he was infringing the express orders of his employers. The employers were convicted and appealed to the Divisional Court.

> It would be fantastic to suppose that a manufacturer, whether a limited company, a firm, or an individual, would, even if he could, always show cars to prospective purchasers himself; and it would defeat the scheme of this legislation if it were open to an employer, whether a company, or a firm, or an individual, to say that although the car was being used under the limited licence in contravention of the conditions upon which it was granted: 'My hand was not the hand that drove the car.' On these facts there ought to have been a conviction of the respondents and also the driver as aider and abettor. (*Per* Lord Hewart, CJ)

Thus, the conviction of Studebakers was affirmed by the Divisional Court.

Comment Note that liability was not affected by the fact that the employee was told not to do the act.

530 *James and Son Ltd v Smee* [1955] 1 QB 78

Under the Motor Vehicles (Construction and Use) Regulations in force at the time the alleged offence occurred, the braking system of a vehicle or trailer used on the road had to be in efficient working order, and further anyone who used or caused or permitted to be used on the road a motor vehicle or trailer where the braking system was not in efficient working order was liable to a fine. James and Son Ltd sent out in the charge of their employee a lorry and trailer the braking system of which was in efficient working order. However, during the course of his rounds the employee had to disconnect the braking system of the trailer and forgot to connect it up again. James and Son were convicted of 'permitting to be used' the trailer in contravention of the regulation then in force. However, their appeal was allowed by the Divisional Court.

> In other words, it is said that in committing the offence of the user in contravention of the regulations he at the same time made his master guilty of the offence of permitting such user. In our opinion this contention is highly artificial and divorced from reality. We prefer the view that before the company can be held guilty of permitting a user in contravention of the regulations it must be proved that some person for whose criminal acts the company is responsible permitted as opposed to committed the offence. There was no such evidence in the present case. (*Per* Parker, J)

531 *Vane v Yiannopoullos* [1965] AC 486

Section 22(1) of the Licensing Act 1961, which was relevant in this case provided, 'If – (*a*) the holder of a Justices' on-licence knowingly sells or supplies intoxicating liquor to persons to whom he is not permitted by the conditions of the licence to sell or supply it . . . he shall be guilty of an offence'. Y was the licensee of a restaurant and had been granted a Justices' on-licence subject to a condition that intoxicating liquor was to be sold only to those who ordered meals. He employed a waitress and he instructed her to serve drinks only to customers who ordered meals but on one occasion whilst Y was in another part of the restaurant the waitress did serve drinks to two youths who had not in fact ordered a meal. Y did not know of that sale. He was charged with knowingly selling intoxicating liquor on the premises to persons to whom he was not permitted to sell contrary to s 22(1)(a) of the Act. The magistrates dismissed the information and the prosecutor appealed eventually to the House of Lords. The appeal of the prosecutor was dismissed and there was therefore no conviction of Y.

> So far, however, as the present case is concerned, I feel no doubt that the decision of the Divisional Court was right. There was clearly no ['knowledge'] in the strict sense proved against the licensee: I agree also with the Lord Chief Justice that there was no sufficient evidence of such ['delegation'] on his part of his powers, duties and responsibilities to render him liable on that ground. I would therefore without hesitation dismiss the appeal. (*Per* Lord Evershed)

Comment Note that Y was on the premises when the drinks were served. Delegation was not, therefore, complete, as it must be.

532 *Ferguson v Weaving* [1951] 1 All ER 412

Section 4 of the Licensing Act 1921, which was relevant in this case, made it an offence for any person, except during permitted hours, to consume intoxicating liquor on any licensed premises. In a large public house of which W was the manager customers were found consuming liquor outside the permitted hours and were convicted of an offence under the section. The evidence did not show that W knew that the liquor was being consumed. It had in fact been supplied to customers by waiters employed by her who had neglected to collect the glasses in time. A charge against W of aiding and abetting the customers' offence was dismissed and the prosecutor appealed. The appeal was dismissed. 'There can be no doubt that this court has more than once laid it down in clear terms that before a person can be convicted of aiding and abetting the commission of an offence he must at least know the essential matters which constitute the offence. . . .' (*Per* Lord Goddard, CJ)

Comment Before a person can be convicted of aiding and abetting an offence, i.e. being a secondary party, he must know of all the essential matters which constitute the offence (see Lord Goddard CJ, in *Johnson v Youden* [1950] 1 KB 544). This is true even of a strict offence. Here there was no knowledge.

SPECIFIC OFFENCES

Murder

533 *R v Dyson* [1908] 2 KB 454

Dyson was charged with manslaughter it being alleged that injuries which he inflicted on his child in November 1906 had caused its death in March 1908. His conviction was quashed. Lord Alverstone, CJ said: 'it is still undoubtedly the law of the land that no person can be convicted of manslaughter where the death does not occur within a year and a day after the injury was inflicted . . .'.

Comment (i) It should be noted that the 'year and a day rule' applied to all homicides but this case is obviously an authority also for murder. It was an ancient rule coming from the days when medical science could not be precise about causation.

(ii) It should be noted that the case still has relevance as an example of a case requiring the consent of the Attorney-General to a prosecution under the Law Reform (Year and a Day Rule) Act 1996, s 2.

Voluntary manslaughter: provocation

534 *R v Camplin* [1978] 2 All ER 168

Paul Camplin was 15 years of age. He went to the house of a Mr K who was in his fifties. While he was there K buggered him in spite of his resistance and after he had finished K laughed at him. Camplin then killed K by splitting his skull with a chapatti pan. He pleaded provocation to reduce a charge of murder to manslaughter. In reaching a decision that he was provoked, the House of Lords said his age must be taken into account. Lord Diplock said that if the jury thinks that the same power of self-control is not to be expected in an ordinary average or normal boy of 15 as in an older person, the boy's age is relevant to his response. A conviction for manslaughter must stand. Camplin's age was relevant.

Comment (i) In *R v Morhall* [1993] 4 All ER 888 the Court of Appeal refused to take into account that the defendant had been glue-sniffing prior to a killing by stabbing and the victim had taunted him about this. This was not found a relevant 'characteristic', in terms of provocation. A conviction of murder must stand. *Camplin* is a different situation. Youth is not self-induced and is a 'characteristic' of each one of us at a certain stage in life (but see (iii) below).

(ii) The decision of the Privy Council in *Luc v The Queen* [1996] 3 WLR 45 is also relevant. It was decided that the *mental condition* of the defendant which impaired his powers of self-control could not be taken into account in provocation. Such a condition could not be attributed to the reasonable man. It should be pleaded as diminished responsibility and succeed or fail on that basis. Since the medical evidence did not establish diminished responsibility, the defendant's conviction for murder stood.

(iii) There was an appeal to the House of Lords in *Morhall* which reversed the Court of Appeal. In cases where a defendant's addiction is the subject of taunts said to constitute provocation, a jury should be directed to take into account the defendant's addiction as a matter going to the gravity of the alleged provocation.

The mere fact that the defendant has a discreditable characteristic does not exclude it from consideration. In the case of glue-sniffing, drug addiction or alcoholism, a distinction must be drawn between, on the one hand, situations where the defendant *is taunted with his addiction*, in which case it may be relevant to take the addiction into account as going to the gravity of the provocation, and on the other *the mere fact that the defendant was intoxicated by alcohol, glue or drugs at the time* since the latter is excluded as a matter of policy (see *R v Morhall* [1995] 3 WLR 330).

(iv) In *R v Roberts* [1990] Crim LR 122 Roberts, who was 23 years old, killed a person because he taunted him about his deafness. It was held that the judge had properly directed the jury to take into account the disability as part of the characteristics of the hypothetical reasonable man.

(v) Again, in *R v Smith (Morgan James)* [2000] 4 All ER 289 the fact that the defendant suffered from depression, which reduced his power of self-control, could said the House of Lords be taken into account as a characteristic of a reasonable person for the purposes of the objective test on a charge of murder.

(vi) *R v Smith (Morgan James)* [2000] 1 AC 146 was not followed by the Privy Council in *Attorney-General for Jersey v Holley* [2005] 2 AC 580. Holley and his girlfriend lived together in Jersey and were alcoholics. Holley killed his girlfriend by striking her a number of times with an axe. The judge did not refer in his summing up to the fact that Holley's alcoholism should be brought into account. What he said to the jury was: 'In your opinion, having regard to the actual provocation and your views of its gravity for the defendant, decide whether a man of the defendant's age, having ordinary power of self-control might have done what the defendant did. If the answer to that question is "Yes" then the verdict is not guilty of murder but guilty of manslaughter. If the answer to that question is "No" then the verdict would be guilty of murder.' The jury convicted Holley of murder.

If we test the facts against the summing up, we shall see that the girlfriend had entered the flat they shared and announced that she had just had sex with another man and then said: 'You haven't got the guts.' Holley, who was going outside to chop wood, then lifted the axe and hit her seven or eight times. The evidence showed that the defendant had drunk a great deal of beer or lager during the day. However, no mention of this is made in the summing up. The standard is the reasonable person not a drunken or alcoholic reasonable person. The Court of Appeal said that the Jersey court should have followed *R v Smith (Morgan James)* (2000) and taken into account the particular characteristics of Holley. However, in *R v James* [2006] 1 All ER 759 the House of Lords preferred *Holley* to its own ruling in *R v Smith (Morgan James)* (2000) and followed Holley. James stabbed his wife to death. She had left home, having formed a relationship with another man. There was psychiatric evidence regarding James but the House of Lords ruled that this should not be taken into account when trying to establish the partial defence of provocation.

The House of Lords followed a persuasive precedent of the Privy Council rather than its own previous judgment in *R v Smith (Morgan James)* (2000). The point of precedent is considered in Chapter 7.

We may conclude, therefore, that special characteristics will not be taken into account except in cases such as *R v Roberts* (1990) (above), where the provocation is directed at the defendant's disability.

535 *R v Johnson (Christopher)* [1989] 1 WLR 740

Johnson killed his victim in a night club. His own behaviour had been unpleasant, resulting in a girlfriend of the victim taunting Johnson calling him a 'white nigger' since he affected a West Indian accent at times. Johnson drew a knife and stabbed the victim because matters were getting more violent and Johnson said he feared that the victim was about to cut him with a glass. A verdict of manslaughter was substituted for one of murder by the Court of Appeal. Watkins, LJ said that whether or not there were elements in Johnson's conduct which justified the conclusion that he started the trouble and induced others including the victim to act as they did, the defence of provocation should nevertheless have been put to the members of the jury and left to them. Since this had not been done, the verdict of murder must be set aside.

536 *R v Thornton* (1991) 141 NLJ 1223

Mrs Thornton was married in 1988. She realised from the start that her husband was a heavy drinker and jealous and possessive. He was violent in the home assaulting Mrs Thornton. In May 1989 he committed a serious assault which led to charges being brought. In June of that year Mrs Thornton told a workmate that she was going to kill her husband. Later that month after a series of rows with her husband in which he called her a whore Mrs Thornton went to the kitchen to calm down. While in the kitchen she picked up a carving knife and sharpened it. She then went back to her husband who was lying on a sofa. She asked him to come to bed but he would not and said he would kill her when she was asleep. She said she would kill him first. He then suggested sarcastically that she should go ahead. She made a downward movement with the knife expecting he would ward it off but it entered his stomach and killed him. She was charged with and convicted of murder. Her appeal to the Court of Appeal was dismissed. It was *held* that since provocation can only be put forward as a defence to a charge of murder if it caused a sudden and temporary loss of self-control on the part of the defendant, prolonged domestic violence does not of itself amount to provocation unless there is a sudden and temporary loss of self-control by the wife.

Comment (i) Although the decision is in some ways an unfortunate one which does not assist the position of the battered wife, there does in all honesty seem to have been a 'cooling-off' period while the wife was in the kitchen and actually sharpening the knife. Some lawyers took the view that in cases such as this the cumulative effect of wife-beating should be taken into account. In other words, there may be a slow wearing down of the wife's self-control.

(ii) There was an appeal to the Court of Appeal (see *R v Thornton* [1996] 2 All ER 1023). The court reiterated the requirement of a sudden and temporary loss of control being clearly anxious not to allow premeditated killings to come under the shelter of provocation. It did, however, somewhat enlarge the defence by accepting the possibility of 'cumulative provocation'. A jury should consider the whole history of a prior abusive relationship between the accused and the victim on which the sudden loss of control was based rather than simply looking at the last provocative act before the killing. This act might be minor in itself but could be 'the last straw which broke the camel's back'. The Court of Appeal ordered a new trial which took place at Oxford Crown Court. The jury substituted a verdict of guilty of manslaughter and sentenced Mrs Thornton to five years' imprisonment. In view of the fact that she had already served five-and-a-half years on the murder conviction, she walked free immediately.

(iii) The principle of a slow wearing down of the accused was raised again in *R v Humphries (Emma)*, *The Independent*, 11 July 1995. H appealed to the Court of Appeal against a conviction of murder on the basis of her defence of provocation. She was 17 at the time of the offence and was described as having explosive, immature and attention-seeking traits. She had worked as a prostitute for her boyfriend who used to beat her and she had cut her wrists on a number of occasions. On the day of the murder she had again cut her wrists and he taunted her saying she had not done a good job of it. She lost control and stabbed and killed him. Her appeal was allowed, and her sentence adjusted to provide for her immediate release. The judge's summing up should have dealt with the victim's behaviour during the whole of her relationship with the victim because the latter's conduct over that period of time was capable of building up and culminating in the final provoking event.

Diminished responsibility: use of alcohol

537 *R v Tandy*, *The Times*, 23 December 1987

Linda Mary Tandy was an alcoholic who drank nine-tenths of a bottle of vodka over part of a day and then strangled her daughter aged 11. They had had a good relationship over the years. She was convicted of murder. The defence of diminished responsibility was not available. Her drinking was not involuntary. She had bought the vodka on Monday but had not started to drink it until the Wednesday of the killing. Her first drink was not involuntary even if later drinking was. This amounted to voluntary drinking and could not amount to a disease of the mind as diminished responsibility required.

538 *R v Gittins* [1984] 3 All ER 252

Gittins killed his wife and raped and killed his step-daughter while suffering from depression *and* the effects of drinking and drugs. He was charged with murder and convicted. He then appealed to the Court of Appeal. His conviction for murder was reduced to manslaughter on the ground of diminished responsibility. The court was careful to point out that normally the taking of drink or drugs would not amount to diminished responsibility, but where other elements were present, such as the mental state of depression in this case which might have been brought on by an extended period of drink and drugs, nevertheless it remained an abnormality of the mind whatever its source and, provided it existed, could be a ground for reducing murder to manslaughter on the grounds of diminished responsibility.

Comment Presumably in the absence of a medically certified mental state of depression, the defendant would not have had the defence of diminished responsibility merely because he was under the influence of drink and drugs at the time.

Involuntary manslaughter by unlawful act

539 *R v Church* [1966] 1 QB 59

Church had an argument with a woman and had a fight with her. She was knocked unconscious and, having failed to revive her, he threw her in a river. She was, in fact, alive at the time and died of drowning. He was convicted of manslaughter and appealed. The problem basically was that he had not killed her in the fight and he did not foresee the risk of death when he threw her in the river because he thought wrongly that she was already dead. Nevertheless, his conviction for involuntary manslaughter was upheld. The court said that his act was unlawful in the sense that throwing a woman into a river deliberately is unlawful even if the defendant did not intend or foresee that death or serious bodily harm would result. Such an act at least created a risk of physical harm and that was enough.

Comment The unlawful act must in general involve the infliction of *physical* as distinct from *emotional* harm. Thus, where in the course of robbing a petrol station the robbers so frighten the attendant that he dies from a heart attack of which neither he nor they knew he was at imminent risk, there can be no conviction of manslaughter (see *R v Dawson* (1985) 81 Cr App R 150).

Statutory offences against the person

540 *Director of Public Prosecutions v K* [1990] 1 All ER 331

K, a 15-year-old schoolboy, left a chemistry class to wash his hands following a spillage of acid. He took a test tube of the acid with him and while in the toilet he heard footsteps approaching and panicked. He poured the acid into a hot air drier. He then returned to his class intending to clean out the drier later. Before he could do so the next user of the drier was squirted in the face by the acid and scarred. K was charged under s 47 of the Offences Against the Person Act 1861. He was reckless in that he had given no thought to the risk of a subsequent use of the machine before he could clean it. *Caldwell* and *Lawrence* were applied. K was convicted (but see now *R v Parmenter* (1991), Case **542** below).

Comment (i) In *R v Spratt* [1991] 1 WLR 1073 the Court of Appeal doubted the above decision. Spratt fired an air pistol from the bedroom window of his flat. Two pellets struck a seven-year-old girl who was playing in the fore-court. He was charged under s 47 of the 1861 Act. He pleaded guilty on legal advice because although he was unaware of the girl's presence he had given no thought to the risk of his action and was, therefore, *Caldwell* reckless. Nevertheless, he appealed against conviction and the Court of Appeal said *Caldwell* recklessness was not enough for the s 47 offence. The *mens rea* of every type of offence against the person under the 1861 Act involved intention or recklessness, i.e. taking the risk of harm ensuing *with foresight* that it might happen. *Caldwell* recklessness was not enough, and this even though s 47 did not use the word 'malice'. The court in *DPP v K* had not been referred to *R v Cunningham* (1957) and the definition of recklessness there. The conviction was quashed. (But see now *R v Parmenter* (1991), Case **542**.)

(ii) In *DPP v Smith (Michael Ross)* [2006] 2 All ER 16 the defendant cut off the complainant's ponytail without her consent with a pair of kitchen scissors. She was his former girlfriend. The issue was whether this had caused 'actual bodily harm' for the purposes of the s 47 offence. The Dudley justices had ruled that the defendant had no case to answer because there was no evidence of bruising, bleeding or cutting of the skin and in the absence of evidence of any psychiatric or psychological harm the facts alleged could not amount to actual bodily harm.

The Queen's Bench Divisional Court, to which the DPP appealed, did not agree. Even if, scientifically speaking, hair above the surface of the skin was dead tissue, it remained part of the body and was intrinsic to each individual. Therefore, the lopping of hair as part of an assault on the victim was capable of amounting to an assault occasioning actual bodily harm.

The case was sent back to the justices with a direction to continue hearing it. It will be appreciated that the fact situation here could be the basis of an action for damages for assault and battery and could be used to illustrate the civil scenario if care is taken to point out that it was a criminal prosecution.

541 *R v Martin* (1881) 8 QBD 54

Just before a theatrical performance came to an end M, intending to terrify people leaving the theatre, put out lights on the staircase which he knew a large number of people would use when leaving the theatre. He then placed an iron bar across an exit door. As a result of his actions several people were hurt as they tried to leave the theatre. M was convicted on a charge of unlawfully and maliciously inflicting grievous bodily harm under s 20 of the Offences Against the Person Act 1861. 'The prisoner . . . acted "unlawfully and maliciously", not that he had any personal malice against the particular individuals

injured, but in the sense of doing an unlawful act calculated to injure, and by which others were in fact injured. The prisoner was most properly convicted.' (*Per* Lord Coleridge, CJ)

Comment (i) This would appear to be an early formulation of *Cunningham* recklessness.

(ii) Did Martin 'inflict' the harm as s 20 of the 1861 Act requires? The Court thought so and yet, oddly enough, would the case not have been better brought under s 18 of the 1861 Act, which only requires the 'causing' of grievous bodily harm? An unresolved problem. Changes in the Act may be required. Perhaps the major offence in s 18 should require an assault and the lesser one in s 20 should not do so.

542 *R v Parmenter* [1991] 2 WLR 408

Parmenter admitted injuring his baby son and was charged amongst other things with inflicting grievous bodily harm contrary to s 20 of the Offences Against the Person Act 1861. The Court of Appeal had eventually to decide upon the *mens rea* for the s 20 offence and the s 47 offence. It *held* as follows:

(*a*) a direction to the jury on the intent necessary to found a conviction of unlawfully and maliciously inflicting grievous bodily harm contrary to s 20 should indicate to the jury that it was necessary that the defendant actually foresaw that some physical harm to some other person would result from his act. A direction that it was sufficient that the defendant ought to or should have foreseen the physical harm was a misdirection;

(*b*) on the suggestion that Parmenter might be convicted on the lesser offence in s 47, the Court of Appeal said no. The necessary *mens rea* for s 47 was intention or subjective (or *Cunningham*) recklessness. Since the trial judge's direction had been objective in form Parmenter's conviction on s 20 was quashed and a s 47 offence could not be substituted.

R v Spratt (1990) was applied.

Comment (i) On appeal to the House of Lords, [1991] 4 All ER 698, their Lordships decided that:

(*a*) in order to establish the offence under s 20, the Crown must prove that the defendant intended or actually foresaw that his act would cause harm. This physical harm need only be of a minor character and it is unnecessary for the Crown to show that the defendant intended or foresaw that his unlawful act might cause physical harm of the gravity described in s 20, i.e. either wounding or grievous bodily harm;

(*b*) in order to establish the offence of assault under s 47, it is sufficient for the Crown to show that the defendant committed an assault; the Crown is not obliged to prove that the defendant intended to cause some actual bodily harm or was reckless as to whether such harm would be caused (*R v Spratt* (1990) was disapproved);

(*c*) a verdict of guilty under s 47 is a permissible alternative to a charge under s 20.

(ii) The House of Lords did not agree entirely with the Court of Appeal as to the *mens rea* required for s 20, and not at all on s 47. The position is, therefore, as stated by the House of Lords.

(iii) The House of Lords' ruling was applied in *R v Rushworth* (*Gary Alan*) (1992) 95 Cr App R 252, where the Court of Appeal decided that the defendant was guilty under s 20 when he attempted, during sexual activities, to insert a vibrator into the complainant's vagina, causing laceration to her vulva and bowel. The jury decided on the evidence that he actually foresaw some physical harm.

543 *R v Belfon* [1976] 3 All ER 46

Belfon attacked a man called Paul Horne with a razor causing him serious injury. He was charged under s 18 of the Offences Against the Person Act 1861. At his trial the judge directed the jury that intention or *Cunningham* recklessness as to the infliction of grievous bodily harm constituted the *mens rea* for an offence under s 18. He was convicted and appealed to the Court of Appeal. His conviction was quashed and a conviction for unlawful wounding under s 20 was substituted. The Court of Appeal laid it down that in directing a jury in relation to an offence under s 18 the judge should direct the jury that what has to be proved is (*a*) the wounding; (*b*) that the wounding was deliberate and without justification; (*c*) that it was committed with intent to cause really serious bodily harm; and (*d*) that the test of intent is subjective.

Sexual offences: rape

544 *R v R* [1991] 4 All ER 482

A husband and wife were having matrimonial problems. The wife left her husband and went to live with her parents. She left a note at the matrimonial home saying she was going to petition for a divorce. Some three weeks later the husband forced his way into the house of his wife's parents who were out at the time and attempted to have sexual intercourse with his wife against her will. In the course of doing so he squeezed her neck and, therefore, assaulted her. He was tried, amongst other things, for attempted rape. His defence was that he could not in law commit rape or attempted rape upon his wife. Her consent was

presumed. He was convicted, the trial judge following an existing rule that rape could take place if the wife had ceased, as in this case, to live with her husband. Nevertheless, the husband appealed saying there could be no rape of a wife in the absence of a court order of divorce or separation or a separation agreement.

The House of Lords eventually heard the appeal. It decided that a husband could rape his wife if he had intercourse with her without her consent even if they were not divorced or separated but were cohabiting. It was unacceptable that by marriage a wife submits to sexual intercourse in all circumstances.

545 *R v Williams* [1923] 1 KB 340

Williams taught singing. He told a 16-year-old female pupil that if she had intercourse with him it would improve her voice. The girl allowed him to have intercourse with her and made no resistance. She believed what he said and in any case was not mature enough to know that he was having sexual intercourse with her. She did not know that that was what they were doing. He was convicted of rape. His appeal was dismissed. Lord Hewart, CJ said: 'She was persuaded to consent to what he did . . . because she thought it was a surgical operation.' Therefore, there was in effect no consent.

Comment A further example of deception nullifying consent is to be found in *R v Tabassum (Navid)*, *The Times*, 26 May 2000 where the Court of Appeal found the defendant guilty of indecent assault where he had, by pretending to be medically qualified, fondled the breasts of three women on the basis that he was demonstrating breast self-examination.

546 *Director of Public Prosecutions v Morgan* [1975] 2 All ER 347

Morgan and his three companions were members of the RAF. Following a drinking session Morgan took the three men home to have sexual intercourse with his wife. He told them she might resist because she was a bit 'kinky' and this was the only way she could get 'turned on'. When they got to Morgan's home Mrs Morgan was in bed asleep. She did not habitually sleep with her husband. She was frog-marched to another bedroom and laid on a double bed; each of her arms was held and her legs were held apart. All three men then had intercourse with her. When they had finished and left the room Morgan had intercourse with her himself. Mrs Morgan immediately left the house and went to a nearby hospital. She said she had done all she could to resist. The three men (not Morgan, who could not commit rape upon his wife in those days) were charged with rape and all four with aiding and abetting the rapes.

The case eventually got to the House of Lords where it was decided that:

(*a*) The crime of rape was committed by having sexual intercourse with a woman with intent to do so without her consent or with reckless indifference as to whether she consented or not. The test of recklessness is subjective and not objective because if the defendant believes the woman is consenting that belief need not be based on *reasonable* grounds.

(*b*) There could have been no subjective belief in the circumstances of this case that Mrs Morgan was consenting and so the convictions for rape and aiding and abetting rape must stand.

Comment The Sexual Offences Act 2003 contains statutory provisions regarding consent. The decision in *Morgan* is replaced by the statutory definition. Under the new provisions, the prosecution must prove that B did not consent and that A did not reasonably believe that B was consenting. An honest but unreasonable belief as to the consent of the victim will no longer entitle the defendant to an acquittal. In deciding whether the defendant's belief in consent is reasonable, the court must have regard to all the circumstances at the time in question, including any steps that the defendant may have taken to establish that the victim did consent to the sexual activity. In addition, the 2003 Act introduces rebuttable and irrebuttable presumptions about consent.

The *Morgan* case is included only to show the previous position and to provide a contrast with current law.

AGE AND RESPONSIBILITY – GENERAL DEFENCES

M'Naghten rules: disease of the mind

547 *R v Kemp* [1956] 3 All ER 249

The accused struck his wife with a hammer without, so he said, being conscious of doing so and was charged with causing grievous bodily harm. He was an elderly man of good character who suffered from arteriosclerosis. Medical opinions differed as to the precise effects of this disease on his mind. It was *held* that, whichever medical opinion was accepted, arteriosclerosis was a disease capable of affecting the mind, and was thus a disease of the mind within the M'Naghten Rules, whether or not it was recognised medically as a mental disease.

Comment In *R v Sullivan* [1983] 2 All ER 673 the House of Lords held that the definition of insanity in *M'Naghten* could apply to a person suffering from epilepsy. Mr Sullivan admitted inflicting grievous bodily harm on a friend of his at a time when he was recovering from a minor epileptic seizure. His defence was automatism which could have resulted in an acquittal but the judge ruled that the defence amounted to one of insanity which would, if successful, have led to Mr Sullivan's immediate detention in a special institution. Mr Sullivan changed his plea to guilty of occasioning actual bodily harm and was convicted and sentenced to probation with medical supervision.

Previously it had been thought that for *M'Naghten* to apply the mind had to be working but not as it should. It seems from this decision that *M'Naghten* applies even if, as in this case, the mind is not working at all.

548 *R v Hennessy* [1989] 1 WLR 287

The defendant was charged with taking a motor vehicle without consent. He suffered from diabetes and had to take insulin every day. He had been having marital and employment problems causing stress and depression and he had not taken his insulin for two or three days before the incident. He claimed that as a result he did not know what he was doing and did not, therefore, have the necessary *mens rea*. The judge took the view that this was a disease of the mind and he was insane within the *M'Naghten* rules. The defendant changed his plea to guilty and then appealed against the insanity ruling. The Court of Appeal *held* that the hyperglycaemia caused by the lack of insulin was a disease of the mind within *M'Naghten*. The defence of automatism was not available. The defendant was insane. The trial judge's ruling was correct.

Comment (i) In *R v Burgess*, *The Times*, 28 March 1991 a man claimed to have been sleepwalking when he wounded a woman. He said he was suffering from non-insane automatism and lacked the necessary *mens rea* for the offence. The Court of Appeal held that he was insane and that an appeal by him against a verdict of not guilty by reason of insanity failed. He was suffering from insane automatism in spite of the transitory nature of the disorder.

(ii) The fact that an epileptic (as in *Sullivan*) and a diabetic (as in *Hennessy*) can be regarded as insane is an illustration of the fact that the test is legal not medical and is based on responsibility for the act in the circumstances of the case.

549 *R v Clarke* [1972] 1 All ER 219

May Clarke was convicted of theft from the International Stores in Leicester. She had put certain items into her shopping bag and not into the wire basket provided by the store which she presented at the check-out. She suffered from diabetes but did not claim not to have taken her insulin. She had not entirely recovered from 'flu and on the Friday previous to the theft her husband had suffered a broken collar bone and she had become, she said, very depressed and forgetful. In her own words, 'Everything seemed to get on top of me.' She pleaded guilty rather than face a decision that she was not guilty by reason of insanity. She appealed against her conviction on the guilty plea. The Court of Appeal *held* that her conviction must be quashed. She had been wrongly advised by the Assistant Recorder that if she did not do so the insanity verdict would be appropriate. It would not have been. The *M'Naghten* rules relating to insanity do not apply to those who retain the powers of reasoning but who in moments of confusion or absent-mindedness fail to use those powers to the full.

550 *R v Windle* [1952] 2 QB 826

The defendant gave his wife a large and fatal dose of aspirin. He was admittedly suffering from mental illness but he did admit he had administered the aspirin and said he supposed he would hang for it as he later was! His only defence was insanity. He was convicted, the trial judge having ruled that there was no evidence to support such a defence. The defence did not go to the jury. Windle appealed and his appeal failed. Lord Goddard, CJ said:

> In the opinion of the court there is no doubt that in the *M'Naghten* rules 'wrong' means contrary to law and not 'wrong' according to the opinion of one man or a number of people on the question of whether a particular act might or might not be justified. In the present case it could not be challenged that the appellant knew that what he was doing was contrary to law, and that he realised what punishment the law provided for murder.

Actus reus: automatism

551 *Hill v Baxter* [1958] 1 All ER 42

The defendant had been charged with dangerous driving and failing to conform with a traffic sign under ss 11 and 49(b) of the Road Traffic Act 1930, respectively. He said in his defence that he had been unconscious at the time because a sudden illness had overtaken him. The magistrates accepted his defence and dismissed the charges and the prosecutor

appealed. The appeal was allowed and the defendant therefore convicted.

> I agree that there may be cases where the circumstances are such that the accused could not really be said to be driving at all. Suppose he had a stroke or an epileptic fit, both instances of what may properly be called acts of God; he might well be in the driver's seat even with his hands on the wheel, but in such a state of unconsciousness that he could not be said to be driving. A blow from a stone or an attack by a swarm of bees I think introduces some conception akin to *novus actus interveniens*. In this case, however, I am content to say that the evidence falls far short of what would justify a court holding that this man was in some automatous state. (*Per* Lord Goddard, CJ)

Comment In *Attorney-General's Reference (No 2 of 1992)*, *The Times*, 31 May 1993 the defendant, who was described as driving without awareness induced by the repetitive stimuli of motorway-driving over a long period, was charged with motor manslaughter and convicted. The Court of Appeal affirmed that conviction and did not accept the defence of automatism. There was no destruction of nor total absence of voluntary control on the part of the defendant in his driving though it was impaired or reduced.

552 *R v Quick* [1973] 3 All ER 347

Quick was a nurse employed at a mental hospital. He assaulted a patient and claimed that he could not remember doing so. He was a diabetic and had taken insulin as recommended by his doctor. He then had a small breakfast and no lunch. He had also been drinking before the assault took place. Medical evidence showed that at the time of the assault he was suffering from a deficiency of blood sugar following the insulin injection. The trial judge ruled that this state could only be relied on to support the defence of insanity. Quick changed his plea to guilty and then appealed against his conviction. The Court of Appeal *held* that the improper functioning of his mind had been caused by an external factor not a disease of the mind. The use of the insulin was that external factor. He was, therefore, entitled to have the defence of automatism put to the jury and since this had not been done his conviction must be quashed.

Comment (i) All that the Court of Appeal was deciding in this case was that the defence of automatism could and should have been put to the jury after proper argument by counsel. The Court of Appeal does indicate that the defence may not have succeeded because the deficiency of blood sugar might very well have been regarded as self-induced. Those who take insulin should eat regularly afterwards. Quick did not. He had also been advised to take a lump of sugar if he felt an attack coming on. He had not done so. However, the conviction had to be quashed because the jury might have accepted the defence. It is important to know that it is available in these circumstances even though it is by no means certain that it will succeed.

(ii) In *Moses v Winder* [1980] Crim LR 232 the defendant had been a diabetic for 20 years. He felt a diabetic attack developing and took a dose of sugar which usually postponed the attacks for about an hour. However, whilst driving home he drove his car on the wrong side of the road, colliding with an oncoming car. He stopped a few minutes later in a daze, examined his car and then drove a further half mile. It was *held* by a Divisional Court that the defendant was nevertheless guilty of driving without due care and attention. His defence of automatism did not succeed and would rarely succeed without medical evidence. The defendant had not taken sufficient precautions to deal with the threat of a diabetic coma.

553 *R v Lipman* [1969] 3 All ER 410

L was charged with murder of a girl but convicted of manslaughter. Both he and the girl had taken LSD together in her room and L said that while under the influence of the drug he had an illusion of being attacked by snakes and that he must have killed the girl during this time. The girl had received two severe blows on the head but the immediate cause of her death was asphyxia as a result of having part of a sheet pushed down her mouth. The Court of Appeal affirmed the conviction, saying that when the killing results from the unlawful act of the accused, no specific intent was to be proved to convict of manslaughter and mental states which are self-induced by drink or drugs are no defence to a charge of manslaughter.

Drunkenness and drugs

554 *Director of Public Prosecutions v Majewski* [1976] 2 All ER 142

There was a disturbance at the Bull public house in Basildon, Essex. Majewski attacked the landlord and two other persons. He also assaulted three police officers. He was charged with assault occasioning actual bodily harm. At his trial he said he did not know what he was doing by reason of drink and drugs. The case eventually reached the House of Lords which ruled that unless the offence charged required a specific intent a drink/drugs defence was not applicable. Since the assaults charged did not require solely

a specific intent (see Chapter 23) the defendant's submissions as to drink and drugs were no defence and his conviction must be upheld.

Comment (i) It seems difficult to find the ingredients of crime in *Lipman* and *Majewski* in terms of the *actus reus* and *mens rea* requirements. Perhaps the law punishes the act of becoming intoxicated on drink or drugs, the punishment being then based on the act which the defendant did while in that state.

(ii) Involuntary intoxication by way of drink or drugs is capable of negativing *mens rea*. In *R v Kingston* [1993] 3 WLR 676 the defendant, a paedophile, was drugged by another man so that the defendant could be photographed in a compromising sexual situation with a boy aged 15 and so that the other man might blackmail him. The defence was that because of the drugs the defendant had no recollection of acting as he did. The defence of involuntary intoxication succeeded in the Court of Appeal. See also *Ross v HM Advocate* (1991) below.

(iii) The House of Lords reversed the decision of the Court of Appeal in *Kingston* (see *The Times*, 22 July 1994). They did not accept that the drugs had sufficiently affected his *intent*. He was still excited by the boy and he acted with the *intent of a paedophile*, i.e. to commit acts of indecency with a young boy. The decision shows how difficult it is, and always has been, to plead involuntary intoxication in crime.

555 *R v Hardie* [1984] 3 All ER 848

Hardie lived with a woman at her flat. The relationship broke down and she insisted that he leave. He was upset and took several tablets of valium, a sedative drug, belonging to the woman. Some hours later he started a fire in the bedroom of the flat while the woman and her daugher were in the sitting room. He was charged with damaging property with intent to endanger life or being reckless as to whether life would be endangered (Criminal Damage Act 1971, s 1(2)). The trial judge said in answer to the defence of no *mens rea* that because the valium was voluntarily self-administered it could not negative *mens rea* and was no defence. Hardie was convicted and appealed. The Court of Appeal decided that although self-induced intoxication from alcohol or a dangerous drug was no defence to crimes involving recklessness because the taking of the alcohol or drugs was itself reckless a drug which was merely soporific was different. The jury should have been asked to consider what effect the valium might have had upon the defendant's ability to appreciate the risk. Since they had not been asked to do so the conviction must be quashed.

556 R v O'Grady [1987] 3 WLR 321

O'Grady and his acquaintances were given to heavy drinking. On the day in question he had drunk at least eight flagons of cider. His companions, Brennan and McCloskey, who had been drinking with him went back to O'Grady's flat. During the night McCloskey attacked O'Grady and in the ensuing fight O'Grady punched McCloskey to death. He put forward self-defence. It seemed from the circumstances that McCloskey's attack was severe but not so severe as to warrant killing him in self-defence. O'Grady asked the court to acquit him because being drunk he had not appreciated the nature of McCloskey's attack. The Court of Appeal heard an appeal by O'Grady against his conviction at his trial of manslaughter. The appeal failed, the Court of Appeal ruling that so far as self-defence is concerned reliance cannot be placed on a mistake as to the nature of the attack induced by voluntary intoxication.

Comment Much depends upon the wording of statutory offences. For example, s 5 of the Criminal Damage Act 1971 requires that a person causing damage to property has a defence if he believed that the owner of the property would have consented to it. The Act says it is immaterial whether the belief is justified if it is honestly held. This means that the test as to belief is subjective. In addition the section does not go on to say 'if it is honestly held other than because of self-induced intoxication'.

In *Jaggard* v *Dickson* [1980] 3 All ER 716 a girl who was drunk broke into a house thinking it was a friend's house which he had said she could use as her own. It was an identical house in the same street but not her friend's. The girl was acquitted of criminal damage because the Divisional Court said if she honestly believed it was her friend's house then the defence in the Act was established even though the honest belief arose from drink. It is doubtful whether there will be much scope to extend this decision into other areas.

557 Attorney-General for Northern Ireland v Gallagher [1963] AC 349

G was convicted of murdering his wife. In his defence he pleaded insanity under the *M'Naghten* rules or, as an alternative, that he was too drunk at the time to form the necessary intent for murder so that he was only guilty of manslaughter. G had shown intention to kill his wife before taking the drink. The case eventually reached the House of Lords where Lord Denning gave a useful summary of the effect of drunkenness when he said:

1. If a man is charged with an offence in which a specific intention is essential (as in murder, though not in manslaughter), then evidence of drunkenness, which renders him incapable of forming that intention is an answer. . . . 2. If a man by drinking brings on a distinct disease of the mind such as *delirium tremens*, so that he is temporarily insane within the M'Naghten Rules, that is to say, he does not at the time know what he is doing or that it is wrong, then he has a defence on the ground of insanity. . . .

However, G's original conviction for murder was upheld because he did not fit the above categories. As Lord Denning said:

My Lords, I think the law on this point should take a clear stand. If a man, whilst sane and sober, forms an intention to kill and makes preparation for it, knowing it is a wrong thing to do, and then gets himself drunk so as to give himself Dutch courage to do the killing, and whilst drunk carries out his intention, he cannot rely on this self-induced drunkenness as a defence to a charge of murder, nor even as reducing it to manslaughter.

558 Ross v HM Advocate, 1991 SLT 564

This was a trial for attempted murder. The evidence was that on the day of the attempted murder the defendant had been drinking lager from a can. He did not know that five or six tablets of temazepam and a quantity of LSD had been squeezed into the can. The defendant drank the lager. Shortly afterwards the defendant started lunging about with a knife and screaming. He injured various people who were strangers to him. On a charge of attempted murder the defendant said that he had no self-control and therefore no *mens rea*. He was nevertheless convicted. He appealed and his appeal was allowed. He should be acquitted because his absence of self-control was not self-inflicted. But see also *R* v *Kingston* (1994), above, where the House of Lords did not apply the *decision* in *Ross* but were able to apply certain of the reasoning in the *Ross* case to the effect that the particular decision should not be of universal application.

Duress

559 R v Gotts [1991] 2 All ER 1

Ben Gotts was charged with the attempted murder of his mother. The mother had left the family home after arguments with the father and gone to a women's aid refuge with two of the younger children. One morning as the mother left the refuge to take one of the children to school Ben then aged 16 armed with a knife supplied by his father ran up behind her and stabbed her. He was charged with attempted murder and wounding with intent. He pleaded duress: that his father had ordered him to kill his mother. The Court of Appeal *held* that duress was not a defence to attempted murder and his appeal was dismissed. There was no verdict on the count relating to wounding with intent.

The decision of the Court of Appeal was affirmed by the House of Lords (see *R* v *Gotts* [1992] 1 All ER 832).

560 *R* v *Hudson* [1971] 2 All ER 244

Two girls aged 17 and 19 were the main witnesses for the prosecution on a charge in Manchester of wounding. At the trial they both failed to identify the defendant Wright. He was acquitted as a result of this. The girls were tried for perjury and put in the defence of duress. They had been approached by a group of men who threatened to 'cut them up' if they 'told on' Wright in court. They were nevertheless convicted and appealed. The appeal turned on the trial judge's direction to the jury that duress can only arise where there is a threat of death or serious personal injury at the moment when the crime is committed. The threat here was to do something in the future. The Court of Appeal said that their convictions must be quashed. Lord Parker, CJ said that the threats in this case were none the less compelling because they could not be executed in the court room if they could be carried out on the streets of Salford the same night.

561 *R* v *Sharp (David)* [1987] 3 WLR 1

David Sharp was involved in the armed robbery of a post office. He participated in the robbery. He was charged with aiding and abetting murder but he was in fact convicted of manslaughter. He claimed that he had not wished to go on with the robbery but had been forced to because a member of the gang to which he belonged which had masterminded the robbery had held a gun to his head to make him proceed. He appealed because the trial judge rejected the defence of duress. The Court of Appeal dismissed the appeal. The defence of duress was not available where, as here, a person had voluntarily and with knowledge of its nature joined a gang which he knew might put pressure on him to commit an offence.

562 *R* v *Shepherd* (1988) 86 Cr App R 47

Shepherd and other persons entered retail premises and stole goods. He was charged with burglary. He said that he had participated willingly at first but later lost his nerve but stayed on because a member of the gang threatened him and his family with violence if he did not continue. The trial judge ruled that the defence of duress was not available because he had voluntarily participated in a criminal act. He appealed and the Court of Appeal *held* that his conviction must be quashed. The defence of duress was available if at the time he joined the gang he did not contemplate that violence would be used against him if he did not continue to participate.

Duress of circumstances

563 *R* v *Martin* [1989] 1 All ER 652

Mr Martin was found guilty of driving whilst disqualified. He appealed on the basis that his wife had suicidal tendencies, and that on the day in question his stepson had overslept and was bound to be late for work and, it was said, at risk of losing his job unless Mr Martin drove him to work. Mr Martin was disqualified from driving but his wife started screaming and beating her head against the wall and threatening suicide unless he drove the stepson to work which he then did. He was stopped and later prosecuted for driving whilst disqualified. His defence was necessity and the Court of Appeal accepted it in this case though referring to the situation as 'duress of circumstances'.

Comment It was held by the Court of Appeal in *R* v *Pommell*, *The Times*, 22 May 1995 that the duress of circumstances defence, though developed in relation to road traffic offences, also applied to other crimes, but not murder, attempted murder and some forms of treason. A person was permitted to break the law to prevent a greater evil from happening to himself or others. P had appealed against conviction for possessing a firearm. The police, having a search warrant, had found him in bed holding a loaded gun which he said he had taken from a visitor to his house the previous night to prevent the visitor from carrying out his threat to kill persons whom he said had killed his friend. He claimed that he intended to take the gun to the police station in the morning. His conviction was set aside and a new trial ordered.

Necessity

564 *R* v *Dudley and Stephens* (1884) 14 QBD 273

A yacht was shipwrecked, and three men and a boy escaped in an open boat. They were adrift for eight days without food when the men killed the boy, who was by then very weak, in order to eat his body and keep themselves alive. They were rescued four days later by a passing ship. They were tried for, and convicted of, murder. It was *held* that there is no principle of law which entitles a man to take the life of an innocent person to save his own. In any case, the death of the men would not have been inevitable, but only probable. Where the offence committed is not a capital offence, the defence of necessity might result in a mitigation of sentence.

Comment (i) It was held in *DPP v Harris*, *The Times*, 16 March 1994, that a police driver could not successfully plead the defence of necessity on a charge of driving without due care and attention when he failed to stop a car, being used for police purposes, at a red light. This would seem to stress the need for an element of threat or danger where the defence is put up (see also *A (children)*, *The Times*, 10 October 2000: necessary to separate conjoined twins: court consents to inevitable death of one).

(ii) The reluctance of our courts to entertain the defence of necessity is also illustrated by *R v Altham*, *The Times*, 1 February 2006.

The defendant suffered pain from a road accident some 15 years before this prosecution was brought. He used cannabis to relieve the pain. He was later prosecuted for the offence of possession of a controlled drug, i.e. cannabis, contrary to s 5(2) of the Misuse of Drugs Act 1971. He was convicted of this offence in Preston Crown Court and appealed to the Court of Appeal. His appeal was dismissed.

His contention that notwithstanding that the cause of his condition was a road accident some 15 years before, the state had an Art 3 human rights obligation to allow him to take any steps necessary to alleviate his condition even though those steps involved breaches of the law was not accepted by the court. The state had done nothing to subject the defendant to either inhuman or degrading treatment and therefore Art 3 was not engaged. Article 3 did not require the state to take any steps to alleviate his condition.

The defence of necessity did not apply because, if it were applied, it would enable individuals to treat themselves by unlawful acts without medical intervention or supervision.

Accordingly, the trial judge was right to hold that the defence of necessity should not be left to the jury.

Note: since the prosecution the defendant has been prescribed another drug which alleviated his pain to such an extent that he no longer uses cannabis.

Mistake

565 *R v Kimber* [1983] 3 All ER 316

Kimber sexually assaulted a woman who was a patient in a mental hospital. He was charged with indecent assault. His defence was that he honestly believed that the woman consented. The woman had been diagnosed as schizophrenic. During the indecent act, which involved the touching of her private parts, she was mumbling all the time giving perhaps to a reasonable person evidence that she was a sick woman. Since the attack took place on the cricket ground near the hospital gardens, it might have led a reasonable person to believe that the sickness was mental and throw doubt upon her consent. The Court of Appeal decided that it was enough if the mistake which Kimber made was to honestly believe that she consented. However, his conviction must stand because no reasonable jury properly instructed that an honest belief was sufficient as a defence could have believed that Kimber could or did honestly believe she consented in the circumstances of the case.

566 *R v Bailey* (1800) 168 ER 651

Bailey, who was the captain of a ship, fired at another ship on the high seas without any justification and wounded one of the sailors on that other ship. He was charged under an Act of Parliament which made such a shooting on the high seas triable and punishable in this country. The following extract from the judgment of the court is relevant:

> It was then insisted that the prisoner could not be found guilty of the offence with which he was charged, because the Act of 39 Geo. 3, c. 37 upon which . . . the prisoner was indicted at this Admiralty Sessions, . . . only received the Royal Assent on 10 May, 1799, and the fact charged in the indictment happened on 27 June in the same year when the prisoner could not know that any such Act existed (his ship the *Langley* being at the time upon the coast of Africa). Lord Eldon told the jury that he was of opinion that he was, in strict law, guilty within the statutes . . . though if the facts laid were proved, though he could not then know that the Act of 39 Geo. 3, c. 37 had passed, and that his ignorance of that fact, could in no other wise affect the case, than that it might be the means of recommending him to a merciful consideration elsewhere should he be found guilty. . . .

Comment At the next Admiralty Sessions Bailey was pardoned.

Self-defence

567 *R v McInnes* [1971] 3 All ER 295

McInnes belonged to a group of youths called 'greasers'. There was a fight between a group of 'greasers' and another group of youths called 'skinheads'. It took place at Platt Fields, Manchester. A skinhead jumped on the defendant's back and his response was to stab the skinhead, which caused his death. The defendant was convicted of murder. He appealed to the Court of Appeal on two main points:

(a) that the trial judge had said that in self-defence cases it was necessary for the defendant to have retreated as far as he could before using the force in self-defence; and

(b) that even if the force used was unreasonable, as it clearly was in this case, a jury could be directed to return a verdict of manslaughter.

On these points it was decided that it was not essential that the defendant should have retreated. Whether he did or not was merely one factor in deciding whether the defence of self-defence succeeded or not. Furthermore, if the defence failed, as it did here, because of lack of reciprocity then it failed altogether. It was not possible for the jury to return a verdict of manslaughter. The defendant's conviction for murder must stand.

Comment (i) The fact that no retreat is merely a factor to be looked at in terms of a plea of self-defence was affirmed again in *R v Bird (Debbie)* [1985] 2 All ER 513, where following a house party the defendant hit the victim in the face with a glass after he slapped her while he was pinning her to the wall. She had not shown an unwillingness to fight but the Court of Appeal said this was not absolutely necessary. Incidentally, the force used here was totally lacking in reciprocity, but the defendant managed to satisfy the court that she did not know she had the glass in her hand and only intended to use her fist.

(ii) The issue of self-defence was raised before the House of Lords in *R v Clegg* [1995] 1 All ER 334. In that case the appellant was a British soldier stationed in Northern Ireland. He was at the relevant time on patrol at a checkpoint when a car drove through it without stopping and in spite of calls for it to stop by soldiers at the checkpoint. The car was stolen. The appellant, believing that the lives of his fellow soldiers were at risk from attack by what appeared to be terrorists in the car, opened fire on it killing the driver and a woman passenger. The evidence showed that the woman had been shot in the back at a time when the car was 50 feet down the road from the checkpoint and when the soldiers could no longer have been in any danger. The appellant was convicted of murder and his defence of self-defence failed. The House of Lords said that a soldier or police officer who, in the course of his duty, killed a person by firing a shot which constituted the use of excessive and unreasonable force in self-defence was guilty of murder and not manslaughter.

The decision states, in effect, that if the force used is unreasonable the defence fails and more importantly that the test of whether the force used was reasonable or not is *objective*. So if the prosecution shows that excessive force was used, the defence fails. The use of excessive force is not to be decided in terms of the defendant's perception of events, which would be a *subjective* test.

The Law Commission has proposed a test in which the key question would be, was the violence used 'reasonable' in the circumstances as the defendant believed them to be? This test is, of course, more objective. Using this test in the *Clegg* case the court would have to decide whether Clegg believed the soldiers still to be at risk. The House of Lords merely decided they were not and that was it. The defence failed. The House of Lords thought that any changes in the law, particularly in connection with the acts of soldiers and policemen, was a matter for Parliament and not the courts. The House of Lords also confirmed that it was no defence for Clegg to say that he was under orders. There is no defence of superior orders in English law.

There was a campaign by the tabloid newspapers in England which resulted in Clegg's release after serving only four years' imprisonment.

(iii) There is a need to look afresh at the law of self-defence. Crime against private property has increased and the police, perhaps because of inadequate funding, are increasingly perceived as ineffective against such crime, leading perhaps to individuals or groups being prepared to use force to defend their homes against crime.

568 Attorney-General's Reference (No 2 of 1983) [1984] 1 All ER 988

The defendant in this case had a shop in an area which had suffered riots and his store had been looted. He was in constant fear of further rioting. He boarded his shop up, bought fire extinguishers and made 10 petrol bombs which he kept upstairs to be used to repel rioters. This was an offence under the Explosive Substances Act 1883. He pleaded self-defence, the problem about that defence being that when he prepared the petrol bombs no attack was taking place. The Court of Appeal *held* on this point that the defence of self-defence was available to go to a jury at least. A person can make preparations for self-defence where there is an apprehension of imminent attack. The issue of reciprocity was not raised, since this was not a trial as such, although the defendant did say he did not intend to throw the bombs at people but to throw them on the pavement in front of his shop to keep the rioters away from it.

569 R v Rose (1884) 15 Cox CC 540

John Rose, who was a very powerful man, was killed by his son, a weakly young man aged 22 years. John Rose had frequently threatened to kill his wife, the young man's mother. On this occasion he violently assaulted her, threatened to cut her throat and said he was going to a bedroom to get a knife which the family knew he kept there. He came back with the knife and grabbed his wife and held her in a position which could have been preparatory to cutting her throat. The son got a gun and shot him dead. He was indicted for manslaughter. He was found not guilty. The judge said that homicide was excusable if the fatal blow (or shot in this case) was necessary for the preservation of the life of another.

Comment (i) This case was decided on common-law principles. Today it provides an example of the possible use of s 3 of the Criminal Law Act 1967.

(ii) Where the defence is raised, as here, in relation to the taking of a person's life, the provisions of Art 2 of the Convention on Human Rights will now be applied. Article 2 is more stringent than s 3. Under Art 2 the force used must be absolutely necessary, and lethal force is likely to be permissible only when acting to defend another from unlawful violence not in the general prevention of crime. Article 2 could well have been satisfied in the *Rose* case.

GLOSSARY OF COMMONLY USED LEGAL WORDS AND PHRASES

accord and satisfaction A phrase used to indicate that a contract which has not been wholly performed is to be treated as discharged by agreement of the parties (*the accord*), this agreement being supported by consideration (*the satisfaction*).

agent A person who is employed by another (called *the principal*) to put that other into a contractual relationship with a third party.

bailment The transfer by one person to another of possession but not ownership of a tangible asset.

bill of exchange A form of credit under which a seller S who has sold goods to a buyer B will draw up a bill of exchange on B, the bill being payable, say, three months hence. If, as is usual, B accepts the bill, he will return it to S who may wait three months before presenting it to B for payment, or alternatively get a bank to pay him so that the bank will present the bill for payment at the end of three months. The price paid for the goods or by the bank for the bill will be adjusted to take into account interest during the waiting period of three months.

case stated An appeal from a magistrates' court to the Divisional Court of Queen's Bench on a point of criminal law. The magistrates state the facts and the Queen's Bench rules on the correctness or otherwise of the law applied by the magistrates.

caveat emptor 'Let the buyer take care' – this implies that the buyer should watch out for any defects in the goods he is buying since, in the absence of misrepresentation by the seller, he will bear the consequences of anything which he fails to notice.

chattel Personal property consisting of a tangible asset, e.g. a watch.

cheque Essentially, a bill of exchange but always drawn on a bank and payable on demand instead of at a fixed or determinable future time.

chose in action An intangible asset such as a claim to money as where A owes money to B. In such a case, the debt is a chose in action. Other forms of property are also included such as copyright in a book and a potential claim on an insurance policy. In essence, a chose in action is a piece of property which the owner has the right to recover by court action if it is withheld.

chose in possession A tangible physical object such as a pen or a book.

conveyance A method by which property, in the main land, is transferred or the document by which this is done.

covenant A promise set out in a deed.

demise The grant of a lease of land. According to the context, it can also mean *death*.

devise A gift of real property by will.

estoppel A rule of evidence by which a party may be prevented from proving what is true because he has previously suggested that it was false and another party has relied on that. Thus A and B who are not partners are present together when A asks X for a loan. X knows B but not A. So A says 'Lend me the money, it will be repaid: B is my partner'. B remains silent and X lends A the money which A cannot repay. B is obliged to repay it since partners are jointly and severally liable for the debts of the firm, and B's silence estops him from denying that he is not A's partner.

ex parte An application in judicial proceedings which as an exception is heard in the absence of an opponent. This is now called a without notice application under the Civil Procedure Rules 1998.

execution The carrying into effect of a court order, e.g. for debt by the bailiffs taking the property of the defendant to sell by public auction in order to pay the claimant what the court has decided he is entitled to.

indictable offence A crime triable by jury either because the law requires it, as in the case of murder, or at the option of the defendant where the offence is triable either summarily or on indictment.

insurable interest The interest which an insured party must have in the subject matter of the policy.

intestate A person is said to die intestate when the death occurs without leaving a will.

laches Unjustifiable delay in bringing a claim to enforce an equitable right.

legacy A gift of personal property by will.

liquidation A process under which a corporate body such as a registered company is dissolved by an administrative procedure laid down by law.

negotiable instrument Personal property in the form of a document the rights in which can be transferred merely by delivering it to another person or by delivery following endorsement. The most common example is a bill of exchange.

parol contract An agreement made by word of mouth.

per In the summary of a case the expression '*per* Bloggs J' may appear. The word '*per*' in this context means 'in the opinion of'.

personal representatives Executors and administrators being persons who deal with the estate of a deceased person.

pledge The giving-up of possession, but not ownership, of goods as security for the future payment of a debt or other obligation.

probate The official recognition by the court that executors have authority to deal with the estate under the will of a dead person.

quantum meruit This phrase is used to indicate an action at law for reasonable payment for work done.

realty Freehold or commonhold interest in land and buildings.

remainder An equitable interest which becomes effective in possession only when the estate of a previous owner expires. In a gift of property 'to A for life remainder to B', B's interest is in remainder and will become effective in possession on the death of A.

reversion If A owns the freehold of Greenacre and grants B a lease of, say, 25 years in Greenacre, the freehold will return to A or his estate if he is dead when the lease expires. Until then, A's interest in Greenacre is in reversion.

simple contract A contract made orally or in writing but not by deed.

specialty contract A contract made by deed.

surety A person who has given a guarantee or indemnity of a debt.

winding-up The liquidation or dissolution of a company.

INDEX

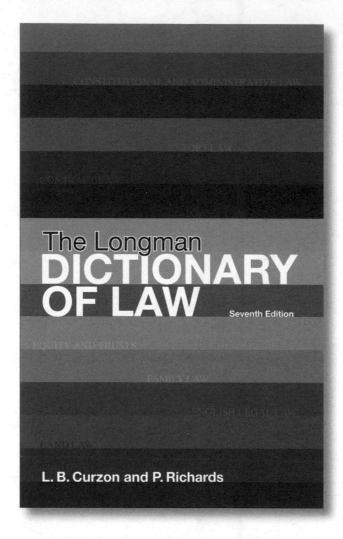